INTERNATIONAL COMMERCIAL ARBITRATION IN NEW YORK

SECOND EDITION

INTERNATIONAL COMMERCIAL ARBITRATION IN NEW YORK

SECOND EDITION

Edited by
James H. Carter
John Fellas

OXFORD
UNIVERSITY PRESS

OXFORD
UNIVERSITY PRESS

Great Clarendon Street, Oxford, OX2 6DP,
United Kingdom

Oxford University Press is a department of the University of Oxford.
It furthers the University's objective of excellence in research, scholarship,
and education by publishing worldwide. Oxford is a registered trade mark of
Oxford University Press in the UK and in certain other countries

First Edition published in 2010
Second Edition published in 2016

Impression: 1

Published in the United States of America by Oxford University Press
198 Madison Avenue, New York, NY 10016, United States of America

British Library Cataloguing in Publication Data
Data available

Library of Congress Control Number: 2016936808

ISBN 978-0-19-875348-3

Printed and bound by
CPI Group (UK) Ltd, Croydon, CR0 4YY

FOREWORD

Gary Born

This study of international commercial arbitration, in New York and under New York law, is of particular quality and importance. Its quality derives from the experience and ability of the New York practitioners and academics who have contributed the book's fourteen chapters, and from the care and detail of their contributions. The study's importance derives from the practical significance of New York, both as a center for international arbitration and as a leading model for the law and practice of international arbitration. Together, these features of James Carter and John Fellas' *International Commercial Arbitration in New York* have made the prior edition of the book essential reading for lawyers, judges, law professors, students, and others, in the United States and elsewhere. This edition is even more impressive.

New York has been a center for the arbitration of disputes—both international and domestic—for centuries. Early Dutch settlers brought the practice of arbitration with them to New Amsterdam, where the absence of established courts and the need for practical, efficient commercial dispute resolution provided fertile ground for arbitration. Later, in the eighteenth century, English and then American colonists continued to use arbitration to resolve their business disputes. These trends continued as New York developed into a center of national and international commerce during the nineteenth century, with arbitration providing a characteristically pragmatic and flexible means of dispute resolution.[1]

The emergence of judicial hostility to arbitration inhibited the use of arbitration in New York, as elsewhere in the United States, during the nineteenth century. As one New York court remarked, one of the "dark chapters in legal history" in the United States involved the treatment of arbitration agreements and awards by U.S. courts during the nineteenth century.[2] Despite that hostility, New York businesses found practical solutions, through trade association rules and otherwise, that enabled them to utilize the arbitral process effectively, even in the absence of judicial support. As a consequence, New York continued to develop as a center for national and international arbitration through the early years of the twentieth century.[3]

---

[1] These developments are described in G. Born, International Commercial Arbitration 41–46 (2d ed. 2014) and William C. Jones, *Three Centuries of Commercial Arbitration in New York: A Brief Survey*, Wash. U. L.Q. 193 (1956).

[2] Robert Lawrence Co. v. Devonshire Fabrics, Inc., 271 F.2d 402, 406 (2d Cir. 1959).

[3] *See* Gary Born, International Commercial Arbitration 41–46 (2d ed. 2014).

The enactment in 1920 of the New York Arbitration Law, which provided for the recognition and enforcement of arbitration agreements and arbitral awards, reversed historic judicial attitudes toward arbitration in New York. The New York legislation also paved the way for enactment of the 1925 United States Arbitration Act (later re-titled the Federal Arbitration Act), which contained similar statutory provisions ensuring the validity and enforceability of agreements to arbitrate and arbitral awards. Together, the New York legislation and the FAA provided an early model for a new generation of arbitration legislation that was enacted in leading commercial jurisdictions around the world (following the 1923 Geneva Protocol on Arbitration Clauses in Commercial Matters and the 1927 Geneva Convention for the Execution of Foreign Arbitral Awards).[4] The two statutes also ushered in a new era of arbitration in New York and the United States, in which New York and other U.S. courts not only abandoned historic hostility to the arbitral process, but began actively to support it.

After World War II, the development of the modern legal framework for international arbitration continued, with the appropriately-named New York Convention (also, occasionally, referred to as the United Nations Convention on the Recognition and Enforcement of Foreign Arbitral Awards). The Convention was the product of extensive collaboration between the international business community and national governments around the world, culminating in three weeks of negotiations in New York in 1958. The resulting treaty has been progressively developed by national legislatures and courts around the world into a global constitutional charter for international commercial arbitration. Together with the efforts of arbitral institutions, businesses, practitioners, and academics, the New York Convention has provided the basis for dramatic growth in the use of arbitration to resolve international commercial disputes. The past sixty years have seen arbitration emerge as the preferred means of dispute resolution for international business and investment transactions, with caseloads at leading institutions increasing ten-fold or more (and new institutions emerging in many commercial centers).

New York has played a central role in the practice of international arbitration—as well as providing the birth-place for contemporary national arbitration legislation and international arbitration treaties. New York law firms have for decades provided a model for international practice, in arbitration and other forms of dispute resolution, as well as corporate and financial matters. It is no coincidence that it was a New York law firm that was enjoined in the 1980s by a Singaporean court from participating in a Singapore-seated international arbitration,[5] nor that it was New York law firms that participated frequently in

---

[4] *See* Gary Born, International Commercial Arbitration 49, 67–68 (2d ed. 2014).

[5] Turner (E. Asia) Pte Ltd v. Builders Fed. (H.K.) Ltd, 5(3) J. Int'l Arb. 139 (Singapore High Ct. 1988).

early ICSID arbitrations.[6] These incidents were the result of decades of leadership by New York law firms and practitioners which, although shared with London, Paris, and other jurisdictions, was nonetheless of fundamental importance to the development of contemporary international commercial arbitration.

At the same time, New York arbitral institutions have also played a key role in the development of international arbitration. The American Arbitration Association, based in New York, and its international arm, the International Centre for Dispute Resolution, have been major forces in the development of modern institutional arbitration. The AAA possesses one of the largest and most substantial caseloads of any arbitral institution in the world, and the ICDR competes on a level playing field with the ICC, SIAC, and other leading international arbitral institutions. More recently, the formation of the New York International Arbitration Center has contributed further weight to New York's institutional presence in the field.

The chapters of this book detail the contributions that New York law and New York courts have made to the international arbitral process, as well as the legal framework for international arbitrations seated in New York or involving issues of New York law. From the subject of international arbitration agreements (including choice-of-law and allocation of competence), to the conduct of arbitral proceedings (including discovery and disclosure and the selection of arbitral tribunals), to the recognition and enforcement of arbitral awards, the book's chapters provide comprehensive and thoughtful discussions of the New York framework for international arbitration. The contributions are uniformly useful and impressive, valuable to both U.S. and foreign practitioners, as well as academics and students.

Like international commercial arbitration itself, and New York's own pivotal role in international arbitration, this book is a work in progress which continues to develop. This is the second edition of *International Commercial Arbitration in New York* and it expands on the book's previous edition, providing a more detailed and comprehensive treatment of the subject and taking into account contemporary developments. Readers from around the world, as well as in New York and the United States, will benefit enormously from this edition and its contributions.

London and Berlin
February 2016

[6] Amco Asia Corp. v. Republic of Indonesia, Award in ICSID Case No. ARB/81/1 of 20 November 1984, 24 Int'l Legal Mat. 1022 (1985); Československa Obchodní Banka AS v. Slovak Republic, Award on Jurisdiction in ICSID Case No. ARB/97/4 of 24 May 1999, 14 ICSID Rev.-For. Inv. L.J. 251, 263 (1999); Swiss Aluminium v. Iceland, Order Noting Discontinuance ICSID Case No. ARB/83/1 of 6 March 1985.

FOREWORD TO THE FIRST EDITION

Gerald Aksen

International commercial arbitration has achieved prominence as the primary method for resolving business disputes. Unlike its domestic counterpart where the main reasons for its use include speed and cost savings, international arbitration is the substitute for the uncertainty and unfamiliarity with foreign courts. The procedure is popular because no one has yet figured out a better method for settling disputes in the context of international commercial relations with a modicum of confidentiality and an effective means of enforcing the resultant decision. Thanks to the success of a number of famous treaties, winning parties can obtain relatively prompt enforcement of foreign arbitral awards with only narrow grounds for review.

The arbitrations are generally held in major commercial cities of the world. New York is featured in this book because it is the center of commercial arbitration in the United States. New York has a well known set of commercial laws, a large cadre of international lawyers well versed in transnational dealings, prominent international academics and many sophisticated arbitrators ready to hear and resolve commercial controversies.

Two leading members of the New York Bar have joined together and invited a dozen or so of their equally prominent colleagues to put together 13 separate legal monologues into a book that is designed to encapsulate the law and practice of international arbitration and how it works in this city. The editors deserve praise for their choice of contributing authors. Included are members of the leading international law firms in New York and a prominent academic. Each has outstanding credentials in the subject matter described.

The common theme is the use of international arbitration in New York. One hopes this will not lead to a sequel from abroad that indicates the downside to placing arbitrations here. The many court citations are from the New York and federal courts, which may have a negative parochial connotation on the international side of the topics. However, the subject matter is relevant whether you are in New York, London or Paris. To this reader, the outstanding feature of the book is the obvious personal experience that each author has brought to bear on his or her selected topic. What a treat to learn about such real world and practical issues such as how to select international arbitrators and court assistance in obtaining interim relief from persons who know whereof they speak. Each separate chapter is a mini-course on the topic. The two overarching issues that attract interest in international arbitration are how to enforce an agreement and the eventual award. There are covered in detail not only with respect to contracts between private parties, but also with sovereigns. Knowing the differences is essential. Most important issues in the life of an international arbitration from drafting the initial arbitration agreement, through the labyrinth of document production to the damages you seek from the tribunal are carefully covered by lawyers who have learned from having been involved with these important and delicate issues. Two unique chapters are included. In the first, the co-editors have provided a useful compendium of the legal environment and institutions involved in New York that help make the big apple a major center for international arbitration. In the other, the book does not shy away from new and undeveloped law. Thus, there is a chapter on Class Action Arbitration ("a relatively recent phenomenon in the United States, but ... expanding at a rapid rate"). Finally, when one needs to know about the thorny and multi faceted issues concerning what is termed "arbitral jurisdiction" ("easily stated, though it is not easily resolved"), the editors have relied upon the ultimate arbiter of American law, the Reporter of the upcoming Restatement of the US Law on International Commercial Arbitration.

The book is right to place an international prominence on New York because the city has been in the forefront of the modern arbitration movement. In 1920, New York was the first state in the United States to pass legislation that overruled the common law hostility toward arbitration. Spurred on by the local business community and the arbitration societies then extant, the legislature enacted a law making agreements to arbitrate future disputes valid, irrevocable and enforceable. New York led the way. Five years later, when Congress enacted the United States Arbitration Act (FAA), the language was borrowed heavily from the pioneering New York law. In 1955 the National Conference of Commissioners on Uniform State Laws promulgated a Uniform Arbitration Act (UAA). Thereafter, the process of arbitral acceptance gained further momentum. By 1958, almost half of the states either adopted the UAA or similar legislation favoring the enforcement of pre-dispute arbitral clauses and limited grounds for review of awards.

In 1958 the single most important event in the life of international arbitration took place. The United Nations, in New York, promulgated the multilateral Convention on the Recognition and Enforcement of Foreign Arbitral Awards. This time it was at the urging of the international business community and such prominent organizations as the International Chamber of Commerce. This treaty did for international contracts what the New York and FAA laws did for domestic contracts. The essence of the UN Convention was to enforce international arbitration clauses and to limit the grounds for review of awards narrowly to due process or public policy type reasons. The Golden Age of International Arbitration was born.

However, the United States was not one of the first to implement the UN Convention. Not until a majority of states had passed the UAA or similar legislation reversing the common law rule of revocability was this possible. Finally, in 1970, the necessary majority was achieved and the Congress enacted Chapter 1 of the FAA in which implementation occurred. Soon after the United States ratified the UN Convention many other countries did the same.

Thereafter, the international arbitration movement took off with an unprecedented fervor: an Inter-American Convention (Panama Convention) was promulgated; bilateral treaties with arbitration became prominent; the rapid globalization of business forged an overnight need for a method of settling international disputes; opening of the Iran-US Claims Tribunal with immediate reliance on international arbitration to resolve claims of American companies against the Government of Iran; the United Nations producing the UNCITRAL Arbitration Rules in 1977 recognizing the value of international ad hoc procedures; followed by the UNCITRAL Model Arbitration Law in 1985 that could easily be adopted wholesale by countries; updating and revising of international rules and procedures by national arbitral institutions; promulgation of new brochures by international law firms identifying the firm experts in the field; growth and development of publications publishing arbitral awards and providing lists of leading lawyers and arbitrators throughout the world; recognition by the International Bar Association that guidelines were needed for uniform rules of evidence (IBA Rules on the Taking of Evidence in International Commercial Arbitration in 1999) and then for advising arbitrators on conflicts (Guidelines on Conflicts of Interest in International Arbitration in 2004); the surge of educational seminars on international arbitration in every major trading country; new arbitral centers created in countries large and small and an outpouring of articles and books on the law and practice of international arbitration. These and many other important factors too numerous to mention have contributed to the Golden Age of International Arbitration.

International Commercial Arbitration in New York will add to the fervor.

FOREWORD TO THE FIRST EDITION

Robert B. von Mehren

For the litigation of commercial disputes, the nations of Europe and North America, over many centuries developed two basic systems: the civil law and the common law. The civil law system, which was adopted and developed by France and the nations of Europe, was a system in which the state played a much larger role than the individual. Judges investigated the facts and managed the trial. The role of the lawyer was reduced to a minimum.

The other basic system was the common law which prevailed in Great Britain and the United States. This system placed the role of fact finding and presentation of the case to the court almost entirely in the hands of the lawyers for the parties. The function of its judges was reduced to instruction of the jury and the presiding over the presentation of the facts and the arguments to the jury.

Arbitration became over time an element of commercial dispute resolution both in Europe and the United States. In civil law countries, the arbitral practice reflected the approach of its courts. The tribunal performed many of the functions that the judge did in a civil trial. As might be expected, in common law countries, the lawyers were generally speaking much more involved in the presentation of the case than in civil law countries.

I. MY INTRODUCTION TO ARBITRATION

I graduated from the Harvard Law School in 1943. After two years of serving as a law clerk to Judge Learned Hand (1946 term) and Justice Stanley F. Reed (1947 term), I married and spent about four months on my honeymoon.[1] I then returned to New York as an associate in Debevoise, Stevenson, Plimpton & Page.

It was in that capacity that I had my first experience with arbitration. Arbitration was not a subject in Harvard Law School's curriculum nor was it often encountered in private commercial practice in New York.

[1] The long honeymoon was based upon my hunch that long vacations were not likely to be frequent in the future. Unfortunately, I was correct!

As time went on, I did some work in the commercial arbitration field. The American Arbitration Association, which was established in 1926, had some commercial arbitrations. Its arbitrators often served pro bono and there were few, if any, international arbitrations heard in New York.[2] This, of course, would all change dramatically. A larger and larger percentage of commercial disputes went to arbitration rather than litigation. More and more lawyers developed arbitral practices. Law Schools offered courses on arbitration. New organizations got into the business of providing arbitration rules and services.

Important factors in these developments were the Federal Arbitration Act of 1925 and the ratification by the Senate in 1970 of the New York Convention of 1958. The ratification of the Convention was of critical importance because it provided for the enforcement of arbitration agreements and awards internationally, thus making arbitral awards easier to enforce abroad than American judicial decisions.

These and other factors resulted in arbitrations becoming more and more important in the areas of domestic and international commercial activity. It also resulted in substantial changes in the practices and procedures of arbitrations. Those are of considerable interest and I shall try to illustrate a few of them by referencing matters in which I have played a role.

II. THE LEGACY FROM LITIGATION

As one might anticipate, arbitration which had existed in a minor role side-by-side with litigation for a long period of time was substantially influenced in its practices for a very long period by the practices of litigation. As one might also expect, the result was that the conduct of arbitrations in civil law countries was in many important respects different from that of common law countries.

A few examples of this are of interest.

A. The Examination of Witnesses

The prevailing practice, when I first became seriously involved in international arbitration conducted in civil law countries, was for the Chairman or, to use the European term, President of the Tribunal, to conduct whatever cross-examination there was to be. In one of my early international arbitrations in Switzerland, the Chairman was a distinguished Dutch Professor and arbitrator. When in the

[2] For a discussion of the Historical Background of arbitration in the United States, *see* Chapter 2, Robert B. von Mehren, et al., AMERICAN ARBITRATION: PRINCIPLES AND PRACTICE (2008).

hearings the time came for cross-examination of the first important witness, he attempted to perform that role. It soon became clear that he could not conduct a meaningful cross. Fortunately, he and I had worked together several times and I urged him to give up cross and let it be done by counsel. He agreed and counsel conducted the cross-examination with much more success.

In my experience, cross-examination is now routinely done by counsel. That is not to say that the arbitrators do not participate in questioning witnesses. They do and often very effectively. But cross in the first instance is conducted by the appropriate counsel. This was, I believe, inevitable once there was a substantial volume of international arbitrations involving civil and common law jurisdictions. The common law solution was the only way in which cross-examination could be conducted where complex factual situations were present. Counsel soon determined that cross was a task for them not the arbitrators.

B. Access to Documents

In some civil law jurisdiction, the internal files of the parties may not be open to discovery. In a major arbitration involving civil law jurisdictions, I was faced with the problem of obtaining access to internal files of the respondent. It appeared to the Tribunal that these files would have information that was essential and would perhaps decide the matter at issue. The Tribunal insisted that its request to see the documents in question be honored. The documents were provided and proved conclusive.

In the matter referred to above, arbitrators from different backgrounds – common law and civil law – joined in the demand for access. That was more than two decades ago. Today the documents would without doubt be produced.

C. Use of Expert Witnesses

In arbitration, which of course, is more flexible than litigation, certain new practices have also been developed relating to the presentation of expert testimony. I believe that I was an arbitrator in one of the first cases in which these new ideas were used. In essence, the concept was that the examination of all the expert witnesses should take place at the same time and that the experts should be free to comment on the responses of their colleagues during the presentation. I have been a party to this practice a number of times and usually it has worked well.

* * * * *

The above examples show the way in which arbitration has developed over the years. It is clear that it has become more like litigation than it was in the 1940s and it is also clear that common law lawyers have played a large role in many of these developments.

We must as a profession recognize that arbitration is not litigation and guard against treating it as litigation. Arbitration, created by the consent of the parties, allows them to settle their disputes without having to meet requirements that must be met in litigation. The process that is created by the consent of the parties is clearly more flexible than that created by legislation and should remain so. We must remember that arbitral jurisdiction is derived from the consent of the parties. The jurisdiction of our courts is fixed by legislation and is necessarily less flexible than that of arbitration.

A review of the Table of Contents will demonstrate that *International Commercial Arbitration in New York* discusses the issues and problems in a comprehensive and thoughtful manner. Its contributors are practitioners or academics who bring experience and scholarship to their contributions. The topics that are discussed are important. Indeed, it is most appropriate that this work should focus on New York which is without doubt the most important and dynamic jurisdiction in the United States dealing with the subject matter of this book. Messers. Carter and Fellas are to be congratulated on their leadership of this important work.

CONTENTS—SUMMARY

Table of Cases xxxiii
Table of Conventions lxv
Table of Legislation lxvii
Table of Arbitral Rules lxxiii
Table of Arbitral Awards lxxvii
List of Contributors lxxxv

Introduction: The New York Arbitration Landscape 1
1. **The Law Applicable to International Arbitration in New York** 17
2. **The Impact of U.S. Litigation** 55
3. **Drafting Considerations for Clauses Designating New York as the Place of Arbitration** 95
4. **The Application of New York Law to Contracts** 115
5. **The Selection of Arbitrators** 143
6. **Jurisdiction: Courts vs. Arbitrators** 171
7. **Enforcing International Arbitration Agreements** 239
8. **Obtaining Preliminary Relief** 297
9. **Discovery** 319
10. **Damages in International Arbitration** 353
11. **Class Action Arbitration** 373
12. **Arbitration Hearings in New York** 421
13. **Challenging and Enforcing International Arbitral Awards in New York** 447
14. **Enforcing Awards Involving Foreign Sovereigns** 507

Appendices
1. Schedule of International Arbitration Conventions 539
2. Federal Arbitration Act 541
3. NY Civil Practice Law and Rules, Article 75 547

4. Supreme Court, New York County Commercial Division, Charles E. Ramos, Justice, International Arbitration Rules (2013) International Arbitration Part Rules—Part 53 553
5. Schedule of Arbitration Rules and Guidelines 555
6. AAA/ABA Code of Ethics for Arbitrators in Commercial Disputes 557
7. Schedule of New York City Bar Association Arbitration Reports 567

Index 569

CONTENTS—DETAILED

Table of Cases xxxiii
Table of Conventions lxv
Table of Legislation lxvii
Table of Arbitral Rules lxxiii
Table of Arbitral Awards lxxvii
List of Contributors lxxxv

Introduction: The New York Arbitration Landscape
James H. Carter and John Fellas

A. Overview of International Arbitration in New York 0.01
1. The Major Arbitral Institutions in New York 0.07
(a) AAA/ICDR 0.08
(b) ICC/SICANA 0.11
(c) CPR 0.13
(d) JAMS 0.16
2. The Court System Supporting Arbitration 0.17
3. The New York International Arbitration Center 0.22
4. Other Supporting Organizations 0.23
(a) The New York International Arbitration Club 0.24
(b) Bar association committees 0.25
(c) The College of Commercial Arbitrators 0.28
(d) Universities 0.29
(e) Consulting firms 0.30
(f) Law firm international groups 0.31
5. Arbitration Hearing Locations 0.32

B. This Book 0.34

1. The Law Applicable to International Arbitration in New York
David M. Lindsey and Yasmine Lahlou

A. Scope of this Chapter 1.01

B. The FAA and How it Works 1.04
1. Fundamental Issues 1.04
(a) What is the FAA? 1.04
(b) Defining preemption 1.06
(c) Jurisdiction of federal courts 1.10

2. FAA Chapter 1: The Federal Law of Arbitration 1.11
(a) Section 1 1.12
(b) Section 2 1.13
(c) Sections 3–4 1.15
(d) Sections 5–6 1.16
(e) Section 7 1.18
(f) Sections 9–13, 16 1.21
3. Chapter 2: The New York Convention 1.30
4. Chapter 3: The Panama Convention 1.34

C. The FAA and the New York State Arbitration Statute 1.36
1. State Law on Court's Authority to Decide Statute of Limitations as Threshold Matter 1.38
2. State Law Limiting Time to Object to Validity of Agreement to Arbitrate 1.40
3. State Law Prohibiting Predispute Arbitration Agreements in Consumer Contracts 1.43

D. Applicable Law Regarding Recognition of Arbitration Agreements under the Conventions 1.44
1. Separability, the Conventions, and the FAA 1.45
(a) Separability doctrine 1.45
(b) The New York Convention 1.48
(c) The FAA 1.54
2. Applicable Law Regarding Formation and Substantive Validity of the Agreement to Arbitrate 1.57
(a) Case Law from the Second Circuit applying law of forum 1.61
(b) Consideration of state contract law principles when applying law of forum in the Second Circuit 1.65
(c) Case law from the Second Circuit applying law of the underlying contract 1.69
(d) Consideration of internationally recognized minimum standards 1.72
3. Applicable Law Regarding Formal Validity of the Agreement to Arbitrate 1.74
4. Applicable Law Regarding Arbitrability 1.79
5. Applicable Law Regarding Interpretation and Scope 1.82
6. Applicable Law Regarding Capacity and Competence 1.83

E. Applicable Law Regarding Recognition and Enforcement of Convention Awards 1.84
1. Application of the Conventions 1.86
2. Nondomestic Awards Rendered in the United States or Pursuant to U.S. Arbitration Law May Be Vacated Under U.S. Arbitration Law 1.88
3. Arbitral Awards Rendered Outside the United States or Pursuant to a Foreign Arbitration Law May Not Be Vacated Under U.S. Arbitration Law 1.95
4. Relevance of New York Arbitration Law to the Arbitral Award 1.100

F. Effective Governing Law Clauses 1.103

2. The Impact of U.S. Litigation
Oliver J. Armas and Thomas N. Pieper

A. Introduction 2.01

B. Overview of U.S. Litigation 2.03
1. The U.S. Legal System: An Adversarial Model 2.04
2. Structure of Courts in the United States 2.08
3. Sources of the Law Governing U.S. Litigation 2.12
(a) The substantive law 2.13
(b) Rules of civil procedure 2.18
(c) Constitutions, rules of evidence, local court, and judge rules 2.21
(d) Ethical obligations and codes 2.24
4. Civil Procedure: A Guide to the Chronology of Litigation 2.26

C. Commencement of the Litigation 2.27
1. Pleadings: The Complaint and Answer 2.28
2. The Court's Authority to Oversee the Litigation: Jurisdiction 2.38
(a) Subject-matter jurisdiction 2.39
(b) Territorial jurisdiction 2.42

D. Procedural Calendar 2.44
1. Managing the Case 2.45
2. Pretrial Conferences 2.46
3. The Scheduling Order 2.50

E. Discovery: Establishing the Facts and Marshaling the Evidence 2.52
1. Discovery in the Adversarial Model 2.55
2. Rules, Methods, and Mechanisms of Discovery in U.S. Litigation 2.57
(a) Federal Rule of Civil Procedure 26 2.59
(b) Depositions, document requests, and third-party subpoenas 2.62
(c) The doctrine of privilege 2.64
3. Expert Discovery 2.68
4. Electronic Discovery 2.71
5. Using the Evidence: The Summary Judgment Motion 2.73

F. Pretrial Matters and Presentation of the Case 2.76

G. Decision and Judgment 2.83
1. Judgment in a Jury Trial 2.85
2. Judgment in a Bench Trial 2.89

H. Costs 2.92

I. Appeals: Challenging the Judgment 2.96
1. The "Final Judgment" Rule 2.98
2. Appeals to Higher Courts 2.99
3. Scope of Appellate Review 2.100

J. Conclusion 2.102

3. Drafting Considerations for Clauses Designating New York as the Place of Arbitration
Paul D. Friedland and Damien Nyer

A. Preliminary Drafting Considerations not Particular to Arbitration in New York 3.04
1. Essential Elements 3.04
2. Recommended Elements 3.08

B. Drafting Considerations Specific to Clauses Providing for Arbitration in New York 3.11
1. The Law Governing Clauses Providing for Arbitration in New York 3.11
2. Jurisdictional Considerations 3.16
(a) *Kompetenz-Kompetenz* 3.16
(b) Arbitral jurisdiction to resolve preliminary issues 3.20
(c) Jurisdiction over nonsignatories 3.24
(d) Validity of sole option clauses 3.26
3. Powers and Duties of the Arbitral Tribunal 3.27
(a) Impartiality of arbitrators 3.27
(b) Allocation of costs and fees 3.29
(c) Punitive damages 3.34
(d) Class proceedings 3.37
4. Arbitral Process 3.38
(a) Discovery 3.38
(b) Consolidation of Proceedings 3.44
(c) Confidentiality 3.49
5. Considerations Relating to Judicial Powers 3.51
(a) Provisional measures 3.51
(b) Modifying the scope of judicial review 3.55
(c) Enforcement of awards 3.58

4. The Application of New York Law to Contracts
David W. Rivkin, Mark W. Friedman, and William H. Taft V

A. Choice-of-Law Rules in New York 4.06

B. Contract Formation 4.12
1. Elements of a Contract 4.14
2. Future Contracts 4.19
3. Authority to Enter Contacts 4.20

C. What Constitutes a Breach 4.22
1. Material Breach 4.23
2. Substantial Performance 4.25
3. Anticipatory Breach and Repudiation 4.26
4. Divisible or Installment Contracts 4.28

D. Consequences of Breach of Contract 4.29
1. Effect on the Performance of the Non-breaching Party 4.29
2. Measure of Damages 4.34
3. Equitable Relief 4.42

E. Claims Ancillary to Breach of Contract 4.45
1. Arbitrability of Ancillary Claims 4.45
2. Claims Ancillary to Breach of Contract under New York Law 4.49
(a) Implied covenant of good faith and fair dealing 4.49
(b) Unjust enrichment 4.51
(c) Fraud in the inducement 4.53
(d) Fraud in the performance 4.55
(e) Third-party beneficiaries 4.57

F. Special Issues Arising under New York Law of Contracts 4.59
1. Merger Clauses 4.60
2. "Best Efforts" vs. "Reasonable Efforts" 4.64
3. Changed Circumstances and *Force Majeure* 4.67

5. The Selection of Arbitrators
James H. Carter

A. Tribunal Structure 5.03
1. Detailed Arbitrator Selection Clauses 5.05
2. Incorporation of Arbitral Rules Governing Tribunal Formation 5.07
(a) ICDR international rules 5.08
(b) AAA commercial rules 5.16
(c) ICC rules 5.19
(d) UNCITRAL rules 5.22
(e) CPR rules 5.24
(f) JAMS rules 5.27
3. Idiosyncratic Appointing Authorities in New York 5.28
4. Dysfunctional Clauses Referring to Nonexistent or Unavailable Institutions 5.29
5. Statutory Default Procedures 5.30

B. Strategy in Selecting Members of a Tripartite Tribunal 5.32
1. Role of the Default Mechanism 5.33
2. Lawyers vs. Nonlawyers 5.35
3. Special Professional Qualifications 5.37
4. Nationality 5.40

C. Neutrality of Party-Appointed Arbitrators 5.43

D. Where to Find Arbitrator Candidates 5.46
1. The CPR Roster 5.47
2. The Energy Arbitrators' List 5.48
3. The JAMS Roster 5.49
4. ICDR 5.50
5. ICC/U.S. Council for International Business 5.51
6. The International Arbitration Club of New York 5.52
7. Lawyer Directories 5.53

E. The Selection Process 5.54
1. Communications with Party-Appointed Arbitrators 5.56
(a) The AAA/ABA Code and AAA Rules 5.57
(b) The Chartered Institute of Arbitrators' Guideline 5.60
(c) Restricted time limits 5.64

2. Role of the Party-Appointed Arbitrators in Selecting a Chairperson 5.66
3. Negotiating Selection of a Chairperson 5.70
4. Convincing the Chairperson Candidate to Serve 5.75
F. Arbitrator Compensation and Conflicts Waivers 5.77
G. Conflicts Checks and Arbitrator Disclosures 5.82
H. Challenges and Replacement of Arbitrators 5.86

6. Jurisdiction: Courts vs. Arbitrators
George A. Bermann

A. Introduction 6.02
1. The Arbitration Agreement 6.02
2. Arbitral Jurisdiction 6.03
3. Policy Dimensions of Arbitral Jurisdiction 6.05
4. *Kompetenz-Kompetenz* and Severability as Guides to Allocating Authority over Arbitral Jurisdiction 6.06
B. The "Arbitral Jurisdiction" Scenarios 6.10
C. Asserting Arbitral Jurisdiction in Judicial Proceedings Prior to Arbitration 6.11
1. Choice of Law Governing Interpretation and Enforcement of the Arbitration Agreement 6.14
2. Severability as a Guide to Validity Questions 6.18
3. *Kompetenz-Kompetenz* and the Arbitrators' Jurisdiction 6.22
(a) Who decides party issues? 6.23
(b) Who decides scope issues? 6.24
(c) Who decides validity issues? 6.25
(d) Who decides arbitrability and "arbitrability-related" issues? 6.26
4. Forum-Specific Issues: When and on What Grounds May Courts Avoid Arbitration of Otherwise Arbitrable Disputes? 6.29
(a) Limitation periods 6.31
(b) Waiver of a party's right to arbitrate the dispute 6.32
(c) Res judicata and collateral estoppel 6.33
5. Appealability of Courts' Arbitral Jurisdiction Determinations 6.35
D. Arbitral Jurisdiction Before the Arbitrators 6.39
1. Procedural Aspects of Arbitrators' Jurisdictional Determinations 6.41
(a) Timing and form of jurisdictional objections 6.42
(b) Deferring the jurisdictional determination and joining it with the merits 6.46
(c) Special jurisdictional procedures for different institutional regimes 6.47
2. Choice of Law Governing Arbitrators' Jurisdictional Determinations 6.48
3. *Kompetenz-Kompetenz* and the Scope and Validity of the Arbitrators' Jurisdiction 6.50
(a) Preclusive effect of prior judicial determinations 6.52
(b) Waiver of jurisdictional challenges 6.55

4. Preclusive Effect of Prior Judicial Determinations on Forum-Specific Issues 6.56
5. Appealability of Interim Arbitral Determinations of Arbitral Jurisdiction 6.60

E. Arbitral Jurisdiction upon Vacatur 6.61
1. Confirmation and Vacatur of Awards Rendered in New York 6.62
2. Law Governing the Interpretation and Validity of the Arbitration Agreement 6.64
3. *Kompetenz-Kompetenz* and Judicial Review upon Vacatur 6.65
(a) Review of the arbitrators' decision as to the parties bound by the agreement 6.68
(b) Review of arbitrators' determination of scope of arbitration agreement 6.72
(c) Review of arbitral determinations of the validity of the arbitration agreement 6.76
(d) Deference in cases where a court compelling arbitration has ruled on the jurisdictional issue 6.86
(e) Waiver of jurisdictional objections by failure to raise them before vacatur 6.90
4. Deference to Arbitrators on Forum-Specific Issues 6.91

F. Arbitral Jurisdiction at Recognition and Enforcement 6.93
1. The Place of Arbitral Jurisdiction in Recognition and Enforcement 6.95
2. Choice of Law Governing the Recognition and Enforcement of an Arbitral Award and Defenses Thereto 6.96
3. *Kompetenz-Kompetenz* and Review of Arbitral Jurisdiction in Recognition and Enforcement Proceedings 6.97
(a) Deference to prior arbitral decision as to the parties bound by the agreement 6.99
(b) Deference to the arbitrators' determination of scope of agreement 6.100
(c) Deference to arbitrators' determination as to validity of agreement 6.102
(d) Deference to arbitrators on arbitrability and "arbitrability-related" issues 6.106
4. Deference to Arbitrators and Vacatur Courts on Forum-Specific Issues 6.107
5. Waiver of Jurisdiction Challenges 6.111

7. Enforcing International Arbitration Agreements
John Fellas and Hagit Elul

A. Proceeding with the Arbitration without Court Intervention 7.04

B. Court Intervention: Introduction 7.08
1. The Federal Policy in Favor of Arbitration and the New York and Panama Conventions 7.14
(a) The federal policy in favor of arbitration 7.14
(b) The New York and Panama Conventions 7.16

2. The Jurisdiction of U.S. Federal Courts 7.19
(a) Subject-matter jurisdiction 7.20
(b) Personal jurisdiction 7.28
3. The Allocation of Power between Arbitrators and Courts 7.29
(a) *Kompetenz-Kompetenz* 7.33
(b) The separability presumption 7.36

C. Reading the *Kompetenz-Kompetenz* Doctrine and the Separability Doctrine Together 7.42
1. Common Arbitrability Issues 7.55
(a) Challenges to the contract 7.57
(b) Nonsignatories 7.63
(c) The scope of an arbitration clause 7.82
(d) Waiver 7.96

D. Court Intervention: Compelling Arbitration 7.98
1. Actions to Compel Arbitration under the Federal Arbitration Act 7.98
2. CPLR § 7503(c) 7.106

E. Court Intervention: Staying Litigation Commenced in the United States in Breach of an Arbitration Clause 7.112
1. Motions to Stay or Dismiss Litigation under the Federal Arbitration Act 7.113
2. The Arbitrability of Claims under U.S. Law 7.121
3. Cases that Include Nonarbitrable Claims 7.124

F. Court Intervention: Antisuit Injunctions 7.129
1. Antisuit Injunctions: An Overview 7.131
2. Circumstances in Which Courts Grant Antisuit Injunctions to Enforce Arbitration Agreements 7.136
3. Circumstances Where Courts Have Denied Antisuit Injunctions in Aid of Arbitration 7.152

G. Damages for Breach of an Arbitration Agreement 7.167

H. Conclusion 7.168

8. Obtaining Preliminary Relief
Robert H. Smit, Tyler B. Robinson, and Janet M. Whittaker

A. Introduction to Preliminary Relief 8.01

B. Preliminary Relief from Arbitral Tribunals in New York 8.05
1. The Authority of Arbitral Tribunals to Issue Preliminary Relief 8.07
(a) Authority derived from the arbitration clause and the chosen arbitration rules 8.09
(b) Authority derived from applicable arbitration law 8.12
2. Preliminary Relief from Arbitral Tribunals: Types of Relief 8.16
3. Preliminary Relief from Arbitral Tribunals: Procedures 8.17
4. Preliminary Relief from Arbitral Tribunals: Judicial Enforcement 8.20
5. Preliminary Relief from an Emergency Arbitrator 8.24

(a) The need for emergency arbitral relief 8.24
(b) Overview of emergency arbitral relief procedures 8.26

C. Preliminary Relief from Courts in Aid of Arbitration 8.32
1. The New York Convention and Preliminary Relief 8.33
2. Preliminary Relief from Federal Court 8.35
3. Preliminary Relief from New York State Courts 8.40
(a) Preliminary relief under NY CPLR § 7502(c) 8.42
(b) Additional requirements for grant of preliminary relief 8.45

9. Discovery
John L. Gardiner, Lea Haber Kuck, and Julie Bédard

A. Introduction 9.01

B. Framework for Discovery in International Arbitrations Venued in New York 9.03
1. Statutory Framework 9.03
(a) The Federal Arbitration Act 9.04
(b) The New York Civil Practice Law and Rules 9.06
2. Courts in New York Support Party Autonomy: Supremacy of the Parties' Agreement on Discovery 9.07
3. In the Absence of an Agreement to the Contrary, Discovery in Arbitration Will Be More Limited than Discovery in Litigation in State or Federal Court 9.11
4. Arbitration Rules and Guidelines 9.13
(a) International Chamber of Commerce 9.15
(b) International Centre for Dispute Resolution 9.17
(c) JAMS/JAMS International Rules on Evidence 9.18
(d) U.N. Commission on International Trade Law 9.21
(e) International Institute for Conflict Prevention and Resolution 9.22
(f) The International Bar Association's Rules on Taking of Evidence in International Commercial Arbitration 9.25
5. The Discretion of the Arbitral Tribunal 9.30

C. Discovery Between the Parties 9.33
1. Document Discovery 9.33
(a) Documents in "hard copy" form 9.33
(b) Electronically stored documents and information 9.39
(c) Consequences of a party's failure to produce documents 9.51
2. Availability of Depositions 9.54
3. Other Discovery Devices 9.55
4. Privilege 9.56
5. Confidentiality 9.59

D. Obtaining Discovery from Nonparties 9.62

E. Discovery from Expert Witnesses 9.71

F. Discovery when Seeking Preliminary Relief in Aid of Arbitration 9.73

G. Discovery in New York in Aid of a Foreign Arbitration 9.74

10. Damages in International Arbitration
Claudia T. Salomon

A. Introduction 10.01
B. Principles Controlling the Proof and Calculation of Damages 10.03
1. Commercial Damages for Breach of Contract 10.03
2. Money Damages vs. Specific Performance 10.06
3. Expectation Damages 10.10
(a) General damages 10.11
(b) Special damages 10.15
(c) Duty to mitigate 10.21
4. Liquidated Damages and Penalties 10.23
5. Punitive Damages 10.27
6. Alternate Theories of Commercial Damages 10.29
(a) Reliance 10.29
(b) Restitution 10.34
7. A Special Case: Demonstrating Damages for Anticipated Future Profits from a Lost Business Opportunity 10.35
C. Calculation of Interest 10.39
1. Prejudgment Interest 10.40
2. Postjudgment Interest 10.46
D. Attorneys' Fees and Costs 10.48
1. Awards of Arbitrator Fees and Costs 10.50
2. Awards of Attorneys' Fees and Costs 10.51

11. Class Action Arbitration
William H. Baker

A. General Principles Governing Class Actions in Courts in the United States 11.04
B. The U.S. Supreme Court's Decision in *Bazzle* 11.08
C. The Class Arbitration Rules Established by the AAA and JAMS Following *Bazzle* 11.29
1. AAA Class Arbitration Rules 11.29
2. JAMS Class Arbitration Rules 11.35
D. The Effect of *Hall St. Associates v. Mattel* on Class Arbitrations 11.37
E. The Different Sources of Law Which One Must Consider in Determining Whether a Silent Arbitration Clause Permits a Class Arbitration 11.48
F. Federal Circuit Court and State Court Decisions Regarding Consolidation of Arbitrations and Class Arbitrations Before *Bazzle* 11.53
G. Clause-Construction Decisions by Arbitral Panels Adjudicating Class Arbitrations After *Bazzle* 11.55

H. The U.S. Supreme Court Decision in *Stolt-Neilsen S.A. v. AnimalFeeds International Corp* 11.65

I. Post-*Stolt-Neilsen* Decisions by Arbitration Tribunals Regarding Whether "Silent Clauses" Permit Class Action Arbitrations 11.71

J. Class-Certification Decisions by Arbitral Tribunals After *Bazzle* 11.73
1. Numerosity 11.76
2. Commonality 11.77
3. Typicality 11.78
4. Adequacy of Class Representative(s) 11.79
5. Adequacy of the Class Representative(s)' Counsel 11.80
6. Substantial Similarity of Arbitration Agreements 11.81
7. Predominance and Superiority of Claims 11.82

K. Arbitral Clauses Prohibiting Class Actions and Public Policy Arguments against Such Clauses Before the Supreme Court Decisions in *AT&T Mobility LLC v. Concepcion* and *American Express Co. v. Italian Colors Restaurant* 11.85

L. Decisions By Courts, Before *AT&T Mobility* and *American Express*, Regarding Whether State Arbitration Laws and Concepts of Public Policy are Preempted by the FAA 11.95

M. The Supreme Court Decisions in *AT&T Mobility* and *American Express* Regarding Whether Clauses Prohibiting Class Arbitrations are Against Public Policy and Whether a State's Public Policy is Preempted by the FAA 11.103

N. Decisions After *AT&T Mobility* and *American Express* Regarding Whether Clauses Prohibiting Class Arbitrations Are Against Public Policy or Whether a State's Public Policy Is Preempted by the FAA 11.110

O. Legislation Regarding Class-Action Arbitrations 11.115

P. Conclusion 11.116

12. Arbitration Hearings in New York
Edward G. Kehoe and Jessica Beess und Chrostin

A. Conducting the Arbitration 12.02
1. Major Arbitral Institutions in New York 12.02
2. Arbitral Tribunals 12.04
(a) Federal and state law 12.05
(b) Institutional rules 12.09
3. Tribunal Secretaries 12.10
(a) Federal and state law 12.11
(b) Institutional rules 12.13

4. Confidentiality and Privacy of Proceedings 12.17
(a) Federal and state law 12.18
(b) Institutional rules 12.21
5. Arbitrators' Lack of Authority to Disqualify Counsel in an Arbitration 12.26

B. Who May Appear to Represent Parties in Arbitration in New York 12.29

C. Witnesses 12.35
1. Written Witness Statements and Extent of Live Direct Testimony 12.36
(a) Federal and state law 12.37
(b) Institutional rules 12.38
2. Expert Witnesses 12.44
3. Depositions 12.49
4. Witness Attendance 12.52
(a) Obligation of a party to produce witnesses 12.53
(b) Subpoenas to compel witness attendance at a hearing 12.58
5. Witness Instructions 12.68
(a) Administering oaths to witnesses 12.69
(b) Adjournment and presence during testimony of other witnesses 12.72
6. Use of Exhibits 12.76
(a) Federal and state law 12.77
(b) Institutional rules 12.78
7. Closing Proceedings and Post-Hearing Submissions 12.82

D. Logistics 12.86
1. Travel, Accommodation, Catering 12.86
(a) Travel to and from New York 12.87
(b) Travel within New York 12.91
(c) Accommodation and entertainment 12.94
(d) Catering 12.97
2. Ancillary Services 12.98

13. Challenging and Enforcing International Arbitral Awards in New York
John V. H. Pierce, Janet R. Carter, and David N. Cinotti

A. Introduction 13.03
1. Options for the "Winner" and the "Loser" in International Arbitration 13.03
2. The Legal Regime Applicable to Actions to Challenge or Enforce International Arbitral Awards in New York 13.07

B. Procedural Issues Involved in Challenging and Enforcing International Arbitral Awards in New York 13.12
1. Actions in the Federal Courts in New York 13.13
(a) General procedural considerations 13.14
(b) Subject-matter jurisdiction 13.29
(c) Personal jurisdiction 13.40

(d) Establishing venue 13.60
(e) Removal of enforcement proceedings from state to federal court 13.65
2. Actions in New York State Courts 13.73
(a) Form and location of action 13.74
(b) Statute of limitations 13.76

C. Substantive Issues Involved in Challenging International Arbitral Awards in New York 13.78
1. Grounds for Nonrecognition under the New York Convention 13.78
(a) Absence of a valid arbitration agreement (Article V(1)(a)) 13.81
(b) Denial of opportunity to present one's case (Article V(1)(b)) 13.96
(c) Excess of authority (Article V(1)(c)) 13.98
(d) Violations of arbitral procedures or the law of the arbitral situs (Article V(1)(d)) 13.101
(e) Awards that are not binding or have been set aside (Article V(1)(e)) 13.104
(f) Awards that address nonarbitrable issues (Article V(2)(a)) 13.106
(g) Awards that violate public policy (Article V(2)(b)) 13.108
2. FAA Chapter 1 Grounds for Vacating International Arbitral Award 13.111
(a) Award procured by corruption, fraud, or undue means (Section 10(a)(1)) 13.113
(b) Partiality or corruption of the arbitrators (Section 10(a)(2)) 13.115
(c) Failure to adjourn or hear evidence; prejudicial misbehavior (Section 10(a)(3)) 13.119
(d) Exceeding jurisdiction (Section 10(a)(4)) 13.124
(e) Manifest disregard of the law 13.126
(f) Public policy 13.135
(g) Sanctions for frivolous attacks on arbitral awards 13.136
3. New York State Law Grounds for Vacating Awards 13.138
4. Choice of Arbitral Law When Resisting Enforcement of an Award Made in the United States 13.142

14. Enforcing Awards Involving Foreign Sovereigns
Brian King and Alexander Yanos

A. Introduction: The Unique Characteristics of Arbitrations Involving Sovereigns 14.01

B. The Legal Regime Applicable to the Enforcement of Arbitral Awards Against Sovereigns in New York 14.04
1. Sovereigns Usually Pay Arbitral Awards 14.05
2. The Recognition of Awards Rendered Against Sovereigns 14.12
(a) Recognition of awards subject to the New York Convention 14.12
(b) Recognition of ICSID awards in the United States is "automatic" 14.15
(c) A potential alternative track: recognition of a foreign court's recognition of the award 14.17

3. Sovereigns Enjoy Significant Immunities With Respect to the Enforcement of Arbitral Awards Against Them 14.19
4. Foreign Sovereigns Are Not Immune From Personal Jurisdiction and Service 14.27

C. Dealing With the Problem of Recalcitrant States 14.31
1. Predispute Protections 14.31
2. Prearbitration Attachment 14.33
(a) The requirement of explicit waiver 14.34
(b) Procedure for prearbitration attachment 14.40
3. Interim Measures from the Arbitral Tribunal 14.41
4. Prerecognition Attachment and Explicit Waiver 14.42
5. Postrecognition Attachment and Execution 14.51
6. What Kind of Assets May Be Attached? 14.56
(a) Debt and property subject to attachment 14.63
(b) Attaching the property of state-owned companies 14.64
(c) Garnishment of royalties or taxes 14.69
(d) Attachment of trust accounts 14.74

Appendices
1. Schedule of International Arbitration Conventions 539
2. Federal Arbitration Act 541
3. NY Civil Practice Law and Rules, Article 75 547
4. Supreme Court, New York County Commercial Division, Charles E. Ramos, Justice, International Arbitration Rules (2013) International Arbitration Part Rules—Part 53 553
5. Schedule of Arbitration Rules and Guidelines 555
6. AAA/ABA Code of Ethics for Arbitrators in Commercial Disputes 557
7. Schedule of New York City Bar Association Arbitration Reports 567

Index 569

TABLE OF CASES

34-35th Corp. v. 1-10 Indus. Associates, LLC 103 A.D.3d 709 (N.Y. App. Div. 2013)..... 10.02
401 Hotel, L.P. v. MTI/ Image Group, Inc., 674 N.Y.S.2d 318 (1st Dep't 1998).......... 10.29
407 E. 61st St. Garage v. Savoy Fifth Ave. Corp., 244 N.E.2d 37 (N.Y. 1968) 4.67
650 Fifth Ave., In Re, No. 08 CIV. 10934 KBF, 2014 WL 1516328 .... 14.59
805 Third Ave. Co. v. M.W. Realty Assoc., 448 N.E.2d 445 (N.Y. 1983)................. 4.20

A. Halcoussis Shipping Ltd. v. Golden Eagle Liberia Ltd., No. 88 CIV. 4500 (MJL), 1989 WL 115941 .... 6.109
A.G. Edwards & Sons v. Lobacz, 831 N.Y.S.2d 346 (App. Div. 2006) 13.140
A.G. Edwards & Sons, Inc. v. McCullough, 967 F.2d 1401 (9th Cir. 1992) 13.113
AAOT Foreign Economic Assoc. (VO) Technostroyexport v. International Dev. and Trade Servs., Inc., 139 F.3d 980 (2d Cir. 1998) 6.111
Abacus Fed. Sav. Bank v. ADT Sec. Servs., Inc., 18 N.Y.3d 675 (2012) 10.26
Abduljaami v. Legalmatch.com, Inc., No. 05 Civ. 94642006, U.S. Dist. LEXIS 26327 (S.D.N.Y. 2006).. 6.19
ABKCO Indus., Inc. v. Apple Films, Inc., 39 N.Y.2d 670 (1976)....................... 14.69
Abram Landau Real Estate v. Bevona, 123 F.3d 69 (2d Cir. 1997) 6.71
Abu Dhabi Comm. Bank PJSC v. Saad Trading, Contracting & Fin. Servs. Co., 986 N.Y.S.2d 454 (1st Dep't 2014) 13.75
ACE Am. Ins. Co., In Re, 6 Misc.3d 1005(A) (N.Y. Sup. Ct. 2004)................ 3.43, 3.40
ACE Capital Re Overseas Ltd. v. Cent. United Life Ins. Co., 307 F.3d 24 (2d Cir. 2002) 4.47, 7.95, 10.49, 13.93
Aceros Pefabricados, SA v. TradeArbed, Inc., 282 F.3d 92 (2d Cir. 2002) 11.15
Acosta v. Master Maint. & Constr., Inc., 52 F. Supp. 2d 699 (M.D. La. 1999)........... 13.72
Acquaire v. Canada Dry Bottling, 906 F. Supp. 819 (E.D.N.Y. 1995).................... 6.20
Action Indus., Inc. v. U.S. Fid. & Guar. Co., 358 F.3d 337 (5th Cir. 2004) 13.145
Adams v. Gillig, 92 N.E. 670 (N.Y. 1910) 4.53
Adams v. Linblad Travel, Inc., 730 F.2d 89 (2d Cir. 1984)...................... 10.03, 10.11
Addressing Sys. & Prods., Inc. v. Friedman, 59 A.D.3d 359 (2009) 10.23
Adler & Shaykin v. Wachner, 721 F. Supp. 472 (S.D.N.Y. 1988)........................ 4.60
Aetna Cas. & Sur. Co. v. LFO Constr. Corp., 615 N.Y.S.2d 389 (1st Dep't 1994) 4.52
Aetna Life & Casualty Co. v. Slekardis, 34 N.Y.2d 182 (1974)........................ 7.107
Af-Cap Inc. v. Chevron Overseas (Congo) Ltd., 475 F.3d 1080 (9th Cir. 2007).....14.59, 14.73
Af-Cap Inc. v. Republic of Congo, 383 F.3d 361 (5th Cir. 2004) 14.69, 14.71
Af-Cap Inc. v. Republic of Congo, 462 F.3d 417 (5th Cir. 2006) 14.61
Ahern v. South Buffalo Ry. Co., 104 N.E.2d 898 (N.Y. 1952), aff'd, 344 U.S. 367 (1953).... 4.14
Ahlstrom Mach. Inc. v. Associated Airfreight Inc., 708 N.Y.S.2d 497 (3d Dep't 2000)..... 4.14
Aioi Nissay Dowa Ins. Co. v. ProSight Specialty Mgmt. Co., No. 12 Civ. 3274 (JPO), 2012 WL 3583176.. 9.59
Aircraft Braking Sys. Corp. v. Local 856, 97 F.3d 155 (6th Cir. 1996)..........6.52, 6.57, 6.91
Albatross S.S. Co. v. Manning Bros., 95 F. Supp. 459 (S.D.N.Y. 1951).................. 8.16
Albrecht Chem. Co. v. Anderson Trading Corp., 84 N.E.2d 625 (N.Y. 1949)............. 4.16
Alexander v. Chesapeake Appalachia, LLC, 839 F. Supp. 2d 544 (N.D.N.Y. 2012) 7.25
Alexander Julian, Inc. v. Mimco, Inc., No. 00 Civ. 4131(DC), 2001 WL 477010........ 13.119
Alexandria Real Estate Equities, Inc. v. Fair, 2011 WL 6015646 (S.D.N.Y. 2011)......... 12.19

Alfa Laval U.S. Treasury Inc. v. Nat'l Union Fire Ins. Co. of Pittsburgh, PA, 857 F. Supp. 2d 404 (S.D.N.Y. 2012). 1.39
Allendale Mut. Ins. Co. v. Bull Data Sys., Inc., 10 F.3d 425 (7th Cir. 1993) 7.133
Alliance Bernstein Inv. Research & Mgmt., Inc. v. Schaffran, 445 F.3d 121 (2d Cir. 2006) 11.14
Allied-Bruce Terminix Cos. v. Dobson, 513 U.S. 265 (1995) 1.04, 6.15, 9.12, 13.07
Allstate Ins. Co. and Global Reinsurance Corp., In Re, 2006 WL 2289999 . . . . . . 3.45
Alvenus Shipping Co. v. Delta Petroleum (U.S.A.), 876 F. Supp. 482 (S.D.N.Y. 1994) 8.34
Am. Centennial Ins. Co. v. Arion Ins. Co., No. 88 Civ. 1665 (RWS), 1990 WL 52295. . . . . 1.94
Am. Centennial Ins. Co. v. Nat'l. Cas. Co., 951 F.2d 207 (6th Cir. 1991) 11.53
Am. Constr. Mach. & Equip. Corp. v. Mechanised Constr. of Pak. Ltd., 659 F. Supp. 426 (S.D.N.Y. 1987), aff'd, 828 F.2d 117 (2d Cir. 1987) 13.61, 13.81
Am. Exp. Fin. Advisors Sec. Litig., In Re, 672 F.3d 113 (2d Cir. 2011). 1.61
Am. Express Bank, Ltd. v. Uniroyal, Inc., 164 A.D.2d, 275 (1st Dep't 1990) 4.03
Am. Express Co. v. Italian Colors Rest., 133 S. Ct. 2304 (2013) 3.37, 9.07, 11.30, 11.105
Am. Indep. Ins. Co. v. Art of Healing Med., P.C., 961 N.Y.S.2d 240 (App. Div. 2013) 9.07
Am. List Corp. v. U.S. News & World Report, Inc., 549 N.E.2d 1161 (N.Y. 1989) 10.15
Am. Med. Sys., In Re, 75 F.3d 1069 (6th Cir. 1996) 11.78
Am. Safety Equip. v. J.P. Maguire & Co., 391 F.2d 821 (2d Cir. 1968) 7.121
American Bureau of Shipping v. Tencara Shipyard S.p.A., 170 F.3d 349 (2d Cir. 1999). 3.24, 7.76
American Const. Machinery & Equipment Corp. Ltd. v. Mechanised Const. of Pakistan Ltd., 659 F. Supp. 426 (S.D.N.Y. 1987) 6.100–6.102
American Home Assurance Co. v. Clearwater Ins. Co., 39 Misc.3d 184, 958 N.Y.S.2d 870 (Sup. Ct. N.Y. Co. 2013). 5.74
Amtel Corp. v. LM Ericsson Telefon, AB, 371 F. Supp. 2d 402 (S.D.N.Y. 2005) 3.39
Andersen Consulting Business Unit Member Firms v. Andersen Worldwide Societe Co-op., No. 98 CIV. 1030 (JGK), 1998 WL 122590 . . . . . . 8.34
Anderson v. SAM Airlines, 939 F. Supp. 167 (E.D.N.Y. 1996). 4.11
Anhui Provincial Import and Export v. Hart Enters. Int'l, 96 Civ. 128 (LAK), 1996 WL 229872 (S.D.N.Y. 1996). 1.96
Answers in Genesis of Kentucky, Inc. v. Creation Ministries Intern., Ltd., 556 F.3d 459 (6th Cir. 2009). 7.133
APL Co. PTE Ltd. v. Blue Water Shipping U.S. Inc. 592 F.3d 108 (2d Cir. 2010) 10.22
Apollo Computer, Inc. v. Berg, 886 F.2d 469 (1st Cir. 1989) 6.54, 6.66, 7.35, 7.68
Apple & Eve, LLC v. Yantai North Andre Juice Co. Ltd., 499 F. Supp. 2d 245 (E.D.N.Y. 2007) 6.16
Application of Corporación Selee de Venezuela, SA v. Selee Corporation, 7 Misc. 3d 1013(A) (N.Y. Sup. Ct. 2005) 1.31
Application of Owl Shipping, LLC, In Re, Civ. Act. No. 15-5655 (AET)(DEA), 2014 WL 5320192. . . . . . 9.77
Applied Energetics, Inc. v. NewOak Capital Markets, LLC, 645 F.3d 522 (2d Cir. 2011). . . 13.45
Applied Indust. Materials Corp. v. Ovalar Makine Ticaret Ve Sanayi, A.S., 492 F.3d 132 (2d Cir. 2007) 5.85, 13.116
Apton v. Barclays Bank, 91 N.Y.S.2d 589 (N.Y. Sup. Ct. 1949) 4.11
Arakawa v. Japan Network Group, 56 F. Supp. 2d 349 (S.D.N.Y. 1999). 1.12
Arbitration Between Douglas Brazell v. American Color Graphics, Inc., 2000 WL 364997 (S.D.N.Y. 2000) 3.39
Arbitration between Halcot Navigation Ltd. Partnership and Stolt-Nielsen Trans. Group, BV, In Re, 491 F. Supp. 2d 413 (S.D.N.Y. 2007) 6.64
Arbitration Between Norfolk S. Corp., Norfolk S. Ry. Co. & Gen. Sec. Ins. Co. & Ace Berm. Ltd., In Re, 626 F. Supp. 2d 882 (N.D. Ill. 2009) 9.77
Arcadian Phosphates, Inc. v. Arcadian Corp., 884 F.2d 69 (2d Cir. 1989) 4.19
Areca, Inc. v. Oppenheimer & Co., Inc., 960 F. Supp. 52 (S.D.N.Y. 1997) 8.18

Argentine Republic v. Nat'l Grid Plc, 2010 U.S. Dist. LEXIS 142052 (D.D.C. June 7, 2010) 14.03
ARI & Co., Inc. v. Regent Int'l Corp., 273 F. Supp. 2d 518 (S.D.N.Y. 2003) 4.50
Arriba Ltd v. Petroleos Mexicanos, 962 F.2d 538 (5th Cir. 1992) 7.75
Arthur Andersen LLP v. Carlisle, 129 S.Ct. 1896 (2009); 556 U.S. 624, 631 (2009) 7.24, 7.70, 7.116
AS v. Storm LLC, 2007 WL 3274699 (S.D.N.Y. 2007). 6.51
Ashland Mgmt. Inc. v. Janien, 624 N.E.2d 1007 (N.Y. 1993); 82 N.Y.2d 395, 404 (2d Cir. 1993). 10.05, 10.36
Astoria Fed. Sav. & Loan Ass'n v. Rambalakos, 372 N.Y.S.2d 689 (2d Dep't 1975) 10.44
Astoria Medical Group v. Health Insurance Plan, 11 N.Y.2d 128 (1962) 3.27
Astra Footwear Industry v. Harwyn International, Inc., 442 F. Supp. 907 (S.D.N.Y. 1978), aff'd 578 F.2d 1366 (2d Cir. 1978). 5.29
Astra Oil Co., Inc. v. Rover Navigation, Ltd., 344 F.3d 276 (2d Cir. 2003). 6.23
AT&T Mobility LLC v. Concepcion, 563 U.S. 333 (2011). 1.08, 3.37, 11.103
AT&T Technologies, Inc. v. Communications Workers of America, 475 U.S. 643 (1986) 6.03, 6.22, 6.25, 6.65, 11.13
Atlas Chartering Servs., Inc. v. World Trade Group, Inc., 453 F. Supp. 861 (S.D.N.Y. 1978) 1.31
Augustea Impb Et Salvataggi v. Mitsubishi Corp., 126 F.3d 95 (2d Cir. 1997) 6.36
Aurelius Capital Partners, LP v. The Republic of Argentina, 584 F.3d 120 (2d Cir. 2009) 14.55–14.57, 14.69
Auten v. Auten, 124 N.E.2d 99 (N.Y. 1954) 4.09
Avant Petroleum, Inc. v. Pecten Arabian Ltd., 696 F. Supp. 42 (S.D.N.Y. 1988) 1.15
Aventine Inv. Mgmt., Inc. v. Can. Imperial Bank of Commerce, 697 N.Y.S.2d 128 (2d Dep't 1999) 4.49
Aviall, Inc. v. Ryder Sys., Inc., 110 F.3d 892 (2d Cir. 1997) 13.115
Avraham v. Shigur Express, Ltd., No. 91 Civ. 1238 (SWK), 1991 U.S. Dist. LEXIS 12267. . . . . 6.101
AXA Equitable Life Ins. Co. v. Kalina, 956 N.Y.S.2d 743 (App. Div. 2012) 9.06
Azavedo v. Royal Caribbean Cruises, Ltd., 4 F. Supp. 3d 1357 (S.D. Fla. 2014) 6.10

B.L. Harbert Int'l, L.L.C. v. Hercules Steel Co., 441 F. 3d 905 (11th Cir. 2006) 1.92, 11.39, 13.136
B-S Steel of Kansas, Inc. v. Texas Industries, Inc., 321 F. Supp. 2d 1214 (D. Kan. 2004) 6.52, 6.87
B.V. v. Conscorcio Barr, S.A., 267 F. Supp. 2d 1335 (S.D. Fla. 2003) 6.63
Baar & Beards, Inc. v. Oleg Cassini, Inc., in re, 282 N.E.2d 624 (N.Y. 1972). 6.111
Babcock v. Jackson, 191 N.E.2d 279 (N.Y. 1963) 4.09
Babcock Borsig AG, In Re, 583 F. Supp. 2d 233 (D. Mass. 2008). 9.77
Baesler v. Cont'l. Grain Co., 900 F.2d 1193 (8th Cir. 1990). 11.53
Bahrain Telecomms. Co. v. Discoverytel, Inc., 476 F. Supp. 2d 176 (D. Conn. 2007). 8.33
Bailey Shipping Ltd. v. American Bureau of Shipping, No. 12 Civ. 5959 (KPF), 2014 WL 1282504 (S.D.N.Y. Mar. 28, 2014) 8.21
Baker Marine (Nig.) Ltd. v. Chevron (Nig.) Ltd., 191 F.3d 194 (2d Cir. 1999) 13.06
Ball v. Cross, 132 N.E. 106 (N.Y. 1921) 4.11
Ballard v. Parkstone Energy, LLC, No. 06 Civ. 13099, 2007 U.S. Dist. LEXIS 86957 (S.D.N.Y Nov. 27, 2007) 6.31–6.32
Banco de Santander Central Hispano, S.A. v. Consalvi International Inc. 425 F. Supp. 2d 421 (S.D.N.Y. 2006) 13.70
Banco de Seguros del Estado v. Mut. Marine Office, Inc., 344 F.3d 255 (2d Cir. 2003) 1.87, 8.14, 13.112, 14.37, 14.41
Bander v. Grossman, 161 Misc. 2d 119 (N.Y. Sup. Ct. 1994) 10.07
Bank Brussels Lambert v. Fiddler Gonzales & Rodriquez, 305 F.3d 120 (2d Cir. 2002) 13.53

Bank Julius Baer & Co. v. Waxfield, Ltd. 424 F.3d 278 (2d Cir. 2005) 13.44
Bank v. WorldCom, Inc., 2002 WL 171629, 2002 N.Y. Slip Op. 40009(U) (N.Y. Sup. Ct. Jan. 24, 2002) 12.07
Barbier v. Shearson Lehman Hutton Inc., 948 F.2d 117 (2d Cir. 1991) 13.142
Barchha v. TapImmune Inc., No. 12 Civ. 8530 (PKC), 2013 WL 120639 (S.D.N.Y. 2013) 8.21
Baronoff v. Kean Development Company, 818 N.Y.S.2d 421 (N.Y. Sup. Ct. 2006) 1.43
Base Metal Trading, Ltd. v. OJSC "Novokuznetsky Aluminum Factory," 283 F.3d 208 (4th Cir. 2002) 13.41, 13.57
Basil Castrovinci Associates, Inc. v. District 65 Pension Plan, 16 A.D.3d 493, 791 N.Y.S. 2d 601 (N.Y. App. Div. 2005) 12.07
Bausch & Lomb Inc. v. Bressler, 977 F.2d 720 (2d Cir. 1992) 4.35–4.36, 10.31, 10.34
Bazak Int'l. Corp. v. Tarrant Apparel Grp., 491 F. Supp. 2d 403 (S.D.N.Y. 2007) 4.13
Bazzle v. Green Tree Fin. Corp., 569 S.E.2d 349 (S.C. 2002) 11.08
Beal v. Stern, 184 F.3d 117 (2d Cir. 1999) 7.135
Bear, Stearns & Co. v. 1109580 Ontario, Inc., 409 F.3d 87 (2d Cir. 2005) 6.91, 13.129
Beatie & Osborn L.L.P. v. Patriotic Sci. Co., 431 F. Supp. 2d 367 (S.D.N.Y. 2006) 4.07
Bechtel do Brasil Construcoes Ltda. v. UEG Araucaria Ltda., 638 F.3d 150 (2d Cir. 2011) 1.39
Becker Autoradio U.S.A. v. Becker Autoradiowerk GmbH, 585 F.2d 39 (3d Cir. 1978) 3.26
Beggs v. Dougherty Overseas, Inc., 287 F.2d 80 (2d Cir. 1961) 10.20
Beiser v. Weyler, 284 F.3d 665 (5th Cir. 2002) 13.69
Bell v. Cendant Corp., 293 F.3d 563 (2d Cir. 2002) 6.15, 6.32, 7.83
Bell Aerospace Co. Div. of Textron v. Local 516, 500 F.2d 921 (2d Cir. 1974) 8.17, 13.120
Benihana of Tokyo, LLC v. Benihana Inc. 2014 WL 3631759 .... 7.91
Benjamin v. Traffic Executive Association Eastern Railroads, 869 F.2d 107 (2d Cir. 1989) 6.33
Berg v. Berg. 926 N.Y.S.2d 568 (N.Y. App. Div. 2011) 10.51
Bergesen v. Joseph Muller Corp., 710 F.2d 928 (2d Cir. 1983) 1.86, 3.59, 6.63, 13.09, 14.12
Berley Indus., Inc. v. City of New York, 385 N.E.2d 281 (1978) 10.02
Bernstein v. Felske, 533 N.Y.S.2d 538 (2d Dep't. 1988) 4.19, 4.64
Bernstein v. On-Line Software Int'l, Inc., 648 N.Y.S.2d 602 (App. Div. 1996) 9.61
Best Concrete Mix Corp. v. Lloyd's of London Underwriters, 413 F. Supp. 2d 180 (E.D.N.Y. 2006) 13.32
Best Van Lines, Inc. v. Walker, 490 F.3d 239 (2d Cir. 2007) 13.53
Betts v. McKenzie Check Advance of Florida, Case No. CL 01-320 AI (Fla. Cir. Ct. 2008) 11.86
BG Group PLC v. Republic of Arg., 134 S. Ct. 1198 (2014) 0.45, 3.20, 11.13, 13.82, 13.89, 14.50
Bi-Econ. Mkt., Inc. v. Harleysville Ins. Co. of N.Y., 886 N.E.2d 127 (N.Y. 2008) 10.04, 10.11, 10.15
Bidermann Indus. Licensing, Inc. v. Avmar N.V., 173 A.D.2d 401, 507 N.Y.S.2d 33 (1st Dep't 1991) 12.27
Biggs v. U.S. Fire Ins. Co., 611 S.W.2d 624 (Tex. 1981) 7.74
Billups v. Bankfirst, 294 F. Supp. 2d 1265 (M.D. Ala. 2003) 11.90
Biotronik A.G. v. Conor Medsystems Ireland, Ltd., 22 N.Y.3d 799 (2014) 10.19
Bippley v. Hollenback, 644 N.Y.S.2d 852, 853–54 (3d Dep't 1996) 10.04
Birch Shipping Corp. v. Embassy of United Republic of Tanzania, 507 F. Supp. 311 (D.D.C. 1980) 14.54, 14.74
Bishop v. Smith Barney Inc., 1998 U.S. Dist. LEXIS 1239, *26 (S.D.N.Y. 1998) 6.34
Bisnoff v. King, 154 F. Supp. 2d 630 (S.D.N.Y. 2001) 13.122
Blinds to Go (U.S.), Inc. v. Times Plaza Dev., L.P., 88 A.D.3d 838, 840, 931 N.Y.S.2d 105 (2011) 10.20, 10.37
Blue Cross & Blue Shield United v. Marshfield Clinic, 152 F.3d 588 (7th Cir. 1998) 9.71
Blue Cross of Cal. v. Superior Court of LA County, 67 Cal. App. 4th 42 (Cal. Ct. App. 1998) 11.53

Blue Ridge Invs., LLC v. Republic of Arg., 902 F. Supp. 2d 367 (S.D.N.Y. 2012), aff'd, 735 F.3d 72 (2d Cir. 2013) 14.15, 14.23, 14.50
Blumenthal v. Merrill Lynch, Pierce, Fenner & Smith, Inc., 910 F.2d 1049 (2d Cir. 1990) 8.35
Bob Schultz Motors, Inc. v. Kawasaki Motors Corp., U.S.A., 334 F.3d 721 (8th Cir. 2002).. 6.85
Bock v. Drexel Burnham Lambert, 143 Misc.2d 542 (N.Y. Sup. Ct. 1989) 3.45
Booth v. Spuyten Duyvil Rolling Mill Co., 60 N.Y. 487 (1875)........................ 10.02
Borden Inc. v. Meiji Milk Products Co., 919 F.2d 822 (2d Cir. 1990)...........3.51, 8.16, 8.33
Borsack v. Chalk & Vermilion Fine Arts Ltd., 974 F. Supp. 293 (S.D.N.Y. 1997)..........1.64, 6.16, 7.24
Botany Industries, Inc. v. New York Joint Bd., Amalgamated Clothing Workers of America, 375 F. Supp. 485 (S.D.N.Y. 1974) 6.97
Bourne v. Walt Disney Co., 68 F.3d 621 (2d Cir. 1995) 4.61
Bowen v. Amoco Pipeline Co., 254 F.3d 925 (10th Cir. 2001).......................... 3.56
BP Exploration Co. (Libya) v. Gov't of the Libyan Arab Republic, 53 I.L.R. 297 (1973)... 14.08
Brandeis Intsel Ltd v. Calabrian Chemicals Corp., 656 F. Supp. 160 (S.D.N.Y. 1987)..1.97, 13.110
Brandon, Jones, Sandall, Zeide, Kohn, Chalal & Musso, P.A. v. MedPartners, Inc., 312 F.3d 1349 (11th Cir. 2002).. 6.10
Braten v. Bankers Trust Co., 456 N.E.2d 802 (N.Y. 1983) 4.61
Breezevale Ltd. v. Dickinson, 262 A.D.2d 248 (N.Y. App. Div. 1999) 14.69
Brener v. Becker Paribas Inc., 628 F. Supp. 442 (S.D.N.Y. 1985)........................ 6.20
Brennan v. Opus Bank, 2015 WL 4731378 (9th Cir. May 8, 2015).......................7.52
Bricklayers & Allied Craftworkers Int'l Union v. Jocanz, Inc., No. 07-2562 (GEB), 2007 WL 1876508 (D.N.J. 2007).. 13.23
Bridas S.A.P.I.C. v. Government of Turkmenistan, 345 F.3d 347 (5th Cir. 2003) 7.74
Bridgestone/Firestone, Inc. v. Recovery Credit Servs., Inc., 98 F.3d 13 (2d Cir. 1996) 4.56
Brink's Inc. v. New York, 717 F.2d 700 (2d Cir. 1983) 10.27
Bristol-Myers Squibb Co. v. SR International Business Insurance Company Ltd., 354 F. Supp. 2d 499 (S.D.N.Y. 2005) 7.95
British Ins. Co. of Cayman v. Water St. Ins. Co., 93 F. Supp. 2d 506 (S.D.N.Y. 2000) 6.92, 8.17, 14.37
Broder v. Cablevision Sys. Corp., 329 F. Supp. 2d 551 (S.D.N.Y. 2004), aff'd, 418 F.3d 187 (2d Cir. 2005).. 4.13
Brown v. W. Ry. Co. of Ala., 338 U.S. 294 (1949) 13.76
Brushton-Moira Cent. Sch. Dist. v. Fred H. Thomas Assoc., P.C., 692 N.E.2d 551 (N.Y. 1998)... 4.34
Bryan v. John Bean Div. of FMC Corp., 566 F.2d 541 (5th Cir. 1978)................... 9.71
Brylgrove Ltd. v. Tompkins, PLC, 568 N.Y.S.2d 799 (1st Dep't 1991) 10.34
Buckeye Check Cashing, Inc. v. Cardegna, 546 U.S. 440, 126 S. Ct. 1204 (2006) 0.41, 1.13, 6.08, 6.15, 6.19, 6.78, 7.39, 11.13, 13.93
Buques Centroamericanos, S.A. v. Refinadora Costarricense de Petroleos, S.A., No. 87 Civ. 3256 (DNE), 1989 U.S. Dist. LEXIS 5429.......................... 6.102, 13.81
Burns Jackson Miller Summit & Spitzer v. Lindner, 451 N.E.2d 459 (N.Y. 1983) 4.57
Burton v. Bush, 614 F.2d 389 (4th Cir. 1980).. 8.38
Bykowsky v. Eskenazi, 72 A.D.3d 590 (N.Y. App. Div. 2010) 10.20

Cabinetree of Wisc., Inc. v. Kraftmaid Cabinetry, Inc., 50 F.3d 388 (7th Cir. 1995)....... 6.10
Cable Connection, Inc. v. DIRECTV, 190 P.3d 586 (Cal. 2008) 1.28
Cable Connections, Inc. v. Hughes Elecs. Corp., AAA Case No. 11-145-00752-04 (2005) 11.54
Cablevision Sys. Corp. v. East Hampton, 862 F. Supp. 875 (E.D.N.Y. 1994), aff'd, 57 F.3d 1062 (2d Cir. 1995)...4.23–4.24
CAE Indus. Ltd. v. Aerospace Holdings Co., 741 F. Supp. 388 (S.D.N.Y. 1989)...... 1.16, 5.30

Caley v. Gulfstream Aerospace Corp., 428 F.3d 1359 (11th Cir. 2005) 11.85
Campaniello Imports Ltd. v. Saporiti Italia S.p.A., 117 F.3d 655 (2d Cir. 1997) 6.20, 7.14, 13.93
Campbell v. Citibank, N.A., 302 A.D.2d 150 (1st Dep't 2003) 10.51
Campeau Corp. v. May Dept. Stores Co., 723 F. Supp. 224 (S.D.N.Y. 1989) 1.15
Can. Life Assurance Co. v. Converium Ruckversicherung (Deutschland) AG, Civ. No. 06-3800 (GEB), 2007 WL 1726565 .... 13.25
Canwest Global Commc'n Corp. v. Mirkaei Tikshoret Ltd., 9 Misc. 3d 845 (N.Y. Sup. Ct. 2005) 3.54
Capgemini v. Sorensen, No. 04 Civ. 7584 (JGK), 2005 WL 1560482 .... 13.99
Carefree Bldg. Prod., Inc. v. Belina, 564 N.Y.S.2d 852 (3d Dep't 1991) 4.25
Cargill Ferrous Int'l v. Sea Phoenix MV, 325 F.3d 695 (5th Cir. 2003) 6.36
Cargill Int'l S.A. v. M/T Pavel Dybenko, 991 F.2d 1012 (2d Cir. 1993) 14.45
Carte Blanche (Singapore) Pte, Ltd v. Diners Club Int'l, Inc., 2 F.3d 24 (2d Cir. 1993) 7.75
Carvel Corp. v. Diversified Mgmt. Grp., Inc., 930 F.2d 228 (2d Cir. 1991) 4.49
Cary Oil Co., Inc. v. MG Ref. & Mktg, Inc., 90 F. Supp. 2d 401 (S.D.N.Y. 2000) ... 4.24, 4.30
Cary Plastic Packaging Corp. v. Merrill, Lynch, Pierce, Fenner & Smith, Inc., 903 F.2d. 176 (1990) 11.07
Caterpillar Inc. v. Williams, 482 U.S. 386 (1987) 13.69
Catlin v. United States, 324 U.S. 229 (1945) 2.98
Cayea v. Lake Placid Granite Co., 665 N.Y.S.2d 127 (3d Dep't 1997) 4.14
Cayuga Harvester, Inc. v. Allis-Chalmers Corp., 465 N.Y.S.2d 606 (4th Dep't 1983) 10.03
CBS Corp. v. WAK Orient Power & Light Ltd., 168 F. Supp. 2d. 403 (E.D. Pa. 2001) 6.99
CD Partners, LLC v. Grizzle, 424 F.3d 795 (8th Cir. 2005) 7.64
CE Int'l Res. Holdings LLC v. S.A. Minerals, Ltd., 2012 U.S. Dist. LEXIS 176158, at *11 (S.D.N.Y. 2012) 3.52
Certain Underwriters at Lloyd's London v. Argonaut Ins. Co., 500 F.3d 571 (7th Cir. 2007) 1.55, 6.64
Champ v. Siegel Trading Co., 55 F.3d 269 (7th Cir. 1995) 11.53
Channel Home Ctrs. v. Grossman, 795 F.2d 291 (3d Cir. 1986) 4.19
Chase Bank USA, N.A. v. Hale, 859 N.Y.S.2d 342 (Sup. Ct. 2008) 9.52
Chelsea Square Textiles v. Bombay Dyeing and Mfg., 189 F.3d 289 (2d Cir. 1999) ... 1.10, 1.67, 6.15, 6.38
Chem. Bank v. Stahl, 712 N.Y.S.2d 452 (1st Dep't 2000) 4.49
Chen-Oster v. Goldman, Sachs & Co., 785 F. Supp. 2d 394 (S.D.N.Y. 2011) 11.85
Chevron Corp., In Re, 633 F.3d 153 (3d Cir. 2011) 9.77
Chicago Typographical Union No. 16 v. Chicago Sun-Times, Inc., 935 F.2d 1501 (7th Cir. 1991) 3.56
China Auto Care, LLC v. China Auto Care (Caymans), 859 F. Supp. 2d 582 (S.D.N.Y. 2012) 7.95
China Minmetals Materials Imp. & Exp. Co. v. Chi Mei Corp., 334 F.3d 274 (3d Cir. 2003) 6.95, 6.102–6.104, 13.94
China Trade & Dev. Corp. v. M.V. Choong Yong, 837 F.2d 33 (2d Cir. 1987) 7.130, 7.134, 8.39
Chios Charm Shipping Co. v. Rionda, No. 93 CIV. 6313 (SS), 1994 U.S. Dist. LEXIS 4571 (S.D.N.Y. 1994) 6.99
Chiron Corp. v. Ortho Diagnostic Sys., Inc., 207 F.3d 1126 (9th Cir. 2000) 6.34, 11.101
Cho v. 401–403 57th Street Realty Corp., 752 N.Y.S.2d 55 (1st Dep't 2002) 4.43
Choctaw Generation Ltd. Partnership v. American Home Assur. Co., 271 F.3d 403 (2d Cir. 2001) 6.23, 6.70, 7.64, 7.78
Choice Hotels Intern., Inc. v. Felizardo, 278 F. Supp. 2d 590 (D.Md. 2003) 6.62
Chromalloy Aeroservices v. The Arab Republic of Egypt, 939 F. Supp. 907 (D.D.C. 1996) 1.98, 13.06
Cia De Navegacion Omsil, S.A. v. Hugo Neu Corporation, 359 F.Supp. 898 (S.D.N.Y. 1973) 3.27

Ciago v. Ameriquest Mortgage Co., 295 F. Supp. 2d 324 (S.D.N.Y. 2003) 9.12
Cingular Cases, In Re, No. D047603 2007 WL 93229 (Cal. Ct. App. 2007)............ 11.86
Circuit City Stores, Inc. v. Adams, 532 U.S. 105 (2001) 1.12, 13.07
Circus Prods., Inc. v. Int'l Impresarios, No. 90 Civ. 0414, 1990 WL 55684 .... 4.48
Citibank v. Plapinger, 485 N.E.2d 974 (N.Y. 1985) 4.63
Citibank, N.A. v. Barclays Bank, PLC, 2013 WL 6153258 (S.D.N.Y. 2013) 10.43
Citifinancial, Inc. v. Newton, 359 F. Supp. 2d 545 (S.D. Miss. 2005)................... 7.35
Citigroup Global Markets, Inc. v. Bacon, 562 F. 3d 349 (5th Cir. 2009) 1.92, 13.133
Citizens Bank v. Alafabco, Inc., 539 U.S. 52 (2003) 7.25, 11.15
City of Newark v. Law Dep't of the City of N.Y., 760 N.Y.S. 2d 431 (N.Y. App. Ct. 2003) 12.20
Clark-Fitzpatrick, Inc. v. Long Island R.R. Co., 516 N.E.2d 190 (N.Y. 1987)............ 4.51
Clark v. Merrill Lynch, Pierce, Fenner & Smith, Inc., 924 F.2d 550 (4th Cir. 1991)........ 6.36
CMS Gas Transmission Company v. Republic of Argentina, No. 08 Civ. 3169 (S.D.N.Y. Apr. 2, 2008) 14.58
Coady v. Ashcraft & Gerel, 223 F.3d 1 (1st Cir. 2000) 6.32
Coady v. Cross Country Bank, Inc., 729 N.W.2d 732 (Wis. Ct. App. 2007)............. 11.86
Coca-Cola Bottling Co. v. Soft Drink & Brewery Workers Union Local 812, 242 F.3d 52 (2d Cir. 2001)... 13.135
Coenen v. R.W. Pressprich & Co., 453 F.2d 1209 (2d Cir. 1972)....................... 6.15
Coffey v. Dean Witter Reynolds, Inc., 891 F.2d 261 (10th Cir. 1989)................... 7.72
Cohan v. Sicular, 625 N.Y.S.2d 278 (2d Dep't 1995)............................... 4.62
Cohen v. S.A.C. Capital Advisors LLC, 11 Misc. 3d 1054(A), 815 N.Y.S. 2d 493, (N.Y. Sup. Ct. 2006).. 1.108
Coimex Trading (Suisse) S.A. v. Cargill Int'l S.A., No. 05 Civ. 2630 (LLS), 2005 U.S. Dist. LEXIS 9784 (S.D.N.Y. May 20, 2005)................................ 1.64
Cole v. Macklowe, 99 A.D.3d 595, 596, 953 N.Y.S.2d 21 (2012) 10.07
Coleman & Co. Secs., Inc. v. Giaquinto Family Trust, 236 F. Supp. 2d 288 (S.D.N.Y. 2002); No. 00 Civ. 1632(DC), 2000 WL 1683450 .... 1.107, 11.49, 13.152
Collins & Aikman Prods. Co. v. Building Sys., Inc., 58 F.3d 16 (2d Cir. 1995) 3.05, 7.55, 7.90, 10.49
Collins v. D.R. Horton, Inc., 505 F.3d 874 (9th Cir. 2007).......................... 11.39
Colon v. R. K. Grace & Co., 358 F.3d 1 (1st Cir. 2003) 6.36
Colonial Co-op. Ins. Co. (Muehlbauer), In Re, 46 A.D.3d 1012 (App. Div. Dec. 6, 2007)... 7.108
Comer v. Micor, Inc., 436 F.3d 1098 (9th Cir. 2006) 7.64
Comisión Ejecutiva, Hidroeléctrica Del Río Lempa v. Nejapa Power Co., No. 08-135-GMS, 2008 WL 4809035 .... 9.77
Commercial Union Ins. Co. v. Lines, 239 F. Supp. 2d 351 (S.D.N.Y. 2002) 9.59
Commissions Imp. Exp. S.A. v. Republic of the Congo, 757 F.3d 321 (D.C. Cir. 2014) 1.08, 14.17
Commonwealth Coatings Corp. v. Cont'l Cas. Co., 393 U.S. 145 (1968) 13.116
Commonwealth Ins. Co. v. Beneficial Corp., No. 87 Civ. 5056 (CSH), 1987 WL 17951 ... 9.12
Compagnie des Bauxites de Guinea v. Ins. Co. of N. America, 651 F.2d 877 (3d Cir. 1981), cert. denied, 457 U.S. 1105 (1982) 7.133, 13.103
Compagnie Noga D'Importation Et D'exp. S.A. v. Russian Fed'n, 361 F.3d 676 (2d Cir. 2004) 6.68, 6.99
Comprehensive Accounting Corp. v. Rudell, 760 F.2d 138 (7th Cir. 1985) 7.06
CompuCredit Corp. v. Greenwood et al., 132 S. Ct. 665 (2012) 0.43
Computer Assocs. Int'l, Inc. v. U.S. Balloon Mfg. Co., Inc., 782 N.Y.S.2d 117 (2d Dep't 2004).. 4.18
Computer Possibilities Unlimited, Inc. v. Mobil Oil Corp., 747 N.Y.S.2d 468 (1st Dep't 2002)... 4.26
COMSAT Corp. v. Nat'l Sci. Found., 190 F.3d 269 (4th Cir. 1999)........... 3.39, 8.38, 9.64
Comverse, Inc. v. American Telecommunications, Inc., 2006 WL 3016315 ....7.165

Concilla v. May, 625 N.Y.S.2d 346 (3d Dep't 1995) 4.14
Concord Reinsurance Co. v. Caja Nacional de Ahorro y Seguro, No. 93 Civ. 6606, 1994 WL 86401 .... 14.29, 14.46
Cong. Secs., Inc. v. Fiserv Secs., Inc., No. 02 Civ. 6593 (JSM), 2003 WL 21664678..... 13.119
Congregation Darech Amuno v. Blasof, 226 A.D.2d 236 (1st Dep't 1996) 8.41
Conn. Bank of Commerce v. Republic of Congo, 309 F.3d 240 (5th Cir. 2002).... 14.58–14.59, 14.72
Consarc Corp. v. Marine Midland Bank, N.A., 996 F.2d 568 (2d Cir. 1993) 4.16
Consolidation Coal Co. v. United Mine Workers of America, 213 F.3d 404 (7th Cir. 2000).. 3.23, 6.34, 6.57
Consorcio Ecuatoriano de Telecomunicaciones S.A. v. JAS Forwarding (USA), Inc., 747 F.3d 1262 (11th Cir. 2014) 9.77
Cont'l Cas. Co. v. Argentine Republic, 893 F. Supp. 2d 747 (E.D. Va. 2012) 14.03
Contec Corp. v. Remote Solution Co., 398 F.3d 205 (2d Cir. 2005)...... 6.66, 7.35, 7.52, 7.66, 11.14, 13.91
Contemporary Mission, Inc. v. Famous Music Corp., 557 F.2d 9182 Fed. R. Evid. Serv. 16 (2d Cir. 1977).. 10.02
ContiChem LPG v. Parsons Shipping Co., Ltd., 229 F.3d 426 (2d Cir. 2000) 3.51
Continental Chartering & Brokerage, Inc. v. T.J. Stevenson & Co., Inc., 678 F. Supp. 58 (S.D.N.Y. 1987) 8.45
Contship Containerlines, Ltd. v. PPG Industries, Inc., 2003 WL 1948807 (S.D.N.Y. 2003).. 3.49, 12.18
Cook Industries, Inc. v. C. Itoh & Co. (America) Inc., 449 F.2d 106 (2d Cir. 1971) 5.81
Cooper v. Ateliers de la Motobécane S.A., 57 N.Y.2d 408 (1982)..............3.51, 8.33, 8.43
Cooper v. QC Fin Services, Inc., 503 F. Supp. 2d 1266 (D. Ariz. 2007) 11.85
Corcoran v. Ardra Ins. Co., 567 N.E.2d 969 (N.Y. 1990)............................ 13.11
Corporacion Mexicana de Mantenimiento Integral ("COMMISA") v. Pemex Exploracion y Produccion ("PEP"), 962 F. Supp. 2d 642 (S.D.N.Y. 2013)................. 1.99, 13.06
Cortez Byrd Chips, Inc. v. Bill Harbert Constr. Co., 529 U.S. 193 (2000).............. 13.23
Cotton v. Slone, 4 F.3d 176 (2d Cir. 1993) 6.36, 7.97
County Natwest Sec. Corp., USA v. Jesup, Josephthal & Co., 180 A.D.2d 468 (1st Dep't 1992) 8.37
County of Sullivan v. Nezelek, Inc., 42 N.Y.2d 123 (NY 1977)....................... 11.50
County of Washington v. Counties of Warren & Washington Indus. Dev. Agency, No. 93-CV-0086, 1997 WL 152001 (N.D. N.Y. Mar. 31, 1997), aff'd, 2 Fed. Appx. 71, (2d Cir. 2001)... 10.02
Cragwood Managers, L.L.C. v. Reliance Ins. Co., 132 F. Supp. 2d 285 (S.D.N.Y. 2001) ... 8.18
Creative Waste Mgmt., Inc. v. Capitol Env't Servs., Inc., 429 F. Supp. 2d 582 (S.D.N.Y. 2006)... 10.02
Credit Suisse First Boston Corp. v. Pitofsky, 824 N.E.2d 929 (N.Y. 2005) 9.07
Creighton Ltd. v. Gov't of Qatar, 181 F.3d 118 (D.C. Cir. 1999)...................... 13.47
Croce v. Kurnit, 737 F.2d 229 (2d Cir. 1984)...................................... 4.04
CSP Techs., Inc. v. Hekal, 869 N.Y.S.2d 449 (App. Div. 2008).......................... 9.06
Cullman Ventura, Inc., In Re, 682 N.Y.S. 2d 391 (NY App. Div. 1998) 11.50
Cunningham v. Citigroup, Inc., No. Civ. 05-3476 2005 WL 3454312 (D.N.J. 2005)..... 11.88
Cuyahoga Equip. Corp., In Re, 980 F.2d 110 (2d Cir. 1992)......................... 13.69
Cyber Media Grp., Inc. v. Island Mortg. Network, Inc., 183 F. Supp. 2d 559 (E.D.N.Y. 2002) 4.50
Czarina, L.L.C. v. W.F. Poe Syndicate, 358 F.3d 1286 (11th Cir. 2004)................ 13.27

D.H. Blair & Co. v. Gottdiener, 462 F.3d 95 (2d Cir. 2006)......................... 13.18
Daebo Int'l Shipping Co. v. Americas Bulk Transp. (BVI) Ltd., No. 12 Civ. 4750 (PAE), 2013 WL 2149591 (S.D.N.Y. 2013) 1.90
Daiei, Inc. v. United States Shoe Corp., 755 F. Supp. 299 (D. Haw. 1991)............... 7.35
Daihitsu Motor Co. v. Terrain Vehicles, Inc., 13 F.3d 196 (7th Cir. 1993)................ 3.60

Daimler AG v. Bauman et al., 134 S.Ct. 746 (2014) 0.47, 13.54
Dalton v. Educ. Testing Serv., 663 N.E.2d 289 (N.Y. 1995). 4.49
Danann Realty Corp. v. Harris, 157 N.E.2d 597 (N.Y. 1959) 4.63
DaPuzzo v. Globalvest Management Company, L.P., 263 F. Supp. 2d 714 (S.D.N.Y. 2003). 1.33, 7.16, 7.20
Dardana Ltd. v. Yuganskneftegaz, 317 F.3d 202 (2d Cir. 2003). 13.5
Daubert v. Merrell Dow Pharmaceuticals, Inc., 509 U.S. 579 (1993) 2.70
David L. Threlkeld & Co. v. Metallgesellschaft Ltd., 923 F.2d 245 (2d Cir. 1991). . . .0.40, 1.64, 4.45, 6.04, 6.06, 6.16, 7.14–7.15
Davis v. A.O. Smith Corp., 262 A.D.2d 752 (3d Dep't 1999). 10.17
De Sapio v. Kohlmeyer, 321 N.E.2d 770 (N.Y. 1974); 35 N.Y.2d 402, 406 (1974) 3.39, 9.06
Dean v. Dean, 149 N.E. 844 (N.Y. 1925); Ball v. Cross, 132 N.E. 106 (N.Y. 1921) 4.11
Dean Witter Reynolds Inc. v. Byrd, 470 U.S. 213 (1985) 1.15, 7.14
Dean Witter Reynolds Inc. v. Trimble, 166 Misc.2d 40 (N.Y. Sup. Ct. 1995) 3.34
Deiulemar Compagnia Di Navigazione S.p.A. v. M/V Allegra, 198 F.3d 473 (4th Cir. 1999). 8.38, 9.64, 11.53
Del Costello v. Int'l Bhd. of Teamsters, 462 U.S. 151 (1983) 7.110
Del E. Webb Constr. v. Richardson Hosp. Auth., 823 F.2d 145 (5th Cir. 1987). 11.53
Del Nero v. Colvin, 111 A.D.3d 1250 (2013) 10.24
Delchi Carrier SpA. v. Rotorex Corp., 71 F.3d 1024 (2d Cir. 1995) 10.14
Delgado v. A. Korenegay Senior House HDFC, No. 07 Civ. 7761 (DC), 2008 WL 748848 . . . . 13.119
Deloitte Noraudit A/S v. Deloitte Haskins & Sells, U.S., 9 F.3d 1060 (2d Cir. 1993). 1.54, 7.14
Delta Mine Holding Co. v. AFC Coal Props., Inc., 280 F.3d 815 (8th Cir. 2001). 13.114
Democratic Republic of Congo v. FG Hemisphere Assocs., LLC, 508 F.3d 1062 (D.C. Cir. 2007) 14.28
Dewan v. Walia, 544 F. App'x 240 (4th Cir. 2013). 1.23
Dexter Bishop Co. v. B. Redmond & Son, Inc., 58 A.D.2d 755 (1st Dep't 1977) 10.07
DFP Mfg. Corp. v. Northrop Grumman Corp., 1999 WL 33458384 (E.D.N.Y. 1999). 4.17
Diamond Waterproofing Systems, Inc. v. 55 Liberty Owners Corp., 4 N.Y.3d 247 (2005) 1.04, 11.49
DiGhello v. Busconi, 673 F. Supp. 85 (D. Conn. 1987). 13.99
Digital Broadcast corp. v. Ladenburg, Thalmann & Co., Inc., 63 A.D.3d 647 (1st Dep't 2009). 10.20, 10.37
DigiTelCom, Ltd. v. Tele2 Sverige AB, 2012 WL 3065345. . . . . 13.136–13.137
DirecTV Latin Am., LLC v. RCTV Int'l Corp., 115 A.D.3d 539, 982 N.Y.S.2d 96 (2014) 10.20
DiRussa v. Dean Witter Reynolds Inc., 121 F.3d 818 (2d Cir. 1997) 9.59
Discover Bank v. Superior Court 113 P.3d 1100 (Cal. 2005) 11.92
District Council No. 9 v. APC Painting, Inc., 272 F. Supp. 2d 229 (S.D.N.Y. 2003). 6.68
Dobco, Inc. v. Mery Gates, Inc., Civ. No. 06-0699 (HAA), 2006 WL 2056799 (D.N.J. 2006). 13.24
Doctor's Associates Inc. v. Casarotto, 517 U.S. 681 (1996) 1.10, 1.75, 6.15, 11.15
Doctor's Associates Inc. v. Distajo, 66 F.3d 438 (2d Cir. 1995) 3.26, 6.10, 7.96, 8.32, 13.145
Doctor's Associates, Inc. v. Jabush, 89 F.3d 109 (2d Cir. 1996) 6.10
Doctor's Associates Inc. v. Stuart, 85 F.3d 975 (2d Cir. 1996) 13.46
Dodge v. Richmond, 196 N.Y.S.2d 477 (1st Dep't 1960), aff'd, 168 N.E.2d 531 (N.Y. 1960). 4.20
Dolgin Eldert Corp., In Re, 286 N.E.2d 228 (N.Y. 1972) 4.19
Dominium Austin Partners, LLC v. Emerson, 248 F.3d 720 (8th Cir. 2001). 11.53
Donald Rubin, Inc. v. Schwartz, 594 N.Y.S.2d 193 (1st Dep't 1993). 10.21
Doscher v. Sobel & Co., No. 14 CV 646(RMB)(GWG), 2014 WL 846773 . . . . 9.59
Downing v. Merrill Lynch, Pierce, Fenner & Smith, Inc., 725 F.2d 192 (2d Cir. 1984). 7.156
Drayer v. Kramer 572 F.2d 348 (2d Cir. 1978). 6.81

Dream Theater, Inc. v. Dream Theater, 124 Cal. App. 4th 547 (2004) 11.14
Drexel Burnham Lambert Inc. v. Ruebsamen, 139 A.D.2d 323 (1st Dep't 1988) . . . 8.37, 13.142
Duferco Int'l Steel Trading v. T. Klaveness Shipping A/S, 333 F.3d 383 (2d Cir. 2003) 8.22, 11.39, 13.127
Dumitru v. Princess Cruise Lines, Ltd., 732 F. Supp. 2d 328 (S.D.N.Y. 2010) 1.31, 6.10
Durant, Nichols, Houston, Hodgson & Cortese-Costa P.C. v. Dupont, 565 F.3d 56 (2d Cir. 2009) 13.29
Durst v. Abrash, 253 N.Y.S.2d 351 (N.Y.A.D. 1 Dept. 1964), aff'd 266 N.Y.S.2d 806 (N.Y. 1965) 6.20
Dynegy Midstream Servs. LP v. Trammochem, 451 F.3d 89 (2d Cir. 2006) 9.68

E.D. Jones & Co. v. American Stock Exchange, LLC, 22 A.D.3d 319 (1st Dep't 2005). 7.110
E.T.I. Euro Telecom International N.V. v. Republic of Bolivia, No. 08 Civ. 4247, 2008 WL 2940583 (S.D.N.Y. July 30, 2008) 14.66
Eagle v. Fred Martin Motor Co., 809 N.E.2d 1161 (Ohio Ct. App. 2004). 11.86
Edelist v. MBNA Am. Bank 790 A.2d 1249 (Del. Super. Ct. 2001) 11.90
Edge Grp. WAICCS LLC v. Sapir Grp. LLC, 705 F. Supp. 2d 304 (S.D.N.Y. 2010) 10.06
Edgewater Const. Co., Inc. v. 81 & 3 of Watertown, Inc., 769 N.Y.S.2d 343 (4th Dep't 2003) 4.25
Educ. Res. Inst., Inc. v. Piazza, 794 N.Y.S.2d 65 (2d Dep't 2005) 4.10
Edward D. Jones & Co., In Re, 10 Misc. 3d 1057(A), 809 N.Y.S. 2d 481 . . . . 1.108
Edward D. Jones & Company v. the American Stock Exchange, LLC, 22 A.D. 3d 319 (N.Y. App. Div. 2005) 1.41
Ehleiter v. Grapetree Shores, Inc., 482 F.3d 207 (3d Cir. 2007) 11.14
El Paso Corp. v. La Comisión Ejecutiva Hidroeléctrica Del Rio Lempa, 341 F. App'x 31 (5th Cir. 2009) 9.77
EM Ltd. v. Republic of Arg., No. 03 CIV. 2507 (TPG), 2009 WL 2568433; 389 Fed. Appx. 38, 42 (2d Cir. 2010) 14.69, 14.76
Emilio v. Sprint Spectrum L.P., 508 F. App'x 3 (2d Cir. 2013) 11.14
Empresa Generadora de Electricidad Itabo, S.A. v. Corporacion Dominica de Empresas Electricas Estatales, 2005 WL 1705080 . . . . .7.103, 7.165
Encyclopaedia Universalis S.A. v. Encyclopaedia Britannica, Inc., 403 F.3d 85 (2d Cir. 2005) 6.03, 6.64, 13.18, 13.81
Endriss v. Eklof Marine Corp., No. 96 Civ. 3137 (KMW), 1998 WL 1085911 . . . . .7.110
Engel (Refco, Inc.), In Re, 746 N.Y.S.2d 826 (N.Y. Supreme Court, NY County 2002) 6.64
Enmon v. Prospect Capital Corp., 675 F.3d 138 (2d Cir. 2012) 13.137
Enron Corp. & Ponderosa Assets L.P. v. Argentine Republic, No. M-82 (S.D.N.Y. Nov. 20, 2007) 14.23
Enron Equip. Procurement Co. v. The M/V TITAN 2, 82 F. Supp. 2d 602 (W.D. La. 1999) 14.38
Epstein v. Kalvin-Miller Int'l, Inc., 139 F.Supp 2d 469 (S.D.N.Y. 2001) 10.45
Equitable Lumber Corp. v. IPA Land Dev. Corp., 344 N.E.2d 391 (N.Y. 1976) 10.24
Erie Railroad Co. v. Tompkins, 304 U.S. 64 (1938) 2.10
Erving v. the Virginia Squires Basketball Club, 349 F. Supp. 716 (E.D.N.Y. 1972) 1.15
ESPN, Inc. v. Office of the Commissioner of Baseball, 76 F. Supp. 2d 383 (S.D.N.Y. 1999) 10.06
Europcar Italia, S.p.A. v. Maiellano Tours, Inc., 156 F.3d 310 (2d Cir. 1998) 6.103, 6.105, 13.105
Evans v. City of Johnstown, 410 N.Y.S.2d 199 (N.Y. Sup. Ct. 1978) 4.52
Exp.-Imp. Bank of the Republic of China v. Grenada, 768 F.3d 75 (2d Cir. 2014) 14.56, 14.73

Fahnestock & Co. v. Waltman, 935 F.2d 512 (2d Cir. 1991) 13.146
Fairchild Corp. v. Alcoa, Inc., 510 F. Supp. 2d 280 (S.D.N.Y. 2007) 13.137
Farago Adver., Inc. v. Hollinger Int'l., Inc., 157 F. Supp. 2d 252 (S.D.N.Y. 2001) 4.14, 4.16

Farash v. Sykes Datatronics, Inc., 452 N.E.2d 1245 (N.Y. 1983) 10.34
Farrell v. Subway Int'l, B.V., 11 CIV. 08 JFK, 2011 WL 1085017 (S.D.N.Y. 2011) 1.73
Favara, Skahan, Tabaczyk, Ltd. v. Ewing, No. 91 Civ. 7878 (JFK), 1992 WL 80659. . . . . . .7.110
Feeney v. Dell Inc., 466 1001 (2013) 11.113
Feinsot v. Burstein, 138 N.Y.S. 185 (1st Dep't 1912) 4.41
Felder v. Casey, 487 U.S. 131 (1988). 13.76
Felts v. CLK Mgmt., 149 N.M. 681 (2011) 11.14
Ferrer v. Preston, 145 Cal. App. 4th 440 (Cal. App. 2006) 6.22
Ferro Corp. v. Garrison Industries, Inc., 927 F. Supp. 234 (N.D. Ohio 1996); 142 F.3d 926 (6th Cir. 1998) 6.78
Fertilizer Corp. of India v. IDI Management, Inc., 517 F. Supp. 948 (S.D. Ohio 1981) 6.101, 13.105
FG Hemisphere Assocs. v. Democratic Republic of Congo, 447 F.3d 835 (D.C. Cir. 2006) 14.25, 14.55, 14.69
FIA Card Servs., N.A. v. Gachiengu, 571 F. Supp. 2d 799 (S.D. Tex. 2008) 6.109
Fiat S.p.A. v. Ministry of Finance and Planning of Republic of Suriname, No. 88 CIV. 6639, 1989 WL 122891 . . . . .6.99, 6.101, 13.99
Fid. Fed. Sav. & Loan Ass'n v. De la Cuesta, 458 U.S. 141 (1982) 11.111
Fielding v. Doctor's Assocs., Inc., 2002 WL 32173569 . . . . 6.78
Figueiredo Ferraz e Engenharia de Projecto Ltda. v. Republic of Peru, 665 F.3d 384 (2d Cir. 2011) (Figueiredo). 13.63, 14.30, 14.55, 14.67
Filanto S.p.A. v. Chilewich, 789 F. Supp. 1229 (S.D.N.Y. 1992) 6.16, 6.36, 8.33
Firchow v. Citibank (South Dakota), N.A., No. B187081 2007 WL 64763 (Cal. Ct. App. 2007) 11.86
Fireman's Fund Ins. Co. v. Cunningham Lindsey Claims Management, 2005 WL 1522783 (E.D.N.Y. 2005) 12.20
First Inv. Corp. of Marshall Islands v. Fujian Mawei Shipbuilding, Ltd., 703 F.3d 742 (5th Cir. 2012) 13.41
First Nat'l City Bank v. Banco Para El Comercio Exterior de Cuba, 462 U.S. 611 (1983) (Bancec) 14.65
First Options of Chicago Inc. v. Kaplan, 514 U.S. 938 (1995) 3.16, 6.06, 6.13, 6.15, 6.22, 6.32, 6.38, 6.64–6.65, 6.71, 6.73, 6.99–6.100, 7.34–7.35, 8.07, 11.12, 11.101, 13.83
First Wall St. Settlement Corp. v. Hart, 590 N.Y.S.2d 81 (1st Dep't 1992) 10.34
Fiser v. Dell Computer Corp. 188 P.3d 1215 (N.M. 2008) 11.87
Fitzpatrick v. Animal Care Hosp., PLLC, 104 A.D.3d 1078, 962 N.Y.S.2d 474 (2013) 10.15
Flagg v. Yonkers Sav. and Loan Ass'n, FA, 396 F.3d 178 (2d Cir. 2005) 1.10
Florasynth, Inc. v. Pickholz, 750 F.2d 171 (2d Cir. 1984) 13.16, 13.74
Flores v. Las Americas Comm., Inc., 218 A.D.2d 595 (1st Dep't 1995) 10.51
Fluor Daniel Intercont'l Inc. v. Gen. Elec. Co., No. 98 Civ. 7181, 1999 WL 637236. . . . . . . 4.46
Flynn v. Labor Ready, Inc., 751 N.Y.S.2d 721 (N.Y. Sup. Ct. 2002) 11.85
Fortune, Alsweet and Eldridge, Inc. v. Daniel, 724 F.2d 1355 (9th Cir. 1983) 6.111
Fotochrome Inc. v. Copal Co., 517 F.2d 512 (2d Cir. 1975) 6.94
Four Seasons Hotels and Resorts, B.V. v. Conscorcio Barr, S.A., 267 F. Supp. 2d 1335, 1340–42 (S.D. Fla. 2003) 6.63
Fourth Ocean Putnam Corp. v. Interstate Wrecking Co., 485 N.E.2d 208 (N.Y. 1985) 4.57
Fradella v. Petricca, 183 F.3d 17 (1st Cir. 1999) 1.24
Franklin Hamilton, LLC. v. Creative Ins. Underwriters, Inc., No. 08 Civ. 7449 (JFK), 2008 WL 4837680 . . . . 13.19
Frater v. Tigerpack Capital, Ltd., No. 98 CIV. 3306 1998 WL 851591 (S.D.N.Y. Dec. 9, 1998) 10.51
Frazier v. CitiFinancial Corp., 604 F.3d 1313 (11th Cir. 2010). 13.133
Freaner v. Valle, No. 11CV1819 JLS (MDD), 2011 WL 5596919 (S.D. Cal. Nov. 17, 2011) 6.10
Freedman v. Chem. Constr. Corp., 372 N.E.2d 12 (N.Y. 1977) 4.07

Freudensprung v. Offshore Tech. Servs., Inc., 379 F.3d 327 (5th Cir. 2004) 13.46
Freund v. Washington Square Press. Inc., 314 N.E.2d 419 (N.Y. 1974) 10.03, 10.10, 10.29
Frontera Res. Azer. Corp. v. State Oil Co. of Azer. Republic, 582 F.3d 393 (2d Cir. 2009) 13.40, 13.58, 14.27
Fruition, Inc. v. Rhoda Lee, Inc., 766 N.Y.S.2d 437 (1st Dep't 2003) 10.02
Frye v. United States, 293 F. 1013 (D.C. Cir. 1923) 2.70
Funnekotter v. Republic of Zimbabwe, No. 09 Civ. 8168 (CM) (Dkt. 11) (S.D.N.Y. Feb. 1, 2010) 14.23

Galleon Syndicate Corp. v. Pan Atl. Grp., Inc., 637 N.Y.S.2d 104 (App. Div. 1996) 9.60
Gambar Enter., Inc. v. Kelly Services, Inc., 418 N.Y.S.2d 818 (4th Dep't 1979) 4.10
Gantt v. Clemson Agric. Coll. of SC, 320 F.2d 611 (4th Cir. 1963) 11.07
Garpeg, Ltd. v. United States, 583 F. Supp. 789 (S.D.N.Y. 1984) 7.132
Garrity v. Lyle Stuart, Inc., 353 N.E.2d 793 (N.Y. 1976); 40 N.Y.2d 354, 356 (1976) 0.50, 3.34, 13.142
Garten v. Kurth, 265 F.3d 136 (2d Cir. 2001) 6.10, 6.38
Gateway Techs, Inc. v. MCI, 64 F.3d 993 (5th Cir. 1995) 3.56
Gatton v. T-Mobile USA, Inc., 61 Cal. Rptr. 3d 344 (Cal. Ct. App. 2007) 11.86
Gau Shan Co. v. Bankers Trust Co., 956 F.2d 1349 (6th Cir. 1992) 7.133
Gay v. Creditinform 511 F.3d 369 (3d Cir. 2007) 11.97
Gen. Elec. Co. v. Deutz AG, 270 F.3d 144 (3d Cir. 2001) 13.89
Generica Ltd. v. Pharm. Basics, Inc., 125 F.3d 1123 (7th Cir. 1997) 13.96
Genesco, Inc. v. T. Kakiuchi & Co. Ltd., 815 F.2d 840 (2d Cir. 1987) 1.64, 6.12, 6.15–6.16, 4.47, 7.14, 7.93
Gentry v. Superior Court, 64 Cal. Rptr. 3d 773 (Cal. Ct. App. 2007); 42 Cal. 4th 443 (Cal. 2007) 11.86, 11.112
Geotech Lizenz AG v. Evergreen Sys., Inc., 697 F. Supp. 1248 (E.D.N.Y. 1988) 13.97
Gerling Global Reins. Corp. v. Home Ins. Co., 752 N.Y.S.2d 611 (1st Dep't 2002) 4.46
Gilmer v. Interstate/Johnson Lane Corp., 500 U.S. 20 (1991) 6.04, 9.12
Giordano v. Mkt. Am., Inc., 941 N.E.2d 727 (N.Y. 2010) 2.70
Glass v. Kidder Peabody & Co., 114 F.3d 446 (4th Cir. 1997) 6.60
Glen Rauch Sec., Inc. v. Weinraub, 768 N.Y.S.2d 611 (App. Div. 2003) 9.06, 9.52
Glencore Grain Rotterdam B.V. v. Shivnath Rai Harnarain Co., 284 F.3d 13.41, 13.50, 13.56
Global Reinsurance Corp.–U.S. Branch v. Argonaut, No. 07 Civ. 8196 (PKC), 2008 WL 126976; 2008 WL 1805459 (S.D.N.Y. 2008) 9.59, 12.19
Global Reinsurance Corp.–U.S. Branch v. Certain Underwriters at Lloyd's, London, 465 F. Supp. 2d 308 (S.D.N.Y. 2006) 5.29
Goel v. Ramachandran, 823 F. Supp. 2d 206 (S.D.N.Y. 2011) 8.34
Goetsch v. Shell Oil Co., 197 F.R.D. 574 (W.D. N.C. 2000) 11.88
Gold v. Deutsche Aktiengesellschaft, 365 F.3d 144 (2d Cir. 2004) 6.64
Goldfinger v. Lisker, 500 N.E.2d 857 (N.Y. 1986) 6.61, 13.140
Goldman v. Architectural Iron Co., 306 F.3d 1214 (2d Cir. 2002) 13.128
Goldman Sachs Execution & Clearing, L.P. v. Official Unsecured Creditors Comm. of Bayou Grp., LLC, 491 F. App'x 201 (2d Cir. 2012) 3.55
Goldman, Sachs & Co. v. Golden Empire Sch. Fin. Auth., 764 F.3d 210 (2d Cir. 2014) 13.44
Goldman, Sachs & Co. v. Griffin, No. 07 Civ. 1313, 2007 U.S. Dist. LEXIS 36674; 2007 WL 147430 (S.D.N.Y. 2007) 1.39, 3.15, 6.31
Gomez v. Bicknell, 756 N.Y.S.2d 209 (2d Dep't 2002) 4.16
Goodstein Constr. Corp. v. City of New York, 604 N.E. 2d 1356 (N.Y. 1992) 10.04
Goodyear Dunlop Tires Operations, S.A. v. Brown, 131 S. Ct. 2846 (2011) 13.54
Gosden v. Elmira City Sch. Dist., 90 A.D.3d 1202 (2011) 10.29
Gotham Boxing Inc. v. Finkel, 856 N.Y.S.2d 498 (Sup. Ct. N.Y. County 2008) 10.29
Gov't of India v. Cargill Inc., 867 F.2d 130 (2d Cir. 1989) 13.126
Gov't of U.K. v. Boeing Co., 998 F.2d 68 (2d Cir. 1993) 11.50

Grad v. Roberts, 198 N.E.2d 26 (N.Y. 1964) 4.49
Granite Partners, L.P. v. Bear, Stearns & Co., Inc., 58 F. Supp. 2d 228 (S.D.N.Y. 1999).... 4.16
Granite Rock Co. v. International Brotherhood of Teamsters, 561 U.S. 287 (2010) ... 7.29, 13.45
Gras v. Associates First Capital Corp., 786 A.2d 886 (N.J. App. Div. 2001) 11.88
Gray v. Conseco, Inc., 2001 U.S. Dist. LEXIS 21696 (C.D. Cal. 2001)................. 11.61
Great E. Sec., Inc. v. Goldendale Invs., Ltd., No. 06 Civ. 6667 DAB, 2006 WL 3851159... 8.21
Great Western Mortgage Corp. v. Peacock, 110 F.3d 222 (3d. Cir. 1997) 1.08
Green Tree Financial Corp. v. Bazzle, 539 U.S. 444 (2003) 0.41, 6.27, 6.58, 11.08
Green Tree Financial Group v. Randolph, 531 U.S. 79 (2000)......................... 6.37
Greenberg v. Bear, Stearns & Co., 220 F.3d 22 (2d Cir. 2000) cert. denied, 531 U.S. 1075 (2001) 11.39
Greenfield v. Philles Records, Inc., 98 N.Y.2d 562 (2002)............................ 4.03
Grenada v. Grynberg, No. 11 Misc. 45 (S.D.N.Y. Apr. 29, 2011)...................... 14.23
Greystone P'ships Grp., Inc. v. Koninklijke Luchtvaart Maatschappij N.V., 815 F. Supp. 745 (S.D.N.Y. 1993)... 4.15
Griffin Indus., Inc. v. Petrojam, Ltd., 58 F. Supp. 2d 212 (S.D.N.Y. 1999).............. 13.121
Grossman v. Lowell, 703 F. Supp. 282 (S.D.N.Y. 1989).............................. 4.64
Grupo Mexicano de Desarrollo, S.A. v. Alliance Bond Fund, Inc., 527 U.S. 308 (1999).... 8.37
Guilford Mills, Inc. v. Rice Pudding, Ltd., 455 N.Y.S.2d 88 (App. Div. 1982) 9.06
Gulf Petro Trading Co. v. Nigerian Nat'l Petroleum Corp., 512 F.3d 742 (5th Cir. 2008).. 13.36
Gutfreund v. Weiner (In Re Salomon Inc. Shareholders Derivative Litig.), 68 F.3d 544 (2d Cir. 1995)... 6.15
Gutierrez v. Autowest, Inc., 7 Cal. Rptr. 3d 267 (Cal. Ct. App. 2003) 11.86
Gvozdenovic v. United Air Lines, 933 F.2d 1100 (2d Cir. 1991) 6.69, 6.71, 7.73

Habitations Ltd. v. BKL Realty Sales Corp., 160 A.D.2d 423 (1st Dep't 1990)........8.37, 8.47
Hackett v. Milbank, Tweed, Hadley & McCloy, 654 N.E.2d 95 (N.Y. 1995) 13.143
Hakala v. Deutsche Bank AG, No. 01 Civ. 3366 (MGC), 2004 WL 1057788 .... 13.113
Hakala v. J.P. Morgan Securities, Inc., 186 Fed. Appx. 131 (2d Cir. 2006) 1.102
Hall Street Associates, L.L.C. v. Mattel, Inc., 552 U.S. 576 (2008); 128 S. Ct. 1396 (2008) 1.13, 1.27, 2.96, 3.56, 6.62, 11.41, 13.132
Hall v. Shearson Lehman Hutton, Inc., 708 F. Supp. 711 (D. Md. 1989)................. 6.20
Hall v. Werthan Bag Corp., 251 F. Supp 184 (M.D. Tenn. 1966) 11.07
Halligan v. Piper Jaffray, Inc 148 F.3d 197 (2d Cir. 1998)........................... 13.131
Hallmark Capital Corp., In Re, 534 F. Supp. 2d 951 (D. Minn. 2007) 9.77
Hamer v. Sidway, 27 N.E. 256 (N.Y. 1891) 4.17
Hamilton v. Accu-Tek, 47 F. Supp. 2d 330 (E.D.N.Y. 1999) 4.11
Hamilton v. McPherson, 28 N.Y. 72 (1863)... 4.37
Hancor, Inc. v. R&R Eng'g Prods., Inc., 381 F. Supp. 2d 12 (D.P.R. 2005).............. 13.24
Harford Accident & Indem. Co. v. Swiss Reinsurance Am. Corp., 246 F.3d 219 (2d Cir. 2001) 6.38
Harris v. Green Tea Fin. Corp., 183 F.3d 173 (3d Cir. 1999) 3.26
Harrison v. Grobe, 790 F. Supp. 443 (S.D.N.Y. 1992), aff'd, 984 F.2d 594 (2d Cir. 1993) ... 4.20
Harry Kolomick Contractors, Inc. v. Shelter Rock Estates, Inc., 567 N.Y.S.2d 845 (2d Dep't 1991) 10.11
Harsco Corp. v. Segui, 91 F.3d 337 (2d Cir. 1996) 4.21
Hartford Accident & Indemnity Co. v. Equitas Reins Ltd., 200 F. Supp. 2d 102 (D. Conn. 2002) 7.103
Hartford Fire Ins. Co. v. Orient Overseas Container Lines Ltd., 230 F.3d 549 (2d Cir. 2000) 4.07
Hausman v. Earlswood Enters., Ltd., No. 95 Civ. 9088 (JSM), 1996 WL 527335 .... 13.51
Hay Group, Inc. v. E.B.S. Acquisition Corp. 360 F.3d 404 (3d Cir. 2004) 3.39, 9.62, 9.65
Health Services Mgmt. Corp. v. Hughes, 975 F.2d 1253 (7th Cir. 1992)...........6.111, 13.18
Heiges v. J.P. Morgan Chase Bank, N.A., 521 F. Supp. 2d 641 (N.D. Ohio 2007)......... 8.07

Helmsley Spear, Inc. v. Local 32 B-32J Service Employees Int'l Union, 1991 U.S. Dist. LEXIS 10298 (S.D.N.Y. 1991) . . . 6.34
Henry v. Murphy, No. M-82, 2002 WL 24307 . . . 6.109, 6.111, 7.25, 13.110
Herman Miller, Inc., In Re, No. 97 Civ. 7878 (SAS), 1998 WL 192213 . . . 1.41
Hines v. Davidowitz, 312 U.S. 52 (1941) . . . 13.143
Hoblock v. Albany County Bd. of Elections, 422 F. 3d 77 (2d Cir. 2005) . . . 2.16
Hoeft v. MVL Group, Inc., 343 F.3d 57 (2d Cir. 2003) . . . 3.57, 11.39, 13.127
Holder v. Gen. Motors Corp., 732 N.Y.S.2d 545 (Sup. Ct. 2001) . . . 13.76
Holy Props. Ltd. v. Kenneth Cole Prods., Inc., 661 N.E.2d 694 (N.Y. 1995) . . . 10.21
Homayouni v. Paribas, 660 N.Y.S.2d 413 (1st Dep't 1997) . . . 4.15
Home Insurance Company v. New England Re. Corp., 1999 WL 681388 (S.D.N.Y. 1999) . . . 3.45
Home Life Ins. Co. v. Kaufman, 547 F. Supp. 833 (S.D.N.Y. 1982) . . . 7.128
Honig v. Comcast of Georgia I, LLC, 537 F. Supp. 2d 1277 (N.D. Ga. 2008) . . . 11.95
Hooper Assocs., Ltd. v. AGS Computers, Inc., 548 N.E.2d 903 (1989) . . . 10.51
Hotchkiss v. National City Bank of New York, 200 F. 287 (S.D.N.Y. 1911) . . . 4.14
Hoteles Condado Beach, La Concha & Convention Ctr. v. Union de Tronquistas Local 901, 763 F.2d 34 (1st Cir. 1985) . . . 13.122
Housekeeper v. Lourie, 333 N.Y.S.2d 932 (1st Dep't 1972) . . . 4.48
Houston Gen. Ins. Co. v. Certain Underwriters at Lloyd's London, No. 02 Civ. 7599 (JSR), 2003 WL 22480058 . . . 13.113
Howsam v. Dean Witter Reynolds, Inc 537 U.S. 79 (2002) . . . 0.41–0.42, 1.36, 3.20, 6.04, 6.08, 6.20, 6.24, 6.30, 6.32, 6.92, 7.29, 7.34, 7.96, 11.12, 13.82
HPD, LLC v. Tetra Techs., Inc., 2012 Ark. 408. . . . 11.14
HSMV Corp. v. ADI Ltd., 72 F. Supp. 2d 1122 (C.D. Cal. 1999) . . . 13.37
Hubbard v. UTZ Quality Foods, Inc., 903 F. Supp. 444 (W.D.N.Y. 1995) . . . 4.28
Hundertmark v. Boston Prof'l Hockey Ass'n, 1996 WL 118538 (E.D.N.Y. 1996) . . . 4.07
Hunter v. Marine Midland Bank, 143 Misc. 2d 697 (N.Y. City Ct. Rochester 1989), aff'd, 48 N.Y.2d 900 (1979) . . . 10.17
Hutcherson v. Sears Roebuck & Co., 793 N.E.2d 886 (Ill. App. Ct. 2003) . . . 11.90
HZI Research Center, Inc. v. Sun Instruments Japan Co., 10 Mealey's Rep. 11 (S.D.N.Y. 1995) . . . 5.29

I. K. Bery, Inc. v. Boody & Co., No. 99 Civ. 10968 (SAS), 2000 WL 218938 (S.D.N.Y. Feb. 23, 2000) . . . 1.41
I/S Stravborg (O. H. Meling, Manager) v. National Metal Converters, Inc., 500 F.2d 424 (2d Cir. 1974) . . . 3.60
Iberia Credit Bureau v. Cingular Wireless, 379 F.3d 159 (5th Cir. 2004) . . . 3.26
Ibeto Petrochem. Indus. Ltd. v. M/T "Beffen," 475 F.3d 56 (2d Cir. 2007) . . . 7.83, 7.91, 7.134, 8.16
IBEW Local 97 v. Niagara Mohawk Power Corp., 143 F.3d 704 (2d Cir. 1998) . . . 13.135
IDS Life Ins. Co. v. SunAmerica, Inc., 103 F.3d 524 (7th Cir. 1996) . . . 7.125
IFC Interconsult, AG v. Safeguard Int'l Partners, LLC, 438 F.3d 298 (3d Cir. 2006) . . . 13.19
Imclone Systems Inc. v. Waksal, 802 N.Y.S. 2d 653 (N.Y. App. Div. 2005) . . . 1.108
In Paduano v. Express Scripts, Inc., 55 F. Supp. 3d 400 (E.D.N.Y. 2014) . . . 7.88
Indu Craft, Inc. v. Bank of Baroda, 47 F.3d 490 (2d Cir. 1995) . . . 4.37
Industrial Risk Insurers v. M.A.N. Gutehoffnungshutte GmbH, 141 F.3d 1434 (11th Cir. 1998) . . . 6.63, 14.12
Infuturia Global Ltd. v. Sequus Pharms., Inc., 631 F.3d 1133 (9th Cir. 2011) . . . 13.69
Ingaseosas Int'l Co. v. Aconcagua Investing Ltd., No. 09-23078-CIV, 2011 WL 500042 . . . 13.37
Ingle v. Circuit City Stores, 328 F.3d 1165 (9th Cir. 2003) . . . 3.26
Ins. Co. of North America v. ABB Power Generation, Inc., 925 F. Supp. 1053 (S.D.N.Y. 1996) question certified 112 F.3d 70 (2d Cir. 1997), certified question answered 690 N.E.2d 1249 (N.Y. 1997) . . . 1.12

Ins. Co. v. Dutcher, 95 U.S. 269 (1877) 4.04
Instituto de Resseguros do Brasil v. First State Ins. Co., 178 A.D.2d 313 (1st Dep't 1991) 3.27
Int'l Brotherhood of Teamsters v. Western Pennsylvania Motor Carriers Ass'n, 574 F.2d 783 (3d Cir. 1978) 6.03
Int'l CableTel Inc. v. Le Groupe Videotron Ltee, 978 F. Supp. 483 (S.D.N.Y. 1997) 4.54
Int'l Components Corp. v. Klaiber, 54 A.D.2d 550 (1st Dep't 1976) 3.40
Int'l Fashion Prods. B.V. v. Calvin Klein, Inc., No. 95-CV-0982 (JFK), 1995 WL 92321 .... 7.135
Int'l Fidelity Ins. Co. v. Rockland, 98 F. Supp. 2d 400 (S.D.N.Y. 2000) 10.20
Int'l Ins. Co. v. Caja Nacional de Ahorro y Seguro, 293 F.3d 392, 399–400 (7th Cir. 2002) 14.43
Int'l Longshoremen's Ass'n v. W. Gulf Mar. Ass'n, 605 F. Supp. 723 (S.D.N.Y. 1985) 9.30
Int'l Minerals & Res., S.A. v. Pappas, 96 F.3d 586 (2d Cir. 1996) 4.07
Int'l Paper Co. v. Schwabedissen Maschinen & Anlagen GmbH, 206 F.3d 411 (4th Cir. 2000) 6.64, 7.69
Int'l Paper Co. v. Suwyn, 966 F. Supp. 246 (S.D.N.Y. 1997) 4.15
Int'l Shipping Co., S.A. v. Hydra Offshore, Inc., 675 F. Supp. 146 (S.D.N.Y. 1987); 875 F.2d 388, 391 n.5 (2d Cir. 1989) 8.34, 13.36
Int'l Standard Elec. Corp. v. Bridas Sociedad Anonima Petrolera, Industrial y Comercial, 745 F. Supp. 172 (S.D.N.Y. 1990) 1.89, 13.36
Integrity Ins. Co., In Liq. v. American Centennial Ins. Co., 885 F. Supp. 69 (S.D.N.Y. 1995) 1.20, 3.39, 3.43, 9.06
Intel Corp. v. Advanced Micro Devices, Inc., 542 U.S. 241 (2004) 2.58, 9.75, 9.77
InterCarbon Berm., Ltd. v. Caltex Trading & Transp. Corp., 146 F.R.D. 64 (S.D.N.Y. 1993) 13.21
InterChem Asia 2000 Pte. Ltd. v. Oceana Petrochemicals AG, 373 F. Supp. 2d 340 (S.D.N.Y. 2005) 9.30, 9.52
Intercontinental Planning, Ltd. v. Daystrom, Inc., 300 N.Y.S.2d 817 (1969) 1.65
Interdigital Communs. Corp. v. Samsung Elecs. Co., No. 06 Civ. 6833, 2007 U.S. Dist. LEXIS 91135 (S.D.N.Y 2007) 6.95, 6.110
Interfilm, Inc. v. Advanced Exhibition Corp., 672 N.Y.S.2d 309 (1st Dep't 1998) 4.35
InterGen N.V. v. Grina, 344 F.3d 134 (1st Cir. 2003) 6.64, 7.69, 7.74, 13.41
International Minerals and Resources, S.A. v. Pappas, 96 F.3d 586 (2d Cir. 1996) 6.17
International Union of Operating Engineers v. Flair Builders, Inc., 406 U.S. 487 (1972) ... 6.34
Interocean Shipping Co. v. National Shipping & Trading Corp., 462 F.2d 673 (2d Cir. 1972) 6.04, 6.20
Iran Aircraft Indus. v. Avco Corp., 980 F.2d 141 (2d Cir. 1992) 13.96
IRB-Brasil Resseguros, S.A. v. Inepar Invs., S.A., 20 N.Y.3d 310 (2012) 4.10
IRB-Brasil Resseguros S.A. v. Portobello Intern. Ltd., 84 A.D.3d 637 (1st Dep't 2011) 10.47
Iskanian v. CLS Transportation Los Angeles, LLC, 59 Cal. 4th 348 (Cal. 2014) 11.112
Island Territory of Curacao v. Solitron Devices, Inc., 356 F. Supp. 1, 12–13 (S.D.N.Y. 1973), aff'd, 489 F.2d 1313 (2d Cir. 1973) 6.20, 7.25
Istithmar World PJSC v. Amato, No. 12 Civ. 7472 (JFK), 2013 WL 66478 .... 9.59

Jacada (Europe), Ltd. v. Int'l Mktg. Strategies, Inc., 401 F.3d 701 (6th Cir. 2005) 6.63
Jackson v. Rent-A-Center West, Inc., 581 F.3d 912 (9th Cir. 2009), rev'd, 130 S. Ct. 2772 (2010) 7.44
Jacob & Youngs v. Kent, 129 N.E. 889 (N.Y. 1921) 4.25
Jacobs v. USA Track & Field, 374 F.3d 85 (2d Cir. 2004) 7.156
Jameson v. Pine Hill Dev., LLC, Civ. A. No. 07-0111-WSB, 2007 WL 623807 .... 8.33
Jarecki v. Moo Louie, 745 N.E.2d 1006 (N.Y. 2001) 4.60
Jean v. Francois, 642 N.Y.S.2d 780 (N.Y. Sup. Ct. 1996) 4.11
Jenkins v. First American Cash Advance of Ga., LLC, 400 F.3d 868 (11th Cir. 2005) 6.27, 11.85, 11.90
JLM Indus. v. Stolt-Nielsen SA, 387 F.3d 163 (2d Cir. 2004) 1.36, 6.27, 6.58

John Hancock Mut. Life Ins. Co. v. Olick, 151 F.3d 132 (3d Cir. 1998). 6.34, 6.57
John Hancock Mut. Life Ins. Co. v. Wilson, 254 F.3d 48 (2d Cir. 2001) 7.34
John Morrell & Co. v. Local 304A United Food & Comm. Workers, 913 F.3d 544 (8th Cir. 1990) 6.57
John Wiley & Sons, Inc. v. Livingston, 376 U.S. 543 (1964) 6.25, 11.13
Johnson v. Summit Equities, Inc., 864 N.Y.S.2d 873 (Sup. Ct. 2008) 13.142
Johnson v. W. Suburban Bank, 225 F.3d 366 (3d Cir. 2000) 6.27, 11.53, 11.85, 11.99
Jones v. Sea Tow Servs. Freeport NY Inc., 30 F.3d 360 (2d Cir. 1994) 13.32
Jonesfilm v. Lions Gate Films, Inc., 65 Fed. Appx. 361 (2d Cir. 2003) 6.37
Joqueviel & Cathala v. Eastern Tanning Co., Inc., 1989 WL 119440, at *5 (E.D.N.Y. 1989) 4.27
Jordache Enter., Inc. v. Global Union Bank, 688 F. Supp. 939 (S.D.N.Y 1988). 10.25
Jorf Lasfar Energy Co. v. AMCI Exp. Corp., No. Civ. A. 05-0423, 2005 WL 3533128. . . . 13.105
Joseph Martin, Jr., Delicatessen, Inc. v. Schumacher, 417 N.E.2d 541 (N.Y. 1981). 4.19
Joseph Muller Corp. Zurich v. Commonwealth Petrochemicals, Inc., 334 F. Supp. 1013 (S.D.N.Y. 1971) 7.98
JSC Surgutneftegaz v. President & Fellows of Harvard Coll., No. 1:04-cv-06069-RMB (RCC), 2005 WL 1863676; 2007 WL 3019234 (S.D.N.Y. 2007). . . .0.36, 1.64, 6.85, 9.60, 11.02, 13.142

Kaepa, Inc. v. Achilles Corp., 76 F.3d 624 (5th Cir. 1996) 7.131, 7.133
Kahn Lucas Lancaster, Inc. v. Lark Int'l Ltd., 186 F.3d 210 (2d Cir. 1999) 1.75, 6.16, 7.24, 13.27
Kaiser v. Fishman, 590 N.Y.S.2d 230 (2d Dep't 1992). 10.39
Kantor v. 75 Worth St., LLC, 95 A.D.3d 718 N.Y.S.2d 245 (2012). 10.20
Kaplan v. Alfred Dunhill of London, Inc., No. 96 Civ. 0258 (JFK), 1996 WL 640901 . . . 13.120
Karaha Bodas Co., L.L.C. v. Perusahaan Pertambangan Minyak Dan Gas Bumi Negara, 190 F. Supp. 2d 936 (S.D. Tex. 2001) 13.103
Karaha Bodas Co., L.L.C. v. Perusahaan Pertambangan Minyak Dan Gas Bumi Negara ("Pertamina"), 313 F.3d 70 (2d Cir. 2002) 14.54, 14.74
Karaha Bodas Co., L.L.C. v. Perusahaan Pertambangan Minyak Dan Gas Bumi Negara, 335 F.3d 357 (5th Cir. 2003) 13.06
Karaha Bodas Co. L.L.C., v. Perusahaan Pertambangan Minyak Dan Gas Bumi Negara, et al., 364 F.3d 274 (5th Cir. 2004) 0.36, 13.36
Karaha Bodas Co., L.L.C. v. Perusahaan Pertambangan Minyak Dan Gas Bumi Negara, 500 F.3d 111 (2d Cir. 2007) 7.134, 7.150, 13.04
Karlan Constr. Co. v. Burdick Assocs. Owners Corp., 560 N.Y.S.2d 480 (App. Div. 1990) 13.74
Kashner Davidson Sec. Corp. v. Mscisz, 531 F.3d 68 (1st Cir. 2008) 11.39
Kasowitz, Benson, Torres & Friedman, LLP v. Duane Reade, 98 A.D.3d 403 (1st Dep't 2012) 4.62
Katz v. Cellco Partnership 794 F.3d 341 (2d Cir. 2015) 7.117–7.118
Katz v. Feinberg, 167 F. Supp. 2d 556 (S.D.N.Y. 2001), aff'd, 290 F.3d 95 (2d Cir. 2002) 6.66, 6.74
Kaye v. Grossman, 202 F.3d 611 (2d Cir. 2000) 4.52
Keating v. Superior Court 31 Cal. 3d 584P. 2d 1192 (Cal. 1982). 11.53, 11.57
Keilly v. Sands Bros., 803 N.Y.S.2d 385 (N.Y. Sup. Ct. 2005) 13.73
Kel Kim Corp. v. Cent. Mkts., Inc., 519 N.E.2d 295 (N.Y. 1987). 4.67
Kelly v. Merrill Lynch, Pierce, Fenner & Smith, Inc., 985 F.2d 1067 (11th Cir.), cert. denied, 510 U.S. 1011 (1993) 6.34, 6.57
Kelly v. Oxford Health Plans (NY), Inc., No. 0602189/2007, 2008 WL 1710739 (N.Y. Sup. Ct. Mar. 19, 2008) 1.108
Kenford Co, Inc. v. Cnty. of Erie, 493 N.E.2d 234 (N.Y. 1986) 4.34, 10.20
Kenford Co, Inc. v. Cnty. of Erie, 537 N.E.2d. 176 (N.Y. 1989) 10.11, 10.15
Kenney, Becker LLP v. Kenney, No. 06 Civ. 2975 (JSR), 2008 WL 681452 . . . . 9.06

Kerr-McGee Refining Corp. v. M.T. Triumph, 924 F.2d 467 (2d Cir. 1991) 6.73
Keytrade USA, Inc. v. Ain Temouchant M/V in rem, 404 F.3d 891 (5th Cir. 2005) 7.69
Keywell Corp. v. Weinstein, 33 F.3d 159 (2d Cir. 1994) 4.53
King v. King, 617 N.Y.S.2d 593 (3d Dep't 1994) 4.15
Kinkel v. Cingular Wireless, LLC, 828 N.E.2d 812 (Ill. App. Ct. 2005) 11.86
Kinoshita, In Re, 287 F.2d 951 (2d Cir. 1961) 3.05, 7.94–7.95
Kirk v. Raymark Indus., Inc., 61 F.3d 147 (3d Cir. 1995) 9.71
Klaxon Co. v. Stentor Elec. Mfg. Co., Inc., 313 U.S. 487 (1941) 1.66, 4.08
Klein v. ATP Flight Sch., LLP, 2014 WL 3013294 .... 7.102
Kleinberg Elec., Inc. v. E-J Elec. Installation Co., 111 A.D.3d 410, 974 N.Y.S.2d 377 (2013) 10.28
Klor's, Inc. v. Broadway-Hale Stores, Inc., 359 U.S. 207 (U.S. 1959) 6.83
Kolel Beth Yechiel Mechil of Tartikov, Inc. v. YLL Irrevocable Trust, 863 F. Supp. 2d 351 (S.D.N.Y 2012) 13.71
Konkar Maritime Enters. v. Compagnie Belge D'Affretement, 668 F. Supp. 267 (S.D.N.Y. 1987) 8.21
Kopple v. Schick Farms, Ltd., 447 F. Supp. 2d 965 (N.D. Iowa 2006) 4.19
Kozera v. Westchester-Fairfield Chapter of Nat'l Elec. Contractors Ass'n, Inc., 909 F.2d 48, 53 (2d Cir. 1990) 6.74
KPMG LLP v. Cocchi, 132 S. Ct. 23 (2011) 0.43
Kramer & Uchitelle, In Re, 48 N.E.2d 493 (N.Y. 1942) 6.20
Krantz v. Chateau Stores of Can. Ltd., 683 N.Y.S.2d 24 (1st Dep't 1998) 4.55
Kremer v. Chemical Construction Corp., 456 U.S. 461 (1982) 6.33
Kristian v. Comcast Corp., 446 F.3d 25 (1st Cir. 2006) 6.85, 11.85, 11.90, 11.93
Kroboth v. Brent, 625 N.Y.S.2d 748 (3d Dep't 1995) 4.64
Krumme v. WestPoint Stevens, Inc., 143 F.3d 71 (2d Cir. 1998) 4.15
Kudler v. Truffelman, 93 A.D.3d 549, leave to appeal denied, 19 N.Y.3d 815 (2012) 10.27
Kulukundis Shipping Co., S/A v. Amtorg Trading Corp., 126 F.2d 978 (2d Cir. 1942) 7.17
Kumho Tire Co. v. Carmichael 2.70
Kyocera Corp. v. Prudential-Bache Trade Servs., Inc., 341 F.3d 987 (9th Cir. 2003) 3.56
Kyung In Lee v. Pacific Bullion (New York) Inc., 788 F. Supp 155 (E.D.N.Y. 1992) 6.20

L.K. Station Grp., LLC v. Quantek Media, LLC, 62 A.D.3d 487 (2009) 10.09
La Société Nationale Pour La Recherche, La Production, Le Transport, La Transformation, et La Commercialisation des Hydrocarbures v. Shaheen Natural Resources Co., 585 F. Supp. 57 (S.D.N.Y. 1983) 6.94, 6.99
Ladau v. Hillier Grp., Inc., 2004 WL 691520, 3 (S.D.N.Y. 2004) 4.15
LaFarge Corp. v. Venezolana de Cementos, S.A., 31 F.3d 70 (2d Cir. 1994) 13.72
LAIF X SPRL v. Axtel S.A. de C.V. 310 F. Supp. 2d 578 (S.D.N.Y. 2004), aff'd, 390 F.3d 194 (2d Cir. 2004) 7.153–7.154
Lakah, In Re, 602 F. Supp. 2d 497 (S.D.N.Y. 2009) 7.69
Lakah v. UBS AG, 996 F. Supp. 2d 250 (S.D.N.Y. 2014) 1.64
Laker Airways Ltd. v. Sabena, Belgian World Airlines, 731 F.2d 909 (D.C. Cir. 1984) 7.130, 7.133
Land of the Free, Inc. v. Unique Sanitation, Inc., 93 N.Y.2d 942 (1999) 7.108
Lander Co. v. MMP Invests., Inc., 107 F.3d 476 (7th Cir. 1997) 13.09
Lann v. U.S. Steel Works Corp., 1 N.Y.S.2d 951 (N.Y. Sup. Ct. 1938) 4.11
Lanvin Inc. v. Colonia, Inc., 739 F. Supp. 182 (S.D.N.Y. 1990) 4.23
Lapina v. Men Women N.Y. Model Mgmt. Inc., 2015 WL 556674 (S.D.N.Y. 2015) 7.69
LaPrade v. Kidder Peabody & Co., 146 F.3d 899 (D.C. Cir. 1998) 6.10
Latham Land I, LLC v. TGI Friday's, Inc., 96 A.D.3d 1327, 948 N.Y.S.2d 147, 151 (2012) 10.10
Lava Trading, Inc. v. Hartford Fire Ins. Co., 365 F. Supp. 2d 434 (S.D.N.Y. 2005) 10.16
Lazard Freres & Co. v. Protective Life Ins. Co., 108 F.3d 1531 (2d Cir. 1997) 4.09

Lea Tai textile Co., Ltd. v. Manning Fabrics, Inc., 411 F. Supp. 1404 (S.D.N.Y. 1975) 5.29
Leadertex, Inc. v. Morganton Dyeing & Finishing Corp., 67 F.3d 20 (2d Cir. 1995).......6.32, 6.38, 7.97
Leavitt-Bernert Tanning Corp. v. Am. Home Assurance Co., 516 N.Y.S.2d 992 (3d Dep't 1987) 4.58
Lebanon Chem. Corp. v. United Farmers Plant Food, Inc., 179 F.3d 1095 (8th Cir. 1999)..... 11.14
Ledee v. Ceramiche Ragno, 684 F.2d 184 (1st Cir. 1982) 1.72
Legion Ins. Co. v. John Hancock Mut. Life Ins. Co., 33 F. App'x 26 (3d Cir. 2002) 9.68
Lehman Bros. v. Minmetals Int'l, 179 F. Supp. 2d 118 (S.D.N.Y. 2000)..... 4.07
LeJacq Pub., Inc. v. Am. Soc'y Contemporary Medicine, Surgery & Ophthalmology, No. 88 Civ. 7242 (MJL), 1989 WL 37673..... 13.51
Leonard v. Terminix Int'l Co., LP, 854 So. 2d 529 (Ala. 2002) 11.86
Lessee, LLC v. Neiman Marcus Grp., Inc., 978 N.Y.S.2d 130 (App. Div. 2013) 9.06
Levitt v. Lipper Holdings, LLC, 2003 U.S. Dist. LEXIS 11411 (S.D.N.Y. 2003) 6.27
Lexington Prods. Ltd. v. B.D. Commc'ns Inc., 677 F.2d 251 (2d Cir. 1982) 4.37
Lian v. First Asset Mgmt., Inc., 273 A.D.2d (1st Dep't 2000) 10.28
Libancell S.A.L. v. The Republic of Lebanon, No. 06 Civ. 2765, 2006 WL 1321328 (S.D.N.Y. 2006)..... 14.49
Liberian E. Timber Corp. v. Republic of Liberia, 650 F. Supp. 73 (S.D.N.Y. 1986); 659 F. Supp. 606 (D.D.C. 1987) 14.55, 14.70, 14.74
Liberty Re (Bermuda) Ltd. v. Transamerica Occidental Life Ins. Co., No. 04 civ. 5044 (NRB), 2005 WL 1216292 ..... 9.59
Libra Bank Ltd. v. Banco Nacional de Costa Rica, S. A., 676 F.2d 47 (2d Cir. 1982)...... 14.36
Libyan Am. Oil Co. (LIAMCO) v. Gov't of the Libyan Arab Republic, 20 I.L.M. 1 (1977) ... 14.08
Liebowitz v. Elsevier Sci. Ltd., 927 F. Supp. 688 (S.D.N.Y. 1996)..... 4.17
Life Ins. Co. of Am. v. Duncanson & Holt, Inc., 228 F.3d 865 (8th Cir. 2000) 9.64
Life Receivables Trust v. Goshawk Syndicate 102 at Lloyd's, 888 N.Y.S.2d 458 (1st Dep't 2009)..... 3.18
Life Receivables Trust v. Syndicate 102 at Lloyd's of London 549 F.3d 210 (2d Cir. 2008) 1.18, 2.63, 3.43, 3.39, 9.05–9.06, 9.65
Lisenba v. California, 314 U.S. 219 (1941)..... 13.119
Livingston v. Assocs. Fin., Inc., 339 F.3d 553 (7th Cir. 2003) 6.27, 11.85
LLC v. Republic of Arg., 902 F. Supp. 2d 367 (S.D.N.Y. 2012), aff'd, 735 F.3d 72 (2d Cir. 2013)..... 14.03
Lloyd's Underwriters v. AO Gazsnabtranzit, No. 00 Civ. 242, 2000 WL 1719493 (N.D. Ga., Nov. 2, 2000)..... 14.53
LNC Invs., Inc. v. Republic of Nicaragua, No. 96 Civ. 6360, 2000 WL 745550 (S.D.N.Y. June 8, 2000) 14.70
Lomax v. Woodmen of World Life Ins. Society 228 F. Supp. 2d 1360 (N.D. Ga. 2002) 11.88
Louis Dreyfus Negoce S.A. v. Blystad Shipping & Trading Inc., 252 F.3d 218 (2d Cir. 2001) 3.05, 4.46, 6.24, 7.91, 7.95
Lourdes Med. Ctr. of Burlington County v. JNESO, No. 04-Civ-4494 (JCL), 2007 WL 1040961 ..... 13.123
Love v. New York, 78 N.Y.2d 540 (1991)..... 10.40
Lovell v. Harris Methodist Health Sys., No. Civ. A. 3:99CV2809G, 2000 WL 351384.... 13.123
Lowden v. T-Mobile USA Inc., 512 F.3d 1213 (9th Cir. 2008) 11.85, 11.101
Lucent Technologies, Inc. v. Tatung Co., No. 02 CIV. 8107, 2003 WL 402539; 379 F.3d 24, 28 (2d Cir. 2004) 13.25, 13.46, 13.117
Lucente v. Int'l Bus. Mach. Corp., 310 F.3d 243 (2d Cir. 2002) 4.29
Ludgate Ins. Co. v. Banco de Seguros del Estado, No. 02 Civ. 3653 (DC), 2003 WL 443584 ..... 13.125
Lugosch v. Pyramid Co. of Onondaga, 435 F.3d 110 (2d Cir. 2006) 9.59
Lumhoo v. Home Depot USA, Inc., 229 F. Supp. 2d 121 (E.D.N.Y. 2002)..... 4.13
Lytle v. Citifinancial Services, Inc., 810 A.2d 643 (Pa. Super. Ct. 2002) 11.86

M&C Corp. v. Erwin Behr GmbH & Co., 87 F.3d 844 (6th Cir. 1996) 13.36
Mace v. Van Ru Credit Corp, 109 F.3d 338 (7th Cir. 1997) 11.08
Mackey v. MBNA America Bank, N.A., 343 F. Supp. 2d 966 (W.D. Wash. 2004) 11.88
MACTEC, Inc. v. Gorelick, 427 F.3d 821 (10th Cir. 2005) 3.57
Magi XXI, Inc. v. Stato Della Citta Del Vaticano, 2008 WL 3895915 (E.D.N.Y. 2008) 5.29
Mallory Factor Inc. v. W. Coast Entm't Corp., No. 99 CIV 4819 (JFK), 1999 WL 1021076 . . . . 9.30
Management & Technical Consultants S.A. v. Parsons-Jurden Intern. Corp., 820 F.2d 1531 (9th Cir. 1987) 6.94, 6.101
Mandarin Trading Ltd. v. Wildenstein, 65 A.D.3d 448 (2009) aff'd, 16 N.Y.3d 173 (2011) 10.34
Mandel v. Household Bank (Nevada), 129 Cal. Rptr. 2d 380 (Cal. Ct. App. 2003) 11.86
Manlius Center Road Corp. v. N.Y., 370 N.Y.S.2d 750 (4th Dep't 1975) 4.34
Manning v. Smith Barney, Harris Upham & Co., 822 F. Supp. 1081 (S.D.N.Y. 1993) . . . 13.137
Marcraft Recreation Corp. v. Frances Devlin Co., Inc., 459 F. Supp. 195 (S.D.N.Y. 1978) 4.51
Marie v. Allied Home Mortgage Corp., 402 F.3d 1 (1st Cir. 2005) 6.32, 11.14
Marine Mgmt., Inc. v. Seco Mgmt. Inc., 574 N.Y.S.2d 207 (2d Dep't, 1991) aff'd, 80 N.Y.2d 886 (1992) 10.47
Marine Trading Ltd. v. Naviera Comercial Naylamp S.A., 879 F. Supp. 389 (S.D.N.Y. 1995) 13.46
Maritime Ventures Int'l, Inc. v. Caribbean Trading & Fidelity Ltd., 689 F. Supp. 1340 (S.D.N.Y. 1988) 6.111
Marmet Health Care Center, Inc. v. Brown, 132 S. Ct. 1201 (2012) 0.43, 10.28
Maryland Cas. Co. v. Realty Advisory Bd. on Labor Relations, 107 F.3d 979 (2d Cir. 1997) 8.36
Master Lease Corp. v. Manhattan Limousine, Ltd. 177 A.D.2d 85 (2d Dep't 1992) 10.18
Master's Choice, Inc. v. Cowie, No. 96-CV-0554E(F), 1997 WL 211368 . . . . 13.113
Mastrobuono v. Shearson Lehman Hutton, Inc., 514 U.S. 52 (1995); 115 S. Ct. 1212, 1219 (1995) 0.50, 1.105, 3.15, 3.34, 6.17, 8.12, 9.07, 9.28, 10.28, 11.49, 13.147
Matarasso v. Continental Casualty Co., 56 N.Y.2d 264 (1982) .1.40, 7.108
Mathews v. Eldridge, 424 U.S. 319 (1976) 13.96
Matter of Diamond Waterproofing Sys., Inc. v. 55 Liberty Owners Corp., 4 N.Y.3d 247 (2005) 3.15, 3.20
Matter of Shomron v. Fuks, 286 A.D.2d 587 (1st Dep't), appeal denied, 97 N.Y.2d 607 (2001) 12.27
Matter of Smith Barney, Harris Upham, & Co. v. Luckie, 85 N.Y.2d 193 (N.Y 1995) 1.108
Matter of Smith Barney Shearson v. Sacharow, 91 N.Y.2d 39 (N.Y 1997) 1.107
Matter of Sojitz Corp. v. Prithvi Info. Solutions Ltd., 921 N.Y.S.2d 14 (1st Dep't 2011) 3.52
Maxwell Commc'n Corp., In Re, 198 B.R. 63 (S.D.N.Y. 1996) 4.14
McCarthy v. Smith Barney Inc., 58 F. Supp. 2d 288 (S.D.N.Y. 1999) 13.113
McConnell v. Commonwealth Pictures Corp., 166 N.E.2d 494 (N.Y. 1960) 4.55
McCreary Tire & Rubber Co. v. CEAT, 501 F.2d 1032 (3d Cir. 1974) 8.33
McDaniel v. Bear Stearns & Co., 196 F. Supp. 2d 343 (S.D.N.Y. 2002) 9.52
McDonald's Corp. v. Hinksman, 1999 WL 441468 . . . . 4.64
McDonnell Douglas Fin. Corp. v. Pa. Power & Light Co., 858 F.2d 825 (2d Cir. 1988) 4.46
MCI Telecommunications Corp. v. Exalon Indus., Inc., 138 F.3d 426 (1st Cir. 1998) 6.68
McKeon v. Van Slyck, 119 N.E. 851 (N.Y. 1918) 4.20
McKesson Automated Healthcare, Inc. v. Brooklyn Hosp. Ctr., 779 N.Y.S.2d 765 (Sup. Ct. 2004) 10.21
McKinley Assocs. v. McKensson HBOC, Inc., 110 F. Supp. 2d 169 (W.D.N.Y. 2000) 10.24
McLeod v. R.B. Hamilton Moving & Storage, 453 N.Y.S.2d 251 (2d Dep't 1982) 10.15
McMahan Sec. Co. v. Forum Capital Mkts., 35 F.3d 82 (2d Cir. 1994) 7.117, 10.49
McQueen-Starling v. Oxford Health Plans, No. 08 Civ. 4885 (JGK), 2009 U.S. Dist. LEXIS 23266 (S.D.N.Y. 2009) 1.29

Meadows Indemnity Co. Ltd. v. Baccala & Shoop Ins. Services, Inc., 760 F. Supp. 1036(E.D.N.Y. 1991) 6.16
Meda Int'l v. Salzman 24 A.D.2d 710 (1st Dep't 1965) 8.49
Medway Power Ltd., In Re, 985 F. Supp. 402 (S.D.N.Y. 1997) 9.76
Meisels v. Uhr, 593 N.E.2d 1359 (N.Y. 1992) 13.141
Mejdrech v. Met-Coif Sys Corp., 319 F.3d 910 (7th Cir. 2003) 11.08
Mencher v. Weiss, 114 N.E.2d 177 (N.Y. 1953) 4.17
Merrill Lynch, Pierce, Fenner & Smith, Inc. v. Adler, 234 A.D.2d 139 (1st Dep't 1996) 3.15, 3.34
Merrill Lynch, Pierce, Fenner & Smith, Inc. v. Bobker, 808 F.2d 930 (2d Cir. 1986) 1.91, 3.55, 13.128
Merrill Lynch, Pierce, Fenner & Smith, Inc. v. Cohen, 62 F.3d 381 (11th Cir. 1995) 11.14
Merrill Lynch, Pierce, Fenner & Smith, Inc. v. Jaros, 70 F.3d 418 (6th Cir. 1995) 6.92
Merrill Lynch, Pierce, Fenner & Smith Inc. v. Lecopulos, 553 F.2d 842 (2d Cir. 1977) 7.28, 13.46
Merrill Lynch, Pierce, Fenner & Smith, Inc. v. McLeod, 622 N.Y.S.2d 954 (N.Y. App. Div. 1995) 7.28
Merrill Lynch, Pierce, Fenner & Smith, Inc. v. Wise Metals Grp., LLC, 798 N.Y.S.2d 14 (1st Dep't 2005) 4.53
Merrill Lynch Investment Managers v. Optibase, Ltd., 337 F.3d 125 (2d Cir. 2003) 7.64
Merritt Hill Vineyards Inc. v. Windy Heights Vineyard, Inc., 460 N.E.2d 1077 (N.Y. 1984) 4.14
Messina & Briante, Inc., v. Blitman Constr. Corp., 32 Misc. 2d 21 (N.Y. Sup. Ct. 1961); aff'd, 19 A.D.2d 862 (2d Dep't 1963), app. dismissed, 14 N.Y.2d 648 (1964) 10.49
Metallgesellschaft A.G. v. M/V Capitan Constante, 790 F.2d 280 (2d Cir. 1986) 6.46, 8.21
Metro. Life Ins. Co. v. Robertson-Ceco Corp., 84 F.3d 560 (2d Cir. 1996) 13.48
Metro. Switch Bd. Mfg. Co., Inc. v. B & G Elec. Contractors, Div. of B & G Indus., Inc., 96 A.D.3d 725 (2012) 10.34
MGM Prods. Group, Inc. v. Aeroflot Russian Airlines, No. 03 Civ. 0500 (RMB), 2003 WL 21108367 . . . . . 13.109
Mgmt. & Tech. Consultants S.A. v. Parsons-Jurden Int'l Corp., 820 F.2d 1531 (9th Cir. 1987) 13.112
Michele Amoruso E Figli v. Fisheries Development Corp., 499 F. Supp. 1074 (S.D.N.Y. 1980) 6.20
Microchip Technology Inc. v. U.S. Philips Corp., 367 F.3d 1350 (Fed. Cir. 2004) 6.20
Micula v. Gov't of Romania, No. 1:14-CV-00600 (APM), 2015 WL 2354310 . . . . . 14.24
Miller v. Benjamin, 617, 37 N.E. 631 (N.Y. 1894) 4.23
Miller v. Flume, 139 F.3d 1130 (7th Cir. 1998) 11.14
Miller v. Worth Capital, Inc., 1998 WL 193213 (S.D.N.Y. 1998) 7.110
Milstein v. Protection One Alarm Services, Inc. 11.80
Miminco, LLC v. Dem. Rep. Congo, 79 F. Supp. 3d 213 (D.D.C. 2015) 14.24
Ministry of Def. of Islamic Republic of Iran v. Gould Inc., 887 F.2d 1357 (9th Cir. 1989) 6.101, 13.34
Mississippi Power Co. v. Peabody Coal Co., 69 F.R.D. 558 (S.D. Miss. 1976) 8.38
Mitsubishi Motors Corp. v. Soler Chrysler-Plymouth, 473 U.S. 614 (1985) 1.13, 4.45, 6.13–6.15, 6.78, 6.82, 6.106, 7.14, 7.122, 9.12, 13.107
Mobil Cerro Negro Ltd. v. Bolivarian Republic of Venezuela, 87 F. Supp. 3d 573 (S.D.N.Y. 2015) 0.48, 14.15, 14.22–14.23, 14.27
Monegasque de Reassurances S.A.M. v. Nak Naftogaz of Ukraine, 311 F.3d 488 (2d Cir. 2002) 13.62, 14.30, 14.55
Morelite Constr. Corp. v. N.Y. City Dist. Council Carpenters Benefit Funds, 748 F.2d 79 (2d Cir. 1984) 13.115
Morgan v. Nikko Sec. Cop. Int'l, 691 F. Supp. 792 (S.D.N.Y. 1992) 7.110
Morgan Servs., Inc. v. Abrams, 801 N.Y.S.2d 457 (4th Dep't 2005) 4.16
Morris v. Morgan Stanley & Co., 942 F.2d 648 (9th Cir. 1991) 6.10

Morton's of Chicago/Great Neck LLC v. Crab House, Inc., 746 N.Y.S.2d 317 (2d Dep't. 2002) 4.16
Moseley v. Electronic & Missile Facilities, Inc., 374 U.S. 167 (1963) 6.20
Moses H. Cone Mem'l Hosp. v. Mercury Const. Corp., 460 U.S. 1 (1983) 1.13, 3.20, 4.45, 6.03, 6.13–6.14, 6.32, 6.64, 6.80, 7.14, 11.13, 13.19
Motorola Credit Corp. v. Kemal Uzan, 388 F.3d 39 (2d Cir. 2004) 1.56, 1.69, 6.17
MQDC, Inc. v. Steadfast Ins. Co., No. CV 2012-1424, 2013 U.S. Dist. LEXIS 172836 . . . . 11.85
Muhummad v. County Bank of Rehobeth Beach, 912 A.2d 88 (N.J. 2006) 11.85–11.86
Mulvaney Mechanical, Inc. v. Sheet Metal Workers Intern. Ass'n, Local 38, 351 F.3d 43 (2d Cir. 2003) 6.30–6.31
Munich Re America Inc. v. Ace Property & Casualty Co., 500 F. Supp.2d 272 (S.D.N.Y. 2007) 12.27
Murphy v. DirecTV, Inc., 724 F.3d 1218 (9th Cir. 2013) 11.111
Murphy v. Gutfreund, 583 F. Supp. 957 (S.D.N.Y. 1984) 10.32
Murray v. Schooner Charming Betsy, 6 U.S. (2 Cranch) 64, 118 (1804) 13.32
Murray Oil Prods. Co. v. Mitsui & Co., 146 F.2d 381 (2d. Cir. 1944) 8.33
Mut. Marine Office, Inc. v. Transfercom Ltd., No. 08 Civ. 10367 (PGG), 2009 WL 1025965 . . . . 9.59

N.Y. Tel. Co. v. Comm'cns Workers of Am. Local 1100, 256 F.3d 89 (2d Cir. 2001) 13.130
Nanosolutions, LLC v. Prajza, 793 F. Supp. 2d 46 (D.D.C. 2011) 6.10
NAS Elec., Inc. v. Transtech Elec. PTE Ltd., 262 F. Supp. 2d 134 (S.D.N.Y. 2003) 4.23
Nat'l Broad. Co., In Re, No. M-77 (RWS), 1998 WL 1994 . . . . 9.76
Nat'l Broad. Co. v. Bear Stearns & Co., In Re, 165 F.3d 184 (2d Cir. 1999) 3.39, 3.43, 9.12, 9.76
Nat'l Cas. Co. v. First State Ins. Group, 430 F.3d 492 (1st Cir. 2005) 13.114
Nat'l Mkt. Share, Inc. v. Sterling Nat'l Bank, 392 F.3d 520 (2d Cir. 2004) 4.37, 10.02
Nat'l Union Fire Ins. Co. v. Belco Petrol. Corp., 88 F.3d 129 (2d Cir. 1996) 6.91
National American Ins. Co. v. Transamerica Occidental Life Ins. Co., 328 F.3d 462 (8th Cir. 2003) 6.32
National Broadcasting Co. v. Bear Stearns & Co 165 F.3d 184 (2d Cir. 1999) 9.76
National Dev. Co. v. Khashoggi, 781 F. Supp. 959 (S.D.N.Y. 1992) 6.55, 6.99
National Oil Corp. v. Libyan Sun Oil Co., 733 F. Supp. 800 (D. Del. 1990) 6.101
National Union Fire Ins. Co. of Pittsburgh v. Belco Petroleum Corp., 88 F.3d 129 (2d Cir. 1996) 6.34
NCR Corp. v. SAC-Co., Inc., 43 F.3d 1076 (6th Cir. 1995) 6.75
NCSPlus Inc. v. WBR Mgmt. Corp., 37 Misc. 3d 227 (N.Y. Sup. Ct. 2012) 10.25
Neptune Maritime, Ltd. v. H&J Isbrandtsen, Ltd., 559 F. Supp. 531 (S.D.N.Y. 1983) 1.16
Neri v. Retail Marine Corp., 285 N.E.2d 311 (N.Y. 1972) 4.39
New Colony Homes, Inc. v. Long Island Prop. Grp., LLC, 803 N.Y.S.2d 615 (2d Dep't 2005) 4.24
New England Energy, Inc. v. Keystone Shipping Co., 855 F.2d 1 (1st Cir. 1988) 11.53
New York v. Oneida Indian Nation, 90 F.3d 58 (2d Cir. 1996) 6.38
New York Water Serv. Corp. v. New York, 163 N.Y.S.2d 538 (1st Dep't 1957) 10.04
Newin Corp. v. Hartford Accident & Indem. Co., 333 N.E.2d 163 (N.Y. 1975) 4.58
Nitro-Lift Technologies LLC v. Howard, 133 S. Ct. 500 (2012) 0.43
NML Capital, Ltd. v. Republic of Arg., 680 F.3d 254 (2d Cir. 2012) 14.56
Norex Petroleum Ltd. v. Access Indus., Inc., 416 F.3d 146 (2d Cir. 2005) 13.64

O'Neill v. Warburg, Pincus & Co., 39 A.D.3d 281 (1st Dep't 2007) 10.20
Oakwood Mobile Homes, Inc., In Re, 987 S.W.2d 571 (Tex. 1999) 6.80
Oberwager v. McKechnie, Ltd., No. 06-2685, 2007 WL 4322982 (E.D. Pa. 2007) 1.24
Oblix, Inc. v. Winiecki, 374 F.3d 488 (7th Cir. 2004) 3.26
Ocean Warehousing B.V. v. Baron Metals & Alloys, Inc., 157 F. Supp. 2d 245 (S.D.N.Y. 2001) 13.07

Odell v. Broadway Condo., 728 N.Y.S.2d 464 (1st Dep't 2001) 4.21
Odfjell ASA v. Celanese AG, 348 F. Supp. 2d 283 (S.D.N.Y. 2004) 9.66
Office of Supply Government of Republic of Korea v. New York Nav. Co., Inc., 469 F.2d 377 (2d Cir. 1972) 6.31
Oh Young Indus. Co. v. E&J Textile Group, Inc., No. B179884, 2005 WL 2470824 . . . . . 7.06
Oil Basins Ltd. v. Broken Hill Proprietary Co. Ltd., 613 F. Supp. 483 (S.D.N.Y. 1985) 7.18, 7.102
Old Colony Trust Co. v. Omaha, 230 U.S. 100 (1913) 4.04
Oldroyd v. Elmira Sav. Bank, 134 F.3d 72 (2d Cir. 1998) 7.117, 7.119, 10.49
Ometto v. ASA Bioenergy Holding A.G., No. 12 CIV 1328, 2013 WL 174259; 549 Fed. Appx. 41 (2d Cir. 2014) 5.85, 13.116
Omstead v. Dell, Inc., 473 F. Supp. 2d 1018 (N.D. Cal. 2007) 11.85
Operadora DB Mex., S.A. de C.V., In Re, No. 6:09-cv-383-Orl-22GJK, 2009 WL 242313 . . . . . 9.77
Orange Chicken, L.L.C. v. Nambe Mills, Inc., No. 00 Civ. 4730, 2000 WL 1858556 (S.D.N.Y. 2000) 6.23
Ore & Chemical Corp. v. Stinnes Interoil, Inc., 611 F. Supp. 237 (S.D.N.Y. 1985) 5.30
Oriental Commercial & Shipping Co., Ltd. v. Rosseel, N.V., 125 F.R.D. 398 (S.D.N.Y. 1989) 3.40
Oriental Republic of Uruguay v. Chemical Overseas Holdings, Inc., No. 05 Civ. 6151 (WHP), 2006 WL 164967 . . . . . 7.35
Orion Shipping & Trading Co. v. Eastern States Petroleum Corp., 312 F.2d 299 (2d Cir. 1963) 1.15, 6.68, 6.70, 6.88
Ortelere v. Teacher's Ret. Bd. of City of New York, 250 N.E.2d 460 (N.Y. 1969) 4.20
Oscar Gruss & Son, Inc. v. Hollander, 337 F.3d 186 (2d Cir. 2003) 10.51
Oscar Prod., Inc. v. Zacharius, 893 F. Supp. 250 (S.D.N.Y. 1995) 4.13
Ottawa Office Integration Inc. v. FTF Bus. Sys., Inc., 132 F. Supp. 2d 215 (S.D.N.Y. 2001) 13.119
Ottley v. Sheepsheard Nursing Homes, 688 F.2d 883 (2d Cir. 1982) 6.05
Overseas Cosmos, Inc. v. NR Vessel Corp., No. 97 Civ. 5898 (DC), 1997 WL 757041 . . . . . 13.81
Oxford Health Plans LLC v. Sutter 133 S.Ct. 2004 (2013) 0.46, 11.25
Oxus Gold PLC, In Re, No. Misc. 06-82, 2006 WL 2927615 . . . . . 9.77

P & P Indus., Inc. v. Sutter Corp., 179 F.3d 861 (10th Cir. 1999) 3.60
P.T. Reasuransi Umum Indon. v. Evanston Ins. Co., No. 92 Civ. 4623, 1992 WL 400733 . . . 13.97
Pac. Reinsurance Mgmt. Corp. v. Ohio Reinsurance Corp., 935 F.2d 1019 (9th Cir. 1991) 8.16, 14.37
PacifiCare Health Sys. v. Bock, 538 U.S. 401 (2003) 0.41, 6.28, 6.78, 6.83
PaineWebber Inc, v. Bybyk, 81 F.3d 1193 (2d Cir. 1996) 1.38, 3.15, 3.19, 3.30, 6.66, 7.35, 11.14, 13.149
Pan Atl. Group, Inc. v. Republic Ins. Co., 878 F. Supp. 630 (S.D.N.Y. 1995) 13.72
Pantzer v. Shields Dev. Co., 660 F. Supp. 56 (D. Del. 1986) 4.19
Paramedics Electromedicina Comercial, Ltda. v. GE Med. Sys. Info. Techs., Inc., 369 F.3d 645 (2d Cir. 2004) 0.41, 7.131, 7.137, 8.39
Parsons & Whittemore Overseas Co. v. Société Generale de l'Industrie du Papier (RAKTA), 508 F.2d 969 (2d Cir. 1974) . . . 1.31, 6.72, 6.94, 6.97, 6.100, 6.102, 6.106, 13.78
Peak v. Northway Travel Trailers Inc., 688 N.Y.S.2d 738 (3d Dep't 1999) 4.40
Pedcor Mgmt. Co. v. Nations Pers. of Tex., 343 F.3d 355 (5th Cir. 2003) 11.53
Pemex-Exploracion y Produccion v. Corporacion Mexicana de Mantenimiento Integral, S. de R.L. de C.V., 13-4022 (2d Cir) 1.99
Perpetual Secs., Inc. v. Tang, 290 F.3d 132 (2d Cir. 2002) 13.29
Perry v. Thomas 482 U.S. 483 (1987) 1.04, 1.08, 1.10, 1.65–1.67, 6.03, 6.15, 11.97
Personalized Media Commc'ns, L.L.C. v. StarSight Telecast Inc., 2000 WL 1457079, 3 (S.D.N.Y. 2000) 4.14
Pesa v. Yoma Dev. Grp., Inc., 18 N.Y.3d 527 (2012) 10.02

Peter F. Gaito Architecture, LLC v. Simone Dev. Corp., 846 N.Y.S.2d 368 (2d Dep't 2007) 4.19
Peters Fabrics, Inc. v. Jantzen, Inc., 582 F. Supp. 1287 (S.D.N.Y. 1984) 5.29
Petrofac, Inc. v. Dynmcdermott Petroleum Operations Co., 687 F.3d 671 (5th Cir. 2012) 11.14
Phibro Energy, Inc. v. Empresa de Polimeros De Sines Sarl, 720 F. Supp. 312 (S.D.N.Y. 1989) 4.70
Phillips P.R. Core, Inc. v. Tradax Petroleum Ltd., 1984 WL 677 .... 4.70
Phoenix Aktiengesellschaft v. Ecoplas, Inc., 391 F.3d 433 (2d Cir. 2004) 3.58–3.60, 7.103
Phoenix Canada Oil Co. Ltd. v. Texaco, Inc., 842 F.2d 1466 (3d Cir. 1988) 7.74
Photopaint Techs., LLC v. Smartlens Corp., 335 F.3d 152 (2d Cir. 2003) 13.14
Pictet Funds (Europe) S.A. v. Emerging Managers Grp., L.P., No. 14-CV-6854 SAS, 2014 WL 6766011 (S.D.N.Y. 2014) 1.41
Pine Valley Productions v. S.L. Collections, 828 F. Supp. 245 (S.D.N.Y. 1993) 1.100
Ping-Kuo Lin v. Horan Capital Mgmt, LLC, No. 14 Civ. 5202 (LLS), 2014 WL 3974585 ... 9.70
Pinnacle Env't Sys, Inc., In Re, 760 N.Y.S.2d 253 (3d Dep't 2003) 3.23
PMC Inc. v. Atomergic Chemetals Corp., 844 F. Supp. 177 (S.D.N.Y. 1994) 1.41
Polin v. Kellwood Co., 103 F. Supp. 2d 238 (S.D.N.Y. 2000) 8.08
Poponin v. Virtual Pro, Inc., 2006 WL 2691418 .... 6.80
Porter Hayden Co v. Century/Mem Co., 136 F.3d 380 (4th Cir. 1998) 11.49
Porzig v. Dresdner, Kleinwort, Benson, N.Am. LLC, 497 F.3d 133 (2d Cir. 2007) 13.127
Positive Software Solutions, Inc. v. New Century Mortgage Corp., 436 F.3d 495 (5th Cir. 2006), rev'd en banc 476 F.3d 278 (5th Cir.), cert. denied, 127 S.Ct. 2943 (2007) 5.43
Postlewaite v. McGraw-Hill, Inc., 333 F.3d 42 (2d Cir. 2003) 6.33
PowerAgent, Inc. v. Elec. Data Sys. Corp., 358 F.3d 1187 (9th Cir. 2004) 6.54
PowerAgent, Inc. v. United States Dist. Court for the N. Dist. of Cal., 210 F.3d 385 (9th Cir. 2000) 6.54
PPG Indus. v. Webster Auto Parts, 128 F.3d 103 (2d Cir. 1997) 6.32
President & Fellows of Harvard Coll. v. JSC Surgutneftegaz, No. 11 168 T 01654 04, Partial Final Award on Claim Construction (Am. Arb. Ass'n 2007) 9.60
Preston v. Ferrer 552 U.S. 346 (2008); 128 S. Ct. 978 (2008) 0.41, 1.54, 6.08, 6.15, 8.13, 13.150
Price v. Socialist People's Libya Arab Jamahiraya, 294 F.3d 82 (D.C. Cir. 2002) 14.27
Prima Paint Corp. v. Flood & Conklin Mfg. Co., 388 U.S. 395 (1967) 0.43, 1.12, 4.47, 6.03, 6.14, 6.19, 7.36, 9.06, 11.13, 11.98, 13.93
Productos Mercantiles e Industriales, S.A. v. Faberge USA, 23 F.3d 41 (2d Cir. 1994) 1.86, 7.18, 13.19
Profilati Italia S.r.l. v. Painewebber Inc., 941 F. Supp. 431 (S.D.N.Y. 1996) 1.15
Progressive Casualty Ins. Co. v. CA Reaseguradora Nacional de Venezuela, 991 F.2d 42 (2d Cir. 1993) 1.66–1.67, 6.04, 6.16, 7.72
Propulsora Ixtapa Sur v. Omni Hotels Franchising Corp., 211 A.D.2d 546 (1st Dep't 1995) 1.41, 7.110–7.111
Prospect Capital Corp. v. Enmon, No. 08 CIV. 3721 (LBS), 2010 WL 907956 .... 13.136
Protective Life Ins. Corp. v. Lincoln Nat'l Life Ins. Corp., 873 F.2d 281 (11th Cir. 1989) 11.53
Prozina Shipping Co. v. Elizabeth-Newark Shipping, Inc., No. 98 Civ. 5834, 1999 WL 705545 .... 13.119
PT Kaltim Prima Coal v. AES Barbers Point, Inc., 180 F. Supp. 2d 475 (S.D.N.Y. 2001) 4.49
Publicis Commc'n v. True N. Commc'ns, Inc., 206 F.3d 725 (7th Cir. 2000) 13.105
Puerto Rico Tel. Co. v. U.S. Phone Mfg. Corp., 427 F.3d 21 (1st Cir. 2005) 3.56

Quaak v. Klynveld Peat Marwick Goerdeler Bedrijfsrevisoren, 361 F.3d 11 (1st Cir. 2004) 7.134
Quackenbush v. Allstate Ins. Co., 517 U.S. 706 (1996) 4.45

Qualcomm Inc. v. Nokia Corp., 466 F.3d 1366 (Fed. Cir. 2006) 7.35, 7.85, 11.14
Quasem Group, Ltd. v. W.D. Mask Cotton Co., 967 F. Supp. 288 (W.D. Tenn. 1997). . . . 6.109
Quick & Reilly v. Jacobson, 126 F.R.D. 24 (S.D.N.Y. 1989) 13.137

R & I Elecs., Inc. v. Neuman, 411 N.Y.S.2d 401 (2d Dep't 1978) 10.14
R.J. O'Brien & Assoc., Inc. v. Pipkin, 64 F.3d 257 (7th Cir. 1995) 7.72
R.M. Perez & Associates, Inc. v. Welch, 960 F.2d 534 (5th Cir. 1992). 6.20
Rachmani Corp. v. 9 E. 96th St. Apartment Corp., 629 N.Y.S.2d 382 (1st Dep't 1995) 4.26
Radin v. Kleinman, 750 N.Y.S.2d 276 (App. Div. 2002). 9.06
Ragan v. AT&T Corp., 355 Ill. App.3d 1143 (Ill. App. Ct. 2005) 6.27
Ragucci v. Professional Constr. Services, 25 A.D. 3d 43 (N.Y. App. Div. 2005) 1.43
Ramos-Santiago v. UPS, 524 F.3d 120 (1st Cir. 2008) 1.92
Randall's Island Family Golf Ctrs., Inc., In Re, 261 B.R. 96 (Bankr. S.D.N.Y. 2001), aff'd, 272 B.R. 521 (S.D.N.Y. 2002). 4.15
Randolph v. Green Tree Fin Corp., Ala., 244 F.3d 814 (11th Cir. 2001). 11.85
Ranieri v. Bell Atlantic Mobile, 304 A.D.2d 353 (N.Y. App. Div. 2003) 6.27, 11.85
RCN Telecom Servs., Inc. v. 202 Centre St. Realty LLC, 419 F. Supp. 2d 553 (S.D.N.Y. 2006). 10.02
Real Color Displays, Inc. v. Universal Applied Technologies Corp., 1998 U.S. App. LEXIS 27791 . . . . 6.78, 6.80
Recold, S.A. de C.V. v. Monfort of Colorado, Inc., 893 F.2d 195 (8th Cir. 1990). 6.16
Red Apple Supermkts./Supermkts. Acquisitions v. Local 338, Retail, Wholesale & Chain Store Food Employees Union, No. 98 Civ. 2303 (LMM), 1999 WL 596273 . . . . 13.113
Red Cross Line v. Atl. Fruit Co., 264 U.S. 109 (1924). 13.140
Redish v. Yellow Transp., Inc., 2008 WL 2572658 (N.D. Tex. June 24, 2008) 2.96
Reed & Martin, Inc. v. Westinghouse Elec. Corp., 439 F.2d 1268 (2d Cir. 1971) 13.51
ReliaStar Life Ins. Co. of N.Y. v. EMC Nat'l Life Co., 564 F.3d 81 (2d Cir. 2009) 2.36, 3.33, 8.14, 9.52
Rembrandt Indus., Inc. v. Hodges Int'l, Inc., 344 N.E.2d 383 (N.Y. 1976). 6.34
Rennick v. O.P.T.I.O.N. Care, Inc., 77 F.3d 309 (9th Cir. 1996) 4.19
Rent-A-Center West, Inc v. Jackson, 561 U.S. 63 (2010); 130 S. Ct. 2722 (2010). 0.44, 1.13, 7.42, 7.58, 11.13
Republic of Arg. v. BG Group PLC, 715 F. Supp. 2d 108 (D.D.C. 2010). 14.03
Republic of Arg. v. Weltover, Inc., 504 U.S. 607 (1992) 14.59
Republic of Argentina v. NML Capital, Ltd , 134 S. Ct. 2250 (2014). 14.57
Republic of Ecuador v. Chevron Texaco Corp., 376 F. Supp. 2d 334 (S.D.N.Y. 2005); 638 F.3d 384 (2d Cir. 2011) 1.64, 6.10, 6.16–6.17, 6.23, 7.52
Republic of Ecuador v. Connor, 708 F.3d 651 (5th Cir. 2013) 9.77
Republic of Ecuador, In Re, 735 F.3d 1179 (10th Cir. 2013) 9.77
Republic of Kazakhstan v. Biedermann Int'l, 168 F.3d 880 (5th Cir. 1999). 3.41, 9.76
Republic of Nicaragua v. Standard Fruit Co., 937 F.2d 469 (9th Cir. 1991) 6.19
Republic of the Philippines v. Westinghouse Elec. Corp., 714 F. Supp. 1362 (D.N.J. 1999) 6.03
Rhone Mediterranee Compagnia Francese di Assicurazioni e Riassicurazoni v. Lauro, 712 F.2d 50 (3d Cir. 1983) 1.72, 6.16
Rintin Corp., S.A. v. Domar, Ltd., 476 F.3d 1254 (11th Cir. 2007) 6.78
Roadway Package Sys., Inc. v. Kayser, 257 F.3d 287 (3d Cir. 2001). 3.56, 11.49
Roberts v. Finger, 15 Misc. 3d 1118(A), 839 N.Y.S.2d 436 (N.Y. Sup. Ct. 2007) 1.108
Roberts v. Karimi, 251 F.3d 404 (2d Cir. 2001) 4.23
Rocanova v. Equitable Life Assurance Soc'y of the United States, 634 N.E.2d 940 (N.Y. 1994). 4.54, 10.05, 10.27
Rochester City Sch. Dist. v. Rochester Teachers Ass'n, 41 N.Y.2d 578 (1977) 8.14
Rollins, Inc. v. Garrett, 176 Fed. Appx. 968 (11th Cir. 2006) 11.85
Rosa Hair Stylists v. Jaber Food Corp., 218 A.D.2d 793 (2d Dep't 1995). 8.48

Rosgoscirc v. Circus Show Corp., 1993 WL 277333 (S.D.N.Y. 1993) 5.29
Roth v. Isomed, Inc., 746 F. Supp. 316 (S.D.N.Y. 1990) 4.17
Rothberg v. Loeb, Rhoades & Co., 445 F. Supp. 1336 (S.D.N.Y. 1978) 7.110
Rourke v. Fred H. Thomas Assocs., 627 N.Y.S.2d 831 (3d Dep't 1995) 10.45
Royal Indem. Co. v. Westinghouse Elec. Corp., 385 F. Supp. 520 (S.D.N.Y. 1974) 10.18
Roz Trading Ltd., In Re, 469 F. Supp. 2d 1221 (N.D. Ga. 2006); No. 1:06-CV-02305-
WSD, 2007 WL 120844 .... 9.77
Rubin v. Soya International Corp., In Re, 457 F. Supp. 2d 191 (S.D.N.Y. 2006) 6.20, 7.58
Rubinstein v. Rubinstein, 23 N.Y.2d 293 (1968) 10.09
Ruppert v. Sec'y of U.S. Dept. of Health & Human Servs., 671 F. Supp. 151
(E.D.N.Y. 1987), rev'd on other grounds, 871 F.2d 1172 (2d Cir. 1989) 4.20
Rush v. Oppenheimer & Co., Inc., 681 F. Supp. 1045 (S.D.N.Y. 1988) 6.20
Rutherford v. Gray Line, Inc., 615 F.2d 944 (2d Cir. 1980) 4.11
Ryan, Beck & Co, LLC v. Fakih, 268 F.Supp.2d 210 (E.D.N.Y. 2003) 6.72

S & R Co. of Kingston v. Latona Trucking, Inc., 159 F.3d 80 (2d Cir. 1998) 6.32, 7.95–7.96, 7.121, 8.32
S.A. Mineracao da Trinidade-Samitri v. Utah Int'l Inc., 576 F. Supp. 566 (S.D.N.Y.
1984), aff'd, 745 F.2d 190 (2d Cir. 1984) 3.05, 7.121
Sabbeth Indus. Ltd. v. Pennsylvania Lumbermens Mut. Ins. Co., 656 N.Y.S.2d 475
(3d Dep't 1997) 10.20
Sablosky v. Edward S. Gordon Co., Inc., 535 N.E.2d 643 (N.Y. 1989) 3.26
Sabo v. Delman, 143 N.E.2d 906 (N.Y. 1957) 4.54
Salim Oleochemicals v. M/V Shropshire, 278 F.3d 90 (2d Cir. 2002) 6.37, 7.117
Salomon, Inc. Shareholders' Derivative Litigation, In Re, 68 F.3d 554
(2d Cir. 1995) 5.29, 6.15
Salvano v. Merrill Lynch, Pierce, Fenner & Smith, Inc., 647 N.E.2d 1298 (N.Y. 1995) ... 13.145
Sammy Line Co. v. Altamar Navegacion, S.A., 605 F. Supp. 72 (S.D.N.Y. 1985) 10.49
Sander v. Savage, 78 N.Y.S. 189 (2d Dep't 1902) 4.20
Sandvik v. Libby, 762 F. Supp. 596 (S.D.N.Y. 1991) 7.110
Sargent v. Paine Webber Jackson & Curtis, Inc., 882 F.2d 529 (D.C. Cir. 1989) 13.17
Sarhank Group v. Oracle Corp., 404 F.3d 657 (2d Cir. 2005) 1.57, 3.16, 6.04, 6.10, 6.17, 6.23, 6.95–6.96, 6.99, 6.102, 7.22, 7.69, 13.27
Satcom Int'l Group PLC v. Orbcomm Int'l Partners, 49 F. Supp. 2d 331 (S.D.N.Y. 1999),
aff'd, 205 F.3d 1324 (2d Cir. 1999) 6.51
Saudi Iron & Steel Co. v. Stemcor USA Inc., No. 97 Civ. 5976 (DLC), 1997
WL 642566 .... 6.106, 13.107, 13.110
Scandinavian Reinsurance Co. v. Saint Paul Fire & Marine Ins. Co., 668 F.3d 60, 71
(2d Cir. 2012) 5.85, 13.37
Scherk v. Alberto-Culver Co., 417 U.S. 506 (1974) 1.13, 6.02, 7.15, 7.17, 7.121, 13.07
Schnabel v. Trilegiant Corp., 697 F.3d 110 (2d Cir. 2012) 9.07
Schneider v. Kingdom of Thailand, 688 F.3d 68 (2d Cir. 2012) 3.18, 13.89
Schneider's Estate, In Re, 96 N.Y.S.2d 652 (N.Y. Sur. Ct. 1950) 4.11
Schoch v. Infousa, Inc., 341 F.3d 785 (8th Cir. 2003) 3.56
Schoenduve Corp. v. Lucent Techs., Inc., 442 F.3d 727 (9th Cir. 2006) 13.123
Schonfeld v. Hilliard, 218 F.3d 164 (2d Cir. 2000) 10.36
Schuman Sons Jewelers, Inc., In Re, 90 F.2d 606 (2d Cir. 1937) 4.04
Schwartz v. Greenberg, 107 N.E.2d 65 (N.Y. 1952) 4.18
Schwartz v. Merrill Lynch & Co., 665 F.3d 444 (2d Cir. 2011) 13.133
Scott v. Cingular Wireless 161 P.3d 1000 (W.A. 2007) 11.86, 11.102
Seattle Totems Hockey Club, Inc. v. Nat'l Hockey League, 652 F.2d 852
(9th Cir. 1981) 7.133
Sec. Ins. Co. of Hartford v. TIG Ins. Co., 360 F.3d 322 (2d Cir. 2004) 1.109, 13.149
Sec. Life Ins. Co. of Am. In Re, 228 F.3d 865 (8th Cir. 2000) 3.39
Sec. Life Ins. Co. of Am. v. Duncanson & Holt, Inc., 228 F.3d 865 (8th Cir. 2000) ... 9.05, 9.68

Seeberger v. McCormick, 175 U.S. 274 (1899) 4.21
Seetransport Wiking Trader Schiffahrtsgesellschaft MBH & Co., Kommanditgesellschaft v. Navimpex Centrala Navala, 989 F.2d 572 (2d Cir. 1993) 6.111, 13.14, 14.14
Seidman v. Indus. Recycling Props., Inc., 106 A.D. 3d 983 (N.Y. App. Div. 2013) 10.04
Sempra Energy Int'l v. Argentine Republic, No. M-82 (S.D.N.Y. Nov. 14, 2007) 14.23
Seven Seas Shipping (UK) Ltd. v. Tondo Limitada, No. 99 Civ. 1164, 2000 WL 60208 (S.D.N.Y. 2000) 14.29
SG Avipro Fin. Ltd. v. Cameroon Airlines, 2005 WL 1353955 . . . . . 7.151
Shaffer v. Heitner 433 U.S. 186 (1977) 13.56
Shanghai Foodstuffs Imp. & Exp. Corp. v. Int'l Chem., Inc., No. 99 Civ. 3320 (RCC), 2004 WL 213019 (S.D.N.Y. 2004) 13.09
Shank/Balfour Beatty v. IBEW Local 99, 497 F.3d 83 (1st Cir. 2007) 11.14
Sharp v. Kosmalski, 351 N.E.2d 721 (N.Y. 1976) 4.52
Shaw Group Inc. v. Triplefine Int'l Corp., 322 F.3d 115 (2d Cir. 2003) . . . 3.18–3.19, 6.15, 6.66, 7.34–7.35, 7.52, 7.167, 10.51, 10.54, 11.14, 13.149
Shea, In Re, 132 N.E.2d 864 (N.Y. 1956) 6.52
Shearson Lehman Hutton, Inc. v. Wagoner, 944 F.2d 114 (2d Cir. 1991) 6.34, 6.92
Shearson/Am. Express Inc. v. McMahon, 482 U.S. 220 (1987) 7.93, 7.123, 11.95
Sherr v. Dell, Inc., No. 05 CV 10097, 2006 WL 2109436 (S.D.N.Y. July 27, 2006) 6.10
Shroyer v. New Cingular Wireless Services, Inc., 498 F.3d 976 (9th Cir. 2007) 11.85, 11.102
Siag v. Arab Republic of Egypt, 2009 WL 1834562 . . . . . 14.23
Siderius, Inc. v. Compania de Acero del Pacifico, S.A., 453 F. Supp. 22 (S.D.N.Y. 1978) 7.25
Siderurgica del Orinoco (Sidor), C.A. v. Linea Naviera De Cabotaje, No. 99 Civ. 0075 (TPG), 1999 WL 632870 . . . . . 7.18, 7.24
Siegel v. Lewis, 358 N.E.2d 484 (N.Y. 1976) 9.07
Silverman v. Benmor Coats, Inc., 461 N.E.2d 1261 (N.Y. 1984) 13.141
Silverman v. Member Brokerage Servs., LLC, 751 N.Y.S.2d 245 (2d Dep't 2002) 4.19
Simply Fit of North America v. Poyner, 579 F. Supp. 2d 371 (E.D.N.Y. 2008) 7.58
Sinochem Int'l Co. v. Malaysia Int'l Shipping Corp., 549 U.S. 422 (2007) 13.62
Sivault Sys., Inc. v. Wondernet, Ltd., No. 05 Civ. 890, 2005 WL 681457 (S.D.N.Y. 2005) 14.40
Skandia America Reinsurance Company v. Caja Nacional de Ahorro y Seguro 1997 WL 278054 . . . . . 14.43–14.44
Slaney v. International Amateur Athletic Federation, 244 F.3d 580 (7th Cir. 2001) . . . 6.104, 13.96
Sleeper Farms v. Agway, Inc., 211 F. Supp. 2d 197 (D. Me. 2002) 7.35
Smiga v. Dean Witter Reynolds, Inc., 766 F.2d 698 (2d Cir. N.Y. 1985) 13.137
Smith Barney Harris Upham & Co. v. Luckie, 85 N.Y.2d 193 (1995) 1.39, 3.15, 3.20, 6.17, 13.148
Smith Barney Shearson Inc. v. Sacharow, 689 N.E.2d 884 (N.Y. 1997); 91 N.Y. 2d 39, 47 (1997) 3.16, 3.19, 6.66, 7.35, 9.07, 10.28, 11.14, 13.149
Smith Barney, Inc. v. Hause, 655 N.Y.S.2d 489 (App. Div. 1997) 13.148
Smith Sarno Inc. v. Sarver, 108 F.3d 92 (6th Cir. 1997) 11.14
Smith v. Gateway, Inc., 2002 WL 1728615 . . . . . 6.78
Smith v. Positive Prods., 419 F. Supp. 2d 437 (S.D.N.Y. 2005) 13.120
Smith/Enron Cogeneration L.P. v. Smith Cogeneration Int'l, Inc., 198 F.3d 88 (2d Cir. 1999) 1.58, 1.62, 4.47, 6.16, 6.64, 7.23, 7.64, 11.15, 13.29
Smoothline Ltd. v. N. Am. Foreign Trading Corp., 249 F.3d 147 (2d Cir. 2001) 6.13
Snowden v. CheckPoint Check Cashing, 290 F.3d 631 (4th Cir. 2002) 6.27, 11.85
Sobel v. Charles Schwab & Co., 828 N.Y.S.2d 720 (App. Div. 2007) 9.06
Soja v. Keystone Trozze, LLC, 106 A.D.3d 1168 (2013) 10.26
Sokoloff v. Harriman Estates Dev. Corp., 754 N.E.2d 184 (N.Y. 2001) 10.06
Sole Resort, S.A. de C.V. v. Allure Resorts Mgmt., LLC, 450 F.3d 100 (2d Cir. 2006) 9.07
Sommer v. Federal Signal Corp, 79 N.Y.2d 540 (1992) 10.26
Somportex Ltd. v. Philadelphia Chewing Gum Corp., 453 F.2d 435 (3d Cir. 1971), cert. denied, 405 U.S. 1017 (1972) 7.132

Sonera Holding B.V. v. Cukurova Holding A.S., 750 F.3d 221 (2d Cir. 2014). 0.47, 13.46, 13.48, 13.54
Sotheby's Int'l Rlty., Inc. v. Relocation Grp., LLC, 588 F. App'x 64 (2d Cir. 2015). 1.92, 13.133
Southland Corp. v. Keating, 465 U.S. 1 (1984) 1.04, 3.13, 6.03, 6.13–6.14, 8.13, 11.98, 13.29
Sovak v. Chugai Pharm. Co., 280 F.3d 1266 (9th Cir. 2002). 13.145
Spahr v. Secco, 330 F.3d 1266 (10th Cir. 2003) 11.14
Spear, Leeds & Kellogg v. Central Life Assur. Co., 85 F.3d 21 (2d Cir. 1996). 7.81
Spector and Specurity Ind. Ltd. v. Torenberg, 852 F. Supp. 201 (S.D.N.Y. 1994) 1.100
Spencer Trask Software & Info. Servs. LLC v. RPost Int'l Ltd., 383 F. Supp. 2d 428 (S.D.N.Y. 2003). 4.56
Sperry Int'l Trade, Inc. v. Gov't of Israel, 689 F.2d 301 (2d Cir. 1982). 8.08, 8.14, 8.21
Sphere Drake Ins. Ltd v. Clarendon Nat'l Ins. Co., 263 F.3d 26 (2d Cir. 2001) 1.31, 7.58, 7.105, 13.92
Sphere Drake Ins. PLC v. Marine Towing Inc., 16 F.3d 666 (5th Cir. 1994). 7.24
Spier v. Calzaturificio Tecnica S.p.A., 663 F. Supp. 871 (S.D.N.Y. 1987). 13.105
Spodek v. Park Prop. Dev. Assocs., 719 N.Y.S.2d 109 (2d Dep't. 2001) 10.39
St. Lawrence Factory Stores v. Ogdensburg Bridge & Port Auth., 13 N.Y.3d 204 (2009). . . . 10.30
St. Paul Fire & Marine Ins. Co. v. York Claims Serv., Inc., 308 A.D.2d 347 (1st Dep't 2003) 8.48
Star Shipping AS. v. China Nat'l Foreign Trade Trans. Corp., [1993] Lloyd's Rep. 445. . . . . 0.35
Startech, Inc. v. VSA Arts, 126 F. Supp. 2d 234 (S.D.N.Y. 2000) 4.17
Starter Corp. v. Converse, Inc., 170 F.3d. 286 (2d Cir. 1999). 4.61
State Farm Mut. Auto. Ins. Co. v. Wernick, 455 N.Y.S.2d 30 (App. Div. 1982) 9.06
Steelworkers v. Enter. Wheel & Car Corp., 363 U.S. 593 (1960). 6.25
Steelworkers v. Warrior & Gulf Navigation Co., 363 U.S. 574 (1960) 6.25
Stefano Berizzi Co. v. Krausz 146 N.E.2d 436 (N.Y. 1925) 13.123
Sternaman v. Metro. Life Ins. Co., 62 N.E. 763 (N.Y. 1902) 4.20
Stillman v. InService America Inc., 738 F.Supp. 2d 480 (S.D.N.Y. 2010). 10.42
Stolt-Nielsen S. A. v. AnimalFeeds Int'l Corp., 559 U.S. 662 (2010). 0.46, 1.23, 3.34, 6.27, 6.58, 7.29, 11.02, 11.24, 11.45, 13.133
Stolt-Nielsen S. A. v. Celanese AG, 430 F.3d 567 (2d Cir. 2005). 9.04, 9.66
Stolt-Nielsen Transp. Group B.V. v. Edible Oil Trading Corp., No. 06 Civ. 0703 (NRB), 2007 WL 194182. . . . . 13.51
Stolt Tankers, Inc. v. Marcus Oil & Chemical, 2001 U.S. Dist. Lexis 19750. . . . . 6.68
Stone & Webster, Inc. v. Triplefine Int'l Corp., 118 F. App'x 546 (2d Cir. 2004) 3.59
Storm LLC v. Telenor Mobile Commc'ns AS, No. 06 Civ. 13157 (GEL), 2006 WL 3735657 . . . . 1.57, 7.151, 8.16
Strauss Paper Co., Inc. v. RSA Exec. Search, Inc., 688 N.Y.S.2d 641 (2d Dep't 1999). 4.64
Suchodolski Assocs., Inc. v. Cardell Fin. Corp., (WHP), 2006 WL 3327625 . . . . .7.151
Sullivan Cnty. v. Edward L. Nezelek Inc., 42 N.Y.2d 123 (1977) 3.45
Sumitomo Corp. v. Parakopi Compania Maritima, S.A., 477 F. Supp. 737 (S.D.N.Y. 1979). . . 7.25
Sunoco, Inc. (R&M) v. Honeywell Int'l, Inc., 2006 U.S. Dist. Lexis 11392 . . . . 6.66, 6.73
Sutter v. Oxford Health Plans, LLC, 227 Fed. Appx. 135 (3d Cir. 2007). 6.91
Swerdloff v. Mobil Oil Corp., 427 N.Y.S.2d 266 (2d Dep't 1980) 10.32
Swift Industries v. Botany Industries, 466 F.2d 1125 (3d Cir. 1972). 6.62
Swift Splash, Ltd. v. Rice Corp., 2010 U.S. Dist. LEXIS 101324 (S.D.N.Y. 2010) 14.40
Swig Weiler & Arnow Mgmt. Co. v. Stahl, 817 F. Supp. 404 (S.D.N.Y. 1993) 4.55
Syncor Int'l Corp. v. McLeland, 1997 WL 452245 (4th Cir. 1997). 3.56
Szczepanek v. Dabek, No. 10-cv-2459(SJF)(ARL), 2011 WL 846193 . . . . 9.52
Szetela v. Discover Bank 118 Cal. Rptr. 2d at 868 (Cal. Ct. App. 2002). 11.85–11.86, 11.91

T. Co Metals, LLC v. Dempsey Pipe & Supply, Inc., 592 F.3d 329 (2d Cir. 2010). 1.94
Tallmadge, In Re, 181 N.Y.S. 336 (N.Y. Sup. Ct. 1919). 4.11

Tassin v. Ryan's Family Steakhouse, Inc., 509 F. Supp. 2d 585 (M.D.La. 2007). 6.10, 6.89
Taylor v. Citibank USA, N.A., 292 F. Supp. 2d 1333 (M.D. Ala. 2003). 11.90
Teamsters, Chauffeurs, Warehousemen & Helpers, Local Union No. 506 v. E.D. Clapp Corp., 551 F. Supp. 570 (S.D.N.Y. 1982). 13.121
Teamsters Local Union No. 764 v. J.H. Merrit & Co., 770 F.2d 40 (3d Cir. 1985) 6.111
Tech. in P'ship, Inc. v. Rudin, 894 F. Supp. 2d 274 (S.D.N.Y. 2012) aff'd, 538 F. App'x 38 (2d Cir. 2013). 7.97
Technologists, Inc. v. MIR's Ltd., 725 F. Supp. 2d 120 (D.D.C. 2010). 13.25
Technostroyexport, In Re, 853 F. Supp. 695 (S.D.N.Y. 1994) 9.13, 9.76
Telcordia Tech, Inc. v. Telkom SA, 458 F.3d 172 (3d Cir. 2006). 13.41
Teledyne, Inc. v. Kone Corp., 892 F.2d 1401 (9th Cir. 1990). 6.20
Telenor Mobile Comms. AS v. Storm LLC, 2007 U.S. Dist. Lexis 81454; 584 F.3d 396 (2d Cir. 2009) 6.64, 6.66, 6.72, 6.74, 13.81, 13.89
Tempo Shain Corp. v. Bertek, Inc., 120 F.3d 16 (2d Cir. 1997). 8.18, 13.119
Terminix Int'l Co., LP v. Palmer Ranch Ltd. P'ship, 432 F.3d 1327 (11th Cir. 2005) 7.35
Terris v. Cummiskey 203 N.Y.S.2d 445 (3d Dep't 1960). 4.53
Terrorist Attacks on Sept. 11, 2001, In Re, 538 F.3d 71 (2d Cir. 2008) 13.53
Tesoro Petroleum Corp. v. Asamera (S. Sumatra) Ltd., 798 F. Supp. 400 (W.D. Tex. 1992). 13.37
Tesoro Petroleum Corp. v. Holborn Oil Co., 145 Misc. 2d 715 (N.Y. Sup. Ct. 1989). 10.13
Texaco Overseas Petroleum Co. (TOPCO) & Cal. Asiatic Oil Co. v. Gov't of the Libyan Arab Republic, 53 I.L.R. 389 (1977) 14.08
Textron, Inc. v. Unisys Corp., 138 Misc.2d 124 (N.Y. Sup. Ct. 1987) 3.40, 3.43
Thai-Lao Lignite (Thailand) Co. Ltd. & Hongsa Lignite (Lao Pdr) Co., Ltd. v. Government of the Lao People's Democratic Republic, 2014 WL 476239 (S.D.N.Y. 2014) 1.99, 13.06, 14.55
The Republic of Ecuador v. Chevron Texaco Corp., 376 F. Supp. 2d 334 (S.D.N.Y. 2005). 1.33
Theis Research, Inc. v. Brown & Bain, 400 F.3d 659 (9th Cir. 2004). 6.78
Thibodeau v. Comcast Corp., 912 A.2d 874 (Pa. Super. Ct. 2006) 11.86
Thomas v. Carnival Corp., 573 F.3d 1113 (11th Cir. 2009). 7.123
Thompson v. Irwin Home Equity Corp., 300 F.3d 88 (1st Cir. 2002). 6.85
Thompson-CSF, S.A. v. American Arbitration Ass'n, 64 F.3d 773 (2d Cir. 1995). 3.24, 6.23, 7.64, 7.69, 7.73
Thyssen, Inc. v. S.S. Fortune Star, 777 F.2d 57 (2d Cir. 1985) 10.05
Thyssen Carbometal Co. v. FAI Energy, Ltd., Civ. No. 89-1695, 1990 U.S. Dist. LEXIS 427 (D.D.C. Jan. 16, 1990) 1.24
Tillman v. Commercial Credit Loans, Inc., 362 N.C. 93, 104; 655 S.E.2d 362 (N.C. 2008) 11.86, 11.114
Timberline Dev. LLC v. Kronman, 702 N.Y.S.2d 237 (1st Dep't 2000). 4.65
Ting v. AT&T, 319 F.3d 1126 (9th Cir. 2003) 6.27, 11.61, 11.85
TMR Energy Ltd v. State Prop. Fund of Ukraine, 411 F.3d 296 (D.C. Cir. 2005) 14.27
Tom Doherty Assocs., Inc. v. Saban Enter., 60 F.3d 27 (2d Cir. 1995) 10.36
Topps Co., v. Cadbury Stani S.A.I.C., 380 F. Supp. 2d 250 (S.D.N.Y. 2005) 10.03
Torrence v. Nationwide Budget Fin., 753 S.E.2d 802 (N.C. Ct. App. 2014) 11.114
Town House Stock LLC v. Coby Housing Corp., 855 N.Y.S.2d 55 (1st Dep't 2008) 4.24
Town of Amherst v. Custom Lighting Servs., L.L.C., No. 07-CV-261S, 2007 U.S. Dist. LEXIS 88296 (W.D.N.Y. 2007) 6.32
Town of Newburgh v. Civil Serv. Employees Ass'n, Inc., 707 N.Y.S.2d 225 (2d Dep't 2000). 3.23
Trans World Metals, Inc. v. Southwire Co., 769 F.2d 902 (2d Cir. 1985). 4.28
Transmarine Seaways Corp. of Monrovia v. Marc Rich & Co. A. G., 408 F. Supp. 352 (S.D.N.Y. 1979) 6.97, 6.102–6.103
Transport Wiking Trader Schiffahrtsgesellschaft MBH & Co., Kommanditgesellschaft v. Navimpex Centrala Navala, 989 F.2d 572 (2d Cir. 1993) 14.18

Transportacion Maritima Mexicana, S.A. v. Companhia de Navegacao Lloyd Brasileiro, 636 F. Supp. 474 (S.D.N.Y. 1983) 6.46, 6.60
Transrol Navagacao S.A. v. Redirekommanditselskaber Merc Scandia XXIX, 782 F. Supp. 848 (S.D.N.Y. 1991) 6.68, 7.06
Trimboli v. Scarpaci Funeral Home, In Re, 326 N.Y.S.2d 227 (2d Dep't 1971) 10.40
Trinity Biotech, Inc. v. Reidy, 665 F. Supp. 2d 377 (S.D.N.Y. 2009) 10.43
Trippe Manufacturing Co. v. Niles Audio Corp., 401 F.3d 529 (3rd Cir. 2005) 7.69
Truck Rent-A-Center, Inc. v. Puritan Farms 2nd, Inc., 361 N.E.2d 1015 (N.Y. 1977) 10.23
Tsadilas v. Providian National Bank 786 N.Y.S. 2d 478 (N.Y. App. Div. 2004) 6.27, 11.60, 11.85
Tube Steel Corp. of Am. v. Chicago Carbon Steel Prods., 319 F. Supp. 1302 (S.D.N.Y. 1970) 13.119
Turtur v. Rothschild Registry Int'l, Inc., 26 F.3d 304 (2d Cir. 1994) 4.07
Tymon v. Linoki, 213 N.E. 2d 661 (N.Y. 1965) 4.16

UHC Mgmt. Co. v. Computer Sew Corp., 148 F.3d 992 (8th Cir. 1998) 11.49
Ukrvneshprom State Foreign Econ. Enter. v. Tradeway, Inc., No. 95 Civ. 10278 (RPP), 1996 WL 107285 . . . . . 1.96, 13.96
Unicorn Bulk Traders Ltd. v. Fortune Maritime Enters., Inc., No. 08 Civ. 9710 (PGG), 2009 WL 125751 . . . . . 8.35
Union Free Sch. Dist. No. 15 v. Lawrence Teachers Ass'n, 822 N.Y.S.2d 767 (App. Div. 2006) 13.140
United Air Lines, Inc. v. Austin Travel Corp., 867 F.2d 737 (2nd Cir. 1989) 10.23
United Equities Co. v. First Nat'l City Bank, 383 N.Y.S.2d 6 (1st Dep't 1976) 4.68
United Kingdom v. Boeing Co., 998 F.2d 68 (2d Cir. 1993) 3.45
United Paperworks Int'l Union, AFL-CIO v. Misco, Inc., 484 U.S. 29, 43, 108 S. Ct. 364, 98 L. Ed. 2d 286 (1987) 8.23
United States v. Carreon-Palacio, 267 F.3d 483 (5th Cir. 2001) 6.20
United States v. Davis, 767 F.2d 1025 (2d Cir. 1985) 7.130
United States v. Eberhard, 2004 WL 616122 . . . . . 7.109
United States v. Panhandle E. Corp., 118 F.R.D. 346 (D. Del. 1998) 3.49, 12.18
United States v. U.S. Gypsum Co., 333 U.S. 364 (1948) 2.101
United States Commodity Futures Trading Comm'n v. Newell, No. 12 C 6763, 2014 WL 4179881 . . . . . 9.71
United States Fire Ins. Co. v. National Gypsum Co., 101 F.3d 813 (2d Cir. 1996), cert. denied, 521 U.S. 1120 (1997) 6.34
United States Titan Inc. v. Guangzhou Zhen Hua Shipping, Co., 241 F.3d 135 (2d Cir. 2001) 6.10, 7.98
United Steelworkers of America v. American Mfg. Co., 363 U.S. 564 (1960) 6.25, 6.60
United Steelworkers of America v. Warrior & Gulf Nav. Co., 363 U.S. 574 (1960) 6.03
Universitas Educ., LLC v. Nova Grp., Inc., No. 11 CIV. 1590, 2013 WL 57892 (S.D.N.Y. Jan. 4, 2013) 13.28
Upper Nyack v. Christian & Missionary Alliance, 540 N.Y.S.2d 125 (Sup. Ct. 1988), aff'd, 547 N.Y.S.2d 388 (2d Dep't 1989) 4.20
US Airways Group, Inc. v. British Airways Plc, 989 F. Supp. 482 (S.D.N.Y. 1997) 4.65

V.S. Int'l, S.A. v. Boyden World Corp., 862 F. Supp. 1188 (S.D.N.Y. 1994) 10.29
Vaden v. Discover Bank, 556 U.S. 49 (2009) 13.29
Vail-Ballou Press, Inc. v. Graphic Comms. Int'l Union/Int'l Brotherhood of Teamsters, Local 898-M, 480 F. Supp. 2d 568 (N.D.N.Y. 2007) 6.73
Van Wagner Advert. Corp. v. S & M Enters., 492 N.E.2d 756 (N.Y. 1986) 10.06
Varley v. Tarrytown Associates, 477 F.2d 208 (2d Cir. 1973) 1.12, 3.58
Vasquez-Lopez v. Beneficial Or., Inc., 152 P.3d 940 (Or. Ct. App. 2007) 11.86
Veleron Holding, B.V. v. Morgan Stanley, No. 12 Civ. 5966 (CM), 2014 WL 1569610 . . . . . 9.59
Venconsul N.V. v. Tim Int'l N.V., No. 03 Civ. 5387 (LTS)(MHD), 2003 WL 21804833 . . . 8.33

Venegas v. Mitchell, 495 U.S. 82 (1990). 2.95
Venus Lines Agency v. CVG Industria Venezolana de Aluminio, C.A., 210 F.3d 1309 (11th Cir. 2000). 14.39
Vera v. Saks & Co., 335 F.3d 109 (2d Cir. 2003) 9.07, 13.67
Victory Transp. Inc. v. Comisaria General de Abastecimientos y Transportes, 336 F.2d 354 (2d Cir. 1964). 13.29
Vigil v. Sears Nat'l. Bank, 205 F. Supp. 2d 566 (E.D. La. 2002) 11.88
Villa Garcia v. Merrill Lynch, Pierce, Fenner and Smith Inc., 833 F.2d 545 (5th Cir. 1987). 6.20
Viorel Micula v. The Government of Romania 14.24
Volt Info. Sciences, Inc. v. Bd. of Trs. of Leland Stanford Junior Univ., 489 U.S. 468 (1989) 0.49, 1.03, 3.14, 6.14, 6.17, 7.14, 9.07, 13.143

W. R. Grace & Co., v. Local 759, International Union 461 U.S. 757 (1983) 6.97
W. Va. ex rel Dunlap v. Berger, 567 S.E.2d 265, 278–79 (W. Va.), cert. denied, 527 U.S. 1087 (2002) 11.86
W.W.W. Assocs., Inc. v. Giancontieri, 77 N.Y.2d 157 (1990) 4.03
Waldman v. Englishtown Sportswear, Ltd., 460 N.Y.S.2d 552 (1st Dep't 1983) 4.51
Walia v. Kiran M. Dewan, CPA, P.A., 134 S. Ct. 1788 (2014). 1.23
Walker Int'l Holdings Ltd. v. Republic of Congo, 395 F.3d 229 (5th Cir. 2004) 14.55
Wallace v. Buttar, 378 F.3d 182 (2d Cir. 2004) 11.39, 13.16, 13.74, 13.128
Warnes, S.A. v. Harvic Int'l, Ltd., 1993 WL 228028 (S.D.N.Y. 1993) 3.06
Washington Mut. Bank v. Crest Mortgage Co., 418 F. Supp. 2d 860 (N.D. Tex. 2006) 3.60
Waterside Ocean Navigation Co. Inc. v. Int'l Navigation Ltd., 737 F.2d 150 (2d Cir. 1984) 13.109
Wathne Imports Ltd. v. PRL USA, Inc., 101 A.D.3d 83 (1st Dep't 2012). 10.20, 10.38
Watts v. Thomas Carter & Sons, 202 N.Y.S. 852 (2d Dep't 1924) 4.15
Waveform Telemedia, Inc. v. Panorama Weather N.A., No. 06 Civ. 5270 CMMDF, 2007 WL 678731 (S.D.N.Y. 2007). 1.94
Webster v. A.T. Kearney, Inc., 507 F.3d 568 (7th Cir. 2007) 13.15
Wechsler v. Hunt Health Sys., Ltd., 330 F. Supp. 2d 383 (S.D.N.Y. 2004) 4.23
Weiner v. McGraw-Hill, Inc., 443 N.E.2d 441 (N.Y. 1982) 4.17
Weiss v. La Suisse, Societe D'Assurances Sur La Vie, 293 F. Supp. 2d 397 (S.D.N.Y. 2003); 141 F. App'x 31, 34 (2d Cir. 2005) 4.11
Weltover, Inc. v. Republic of Arg., 941 F.2d 145, 150 (2d Cir. 1991) aff'd, 504 U.S. 607, 112 S. Ct. 2160, 119 L. Ed. 2d 394 (1992). 14.59
Westerbeke Corp. v. Daihatsu Motor Co., 304 F.3d 200 (2d Cir. 2002) 8.22, 10.36, 11.39, 13.124
Westmoreland Capital Corp. v. Findlay, 100 F.3d 263 (2d Cir. 1996) 7.109
Weyerhaeuser Co. v. W. Seas Shipping Co., 743 F.2d 635 (9th Cir. 1984). 11.53
Whirlpool Corp. v. Philips Elecs., N.V., 848 F. Supp. 474 (S.D.N.Y. 1994) 13.99
Whitney v. Alltel Commc'ns, Inc., 173 S.W.3d 200, 313014 (Mo. Ct. App. 2005) 11.86
Whitney v. Stearns, 16 Me. 394 (1839) 4.17
Wien & Malkin LLP v. Helmsley-Spear, Inc., 783 N.Y.S. 2d 339 (NY App. Div. 2004); 846 N.E.2d 1201 (N.Y. 2006). 11.15, 13.140
Wilko v. Swan 346 U.S. 427 (1953) 3.55, 6.82, 7.121, 11.42, 13.126
Willeminjn Houdstermcatschappi v. Standard Microsystems, Corp., 103 F.3d 9 (2d Cir. 1997) 6.10, 6.61–6.62
Wilmot v. State, 297 N.E.2d 90 (N.Y. 1973). 10.21
Wilson Electrical Contractors, Inc. v. Minotte Contracting Corp., 878 F.2d 167 (6th Cir. 1989). 3.26
Wine & Spirits of Am., Inc. v. Impact Envtl. Eng'g, PLLC, 104 A.D.3d 613 (N.Y. App. Div. 2013). 10.26
Wing v. Cingular Wireless, LLC, No. A105906 2005 WL 1168363 . . . . 11.88
Wis. Auto Title Loans, Inc. v. Jones, 714 N.W.2d 155 (Wis. 2006). 11.86

Wood v. Lucy, Lady Duff-Gordon, 118 N.E. 214 (N.Y. 1917) 4.64
Woodling v. Garrett Corp., 813 F.2d 543 (2d Cir. 1987) 4.10
World Brilliance Corp. v. Bethlehem Steel Co., 342 F.2d 362 (2d Cir. 1965) 1.17
World-Link, Inc. v. Mezun.com, Inc., 827 N.Y.S.2d 642 (Sup. Ct. 2006) 13.76
World-Wide Volkswagen Corp. v. Woodson, 444 U.S. 286 (1980) 2.42, 13.53
WorldCrisa Corp. v. Armstrong 129 F.3d 71 (2d Cir. 1997) 7.55, 7.90, 7.126
Wornow v. Register.com, Inc., 778 N.Y.S.2d 25 (1st Dep't 2004) 4.50
Wright v. SFX Entm't Inc., No. 00 Civ. 5354, 2001 WL 103433 .... 7.58
Wyatt v. Fulrath, 239 N.Y.S.2d 486 (N.Y. Sup. Ct. 1963) 4.11
Wynn Resorts v. Atl.-Pac. Capital, Inc. 497 F. App'x 740 (9th Cir. 2012) 11.14

X.L.O. Concrete Corp. v. John T. Brady and Co., 482 N.Y.S.2d 476 (1st Dep't 1984) aff'd, 489 N.E.2d 768, 768 (N.Y. 1985) 10.24
Xpedior Creditor Trust v. Credit Suisse First Boston (USA) Inc., 341 F. Supp. 2d 258 (S.D.N.Y. 2004) 10.02

Y & A Group Sec. Litigation, In Re, 38 F.3d 380 (8th Cir. 1994) 6.34
Yahoo v. Microsoft 983 F. Supp. 2d 310 (S.D.N.Y. 2013) 8.31
Yasuda Fire & Marine Ins. Co. of Europe v. Continental Cas. Co., Ltd., 37 F.3d 345 (7th Cir. 1994) 8.16
Yonir Techs., Inc. v. Duration Sys. (1992) Ltd., 244 F. Supp. 2d 195 (S.D.N.Y. 2002) 8.16, 13.121
York Hannover Holding A.G. v. Am. Arbitration Ass'n, No. 92 Civ. 1643 (CSH), 1993 WL 159961 .... 13.118
Yukos Capital S.A.R.L. v. Samaraneftegaz, No. 13-3357, 2014 WL 5572696 .... 13.110
Yusuf Ahmed Alghanim & Sons v. Toys "R" Us, Inc., 126 F.3d 15 (2d Cir. 1997) 1.89, 6.63, 6.107, 6.110, 7.18, 13.05, 13.36, 14.12

Zeiler v. Deitsch, 500 F.3d 157 (2d Cir. 2007) 13.111, 14.12
Zim Israel Navigation Co. v. Sealanes Int'l, Inc., 17 A.D. 2d. 393 (N.Y. App. Div. 1962) 1.19
Zubulake v. UBS Warburg LLC, 217 F.R.D. 309 (S.D.N.Y. 2003) 2.72, 9.39
Zullo v. Varley, 868 N.Y.S.2d 290 (2d Dep't 2008) 4.27

TABLE OF CONVENTIONS

Convention on the Recognition and Enforcement of Foreign Arbitral Awards (New York Convention), adopted 10 June 1958, entered into force 7 June 1959, 21 U.S.T. 2517, 2521, 330 U.N.T.S. 3.44
Art. I(1) 6.63, 13.09
Art. I(3) 7.16, 13.33
Art. II 6.95, 6.104, 13.40, 13.62, 13.79, 13.81
Art. II(1) 1.46, 1.48, 1.74–1.75, 1.79, 6.104
Art. II(2) 1.46, 1.74, 1.76, 6.104
Art. II(3) 1.02, 1.49, 1.51, 1.57, 1.59, 1.72, 6.14, 6.16, 6.25, 7.16, 8.33
Art. III 13.40, 13.62, 13.79
Art. IV 13.78
Art. IV(1)(a) 13.27
Art. V 1.02, 1.50, 1.52, 1.90, 1.95–1.97, 6.03, 6.16, 6.63, 6.94–6.95, 6.102, 6.104, 13.35, 13.40, 13.79, 13.111, 14.12
Art. V(1) 1.46, 1.84, 13.79
Art. V(1)(a) 1.50–1.52, 1.83, 6.96, 6.97, 6.100, 6.102, 6.104–6.106, 13.79, 13.81, 13.83, 13.88, 13.94–13.95, 13.99
Art. V(1)(b) 1.96, 6.97, 13.79, 13.96–13.97, 13.112
Art. V(1)(c) 6.95–6.97, 6.100–6.101, 12.12, 13.79, 13.82, 13.98–13.100, 13.112, 13.125
Art. V(1)(d) 6.97, 13.79, 13.101–13.102, 13.118
Art. V(1)(e) 1.89, 1.98, 6.63, 6.97, 13.39, 13.79, 13.104–13.105, 13.111
Art. V(2) 6.96, 6.99, 6.102–6.103, 13.79, 13.106
Art. V(2)(a) 1.48, 1.79, 1.81, 6.97, 6.99, 6.106, 13.82, 13.106–13.107
Art. V(2)(b) 6.96–6.97, 6.102–6.104, 6.106, 13.108, 13.110, 13.112, 13.135
Art. V(3) 6.102
Art. V(e) 6.105
Art. VI 13.105, 14.43, 14.45, 14.47, 14.50
Art. VII 1.98
Art. VII(1) 1.35, 13.142

Convention on the Settlement of Investment Disputes Between States and Nationals of Other States (ICSID Convention or Washington Convention) (18 March 1965) 17 U.S.T. 1270, 575 U.N.T.S. 159, entered into force 14 October 1966
Art. 39(6) 14.32–14.33
Art. 41(2) 6.42, 6.46
Art. 54 . . . . 14.15, 14.24
Art. 54(1) 14.22
Art. 54(2) 14.16

Geneva Convention on the Execution of Foreign Arbitral Awards, signed 26 September 1927, 92 L.N.T.S. 301 . . . . 13.04, 13.104

Hague Convention on the Service Abroad of Judicial and Extrajudicial Documents in Civil or Commercial Matters, 15 November 1965, 20 U.S.T. 361, 658 U.N.T.S. 263 . . . . . 2.28, 14.28

Inter-American Convention on International Commercial Arbitration of 1975, OAS/SERA20 (SEPEF), 14 I.L.M. 336 (1975), January 30, 1975 (Panama Convention), entry into force for the United States on 27 October 1990
Art. 1 . . . . 1.74
Art. 1(c) 6.100
Art. 3 . . . . 7.101, 7.104, 7.107
Art. 4 . . . . 1.84
Art. 5 . . . . 6.94, 6.97
Art. 5(1) 1.84
Art. 5(1)(a) 6.106
Art. 5(1)(b) 13.112

Art. 5(1)(c) 13.112
Art. 5(1)(d) 13.118
Art. 5(1)(e) 1.89, 13.39
Art. 5(2)(a) 6.97, 6.106
Art. 5(2)(b) 6.97, 13.112, 13.135
UN Convention on Contracts for the International Sale of Goods (adopted 11 April 1980, entered into force 1 January 1988) 1489 UNTS 3 ('CISG') 4.02
Vienna Convention on Diplomatic Relations (adopted 18 April 1961, entered into force 24 April 1964) 500 UNTS 95 (VCDR) 14.74

TABLE OF LEGISLATION

Age Discrimination in Employment Act of 1967, Pub. L. No. 90-202 . . . . 6.04
Arbitration Fairness Act of 2013, introduced on 7 May 2013, not enacted 11.115
Clayton Antitrust Act of 1914 (Pub. L. 63–212, 38 Stat. 730, enacted October 15, 1914)
§ 12 . . . . 13.52
Credit Repair Organizations Act (1996) 0.43
Fair Credit Billing Act of 1974 (codified at 15 U.S.C. § 1601 *et seq.*). 11.90
Fair Debt Collection Practices Act of 1977 (Pub. L. 95-109; 91 Stat. 874, codified as 15 U.S.C. § 1692 – 1692p, approved on September 20, 1977). 11.07
Federal Rules of Civil Procedure (F.R.C.P.), established 1938
F.R.C.P. 4 . . . . 2.28
F.R.C.P. 4(e) 2.28
F.R.C.P. 4(f) 2.28, 13.25
F.R.C.P. 4(h)(2) 13.25
F.R.C.P. 4(k)(1)(C) 13.51
F.R.C.P. 4(k)(2) 13.50
F.R.C.P. 5 . . . . 2.28
F.R.C.P. 8(a) 2.30–2.31
F.R.C.P. 8(a)(2) 2.30
F.R.C.P. 8(b) 2.32
F.R.C.P. 8(b)(6) 2.32
F.R.C.P. 8(c) 2.33
F.R.C.P. 9 . . . . 2.30
F.R.C.P. 10 . . . . 2.30
F.R.C.P. 11 . . . . 2.95, 13.137
F.R.C.P. 11(a) 2.36
F.R.C.P. 11(b)(1) 2.36
F.R.C.P. 11(b)(2) 2.36
F.R.C.P. 11(b)(3) 2.36
F.R.C.P. 11(b)(4) 2.36
F.R.C.P. 11(c) 2.36
F.R.C.P. 12(b) 2.34–2.35, 13.19
F.R.C.P. 12(e) 2.31
F.R.C.P. 12(g) 2.35
F.R.C.P. 12(h)(1) 2.35
F.R.C.P. 14 . . . . 2.34
F.R.C.P. 15 . . . . 2.30
F.R.C.P. 16 . . . . 2.50
F.R.C.P. 16(1) 2.49
F.R.C.P. 16(2)(c)(A) 2.48
F.R.C.P. 16(2)(c)(B) 2.48
F.R.C.P. 16(2)(c)(C) 2.48
F.R.C.P. 16(2)(c)(D) 2.48
F.R.C.P. 16(2)(c)(E) 2.48
F.R.C.P. 16(2)(c)(F) 2.48
F.R.C.P. 16(2)(c)(G) 2.48
F.R.C.P. 16(2)(c)(H) 2.48
F.R.C.P. 16(2)(c)(I) 2.48
F.R.C.P. 16(2)(c)(J) 2.48
F.R.C.P. 16(2)(c)(K) 2.48
F.R.C.P. 16(2)(c)(L) 2.48
F.R.C.P. 16(2)(c)(M) 2.48
F.R.C.P. 16(2)(c)(N) 2.48
F.R.C.P. 16(2)(c)(O) 2.48
F.R.C.P. 16(2)(c)(P) 2.48
F.R.C.P. 16(a) 2.47–2.48
F.R.C.P. 16(a)(3) 6.37
F.R.C.P. 16(b) 2.45, 2.46, 2.50–2.51
F.R.C.P. 16(b)(2) 2.50
F.R.C.P. 16(b)(3) 2.51
F.R.C.P. 16(b)(4) 2.51
F.R.C.P. 16(c) 2.47
F.R.C.P. 16(d) 2.61
F.R.C.P. 16(e) 2.46, 2.76
F.R.C.P. 16(f) 2.47, 2.49
F.R.C.P. 19 . . . . 2.34
F.R.C.P. 19(a) 2.34
F.R.C.P. 19(a)(1) 2.34
F.R.C.P. 23 . . . . . . 2.34, 11.04, 11.32, 11.73
F.R.C.P. 23(a) 11.04, 11.36, 11.73
F.R.C.P. 23(b) 11.04, 11.36, 11.73, 11.77, 11.82
F.R.C.P. 23(b)(2) 11.05
F.R.C.P. 23(b)(3) 11.04–11.05
F.R.C.P. 23(c) 11.05
F.R.C.P. 23(c)(2)(B) 11.05
F.R.C.P. 23(h) 11.06
F.R.C.P. 24 . . . . 2.34
F.R.C.P. 26 . . . . .2.59, 2.65, 2.71, 9.71
F.R.C.P. 26(a) 9.34
F.R.C.P. 26(a)(1)(A) 2.61
F.R.C.P. 26(a)(2) 2.69

F.R.C.P. 26(a)(2)(B). 2.69
F.R.C.P. 26(b) 2.59
F.R.C.P. 26(b)(1) 2.59, 9.48
F.R.C.P. 26(b)(2)(B) 2.69, 2.72, 9.47
F.R.C.P. 26(b)(2)(C) 9.47
F.R.C.P. 26(b)(3) 2.66
F.R.C.P. 26(b)(4)(B) 9.71
F.R.C.P. 26(b)(4)(C) 9.71
F.R.C.P. 26(b)(5) 2.65, 2.67, 2.71
F.R.C.P. 26(b)(5)(B) 2.67, 2.71
F.R.C.P. 26(c). 2.60, 9.48
F.R.C.P. 26(d) 2.61
F.R.C.P. 26(e). 2.62
F.R.C.P. 26(f). 2.46, 2.50, 2.61
F.R.C.P. 26(g) 2.36
F.R.C.P. 29(b) 2.46
F.R.C.P. 30. . . . . 2.63, 9.54
F.R.C.P. 31 . . . . 9.54
F.R.C.P. 32. . . . . 2.63, 12.49
F.R.C.P. 33. . . . . 2.71, 9.55
F.R.C.P. 34. . . . . 2.71
F.R.C.P. 34(a)(1)(A). 9.39
F.R.C.P. 34(b)(1) 9.37
F.R.C.P. 34(b)(1)(A) 2.63
F.R.C.P. 34(b)(2)(E) 9.47
F.R.C.P. 36. . . . . 9.55
F.R.C.P. 37. . . . . 2.56, 2.65
F.R.C.P. 37(b) 2.95
F.R.C.P. 38(b) 2.17
F.R.C.P. 38(d) 2.17
F.R.C.P. 45 . . . . 2.71, 12.59
F.R.C.P. 45(a). 2.63
F.R.C.P. 45(a)(2) 9.69
F.R.C.P. 45(b) 9.68
F.R.C.P. 45(b)(2) 9.68, 12.61
F.R.C.P. 45(b)(3) 12.61
F.R.C.P. 45(c). 9.69
F.R.C.P. 48. . . . . 2.85
F.R.C.P. 49(a). 2.85
F.R.C.P. 49(b) 2.85
F.R.C.P. 50(a). 2.87, 2.90
F.R.C.P. 50(a)(1) 2.87
F.R.C.P. 52(a). 2.89
F.R.C.P. 52(a)(6) 2.89
F.R.C.P. 52(c). 2.90
F.R.C.P. 54(d)(1) 2.94
F.R.C.P. 54(d)(2) 2.95
F.R.C.P. 56. . . . . 2.74, 13.19
F.R.C.P. 56(a). 2.74
F.R.C.P. 56(b) 2.74
F.R.C.P. 56(d) 2.75
F.R.C.P. 58. . . . . 2.83
F.R.C.P. 59(a)(1) 2.88
F.R.C.P. 59(a)(1)(B). 2.90
F.R.C.P. 59(a)(2) 2.90
F.R.C.P. 62(a). 14.25
F.R.C.P. 64. . . . . 8.37, 14.60
F.R.C.P. 64(a). 8.37
F.R.C.P. 65 . . . . 8.35
F.R.C.P. 65(b)(1)(A) 8.35
F.R.C.P. 65(d) 2.84
F.R.C.P. 69 . . . . 14.60
F.R.C.P. 69(a)(1) 13.28
F.R.C.P. 69(a)(2) 13.28
F.R.C.P. 81(a)(6) 13.19
F.R.C.P. 81(c) 13.20
Labor Management Relations Act of 1947 "Taft–Hartley Act" (80 H.R. 3020, Pub. L. 80–101, 61 Stat. 136, enacted June 23, 1947) 13.135
New York Civil Practice Law and Rules (N.Y. C.P.L.R.) (2009)
Art. 2. . . . . 2.29
Art. 9. . . . . 2.34
Art. 45. . . . . 2.22
Art. 52. . . . . 13.28
Art. 54. . . . . 14.23
Art. 62. . . . . 8.45–8.46
Art. 63. . . . . 8.45, 8.48
Art. 75. . . . . 1.05, 1.36, 3.12, 3.14, 8.41–8.42, 9.03, 13.141
Art. 81. . . . . 2.94
Art. 82. . . . . 2.94
Art. 83. . . . . 2.94
Art. 84. . . . . 2.94
Art. 85. . . . . 2.94
Art. 86. . . . . 2.94
§ 75 . . . . 9.03
§ 101 . . . . 2.20
§ 102 . . . . 2.20
§ 302 . . . . 2.43
§ 302(a). 13.49
§ 302(a)(1). 13.49
§ 2302(a). 9.06
§ 3101 . . . . 2.59
§ 3101(a) 2.59
§ 3101(b). 2.65
§ 3101(c) 2.66
§ 3101(d)(1). 2.69
§ 3102 . . . . 2.63
§ 3102(c) 9.06, 9.73
§ 3103 . . . . 2.60
§ 3106 . . . . 9.54
§ 3107 . . . . 9.54
§ 3108 . . . . 9.54
§ 3109 . . . . 9.54
§ 3110 . . . . 9.54
§ 3111 . . . . 9.54

§ 3112 . . . . 9.54
§ 3113 . . . . 9.54
§ 3114 . . . . 9.54
§ 3115 . . . . 9.54
§ 3116 . . . . 9.54
§ 3117 . . . . 9.54
§ 3117(a) 2.63, 12.49
§ 3120 . . . . 2.63, 9.39
§ 3120(1) 9.37
§ 3120(2) 9.37
§ 3123 . . . . 9.55
§ 3130 . . . . 9.55
§ 3131 . . . . 9.55
§ 3132 . . . . 9.55
§ 3133 . . . . 9.55
§ 3212 . . . . 2.34, 2.74
§ 3401 . . . . 2.46
§ 3404 . . . . 2.45
§ 4101 . . . . 2.17
§ 4102 . . . . 2.17
§ 4111 . . . . 2.85
§ 5001(a) 10.42
§ 5001(b) 10.43
§ 5003 . . . . 10.46
§ 5004 . . . . 10.44
§ 5201 . . . . 14.16
§ 5201(a) 14.63
§ 5201(b) 14.63
§§ 5201–5253 . . . . 13.28
§ 5205 . . . . 14.63
§ 5206 . . . . 14.63
§ 5222 . . . . 13.28
§ 5223 . . . . 13.28
§ 5224 . . . . 13.28
§ 5228 . . . . 13.28
§ 5230 . . . . 13.28
§ 5232 . . . . 13.28
§ 5233 . . . . 13.28
§ 5236 . . . . 13.28
§ 5237 . . . . 13.28
§ 5302 . . . . 14.17
§ 5402 . . . . 14.23
§ 5403 . . . . 14.23
§ 5501 . . . . 2.11
§ 5515 . . . . 2.99
§ 5601 . . . . 2.11, 2.99
§ 5602 . . . . 2.99
§ 5701 . . . . 2.98
§ 6201 . . . . 8.37, 8.45–8.47
§ 6201(3) 8.37, 8.47, 14.40
§ 6202 . . . . 14.63
§ 6212(a) 14.40
§ 6301 . . . . 8.48
§ 6311 . . . . 8.48
§ 7501 . . . . 3.58
§ 7502 . . . . 3.51, 13.72–13.74
§ 7502(a) 13.74
§ 7502(b) 1.38–1.39, 3.20, 6.92
§ 7502(c) 3.52, 8.37, 8.42–8.45, 8.47, 14.40
§ 7503 . . . . 7.106, 13.141
§ 7503(c) 1.40, 1.41, 7.106–7.111, 13.141
§ 7504 . . . . 12.07, 13.141
§ 7505 . . . . 3.39, 9.06, 12.62, 12.71, 13.141
§ 7506 . . . . 12.32, 12.70, 13.141
§ 7507 . . . . 13.141
§ 7508 . . . . 13.141
§ 7509 . . . . 1.100, 13.02, 13.11, 13.141
§ 7510 . . . . 6.62, 13.02, 13.11, 13.76
§ 7511 . . . . 1.100, 1.102, 13.02, 13.11, 13.77, 13.140, 13.143
§ 7511(a) 13.74, 13.77
§ 7511(b) 6.62
§ 7511(b)(1) 6.62, 13.138, 13.140
§ 7511(b)(iv) 13.141
§ 7513 . . . . 3.30, 10.49
New York General Business Law
§ 399-c 1.43
New York Uniform Commercial Code (N.Y.U.C.C.) (2010)
§ 1-105(1) 13.31
§ 2-105(1) 4.02
§ 2-207 . . . . 4.15
§ 2-508 . . . . 4.32
§ 2-A-508 . . . . 4.39
§ 2A-509 . . . . 4.31
§ 2-A-523 . . . . 4.39
§ 2-601 . . . . 4.31
§ 2-608 . . . . 4.31–4.32
§ 2-612 . . . . 4.28
§ 2-612(2) 4.33
§ 2-612(3) 4.33
§ 2-615 . . . . 4.67
§ 2-706(1) 4.39
§ 2-708 . . . . 4.39
§ 2-708(2) 4.39
§ 2-709(1)(b) 4.39
§ 2-710 . . . . 4.39
§ 2-712 . . . . 4.40
§ 2-713 . . . . 4.40
§ 2-714 . . . . 4.39
§ 2-714(1) 4.31
§ 2-715 . . . . 4.40
§ 2-716 . . . . 4.43
§ 2-716(1) 10.07
§ 2-716(2) 10.07
§ 2-719(3) 10.18

Racketeer Influenced and Corrupt Organizations Act (RICO) of 1970 (Pub. L. 91–452, 84 Stat. 922, enacted 15 October 1970) 0.41, 6.28, 7.93
Revised Uniform Arbitration Act (2000)
§ 6(c) 11.13
Rules Enabling Act of 1934 (ch. 651, Pub. L. 73–415, 48 Stat. 1064, enacted 19 June, 1934) 2.20
Seaman's Wage Act of 1880 (Pub. L. 114–38). 7.123
Sherman Antitrust Act of 1890 (26 Stat. 209, 15 U.S.C. §§ 1–7) 6.58, 6.81
Truth in Lending Act (TILA), enacted 29 May 1968 (Pub. L. 90–321), effective July 1, 1969 . . . . 11.53
Uniform Enforcement of Foreign Judgments Act (UEFJA) of 1948, amended 1964 . . . . 14.23
Uniform Foreign-Country Money Judgments Recognition Act (UFCMA) of 1962, amended 2005 . . . . 1.08, 14.17

UNITED STATES CODE (U.S.C)

Title 9 (9 U.S.C.) U.S. Federal Arbitration Act (FAA)
Ch 1. . . . . 1.11–1.29, 1.85, 1.97, 1.101, 6.51, 6.63–6.64, 6.73, 7.18, 7.20, 7.99, 7.113–7.114, 8.33, 9.63, 13.05, 13.07, 13.14, 13.18, 13.23, 13.27, 13.29, 13.61, 13.111–13.137, 13.140, 13.145
Ch 2. . . . . 1.04, 1.30–1.33, 1.63, 1.65–1.66, 3.12, 3.52, 6.14, 6.16, 7.17–7.18, 7.20, 7.100, 7.102, 7.105, 7.113, 8.13, 9.63, 11.15, 13.07, 13.09, 13.21, 13.26, 13.37, 13.51, 13.68, 13.87, 13.89–13.90
Ch 3. . . . . 1.04, 1.34–1.35, 1.66, 1.84, 3.12–3.13, 7.17–7.18, 7.20, 7.102, 7.113, 8.13, 8.34, 13.26, 13.51, 13.65, 13.87, 13.90
§ 1 . . . . 1.01, 1.12, 1.77, 3.12, 6.14, 7.25, 9.03, 9.63, 11.95, 13.07, 13.10, 13.21
§ 1 *et seq* 4.45, 11.19, 11.65, 14.15
§§ 1–307. . . . . 13.02
§ 2 . . . . 1.01, 1.12–1.14, 1.47, 1.54, 3.12, 6.03, 6.14–6.15, 6.25, 6.27, 7.48, 7.58, 9.03, 9.63, 11.48, 11.95–11.99, 13.07
§ 3 . . . . 1.01, 1.15, 3.12, 6.14, 6.19, 7.18, 7.24, 7.86–7.88, 7.114, 7.116–7.119, 7.128, 9.03, 9.63
§ 4 . . . . 1.01, 1.15, 3.12, 6.02, 6.11, 6.14, 6.19, 7.99, 7.102, 7.105, 7.109, 9.03, 9.63, 11.53, 13.29, 13.92
§ 5 . . . . . . 1.01, 1.16, 3.09, 3.12, 5.30, 6.14, 9.03, 9.63, 12.05, 12.07
§ 6 . . . . 1.01, 1.16–1.17, 3.12, 6.14, 9.03, 9.63, 13.18
§ 7 . . . . . . 1.01, 1.18–1.20, 2.63, 3.12, 9.04, 3.39, 6.14, 9.03, 9.04, 9.51, 9.63–9.65, 9.70, 12.59–12.60, 12.62–12.63
§ 8 . . . . 1.01, 3.12, 6.14, 9.03, 9.63
§ 9 . . . . 1.01, 1.21–1.29, 1.31, 3.12, 3.58–3.59, 6.14, 6.62, 6.109, 8.21, 9.03, 9.63, 11.44, 13.07, 13.14, 13.21–13.26, 13.51–13.52, 14.12–14.13
§ 10 . . . . . . 1.01, 1.21–1.29, 1.91, 2.96, 3.12, 5.91, 6.03, 6.14, 6.62, 8.22, 9.03, 9.63, 11.38, 11.41, 11.44–11.45, 13.07, 13.61, 13.77, 13.84, 13.133, 13.143
§ 10(a) 3.55, 6.62, 6.72, 13.111
§ 10(a)(1). 13.119
§ 10(a)(2). 13.115
§ 10(a)(3). 12.37, 13.112
§ 10(a)(4). 11.45, 12.11, 13.99, 13.112, 13.124–13.125
§ 11 . . . . 1.01, 1.21–1.29, 2.96, 3.12, 6.14, 8.22, 9.03, 9.63, 11.38, 11.41, 13.07, 13.26
§ 12 . . . . 1.01, 1.21–1.29, 3.12, 6.14, 9.03, 9.63, 13.15, 13.17, 13.21–13.26, 13.77
§ 13 . . . . 1.01, 1.21–1.29, 3.12, 6.14, 9.03, 9.63, 13.27
§ 14 . . . . . . 1.01, 1.26, 3.12, 6.14, 9.03, 9.63
§ 15 . . . . 1.01, 1.26, 9.03, 9.63
§ 16 . . . . . 1.01, 1.26, 6.35–6.36, 9.03, 9.63
§ 16(a)(1). 6.36
§ 16(a)(1)(A) 6.36
§ 16(a)(1)(B) 6.36
§ 16(a)(1)(C). 1.26, 6.36
§ 16(a)(3). 6.37
§ 16(b). 1.26
§ 16(b)(3) 6.36
§ 201 . . . . . 1.01, 1.30, 3.12, 6.14, 7.17, 8.33, 9.03, 9.63, 13.07, 14.12
§§ 201–307. . . . . 8.13
§ 202 . . . . 1.01, 1.30, 3.12, 3.13, 6.14, 7.21, 7.27, 8.33, 9.03, 9.63, 13.07, 13.09, 13.31–13.32, 14.12
§ 203 . . . . 1.01, 1.10, 1.30, 1.32, 1.61, 1.66, 3.12, 6.14, 7.20, 8.33, 9.03, 9.63, 13.07, 13.29–13.38, 13.68, 14.12, 14.13

§ 204 . . . . 1.01, 1.30, 3.12, 6.14, 8.33, 9.03, 9.63, 13.07, 13.60, 14.13
§ 205 . . . . 1.01, 1.10, 1.30, 1.32, 1.61, 1.66, 3.12, 3.13, 6.14, 7.20, 8.33, 9.03, 9.63, 13.07, 13.11, 13.13, 13.37–13.38, 13.65, 13.67–13.68, 13.72, 14.12
§ 206 . . . . .1.01, 1.26, 1.30, 3.12, 6.14, 6.17, 7.102, 8.33, 9.03, 9.63, 13.07, 14.12
§ 207 . . . . 1.01, 1.21, 1.30, 1.31, 1.84, 3.12, 6.14, 6.93–6.94, 6.110, 8.33, 9.03, 9.63, 13.07, 13.76, 13.111, 14.12
§ 208 . . . . 1.01, 1.30, 1.31, 3.12, 3.13, 6.14, 7.18, 7.113, 8.33, 9.03, 9.63, 13.07, 13.18, 13.21, 13.51, 14.12
§ 301 . . . . .1.01, 3.12, 6.14, 7.17, 8.34, 9.03, 9.63, 13.07
§ 302 . . . . .1.01, 1.10, 1.31, 1.61, 1.66, 3.12, 6.14, 7.18, 7.20–7.21, 8.34, 9.03, 9.63, 13.07, 13.11, 13.13, 13.29–13.31, 13.34–13.35, 13.37–13.38, 13.65, 13.76
§ 303 . . . . .1.01, 3.12, 6.14, 7.101–7.102, 8.34, 9.03, 9.63, 13.07
§ 304 . . . . 1.01, 3.12, 6.14, 8.34, 9.03, 9.63, 13.07, 13.33
§ 305 . . . . 1.01, 1.35, 3.12, 6.14, 7.23, 8.34, 9.03, 9.63, 13.07, 13.34
§ 305(1) 13.10
§ 305(2) 1.35
§ 306 . . . . 1.01, 3.12, 6.14, 8.34, 9.03, 9.63, 13.07
§ 307 . . . . 1.01, 1.31, 3.12, 3.13, 6.14, 6.36, 7.18, 8.34, 9.03, 9.63, 13.07, 13.18, 13.21, 13.51
Title 15 (15 U.S.C.)
§ 22 . . . . 13.52
§ 77v(a) 13.52
Title 22 (22 U.S.C.)
§ 1650a 14.15, 14.22, 14.24
Title 28 (28 U.S.C.) Foreign Sovereign Immunities Act (FSIA)
Pt IV 2.08
§ 1251 . . . . 2.10, 2.40
§ 1253 . . . . 2.10
§ 1254 . . . . 2.10
§ 1257 . . . . 2.09–2.10
§ 1258 . . . . 2.10
§ 1259 . . . . 2.10
§ 1260 . . . . 2.10
§ 1291 . . . . 2.98
§ 1292 . . . . 2.98, 6.36
§ 1292(b) .6.35–6.36
§ 1295 . . . . 2.10
§ 1330 . . . . 13.29
§ 1330(a) 14.13
§ 1330(b) 14.27
§ 1331 . . . . 7.20, 13.29, 13.37
§ 1332 . . . . 7.20
§ 1332(a) 2.41
§ 1334(b) 13.69
§ 1367 . . . . 14.18
§ 1367(a) 13.38, 14.18
§ 1391 . . . . 13.61
§ 1446(b) 13.72
§ 1447(d) 13.72
§ 1603 . . . . 14.01, 14.19
§ 1603(d) 14.59
§ 1605 . . . . 13.29
§ 1605(a) 14.62
§ 1605(a)(1) 14.14, 14.17
§ 1605(a)(6)(B) 14.13
§ 1606 . . . . 13.29
§ 1607 . . . . 13.29
§ 1608 . . . . 14.27
§ 1608(a) 14.27, 14.29
§ 1608(a)(1) 14.29
§ 1608(e) 14.25
§ 1609 . . . . 14.01
§ 1610 . . . . 14.19, 14.45
§ 1610(a) 14.19, 14.52, 14.56
§ 1610(a)(1) 14.54
§ 1610(a)(6) 14.49
§ 1610(b) 14.19, 14.52, 14.58
§ 1610(b)(1) 14.54
§ 1610(c) 14.19, 14.20, 14.25, 14.55
§ 1610(d) 14.19, 14.34, 14.42, 14.46
§ 1611 . . . . 14.45
§ 1782 . . . . 9.02, 9.74, 9.77
§ 1782(a) 2.58, 9.75
§ 1783 . . . . 12.61
§ 1783(a) 12.61
§ 1920 . . . . 2.94
§ 1927 . . . . 13.137
§ 2071 . . . . 2.20
§ 2072 . . . . 2.20
§ 2073 . . . . 2.20
§ 2074 . . . . 2.20
§ 2342 . . . . 2.10
Title 42 (42 U.S.C.)
§ 1988 . . . . 2.95

TABLE OF ARBITRAL RULES

American Arbitration Association (AAA) Commercial Arbitration Rules and Mediation Procedures, rules amended and effective October 1, 2013
- Rule 3 .... 11.31
- Rule 4 .... 11.32
- Rule 4(a)(2) 11.77
- Rule 4(a)(3) 11.78
- Rule 4(a)(4) 11.79
- Rule 4(a)(6) 11.81
- Rule 4(b) 11.77, 11.82
- Rule 5 .... 11.32
- Rule 7 .... 11.33, 13.91
- Rule 7(a) 6.42
- Rule 12 .... 5.16
- Rule 13 .... 5.16
- Rule 14 .... 5.17
- Rule 15 .... 5.18
- Rule 18(a) 5.44
- Rule 18(b) 5.44, 5.90
- Rule 19(a) 5.58, 5.67
- Rule 19(b) 5.44
- Rule 22 .... 9.34
- Rule 22(b)(iii) 9.35
- Rule 37 .... 8.10, 14.33
- Rule R-52(c) 3.60
- Art. 13(6) 5.58
- Art. 19(3) 6.42
- Art. 24 .... 8.07

IBA Rules on the Taking of Evidence in International Arbitration, International Bar Association, adopted by a resolution of the IBA Council, 29 May 2010
- Preamble 9.25
- Art. 1 .... 9.43
- Art. 2(1) 9.44
- Art. 2(2) 9.27
- Art. 3 .... 9.34
- Art. 3(1) 9.28
- Art. 3(2) 9.34
- Art. 3(3) 9.26
- Art. 3(3)(a) 9.35, 9.44
- Art. 3(3)(b) 9.35
- Art. 3(3)(c) 9.35
- Art. 3(3)(c)(i) 9.35
- Art. 3(3)(c)(ii) 9.35
- Art. 3(4) 9.28
- Art. 3(5) 9.28
- Art. 3(6) 9.28
- Art. 3(7) 9.28
- Art. 3(9) 9.62
- Art. 3(12)(b) 9.44
- Art. 4 .... 9.33, 9.43
- Art. 9(2) 9.28, 9.36, 9.57
- Art. 9(2)(a) 9.57
- Art. 9(2)(b) 9.57
- Art. 9(2)(c) 9.57
- Art. 9(2)(d) 9.57
- Art. 9(2)(e) 9.57
- Art. 9(2)(f) 9.57
- Art. 9(2)(g) 9.57
- Art. 9(3) 9.57
- Art. 9(5) 9.52
- Art. 9(7) 9.44

International Centre for Dispute Resolution (ICDR) Arbitration Rules (or American Arbitration Association (AAA) International Arbitration Rules), latest edition entry into force 1 June 2014
- Rule 18(c) 5.88
- Rule 25 .... 12.45
- Art. 2 .... 2.27
- Art. 6 .... 8.29
- Art. 6(2) 8.29
- Art. 8 .... 3.48
- Art. 11 .... 5.08, 5.86
- Art. 12 .... 5.09
- Art. 12(4) 5.15
- Art. 12(5) 5.12
- Art. 12(6) 5.10
- Art. 13(1) 3.28, 5.44
- Art. 13(6) 5.67
- Art. 14(1) 5.86
- Art. 14(3) 5.86
- Art. 16 .... 12.33
- Art. 19 .... 13.91
- Art. 20 .... 2.18, 12.45, 12.78

Art. 20(1) 2.22, 9.17, 12.78
Art. 20(2) 2.44
Art. 20(3) 2.73
Art. 20(4) 9.17, 12.54, 12.78
Art. 20(7) 9.52
Art. 21(1)........................... 9.41
Art. 21(3) 9.34
Art. 21(4) 9.17
Art. 21(6) 9.41
Art. 21(8) 9.41
Art. 21(9) 9.52
Art. 21(10).............. 9.54–9.55, 12.50
Art. 22.............................. 9.58
Art. 23(1) 12.39
Art. 23(3) 12.74
Art. 23(4) 12.38
Art. 23(6) 9.60
Art. 24.............................. 8.07
Art. 24(3) 8.32
Art. 25.............................. 2.68
Art. 27............................. 12.83
Art. 30............................. 12.22
Art. 31.............................. 2.16
Art. 31(5) 2.84, 3.35
Art. 33.............................. 2.91
Art. 34.............................. 3.31
Art. 37............................. 12.21
Art. 37(1).......................... 12.22

International Centre for Settlement of Investment Disputes (ICSID) Arbitration Rules, adopted on September 25, 1967 and effective as of January 1, 1968
Rule 39(6).......................... 14.33
Art. 41(2) 6.42

International Chamber of Commerce (ICC) Rules of Arbitration, current rules in force as from 1 January 2012
App. IV................ 8.28, 9.15, 12.43
Rule 35 .... 2.96
Art. 2(1)............................ 8.28
Art. 4............................... 2.27
Art. 6(2) 6.42, 7.35
Art. 6(3) 3.16, 6.42, 7.05, 13.91
Art. 6(4) 6.41, 6.47, 6.50
Art. 12.............................. 5.19
Art. 14.............................. 5.89
Art. 15.............................. 5.89
Art. 19.............................. 9.15
Art. 21.............................. 2.16
Art. 22(1) 12.81
Art. 22(3) 9.60, 12.25
Art. 22(4) 9.15, 12.81
Art. 23(4) 12.67
Art. 24.............................. 2.44
Art. 24(1) 9.15
Art. 25..................... 12.43, 12.48
Art. 25(1) 9.15, 9.58
Art. 25(2) 12.43
Art. 25(3) 12.43, 12.67
Art. 25(4) 12.48
Art. 25(5) 9.15, 9.58
Art. 26(3) 9.60
Art. 27............................. 12.85
Art. 28(1) 8.07, 8.09
Art. 28(2) 8.32
Art. 29................ 1.24, 8.24, 8.28
Art. 29(3) 8.28
Art. 29(6) 8.28
Art. 31(3) 13.14
Art. 35...................... 2.91, 6.49
Art. 37(4) 3.31

International Institute for Conflict Prevention and Resolution (CPR), Rules for Administered Arbitration of International Disputes (2013), effective 1 December 2014
Rule 4 .... 12.34
Rule 9.3.................... 9.23, 12.46
Rule 11 .... 9.22, 12.23
Rule 12 .... 12.40, 12.65, 12.79
Rule 12.2 .... 12.79
Rule 12.3 .... 12.46, 12.55
Rule 12.4........................... 12.74
Rule 16 .... 12.55
Rule 20 .... 12.23
Art. 13(2) 8.32

International Institute for Conflict Prevention and Resolution (CPR), Rules for Non-Administered Arbitration of International Disputes, effective 1 November 2007
Rule 5.4............................. 5.25
Rule 7.4............................. 5.58
Rule 9.1............................. 9.23
Rule 9.2............................. 9.23
Rule 9.3(a) 9.23
Rule 11 .... 9.23, 9.58, 12.23
Rule 13.1............................ 8.07
Rule 14 .... 8.30
Art. 9(2) 9.23
Art. 9(3) 9.23
Art. 9(3)(a) 9.23
Art. 11...................... 9.23, 9.58
Art. 14.............................. 8.30
Art. 14(5) 8.26

JAMS (formerly, Judicial Arbitration and Mediation Services) Class Action Procedures (2005), effective 1 May 2009
Rule 1 .... 11.35
Rule 2 .... 11.35
Rule 3 .... 11.35
Rule 3(b) 11.82
Rule 4 .... 11.35
Rule 4(7) 11.36
Rule 5 .... 11.35
Rule 6 .... 11.36
JAMS (formerly, Judicial Arbitration and Mediation Services) International Arbitration Rules, effective 1 August 2011
Rule 15 .... 12.80
Rule 18 .... 2.73
Art. 14.2 .... 12.66
Art. 16 .... 12.24
Art. 19 .... 12.33
Art. 22(2) 12.47
Art. 23 .... 12.41, 12.47
Art. 23(4) 12.75
Art. 24 .... 12.41, 12.47
Art. 24(2) 12.66
Art. 24(5) 12.42
Art. 24(6) 12.75
Art. 24(7) 12.47
Art. 25 .... 12.80
Art. 25(2) 9.18, 12.56
Art. 25(4) 9.18
Art. 29 .... 12.84
JAMS (formerly, Judicial Arbitration and Mediation Services) Streamlined Arbitration Rules and Procedures, effective 1 July 2014
Rule 13 .... 12.80
Rule 17(e) 12.49
London Court of International Arbitration (LCIA) Arbitration Rules, current rules effective 1 October 2014
Art. 15(2) 7.05
Art. 15(3) 7.05
Art. 15(4) 7.05
Art. 15(5) 7.05
Art. 15(6) 7.05
Art. 15(8) 7.05
Art. 19(1) 2.73
Art. 22 .... 9.14
Art. 23 .... 13.91
Art. 23(1) 6.42
Art. 23(3) 6.42
Art. 25(3) 14.33
Art. 26(2) 13.14
Art. 30 .... 3.50
Art. 30(1) 9.60
Permanent Court of Arbitration (PCA) Arbitration Rules, current rules effective 17 December 2012
Art. 26(9) 14.33
Rules of the Arbitration Institute of the Stockholm Chamber of Commerce (SCC), entered into force 1 January 2010
Art. 32 .... 14.33
Swiss Rules of International Arbitration, Swiss Chambers' Arbitration Institution, adopted 2004, revised 1 June 2012
Art. 15(2) 2.73
UNCITRAL Arbitration Rules (revised), UN Doc A/65/465; 53rd session, UN General Assembly 65/22, entered into force 15 August 2010
Art. 6 .... 5.23
Art. 8(2) 5.22
Art. 9(3) 5.22
Art. 16(2) 6.43
Art. 21 .... 6.42
Art. 21(3) 6.42
Art. 23 .... 13.91
Art. 26 .... 8.11
Art. 26(1) 8.07
Art. 27 .... 9.21
Art. 32(4) 13.14
Art. 38 .... 2.91

TABLE OF ARBITRAL AWARDS

A

Adame v. Fleetwood Enterprises, Inc.,
AAA Case No. 11 181 01292 07 (Mar. 11, 2008) 11.62
Addleman v. The Ryland Group, Inc.,
AAA Case No. 11 181 001524 05 (Sept. 15, 2005) 11.62
Alam v. Charter,
AAA Case No. 73 160 00378 12 (Sept. 26, 2013) 11.71
Alexander v. GMRI, Inc.,
AAA Case No. 11 160 02018 05 (June 20, 2005) 11.62
Ali v. Morton's of Chicago/Sacramento, Inc.,
AAA Case No. 11 160 02015 05 (Mar. 22, 2006) 11.61
Allen v. Sport & Fitness Clubs of Am., Inc.,
AAA Case No. 11 160 03041 04 (Apr. 13, 2005) 11.61
Almaraz v. Newbridge College,
AAA Case No. 11 434 02001 08 (Jul. 6, 2010) 11.74
Anderson v. Check 'N Go of California, Inc.,
AAA Case No. 11 160 03021 04 (June 20, 2005 .... 11.61
Armstrong v. Ameriquest Mortgage Co.,
AAA Case No. 11 160 Y 01652 06 (May 23, 2007) 11.61
Associated Pathology Consultants,
S.C. v. United Healthcare of Illinois, Inc.,
AAA Case No. 11 195 00971 06 (Feb. 25, 2008) 11.74
Awe v. I & M Rail Link, LLC,
AAA Case No. 11 160 00026 05 (May 24, 2005) 11.62
Awe v. I&M Rail Link, LLC,
AAA Case No. 11 160 00026 05 (June 23, 2006) 11.74

B

Baer v. TruGreen,
AAA Case No. 14 160 01482 12 (Jul. 22, 2013) 11.71
Bagpeddler.com v. U.S. Bancorp,
AAA Case No. 11 181 00322 04 (Sept. 2, 2004) 11.02, 11.62
Bagpeddler.com v. U.S. Bancorp,
AAA Case No. 11 181 00322 04 (May 4, 2007) 11.74, 11.80–11.81, 11.83
Bandler v. Charter One Bank, N.A.,
AAA Case No. 11 148 02801 04 (Sept. 3, 2006) 11.62
Barton v. Cottage Homesteads of Am., Inc.,
AAA Case No. 11 115 02967 04 (May 11, 2005) 11.62, 11.74, 11.80–11.81
Beazury v. Arbor Homes, LLC,
AAA Case No. 11 148 02161 04 (Jan. 31, 2005) 11.62
Beery v. Quest Diagnostics,
AAA Case No. 32 160 00323 13 (Feb. 11, 2014) 11.71
Benjamin Clark, III v. CHDP Condo LLC,
AAA Case No. 11 115 Y 01921 09 (Jul. 22, 2010) 11.71

Betts v. Fastfunding,
AAA Case No. 33 516 00012 13 (Aug. 21, 2013) 11.71
Blackwell v. 24 Hour Fitness USA, Inc.,
AAA Case No. 11 196 02299 07 (June 20, 2008) 11.62
Brown v. Cellco P'ship,
AAA Case No. 11 494 01274 05 (Sept. 15, 2005) 11.62
Brown v. Cellco P'ship,
AAA Case No. 11 494 01274 05 and 11 494 0032 05 (Oct. 1, 2008) 11.74
Bryant v. Joel Antunes, LLC,
AAA Case No. 111 160 01783 05 (Sept. 17, 2007) 11.74, 11.76
Budner v. Oats,
AAA Case No. 11 181 00828 04 (Dec. 20, 2004) 11.62

C

Cable Connections, Inc. v. Directu, Inc.,
AAA Case No. 11 145 00752 04 (Mar. 10, 2005) 11.61
Cable Connections, Inc. v. Hughes Elecs. Corp.,
AAA Case No. 11 145 00752 04 (Feb. 2, 2005) 11.54
CBR Enterprises, LLC v. Blimpie Int'l, Inc.,
(AAA Case Pending) 11.02
Chae v. Western,
AAA Case No. 11 160 424 11 (Sept. 30, 2011) 11.71
Champion Ford Lincoln Mercury, Inc. v. Dealer Computer Svcs., Inc.,
AAA Case No. 11 117 01935 06 (June 6, 2007) 11.62
Chavez v. 3P,
AAA Case No. 11 145 Y 1839 07 (Jul. 12, 2009) 11.74
Chavez v. Rent-A-Center, Inc.,
AAA Case No. 11 160 01817 04 (Aug. 18, 2005) 11.74, 11.76
CK Food v. Restaurant,
AAA Case No. 11 117 00839 12 (Jul. 10, 2013) 11.74
Cole v. Long John Silver's Rest., Inc.,
AAA Case No. 11 160 00194 04 (June 15, 2004) 11.61, 11.74
Cole v. Long John Silver's Rest., Inc.,
AAA Case No. 11 160 00194 04 (Oct. 7, 2010) 11.74, 11.78, 11.83
Cook v. Rent-A-Center, Inc.,
AAA Case No. 11 160 01815 04 (Sept. 19, 2005) 11.62
Cordova v. United,
AAA Case No. 73 516 Y 000065 13 (Aug. 29, 2013) 11.71
Cotton v. Rent-A-Center, Inc.,
AAA Case No. 11 160 01819 04 (Aug. 12, 2005) 11.62
Crawford v. Labor Ready Northwest, Inc.,
AAA Case No. 11 160 02264 06 (June 20, 2007) 11.62
Cummings v. AT&T Corp.,
AAA Case No. 11 181 02586 04 (Mar. 3, 2006) 11.60
Cummings v. Florida Mag Enter., Inc.,
AAA Case No. 11 188 00203 07 (July 31, 2007) 11.74, 11.76–11.77, 11.81
Curtis Hanna v. Pizza Hut Inc.,
AAA Case No. 33 160 00281 12 (Jul. 23, 2013) 11.71

D

Danielle Demetriou v. Earthlink, Inc.,
AAA Case No. 11 117 00273 10 (Sept. 1, 2010) 11.71
David Godina v. Countrywide Financial Corp.,
AAA Case No. 11 160 01857 06 (Oct. 24, 2008) 11.74

David Rivera v. Corinthian College, Inc.,
AAA Case No. 11 434 1075 08 (Sep. 11, 2009) 11.61
Dealer Computer Svcs., Inc. v. Randall Ford, Inc.,
AAA Case No. 11 117 Y 002788 06 (June 2, 2008)................................ 11.61
Duran v. Western Exterminator,
AAA Case No. 11 160 002055 08 (May 20, 2010)................................ 11.74

E

Emergency v. Proassurance,
AAA Case No. 11 195 Y 01789 10 (Apr. 2, 2011)................................. 11.71

F

Fannan v. Technisource, Inc.,
AAA Case No. 11 160 01881 06 (Feb. 25, 2007) 11.61
Flaxman v. Terminex, Inc.,
AAA Case No. 11 434 00701 07 (Jan. 14, 2008)............................11.61, 11.74
Flaxman v. Terminix,
AAA Case No. 11 434 00701 07 (Jul. 25, 2011)................................. 11.74
Fortuna v. Snap-on Tools Co., LLC,
AAA Case No. 11 114 01818 04 (Aug. 12, 2005)................................. 11.62
Fox Valley Ford v. Dealer Computer Svcs., Inc.,
AAA Case No. 11 117 01929 06 (Nov. 9, 2007)................................. 11.62
Francis v. United El Segundo,
AAA Case No. 11 160 00267 07 (April 30, 2007)................................ 11.62
Francis v. United El Segundo,
AAA Case No. 11 160 00267 07 (Jun. 22, 2010)............................11.71, 11.74

G

Garcia-Herman v Greystar,
AAA Case No. 73 160 00378 12 (Oct. 11, 2013)................................. 11.71
Garrett v. Rollins, Inc.,
AAA Case No. 11 181 01663 04 (Mar. 23, 2005)................................. 11.62
Garrett v. Rollins, Inc.,
AAA Case No. 11 181 01663 04 (July 14, 2006) 11.74
Goldstein v. Ibase Consulting of Fairfield County, LLC,
AAA Case No. 11 160 02760 03 (Mar. 29, 2004) 11.61
Gonzalez and Brand,
AAA Case No. 70 160 000270 13 (Oct. 15, 2013)................................ 11.71
Gonzalez v. MMM,
AAA Case No. 32 187 Y 000450 12 (Aug. 15, 2013).............................. 11.71
Grayson v. Rent-A-Center, Inc.,
AAA Case No. 11 160 01823 04 (Aug. 8, 2005).................................. 11.61
Groves v. Hemet Manufacturing Co, Inc.,
AAA Case No. 11 160 00194 05 (Nov. 8, 2005).................................. 11.61
Groves v. Hemet Manufacturing Co, Inc.,
AAA Case No. 11 160 00194 05 (May 30, 2007)...........................11.74, 11.76
Guzman and AIMCO River Club, LLC,
AAA Case No. 18 526 Y 000120 13 (Dec. 4, 2013)............................... 11.71

H

Hamilton v. Rent-A-Center, Inc.,
AAA Case 11 160 01825 04 (Oct. 21, 2004)..................................11.61–11.62
Hamilton v. Rent-A-Center, Inc.,
AAA Case No. 11 160 0182 04 (Mar. 10, 2005).................................. 11.61

Harding v. Midsouth,
AAA Case No. 69 516 Y 00219 12 (Aug. 29, 2013) 11.71
Haro v. NCR Corp.,
AAA Case No. 111 160 1962 05 (Nov. 9, 2007) 11.74, 11.77–11.79
Harris v. Tele Tech Holdings, Inc.,
AAA Case No 11 160 02701 04 (Dec. 16, 2005) 11.62
Harvard Coll. v. JSC Surgutneftegaz,
AAA Case No. 11 168 T 01654 04 (Aug. 1, 2007) 11.62
Hausner v. United Healthcare of Texas, Inc.,
AAA Case No. 11 193 Y 00447 07 (Oct. 19, 2007) 11.62
Hayes v. M.S. Carriers, Inc.,
AAA Case No. 11 118 02907 04 (June 15, 2005) 11.61
Hayes v. M.S. Carriers, Inc.,
AAA Case No. 11 118 02907 04 (June 26, 2006) 11.74, 11.77–11.78, 11.83
Hearthside Rest., Inc. v. Quest Dex, Inc.,
AAA Case No. 1I 147 00357 04 (Sept. 2, 2004) 11.62
Her v. Club One,
AAA Case No. 74 160 01109 12 (Jul. 29, 2013) 11.71
Herbert Kirsh v. Finova Group, Inc.,
AAA Case No. 11 148 Y 01381 07 (Nov. 4, 2008) 11.74
Herbert Kirsh v. Finova Group, Inc.,
AAA Case No. 11 148 Y 01381 07 (Sep. 18, 2009) 11.74
Herman Benson v. Credit Solutions of America,
AAA Case No. 11 160 M 02281 08 (Jul. 6, 2010) 11.71
Hernandez v. Teletech,
AAA Case No. 11 160 01892 06 (Jun. 8, 2009) 11.74
Hlas v. Menard,
AAA Case No. 11 160 00131 07 (June 29, 2007) 11.61
Hobby v. Snap-on-Tools Co, LLC,
AAA Case No. 11 114 01884 04 (June 8, 2005) 11.62
Hoffman v. Arthur Anderson LLP,
AAA Case No. 11 180 01410 05 (Jul. 23, 2006) 11.62

J
Jock v. Sterling,
AAA Case No. 11 160 00655 08 (Mar. 8, 2010) 11.74
John Flores v. Arakelian Enterprises, Inc.,
AAA Case No. 11 160 02637 05 (Dec. 29, 2008) 11.74
John Ivan Sutter v. Limited Health Care Insurance Company,
AAA Case No. 11 195 02075 06 . . . . 11.57
John Lear v. Neil Jones Food Company, Inc.,
AAA Case No. 74 154 Y 00238 11 (Aug. 18, 2013) 11.74
Johnson v. Morton's Rest. Group,
AAA Case No. 11 160 01513 05 (June 27, 2007) 11.74, 11.79
Jones v. Amerix,
AAA Case No. 11 181 00295 05 (Apr. 11, 2014) 11.74
Jones v. Genus Credit Mgmt. Corp.,
AAA Case No. 11 181 00295 05 (Oct. 13, 2005) 11.62
Jones v. Genus Credit Mgmt. Corp.,
AAA Case No. 11 181 00295 05 (May 7, 2009) 11.74
Jones, et al. v. Genus Credit Mgmt. Corp.,
AAA Case No. 11 181 00295 05 (Apr. 30, 2014) 11.74
Jost v. Sizzler USA Restaurants, Inc.,
AAA Case No. 11 160 01721 05 (Oct. 25, 2006) 11.61

K

Kaplan v. Citibank, N.A.,
AAA Case No. 111 148 1007 07 (June 4, 2008) 11.74
Kinkel v. Cingular Wireless, LLC,
AAA Case No. 11 494 02 646 06 (Oct. 12, 2007) 11.62
Kissel v. Sirius XM,
AAA Case No. 13 516 00198 13 (Dec. 6, 2013) 11.71
Knudsen v. North Motors,
AAA Case No. 11 155 02699 09 (May 18, 2010) 11.71
Krastel v. TES Franchising, LLC,
AAA Case No. 11 114 00320 05 (July 7, 2006) 11.61

L

Laverne Jones, et al. v. Genus Credit Management Corporation,
AAA Case No. 11 181 00295 05 (Apr. 30, 2014) 11.74
Le v. Toshiba Am. Info. Sys, Inc.,
AAA Case No. 11 160 02033 04 (Mar. 7, 2005) 11.62
Lear v. Neil Jones Food Co.,
AAA Case No. 74 154 00238 11 (Jul. 18, 2013) 11.74
Levitt v. Lipper Holdings, LLC,
AAA Case No. 11 168 00663 04 (May 20, 2005) 11.62
Levitt v. Lipper Holdings,
AAA Case No. 11 168 00663 04 (Mar. 18, 2008) 11.74
Louisiana Health Svc. Indemn. Co. v. DVA Renal Healthcare, Inc.,
AAA Case No. 11 193 02297 06 (Oct. 5, 2007) 11.62
Luis Maldonado and others v. Callahan's Express Delivery Inc.,
AAA Case No. 33 523 00375 13 (Apr. 18, 2014) 11.71
Lynn Grande v. Lawrence Recruiting Specialists Inc. d/b/a LRS Healthcare,
AAA Case No. 57 160 00080 13 (Dec. 20, 2013) 11.71

M

Mary Karen Hoffman and Timothy Lamagna,
AAA Case No. 55 160 00251 12 (Apr. 18, 2014) 11.71
Maslo v. Oake Pointe Country Club, Inc.,
AAA Case No. 11 181 002243 06 (May 9, 2008) 11.74, 11.77, 11.79, 11.80, 11.83
Maslo v. Oake Pointe Country Club, Inc.,
AAA Case No. 11 181 02243 06 (Jun. 15, 2010) 11.71
MB & CO., LTD. v. Charter One Bank, N.A.,
AAA Case No. 11 148 02801 04 (Apr. 24, 2014) 11.74
McCalley v. NVR,
AAA Case No. 11 110 01323 09 (Feb. 10, 2011) 11.71
McCullough v Terminal,
AAA Case No. 31 160 00371 12 (Sept. 17, 2013) 11.71
McGraw v. Morton's Rest. Group, Inc.,
AAA Case No. 11 60 02171 06 (April 18, 2008) 11.74, 11.78, 11.81
Medina v. GMRI, Inc.,
AAA Case No. 11 160 02409 04 (July 20, 2005) 11.61
Michael Mensch v. Alta Colleges, Inc.,
AAA Case No. 11 516 00995 09 (Jul. 16, 2010) 11.71
Milstein v. Protection One Alarm Servus, Inc.,
AAA Case No. 11 110 00270 04 (Oct. 11, 2004) 11.61
Milstein v. Protection One Alarm Services, Inc.,
AAA Case No. 11 110 00270 04 (May 12, 2005) 11.74, 11.79–11.81
Misty Owens et al. v. Automobile Protection Corp.,
AAA Case No. 11 188 01140 05 (Jul. 19, 2010) 11.74

Mitchell v. GMRI, Inc.,
AAA Case No. 11 160 02939 03 (June 10, 2005) 11.61
Morton v. Championcomm.net of Tuscaloosa, Inc.,
AAA Case No. 11 199 00704 07 (Dec. 26, 2007) 11.62
Muhammad v. Delaware Title Loans Inc.,
AAA Case No. 18 434 00804 13 (Feb. 10, 2014) 11.71
Murdock v. Thomas,
AAA Case No. 11 148 Y 01805 07 (Sep. 4, 2009) 11.74
Murdock v. Thomas,
AAA Case No. not available (May 2, 2011) 11.74

N
Nichols v. Fanfare Media Works, Inc.,
AAA Case No. 11 160 Y 01780 06 (June 14, 2007) 11.61

O
Olson v. Rent-A-Center, Inc.,
AAA Case No. 11 160 01831 04 (Oct. 21, 2005) 11.61
Orea v. Tavistock Restaurants LLC,
AAA Case No. 11 160 01982 06 (March 2, 2007) 11.61
Ormiston v. Red Bull,
AAA Case No. 72 160 01077 12 (Apr. 18, 2014) 11.71
Ortiz v. Clougherty Packaging Co. LLC,
AAA Case No. 11 160 01241 09 (Apr. 5, 2010) 11.61

P
Pamela Herrington and others v. Waterstone Mortgage Corporation,
AAA Case No. 51 160 00393 12 (Mar. 4, 2014) 11.74
Parham v. Am. Bankers Ins. Co. of Florida,
AAA Case No. 11 195 00157 07 (July 30, 2007) 11.59
Partners Two, Inc. v. Adecco N. Am., LLC,
AAA Case No. 11 114 03042 04 (May 14, 2007) 11.74, 11.76
Paul Holland v. ECPI College of Technology,
AAA Case No. 11 434 001716 08 (Oct. 22, 2009) 11.74
Petsch v. Orkin Exterminating Co. v. Rollins, Inc.,
AAA Case No. 11 181 02541 04 (Aug. 31, 2005) 11.62
Price v. NCR, AAA Case No. 51 160 908 12 (Oct. 24, 2013) 11.71

R
Rhodes Colleges, Inc. v. Michael Satz,
AAA Case No. 11 18102217 04 (June 23, 2005) 11.62
Rich v. Rent-A-Center, Inc,
AAA Case No. 11 160 01833 04 .... 11.56
Rivera et al. v. Corinthian Colleges,
AAA Case No. 11 434 1075 08 (Nov. 1, 2011) 11.71
Rubio's v. Larke Holden,
AAA Case No. 11 160 02787 05 (May 12, 2010) 11.74
Rubio's v. Larke Holden,
AAA Case No. 11 160 02787 05 (Jul. 28, 2010) 11.74

S
Salcedo v. Cintas Corp.,
AAA Case No. 11 160 00018 06 (Aug. 16, 2006) 11.61
Sanchez v. Corinthian Colleges, Inc.,
AAA Case No. 11 181 00286 5 (Nov. 15, 2005) 11.61

Savaria v. Steiner,
AAA Case No. 12 460 454 12 (Oct. 30, 2013) 11.71
Scher v. Oxford Health Plans, Inc.,
AAA Case No. 11 193 00548 05 (Mar. 7, 2006) 11.40, 11.57, 11.62
Scher v. Oxford Health Plans,
AAA Case No. 11 193 00548 05 (Sept. 12, 2008) 11.74
Sidhu v. GMRI, Inc.,
AAA Case No. 11 160 02273 04 (June 10, 2005) 11.61
Smith v. Tele Tech Holdings, Inc.,
AAA Case No. 11 160 02726 04 (Apr. 12, 2005) 11.62
AAA Case No. 11 160 02726 04 (Dec. 26, 2006) 11.74, 11.83
Spalding v. Glass Lewis,
AAA Case No. 11 160 00078 11 (Jul. 7, 2011) 11.71
Spradlin v. Trump,
AAA Case No. 11 115 Y 01846 09 (Aug. 10, 2010) 11.71
Stokes v. AWSM Technology, LLC,
AAA Case No. 11 147 02374 06 (June 22, 2007) 11.62
Sutter v. Oxford Health Plans, Inc.,
AAA Case No. 18 193 20593 02 (Sept. 23, 2003) 11.62
SWLA Hospital Assoc. v. Corvel Corp.,
AAA Case No. 11 193 02760 06 (Sept. 3, 2010) 11.71

T

Tarek, LLC v. Kinkade,
AAA Case No. 11 Y 114 00578 04 (Apr. 1, 2005) 11.74, 11.77–11.79, 11.83–11.84
Terrapin Express, Inc. v. Airborne Express, Inc.,
AAA Case No. 11 199 01536 05 (May 9, 2006) 11.62
Thomas v. SoutherLinc,
AAA Case No. 11 494 01518 08 (Jun. 24, 2010) 11.74
Thomas Bundy v. Countrywide Financial Corp.,
AAA Case No. 11 160 01858 06 (Oct. 24, 2008) 11.74
Timothy A. v. American Dairy Queen Corp.,
AAA Case No. 65 114 00016 13 (Feb. 18, 2014) 11.71
Tomeldon Co., Inc. v. Medco Health Solutions, Inc.,
AAA Case No. 11 193 00546 06 (Nov. 22, 2006) 11.62
Toney C. Giles v. Legal Helpers Debt Resolution, PLLC,
AAA Case No. 11 194 01162 13 (Mar. 16, 2014) 11.71
Travis v. Rhodes Colleges, Inc,
AAA Case No. 11 199 01827 06 (June 26, 2007) 11.62

W

Walters v. Palm Harbor Homes, Inc.,
AAA Case No. 11 421 002782 06 (Jan. 17, 2008) 11.62
Warrior Transportation v. FFE Transportation Services, Inc.,
AAA Case No. 11 118 00365 05 (Aug. 18, 2005) 11.58, 11.62
Weller v. Sprint Commc'n Co., L.P.,
AAA Case No. 11 181 00070 06 (May 22, 2007) 11.74, 11.79
Wolf v. Lakewood Homes, Inc.,
AAA Case No. 11 181 02243 06 (Mar. 2, 2007) 11.78, 11.80
Wolf v. Lakewood Homes, Inc.,
AAA Case No. 111 181 Y 01244 06 (Mar. 6, 2007) 11.74

X

XM v. Enderlin,
AAA Case No. 11 181 00989 06 (Jul. 30, 2009) 11.74

Z

Zacharias v. Cypress Communications, Inc,
AAA Case No. 11 181 00004 06 (Nov. 27, 2006) 11.62
Zobrist v. Verizon Wireless,
AAA Case No. 11 494 01274 05, 11 494 0032 05 (Mar. 10, 2008) 11.84

LIST OF CONTRIBUTORS

Oliver J. Armas is the managing partner of the New York office of Hogan Lovells US LLP. He handles complex domestic and international disputes. He has an active trial practice in U.S. federal and state courts, and routinely represents foreign and domestic clients in arbitrations before the ICC, AAA/ICDR, LCIA, ICSID, and other arbitral tribunals. Ollie sits often as an arbitrator. Because he is fluent in Spanish (and can understand Portuguese), Ollie routinely counsels clients on matters involving Latin America. He has acted as a legal expert in certain aspects of U.S. law in foreign proceedings (e.g., Mexico and Peru), and has supervised litigation and conducted FCPA investigations in almost every country in Latin America.

William H. Baker is an independent mediator and arbitrator with a website at www.bakeradr.com. Before becoming a neutral, he practiced intellectual property litigation and international arbitration at a major New York firm. He has been listed in Best Lawyers in America for International Arbitration every year since 2010 and is also listed by Corporate America Legal Elite as Best in Intellectual Property Litigation—New York. He served as an adjunct professor at Cardozo Law School for five years, where he taught a course on international arbitration and mediation. He has served on several class action arbitration panels and has written and spoken frequently on the topic of class action arbitrations. Mr. Baker is a graduate of Yale University and Harvard Law School.

Julie Bédard is a partner at Skadden, Arps, concentrating on international litigation and arbitration. She regularly advises clients on the drafting of dispute resolution clauses and has served as counsel in international arbitration proceedings held under the auspices of the ICC, the AAA, the ICDR, and ICSID. In 2015, Ms. Bédard was named one of Latin America's "Top Female Lawyers" by Latinvex magazine. She has repeatedly been listed in *Chambers Global*, *Chambers USA*, *Global Arbitration Review's International Who's Who of Commercial Arbitration*, *Chambers Latin America*, and *The Best Lawyers in America*. In addition, Ms. Bédard was selected by Harvard Law School as an honoree for its second annual International Women's Day Exhibition in 2015.

Jessica Beess und Chrostin is an associate in the New York office of King & Spalding LLP. Ms. Beess und Chrostin's practice focuses on international commercial and investment arbitration, and she represents clients in international energy, construction, telecommunications, and pharmaceutical disputes. Ms.

Beess und Chrostin received her B.A. *cum laude* from Columbia University and her J.D. *cum laude* from Harvard Law School.

George A. Bermann is the Jean Monnet Professor of EU Law, Walter Gellhorn Professor of Law, and director of the Center for International Commercial and Investment Arbitration at Columbia University. He is an affiliated professor at the Institut d'études politiques, Paris, and a visiting professor at the Collège d'Europe, Bruges. He is president of the Académie internationale de droit comparé, past president of the American Society of Comparative Law, past editor-in-chief of the *American Journal of Comparative Law*, and a member of the New York City Bar Committee on International Commercial Dispute Resolution. He practices as an international arbitrator, and is on the governing board of the ICC International Court of Arbitration, and is the editor-in-chief of the *American Review of International Arbitration*. He received his J.D. from Yale Law School in 1971, and is the author of numerous books and articles.

James H. Carter is senior counsel in the New York office of Wilmer Culter Pickering Hale and Dorr LLP, where he serves as counsel and as an arbitrator. Mr. Carter has participated in more than 150 international commercial and investment arbitration cases. He previously was a partner of Sullivan & Cromwell LLP in New York, specializing in international arbitration. He has served as Chair of the Board of Directors of the American Arbitration Association, President of the American Society of International Law, Chair of the American Bar Association Section of International Law, and a member of the London Court of International Arbitration. Mr. Carter is Chairperson of the New York International Arbitration Center, a member of the Court of Arbitration for Sport, and a graduate of Yale College and Yale Law School.

Janet R. Carter is counsel in the New York office of Wilmer Cutler Pickering Hale and Dorr LLP, focusing on international arbitration and international litigation. She has acted as counsel in cases under the ICC, ICDR/AAA, and JAMS rules, in arbitrations sited in the U.S., Europe, Asia, as well as maintaining a practice in litigation involving the application of international and foreign law in U.S. courts. She has served on the Arbitration Committee of the New York City Bar Association and on the Programs Committee of the New York International Arbitration Center. She previously served as law clerk to Justice Sandra Day O'Connor of the U.S. Supreme Court and Judge Richard Posner of the U.S. Court of Appeals for the Seventh Circuit. She is a graduate of the University of Otago and New York University School of Law.

David N. Cinotti is counsel in the New York office of Venable LLP, where he focuses on international commercial and investor–state arbitration and the resolution of international disputes in U.S. courts. He has served as counsel in arbitrations before ICSID, ICDR/AAA, and JAMS tribunals, and he has substantial experience litigating matters collateral to international arbitration, including the enforcement of international arbitration agreements and awards. He serves as an adviser to a mission to the United Nations, at meetings of UNCITRAL Working Group II (Arbitration and Conciliation), and the Sixth Committee of the General Assembly. Before joining Venable, he was a law clerk to the Hon. Joseph M. McLaughlin of the U.S. Court of Appeals for the Second Circuit, an associate at Wilmer Cutler Pickering Hale and Dorr LLP, and a law clerk to the Hon. Richard Conway Casey of the U.S. District Court for the Southern District of New York. Mr. Cinotti received his J.D. from Georgetown University Law Center and his B.A. from the College of the Holy Cross.

Hagit Elul is a partner in the Litigation, International Arbitration and Alternative Dispute Resolution, and Appellate groups at Hughes Hubbard & Reed LLP. She has served as counsel in arbitrations under all major institutional rules and has represented international clients in a wide array of contract and licensing disputes involving financial services, energy, pharmaceutical, construction, and professional services. Among other activities, she is the chair of the international section of the New York City Bar Association federal courts committee and an officer of the arbitration commission of AIJA, the International Association of Young Lawyers. Hagit writes and speaks widely on the subjects of arbitration and international arbitration. She was shortlisted on Global Arbitration Review's 45 under 45 international arbitration practitioners and has been recognized as "one to watch" and a rising star among women in international arbitration by Global Arbitration Review.

Hagit graduated from the University of California at Berkeley and received her law degree with honors from Columbia Law School. After law school she clerked for the United States District Court, District of New Mexico.

John Fellas is a partner in the New York office of Hughes Hubbard & Reed LLP. He is Co-Chair of the firm's International Arbitration and Dispute Resolution Practice and Co-Chair of the International Practice, and focuses on the areas of international litigation and arbitration. Mr. Fellas has practiced in both the U.S. and England and, as well as being a member of the New York Bar, he is also a Solicitor of the Supreme Court of England and Wales. He has served as counsel, and as chair, sole arbitrator, and co-arbitrator, in arbitrations under the AAA, ICC, and ad hoc rules. He has been recognized for his practice in international arbitration by: *Who's Who Legal—The International Who's Who Of Business Lawyers*; *Chambers USA—Guide to America's Leading Business Lawyers*; *Chambers Global*; *The Best Lawyers In America*; *Euromoney Expert Guides—Best of the Best USA*. He received a B.A. (Hons.) from the University of Durham, England, and both an L.L.M. and an S.J.D. from the Harvard Law School.

Paul D. Friedland has been global head of the 2015 No. 1 ranked White & Case International Arbitration practice group since 2002. He is widely recognized as one of the world's leading authorities on international arbitration. Paul has served as counsel or as arbitrator in numerous international arbitrations, both commercial and investor–state. Paul's leadership positions include: American Arbitration Association (Executive Committee, 2011–14, Chair of Law Committee, 2008–14, Chair of Subcommittee on ICDR Rules revision, 2013–14); International Bar Association (Arbitration Committee Co-Chair, 2014–15); Singapore International Arbitration Centre (Court member, since 2013); and London Court of International Arbitration (Court member, 2006–10).

Mark W. Friedman is a litigation partner in the New York office of Debevoise & Plimpton LLP. He has broad experience in civil and criminal matters, with a concentration on international arbitration and litigation. He has acted as counsel or arbitrator in disputes under the rules of the LCIA, ICC, AAA, ICDR, CPR, UNCITRAL, and ICSID. Mr. Friedman has been ranked as a leading individual by *Chambers Global*, *Chambers UK*, *Chambers USA*, *The International Who's Who of Commercial Arbitration*, *The International Who's Who of Commercial Litigation*, *PLC Which Lawyer? Yearbook*, and *Legal Experts*. Among other positions, he is a Vice President of the ICC Court of Arbitration, a member of the editorial board of *Dispute Resolution International*, and was previously Co-Chair of the International Bar Association's Arbitration Committee, member of the Court of the London Court of International Arbitration, Vice-Chair of the International Dispute Resolution Committee of the International Section of the American Bar Association, and co-rapporteur of the International Law Association's Commercial Arbitration Committee. Mr. Friedman received his B.A. *summa cum laude* from the University of Massachusetts in 1988 and his J.D. from Yale Law School in 1991.

John L. Gardiner is global co-head of Skadden's International Litigation and Arbitration Group. He concentrates his practice in the resolution of complex, high-exposure, multijurisdictional disputes before leading arbitral institutions as well as before federal and state courts in the United States. Mr. Gardiner repeatedly has been listed in *Chambers Global: The World's Leading Lawyers for Business*, *The Best Lawyers in America*, *International Who's Who of Commercial Arbitration*, and *Chambers USA: America's Leading Lawyers for Business*. Mr. Gardiner also has acted as arbitrator in complex international corporate disputes and as mediator in intricate corporate and partnership separation situations. He has participated as counsel in many successful mediations and expert proceedings both internationally and domestically.

Edward G. Kehoe is the co-head of King & Spalding's International Arbitration Practice, and a member of the firm's management committee. Mr. Kehoe has more than twenty-five years of experience in business arbitration and litigation, and for each year since 2007, Mr. Kehoe has been recognized in *Chambers USA* as one of the top lawyers for international arbitration, and is ranked as a top lawyer by *Chambers Global* and by *Legal 500* for international arbitration. He is a Fellow of the Litigation Counsel of America, Trial Lawyer Honorary Society. In addition to serving as counsel, Mr. Kehoe sits as an arbitrator and is listed as an arbitrator on the Panel of Neutrals for the International Centre for Dispute Resolution. He is a frequent writer and lecturer on international arbitration issues, and is a member of the board of editors of *Global Arbitration Review* and on the advisory board of the Institute for Transnational Arbitration.

D. Brian King is a New York-qualified lawyer and partner in the Freshfields Bruckhaus Deringer dispute resolution practice, resident in New York. Brian headed the international arbitration group in the firm's Amsterdam office for seven years before moving back to New York in 2007. Brian's practice focuses on acting as counsel and arbitrator in international commercial and investment arbitrations before the ICSID, ICC, LCIA, ICDR and other arbitral institutions. Brian graduated first in his class at the New York University School of Law in 1990, having received a degree in politics and economics (*summa cum laude*) from Princeton University in 1985. Among other professional affiliations, Brian is an Adjunct Professor at the N.Y.U. School of Law. He speaks English and Dutch and reads Spanish and French.

Lea Haber Kuck is a partner in Skadden's International Arbitration and Litigation Group. She concentrates her practice on the resolution of complex disputes arising out of international business transactions. She represents clients in federal and state courts in the United States, as well as in international arbitrations conducted under UNCITRAL, ICC, ICDR, LCIA, and other arbitration rules.

Ms. Kuck regularly advises clients on a variety of issues relating to international dispute resolution, including forum selection, jurisdiction, service of process, extraterritorial discovery, and enforcement of judgments, as well as the drafting of arbitration, dispute resolution, and choice-of-court clauses. She is a member of the Skadden team that was named the 2013 "Law Firm of the Year: Dispute Resolution" by *Chambers Global*.

Yasmine Lahlou is a partner at Chaffetz Lindsey LLP. She advises and represents U.S. and international clients on a range of commercial disputes in both international arbitration and litigation proceedings. Initially trained in Paris and admitted in New York, Yasmine is experienced in civil and common law systems. Yasmine has represented clients in arbitration proceedings conducted under the ICC, ICDR, LCIA, UNCITRAL, and ad hoc rules. She has acted as a sole and co-arbitrator in ICC and Stockholm Chamber of Commerce (SCC) arbitrations.

David M. Lindsey is a founding partner in the law firm Chaffetz Lindsey LLP in Manhattan, a boutique commercial litigation and international arbitration firm established in 2009. In his twenty-eight-year career, he has acted for clients in major disputes arising out of jurisdictions around the world, much of it relating to the power and oil and gas sectors. David has represented foreign sovereigns, including foreign central banks, in U.S. courts, including in cases arising from the terrorism exception to the U.S. Foreign Sovereign Immunities Act. He is co-editor of *International Arbitration in Latin America* (Kluwer 2002) (2d ed. forthcoming) and has had extensive experience representing clients in the region. He is regularly listed by peers as a leader in the field of international arbitration in publications such as *Chambers* (Global, USA, and Latin America editions), *Legal 500*, *Best Lawyers in America*, *Super Lawyers*, *Benchmark*, and *Who's Who.* He sits as arbitrator, both as party-appointed arbitrator and presiding arbitrator, and regularly speaks at conferences on international arbitration. David is also an experienced U.S. litigator and has tried commercial cases in U.S. state and federal courts. He was previously a partner in the New York office of Clifford Chance and led the firm's international arbitration practice in the Americas from 1999 to 2009. From 1988 to 1999, he was at Steel Hector & Davis, a leading Miami firm, in their Miami and London offices. He is licensed to practice in New York, Washington, D.C., and Florida.

Damien Nyer is an associate in White & Case's New York office where his practice focuses on international arbitration. Mr. Nyer has experience representing governments, international organizations, and private parties in both institutional and ad hoc arbitral proceedings. He is the current Co-Chair of Young ICCA (International Council for Commercial Arbitration) and was the Secretary of the International Bar Association's Taskforce on International Arbitration Clauses. Prior to joining White & Case in New York, Mr. Nyer trained in the international arbitration group of the firm's Paris office. Mr. Nyer holds both common-law and civil-law degrees.

Thomas N. Pieper is counsel at Hogan Lovells in New York. He focuses on complex international dispute resolution, with a particular emphasis on European and Latin American parties. He has successfully represented foreign and domestic clients in large international cases before German, Mexican, and U.S. courts, as well as in international arbitrations, both before arbitral organizations and in ad hoc proceedings. An important component of his work is the drafting of proper dispute resolution clauses. Thomas also represents clients in regulatory matters, including FCPA-related investigations, and assists with transactional issues.

John V. H. Pierce is the head of the international arbitration practice in the New York office of Wilmer Cutler Pickering Hale and Dorr LLP. Recognized by *Chambers* as "a crucial figure in the firm's global arbitration practice," Mr. Pierce represents clients in international arbitration matters in venues around the world, under both civil and common law regimes, and under the rules of all major arbitral institutions. Mr. Pierce has represented European, U.S., Latin American, and other companies in a wide range of industries and sectors, in arbitrations sited in Latin America, the U.S., Europe, and Asia. He has particular experience in international joint venture, M&A, shareholder, pharmaceutical, electronics, telecommunications, transportation, financial services, and agency disputes.

In addition to his work as counsel, Mr. Pierce sits as an arbitrator in international disputes, and he is a frequent writer and speaker on issues of international arbitration and dispute resolution. He is a Board Member and member of the Programs Committee of the New York International Arbitration Center, a founding member of the International Arbitration Club of New York, a member of the International Commercial Dispute Resolution Committee at the Association of the Bar of the City of New York, and a member of the Council on Foreign Relations. He is an honors graduate of Georgetown University's School of Foreign Service, the Institut d'études politiques de Paris, and the Georgetown University Law Center. He was also Jean Monnet Fellow at the École polytechnique and a Young Leader of the American Council on Germany.

David W. Rivkin is Co-Chair of Debevoise & Plimpton's International Dispute Resolution Group and President of the International Bar Association. A litigation partner in the firm's New York and London offices, Mr. Rivkin has broad experience in the areas of international litigation and arbitration. He has handled international arbitrations throughout the world and before virtually every major arbitral institution, including the ICC, AAA, LCIA, ICSID, IACAC, and the Stockholm Chamber of Commerce. Mr. Rivkin also represents European, Latin American, and Asian companies in transnational litigation in the United States, including the enforcement of arbitral awards and arbitration agreements. Mr. Rivkin is Vice Chair of the Arbitration Institute of the Stockholm Chamber of Commerce and immediate past President of the North American Users' Council of the LCIA. He is a member of the Council of the American Law Institute, for which he is an Adviser to the Restatement of the Law of International Arbitration, and a Councillor to the Restatement of Foreign Relations Law. He held leadership positions within the ABA's Litigation Section for twenty years, including five years as Co-Chair of the International Litigation Committee and a member of the Section's Council and its Director of Divisions. He is a Fellow of the London-based Chartered Institute of Arbitrators; a Fellow of the College of Commercial Arbitrators; a member of the Commission on Settlement in International Arbitration of the Centre for Effective Dispute Resolution (CEDR); a member of the Centro Internacional de Arbitraje, Mediacion y Negociacion of the Instituto Universitario de Estudios Europeas, Universidad de San Pablo in Madrid; and a member of the Association of the Bar of the City of New York.

Tyler B. Robinson is a partner in the Litigation Department of Simpson Thatcher & Bartlett LLP, based in the London office. He represents clients in a wide variety of complex commercial disputes, focusing on international arbitration and international litigation. Mr. Robinson received his J.D. from the University of Michigan Law School.

Claudia T. Salomon is a partner in the New York office of Latham & Watkins LLP and global Co-Chair of the firm's International Arbitration Practice. Her practice is focused on complex international disputes and she is recognized as a leading international arbitration attorney by *Chambers USA*, *The Legal 500*, *Who's Who Legal*, and *Best Lawyers*. Ms. Salomon is a leading advocate in significant investor treaty arbitration and international commercial arbitration cases. She has experience handling cases under all of the major arbitral rules, in venues around the globe, under common law and civil law. Ms. Salomon also litigates in connection with arbitration, including enforcing arbitral awards worldwide and obtaining emergency relief. Ms. Salomon is the U.S. member of the ICC International Court of Arbitration and serves as the Co-Chair of the ICC Taskforce on Financial Institutions and International Arbitration. She is a frequent speaker and writer on international arbitration and is the co-editor of *Choice of Venue in International Arbitration*, published by Oxford University Press.

Robert H. Smit is a Partner at Simpson Thacher & Bartlett LLP in the firm's Litigation Department, where he Co-Chairs the Firm's International Arbitration and Dispute Resolution Practice. He represents clients in a wide range of complex commercial litigations and arbitrations. Rob has regularly served as arbitrator in significant international arbitrations, and is listed as one of the leading international arbitration lawyers in the world by *Chambers Global*, *Chambers USA*, *International Who's Who of Business Lawyers*, *Law Business Research*, *Legal Media Group Expert Guides*, Euromoney's *Benchmark Litigation*, and *PLC Global Counsel* Handbooks. Rob is Adjunct Professor of International Arbitration at Columbia Law School; Co-Editor-in-Chief of the *American Review of International Arbitration*; and Member of the ICC Commission on Arbitration.

William H. Taft V has been a partner in the Litigation Department of the New York office of Debevoise & Plimpton LLP since 2005. His practice focuses on commercial and corporate governance litigation and international arbitration. From 2004 to 2005, Mr. Taft clerked for the Hon. Samuel A. Alito, Jr., when Justice Alito served on the U.S. Court of Appeals for the Third Circuit. Mr. Taft received a J.D. *cum laude* from New York University School of Law in 2004, and a B.A. in History from Yale University in 2000.

Janet M. Whittaker is counsel at Simpson Thacher & Bartlett LLP, where she specializes in international arbitration and litigation. She has significant experience of arbitrating and litigating cross-border disputes within the United States and in overseas jurisdictions. Janet has handled international commercial and investment arbitrations under the rules of the LCIA, ICC, AAA, UNCITRAL, and ICSID. She has advised government representatives on negotiating and drafting investment treaties and investors about structuring agreements to achieve protection for overseas investments. Ms. Whittaker frequently advises clients on issues relating to foreign sovereign immunities and international human rights law. She also sits as arbitrator.

Ms. Whittaker previously served as legal counsel at ICSID. She also practiced international arbitration and acted as counsel in cases before English courts. She has been a lecturer in International Arbitration at Stanford Law School and taught European Law at University College London. Ms. Whittaker is recognized by *Who's Who Legal* as a leading arbitration lawyer.

Alexander Yanos is a litigation partner in the New York office of Hughes Hubbard & Reed LLP and co-chairs the firm's Treaty Arbitration practice group. His practice focuses on complex disputes, particularly international disputes, both in court and before arbitral tribunals. Mr. Yanos's arbitration practice includes commercial, financial, and treaty-based disputes, particularly in the energy and mining sectors and in Latin America. He has acted in matters before nearly every international arbitration tribunal, including the International Centre for Settlement of Investment Disputes, the International Chamber of Commerce, the London Court of International Arbitration, the American Arbitration Association, the Hong Kong International Arbitration Centre, the Inter-American Commercial Arbitration Commission, the International Court of Justice, and the Stockholm Chamber of Commerce. Mr. Yanos received his B.A. *magna cum laude* from Princeton University, and his J.D. from the Columbia University Law School.

INTRODUCTION

The New York Arbitration Landscape

James H. Carter and John Fellas

A. **Overview of International Arbitration in New York** 0.01
1. The Major Arbitral Institutions in New York 0.07
(a) AAA/ICDR 0.08
(b) ICC/SICANA 0.11
(c) CPR 0.13
(d) JAMS 0.16
2. The Court System Supporting Arbitration 0.17
3. The New York International Arbitration Center 0.22
4. Other Supporting Organizations 0.23
(a) The New York International Arbitration Club 0.24
(b) Bar association committees 0.25
(c) The College of Commercial Arbitrators 0.28
(d) Universities 0.29
(e) Consulting firms 0.30
(f) Law firm international groups 0.31
5. Arbitration Hearing Locations 0.32
B. **This Book** 0.34

A. OVERVIEW OF INTERNATIONAL ARBITRATION IN NEW YORK

New York City is the center of international commercial arbitration in the United States. Approximately 30 percent of the more than 1000 American Arbitration Association (AAA) commercial arbitration cases filed each year that are defined by the AAA as international and are located in the United States designate New York as the arbitration site. New York is by far the leading venue, with more than double the number of cases heard than in any other U.S. city.[1] AAA international cases most often involve at least one U.S. party, and some of those cases are primarily between two U.S. parties but are classified by the AAA as international because the parties include a subsidiary or joint venture incorporated elsewhere. The cases located in New York, however, tend to involve at least one **0.01**

[1] Information supplied by the American Arbitration Association's International Dispute Resolution Centre, on file with the authors. In 2013, parties in 31% of new ICDR cases in the U.S. (333 of 1,076) selected New York as the venue.

primary nondomestic party and represent a significant portion of matters with larger amounts in dispute.

0.02 The International Chamber of Commerce (ICC)'s International Court of Arbitration, with a much smaller U.S.-sited caseload, has administered on average about 50 percent of these U.S. cases in New York. New York in recent years typically has ranked sixth worldwide among the most popular cities for ICC cases (behind only Paris, London, Geneva, Zurich, and Singapore) and is more popular than any other U.S. venue.[2]

0.03 Although other verifiable arbitration statistics are notoriously elusive, there is no reason to believe that the percentage of U.S. ad hoc international commercial arbitrations based in New York differs from this 30–50 percent range, and anecdotal evidence indicates that they also tend to include many of the larger cases. The Fulbright Annual Litigation Trends Survey Report for 2013,[3] based on data from 392 in-house attorneys, predominantly from the U.S. and the United Kingdom, found that 43 percent of the U.K. respondents preferred New York over all other U.S. cities and that the largest share of the U.S. respondents, 27 percent, considered New York the preferred site.

0.04 We therefore estimate that New York is the home of not less than one-third of all significant international commercial arbitrations in the country, with the balance of international cases distributed widely among a number of other U.S. venues. Also, New York frequently is the venue of convenience for hearings in arbitrations with a technical site in some other part of the world.

0.05 New York's role as a financial and legal capital leads to the choice of New York governing law for many commercial documents, often resulting in a choice of New York as the venue for any disputes arising from those documents. When the International Swaps and Derivatives Association (ISDA) released six model arbitration clauses in 2013 for use with its global standard form agreements for documenting financial derivatives transactions, for example, two of them provided for U.S. alternatives, in both instances suggesting New York law and an arbitral seat in New York (one clause specified AAA/ICDR Rules, the other specified ICC Rules).

0.06 The city's leading position in international commercial arbitration also derives from the facts that a number of leading arbitration institutions are based

[2] The ICC's Statistical Report is published annually in the ICC International Court of Arbitration Bulletin and is available in the ICC's Dispute Resolution Library, http://www.iccdrl.com. The U.S. caseload for the ICC is important but remains relatively small: e.g., fifty-eight cases in 2014 (twelve in New York City), thirty-eight cases in 2013 (twenty-four in New York City), forty-one cases in 2012 (twenty-two in New York City), forty-eight cases in 2011 (twenty in New York City), forty-four cases in 2010 (twenty-three in New York City).

[3] Available at http://www.LitigationTrends.com.

in New York, the local court system strongly supports international arbitration, and the community of supporting organizations, such as the New York International Arbitration Center, bar associations, universities and others is quite strong.

1. The Major Arbitral Institutions in New York

New York is a hub of international commercial arbitration in large part because of the administering institutions with operations based in the city. **0.07**

(a) AAA/ICDR The AAA, formed in 1926 as a not-for-profit corporation, is **0.08** the flagship U.S. alternative dispute resolution organization and maintains its headquarters in New York. The AAA has twenty-three offices or affiliates, located throughout the United States and in Mexico, Singapore and Bahrain. It offers a full range of arbitration and mediation services, as well as election monitoring, disaster-related claims programs, and other specialized training and other services. The AAA administers more than 200,000 cases each year, involving consumer and employee claims as well as business-to-business disputes. Its Web site is http://www.adr.org.

The AAA administers its international caseload through a separate division, the **0.09** International Centre for Dispute Resolution (ICDR), which manages most of the AAA international cases from its New York office at 120 Broadway. The ICDR also has offices in Mexico City, Singapore and Seoul and a cooperative venture in Bahrain, as well as case management teams in Houston and Miami. In 2015, it began an ICDR Canada service.

In 2013, the ICDR administered 1165 new cases, in 89 of which, parties re- **0.10** quested venues outside the United States. The ICDR has a staff of 30, including attorneys with language skills in at least thirteen languages. Most ICDR cases are administered under either the ICDR's International Arbitration Rules (revised in 2014) or the AAA's Commercial Arbitration Rules (revised in 2013).

(b) ICC/SICANA The ICC is based in Paris, but in 2014 it began to admin- **0.11** ister all of its North American cases from a regional office in New York, known as SICANA, Inc. (for "Secretariat of the International Court of Arbitration, North America") located at 1212 Avenue of the Americas, where ICC Team 9 is based. The ICC administers more than seven hundred commercial and investment arbitration cases filed each year worldwide. Its Web site is http://www.iccwbo.org.

The U.S. National Committee of the ICC is the Arbitration Committee of the **0.12** U.S. Council for International Business (U.S. Council), a broad-based business advocacy organization whose offices also are in New York at 1212 Avenue of the Americas. The Arbitration Committee is administered by a U.S. Council employee, the Director of Arbitration and Alternative Dispute Resolution, North

America. The U.S. Council Arbitration Committee supports the ICC Court by making nominations of arbitrators when requested and by promoting ICC arbitration in the United States. Its Web site is http://www.uscib.org.

0.13 *(c) CPR* The International Institute for Conflict Prevention & Resolution (CPR) is a nonprofit business-to-business dispute resolution membership organization supported by a number of leading corporations and law firms. It pursues an agenda of research on alternative dispute resolution techniques, as well as ADR education and advocacy. CPR also provides commercial arbitration services.

0.14 In 2013, CPR for the first time issued Administered Arbitration Rules broadly similar to those of other international arbitration organizations and began the administration of both domestic and international arbitration cases in which the parties select those rules. Prior to that time, CPR cases could be brought only under what were, in effect, "semi-administered" procedures that did not include continuing administrative services as a case progresses but did provide parties with access to limited CPR administrative services in connection with arbitrator appointments and challenge procedures at the start of a case. Under those earlier CPR rules, which also remain available for use, the arbitrators collect and manage financial deposits from the parties in CPR arbitrations, as is the case in ad hoc arbitrations.

0.15 Because, until recently, it did not provide administrative services and might not be asked to assist in the appointment process, CPR has not had records showing how many arbitrations proceed using its rules. CPR historically has provided appointment services in approximately one hundred arbitration cases each year, a limited number of which are categorized as international. The most common venue is New York City. CPR's headquarters are in New York at 30 E. 33rd Street. Its Web site is http://www.cpradr.org.

0.16 *(d) JAMS* Formerly known as the Judicial Arbitration and Mediation Service, JAMS is a for-profit U.S. provider of ADR services in the United States, based in Irvine, California. It offers arbitration and mediation services exclusively from its own roster of retired judges and litigation attorneys. JAMS has an office and hearing facilities in New York at 620 Eighth Avenue. Its Web site is http://www.jamsadr.com. JAMS has both domestic and international arbitration rules and a roster of potential arbitrators in the New York area, some of whom are specialists in international matters.

2. The Court System Supporting Arbitration

0.17 Both U.S. federal and New York State law are strongly pro-arbitration. Courts in both systems refer regularly to the efficiencies realized by honoring parties' decisions to refer disputes to private resolution systems, and they apply the laws restricting judicial review of arbitral awards to avoid undermining the arbitration process. New York courts also are mindful that New York's role as a center of financial and business transactions is strengthened by the dependability of its international commercial arbitration laws.

In the U.S. federal system, the courts of first instance are called district courts. Each state has at least one district court, with some states having as many as four, each with jurisdiction over a particular part of the state. New York State has four separate federal judicial districts, with two covering New York City: the Southern District of New York, which has the largest civil caseload in the country, with forty-four district court judges, covering Manhattan, the Bronx, and several counties to the immediate north; and the Eastern District of New York, with twenty-seven district court judges, covering Brooklyn, Queens, and the remainder of Long Island. The judges of these courts hear a significant number of arbitration cases, both international and domestic, and are familiar with most of the issues that typically arise. **0.18**

Appeals from district courts are taken to circuit courts, which are intermediate courts of appeals. There are twelve circuit courts, eleven with jurisdiction over appeals from particular states, and one, the Court of Appeals for the Federal Circuit, with jurisdiction over appeals in patent cases. The Court of Appeals for the Second Circuit hears appeals from cases decided by New York federal district courts, and its decisions are binding on those courts. The decisions of other New York federal district courts and of other circuit courts of appeals are not binding on New York federal district courts, but constitute only persuasive authority. The appeals court of last resort is the U.S. Supreme Court. **0.19**

Litigated matters in the New York State courts involving arbitration typically are brought in the Supreme Court (which is not, in fact, the court of last resort but instead a trial level court) for New York County, whose jurisdiction encompasses Manhattan and the Bronx. That court has a separate Commercial Division, with nine judges, who have special expertise in business disputes. **0.20**

In 2013, the Commercial Division designated one of its members to handle all matters involving international arbitration and issued "International Arbitration Part Rules"[4] describing how such cases may be brought and heard on an expedited basis. A number of applications under these rules have involved requests that the Court issue orders of attachment or other provisional remedies in aid of arbitration. **0.21**

3. The New York International Arbitration Center

The New York International Arbitration Center (NYIAC) is a not-for-profit corporation that does not administer cases but instead promotes New York as a place **0.22**

[4] Appendix 4 of this book.

to hold international arbitration hearings and related meetings and events. It offers multiple hearing room facilities with video link and language interpretation capabilities, available to users of any type of administered or ad hoc arbitration, located at 150 East 42nd Street. The rooms can accommodate large hearings of up to 45 people. NYIAC also organizes educational programs on dispute resolution subjects and provides programs for the New York judiciary. It is supported by 39 leading law firms and two sections of the New York State Bar Association. NYIAC's Web site is http://nyiac.org.

4. Other Supporting Organizations

0.23 The New York international commercial arbitration community includes a large number of lawyers and others actively involved in supporting the development of arbitration law and practice. The extensive U.S. domestic arbitration practice in New York provides a deep reservoir of expertise from which international arbitration practitioners benefit. These lawyers see each other regularly at bar association and other meetings, resulting in a high degree of interaction, more typical of a specialized bar than the relative anonymity of much of New York City law practice.

0.24 *(a) The New York International Arbitration Club* The New York International Arbitration Club is an association of lawyers and arbitrators active in international arbitration in New York. It promotes best practices in arbitration, provides a forum for discussion within that community of current topics and publishes materials on its Web site, http://arbitrationclub.org. Its list of members is a source of names often considered by parties seeking to appoint arbitrators in New York cases.

0.25 *(b) Bar association committees* Many U.S. bar associations have committees devoted primarily or exclusively to international commercial arbitration. In New York, both the New York City Bar Association and the New York State Bar Association sponsor such committees.

0.26 The New York City Bar Association has both an International Commercial Disputes Committee and an Arbitration Committee. Both groups publish reports on arbitration issues, and the International Commercial Disputes Committee has proposed and successfully promoted the amendment of New York State arbitration legislation.[5] The New York State Bar Association's International Section and Dispute Resolution Section both also have active International Arbitration Committees.

[5] *See* Amendment of New York Civil Practice Law and Rules Section 7502(c) to Permit Attachments and Preliminary Injunctions in Connection with National and International Arbitrations, Committee Report available at http://www.nycbar.org/Publications/reports.

Members of the New York arbitration community are active, too, in the American Bar Association International Law Section's International Commercial Disputes Committee, the Dispute Resolution Section's International Committee and the Litigation Section's International Arbitration Committee, as well as in the International Bar Association's Arbitration Committee. **0.27**

(c) The College of Commercial Arbitrators The College of Commercial Arbitrators (CCA) is a national association of experienced commercial arbitrators, which promotes professionalism and ethical practice in commercial arbitration, including international arbitrations in the U.S., and provides training and best practices materials. A number of New York arbitrators are active in its leadership. **0.28**

(d) Universities The New York metropolitan area is the home of a dozen university law schools, many of which offer courses or seminars in international commercial arbitration. Faculty members at these schools are active as arbitrators and as members of the bar association committees that develop reports and policy statements. New York University School of Law and Columbia University's Law School, in particular, maintain extensive libraries of arbitration materials. **0.29**

(e) Consulting firms A number of accounting and other professional firms with offices in New York have groups of professionals, including economists, accountants, and others, who specialize in providing services to counsel in international commercial arbitration proceedings. **0.30**

(f) Law firm international groups New York City is home to or an important office location for almost all of the largest U.S. law firms, all of which are involved in international arbitrations with at least some regularity. Non-U.S. law firms with an international practice also are present in large numbers. Some of these law firms have organized arbitration or international arbitration groups specializing in this area of practice. **0.31**

5. Arbitration Hearing Locations

In addition to NYIAC's facilities at 150 East 42nd Street, which are available for any type of arbitration, the ICDR maintains a number of hearing rooms, including rooms with video link capabilities, at its midtown dispute resolution center also located at 150 East 42nd Street. Although the rooms are primarily for ICDR cases, they are available for rental by parties seeking a hearing room in other cases. In addition, JAMS has hearing facilities at 620 Eighth Avenue, and the New York City Bar Association maintains hearing rooms at its building at 42 West 44th Street that may be rented for arbitration hearings. **0.32**

Many international arbitration hearings in New York take place either in the offices of law firms with which a member of the tribunal may be affiliated or at the offices of counsel for one of the parties. Hotel facilities also are widely available and sometimes used for this purpose. **0.33**

B. THIS BOOK

0.34 This book is about both the practicalities and the law of international commercial arbitration in New York City, focused primarily on disputes arising from business-to-business transactions of all sorts that are defined as international. An arbitration in the United States usually is considered "international" by arbitration institutions and courts if there are one or more non-U.S. nationals among the parties or if the dispute is between U.S. nationals but arises from a transaction in international commerce. New York is home to specialized varieties of international commercial dispute resolution, such as maritime arbitration, which fit within this definition but are the subjects of their own detailed studies and thus are not treated here. Commercial disputes in New York sometimes include governments and parastatal organizations as parties, and this book discusses those matters. New York also is the site of investment arbitrations, particularly in cases brought under the United Nations Commission on International Trade Law (UNCITRAL) Arbitration Rules. The primary focus of this book, however, is upon international commercial arbitration in New York, between and among business entities arising from commercial settings, with discussion from time to time of other aspects of the New York arbitration landscape.

0.35 The place of arbitration, together with such matters as the rules under which it is conducted and the identity of the arbitrators, are among the important factors that will affect how an arbitration will proceed. Without trying to rank the degree to which different elements of the arbitration process might shape it, the place of arbitration is, in any view, significant.[6]

0.36 It is conventional wisdom that the difference between an arbitral seat, like New York, that is in a country that is a party to the New York or Panama Conventions, and one that is not is of critical significance, since, as a general matter, only in the former case will the parties to the arbitration be able to obtain the benefits of those Conventions. But this does not distinguish New York—the focus of this book—from any other city in any of the 156 countries that are parties to the Conventions. Beyond the ability to obtain the benefits of the New York or Panama Conventions, the place of arbitration will determine not only the procedural law under which an arbitration takes place,[7] but also what might be referred to as the dispute resolution culture in which it takes place.

[6] As the English Court of Appeal has stated: "In international commercial arbitration, the place or seat of arbitration is of paramount importance." Star Shipping AS. v. China Nat'l Foreign Trade Trans. Corp., [1993] Lloyd's Rep. 445.

[7] JSC Surgutneftegaz v. President and Fellows of Harvard College, 2005 WL 1863676 (Aug. 3, 2005) ("The situs of the arbitration is of critical importance because the law of the jurisdiction in which the arbitration is conducted ordinarily provides the procedural law of the arbitration") *aff'd*, 167 Fed.Appx. 266 (2d Cir. 2006); Karaha Bodas Co. L.L.C., v. Perusahaan Pertambangan Minyak Dan Gas Bumi Negara, et al., 364 F.3d 274, 291 (5th Cir. 2004) ("Under the New York

With respect to the latter issue, since the participants in an arbitration proceeding—the parties, the lawyers representing the parties, and the arbitrators—will likely, although not inevitably, be disproportionately based in the place or country of the arbitration, they will likely come to the arbitration with some shared approaches to dispute resolution. In this context, it is worth emphasizing that in New York (and the United States more generally), as opposed to other prominent centers of international arbitration, such as Paris or London, lawyers who practice in the field of international commercial arbitration rarely do so exclusively. It is more common for lawyers who practice international commercial arbitration in New York also to practice commercial litigation more generally, although some do focus on international arbitration alone, especially in the field of treaty arbitration. **0.37**

For the most part, therefore, the views of the New York-based participants in international arbitration—arbitration counsel and arbitrators—have been forged in the crucible of the U.S. system of civil litigation—a system that is adversarial, includes notice pleadings rather than the more substantive pleadings used in civil law jurisdictions, broad discovery, depositions, party-appointed experts, dispositive motions, live direct testimony, often aggressive cross-examination at trial, and the device of the class action. This "legal baggage," which New York lawyers may bring with them to an international arbitration proceeding and which is discussed in more detail in Chapter 2, has led some to bemoan the "Americanization" of international arbitration.[8] Indeed, this Americanization has spawned class arbitration in the United States—an arbitration proceeding in which the claimant brings a claim not only on behalf of herself, but also on behalf of others—which is discussed in Chapter 11.[9] **0.38**

But the influences have also run the other way, through "cross-pollination," to borrow Rusty Park's felicitous term.[10] This cross-pollination has produced a hybrid set of converging practices in international arbitration that are the product of different legal traditions.[11] Experienced practitioners and arbitrators in New York, which includes all the contributors to this book, will not **0.39**

Convention, an agreement specifying the place of the arbitration creates a presumption that the procedural law of that place applies to the arbitration.").

[8] *See* Lucy Reed and Jonathan Sutcliffe, *The "Americanization" of International Arbitration?*, 16 Int'l Arb. Rep. 37, 42 (2001).

[9] Not everyone laments the use of prototypically American litigation practices in arbitration. Thus, with respect to class arbitration, international arbitrators based in Europe have raised the question of whether the device of the class arbitration merits being adopted more generally. *See* Bernard Hanotiau, Complex Arbitrations: Multiparty, Multicontract, Multi-Issue, and Class Actions 257–79 (2005).

[10] *See* William W. Park, *Arbitration Procedural Matrix*, in Arbitration of International Business Disputes 121 (2d ed. 2012).

[11] *See* Siegfried H. Elsing and John M. Townsend, *Bridging the Common Law–Civil Law Divide in International Arbitration*, 18 Arb. Int'l 59, 59 (2002).

approach an international arbitration proceeding with the expectation that it will resemble a U.S. civil litigation. Rather, they will be familiar with the practices commonly used in international arbitration proceedings, such as having the direct testimony of a witness submitted in writing, foregoing depositions, and limiting disclosure to that permitted under the International Bar Association (IBA) Rules for the Taking of Evidence in International Arbitration. Having said this, it is not infrequent that one encounters New York commercial litigators as counsel in their first international arbitration proceeding, who approach it as if it were the same as a U.S.-style litigation, only before a different audience. Moreover, where both parties to an international arbitration sited in New York are represented by U.S. counsel, such counsel may both wish to adopt certain U.S. litigation devices, such as depositions, in the arbitration even though they are not generally used in international arbitration proceedings.

0.40 As noted, the place of arbitration determines the procedural law governing the arbitration. This affects such matters as the appropriate allocation of jurisdiction between courts and arbitrators on various issues, whether local law supports the arbitration process by, for example, naming arbitrators where there is no mechanism for their selection, enforcing agreements to arbitrate, granting preliminary relief in aid of arbitration, or assisting in the taking of evidence for use in the arbitration. As a general matter, New York courts and other courts in the United States are very supportive of international arbitration, based on the federal policy in its favor, which, according to the courts, applies with greater force to international arbitration. The Court of Appeals for the Second Circuit has described this policy in the following way:

> As a point of departure, we note that federal policy strongly favors arbitration as an alternative dispute resolution process. While it is still the rule that parties may not be compelled to submit a commercial dispute to arbitration unless they have contracted to do so, federal arbitration policy requires that "any doubts concerning the scope of arbitrable issues should be resolved in favor of arbitration."
>
> The policy in favor of arbitration is even stronger in the context of international business transactions. Enforcement of international arbitral agreements promotes the smooth flow of international transactions by removing the threats and uncertainty of time-consuming and expensive litigation. The parties may agree in advance as to how their disputes will be expeditiously and inexpensively resolved should their business relationship sour. Stability in international trading was the engine behind the Convention on the Recognition and Enforcement of Foreign Arbitral Awards. This treaty—to which the United States is a signatory—makes it clear that the liberal federal arbitration policy applies with special force in the field of international commerce.[12]

[12] David L. Threlkeld & Co., Inc. v. Metallgesellschaft Ltd. (London), 923 F.2d 245, 248 (2d. Cir. 1991) (internal citations omitted).

Some version of this language appears numerous times in reported decisions by U.S. courts.

The favorable attitude of U.S. courts to arbitration can be illustrated by examining the device of the antisuit injunction. New York federal courts routinely exercise the authority to enjoin litigation brought in another country in breach of an arbitration clause requiring arbitration in New York.[13] Moreover, the general trend in the recent cases decided by the U.S. Supreme Court has been to limit court interference in the arbitration process and to resolve questions about the allocation of authority between courts and arbitrators in favor of arbitrators.[14] **0.41**

Indeed, since the publication of the first edition of this book, the United States Supreme Court has continued to resolve questions about the allocation of authority between courts and arbitrators in favor of arbitrators. Some years ago, the Supreme Court began to rely on the metaphor of a "gateway"—which calls to mind a gate through which a party must pass in order to proceed with an arbitration on the merits—in addressing questions about the allocation of authority between arbitrators and courts. In *Howsam v. Dean Witter Reynolds, Inc.*, 123 S. Ct. 588, 592 (2002), Justice Breyer, writing for the Court, stated that use of the phrase a "question of arbitrability" should be limited to gateway matters decided by a court rather than by an arbitrator. This, of course, raises the question of how to distinguish between issues for the court and issues for the arbitrator. Justice Breyer stated that it is necessary to look at the expectations of the parties: "the Court has found the phrase [a question of arbitrability] applicable in the kind of narrow circumstance where contracting parties would likely have expected a court to decide the gateway matter" and "*not* applicable ... where parties would likely expect that an arbitrator would decide the gateway matter." Id. **0.42**

Since the publication of the first edition, the Court has continued to rely on the gateway metaphor and, where the Court has itself addressed a gateway matter, it has generally required arbitration in the face of an objection that the arbitration **0.43**

---

[13] Paramedics Electromedicina Comercial, Ltda. v. GE Medical Systems Information Technologies, Inc., 2003 WL 23641529 (S.D.N.Y. June 4), *aff'd*, 369 F.3d 645 (2d Cir. 2004). For a discussion of the device of the antisuit injunction in the arbitration context, *see* Chapter 7 of this book.

[14] Preston v. Ferrer, 128 S. Ct. 978 (2008) (when parties agree to resolve all disputes arising under a contract, questions concerning the validity of the entire contract are to be resolved by an arbitrator not by a court); Buckeye Check Cashing v. Cardegna, 546 U.S. 440 (2006) (assertion that contract void on ground of illegality to be determined by arbitrator rather than court); Green Tree Financial Corp. v. Bazzle, 543 U.S. 444 (2003) (plurality opinion holding that arbitrators, rather than courts, should decide whether arbitration agreement permits class action); Pacificare Health Systems v. Book, 538 U.S. 401 (2003) (whether or not claims under the Racketeer Influenced and Corrupt Organizations Act (RICO) were arbitrable for arbitrator, rather than court, to consider in first instance); Howsam v. Dean Witter Reynolds, Inc., 537 U.S. 79 (2002) (holding that procedural questions, such as contractual time limits for asserting claims contained in arbitral rules, are presumptively for an arbitrator, not a court, to decide).

of a particular claim is barred by a state statute.[15] More significantly, the Supreme Court has gone further and over the last several years has granted more authority to arbitrators to resolve questions of who should decide a particular gateway matter and, to make it harder, in some circumstances, to argue that certain of those questions should be resolved by courts.

0.44 The question of who should decide a particular gateway matter has always been animated by two principles, the separability doctrine[16] and what, borrowing from the Supreme Court, we may call the delegation doctrine.[17] In *Rent-A-Center West, Inc. v. Jackson*, 130 S. Ct. 2722 (2010), Justice Scalia, writing for the majority, took matters further by conjoining the separability doctrine from *Prima Paint* and the delegation doctrine from *First Options* in a manner that makes it easier to argue that the arbitrator stands as the gatekeeper for particular issues. In particular, when a party resists arbitration in a case where the arbitration agreement contains a provision that clearly and unmistakably delegates to the arbitrator the authority to resolve questions about the validity of that agreement (the delegation doctrine of *First Options*), *Rent-A-Center* holds that those questions must be resolved by an arbitrator unless the party challenges the validity of the delegation provision itself (the separability doctrine of *Prima Paint*). But it is inevitably more difficult to challenge a delegation provision in an arbitration clause specifically—to argue that that specific, narrow provision was procured by fraud or is unconscionable, for example—than it is to challenge the arbitration clause in its entirety.

---

[15] In recent cases, the Court has shown no hesitation in holding that state laws deeming certain subjects not to be arbitrable are preempted by the FAA, reasoning that "[w]hen state law prohibits outright the arbitration of a particular type of claim, the analysis is straightforward: The conflicting rule is displaced by the FAA." Marmet Health Care Center, Inc. v. Brown, 132 S. Ct. 1201, 1204 (2012) (striking down West Virginia statute barring the arbitration of personal injury or wrongful death claims against nursing homes) (citation omitted). Similarly, it found a federal statute to be silent on whether it bars the resolution of claims in arbitration, and thus required claims to proceed in arbitration. CompuCredit Corp. v. Greenwood et al., 132 S. Ct. 665 (2012) (disclosure provision of Credit Repair Organizations Act requiring credit repair organizations to provide consumers with statement "[y]ou have a right to sue ..." "insufficient to override mandate of FAA that arbitration agreements be enforced according to their terms"). The Court has also cautioned lower courts to examine a complaint with care to assess whether any of the claims set forth therein is subject to arbitration, since a lawsuit that has both arbitrable and non-arbitrable claims must proceed to arbitration even if the result is piecemeal litigation. KPMG LLP v. Cocchi, 132 S. Ct. 23 (2011).

[16] This was most famously articulated in Prima Paint Corp. v. Flood & Conklin Mfg. Co., 388 U.S. 395 (1967) and holds that an arbitration clause is separate from the contract in which it is contained, and that attacks on the validity of the entire contract are to be resolved by the arbitrator, whereas attacks on the arbitration clause itself are to be resolved by the court. In one recent case, the Court reaffirmed that principle. Nitro-Lift Technologies LLC v. Howard, 133 S. Ct. 500 (2012) (assertion that non-competition provision in employment contract void under Oklahoma law should be resolved by arbitrator since challenge was not to the arbitration provision specifically, but to the contract as a whole).

[17] This was most famously articulated in *First Options*, which held that where parties have "clearly and unmistakably" delegated to an arbitrator the authority to resolve a gateway question, for example, the validity of a contract, that is a question for the arbitrator rather than the court.

Since the first edition of the book was published, the Supreme Court has also heard its first bilateral investment treaty case.[18] While the primary focus of this book is on commercial arbitration rather than treaty arbitration, in a 7-2 decision, the majority in the *BG* case explicitly took the same approach to the interpretation of the treaty as it would have done had it been faced with a commercial contract. Thus, its approach is instructive for commercial cases. In *BG*, the majority, again, showed a willingness to allocate to arbitrators rather than courts the authority to resolve gateway issues, holding that it is for arbitrators, rather than courts, to decide whether a provision in the UK–Argentina bilateral investment requiring litigation as a precondition to the commencement of arbitration was satisfied. **0.45**

Since the last edition of this book, the law on class arbitration has been addressed by the Supreme Court several times and has gone through a roller coaster ride, from being apparently killed off in *Stolt-Nielsen S.A. v. AnimalFeeds International Corp.*,[19] to getting a new lease of life in *Oxford Health Plans LLC v. Sutter.*[20] These developments will be addressed in more detail in Chapter 11. **0.46**

There has also been one development, in the *Daimler* case,[21] that appears to have had the effect of making it more difficult to enforce international awards in the United States. The development is not specific to arbitration as such, but relates to a decision by the Supreme Court to heighten the standards for the assertion of personal jurisdiction over a defendant in US courts. Because an award creditor must establish personal jurisdiction over an award debtor to enforce an arbitral award in the US, including an award under the New York Convention, the tightening of standards inevitably makes it harder to enforce an award. In fact, in one recent case, the Second Circuit reversed a decision by the District Court of the Southern District of New York enforcing an arbitration award, precisely based on the decision in *Daimler*.[22] This issue will be explored in more detail in Chapter 13. **0.47**

Finally, it is worth mentioning that a recent decision of the District Court for the Southern District of New York confirmed that parties may use a streamlined procedure for the enforcement of awards rendered under the auspices of the International Centre for the Settlement of Investment Disputes, better known as ICSID.[23] This decision will be discussed in Chapter 14. **0.48**

* * *

---

[18] BG Group PLC v. Republic of Argentina, 134 S. Ct. 1198 (2014)

[19] 130 S. Ct. 1758 (2010)

[20] 133 S. Ct. 2004 (2013)

[21] Daimler AG v. Bauman et al., 134 S. Ct. 746 (2014).

[22] Sonera Holding BV v. Çukurova Holding AS, 750 F.3d 221, *cert. denied*, 189 L.Ed.2d 837 (2014).

[23] Mobil Cerro Negro, Ltd. et al. v. Bolivarian Republic of Venezuela, 2015 WL 631409 (SDNY Feb. 13, 2015).

0.49 As with many areas of law in the United States, the law applicable to international arbitrations sited in New York is complicated by the fact that two different overlapping bodies of law apply—federal law and state law. This complexity is compounded by the fact that two overlapping Conventions, the New York Convention and the Panama Convention, also apply to arbitrations sited in New York. Thus, the Federal Arbitration Act, which, among other things, implements each of the Conventions, applies to international arbitrations sited in New York, as does New York state arbitration law to the extent that it is not preempted by federal law.[24] The relationship between federal arbitration and state arbitration law, as well as the New York and Panama Conventions, is the subject of Chapter 1.

0.50 The fact that two overlapping bodies of law apply to arbitrations sited in New York can make a difference even to such matters as the drafting of an arbitration clause, the topic of Chapter 3. Thus, while New York state law prohibits arbitrators' from awarding punitive damages,[25] the U.S. Supreme Court has held that this prohibition is preempted by federal law,[26] so that in an international arbitration sited in New York, arbitrators are empowered to award punitive damages unless the parties agree otherwise.

0.51 In addition to the topics mentioned previously, this book also considers the law and practices applicable to arbitrations sited in New York on such matters as the selection of arbitrators (Chapter 5), the law relating to the allocation of jurisdiction between courts and arbitrators (Chapter 6), the enforcement of agreements to arbitrate (Chapter 7), obtaining preliminary relief in aid of arbitration (Chapter 8), disclosure (Chapter 9), class arbitration (Chapter 11), the standards for vacatur of an award rendered in New York, as well for the enforcement of an international award by New York courts (Chapter 13), and the special considerations involved in enforcing arbitral awards against foreign sovereigns (Chapter 14). In addition, since many contracts calling for arbitration in New York are governed by New York law, the book also addresses New York law applicable to contracts, expanded since the first edition (Chapter 4), and New York law on damages (Chapter 10). This book also considers certain situations in which New York courts will provide assistance in aid of an arbitration taking place outside the United States, on such issues as the granting of preliminary relief by New York courts in aid of an international arbitration

[24] Volt Info Sciences, Inc. v. Bd. of Trustees, 489 U.S. 468, 477 (U.S. 1989) ("The FAA contains no express pre-emptive provision, nor does it reflect a congressional intent to occupy the entire field of arbitration. But even when Congress had not completely displaced state regulation in an area, state law may nonetheless be preempted to the extent that it actually conflicts with federal law.").

[25] Garrity v. Lyle Stuart, Inc., 353 N.E.2d 793, 797 (1976) ("The law does not and should not permit private persons to submit themselves to punitive sanction of the order reserved to the State.").

[26] Mastrobuono v. Shearson Lehman Hutton, Inc., 514 U.S. 52 (1995).

venued elsewhere (Chapter 8.C), the taking of evidence for use in an arbitration taking place elsewhere (Chapter 9.G), and the enforcement by New York courts of arbitral awards rendered outside the United States (Chapters 13 and 14). This second edition of the book also includes a new chapter, addressing the holding of arbitration hearings in New York (Chapter 12). The law is stated as of January 1, 2015.

1

THE LAW APPLICABLE TO INTERNATIONAL ARBITRATION IN NEW YORK

David M. Lindsey and Yasmine Lahlou[1]

A. Scope of this Chapter 1.01

B. The FAA and How it Works 1.04

1. Fundamental Issues 1.04
   - (a) What is the FAA? 1.04
   - (b) Defining preemption 1.06
   - (c) Jurisdiction of federal courts 1.10
2. FAA Chapter 1: The Federal Law of Arbitration 1.11
   - (a) Section 1 1.12
   - (b) Section 2 1.13
   - (c) Sections 3–4 1.15
   - (d) Sections 5–6 1.16
   - (e) Section 7 1.18
   - (f) Sections 9–13, 16 1.21
3. Chapter 2: The New York Convention 1.30
4. Chapter 3: The Panama Convention 1.34

C. The FAA and the New York State Arbitration Statute 1.36

1. State Law on Court's Authority to Decide Statute of Limitations as Threshold Matter 1.38
2. State Law Limiting Time to Object to Validity of Agreement to Arbitrate 1.40
3. State Law Prohibiting Predispute Arbitration Agreements in Consumer Contracts 1.43

D. Applicable Law Regarding Recognition of Arbitration Agreements under the Conventions 1.44

1. Separability, the Conventions, and the FAA 1.45
   - (a) Separability doctrine 1.45
   - (b) The New York Convention 1.48
   - (c) The FAA 1.54
2. Applicable Law Regarding Formation and Substantive Validity of the Agreement to Arbitrate 1.57
   - (a) Case law from the Second Circuit applying law of forum 1.61
   - (b) Consideration of state contract law principles when applying law of forum in the Second Circuit 1.65
   - (c) Case law from the Second Circuit applying law of the underlying contract 1.69
   - (d) Consideration of internationally recognized minimum standards 1.72
3. Applicable Law Regarding Formal Validity of the Agreement to Arbitrate 1.74
4. Applicable Law Regarding Arbitrability 1.79
5. Applicable Law Regarding Interpretation and Scope 1.82
6. Applicable Law Regarding Capacity and Competence 1.83

[1] The authors thank their colleagues, Gretta L. Walters and Farrell A. Brody, who assisted with this chapter.

E. **Applicable Law Regarding Recognition and Enforcement of Convention Awards** 1.84
1. Application of the Conventions 1.86
2. Nondomestic Awards Rendered in the United States or Pursuant to U.S. Arbitration Law May Be Vacated Under U.S. Arbitration Law 1.88
3. Arbitral Awards Rendered Outside the United States or Pursuant to a Foreign Arbitration Law May Not Be Vacated Under U.S. Arbitration Law 1.95
4. Relevance of New York Arbitration Law to the Arbitral Award 1.100

F. **Effective Governing Law Clauses** 1.103

A. SCOPE OF THIS CHAPTER

1.01 This chapter focuses on the applicable arbitration law in the context of arbitration agreements and awards that fall under the New York Convention or the Panama Convention,[2] and how those two treaties interact with the U.S. Federal Arbitration Act (FAA),[3] New York state law, and, possibly, foreign law in the context of international arbitration in New York. We first summarize the FAA and explain the FAA's preemption of state law that is inconsistent with the FAA, which is important to understand even though FAA preemption plays a larger role in domestic FAA arbitration than it does in international arbitration in New York.

1.02 We then discuss application of the Conventions and the difficult issues that can arise when determining the applicable law. In particular, we focus on the choice of law issues that arise when enforcing the agreement to arbitrate under Article II of the New York Convention. U.S. courts have struggled to employ a consistent choice of law analysis when interpreting the "null and void" provisions in Article II(3) of the Convention. While that struggle is not unique to U.S. courts, the analysis in the United States is made more difficult by the uncertainty surrounding the role of state law. Of course, we also discuss choice of law issues in the context of enforcing Convention awards under Article V, which generally are not as complex as those under Article II.

1.03 We conclude the chapter with some suggestions on how to simplify the analysis by specifying the law applicable to the agreement to arbitrate in the agreement itself.[4] In theory, parties have the autonomy to choose the law that will govern

[2] The 1958 U.N. Convention on the Recognition and Enforcement of Foreign Arbitral Awards (New York Convention) and the 1975 Inter-American Convention on International Commercial Arbitration (Panama Convention) are referenced generally in this chapter as "the Conventions" and agreements and awards covered by the Conventions are referenced as "Convention agreements" or "Convention awards." If necessary to show a distinction between the two Conventions, they will be referred to separately. *See* 9 U.S.C. §§ 201–08, 301–07.

[3] 9 U.S.C. §§ 1–16.

[4] Issues regarding choice of law can arise in numerous instances during the course of arbitral proceedings and this chapter does not attempt to address all of those. Choice of law or applicable law is discussed in other chapters in this book where necessary with respect to particular topics. *See* in particular Chapter 4.A, Chapter 6.C.1, Chapter 6.D.2, Chapter 6.E.2, Chapter 6.F.2.

their arbitration agreement, and courts will typically enforce that choice if it is clearly set forth in the agreement.[5]

B. THE FAA AND HOW IT WORKS

1. Fundamental Issues

(a) What is the FAA? The FAA is the principal law on arbitration in the United States for both domestic and international arbitration. Over the last more than forty years, the U.S. Supreme Court has defined the scope of the FAA so broadly that few arbitrations seated in the United States fail to come under its umbrella.[6] Particularly relevant to the international focus of this book, any arbitration seated in New York that includes a foreign party, applies foreign law to the underlying agreement, or involves performance of a contract outside the United States, will fall within the scope of Chapter 2 or 3 of the FAA, which codify U.S. ratification of the New York and Panama Conventions, respectively. Chapters 2 and 3 also apply to the recognition and enforcement of Convention awards in the United States. **1.04**

The FAA, however, is not the sole statutory authority governing arbitration in the United States that could have an impact on arbitrations covered by the Conventions. Individual states, including New York, have their own arbitration statutes, and now at least twelve states have their own international arbitration statutes.[7] Obviously there will be conflicts between the laws affecting arbitration enacted by each of the individual states and the federal government. This is resolved by the preemption doctrine. **1.05**

(b) Defining preemption The FAA was enacted pursuant to Congress' powers under the Commerce Clause of the U.S. Constitution.[8] That grant of power by the Constitution to Congress to regulate interstate commerce allows Congress **1.06**

---

[5] Volt Info. Sciences, Inc. v. Bd. of Trs. of Leland Stanford Junior Univ., 489 U.S. 468 (1989).

[6] *See, e.g.*, Allied-Bruce Terminix Companies, Inc. v. Dobson U.S.A., 513 U.S. 265, 273 (1995); Perry v. Thomas, 482 U.S. 483, 490 (1987); Southland Corp. v. Keating, 465 U.S. 1, 14–15 (1984); *see also* Diamond Waterproofing Systems, Inc. v. 55 Liberty Owners Corp., 4 N.Y.3d 247 (2005) (New York's highest state court, the New York Court of Appeals, recognizing the broad scope of the FAA).

[7] New York Civil Practice Law & Rules (CPLR), Article 75. The states that have adopted international arbitration laws include California, Colorado, Connecticut, Florida, Georgia, Hawaii, Illinois, Maryland, North Carolina, Ohio, Oregon, and Texas.

[8] The Supremacy Clause of the U.S. Constitution establishes that federal law is the supreme law of the land, but only with respect to those powers specifically granted under the Constitution. All other powers of government remain with the individual states. One of the most comprehensive grants of power to the federal government is found under the Constitution's Commerce Clause, which gives Congress the authority to pass laws regulating interstate or international commerce. U.S. Const. art. IV, § 2.

to preempt all state laws on the same subject or allow state laws to coexist with federal laws on the subject, as long as those state laws are not inconsistent with the policies behind the federal laws.

1.07 The Supreme Court has held that the FAA "contains no express pre-emptive provision, nor does it reflect a congressional intent to occupy the entire field of arbitration."[9] Therefore, the FAA does not automatically preempt all state arbitration laws. As a general matter, the Supreme Court has applied the FAA to preempt only those state laws that undermine the FAA's goal of ensuring that private arbitration agreements are enforced according to their terms.[10] More precisely, state law will be preempted "to the extent that it *actually conflicts* with federal law."[11]

1.08 It is not always clear when the FAA preempts state arbitration law on a specific issue or whether state law may be applicable in addition to the FAA. The FAA clearly preempts state laws that interfere with the enforceability of agreements to arbitrate, such as subjecting the validity of arbitration agreements to conditions other than those applicable to other contract terms[12] or by requiring parties who have agreed to arbitrate to appear instead before a judicial forum.[13] Such laws are in actual conflict with the FAA. Some courts, focusing on the issue of enforceability, have expressed the view that the FAA has only a narrow preemptive effect,[14] and "in the absence of a state law which discourages the enforcement of arbitration agreements, no question of preemption, as such, is presented."[15]

---

[9] *Volt Info. Sciences*, 489 U.S. at 477.

[10] *Id.* at 477–78.

[11] *Id.* at 477 (emphasis added).

[12] *Allied-Bruce Terminix Cos.*, 513 U.S. 265. The U.S. Supreme Court has reversed lower court decisions that altered the terms of arbitration agreements under state law unconscionability principles, holding that those principles stand "as an obstacle to the accomplishment and execution of the full purposes and objectives of Congress" and are therefore preempted by the FAA. AT&T Mobility LLC v. Concepcion, 563 U.S. 333, 352 (2011) (citation omitted).

[13] *Volt Info. Sciences, Inc.*, 489 U.S. at 478 ("In recognition of Congress' principal purpose of ensuring that private arbitration agreements are enforced according to their terms, we have held that the FAA pre-empts state laws which 'require a judicial forum for the resolution of claims which the contracting parties agreed to resolve by arbitration.' ") (*quoting Southland Corp.*, 465 U.S. at 10); Perry v. Thomas, 482 U.S. at 490 (finding that an employment application arbitration provision preempted a state statute that rendered private agreements to arbitrate certain wage collection claims unenforceable).

[14] Great Western Mortgage Corp. v. Peacock, 110 F.3d 222, 230 (3d. Cir. 1997).

[15] *Id.* at 231. One U.S. court upheld a party's attempt to circumvent the FAA's three-year time limitation to enforce a foreign award by having it first recognized in England and thereafter seeking to enforce the English court judgment under the Uniform Foreign-Country Money Judgments Recognition Act (UFCMA). The United States Circuit Court for the District of Columbia held that the FAA's three-year statute of limitations on confirmation actions for foreign arbitral awards established a "floor but not a ceiling" on the time limit for confirmation and that the UFCMA was not pre-empted by the FAA because its fifteen-year limitation period actually afforded greater protection to arbitral awards. Accordingly, the award creditor was not precluded from obtaining recognition and enforcement in the United States of a 2009 English court judgment, which, in turn, enforced an ICC arbitration award issued in 2000. Commissions Imp. Exp. S.A. v. Republic of the Congo, 757 F.3d 321, 328, 333 (D.C. Cir. 2014).

Other courts may take a more nuanced view as to whether, and to what extent, state arbitration laws may apply in addition to the FAA in an arbitration proceeding governed by the FAA. This is particularly relevant when questions of procedure rather than enforceability arise. More specifically, even where an agreement to arbitrate has been fully enforced and the parties have begun proceedings before an arbitrator, the parties' expectations still may differ as to whether state procedural rules will influence their proceeding under the FAA and the extent to which those state laws are preempted. This view is consistent with the Supreme Court's statement that the FAA does not favor arbitration under any set of *procedures*, leaving states free to develop their own pro-arbitration procedures.[16] **1.09**

(c) Jurisdiction of federal courts Importantly, the FAA grants original jurisdiction to the federal district courts over all matters arising from Convention agreements and awards but grants no such jurisdiction for matters arising from domestic FAA arbitrations or non-Convention international arbitrations.[17] This allows parties whose arbitration is governed by the Conventions to avoid state courts and many of the potential problems that might arise under FAA preemption. FAA preemption, however, remains important for Convention agreements and awards because, among other things, state contract law may apply to issues regarding the arbitration agreement's formation and substantive validity.[18] Some state contract law in this context may be preempted, employing the same preemption principles that would apply in the domestic context. **1.10**

2. FAA Chapter 1: The Federal Law of Arbitration

Chapter 1 was enacted in 1925 and was based on the New York arbitration law that had come into existence just five years earlier, in 1920. In essence, Chapter 1 applies to domestic arbitrations governed by the FAA. Chapter 1 consists of sixteen sections and contains the FAA's core substantive provisions, such as the enforceability of agreements to arbitrate future disputes, procedures to enforce the right to arbitrate a dispute, and limited court review. The provisions in Chapter 1 are typically the provisions at issue in any analysis of FAA preemption of state law.[19] **1.11**

---

[16] *Volt Info. Sciences, Inc.*, 489 U.S. at 476.

[17] 9 U.S.C. §§ 203, 205, 302. As described in more detail herein, no provision of the FAA grants subject-matter jurisdiction to the federal courts over domestic FAA arbitrations. As a result, to the extent a court is necessary, matters arising from most domestic FAA arbitrations must be heard in state, as opposed to federal, court.

[18] *See, e.g.*, Chelsea Square Textiles v. Bombay Dyeing and Mfg., 189 F.3d 289, 295–96 (2d Cir. 1999) (*citing* Perry v. Thomas, 482 U.S. at 492 n.9 and Doctor's Assocs., Inc. v. Casarotto, 517 U.S. 681, 687 (1996)).

[19] Chapter 1 has not changed significantly since 1925, although some sections have been added and some modified. A reader not familiar with the FAA will have some difficulty understanding its meaning by simply reading its terms. The precise meaning of the FAA's provisions is found in the literally thousands of federal cases that have interpreted the FAA, especially the case law since the early 1980s. For example, there is no mention of the strong federal policy in favor of arbitration in the FAA. That articulation is found only in the case law.

1.12 *(a) Section 1* The FAA applies to arbitration agreements in "maritime transactions" and "contract[s] evidencing a transaction involving commerce."[20] Section 1 of the FAA defines commerce as "commerce among the several States or with foreign nations, or in any territory of the United States or in the District of Columbia, or between any such Territory and another, or between any such Territory and any State or foreign nation, or between the District of Columbia and any State or Territory or foreign nation[.]"[21] Courts have construed this as a reference to interstate and foreign commerce.[22] Thus, the FAA was enacted pursuant to Congress' power under the Commerce Clause of the U.S. Constitution to regulate interstate and foreign commerce in the United States,[23] and the Supreme Court has held that Congress intended to exercise that power as broadly as possible.[24] The Supreme Court has also held that Chapter 1's exclusion of "contracts of employment of seamen, railroad employees, or any other class of workers engaged in foreign or interstate commerce" shall be confined exclusively to employment contracts for transportation workers.[25]

1.13 *(b) Section 2* Section 2 of the FAA is perhaps the most important provision in the statute. It was adopted to bolster the enforceability of arbitration agreements and provides that any "written provision" evidencing an intention to submit existing or future disputes to arbitration "shall be valid, irrevocable, and enforceable, save upon such grounds as exist at law or in equity for the revocation of any contract."[26] When interpreting this provision, the Supreme Court has held that Congress enacted the FAA to "replace judicial indisposition to arbitration with 'a national policy favoring arbitration and plac[ing] arbitration agreements on equal footing with all other contracts.'"[27] The scope of arbitrable issues is decided with a "healthy regard" for the strong federal policy in favor of arbitration, and "any doubts concerning the scope of arbitrable issues should be resolved in favor of arbitration, whether the problem at hand is the construction of the contract language itself or an allegation of waiver, delay, or a like defense to arbitrability."[28]

[20] 9 U.S.C. § 2.

[21] 9 U.S.C. § 1.

[22] *Allied-Bruce Terminix Cos.*, 513 U.S. at 274. *See* Varley v. Tarrytown Assocs., Inc., 477 F.2d 208 (2d Cir. 1973); Ins. Co. of North America v. ABB Power Generation, Inc., 925 F. Supp. 1053 (S.D.N.Y. 1996), *question certified* 112 F.3d 70 (2d Cir. 1997), *certified question answered* 690 N.E.2d 1249 (N.Y. 1997).

[23] Prima Paint Corp. v. Flood & Conklin Mfg. Co., 388 U.S. 395, 405 (1967).

[24] *Allied-Bruce Terminix Cos.*, 513 U.S. at 277.

[25] Circuit City Stores, Inc. v. Adams, 532 U.S. 105 (2001). *See* Arakawa v. Japan Network Group, 56 F. Supp. 2d 349 (S.D.N.Y. 1999). In other words, unlike the case in many other countries such as the United Kingdom and Germany, employment disputes not expressly excluded by the FAA can be subject to arbitration.

[26] 9 U.S.C. § 2.

[27] Hall Street Assocs. L.L.C. v. Mattel, 128 S. Ct. 1396, 1402 (2008) (*quoting* Buckeye Check Cashing, Inc. v. Cardegna, 546 U.S. 440, 443 (2006)).

[28] *Moses H. Cone Mem'l Hosp.*, 460 U.S. at 24–25; Mitsubishi Motors Corp. v. Soler Chrysler-Plymouth, Inc., 473 U.S. 614, 629–31 (1985); Scherk v. Alberto-Culver Co., 417 U.S. 506, 516–18 (1974). Relatedly, the Supreme Court has held that under Section 2 of the

The Supreme Court has also held that the FAA's provisions on regulating the enforcement of agreements to arbitrate arising out of contracts involving interstate or international commerce creates a body of substantive federal law. As such, the FAA applies in both federal and state courts pursuant to Congress' authority under the Commerce Clause.[29] **1.14**

(c) Sections 3–4 Section 3 of the FAA requires generally that upon the application by a party, the courts must stay proceedings pending before them if the subject matter of those proceedings is arbitrable and governed by a written arbitration agreement.[30] The corollary of Section 3 is found in Section 4 of the FAA, which allows a party aggrieved by the other side's failure, neglect, or refusal to submit a dispute to arbitration, to seek from the court an order compelling the other side to arbitrate.[31] **1.15**

(d) Sections 5–6 Section 5 grants courts, upon the application of any party to the dispute, the power to appoint arbitrators where the parties have failed to agree on a method to appoint arbitrators or have otherwise failed to constitute the tribunal for any reason.[32] **1.16**

Section 6 allows applications under the FAA to be treated as motions rather than parties having to initiate formal proceedings with a complaint. This was intended to provide a mechanism for the courts to act swiftly to avoid impeding the arbitral proceedings.[33] **1.17**

(e) Section 7 Pursuant to Section 7 of the FAA, arbitrators are empowered to issue subpoenas to third parties to require them to appear as witnesses or to produce documents at a hearing before the arbitral tribunal. It also gives the federal court of the district where the arbitral tribunal is seated the power to enforce these subpoenas.[34] The Second Circuit Court of Appeals, the federal appellate **1.18**

FAA, where a contract incudes a specific agreement that the arbitrator will determine the enforceability of the agreement, if a party challenges specifically the validity of the agreement to arbitrate at issue, the federal court must consider the challenge before ordering compliance with the agreement, but if a party challenges the enforceability of the agreement as a whole, the challenge is to be decided by the arbitrator. Rent-A-Ctr., W., Inc. v. Jackson, 561 U.S. 63, 64 (2010).

[29] *Southland Corp.*, 104 S. Ct. 852.

[30] 9 U.S.C. § 3; Profilati Italia S.r.l. v. Painewebber Inc., 941 F. Supp. 431 (S.D.N.Y. 1996); Erving v. the Virginia Squires Basketball Club, 349 F. Supp. 716 (E.D.N.Y. 1972); Campeau Corp. v. May Dept. Stores Co., 723 F. Supp. 224 (S.D.N.Y. 1989).

[31] 9 U.S.C. § 4; Dean Witter Reynolds Inc. v. Byrd, 470 U.S. 213 (1985); Orion S & T Co. v. Easter States Petro. Corp. of Panama, 284 F.2d 419 (2d Cir. 1960); Avant Petroleum, Inc. v. Pecten Arabian Ltd., 696 F. Supp. 42 (S.D.N.Y. 1988). Sections 3 and 4 of the FAA are discussed in more detail in Chapter 7.

[32] 9 U.S.C. § 5; Neptune Maritime, Ltd. v. H&J Isbrandtsen, Ltd., 559 F. Supp. 531, 533 (S.D.N.Y. 1983); CAE Indus. Ltd. v. Aerospace Holdings Co., 741 F. Supp. 388, 392 (S.D.N.Y. 1989).

[33] 9 U.S.C. § 6; World Brilliance Corp. v. Bethlehem Steel Co., 342 F.2d 362 (2d Cir. 1965).

[34] 9 U.S.C. § 7.

court whose jurisdiction includes New York, has held that this provision must be read narrowly and according to its terms.[35]

1.19 The application of a state's arbitration law may be triggered because the arbitration has its seat in that state.[36] For instance, where New York is the seat of an arbitration, one party may want to take advantage of state arbitration laws allowing depositions of nonparty witnesses, while the counterparty may rely on the FAA, which generally disallows such depositions.

1.20 In *Integrity Insurance Co. v. American Centennial Insurance Co.*,[37] an arbitrator had compelled a nonparty to appear at a prehearing deposition, and the court was tasked with deciding whether that arbitrator's subpoena had been valid under the FAA. However, the court acknowledged in a footnote that "[t]he arbitrators are sitting in New York, which grants arbitrators authority to issue subpoenas."[38] Without deciding on the parties' rights under New York arbitration law, the court stated that the FAA applies where federal subject-matter jurisdiction is present and when the underlying transaction between the parties involved interstate commerce.[39] The court concluded its footnote on New York law by implying that the state law, insofar as it expanded the arbitrator's power to order discovery, was actually in conflict with the FAA: "The FAA would therefore prevail over any inconsistent state arbitration statute."[40] The court provided no further explanation as to whether and how the New York law conflicted with the FAA's goal of ensuring that private arbitration agreements are enforced. Nor is it certain that other courts will agree that more expansive discovery rights under state law would be preempted by the FAA's narrow discovery provisions found in Section 7 of Chapter 1 of the FAA.[41]

(f) Sections 9–13, 16

(I) THE PROVISIONS

1.21 Section 9 requires U.S. courts to enforce an arbitration award, unless there are grounds to vacate, modify, or correct the award under either Section 10 or 11 of the FAA, provided that the application to enforce the award is brought within one year after the award is made. This provision gives territorial jurisdiction to

[35] Life Receivables Trust v. Syndicate 102 at Lloyd's of London, 549 F.3d 210 (2d Cir. 2008); *see* Chapter 9.D of this book.

[36] Under the New York arbitration statute, New York courts have jurisdiction to enforce it if the agreement provides for arbitration in New York, either expressly or by necessary implication. Zim Israel Navigation Co. v. Sealanes Int'l, Inc., 17 A.D. 2d. 393 (N.Y. App. Div. 1962).

[37] Integrity Ins. Co. v. American Centennial Ins. Co., 885 F. Supp. 69 (S.D.N.Y. 1995), *abrogated in part by Life Receivables Trust*, 549 F.3d 210.

[38] *Integrity Ins. Co.*, 885 F. Supp. at 71 n.3.

[39] *Id.* (citations omitted).

[40] *Id.* (citation omitted).

[41] 9 U.S.C. § 7.

the court agreed upon by the parties or the court sitting in the district where the award was made.[42]

Under Section 10 of the FAA, an award may be vacated where (1) it was procured by fraud, corruption, or undue means; (2) there was evident partiality or corruption in some or all of the arbitrators; (3) the arbitrators were guilty of misconduct in refusing to postpone the hearing; or (4) the arbitrators exceeded their powers. A court that vacates an award has the discretion to direct a rehearing before the arbitral tribunal, provided the time within which the arbitration agreement required the award to be made has not expired.[43] **1.22**

Pursuant to Section 11 of the FAA, an award may be modified or corrected for: (1) evident material miscalculation; (2) evident material mistake; (3) dealing with matters not submitted to the arbitrators; or (4) imperfections not affecting the merits of the award. The U.S. Supreme Court has held that these are the exclusive grounds available to vacate, modify, or correct an award under the FAA and that, contrary to some longstanding practices, parties may not contractually agree to add to them.[44] **1.23**

Section 12 requires that a motion to vacate, modify, or correct an award be served on the opposing side within three months after the award is made.[45] This time period is not tolled by an application to the arbitral tribunal to correct or interpret an award under the rules applicable to that arbitration.[46] As an example, in an International Chamber of Commerce (ICC) arbitration seated in New York, the three-month period within which to petition a court to vacate an award begins to run from the time the award was made, no matter if a party seeks correction or interpretation of the award under Article 29 of the ICC Rules. This timing may require a party to seek correction or interpretation of an award while, essentially in parallel court proceedings, also seeking to vacate the award with respect to the same subject matter, **1.24**

---

[42] 9 U.S.C. § 9; *see also* 9 U.S.C. § 207 (three-year time limit for Convention awards). Section 9 of the FAA is discussed in more detail in Chapter 13B.

[43] 9 U.S.C. § 10. Section 10 of the FAA is discussed in more detail in Chapter 13.C.2..

[44] 9 U.S.C. § 11; *Hall Street*, 128 S. Ct. 1396. As discussed in Chapter 13.C.2(e), there is a split of authority among the federal intermediate appellate courts whether the judicial standard of review called "manifest disregard of the law" still applies at all in the United States and, if it does, whether it would apply to a Convention award. In the Second Circuit, the law is that if the Convention award is otherwise subject to U.S. vacatur law under the Conventions, as opposed to merely recognition and enforcement proceedings in the United States, then the FAA's vacatur standards apply, including manifest disregard of the law. Despite recent opportunities to do so, the U.S. Supreme Court has declined to clarify whether manifest disregard of the law is an appropriate standard of review for any FAA award. *See* Stolt Nielsen SA v. AnimalFeeds Int'l Corp., 559 U.S. 662, 672 n.3 (2010); *see also* Dewan v. Walia, 544 F. App'x 240, 241 (4th Cir. 2013), *cert. denied sub nom.* Walia v. Kiran M. Dewan, CPA, P.A., 134 S. Ct. 1788 (2014).

[45] 9 U.S.C. § 12.

[46] Thyssen Carbometal Co. v. FAI Energy, Ltd., Civ. No. 89-1695, 1990 U.S. Dist. LEXIS 427 (D.D.C. Jan. 16, 1990); Fradella v. Petricca, 183 F.3d 17, 20 (1st Cir. 1999); Oberwager v. McKechnie, Ltd., No. 06-2685, 2007 WL 4322982, at *5 (E.D. Pa. Dec. 10, 2007).

or otherwise risk losing the right to seek vacatur. In that circumstance, if an arbitral tribunal's decision on an ICC Article 29 application may impact a court's consideration of a pending petition to vacate, that court will typically stay its hand until the arbitral tribunal considers and finally decides the matters before it.[47]

1.25 Section 13 lists the various documents that an applicant must file with the court in support of its motion for an order confirming, modifying, or correcting an award for the entry of judgment on the order. The section also provides that judgment on the award is vested with the same force and effect as any other judgment issuing from that court.[48]

1.26 Section 16 addresses a party's right to appeal an order from a federal district court to the federal appellate, or circuit, court. Specifically in reference to orders concerning motions to compel arbitration in the context of the Conventions, an order denying a motion to compel arbitration pursuant to the Conventions is immediately appealable to the federal circuit court, but an order granting a motion to compel arbitration in that instance may not be appealed because it is deemed to be an interlocutory order of the district court.[49]

(II) *HALL STREET* AND *CABLE CONNECTION*

1.27 One sentence in a landmark Supreme Court decision, *Hall Street Associates, L.L.C. v. Mattel, Inc.*,[50] seemingly resurrected state vacatur laws. Based on *Hall Street*, parties arguably may apply state law to vacatur, which in turn may allow broader court review of arbitral awards than that allowed under the FAA.[51]

1.28 The California Supreme Court quickly took advantage of this opening when rendering its decision in *Cable Connection, Inc. v. DIRECTV, Inc.*, which held that in a California state court, an FAA-governed arbitration award may be reviewed under more expansive judicial standards if the parties had agreed to such a procedure in their agreement to arbitrate.[52] It is nevertheless unlikely that a federal court would apply expanded review under state law. Therefore, this potentially expanded review has not generally impacted the review of international arbitral awards. However, for those domestic FAA arbitrations lacking grounds to establish federal court jurisdiction, this could lead to broader review by state courts, depending on the applicable state law.

---

[47] *Thyssen Carbometal Co.*, 1990 U.S. Dist. LEXIS 427, at *9–10.

[48] 9 U.S.C. § 13; *see* Chapter 13 of this book.

[49] 9 U.S.C. § 16(a)(1)(C) and (b); *see also* 9 U.S.C. § 206 (addressing orders to compel arbitration of dispute governed by the New York Convention). Section 14 provides that the FAA does not apply to contracts entered before 1925 and Section 15 provides that the Act of State doctrine does not apply. 9 U.S.C. §§ 14–15. Sections 14 and 15 of the FAA are not relevant to the subject matter of this chapter.

[50] *Hall Street*, 128 S. Ct. 1396.

[51] *Id.* at 1406.

[52] Cable Connection, Inc. v. DIRECTV, 190 P.3d 586 (Cal. 2008).

A New York federal court has rejected applying state law standards of review to a domestic FAA arbitration award. In an action to vacate a domestic award not governed by the Conventions, a federal trial court in New York held that, under *Hall Street*, agreements incorporating a state law standard of review would not be enforceable in federal court under the FAA "because contracting around the FAA is precisely the maneuver prohibited by *Hall Street* and the cases in this Circuit interpreting it."[53] The court noted that in *Cable Connection*, the California Supreme Court "explicitly relied on the notion that 'the United States Supreme Court does not read the FAA's procedural provisions to apply to *state court* proceedings.'"[54] **1.29**

3. Chapter 2: The New York Convention

The New York Convention was added to the FAA in 1970 as a new Chapter 2 rather than being incorporated within the original FAA (now Chapter 1) because the drafters believed that incorporating the Convention into the core of the FAA would require so many minor changes differentiating Convention and non-Convention matters that the text would be too confusing. A new Chapter 2 was therefore created, consisting of Sections 201–08.[55] **1.30**

Section 208, and the corresponding provision found in Section 307 of Chapter 3 for the Panama Convention, provide that Chapter 1 of the FAA also applies to proceedings under Chapters 2 and 3, to the extent Chapter 1 is not in conflict with Chapters 2 and 3 or the corresponding Conventions.[56] Thus, U.S. state and federal courts must enforce valid Convention agreements, refer parties to arbitration in those cases, and recognize and enforce valid Convention awards, but Section 9's one-year time limit for recognition and enforcement of a valid award is replaced by Section 207's three-year limit for Convention awards.[57] **1.31**

---

[53] McQueen-Starling v. Oxford Health Plans, No. 08 Civ. 4885 (JGK), 2009 U.S. Dist. LEXIS 23266, at *23 (S.D.N.Y. Mar. 20, 2009). The parties' agreement did not refer to New York arbitration law but instead allowed the court to apply the same standard of review "as that applied by an appellate court reviewing the decision of a trial court sitting without a jury." The language used in the decision nevertheless evinces the court's clear intent that its holding would apply to any agreement seeking to vary the grounds to vacate an award under the FAA.

[54] *Id.* at *22 (emphasis added).

[55] 9 U.S.C. §§ 201–08. *See* Testimony of Richard D. Kearney of the Office of Legal Advisor of the U.S. Department of State before the Senate Committee on Foreign Relations, Feb. 9, 1970, Hearings before Senate Com. on Foreign Relations on Sen. No. 3274, 91st Cong., 2d Sess., Appendix to Sen. Rep. No. 91-702, p. 5 (1970).

[56] 9 U.S.C. § 208 and § 307. *See* Parsons & Whittemore Overseas Co., Inc. v. Société Générale de l'Industrie du Paper (RAKTA), 508 F.2d 969, 973 (2d Cir. 1974); Sphere Drake Ins. Ltd v. Clarendon Nat'l Ins. Co., 263 F.3d 26, 30 n.2 (2d Cir. 2001); Atlas Chartering Servs., Inc. v. World Trade Group, Inc., 453 F. Supp. 861, 863 (S.D.N.Y. 1978); Application of Corporación Selee de Venezuela, SA v. Selee Corporation, 7 Misc. 3d 1013(A) (N.Y. Sup. Ct. 2005).

[57] 9 U.S.C. §§ 9, 207; *see also* 9 U.S.C. § 302 (incorporating by reference Section 207 into Chapter 3). However, a federal court in New York concluded that Chapter 1's exemption from arbitration for seamen's employment contracts did not apply to remove a written commercial arbitration agreement, between a Romanian crew member on a cruise ship and his employer cruise line, from the statutes implementing the New York Convention, because the legislation

1.32 As mentioned previously, Section 203 provides that an action or proceeding falling under the Convention shall be deemed to be an action or proceeding arising under the laws and treaties of the United States and that the federal district courts shall have original jurisdiction over any such action or proceeding, regardless of the amount in controversy.[58] Section 205 further provides that if a party files such an action or proceeding in a state court, the defendant may remove the action to a federal court at any time before the trial.[59] In the context of an action arising under the treaties of the United States, a federal court is unlikely to find that the parties intended to apply state arbitration law unless the agreement to arbitrate states in very clear terms that state law shall apply.[60]

1.33 Actions that do not fall within the coverage of the Conventions do not have a basis for federal court jurisdiction under Chapter 1, which does not provide an independent basis for federal court jurisdiction to enforce an arbitration agreement or award. In such an action, litigants seeking to rely on the FAA in federal court must satisfy the jurisdictional requirements of the amount in controversy and diversity of citizenship, or demonstrate the existence of some other independent basis of subject-matter jurisdiction, before a federal court can validly entertain an application for any remedy authorized by the FAA.[61]

4. Chapter 3: The Panama Convention

1.34 Chapter 3 of the FAA, adopted in 1990, implements the Panama Convention, which embodies the same objectives as the New York Convention but on a

implementing the Convention included specific references to FAA provisions and made no reference to exemption for seamen's employment contracts. *See* Dumitru v. Princess Cruise Lines, Ltd., 732 F. Supp. 2d 328, 338 (S.D.N.Y. 2010).

[58] 9 U.S.C. § 203.

[59] 9 U.S.C. § 205.

[60] New York state courts have concurrent jurisdiction with the New York federal courts to enforce the provisions of the New York and Panama Conventions. Therefore, the parties could prosecute their case with respect to the Conventions entirely before New York state courts if they wish to do so. The New York Supreme Court, which is the New York state court of first instance with general jurisdiction, has a well-qualified commercial bench in Manhattan capable of addressing the issues raised by counsel with respect to the Conventions. No matter, a foreign party or even a party from another U.S. state may wish to have their case heard in the federal courts because the federal judiciary has more experience in enforcing U.S. treaties and U.S. federal law. In addition, there may be procedural differences between the state and federal courts that may or may not favor a party. This analysis must be carefully made, especially in light of the California Supreme Court decision in *Cable Connection.*

[61] *Moses H. Cone Mem'l Hosp.*, 460 U.S. at 26 n.34, *cited by* DaPuzzo v. Globalvest Mgmt. Co., LP, 263 F. Supp. 2d 714, 722 (S.D.N.Y. 2003). *See also* The Republic of Ecuador v. ChevronTexaco Corp., 376 F. Supp. 2d 334, 347 (S.D.N.Y. 2005) ("Defendants' suggestion that the mere applicability of the federal substantive law of arbitration would be sufficient to provide federal-question jurisdiction ... is incorrect, however. The original FAA, now Chapter 1 of that statute, 'creates a body of federal substantive law establishing and regulating the duty to honor an agreement to arbitrate, yet ... does not create any independent federal-question jurisdiction[.]' Thus, whether federal-question jurisdiction exists depends upon whether either the New York or the Inter-American Convention ... applies.") (internal citations omitted).

regional basis covering nearly all of the Americas.[62] Chapter 3 consists of Sections 301–07. Section 302 of Chapter 3 incorporates by reference the main provisions of Chapter 2 (including federal court subject-matter jurisdiction) and the two Conventions are very similar, although not identical.

The Panama Convention is presumed to apply in place of the New York Convention under Section 305 in the following circumstance: **1.35**

> When the requirements for application of both the [Panama Convention] and the [New York Convention] are met, determination as to which Convention applies shall, unless otherwise expressly agreed, be made as follows:
> 1. If a majority of the parties to the arbitration agreement are citizens of a State or States that have ratified or acceded to the [Panama Convention] and are member States of the Organization of American States, the [Panama Convention] shall apply.
> 2. In all other cases the [New York Convention] shall apply.

In addition, Article VII(1) of the New York Convention states:

> The provisions of the present Convention shall not affect the validity of multilateral or bilateral agreements concerning the recognition and enforcement of arbitral awards entered into by the Contracting States nor deprive any interested party of any right he may have to avail himself of an arbitral award in the manner and to the extent allowed by the law or the treaties of the country where such award is sought to be relied upon.

Thus, the Panama Convention shall apply over the New York Convention in a U.S. court if a majority of the parties to the arbitration agreement are citizens of a country that has ratified the Panama Convention, pursuant to Section 305(2) of the FAA. Section 305 also makes clear that the parties could agree to apply the New York Convention in any event.[63]

C. THE FAA AND THE NEW YORK STATE ARBITRATION STATUTE

Under the New York state arbitration statute,[64] courts play a greater gatekeeper role than under the FAA. The FAA requires that once a court has determined **1.36**

---

[62] Act of August 15, 1990, Pub. L. No. 101-369, 1990 U.S.C.C.A.N. (104 Stat. 448) 675; Section 3 of Pub. L. No. 101-369 provided that "This Act shall take effect upon the entry into force of the Inter-American Convention on International Commercial Arbitration, with respect to the United States [.]" The Convention entered into force for the United States on Oct. 27, 1990. As of September 2015, nineteen nations in the Americas had ratified the Convention: Argentina, Bolivia, Brazil, Chile, Colombia, Costa Rica, the Dominican Republic, Ecuador, El Salvador, Guatemala, Honduras, Mexico, Nicaragua, Panama, Paraguay, Peru, the United States, Uruguay, and Venezuela.

[63] Nineteen states in the Americas have ratified the Panama Convention. http://www.oas.org/juridico/english/sigs/b-35.html. Each one is also a contracting state to the New York Convention. http://www.uncitral.org/uncitral/en/uncitral_texts/arbitration/NYConvention_status.html.

[64] The New York arbitration law has been amended substantially since 1920 and is now found at Article 75 of New York's Civil Practice Law & Rules. NY CPLR Chap. 8, Article 75, Arbitration.

that parties have agreed to arbitrate a dispute and that the subject matter of a dispute is arbitrable, the court must refer those parties to arbitration.[65] Further, threshold issues such as allegations of "waiver, delay, or like defense[s] to arbitrability" are presumed to be for the arbitrators.[66] Conversely, the New York state arbitration statute reserves many such decisions for the courts. To the extent that the New York state provisions are found to be inconsistent with the FAA and the strong federal policy in favor of arbitration, those provisions will likely be preempted by the FAA.

1.37 The case law addressing whether specific provisions of the New York arbitration statute are preempted by the FAA is not always consistent. If, however, an arbitration falls within the scope of the Conventions, federal court decisions are more relevant because federal courts have subject-matter jurisdiction over all such matters and federal courts will not be inclined to follow state court decisions in the face of adverse federal case law. The following are examples where the FAA may preempt New York state arbitration law.

1. State Law on Court's Authority to Decide Statute of Limitations as Threshold Matter

1.38 Under Section 7502(b) of the New York CPLR, courts in New York may stay an arbitration at the very early stages and decide, as a threshold issue, whether the claim sought to be arbitrated would be barred by the applicable statute of limitations.[67] If the moving party fails to seek the stay within twenty days of service of a demand for arbitration, the moving party may still raise the issue with the arbitral tribunal. The arbitrators' decision, however, will be a matter within their sole discretion and may not serve as grounds to vacate or set aside the eventual award.[68] The issue arises whether this New York state law, which essentially gives the courts, not the arbitrators, the authority to determine the threshold question of whether a claim is time-barred, is preempted by the FAA. Under the FAA, such issues are presumably for the arbitrators to decide.[69]

The New York arbitration law was the first of its kind in the country and was considered groundbreaking at the time. *See Southland Corp.*, 465 U.S. at 34.

[65] JLM Indus. v. Stolt-Nielsen SA, 387 F.3d 163, 169 (2d Cir. 2004). Where parties agree to arbitrate "gateway questions of arbitrability," such issues are for the arbitrators, rather than the courts, to decide. *Rent-A-Ctr.*, 561 U.S. at 68–69.

[66] Howsam v. Dean Witter Reynolds, Inc., 537 U.S. 79, 83–84 (2002) (*citing Moses H. Cone Mem'l Hosp.*, 460 U.S. at 24–25) (The Court found "a gateway dispute about whether the parties are bound by a given arbitration clause raised a 'question of arbitrability' for a court to decide, [but] the phrase 'question of arbitrability [is] *not* applicable in other kinds of general circumstance where parties would likely expect that an arbitrator would decide the gateway matter" and noted that "the presumption is that the arbitrator should decide 'allegation[s] of waiver, delay, or a like defense to arbitrability.' ").

[67] N.Y. CPLR § 7502(b).

[68] *Id.*

[69] Painewebber v. Bybyk, 81 F.3d 1193 (2d Cir. 1996).

The New York Court of Appeals, New York's highest court, held that the New York rule was "not inimical to the policies of the FAA" and was therefore not preempted by it.[70] A federal court, however, later held that the New York Court of Appeals' decision was contrary to and preempted by the FAA, because as a matter of federal policy, any doubts concerning the scope of arbitrable issues should be resolved in favor of arbitration.[71] Thus, at least in a New York federal district court, Section 7502(b) of the New York CPLR is likely preempted by the FAA. **1.39**

2. State Law Limiting Time to Object to Validity of Agreement to Arbitrate

Under Section 7503(c) of the New York CPLR, a party served with a demand to arbitrate has twenty days after service to seek a stay of the arbitration or will otherwise be precluded from later denying the validity or compliance with the arbitration agreement or asserting in court that the claim is time-barred.[72] This rule prohibits parties from objecting to the validity of, or compliance with, the arbitration agreement past the twenty-day deadline. This appears to be inconsistent with the FAA, which allows the arbitrators to decide such claims and puts no explicit time limit on when the matters may be raised. **1.40**

A federal trial court in New York noted that "[t]he law in this Circuit is not settled on the applicability of CPLR §7503(c) in cases arising under the FAA."[73] Some federal trial courts held that since the FAA does not provide for a comparable time limitation, Section 7503(c) is inapplicable to arbitrations under the FAA.[74] Predictably, other judges relied on the same rationale to hold that Section 7503(c) applied to actions governed by the FAA.[75] The same divide exists at the **1.41**

[70] Smith Barney, Harris Upham, & Co. v. Luckie, 85 N.Y.2d 193, 206 (1995).

[71] Goldman Sachs & Co. v. Griffin, No. 07 Civ. 1313 (LMM), 2007 WL 1467430 (S.D.N.Y. May 16, 2007) (*citing to Moses H. Cone Mem'l Hosp*, 460 U.S. at 24–25). *See also* Bechtel do Brasil Construcoes Ltda. v. UEG Araucaria Ltda., 638 F.3d 150, 158 (2d Cir. 2011) (declining to find that timeliness issues could be decided by a court where party agreement on this point was "ambiguous"); Alfa Laval U.S. Treasury Inc. v. Nat'l Union Fire Ins. Co. of Pittsburgh, PA, 857 F. Supp. 2d 404, 417 (S.D.N.Y. 2012) ("given the strong presumption that timeliness issues are for the arbitrators, along with the conclusion that the parties' timeliness dispute falls within the scope of the arbitration clause, a general choice of law clause does little to support the plaintiffs' argument that the statute of limitations question is for the Court.").

[72] NY CPLR § 7503(c). The New York Court of Appeals held this time limit does not apply if "the parties never agreed to arbitrate, as distinct from situations in which there is an agreement to arbitrate which is nevertheless claimed to be invalid or unenforceable because its conditions have not been complied with." Matarasso v. Continental Casualty Co., 56 N.Y.2d 264, 266 (1982). *See also* discussion of CPLR § 7503(c) in Chapter 7.D.2.

[73] I. K. Bery, Inc. v. Boody & Co., No. 99 Civ. 10968 (SAS), 2000 WL 218938 (S.D.N.Y. Feb. 23, 2000).

[74] *See, e.g.*, PMC Inc. v. Atomergic Chemetals Corp., 844 F. Supp. 177, 182 (S.D.N.Y. 1994).

[75] *See, e.g., In re* Herman Miller, Inc., No. 97 Civ. 7878 (SAS), 1998 WL 192213, at *3 (S.D.N.Y. Apr. 21, 1998). In an international dispute, a federal trial court also ruled that where the dispute pertains to the existence of an agreement to arbitrate, as opposed to its validity, Section 7503(c)

state court level, where some judges find the New York state rule to be inapplicable under the FAA,[76] and others apply it with the FAA.[77]

1.42 The trend in the law indicates that such state law rules will not be enforced in a federal court, although the issue should not be overlooked. In fact, parties rarely raise either Section 7502(b) or Section 7503 in the context of an international arbitration in New York.

3. State Law Prohibiting Predispute Arbitration Agreements in Consumer Contracts

1.43 New York law prohibits the inclusion of mandatory arbitration agreements in contracts for the sale or purchase of consumer goods that require consumers to submit future disputes to arbitration.[78] If the transaction affects interstate or foreign commerce, however, the FAA preempts such law.[79]

D. APPLICABLE LAW REGARDING RECOGNITION OF ARBITRATION AGREEMENTS UNDER THE CONVENTIONS

1.44 Before addressing the choice of law analyses employed by New York federal courts when enforcing Convention agreements, we summarize the separability doctrine and relevant portions of the Conventions and the FAA in order to put the courts' decisions in some context.

1. Separability, the Conventions, and the FAA

1.45 *(a) Separability doctrine* The agreement to arbitrate is treated as an agreement that is separate from, although clearly related to, the underlying contract.

---

does not apply. Pictet Funds (Europe) S.A. v. Emerging Managers Grp., L.P., No. 14-CV-6854 SAS, 2014 WL 6766011, at *7 (S.D.N.Y. Dec. 1, 2014).

[76] Edward D. Jones & Company v. the American Stock Exchange, LLC, 22 A.D. 3d 319, 320 (N.Y. App. Div. 2005).

[77] Propulsora Ixtapa Sur, S.A. de C.V. v. Omni Hotels Franchising Corp., 211 A.D. 2d 546, 548 (N.Y. App. Div. 1995) ("Equally devoid of merit is petitioner's contention, which is raised for the first time on appeal, that the twenty-day limitations period set forth in CPLR 7503(c) is preempted by the [FAA]. Federal law in the field of arbitration pre-empts state law only to the extent that the two bodies of law conflict ... In the matter at bar, no conflict exists as the FAA is silent on the issue of limitations periods whereas CPLR 7503(c), the applicability of which was specifically endorsed by both parties, provides that a petition must be brought within twenty days, and in such a circumstance, a court applying federal law would utilize the restrictive period.").

[78] CLS Gen Bus Law § 399-c; Ragucci v. Professional Constr. Services, 25 A.D. 3d 43 (N.Y. App. Div. 2005).

[79] Baronoff v. Kean Development Company, 818 N.Y.S.2d 421, 425 (N.Y. Sup. Ct. 2006) ("While the Federal Arbitration Act may in some cases preempt a state statute such as Section 399-c, it may only do so in transactions "affecting commerce.")

The separability doctrine protects an important characteristic of the arbitration agreement—it can stand on its own validity, even if the underlying contract falls away.[80]

Provisions in both the New York Convention and the FAA support the doctrine, although neither the Convention nor the FAA explicitly requires its application. Articles II and V of the New York Convention refer to the agreement to arbitrate as separate from other agreements. Article II(2) refers to agreements to arbitrate, including an arbitral clause in a contract or an arbitration agreement. Article II also speaks of a writing requirement and certain presumptions that cannot be referring to the underlying contract. Additionally, Article II(1) requires contracting states to recognize and give effect to the parties' arbitration agreements, which inherently includes recognizing the arbitration agreement's nature as separate from the underlying contract. Article V(1)(a) most clearly foresees a different law applying to the agreement to arbitrate and treats the agreement to arbitrate separately from the underlying contract.[81] **1.46**

Section 2 of the FAA refers to "[a] written provision in … a contract evidencing a transaction involving commerce to settle by arbitration a controversy thereafter arising out of such contract … shall be valid, irrevocable, and enforceable …" So the FAA seems to have supported the notion of separability from the time of its origins in 1925.[82] In 1967, the U.S. Supreme Court held that as a matter of federal law, an agreement to arbitrate is presumed to be separate from the underlying contract in any transaction falling within the FAA's coverage. As previously mentioned, the FAA applies to any transaction that "affects" interstate or international commerce, which is an extremely broad standard that captures nearly every significant business transaction in the United States.[83] Thus, the separability doctrine is alive and well in the United States. **1.47**

(b) The New York Convention[84] Article II of the New York Convention directly addresses recognition of agreements to arbitrate and referral of those matters to arbitration. Specifically, Article II(1) of the New York Convention provides that each contracting state *shall* recognize an agreement in writing to arbitrate differences between parties regarding a defined legal relationship that is capable of being settled by arbitration. This paragraph (1) includes an arbitrability requirement that is repeated later in the context of enforcing arbitral awards in Article V(2)(a) of the Convention. **1.48**

---

[80] For a more detailed discussion of the separability doctrine, *see* Chapter 6.A.4, Chapter 6.C.2, Chapter 7.B.3(b) of this book; *see also* Gary B. Born, International Commercial Arbitration, Vol. 1, 349–52 (2d ed. 2014) (Born addresses the separability doctrine in great detail throughout Chapter 3 of his treatise, 349–471).

[81] *Id.* at 354–56.

[82] *Id.* at 365.

[83] *See Allied-Bruce Terminex Cos.*, 513 U.S. at 277 (applying FAA to full extent as allowed under Commerce Clause of the U.S. Constitution).

[84] The same analysis applies to arbitral agreements governed by the Panama Convention.

1.49 The choice of law issue that has caused the most difficulty for courts of contracting states, and certainly U.S. courts, is found in Article II(3) where the Convention requires the court of a contracting state to "refer the parties to arbitration, unless it finds that the *said agreement is null and void*, inoperative or incapable of being performed."[85] There is no explicit guidance in the Convention as to any choice of law analysis to determine the applicable law for defining "null and void."

1.50 By comparison, Article V of the Convention, concerning recognition and enforcement of arbitral awards, provides fairly certain guidance for a choice of law scheme applicable to agreements to arbitrate. Article V(1)(a) states clearly that recognition and enforcement of an arbitral award may be refused if the arbitration agreement referred to in Article II "is not valid under the law to which the parties have subjected it or, failing any indication thereon, under the law of the country where the award was made." In other words, at least at the award enforcement stage, the choice of law for arbitration agreements is relatively simple. The applicable law is the law that the parties have agreed shall apply to the agreement to arbitrate and, failing any such indication, then the law of the seat of the arbitration shall apply.

1.51 The references to "null and void" in Article II(3) and to "invalid" in Article V(1)(a) are similar and refer principally to defenses such as form, illegality, unconscionability, fraud, duress, and other generally recognized defenses to the enforcement of contracts. Article II naturally would focus more on cases where the agreement to arbitrate was defective from the outset as a result of issues such as lack of consideration, fraud, duress, and illegality.[86]

1.52 Even though the defenses that would apply in both instances are nearly the same, U.S. courts have frequently refused to apply Article V(1)(a)'s choice of law analysis to Article II cases. First, at the time of enforcement of the agreement, it is certainly conceivable that not only have the parties not agreed on the law applicable to the agreement to arbitrate (they rarely have), but there may not be a designated seat of the arbitration. It is not out of the ordinary in many contracts to have a seat that is not specifically identified or even referenced in an agreement to arbitrate. In addition, had the drafters of the Convention wanted Article V(1)(a)'s choice of law provision to apply to an agreement to arbitrate at the stage of enforcement of the agreement under Article II, as opposed to the stage of enforcement of the award under Article V, they could have easily added a sentence providing for exactly that. So U.S. courts, when interpreting the Convention, have held that Article V's choice of law rules were not meant to apply to Article II and, in fact, in many situations when enforcement of the agreement to arbitrate is sought, it would not be possible to apply those choice of law rules to Article II.[87]

---

[85] Emphasis added.

[86] Gary B. Born, International Arbitration in the United States 301 (1994).

[87] Born, International Commercial Arbitration at 564–65, 570–73.

This leaves essentially no guidance within the Convention itself regarding the choice of law rules that should apply to "null and void" under Article II(3), except of course the overriding Convention policy in favor of enforcing agreements to arbitrate.[88] **1.53**

(c) The FAA Nor does the FAA provide explicit guidance regarding choice of law rules for Convention agreements. The FAA does, however, provide a strong federal policy in favor of enforcing agreements to arbitrate, a policy that has particular force in the context of the Conventions.[89] Section 2's substantive law granting a presumption in favor of the enforceability of an agreement to arbitrate effectively preempts a wide range of U.S. state laws found to be inconsistent with the terms of the FAA and the strong federal policy in favor of arbitration that Congress intended when it enacted the FAA.[90] The volume of federal common law in the domestic context that has developed under the FAA, and the strong federal policy in favor of arbitration, has undoubtedly influenced the judiciary sitting in the United States today. Since the early 1980s, the U.S. Supreme Court has repeatedly stricken state laws on a wide range of issues found to be inconsistent with the FAA,[91] and has broadened the scope of arbitrability to include potentially any claim between commercial parties. Nearly every judge on the bench today would have started his or her judicial career after *Moses H. Cone Memorial Hospital*[92] and the relevant Supreme Court cases that followed shortly thereafter. **1.54**

That influence may be one reason why U.S. courts tend to apply the law of the forum, namely the FAA, to questions regarding enforcement of a Convention agreement.[93] Some U.S. courts are also less willing to look to state contract law principles in the context of the Conventions, based in part on their having subject-matter jurisdiction over matters relating to the Conventions. Perhaps the experiences of applying FAA preemption domestically has also led some U.S. courts, when determining the meaning of Article II(3)'s "null and void" provision, to apply only internationally recognized defenses such as duress, mistake, fraud, or waiver, and to disregard foreign laws that single out arbitration agreements or **1.55**

[88] As mentioned previously, the Panama Convention would be interpreted to have the same effect in U.S. courts. *See* Section B.4 of this chapter.

[89] Deloitte Noraudit A/S v. Deloitte Haskins & Sells, U.S., 9 F.3d 1060, 1063 (2d Cir. 1993) (stating that the strong federal policy in favor of arbitration "is even stronger in the context of international transactions").

[90] *Mitsubishi Motors Corp*, 473 U.S. at 625.

[91] *Southland Corp.*, 465 U.S. 1; *Doctor's Assocs.*, 517 U.S. 681; *Buckeye Check Cashing*, 546 U.S. 440; Preston v. Ferrer, 128 S. Ct. 978 (2008).

[92] *Moses H. Cone Mem'l Hosp.*, 460 U.S. 1.

[93] Certain Underwriters at Lloyd's London v. Argonaut Ins. Co., 500 F.3d 571, 577–78 (7th Cir. 2007) ("We note, however, that, when our sister circuits have been confronted with issues relating to agreements under the Convention—whether the question be arbitrability or enforcement or some other question—they appear to have resolved those issues by employing federal rules of decision, particularly when the parties have not provided otherwise by their contract.").

that are otherwise idiosyncratic and not widely followed internationally. Some have also shown a willingness to follow the validation principles endorsed by some commentators whereby the reviewing court would apply a choice of law analysis that would seek to avoid those laws invalidating an agreement to arbitrate in favor of those laws that would enforce the agreement.[94]

1.56 In summary, U.S. courts give significant weight to the policies behind the FAA and the Conventions, and tend to apply the forum's law, i.e., the FAA, on these issues. In a U.S. court, reliance on foreign law to argue that a Convention agreement should not be enforced often fails if that same agreement would be enforceable under the FAA.[95]

2. Applicable Law Regarding Formation and Substantive Validity of the Agreement to Arbitrate

1.57 There is surprisingly little case law in the United States defining the choice of law analysis used to interpret the "null and void" provisions in Article II(3) and the other enforcement issues generally. In addition, many U.S. court decisions provide little or no explanation or analysis of the law chosen, especially where a U.S. federal court simply applies the FAA and the common law derived from the FAA.[96] Indeed, even the Second Circuit Court of Appeals and the district courts within the circuit, which have been the source of more U.S. jurisprudence on international arbitration than any of the other U.S. circuit courts, have rendered relatively few cases addressing choice of law for enforcement of Convention agreements.[97]

1.58 In addition, the Second Circuit's decisions in this area have not been consistent. While the weight of case law suggests that courts will apply the law of the forum (i.e., the FAA), some courts have chosen the law of the underlying contracts.[98]

[94] Born, International Commercial Arbitration, at 541–48.

[95] That is not to say that a federal court will never apply foreign law to reject enforcement of a Convention agreement. *See, e.g.*, Motorola Credit Corp. v. Kemal Uzan, 388 F.3d 39, 50–51 (2d Cir. 2004) (applying Swiss law of underlying contracts to question of existence of Convention agreement to arbitrate). The facts of *Motorola Credit Corp.*, however, were somewhat unusual.

[96] Sarhank Group v. Oracle Corp., 404 F.3d 657, 661 (2d Cir. 2005); Storm LLC v. Telenor Mobile Commc'ns AS, 06 Civ. 13157 (GEL), 2006 U.S. Dist. LEXIS 90978, at *24 n.4 (S.D.N.Y. Dec. 15, 2006).

[97] The U.S. Court of Appeals for the Second Circuit is one of thirteen intermediate appellate courts in the United States. Its territory includes the states of New York, Connecticut, and Vermont, and it has appellate jurisdiction over the six federal district courts in those states, including the District Court for the Southern District of New York in Manhattan. For a comparison of the number of Convention award cases estimated to have been handled by each of the circuits since the 1960s, *see* Christopher A. Whytock, *The Arbitration-Litigation Relationship in Transnational Dispute Resolution: Empirical Insights from the U.S. Federal Courts*, Vol. 2, No. 5 World Arbitration & Mediation Review 39 (2008).

[98] *See, e.g.*, Smith/Enron Cogen. Ltd. P'ship, Inc., v. Smith Cogen. Int'l, Inc., 198 F.3d 88, 96 (2d Cir. 1999) (underlying contracts governed by Texas law; court applied federal common

U.S. jurisprudence provides yet another choice of law hurdle: whether to apply state contract law (or perhaps even foreign law as a result of conflict of law rules) in the context of applying the FAA as the law of the forum.[99] Again, the case law in the Second Circuit is not consistent in this area.

The encouraging news for a party seeking enforcement is that U.S. courts are pro-enforcement. This is true around the country generally and certainly in New York. A party should be prepared to argue both the law under the FAA as well as the law of the underlying agreement, as necessary. Parties should also be prepared to apply New York state conflict of law rules (discussed below) in the event that the court decides to apply state contract law to a contract formation issue. Finally, U.S. courts generally have not applied the law of the seat of the arbitration to determine enforcement of a Convention agreement under Article II. Most Second Circuit decisions do not even mention the law of the seat, other than in the context of applying state conflict of law rules and establishing contacts with the jurisdiction.[100] **1.59**

Discussed later are examples of the case law from the Second Circuit and district courts within the Second Circuit. **1.60**

(a) Case law from the Second Circuit applying law of forum As previously mentioned, applying the law of the forum can increase complexity in the United States because of the FAA preemption issues and the Supreme Court case law directing lower courts to use state contract law principles to decide matters concerning the formation and substantive validity of the agreement to arbitrate.[101] Some courts, however, have disregarded the notion of applying state contract law in the context of Convention agreements because of the nature of the federal courts' jurisdiction. Because the federal courts have subject-matter jurisdiction over all matters relating to Convention agreements and awards under Sections 203, 205, and 302 of the FAA, the courts have held that federal common law, not state law, governs the interpretation and application of those provisions.[102] **1.61**

law to all questions of enforcement of Convention agreement to arbitrate including existence of agreement and waiver); *Motorola Credit Corp.*, 388 F.3d at 50–51 (applied Swiss law of underlying contracts to question of existence of Convention agreement).

[99] *See, e.g., Sarhank Group*, 404 F.3d at 662 ("American federal arbitration law" controls whether Convention agreement existed); *Chelsea Square Textiles*, 189 F.3d at 295–96 (applying state contract law principles to question of existence of Convention agreement).

[100] The apparent lack of interest in applying the law of the seat to enforcement of an agreement to arbitrate under Article II(3) of the New York Convention is curious, given that it is the preferred analysis in some other jurisdictions and also by some leading commentators. *See* Born, International Commercial Arbitration, at 524–25.

[101] *See Perry*, 482 U.S. at 492.

[102] *In re* Am. Exp. Fin. Advisors Sec. Litig., 672 F.3d 113, 127 (2d Cir. 2011) ("The FAA creates a body of federal substantive law of arbitrability, applicable to any arbitration agreement within the coverage of the Act.") (quotation omitted).

1.62 The leading case, *Smith/Enron Cogeneration Ltd. P'ship, Inc. et al., v. Smith Cogeneration Int'l, Inc.* (hereafter *Smith/Enron*),[103] is often cited for this proposition. In *Smith/Enron*, the agreement provided for arbitration in New York.[104] The agreement included a governing law provision calling for Texas law to govern interpretation of the agreement's terms. With respect to arbitration, the agreement included a provision that arbitration "shall for all purposes be governed by, and construed and enforced in accordance with," the FAA.[105]

1.63 The Second Circuit Court of Appeals first addressed the choice of law issues. The defendant, Smith Cogeneration Int'l, Inc. (SCI), which was fighting enforcement of the Convention agreement, argued that state contract law principles generally apply to the issue of whether an agreement was made. SCI then argued that the court should apply New York state conflict of law rules, which, according to SCI, would call for the court to apply the law of the Turks and Caicos Islands to the issue of whether there was an enforceable agreement to arbitrate. SCI alternatively argued that the relevant underlying partnership agreement called for Turks and Caicos Islands law to apply to issues regarding formation and organization of the partnership.[106] Noting that the matter had little connection to New York and that the agreement itself called for application of the FAA, the Second Circuit rejected both of SCI's arguments and held, "When we exercise jurisdiction under Chapter 2 of the FAA, we have compelling reasons to apply federal law, which is already well-developed, to the question of whether an agreement to arbitrate is enforceable."[107] The court also noted that no party was domiciled in New York and that there was no indication that either party contemplated application of New York law. The only connection to New York was that it was the seat of arbitration. Interestingly, the court noted that neither party argued for application of Texas law, the governing law of the underlying agreement.[108]

1.64 The Second Circuit's decision in *Smith/Enron* is the majority rule currently in the Second Circuit, to the extent there is one.[109] Other courts have generally applied federal law to decide the enforceability of Convention agreements.[110] It is interesting to note, however, that the court in *Smith/Enron* did not say that it was required to apply federal law and, in fact, did go through some analysis regarding the parties' contacts with New York that was not necessary if federal law automatically applied to the issue.

[103] 198 F.3d 88 (2d Cir. 1999).

[104] *Id.* at 90.

[105] *Id.* at 96.

[106] *Id.*

[107] *Id.* (citing cases).

[108] *Id.*

[109] Republic of Ecuador v. Chevron Corp., 638 F.3d 384, 392 (2d Cir. 2011) (affirming *Smith/Enron*'s holding that federal law applies where there is "little connection to the forum").

[110] *See, e.g.*, Lakah v. UBS AG, 996 F. Supp. 2d 250, 260 (S.D.N.Y. 2014) (applying federal law to determine the enforceability of an arbitration agreement where the dispute had little connection

(b) Consideration of state contract law principles when applying law of forum in the Second Circuit Several decisions within the Second Circuit have done what the court in *Smith/Enron* refused to do: apply the law of the forum, *i.e.*, the FAA, but follow the U.S. Supreme Court's directions in *Perry v. Thomas*[111] to apply state contract law principles with respect to the formation of the agreement to arbitrate. Application of state law typically begins with employing that state's conflict of law analysis, which may lead to the application of another state's contract law principles, or perhaps foreign law.[112] New York uses the "interest analysis" to decide conflict of law issues involving contract disputes, which seeks to apply "the law of the jurisdiction having the greatest interest in the litigation."[113] This analysis will consider, for example, the domicile of the parties, the place where the agreement was executed, and the place of performance.[114] **1.65**

In *Progressive Cas. Ins. Co. v. Reaseguradora Nacional de Venezuela*,[115] the court held that state contract law principles must be followed when interpreting the enforceability of an agreement to arbitrate, and applied New York state law after conducting a conflict of law analysis under New York's "interest analysis." The court acknowledged that the matter fell under Chapter 2 of the FAA, and then applied state law under the formula provided in *Perry v. Thomas*. The court, however, seems to have mistakenly believed that it had only diversity jurisdiction and cited the authority for applying state law as if it was sitting in diversity.[116] The court seems to have missed the fact that it had explicit original jurisdiction **1.66**

---

to New York and "[a]ll the relevant events occurred in Egypt"); *Sarhank Group*, 404 F.3d at 662 (applying federal law to determine whether nonsignatory should have been compelled to arbitrate an Egyptian law dispute in Egypt); David L. Threlkeld & Co., Inc. v. Metallgesellschaft Limited (London), 923 F.2d 245, 249–50 (2d Cir. 1991) (applying federal common law to determine validity of arbitration provision and preempting state law that singles out arbitration agreements); Genesco, Inc. v. T. Kakiuchi & Co., 815 F.2d 840, 845–46 (2d Cir. 1987) (applying federal common law to Convention case); JSC Surgutneftegaz v. President and Fellows of Harvard Coll., No. 04 Civ 6069 (RCC), 2005 WL 1863676, at *2 (S.D.N.Y. Aug. 3, 2005) (federal, not state, law applies to motion to stay arbitration governed by New York Convention); *The Republic of Ecuador*, 376 F. Supp. 2d at 356 (following *Sarhank* and holding that federal common law applied where enforcement sought against nonsignatory); Coimex Trading (Suisse) S.A. v. Cargill Int'l S.A., No. 05 Civ. 2630 (LLS), 2005 U.S. Dist. LEXIS 9784 (S.D.N.Y. May 20, 2005) (holding that determination of whether agreement to arbitrate exists is a matter of federal law, not state law); Borsack v. Chalk & Vermillion Fine Arts, Ltd., 974 F. Supp. 293, 299 n.5 (S.D.N.Y. 1997) (applying federal law to questions of enforceability of agreement to arbitrate when court has jurisdiction under Chapter 2 of FAA).

[111] *Perry*, 482 U.S. at 492 n.9.

[112] *Smith/Enron Cogen. Ltd P'ship, Inc.*, 198 F.3d at 96.

[113] Intercontinental Planning, Ltd. v. Daystrom, Inc., 300 N.Y.S.2d 817, 825 (1969).

[114] *Id.*

[115] 991 F.2d 42, 45–46 & n.6 (2d Cir. 1993).

[116] *Id.* at 45–46 & n.6. When a federal court has diversity jurisdiction, as opposed to federal question jurisdiction, it must apply the choice of law rules of the state in which the action was brought. Klaxon Co. v. Stentor Elec. Mfg. Co., 313 U.S. 487, 496 (1941). In the context of domestic FAA arbitration matters brought before federal courts, diversity jurisdiction is the only way

under Section 203 of the FAA's Chapter 2 and did not need to refer to diversity standards.[117]

1.67 In a subsequent Second Circuit case, *Chelsea Square Textiles v. Bombay Dyeing and Mfg.*,[118] Chelsea Square argued that the arbitration clause on the back of a document was illegible and therefore it never could have agreed to arbitrate. The Second Circuit held, citing *Perry v. Thomas*[119] and *Progressive Cas. Ins. Co*,[120] that the district court properly looked to New York state law when determining whether the parties entered into an agreement to arbitrate.

1.68 The decision in *Chelsea Square Textiles* provided some clarity in that diversity jurisdiction played no role in the court's decision to apply state law, and it cited *Progressive Cas. Ins. Co.* in support of the proposition to apply state law in the context of Section 203 jurisdiction. This provides some assurance that these two cases remain good law, even though they seem to conflict with *Smith/Enron* and the line of cases applying only federal law.[121]

1.69 *(c) Case law from the Second Circuit applying law of the underlying contract* At least two decisions from the Second Circuit have applied the governing law of the underlying contract to the agreement to arbitrate as well. In *Motorola Credit Corp. v. Kemal Uzan*,[122] the Second Circuit affirmed the district court's denial of the defendants' motion to compel arbitration. The defendants sought to have U.S. federal law apply, which was more likely to allow nonparties to enforce the agreement to arbitrate against a party that had signed the agreement. The defendants cited *Smith/Enron* to argue in favor of applying U.S. federal law, but the

to have the matter heard by a federal court. Thus, U.S. courts will be comfortable with applying state law in that circumstance, but those cases never involve Chapters 2 and 3 of the FAA, which provide federal court jurisdiction under sections 203, 205, and 302. 9 U.S.C. §§ 203, 205, 302.

117 For a detailed discussion on the impact that the nature of the court's jurisdiction can have on the choice of law analysis in the United States, *see The Republic of Ecuador*, 376 F. Supp. 2d 334 (applying federal law to enforcement of agreement against nonparty).

118 189 F.3d at 295–96.

119 *Perry*, 482 U.S. at 492 n.9.

120 *Progressive Cas. Ins. Co*, 991 F.2d at 45–46 & n.6.

121 The Second Circuit's decision in *Smith/Enron Cogen. Ltd P'ship*, 198 F.3d at 95–96 (federal law applies to enforcement of Convention agreements), was decided only seven months after *Chelsea Square Textiles*, 189 F.3d at 295–96 (state contract law applies to determine whether parties entered into a Convention agreement), albeit by a different panel of judges. The conflicting analysis by the same court on very similar issues is puzzling. The court in *Smith/Enron* did mention that none of the parties were domiciled in New York and that the only connection to New York was that it was the seat of arbitration. However, if, as the court held, federal law applies to enforcing Convention agreements, there was no need for the court to consider the parties' contacts with New York. The court also mentioned that the parties did not seek to apply Texas law, which was the law of the underlying contract. The court rejected applying Turks and Caicos Islands law, but without any substantive analysis other than to say that there are compelling reasons to apply federal law when determining enforceability of a Convention agreement. Perhaps if the parties in *Smith/Enron* had closer connections to New York, the court may have given stronger consideration to applying New York state contract law rather than federal law.

122 *Motorola Credit Corp.*, 388 F.3d at 50–51.

court rejected the use of *Smith/Enron* as precedent on this point because, according to the court, the parties in *Smith/Enron* never asked the court to apply the law of the underlying contract, which was Texas law. The court then held that if the defendants wanted the benefit of the contracts, they had to take the governing law provisions that came with them. The court also said that this rule would help prevent forum shopping as well.[123]

The court provided little analysis for its decision, and while the court could correctly conclude there was no definite law in the Second Circuit that required enforcement, the decision was a departure from past Second Circuit decisions where the underlying contract's governing law clause rarely played a role. Both the circuit court and the trial court seemed keen to keep the defendants in the U.S. court.[124] **1.70**

This approach was long favored in England, but disfavored by some who believe it runs against the notion of separability to have a presumption that the law of the underlying contract prevails.[125] The decisions in *Sphere Drake* and *Motorola* go against the weight of authority in the circuit, and the unusual facts in both cases may further isolate their holdings. Nonetheless, a party should be prepared to argue the issue if making submissions to the court. **1.71**

(d) Consideration of internationally recognized minimum standards Two federal appellate court decisions get considerable attention from commentators, although they seem to get only limited attention in Second Circuit decisions. *Rhone Mediterranee Compagnia Francese di Assicurazioni e Riassicurazoni v. Lauro*[126] was decided by the Third Circuit in 1983 and *Ledee v. Ceramiche Ragno*[127] was decided by the First Circuit a year earlier in 1982. Essentially, the holdings in these two cases are that under the New York Convention, an agreement to arbitrate is "null and void" only if it is subject to internationally recognized defenses such as fraud, duress, mistake, or waiver, or when it violates the most fundamental policies of the forum state. The cases hold that the "null and void" provisions in Article II(3) of the Convention must be read narrowly. The courts based their decisions largely on the clear policy behind the Convention in support of arbitration and enforcing agreements to arbitrate. In *Rhone*, the court held that the **1.72**

---

[123] *Id.*

[124] The court relied on the U.S. Supreme Court's decision in *Volt Info. Sciences*, 489 U.S. 468, where the Court affirmed a California Supreme Court decision that by including a broad California governing law provision, the parties intended to apply California's arbitration laws as well. The court also relied on *Sphere Drake Ins. Ltd*, 263 F.3d 26, where the Second Circuit applied the law of the underlying contract to the agreement to arbitrate because the FAA does not preempt choice of law clauses, citing *Volt*.

[125] Born, International Commercial Arbitration, at 514.

[126] Rhone Mediterranee Compagnia Francese di Assicurazioni e Riassicurazoni v. Lauro, 712 F.2d 50, 53–54 (3d Cir. 1983).

[127] Ledee v. Ceramiche Ragno, 684 F.2d 184, 187 (1st Cir. 1982).

Italian law (Italy was the seat) requiring an odd number of arbitrators, instead of the even number as stated in the agreement to arbitrate at issue, was not sufficient grounds to refuse enforcement of the agreement. The court found that such a rule was not internationally recognized and therefore could not trump the policies in favor of arbitration under the Convention. Nor did enforcement of the agreement violate any fundamental policies of the enforcement forum, which was the United States.[128]

1.73 In his treatise on international arbitration, Gary Born encourages an even broader international practice, called the *validation principle*, that calls upon judges and arbitrators to review the possible applicable law choices and always choose the law that would validate the agreement to arbitrate, no matter if the choice of law analysis may point in another direction.[129]

3. Applicable Law Regarding Formal Validity of the Agreement to Arbitrate

1.74 Contracting states generally look to the plain language of the Conventions to determine the formal validity of the agreement to arbitrate.[130] Article II(1) requires that the Convention agreement be in writing. Article II(2) states that " 'agreement in writing' *shall* include an arbitral clause in a contract or an arbitration agreement, *signed by the parties or contained in an exchange of letters or telegrams*."[131]

1.75 U.S. courts, like the courts in nearly all other jurisdictions, have held that Articles II(1) and (2) establish the maximum standard for formal validity. That is, a contracting state cannot create formal validity requirements that are more stringent than those found in Article II.[132] These requirements are more stringent than those applicable to non-Convention arbitration agreements in the United States, but must be met to qualify for treatment as a Convention agreement.[133]

---

[128] *Rhone Mediterranee*, 712 F.2d at 53–54.

[129] Born, International Commercial Arbitration, at 541–48. At least one federal district court in New York has applied this principle to validate a forum selection clause in an arbitration agreement under federal common law, where the petitioner argued that the parties' choice of substantive law (the law of Liechtenstein) invalidated the provision. Farrell v. Subway Int'l, B.V., 11 CIV. 08 JFK, 2011 WL 1085017, at *3 (S.D.N.Y. Mar. 23, 2011) ("In this case, deferring to the Agreement's choice of law could result in the Court disregarding the agreed-upon forum selection clause, a result that encourages forum shopping and destroys any predictability of forum for the parties.").

[130] "Formal validity" refers to matters such as the writing requirement in Article II of the New York Convention. This is in contrast to the immediately preceding section that addressed "substantive validity," such as whether the agreement to arbitrate is "null and void" under Article II(3).

[131] Emphasis added. Article I of the Panama Convention is substantially the same.

[132] Given that this standard is higher than the standard that would otherwise apply in the United States, and given that the Supreme Court in Doctor's Assoc., Inc. v. Cassarotto, 517 U.S. 681 (1996) held that state law formal validity requirements that single out arbitration agreements are preempted, it is unlikely that restrictions beyond those established in Article II will be created in the United States.

[133] Kahn Lucas Lancaster, Inc. v. Lark Int'l Ltd., 186 F.3d 210 (2d Cir. 1999).

Authority in the Second Circuit holds that Article II also creates a minimum standard whereby agreements to arbitrate that do not meet these standards should not be recognized as Convention agreements.[134] **1.76**

In the context of non-Convention arbitral agreements, or if the Convention standards are not met when determining whether to enforce a nondomestic agreement, U.S. courts generally will apply the law of the forum if the seat of the arbitration is located within the national territory for that court. For example, a U.S. court would likely enforce a nondomestic agreement to arbitrate that does not meet the Convention standards in paragraphs (1) and (2) of Article II, but does meet the lower standard for formal validity under the FAA, as long as the seat of arbitration is in the United States.[135] Of course, the resulting award will not be deemed a Convention award if it failed to meet the formal validity requirements in Article II. **1.77**

If the arbitration agreement calls for a seat outside the United States, then, according to Gary Born's treatise, the U.S. court would likely apply the same choice of law analysis that it would apply in the context of determining the applicable law governing the substantive validity of the agreement to arbitrate. There is, however, little case law to guide the court, and the FAA is silent.[136] **1.78**

4. Applicable Law Regarding Arbitrability

At the award enforcement stage, Article V(2)(a) of the New York Convention explicitly mentions that a contracting state may refuse enforcement of an award if "the subject matter of the difference is not capable of settlement by arbitration under the law of that country." Clearly the law of the forum would apply to that analysis.[137] Article II(1) also allows a court in a contracting state to refuse to recognize a Convention agreement to arbitrate if the subject matter of the dispute is not "capable of settlement by arbitration." In Article II(1), there is no mention as to what law should govern. **1.79**

---

[134] *Id.; but see* Born, International Commercial Arbitration, at 618–19 (Born suggests that the better reading of Article II(2) is that it does not establish a minimum standard and suggests that the more modern trend is to interpret the provision as not establishing a minimum standard. For now, however, the reader should assume that it does provide a minimum standard in the United States).

[135] *Id.* at 620–21 (*citing* 9 U.S.C. § 1).

[136] *Id.* at 621–22 (citing treatises but no case law; also stressing use of validation principle if Conventions not applicable). The authors of this chapter could find no case law in the United States on point, but Born's thesis that a U.S. court would likely follow the same choice of law analysis that it would in the context of enforcing an agreement to arbitrate seems to be the likely outcome. As stated previously, the courts in the Second Circuit typically apply the law of the forum, and, in addition, typically apply federal law rather than state conflict rules to determine an applicable contract law. Thus, the outcome would likely be the same, although the case law previously discussed showed just how inconsistent the analysis can be.

[137] *Scherk*, 417 U.S. at 519 n.14 (law of place where enforcement of award is sought governs arbitrability under Article V(2)(a)).

1.80 In the United States, and in most jurisdictions, the court applying Article II(1)'s provisions regarding arbitrability will apply the law of the forum to determine arbitrability. The Supreme Court said in *Mitsubishi* that the United States must apply "federal substantive law of arbitrability" that applies to any Convention agreement.[138] In the United States, the courts will apply federal, not state, law to determine arbitrability and the Supreme Court in *Mitsubishi* and *Scherk* made very clear that notions of arbitrability or public policy as defenses to enforcement of arbitration agreements or awards must be very narrowly defined.[139]

1.81 U.S. courts have shown a willingness to enforce agreements to arbitrate even though the subject matter of those agreements may not be arbitrable or may be against the public policy of another Convention jurisdiction. Instead, the U.S. courts look at the strong public policy in the United States in favor of arbitration and enforce the agreement to arbitrate.[140] Of course, the other jurisdiction will be free to refuse enforcement of an award under Article V(2)(a).[141]

5. Applicable Law Regarding Interpretation and Scope

1.82 Matters of interpretation and scope of the Convention agreement are strictly matters of federal law under the FAA and not state law.[142] The U.S. Supreme Court in *Mitsubishi* applied federal law with its strong presumption in favor of arbitration even though the arbitration was seated in Japan and was to be governed by Japanese or Swiss law.[143] The Court's decision in *Mitsubishi* is now well-established law in the United States.

6. Applicable Law Regarding Capacity and Competence

1.83 Article V(1)(a) specifically provides that proof of a party's incapacity is grounds to refuse enforcement of a Convention award. The provision also states "under the law applicable to them." Thus, U.S. courts will apply the law of the domicile for individuals and, in the case of a juridical person, they will apply the law of the place of incorporation or the law of the principal place of business.[144]

---

[138] *Mitsubishi*, 473 U.S. at 626.

[139] *Id.; Scherk*, 417 U.S. 506.

[140] *Ledee*, 684 F.2d at 184; *JSC Surgutneftegaz*, 2005 WL 1863676, at *2.

[141] The Second Circuit has similarly limited defenses based on notions of public policy. *See Parsons & Whittemore Overseas*, 508 F.2d at 974. In that case, the Second Circuit limited public policy to notions of international public policy rather than national public policy. It is very difficult to prove such a case.

[142] *Mitsubishi Motors Corp.*, 473 U.S. at 626.

[143] *Id.* at 614.

[144] Born, International Commercial Arbitration, at 625–34.

E. APPLICABLE LAW REGARDING RECOGNITION AND ENFORCEMENT OF CONVENTION AWARDS

Both the New York and Panama Conventions require signatory states to recognize arbitral awards that fall within the Conventions.[145] Both Conventions, however, list a limited number of grounds whereby a court *may* deny recognition and enforcement of an international arbitral award. In keeping with its pro-arbitration objectives, Section 207 of the FAA, which applies to awards under both Conventions,[146] provides that a court "*shall* confirm" awards "*unless* it finds one of the grounds for refusal or deferral of recognition or enforcement of the award specified in the said Convention."[147] **1.84**

The similarly narrow grounds to vacate arbitral awards under FAA Chapter 1 may also apply to nondomestic awards issued in, or under the arbitral law of, the United States. **1.85**

1. Application of the Conventions

The New York Convention applies to arbitral awards (1) made in a Convention country outside the country where enforcement is sought, or (2) "not considered as domestic awards in the country where enforcement is sought."[148] In *Bergesen v. Joseph Muller Corp.*, the Second Circuit held that the Convention applied to an award made in the United States between two foreign nationals because such award was nondomestic under the Convention: "We adopt the view that awards 'not considered as domestic' denotes awards which are subject to the Convention not because made abroad, but because made within the legal framework of another country, e.g., pronounced in accordance with foreign law or involving parties domiciled or having their principal place of business outside the enforcing jurisdiction."[149] **1.86**

---

[145] Article III of the New York Convention provides that "[e]ach contracting State shall recognize arbitral awards as binding and enforce them in accordance with the rules of procedure of the territory where the award is relied upon, under the conditions laid down in the following articles[.]" Article 4 of the Panama Convention provides that "[a]n arbitral decision or award that is not appealable under the applicable law or procedural rules shall have the force of a final judicial judgment. Its execution or recognition may be ordered in the same manner as that of decisions handed down by national or foreign ordinary courts, in accordance with the procedural laws of the country where it is to be executed and the provisions of international treaties." The general topic of the enforcement of arbitral awards is dealt with in detail in Chapter 13.

[146] Pursuant to 9 USC § 302, 9 USC §207 is incorporated into Chapter 3 of the FAA.

[147] 9 USC § 207 (emphasis added). Finally, both Conventions presume the validity of arbitral awards and put the burden of proving the existence of grounds of nonrecognition on the party resisting recognition or enforcement of the award. *See* Article V(1) of the New York Convention and Article 5(1) of the Panama Convention.

[148] Article I(1).

[149] 710 F.2d 929, 932 (2d Cir. 1983). *See* Productos Mercantiles Industriales S.A. v. Faberge USA Inc., 23 F.3d 41, 45 (2d Cir. 1994) (applying the same principle under the Panama Convention).

1.87 Similarly, the Panama Convention applies to: (1) awards "made in the territory of a foreign state" that has ratified the Convention,[150] and (2) nondomestic awards made in the United States.[151]

2. Nondomestic Awards Rendered in the United States or Pursuant to U.S. Arbitration Law May Be Vacated Under U.S. Arbitration Law

1.88 Nondomestic arbitral awards issued by a tribunal seated in the United States or made pursuant to U.S. arbitration law may be vacated under U.S. arbitration law.

1.89 Although neither Convention directly addresses actions to vacate arbitral awards, both provide that a court may refuse to confirm an award that has been vacated or suspended by a competent authority of the country in which, or under the law of which, that award was made.[152] The "law" referred to is the arbitration law, not the substantive law that applied to the dispute.[153]

1.90 The Second Circuit has held that, under the New York Convention, the state in which, or under the law of which, the award is made, is free to set aside or modify an award in accordance with its domestic arbitral law and its full panoply of express and implied grounds for relief.[154] This is to be contrasted with actions for *enforcement* of awards, in which the state may refuse to enforce the award only on the grounds explicitly set forth in Article V of the Convention.[155]

1.91 This means that U.S. courts may vacate awards made in the United States relying on the grounds listed in Section 10 of the FAA, i.e., where (1) the award was procured by fraud, corruption, or undue means; (2) there was evident partiality or corruption in some or all of the arbitrators; (3) the arbitrators were guilty of

150 9 USC § 304.

151 Banco de Seguros del Estado v. Mutual Marine Offices, Inc., 230 F. Supp. 2d 362 (S.D.N.Y. 2002).

152 *See* Article V(1)(e) of the New York Convention and Article 5(1)(e) of the Panama Convention.

153 Int'l Standard Elec. Corp. v. Bridas Sociedad Anonima Petrolera, Industrial y Comercial, 745 F. Supp. 172 (S.D.N.Y. 1990) ("We conclude that the phrase in the Convention '[t]he country under the laws of which the award was made' undoubtedly referenced the complex thicket of the *procedural* law of arbitration obtaining in the numerous and diverse jurisdictions of the dozens of nations in attendance at the time the Convention was being debated.")(emphasis in original); Yusuf Ahmed Alghanim v. Toys "R" Us, Inc., 126 F.3d 15, 21 n.3 (2d Cir. 1997) (*quoting* Albert Jan van den Berg, The New York Convention of 1958: Towards a Uniform Judicial Interpretation 28 (1981)) ("we note that Article V(i)(e) specifically contemplates the possibility that an award could be rendered in one state, but under the arbitral law of another state ... This situation may be so rare as to be a 'dead letter.'").

154 *Yusuf Ahmed Alghanim*, 126 F.3d at 23; Daebo Int'l Shipping Co. v. Americas Bulk Transp. (BVI) Ltd., No. 12 Civ. 4750(PAE), 2013 WL 2149591, at *5–6 (S.D.N.Y. May 17, 2013).

155 *Yusuf Ahmed Alghanim*, 126 F.3d at 23; *Daebo Int'l Shipping*, 2013 WL 2149591 at *6.

misconduct in refusing to postpone the hearing; or (4) the arbitrators exceeded their powers.[156] In addition to these express grounds, federal courts in New York had long held that an award could be vacated for "manifest disregard of the law" by arbitrators.[157]

The Second Circuit reaffirmed the applicability of the manifest disregard of the law standard in *Sotheby's Int'l Rlty., Inc. v. Relocation Grp., LLC*, despite the language in the U.S. Supreme Court's decision in *Hall Street* holding that nonstatutory bases for vacatur are not allowed under the FAA.[158] In *Hall Street*, a domestic arbitration dispute, the Supreme Court held that the statutory grounds to vacate an arbitral award are exclusive and that parties cannot expand those grounds by contract. In passing, the Court expressed skepticism as to the survival of the "manifest disregard of the law" doctrine.[159] While the Second Circuit has affirmed the continuing viability of the manifest disregard standard, it also has affirmed the exceptionally narrow grounds for vacatur under that standard.[160] **1.92**

Recognition and enforcement of nondomestic awards rendered in the United States or under U.S. arbitral law may be further challenged under the limited grounds listed in the Conventions, discussed in Section 3 below. **1.93**

U.S. arbitration law may also be relevant to the arbitrators' authority to correct or modify their award after it has been issued. While the FAA is silent on this issue, U.S. courts have repeatedly upheld the *functus officio* doctrine, whereby the arbitrators' mandate and authority definitively cease when they issue their award.[161] Nevertheless, if an award fails to address all issues properly submitted, or if the award fails to have completely adjudicated an issue, the tribunal may supplement the original award to address those issues so that the tribunal's duties are fully and finally finished.[162] This exception to the *functus officio* doctrine is intended to ensure that the ultimate award fully and finally decides all matters properly presented in the arbitration. **1.94**

---

[156] 9 USC § 10.

[157] Merrill Lynch, Pierce, Fenner, & Smith Inc. v. Bobker, 808 F.2d 930, 936 (2d Cir. 1986).

[158] 588 F. App'x 64, 65 (2d Cir. 2015); *contra* Citigroup Global Markets, Inc. v. Bacon, 562 F. 3d 349 (5th Cir. 2009); Ramos-Santiago v. UPS, 524 F.3d 120 (1st Cir. 2008).

[159] *Hall Street*, 128 S. Ct. at 1404.

[160] *Sotheby's Int'l Rlty.*, 588 F. App'x at 65; *see also* B.L. Harbert Int'l, LLC v. Hercules Steel Co., 441 F. 3d 905, 913 (11th Cir. 2006) (the court warned litigants they will be sanctioned for bringing baseless claims of manifest disregard in seeking to vacate arbitral awards).

[161] Am. Centennial Ins. Co. v. Arion Ins. Co., No. 88 Civ. 1665 (RWS), 1990 WL 52295, at *5 (S.D.N.Y. Apr. 13, 1990).

[162] T.Co Metals, LLC v. Dempsey Pipe & Supply, Inc., 592 F.3d 329, 342 (2d Cir. 2010) (explaining that an arbitrator has "inherent authority [that] applies narrowly to clerical mistakes or obvious errors in arithmetic computation") (internal citation omitted); Waveform Telemedia, Inc. v. Panorama Weather N.A., No. 06 Civ. 5270 CMMDF, 2007 WL 678731, at *6–7 (S.D.N.Y. Mar. 2, 2007) (recognizing three exceptions to *functus officio* doctrine including tribunal's post-award authority to supplement).

3. Arbitral Awards Rendered Outside the United States or Pursuant to a Foreign Arbitration Law May Not Be Vacated Under U.S. Arbitration Law

1.95 In an action to confirm awards rendered in, or under the arbitration law of, a foreign jurisdiction, the grounds for relief enumerated in Article V of the New York Convention are the only grounds available for setting aside an award.[163]

1.96 Under the New York Convention, a court *may* refuse to recognize and enforce a foreign arbitral award if (1) the parties to the arbitration agreement were under some incapacity, or the said agreement is not valid under the law; or (2) the party against whom the award is invoked was not given proper notice of the appointment of the arbitrator or of the arbitration proceedings;[164] or (3) the award deals with a difference not contemplated by or not falling within the terms of the submission to arbitration, or it contains decisions on matters beyond the scope of the submission to arbitration; or (4) the composition of the arbitral authority or the arbitral procedure was not in accordance with the agreement of the parties; or (5) the award has not yet become binding on the parties, or has been set aside or suspended by a competent authority of the country in which, or under the law of which, that award was made. Enforcement may also be refused if "[t]he subject matter of the difference is not capable of settlement by arbitration," or if "recognition or enforcement of the award would be contrary to the public policy"[165] of the country in which enforcement or recognition is sought.[166]

1.97 Courts in New York have consistently held that in actions to confirm an award rendered in, or under the law of, a foreign jurisdiction, the grounds listed in Article V are the exclusive grounds available to deny confirmation of an arbitral award.[167] The Second Circuit had expressly rejected the availability of the "manifest disregard of the law" doctrine.

---

[163] *Yusuf Ahmed Alghanim*, 126 F.3d at 20. Article V of the New York Convention is discussed in more detail in Chapter 13.C.

[164] A court held that successful reliance on this provision requires a showing that the arbitration was conducted in violation of the United States' standards of due process of law. *Parsons & Whittemore Overseas*, 508 F.2d at 975; *see also* Anhui Provincial Import and Export v. Hart Enters. Int'l, 96 Civ. 128 (LAK), 1996 WL 229872, at *3 (S.D.N.Y. May 7, 1996) (to comport with due process, parties to an arbitration must be given "notice reasonably calculated" to inform them of the proceedings and "an opportunity to be heard"); Ukrvneshprom State Foreign Econ. Enter. v. Tradeway, Inc., 95 Civ. 10278 (RPP), 1996 WL 107285, at *5 (S.D.N.Y. Mar. 11, 1996) (party relying on Article V(1)(b) defense "must establish that it was denied the opportunity to be heard at a meaningful time or in a meaningful manner").

[165] The Court of Appeals for the Second Circuit held that the New York Convention's public policy defense must be "construed narrowly. Enforcement of foreign arbitral awards may be denied only where enforcement would violate the forum state's most basic notions of morality and justice." *Parsons & Whittemore Overseas*, 508 F.2d at 974.

[166] New York Convention, Article V.

[167] *Yusuf Ahmed Alghanim*, 126 F.3d at 23; *International Standard Elec. Corp.*, 745 F. Supp. at 181–82; Brandeis Intsel Ltd v. Calabrian Chemicals Corp., 656 F. Supp. 160, 165 (S.D.N.Y. 1987) ("'[M]anifest disregard' of law, whatever the phrase may mean, does not rise to the level

Nevertheless, the FAA may become relevant when a party seeks to enforce in the United States an award that has been vacated by the courts of the state where, or under the law of which, the award was made. Indeed, while Article V(1)(e) of the New York Convention gives U.S. courts discretion to enforce such an award, Article VII reserves the application of the arbitration law of the forum and provides that the Convention "shall not deprive any interested party of any right he may have to avail himself of an arbitral award in the manner and to the extent allowed by the law ... of the country where such award is sought to be relied upon." Accordingly, in an action to enforce in the United States an award that had been vacated by the courts in Egypt, where the award had been made, a federal trial court in the District of Columbia relied on Article VII of the Convention and held that "under the Convention, [petitioner] maintains all rights to the enforcement of this Arbitral Award that it would have in the absence of the Convention. Accordingly, the Court finds that, if the Convention did not exist, the [FAA] would provide [the petitioner] with a legitimate claim for enforcement of this arbitral award."[168] Having found no ground to deny recognition and enforcement of the award under the FAA, the court held that "as a matter of U.S. law, the award is proper."[169] **1.98**

More recently, however, a federal district court in New York vacated its own judgment granting recognition to an award made in Malaysia, on the ground that, subsequent to entry of that judgment, the competent Malaysian court had vacated the award. The court held that the Malaysian court judgment should be respected in the absence of extraordinary circumstances that would render non-recognition of the award a violation of fundamental U.S. public policy.[170] Although this has emerged as the dominant position in the United States, some judges are still reluctant to respect a foreign court's vacatur, where the foreign vacatur is perceived to prejudice a party's rights. For instance, a federal district court in New York confirmed a $400 million arbitral award in favor of COMMISSA, a Mexican subsidiary of the United States company KBR against PEMEX-Exploración y Producción, an instrumentality of Mexico, even though the award had been vacated at the arbitral seat in Mexico City.[171] The court found that the Mexican court had retroactively applied a Mexican law rendering certain types of claim non-arbitrable. The court **1.99**

of contravening 'public policy,' as that phrase is used in Article V of the Convention. Nor, unlike proceedings under Chapter 1 of the Federal Arbitration Act, can manifest disregard of law be urged as an independent ground for vacating an award falling within the Convention.").

[168] Chromalloy Aeroservices v. The Arab Republic of Egypt, 939 F. Supp. 907, 910 (D.D.C. 1996).

[169] *Id.* at 911. The impact of the *Chromalloy* decision has been curtailed by subsequent court decisions, as explained in Chapter 13.C.1(e).

[170] Thai-Lao Lignite (Thailand) Co. v. Government of the Lao People's Democratic Republic, 997 F.Supp.2d 214, 227 (S.D.N.Y. 2014).

[171] Corporación Mexicana de Mantenimiento Integral, S. de R.L. de C.V. v. PEMEX-Exploración y Producción, 962 F. Supp. 2d 642, 661 (S.D.N.Y. 2013).

found that because the law was not in force at the time the parties entered arbitration, it therefore interfered with the parties' legitimate expectations. As a result, the vacatur judgment "violated basic notions of justice" and the court confirmed the award and declined to defer to the Mexican court's annulment.[172]

4. Relevance of New York Arbitration Law to the Arbitral Award[173]

1.100 The New York arbitration statute expressly allows the parties to ask arbitrators to modify or correct their award under certain conditions.[174] The FAA is silent on the arbitrators' authority to modify their award. Federal trial courts in New York have held that those provisions of the New York statute are not preempted by the FAA,[175] including with respect to a Convention award.[176] This is consistent with the general understanding that preemption is generally triggered when state law impairs the enforcement of arbitration agreements and arbitration awards, not necessarily when state law purports to govern the arbitral process.[177]

1.101 Again, as a practical matter, federal courts have repeatedly held that a party's application to the arbitrators to have the award modified does *not* toll the three-month limitation to move to vacate an award under Chapter 1 of the FAA.[178] Accordingly, litigants must seek both remedies in parallel in order to preserve their right to move to vacate the award under the FAA while their motion to modify it is pending.

1.102 With respect to the time limit to move to vacate arbitral awards, the FAA requires that a notice to vacate be served on the other party within three months after receipt of the award,[179] while the New York statute requires an application to vacate to be made within ninety days after delivery of the award.[180] Federal courts in New York have generally applied the FAA and paid little attention to the New York rule. The Second Circuit nevertheless held, in a unique decision, that the New York ninety-day time limit applied to the filing of the motion, while

[172] At the time of publication of this book, the Mexican state oil company's appeal of this decision was pending before the U.S. Court of Appeals for the Second Circuit following oral arguments made on November 20, 2014. *See* Pemex-Exploración y Producción v. Corporación Mexicana de Mantenimiento Integral, S. de R.L. de C.V., 13-4022 (2d Cir).

[173] *See supra* at Section C.

[174] NY CPLR 7509 and 7511. Parties may ask arbitrators to modify their award where (1) there was a miscalculation of figures or a mistake in the description of any person, thing, or property referred to in the award; or (2) the arbitrators have awarded upon a matter not submitted to them and the award may be corrected without affecting the merits of the decision upon the issues submitted; or (3) the award is imperfect in a matter of form, not affecting the merits of the controversy.

[175] Pine Valley Productions v. S.L. Collections, 828 F. Supp. 245, 248 (S.D.N.Y. 1993).

[176] Spector and Specurity Ind. Ltd. v. Torenberg, 852 F. Supp. 201, 206–07 (S.D.N.Y. 1994).

[177] *Pine Valley Productions*, 828 F. Supp. at 248 (citing *Volt Info. Sciences*, 489 U.S. at 476–77).

[178] *Thyssen Carbometal Co.*, 1990 U.S. Dist. LEXIS 427, at *8–9; *Fradella*, 183 F.3d at 20; *Oberwager*, 2007 WL 4322982, at *5.

[179] 9 USC §12.

[180] N.Y. CPLR §7511.

the three-month deadline applied to service of said motion on the other side.[181] Litigants should therefore be careful to comply with both deadlines.[182]

F. EFFECTIVE GOVERNING LAW CLAUSES

Agreements to arbitrate are almost always found as a clause or section of a much larger commercial contract between the parties. Such commercial contracts ordinarily have governing law provisions that may govern, among other things, the formation, execution, performance, termination, interpretation, and enforcement of the contract. Depending on how broadly the governing law provision is drafted, it may govern disputes arising out of or relating to the contract as well, such as related tort claims like fraud. These governing law clauses should be drafted with more care than is often provided during contract negotiations.[183] **1.103**

The arbitration clause within the larger commercial contract rarely specifies its governing law. This leaves open the question whether, for instance, the parties intended the contract's overall governing law provision to apply, or whether the law of the seat should apply to the arbitration clause. Because of the unique nature of the FAA's application over state arbitration law, this is a thorny issue in the United States. For instance, if the underlying contract provides a broad governing law provision applying New York state law to the contract and all its terms, does that indicate the parties' intention to displace the FAA entirely in favor of state arbitration law? The answer is no, but with a caveat, according to a line of New York state case law. Even though federal courts have refused to follow this line of law, and parties to a New York or Panama Convention arbitration will have access to federal court, this line of state cases is important to understand and sheds additional light on the inherent tension between the FAA and New York state arbitration law.[184] **1.104**

New York federal courts have held, as have most U.S. federal courts, that a general governing law clause in a commercial contract does not indicate the parties' intention to displace the FAA. In a leading U.S. Supreme Court case, *Mastrobuono v. Shearson Lehman Hatton Inc.*,[185] a securities broker's contract with its customer provided for New York law to govern and that all disputes were to be arbitrated in New York under the rules of the National Association of Securities Dealers (NASD).[186] The issue in the case was whether the arbitrators could award punitive damages, something arbitrators could not do under **1.105**

[181] Hakala v. J.P. Morgan Securities, Inc., 186 Fed. Appx. 131, 133 (2d Cir. 2006).

[182] *See* Chapter 13.B.1 of this book.

[183] The drafting of arbitration clauses is discussed in more detail in Chapter 3.

[184] *See* 2 N.Y.Prac., Comm. Litig. in New York State Courts 12:14 (West 2d ed.) (description of issue generally under New York law).

[185] Mastrobuono v. Shearson Lehman Hatton Inc., 514 U.S. 52 (1995).

[186] The NASD is now known by the acronym FINRA.

New York arbitration law, but were allowed to do under the FAA. The Supreme Court found that the contract did not explicitly adopt New York arbitration law and explicitly adopted NASD rules, which do not restrict an arbitrator's ability to award punitive damages. The Court held that the contract was ambiguous and that such ambiguity must give way to the federal policy in favor of arbitration and the FAA. The Court held that the award including punitive damages should have been enforced.

1.106 The Court sought to distinguish its 1989 decision in *Volt*, where the Court gave some deference to the California Supreme Court's interpretation of its own state law.[187] The decision in *Volt* also merely delayed an arbitration, whereas in *Mastrobuono* the arbitrators would have been forever denied the ability to render punitive damages. Finally, the agreement in *Volt* was truly at arm's length and a stronger argument could be made that the parties intended California law to apply, whereas in *Mastrobuono* the agreement was a standard-form NASD agreement that required arbitration of all disputes with brokerage customers.

1.107 Subsequent federal decisions have further clarified the matter. New York federal courts, for instance, have held that a general governing law clause in a contract does not indicate that the parties intended that law to govern the arbitration clause itself in place of the FAA.[188] That is, a New York governing law clause found in the underlying contract does not govern the arbitration clause if that clause would otherwise be governed by the FAA, unless the parties show a clear indication that they intended New York state arbitration law to govern in place of the FAA.

1.108 New York federal courts have rejected an interpretation of the FAA by New York state courts on a related matter. The New York Court of Appeals, New York's highest state court and the highest judicial authority on matters of New York law, has held that where a governing law clause states that New York law governs the contract "and its enforcement," the FAA does not preempt New York arbitration law requiring that statutory time limits be decided by a court, not an arbitrator, in the first instance.[189] New York courts have applied this analysis beyond the

---

[187] *Mastrobuono*, 514 U.S. at 60 n.4.

[188] *Goldman Sachs*, 2007 WL 1467430, at *4; *Painewebber*, 81 F.3d at 1198; Coleman & Co. Sec., Inc. v. Giaquinto Family Trust, No. 00 Civ. 1632 (DC), 2000 WL 1683450, at *2–4 (S.D.N.Y. Nov. 9, 2000); *see also* Matter of Smith Barney Shearson v. Sacharow, 91 N.Y.2d 39, 47 (N.Y 1997).

[189] *See* Matter of Smith Barney, Harris Upham, & Co. v. Luckie, 85 N.Y.2d 193, 206 (N.Y 1995); *Diamond Waterproofing Systems*, 4 N.Y. 3d at 253 ("A choice of law provision, which states that New York law shall govern both 'the agreement and its enforcement' adopts as 'binding New York's rule that threshold Statute of Limitations questions are for the courts.' ") (*quoting Luckie*, 85 N.Y. 2d at 202); *see also* Imclone Systems Inc. v. Waksal, 802 N.Y.S. 2d 653, 654 (N.Y. App. Div. 2005) (finding FAA not displaced because generic governing law provision did not include "enforcement"); *In re* Edward D. Jones & Co., 10 Misc. 3d 1057(A), 809 N.Y.S. 2d 481, at *2 (N.Y. Sup. Ct. 2005) (failure to include "enforcement" in governing law clause meant that statute of limitations issue for arbitrator under FAA rather than for court under New York state arbitration law); Kelly

arbitrability of a statute of limitations issue.[190] However, as previously mentioned, New York federal courts have refused to follow this line of New York state cases.[191]

Unfortunately, the federal appellate court in New York has added another level of complexity regarding the applicable law of arbitration. In *Security Insurance of Hartford v. TIG Insurance*, the parties included a generic California governing law provision in their agreement. The Second Circuit attempted to determine how a California court would interpret the parties' intent with respect to the scope of the governing law provision and found that unlike New York governing law provisions, which are read narrowly, California law reads such provisions broadly.[192] Thus, sophisticated parties would have intended that such a governing law provision would include the entire agreement, including the arbitration clause, and displace the FAA in favor of California arbitration law.[193] This case is a reminder of the importance of careful drafting and understanding the impact of selecting a particular governing law. **1.109**

Depending on the specific circumstances of individual transactions, parties may wish to consider addressing some of these uncertainties by stating as clearly as possible in their arbitration agreement that the parties intend for the FAA to apply to all aspects of the arbitration to the exclusion of any inconsistent state laws. If the parties wish for New York state arbitration law to apply in place of the FAA, they must say so expressly and clearly in the arbitration clause itself to avoid any ambiguity.[194] These decisions, however, should not be taken lightly and should be made only after careful consideration of the potential unintended consequences of an overly detailed arbitration clause. Advice from counsel experienced in these matters when drafting the arbitration provisions is important to avoid surprises once a dispute arises. **1.110**

v. Oxford Health Plans (NY), Inc., No. 0602189/2007, 2008 WL 1710739 (N.Y. Sup. Ct. Mar. 19, 2008) (governing law clause stating it governs "in all respects" would include enforcement and therefore statue of limitations issue is for court, rather than arbitrator to decide).

[190] *See* Cohen v. S.A.C. Capital Advisors LLC, 11 Misc. 3d 1054(A), 815 N.Y.S. 2d 493, at *7 (N.Y. Sup. Ct. 2006) (refusing to order consolidation of arbitrations under New York arbitration law because governing law clause did not explicitly provide that New York law governed enforcement); Roberts v. Finger, 15 Misc. 3d 1118(A), 839 N.Y.S.2d 436, at *6 (N.Y. Sup. Ct. 2007) (governing law provision including enforcement showed parties' intent to apply New York, rather than FAA, judicial review standards for arbitral awards).

[191] *See Goldman Sachs*, 2007 WL 1467430, at *4 (holding that New York Court of Appeals' rulings in *Diamond Waterproofing Systems* and *Luckie* were contrary to and preempted by the FAA).

[192] Security Ins. Co. of Hartford v. TIG Ins. Co., 360 F.3d 322, 328–29 (2d Cir. 2004).

[193] *Id.* at 328.

[194] *See* Flagg v. Yonkers Sav. and Loan Ass'n, FA, 396 F.3d 178, 186 (2d Cir. 2005) ("While contracts may incorporate particular laws as contract terms, the contract must do so with specificity. General choice of law provisions do not accomplish this task."). Governing law provisions should be precisely worded or otherwise risk unintended effects. For example, it is not sufficient to state simply that both the FAA and New York state arbitration law will apply because the court may then seek to harmonize the two laws, rather than apply the preemptive effect of the FAA over inconsistent state law. *See, e.g., Coleman & Co. Sec.*, 2000 WL 1683450, at *4 (holding that the New York rule limiting arbitrators' authority to decide statute of limitations applied where second choice of law provision provided that both FAA and New York state law were to apply to any arbitration under the contract).

2

THE IMPACT OF U.S. LITIGATION

Oliver J. Armas and Thomas N. Pieper[1]

A. Introduction	2.01
B. Overview of U.S. Litigation	2.03
1. The U.S. Legal System: An Adversarial Model	2.04
2. Structure of Courts in the United States	2.08
3. Sources of the Law Governing U.S. Litigation	2.12
(a) The substantive law	2.13
(b) Rules of civil procedure	2.18
(c) Constitutions, rules of evidence, local court, and judge rules	2.21
(d) Ethical obligations and codes	2.24
4. Civil Procedure: A Guide to the Chronology of Litigation	2.26
C. Commencement of the Litigation	2.27
1. Pleadings: The Complaint and Answer	2.28
2. The Court's Authority to Oversee the Litigation: Jurisdiction	2.38
(a) Subject-matter jurisdiction	2.39
(b) Territorial jurisdiction	2.42
D. Procedural Calendar	2.44
1. Managing the Case	2.45
2. Pretrial Conferences	2.46
3. The Scheduling Order	2.50
E. Discovery: Establishing the Facts and Marshaling the Evidence	2.52
1. Discovery in the Adversarial Model	2.55
2. Rules, Methods, and Mechanisms of Discovery in U.S. Litigation	2.57
(a) Federal Rule of Civil Procedure 26	2.59
(b) Depositions, document requests, and third-party subpoenas	2.62
(c) The doctrine of privilege	2.64
3. Expert Discovery	2.68
4. Electronic Discovery	2.71
5. Using the Evidence: The Summary Judgment Motion	2.73
F. Pretrial Matters and Presentation of the Case	2.76
G. Decision and Judgment	2.83
1. Judgment in a Jury Trial	2.85
2. Judgment in a Bench Trial	2.89
H. Costs	2.92
I. Appeals: Challenging the Judgment	2.96
1. The "Final Judgment" Rule	2.98
2. Appeals to Higher Courts	2.99
3. Scope of Appellate Review	2.100
J. Conclusion	2.102

[1] This Chapter was prepared with the invaluable assistance of Samuel L. Zimmerman, a member of the International Dispute Resolution group at Hogan Lovells US LLP. The Hon. George Bundy Smith assisted with a prior version of this chapter.

A. INTRODUCTION

2.01 For lawyers from the United States, involvement in the field of international arbitration often follows or complements practice in litigation.[2] U.S.-trained lawyers acting as counsel or arbitrators in international arbitration will naturally bring with them into the arbitration certain expectations that flow from their U.S. litigation experience, which may differ from those of their non-U.S. trained colleagues. U.S. lawyers' expectations, their U.S. "litigation baggage," is a direct product of the adversarial model employed by the U.S. common-law legal system. In the adversarial model, the lawyers take control of the litigation as advocates, rather than the judge. U.S. lawyers are accustomed to lax pleading requirements in which the complaint that commences the action usually only sets forth the most basic allegations. U.S. litigators are highly involved in case management. They help the court develop the litigation schedule, and are empowered to seek redress if their opponent does not adhere to it. They typically conduct (sometimes extensive) discovery in which the lawyers seek to uncover crucial information regarding the underlying facts of the dispute from the opposing party or third parties. Such discovery includes depositions (sworn interviews of witnesses) and document requests. The lawyers will often learn that the case as pleaded is not the case that will ultimately go to trial because the facts uncovered through discovery alter the landscape of the litigation. They will often pursue early resolution of the case through dispositive motion practice. If trial is ultimately necessary, U.S. lawyers will expect to be able to prepare their witnesses for trial and that the evidence will be driven by witness testimony. Following trial, U.S. litigators will anticipate post-trial motions and appeals where the judgment may be altered or overturned and they will expect that each party will bear most of their own litigation costs with only certain exceptions. These expectations and practices are reinforced and facilitated by procedural rules designed to ensure that the litigation is orderly and fairly conducted. These rules serve as a road map into the U.S. litigation system.

2.02 In short, non-U.S. litigators should not be surprised if their U.S. counterpart expects that the lawyers will play a greater role in the arbitration, rather than the arbitrator. U.S. litigators will seek to be more involved in case management, feel greater entitlement to broad discovery, and prepare for a witness-oriented hearing. This chapter will provide an account of some of the salient aspects of the U.S. legal system that will help non-U.S. readers identify the impact of this background and the litigation baggage U.S. lawyers may bring to an international arbitration, by walking through the typical stages of a U.S. litigation and explaining how a U.S. litigator may approach and react during each. This chapter will also address baggage that U.S. lawyers may carry over from their experiences

[2] Many Latin American arbitrators, as a contrasting example, have a transactional background.

in domestic arbitrations, which includes a prior practice of arbitrators acting as advocates, and a legal climate where almost any dispute is actionable.

B. OVERVIEW OF U.S. LITIGATION

This section focuses on the basic steps involved in litigation within the U.S. It will endeavor to provide an overview of U.S. court litigation, with the goal of familiarizing those who have not been exposed to significant U.S. litigation with core litigation procedures. Accordingly, this section will break down U.S. litigation into its component parts, thereby giving the reader a window into the fundamental aspects, and the checks and balances of, the U.S. litigation process.[3] **2.03**

1. The U.S. Legal System: An Adversarial Model

The U.S. legal system is structured around an adversarial paradigm, which is the basis of both the federal and state court systems.[4] It is premised on the theory that justice is better served when the parties control the litigation. This results in the attorneys acting as the main driving forces behind the litigation, as advocates for the parties they represent.[5] **2.04**

By contrast, in civil law countries, the judge presiding over the case bears more responsibility in determining how the litigation proceeds and ultimately resolving the litigation. Judges in civil law systems accomplish this by actively conducting independent inquiries into the facts of a case and otherwise asserting more authority over the entire litigation process. Historically, in an adversarial system, the judge functions more as a referee or neutral observer and is mostly charged with regulating the proceedings when disputes between the parties make it necessary.[6] Except when judicial intervention is necessary, the judge remains content to let the lawyers run the show, and will normally only rule on matters affecting the case when the advocates make motions, objections, or otherwise **2.05**

---

[3] Later sections of this chapter will provide greater detail about certain aspects or steps in the process as they may have particular relevance when juxtaposed with international arbitration procedures.

[4] For discussion regarding the federal and state court systems, *see* Section B.2 of this chapter.

[5] The *adversary system* is defined as "a procedural system, such as the Anglo-American legal system, involving active and unhindered parties contesting with each other to put forth a case before an independent decision-maker." Bryan A. Garner, Black's Law Dictionary (10th ed. 2014).

[6] Notably, in the domestic arbitration setting in the United States, there has been a shift away from having party-appointed arbitrators that function as advocates, and they are now required to provide neutral and objective oversight—similar to the role of judge in the U.S. litigation system. The exception to this current rule is the so called "Canon X" arbitrator. The Canon X arbitrator is allowed to be predisposed toward the party that appointed him or her, but must abide by all of the other ethical rules. *See* American Arbitration Association, *The Code of Ethics for Arbitrators in Commercial Disputes* (effective March 1, 2004).

petition the court. Generalizations and prior assumptions about the adversarial system are becoming less true today as judicial relief grows more expansive, and judges are empowered to function more actively in the litigation. For example, in New York, court rules, such as the Rules of the Chief Administrator of the Courts, spell out procedures for moving cases along expeditiously. Nevertheless, the underlying adversarial nature of the U.S. system remains its defining characteristic.

2.06 Much of the baggage that is carried by U.S. litigators is attributable to the adversarial model of the U.S. court system, as litigators within it are accustomed to being in control of the litigation to a degree not present in the civil law systems. In an adversarial system, to be assured that the litigation will be properly pursued, the attorneys themselves are charged with bearing the heavy responsibility for taking action to move the litigation forward in a favorable and competent fashion. This obligation includes attending and preparing for pretrial conferences, reviewing and producing relevant documents to the other party, identifying and taking depositions, preparing witnesses for testimony, deciding what dispositive motions to bring and legal arguments to make, deciding whether to settle, conducting examinations of witnesses at trial, raising objections and making arguments in open court, and determining what other evidence to present at trial.[7]

2.07 The fact that most cases never make it to trial furthers the predominance of counsel's actions as opposed to the court's intervention. Only a very small percentage of litigations in the United States actually proceed through every step of the process to terminate at the final judgment phase. A study by the National Center for State Courts (NCSC) revealed that the overall rate of cases disposed through trial was about 3 percent overall and 2 percent in contract cases.[8] That means that 97–98 percent of all civil cases are settled out of court by agreement of the parties prior to judgment. Even if the case makes it all the way through trial, the judge's role still remains relatively passive.[9] U.S.-trained arbitrators may likewise remain somewhat passive and expect counsel for parties in the arbitration to engage in more proactive advocacy.

2. Structure of Courts in the United States

2.08 The court system in the United States is bifurcated at the first and most fundamental level between the federal courts and the state courts.[10] Indeed, each and

[7] Even though the nature of the system is adversarial, a court may direct the parties to see if issues can be narrowed or if the case can be settled. *See, e.g.*, Fed. R. App. P. 33.

[8] *See* U.S. Department of Justice, Office of Justice Programs, *Civil Justice Survey of State Courts 2005*, at 9 *available at* http://www.bjs.gov/content/pub/pdf/cbjtsc05.pdf.

[9] Note that judges in criminal trials in New York may question the prospective jurors. N.Y. C.P.L § 270.15 (McKinney 2014). Similar developments are taking place in civil trials as well.

[10] In both the state and federal governments, the court system represents one branch of a three-branched, or tripartite, form of government where each branch (judicial, legislative, and executive) acts as a check and balance on the others. This fundamental characteristic of U.S. government is known as the separation of powers.

every one of the fifty U.S. states (and the District of Columbia) has its own unique and autonomous legal system, operating parallel to the federal court system.[11] This structure—individual state courts and separate federal courts—originates from the U.S. Constitution and the sovereignty the states maintain under the Tenth Amendment. *See* U.S. Constitution Amendment X.

The court systems employed by most of the states are generally three-tiered, comprising a trial court level with numerous trial courts, an initial appellate court level with a few courts, and a court at the highest tier that is the court of last resort.[12] In New York State, for example, the trial courts, at the lowest tier, are known (somewhat confusingly) as the Supreme Court. The court of initial appellate review is the Appellate Division of the Supreme Court, which is divided into four departments (First, Second, Third, and Fourth) that hear appeals based upon geographical locations within the state. The New York State Court of Appeals, sitting in the capital at Albany, is at the top of the New York court system. Following a decision by the New York State Court of Appeals, a party may ask the Supreme Court of the United States to review the case under 28 U.S.C. § 1257.[13] **2.09**

The federal court system is similarly organized in this three-tiered structure. The district courts, scattered throughout the United States and its territories, function as the trial courts.[14] This is where judicial cases originate in the federal system.[15] At the second tier are the U.S. Court of Appeals courts, also known as the *circuit* **2.10**

[11] U.S. litigators normally practice in both state courts and federal courts and must be admitted or licensed by the bar of these respective courts. The choice to bring litigation in a state court or a federal court is often dictated by whether a particular court has jurisdiction, or authority, to hear the case. *See* Section C.2 *infra*. The U.S. Constitution and other federal statutes limit the jurisdiction of the federal courts. *See* Title 28, U.S.C. Part IV. By contrast, state courts have greater "general" jurisdiction to hear a wide array of disputes. If both a state and federal court has jurisdiction, then the decision which court to commence the action in becomes mostly tactical. As to jurisdiction related to arbitration matters (e.g., compel arbitration, enforce awards, etc.), see Chapter 6 and Chapter 7 of this book.

[12] For a detailed, interactive map of states' respective judicial systems, see the State Court Structure Charts published by the Court Statistics Project (CSP)—a joint project of the National Center for State Courts (NCSC) and the Conference of State Court Administrators (COSCA)—*available at* http://www.courtstatistics.org/Other-Pages/State_Court_Structure_Charts.aspx.

[13] In New York, as with other states, there are additional trial courts with more particularized functions than the Supreme Courts, such as family courts (resolving matrimonial matters), surrogates courts (dealing with probate and estates), and others. To the extent that this chapter references New York State courts, the focus of the discussion here is on the primary trial courts, the Supreme Court and the County Courts which have the broadest jurisdiction and are governed by New York Civil Practice Law and Rules. For more discussion regarding court jurisdiction, see Section C.2 of this chapter.

[14] There are 94 federal judicial districts, including at least one district in each state, the District of Columbia, and Puerto Rico. Three U.S. territories (the Virgin Islands, Guam, and the Northern Mariana Islands) have district courts that hear federal cases, including bankruptcy cases. The Administrative Office of U.S. Courts has published a printable map, available at www.uscourts.gov/file/document/us-federal-courts-circuit-map.

[15] There are a few exceptions, such as the review of federal administrative body rulings.

courts, of which there are eleven numbered courts, as well as the Court of Appeals for the District of Columbia, and the Federal Circuit,[16] all of which are responsible for initial review of the district courts' decisions. The U.S. Supreme Court rests at the apex of the federal judicial court system.[17] Although the federal courts have their own procedural laws (*see* Section B.3 *infra*), under the doctrine first established by the U.S. Supreme Court in *Erie Railroad Co. v. Tompkins*, 304 U.S. 64 (1938), when the federal courts have diversity jurisdiction (*see* Section C.2 of this chapter, *infra*, discussing jurisdiction), they apply the substantive common law of the appropriate state. This is not unlike the application of state or national substantive law in the international arbitration context, and U.S.-trained arbitrators and counsel will likely be accustomed to this practice.

2.11 Although the U.S. litigation experience can potentially involve each tier of the state or federal court system in which a particular case has been initiated, the lion's share of that experience will, with limited exception, take place at the lowest tier, trial-court level. It is at this level that the case moves through the main components of the litigation. The function of the middle- and top-tier courts is generally limited to review of what transpired at the trial court level for a determination of whether the trial court result was correct or whether it was in error. See, for example, N.Y. CPLR §§ 5501, 5601 (defining the scope of the appellate division's and Court of Appeals' review authority, respectively).

3. Sources of the Law Governing U.S. Litigation

2.12 There are multiple sources of law that govern U.S. litigation, including the substantive common law, rules of civil procedure, state and federal constitutions and statutes, rules of evidence, local court and individual judge rules, and ethical codes. All of these rules are designed to allow attorneys certain liberties in conducting the litigation, while also supplying needed checks and balances so that overzealous attorneys cannot run roughshod over an opponent. Fairness and justice work in favor of a structured litigation approach. The rules of civil procedure are the most important to understanding the core processes of U.S. litigation, although there are numerous other procedural rules that govern the U.S. litigation process and of which a litigant and his attorney must be aware in order to know how to interface properly with the court and with the adversary.

---

[16] Just as with the district courts, the numbered circuit courts are located throughout the United States and are responsible for review of the district courts within their legislatively assigned geographic areas. The Court of Appeals for the District Court of Columbia (the D.C. Circuit) reviews decisions from D.C.'s federal district court and, like all circuit courts, may also review administrative agency action. *See* 28 U.S.C. § 2342. The Federal Circuit handles appeals only on certain specific matters such as patent litigation and appeals from the Court of Federal Claims. *See* 28 U.S.C. § 1295.

[17] Notably, the U.S. Supreme Court may also hear appeals, at its discretion, from the states' highest courts. *See* 28 U.S.C. §§ 1251, 1253–54, 57–60.

(a) The substantive law While civil-law arbitrators are said to adhere more closely to the precise terms of a contract or statutory regime (and, thus, are sometimes labeled as "strict constructionists"), oftentimes U.S. arbitrators are said to look at underlying equitable considerations, i.e., trying to achieve the "fairest" result.[18] An explanation for this difference is that U.S. arbitrators are trained to apply the substantive law in a common-law system in which greater importance is placed on case law precedent and equitable outcomes. **2.13**

(I) THE COMMON LAW

Much of the law that determines the substantive outcome of U.S. litigation— which party is "right" and which is "wrong"—rests in the law known as the *common law*. This is the judicial form that traces its historical roots to England and is now practiced in most English-speaking countries today.[19] Under the common-law system, the rules of law and the substantive legal doctrines predominately reside in and originate from the outcomes of court cases, not from legislatively enacted statutes or constitutions. *See* GARNER, BLACK'S LAW DICTIONARY (10th ed. 2014) ("common law"). In other words, prior court cases function as precedents upon which subsequent courts can (and must) base their decisions. This concept is also known as the doctrine of *stare decisis*, which means that courts must follow earlier court decisions when the same legal points arise. *See* GARNER, LACK'sawDICTIONARY (10th ed. 2014) ("*stare decisis*"). The court's resolution of disputes through the adversarial model generates the common law, which is promulgated in the form of published court decisions. **2.14**

The court cases out of which this common law flows must be governed by definitive rules that clearly articulate the contours of the litigation and allow the parties to form reasonable expectations about how the litigation will proceed. The application of such rules is designed to provide the fairest and most just result for the parties, as the ultimate (and idyllic) goal of U.S. litigation is to obtain a truly equitable outcome.[20] **2.15**

(II) EQUITY

The U.S. legal system's focus on providing a fair or equitable outcome relates to a form of remedy developed by early English courts and known in the United States **2.16**

---

[18] Such generalizations are certainly not necessarily applicable to any particular arbitrator, and either approach may be better for a client, depending on the circumstances of the particular dispute in arbitration.

[19] *See* Siegfried H. Elsing and John M. Townsend, *Bridging the Common Law Civil Law Divide in Arbitration*, ARBITRATION INT'L, Vol. 18, No. 1 (2002). These historic English roots of the common law, in which terms and precedent are mostly in the English language, may be a reason why many U.S. litigators harbor an expectation that litigants, documents, and proceedings be in English. Of course, that expectation often goes unfulfilled in international arbitration.

[20] The U.S. litigator's focus on equity and arriving at what is "fair" likely remains an expectation for anyone with a U.S. litigation background operating in an arbitration context.

as *equitable relief*.[21] Courts developed equitable remedies when monetary damages were insufficient. Accordingly, in order to be entitled to an equitable remedy, such as an injunction, there must be the danger of "irreparable harm" that money damages cannot correct. *See Hoblock v. Albany County Bd. of Elections*, 422 F. 3d 77, 96–97 (2d Cir. 2005).

2.17 As this form of relief developed in the English courts, it initially resulted in the development of two parallel court systems—those of equity and those at law. The American colonies modeled their legal system on this bifurcated English system. The two systems soon merged into one single court that could handle both actions at law and actions in equity. However, because actions brought for equitable remedies had historically only been handled by a judge, under the Seventh Amendment of the U.S. Constitution the right to a jury trial only exists in "suits at common law," i.e., those that seek money damages. *See* U.S. Constitution Amendment VII.[22] Therefore, if the aggrieved party seeks only equitable relief, there is no constitutional right to a jury.[23] When both legal and equitable demands are asserted in the same action, however, the legal claims are tried by the jury.

2.18 *(b) Rules of civil procedure* Under most international arbitration rules, the arbitrators enjoy great freedom as to the procedural management and scheduling of the case. As long as certain minimum due process standards are observed, the arbitrators are relatively free to manage the arbitration however they deem appropriate under the circumstances of the arbitration in question.[24] In doing so, the

[21] It should be recognized that in U.S. litigation, seeking "equitable" relief does not mean that case-law precedent has less significance or effect. The basic characteristics of the common-law system persist in actions based in equity. It should also be noted that a U.S. court granting "equitable" relief is different from the arbitrator acting as an *amiable compositeur* or *ex aequo et bono. See, e.g.*, Article 21 of the International Chamber of Commerce (ICC) Rules; Article 31 of the International Centre for Dispute Resolution Rules.

[22] The Seventh Amendment does not provide a right to a trial by jury when in a state court, but almost all states have equivalent provisions in their respective constitutions. *See, e.g.*, N.Y. Const. art. I, § 2; *see also* N.Y. CPLR §§ 4101, 4102. In federal court, Federal Rule of Civil Procedure 38 requires that the party seeking the jury trial must serve a demand for such on the opposing party or the right is waived. Fed. R. Civ. P. 38(b), (d).

[23] The complexity of relief requested and other factors have resulted in the expansion of the right to a jury trial in U.S. litigation beyond the historical requirement that it be an action at common law. For discussion of what a "jury trial" entails, see Section F of this chapter.

[24] *See, for example*, Art. 20 of the ICDR Rules:

1. Subject to these Rules, the arbitral tribunal may conduct the arbitration *in whatever manner it considers appropriate*, provided that the parties are treated with equality and that each party has the right to be heard and is given a fair opportunity to present its case.
2. The tribunal shall conduct the proceedings with a view to expediting the resolution of the dispute. The tribunal may, promptly after being constituted, conduct a preparatory conference with the parties for the purpose of organizing, scheduling, and agreeing to procedures, including the setting of deadlines for any submissions by the parties. In establishing procedures for the case, the tribunal and the parties may consider how technology, including electronic communications, could be used to increase the efficiency and economy of the proceedings.

arbitrators are often inspired and guided by the procedural rules of their home jurisdiction, to which they are naturally accustomed. It is before this background that we now examine the procedural rules as applied in the United States.

The U.S. court system, from the federal to the state courts, employs detailed procedural rules which litigants, their attorneys, and, the courts themselves must follow. Appropriately, these positive procedural rules of civil litigation are generically referred to as the *rules of civil procedure.* **2.19**

Each state court system has its own respective rules of civil procedure. In New York, these rules are the New York Civil Practice Law and Rules (N.Y. CPLR).[25] In the federal judicial system, the Federal Rules of Civil Procedure (FRCP) govern the procedure of civil litigation. In most of the states and the federal courts these procedural rules are adopted and implemented through a formal process authorized by statute.[26] In a minority of states, including New York with the CPLR, the civil procedure itself is a statutory code. N.Y. CPLR § 102.[27] **2.20**

(c) Constitutions, rules of evidence, local court, and judge rules Aside from the common law and the procedural rules, there is a large body of legislatively enacted law, including the U.S. Constitution, state constitutions, and other regulations, that influence U.S. litigation and rules of civil procedure. Indeed, both the federal and state rules of civil procedure must adhere to federal and relevant state constitutions. **2.21**

In addition to their respective rules of civil procedure, the U.S. courts also employ other rules intended to guide the litigation process. Such rules and regulations include rules of evidence,[28] which govern how evidence is properly presented at trial for consideration by the trier of fact, and local court rules and procedures promulgated by and unique to the specific court in question.[29] Individual judges **2.22**

> 3. The tribunal may decide preliminary issues, bifurcate proceedings, direct the order of proof, exclude cumulative or irrelevant testimony or other evidence, and direct the parties to focus their presentations on issues whose resolution could dispose of all or part of the case.

[25] The N.Y. CPLR arbitration rules are discussed in Chapter 1 of this book.

[26] In the federal court system, the Rules Enabling Act authorizes the Supreme Court to make the federal courts' procedural rules. 28 U.S.C. §§ 2071–74.

[27] The N.Y. CPLR was first adopted in 1962 and it represents the primary source of the law of civil litigation in New York, and it succeeds the Civil Practice Act. *See* N.Y. CPLR § 101. The N.Y. CPLR governs the major New York trial courts—the Supreme Courts and the County Courts, while other courts, such at the surrogate's court, civil courts, and family courts, are subject to other legislation which is guided by the CPLR. *See, e.g.*, New York City Civil Court Act (commonly cited as CCA).

[28] The federal courts rely upon the Federal Rules of Evidence, which are entirely separate from the Federal Rules of Civil Procedure. Notably, New York State does not have a code of evidence. Although one was proposed a number of years ago, it was never adopted. New York does have some evidence rules, but they should not be taken as a code of evidence. *See* N.Y. CPLR art. 45.

[29] For example, the Supreme Court of New York County has its own Rules of the Justices, which provide the general rules for that court and the individual rules of the numerous justices

within the courts also utilize a personal set of rules that parties are to follow when the litigation has been assigned to that judge.[30] Among all of these rules are often detailed (and somewhat draconian) requirements regarding paper submissions presented to the court, including page and word limits, font and type requirements, restrictions on how a submission is to be bound or numbered, heading and subheading rules, and many others.[31] U.S.-trained arbitrators may utilize similar rules to help ensure that parties have equal opportunity to present their case. *See* ICDR Rules art. 20(1). Appellate-level courts also have their own procedural rules that govern how appeals are to be handled by such courts. See, for example, Federal Rules of Appellate Procedure. Parties in arbitration should not be surprised if a U.S.-trained arbitrator imposes detailed instructions regarding procedural matters.

2.23 Technological advancements have changed the way counsel and the court interface, and electronic filing of court papers has become increasingly the norm. Many courts have adopted procedural rules related to the proper ways for parties to submit papers electronically. New York State has implemented the New York State Court E-Filing (NYSCEF) system in many of its Supreme Courts.[32] Many international arbitration bodies, such as the International Centre for Dispute Resolution, also increasingly utilize electronic case management technologies and procedures.

2.24 *(d) Ethical obligations and codes* Another source of considerable baggage for U.S. lawyers is that they are expected to adhere to strict ethical standards that govern the way they interact with their clients, opposing parties, opposing counsel, the court, jurors, the media, former clients, and even their own colleagues. The American Bar Association and the states have adopted such ethical rules. *See* Am. Bar Ass'n, *Model Rules of Professional Conduct and Code of Judicial Conduct* (1992); *Disciplinary Rules of the Code of Professional Responsibility*, 22 NYCRR Part 1200 (New York).[33] These rules have been promulgated to help attorneys

that preside within it. *See* New York County, Supreme Court, Civil Branch, Rules of the Justices (as amended), *available at* http://www.nycourts.gov/courts/1jd/supctmanh/Uniform_Rules.pdf.

[30] The rules of individual courts and judges cannot alter or vary the overarching rules of civil procedure that govern all the courts of the court system in which such courts or judges operate. Nevertheless, there can arise some confusion for litigants and their attorneys when the idiosyncratic rules of a particular court or a particular judge vary greatly from those of another court with which they are more familiar.

[31] *See, e.g.*, Local Rules of the United States District Courts for the Southern and Eastern Districts of New York (as amended), *available at* http://www.nysd.uscourts.gov/rules/rules.pdf. These rules vary from court to court, and failure to abide by the court's regulations can result in the rejection of a submitted paper (and much embarrassment for the guilty attorney).

[32] *See* NYSCEF, https://iapps.courts.state.ny.us/fbem/mainframe.html.

[33] Violations of state ethical rules can result in serious sanctions or penalties for violators, including suspension of an attorney's license to practice or even disbarment. The risk of such penalties provides a strong incentive for attorneys to adhere to the ethical obligations imposed by their respective state rules or codes, and also can have significant impact on how or whether an attorney chooses to proceed with a particular litigation or party.

and their clients understand what is expected of attorneys as representatives of and advocates for those clients, as well as to make certain that attorneys treat one another (and the judicial process) with the proper respect and decorum. These rules include the important obligation to avoid conflicts of interest (including when representation of one client is adverse to the representation of another) and to provide clients with zealous and competent representation.

U.S. lawyers, in their roles as the litigation conductors, are obligated to advise the court of material facts and of controlling case precedent so that the court can make informed rulings about the case. *See* 22 NYCRR § 1200.37 (Disciplinary Rules). This includes those court rulings that are adverse to the party's position. Another important ethical responsibility is to avoid ex parte communications with the court. This means the opposing party must be copied in on any letters to the court or otherwise be privy to communications with the court, so that each party has a fair opportunity to be heard. *See* 22 NYCRR § 1200.41. U.S. litigators expect these discrete ethical obligations to be followed in the arbitration context, and would feel uncomfortable with, for example, ex parte communications with an arbitrator. Likewise, a U.S. arbitrator would react negatively if a party failed to identify relevant adverse case law that was directly on point. Instead, he would expect the party to have attempted to distinguish it or to explain why it should not be applied in the arbitration. **2.25**

4. Civil Procedure: A Guide to the Chronology of Litigation

Using the FRCP (and, when appropriate or otherwise noteworthy, the N.Y. CPLR) as our procedural roadmap,[34] the phases of the standard U.S. litigation can be classified and summarized as follows: **2.26**

- *Commencement of the Litigation*: To commence a lawsuit, the plaintiff files a "complaint" with the court (thereby obtaining an index number) and serves it (along with a summons) upon the defendant(s).[35] The complaint states the relief plaintiff is seeking (monetary or equitable) and provides, in numbered paragraphs, the general basis for why such relief should be granted. It is not necessary (other than in a few exceptions) to allege detailed facts or attach documents to the complaint.

  After being served with the complaint, the defendant will have a period of time, again set by the applicable civil procedure rules, to respond by filing and serving another pleading called the *answer* or, instead, by responding with a

[34] Of course, not all litigations proceed in identical fashion, and the rules of civil procedure in both the federal and state courts contemplate any number of ways in which a litigation could deviate from the more common path.

[35] *Service* or *service of process* is the act of formally delivering to the opposing party the official document in question, such as the complaint. *See* Section C *infra*. In the United States, service is effected by the parties, not by the court.

dispositive motion.[36] In the answer, the defendant addresses all of the complaint's numbered paragraphs setting forth the basis for relief by (i) denying, or (ii) admitting the truth of the statement, (iii) stating that defendant does not have enough information to know if the statement is correct or not, or (iv) taking the position that the statement contains a conclusion of law to which no response is required. Again, the answer need not attach documents or written statements, but must only adhere to technical form requirements that do not mandate the inclusion of significant substantive materials.

- *Procedural Calendar*: Once the action has been commenced, and once it is clear that early dispositive motions will not dispense with the action, then the parties will begin to fashion a timetable under which the litigation will proceed.[37] The schedule is determined in large part by the parties' attorneys with supervision by the court. It is the attorneys' responsibility to propose a reasonable litigation schedule, while the judge must ensure that the schedule is followed. As the case proceeds, and circumstances change, the dates established in the scheduling order may be adjourned for good cause shown or when the parties agree.
- *Discovery: Establishing the Facts and Marshaling the Evidence*: After the schedule has been determined, the parties will begin the often labor-intensive process of gathering the facts that gave rise to and impact the claims brought in the complaint. This means that the case develops as it proceeds because as background information is acquired, the litigation takes shape accordingly. Discovery allows the parties to build their case and to avoid surprise. It is the attorneys' responsibility to actively seek discovery and to appropriately and timely respond to the discovery requests of the other party. This fact gathering is accomplished through several procedural mechanisms including document requests, depositions, subpoenas, and expert witness reports and disclosures, among others.[38]
- *Pretrial Matters and Presentation of the Case*: Once all the facts have been gathered and the discovery phase has come to a close, the parties are ready to move to the pretrial and trial portion of the litigation. The pretrial phase often entails one or both parties making a motion for the case to be resolved on the evidence gathered during discovery. *See* Section F *infra*. If the court determines that there are issues of fact for which a trial is required, then the litigants must engage in the trial process, which itself encompasses multiple stages with unique challenges.

---

[36] The most common early dispositive motions include the motion to dismiss the complaint (*see* Section C *infra*). Another major dispositive motion is the summary judgment motion, discussed in Section E.5 of this chapter.

[37] In New York, the filing of a lawsuit as such does not lead to a judge being assigned to the case, and thus does not cause a judge to intervene. Instead, a party must file a so-called Request for Judicial Intervention (RJI) to ask a judge to intervene in a case.

[38] *See* Section E of this chapter. Cases often settle before discovery is complete.

- *Decision and Judgment*: After the parties have had the opportunity to present all of their arguments and defenses at trial, the court or the jury will be charged with deciding which party should prevail based on the facts they have heard and the law that governs. In determining which party will prevail, the judge or jury must carefully consider all the evidence they have heard during the trial, and then must arrive at a fair and judicious outcome in light of the applicable legal doctrines.
- *Costs*: There are only nominal upfront court costs in U.S. litigation.[39] At the end of litigation, each party normally pays their own legal fees. Only under certain circumstances does the losing party pay the winning party's attorneys' fees. There are, however, certain costs that can be charged to the losing party under various federal rules and statutes.
- *Appeals: Challenging the Judgment*: After the judge or jury has reached a verdict and issued a decision, the losing party (or, under certain circumstances, a party that has not won everything it was seeking) may pursue a challenge of that decision in the form of an appeal to the second-tier review courts and, perhaps, eventually even to the top tier.

Greater detail regarding the salient points of these steps and the federal and New York civil procedure rules that govern them are discussed below.

C. COMMENCEMENT OF THE LITIGATION

Commencing an international arbitration is a relatively simple procedure. While terminology may vary, depending on the governing rules,[40] the method is basically the same: preparation of a modest paper that sets forth that the initiating party is invoking an arbitration clause or agreement and contains a brief description of the dispute and the relief sought is generally technically sufficient. Such an approach may be somewhat foreign in common-law systems where pleadings often require great detail. But for the U.S.-trained arbitrator, this simple, minimalistic approach is a familiar concept given the "notice pleading" standards, under which commencing litigation in the U.S. generally only requires filing and serving a complaint providing notice to the opposing party of the issues and basic facts to be litigated. **2.27**

[39] In the United States, the fees required to initiate an action are fixed, and do not increase when the plaintiff seeks greater monetary relief. The filing fee for an action in federal court is $350. *See* 28 U.S. Code § 1914. In the New York County Supreme Court, for example, the filing fee (to obtain an index number) is $210 (plus $65 if a jury trial is demanded), the fee for an RJI is $95, and the fee for any motion brought is $45. New York County, Civil Branch, Court Fees, *available at* http://nycourts.gov/forms/filingfees.shtml.

[40] *See* Art. 2 of the ICDR Rules: "Notice of Arbitration"; Art. 4 of the ICC Rules: "Request for Arbitration."

1. Pleadings: The Complaint and Answer

2.28 In federal court, the litigation begins when the plaintiff files a complaint.[41] The complaint, along with a summons (a form provided by the court that notifies the defendant that he is being hailed into court) must then be served, or formally delivered, to the defendant. Fed. R. Civ. P. 4 and 5.[42] The requirement of proper service of the summons and complaint is designed to ensure that the defendant is put on notice that the plaintiff has brought a claim and that he is to report to court.

2.29 The litigation must be initiated before a period of time, known as the statute of limitations, has expired, otherwise the lawsuit will be time-barred and the litigant will be unable to attain relief he otherwise might have won.[43] Although there has been debate, state statutes of limitations are often treated as substantive law rather than procedural. Accordingly, the federal courts, which do not have their own statutes of limitations, will borrow those of the states when not inconsistent with policies underlying federal law.

2.30 The complaint is a pleading that must be drafted in conformity with the rules of civil procedure, but it is not necessary (other than with a few exceptions) to allege detailed facts or to attach documents to the complaint. In the federal court system, the main requirement is that the complaint contain "a short and plain statement of the claim showing that the pleader is entitled to relief." Fed. R. Civ. P. 8(a)(2).[44] This simple drafting requirement is called *notice pleading*, the purpose of which is to provide the defendant with notice of the claims and defenses. This can lead to terse complaints containing the bare minimum required facts. The complaint need not provide any evidence (although some states require that for claims based on breach of contract, a copy of the contract

---

[41] In some states, the action is commenced upon the service, not the filing, of the complaint.

[42] In the federal courts, as well as in many states, service of the summons can be accomplished by an attorney or someone authorized by statute and designated by the attorney for service, and it may be done by mail. When serving an individual in the United States, Rule 4 incorporates by reference the service requirements of the state in which the district court is located or where service is made. Fed. R. Civ. P. 4(e). Note that service of the summons abroad must adhere to the Hague Convention on the Service Abroad of Judicial and Extrajudicial Documents. Fed. R. Civ. P. 4(f).

[43] The statute of limitations varies depending on the claim in question and the court in which the claim is to be brought. *See, e.g.*, N.Y. CPLR art. 2, "Limitations of Time." Of course, sometimes litigants commence the action only to find later that their action was already time-barred by the applicable statute of limitations when the defendant moves to dismiss the action. This is discussed later in this chapter.

[44] Fed. R. Civ. P. 10 sets forth the form requirements for the complaint (and the answer). Pleadings must have a caption, which is the official title of the action, and the allegations must be delineated in separate paragraphs "each limited to a single set of circumstances." Presenting the allegations in this way allows later pleadings to refer to the allegations by easily identifiable paragraphs. For certain types of claims, however, there are more particularized rules beyond simple notice pleading that must be followed. *See* Fed. R. Civ. P. 9. Pleadings can be amended to correct errors or to modify allegations if new facts are discovered. Fed. R. Civ. P. 15.

be attached to the complaint), and, often, the complaint does not even tell a complete story.

In sum, the complaint must only state the basis of the court's jurisdiction and the claim, and make a demand for relief. Fed. R. Civ. P. 8(a). With regard to the relief, however, there is no requirement that the plaintiff state a specific amount of damages he seeks as relief, other than to state that the amount exceeds some threshold number in order to show that the court has jurisdiction over the matter, such as $75,000 in federal diversity actions (*see* Section C.2(a), *infra*). Still, the complaint must state enough facts to demonstrate the basic elements of the claim, and it also must be sufficiently clear and unambiguous for the defendant to understand the basis for the complaint.[45] **2.31**

In responding to the complaint, the defendant must "state in short and plain terms its defenses to each claim asserted against it" and admit or deny the allegations, or state that it lacks knowledge to form a belief about the truth of the allegation. Fed. R. Civ. P. 8(b).[46] These statements will correspond to the delineated paragraphs in the complaint. If the answer fails to deny an allegation, with the exception of the amount of damages claimed, it is deemed admitted, but if no response is required, the allegation is deemed denied. Fed. R. Civ. P. 8(b)(6). Therefore, in responding to allegations, the safer practice is for the answer to deny the allegation (to the extent denial can be done in good faith), or else risk possibly harmful admission. This differs from the practice under some arbitration rules where failure to respond expressly to an allegation is treated as a denial, not an admission. **2.32**

The answer must also include defenses, called *affirmative defenses*, in which the defendant raises new facts or arguments that will defeat the plaintiff's claims, even if all the allegations of the complaint are also true. The federal rules provide a list of these defenses, which include, for instance, estoppel, laches (delay in bringing claim without good cause), and statute of limitations. Fed. R. Civ. Pro. 8(c). If the answer fails to assert such defenses, then they will be deemed waived. In addition, the answer may assert counterclaims against the plaintiff, which are subject to the same requirements as the complaint. The plaintiff must likewise answer as Rule 8 instructs. The terseness and simplicity of pleadings in U.S. litigation also means that an arbitrator with a U.S. litigation background will not be shocked by, and may even expect, a demand for arbitration that is not comprehensive or detailed. Nevertheless, while the claimant may not be *obligated* to submit such detail, the arbitrator will certainly appreciate a cohesive story, and **2.33**

[45] If a complaint is overly vague or ambiguous, the defendant can move for a more definite statement under Fed. R. Civ. P. 12(e).

[46] The defendant may also take the position that the statement made in the complaint contains a legal conclusion to which no response is required.

the claimant may not have another opportunity to tell his story as he can in the statement of claim.

2.34 In lieu of answering the complaint, the defendant may respond with a dispositive motion to dismiss the complaint on the ground that there exists some defect. *See* Fed. R. Civ. P. 12(b), *see also* N.Y. CPLR § 3212. Grounds for such motions include:

(1) lack of subject-matter jurisdiction (i.e., the court is not authorized to hear the case);
(2) lack of personal jurisdiction (i.e., the court has no authority over the defendant);
(3) improper venue;[47]
(4) insufficient process (i.e., the document itself does not meet the requirements of Rule 4(a)(1));
(5) insufficient service of process (defendant asserts that the complaint was not properly served under Rule 4);
(6) failure to state a claim upon which relief can be granted (defendant argues that even if all the allegations contained in the complaint are true, they are insufficient to entitle the plaintiff to any relief);
(7) failure to join a party under Rule 19.[48]

2.35 Failure to bring a Rule 12(b) motion on grounds of lack of personal jurisdiction, improper venue, insufficiency of process, or insufficiency of service prior to answering the complaint will result in their waiver and the defendant will be unable

[47] Another motion that is similar to a motion for change of venue, in that it also alleges that the selected court is improper, is called the motion for "*forum non conveniens.*" In these motions, the defendant argues that although the court may technically have jurisdiction, there is another court before which the case would be more appropriately held.

[48] Fed. R. Civ. P. 19 mandates that certain persons (or entities) be joined or brought into the litigation as a "required party" if doing so would not destroy the subject-matter jurisdiction of the court. Fed. R. Civ. P. 19(a)(1). Such persons should be made part of the litigation because, in their absence, the court could not provide complete relief to the existing parties, or the person to be joined has an interest in the action such that the person's absence would impair the person's ability to protect the interest or leave an existing party at risk of incurring multiple or inconsistent obligations. Fed. R. Civ. P. 19(a)(1).

Third parties may also enter the litigation through other mechanisms. These include impleader, where the plaintiff or the defendant serves a third-party complaint on an outsider, forcing the outsider to join the litigation. Fed. R. Civ. P. 14. Another method is by intervention, where an outside party petitions to come into the litigation because the outsider has some interest or right that will be affected by the litigation. Fed. R. Civ. P. 24. The underlying goal of the ability to bring multiple parties into the same action when their claims are related is that it provides for greater judicial economy by allowing the courts to dispense with multiple disputes simultaneously. The type of litigation wherein the largest numbers of parties may participate is the class action suit allowed under Fed. R. Civ. P. 23. These are actions in which many individuals claiming to have been injured by the same or similar conduct by a single or a few defendants bring their claims together in one single, omnibus action. Many states also have procedures allowing for class action suits. *See, e.g.*, N.Y. CPLR art. 9.

to raise them later in the litigation. Fed. R. Civ. P. 12(g), (h)(1). If these motions are denied, the defendant must answer the complaint.

Pleadings, and other written papers submitted to the court, are subject to signature requirements under Rule 11, which mandates that at least one attorney of record sign the pleading (or the party, if unrepresented by counsel). Failure to sign will result in the court striking the pleading. Fed. R. Civ. P. 11(a).[49] Presenting a signed paper to the court serves as a representation that "to the best of the person's knowledge, information, and belief" it is not presented for an improper purpose (such as to harass, cause unnecessary delay, or needlessly increase the cost of litigation); the claims and defenses are warranted by existing law or by a nonfrivolous argument for modifying existing law; the factual contentions have evidentiary support (or will likely have evidentiary support after discovery); and the denials are warranted on the evidence or information known. Fed. R. Civ. P. 11(b)(1)–(4). Bringing frivolous claims, making known false representations to the court, or otherwise violating Rule 11 can result in serious sanctions, including an order to pay the other party's reasonable attorneys' fees. Fed. R. Civ. P. 11(c). Although sanctions for frivolous claims or false representations may not be available in arbitration per se,[50] arbitrators will rightly hold the parties to that standard. A party that fails to meet that standard will surely lose valuable credibility with the arbitrator, perhaps the most important asset in an international arbitration. **2.36**

The relatively lax notice pleading requirements, and the accepted minimal approach in submitting the answer to the complaint, is the reason the subsequent discovery phase is so crucial to the overall U.S. litigation process. *See* Section E of this chapter, *infra*. **2.37**

2. The Court's Authority to Oversee the Litigation: Jurisdiction

In order for a U.S. court to have authority to oversee an action, that court must have jurisdiction. The jurisdictional requirement takes two forms: subject-matter jurisdiction and territorial jurisdiction. **2.38**

(a) Subject-matter jurisdiction A court has subject-matter jurisdiction when it is competent to hear the case, having been vested with authority over the type of matter or claim being asserted. State court systems in the United States **2.39**

---

[49] Under local court rules, some papers may be submitted electronically with an electronic signature. Discovery documents, such as requests and disclosures, must also be signed pursuant to Rule 26. Fed. R. Civ. P. 26(g).

[50] But note that a U.S. appellate court in New York affirmed an award for attorneys' fees, arbitrator's fees and costs as a "sanction" for failing to arbitrate in good faith, despite a provision in the underlying contract that each party would bear its own expenses. *See ReliaStar Life Insurance Co. of New York v. EMC National Life Co. ("ReliaStar")*, 564 F.3d 81 (2d Cir. 2009); Wilkinson/Pieper, Arbitrators Have the Power to Award Fees and Costs Notwithstanding Contractual Provision Providing that Each Party Bear its Own Expenses, *International Bar Association's Arbitration News*, Vol. 15, No. 1.

typically have a court of "general jurisdiction" that has broad competence with few limitations.[51] General-jurisdiction courts are also normally the courts of original jurisdiction, meaning that they are the courts in which actions are first brought. Courts of appellate jurisdiction predominately hear cases that have been brought up from courts of original jurisdiction on appeal.

2.40 In the federal system, Article III of the U.S. Constitution defines the subject-matter jurisdiction of the federal courts and further provides authority to Congress to establish inferior courts (*i.e.*, those courts beneath the U.S. Supreme Court). District courts are the courts of original jurisdiction in the federal system. The exception is that the U.S. Supreme Court has original jurisdiction over cases affecting ambassadors or other foreign officials and those in which a U.S. state is a party. *See* 28 U.S.C. § 1251. Federal courts have original jurisdiction over cases arising under the Constitution or other laws of the United States (federal question jurisdiction); over admiralty and maritime cases; over controversies in which the United States itself is a party; over cases between citizens of different states (diversity jurisdiction); over cases between citizens of the same state claiming lands under grants of different states; over cases between a state or its citizens and foreign states or their citizens; and over bankruptcy cases.[52] There are two special trial courts with nationwide jurisdiction over certain types of cases: (1) the Court of International Trade, located in New York City, addresses cases involving international trade and customs issues; and (2) the U.S. Court of Federal Claims has jurisdiction over most claims for money damages against the United States, disputes over federal contracts, unlawful takings of private property by the federal government, and a variety of other claims against the United States.

2.41 The litigation in federal courts is most commonly based on federal-question or diversity jurisdiction. Note that in diversity cases, however, there must be complete diversity between the parties (i.e., none of the plaintiffs can share citizenship of a state in common with any of the defendants)[53] and the amount in controversy must exceed $75,000 in order for the federal court to have jurisdiction. 28 U.S.C. § 1332(a).

2.42 *(b) Territorial jurisdiction* The state courts must possess territorial jurisdiction in order to satisfy the requirements of the Due Process Clause of the Fourteenth Amendment, while the federal courts must abide by the Due Process Clause of the Fifth Amendment. In essence, this means that in order for the court to

[51] In New York, the court of general jurisdiction is the Supreme Court, which handles the majority of civil and criminal actions in New York.

[52] Bankruptcy courts are separate units of the district courts. Bankruptcy cases cannot be filed in a state court.

[53] There is no diversity jurisdiction if none of the parties is from the United States. This leads to the perhaps surprising result that, unless there is some independent federal jurisdiction, two non-U.S. parties can sue each other only in state court, not in federal court.

exercise some authority over a person such that that person is bound by its rulings, that person must have some minimum contacts with the territory in which that court sits. *See World-Wide Volkswagen Corp. v. Woodson*, 444 U.S. 286, 291–92 (1980).

There are three historical ways in which the court can satisfy the territorial jurisdiction requirement. It may have *in personam* jurisdiction over the defendant himself. This type of jurisdiction can be found when the defendant is domiciled in the territory in question, has engaged in business in the territory, or committed a wrong in the territory that gives rise to the action. Most states have enacted "long-arm" statutes, which establish the circumstances under which courts within the state can properly and constitutionally exercise *in personam* jurisdiction over individuals outside the state. In addition to *in personam* jurisdiction, due process may be satisfied if the court has *in rem* or *quasi in rem* jurisdiction. See, for example, N.Y. CPLR § 302. For *in rem* jurisdiction, the court has authority over some thing or property that is located within the forum and its adjudication as to that property has effect as to any person that may have had a right or interest in that property, no matter where the person may be. Similarly, with *quasi in rem* jurisdiction, the court exercises authority over some thing, or "*res*," present in the territory, but it can also be used as a device to adjudicate personal obligations of specific individuals outside the state. **2.43**

D. PROCEDURAL CALENDAR

Establishing a schedule for the arbitration is a valuable way for the arbitrator to exercise control over the proceedings.[54] U.S.-trained arbitrators and advocates will be particularly accustomed to scheduling orders designed to facilitate the expeditious resolution of the matter given that in the U.S. advocacy system, lawyers are charged with proactively assisting the court in developing and maintaining a litigation schedule. In the U.S. system where heavy case loads clutter and stall the dockets (i.e. the calendar of pending cases) in most courts, advocates recognize that case management is essential to the efficient and timely administration of justice. Even where cluttered dockets are of no concern, the appreciation for scheduling orders and vigilant case management will be applied equally in the arbitration setting. **2.44**

1. Managing the Case

Establishing a procedural calendar is crucial to any U.S. litigation because it helps ensure that the parties (and their counsel) move through the various litigation **2.45**

[54] *See, e.g.*, Article 24 of the ICC Rules; Article 20(2) of the ICDR Rules.

phases expeditiously. Heavy workloads for both the courts and the attorneys, along with the frequent and growing complexity of U.S. litigation, can cause delay in the progress of the action. In response, the overburdened system has led courts to the "managerial judge" approach.[55] This managerial approach, fostered by the application of procedural rules discussed later, is one in which the judge is encouraged to set clear timetables for the litigation and to exercise increased supervision. Still, the adversarial nature of the U.S. system continues to cling to the expectation that counsel will be proactive in helping the court determine the litigation schedule. This occurs by conducting an analysis of how much discovery will be required, what issues will be tried, what motions will be made, and other issues. Attorneys must remain diligent because U.S. courts have a low tolerance for lethargic case prosecution, and may even dismiss actions that are not being pursued any further. See, for example, N.Y. CPLR § 3404.

2. Pretrial Conferences

2.46 The FRCP contain two primary rules governing the issuance and the purpose of a litigation schedule—Rule 16(b) and Rule 26(f).[56] Of these rules, Rule 16 is the overarching federal rule addressing pretrial conferences, scheduling, and calendar management.[57] These help the parties and the court determine an appropriate calendar for the action in question.[58]

2.47 One key way in which the court can oversee the progress of the case is by holding pretrial conferences. Fed. R. Civ. P. 16(a), (c). These conferences are attended by the attorneys (and, occasionally, the parties themselves) with a trial judge or magistrate judge[59] present to direct and mediate the meeting. Although a judge is present, it remains the attorneys' duty to prepare adequately for the conference such that they can properly advise the court. *See* Fed. R. Civ. P. 16(f).

2.48 Rule 16(a) identifies the various purposes of pretrial conferences as follows: "(1) expediting disposition of the action; (2) establishing early and continuing control

---

[55] Although there are procedural rules in place for establishing and maintaining a tight litigation calendar, there can be great disparity in how effectively the courts can manage their cases, particularly when the court in question is exceptionally busy or when cases are uniquely complex.

[56] Rule 29(b) is also relevant in that it requires court approval if discovery would interfere with the scheduling order issued pursuant to Rule 16(b).

[57] Rule 16(e) deals with the final pretrial conference, as discussed in Section F of this chapter.

[58] In the New York trial courts, N.Y. CPLR § 3401 authorizes the chief administrator of the courts to adopt rules regulating the calendar, which has been done with Uniform Rules for the New York State Trial Courts § 202.22. In addition, Uniform Rules of Trial Courts § 202.26 sets forth the pretrial conference requirement. These rules function similarly to Rule 16 of the Federal Rules and allow the judge to "establish such calendars of cases as the judge shall deem necessary or desirable for proper case management." 22 NYCRR § 202.22(a).

[59] Federal magistrate judges are appointed by district court judges to serve in a U.S. district court for eight years. Magistrate judges are authorized to handle trials on consent of the parties or other matters with oversight by a district judge. *See* Federal Magistrate Judges Association, http://www.fedjudge.org/.

so that the case will not be protracted because of lack of management; (3) discouraging wasteful pretrial activities; (4) improving the quality of the trial through more thorough preparation; and (5) facilitating settlement." Fed. R. Civ. P. 16(a). In the federal courts, there has been a push toward settlement as a main goal of the pretrial conference, although generally improving the quality and simplifying the trial process is also valued.[60] In order to provide the court with broad pretrial conference authority to meet these goals, Rule 16 sets forth a host of matters appropriately considered at pretrial conferences, including: "formulating and simplifying the issues and eliminating frivolous claims or defenses"; amending pleadings; "obtaining admissions and stipulations about facts and documents to avoid unnecessary proof, and ruling in advance on the admissibility of evidence"; determining if summary judgment is appropriate under Rule 56; controlling and scheduling discovery; settling the case; "adopting special procedures for managing potentially difficult or protracted actions"; "facilitating in other ways the just, speedy, and inexpensive disposition of the action"; and many others. Fed. R. Civ. P. 16(2)(c)(A)–(P).

When the court schedules a conference under Rule 16, it is mandatory that the **2.49** parties attend through an attorney authorized to make stipulations and admissions on their behalf. The court may even require that the party or a representative be reasonably available to consider possible settlement. Fed. R. Civ. P. 16(1).[61] Rule 16 also authorizes the court to hold a special "Final Pretrial Conference" as close to the trial date as possible and issue related orders. This topic is discussed in Section F of this chapter.

3. The Scheduling Order

In addition to pretrial conferences, Rule 16 mandates that the court issue **2.50** an order that will guide the timing of the litigation. Pursuant to Rule 16(b), the judge must issue the case scheduling order "as soon as practicable, but in any event within the earlier of 120 days after any defendant has been served

[60] The rule has been successful in facilitating settlements. The Advisory Committee Notes to the 1983 amendment to Rule 16 stated:

> In many respects, the rule has been a success. For example, there is evidence that pretrial conferences may improve the quality of justice rendered in the federal courts by sharpening the preparation and presentation of cases, tending to eliminate trial surprise, and improving as well as facilitating the settlement process ... Empirical studies reveal that when a trial judge intervenes personally at an early stage to assume judicial control over a case and to schedule dates for completion by the parties of the principal pretrial steps, the case is disposed of by settlement or trial more efficiently and with less cost and delay than when the parties are left to their own devices.

[61] If a party or its attorney fails to attend a pretrial conference without first obtaining permission from the court, that party may be sanctioned under Rule 16(f), and may be ordered to pay the associated costs incurred by the other party (e.g., attorneys' fees for cost of attorney wasting time preparing for the conference).

with the complaint or 90 days after any defendant has appeared." Fed. R. Civ. P. 16(b)(2). Prior to the court issuing the scheduling order, however, the parties must first attend a discovery conference. Fed. R. Civ. P. 26(f).[62] After the parties have attended the discovery conference and have had a chance to develop a general sense of how much discovery will be necessary and how the litigation should proceed relative to the parties' expected needs, the parties must then submit a report of their contemplated discovery plan to the court. Fed. R. Civ. P. 26(f); Advisory Committee Notes to the 1983 Amendment to Fed. R. Civ. P. 16. The report will help the court construct the scheduling order it issues under Rule 16.

2.51 The court has broad authority under Rule 16(b) to fashion a procedural calendar that makes sense for the litigation.[63] Importantly, the schedule can only be modified "for good cause and with the judge's consent." Fed. R. Civ. P. 16(b)(4). Courts usually grant permission to deviate from the scheduling order (know as "adjournment") only if and when there is good cause or the parties otherwise agree.

E. DISCOVERY: ESTABLISHING THE FACTS AND MARSHALING THE EVIDENCE

2.52 One of the areas where the civil-law and common-law traditions arguably differ the most is in the uncovering and taking of evidence. In the U.S. courts, the process by which parties exchange information (usually in response to a demand from the opposing party to supply such information) is known as *discovery*. In the United States, counsel depend heavily on discovery to develop their case and support their clients' arguments. Internationally, by contrast, the concept of *discovery* is often considered so taboo that it is more often termed *disclosure*. But over the years, international arbitration practitioners have tried to find some middle ground. The IBA Rules on the Taking of Evidence in International Commercial Arbitration[64] have been of significant help in that regard.

[62] For more detailed discussion regarding the discovery conference and other discovery procedures, see Section E of this chapter.

[63] Rule 16(b)(3) sets forth the required and permissible contents of the order. Fed. R. Civ. P. 16(b)(3). The order must limit the time to join other parties, amend the pleadings (*see* Section C *infra*), complete discovery, and file motions. The order may also: modify the timing of disclosures under Rule 26; modify the extent of discovery; provide for disclosure or discovery of electronically stored information; include any agreements the parties reach for asserting claims of privilege or of protection as trial-preparation material after information is produced. *Id.* at (B); *see also* Section E *infra*.

[64] The Revised IBA Rules in Taking of Evidence were adopted in May 2010, updating the IBA Rules of Evidence originally published in 1999 (which in turn had replaced the 1983 IBA Supplementary Rules Governing the Presentation and Reception of Evidence in International Commercial Arbitration).

The reality is that there has even been a general shift toward more discovery/disclosure in recent years. Electronic discovery (*see* Section E.4 *infra*) has also become more prevalent as it becomes the norm in U.S. litigation. Parties should remember that it is not discovery itself, but the abuse of discovery, that is the problem. As the shift toward more discovery continues, a better understanding of how the discovery process actually works in the U.S. is helpful to develop an appreciation of the potential benefits of broader discovery in the arbitration setting. **2.53**

This phase of the litigation process can be time-consuming and expensive, but it is essential. The facts gathered through this process are the evidentiary bricks that will build the parties' respective arguments. A party that is particularly successful in obtaining supporting evidence for its case may prevail in a pretrial motion for summary judgment or will have leverage to pressure the opposing party to settle the case favorably. **2.54**

1. Discovery in the Adversarial Model

With its lax pleading requirements, where only the most material facts are required in order to state a claim, U.S. courts have, by necessity, developed discovery procedures designed to help prevent surprise, preserve evidence that may not otherwise later be available at trial, and assist each party with the development of their case and arguments. In general, the trend has been to expand the area of material that is discoverable (i.e. which must be provided to the opposing party) in order to help the court and the parties more completely understand and refine the case. Although the ostensible goal is that discovery will help avoid surprise at trial and to make the outcome fair and just, the underlying adversarial model persists in exerting its influence. Parties continue to resist providing the other side with information when possible in order to maintain a tactical advantage at later stages of the litigation. This proclivity to resist discovery may lead to a contentious discovery phase that can delay the case and require significant intervention from the court. **2.55**

To balance against parties' desire to avoid disclosure when possible, the rules of civil procedure provide the court with authority to compel disclosure when a party is recalcitrant and, under certain circumstances, to impose sanctions for discovery failures. *See* Fed. R. Civ. P. 37. This authority underscores the importance of discovery in the U.S. adversarial system. **2.56**

2. Rules, Methods, and Mechanisms of Discovery in U.S. Litigation

In international arbitration, the general approach is that requests for the production of documents must be narrow and highly specific.[65] Broad disclosure ("any **2.57**

[65] Discovery in international arbitration is discussed in more detail in Chapter 9. The limited nature of discovery in international arbitration is illustrated by Article 3(3) of the IBA Evidence

and all documents") is generally disfavored, and the use of such language will often result in objections by the opposing party. Similarly, depositions are rarely taken in the international arbitration context.

2.58 Still, despite the general trend against broad disclosure in international arbitration, U.S.-trained arbitrators are accustomed to these types of discovery mechanisms and may be more inclined to allow them, particularly if both sides are represented by U.S. counsel. U.S.-style discovery may also arise in the context of 28 U.S.C. § 1782(a),[66] a federal statute allowing discovery in assistance to "a foreign or international tribunal."[67] In any event, a closer analysis may help the reader to understand the common expectations of a U.S. practitioner with regard to discovery.

2.59 *(a) Federal Rule of Civil Procedure 26* The Federal Rules of Civil Procedure contain several rules governing discovery in the federal courts. Predominant among these rules is Rule 26, which is a comprehensive rule addressing many aspects of the discovery process. *See* Fed. R. Civ. P. 26. The federal rules provide for a broad and far-reaching scope of discoverable material.[68] Rule 26(b) defines

---

Rules, which provides: "A Request to Produce shall contain: (a) (*i*) a description of a requested document sufficient to identify it, or *(ii)* a description in sufficient detail (including subject matter) of a narrow and specific requested category of Documents that are reasonably believed to exist; in the case of Documents maintained in electronic form, the requesting Party may, or the Arbitral Tribunal may order that it shall be required to, identify specific files, search terms, individuals or other means of searching for such Documents in an efficient and economical manner; (b) a statement as to how the Documents requested are relevant to the case and material to its outcome; and (c) *(i)* a statement that the Documents requested are not in the possession, custody or control of the requesting Party or a statement of the reasons why it would be unreasonably burdensome for the requesting Party to produce such Documents, and *(ii)* a statement of the reasons why the requesting Party assumes the Documents requested are in the possession, custody or control of another Party."

[66] "Assistance to foreign and international tribunals and to litigants before such tribunals: (a) The district court of the district in which a person resides or is found may order him to give his testimony or statement or to produce a document or other thing for use in a proceeding in a foreign or international tribunal, including criminal investigations conducted before formal accusation. The order may be made pursuant to a letter rogatory issued, or request made, by a foreign or international tribunal or upon the application of any interested person and may direct that the testimony or statement be given, or the document or other thing be produced, before a person appointed by the court. By virtue of his appointment, the person appointed has power to administer any necessary oath and take the testimony or statement. The order may prescribe the practice and procedure, which may be in whole or part the practice and procedure of the foreign country or the international tribunal, for taking the testimony or statement or producing the document or other thing. To the extent that the order does not prescribe otherwise, the testimony or statement shall be taken, and the document or other thing produced, in accordance with the Federal Rules of Civil Procedure.

A person may not be compelled to give his testimony or statement or to produce a document or other thing in violation of any legally applicable privilege." 28 U.S.C. § 1782(a).

[67] Since the U.S. Supreme Court left the issue open in Intel Corp. v. Advanced Micro Devices, Inc., 542 U.S. 241 (2004), it is not clear whether this language includes international arbitral tribunals. This is discussed in more detail in Chapter 9.G of this book.

[68] Many states, including New York, have also implemented procedural rules that create the presumption of discoverability with certain exceptions such as privileged information. *See* N.Y. CPLR § 3101.

what is discoverable in a federal litigation, stating that a party may discover any matter that is not protected by privilege (*see* Sub-sub-section (c)) and which is "relevant to any party's claim or defense" and is reasonably calculated to lead to the discovery of admissible evidence. Fed. R. Civ. P. 26(b)(1). In New York, discovery is governed by several procedural rules, and N.Y. CPLR § 3101 functions similarly to Rule 26 by establishing the scope of permissible discovery. It allows "full disclosure of all matter material and necessary in the prosecution or defense of an action, regardless of burden of proof." N.Y. CPLR § 3101(a). Under this language and corresponding New York case law, discovery in New York is broad.

Although there is the presumption of broad discovery under these standards, the court may nevertheless limit or otherwise restrict discovery when a party seeks a protective order for good cause shown under FRCP 26(c) in the federal system, and N.Y. CPLR § 3103 in New York. Under Rule 26(c), protective orders may be issued on such grounds as "annoyance, embarrassment, oppression, or undue burden or expense," but such orders are issued sparingly in light of the presumption of discoverability. **2.60**

In order to expedite the litigation process, Rule 26 also mandates that the parties provide certain basic information to each other in an *initial disclosure*, which must be done without awaiting a formal discovery request from the opposing party. Fed. R. Civ. P. 26(a)(1)(A). These disclosures are intended to provide the opposing side with the most fundamental facts about the case (which probably are not included in the pleadings). Initial disclosures might include, for example, the identity of individuals likely to have discoverable information and documents in the disclosing party's possession that may be used to support that party's claims or defenses. Fed. R. Civ. P. 26(a)(1)(A). This requirement compensates for the lack of information resulting from the lax notice pleading standards. Rule 26 also mandates that the parties attend an early discovery conference. Fed. R. Civ. P. 26(f).[69] *See also* discussion regarding Fed. R. Civ. P. 16, Section D, *supra*. **2.61**

(b) Depositions, document requests, and third-party subpoenas There are several discovery devices that are regularly used in U.S. litigation to obtain information from the opposing party. Other than the initial disclosures required under Rule 26, the discovery process generally involves each party submitting requests to the other party that define (typically in broad terms) the scope and nature of what they are seeking, or may specify a particular individual from whom they would like information. Once a party has been served with a discovery request, it is obligated to respond to that request completely and fully, and must continue to supplement with newly uncovered information if necessary. *See* Fed. R. Civ. P. 26(e). **2.62**

[69] Neither party may seek discovery from the opposing party until after the Rule 26(f) conference is held. *See* Fed. R. Civ. P. 26(d).

2.63 The main mechanisms for obtaining information from the opposing party are by taking depositions and issuing document requests or requests for production. See, for example, N.Y. CPLR § 3102 (naming methods of obtaining discovery under New York procedure). In addition, information that is relevant to the litigation may also be obtained from nonparties by attorney-issued third-party subpoenas. The most common discovery devices are:

- *Depositions*: These are interviews in which the witness testifies under oath in response to questions posed by the party seeking the discovery from the witness. The dialogue is officially recorded by a court reporter (and, if a party elects, also by video). Depositions give parties the important opportunity to find out what potential trial witnesses would say if they testified at trial. *See generally* Fed. R. Civ. P. 30. In addition, deposition transcripts can be used under certain circumstances at trial, such as to impeach the witness if he contradicts the deposition testimony. *See* Fed. R. Civ. P. 32; N.Y. CPLR § 3117(a) (listing uses of deposition testimony).
- *Requests for Production*: These are documents served upon the opposing party that compel the party to produce particular documents or materials relevant to the claims or defenses asserted in the litigation. *See* N.Y. CPLR § 3120. Such requests may be of a general or a specific nature, but must describe with "reasonable particularity each item or category of items to be inspected." Fed. R. Civ. P. 34(b)(1)(A).
- *Third-party subpoenas*: In order to compel third parties to produce documents or provide deposition testimony that is relevant to the proceedings, parties seeking such disclosure must utilize subpoenas issued by the court. See, for example, N.Y. CPLR § 3120 (subpoenas *duces tecum* for documents). These subpoenas direct third parties to submit to disclosure that they would otherwise not be required to make, insofar as they are not participants in the litigation. *See* Fed. R. Civ. P. 45(a). In the international arbitration setting, there is some authority under the Federal Arbitration Act to compel nonparties to provide testimony or other evidence, but that power is not nearly as robust as the power to subpoena. *See* 9 U.S.C. § 7; *see also Life Receivables Trust v. Syndicate 102 at Lloyd's of London*, No. 07-1197-cv, 2008 WL 497850 (2d Cir. 2008) (holding that the Federal Arbitration Act does not authorize an arbitrator to compel pre-hearing document discovery from nonparties to the arbitration).

2.64 *(c) The doctrine of privilege* Privilege is a protection against discovery requests that seek to uncover confidential communications or attorney work product. Since the civil-law system has such limited discovery to begin with, there was no need to develop the concept of privilege.[70] As such, there is a constant struggle in

[70] All legal systems, including civil law countries, however, have regulations regarding professional secrecy, including ethical obligations imposed by the local bar.

international disputes (and international arbitration is no exception) as to whether communications involving non-U.S. lawyers are privileged at all. A closer look at the U.S. conception and application of privilege is helpful in understanding this struggle and the importance of privilege when broad discovery is allowed.

The doctrine of privilege is an essential and virtually universal shield within the U.S. court system against expansive discovery. The concept of *privilege* includes, perhaps most importantly, the attorney-client privilege and the work-product doctrine. Federal courts adopt the privilege rules of the states through Federal Rule of Evidence 501, but the generic concept of privilege is referenced throughout the Federal Rules of Civil Procedure. See, for example, Fed. R. Civ. P. 26. Privileged information is exempt from discovery, acting to check or counterbalance the otherwise wide berth that attorneys have to seek discovery from the opposing party.[71] In New York, CPLR § 3101(b) provides that "privileged matter shall not be obtainable." **2.65**

The attorney-client privilege makes confidential communications between lawyers and their clients, in which lawyers provide legal advice, off limits. Indeed, attorneys are under an ethical obligation to maintain confidential any privileged communications they have had with their clients. Except in a few narrow circumstances, attorneys can only divulge such confidences if first given express permission from the client. See, for example, 22 NYCRR § 1200.19. The work-product doctrine guards documents or materials created by the lawyer that contain his mental impressions of the case prepared in anticipation of litigation. The work-product doctrine allows attorneys to work without fear that the material they produce in preparation for litigation will be subject to disclosure to their adversary unless the adversary can show substantial need for the material and that it cannot be obtained from other sources. *See* Fed. R. Civ. P. 26(b)(3); *see also* N.Y. CPLR § 3101(c) ("The work product of an attorney shall not be obtainable."). **2.66**

Privilege can be waived, however, and once privileged information has been divulged, privilege is likewise waived as to any communication regarding the same information.[72] This is an "all or nothing" approach that prevents parties from **2.67**

[71] Under Fed. R. Civ. P. 26(b)(5), whenever documents or other materials are withheld on the basis of privilege, a log must be created and provided to the other side which will allow the opposing party to evaluate the claim. If the requesting party has reason to believe that materials should not be protected by privilege, they may bring a motion to compel their production under Fed. R. Civ. P. 37. The court will then evaluate the documents *in camera*, or in private, to determine if indeed they are protected as privileged.

[72] In contrast to voluntary disclosure of privileged information, the impact of inadvertent disclosure and whether it results in complete waiver has been treated differently by various courts. Some courts treat this as waiver, while others do not. Still others look more closely to the particular circumstances of the disclosure to see if there has been a waiver. When privileged documents are inadvertently disclosed, the disclosing party must immediately notify the other party who must then follow the procedure outlined in Fed. R. Civ. P. 26(b)(5)(B), which is designed to safeguard the content of the material until the court can decide how the parties should proceed.

unfairly asserting the doctrine in order to gain a strategic advantage. For example, a party cannot selectively divulge only those communications that are helpful to the disclosing party's case, while claiming privilege over other related communications that may be harmful.

3. Expert Discovery

2.68 In international arbitration, the use of experts is widespread. Arbitrators rarely appoint independent experts, although permitted by most rules, such as Article 25 of the ICDR Rules. In most cases, the arbitral tribunal relies on the expert(s) retained by the parties—who are cross-examined by the other side and questioned by the arbitrators.[73] For a U.S.-trained arbitrator, utilization of experts by parties and the cross-examination of experts will be a familiar scenario given the frequent reliance on experts in U.S. litigation.

2.69 Just as in international arbitration, in much U.S. litigation the nature of the claims requires that an expert provide analysis to enable the party to prove its claim on the merits or to establish the amount of damages to be awarded. In order for the parties to be able to anticipate what their respective experts will present to the judge and jury, pretrial discovery is essential. In federal court, FRCP 26(a)(2) governs expert discovery, while CPLR § 3101(d)(1) controls in New York. In federal court, parties intending to use an expert witness must provide the other party with a written report that explains who the expert is and what conclusions he has drawn, among others. Fed. R. Civ. P. 26(a)(2)(B).

2.70 In U.S. litigation, a party may challenge the other side's expert's qualification to testify as an expert. This is usually done by way of a motion *in limine*. The court will then conduct a hearing—in federal court called a "Daubert challenge"[74]—to determine the validity and admissibility of the expert's testimony. The expert, subject to cross-examination by counsel, has to demonstrate that his or her methodology and reasoning are scientifically valid and can be applied to the facts of the case.[75] While *Daubert* hearings are sometimes used in U.S. domestic arbitration,

[73] A recent development in this area has been the practice of "hot-tubbing" in which opposing expert witnesses are heard together or even given the opportunity to question each other directly.

[74] The term stems from a 1993 U.S. Supreme Court case, Daubert v. Merrell Dow Pharmaceuticals, Inc., 509 U.S. 579 (1993).

[75] In *Daubert*, the U.S. Supreme Court articulated several factors for the admissibility of scientific expert testimony, including whether it can be, and has been, tested; whether it has been subjected to peer review and publication; its known or potential rate of error; the existence and maintenance of standards controlling its operation; and whether it is generally accepted in the relevant scientific community. *Daubert*, 509 U.S. at 593–94. In Kumho Tire Co. v. Carmichael, the U.S. Supreme Court extended *Daubert's* general holding to non-scientific expert testimony. Prior to *Daubert*, the so-called *Frye* test provided that expert opinion based on a scientific technique is admissible only where the technique is generally accepted as reliable in the relevant scientific community. *See* Frye v. United States, 293 F. 1013 (D.C. Cir. 1923). The *Frye* test is still applied by several state courts, including New York. *See* Giordano v. Mkt. Am., Inc., 941 N.E.2d 727, 733 (N.Y. 2010).

they are virtually unheard of in international arbitration. The tribunal would simply not give much weight to an expert's testimony if it comes to the conclusion that the methodology cannot be trusted.

4. Electronic Discovery

Electronic discovery, sometimes called *e-discovery*, is the discovery of electronic or digital files, often in the form of e-mails, databases, and essentially any type of file format that is created by or stored on computer hardware. The advent of the digital age, and the explosion in the use of electronic methods of document creation and retention, has had a dramatic impact on the discovery process in U.S. litigation. The impact of the trend toward electronic document production has been significant enough that in 2006, the Federal Rules of Civil Procedure were amended to address particular electronic discovery considerations.[76] The amendments, which altered Fed. R. Civ. P. 26, 33, 34, 45, among others, create a comprehensive framework to provide much-needed guidance to litigants, who must inevitably deal with electronic data when engaging in the discovery process. The new rules also include new protections and protocols regarding privileged information, recognizing that the production of electronic files makes it more difficult to identify privileged information prior to disclosure. *See* Fed. R. Civ. P. 26(b)(5)(b). The new rule (also discussed in Section E.2(c) of this chapter) creates the obligation to promptly destroy any inadvertently produced information as soon as a party is notified of the error by the producing party. **2.71**

The costs of electronic discovery are incurred by the party producing the material, not by the party making the request. However, under a still developing body of law, the federal courts will employ a multifactor analysis to determine whether the costs of producing electronic data should be shifted to or shared by the requesting party, usually when the cost is overly burdensome. *See Zubulake v. UBS Warburg LLC*, 217 F.R.D. 319 (S.D.N.Y. 2003). The new federal rules regarding electronic discovery recognize that electronic discovery presents unique expense considerations, and include provisions allowing the judge to place conditions on such discovery, such as fee-shifting. *See* Fed. R. Civ. P. 26(b)(2)(B). **2.72**

5. Using the Evidence: The Summary Judgment Motion

Efficiency is one of the stated goals of international arbitration. For example, Article 20(3) of the ICDR Rules allows the arbitrators to "direct the parties to focus their presentations on issues whose resolution could dispose of all or part of the case." But few arbitration rules allow the arbitrators to decide the case without **2.73**

[76] The new rules became effective December 1, 2006. An amendment to Rule 26 became effective on December 1, 2010. Stylistic changes to Rules 33 and 34 became effective on December 1, 2007. An amendment to Rule 45 became effective on December 1, 2013.

first holding a hearing on the merits.[77] Dispositive motions, such as summary judgment motions, are not the norm in the international arbitration context. The JAMS rules, for example, illustrate the novelty of resolution by dispositive motion in the arbitration environment. While Rule 18 of the JAMS Comprehensive Arbitration Rules and Procedures[78] specifically allows for motions for summary disposition, the International Arbitration Rules of the same institution do not contain a similar rule.

2.74 So what exactly are dispositive motions, and what is their purpose in U.S. litigation? Let us examine the motion for summary judgment. The summary judgment motion is the first significant opportunity the parties have to utilize the evidence they have gathered during discovery. At the close of discovery, but before the parties begin to prepare for trial, at least one of the parties, but often both, will bring a motion for summary judgment. These motions typically include many exhibits of the evidence that has been gathered, and argue that there is no disputed issue of material fact for which a trial is necessary, allowing the court to determine the merits as a matter of law. In the federal courts, these motions are brought pursuant to Federal Rule of Civil Procedure 56, and in New York such motions are governed by N.Y. CPLR § 3212.[79]

2.75 The primary purpose of summary judgment motions is to seek early resolution of the case by allowing the judge to determine if there is any need for a trial based on the evidence that has been collected during discovery. If the court concludes upon evaluation of the evidence that there is no need for a trial, it can determine which party should prevail as a matter of law. If the court is able to conclude certain questions of law, it can determine which facts are not genuinely in dispute, thereby simplifying the issues addressed at any subsequent trial. Fed. R. Civ. P. 56(d).

---

[77] *See, e.g.*, Art. 15(2) of the Swiss Arbitration Rules: "After consulting with the parties, the arbitral tribunal may also decide to conduct the proceedings on the basis of documents and other materials." Article 19(1) of the LCIA Rules, on the other hand, establishes a party's right to a hearing: "Any party which expresses a desire to that effect has the right to be heard orally before the Arbitral Tribunal on the merits of the dispute, unless the parties have agreed in writing on documents-only arbitration."

[78] Rule 18. Summary Disposition of a Claim or Issue:

> (a) The Arbitrator may permit any Party to file a Motion for Summary Disposition of a particular claim or issue, either by agreement of all interested Parties or at the request of one Party, provided other interested Parties have reasonable notice to respond to the request.

[79] Pursuant to Rule 56 of the Federal Rules of Civil Procedure, a summary judgment motion can be brought prior to the close of discovery. Fed. R. Civ. P. 56(a)–(b). However, the court's willingness to grant summary judgment is often enhanced when all discovery has been closed and at which time the court has a complete picture of the available evidence. With all the evidence gathered during discovery before it, the court can better decide if there are indeed any facts in dispute such that a trial is necessary.

F. PRETRIAL MATTERS AND PRESENTATION OF THE CASE

Once all discovery has closed, and if the case survives any summary judgment motions, it will proceed to the long-awaited trial. In federal court, the first step is that the court will hold the "final pretrial conference." The final pretrial conference is important because the case that goes to trial is often quite different from what the parties may have expected at the outset of the litigation, due to information gathered during the discovery process. This conference is designed to streamline the trial by establishing what issues remain for the trier of fact. In federal court, the final pretrial conference is held to "formulate a trial plan, including a plant to facilitate the admission of evidence," and the conference "must be held as close to the start of the trial as is reasonable." Fed. R. Civ. P. 16(e). Prior to the conference, judges will often require the parties to submit detailed information in a joint pretrial order that sets forth the witnesses they intend to call for testimony and the evidence upon which they will rely. In this way, the court and the parties are more aware of what to expect at trial. This process of conferring and exchanging witness and exhibit lists is similar to prehearing conferences often held in the arbitration setting, which are also intended to simplify the hearing process. **2.76**

Following the final pretrial conference, the parties will make final preparation for the trial by readying exhibits and evidence for submission, creating opening statement and examination outlines, and making demonstrative exhibits to use during witness presentations. U.S.-trained arbitrators are likely accustomed to demonstrative devices, while those from a civil-law background may find such tools unnecessary. The parties will also often spend considerable time in preparing their respective witnesses to give trial testimony.[80] This essential trial preparation can be time-intensive work for the U.S. litigator, especially if the discovery process involved many depositions, experts, and voluminous document productions. All of these materials must be marshaled by the attorneys and utilized in support of the party's case at trial. **2.77**

The trial itself will either be a bench trial, in which the judge acts as the trier of fact, or a jury trial, in which members of the community will be called upon to serve as jurors and to make the fact determinations. **2.78**

With a jury trial, there are typically many more phases of the trial because the presence of the jury requires special attention. First, the jury must be selected **2.79**

[80] Although in some civil law countries the idea of preparing a witness before testimony may be virtually unheard of, or at least seriously frowned upon, it is a crucial trial preparation activity in the United States.

through the process known as *voir dire*. This involves the attorneys, again in their active role, posing questions to potential members of the jury and deciding, based on the answers they receive, which individuals should ultimately compose the jury. After the jury is selected, the court administers an oath in which the jurors swear or affirm to abide by the court's instructions.[81]

2.80 The attorneys for the parties will then deliver their opening statements. This is the first opportunity the trial lawyer has to explain to the jury (or to the judge in a bench trial) why his client should prevail. The parties will then call witnesses and conduct direct examination of such witnesses (including any experts), followed by opposing counsel having the opportunity to cross-examine such witnesses. Throughout the witness process, the parties will present documentary or other evidence. In U.S. litigation, witnesses are the key mechanism through which the party's case is presented, whereas civil law courts and, to some extent, international arbitral tribunals tend to place more focus on documents.

2.81 The submission of evidence must comply with the Federal Rules of Evidence in order for the evidence to be admissible. This means that documents must be properly authenticated by witnesses, and the witnesses themselves cannot testify as to what a third person outside court said (this is known as *hearsay*) except under certain specific circumstances. It is the judge's responsibility to make rulings on whether evidence is admissible under these rules. If evidence is not admitted, it cannot be considered by the jury. After the plaintiff presents its case in full, the defense will then present its evidence and witnesses.

2.82 After each side has presented all of its evidence in support of its case, the attorneys will present their respective closing arguments. In a jury trial, before making the closing arguments, the court and the parties first hold a conference outside the presence of the jury to determine what issues should actually be presented to the jury for a determination. With the closing arguments, the attorney's goal is to provide the jury with a clear summary of what the evidence has shown and why the other party has failed to put forth a winning case. The judge will then administer instructions to the jury so that the jury has a guide on how to apply the facts to the law. The jury will then be isolated to engage in their deliberations.

G. DECISION AND JUDGMENT

2.83 After the parties have presented all of their evidence, either the judge (in a bench trial) or the jury will be tasked with weighing that evidence in light of the law and determining which party should prevail, ultimately rendering a final decision.

[81] During *voir dire*, the prospective jurors would have sworn merely to tell the truth in response to the questions asked.

This is the determination of the merits of the action. The official pronouncement of this decision on the merits is termed the *judgment.*[82]

Along with deciding which party wins, in most actions, the judge or jury will simultaneously determine the damages to be awarded (unless the damages determination has been bifurcated from the determination on the merits).[83] In U.S. litigation, the recoverable damages vary depending on the nature of the action, with the primary purpose being to compensate the aggrieved party for its loss. The plaintiff must have suffered some harm capable of being monetarily quantifiable, but it need not be precisely calculated. In contract actions, this means giving the winning party the "benefit of his bargain" (*see* Restatement (Second) of Contracts § 347 (1981)), whereas, in tort actions, damages are designed to make the injured party "whole." *See* Restatement (Second) of Torts § 901 (1979). Punitive damages or exemplary damages, designed to punish a party for especially egregious or malicious behavior, may also be available in tort actions. Under certain statutes, treble damages may be available if the legislature has determined that any award under that statute should be tripled, as an extra deterrent and to benefit the public. In international arbitration, such damages that go beyond mere compensation are usually disfavored.[84] **2.84**

1. Judgment in a Jury Trial

After the jury is charged with the jury instructions and the jurors have engaged in their private deliberations, they will render a verdict.[85] In federal court, the jury must arrive at a unanimous verdict in which all of the jurors have participated. Fed. R. Civ. P. 48. The jury may issue its verdict under several different verdict types. These are a *General Verdict*, or, under Rule 49, a *Special Verdict* or a *General Verdict with Special Interrogatories*. Fed. R. Civ. P. 49(a)–(b).[86] In the General Verdict, the jury will indicate the party for which it has found favorably and state the damages to be awarded, but will provide no explanation as to the basis of its findings and award. By contrast, verdicts rendered as Special Verdicts or General Verdicts with Interrogatories require the jury to be more specific. In **2.85**

---

[82] In the federal system, Fed. R. Civ. P. 58 directs that judgments be entered with the district court by the court clerk.

[83] Note that if the prevailing party is seeking equitable relief, such as a permanent injunction, the judge must issue and construct the relief, not the jury. *See* Fed. R. Civ. P. 65(d). Again, this allocation of authority finds its roots in the historical separation between remedies "at law" (*i.e.*, monetary damages), and remedies in equity. *See Section* B.3.II *supra.*

[84] *See, e.g.*, Article 31(5) of the ICDR Rules ("Unless the parties agree otherwise, the parties expressly waive and forego any right to punitive, exemplary or similar damages unless applicable law(s) requires that compensatory damages be increased in a specified manner. This provision shall not apply to an award of arbitration costs to a party to compensate for misconduct in the arbitration.")

[85] The verdict form will have been negotiated and finalized by the parties and the judge at a charging conference held before the jury is read the jury instructions.

[86] New York State employs these generic types of verdict forms as well. N.Y. CPLR § 4111.

Special Verdicts, the jury is required to answer discrete questions regarding each issue of fact. In the General Verdict with Interrogatories the jury will first provide a general verdict, but will also answer questions designed to supply the basis for the verdict.

2.86 After the jury renders its verdict, the losing party may want to bring several kinds of post-trial motions to the trial court in order to attempt to get the verdict set aside or otherwise altered. In the federal courts, such post-trial motions include a motion for judgment as a matter of law under Rule 50(b) and a motion for a new trial under Rule 59.[87] These motions allow the trial court to exercise some control over the outcome of the case, even when the jury has been the trier of fact, if the court determines evidence could only support one result in the case or that the jury engaged in misconduct.

2.87 In a Rule 50(b) motion, the party asserts that, based on the evidence presented, a "reasonable" jury would not have a "legally sufficient basis to find for the part on that issue." Fed. R. Civ. P. 50(a)(1).[88] Thus, the court may undo the jury verdict when it is against the weight of the evidence.

2.88 In a jury trial, the trial court may order a new trial "for any reason for which a new trial has heretofore been granted in an action at law in federal court." Fed. R. Civ. P. 59(a)(1).[89] Such grounds for a new trial are numerous, but most commonly include errors in the jury's evaluation of the evidence and errors in the trial process itself. An error in evaluating the evidence may be indicated by the jury awarding excessive damages, while a process error is evident if it is discovered that the jury has engaged in misconduct or if the verdict is irreconcilably inconsistent. If these motions fail, then the jury's verdict stands.

2. Judgment in a Bench Trial

2.89 Trials may be held before a judge only if the parties waive their right to a jury trial or if the action is only one in equity. The judge in a bench trial is required to articulate findings of fact and conclusions of law, either orally in open court or in written form. Fed. R. Civ. P. 52(a). This requirement contrasts sharply with the verdict issued by a jury, which can be vague, particularly in the case of the general verdict. These findings can only be overturned by an appellate court if they are "clearly erroneous." Fed. R. Civ. P. 52(a)(6). This is discussed in Section I.3 of this chapter.

[87] These motions are distinct from the process by which a losing party will challenge the decision in a higher court. *See* Section I of this chapter.

[88] The Rule 50(b) postverdict motion is commonly referred to as motions for *judgment n.o.v.* (from the Latin "non obstante veredicto" or judgment notwithstanding the verdict). A party moving under Rule 50(b) must have brought a Rule 50(a) motion for a directed verdict at the close of all of its evidence but before the jury rendered the verdict.

[89] Motions for a new trial must be made within ten days after entry of the judgment.

Unlike the availability of a Rule 50 motion in a jury trial,[90] the primary motion available to alter the judgment following a bench trial is the Rule 59 motion for a new trial. Fed. R. Civ. P. 59(a)(1)(B), (a)(2). Under Rule 59(a)(2), the court may "open the judgment if one has been entered, take additional testimony, amend findings of fact and conclusions of law or make new ones, and direct the entry of a new judgment."[91] **2.90**

In the international arbitration context, there is no equivalent to these post-determination motions. However, arbitration regimes usually do allow for post-award corrections and interpretations within a certain time limit, usually thirty days after the arbitrators have made their "final" determination. See, for example, Article 33 of the ICDR Rules, Article 35 of the ICC Rules, and Article 38 of the UNCITRAL Rules. **2.91**

H. COSTS

Frequently, the arbitration clause itself directs the arbitrators as to how costs should be assessed and allocated among the parties.[92] In the event that the clause is silent, however, many, if not most, arbitration rules give the arbitrators full discretion to fix and apportion the costs of the arbitration between the parties. In such a situation, the arbitrators often resort to their own law. In that regard, the practice a U.S.-trained arbitrator is accustomed to may be very different from that of a civil-law arbitrator, or even that of an English colleague. As such, post-litigation cost allocation in the U.S. system deserves a closer look. **2.92**

Litigation anywhere can be expensive, but the adversarial system in the United States can make litigation particularly expensive, especially if the case is complex or the discovery process becomes contentious. Although court fees and costs are typically minimal,[93] attorneys' fees, whether charged on an hourly or contingency basis, along with the cost of disbursements (experts, translations, document production/copying) can be considerable. **2.93**

The U.S. court system employs a unique approach to cost allocation that requires each party to bear its own costs (including attorneys' fees), regardless of the litigation outcome. This practice of precluding fee shifting is known as the *American rule*, and it has long been applied in the United States. In the federal courts, some minor costs under Federal Rule of Civil Procedure 54(d)(1) are to be paid by the losing **2.94**

[90] Notably, however, under Rule 52(c), at the close of all of a party's evidence in a bench trial, the party may move the court for a directed verdict just as is done in a jury trial under Rule 50(a). Fed. R. Civ. P. 52(c), 50(a).

[91] Under Rule 59(d), the court may also order a new trial for any reason that would justify granting one, even if neither party moved for a new trial.

[92] For a discussion of how to draft an arbitration clause to allow arbitrators to award fees to the prevailing party in an arbitration, see Chapter 3.B of this book.

[93] *See supra* note 39.

party, and the successful party may recover such costs (other than attorneys' fees). Fed. R. Civ. P. 54(d)(1).[94] Such recoverable costs are limited,[95] and they are normally negligible relative to the expense it would require to bring a motion for such costs.

2.95 Typically, the largest part of the expenses a party incurs over the course of the litigation will be for its attorneys' fees.[96] There are several general categories of exceptions to the American rule with regard to attorneys' fees that allow the prevailing party to collect them. These exceptions occur most frequently when: (1) the litigation involves a contract in which the parties have expressly agreed that the losing party will pay the attorneys' fees of the prevailing party; (2) the litigation results in a "common fund" for the prevailing side out of which a percentage of the award may be assigned to cover the fees of the successful attorneys; (3) a specific statute allows for fee shifting;[97] or (4) the litigation was brought frivolously by the losing party with no sound basis in law or fact.[98] Whenever attorneys' fees are sought after judgment is entered, the prevailing party must do so by bringing a motion pursuant to Rule 54(d)(2). The limited circumstances under which attorneys' fees can be collected in the United States contrasts sharply with almost all other countries (even England), where the ability of the prevailing party to collect fees is presumed and is viewed to have a beneficial deterrent effect against groundless claims.

I. APPEALS: CHALLENGING THE JUDGMENT

2.96 One of the hallmarks of arbitration is its nearly absolute finality: typically, the arbitration award is binding upon the parties and cannot be altered in any substantive way. Accordingly, arbitration rules usually only allow for corrections of clerical,

---

[94] Many federal district courts also have their own rules regarding taxable costs. *See, e.g.*, Local Rules for the U.S. District Courts for the Southern and Eastern Districts of New York, Local Rule 54.1 (2013). In the New York State courts, several articles of the N.Y. CPLR govern costs, and they generally allow costs to the party in whose favor a judgment is entered (with the exception of attorneys' fees). *See* N.Y. CPLR arts. 81–86.

[95] *See* 28 U.S.C. § 1920. However, even these fees can be substantial given the right circumstances.

[96] Normally included as part of the cost of attorneys' fees are the disbursements (document copying and retrieval, translations, data restoration) that the attorney paid to accomplish litigation activities in the discovery process, for example, and which is passed on to the paying client. The cost of discovery, which in the electronic data age can be significant, and the circumstances under which this cost can be shifted, is discussed in Section E.4 of this chapter.

[97] One prominent example is 42 U.S.C. § 1988, which allows shifting of attorneys' fees (including expert fees) in the court's discretion, when the plaintiff has succeeded in bringing an action to vindicate civil rights under various civil rights statutes. There are dozens of other federal statutes that allow shifting of attorneys' fees. Any attorneys' fees awarded must be "reasonable." *See generally* Venegas v. Mitchell, 495 U.S. 82 (1990).

[98] As noted in Section C of this chapter, such a sanction would be recoverable pursuant to Fed. R. Civ. P. 11, but motions seeking such sanctions are not often granted. Note also that other rules allow for costs, including attorneys' fees, to be collected as a sanction. *See* Fed. R. Civ. P. 37(b) (allowing collection of reasonable attorneys' fees for various discovery abuses).

computational, or typographical errors (e.g., ICC Rule 35), but not for de novo or plenary review of the award on the merits. There are only a few circumstances in which a party can request a court to vacate an award.[99] As the U.S. Supreme Court recently held, these grounds are exclusive and may not be expanded by mutual agreement of the parties.[100] The parties are free, however, to provide for a review within the arbitral process by an "appellate" arbitration panel.[101]

By striking contrast, in U.S. litigation, the availability of appellate review at the secondary level is a virtual given in all but the narrowest of circumstances. This section takes a closer look at the appellate process in the United States and in New York. **2.97**

1. The "Final Judgment" Rule

Following the judgment, a litigant may want to submit the lower court's disposition of the litigation to a higher court for review.[102] By statute, in order to bring an appeal in the federal system, the trial court must have made and entered a "final" judgment. 28 U.S.C. § 1291.[103] Such a final judgment "ends the litigation on the merits and leaves nothing for the court to do but execute the judgment." *Catlin v. United States*, 324 U.S. 229, 233 (1945). By requiring the decision to be final, the circuit courts are able to limit the number of appeals, making both appeals and district court proceedings more efficient.[104] **2.98**

2. Appeals to Higher Courts

In the federal and state systems, a litigant has a right to appeal to the first appellate level (the circuit courts in the federal system).[105] Appeals from these intermediate **2.99**

---

[99] *See* 9 U.S.C. §§ 10–11. Grounds include: where the award was procured by corruption, fraud, or undue means; where there was evident partiality or corruption in one or more of the arbitrators; where the arbitrators were guilty of misconduct in refusing to postpone the hearing, upon sufficient cause shown, or in refusing to hear evidence pertinent and material to the controversy; or of any other misbehavior by which the rights of any party have been prejudiced; or where the arbitrators exceeded their powers, or so imperfectly executed them, that a mutual, final, and definite award upon the subject matter submitted was not made. These grounds are discussed in detail in Chapter 13.C.

[100] Hall Street Associates, L.L.C. v. Mattel, Inc., 128 S. Ct. 1396 (2008).

[101] *See* Redish v. Yellow Transp., Inc., 2008 WL 2572658 (N.D. Tex. June 24, 2008). Some arbitral institutions, such as the International Institute for Conflict Prevention & Resolution (CPR), JAMS and the AAA offer appellate procedures.

[102] A party bringing an appeal is called the *appellant*, while the other party is the *respondent*. In order to be entitled to bring an appeal, the appellant must have been aggrieved or adversely affected by the lower court's ruling.

[103] Some states, including New York, allow appeals to the intermediate appellate court (in New York, the Appellate Division of the Supreme Court), from non-final rulings. Such appeals are called *interlocutory appeals*. *See* N.Y. State Const., art. VI, § 4(k); N.Y. CPLR § 5701. Although they are disfavored and allowed sparingly, the federal courts also allow interlocutory appeals in a narrow set of circumstances. *See* 28 U.S.C. § 1292. The collateral order doctrine also allows interlocutory appeals from orders that are incidental to the merits of the case and which would not be preserved on review from a final order.

[104] Fed. R. Civ. P. 58 mandates that judgments be set forth on a separate document.

[105] Appeals in most jurisdictions are governed by separate procedural rules which often include local rules of the appellate court in question. The procedure for appeals in the federal courts is

level courts to the highest courts are generally not as of right, except for limited circumstances, such as capital punishment cases. See, for example, N.Y. CPLR §§ 5601, 5602. Appeal from a circuit court to the U.S. Supreme Court is by permission, or on *certiorari*. The Supreme Court will grant *certiorari* to resolve conflicts between circuit courts or conflicts between state courts of last resort, conflicts on federal questions (*i.e.*, federal statutes and the U.S. Constitution), conflicts between prior U.S. Supreme Court rulings, and others. It is important to recognize that with a few exceptions the appeal court's review is limited to only those facts and those arguments that were made, or "preserved," at the trial-court level, and which have been presented for review to the appellate court in the notice of appeal.

3. Scope of Appellate Review

2.100 Depending on what is being challenged, the appellate court will have varying degrees of review power over the findings of the trial court and/or jury known as the *standard of review*.[106] These indicate the level of deference the reviewing court will show to the lower court's findings. The several standards of review can be placed along a scale or spectrum from most authority to review to no review whatsoever. The greater the reviewing court's review authority, the greater the likelihood that the lower court will be reversed on appeal. The standard applied by the reviewing court depends on the substance of what is being reviewed, which can be generally summarized as greater deference being shown toward findings of fact and less deference toward the judge's rulings on questions of law.

2.101 The broadest standard of review is *de novo* review (Latin for "anew"), which is commonly applied to review of questions of law. Under this standard, the reviewing court is not bound by the trial court's findings and can look at the case "from scratch." Factual findings made by the court (as opposed to the jury) are typically reviewed under the "clearly erroneous" standard. A finding is clearly erroneous when "although there is evidence to support it, the reviewing court on the entire evidence is left with a definite and firm conviction that a mistake has been committed." *United States v. U.S. Gypsum Co.*, 333 U.S. 364, 395 (1948). The next standard, which represents a wide degree of deference, is the "abuse of discretion" standard. When an appellate court reviews for abuse of discretion, it seeks to determine if the trial court improperly applied its discretion in arriving

set forth in the Federal Rules of Appellate Procedure. From a procedural perspective, the most essential requirement in any jurisdiction is to file a notice of appeal within the prescribed period of time, which informs the lower court that the party intends to appeal its ruling to the higher court. *See* Fed. R. App. P. 3; N.Y. CPLR § 5515. Other standard procedural steps include preparing and sending the record or parts of the record to the appellate court, briefing the arguments, and presenting oral argument (if granted).

[106] Although at the trial court level the litigation is normally presided over by only one judge, appeals are handled by a panel of judges of varying numbers depending on the jurisdiction.

at the disposition. Finally, the most deferential level of appellate review along the spectrum (aside from no review) is the "reasonableness" standard. This standard is applied to review findings made by the jury. This standard asks if it was reasonable for the jury to reach its conclusion. While theoretically highly deferential, it may nevertheless result in reversals when the jury has made excessive monetary awards.

J. CONCLUSION

The essence of U.S. litigation is the adversarial model, and the related emphasis **2.102** on attorney control (although there has been a shift toward more control by the judge) and active attorney case management. Also important are: broad discovery in the form of document requests, depositions, subpoenas, etc.; dispositive motions; witness-oriented presentation; and limited cost-shifting. The U.S. litigation background of an arbitrator or counsel in an international arbitration can impact how that arbitration is conducted or how such participants expect it to be conducted. Nevertheless, U.S.-trained arbitrators and counsel are not oblivious to the fact that arbitration is not litigation and that different rules apply. It remains that for non-U.S. litigators representing a client in an international arbitration, and especially for those from a civil law background, certain advantages may be achieved by remembering the more salient aspects of the U.S. litigation system that could creep into the arbitration when the participants bring along their U.S. litigation baggage.

3

DRAFTING CONSIDERATIONS FOR CLAUSES DESIGNATING NEW YORK AS THE PLACE OF ARBITRATION

Paul D. Friedland and Damien Nyer[1]

A. Preliminary Drafting Considerations not Particular to Arbitration in New York	3.04
1. Essential Elements	3.04
2. Recommended Elements	3.08
B. Drafting Considerations Specific to Clauses Providing for Arbitration in New York	3.11
1. The Law Governing Clauses Providing for Arbitration in New York	3.11
2. Jurisdictional Considerations	3.16
(a) *Kompetenz-Kompetenz*	3.16
(b) Arbitral jurisdiction to resolve preliminary issues	3.20
(c) Jurisdiction over nonsignatories	3.24
(d) Validity of sole option clauses	3.26
3. Powers and Duties of the Arbitral Tribunal	3.27
(a) Impartiality of arbitrators	3.27
(b) Allocation of costs and fees	3.29
(c) Punitive damages	3.34
(d) Class proceedings	3.37
4. Arbitral Process	3.38
(a) Discovery	3.38
(b) Consolidation of proceedings	3.44
(c) Confidentiality	3.49
5. Considerations Relating to Judicial Powers	3.51
(a) Provisional measures	3.51
(b) Modifying the scope of judicial review	3.55
(c) Enforcement of awards	3.58

This chapter offers recommendations for drafting arbitration clauses that provide for international arbitration in New York. **3.01**

Section A addresses preliminary issues that, irrespective of the chosen seat of arbitration, must be considered. The literature on this topic is extensive, and Section A is therefore only summary. The basic rule when drafting an arbitration clause is to start with a model clause.[2] This is so whether or not the clause provides for arbitration in New York. **3.02**

[1] The authors wish to thank Jaroslav Kudrna of White & Case LLP's International Arbitration Group for his assistance in updating this chapter.

[2] *See generally* International Bar Association, IBA Guidelines for Drafting International Arbitration Clauses (2010), Paul Friedland, Arbitration Clauses for International Contracts, 1–5 (2d ed. 2007).

3.03 Section B, which comprises the bulk of this chapter, discusses considerations that are specific to arbitration clauses designating New York as place of arbitration, and offers proposed wording.[3]

A. PRELIMINARY DRAFTING CONSIDERATIONS NOT PARTICULAR TO ARBITRATION IN NEW YORK

1. Essential Elements

3.04 Regardless of the seat of arbitration and the applicable arbitration law, there are three elements that are necessary to an effective arbitration clause: (1) an appropriately defined scope, which in most instances will be broad; (2) a clear designation of arbitration as the agreed dispute resolution mechanism; and (3) an unambiguously binding undertaking to arbitrate. Parties can ensure that these three objectives are met by using the model clauses recommended by the leading arbitral institutions, such as the International Chamber of Commerce (ICC), the International Centre for Dispute Resolution (ICDR) of the American Arbitration Association (AAA), or the London Court of International Arbitration (LCIA), all of whom make their model clauses available on their Web sites.[4]

3.05 **Scope**. Absent special circumstances, the scope of disputes to be submitted to arbitration should be broad. Courts in New York have been liberal in their interpretation of the ambit of arbitration clauses, but an unnecessarily narrow scope remains an invitation to dispute over whether a given fact-pattern is to be submitted to arbitration.[5] The language in the model clauses of the leading arbitral institutions should be used. For example, the ICDR's model clause for international contracts recommends the following language: "any claim or controversy *arising out of or relating to* this contract ..."[6] This language has been tested and given a broad interpretation.[7] Narrower clauses (e.g., "all disputes arising under

[3] The clauses presented in this chapter are largely based on the recommended clauses presented in Paul Friedland, Arbitration Clauses for International Contracts (2d ed. 2007).

[4] The ICC model clauses are available at http://www.iccwbo.org/court/arbitration. The ICDR model clauses are available at https://www.icdr.org. The LCIA model clauses are available at http://www.lcia.org.

[5] *See, e.g.*, Louis Dreyfus Negoce S.A. v. Blystad Shipping & Trading Inc., 252 F.3d 218 (2d Cir. 2001) (holding that a clause in a charter party mandating arbitration of "[a]ny dispute arising from the making, performance or termination of this Charter Party" was sufficiently broad to cover disputes arising under collateral letters of indemnity that included a choice-of-forum clause designating the High Court in London).

[6] ICDR, Guide to Drafting International Dispute Resolution Clauses, available at www.icdr.org (emphasis added).

[7] Collins & Aikman Prods. Co. v. Building Sys., Inc., 58 F.3d 16, 20 (2d Cir. 1995) (finding that the language "[a]ny claim or controversy arising out of or relating to this agreement shall be settled by arbitration" suggested a broad arbitration clause).

this contract" or "all disputes arising out of this contract") should be avoided as they have, at times, given rise to disputes.[8]

Arbitration as the designated dispute settlement method. In a surprising number of cases, parties fail either clearly to identify arbitration as the agreed dispute settlement mechanism or, where an arbitral institution is selected, to identify this institution properly. Courts in New York will exercise common sense to try to remedy such drafting deficiencies,[9] in which event poor drafting will have resulted in costs and delays that could have been avoided. **3.06**

Exclusivity. The arbitration clause must set forth a binding undertaking to arbitrate disputes with arbitration being the exclusive recourse in case of dispute. A common error is to provide that any dispute which cannot be settled by negotiation "may" be submitted to arbitration. **3.07**

2. Recommended Elements

Irrespective of the seat of arbitration, there are elements that contracting parties *should* consider when drafting an arbitration clause. Although failure to include these elements will not result in an unenforceable arbitration clause, their omission may cause delay and added expense. **3.08**

The most important recommended element is an appropriate mechanism for appointing (and replacing) arbitrators. Where administered arbitration is chosen, this mechanism will be provided by the arbitral rules of the institution, and reference to these rules will suffice. Where the parties have opted for non-administered arbitration, the appointment mechanism should be spelled out in the arbitration clause itself,[10] notwithstanding that, under both U.S. federal law and New York law, courts in New York are empowered to fill in the gap and to appoint arbitrators.[11] **3.09**

For international contracts, the parties should additionally specify the language of the proceedings. Absent party agreement, this point will be decided by the arbitrators, who will usually opt for the language of the contract. Any uncertainty and cost in this regard can be avoided by appropriate drafting. **3.10**

---

[8] *In re* Kinoshita & Co., 287 F.2d 951, 953 (2d Cir. 1961) (suggesting that the language "arising under" was not sufficiently broad to encompass dispute or controversy about alleged fraudulent inducement to enter into the contract); *but see* S.A. Mineracao Da Trinidade-Samitri v. Utah Int'l, Inc., 745 F.2d 190 (2d Cir. 1984) (limiting *Kinoshita* to its precise facts).

[9] *See, e.g.*, Warnes, S.A. v. Harvic Int'l, Ltd., 1993 WL 228028 (S.D.N.Y. 1993) (interpreting a clause designating "the New York Commercial Arbitration Association" as meaning the American Arbitration Association in New York).

[10] This can easily be done by referring in the arbitration clause to a set of non-administered arbitration rules, *e.g.*, the U.N. Commission on International Trade Law (UNCITRAL) Arbitration Rules, which provide a default mechanism for appointment and replacement of arbitrators.

[11] Section 5 of the Federal Arbitration Act, and § 7504 of the New York Civil Procedure Law and Rules.

B. DRAFTING CONSIDERATIONS SPECIFIC TO CLAUSES PROVIDING FOR ARBITRATION IN NEW YORK

1. The Law Governing Clauses Providing for Arbitration in New York

3.11 Arbitration practitioners will be familiar with the distinction between the law governing the substantive provisions of the contract and the merits of a subsequent dispute (*substantive law*) and the law governing the arbitration agreement and the conduct of subsequent arbitration proceedings (*arbitration law*).

3.12 As explained in Chapter 1 of this book, the arbitration law applicable to arbitrations located in New York stems from the Federal Arbitration Act (FAA),[12] the 1958 New York Convention on the Recognition and Enforcement of Foreign Arbitral Awards (New York Convention), and the 1975 Inter-American Convention on International Commercial Arbitration (Panama Convention), which are implemented in and through Chapters 2 and 3 of the FAA respectively[13] and Article 75 of the New York Civil Practice Law and Rules (CPLR), which is the arbitration law of the State of New York.

3.13 The first place to look for the law pertaining to *international* arbitration agreements is the New York Convention[14] and, where applicable, the Panama Convention.[15] In addition, the general provisions found in Chapter 1 of the FAA are applicable to international arbitration agreements to the extent that they do not conflict with the provisions of the New York Convention and, where applicable, of the Panama Convention.[16] In matters involving international arbitration agreements, the provisions of the CPLR will be applicable in only a limited set of circumstances and only to the extent that they are consistent with the FAA.[17] Insofar as

[12] 9 U.S.C. §§ 1–14.

[13] 9 U.S.C. §§ 201–208 and 9 U.S.C. §§ 301–307.

[14] Under § 202 of the FAA, the New York Convention is applicable to "an arbitration agreement or award arising out of a legal relationship, whether contractual or not, which is considered as commercial" except where the relationship is between U.S. citizens and does not involve property located abroad, does not envisage performance or enforcement abroad, and does not have some other reasonable relation with one or more foreign states.

[15] Under Chapter 3 of the FAA, the Panama Convention is applicable where the New York Convention would be applicable under § 202 of the FAA and where "a majority of the parties to the arbitration agreement are citizens of a State or States that have ratified or acceded to the Inter-American Convention and are member States of the Organization of American States ..."

[16] FAA, § 208 and § 307.

[17] The CPLR will be applicable in the rare case where an action to enforce the arbitration agreement is brought in New York state courts and not removed to the federal courts pursuant to § 205 of the FAA. In this case, the CPLR will only be applicable to the extent that its provisions are consistent with and not preempted by federal law. *See* Southland Corp. v. Keating, 465 U.S. 1, 16 (1984) (holding that the FAA creates a body of federal substantive law applicable in state and federal courts).

relevant to drafting, the differences between the CPLR and the FAA are pointed out in the remainder of this text.

Parties to an arbitration agreement are free to choose both the applicable substantive law and the applicable arbitration law.[18] Where the parties wish to assure that the FAA will govern the arbitration agreement and any subsequent arbitration, the following language can be used: **3.14**

> This arbitration agreement and any arbitration shall be governed by the United States Federal Arbitration Act to the exclusion of state law inconsistent therewith.

Conversely, if the parties want New York arbitration law (Article 75 of the CPLR) to be the governing arbitration law, the following language can be used:

> This arbitration agreement and any arbitration shall be governed by New York's Civil Practice Law and Rules.

Generally, a clause providing that the laws of New York (or another jurisdiction) shall govern the contract will not be interpreted as requiring application of New York (or another forum's) arbitration law. Rather, the clause will be read as referring solely to the substantive law.[19] Where, however, a clause provides that "the laws of the state of New York govern the contract and *its enforcement*," the law is unsettled whether this makes New York arbitration law applicable. The New York Court of Appeals, the highest state court in New York, has held that such language *did* call for application of the provisions of the CPLR.[20] By contrast, the U.S. Court of Appeals for the Second Circuit (the highest federal court in the circuit that encompasses the State of New York), has held the opposite.[21] To avoid uncertainty, the quoted language (providing for New York law to govern the "contract and its enforcement") should be avoided, and the choice of substantive law clause should be separate from the arbitration clause. **3.15**

---

[18] Volt Information Sciences, Inc. v. Board of Trustees of Leland Stanford Junior Univ., 489 U.S. 468, 476 (1989) ("There is no federal policy favoring arbitration under a certain set of procedural rules; the federal policy is simply to ensure the enforceability, according to their terms, of private agreements to arbitrate.").

[19] Mastrobuono v. Shearson Lehman Hutton, Inc., 115 S. Ct. 1212, 1219 (1995) (finding that a choice-of-law clause providing that a contract "shall be governed by the laws of the State of New York" encompassed only "substantive principles that New York courts would apply, but not ... special rules limiting the authority of arbitrators.").

[20] Matter of Diamond Waterproofing Sys., Inc. v. 55 Liberty Owners Corp., 4 N.Y.3d 247, 253 (2005) ("A choice of law provision, which states that New York law shall govern both 'the agreement and its *enforcement*,' adopts as binding New York's rule that threshold Statute of Limitations questions are for the courts."); Merrill Lynch, Pierce, Fenner, & Smith v. Adler, 234 A.D.2d 139 (1st Dep't 1996) (similar); *see also* Smith Barney, Harris Upham & Co., Inc. v. Luckie, 85 N.Y.2d 193 (1995).

[21] Painewebber Incorporated v. Bybyk, 81 F.3d 1193 (2d Cir. 1996) (rejecting the argument that because the agreement provided that it and its enforcement "shall be governed by the laws of the State of New York," the CPLR's rule regarding the nonallocation of attorneys' fees was applicable). This decision was most recently followed by the Southern District of New York in Goldman, Sachs & Co. v. Griffin, 2007 WL 147430 (S.D.N.Y. 2007).

2. Jurisdictional Considerations

3.16 *(a)* Kompetenz-Kompetenz Under the principle of *Kompetenz-Kompetenz*, arbitrators are empowered to decide their own jurisdiction.[22] This principle is reflected in the rules of the leading arbitral institutions[23] and is recognized by the laws of many countries.[24] The law in the United States is, however, partially at odds with international practice. Under the FAA, questions of arbitral jurisdiction[25] can be referred to arbitrators only if there is "clear and unmistakable" evidence that the parties intended that arbitrators decide these questions.[26] New York arbitration law follows the same rule.[27]

3.17 The significance of the distinction between the United States and international practice can be, and is, often overstated. Internationally, like in the United States, courts have the final say on arbitral jurisdiction. The difference is one of timing: internationally, arbitrators are generally empowered to rule first on their own jurisdiction, with courts reviewing disputes about jurisdiction only after an arbitration is completed; in the United States, parties can go to courts at the outset of an arbitration.

3.18 In any event, federal and state courts in New York have been liberal in finding "clear and unmistakable" evidence of the parties' intent to submit jurisdictional issues to the arbitrators. The reference in the arbitration agreement to arbitration rules that empower arbitrators to decide questions of arbitral jurisdiction (as most arbitration rules do) will suffice. For example, the ICC Rules of Arbitration, the AAA Commercial Arbitration Rules and the UNCITRAL Arbitration Rules have

---

[22] For a detailed discussion of this doctrine, *see* Chapter 6.A.4 of this book.

[23] *See, e.g.*, ICC Rules of Arbitration (2012), Art. 6(3).

[24] For a comparative account of national laws, *see* Jean-François Poudret and Sébastien Besson, Comparative Law of International Arbitration, 384 *et seq.* (2007).

[25] The terminology used by courts in the United States is liable to confuse foreign practitioners. In the United States, courts use the term "arbitrability" to refer to any one or all of the following: (1) the existence of an arbitration agreement; (2) the competence of the arbitral tribunal; or (3) the subject matters that can properly be settled by arbitration. *See* William Park, *Kompetenz-Kompetenz: The Arbitrability Dicta in First Options* in Arbitration of International Business Disputes, 88 (2006). Outside the United States, only the third topic would be referred to as "arbitrability." *See* Emmanuel Gaillard and John Savage, Fouchard Gaillard Goldman on International Commercial Arbitration, 312 *et seq.* (1998).

[26] First Options of Chicago, Inc. v. Kaplan, 514 U.S. 938 (1995) ("Courts should not assume that the parties agreed to arbitrate arbitrability unless there is 'clea[r] and umistakabl[e]' evidence that they did so."); *see also* Sarhank Group v. Oracle Corporation, 404 F.3d 657 (2d Cir. 2005) (when there is no clear and unmistakable evidence of intent to permit the arbitrator to decide issues of arbitral jurisdiction, the district court is not bound by the arbitrator's decision).

[27] Smith Barney Shearson Inc. v. Sacharow, 91 N.Y.2d 39 (1997) (the courts will recognize and enforce an agreement to arbitrate questions of arbitrability when the parties have clearly and unmistakably so provided).

all been found to constitute an agreement to submit issues of jurisdiction to the arbitrators.[28]

Even absent such incorporation by reference, there is also authority that an agreement to submit "all and any disputes" to arbitration sufficiently evidences the parties' intent to have arbitrators decide jurisdictional questions.[29] As the case law is scant, if parties wish to empower the arbitrators to decide questions of arbitral jurisdiction and have not incorporated arbitration rules that provide so or wish to leave no doubt, the following language can be used: 3.19

> The arbitral tribunal shall have the power to rule upon any challenge to its jurisdiction.

Conversely, if the parties wish to assure that courts will decide questions of arbitral jurisdiction, the following language can be used:

> Any challenge to arbitral jurisdiction is to be submitted to the federal courts in the Southern District of New York.

(b) Arbitral jurisdiction to resolve preliminary issues The question of whether courts or arbitrators are to decide threshold issues such as the timeliness of claims (for example, compliance with statutes of limitations or contractual time limitations, laches) has generated case law in the United States. Under the FAA, these threshold issues are generally for the arbitrators to decide.[30] By contrast, under New York arbitration law, issues of compliance with statutory time limitations (as opposed to contractual ones) are for the courts to decide.[31] The New York rule has, however, been held inapplicable to arbitrations governed by the FAA located in New York.[32] 3.20

---

[28] Shaw Group Inc. v. Triplefine Intern. Corp., 322 F.3d 115 (2d Cir. 2003) (ICC rules); Schneider v. Thailand, Case No. 11-1458 (2d Cir. Aug. 8, 2012) (UNCITRAL rules); Life Receivables Trust v. Goshawk Syndicate 102 at Lloyd's, 888 N.Y.S.2d 458 (1st Dep't 2009) (AAA rules).

[29] Painewebber Incorporated v. Bybyk, 81 F.3d 1193, 1199–200 (2d Cir. 1996) (holding that the language "[a]ny and all controversies" was sufficiently broad to evidence an intent to arbitrate issues of arbitrability); *see also* Shaw Grp. Inc. v. Triplefine Intern. Corp., 322 F.3d 115, 121–22 (2d Cir. 2003) (suggesting that the reference to "all disputes" in the arbitration clause is sufficient to evidence the parties' intent to arbitrate arbitrability); Smith Barney Shearson Inc. v. Sacharow, 91 N.Y.2d 39 (1997) (language providing for "[a]ny and all controversy" between the parties to be settled by arbitration is sufficiently "plain and sweeping" to indicate an intent to arbitrate arbitrability).

[30] BG Group PLC v. Republic of Arg., 134 S. Ct. 1198, 1207 (2014) (disputes about the meaning and application of procedural preconditions to arbitration are for the arbitrators to decide); Howsam v. Dean Witter Reynolds, Inc., 537 U.S. 79 (2002) (interpretation of NASD rule imposing six-year time limit for arbitration was a matter presumptively for the arbitrator, not for the court); Moses H. Cone Memorial Hospital v. Mercury Constr. Corp., 460 U.S. 1 (1983) (allegations of waiver, delay, or a like defense to arbitrability are for the arbitrators to decide).

[31] CPLR § 7502(b); *see, e.g.*, Smith Barney, Harris Upham & Co. v. Luckie, 85 N.Y.2d 193, 202 (1995) ("Clearly, under New York law, *statutory* time limitations questions ...—as opposed to *contractual* time limitations agreed upon by the parties—are for the courts, not the arbitrators.").

[32] Matter of Diamond Waterproofing Sys., Inc. v. 55 Liberty Owners Corp., 4 N.Y.3d 247, 253 (2005) (suggesting that the New York rule would be applicable only where the parties have agreed that "the laws of the State of New York shall govern their agreement and *its enforcement*.").

3.21 Given this state of the law, in the rare case where the parties want to clarify the respective roles of the arbitrators and courts regarding threshold issues, appropriate language can be added to the arbitration clause. If their wish is for arbitrators to decide these issues, the following language can be used:

> The arbitrators shall have the discretion to hear and determine in a preliminary phase of the arbitration, in accordance with such procedure as the arbitrators may deem appropriate, any issue asserted by any party to be dispositive of any claim or counterclaim, in whole or part, including any defense that any claim or counterclaim is not timely by reason of statute of limitations, contractual limitations period, or laches, and the arbitrators may render an award on such issue.

3.22 Conversely, if parties want the courts to decide a designated category of threshold issues (here, timeliness issues), the following language can be used:

> Determination of whether a claim or counterclaim is timely under this Agreement or the applicable law is an issue that shall be determined by a court of competent jurisdiction, and not by the arbitrators.

3.23 A related issue that has been the subject of case law in the United States is who decides the preclusive effect of a prior related award (res judicata). Under the FAA, this question is for the arbitrators to decide.[33] New York state courts are divided on this issue, some holding that the res judicata effect of prior awards is a question for the courts.[34] If the parties have concerns about this subject, the provisions presented above can be adapted to clarify the applicable rule.

3.24 *(c) Jurisdiction over nonsignatories* Courts in the United States have extended the effect of arbitration agreements to nonsignatories under a variety of now well-established contractual and legal theories.[35] Federal and state courts in New York have applied these norms, and the situation in New York is not distinct.[36]

3.25 If parties wish to ensure that affiliates and related parties will not be bound, the following language could be used: "This arbitration agreement binds only the signatories hereto."

---

[33] Consol. Coal Co. v. United Mine Workers of America, District 12, Local Union 1545, 213 F.3d 404, 408–09 (7th Cir. 2000) ("The res judicata effect of a judicial decision merely confirming an arbitral award is extremely limited. All it amounts to is a determination that there is no basis for upending *that* award; the effect on subsequent awards must be left to the arbitrators who make them.").

[34] *In re* Pinnacle Env't Sys, Inc., 760 N.Y.S.2d 253 (3d Dep't 2003) (holding that a court, not an arbitrator, should decide the preclusive effect of a prior award), *but see* Town of Newburgh v. Civil Serv. Employees Ass'n, Inc., 707 N.Y.S.2d 225 (2d Dep't 2000) (holding the opposite).

[35] Larry Edmonson, ed., Domke on Commercial Arbitration, §§ 13.1 *et seq.* (3d ed. 2007).

[36] American Bureau of Shipping v. Tencara Shipyard S.p.A., 170 F.3d 349, 352 (2d Cir. 1999) (explaining that nonsignatories may be bound under five different theories: (1) incorporation by reference; (2) assumption; (3) agency; (4) veil-piercing/alter ego; and (5) estoppel). *See also* Thomson-CSF, S.A. v. American Arbitration Ass'n, 64 F.3d 773 (2d Cir. 1995) (similar). For a discussion of the circumstances in which nonsignatories may be bound by, or rely upon, arbitration agreements, *see* Chapter 7.C.1(b) of this book.

(d) Validity of sole option clauses Some contracting parties (typically lenders) have the bargaining power to impose arbitration upon the other contracting party while reserving to themselves the option of choosing between arbitration and litigation after a dispute arises. These asymmetrical, or sole option, arbitration clauses are generally valid and enforceable in commercial agreements under both the FAA[37] and New York law.[38] **3.26**

3. Powers and Duties of the Arbitral Tribunal

(a) Impartiality of arbitrators A distinguishing feature of U.S. arbitration practice, as compared to international practice, is that, traditionally, party-appointed arbitrators in the United States need not be impartial or neutral. Federal and state courts in New York have relied upon this distinction to deny actions to disqualify arbitrators or to reject actions to vacate awards on the basis of bias.[39] **3.27**

International arbitration rules generally require neutrality or impartiality by all arbitrators, including party-appointed ones.[40] Where the parties choose not to adopt arbitration rules that require impartiality on the part of all arbitrators and this aspect of U.S. arbitration practice is a concern, the following language can be used: "All arbitrators shall be impartial." **3.28**

(b) Allocation of costs and fees In most countries, costs (administrative expenses and other expenses such as stenographic costs) and attorneys' fees incurred in **3.29**

[37] *See, e.g.*, Oblix, Inc. v. Winiecki, 374 F.3d 488, 490–91 (7th Cir. 2004) (concluding that an asymmetrical arbitration agreement is enforceable); Harris v. Green Tea Fin. Corp., 183 F.3d 173, 183 (3d Cir. 1999) ("[T]he mere fact that [one party] retains the option to litigate some issues in court, while the [other] must arbitrate all claims does not make the arbitration agreement unenforceable."); Doctor's Associates, Inc. v. Distajo, 66 F.3d 438 (2d Cir. 1995) (enforcing agreement that required franchisees to submit to arbitration while reserving to franchiser the right to seek summary eviction against the franchisees); Wilson Electrical Contractors, Inc. v. Minotte Contracting Corp., 878 F.2d 167, 168 (6th Cir. 1989) (enforcing clause that provided for arbitration "at the election of Contractor"); Becker Autoradio U.S.A. v. Becker Autoradiowerk GmbH, 585 F.2d 39, 47 n. 15 (3d Cir. 1978) (enforcing asymmetrical clause); ***but see*** Iberia Credit Bureau v. Cingular Wireless, 379 F.3d 159, 171 (5th Cir. 2004) (refusing to enforce an asymmetrical clause in a consumer contract); Ingle v. Circuit City Stores, 328 F.3d 1165, 1174 (9th Cir. 2003) (refusing to enforce an asymmetrical clause in an employment contract).

[38] Sablosky v. Edward S. Gordon Co., Inc., 535 N.E.2d 643 (N.Y. 1989) (enforcing asymmetrical clause under New York law).

[39] Instituto de Resseguros do Brasil v. First State Ins. Co., 178 A.D.2d 313 (1st Dep't 1991) (holding that a party designated member of a tripartite arbitration tribunal is not expected to be neutral in the same sense as a judge or arbitral umpire); Cia De Navegacion Omsil, S.A. v. Hugo Neu Corporation, 359 F.Supp. 898, 899 (S.D.N.Y. 1973) ("As everyone knows, the party's named arbitrator in this type of tribunal is an amalgam of judge and advocate."); Astoria Medical Group v. Health Insurance Plan, 11 N.Y.2d 128, 134 (1962) ("Arising out of the repeated use of the tripartite arbitral board, there has grown a common acceptance of the fact that the party-designated arbitrators are not and cannot be 'neutral,' at least in the sense that the third arbitrator or a judge is.").

[40] *See, e.g.*, ICDR International Arbitration Rules (2014), Art. 13(1), which provides that "[a]rbitrators acting under these Rules shall be impartial and independent ..."

litigation or arbitration are allocated at the end of the proceedings, with the losing party typically obliged to pay part or all of the prevailing party's expenses. The United States stands apart. Under the so-called *American Rule*, each party generally bears its own costs and attorneys' fees regardless of the outcome of the proceedings.[41]

3.30 The FAA is silent on the issue of costs. By contrast, New York arbitration law explicitly disallows the allocation of attorneys' fees absent specific language to this effect in the arbitration agreement.[42] The New York rule has, however, been held inapplicable to international arbitrations or other arbitrations subject to the FAA located in New York.[43] Arbitrators are thus free to award costs in international arbitrations located in New York.

3.31 While the American Rule does not govern international arbitral proceedings in New York, the U.S. practice may inhibit arbitrators sitting in New York from allocating fees and expenses. This may be so even where the parties select arbitral rules (such as the ICC Rules of Arbitration or the ICDR International Arbitration Rules) that empower arbitrators to allocate costs and fees.[44]

3.32 Accordingly, if parties choosing New York as seat of arbitration want the arbitrators to have the discretion to allocate costs and fees, they should so provide in their arbitration clause. The following language can be used:

> The arbitrators are authorized to include in their award an allocation to any party of such costs and expenses, including attorneys' fees, as the arbitrators shall deem reasonable.

3.33 Conversely, as the FAA contains no prohibition on allocating costs and attorneys' fees, if the parties wish to ensure that arbitration costs will be shared equally and that each party will bear its own attorneys' fees and costs (and thereby override the grant of authority, for example in the ICDR International Arbitration Rules), the following language should be added to the arbitration clause:

> All costs and expenses of the arbitrators [and the arbitral institution] shall be borne by the parties equally; each party shall bear the costs and expenses, including attorneys' fees, of its own counsel, experts, witnesses and preparation and presentation of its case.[45]

---

[41] *See* discussion in Chapter 2.H of this book.

[42] CPLR, § 7513.

[43] Painewebber Inc, v. Bybyk, 81 F.3d 1193. (2d Cir. 1996) (New York rule not applicable to FAA arbitration in New York, and this despite the New York choice of law provision in the contract).

[44] ICC, Rules of Arbitration (2012), Art. 37(4); ICDR, International Arbitration Rules (2014), Art. 34.

[45] In ReliaStar Life Ins. Co. of New York v. EMC National Life Company, 564 F.3d 81, 88–89 (2d Cir. 2009), the Court of Appeals for the Second Circuit held that such a clause did not prevent the arbitrators from awarding costs as a sanction against a party that the arbitrators determined had failed to arbitrate in good faith.

(c) Punitive damages A well-known distinction of U.S. litigation is the availability of punitive damages in commercial cases. Under the FAA, arbitrators are empowered to award punitive damages.[46] By contrast, arbitrators have no such authority under New York arbitration law, and this is so even if the parties seek to confer such authority on the arbitrators.[47] The New York prohibition is, however, not applicable to international arbitrations located in New York (even where the contract is governed by New York law).[48] **3.34**

In practice, the authors are not aware of any international arbitration case in New York where punitive damages have been awarded. The theoretical availability of punitive damages remains a cause of concern for some foreign parties choosing New York as their seat of arbitration. Taking this concern into consideration, the AAA/ICDR amended its International Arbitration Rules to prohibit awards of punitive damages absent party agreement.[49] The rules of other institutions do not include similar prohibitions. Where the subject of punitive damages is not addressed in the chosen arbitral rules, the matter can be addressed in the arbitration clause. To disable the arbitrators from awarding punitive damages, the following sentence can be added to the arbitration clause: **3.35**

> The arbitrators are not empowered to award punitive damages, and each party hereby waives any right to seek or recover punitive damages with respect to any dispute resolved by arbitration.

Conversely, parties to an arbitration agreement who wish to confirm the arbitrators' power to grant punitive damages could use the following language: "The arbitrators shall be empowered to award punitive damages in appropriate cases." **3.36**

(d) Class proceedings The availability of class proceedings in arbitration is a hotly debated issue in the United States. The silence of an arbitration clause on the topic of class proceedings is generally not considered as evidencing that the parties consent to participate in such proceedings,[50] but, given the uncertainty **3.37**

---

[46] Mastrobuono v. Shearson Lehman Hutton, Inc., 514 U.S. 52, 60 (1995) (FAA preempts New York rule prohibiting arbitrators from awarding punitive damages).

[47] Garrity v. Lyle Stuart, Inc., 40 N.Y.2d 354, 356 (1976) ("An arbitrator has no power to award punitive damages, even if agreed upon by the parties.").

[48] Mastrobuono v. Shearson Lehman Hutton, Inc., 514 U.S. 52, 60 (1995) (New York choice-of-law provision is not "an unequivocal exclusion of punitive damages claims."); Merrill Lynch, Pierce, Fenner & Smith, Inc. v. Adler, 234 A.D.2d 139 (1st Dep't 1996) (following *Mastrobuono*); *but see* Dean Witter Reynolds Inc. v. Trimble, 166 Misc.2d 40 (N.Y. Sup. Ct. 1995) (holding that the New York prohibition on punitive damages would be applicable where the contract requires arbitration in New York).

[49] Article 31(5) of the ICDR International Arbitration Rules (2014) reads in relevant part: "Unless the parties agree otherwise, the parties expressly waive and forego any right to punitive, exemplary or similar damages unless any applicable law(s) requires that compensatory damages be increased in a specified manner."

[50] Stolt-Nielsen S.A. v. AnimalFeeds Int'l Corp., 130 S. Ct. 1758, 1775 (2010) ("[T]he panel regarded the agreement's silence on the question of class arbitration as dispositive. The panel's conclusion is fundamentally at war with the foundational FAA principle that arbitration is a matter of consent.").

of the case law, parties wishing to ensure that class arbitration is excluded would be well-advised to do so expressly (for example, by stating in their clause that "there shall be no class action arbitration").[51] The enforceability of such waivers of class proceedings has been upheld by the U.S. Supreme Court.[52] In *American Express*, the Supreme Court held that, under the FAA, courts were not allowed to disregard a contractual waiver of class arbitration on the basis that the cost to plaintiffs of individually arbitrating the claims would exceed the potential recovery.[53] The U.S. Supreme Court has also ruled that the FAA preempts any state law that would require class arbitration where an arbitration agreement excludes it.[54] Conversely, parties wishing to provide for class arbitration should consent expressly in the arbitration clause (for example, by including the following language: "The parties agree that class action arbitration shall be available under this clause"). Such parties may also wish to incorporate by reference into their arbitration clause the AAA's Supplementary Rules for Class Arbitration, which provide a mechanism for the administration of class arbitration.[55]

4. Arbitral Process

3.38 *(a) Discovery* Extensive discovery—wide-ranging document disclosure and pretrial depositions and interrogatories of parties and nonparties—is the hallmark of U.S. litigation.[56] This practice is of concern to many parties considering New York as place of arbitration.

3.39 This concern is misguided because international arbitrators sitting in New York need not, and generally do not, follow U.S. litigation standards regarding discovery.[57] As a matter of law, the arbitrators' power to compel prehearing discovery in arbitrations located in New York is limited.[58] Courts in New York have

[51] Paul Friedland, *The Impact of Stolt-Nielsen on Drafting Arbitration Clauses*, Kluwer Arbitration Blog (June 25, 2010).

[52] Am. Express Co. v. Italian Colors Rest., 133 S. Ct. 2304 (2013).

[53] *Id.* at 2309 ("No contrary congressional command requires us to reject the waiver of class arbitration here.").

[54] AT&T Mobility LLC v. Conception, 131 S. Ct. 1740, 1748–1751 (2011).

[55] *Id.*

[56] For a discussion of how discovery operates in the U.S. system of civil litigation, *see* Chapter 2.E of this book.

[57] For a discussion of discovery procedures in an international arbitration seated in New York, *see* Chapter 9 of this book.

[58] Section 7 of the FAA provides that "[t]he arbitrators ... may summon in writing any person to attend before them or any of them as a witness and in a proper case to bring with him or them any book, record, document, or paper which may be deemed material as evidence in the case." For the way this provision has been interpreted, *see generally* Paul Friedland and Lucy Martinez, *Arbitral Subpoenas under U.S. Law and Practice*, 14 Am. Rev. Int'l Arb. 197 (2003). Under § 7505 of the CPLR, arbitrators are granted power to issue subpoenas. This provision has, however, been limited to the procuring of evidence at the hearing, i.e., to compel attendance at the hearing, *see* De Shapiro v. Kohlmeyer, 35 N.Y.2d 402, 406 (1974) ("Under the CPLR, arbiters do not have the power to direct the parties to engage in disclosure proceedings.").

recognized the arbitrators' power to order document disclosure from parties,[59] but not from nonparties.[60] Although doubts remain as to whether arbitrators have the authority to compel pre-hearing depositions of parties,[61] there is significant authority for the proposition that arbitrators cannot require depositions of *nonparties.*[62]

The *courts'* authority to compel discovery in aid of arbitration proceedings is also extremely limited. As a general rule, federal and state courts in New York will not intervene in arbitration proceedings to order disclosure of documents or other forms of discovery absent "extraordinary circumstances."[63] There is some authority in New York for the proposition that parties could, by agreement, waive this requirement and agree, for example, to discovery of third parties.[64] **3.40**

If discovery remains a concern, parties choosing New York as seat of arbitration may specify the rules applicable to discovery in their arbitration clause. Under the FAA, they are free to specify both the discovery that is permissible between them and the powers of the arbitrator respecting such discovery.[65] Parties seeking to **3.41**

[59] *See, e.g.*, Integrity Ins. Co., In Liq. v. American Centennial Ins. Co., 885 F. Supp. 69, 72 (S.D.N.Y. 1995) (although § 7 of the FAA "speaks only to the arbitrators' power to summon a witness to 'attend before them,' *i.e.* at the hearing, the courts have permitted arbitrators to order prehearing discovery of *parties.*") (Emphasis in original); *see also* Arbitration Between Douglas Brazell v. American Color Graphics, Inc., 2000 WL 364997 at *2 (S.D.N.Y. 2000) ("Section 7 has been interpreted by courts in this district to include pre-hearing discovery among parties.")

[60] Life Receivables Trust v. Syndicate 102 at Lloyd's of London, 549 F.3d 210 (2d Cir. 2008) (finding that §7 of the FAA does not enable arbitrators to issue prehearing document subpoenas to entities not parties to the arbitration proceeding). This interpretation of the FAA has been adopted in several other federal circuits. *See* COMSAT Corp. v. Nat'l Sci. Found., 190 F.3d 269 (4th Cir. 1999) and Hay Grp., Inc. v. E.B.S. Acquisition Corp., 360 F.3d 404 (3d Cir. 2004); *but see In re* Sec. Life Ins. Co., 228 F.3d 865, 871 (8th Cir. 2000) (the power to compel document disclosure from third parties is "implicit in an arbitration panel's power to subpoena relevant documents for production at a hearing ...").

[61] In Nat'l Broad. Co., Inc. v. Bear Stearns & Co., Inc. 165 F.3d 184, 187 (2d Cir. 1999), the Second Circuit noted that "open questions remain as to whether § 7 [of the FAA] may be invoked as authority for compelling pre-hearing depositions ..." The Court, however, eschewed deciding the question.

[62] Amtel Corp. v. LM Ericsson Telefon, AB, 371 F. Supp. 2d 402, 403 (S.D.N.Y. 2005) ("The weight of judicial authority favors the view that the Federal Arbitration Act ... does not authorize arbitrators to issue subpoenas for discovery depositions against third parties."); Integrity Ins. Co., v. Am. Centennial Ins. Co., 885 F. Supp. 69 (S.D.N.Y. 1995) ("[A]n arbitrator does not have the authority [under the FAA] to compel nonparty witness to appear for pre-arbitration depositions.")

[63] *See, e.g.*, Oriental Commercial & Shipping Co., Ltd. v. Rosseel, N.V., 125 F.R.D. 398, 400 (S.D.N.Y. 1989) ("As a general rule, the discovery provisions of the Federal Rules of Civil Procedure are not available as an incident to an arbitration proceeding... However, discovery 'in aid of arbitration' is permitted by the courts where a movant can demonstrate 'extraordinary circumstances.' "); Int'l Components Corp. v. Klaiber, 54 A.D.2d 550, 551 (1st Dep't 1976) ("The court's power to direct disclosure should not be granted in arbitration proceedings except under extraordinary circumstances.").

[64] *In re* ACE Am. Ins. Co., 6 Misc.3d 1005(A) (N.Y. Sup. Ct. 2004) (special circumstances need not be present to obtain deposition of third party where both parties to the arbitration stipulated to the discovery); Textron, Inc. v. Unisys Corp., 138 Misc.2d 124 (N.Y. Sup. Ct. 1987) (same).

[65] Republic of Kazakhstan v. Biedermann Int'l, 168 F.3d 880, 883 (5th Cir. 1999) ("[A]s a creature of contract, both the substance and procedure for arbitration can be agreed upon in advance.

limit the scope of discovery to the disclosure of documents between them could use the following language:

> The parties shall be entitled to reasonable production of relevant, non-privileged documents, carried out expeditiously. If the parties are unable to agree upon same, the arbitral tribunal shall have the power, upon application of any party, to make all appropriate orders for production of documents by any party. There shall be no other form of discovery, including discovery depositions.

3.42 Where the parties wish to provide for U.S. litigation-style discovery, the following provision could be used:

> The parties shall allow and participate in discovery in accordance with the United States Federal Rules of Civil Procedure. Unresolved discovery disputes shall be submitted to the arbitrator(s).

3.43 It remains uncertain whether this language would be sufficient to allow broad discovery of third parties. Contracting parties cannot by agreement expand the power of the *arbitrators* to compel nonparties to participate in the prehearing discovery process, notably to participate in prehearing depositions.[66] There is, however, some authority in New York supporting the view that parties to an arbitration agreement could agree to turn to the *courts* to obtain prehearing depositions of third parties.[67]

3.44 *(b) Consolidation of proceedings* Absent party consent, consolidation of related arbitral proceedings can give rise to insuperable difficulties. This is a disadvantage of arbitration as compared to litigation in projects involving multiple contracts and parties.

3.45 Although court-ordered consolidation is possible under the FAA, parties choosing New York as the seat of arbitration should be aware that judicial assistance will not necessarily be available. The Second Circuit, as a majority of the other federal circuits, considers that courts have no authority under the FAA to consolidate related arbitral proceedings absent party consent.[68] The case law is scant,

---

The parties may pre-arrange discovery mechanisms directly or by selecting an established forum or body of governing principles in which the conventions of discovery are settled.").

[66] Nat'l Broad. Co., Inc. v. Bear Stearns & Co., Inc., 165 F.3d 184, 187 (2d Cir. 1999) ("If discovery were to be obtained from … third parties … the authority to compel their participation would have to be found in a source other than the parties' arbitration agreement."); Integrity Ins. Co. v. Am. Centennial Ins. Co., 885 F. Supp. 69, 71 (S.D.N.Y. 1995) ("Because the parties to a contract cannot bind non-parties, they certainly cannot grant such authority to an arbitrator. Thus, an arbitrator's power *over non-parties* derives solely from the FAA."). *See also* Life Receivables Trust v. Syndicate 102 at Lloyd's of London, 549 F.3d 210, 218 (2d Cir. 2008) (similar).

[67] *In re* ACE Am. Ins. Co., 6 Misc.3d 1005(A) (N.Y. Sup. Ct. 2004) (special circumstances need not be present to obtain deposition of third party where both parties to the arbitration stipulated to the discovery); Textron, Inc. v. Unisys Corp., 138 Misc.2d 124 (N.Y. Sup. Ct. 1987) (same).

[68] United Kingdom v. Boeing Co., 998 F.2d 68, 74 (2d Cir. 1993) ("[T]he district court cannot consolidate arbitration proceedings arising from separate agreements to arbitrate, absent the parties' agreement to allow such consolidation."); *see also In re* Allstate Ins. Co. and Global Reinsurance Corp., 2006 WL 2289999 (S.D.N.Y. 2006) (applying *Boeing* and refusing to order

but suggests that this is so even though consolidation can be ordered absent party consent under New York arbitration law.[69]

As a result, parties who anticipate the need for consolidation are left with three options. First, they can explicitly consent in their arbitration agreement to judicial consolidation of related proceedings. The drawback of this approach, however, is that it frustrates the purpose of choosing to arbitrate in the first place, i.e., to avoid being drawn into court proceedings. **3.46**

The second option is to spell out a mechanism for parties or arbitrators to consolidate related proceedings. This option will require a significant drafting effort, as multiple scenarios and technicalities must be taken into account. Readers should refer to specialized works on the issue.[70] The best way is to do so in a stand-alone arbitration protocol signed by all parties to all related agreements. Where that is done, there should be no need for consolidation orders by arbitrators or judges. Absent a single arbitration agreement, the arbitration clauses of the several related agreements must include complementary and cross-referenced consolidation provisions. The drafting considerations are not particular to New York arbitration. **3.47**

The third option is to select arbitration rules that include a procedure for consolidation. The ICDR International Arbitration Rules for example provide that the ICDR may, at the request of a party, appoint a "consolidation arbitrator" who will have the power to consolidate two or more arbitrations pending under the ICDR Rules, or the ICDR Rules and other arbitration rules administered by the AAA or ICDR if certain requirements are met.[71] **3.48**

(c) Confidentiality Confidentiality of arbitral proceedings and awards is one of the enduring myths surrounding international arbitration.[72] In the United States, **3.49**

consolidation absent party consent, but referring the parties to an arbitration panel to determine whether consolidation would be appropriate).

[69] Sullivan Cnty. v. Edward L. Nezelek Inc., 42 N.Y.2d 123 (1977) ("[P]arties signing an agreement to arbitrate must be held to do so in contemplation of the announced authority of the courts in proper cases to direct consolidation."). Prior to the Second District's decision in *Boeing*, the New York Supreme Court had found this rule applicable to proceedings governed by the FAA. *See* Bock v. Drexel Burnham Lambert, 143 Misc.2d 542 (N.Y. Sup. Ct. 1989). After *Boeing*, this approach would, however, appear to be no longer applicable. *See* Home Insurance Company v. New England Re. Corp., 1999 WL 681388 (S.D.N.Y. 1999) ("[A]ny New York arbitration law that permits consolidation without the consent of all parties would conflict with federal law as pronounced by the Second Circuit and be preempted.").

[70] *See, e.g.*, Paul Friedland, Arbitration Clauses for International Contracts, 135 *et seq.* (2d ed. 2007).

[71] Article 8 of the ICDR International Arbitration Rules. The requirements are that "a. the parties have expressly agreed to consolidation; or b. all of the claims and counterclaims in the arbitrations are made under the same arbitration agreement; or c. the claims, counterclaims, or setoffs in the arbitrations are made under more than one arbitration agreement; the arbitrations involve the same parties; the disputes in the arbitrations arise in connection with the same legal relationship; and the consolidation arbitrator finds the arbitration agreements to be compatible." *Id.*

[72] Confidentiality should be distinguished from privacy. Arbitration ensures privacy in the sense that arbitral proceedings, unlike court proceedings, are and remain private. Confidentiality

the few cases that have addressed the issue have held that no duty of confidentiality exists absent party agreement.[73] Parties choosing New York as seat of arbitration should not expect the proceedings and award to be confidential unless they expressly provide so.

3.50 If confidentiality is an issue, either because a party wishes to keep the subject matter of the contract confidential (e.g., because it involves trade secrets) or because it is anticipated that disclosure of the arbitration proceedings would be prejudicial to its business interests, this should be addressed at the drafting stage. This can be done in one of two ways. First, the parties can agree to arbitration in New York under the rules of an institution that provides for confidentiality, for example, the Arbitration Rules of the LCIA.[74] Second, the parties can include a confidentiality clause in their arbitration agreement. The following language, adapted from the LCIA rules, could be used:

> The parties and the arbitrators shall keep confidential all awards in the arbitration, together with all materials in the proceedings created for the purpose of the arbitration and all other documents produced by another party in the proceedings not otherwise in the public domain, save and to the extent that disclosure may be required of a party or arbitrator by legal duty, to protect or pursue a legal right or to enforce or challenge an award in legal proceedings before a court or other judicial authority.

5. Considerations Relating to Judicial Powers

3.51 *(a) Provisional measures* Whether courts in New York have the authority to grant provisional measures (e.g., preliminary injunctions or attachments) in aid of international arbitral proceedings used to be a vexed topic.[75] In its 1982 decision in *Cooper v. Ateliers de la Motobécane S.A.*, the New York Court of Appeals interpreted the New York Convention as barring courts from granting such relief in international cases.[76] The *Cooper* decision was followed by state and, to an extent, federal courts in New York.[77]

---

refers to restrictions on the disclosure that the parties or counsel can make regarding the arbitration. Arbitration's privacy permits, but does not mandate, confidentiality.

[73] United States v. Panhandle E. Corp., 118 F.R.D. 346 (D. Del. 1998) (arbitration proceedings not confidential where there was no evidence that the parties had, in fact, agreed to hold the proceedings in confidence); Contship Containerlines, Ltd. v. PPG Industries, Inc., 2003 WL 1948807 (S.D.N.Y. 2003) (ordering production of documents relating to foreign arbitral proceedings despite allegation that such proceedings were covered by an implied duty of confidentiality).

[74] LCIA Arbitration Rules (1998), Art. 30; LCIA Arbitration Rules (2014), Art. 30.

[75] *See generally* Chapter 8 of this book.

[76] 57 N.Y.2d 408 (1982). *See* discussion in Chapter 8.C.3 of this book.

[77] Federal courts in New York were bound by *Cooper* when asked to order provisional remedies under the CPLR. ContiChem LPG v. Parsons Shipping Co., Ltd., 229 F.3d 426 (2d Cir. 2000) (refusing to order attachment under CPLR 7502 in aid of arbitral proceedings in London). Federal courts in New York, however, have interpreted the New York Convention as not limiting their equitable power to grant preliminary injunctions in aid of arbitral proceedings. *See* Borden Inc. v. Meiji Mills Prods. Co., 919 F.2d 822 (2d Cir. 1990) (confirming a preliminary injunction

In 2005, the New York legislature amended the CPLR and explicitly authorized New York courts to order attachments and preliminary injunctions in aid of arbitral proceedings subject to the New York Convention.[78] While some have questioned whether the New York legislature was competent to overrule *Cooper* (absent a decision of the New York Court of Appeals or of the Supreme Court of the United States),[79] New York courts now routinely order provisional measures (including attachments) in aid of international arbitrations seated in New York.[80] Furthermore, New York courts are also willing to enforce provisional measures ordered by arbitrators including provisional measures, such as Mareva-type injunctions, that would not be available in court.[81] **3.52**

If the availability of provisional measures remains a concern, parties may contractually assuage any judicial concerns that a court order of provisional relief would be inconsistent with the arbitration agreement. To this end, the following language can be added to the arbitration agreement: **3.53**

> Nothing in this Agreement shall prevent either party from seeking provisional measures from any court of competent jurisdiction, and any such request shall not be deemed incompatible with the agreement to arbitrate or a waiver of the right to arbitrate.

There is some authority in New York that similar language would be effective and not inconsistent with *Cooper*.[82] **3.54**

---

granted pending arbitration of a trademark dispute between a U.S. licensor and a Japanese licensee subject to the New York Convention).

[78] Section 7502(c) of the CPLR reads as follows: "The Supreme Court ... may entertain an application for an order of attachment or for a preliminary injunction in connection with an arbitration that is pending or that is to be commenced inside or outside this state, whether or not it is subject to the United Nations convention on the recognition and enforcement of foreign arbitral awards, but only upon the ground that the award to which the applicant may be entitled may be rendered ineffectual without such provisional relief ..."

[79] By amending § 7502(c) of the CPLR, the New York legislature, arguably, purported to interpret federal law (Chapter 2 of the FAA implementing the New York Convention), an exercise that it was incompetent to perform. At most, the New York legislature's action is an invitation to the New York Court of Appeals to reconsider *Cooper*. *See* Robert P. Knapp III, *New CPLR 7502(c): Can Legislature Interpret Federal Law for N.Y.?* N.Y.L.J. 4 (July 25, 2006). *See* discussion in Chapter 8.C.3 of this book.

[80] *See, e.g.*, Matter of Sojitz Corp. v. Prithvi Info. Solutions Ltd., 921 N.Y.S.2d 14 (1st Dep't 2011) (holding that "pursuant to CPLR 7502 (c), a preaward attachment in international arbitration is proper; that is, debt owed by an entity domiciled within this state to the party against whom the award is sought may be attached.").

[81] CE Int'l Res. Holdings LLC v. S.A. Minerals, Ltd., 2012 U.S. Dist. LEXIS 176158, at *11 (S.D.N.Y. 2012) (confirming and enforcing an interim award enjoining a party from transferring any assets located anywhere in the world absent posting of adequate security).

[82] Canwest Global Commc'n Corp. v. Mirkaei Tikshoret Ltd., 9 Misc. 3d 845, 866 (N.Y. Sup. Ct. 2005) ("The injunctive relief carve-out, contractually agreed upon by the parties herein, does not frustrate the purpose of the UN Convention, but supports the goal of 'minimiz[ing] the uncertainty of enforcing arbitration agreements and to avoid the vagaries of foreign law for international traders' [announced in *Cooper*].").

3.55 *(b) Modifying the scope of judicial review* Section 10(a) of the FAA sets forth the grounds upon which courts may vacate arbitral awards. Courts have also recognized "implied" grounds of vacatur, most notably "manifest disregard of the law" by the arbitrators.[83] A question that has received considerable attention in the United States is whether parties may by contract modify the scope of judicial review of an arbitral award.

3.56 In its recent decision in *Hall Street Associates v. Mattel, Inc.*, the Supreme Court of the United States held that the grounds for vacatur set forth in the FAA are exclusive and that it is not open to parties to stipulate additional grounds.[84] In this decision, the Supreme Court resolved a split among U.S. federal circuit courts.[85]

3.57 A related issue is whether grounds for vacating awards can be excluded by contract. This question was not addressed by the Supreme Court in its recent decision, but the import of *Hall Street* is that parties would lack such power. There is authority in the Second Circuit for the proposition that parties cannot limit the grounds for vacatur.[86]

3.58 *(c) Enforcement of awards* Section 9 of the FAA provides that a court may confirm an award "if the parties in their agreement have agreed that a judgment of the court shall be entered upon the award made pursuant to the arbitration." Interpreting this language, some courts in New York have held that they have no

---

[83] Wilko v. Swan, 346 U.S. 427, 436–37 (1953) ("[T]he interpretations of the law by the arbitrators in contrast to manifest disregard are not subject, in the federal courts, to judicial review for error in interpretation."). *See also* Merrill Lynch, Pierce, Fenner & Smith, Inc. v. Bobker, 808 F.2d 930, 933 (2d Cir. 1986) ("'Manifest disregard of the law' by arbitrators is a judicially-created ground for vacating their arbitration award, which was introduced by the Supreme Court in *Wilko v. Swan*."). *See also* Goldman Sachs Execution & Clearing, L.P. v. Official Unsecured Creditors Comm. of Bayou Grp., LLC, 491 F. App'x 201 (2d Cir. 2012) (confirming that manifest disregard remains a valid ground for vacating arbitration awards). For a detailed discussion of the doctrine of "manifest disregard," and its continued viability, see Chapter 14.C.2(c) of this book.

[84] Hall Street Associates v. Mattel, Inc., 552 U.S. 576 (2008). *See* Chapter 14.C.2(c) of this book.

[85] Kyocera Corp. v. Prudential-Bache Trade Servs., Inc., 341 F.3d 987 (9th Cir. 2003); Schoch v. Infousa, Inc., 341 F.3d 785, 789 n.3 (8th Cir. 2003) (expressing skepticism as to whether parties can heighten the standard of review); Bowen v. Amoco Pipeline Co., 254 F.3d 925 (10th Cir. 2001); Chicago Typographical Union No. 16 v. Chicago Sun-Times, Inc., 935 F.2d 1501, 1504–05 (7th Cir. 1991) (stating in dicta that "[p]arties cannot contract for *judicial* review of [an] award; federal jurisdiction cannot be created by contract."). *But see* Puerto Rico Tel. Co. v. U.S. Phone Mfg. Corp., 427 F.3d 21 (1st Cir. 2005), *abrogated by* Hall Street Assocs. v. Mattel, Inc., 552 U.S. 576 (2008); Roadway Package Sys., Inc. v. Kayser, 257 F.3d 287 (3d Cir. 2001), *abrogated by* Hall Street Assocs. v. Mattel, Inc., 552 U.S. 576 (2008); Syncor Int'l Corp. v. McLeland, 1997 WL 452245 (4th Cir. 1997), *abrogated by* Hall Street Assocs. v. Mattel, Inc., 552 U.S. 576 (2008); Gateway Techs, Inc. v. MCI, 64 F.3d 993 (5th Cir. 1995), *abrogated by* Hall Street Assocs. v. Mattel, Inc., 552 U.S. 576 (2008).

[86] Hoeft v. MVL Group, Inc., 343 F.3d 57, 64 (2d Cir. 2003) ("Since federal courts are not rubber stamps, parties may not, by private agreement, relieve them of their obligation to review arbitration awards for compliance with §10(a) [of the FAA]."). It has, however, been held that parties can limit appellate review of the district court's review of an award, *see* MACTEC, Inc. v. Gorelick, 427 F.3d 821, 829 (10th Cir. 2005).

jurisdiction to enforce arbitral awards absent an indication of the parties' intent to have a court enter judgment upon the award.[87]

It is doubtful that the FAA requirement applies to international arbitration. The U.S. Court of Appeals for the Second Circuit (the highest federal court in New York) has held that the FAA requirement of consent to entry of judgment does not apply to awards enforced under the New York Convention,[88] including international arbitration awards made in the United States.[89] **3.59**

There is, moreover, authority for the proposition that an arbitration clause stating that awards shall be "*final*" or that disputes shall be "*finally*" settled by arbitration is sufficient to satisfy the FAA requirement.[90] The case law also suggests that arbitration agreements calling for arbitration under the AAA Commercial Arbitration Rules, which explicitly provide for consent to entry of judgment,[91] would be sufficient to satisfy the FAA requirement.[92] **3.60**

To avoid uncertainty as to the ultimate enforceability of the award, where New York is the place of arbitration, it remains advisable to add language to the arbitration agreement empowering the courts to enter judgment upon the award (a so-called "entry-of-judgment" provision). The following language can be used: "Judgment upon any award(s) rendered by the arbitrators may be entered in any court having jurisdiction thereof." **3.61**

---

[87] *See* Phoenix Aktiengesellschaft v. Ecoplas, Inc., 391 F.3d 433, 436 (2d Cir. 2004) (9 U.S.C. § 9 "requires prior consent to confirmation by both parties."); Varley v. Tarrytown Associates, 477 F.2d 208 (2d Cir. 1973) (no jurisdiction to confirm arbitration award and enter judgment on the award where contract does not explicitly provide that judgment could be entered upon an arbitration award). New York arbitration law, by contrast, does not require consent to entry of judgment. Section 7501 of the CPLR provides that an arbitration agreement "confers jurisdiction on the courts of the state to enforce it and to enter judgment on an award."

[88] Phoenix Aktiengesellschaft v. Ecoplas, Inc., 391 F.3d 433, 436 (2d Cir. 2004) (9 U.S.C. § 9 not applicable to New York Convention awards).

[89] Stone & Webster, Inc. v. Triplefine Int'l Corp., 118 F. App'x 546, 548–49 (2d Cir. 2004) (9 U.S.C. § 9 not applicable to enforcement of an award rendered in New York in a dispute opposing U.S. and Taiwanese corporations concerning a contract to be performed in Taiwan) referring to Bergersen v. Joseph Muller Corp., 710 F.2d 928, 932 (2d Cir. 1983) (award rendered in New York City between two foreign entities is a "nondomestic award" for the purposes of the New York Convention).

[90] I/S Stravborg (O. H. Meling, Manager) v. National Metal Converters, Inc., 500 F.2d 424, 425–27 (2d Cir. 1974) (holding that the FAA requirement was satisfied in light of the provision that the decisions of the arbitrators "shall be final"); Phoenix Aktiengesellschaft v. Ecoplas, Inc., 391 F.3d 4333, 437 (2d Cir. 2004) (suggesting obiter that the "final" language could be sufficient); Daihitsu Motor Co. v. Terrain Vehicles, Inc., 13 F.3d 196, 207 (7th Cir. 1993) (FAA requirement is satisfied where the agreement provides that "any given dispute … would be 'finally settled' by arbitration").

[91] Rule R-52(c) of the AAA Commercial Arbitration Rules (2013) reads: "Parties to an arbitration under these rules shall be deemed to have consented that judgment upon the arbitration award may be entered in any federal or state court having jurisdiction thereof." It should be noted that the AAA International Arbitration Rules (2014) do not contain any similar language.

[92] *See, e.g.*, P & P Indus., Inc. v. Sutter Corp., 179 F.3d 861, 866–67 (10th Cir. 1999); Washington Mut. Bank v. Crest Mortgage Co., 418 F. Supp. 2d 860 (N.D. Tex. 2006).

4

THE APPLICATION OF NEW YORK LAW TO CONTRACTS

David W. Rivkin, Mark W. Friedman, and William H. Taft V[1]

A. Choice-of-Law Rules in New York	4.06
B. Contract Formation	4.12
1. Elements of a Contract	4.14
2. Future Contracts	4.19
3. Authority to Enter Contacts	4.20
C. What Constitutes a Breach	4.22
1. Material Breach	4.23
2. Substantial Performance	4.25
3. Anticipatory Breach and Repudiation	4.26
4. Divisible or Installment Contracts	4.28
D. Consequences of Breach of Contract	4.29
1. Effect on the Performance of the Non-breaching Party	4.29
2. Measure of Damages	4.34
3. Equitable Relief	4.42
E. Claims Ancillary to Breach of Contract	4.45
1. Arbitrability of Ancillary Claims	4.45
2. Claims Ancillary to Breach of Contract under New York Law	4.49
(a) Implied covenant of good faith and fair dealing	4.49
(b) Unjust enrichment	4.51
(c) Fraud in the inducement	4.53
(d) Fraud in the performance	4.55
(e) Third-party beneficiaries	4.57
F. Special Issues Arising under New York Law of Contracts	4.59
1. Merger Clauses	4.60
2. "Best Efforts" vs. "Reasonable Efforts"	4.64
3. Changed Circumstances and *Force Majeure*	4.67

Arbitrations in New York often, but not always, concern contracts governed by New York law. This chapter provides a brief overview of some basic principles of New York law that are relevant to the interpretation and enforcement of contracts. **4.01**

New York contract law is derived from common law, statutes, and administrative sources. New York's common law, which generally follows the Second Restatement of the Law of Contracts, published by the American Law Institute, will typically apply to contracts for services, real property, and non-goods personal property.[2] The Uniform Commercial Code (U.C.C.), whose original **4.02**

[1] The authors thank Matthew Hartz for his editing and research assistance in the creation of this chapter.

[2] The Restatement presents a lengthy and intense analysis of common-law precedent by legal scholars, and because of its pedigree, it is often given considerable deference by New York judges

articles have been adopted in nearly every state, including New York, will typically apply to contracts for the sale or of goods.[3] The U.C.C. deals primarily with transactions involving personal property rather than real property: Article 1 of the U.C.C. contains general contractual provisions and definitions used in the code; Article 2 governs sales contracts; and Article 9 governs secured transactions, or contracts assigning the rights to payment in security interest agreements.[4] New York also derives provisions of its contract laws from the New York General Obligations Law,[5] various state administrative laws,[6] and international treaties, including the U.N. Convention on Contracts for the International Sale of Goods.[7]

4.03 The core principle of contract interpretation in New York is that the intent of the parties should control the interpretation of the contract.[8] New York courts recognize that clear and unambiguous contract language should be enforced according to its plain meaning since such language is the best evidence of the parties' intent.[9] Furthermore, contracts are read in their entirety and as a whole, such that each part is understood in reference to the context of the entire contract.[10] Moreover, New York courts strictly follow the "parol evidence rule," which prohibits consideration of extrinsic evidence of prior negotiations, representations, and inconsistent understandings in analyzing the meaning of unambiguous contract language.[11] These principles guide New York courts in evaluating all aspects

---

facing decisions that turn on technical points of contract law. *See* Restatement (Second) of Contracts (2006).

[3] Under the U.C.C., *goods* include tangible, movable objects, including "unborn young animals," "growing crops," and "things attached to realty," but excluding the money with which the buyer is paying for goods. N.Y.U.C.C. § 2-105(1) (2005).

[4] N.Y.U.C.C. (2005).

[5] *See* Section A of this chapter.

[6] *See* New York Contract Law (Glen Banks ed., 2006).

[7] The U.N. Convention on Contracts for the International Sale of Goods (CISG) applies to contracts for the sale of goods between a resident of the United States and a resident of another country. This treaty was adopted by the United States on April 11, 1980. *See* 52 C.F.R. §§ 6262, 6264–6280 (1987).

[8] *See* 11 Williston On Contracts § 30:2 (4th ed.) (2014) ("In the interpretation, and ultimately, in the construction of contracts as well, the avowed purpose and primary function of the court is to ascertain the intention of the parties."); Am. Express Bank, Ltd. v. Uniroyal, Inc., 164 A.D.2d, 275, 277 (1st Dep't 1990) ("In interpreting a contract, the intent of the parties governs.").

[9] *See* Greenfield v. Philles Records, Inc., 98 N.Y.2d 562, 569 (2002) ("The best evidence of what parties to a written agreement intend is what they say in their writing. Thus, a written agreement that is complete, clear and unambiguous on its face must be enforced according to the plain meaning of its terms.").

[10] *See* 11 Williston On Contracts § 32:5 (4th ed. 2014) ("A contract will be read as a whole and every part will be read with reference to the whole.").

[11] *See* W.W.W. Assocs., Inc. v. Giancontieri, 77 N.Y.2d 157 (1990) ("A familiar and eminently sensible proposition of law is that, when parties set down their agreement in a clear, complete document, their writing should as a rule be enforced according to its terms. Evidence outside the four corners of the document as to what was really intended but unstated or misstated is generally inadmissible to add to or vary the writing.").

of contracts, from complex multi-part instruments to specific provisions of basic agreements. These principles establish the foundation for New York courts engaging in contract interpretation, and courts will strive to ensure that the parties' intentions at the time of contracting, as best evidenced by the agreed written document, are enforced according to their clear terms.

Unlike some foreign jurisdictions, New York courts afford substantial weight to contracting parties' practical construction or performance when interpreting contracts.[12] As reflected in the Restatement, New York courts will generally find that, if the words of the contract are not clear, "the parties to an agreement know best what they meant, and their action under it is often the strongest evidence of their meaning."[13] Any New York contract should be construed with this rule of interpretation in mind. **4.04**

A chapter like this obviously cannot cover all aspects of New York law, so it focuses on important principles and those areas where New York law may differ from foreign jurisdictions. This chapter begins by addressing New York choice-of-law rules. Next, it turns to the elements of a contract and the New York laws and presumptions regarding contract formation. The chapter then examines the elements and consequences of a breach of contract, before turning to a number of claims ancillary to a contractual breach. The chapter concludes with some special issues that may arise under New York contract law. **4.05**

A. CHOICE-OF-LAW RULES IN NEW YORK

The laws and presumptions that govern contracts differ among the fifty states. When evaluating American contracts, a practitioner must first consider which state's laws to apply to a contract's interpretation. While New York choice-of-law precedent is not binding on arbitrations held in New York, arbitrators will usually apply the same principles. **4.06**

[12] *See* 11 Williston on Contracts § 32:14 (4th ed. 2008) ("An important aid in the interpretation of contracts is the practical construction placed on the agreement by the parties themselves."); Restatement (Second) of Contracts § 202 cmt. g (2006) ("The parties to an agreement know best what they meant, and their action under it is often the strongest evidence of their meaning."). This rule stems from long-standing precedent to consider the conduct of the parties in resolving ambiguities in contractual language. *See* Ins. Co. v. Dutcher, 95 U.S. 269, 273 (1877) ("the practical interpretation of an agreement by a party to it is always a consideration of great weight. The construction of a contract is as much a part of it as anything else. There is no surer way to find out what parties meant, than to see what they have done."); Old Colony Trust Co. v. Omaha, 230 U.S. 100, 118 (1913) ("generally speaking, the practical interpretation of a contract by the parties to it for any considerable period of time before it comes to be the subject of controversy is deemed of great, if not controlling, influence.").

[13] Restatement (Second) of Contracts § 202, cmt. g (2006). *See* Croce v. Kurnit, 737 F.2d 229, 235 (2d Cir. 1984); *In re* Schuman Sons Jewelers, Inc., 90 F.2d 606, 607 (2d Cir. 1937).

4.07 A court's application of a state's law often flows from a choice-of-law clause, under which parties to a contract elect to have their agreement governed by the laws of a particular jurisdiction. New York courts tend to defer to choice-of-law clauses.[14] Historically, courts have disregarded choice-of-law clauses only where there is no reasonable basis for the choice of law, or where giving effect to the choice-of-law clause would violate a fundamental public policy of another state with a materially greater interest in the dispute.[15]

4.08 New York law provides for the enforcement of a choice of New York law for certain high-value contracts. New York General Obligations Law §5-1401 allows parties to choose New York law for contracts where the value exceeds $250,000, even where there is no relationship between the contract and the state of New York.[16] Arbitrators generally follow this provision, even though some federal courts may not recognize it because of federal jurisdictional issues.[17]

4.09 In the absence of a choice-of-law provision, New York courts and arbitrators sitting in New York determine the governing law of a contract by applying a "center of gravity" or "significant contacts" test. Under this test, the state's law that is most closely connected to the contract will govern the contract.[18] Factors relevant to this determination include "the place of contracting, the places of negotiation and performance, the location of the subject matter, and the domicile or place of business of the contracting parties," as well as public policy concerns.[19] New York

[14] Freedman v. Chem. Constr. Corp., 372 N.E.2d 12, 15 n.* (N.Y. 1977) ("As a general matter, the parties' manifested intentions to have an agreement governed by the law of a particular jurisdiction are honored."); Turtur v. Rothschild Registry Int'l, Inc., 26 F.3d 304, 310 (2d Cir. 1994); Hundertmark v. Boston Prof'l Hockey Ass'n, 1996 WL 118538, *4 (E.D.N.Y. 1996) ("choice of law clauses are routinely enforced so long as there is a reasonable basis for the choice or the state whose law is selected has sufficient contacts with the transaction.").

[15] Beatie & Osborn L.L.P. v. Patriotic Sci. Co., 431 F. Supp. 2d 367 (S.D.N.Y. 2006); Hartford Fire Ins. Co. v. Orient Overseas Container Lines Ltd., 230 F.3d 549, 556 (2d Cir. 2000) ("New York law is clear in cases involving a contract with an express choice-of-law provision: Absent fraud or a violation of public policy, a court is to apply the law selected in the contract as long as the state selected has sufficient contacts with the transaction."); Int'l Minerals & Res., S.A. v. Pappas, 96 F.3d 586, 592 (2d Cir. 1996); *see also* Restatement (Second) Conflict of Laws § 187(2) (2006).

[16] This provision includes transactions covered by the U.C.C.; but excludes contracts for labor or personal services, transactions for personal, family or household services, and those transactions for which the applicable law is otherwise specified under § 1-105(2) of the U.C.C. N.Y. GEN. OBLIG. LAW § 5-1401 (2005).

[17] Lehman Bros. v. Minmetals Int'l, 179 F. Supp. 2d 118, 135 (S.D.N.Y. 2000) ("[t]he power of courts to enforce [the parties' choice of New York law], however, remains restricted within constitutional bounds."). On the application of state conflict of laws rules by federal courts, *see* Klaxon Co. v. Stentor Elec. Mfg. Co., Inc., 313 U.S. 487, 496 (1941).

[18] *See, e.g.*, Auten v. Auten, 124 N.E.2d 99 (N.Y. 1954) (adopting the "center of gravity" test to determine the governing law of a contract, and explaining that this " 'center of gravity' or 'grouping of contacts' theory of the conflict of laws emphasizes the law of the place which has the most significant contacts with the matter in dispute."); Lazard Freres & Co. v. Protective Life Ins. Co., 108 F.3d 1531, 1539 (2d Cir. 1997); Babcock v. Jackson, 191 N.E.2d 279, 282 (N.Y. 1963).

[19] *Lazard Freres*, 108 F.3d at 1539.

courts tend to give particular weight to the place of contracting and place of performance of the contract.[20]

In New York, the choice of law has the effect of importing a state's substantive laws for contract interpretation. Because the choice of law includes only the state's substantive and not its procedural law, the choice of law does not adopt that state's arbitration law.[21] **4.10**

New York courts are inconsistent in determining whether the conflicts of law rules of the chosen state apply, which can lead to issues of *renvoi*—the problem arising when one state's rule on conflicts of law refers a case to the law of another state, and that second state's conflict-of-law rule refers the case back to the law of the first state, or to an unrelated third state.[22] A number of New York courts have simply rejected the application of the doctrine of renvoi outright;[23] others have stated that renvoi is generally not favored in New York;[24] while other courts have in fact applied the doctrine. Cases in which renvoi has been applied include those dealing with divorce[25] and disposition of an estate.[26] Some courts have simply avoided the issue by concluding that the same law would be applicable **4.11**

---

[20] *Id.*

[21] *See, e.g.*, Educ. Res. Inst., Inc. v. Piazza, 794 N.Y.S.2d 65, 66 (2d Dep't 2005) ("New York courts ... apply contractual choice of law clauses only to substantive issues"); Woodling v. Garrett Corp., 813 F.2d 543, 551 (2d Cir. 1987) ("The contractual choice of law provision is deemed to import only substantive law ... not procedural law."); Gambar Enter., Inc. v. Kelly Services, Inc., 418 N.Y.S.2d 818, 822 (4th Dep't 1979) (interpreting a contractual clause specifying the law of Michigan as the governing law of the contact as only applying to the substantive law, and proceeding to apply the procedural law of New York); *see also* IRB-Brasil Resseguros, S.A. v. Inepar Invs., S.A., 20 N.Y.3d 310 (2012) (holding that a contract with a choice of law provision for New York law must be enforced under New York substantive law even if New York's conflict-of-laws rules would not provide that result).

[22] *See* Black's Law Dictionary (8th ed. 2004) (defining "renvoi").

[23] *See, e.g., In re* Tallmadge, 181 N.Y.S. 336, 345 (N.Y. Sup. Ct. 1919) ("renvoi is no part of the New York law"); Lann v. U.S. Steel Works Corp., 1 N.Y.S.2d 951, 956 (N.Y. Sup. Ct. 1938) ("To adopt any other view would involve acceptance of the 'renvoi' doctrine, which has been rejected almost unanimously."); Wyatt v. Fulrath, 239 N.Y.S.2d 486, 493 (N.Y. Sup. Ct. 1963) ("The plaintiff's claim is based on the renvoi doctrine, which is not followed in New York"); Apton v. Barclays Bank, 91 N.Y.S.2d 589, 591 (N.Y. Sup. Ct. 1949) ("the so-called rule of 'renvoi' ... has been consistently and universally rejected in this Country and, of more pertinence here, in this State."); Weiss v. La Suisse, 141 F. App'x 31, 34 (2d Cir. 2005); Weiss v. La Suisse, 313 F. Supp. 2d 241, 244 (S.D.N.Y. 2004) ("It is settled law that New York courts look to New York and not foreign conflicts provisions in order to avoid the prospect of renvoi."); Anderson v. SAM Airlines, 939 F. Supp. 167, 175 (E.D.N.Y. 1996) ("Under New York law, the court ignores the conflicts laws of another jurisdiction, and imports only the substantive law, so as to avoid the dreaded renvoi.").

[24] Jean v. Francois, 642 N.Y.S.2d 780, 781–82 (N.Y. Sup. Ct. 1996) ("New York courts generally disfavor the renvoi doctrine"); Weiss v. La Suisse, Societe D'Assurances Sur La Vie, 293 F. Supp. 2d 397, 402 (S.D.N.Y. 2003) ("applying Plaintiff's logic would draw the case into the renvoi 'bog' generally disfavored by New York courts.").

[25] Dean v. Dean, 149 N.E. 844 (N.Y. 1925); Ball v. Cross, 132 N.E. 106 (N.Y. 1921).

[26] *In re* Schneider's Estate, 96 N.Y.S.2d 652 (N.Y. Sur. Ct. 1950) (suggesting that renvoi should be applied except where it would violate public policy or where theoretical possibility of endless chain of re-reference becomes an actuality).

whether New York conflicts of law rules were applied or those of the other state in question.[27]

B. CONTRACT FORMATION

4.12 Once a determination is made as to which state's laws govern the interpretation of a contract, it must then be determined whether there is in fact a contract to interpret. Arbitrators may be guided by the contract principles of the state whose law governs the contract.

4.13 New York recognizes a contract as "a promise or a set of promises for the breach of which the law gives a remedy, or the performance of which the law in some way recognizes as a duty."[28] Under New York law, not all promises are contracts. To rise to the level of contractual obligation, a promise must consist of a definite *offer* by one party that is *accepted* by another in return for *consideration*.[29] A promise that meets these criteria may create legally binding obligations between the parties. Courts and arbitrators in New York will examine the totality of a party's express deeds and acts, the situation of both parties, the attendant circumstances, and both parties' objectives to determine whether a contract was executed and whether it is enforceable.[30]

1. Elements of a Contract

4.14 **Offer**: An offer is an act on the part of one party (the *promisor*) that creates a power of acceptance in the other party (the *promisee*).[31] An offer must create a reasonable expectation in the promisee that the promisor is willing to enter into a contract on the basis of his or her offered terms.[32] The offer must be definite and certain,[33] and it must contain an express or implied promise, undertaking, or

---

27 Rutherford v. Gray Line, Inc., 615 F.2d 944, 947 (2d Cir. 1980) ("Even if the New York courts did look to the whole law, however, we believe a Pennsylvania court would follow its own substantive law"); Hamilton v. Accu-Tek, 47 F. Supp. 2d 330, 342 (E.D.N.Y. 1999) ("Renvoi need not be considered because California law also governs under California's choice of law rules.").

28 Restatement (Second) of Contracts §1 (2006).

29 *See, e.g.*, Broder v. Cablevision Sys. Corp., 329 F. Supp. 2d 551, 556 (S.D.N.Y. 2004), *aff'd*, 418 F.3d 187 (2d Cir. 2005); Lumhoo v. Home Depot USA, Inc., 229 F. Supp. 2d 121, 161 (E.D.N.Y. 2002); Oscar Prod., Inc. v. Zacharius, 893 F. Supp. 250, 255 (S.D.N.Y. 1995); Restatement (Second) of Contracts §§ 24, 50, 71 (2006).

30 Bazak Int'l. Corp. v. Tarrant Apparel Grp., 491 F. Supp. 2d 403, 408 (S.D.N.Y. 2007).

31 Farago Adver., Inc. v. Hollinger Int'l., Inc., 157 F. Supp. 2d 252, 258 (S.D.N.Y. 2001); *see also* Restatement (Second) of Contracts § 22(1) (2006).

32 *See* Ahern v. South Buffalo Ry. Co., 104 N.E.2d 898, 907 (N.Y. 1952), *aff'd*, 344 U.S. 367 (1953) (*quoting* Hotchkiss v. National City Bank of New York, 200 F. 287, 293 (S.D.N.Y. 1911)).

33 Ahlstrom Mach. Inc. v. Associated Airfreight Inc., 708 N.Y.S.2d 497, 499 (3d Dep't 2000); Concilla v. May, 625 N.Y.S.2d 346 (3d Dep't 1995); *In re* Maxwell Commc'n Corp., 198 B.R. 63, 67–68 (S.D.N.Y. 1996).

commitment to enter into a contract.[34] Technical language such as "I offer" or "I promise" is useful, but it is not necessary to create a binding obligation. Indeed, there is no particular requirement covering the form or content of an offer; rather, New York law requires only that at the minimum a valid offer must include the identity of the parties and a sufficient description of the subject matter.[35]

Acceptance: Acceptance is a promisee's formal assent to the terms of an offer. An acceptance must be clear, unambiguous, and unequivocal.[36] Generally at common law, it is required that an acceptance "mirror" the offer; if the acceptance varies even slightly from the offer, the qualified response operates as a rejection and termination of the initial offer.[37] However, contracts governed by the U.C.C. do not require such rigid acceptance.[38] Under the U.C.C., an acceptance that contains immaterial deviations may still be valid and may create contractual obligations including the deviated terms.[39] Once an offer is rejected, the offer is extinguished and is not a legally cognizable basis for conduct.[40] **4.15**

The form of an acceptance depends on the terms of the offer. The promisor may, in his or her offer, dictate the manner by which the promisee may accept to create a binding contract. If the promisor makes a unilateral offer, the promisee's conduct can serve as an acceptance and thereby give rise to contractual obligations.[41] Alternatively, the promisor may require acceptance to be in writing, in which case only a written acceptance forms a contract.[42] Absent any express direction, an oral acceptance to a written contract can create a binding contract,[43] as can a promisee's silence where appropriate.[44] If the promisor makes delivery an **4.16**

---

34 Restatement (Second) of Contracts §2 (2006); Merritt Hill Vineyards Inc. v. Windy Heights Vineyard, Inc., 460 N.E.2d 1077 (N.Y. 1984).

35 Personalized Media Commc'ns, L.L.C. v. StarSight Telecast Inc., 2000 WL 1457079, 3 (S.D.N.Y. 2000); Cayea v. Lake Placid Granite Co., 665 N.Y.S.2d 127, 128 (3d Dep't 1997).

36 King v. King, 617 N.Y.S.2d 593, 593 (3d Dep't 1994); Krumme v. WestPoint Stevens, Inc., 143 F.3d 71, 83 (2d Cir. 1998); Int'l Paper Co. v. Suwyn, 966 F. Supp. 246, 253 (S.D.N.Y. 1997).

37 Restatement (Second) of Contracts §58 (2006); Homayouni v. Paribas, 660 N.Y.S.2d 413, 414 (1st Dep't 1997); Watts v. Thomas Carter & Sons, 202 N.Y.S. 852 (2d Dep't 1924).

38 "A definite and seasonable expression of acceptance or a written confirmation which is sent within a reasonable time operates as an acceptance even though it states terms additional to or different from those offered or agreed upon, unless acceptance is expressly made conditional on assent to the additional or different terms." N.Y.U.C.C. §2-207 (2005).

39 Ladau v. Hillier Grp., Inc., 2004 WL 691520, 3 (S.D.N.Y. 2004); *In re* Randall's Island Family Golf Ctrs., Inc., 261 B.R. 96, 100 (Bankr. S.D.N.Y. 2001), *aff'd*, 272 B.R. 521 (S.D.N.Y. 2002).

40 Greystone P'ships Grp., Inc. v. Koninklijke Luchtvaart Maatschappij N.V., 815 F. Supp. 745, 753 (S.D.N.Y. 1993).

41 Consarc Corp. v. Marine Midland Bank, N.A., 996 F.2d 568, 573 (2d Cir. 1993).

42 *See, e.g.*, Farago Adver., Inc. v. Hollinger Int'l., Inc., 157 F. Supp. 2d 252, 258 (S.D.N.Y. 2001); Granite Partners, L.P. v. Bear, Stearns & Co., Inc., 58 F. Supp. 2d 228, 250 (S.D.N.Y. 1999).

43 Tymon v. Linoki, 213 N.E. 2d 661, 662, 665 (N.Y. 1965); Morton's of Chicago/Great Neck LLC v. Crab House, Inc., 746 N.Y.S.2d 317, 319 (2d Dep't 2002).

44 Albrecht Chem. Co. v. Anderson Trading Corp., 84 N.E.2d 625 (N.Y. 1949); *contra* Gomez v. Bicknell, 756 N.Y.S.2d 209 (2d Dep't 2002).

essential element of contract formation, a contract is not formed until delivery is completed, even if the offer has already been accepted.[45]

4.17 **Consideration**: A properly executed contract is invalid if it lacks consideration.[46] Consideration is a bargained-for exchange that constitutes a benefit to the promisor or a detriment to the promisee.[47] Consideration can be something that is promised, acted upon, forborne, or suffered by a party,[48] or can be a benefit that flows to an unrelated party.[49] As a general rule, courts and arbitrators will not inquire as to the value of consideration; it is said that even a peppercorn—symbolic of something trifling in value—can be consideration as long as it is bargained for.[50] A tribunal's inquiry as to contract formation is limited to the question whether there was in fact consideration and whether the consideration was adequate (i.e., whether each party received something of value).[51]

4.18 These three elements—offer, acceptance, and consideration—form the fundamental basis of enforceable contracts.[52] However, even a properly formed contract is unenforceable without a meeting of the minds of the two parties on the essential terms of the agreement.[53] Whether a meeting of the minds has occurred is a subjective inquiry as to whether the parties both gave their mutual assent to be bound by the bargained-for essential terms. Without mutual consent, there is no contract as a matter of law.[54]

2. Future Contracts

4.19 Future contracts, in which an agreement is made to contract at some point in the future, look remarkably similar to valid contracts. However, future contracts are not considered to be contracts.[55] A promise to agree in the future inherently

---

[45] Morgan Servs., Inc. v. Abrams, 801 N.Y.S.2d 457 (4th Dep't 2005).

[46] DFP Mfg. Corp. v. Northrop Grumman Corp., 1999 WL 33458384 (E.D.N.Y. 1999); Liebowitz v. Elsevier Sci. Ltd., 927 F. Supp. 688, 703 (S.D.N.Y. 1996); *see also* Roth v. Isomed, Inc., 746 F. Supp. 316, 319 (S.D.N.Y. 1990).

[47] Weiner v. McGraw-Hill, Inc., 443 N.E.2d 441, 444 (N.Y. 1982); Startech, Inc. v. VSA Arts, 126 F. Supp. 2d 234, 237 (S.D.N.Y. 2000).

[48] Weiner v. McGraw-Hill, Inc., 443 N.E.2d 441 (N.Y. 1982); Hamer v. Sidway, 27 N.E. 256, 257 (N.Y. 1891).

[49] Mencher v. Weiss, 114 N.E.2d 177, 181 (N.Y. 1953).

[50] *See* Whitney v. Stearns, 16 Me. 394, 397 (1839) ("A cent or a pepper corn ... would constitute a valuable consideration.").

[51] Banks, *supra* note 5, § 2:28.

[52] Certain contracts are governed by more specific rules; for example, the Statute of Frauds requires that certain contracts (such as for the sale of land and for contracts that cannot be completed within one year) be in writing. For a discussion of the Statute of Frauds and its relation to specific contracts, *see Commercial Litigation in New York State Courts*, 4 N.Y. Prac. § 59:22 (2d ed.) (Robert L. Haig, ed., 2004).

[53] Computer Assocs. Int'l, Inc. v. U.S. Balloon Mfg. Co., Inc., 782 N.Y.S.2d 117 (2d Dep't 2004).

[54] Schwartz v. Greenberg, 107 N.E.2d 65 (N.Y. 1952).

[55] Bernstein v. Felske, 533 N.Y.S.2d 538, 540 (2d Dep't 1988) ("it is well settled that a mere agreement to agree, in which a material term is left for future negotiations, is unenforceable.").

precludes a binding agreement to the same bargain at the present time. Under New York law, such indefinite "agreements to agree" are generally not enforced, as the parties by their words make clear that there is no present intent to be bound, that they intend to be bound only in the future, and then only if they subsequently reach an agreement with respect to the unsettled terms.[56]

3. Authority to Enter Contacts

Although individuals differ markedly in their ability to represent their own interests in the bargaining process, the freedom to bind oneself to contractual obligations is broad. Only in limited instances is that freedom restricted because a lack of competency renders a party unable to participate meaningfully in the bargaining process.[57] Lack of mental capacity,[58] infancy,[59] and in some instances intoxication[60] are grounds to limit an individual's authority to enter into contracts. Outside of these limited circumstances, individuals have the authority **4.20**

[56] Joseph Martin, Jr., Delicatessen, Inc. v. Schumacher, 417 N.E.2d 541, 544 (N.Y. 1981); *In re* Dolgin Eldert Corp., 286 N.E.2d 228, 234 (N.Y. 1972). Similarly, in the context of real estate transactions, letters of intent to enter into a contract at some point in the future, are also unenforceable. *See* Rennick v. O.P.T.I.O.N. Care, Inc., 77 F.3d 309, 315 (9th Cir. 1996), *cert. denied*, 519 U.S. 865 (1996); Kopple v. Schick Farms, Ltd., 447 F. Supp. 2d 965, 974 (N.D. Iowa 2006); Pantzer v. Shields Dev. Co., 660 F. Supp. 56, 60 (D. Del. 1986); Channel Home Ctrs. v. Grossman, 795 F.2d 291, 298 (3d Cir. 1986). Memoranda of intent also fall in this category, and are similarly unenforceable. *See* Peter F. Gaito Architecture, LLC v. Simone Dev. Corp., 846 N.Y.S.2d 368 (2d Dep't 2007) (no enforceable obligation arose out of preliminary memorandum of understanding which plaintiff had sent to defendant by e-mail, given an unsigned draft agreement which had been the subject of negotiations between the parties evincing the parties' intent not to be bound until the execution of a formal contract); Silverman v. Member Brokerage Servs., LLC, 751 N.Y.S.2d 245 (2d Dep't 2002) (signed memorandum of understanding between employer and employee providing that they would execute more formalized settlement agreement regarding breach of employment contract claim was not enforceable contract; parties did not simply contemplate more formal agreement, but required execution of such agreement to trigger certain obligations); Arcadian Phosphates, Inc. v. Arcadian Corp., 884 F.2d 69 (2d Cir. 1989) (plaintiff's partial performance did not result in memorandum of understanding being an enforceable contract but was held to possibly form the basis for compensable claim of promissory estoppel). Some future contracts give rise to an equitable duty to negotiate in good faith. Typically, a party claiming a breach of such a duty is entitled only to recover for any costs incurred in reliance on the other party's good faith, but may not recover for the expected benefit of the contract that was subject to the negotiations.

[57] Melvin Aron Eisenberg, *The Limits of Cognition and the Limits of Contract*, 47 Stan. L. Rev. 211 (1995).

[58] Ortelere v. Teacher's Ret. Bd. of City of New York, 250 N.E.2d 460, 462 (N.Y. 1969); Harrison v. Grobe, 790 F. Supp. 443, 447 (S.D.N.Y. 1992), *aff'd*, 984 F.2d 594 (2d Cir. 1993).

[59] Ruppert v. Sec'y of U.S. Dept. of Health & Human Servs., 671 F. Supp. 151, 184–85 (E.D.N.Y. 1987), *rev'd on other grounds*, 871 F.2d 1172 (2d Cir. 1989).

[60] Cases in which intoxication renders a party incapacitated may be voided. Sander v. Savage, 78 N.Y.S. 189 (2d Dep't 1902). Not every degree of addiction or intoxication will render a person incompetent. Consequently, the rule has developed in the majority of jurisdictions that the affected person must be so far intoxicated or so chronically affected by alcohol or drugs as to be incapable in fact of understanding the nature of the transaction in which he engaged. *See* Restatement (Second) of Contracts § 16 (2006); McKeon v. Van Slyck, 119 N.E. 851 (N.Y. 1918).

to bind themselves to most contracts, so long as the contract is not illegal,[61] fraudulent,[62] induced by duress,[63] or, in some cases, against public policy.[64]

4.21 The authority to contract also extends to the ability to bind others to contracts. Principles of agency permit an agent to bind his principal to a contract.[65] A principal will be imputed liability for a contract when its agent has actual, apparent, or implied authority.[66] For example, a corporation's president is ordinarily presumed to have the power to make contracts pertaining to the business of the corporation, so such contracts are typically within the apparent scope of a president's authority.[67]

C. WHAT CONSTITUTES A BREACH

4.22 To bring a claim for breach of contract in New York, a plaintiff must plead and prove (1) the existence of a contract between plaintiff and defendant, (2) plaintiff's complete and adequate performance of his or her obligations under the contract, (3) breach of the contractual terms by the defendant, and (4) damages as a result of the breach.[68] A breach of contract occurs when a party to a contract commits an act in violation of its terms.[69] A breach can be total, impairing the entire contract, or merely incidental to the contract, and it will entitle the non-breaching party to damages.

1. Material Breach

4.23 A breach is material if it is so substantial that it defeats the purpose of the transaction.[70] A material breach can justify the non-breaching party's suspension of his or her own performance of the contract,[71] and when not cured, will completely relieve the non-breaching party from that party's performance obligations under the contract.[72] For a breach to be material, the departure from the terms of the

---

[61] Dodge v. Richmond, 196 N.Y.S.2d 477 (1st Dep't 1960), *aff'd*, 168 N.E.2d 531 (N.Y. 1960); Sternaman v. Metro. Life Ins. Co., 62 N.E. 763 (N.Y. 1902).

[62] Upper Nyack v. Christian & Missionary Alliance, 540 N.Y.S.2d 125, 130 (Sup. Ct. 1988), *aff'd*, 547 N.Y.S.2d 388 (2d Dep't 1989).

[63] 805 Third Ave. Co. v. M.W. Realty Assoc., 448 N.E.2d 445, 447 (N.Y. 1983).

[64] Restatement (Second) of Contracts § 178 (2006).

[65] Restatement (Third) of Agency §§ intro., 1 (2006).

[66] Seeberger v. McCormick, 175 U.S. 274, 279–80 (1899).

[67] *See* Odell v. Broadway Condo., 728 N.Y.S.2d 464 (1st Dep't 2001).

[68] *See* Harsco Corp. v. Segui, 91 F.3d 337, 348 (2d Cir. 1996). If a contract includes an enforceable liquidated damages provision, the plaintiff will have no duty to prove affirmative damages.

[69] Banks, *supra* note 5, § 17:2.

[70] *Id.*, § 17:10.

[71] Lanvin Inc. v. Colonia, Inc., 739 F. Supp. 182, 195 (S.D.N.Y. 1990).

[72] *See* Cablevision Sys. Corp. v. East Hampton, 862 F. Supp. 875, 885 (E.D.N.Y. 1994), *aff'd*, 57 F.3d 1062 (2d Cir. 1995); NAS Elec., Inc. v. Transtech Elec. PTE Ltd., 262 F. Supp. 2d 134 (S.D.N.Y. 2003).

contract or defects of performance must so pervade the contract or have been so essential to the contract as to substantially defeat the parties' objective in making the contract.[73] In determining whether a breach is material, no single factor is determinative. New York follows the Restatement § 241 for common-law contracts, by examining (1) the extent to which the injured party will be deprived of the benefit which [he] reasonably expected; (2) the extent to which the injured party can be adequately compensated for the part of that benefit of which he will be deprived; (3) the extent to which the party failing to perform or to offer to perform will suffer forfeiture; (4) the likelihood that the party failing to perform or to offer to perform will cure his failure, taking account of all the circumstances, including any reasonable assurances; and (5) the extent to which the behavior of the party failing to perform or to offer to perform comports with standards of good faith and fair dealing.[74] In order to sustain a claim for breach of contract, the plaintiff must prove that he has performed his obligations under the terms of the agreement, and that he was "ready, willing and able to do all the contract required of it."[75]

For example, New York courts have found that the following occurrences constituted material breaches of a contract: the failure to tender purchase price on a closing date[76]; the failure to maintain financial hedges, as expressly provided for in contract between plaintiff and defendant[77]; and the failure to render performance on a specified date where "time is of the essence."[78] By contrast, where a provider of cable television services had breached the contractual terms of its Franchise Agreement by raising its rates two days before the contractually designated date, this was an "insignificant" breach given the nine-year duration of the franchise, with a "negligible" impact, not rising to a material breach as a matter of law.[79] **4.24**

2. Substantial Performance

The equitable rule of substantial performance is the other side of the same coin. This rule allows a party that performs first to enforce a contract if the primary **4.25**

[73] *See Cablevision Sys. Corp.*, 862 F. Supp. at 885 (E.D.N.Y. 1994), *aff'd*, 57 F.3d 1062 (2d Cir. 1995) (*citing* Miller v. Benjamin, 617, 37 N.E. 631 (N.Y. 1894)).

[74] Wechsler v. Hunt Health Sys., Ltd., 330 F. Supp. 2d 383 (S.D.N.Y. 2004) (*citing* Restatement (Second) of Contracts §241(a) (2006)). By contrast, the U.C.C. does not rely on a test of materiality. Any deviation from the goods demanded in the contract is considered a breach of the perfect tender rule, and permits the buyer to treat that deviation as a breach of contract, save for certain exceptions. The perfect tender rule is discussed in greater detail in Section D.1 of this chapter.

[75] Roberts v. Karimi, 251 F.3d 404, 407 (2d Cir. 2001).

[76] Town House Stock LLC v. Coby Housing Corp., 855 N.Y.S.2d 55 (1st Dep't 2008).

[77] Cary Oil Co., Inc., v. MG Ref. & Mktg., Inc., 90 F. Supp. 2d 401, 408 (S.D.N.Y. 2000).

[78] New Colony Homes, Inc. v. Long Island Prop. Grp., LLC, 803 N.Y.S.2d 615 (2d Dep't 2005).

[79] Cablevision Sys. Corp. v. East Hampton, 862 F. Supp. 875, 885 (E.D.N.Y. 1994), *aff'd*, 57 F.3d 1062 (2d Cir. 1995).

purpose of the contract has been fulfilled in good faith and the alleged breach is trivial.[80] In evaluating whether a party has substantially performed under a contract, New York law weighs "the purpose to be served, the desire to be gratified, the excuse for deviation from the letter, [and] the cruelty of enforced adherence."[81] For example, in *Edgewater*, after discovering that a subcontractor had failed to install $619.20 worth of a horizontal wall reinforcement during construction, the plaintiff brought a claim for breach of contract, which would incidentally force the defendant to rebuild the foundation at a cost of over $500,000. The court held that where the record established that the breach was the result of mere oversight on the part of the subcontractors and did not damage the structural integrity of the building, the contractors had substantially performed under the contract. Practitioners should note, however, that the bar for substantial performance is relatively high in New York, with courts generally requiring 75 percent or more completion of performance in order to meet the standard.[82]

3. Anticipatory Breach and Repudiation

4.26 A contract is not breached as a matter of law until the time set for performance has expired, unless that breach is anticipatory.[83] An anticipatory breach of contract arises when there is a present duty of performance and one party anticipatorily repudiates a contractual obligation through words or acts evincing an intention to refuse performance in the future.[84] When there has been anticipatory repudiation of a contract by one party, the other party has an immediate right to sue for total breach and is discharged from rendering performance under the contract in the future.[85]

4.27 Under New York law, a repudiation can either be express or implied. An express repudiation is defined as a clear, positive, and unequivocal refusal to perform, while an implied repudiation is inferred from conduct making substantial performance impossible.[86] Accordingly, New York courts have found anticipatory repudiation when a party refused to complete a contract except upon new terms not included in the original contract[87] or where a party indicated delay in a contract where time is of the essence.[88]

---

[80] Banks, *supra* note 5, §17:14.

[81] Edgewater Const. Co., Inc. v. 81 & 3 of Watertown, Inc., 769 N.Y.S.2d 343 (4th Dep't 2003) (*citing* Jacob & Youngs v. Kent, 129 N.E. 889, 891 (N.Y. 1921)).

[82] *See, e.g.*, Carefree Bldg. Prod., Inc. v. Belina, 564 N.Y.S.2d 852 (3d Dep't 1991).

[83] Rachmani Corp. v. 9 E. 96th St. Apartment Corp., 629 N.Y.S.2d 382, 383–84 (1st Dep't 1995).

[84] 22 N.Y. JUR. 2d *Contracts* § 454 (2008).

[85] Computer Possibilities Unlimited, Inc. v. Mobil Oil Corp., 747 N.Y.S.2d 468, 475 (1st Dep't 2002).

[86] Banks, *supra* note 5, § 17:7.

[87] Joqueviel & Cathala v. Eastern Tanning Co., Inc., 1989 WL 119440, at *5 (E.D.N.Y. 1989).

[88] Zullo v. Varley, 868 N.Y.S.2d 290, 292 (2d Dep't 2008).

4. Divisible or Installment Contracts

An installment contract, within the meaning of the U.C.C. § 2-612(1), is one that "requires or authorizes the delivery of goods in separate lots to be separately accepted." In practice, this means that New York courts treat such contracts as a series of separate contracts. Therefore, breach of one part of the contract does not necessarily breach the entire contract, unless the breach substantially impairs the contract as a whole. For example, in *Trans World Metals, Inc. v. Southwire Co.*, the court found that where the parties had entered into an installment contract for the monthly delivery of aluminum, defendant's failure to deliver several installments on time did not substantially impair the contract as a whole.[89] Substantial impairment of an installment contract can turn not only on factors such as time and payment, but also the quality, quantity, and assortment of goods, in light of the specific purposes of the contract.[90] For example, in another installment contract case, the court found that a seller's failure to meet the proper color standard for a shipment of potatoes, where the "quality standards" in this contract were "set forth with great specificity," substantially impaired the value of the whole contract.[91] **4.28**

D. CONSEQUENCES OF BREACH OF CONTRACT

1. Effect on the Performance of the Non-breaching Party

Under New York law, a breach of contract may excuse the non-breaching party from any further performance under the contract. If the non-breaching party believes that there has been a material breach of the contract, it has a right of election. It may stop performance, terminate the contract, and sue for damages for total breach. Alternatively, it may continue performance under the contract and sue for the partial damages caused by the breach. The injured party may not claim damages for total breach and continue to demand performance, as such a claim replaces the remaining substantive rights under the contract.[92] This right of election is equally applicable when the breach arises from an anticipatory repudiation of the contract.[93] **4.29**

New York law provides some mitigation to the rule of unilateral election by the non-breaching party. The injured party can elect to terminate the contract only if the breaching party fails to cure the breach within a reasonable amount of time, where a cure is possible,[94] and the breaching party may be entitled to restitution **4.30**

[89] Trans World Metals, Inc. v. Southwire Co., 769 F.2d 902, 904 (2d Cir. 1985).
[90] N.Y.U.C.C. § 2-612 cmt. 4 (2005).
[91] Hubbard v. UTZ Quality Foods, Inc., 903 F. Supp. 444, 451 (W.D.N.Y. 1995).
[92] Banks, *supra* note 5, § 17:13.
[93] Lucente v. Int'l Bus. Mach. Corp., 310 F.3d 243 (2d Cir. 2002).
[94] Cary Oil Co., Inc. v. MG Ref. & Mktg, Inc., 90 F. Supp. 2d 401 (S.D.N.Y. 2000).

for any benefit it conferred upon the non-breaching party either through partial performance or by reliance.[95] Finally, contract forfeiture may be avoided if the contract is found to be divisible. The court "will then allow pro rata recovery based on the contract price for the proportion of the performance rendered."[96]

4.31 The U.C.C. adopts a different rule from the common law. The perfect tender rule allows the buyer to reject performance "if the goods or the tender of delivery fail in any respect to conform to the contract."[97] Where nonconforming goods have been tendered, the buyer has the right either to reject all of them, to accept all of them, or to accept some of the commercial units and reject the others.[98] If the buyer accepts the goods, it may revoke that acceptance upon later discovery of nonconformity.[99] Whichever option the buyer chooses, it can seek damages for any loss resulting from the seller's breach.[100]

4.32 The harsh impact of this rule on the seller is softened somewhat by related provisions of the U.C.C. When a buyer has accepted goods, it may only revoke that acceptance if the nonconformity of the goods "substantially impairs" their value.[101] Further, the seller has the right to cure the nonconformity after the buyer has rejected the goods if the time for performance has not yet expired, and even after this time has expired in limited circumstances.[102]

4.33 Under the UCC, where the contract is an installment contract, the perfect tender rule described above does not apply. A buyer may only reject an installment of goods if the nonconformity "substantially impairs" the value of that installment and cannot be cured. If the nonconformity does not impair the value of the whole contract, and the seller gives adequate assurance that it will cure the defect, the buyer must accept the installment.[103] A breach of the whole contract giving rise to a right to cancel the contract will only be found where a nonconformity in one or more installments "substantially impairs" the value of the whole contract. Even in this latter situation, the buyer will be found to have "reinstated" the contract if it accepts a nonconforming installment without seasonably notifying the seller of cancellation, if it brings an action with respect to only past installments, or if it demands performance as to future installments.[104]

---

[95] Banks, *supra* note 5, § 17:13.
[96] E. Allan Farnsworth, Farnsworth on Contracts § 8:13 (3d ed. 2008).
[97] N.Y.U.C.C. § 2-601 (2005). Article 2A covering the lease of goods follows the same rule, *see* N.Y.U.C.C. § 2A-509 (2005).
[98] N.Y.U.C.C. § 2-601 (2005).
[99] N.Y.U.C.C. § 2-608 (2005).
[100] N.Y.U.C.C. § 2-714(1) (2005).
[101] N.Y.U.C.C. § 2-608 (2005).
[102] N.Y.U.C.C. § 2-508 (2005).
[103] N.Y.U.C.C. § 2-612(2) (2005).
[104] N.Y.U.C.C. § 2-612(3) (2005).

2. Measure of Damages

An award of damages[105] is the most common form of judicial relief for a breach of contract. In New York, courts ordinarily award damages based upon the injured party's expectations when it had entered into the contract.[106] The injured party is awarded a sum of money that will, so far as is possible, put it in the position in which it would have been if the contract had been performed according to its terms. The general measure is the difference between the value of what has been received by the plaintiff under the contract and the value of what would have been received if the contract been performed.[107] This value is measured at the date of the breach.[108] The fact that an element of the damage will be incurred in the future does not prevent its recovery,[109] and the loss of future profits resulting from the breach is recoverable so long as it was caused by the breach, can be established with reasonable certainty, and was within the contemplation of the parties at the time of contracting.[110] **4.34**

Although expectation damages are the norm in New York, the law recognizes and awards reliance damages in appropriate cases, such as when the plaintiff is unable to calculate expectation damages with certainty. The reliance measure aims to put the injured party back in the position in which it would have been if the contract had not been made.[111] An award of reliance damages permits a plaintiff to recover any expenses it incurred in preparation for performance and partial performance of a contract, as well as other foreseeable expenses incurred in reliance on the contract.[112] Reliance damages are not permitted when they would put the plaintiff in a better position than if the contract had been performed; if it is established that the plaintiff's losses on full performance would have equaled or exceeded its reliance expenditures, the plaintiff cannot recover under a reliance theory.[113] Damages for loss of profits cannot be recovered in addition to reliance damages.[114] **4.35**

A plaintiff may also recover damages for breach of contract under a theory of restitution, by which the plaintiff recovers the value of any benefit it conferred upon the breaching party by way of part performance or reliance on the contract, less the reasonable value of any counter-performance it received.[115] The reasonable **4.36**

---

105 The topic of damages in dealt with in more detail in Chapter 10 of this book.
106 Farnsworth, *supra* note 96, § 12.1.
107 Banks, *supra* note 5, §§ 23:2, 23:26.
108 Brushton-Moira Cent. Sch. Dist. v. Fred H. Thomas Assoc., P.C., 692 N.E.2d 551 (N.Y. 1998).
109 Manlius Center Road Corp. v. N.Y., 370 N.Y.S.2d 750 (4th Dep't 1975).
110 Kenford Co, Inc. v. Cnty. of Erie, 493 N.E.2d 234, 235 (N.Y. 1986).
111 Farnsworth, *supra* note 96, § 12.1.
112 Bausch & Lomb, Inc. v. Bressler, 977 F.2d 720, 729 (2d Cir. 1992).
113 *Id.*
114 Interfilm, Inc. v. Advanced Exhibition Corp., 672 N.Y.S.2d 309 (1st Dep't 1998).
115 Banks, *supra* note 5, § 23:35.

value of the benefit unjustly received, and not the contract price, determines the amount of the award. Unlike reliance damages, restitution damages are available even if the plaintiff would have lost money had the contract been fully performed.[116]

4.37 The award of damages is subject to a number of general principles. In New York, damages are offset by any amount that the plaintiff has saved as a result of the breach.[117] The plaintiff must prove that the defendant's breach caused the claimed damages, and it must prove the existence of damages.[118] However, "scientific rigor" in the calculation of damages that will be incurred in the future is not required.[119] A party injured by a breach of contract is under a duty to mitigate its damages and, if, through willfulness or negligence, it allows damages to be unnecessarily enhanced, the increased loss will fall upon it.[120] Punitive damages are generally not available for breach of contract.[121] Consequential damages, which seek to compensate a plaintiff for any losses in addition to the value of the promised performance, may only be recovered if, at the time of the execution of the contract, it was reasonably foreseeable to the defendant that such damages would flow from its breach.[122]

4.38 When the parties have agreed on a measure of damages to be applied in the event of breach, courts in New York will generally respect that agreement. However, courts may refuse to uphold a liquidated damages provision if it is found to be unconscionable and against public policy by imposing a penalty on the breaching party.[123]

4.39 The U.C.C. provides for specific remedies when a sale of goods contract has been breached.[124] If the buyer has breached the contract, the seller may resell the goods in good faith and in a commercially reasonable manner and recover from the buyer the difference between the contract price and the resale price.[125] A seller that does not act in a commercially reasonable manner, or fails to resell the goods, is only entitled to recover the difference between the contract price and the market value of the goods at the time and place of tender.[126] The seller may be able to recover the full contract price from the buyer if it is unable, after reasonable effort, to resell the goods at a reasonable price, or if the circumstances

[116] Bausch & Lomb, Inc. v. Bressler, 977 F.2d 720, 730 (2d Cir. 1992).
[117] Indu Craft, Inc. v. Bank of Baroda, 47 F.3d 490, 495 (2d Cir. 1995).
[118] Nat'l Mkt. Share, Inc. v. Sterling Nat'l Bank, 392 F.3d 520 (2d Cir. 2004).
[119] Lexington Prods. Ltd. v. B.D. Commc'ns Inc., 677 F.2d 251, 253 (2d Cir. 1982).
[120] Hamilton v. McPherson, 28 N.Y. 72 (1863).
[121] Banks, *supra* note 5, § 22:32.
[122] *Id.*, § 22:18.
[123] *Id.*, §§ 22:35–43.
[124] *See also* N.Y.U.C.C. §§ 2-A-508, 2-A-523 (2005) (remedies available in a contract for the lease of goods).
[125] N.Y.U.C.C. § 2-706(1) (2005).
[126] N.Y.U.C.C. § 2-708 (2005).

reasonably indicate that such effort would be unavailing.[127] Finally, even if the seller has resold the goods that the breaching buyer was under an obligation to buy, the seller is entitled to the benefit of both the breached bargain *and* the resale if it would have made *both* sales if the buyer had not breached the contract.[128] The seller is also entitled to incidental damages arising from the breach.[129]

The buyer also has a number of remedies available under the U.C.C. when the seller breaches the contract. If the buyer chooses to accept the goods, it may only recover damages resulting in the ordinary course of events from the seller's breach,[130] such as the cost of repairing the goods. However, if the buyer accepts and proves that what it received was essentially worthless (and returns the goods), it may recover the full amount paid.[131] If the buyer refuses the goods or revokes its acceptance, it may "cover" by purchasing substitute goods in good faith and without unreasonable delay. It is then entitled to claim from the seller the difference between the contract price and the substitute contract price.[132] If the buyer does not act in good faith, or does not purchase substitute goods, it is entitled to the difference between the market price of the goods and the contract price.[133] The buyer is also entitled to incidental damages.[134] **4.40**

As an alternative to proving actual damages, in cases with contracts that include liquidated damages provisions, a non-breaching party may be entitled to liquidated damages. Under New York law, parties may decide at the time of contracting that, upon a breach of the contract, the non-breaching party shall be entitled to receive a stipulated sum of money as liquidated damages. New York courts will generally enforce a liquidated damages provision, provided it was fairly negotiated, the stipulated sum bears a reasonable proportion to the anticipated harm in the event of a breach, and the probable actual loss is difficult or impossible to estimate.[135] **4.41**

3. Equitable Relief

As an alternative to seeking damages, a non-breaching party may seek the equitable remedy of specific performance or injunctive relief. Specific performance aims to give the injured party the very performance that was promised under the contract.[136] In the context of claims for breach of contract, this relief takes two **4.42**

[127] N.Y.U.C.C. § 2-709 (1) (b) (2005).
[128] N.Y.U.C.C. § 2-708 (2); *see also* Neri v. Retail Marine Corp., 285 N.E.2d 311 (N.Y. 1972).
[129] N.Y.U.C.C. § 2-710 (2005).
[130] N.Y.U.C.C. § 2-714 (2005).
[131] Peak v. Northway Travel Trailers Inc., 688 N.Y.S.2d 738, 740 (3d Dep't 1999).
[132] N.Y.U.C.C. § 2-712 (2005).
[133] N.Y.U.C.C. § 2-713 (2005).
[134] N.Y.U.C.C. § 2-715 (2005).
[135] *See* Feinsot v. Burstein, 138 N.Y.S. 185 (1st Dep't 1912) (recognizing that when a liquidated damages sum was in reasonable proportion to the probable damages from breach, the court is bound to enforce the terms of the liquidated damages provision).
[136] Farnsworth, *supra* note 96, §§ 12.1, 12.4–12.6.

forms: specific performance and injunction. In addition, the injured party may be entitled to seek interim relief.

4.43 Specific performance compels the promisor to render the promised performance. This remedy is rarely provided. It is available if there is a valid contract, the plaintiff has substantially performed under the contract and is willing and able to perform its remaining obligations, the defendant is able to perform its obligations, and the plaintiff has no adequate remedy at law.[137] However, specific performance tends to be an appropriate remedy only if compelling performance does not impose a "disproportionate or inequitable burden" on the breaching party.[138] For contracts governed by the U.C.C., the buyer may demand specific performance of a sale of goods contract in certain circumstances.[139]

4.44 The issue of injunctions by arbitrators or by courts in aid of arbitration is discussed in Chapter 8 of this book, so it will not be covered here.

E. CLAIMS ANCILLARY TO BREACH OF CONTRACT

1. Arbitrability of Ancillary Claims

4.45 When a dispute arises from a contractual relationship, it is not unusual for one or both parties to assert—in addition to claims for breach of contract—ancillary claims arising from the same facts, such as breach of fiduciary duties or breach of the implied covenant of good faith. When these claims are asserted, a question arises as to whether they are subject to arbitration, or must be litigated in a separate court proceeding. The Federal Arbitration Act (FAA)[140] reflects, in the words of the U.S. Supreme Court, an "emphatic federal policy in favor of arbitral dispute resolution."[141] The FAA mandates that, "as a matter of federal law, any doubts concerning the scope of arbitrable issues should be resolved in favor of arbitration."[142] Accordingly, the U.S. Court of Appeals for the Second Circuit, which includes New York, strives to "construe arbitration clauses as broadly as possible."[143] In doing so, it has often found that claims related to, though not directly arising under, a contract containing an arbitration clause are arbitrable.[144]

[137] Banks, *supra* note 5, 18:19.

[138] Cho v. 401–403 57th Street Realty Corp., 752 N.Y.S.2d 55, 57 (1st Dep't 2002).

[139] N.Y.U.C.C. § 2-716 (2005).

[140] *See* 9 U.S.C. § 1 *et seq.* (2008).

[141] Quackenbush v. Allstate Ins. Co., 517 U.S. 706, 729 (1996) (*quoting* Mitsubishi Motors Corp. v. Soler Chrysler-Plymouth, Inc., 473 U.S. 614, 631 (1985)).

[142] Moses H. Cone Mem'l Hosp. v. Mercury Constr. Corp., 460 U.S. 1, 24–25 (1983).

[143] David L. Threlkeld & Co. v. Metallgesellschaft Ltd., 923 F.2d 245, 250 (2d Cir. 1991) (internal quotations omitted).

[144] *Id.* at 251.

In considering whether a claim ancillary to breach of contract is arbitrable, the Second Circuit undertakes a two-part inquiry.[145] First, it determines whether the arbitration clause is broad or narrow.[146] If the arbitration clause is narrow, a collateral matter will generally be outside its purview. If the arbitration clause is broad, on the other hand, "there arises a presumption of arbitrability, and arbitration of even a collateral matter will be ordered if the claim alleged implicates issues of contract construction or the parties' rights and obligations under it."[147] **4.46**

Under this liberal standard, many claims ancillary to breach of contract have been found arbitrable. In *ACE Capital*, the Second Circuit determined that a claim for rescission based on fraudulent inducement was arbitrable pursuant to an arbitration clause in the contested contract.[148] Likewise, extra-contractual claims such as unjust enrichment may be arbitrable when predicated on duties connected to a contract with a broad arbitration clause.[149] Even a third-party beneficiary of a contract may "compel arbitration with a signatory ... when the issues the nonsignatory is seeking to resolve in arbitration are intertwined with the agreement that the [signatory] has signed."[150] **4.47**

Claims of breach of implied covenant of good faith and fair dealing and of fraud in the performance have also been held arbitrable. As one Southern District of **4.48**

---

[145] *See* Louis Dreyfus Negoce S.A. v. Blystad Shipping & Trading Inc., 252 F.3d 218, 224 (2d Cir. 2001) (outlining this test). For a discussion of how courts go about determining the scope of an arbitration clause, *see also* Chapter 7.C.1(c) of this book.

[146] *See, e.g.*, McDonnell Douglas Fin. Corp. v. Pa. Power & Light Co., 858 F.2d 825, 832 (2d Cir. 1988) ("In construing arbitration clauses, courts have at times distinguished between 'broad' clauses that purport to refer all disputes arising out of a contract to arbitration and 'narrow' clauses that limit arbitration to specific types of disputes."); *see also* Gerling Global Reins. Corp. v. Home Ins. Co., 752 N.Y.S.2d 611, 618 (1st Dep't 2002) (employing the Second Circuit's test for the breadth of an arbitration clause). Note that the language of the arbitration clause frequently determines the breadth of its scope. For example, language such as "in connection with" and "arising in connection with" have been found to indicate more expansive arbitration clauses. *See, e.g.*, Fluor Daniel Intercont'l Inc. v. Gen. Elec. Co., No. 98 Civ. 7181, 1999 WL 637236, at *7 (S.D.N.Y. 1999) ("The phrase 'arising out of, under, or in connection with' is prototypical of a broad arbitration clause.").

[147] *Louis Dreyfus Negoce S.A.*, 252 F.3d at 224 (internal quotations omitted).

[148] ACE Capital Re Overseas Ltd. v. Cent. United Life Ins. Co., 307 F.3d 24, 33–34 (2d Cir. 2002). Note, however, that "[i]f the claim is fraud in the inducement of the arbitration clause itself—an issue which goes to the 'making' of the agreement to arbitrate—the federal court may proceed to adjudicate it" rather than send it to arbitration. *Id.* at 29 (*quoting* Prima Paint Corp. v. Flood & Conklin Mfg. Co., 388 U.S. 395, 403–04 (1967)). *See also* Banks, *supra* note 5, § 5:5 ("Where no claim is made that the fraud was directed at the arbitration clause itself, a broad arbitration clause ... will be held to encompass arbitration of the claim that the contract was induced by fraud.").

[149] Genesco, Inc. v. T. Kakiuchi & Co., 815 F.2d 840, 856–57 (2d Cir. 1987); *see also id.* at 846 ("In determining whether a particular claim falls within the scope of the parties' arbitration agreement, we focus on the factual allegations in the complaint rather than the legal causes of action asserted.").

[150] Smith/Enron Cogeneration Ltd. P'ship v. Smith Cogeneration Int'l, Inc., 198 F.3d 88, 98 (2d Cir. 1999) (internal citations and quotations omitted).

New York case has noted, "Any dispute over the implied covenant of good faith in a contract is, by its nature, a dispute regarding that contract. Thus, where … disputes arising out of a contract are arbitrable, then a disagreement regarding the covenant of good faith is arbitrable."[151] Similarly, courts have held that "[g]enerally, … fraud in the performance of a contract is arbitrable under a broad arbitration clause contained in the contract."[152]

2. Claims Ancillary to Breach of Contract under New York Law

4.49 *(a) Implied covenant of good faith and fair dealing* Every New York contract contains an implied covenant of good faith and fair dealing. The covenant includes "an implied undertaking on the part of each party that he will not intentionally and purposely do anything to prevent the other party from carrying out the agreement on his part."[153] However, "the duty cannot be used to create independent obligations beyond those agreed upon and stated in the express language of the contract; it cannot add to, detract from, or alter the terms of the contract itself."[154]

4.50 As a preliminary matter, a claim for breach of the implied covenant requires that there be a valid contract or other beneficial relationship between the parties.[155] The claim cannot be based on the same facts as a corresponding claim for breach of contract, or it will be dismissed as duplicative.[156] Likewise, there can be no claim for breach of the implied covenant if the plaintiff has already received full benefit under the agreement.[157]

4.51 *(b) Unjust enrichment* The doctrine of unjust enrichment is "based on the equitable principle[] that a person shall not be allowed to enrich himself unjustly at

[151] Circus Prods., Inc. v. Int'l Impresarios, No. 90 Civ. 0414, 1990 WL 55684, at *3 (S.D.N.Y. 1990).

[152] Housekeeper v. Lourie, 333 N.Y.S.2d 932, 935 (1st Dep't 1972).

[153] Carvel Corp. v. Diversified Mgmt. Grp., Inc., 930 F.2d 228, 330 (2d Cir. 1991) (*quoting* Grad v. Roberts, 198 N.E.2d 26, 28 (N.Y. 1964)). The obligation also encompasses "any promises which a reasonable person in the position of the promisee would be justified in understanding were included." Dalton v. Educ. Testing Serv., 663 N.E.2d 289, 291 (N.Y. 1995) (internal quotations omitted). The defendant has breached the covenant if it "prevent[ed] the [plaintiff] from carrying out the agreement," Chem. Bank v. Stahl, 712 N.Y.S.2d 452, 462 (1st Dep't 2000), or if it "sought to … withhold [contract] benefits from the plaintiff." Aventine Inv. Mgmt., Inc. v. Can. Imperial Bank of Commerce, 697 N.Y.S.2d 128, 130 (2d Dep't 1999).

[154] PT Kaltim Prima Coal v. AES Barbers Point, Inc., 180 F. Supp. 2d 475, 483 (S.D.N.Y. 2001) (internal quotations omitted).

[155] Cyber Media Grp., Inc. v. Island Mortg. Network, Inc., 183 F. Supp. 2d 559, 582 (E.D.N.Y. 2002).

[156] *See* ARI & Co., Inc. v. Regent Int'l Corp., 273 F. Supp. 2d 518, 522 (S.D.N.Y. 2003) ("New York law does not recognize a separate cause of action for breach of the implied covenant of good faith and fair dealing when a breach of contract claim, based upon the same facts, is also pled.") (internal quotations omitted).

[157] *See* Wornow v. Register.com, Inc., 778 N.Y.S.2d 25, 27 (1st Dep't 2004).

the expense of another."[158] Under this theory, recovery "is not contingent upon the existence of an express or even an implied agreement."[159] Indeed, the existence of a valid agreement covering the issue in dispute will preclude a claim for unjust enrichment.[160] If there is no contract covering the particular subject matter, equitable relief may be available if the "defendants have taken certain benefits from plaintiff without providing appropriate compensation therefor."[161]

A New York plaintiff seeking to recover for unjust enrichment must establish "(1) that the defendant benefited (2) at the plaintiff's expense and (3) that equity and good conscience require restitution."[162] If this showing is made, the possible injuries that the doctrine may redress are nearly infinite. As one court explained, "Unjust enrichment is exactly what it seems to be ... A defendant can be enriched by the receipt of money or its equivalent, or by being saved from expense or loss."[163] The unjust enrichment claim does not even require that the party unfairly benefited have taken an active role in securing the benefit.[164] Rather, courts examine the conveyance "not literally or irrespective of its setting, but sensibly and broadly with all its human implications."[165] **4.52**

(c) Fraud in the inducement In New York, a fraudulently induced contract is subject to rescission and is unenforceable by the culpable party.[166] In order to show fraud in the inducement, the plaintiff must allege "a material representation, known to be false, made with the intention of inducing reliance, upon which the victim actually relies, consequentially sustaining a detriment."[167] He or she must also show that reliance was reasonable under all the circumstances. For example, "[w]hen a party is aware of circumstances that indicate certain representations **4.53**

[158] Waldman v. Englishtown Sportswear, Ltd., 460 N.Y.S.2d 552, 556 (1st Dep't 1983).

[159] Marcraft Recreation Corp. v. Frances Devlin Co., Inc., 459 F. Supp. 195, 197 (S.D.N.Y. 1978). In fact, "[t]he existence of a valid and enforceable written contract governing a particular subject matter ordinarily precludes recovery in quasi contract for events arising out of the same subject matter." Clark-Fitzpatrick, Inc. v. Long Island R.R. Co., 516 N.E.2d 190, 193 (N.Y. 1987).

[160] Clark-Fitzpatrick, Inc. v. Long Island R.R. Co., 70 N.Y.2d 382, 388 (1987).

[161] *Marcraft Recreation*, 459 F. Supp. at 197.

[162] Kaye v. Grossman, 202 F.3d 611, 616 (2d Cir. 2000).

[163] Evans v. City of Johnstown, 410 N.Y.S.2d 199, 203 (N.Y. Sup. Ct. 1978).

[164] Aetna Cas. & Sur. Co. v. LFO Constr. Corp., 615 N.Y.S.2d 389, 391 (1st Dep't 1994).

[165] Sharp v. Kosmalski, 351 N.E.2d 721, 724 (N.Y. 1976) (internal quotations omitted).

[166] Merrill Lynch, Pierce, Fenner & Smith, Inc. v. Wise Metals Grp., LLC, 798 N.Y.S.2d 14, 16 (1st Dep't 2005); *see also* Adams v. Gillig, 92 N.E. 670, 671 (N.Y. 1910) ("Any statement of an existing fact material to the person to whom it is made that is false and known by the person making it to be false and which is made to induce the execution of a contract, and which does induce the contract, constitutes a fraud that will sustain an action to avoid the contract if the person making it is injured thereby.").

[167] *Merrill Lynch*, 798 N.Y.S.2d at 16. The scienter (which is a term of art in United States law for the knowledge or intent of the alleged fraudster) required to show fraudulent inducement is frequently at issue. For example, in Terris v. Cummiskey, the Appellate Division noted: "Fraud includes pretense of knowledge when there is none and if a statement is recklessly made without knowledge or without genuine belief in its truth the statement may be actionable." 203 N.Y.S.2d 445, 446 (3d Dep't 1960).

may be false, that party cannot reasonably rely on those representations, but must make additional inquiry to determine their accuracy."[168]

4.54 One of the main concerns of the courts with respect to fraudulent inducement actions has been to prevent plaintiffs from elevating every breach of contract case into a case for fraud merely by alleging intent not to perform. Courts are split as to whether a plaintiff may establish the material misrepresentation necessary to show fraud merely by proving that the defendant signed the contract with no intention of meeting his or her obligations.[169] Other decisions have attempted to reconcile this confusion by adding an additional inquiry: whether the misrepresentation is "collateral or extraneous to the contract."[170]

4.55 *(d) Fraud in the performance* Under New York law, "fraud in the performance of a contract renders the contract unenforceable."[171] However, as with fraudulent inducement, "[a] cause of action for fraud does not arise when the only fraud charged relates to a breach of contract."[172]

4.56 The Second Circuit has identified three situations in which a plaintiff may allege both fraud in the performance and breach of contract without introducing redundancy into the complaint: (1) where there is a "legal duty separate from the duty to perform under the contract"; (2) where there is a "fraudulent misrepresentation collateral or extraneous to the contract"; and (3) where the plaintiff "seek[s] special damages that are caused by the misrepresentation and unrecoverable as contract damages."[173] Likewise, as the Southern District has noted, "to sustain an action for fraud, there must be some actual loss incurred as a direct result of the wrong by the [plaintiff], and in an action for damages, the plaintiff must make a showing of some concrete pecuniary loss."[174]

[168] Keywell Corp. v. Weinstein, 33 F.3d 159, 164 (2d Cir. 1994).

[169] *See* Int'l CableTel Inc. v. Le Groupe Videotron Ltee, 978 F. Supp. 483, 486–87 (S.D.N.Y. 1997) (*comparing* Rocanova v. Equitable Life Assurance Soc'y of U.S., 634 N.E.2d 940, 944 (N.Y. 1994) ("a contract action cannot be converted to one for fraud merely by alleging that the contracting party did not intend to meet its contractual obligations") with Sabo v. Delman, 143 N.E.2d 906, 908 (N.Y. 1957) ("if a promise was actually made with a preconceived and undisclosed intention of not performing it, it constitutes a misrepresentation of a material existing fact upon which an action for rescission may be predicated" (internal quotations omitted))).

[170] *Int'l CableTel*, 978 F. Supp. at 487 (internal quotations omitted).

[171] Swig Weiler & Arnow Mgmt. Co. v. Stahl, 817 F. Supp. 404, 407 (S.D.N.Y. 1993); *see also* McConnell v. Commonwealth Pictures Corp., 166 N.E.2d 494, 497 (N.Y. 1960) ("[W]e in New York deny awards for the corrupt performance of contracts even though in essence the contracts are not illegal.").

[172] Krantz v. Chateau Stores of Can. Ltd., 683 N.Y.S.2d 24, 25 (1st Dep't 1998) (internal quotations omitted).

[173] Bridgestone/Firestone, Inc. v. Recovery Credit Servs., Inc., 98 F.3d 13, 20 (2d Cir. 1996) (*citing* New York cases).

[174] Spencer Trask Software & Info. Servs. LLC v. RPost Int'l Ltd., 383 F. Supp. 2d 428, 454 (S.D.N.Y. 2003).

(e) Third-party beneficiaries The New York Court of Appeals has held that a non-party to a contract may nonetheless enforce the agreement if he or she can establish: "(1) the existence of a valid and binding contract between other parties, (2) that the contract was intended for his benefit and (3) that the benefit to him is sufficiently immediate, rather than incidental, to indicate the assumption by the contracting parties of a duty to compensate him if the benefit is lost."[175] For a party to be considered an intended beneficiary, the performance of the underlying promise must "satisfy an obligation of the promisee to pay money to the beneficiary," or the contract must otherwise show that the promisee intended to confer the benefit of the agreement on the third party.[176] **4.57**

New York courts do not require the third-party beneficiary to be named by the contract.[177] To determine whether a nonparty is a third-party beneficiary, courts may consider the circumstances surrounding the contract, including "whether manifestation of the intention of the promisor and promisee is sufficient, in a contractual setting, to make reliance by the beneficiary both reasonable and probable."[178] However, "[a] party who seeks the status of a third-party beneficiary under a contract has the burden of demonstrating that he has enforceable rights thereunder," and courts will not invent rights not intended by the contracting parties.[179] **4.58**

F. SPECIAL ISSUES ARISING UNDER NEW YORK LAW OF CONTRACTS

In addition to the considerations outlined above regarding contract formation, breach of contract, relief available in the event of a breach, and claims ancillary to the breach of a contract, a practitioner should be aware of several other special issues under New York contract law. They include: (1) the effect of merger clauses; (2) the requirements of best efforts versus reasonable efforts; and (3) the doctrine of changed circumstances and *force majeure*. Although each subject could fill its own individual chapter, the most relevant and significant aspects of these issues are outlined as follows. **4.59**

1. Merger Clauses

A merger clause, also known as an integration clause, typically states that the writing in which the contract is memorialized contains the entire contract and **4.60**

[175] Burns Jackson Miller Summit & Spitzer v. Lindner, 451 N.E.2d 459, 469 (N.Y. 1983).
[176] Fourth Ocean Putnam Corp. v. Interstate Wrecking Co., 485 N.E.2d 208, 212 (N.Y. 1985) (*quoting* the Restatement (Second) of Contracts).
[177] Newin Corp. v. Hartford Accident & Indem. Co., 333 N.E.2d 163, 168 (N.Y. 1975).
[178] *Fourth Ocean Putnam Corp.*, 485 N.E.2d at 212 (internal quotations omitted).
[179] Leavitt-Bernert Tanning Corp. v. Am. Home Assurance Co., 516 N.Y.S.2d 992, 995 (3d Dep't 1987).

that no additional representations have been made.[180] Such a clause integrates the contract negotiations into the signed contract and attests that the written document contains the full extent of the parties' agreement. The purpose of such a clause relates to the parol evidence rule, which generally bars parties from offering evidence of previous negotiations to contradict or to modify the written contract.[181] A merger clause demonstrates the parties' intent for the written contract to represent the full extent of their agreement and prevents the submission of evidence to the contrary.

4.61 In the absence of a merger clause, the court will read the written agreement in light of the relevant circumstances to determine if the parties intended for their contract to represent the full extent of their agreement.[182] Specifically, the court examines whether "the writing completely and accurately embodies all of the mutual rights and obligations of the parties."[183] In making that determination, the court relies on the following factors: (1) whether the written agreement explicitly refers to an oral agreement; (2) whether the oral agreement is the type typically reduced to writing; (3) whether the parties were represented by attorneys when they bargained for and entered the agreement; (4) how thoroughly the parties negotiated the agreement; and (5) whether the contract contains any language suggesting that it contains the full agreement between the parties.[184]

4.62 If the court concludes the document is fully integrated, that finding bars the admission of negotiations or agreements that vary or are inconsistent with the terms of the contract, including any oral agreements, even if the contract lacks an integration clause.[185] However, an integrated contract does not provide a complete bar to extrinsic evidence: parties may submit evidence to explain or elaborate on the terms of the contract so long as their interpretations are not inconsistent with the terms of the contract. Parol evidence is also admissible to demonstrate fraud in the inducement of the contract even when a merger clause exists.[186]

4.63 New York makes an unusual distinction in this area. Under New York law, a merger clause's ability to exclude parol evidence depends on the specificity of the clause itself. A general or vague merger clause—one that does not specifically disclaim reliance on representations made while negotiating the contract—will not

[180] Banks, *supra* note 5, § 8:18.

[181] Jarecki v. Moo Louie, 745 N.E.2d 1006, 1009 (N.Y. 2001); *see also* Adler & Shaykin v. Wachner, 721 F. Supp. 472, 476 (S.D.N.Y. 1988).

[182] Bourne v. Walt Disney Co., 68 F.3d 621, 627 (2d Cir. 1995); *see also* Braten v. Bankers Trust Co., 456 N.E.2d 802, 805 (N.Y. 1983).

[183] *Alder & Shaykin*, 721 F. Supp. at 476.

[184] Banks, *supra* note 5, § 8:18; *see also* Starter Corp. v. Converse, Inc., 170 F.3d. 286, 295 (2d Cir. 1999); *Braten*, 456 N.E.2d at 805.

[185] *Alder & Shaykin*, 721 F. Supp. at 477; Kasowitz, Benson, Torres & Friedman, LLP v. Duane Reade, 98 A.D.3d 403, 405 (1st Dep't 2012).

[186] Corbin On Contracts § 28.21 (Mathew Bender & Co., Inc., 2008); Cohan v. Sicular, 625 N.Y.S.2d 278, 279–80 (2d Dep't 1995).

by itself bar parol evidence of misrepresentations.[187] To prevent the use of such evidence, parties should explicitly state that they are not relying on representations previously made or agree that the contract is "absolute or unconditional."[188] The distinction complicates the drafting of merger clauses, so that parties should be as thorough as possible when doing so.

2. "Best Efforts" vs. "Reasonable Efforts"

As noted above, implicit in every agreement is the requirement that the parties perform their contractual obligations in good faith. The good faith obligation requires a reasonable effort to perform the contract.[189] Parties sometime choose to require a higher degree of diligence and require one or both of them to make "best efforts" to perform their obligations. This more substantial obligation "requires that plaintiffs pursue *all* reasonable methods for obtaining" the promised result.[190] The extent of a best efforts obligation depends on the explicit language creating the duty and how clearly the contract articulates what is expected of a party.[191] An obligation to employ best efforts may also be implied through the circumstances of the agreement. If the best efforts obligation is implied, the extent of the obligation is more difficult to ascertain.[192] **4.64**

Whether or not a party has met a "best efforts" obligation is a question of fact, but the criteria by which New York courts evaluate best efforts obligations are not always clear.[193] Generally, New York courts require concrete, objective criteria against which the conduct may be judged.[194] However, the absence of explicit criteria may not defeat the enforcement of a best efforts provision.[195] Courts have enforced such clauses by employing one or more of the following analyses: considering the circumstances surrounding the parties' understanding of the best efforts clause; comparing the performance at issue with that of a reasonable **4.65**

[187] Corbin, *supra* note 186, § 28.21; *see also* Danann Realty Corp. v. Harris, 157 N.E.2d 597, 598–99 (N.Y. 1959) (noting "the fundamental principle that a general merger clause is ineffective to exclude parol evidence to show fraud in inducing the contract").

[188] Corbin, *supra* note 186, § 28.21; Citibank v. Plapinger, 485 N.E.2d 974, 974 (N.Y. 1985).

[189] Banks, *supra* note 5, § 28:14; *see also* Wood v. Lucy, Lady Duff-Gordon, 118 N.E. 214, 215 (N.Y. 1917).

[190] Kroboth v. Brent, 625 N.Y.S.2d 748, 749 (3d Dep't 1995) (emphasis added); Grossman v. Lowell, 703 F. Supp. 282, 284 (S.D.N.Y. 1989).

[191] Strauss Paper Co., Inc. v. RSA Exec. Search, Inc., 688 N.Y.S.2d 641, 642 (2d Dep't 1999) ("it is essential that the agreement also contain clear guidelines against which to measure such efforts in order for such clause to be enforced.").

[192] *See* Bernstein v. Felske, 533 N.Y.S.2d 538 (2d Dep't 1988).

[193] McDonald's Corp. v. Hinksman, 1999 WL 441468, at *12 (E.D.N.Y. 1999) ("The standard applied under New York law to establish whether a party has fulfilled its obligation under a 'best efforts' clause is murky."); *Kroboth*, 625 N.Y.S.2d at 750 (whether best efforts obligation has been satisfied "almost invariably" involves a question of fact).

[194] Timberline Dev. LLC v. Kronman, 702 N.Y.S.2d 237, 239–40 (1st Dep't 2000).

[195] US Airways Group, Inc. v. British Airways Plc, 989 F. Supp. 482, 491 (S.D.N.Y. 1997).

comparable party; or determining whether the party used all reasonable methods in pursuit of the contract goals.[196]

4.66 In general, if parties intend to elevate the standard by which a party's conduct is reviewed—requiring that the party employ best efforts instead of reasonable efforts—they should define what "best efforts" means in the context of their agreement. Giving a court clear guidelines against which it can ultimately compare the behavior of the parties will create a more easily enforceable standard of conduct.

3. Changed Circumstances and *Force Majeure*

4.67 Under New York law, a change in circumstances rarely excuses performance. Even if impractical, a party must generally perform his or her obligation under the contract or pay damages. New York will only excuse performance in case of "impossibility."[197] To allow flexibility for a change in circumstances, parties may include in their common-law contract a *force majeure* clause to allocate risk in the event that outside circumstances prevent performance or make it impractical.[198] The basics of the *force majeure* clause have also been incorporated into the U.C.C. § 2-615. Under Section 2-615, a seller who is unable to deliver goods because of a contingency that makes the terms of the contract impossible to fulfill is excused from his obligation, but must notify the buyer of the delay or nondelivery.[199]

4.68 A *force majeure* clause explicitly forgives nonperformance if certain circumstances outside the control of the parties occur. Events covered are typically of a calamitous or sporadic nature, such as natural disasters or national emergencies.[200] The purpose of such a clause "is to limit damages where the reasonable expectation of the parties and the performance of the contract have been frustrated by circumstances beyond the control of the parties."[201] In such an instance, both parties' obligations under the contract are excused.[202]

---

[196] Banks, *supra* note 5, § 28:16.

[197] Kel Kim Corp. v. Cent. Mkts., Inc., 519 N.E.2d 295, 296 (N.Y. 1987) ("Impossibility excuses a party's performance only when the destruction of the subject matter of the contract or the means of performance makes performance objectively impossible. Moreover, the impossibility must be produced by an unanticipated event that could not have been foreseen or guarded against in the contract."); 407 E. 61st St. Garage v. Savoy Fifth Ave. Corp., 244 N.E.2d 37 (N.Y. 1968) ("[W]here impossibility or difficulty of performance is occasioned only by financial difficulty or economic hardship, even to the extent of insolvency or bankruptcy, performance of a contract is not excused.").

[198] *See* Black's Law Dictionary (8th ed. 2004) (defining *force-majeure* clause as: "[a] contractual provision allocating the risk if performance becomes impossible or impracticable, esp. as a result of an event or effect that the parties could not have anticipated or controlled."); Corbin, *supra* note 186, § 74.19.

[199] *See* N.Y.U.C.C. § 2-615 (2005).

[200] United Equities Co. v. First Nat'l City Bank, 383 N.Y.S.2d 6, 9 (1st Dep't 1976).

[201] *Id.*

[202] Farnsworth, *supra* note 96, § 9.9.

Parties may use a *force majeure* clause in other ways. For example, a *force majeure* clause may limit damages if events frustrate the reasonable expectations of the parties. In that instance, the clause may not be used to give a party greater profit than originally expected under the contract.[203] They may even be used inversely to their original purpose; parties may include language that specifically denies excusing performance based on *force majeure* events.[204] Finally, unless the effect of a *force majeure* event is permanent, for example the destruction of a unique good to be sold, a *force majeure* clause will generally not excuse performance, but simply permit delay in performance until the effects of the *force majeure* event abate. **4.69**

The scope of a *force majeure* clause under New York law is traditionally very limited and provides a "narrow defense."[205] To claim *force majeure* as a defense to excuse a party's performance, the clause must explicitly consider the actual event that prevents performance or one identical in character or class.[206] Difficulty with performance or "mere impracticability" will not excuse performance.[207] Consequently, parties should draft *force majeure* clauses with as much specificity as possible. **4.70**

---

[203] *United Equities*, 383 N.Y.S.2d at 9.

[204] Banks, *supra* note 5, § 20:14.

[205] *Kel Kim Corp.*, 519 N.E.2d at 296.

[206] *Id.* at 902–03; Phibro Energy, Inc. v. Empresa de Polimeros De Sines Sarl, 720 F. Supp. 312, 318 (S.D.N.Y. 1989). Corbin, *supra* note 186, § 74.19; *see also* Phillips P.R. Core, Inc. v. Tradax Petroleum Ltd., 1984 WL 677, at *4 (S.D.N.Y. 1984).

[207] *Kel Kim Corp.*, 519 N.E.2d at 296.

5

THE SELECTION OF ARBITRATORS

James H. Carter

A. **Tribunal Structure** 5.03
  1. Detailed Arbitrator Selection Clauses 5.05
  2. Incorporation of Arbitral Rules Governing Tribunal Formation 5.07
    (a) ICDR international rules 5.08
    (b) AAA commercial rules 5.16
    (c) ICC rules 5.19
    (d) UNCITRAL rules 5.22
    (e) CPR rules 5.24
    (f) JAMS rules 5.27
  3. Idiosyncratic Appointing Authorities in New York 5.28
  4. Dysfunctional Clauses Referring to Nonexistent or Unavailable Institutions 5.29
  5. Statutory Default Procedures 5.30

B. **Strategy in Selecting Members of a Tripartite Tribunal** 5.32
  1. Role of the Default Mechanism 5.33
  2. Lawyers vs. Nonlawyers 5.35
  3. Special Professional Qualifications 5.37
  4. Nationality 5.40

C. **Neutrality of Party-Appointed Arbitrators** 5.43

D. **Where to Find Arbitrator Candidates** 5.46
  1. The CPR Roster 5.47
  2. The Energy Arbitrators' List 5.48
  3. The JAMS Roster 5.49
  4. ICDR 5.50
  5. ICC/U.S. Council for International Business 5.51
  6. The International Arbitration Club of New York 5.52
  7. Lawyer Directories 5.53

E. **The Selection Process** 5.54
  1. Communications with Party-Appointed Arbitrators 5.56
    (a) The AAA/ABA Code and AAA Rules 5.57
    (b) The Chartered Institute of Arbitrators' Guideline 5.60
    (c) Restricted time limits 5.64
  2. Role of the Party-Appointed Arbitrators in Selecting a Chairperson 5.66
  3. Negotiating Selection of a Chairperson 5.70
  4. Convincing the Chairperson Candidate to Serve 5.75

F. **Arbitrator Compensation and Conflicts Waivers** 5.77

G. **Conflicts Checks and Arbitrator Disclosures** 5.82

H. **Challenges and Replacement of Arbitrators** 5.86

5.01 The most important step in any arbitration is selection of the arbitrators. It presents a challenge, at the outset of a proceeding, to counsel's strategic thinking: how to obtain a tribunal that will be both fair and favorable? As one practitioner puts it,

> A party's goal should be the appointment of an arbitral tribunal, a majority (at least) of whose members, while being independent and impartial as regards the parties (as required by the relevant arbitration rules and law), will at the same time be well disposed towards, or sympathetic to, or at the very least receptive to that party's position.[1]

5.02 Pursuit of this goal requires study of the applicable arbitration tribunal structure, development of a strategy, and knowledge about potential arbitrators.

A. TRIBUNAL STRUCTURE

5.03 The process begins with a study of the applicable tribunal structure dictated by the parties' arbitration agreement. International arbitral tribunals in New York, as elsewhere, most often are made up of three members. The typical arbitration clause or agreement for arbitration in New York provides for what is sometimes called a tripartite tribunal: each party or group of parties is to select one arbitrator, and a third arbitrator—the chair of the tribunal—is to be chosen by agreement of the first two arbitrators, or by agreement of the parties, or is to be selected by an arbitral or other institution. Alternatively, the arbitration clause may specify a sole arbitrator, in which case he or she will be selected in the manner provided by the clause, as supplemented by any applicable arbitration rules.

5.04 The tripartite selection system, allowing each party to appoint an arbitrator and typically permitting both parties to have a role in choosing the third, is intended to give each side a degree of confidence in the tribunal at the outset as a result of having participated in its formation. This tends to mitigate natural litigiousness somewhat and induce cooperation when the tribunal sets the initial procedural directions. The system's principal practical drawbacks, discussed below, are that (1) the rules and ethical principles applicable to the selection of the party-appointed arbitrators are not entirely clear, and (2) the actual process for selecting a third arbitrator "by agreement" tends to be murky.

[1] Christopher R. Seppälä, *Obtaining the Right International Arbitral Tribunal: A Practitioner's View*, 22 Mealey's Int'l Arb. R. 26 (Oct. 2007), also published in 25 Int'l Construction L. Rev. 198 (2008). Although this goal is hardly a secret, open discussion of it is relatively scarce. *See* Ahmed S. El-Kosheri and Karim Y. Yonsset, *The Independence of International Arbitrators: An Arbitrator's Perspective*, ICC Court of Arb. Bull. 2007 Spec. Supp. 43, 48–49 (2008); Doak Bishop and Lucy Reed, *Practical Guidelines for Interviewing, Selecting, and Challenging Party-Appointed Arbitrators in International Commercial Arbitration*, 14(4) Arb. Int'l 395 (1998); James H. Carter, *The Selection of Arbitrators*, 5 Am. Rev. Int'l Arb. 84 (1994).

1. Detailed Arbitrator Selection Clauses

Arbitration clauses sometimes specify the sequence and timing of arbitrator selection in detail, with various steps to occur within a few days of each other. Unfortunately, drafters of such clauses often are not experienced in the litigation of actual arbitral disputes and take the idea that arbitration is to be expeditious as their guiding star. This often leads to clause language providing unrealistically short time limits for arbitrator selection, which may require extension by agreement when a dispute arises. Arbitration rules suffer to a lesser extent from this difficulty and generally have been drafted to arrive at a compromise between desired expedition and the realities of practice. **5.05**

Detailed arbitration clauses also may contain requirements that only persons with certain attributes may serve, thus limiting the available universe of candidates. **5.06**

2. Incorporation of Arbitral Rules Governing Tribunal Formation

Other arbitration clauses incorporate arbitral rules without saying anything further concerning arbitrator selection, thereby electing the default selection mechanism contained in those rules to cover situations in which the parties' agreement is silent on method of appointment. It therefore is important to be familiar with the default provisions of the rules most likely to be selected for international arbitrations in New York. **5.07**

(a) ICDR international rules The American Arbitration Association (AAA)'s International Centre for Dispute Resolution (ICDR) International Arbitration Rules (2014) provide that, if the parties have not agreed on a number of arbitrators, a sole arbitrator will be appointed unless the administrator determines that three arbitrators are appropriate "because of the size, complexity or other circumstances of the case."[2] In practice, ICDR administrative staff normally will discuss with counsel how many arbitrators should be selected and in the absence of agreement will interpret this rule to provide for three arbitrators if the amount claimed is at least $1 million. **5.08**

Whether the tribunal is to be one arbitrator or three, the International Rules invite the parties to agree on a procedure for appointing arbitrators; but if they have not done so within a forty-five-day period from the commencement of the arbitration, the ICDR administrator, at the request of a party, will appoint all of the arbitrators and designate the presiding arbitrator.[3] This provides a strong incentive for parties who have not done so in their arbitration clause to agree on an appointment method after the arbitration has commenced. The usual result **5.09**

[2] ICDR International Arbitration Rules, Art. 11, *available at* http://go.adr.org/icdrrules.
[3] *Id.*, Art. 12.

is agreement that each side will appoint one arbitrator and those two arbitrators may select the chairman.

5.10 If there is no agreement on a method of arbitrator selection, Article 12(6) defines the ICDR list method, under which the staff provides the parties with a list of possible arbitrators from which each may strike a designated number of names and number the remaining names in order of preference. If a sole arbitrator or chairman is to be appointed, the list usually includes ten names, accompanied by brief resumes of each candidate. If the list is to be used to select three arbitrators, it normally includes fifteen names, with resumes. The administrator may discuss types of arbitrators who might be included, but not specific arbitrator names, with counsel for each party separately before making up the list. Each party returns its copy of the list to the ICDR in confidence within fifteen days and the administrator tallies the votes to determine who will be approached to form the tribunal. The ICDR will approach the top-ranking candidate or candidates, who will not have known of the process until that point. If one or more of them is unable or unavailable to serve, the ICDR will contact the next-ranking candidate from the list. Occasionally an initial list may not be sufficient, in which case the ICDR may provide a second list. If the parties fail to agree, the rules give the ICDR the right to make an appointment unilaterally without the submission of additional lists.[4]

5.11 If the AAA appoints all three arbitrators, either the arbitrators decide which of them will be chairperson or, if they request, the ICDR staff will choose the chairperson.

5.12 The ICDR International Rules cover the multiparty situation by stating that, if the parties have not agreed otherwise within forty-five days after commencement of the arbitration and the notice of arbitration names two or more claimants or two or more respondents, the administrator will appoint all of the arbitrators.[5] This also provides an incentive for the parties to reach agreement.

5.13 The AAA maintains an extensive database of potential arbitrators from which its lists are composed. AAA arbitrators, all of whom must undergo AAA-organized training courses and updates, total approximately 7,300. There are regional panels for various parts of the United States and a separate National Panel, as well as an International Panel of approximately 650 arbitrators, two-thirds of whom are located outside the U.S. Lists of arbitrators prepared by the ICDR normally are drawn from the International Panel, although other names may be added where special credentials are required, such as a certain industry expertise.

5.14 The AAA offers an "Enhanced Neutral Selection Process for Large Complex Cases," available in international as well as U.S. domestic cases for which the

---

[4] *Id.*, Art. 12(6)

[5] *Id.*, Art. 12(5)

parties elect to include AAA "Large, Complex Case Procedures." The AAA will provide the parties with an early, initial sample of arbitrator resumes based on the qualifications requested by the parties and receive feedback from counsel on the type of arbitrators preferred before preparing a final list of arbitrators from which the parties may select through the strike process. Additional steps also are available: the AAA is prepared to work with the parties to develop an interview protocol for a telephone conference or written questions to prospective arbitrators and to pre-screen a limited number of selected potential arbitrators for freedom from conflicts.

The ICDR International Rules contain no limitations concerning nationality of arbitrators, but at the request of a party or on their own initiative administrators "may" appoint nationals of a country other than that of any of the parties.[6] **5.15**

(b) AAA commercial rules The AAA's Commercial Arbitration Rules (2013), specified by parties in about 40 percent of ICDR international cases,[7] outline their default selection procedure in greater detail. If the parties have not agreed otherwise, immediately after the filing of the arbitration demand and answering statement, the ICDR will send simultaneously to each party an identical list of ten names (unless the AAA decides that a different number is appropriate) from its International Roster. The parties then have fourteen days from the transmittal date within which to strike names objected to and number remaining names in order of preference. Arbitrators are selected based on mutual preference.[8] The Commercial Rules also provide expressly for direct appointment of an arbitrator by a party if the agreement calls for such selection, and upon request the ICDR will provide a list of potential arbitrators for a party's consideration.[9] The Enhanced Selection Process also is available as part of the procedures for Large, Complex Cases heard under the Commercial Rules. **5.16**

Like the International Rules, the Commercial Rules allow the party-appointed arbitrators to select the chairperson if authorized by the parties but permit the AAA staff to select the chairperson (in practice, the parties participate in this through the list procedure) if the two party-appointed arbitrators or the parties are unable to do so within specified time limits.[10] **5.17**

The Commercial Arbitration Rules provide that, where the parties are nationals of different countries, the AAA, at the request of any party or on its own **5.18**

[6] *Id.*, Art. 12(4).

[7] The AAA also administers cases in New York under UNCITRAL Arbitration Rules and under the Inter-American Arbitration Commission (IACAC) Rules, the Commercial Arbitration and Mediation Center for the Americas (CAMCA) Arbitration Rules, and specialized AAA rules such as those for the construction and real estate industries, *all available at* http://www.adr.org.

[8] AAA Commercial Arbitration Rules, R-12.

[9] *Id.*, Rule 13.

[10] *Id.*, Rule 14.

initiative, "may" appoint as arbitrator a national of a country other than that of any of the parties.[11]

5.19 *(c) ICC rules* The International Chamber of Commerce's International Rules (2012) also provide for a sole arbitrator unless the ICC Court decides that there shall be three arbitrators, which it does for all larger cases.[12] The ICC default procedure for three-arbitrator cases authorizes each side to choose one arbitrator and calls for the ICC to select the chairperson unilaterally. However, if requested to do so by the parties, the ICC Secretariat will allow a reasonable period of time for the parties to try to agree on the third arbitrator before exercising its institutional appointment right. If it appoints, the ICC Court in Paris, operating on the recommendation of its Secretariat, which has a branch located in New York called SICANA, Inc. (for "the Secretariat of the International Court of Arbitration, North America"), names a single individual as chairperson without giving the parties or their counsel any choice among candidates. The Secretariat will consider the parties' suggestions regarding appropriate nationality and other characteristics of the tribunal chairperson, and in the absence of agreement otherwise the ICC will choose a chairperson of a nationality other than that of either of the parties. Recent ICC statistics[13] show that the nationality of chairpersons appointed or confirmed by the ICC worldwide is most frequently (in order): British, Swiss, French, American, and German; but the choice in a particular case will depend on the site of arbitration, the governing law, and the nationalities of the parties involved.

5.20 When called on to appoint an arbitrator in an ICC arbitration in New York, the ICC Court initially determines what nationality arbitrator should be chosen. If the ICC is to appoint a chairperson, the Court typically turns to a National Committee of a country different from that of any of the parties. The National Committee, after appropriate dialogue with the Secretariat, proposes the name of a person to serve. The ICC Court then considers the proposed candidate and his or her qualifications and statement of independence and, assuming no difficulties, makes the appointment.[14]

5.21 If the arbitrator is to be of U.S. nationality, the ICC consults its U.S. National Committee, which is the Arbitration Committee of the United States Council for International Business (USCIB), headquartered in New York City. That committee has a database of 2,600 names, and the ICC will supply lists of names from it to parties for consideration if requested to do so. If the committee is requested

---

[11] *Id.*, Rule 15.

[12] ICC Arbitration Rules, Art. 12. As a guideline, the ICC will specify three arbitrators in a case involving a demand for $5 million or more.

[13] *E.g.*, ICC Int'l Court of Arb. Bull. 25(1) 7–8 (2014).

[14] Jennifer Kirby, *The ICC Court: A Behind-the-Scenes Look*, 16(2) ICC Int'l Court of Arb. Bull. 9, 15 (2005); Anne Marie Whitesell, *Independence in ICC Arbitration: ICC Court Practice Concerning the Appointment, Confirmation, Challenge, and Replacement of Arbitrators*, ICC Int'l Court of Arb. Bull. 2007 Spec. Supp. 7, 11–14 (2008).

to nominate, the USCIB Executive Director identifies six to ten names from the database, and the committee considers those and other names suggested by its members and selects a candidate. In practice, only about fifteen to twenty-five arbitrators are nominated each year by the U.S. National Committee.

(d) UNCITRAL rules The U.N. Commission on International Trade Law (UNCITRAL) Arbitration Rules (2010) do not provide for the administrative services of an arbitral institution, so their default provisions first require selection of an arbitral institution to serve as Appointing Authority. The Appointing Authority may be, and usually is, named by the parties in their arbitration clause. The Appointing Authority must use a list procedure, sending the parties a list of names of possible arbitrators (again, sometimes after some input from the parties regarding nationality and other characteristics) and asking them to return the lists simultaneously, numbering the candidates in order of preference.[15] The most frequently named Appointing Authority for UNCITRAL Rules arbitration in New York is the American Arbitration Association, and in practice this means appointment by the ICDR, using its normal list procedure.[16] Each year the ICDR administers approximately thirty-five cases under the UNCITRAL Rules. **5.22**

In the absence of a choice in the clause, and failing subsequent agreement, an Appointing Authority will be selected by the Permanent Court of Arbitration (PCA) in The Hague.[17] The PCA makes only a handful of designations of Appointing Authorities each year for cases in the United States, normally choosing an institution (but occasionally an individual) with international expertise and a presence at the arbitration site. The PCA occasionally itself is named as Appointing Authority for UNCITRAL Rules cases in the United States. **5.23**

(e) CPR rules The International Institute for Conflict Prevention and Resolution (CPR) publishes rules for both administered and non-administered arbitration of international disputes, each with a domestic equivalent.[18] The default rules for cases with "international" attributes are the CPR Rules for Administered International Disputes. All provide as a default that, if the appointment method is not specified by agreement, each of the parties shall appoint one arbitrator and may agree that the two arbitrators shall select a third arbitrator. The CPR domestic rules require that any arbitrator appointed by CPR, as opposed to an arbitrator appointed directly by a party, must be a member of the CPR Panels of Distinguished Neutrals unless otherwise agreed; but the CPR international rules **5.24**

---

[15] UNCITRAL Arbitration Rules, Arts. 8(2) (sole arbitrator), 9(3) (arbitral panel), *available at* http://www.uncitral.org.

[16] The AAA publishes *Procedures for Cases Under the UNCITRAL Arbitration Rules, available at* http://www.adr.org.

[17] UNCITRAL Arbitration Rules, Art. 6.

[18] The CPR-administered rules became effective in 2013 (domestic) and 2014 (international). All CPR rules are available at http://www.cpradr.org.

contain greater flexibility. CPR maintains a Global Panel composed of neutrals located outside the U.S., a Cross Border Panel with names of North American-based arbitrators experienced in transnational disputes, a National Panel, and various regional and specialized panels.

5.25 The CPR rules include a unique provision by which, if the parties have agreed on a Tribunal consisting of three arbitrators, two of whom are to be designated by the parties without knowing which party designated each of them, CPR will approach the designated arbitrators on a "blind" basis and arrange for their retention without disclosing to any arbitrator which party selected that arbitrator.[19]

5.26 CPR's practice is to appoint by a list procedure, normally prescreening the candidates on the lists supplied to the parties to determine their availability and absence of conflicts before listing them for ranking by the parties. This contrasts with the AAA/ICDR list procedure, which ordinarily does not involve prescreening of candidates. As a result of the prescreening process, CPR arbitrator lists normally are relatively short and may contain as few as five names if a sole arbitrator is to be selected or seven if three arbitrators are called for.

5.27 *(f) JAMS rules* JAMS, originally known as Judicial Arbitration and Mediation Associates, Inc., administers some international cases in New York. It operates primarily under its Comprehensive Arbitration Rules and Procedures (2014) and also has a separate set of International Rules. Both honor any method of arbitrator selection agreed by the parties and include a list and strike method (using a list drawn from JAMS' own group of arbitrators) as the default mechanism.

3. Idiosyncratic Appointing Authorities in New York

5.28 Occasionally, arbitration agreements calling for arbitration in New York designate a New York bar association or other nonspecialist institution, or even a specified individual, rather than a professional arbitral organization, to select arbitrators. The President of the New York City Bar Association[20] is named and called upon to act in this capacity in a few cases each year. Such organizations typically have no extensive list of potential arbitrators available, lack a body of administrative expertise, and are not well prepared to appoint arbitrators; but they usually manage to do so rather than see the parties' intentions frustrated. The extent of party input into the procedure depends largely on the individual practices of those making the appointments.

---

[19] CPR Domestic Rule 5.4, International Rule 5.4.

[20] This association's formal name is The Association of the Bar of the City of New York, and that name appears in some clauses. It has an active role in mediation and arbitration of disputes among lawyers, the rules for which are available at http://www.nycbar.org/Publications/lawyerdisp.

4. Dysfunctional Clauses Referring to Nonexistent or Unavailable Institutions

Occasionally arbitration clauses provide for appointment of arbitrators by nonexistent entities, such as the "College of Arbiters," or appointment by entities that have ceased to or will not act as an appointing authority. New York courts faced with such dysfunctional clauses sometimes have appointed an arbitrator for the parties,[21] or interpreted the clauses to apply to an institution with a name similar to the one used in the clause, on the assumption that this was what the parties intended.[22] On other occasions, New York courts have held that the clause is unenforceable.[23] In the "College of Arbiters" case, the court held that the term referred to a generic arbitral panel, which the clause contemplated by providing for a traditional tripartite appointment system with two party-appointed arbitrators and a "neutral."[24] **5.29**

5. Statutory Default Procedures

If the arbitration agreement makes no reference to any rules, the default procedures for arbitrator appointment will be found in applicable arbitration statutes. The Federal Arbitration Act provides that, if no method for naming arbitrators is specified, or if a method is specified but not followed, or "if for any other reason there shall be a lapse in the naming of an arbitrator or arbitrators or umpire, or in filling a vacancy," either party may apply to a U.S. federal district court to make the appointment.[25] Federal courts in New York receive occasional applications to appoint arbitrators under this provision, but they maintain no roster of arbitrators and have no standing procedures for making appointments. The choice is **5.30**

[21] Global Reinsurance Corp.–U.S. Branch v. Certain Underwriters at Lloyd's, London, 465 F. Supp. 2d 308, 310–11 (S.D.N.Y. 2006); Rosgoscirc v. Circus Show Corp., 1993 WL 277333 (S.D.N.Y. 1993); Astra Footwear Industry v. Harwyn International, Inc., 442 F. Supp. 907, 910 (S.D.N.Y. 1978), *aff'd* 578 F.2d 1366 (2d Cir. 1978).

[22] HZI Research Center, Inc. v. Sun Instruments Japan Co., 10 Mealey's Rep. 11 (S.D.N.Y. 1995) (appointing the AAA where the arbitration agreement allowed for "the American or the Japanese Arbitrator Society").

[23] *In re* Salomon, Inc. Shareholders' Derivative Litigation, 68 F.3d 554, 560–61 (2d Cir. 1995) (holding a clause null where the parties bargained for arbitration under the rules of an institution that was not available to them); Lea Tai textile Co., Ltd. v. Manning Fabrics, Inc., 411 F. Supp. 1404 (S.D.N.Y. 1975) (finding a clause unenforceable because it is impossible to determine what the parties intended). *But see* Peters Fabrics, Inc. v. Jantzen, Inc., 582 F. Supp. 1287, 1291 (S.D.N.Y. 1984) (competing forms providing different arbitral institutions, but with relatively similar rules, held to constitute agreement to arbitrate).

[24] Magi XXI, Inc. v. Stato Della Citta Del Vaticano, 2008 WL 3895915 (E.D.N.Y. 2008) (parties then agreed to abandon right to arbitration, 818 F.Supp.2d 597).

[25] 9 U.S.C. § 5. The New York State arbitration statute, Civil Practice Law & Rules Section 7504, provides similar authority for a state court to make arbitrator appointments. However, as discussed in Chapters 7 and 13 of this book, most litigation arising in connection with international arbitrations in New York occurs in federal courts. *See also* CAE Industries Ltd. v. Aerospace Holdings Co., 741 F. Supp. 388, 393 (S.D.N.Y. 1989) (naming a sole arbitrator where the arbitration agreement was silent as to the appointment of arbitrators); Ore & Chemical Corp. v. Stinnes Interoil, Inc., 611 F. Supp. 237, 240–41 (S.D.N.Y. 1985) (same).

thus subject to the discretion of the individual judge to whom the application may be assigned,[26] who typically will think first of retired judges or others known personally to him or her. Some judges give the parties a role in suggesting or considering candidates, but others do not.

5.31 In 2013, the Commercial Division of the New York State Supreme Court for New York County (a trial level court with jurisdiction over Manhattan) designated a single judge to preside over all international commercial disputes in that court. The court has promulgated rules[27] under which it will appoint arbitrators if requested, either from a list or source agreed by the parties or from the Unified Court System's Fiduciary Eligibility List.

B. STRATEGY IN SELECTING MEMBERS OF A TRIPARTITE TRIBUNAL

5.32 The key to success in selecting a tripartite tribunal is choosing the proper party-appointed arbitrator. The goal in selecting a party-appointed arbitrator, like any other arbitrator, should be to choose someone who will be perceived to be and will be independent of the appointing party and its counsel and also is likely to be sympathetic to or at least understanding of the type of arguments the party will advance in the case. In addition, the party-appointed arbitrator should be a person who is able to perform effectively in the process of selecting a chairperson, if the structure of the arbitration gives party-appointees a role in that process, and should have personal qualities likely to make him or her effective in interactions with the chairperson.

1. Role of the Default Mechanism

5.33 When thinking about a party-appointed arbitrator, it is useful to bear in mind the relevant default provisions, discussed above, for selecting a chairperson. If the parties or the two party-appointed arbitrators, as the case may be, fail to agree on a chairperson, the relevant default selection mechanism will come into play; and it may be possible to predict, at least to some extent, what type of chairperson that process will produce. Knowledgeable parties will negotiate the selection of the chairperson themselves, if possible, rather than take the increased risk of the unknown inherent in the default mechanisms. They often do so against the background of their assessment of what type of arbitrator the default mechanism is most likely to yield—in recognition of the risk that, if the negotiating process does not offer a better candidate, the chairperson, in all likelihood, will have a profile similar to that of the "default chairperson."

[26] Such applications are assigned to judges on a random basis.
[27] Appendix 4 of this book.

For example, counsel may calculate that the default chairperson in an international case sited in New York, with a choice of New York governing law in the agreement and a New York court making the appointment, is likely to be a New York lawyer. If so, the parties are likely to agree on such a person because either side, by withholding agreement, could bring about that result in any case. On that assumption, counsel might then think of what type of party-appointed arbitrator should be chosen. What sort of arbitrator is likely to be effective in negotiating against this default profile to get a good chairperson and then working effectively with such a chairperson? **5.34**

2. Lawyers vs. Nonlawyers

Most party-appointed arbitrators in international commercial cases in New York are lawyers, including both practitioners and academic lawyers. This is not because lawyers necessarily are wiser than nonlawyers but, rather, is largely a result of the "default chairperson" principle. The chairperson of a tribunal in a general commercial dispute arising out of a contractual relationship of any complexity almost certainly will be a lawyer, since he or she must manage what is likely to be a reasonably formal arbitral procedure; and another lawyer is more likely to be able to understand the thinking of such a chairperson than is a potential arbitrator without legal training. This widespread practice of appointing a lawyer as party-appointed arbitrator also is based on the fact that failure to name a lawyer would give the opposing party the chance to do so, potentially isolating the nonlawyer on the tribunal. **5.35**

Some international arbitrations in New York, such as maritime cases, normally are heard by "commercial men" rather than lawyers; and sometimes a clause will specify a nonlawyer credential, such as that all arbitrators be present or former insurance or reinsurance executives. But nonlawyer businessmen or women rarely are selected to preside over general commercial cases heard in New York by AAA, ICC, or similar tribunals. As a result, typically either all three arbitrators are persons trained as lawyers, whether or not they have other credentials, or all three are nonlawyers. **5.36**

3. Special Professional Qualifications

Sometimes, arbitration clauses provide that all of the arbitrators, or perhaps only the chairperson, must be experienced in a particular industry, or have held a specified rank at a particular type of company, or have been engaged in the practice of a profession for a specific period of time. These arbitrators of course may also be lawyers. Sometimes clauses go so far as to require that arbitrators be former judges of a particular court.[28] **5.37**

[28] Under U.S. law, sitting judges and "senior status" judges still receiving government pay and available for judicial duties may not accept employment as arbitrators in private commercial matters. *See, e.g.*, New York Constitution, Art. 6, § 20. Retired judges may do so.

5.38 Restrictions of this type are problematic, because they tend to limit the universe from which parties and counsel may select arbitrators and because they tend to inject ambiguity regarding the qualifications necessary. For example, a clause might require that the members of an arbitral tribunal all be attorneys experienced in the aviation industry. But panels classified as aviation specialists by arbitral institutions may contain primarily attorneys experienced in aircraft accident cases, which may be a different expertise from that needed for a contract dispute between two airline companies. Similarly, a requirement that all of the arbitrators or the chairperson be former judges may restrict the available candidate pool to a handful of individuals, not all of whom may be available. Counsel faced with clauses of this type may wish to engage in discussions with opposing counsel concerning waiver or loosening of such restrictions.

5.39 Even in the absence of contractual limitations, it is proper to think about the qualifications appropriate for arbitrators in the particular case. Some arbitrations seem well suited to lawyers, whether or not former judges, with a range of experience in commercial dealings. Others may be better suited to legal specialists in a particular subject or, if all arbitrators are to be nonlawyers, for persons with backgrounds in accounting or some other profession.

4. Nationality

5.40 Nationality of the party-appointed arbitrator is also of importance in considering strategy. Sometimes a party in international arbitration nominates an arbitrator of the party's nationality, thereby assuring that at least one tribunal member will be likely to understand and appreciate that party's arguments. In such a situation, the party's expectation may be that the other party will do the same and that the chairperson will have a third nationality. While that pattern is found in international arbitrations in New York, it often is not followed and instead an American lawyer is appointed by the non-U.S. party, at least where New York or another U.S. law is the governing law, because of the likelihood that the chairperson will be a New York or other American lawyer.

5.41 Again, the default chairperson logic is at work. If he or she is likely to be a New York lawyer, another American lawyer is likely to have some degree of intellectual rapport with the chairperson. If the party-appointed arbitrator is trained in New York law, this provides a further point of potential common background with the likely chairperson. And if it turns out that the chairperson is not American, he or she nevertheless remains likely to be a lawyer; and then the party-appointed arbitrator may have the advantage of being able to bring New York law expertise to the assistance of the chairperson. All of this may incline a non-U.S. party to appoint an American arbitrator.

As noted previously, however, some arbitral rules and institutional practices require or at least presume that a chairperson be of a nationality different from that of any of the parties, if a party so prefers. **5.42**

C. NEUTRALITY OF PARTY-APPOINTED ARBITRATORS

A party-appointed international arbitrator ordinarily must be neutral as a requirement of most institutional or ad hoc arbitration rules. The party-appointed arbitrator's role nevertheless may be confusing because of the history of the party appointment practice in U.S. domestic arbitration, where party-appointed arbitrators sometimes have been considered advocates rather than neutrals. The "partisan" or "nonneutral" arbitrator has not been customary in international arbitration in the United States, however, and since 2004 the American Arbitration Association/American Bar Association Code of Ethics for Arbitrators in Commercial Matters (AAA/ABA Code of Ethics)[29] has helped to clarify the situation by prescribing a presumption that party-appointed arbitrators in all commercial matters, whether international or domestic, will be neutral unless there is specific agreement to the contrary. **5.43**

Arbitration rules typically used in New York are consistent with this presumption of neutrality for all members of the arbitral tribunal. For example, the ICDR International Arbitration Rules state that "[a]rbitrators acting under these Rules shall be impartial and independent,"[30] and the AAA Commercial Arbitration Rules similarly state that "[a]ny arbitrator shall be impartial and independent."[31] However, consistent with the AAA/ABA Code of Ethics, the Commercial Rules allow the parties to agree to treat party-appointed arbitrators as "non-neutral."[32] Non-neutral arbitrators may be predisposed toward the party appointing them and may have ex parte communications with that party if the intent to do so is disclosed prior to the occurrence of such communications. Nevertheless, where the parties have so agreed, the AAA "shall as an administrative practice suggest to the parties" that they agree further that Rule 19(a) (limiting ex parte communications after the tribunal is appointed) "should nonetheless apply prospectively."[33] **5.44**

---

[29] Code of Ethics for Arbitrators in Commercial Disputes (2004), Appendix 6 of this book. Ethical Codes are not binding on courts but often are cited as "highly significant." *E.g.*, Positive Software Solutions, Inc. v. New Century Mortgage Corp., 436 F.3d 495, 503 n.43 (5th Cir. 2006), rev'd en banc 476 F.3d 278 (5th Cir.), cert. denied, 127 S.Ct. 2943 (2007).

[30] ICDR International Arbitration Rules, Art. 13(1).

[31] AAA Commercial Arbitration Rules, R-18(a).

[32] *Id.*, Rule 18(b).

[33] *Id.*, Rule 19(b). This suggestion usually is made immediately prior to the initial conference among the arbitrators and counsel, so that the chairperson can raise the issue at that conference.

5.45 U.S. case law continues to support the validity of the concept of the nonneutral arbitrator but increasingly has recognized that the presumption now enshrined in the AAA/ABA Code of Ethics is sensible and provides a practical guide for use in determining whether or not parties intend arbitrators to be impartial and independent. Accordingly, all international arbitrators in New York should be impartial and independent.

D. WHERE TO FIND ARBITRATOR CANDIDATES

5.46 Often consulting a list of possible arbitrators stimulates thinking about candidates. Arbitration organizations maintain rosters of specialist arbitrators in a number of areas, and some of these lists are available publicly. Other types of list also are generally available, and arbitral institutions may make lists of suggested arbitrators available on request for party consideration, as described above.

1. The CPR Roster

5.47 The International Institute for Conflict Prevention and Resolution (CPR) maintains lists of potential arbitrators on its Web site,[34] most of which are available only through passwords available to CPR members. CPR's National Panel lists fifty-four arbitrators, all based in the U.S., while its Global Panel contains names of eighty individuals, primarily located in the U.S., Canada, or Mexico, and its Cross-Border Panel contains seventy names of arbitrators, all located outside the U.S. CPR has industry specialist panels for subjects such as banking, energy, and insurance. There are also general arbitrator lists for a number of specific foreign countries and lists organized by U.S. state, including one hundred three names of arbitrators in New York State.

2. The Energy Arbitrators' List

5.48 The ICDR makes available an electronic list of more than one hundred peer-reviewed arbitrators experienced in energy disputes, which is searchable by name, nationality, country of residence, language capability, and key words relating to their type of energy industry experience.[35]

3. The JAMS Roster

5.49 JAMS also makes available lists of its arbitrators,[36] twenty-five of whom are identified as U.S./Canada-based international arbitration specialists, and individuals also are listed for several foreign countries.

[34] Http://www.cpradr.org.
[35] Http//energyarbitratorslist.icdr.org.
[36] Http://www.jamsadr.com.

4. ICDR

The larger arbitration organizations active in international arbitration in New York, the ICDR and the ICC, do not publish lists of potential arbitrators, except for the ICDR's Energy Arbitrators' List. The ICDR nevertheless will provide sample arbitrator names and resumes as part of its Enhanced Neutral Selection Process. **5.50**

5. ICC/U.S. Council for International Business

The ICC's local affiliate, the U.S. Council for International Business's Arbitration Committee, maintains a proprietary Arbitrator/Mediator/Expert Database on its website,[37] into which members may input their resume data, for use by the U.S. National Committee when it makes arbitrator nominations. Lists of sample names will be made available by the USCIB. **5.51**

6. The International Arbitration Club of New York

The International Arbitration Club of New York is composed of leading counsel, arbitrators and academics active in the New York international arbitration community. It publishes a list of members on its Web site, www.arbitrationclub.org. **5.52**

7. Lawyer Directories

In addition to these listings, a number of published directories of "leading" lawyers include sections on international arbitration that may provide information on lawyers active as both counsel and arbitrators. Among these are the directories published by Chambers U.S.A.,[38] Law Business Research's *Who's Who Legal*,[39] and the *Legal 500: United States* volume.[40] Similarly, directories of members of arbitration associations such as the London Court of International Arbitration (LCIA), the Association Suisse de l'Arbitrage (ASA), the International Council for Commercial Arbitration (ICCA) and the International Arbitration Institute (IAI) are useful sources of information about arbitrators. **5.53**

E. THE SELECTION PROCESS

It is essential to know as much as possible about any person being considered for arbitrator appointment. But unlike judges, most arbitrators do not have a body **5.54**

---

[37] Http://www.uscib.org.

[38] CHAMBERS U.S.A.: AMERICA'S LEADING LAWYERS FOR BUSINESS, published annually.

[39] LAW BUSINESS RESEARCH LTD., WHO'S WHO LEGAL: THE INTERNATIONAL WHO'S WHO OF BUSINESS LAWYERS, published annually.

[40] JOHN PRITCHARD, THE LEGAL 500: UNITED STATES, published annually.

of published work showing examples of their approaches to problems of contract interpretation. How, then, does counsel form a view regarding how a potential arbitrator might think about the issues in a case?

5.55 Arbitrators often are selected based on counsel's prior experience with them, in one connection or another, which has given a window into the nature of their thinking. Sometimes, in the absence of such information, counsel may select simply on the basis of the arbitrator's reputation. The selection may be made without any contact with the prospective arbitrator; but typically counsel prefer to interview one or more arbitrator candidates to determine "first-hand, what a prospective arbitrator's actual experience, commitment and availability are."[41] The rules governing such arbitrator "beauty contests" are addressed, to some extent, by the AAA/ABA Code of Ethics and some arbitration rules.

1. Communications with Party-Appointed Arbitrators

5.56 The issues that most often cause confusion in the appointment process are interviews with prospective arbitrators and discussions with a party-appointed arbitrator, usually after appointment, about the identity of a possible tribunal chairperson.

5.57 *(a) The AAA/ABA Code and AAA Rules* The AAA/ABA Code of Ethics, in effect in its present form since 2004, provides for both of these types of communications between party/counsel and prospective arbitrator/appointed arbitrator, as follows:

> CANON III. AN ARBITRATOR SHOULD AVOID IMPROPRIETY OR THE APPEARANCE OF IMPROPRIETY IN COMMUNICATING WITH PARTIES.
>
> * * *
>
> B. An arbitrator or prospective arbitrator should not discuss a proceeding with any party in the absence of any other party, except in any of the following circumstances:
> (1) When the appointment of a prospective arbitrator is being considered, the prospective arbitrator:
> a. May ask about the identities of the parties, counsel, or witnesses and the general nature of the case; and
> b. May respond to inquiries from a party or its counsel designed to determine his or her suitability and availability for the appointment. In any such dialogue, the prospective arbitrator may receive information from a party or its counsel disclosing the general nature of the dispute but should not permit them to discuss the merits of the case.

---

[41] Gary B. Born, International Commercial Arbitration § 12.03[A] at 1686 (2d ed. 2014) ("Likewise, pre-dispute contacts perform the legitimate function of reminding the co-arbitrator of the seriousness of his or her mandate.").

(2) In an arbitration in which the two party-appointed arbitrators are expected to appoint the third arbitrator, each party-appointed arbitrator may consult with the party who appointed the arbitrator concerning the choice of the third arbitrator.

* * *

(4) In an arbitration involving party-appointed arbitrators, each party-appointed arbitrator may consult with the party who appointed the arbitrator concerning the status of the arbitrator (i.e., neutral or non-neutral), as contemplated by paragraph C of Canon IX.

* * *

The AAA has incorporated this standard in the most recent revisions of its arbitration rules. Article 13(6) of the International Rules provides that communications with a prospective arbitrator should be limited to advising the candidate of "the general nature of the controversy and of the anticipated proceedings" and discussing "the candidate's qualifications, availability, or impartiality and independence in relation to the parties" and "the suitability of candidates for selection as a presiding arbitrator where the parties or party-appointed arbitrators are to participate in that selection." The same language appears in the Commercial Rules, R-19(a).[42] **5.58**

When interviewing an arbitrator candidate, where should one draw the dividing line between a proper disclosure by counsel of the "general nature of the controversy" and what the Code calls an improper discussion of the "merits of the case" with the candidate? The Code does not explain further or provide examples, but the distinction it seeks to make is essentially between a description of the case by counsel, which is necessary and inevitably will involve some exposition of the issues as counsel believes them to be seen by each side, and an attempt to draw the prospective arbitrator into an expression of views as to how the matter might be resolved. **5.59**

(b) The Chartered Institute of Arbitrators' Guideline Another approach to controlling the content of arbitrator interviews is the Chartered Institute of Arbitrators' Practice Guideline 16,[43] which suggests the following parameters for arbitrator interviews (emphasis added): **5.60**

- In agreeing to be interviewed, the prospective arbitrator should make the basis upon which the interview is to be conducted, whether such is to be these guidelines or otherwise, wholly clear *and in writing* to the interviewing party.
- The interviewee arbitrator should be permitted to be accompanied by a secretary or pupil or other assistant to *take a note of proceedings*.

---

[42] *Compare* CPR Administered International Rule 7.4; IBA Guidelines on Conflicts of Interest in International Arbitration ("IBA Guidelines"), Green List 4.5.1 (2014), *available at* http://www.ibanet.org.

[43] Published in Contemporary Issues in International Arbitration and Mediation 214–16 (Arthur W. Rovine ed., 2008), and in Hew R. Dundas, *The Chartered Institute Good Practice Guidelines: Guideline on the Interviewing of Prospective Arbitrators*, 2(2) Disp. Res. Int'l. 276, 281 (2008).

- Either a tape recording or a detailed arbitrator's file note should be made of the interview *and the tape or the file note disclosed to the other side in the dispute, and to the appointing body*, at the earliest available opportunity.
- The interview should be conducted in a professional manner in a business location, and *not over drinks or a meal.*
- A time limit should be agreed for the interview.

As regards the substance of an arbitrator interview, the Chartered Institute Guideline 16 expressly permits discussion of:

(i) the names of the parties in dispute and any third parties involved or likely to be involved;
(ii) the *general nature* of the dispute;
(iii) *sufficient detail, but no more than necessary*, of the project to enable both interviewer and interviewee to assess the latter's suitability for the appointment;
(iv) the expected timetable of the proceedings;
(v) the language, governing law, seat of and rules applicable to the proceedings if agreed, or the fact that some or all of these are not agreed; and
(vi) the interviewee's experience, expertise and availability.

Conversely, the Guideline specifies certain "no-nos" that may *not* be discussed, either directly or indirectly:

(i) the *specific circumstances or facts* giving rise to the dispute;
(ii) the *positions or arguments* of the parties;
(iii) the *merits* of the case.

5.61 Questions may be asked to test the candidate's knowledge and understanding of (1) the nature and type of project in question; (2) the particular area of law applicable to the dispute; (3) arbitration law, practice, and procedure. However, "such questions should be general in nature and neutrally put in order to test the interviewee and should not be put in order to ascertain his/her views or opinions on matters which may form part of the case."

5.62 Some elements of this guideline, such as the portions italicized above, vary considerably from common practice in New York and have been widely criticized. One New York lawyer has commented:

> First, it is not clear there is a pressing need for regulation of the arbitrator interview process. I am not aware of a great tide of challenges to arbitrators or awards based on the fact or contents of arbitrator interviews. If that is factually correct, one has to wonder what mileage we get by fixing something that, while perhaps inelegant and lacking in uniformity, nevertheless is not broken.
>
> Additionally, it seems fair to ask how much damage can actually be done in a pre-appointment interview. Between such an interview and an ultimate award a lot happens that is likely to blunt the impact even of comments that go too far. After the interview the arbitrator typically has to swear an oath or sign an undertaking attesting to his or her independence or impartiality, and thereafter during the proceedings

must in fact conduct him or herself accordingly. These are powerful safeguards against partisanship, and it is difficult to imagine that discussion in an interview of topics the Guidelines forbid would materially undermine these safeguards.

In addition to these duties, which an arbitrator assumes when he or she accepts the appointment, during an arbitration, parties submit arguments and evidence, witnesses testify, legal authorities are discussed, deliberations occur and time passes (in some cases, much more time than is desirable.) We might then reasonably wonder whether comments made in a pre-appointment interview have any bearing at all on an award decided after a contested proceeding that lasts a couple of years. Even if the interviewing lawyer described some of the facts of the case as he understood them at that time, it seems that any reasonably competent arbitrator is far more likely to rely on the facts actually presented during the arbitration rather than on the preliminary description provided in the interview, if he or she even remembers the interview at all.

To put the point more sharply: an arbitrator who believes in the process and the fundamental requirement to remain impartial is unlikely to need detailed guidelines; one who does not and is prepared to be a partisan is unlikely to heed them.[44]

In addition, specifying detailed requirements in mandatory language may cause an increase in challenges to arbitrators after awards, a result to be avoided if possible. **5.63**

(c) Restricted time limits One experienced New York arbitrator has proposed procedural guidelines designed to control the setting of and minimize the extent of contact during such an interview, which is another way of avoiding too much dialogue about the "merits of the case." He generally refuses interviews entirely where the party is a U.S. or multinational company but does consent to them in the case of a foreign party relatively unfamiliar with the international arbitral process. This arbitrator then limits the interview to thirty minutes, permits only counsel to pose questions, and refuses to look at the contract at issue.[45] **5.64**

These are the practices of a particular arbitrator that may recommend themselves, or not, to others. New Yorkers tend to be eclectic in their interviewing practices, within the contours of the AAA/ABA Code of Ethics. **5.65**

2. Role of the Party-Appointed Arbitrators in Selecting a Chairperson

The typical tripartite tribunal clause, and many arbitration rules, provide for appointment of the chairperson by the two party-appointed arbitrators. Less frequently, the clause may specify that the chairperson is to be selected jointly by the parties. In practice, however, the chairperson selection process works best if it is a four-way communication between and among the parties, normally through their counsel, and the party-appointed arbitrators. Ultimately, all four should be satisfied with the identity of the chairperson. **5.66**

[44] Mark W. Friedman, *Regulating Judgment: A Comment on the Chartered Institute of Arbitrators' Guidelines on the Interviewing of Prospective Arbitrators*, 2(2) Disp. Res. Int'l 288, 292–93 (2008).

[45] Gerald Aksen, *The Tribunal's Appointment* in The Leading Arbitrator's Guide to International Arbitration, 31, 35–36 (Lawrence W. Newman and Richard D. Hill eds., 2004).

5.67 Although views among practitioners differ, the majority view in New York appears to be that the process by which two parties and their counsel work with party-appointed arbitrators to select a chairperson requires both reasonable transparency and also sufficient room for some ex parte discussions between counsel and the arbitrator he or she has appointed.[46] The need for transparency regarding how the process is to operate is obvious: each side should be playing by the same rules. If counsel for a party and one arbitrator are communicating about the names of possible chairpersons, as paragraph B(4) of the AAA/ABA Code, quoted previously, and the AAA rules contemplate they normally will, the other party should expect to enjoy the same opportunity. Conversely, if there is intended to be some restriction on such communication, which would be the exception under the Code, that also should be clearly understood.

5.68 The logic behind permitting and even encouraging some communication on a private basis between one party's counsel and a party-appointed arbitrator about potential chairpersons may not be immediately apparent. It begins with the assumption that, in many cases, the two opposing counsel and the two party-appointed arbitrators may not be acquainted with one another when the arbitration begins and may not have a large universe of common professional colleagues to which they naturally would turn for arbitrator names. If this is the case, a common exploratory process must be devised to determine whether they can find and agree on such a universe, albeit small, from which to choose a chairperson. If they fail in this, as sometimes happens, a default process involving arbitral rules and institutions of the sort discussed above may have to fill the void.

5.69 The chances of finding such a common universe of candidates are increased by discussion initially between one side's counsel and the corresponding party-appointed arbitrator. Each normally will bring some ideas to the table, and often a discussion of specific names will disclose conflicts involving this or that person that might be known to either counsel or the appointed arbitrator but not the other. For example, the party-appointed arbitrator might be serving in another arbitration at the time with a suggested candidate, making him or her less likely to be acceptable to the other party.

3. Negotiating Selection of a Chairperson

5.70 In addition, there must be a process by which the two counsel, or the two arbitrators, begin a dialogue about identity of the chairperson. There is a danger that, initially, each party may lack confidence that someone suggested by the other party would be sufficiently neutral. Until each side has put forward some names,

[46] Seppälä, *supra* note 1; *contra*, Aksen, supra note 45; *see* ICDR International Arbitration Rules, Art. 13(6) and AAA Commercial Rule R-19(a) (permitting ex parte communications "to discuss the suitability of candidates for selection as a presiding arbitrator where the parties or party-appointed arbitrators are to participate in that selection.") Born, *supra* note 41 § 2.03[C].

neither is likely to know whether there is a common perception of the type of person who would be appropriate as chairperson. The difficulty, then, is in initiating the process.

One way to start the process is to ask the administering institution, if there is one, to supply the party-appointed arbitrators or counsel with a list of possible chairpersons for their consideration but without any obligation that they select from that list. Administering institutions generally are willing to provide such lists, and the ICDR sometimes does so without being asked. **5.71**

The two arbitrators or counsel then face a different version of the "who goes first" problem. Whether the names are drawn from an institution's suggested list or from the two sides' own imaginations, a small universe of names must be prepared and some method must be devised for coming to agreement on an individual. One way to do this is for each side to exchange a specific number of names, say two or three, either drawn from an institutional list or not, which will make up a universe of candidates who might be appropriate. There need not be any agreement that the ultimate selection must be made from those names, but such a process may yield one or more names common to both lists and suggest a priority of selection. If it does not, the process still might stimulate each side to consider names that had not occurred to them but could be acceptable. Dialogue between the two party-appointed arbitrators and counsel for each side stimulates this process. **5.72**

The ranking of names on such a short list still might remain difficult, particularly if the two sides prefer different types of candidates. One way to deal with this is to suggest that each side rank the arbitrators on the short list that the two sides have assembled, without binding effect, and exchange those rankings just as they would rank names from, for example, an ICDR list when submitting rankings to the ICDR. This allows the arbitrators and counsel to assess any common denominator that may exist, such as each side having a different preferred first choice but each ranking another name as their second choice, thus yielding a possibility of agreement. It also can be done "without prejudice": if the process results in what either side sees as an absence of consensus, the parties are free to start over with different names or allow an institution to submit a list for binding ranking or otherwise proceed with default selection procedures. In most instances, the parties and counsel are able to reach agreement through such a process. **5.73**

Sometimes the process results in a narrowing of the list to only two finalists, perhaps by letting each party select one from an appropriately winnowed short list proposed by the other party. The choice then may be made by a simple coin toss—a process that a New York court has approved.[47] **5.74**

[47] American Home Assurance Co. v. Clearwater Ins. Co., 39 Misc.3d 184, 958 N.Y.S.2d 870 (Sup. Ct. N.Y. Co. 2013) (also discussing role of an "umpire").

4. Convincing the Chairperson Candidate to Serve

5.75 If the two party-appointed arbitrators and counsel are able to agree on a preferred candidate for chairperson, the ideal way to persuade the candidate to serve is for the two arbitrators to place a joint telephone call to him or her to announce the news and urge acceptance. Unless there is a conflict, most arbitrators approached in this fashion will be inclined to accept.

5.76 Beauty contests for prospective presiding arbitrators should be avoided if possible. Although some contact between counsel and party-appointed arbitrators is necessary and appropriate, notification of the chairperson by the two arbitrators assures that he or she will not have had contact with the parties' representatives, which tends to add to party confidence in neutrality of the tribunal. This process also avoids creating a group of chairperson candidates not selected, who perhaps might be less than enthusiastic about serving in another matter if approached by the same counsel.

F. ARBITRATOR COMPENSATION AND CONFLICTS WAIVERS

5.77 Arbitrators in international commercial matters heard in New York typically are compensated on an hourly basis, which is the norm for ICDR, CPR, and ad hoc proceedings. Arbitrator compensation in ICC cases is the exception, since it is based on a formula taking into account the amount in dispute and also the number of hours worked. Hourly rates charged by experienced commercial arbitrators in New York can vary widely in the range from $400 to $1,200.

5.78 The ICDR and the ICC collect deposits from the parties and pay arbitrators from those deposits, and CPR provides this service for its administered cases. In CPR Non-Administered Rules cases, as in ad hoc cases, the chairperson of the tribunal may administer an escrow account from which arbitrators are paid. However, it is accepted that, in situations where the rules are not to the contrary,[48] arbitrators in New York who are party-appointed may be compensated directly by the party appointing them. The AAA/ABA Code of Ethics provides expressly that such payments are not improper, in paragraph B(3) of Canon III:

> In an arbitration involving party-appointed arbitrators, each party-appointed arbitrator may consult with the party who appointed the arbitrator concerning arrangements for any compensation to be paid to the party-appointed arbitrator. Submission of routine written requests for payment of compensation and expenses

[48] The ICC Rules, for example, prohibit this practice.

in accordance with such arrangements and written communications pertaining solely to such requests need not be sent to the other party.

Arbitrators sometimes charge "cancellation fees," payable when an arbitration is settled and the arbitrator has allocated future time to that matter that he or she expects will not be filled by another matter. Such fee arrangements are not common in New York, but they are not unknown. If arbitrators do contemplate charging such a cancellation fee, it should be disclosed as part of the fee arrangement at the outset of an arbitration. **5.79**

An arbitrator who is a member of large law firm may confront conflicts issues if he or she accepts an arbitrator appointment and the law firm thereafter becomes involved in a transaction or litigation including one of the parties to the arbitration. To provide for such possibilities, some arbitrators in New York request an advance conflict waiver from the appointing party or parties, the terms of which provide that any such future engagement by the arbitrator's law firm will not constitute a basis for challenge to the arbitrator or for a claim of conflict on the part of the law firm, so long as the future matter is unrelated to the issues in dispute in the arbitration and the arbitrator is not personally involved in it. The language of some waiver declarations or agreements provides that the arbitrator will not undertake to monitor and advise the parties of future law firm engagements that fall within certain parameters. **5.80**

Arbitrators who are lawyers are not the representatives of the parties appointing them and do not undertake fiduciary obligations toward them. The status of such advance conflict waivers, entered into or accepted voluntarily by parties in commercial arbitrations who are represented and advised by their own counsel, has not been litigated in New York courts. Although some arbitral institutions and the IBA Guidelines on Conflicts of Interest in International Arbitration take the position that an ongoing duty of disclosure may not be waived entirely,[49] present federal arbitration law as applied in New York does not provide affirmative support for a limitation on party autonomy concerning waivers. **5.81**

[49] IBA Guidelines, Explanation to General Standard 3(b) ("The Guidelines, however, do not otherwise take a position as to the validity and effect of advance declarations or waivers, because the validity and effect of any advance declaration or waiver must be assessed in view of the specific text of the advance declaration or waiver, the particular circumstances at hand and the applicable law."); Catherine A. Rogers, Ethics in International Arbitration §§ 9.25–9.35 (2014) (role of arbitrators as "adjudicators" leads to the conclusion that "parties cannot waive in an arbitration agreement the right to have a neutral or impartial decision-maker" and that this fundamental principle limits advance conflicts waivers that would "assign a role that is inconsistent with adjudication."); *but see* Cook Industries, Inc. v. C. Itoh & Co. (America) Inc., 449 F.2d 106, 107–08 (2d Cir. 1971) ("[A party] cannot remain silent, raising no objection during the course of the arbitration proceeding, and when an award adverse to him has been handed down complain of a situation of which he had knowledge from the first.").

G. CONFLICTS CHECKS AND ARBITRATOR DISCLOSURES

5.82 The AAA/ABA Code of Ethics and all international arbitration rules require arbitrators to disclose any interest or relationship that might be perceived as likely to affect their impartiality. The AAA/ABA Code of Ethics provides as follows:

> CANON II. AN ARBITRATOR SHOULD DISCLOSE ANY INTEREST OR RELATIONSHIP LIKELY TO AFFECT IMPARTIALITY OR WHICH MIGHT CREATE AN APPEARANCE OF PARTIALITY.
>
> A. Persons who are requested to serve as arbitrators should, before accepting, disclose:
>   (1) Any known direct or indirect financial or personal interest in the outcome of the arbitration;
>   (2) Any known existing or past financial, business, professional or personal relationships which might reasonably affect impartiality or lack of independence in the eyes of any of the parties. For example, prospective arbitrators should disclose any such relationships which they personally have with any party or its lawyer, with any co-arbitrator, or with any individual whom they have been told will be a witness. They should also disclose any such relationships involving their families or household members or their current employers, partners, or professional or business associates that can be ascertained by reasonable efforts;
>   (3) The nature and extent of any prior knowledge they may have of the dispute; and
>   (4) Any other matters, relationships, or interests which they are obligated to disclose by the agreement of the parties, the rules or practices of an institution, or applicable law regulating arbitrator disclosure.
>
> B. Persons who are requested to accept appointment as arbitrators should make a reasonable effort to inform themselves of any interests or relationships described in paragraph A.
>
> C. The obligation to disclose interests or relationships described in paragraph A is a continuing duty which requires a person who accepts appointment as an arbitrator to disclose, as soon as practicable, at any stage of the arbitration, any such interests or relationships which may arise, or which are recalled or discovered.
>
> D. Any doubt as to whether or not disclosure is to be made should be resolved in favor of disclosure.
>
> E. Disclosure should be made to all parties unless other procedures for disclosure are provided in the agreement of the parties, applicable rules or practices of an institution, or by law. Where more than one arbitrator has been appointed, each should inform the others of all matters disclosed.[50]

* * *

5.83 In order to make appropriate disclosures, a prospective arbitrator who is a member of an organization normally must conduct a conflicts check. It is important

[50] *Compare* IBA Guidelines, General Standards 3, 6, 7.

that counsel provide prospective arbitrators with the names of all parties and other potentially involved entities, including identification of corporate parent relationships.

The ICDR provides arbitrators with a questionnaire, which it invites them to supplement with disclosures to the extent that any are to be made. The ICC provides prospective arbitrators with a simpler questionnaire, asking them to determine whether they have or do not have any relationships to disclose and inviting them to describe their relationships if they exist. CPR follows a similar questionnaire approach. If there are disclosures, each institution provides a copy of the disclosure statement to counsel and invites them to comment within a specified period of time. **5.84**

The Second Circuit has interpreted the Federal Arbitration Act to impose an affirmative obligation on prospective arbitrators to search their records for and disclose all "nontrivial" conflicts if the arbitrator has reason to believe that such a conflict of interest might exist.[51] The court nevertheless cautioned: **5.85**

> We emphasize that we are *not* creating a free-standing duty to investigate. The mere failure to investigate is not, by itself, sufficient to vacate an arbitration award. But, when an arbitrator knows of a potential conflict, a failure to either investigate or disclose an intention not to investigate is indicative of evident partiality.[52]

The Second Circuit also has confirmed that even an allegedly "careless" conflicts check, which failed to disclose a "nontrivial conflict" that an arbitrator in fact did not know of and therefore failed to disclose, does not "rise to the level of willful blindness" or provide a basis for setting aside an award as evident partiality.[53]

H. CHALLENGES AND REPLACEMENT OF ARBITRATORS

Arbitration rules, where applicable, specify the procedures for challenge to and, if the challenge is successful, replacement of an arbitrator. The ICDR International Arbitration Rules permit a challenge "whenever circumstances exist that give rise to justifiable doubts as to the arbitrator's impartiality or independence."[54] The challenge must be made within fifteen days after notice of the appointment or after the circumstances giving rise to the challenge became known to the party. The ICDR administrator notifies the other party or parties and the arbitrator of **5.86**

---

[51] Applied Indust. Materials Corp. v. Ovalar Makine Ticaret Ve Sanayi, A.S., 492 F.3d 132 (2d Cir. 2007); *see also* Scandinavian Reinsurance Co. v. Saint Paul Fire and Marine Ins. Co., 668 F.3d 60 (2d Cir. 2012).

[52] 492 F.3d at 138.

[53] Ometto v. ASA Bioenergy Holding A.G., 549 Fed. Appx. 41 (2d Cir. 2014).

[54] ICDR International Arbitration Rules, Art. 14(1).

the challenge and permits a response from the other parties. At the administrator's discretion, the arbitrator also may be asked to submit information relevant to a challenge. If all parties do not agree to accept the challenge, and if the arbitrator does not choose to withdraw,[55] the ICDR "in its sole discretion shall make the decision on the challenge."[56] If a challenge is successful, a replacement arbitrator is appointed using the procedures that were followed when that arbitrator was appointed initially.[57]

5.87 The ICDR receives about forty-five arbitrator challenges per year, of which approximately twenty-five percent are successful.

5.88 In domestic AAA cases, arbitrator challenges in large, complex cases are considered by the AAA's Administrative Review Council (the "ARC"), which consists of at least five voting members of AAA supervisory administrative staff and a member of the AAA legal department, consulting others as they consider necessary. The AAA has published "review standards" for these challenges, which state that removal is based on a weighing of four aspects of a suggested conflict: whether it is "direct, continuing, substantial, recent." The determination is based on whether the disclosed conflict "creates, to a reasonable person, the appearance that an award would not be fairly rendered." If a party raises a potential conflict not previously disclosed, before considered an objection the AAA will ask the arbitrator to make a supplemental disclosure to the parties regarding the new issue. ARC administrative procedures do not apply at present to ICDR cases, but the standards for disqualification are similar. Decisions to disqualify an arbitrator do not contain any statement of reasons, and they are not published. The AAA Commercial Arbitration Rules state that AAA determinations regarding arbitrator disqualifications "shall be conclusive."[58]

5.89 Other international arbitration rules are broadly similar.[59]

5.90 However, as discussed previously, the AAA Commercial Arbitration Rules make an exception to the normal grounds for disqualification where the parties have

---

[55] An arbitrator considering whether to withdraw might be guided by Canon II, Paragraph G(2) of the AAA/ABA Code of Ethics, which states that an arbitrator challenged by one party should withdraw unless:

> In the absence of applicable procedures, if the arbitrator, after carefully considering the matter, determines that the reason for the challenge is not substantial, and that he or she can nevertheless act and decide the case impartially and fairly.

[56] ICDR International Rules, Art. 14(3).

[57] *Id.*, Art. 11.

[58] *Id.*, R-18(c).

[59] *E.g.*, ICC Rules, Art. 14 (thirty days for challenges), Art. 15 (ICC Court also may replace arbitrator on its own initiative and in all replacements has discretion to decide whether or not to follow original nominating process). Beginning in 2015, the ICC will provide reasons for administrative decisions, including rulings on arbitrator challenges, to parties (but not to the public), upon their joint request and subject to payment of an additional fee.

agreed in writing that the two arbitrators appointed by the parties are to be "non-neutral," in which case "such arbitrators need not be impartial or independent and shall not be subject to disqualification for partiality or lack of independence."[60]

In the absence of applicable rules governing challenges and replacement, as a practical matter judicial challenges to the qualifications of an arbitrator in an international arbitration in New York usually must await an award. The Federal Arbitration Act does not contain any provisions addressing pre-award disqualification. Rather, arbitrator misconduct is a basis for an application to vacate an award at the conclusion of the proceeding.[61] **5.91**

New York's state arbitration law, by contrast, has been interpreted to permit applications to New York state courts challenging the independence of an arbitrator and seeking his or her removal at any time. But in an international matter, as is discussed in Chapter 1 of this book, the Federal Arbitration Act permits a party to remove an action commenced in a New York state court to a federal court, which then will apply Federal Arbitration Act standards and ordinarily decline to hear a challenge to an arbitrator prior to the entry of an award. **5.92**

The fact that an arbitral institution has rejected a challenge to an arbitrator under its rules, however nominally dispositive they may be, does not bar a judicial challenge to the arbitrator. As a practical matter, however, courts are reluctant to second-guess administrative decisions on disqualification applications in the absence of unusual circumstances. **5.93**

---

[60] AAA Commercial Arbitration Rules, R-18(b).

[61] 9 U.S.C. § 10. *See* Chapter 13.C of this book.

6

JURISDICTION
Courts vs. Arbitrators

George A. Bermann

A. **Introduction** 6.02
1. The Arbitration Agreement 6.02
2. Arbitral Jurisdiction 6.03
3. Policy Dimensions of Arbitral Jurisdiction 6.05
4. *Kompetenz-Kompetenz* and Severability as Guides to Allocating Authority over Arbitral Jurisdiction 6.06

B. **The "Arbitral Jurisdiction" Scenarios** 6.10

C. **Asserting Arbitral Jurisdiction in Judicial Proceedings Prior to Arbitration** 6.11
1. Choice of Law Governing Interpretation and Enforcement of the Arbitration Agreement 6.14
2. Severability as a Guide to Validity Questions 6.18
3. *Kompetenz-Kompetenz* and the Arbitrators' Jurisdiction 6.22
   (a) Who decides party issues? 6.23
   (b) Who decides scope issues? 6.24
   (c) Who decides validity issues? 6.25
   (d) Who decides arbitrability and "arbitrability-related" issues? 6.26
4. Forum-Specific Issues: When and on What Grounds May Courts Avoid Arbitration of Otherwise Arbitrable Disputes? 6.29
   (a) Limitation periods 6.31
   (b) Waiver of a party's right to arbitrate the dispute 6.32
   (c) Res judicata and collateral estoppel 6.33
5. Appealability of Courts' Arbitral Jurisdiction Determinations 6.35

D. **Arbitral Jurisdiction Before the Arbitrators** 6.39
1. Procedural Aspects of Arbitrators' Jurisdictional Determinations 6.41
   (a) Timing and form of jurisdictional objections 6.42
   (b) Deferring the jurisdictional determination and joining it with the merits 6.46
   (c) Special jurisdictional procedures for different institutional regimes 6.47
2. Choice of Law Governing Arbitrators' Jurisdictional Determinations 6.48
3. *Kompetenz-Kompetenz* and the Scope and Validity of the Arbitrators' Jurisdiction 6.50
   (a) Preclusive effect of prior judicial determinations 6.52
   (b) Waiver of jurisdictional challenges 6.55
4. Preclusive Effect of Prior Judicial Determinations on Forum-Specific Issues 6.56
5. Appealability of Interim Arbitral Determinations of Arbitral Jurisdiction 6.60

E. **Arbitral Jurisdiction upon Vacatur** 6.61
1. Confirmation and Vacatur of Awards Rendered in New York 6.62
2. Law Governing the Interpretation and Validity of the Arbitration Agreement 6.64

3. *Kompetenz-Kompetenz* and Judicial Review upon Vacatur 6.65
   (a) Review of the arbitrators' decision as to the parties bound by the agreement 6.68
   (b) Review of arbitrators' determination of scope of arbitration agreement 6.72
   (c) Review of arbitral determinations of the validity of the arbitration agreement 6.76
   (d) Deference in cases where a court compelling arbitration has ruled on the jurisdictional issue 6.86
   (e) Waiver of jurisdictional objections by failure to raise them before vacatur 6.90
4. Deference to Arbitrators on Forum-Specific Issues 6.91

F. Arbitral Jurisdiction at Recognition and Enforcement 6.93
1. The Place of Arbitral Jurisdiction in Recognition and Enforcement 6.95
2. Choice of Law Governing the Recognition and Enforcement of an Arbitral Award and Defenses Thereto 6.96
3. *Kompetenz-Kompetenz* and Review of Arbitral Jurisdiction in Recognition and Enforcement Proceedings 6.97
   (a) Deference to prior arbitral decision as to the parties bound by the agreement 6.99
   (b) Deference to the arbitrators' determination of scope of agreement 6.100
   (c) Deference to arbitrators' determination as to validity of agreement 6.102
   (d) Deference to arbitrators on arbitrability and "arbitrability-related" issues 6.106
4. Deference to Arbitrators and Vacatur Courts on Forum-Specific Issues 6.107
5. Waiver of Jurisdiction Challenges 6.111

6.01 The problem of arbitral jurisdiction, while easily stated, is not easily resolved: What is the optimal allocation of authority between courts and arbitrators in interpreting an arbitration agreement and determining whether it is valid, applicable and enforceable? This chapter assesses the allocation of authority in New York, a matter largely governed, in view of its subject, by federal law. It examines the different scenarios in which the question arises, attempting to describe the degree of independent judgment or deference that courts and arbitrators exercise in each scenario.

A. INTRODUCTION

1. The Arbitration Agreement

6.02 Arbitration agreements are a type of forum selection clause that "specify an arbitral forum for resolution of differences" between the parties.[1] While forum selection clauses may be of a "derogation" nature (i.e., may designate an exclusive forum for the resolution of covered disputes)[2] or of a "prorogation" nature (i.e.,

[1] Scherk v. Alberto-Culver Co., 417 U.S. 506, 529 (1974). The draft Restatement of the U.S. Law of International Commercial Arbitration (Tentative Draft No. 4, April 17, 2015) ("Draft Restatement") defines an "international arbitration agreement" as "an 'arbitration agreement' that related to a defined legal relationship of a commercial nature having a nexus (with one or more foreign states." (§1.1.))

[2] *See* James P. George, *International Parallel Litigation: A Survey of Current Conventions and Model Laws*, 37 Tex. Int'l L.J. 499, 539 (2003) (explaining difference between derogation and prorogation clauses).

merely identify a possible forum),[3] arbitration clauses are ordinarily deemed to have an exclusive character.[4]

2. Arbitral Jurisdiction

Determining the existence and scope of arbitral jurisdiction is crucial to the legitimacy of arbitration which, after all, is "a matter of contract."[5] An arbitrator who proceeds in the absence of consent is effectively an "officious intermeddler,"[6] and an award not based upon a valid submission of the dispute to arbitration may be susceptible to vacatur or denial of recognition or enforcement.[7] It follows that a court, if called upon to enforce an arbitration agreement or award, should first assure itself that the parties could—and, indeed, did—consent to arbitral jurisdiction.[8] The more difficult questions are when such judicial inquiry should occur,[9] how vigorous it should be,[10] and what issues fall within its scope.[11] While federal law, in particular the Federal Arbitration Act and the New York Convention, provides the general framework for answering these questions in the context of international commercial arbitration,[12] it does not satisfactorily answer all these questions. **6.03**

---

[3] *Id.*

[4] The Federal Arbitration Act, which requires courts to refer parties to arbitration if there is a valid arbitration agreement, is premised on the notion that derogation arbitration clauses are the default rule. *See* 9 U.S.C. § 4 (2000); *cf.* N.C.P.C. art. 1458 (stating French rule, which is that court must refer parties to arbitration unless the arbitration agreement is *manifestement nulle*, or clearly void). The UNCITRAL Model Law rests on a similar premise. *See* UNCITRAL Model Law § 8(1) ("A Court before which an action is brought in a matter which is the subject of an arbitration agreement shall ... refer the parties to arbitration unless it finds that the agreement is null and void, inoperative or incapable of being performed.").

[5] United Steelworkers of America v. Warrior & Gulf Nav. Co., 363 U.S. 574, 582 (1960).

[6] William W. Park, *Determining Arbitral Jurisdiction: Allocation of Tasks Between Courts and Arbitrators*, 8 Am. Rev. Int'l Arb. 133, 134 (1997).

[7] *See* Federal Arbitration Act, 9 U.S.C. § 10 (2000) (enumerating grounds upon which courts may vacate an award); Convention on the Recognition and Enforcement of Foreign Arbitral Awards, art. V, June 10, 1958, 21 U.S.T. 2517, 2521, 330 U.N.T.S. 3, 44 [hereinafter New York Convention] (enumerating grounds for nonrecognition and nonenforcement). *See* Chapter 13 of this book.

[8] *See, e.g.*, AT&T Technologies, Inc. v. Communications Workers of America, 475 U.S. 643, 649 (1986) (labeling the arbitral jurisdiction issue as one that is "undeniably ... for judicial determination").

[9] *See* Alan Scott Rau, *Everything You Really Need to Know About "Separability" in Seventeen Simple Propositions*, 14 Am. Rev. Int'l Arb. 1, 93–94 (2003) (labeling "the rule of *compétence/compétence* ... a timing mechanism").

[10] *See* Int'l Brotherhood of Teamsters v. Western Pennsylvania Motor Carriers Ass'n, 574 F.2d 783, 787 (3d Cir. 1978) (stating that "decision by an arbitrator that he has authority to decide a dispute is subject to a much broader and more rigorous judicial review" than the review of the merits).

[11] *Compare* Prima Paint v. Flood & Conklin Mfg. Co., 388 U.S. 395, 403–04 (1967) (stating that claim that entire contract was fraudulently induced should be decided by arbitrators) *with* Republic of the Philippines v. Westinghouse Elec. Corp., 714 F. Supp. 1362, 1369 (D.N.J. 1999) (deciding a claim of fraudulent inducement that went to the entire contract).

[12] *See* Moses H. Cone Memorial Hospital v. Mercury Construction Corp., 460 U.S. 1, 24 (1983) (concluding that Federal Arbitration Act creates "body of federal substantive law of arbitrability, applicable to any arbitration agreement within the coverage of the Act"); Encyclopaedia Universalis S.A. v. Encyclopaedia Britannica, Inc., 403 F.3d 85, 90 (2d Cir.

6.04 *Arbitral jurisdiction* denotes the authority of arbitrators to entertain and authoritatively resolve a legal controversy. Questions of arbitral jurisdiction include *party* questions (whether certain parties, including notably nonsignatories, agreed to arbitrate),[13] *scope* questions (whether the arbitration agreement encompasses the dispute at hand),[14] and *validity* questions.[15] *Validity* refers to such questions as whether fraud, mistake, unconscionability, lack of capacity, and the like, vitiate the putative meeting of the minds with respect to the arbitration agreement. Related to the validity of the agreement is the question whether the substantive law that creates the cause of action or underlying public policy permits arbitration, i.e., "whether, under applicable law, a dispute is susceptible of arbitration at all."[16] Unfortunately, case law often uses the term *arbitrability* to cover all the questions listed above,[17] whereas commentators often use that term to refer specifically to the last-mentioned question. We will here avoid using the term "arbitrability" in its narrow sense, referring instead to *arbitral jurisdiction* to cover all the questions above. The one exception will be our use of the term "arbitrability-related," which (as Section E of this chapter will explain in greater detail) refers to challenges to the arbitration agreement that entail public policy claims.

2005) (applying the New York Convention grounds on review of district court refusal to confirm an arbitral award). New York contract law is relevant to the questions of interpretation and validity and may be applicable to the extent that it is not inconsistent with the federal policy in favor of arbitration. *See, e.g.*, Perry v. Thomas, 482 U.S. 483, 489–90 (1987) (stating that Section 2 of the FAA directs courts to look to state law on issues of construction of arbitration agreement); Southland Corp. v. Keating, 465 U.S. 1, 11–12 (1984) (holding that Section 2 of the FAA preempts California law that disfavors judicial resolution of certain claims). *See also* Chapter 1 of this book.

[13] *See, e.g.*, Sarhank Group v. Oracle Corp., 404 F.3d 657, 662–63 (2d Cir. 2005) (reversing district court for failing to determine if party resisting confirmation of award had "agreed to arbitrate, by its actions or inaction"). A court, of course, will also confirm that an agreement exists at all, in addition to determining who are the parties to that agreement. *See, e.g.*, Interocean Shipping Co. v. Nat'l Shipping & Trading Co., 462 F.2d 673 (2d Cir. 1972). *See* Chapter 7.C.1(b) of this book.

[14] *See, e.g.*, Progressive Casualty Ins. Co. v. C.A. Reaseguradora Nacional de Venezuela, 991 F.2d 42, 48 (2d Cir. 1993) (considering motion to compel arbitration and ruling that claims were within scope of arbitration agreement). *See* Chapter 7.C.1(c) of this book.

[15] *See, e.g.*, David L. Threlkeld & Co. v. Metallgesellschaft Ltd. (London), 923 F.2d 245, 249 (2d Cir. 1991) (considering challenges to arbitration agreement based on unconscionability and state law that precluded arbitration of certain types of claims). *See* Chapter 7.C.1(a) of this book.

[16] Hans Smit, *The Arbitration Clause: Who Determines Its Validity and Its Personal and Subject Matter Reach?*, 6 Am. Rev. Int'l Arb. 395, 396 (1995). For example, one might ask whether a claim involving the Age Discrimination in Employment Act (ADEA) can be decided by arbitration, or whether the policies underlying the Act preclude such an allocation of authority. The Supreme Court concluded in 1991 that an ADEA claim was in fact "arbitrable." Gilmer v. Interstate/Johnson Lane Corp., 500 U.S. 20, 26–27 (1991). *See* Chapter 7.D.2 of this book.

[17] First Options of Chicago, Inc. v. Kaplan, 514 U.S. 938, 944–45 (1995). The Court attempted to refine matters in Howsam v. Dean Witter Reynolds, Inc., 537 U.S. 79, 79 (2002), by referring to arbitrability questions as those bearing on "gateway" matters the parties would likely expect a court to resolve. *See* Chapter 7.D.2 of this book.

3. Policy Dimensions of Arbitral Jurisdiction

With this understanding of terminology, we begin with the "stakes" of the discussion. Delineating arbitral jurisdiction requires a balance between enforcing an agreement to arbitrate (thus preserving the integrity of the arbitral process) on the one hand, and protecting parties from being bound by arbitration agreements to which they did not agree or by which for some other good reason they should not be bound (thus preserving the principle of consent), on the other. Precisely because arbitration is a matter of party consent,[18] courts show some wariness about leaving questions of arbitral jurisdiction completely to the arbitrators who, after all, may have a vested interest in affirming their authority to proceed.[19] The question arises not only when courts are asked to enforce an agreement to arbitrate, but also when they are called upon to confirm, vacate, recognize, or enforce the resulting award. Indeed, one reason for courts to make an arbitral jurisdiction inquiry at the outset would be to avoid the spectacle of parties engaging in long and costly arbitral proceedings, only to produce an award that proves later to be vulnerable to vacatur or a denial of enforcement.[20] On the other hand, there is good reason to give arbitrators substantial freedom to independently determine their own authority, for if concern over protecting party consent creates too steep barriers to arbitration, the attractiveness and availability of the arbitration alternative could be substantially lessened.[21] **6.05**

4. *Kompetenz-Kompetenz* and Severability as Guides to Allocating Authority over Arbitral Jurisdiction

These policy dilemmas find legal expression in both the doctrines of *Kompetenz-Kompetenz* and severability. The former recognizes the power of arbitrators to decide the existence and scope of their own jurisdiction, but it also raises the question of the extent to which courts owe deference to arbitrators on issues of arbitral jurisdiction.[22] While U.S. courts are not likely to invoke *Kompetenz-Kompetenz* **6.06**

---

[18] *Cf.* John J. Barcelo III, *Who Decides the Arbitrators' Jurisdiction? Separability and Competence-Competence in Transnational Perspective*, 36 Vand. J. Transnat'l L. 1115, 1119 (2003) ("[O]f course arbitration is not the holy grail.... A party should be entitled to its day in court unless it has agreed to arbitrate.").

[19] *Cf.* Ottley v. Sheepsheard Nursing Homes, 688 F.2d 883, 898 (2d Cir. 1982) (Newman, J., dissenting) (arguing that courts should not "leave to the unfettered discretion of an arbitrator" questions of arbitral jurisdiction because of "the obvious self-interest of an arbitrator").

[20] *See* William W. Park, *Duty and Discretion in International Arbitration*, 93 Am. J. Int'l L. 805, 808–09 (1999) (noting that judicial review of arbitral awards is likely to occur, and considering policy implications).

[21] John J. Barcelo III, *Who Decides the Arbitrators' Jurisdiction? Separability and Competence-Competence in Transnational Perspective*, 36 Vand. J. Transnat'l L. 1115, 1118–19 (2003) (arguing that the "greater the number" of possible jurisdictional objections before arbitration can proceed, "the greater the potential for disruption of the arbitration process").

[22] William W. Park, *Determining Arbitral Jurisdiction: Allocation of Tasks Between Courts and Arbitrators*, 8 Am. Rev. Int'l Arb. 133, 140–41 (1997) (defining *Kompetenz-Kompetenz*).

by name, the underlying notion is alive and well, as shown by the courts' demonstrated willingness to resolve close questions of the scope of the arbitration agreement in favor of arbitration.[23]

The Draft Restatement notes:

> § 2-8. Competence of the Tribunal to Determine its Own Jurisdiction
>
> Unless the arbitration agreement provides otherwise, an arbitral tribunal may rule on issues relating to its own jurisdiction, including but not limited to the existence, validity, or scope of an international arbitration agreement.

6.07 The severability doctrine comes at the problem of arbitral jurisdiction from a different angle. Under this notion, the existence and validity of the arbitration agreement are to be addressed independently of the existence and validity of the contract in which the agreement is found (the *container contract*). Thus the container contract's invalidity or unenforceability will not in principle affect the arbitration agreement's validity or enforceability, meaning that the arbitral tribunal may rule the container contract invalid without automatically undermining its jurisdiction to do so. More generally, challenges to the container contract will ordinarily be for the arbitrators to decide, while those addressed to the arbitration agreement itself, independent of the container contract, are left to the courts.[24]

6.08 The severability doctrine seems today very much intact, having been reaffirmed in principle by the U.S. Supreme Court in its recent *Buckeye* decision.[25] Still, in *Buckeye*, the Court also implied—without, however, holding—that challenges to the container contract's very existence, as opposed to its validity, may be for the courts, rather than arbitrators, to decide. On the other hand, the Court has suggested that some arbitration-specific questions are so procedural in nature that the parties should be assumed to have intended for the arbitrators to resolve them.[26] In these ways, the severability's precise contours have been modified by recent decisions at the highest judicial level in the United States.[27]

6.09 Because notions of *Kompetenz-Kompetenz* and severability continue to guide thinking about arbitral jurisdiction, they will recur in the more detailed discussion to follow. But, experience shows that analysis and outcome in concrete cases

---

[23] *See, e.g.*, First Options of Chicago v. Kaplan, 514 U.S. 938, 944 (1995) (stating traditional presumption in favor of arbitration on questions of scope of arbitration agreement, but reversing presumption with respect to whether parties had agreed to arbitrate the propriety of arbitral jurisdiction); David L. Threlkeld & Co. v. Metallgesellschaft Ltd., 923 F.2d 245, 252 (2d Cir. 1991) (stating traditional presumption).

[24] *See* discussion Section C.2 of this chapter.

[25] Buckeye Check Cashing v. Cardegna, 546 U.S. 440 (2006).

[26] The Court has referred to these as issues of "procedural arbitrability." Howsam v. Dean Witter Reynolds, Inc., 537 U.S. 79, 85 (2002); *see also infra* note 99 and accompanying text.

[27] The Court's recent decision in Preston v. Ferrer, 128 S. Ct. 978, 981, (2008) reaffirmed the validity of *Buckeye* and applied its principles to reject a state law requirement of exhaustion of administrative remedies before one can request arbitration under an arbitration agreement.

depend very much on the time when the question of arbitral jurisdiction—and of the respective role of courts and arbitrators in deciding it—arises for decision. This chapter accordingly now turns to the distinctive moments at which arbitral jurisdiction issues are likely to surface.

B. THE "ARBITRAL JURISDICTION" SCENARIOS

6.10 Disputes over arbitral jurisdiction may arise at various points in the life of a dispute that is arguably subject to arbitration. First, parties may seek at the outset of litigation (a) to institute action in court on a claim that is potentially subject to arbitration, and even enjoin ongoing or imminent arbitral proceedings on that claim;[28] (b) to stay ongoing litigation and compel arbitration precisely where the opposing party has sought to prosecute its claim in court;[29] or (c) to compel arbitration in the first instance even where neither party has sought to litigate the dispute.[30] Second, these issues may be raised before the arbitrators,

[28] *See, e.g.*, Republic of Ecuador v. ChevronTexaco Corp., 376 F. Supp. 2d 344, 365 (S.D.N.Y. 2005) (plaintiff sought permanent stay of arbitration on the grounds they "never agreed to arbitrate").

[29] *See, e.g.*, Garten v. Kurth, 365 F.3d 136 (2d. Cir. 2001); Sherr v. Dell, Inc., No. 05 CV 10097, 2006 WL 2109436 (S.D.N.Y. July 27, 2006). As set forth in the Reporters' Notes on the Draft Restatement:

> A "stay" is a ruling that suspends an existing lawsuit. It is ordinarily sought by the defendant. See Nanosolutions, LLC v. Prajza, 793 F. Supp. 2d 46 (D.D.C. 2011). Unlike dismissals, stays involve the maintenance of jurisdiction by the court. Retained jurisdiction in turn facilitates post-stay judicial supervision relative to the arbitration. See, e.g., Brandon, Jones, Sandall, Zeide, Kohn, Chalal & Musso, P.A. v. MedPartners, Inc., 312 F.3d 1349, 1355 (11th Cir. 2002) (district court retained jurisdiction to confirm the arbitration award and to award attorney's fees); LaPrade v. Kidder Peabody & Co., 146 F.3d 899, 892 (D.C. Cir. 1998) (retaining jurisdiction after stay enabled court to issue sanctions for litigant attempts to thwart arbitration); Morris v. Morgan Stanley & Co., 942 F.2d 648 (9th Cir. 1991) (retaining jurisdiction allowed court to dismiss case on the merits for failure to prosecute the arbitration).
>
> A stay is a form of indirect enforcement; it eliminates access to the court granting the stay, and to that extent curtails the plaintiff's options. LaPrade, 146 F.3d at 903 (a district court stay instructs plaintiff, in effect, that it may not litigate claims directly in court, but could only arbitrate them or abandon them); Cabinetree of Wisc., Inc. v. Kraftmaid Cabinetry, Inc., 50 F.3d 388, 389 (7th Cir. 1995) ("[A] defendant who wants arbitration is often content with a stay, since that will stymie the plaintiff's effort to obtain relief unless he agrees to arbitrate.").
>
> (§2.1)

[30] *See, e.g.*, U.S. Titan, Inc. v. Guangzhou Zhen Hua Shipping Co., Ltd., 241 F.3d 135 (2d Cir. 2001); Doctor's Associates, Inc. v. Jabush, 89 F.3d 109 (2d Cir. 1996) (plaintiff sought to compel arbitration against certain defendants who had threatened to but had not filed claims in court). As set forth in the Reporter Notes to the Draft Restatement:

> [A]n order compelling arbitration affirmatively directs the parties to arbitrate in accordance with the agreement to arbitrate. See, e.g., Azavedo v. Royal Caribbean Cruises, Ltd., 4 F. Supp. 3d 1357, 1361 (S.D. Fla. 2014) (defendant's motion to compel granted: "[t]he parties shall submit to binding arbitration in accordance with the arbitration clauses"); Freaner v. Valle, No. 11CV1819 JLS (MDD), 2011 WL 5596919

either in the first instance or following a court order compelling arbitration.[31] Where arbitration has been compelled by court order (and a court has accordingly to some extent spoken to the arbitral jurisdiction issue), the arbitrators may afford varying levels of deference to the court's determinations of arbitral jurisdiction.[32] Third, these issues may be raised after an arbitral award has been issued, when a party asks a court to confirm or set aside the award.[33] Finally, a court may be asked to revisit the issue of arbitral jurisdiction by a party seeking to resist judicial recognition or enforcement of a final arbitral award.[34]

C. ASSERTING ARBITRAL JURISDICTION IN JUDICIAL PROCEEDINGS PRIOR TO ARBITRATION

6.11 We begin with the scenario in which a party brings to court a claim that is arguably subject to arbitration, and its opponent objects to judicial jurisdiction on the basis of an arbitration agreement, possibly even asking the court to compel arbitration. The plaintiff may respond by seeking to enjoin arbitration. In New York, for example, a court may compel arbitration under either FAA § 4 or N.Y. Civ. Prac. L. & R. § 7503.[35] At this early stage, we already come upon the guideposts of *Kompetenz-Kompetenz* and severability. We also encounter difficult choice of law issues, issues that will not become any easier at later stages.

6.12 When asked to enforce an arbitration agreement (i.e., to decide whether arbitral jurisdiction exists), New York courts must first decide which body, or more likely bodies, of substantive law govern the determination of arbitral jurisdiction. Next, the courts will proceed under that law to determine (a) whether the parties agreed to arbitrate, (b) whether the parties intended the particular issues at hand to be arbitrated, and (c) if statutory claims are involved, whether they may be adjudicated by arbitration (i.e., the "arbitrability" question, narrowly construed).[36]

(S.D. Cal. Nov. 17, 2011) (The parties "shall select an arbitrator pursuant to the AAA rules" and "shall notify the court within thirty days of the completion of arbitration.").

...

A defendant may request both a stay and an order compelling arbitration; the two remedies are often given together. See Dumitru v. Princess Cruise Lines, Ltd., 732 F. Supp. 2d 328 (S.D.N.Y. 2010) (plaintiff compelled to submit claims to arbitration; case stayed, but administratively closed, pending arbitral resolution).

(§2.1).

[31] *See, e.g.*, Tassin v. Ryan's Family Steakhouse, Inc., 509 F. Supp. 2d 585, 592 (M.D.La. 2007).

[32] *See* discussion Section D of this chapter.

[33] *See* Willeminjn Houdstermcatschappi v. Standard Microsystems, Corp., 103 F.3d 9, 12 (2d Cir. 1997).

[34] *See* Sarhank Group v. Oracle Corp., 404 F.3d 657 (2d Cir. 2005).

[35] *See supra* note 28 and accompanying text (discussing compulsion of arbitration). *See also* Chapter 1 of this book.

[36] *See* Genescro, Inc. v. T. Kakiuchi & Co., 815 F.2d 840, 844 (2d Cir. 1987).

A court may also consider the "arbitrability-related" claims we noted previously, as well as what we will define below as "forum-specific" issues involving procedural failures barring arbitration.

Eventually, the court will decide whether to enforce or deny arbitration, based not only on what it has read and heard, but also in consideration of potentially conflicting foundational principles like the federal presumption in favor of arbitration[37] and the necessity of effectuating party intent.[38] The way the court frames its holding, both substantively and procedurally,[39] will in turn have significant implications for the appealability of the decision and the level of deference granted to its determinations in subsequent arbitral and judicial proceedings.[40] **6.13**

1. Choice of Law Governing Interpretation and Enforcement of the Arbitration Agreement

Even at this threshold stage, complicated choice of law issues, involving the interaction of state, federal, and international legal norms, may arise concerning the interpretation and enforcement of an arbitration agreement.[41] In the United States, the substantive legal framework governing arbitration is overwhelmingly one of federal law binding on federal and state courts:[42] the Federal Arbitration **6.14**

[37] Mitsubishi Motors Corp. v. Soler Chrysler-Plymouth, Inc., 473 U.S. 614, 631 (1985); Southland Corp. v. Keating, 465 U.S. 1, 10 (1984); Moses H. Cone Mem'l Hosp. v. Mercury Constr. Corp., 460 U.S. 1, 24 (1983). The presumption in favor of arbitration applies with "special force in the field of international commerce." Mitsubishi Motors Corp., 473 U.S. at 631, *accord* Smoothline Ltd. v. N. Am. Foreign Trading Corp., 249 F.3d 147, 153 (2d Cir. 2001).

[38] *See* First Options of Chicago, Inc. v. Kaplan, 514 U.S. 938 (1995).

[39] *See* discussion Section D of this chapter.

[40] *See* discussion Section C.5 of this chapter.

[41] *See* Piero Bernardini, *Arbitration Clauses: Achieving Effectiveness in the Law Applicable to the Arbitration Clause*, in Improving the Efficiency of Arbitration Agreements and Awards: 40 Years of Application of the New York Convention 197, 199 (Albert Jan van den Berg ed., 1999) ("The determination of the law applicable to the substance of the arbitration clause is certainly a more complex task than determining the law governing the contract. This is due to the many effects of the clause, which are both of a substantive nature (the parties' obligation to refer their disputes to arbitration and to accept the award as binding upon them; the so-called *positive effect*) and a procedural nature (the derogation to the otherwise natural jurisdiction of a national court with the resulting court's duty of abstention, as provided by Art. II(3) of the New York Convention; the so-called *negative effect*)."); Marc Blessing, *The Law Applicable to the Arbitration Clause and Arbitrability*, in Improving the Efficiency of Arbitration Agreements and Awards: 40 Years of Application of the New York Convention 168, 169–70 (Albert Jan van den Berg ed., 1999) (enumerating nine legal theories that could conceivably be applied to an arbitration agreement).

[42] *See* Prima Paint Corp. v. Flood & Conklin Mfg. Co., 388 U.S. 395, 399–400 (1967); Moses H. Cone Memorial Hosp. v. Mercury Const. Corp., 460 U.S. 1, 24–25 (1983) (Section 2 of the FAA "create[s] a body of federal substantive law of arbitrability, applicable to any arbitration agreement within the coverage of the Act"); Southland Corp. v. Keating, 465 U.S. 1, 12 (1985) (reaffirming *Moses* as to Sections 1 and 2 of the FAA); Mitsubishi Motors Corp. v. Soler Chrysler-Plymouth, Inc., 473 U.S. 614, 626 (1985); Volt Information Sciences, Inc. v. Board of Trustees of Leland Stanford Junior University, 489 U.S. 468, 477 n.6 (1989) (reaffirming that Sections 1 and 2 of the FAA are substantive federal law but refusing to answer whether Sections 3 and 4 are similarly applicable).

Act (FAA),[43] the New York Convention,[44] and the Panama Convention.[45] This federal framework provides formal and substantive requirements for enforcing arbitration agreements and awards. Determining which statutory framework to apply is only the first step. At each stage of the analysis—when evaluating the existence, validity, scope, and enforceability of the agreement—a court may apply a different body of law, as neither the FAA nor the New York Convention provides a substantive solution or even much guidance as to the law to be applied.[46] While some trends may be ascertained, there is sufficient variation to prevent identifying a dominant approach.

6.15 In "domestic" cases governed by the FAA, we observe a general tendency among courts to apply federal law to determine whether the FAA applies in the first instance and to answer questions of the interpretation, construction and scope of the agreement once it is determined that the FAA applies.[47] However, courts will generally apply the otherwise applicable state contract law—with the exception of state law singling out arbitration agreements for negative treatment[48]—to evaluate the formation, existence and validity of the arbitration agreement.[49] Prior to

[43] FAA 9 U.S.C. §§ 1–16 (2000) (applies generally to agreements and awards affecting interstate or foreign commerce).

[44] The New York Convention is codified in Chapter 2 of the Federal Arbitration Act at 9 U.S.C. §§ 201–08 (2000).

[45] Inter-American Convention on International Commercial Arbitration, Jan. 30, 1975, 104 Stat. 449, Pan-Am. T.S. 42 [hereinafter Panama Convention]. The Panama Convention is codified at 9 U.S.C. §§ 301–07 (2000). For a detailed analysis of the relevant state and federal law, *see generally* Chapter 1 of this book.

[46] *See* Julian D.M. Lew, *The Law Applicable to the Form and Substance of the Arbitration Clause*, in Improving the Efficiency of Arbitration Agreements and Awards: 40 Years of Application of the New York Convention 114, 119 (Albert Jan van den Berg ed., 1999) (the requirements of formal and substantial validity are "not necessarily governed by the same law").

[47] *See, e.g.*, Mitsubishi Motors Corp. v. Soler Chrysler-Plymouth, Inc., 473 U.S. 614, 625–27 (1985); Gutfreund v. Weiner (*In re* Salomon Inc. Shareholders Derivative Litig.), 68 F.3d 544, 559 (2d Cir. 1995) (*quoting* Coenen v. R.W. Pressprich & Co., 453 F.2d 1209, 1211 (2d Cir. 1972) ("Once a dispute is covered by the [FAA] federal law applies to all questions of interpretation, construction, validity, revocability, and enforceability.") *cert. denied* 406 U.S. 949 (1972)).

[48] Allied-Bruce Terminix Cos. v. Dobson, 513 U.S. 265, 281 (1995) ("What states may not do is decide that a contract is fair enough to enforce all its basic terms ... but not fair enough to enforce its arbitration clause."). The FAA's displacement of conflicting state law has been repeatedly reaffirmed by the Supreme Court. *See, e.g.*, Preston v. Ferrer, 128 S. Ct. 978, 983 (2008); Buckeye Check Cashing, Inc. v. Cardegna, 546 U.S. 440, 445–46 (2006); Doctor's Assocs., Inc. v. Casarotto, 517 U.S. 681, 684–85 (1996); Perry v. Thomas, 482 U.S. 483, 489 (1987).

[49] *See, e.g.*, Perry v. Thomas, 482 U.S. 483, 492 n.9 (1987) ("Thus, state law ... is applicable if that law arose to govern issues concerning the validity, revocability, and enforceability of contracts generally."); First Options of Chicago, Inc. v. Kaplan, 514 U.S. 938, 944 (1995) ("when deciding whether parties agreed to arbitrate a certain matter (including arbitrability), courts generally ... should apply ordinary state-law principles that govern the formation of contracts"); Bell v. Cendant Corp., 293 F.3d 563 (2d Cir. 2002) (*citing First Options*) ("because an agreement to arbitrate is a creature of contract ... the ultimate question of whether the parties agreed to arbitrate is determined by state law."); Shaw Group, Inc. v. Triplefine Int'l Corp., 322 F.3d 115, 120 (2d Cir. 2003); Chelsea Square Tiles, Inc. v. Bombay Dyeing & Mfg. Co., 189 F.3d 289, 295 (2d Cir. 1998).

the Supreme Court rulings in the *Perry*[50] and *First Options*[51] cases, many courts held that federal law completely displaced state law, governing all aspects of the arbitrability analysis, including any defenses contained in FAA § 2's "savings clause."[52] This approach has arguably lost much of its appeal post-*First Options*,[53] though it is unclear whether it can definitively be termed obsolete.

In "international" cases governed by the New York Convention, four main approaches may be distinguished according to the courts' interpretation of the scope of the "null and void" proviso in the Convention's Article II(3) and their willingness to read into it the choice of law guidance found in Article V of the Convention governing recognition and enforcement of arbitral awards. First, some courts have held that uniform international legal standards, as established by the Convention, should govern not only the scope and application of the Convention, but also the formation, validity, and enforceability of the arbitration agreement, including any grounds that may fall within Article II's "null and void" exception.[54] Second, some courts, while generally applying uniform international standards to the analysis of arbitral jurisdiction, nevertheless read the "null and void" proviso in conjunction with the forum policy limitations in Article V, so as to include defenses available not only under uniform international standards but also under forum law.[55] Third, some courts apply uniform international standards to determine the applicability of the Convention, but general federal common law to questions of the formation, validity, and enforceability of the arbitration agreement; in this way, the "null and void" proviso operates to preserve defenses available under federal common law.[56] Fourth, a very small number of courts, **6.16**

[50] Perry v. Thomas, 482 U.S. 483 (1987).

[51] First Options of Chicago, Inc. v. Kaplan, 514 U.S. 938 (1995).

[52] *See, e.g.*, Genesco, Inc. v. T. Kakiuchi & Co., Ltd., 815 F.2d 840, 845 (2d Cir. 1987).

[53] Gary B. Born, International Civil Litigation in United States Courts, at 1092 n.68 (2007).

[54] *See* Kahn Lucas Lancaster v. Lark Int'l, 186 F.d 210, 218–19 (2d Cir. 1999) (applying U.S. treaty construction principles to interpret and apply the Convention requirement of an "arbitral clause in a contract ... signed by the parties."); Apple & Eve, LLC v. Yantai North Andre Juice Co. Ltd., 499 F. Supp. 2d 245, 248 (E.D.N.Y. 2007) ("The limited scope of the Conventions' null and void clause must be interpreted to encompass only those situations—such as fraud, mistake, duress, and waiver—that can be applied neutrally on an international scale.") (internal citations omitted).

[55] *See* Meadows Indemnity Co. Ltd. v. Baccala & Shoop Ins. Services, Inc., 760 F. Supp. 1036, 1043 (E.D.N.Y. 1991) (explaining that the "null and void" exception may be used to preclude enforcement of an arbitration agreement that is either "subject to an internationally recognized defense such as duress, mistake, fraud, or waiver" or "contravenes fundamental policies of the forum state.") (*quoting* Rhone Mediterranee v. Lauro, 712 F.2d 50 (3d Cir. 1983)).

[56] *See, e.g.*, Smith/Enron Cogeneration Ltd. Partnership, Inc. v. Smith Cogeneration Intern., Inc., 198 F.3d 88, 96 (2d Cir. 1999) ("When we exercise jurisdiction under Chapter 2 of the FAA, we have compelling reasons to apply federal law ... to the questions of whether an agreement to arbitrate is enforceable ... proceeding otherwise would introduce a degree of parochialism and uncertainty into international arbitration that would subvert the goal of simplifying and unifying international arbitration law.") (*citing* David L. Threlkeld & Co., Inc. v. Metallgesellschaft Ltd. (London), 923 F.2d 245, 249–50 (2d Cir. 1991); Genesco, Inc. v. T. Kakiuchi & Co., Ltd., 815 F.2d 840, 845 (2d Cir. 1987) (whether a party was "bound by the arbitration clause ... is determined under

and not without criticism,[57] seem to have transplanted the choice of law reasoning from "domestic" FAA cases to those under the Convention. These courts apply federal law to a number of issues, including the scope of the agreement to arbitrate, but apply state contract law to determine whether an agreement to arbitrate exists for purposes of the Convention.[58]

6.17 When there is a valid choice of law clause, courts seem generally willing to apply it but only to determine the existence, formation, and validity of the arbitration agreement.[59] (Rarely, the parties will have designated a different law to govern the arbitration agreement from the law chosen to govern the contract as a whole. In that event, the former law will presumably govern these questions.) However, in certain instances, particularly in international cases where nonsignatories are involved,[60] or where the chosen law is adverse to arbitration or public policy, courts may refuse to enforce the choice of law clause or may enforce only the nonoffending "substantive" law of the chosen law.[61]

federal law, which comprises generally accepted principles of contract law."); Republic of Ecuador v. ChevronTexaco Corp., 376 F. Supp. 2d 344, 365 (S.D.N.Y. 2005) (applying the "*Coenen* rule"); Borsack v. Chalk & Vermilion Fine Arts, Ltd., 974 F. Supp. 293, 299 n.5 (S.D.N.Y. 1997)); Filanto S.p.A. v. Chilewich, 789 F. Supp. 1229, 1235–36 (S.D.N.Y. 1992).

[57] *Filanto SpA*, 789 F. Supp. at 125–36 (discussing whether it is proper to apply state or federal law to questions of the existence of an agreement to arbitrate under the Convention, holding that federal law applies).

[58] *See, e.g.*, Recold, S.A. de C.V. v. Monfort of Colorado, Inc., 893 F.2d 195, 197 n.6 (8th Cir. 1990). *See also* Progressive Cas. Ins. Co. v. C.A. Reaseguradora Nacional De Venezuela, 991 F.2d 42, 46 (2d Cir. 1993).

[59] *See* International Minerals and Resources, S.A. v. Pappas, 96 F.3d 586, 592 (2d Cir. 1996) ("New York law is unambiguous in the area of express choice of law provisions in a contract… '[A]bsent fraud or violation of public policy, contractual selection of governing law is generally determinative so long as the State selected has sufficient contacts with the transaction.' ") (internal citations omitted).

[60] *Compare* Sarhank Group v. Oracle Corp., 404 F.3d 657 (2d Cir. 2005) (held that on remand the district court must decide whether the nonsignatory party was properly bound by the arbitration agreement under general federal law, notwithstanding an Egyptian choice of law clause, before ruling on a motion for recognition and enforcement) *with* Motorola Credit Corp. v. Uzan, 388 F.2d 39 (2d Cir. 2004) (nonsignatory defendants sought to compel arbitration against signatory plaintiffs pursuant to 9 U.S.C. § 206, which instructs courts to compel arbitration "in accordance with the agreement," which contained a Swiss law choice of law clause. The Second Circuit held that the district court correctly applied Swiss law to determine the validity of the agreement and to deny the nonsignatory defendants' motion to compel arbitration. "In short, if defendants wish to invoke the arbitration clauses in the agreements at issue, they must also accept the Swiss choice-of-law clauses that govern those agreements."). *See also* Republic of Ecuador v. ChevronTexaco Corp., 376 F. Supp. 2d 334, 355 (S.D.N.Y. 2005) (attempting to reconcile *Sarhank* and *Uzan* on the grounds that "a choice-of-law clause will govern where a nonsignatory to a particular arbitration agreement seeks to enforce that agreement against a signatory, but not where a signatory seeks to enforce the agreement against a nonsignatory").

[61] *See* Volt Information Sciences, Inc. v. Board of Trustees of Stanford Junior University, 489 U.S. 468 (1989); Smith Barney Harris Upham & Co. v. Luckie, 85 N.Y.2d 193 (1995) (following *Volt*). *But see* Mastrobuono v. Shearson Lehman Hutton, Inc., 514 U.S. 52, 63–64 (1995) ("We think the best way to harmonize the choice-of-law provision with the arbitration provision is to read "the laws of the State of New York" to encompass substantive principles that New York courts would apply, but not to include special rules limiting the authority of arbitrators.").

2. Severability as a Guide to Validity Questions

As noted earlier, the severability doctrine[62] "refers to the separability or independence of the arbitration agreement in relation to the main ... contract."[63] Because they are treated as two independent contracts,[64] the invalidity of the one does not automatically entail the invalidity of the other.[65] In order to understand the discussion that follows in the next section, where we explore the degree of independent judgment courts exercise at the stage of compelling arbitration, it is necessary to explore severability in more detail. **6.18**

The doctrine of severability serves as both a rule of contract interpretation and as a default division of decision-making authority between courts and arbitrators, which may be altered by the parties.[66] This "universally recognized"[67] doctrine was first established by the Supreme Court as a matter of federal law under the FAA in the *Prima Paint* case.[68] According to the Court, the arbitration clause is analytically separate from the container contract.[69] By way of corollary, unless the parties have specified otherwise, a challenge to the arbitration that runs equally to the container contract must be decided by the arbitrators in the first instance; **6.19**

---

[62] Or *separability*, as it is often called. It is also discussed in Chapter 1.D.1 and Chapter 7.B.3(b) of this book.

[63] Antonias Dimolitsa, *Separability and Kompetenz-Kompetenz*, in IMPROVING THE EFFICIENCY OF ARBITRATION AGREEMENTS AND AWARDS: 40 YEARS OF APPLICATION OF THE NEW YORK CONVENTION 217, 218 (Albert Jan van den Berg ed., 1999).

[64] A container contract (or *main contract*) governing the commercial relationship between the parties, and an arbitration agreement (or *secondary contract*) governing the resolution of disputes that may arise from the container contract. Alan Redfern and Martin Hunter, LAW AND PRACTICE OF INTERNATIONAL COMMERCIAL ARBITRATION 3–61 (4th ed. 2004).

[65] The practical benefit of this doctrine, for arbitrators, is that it protects their jurisdictional authority, which stems from the arbitration agreement, in the event they find that the container contract is invalid and unenforceable.

[66] For example, in the United States, the doctrine of severability is applied as a general presumption to delineate those issues that are to be decided by the court and those which are for the arbitrators. *See* Prima Paint Corp. v. Flood & Conklin Mfg. Co., 388 U.S. 395, 403–04 (1967); Buckeye Check Cashing, Inc. v. Cardegna, 546 U.S. 440, 445–46 (2006). This presumption, however, can, in principle, be expressly altered by the parties in the terms of their arbitration agreement. El Hoss Engineering & Transport Co. v American Independent Oil Co., 289 F.2d 346, 250 (2d Cir. 1961) ("Although the U.S. Arbitration Act looks favorably upon arbitration it does not dictate that we should disregard parties' contractual agreements that contain specific language outlining the boundaries of the areas intended to be arbitrable areas."). The doctrine of severability should not be confused with the doctrine of *Kompetenz-Kompetenz*. *See* discussion in Sections A and D of this chapter.

[67] Antonias Dimolitsa, *Separability and Kompetenz-Kompetenz*, in IMPROVING THE EFFICIENCY OF ARBITRATION AGREEMENTS AND AWARDS: 40 YEARS OF APPLICATION OF THE NEW YORK CONVENTION 217, 223 (Albert Jan van den Berg ed., 1999). *See also* Alan Redfern and Martin Hunter, LAW AND PRACTICE OF INTERNATIONAL COMMERCIAL ARBITRATION 3-61–3-64 (4th ed. 2004).

[68] Prima Paint Corp. v. Flood & Conklin Mfg. Co., 388 U.S. 395, 403–04 (1967). While the FAA does not expressly codify the doctrine of severability, the Court in *Prima Paint* found that the doctrine of severability could be sustained by the statutory language in 9 U.S.C. § 4 and extended to 9 U.S.C. § 3. *See also* Buckeye Check Cashing, Inc. v. Cardegna, 546 U.S. 440, 445–46 (2006).

[69] *Prima Paint Corp.*, 388 U.S. at 403–04; *Buckeye Check Cashing, Inc.*, 546 U.S. at 445–46.

only a challenge to the arbitration clause as such will be decided by the court at this early stage.[70] The mere fact that a party's complaint alleges that its challenge relates solely to the arbitration clause will not be dispositive.[71] There must be sufficient facts specifically connecting the alleged defects to the arbitration clause.[72]

6.20 At the same time, the severability doctrine may be subject to two exceptions, albeit exceptions not universally accepted by the courts. On the one hand, if the challenge goes to the very existence of the container contract,[73] as opposed to its validity or enforceability,[74] it may be treated as one for the court to decide in the first instance. The reasoning would be that if the container contract never even came into being, it would be illogical and unfair to enforce its arbitration agreement under the pretense of effectuating party intent. On the other hand, even when a challenge is indeed directed to the arbitration clause alone, it may be based upon what the Supreme Court has described as largely forum-specific procedural rules; in that event, courts may want to leave these issues to the arbitrators, who are, after all, the forum-specific decision-makers, based on an assumption that the parties can reasonably be presumed to have allocated authority over these issues to the arbitrators.[75] We will explore these forum-specific questions in more detail later. For now, it is important to note that even these apparent exceptions tend to break down at the margins,[76] making it difficult to predict with certainty how different courts will treat any particular set of facts.

[70] *Id.*

[71] Abduljaami v. Legalmatch.com, Inc., No. 05 Civ. 94642006, U.S. Dist. LEXIS 26327, at *13–14 (S.D.N.Y. Apr. 2006).

[72] *Id.*

[73] The dictum in *Buckeye* tends to support this outcome. *Buckeye Check Cashing, Inc.*, 546 U.S. at 444 n.1. *See also* Interocean Shipping Co. v. National Shipping & Trading Corp., 462 F.2d 673, 676 (2d Cir. 2972); Petition of Kinoshita & Co., 287 F.2d 951, 953 (2d Cir. 1961); Microchip Technology Inc. v. U.S. Philips Corp., 367 F.3d 1350, 1358 (Fed. Cir. 2004). *But see* Republic of Nicaragua v. Standard Fruit Co., 937 F.2d 469 (9th Cir. 1991); U.S. v. Carreon-Palacio, 267 F.3d 483, 491–92 (5th Cir. 2001); Teledyne, Inc. v. Kone Corp., 892 F.2d 1401, 1410 (9th Cir. 1990).

[74] *See, e.g., Buckeye Check Cashing, Inc.*, 546 U.S. at 445–46; Island Territory of Curacao v. Solitron Devices, Inc., 489 F.2d 1313 (2d Cir. 1973); Rubin v. Sona Int'l Corp., 457 F. Supp. 2d 191, 195–96 (S.D.N.Y. 2006). *But see* Durst v. Abrash, 253 N.Y.S.2d 351 (N.Y.A.D. 1 Dept. 1964), *aff'd* 266 N.Y.S.2d 806 (N.Y. 1965); *In re* Kramer & Uchitelle, 48 N.E.2d 493 (N.Y. 1942). Though it is unlikely that these latter cases have survived *Buckeye.*

[75] *See* Howsam v. Dean Witter Reynolds, 537 U.S. 79, 86 (2002) ("parties to an arbitration contract would normally expect a forum-based decision-maker to decide forum-specific procedural gateway matters"). For a more detailed discussion of issues falling within this second exception that we have termed "forum specific issues," *see* discussion at Section C.3 of this chapter.

[76] For example, many courts hold that a claim of fraudulent inducement must be confined to the arbitration clause in order to be entitled to judicial adjudication. *See, e.g.*, Moseley v. Electronic & Missile Facilities, Inc., 374 U.S. 167 (1963); Campaniello Imports, Ltd. v. Saporiti Italia S.p.A., 117 F.3d 655, 667 (2d Cir. 1997) ("We believe that the only way to reconcile Prima Paint with Moseley is to require some substantial relationship between the fraud or misrepresentation and the arbitration clause in particular."); Michele Amoruso E Figli v. Fisheries Development Corp., 499 F. Supp. 1074 (S.D.N.Y. 1980) (there was only an arbitration clause at issue in this case, no *container contract*); Brener v. Becker Paribas Inc., 628 F. Supp. 442, 446 (S.D.N.Y. 1985). However, some courts are willing to hear fraudulent inducement claims that apply to the *container contract*, which contains the

The Draft Restatement describes the severability doctrine in the following way: **6.21**

§ 2-7. Separability of the Arbitration Agreement

(a) An international arbitration agreement is presumed to be separable from the contract in which it is found.

(b) As a consequence of the separability of an international arbitration agreement:

  (1) the arbitration agreement can be enforced notwithstanding the invalidity or unenforceability of the underlying contract;

  (2) the decision making authority as between arbitrators and courts can be allocated as specified in §§ 2-12 through 2-21; and

  (3) the laws and rules applicable to the arbitration agreement can differ from those governing the underlying contract.

(c) The presumption of separability may be overcome by agreement of the parties.

(§2.7)

3. *Kompetenz-Kompetenz* and the Arbitrators' Jurisdiction

6.22 Putting severability aside, it will be useful at this point to distinguish among the various issues that may be raised in connection with challenges to enforceability of the arbitration agreement. It is commonly asserted, in very general terms, that the issue of arbitral jurisdiction is "undeniably an issue for judicial determination,"[77] which at a minimum includes some level of judicial inquiry into what we have referred to as "party," "scope," and "validity" questions, as well as whether the dispute

---

arbitration clause. *See, e.g.*, Rush v. Oppenheimer & Co., Inc., 681 F. Supp. 1045, 1053 (S.D.N.Y. 1988) ("Thus, *Prima Paint* requires a federal court to resolve allegations of fraud that pertain to both the principal agreement as a whole and the arbitration agreement in particular."). Similarly, many courts have held that allegations of fraud in the factum of the *container contract* challenge the very existence of the contract and thereby require judicial review. *See* Acquaire v. Canada Dry Bottling, 906 F. Supp. 819 (E.D.N.Y. 1995); Kyung In Lee v. Pacific Bullion (New York) Inc., 788 F. Supp 155, 156–57 (E.D.N.Y. 1992) (concerning issue of fraudulently obtained signature). Other courts, on the other hand, send fraudulent inducement claims to the arbitrators. *See, e.g.*, R.M. Perez & Associates, Inc. v. Welch, 960 F.2d 534, 539 (5th Cir. 1992) (on a motion confirming arbitral award, holding in part that "plaintiffs' allegations that they did not read or understand the documents and that Welch did not explain the documents to them does not allege fraud in the making of the arbitration agreements, but goes to the formation of the entire contracts. Therefore, the allegations are arbitrable."); Villa Garcia v. Merrill Lynch, Pierce, Fenner and Smith Inc., 833 F.2d 545 (5th Cir. 1987); Hall v. Shearson Lehman Hutton, Inc., 708 F. Supp. 711 (D. Md. 1989) (purported forged signature on the arbitration agreement would *not* bar arbitration of the claim: "A forged signature ordinarily voids a transaction just as fraudulently induced entry into the transaction voids it. The Court notes that, although the evidence before it indicates that Mr. Hall might not have personally signed the client agreement, there remain open questions regarding whether he gave implied authority to someone else to sign it for him and/or whether he ratified it, even if he did not sign it … These open questions may be presented to the arbitrator under …") (internal citations omitted). These cases have, however, tended to be widely criticized.

[77] AT&T Technologies, Inc. v. Communications Workers of America, 475 U.S. 643, 649 (1986); *see also* Alan Scott Rau, *Arbitral Jurisdiction and the Dimensions of "Consent,"* Univ. of Texas Law: Law and Economics Research Paper No. 103 (2007), *available at* SSRN: http://ssrn.com/ abstract=1081616; Alan Scott Rau, *Everything You Really Need to Know About "Separability" in Seventeen Simple Propositions*, 14 Amer. Rev. Int'l Arb. 1, 5 (2003).

is capable of settlement through arbitration as a matter of statutory law or public policy. Although the notion of *Kompetenz-Kompetenz* will have a general impact on the analysis of who decides, a court's readiness to enter at the outset upon the terrain to make its own determination of arbitral jurisdiction may vary with the particular jurisdictional aspect in issue. Following is a summary of what appear to be the dominant judicial approaches to these four central arbitral jurisdiction issues.[78]

6.23 *(a) Who decides party issues?* When the question is brought before them at the outset, New York courts will generally make a preliminary inquiry into which parties are bound by the arbitration agreement under the applicable contract law, doing so as an integral part of determining whether there is an agreement to arbitrate in the first place.[79] Where a nonsignatory is involved, courts will engage in more rigorous analysis to determine whether that party can invoke or be bound by the agreement under general principles of contract law.[80] They will analyze the question under one of the five common legal theories for binding non-signatories recognized by the Second Circuit: (1) incorporation by reference; (2) assumption; (3) agency; (4) veil-piercing/alter ego; and (5) estoppel.[81] On occasion, a court may permit a nonsignatory to compel arbitration against a signatory under a theory of estoppel,[82] and to apply the arbitration agreement's chosen law, if one exists.[83] On the other hand, where a signatory seeks to bind a nonsignatory, New York courts are more likely to analyze the question under state or federal

[78] Where the parties have clearly allocated decision-making authority in a different manner, their intent will presumably be enforced, but, in the absence of a clear agreement to the contrary, courts will resolve any doubts in favor of arbitration pursuant to the federal presumption in favor of arbitration. *See* First Options of Chicago, Inc. v. Kaplan, 514 U.S. 938 (1995). For an example of a broad clause conferring jurisdiction on arbitrators, *see* Ferrer v. Preston, 145 Cal. App. 4th 440, 449 (Cal. App. 2006) (The arbitration provision provides, "In the event of any dispute under or relating to the terms of this agreement, *or the breach, validity, or legality thereof*, it is agreed that the same shall be submitted to arbitration ..."). The doctrine is also discussed in Chapter 7.B.3(a) of this book.

[79] "Under American law, whether a party has consented to arbitrate is an issue to be decided by the Court in which enforcement of an award is sought ... the court decides, based on general principles of domestic contract law, whether the parties agreed to submit the issue of arbitrability to the arbitrators." Sarhank Group v. Oracle Corp., 404 F.3d 657, 661 (2d Cir. 2005) (*citing First Options, Inc.*, 514 U.S. at 943).

[80] Orange Chicken, L.L.C. v. Nambe Mills, Inc., No. 00 Civ. 4730, 2000 WL 1858556, at *4–7 (S.D.N.Y. Dec. 19, 2000) (affirming that the court must determine whether nonsignatories can be bound by the arbitration agreement). For a more detailed analysis, *see* Chapter 7.C.1(b) of this book. *See also* Section C.1 of this chapter (discussing choice of law issues).

[81] Thomson-CSF, S.A. v. American Arbitration Ass'n, 64 F.3d 773, 776–80 (2d Cir. 1995). Note that the precise legal doctrines may vary depending on the applicable law. *See* discussion in Section C.1 of this chapter.

[82] *See* Astra Oil Co., Inc. v. Rover Navigation, Ltd., 344 F.3d 276, 279, 281 (2d Cir. 2003); Choctaw Generation Ltd. Partnership v. American Home Assur. Co., 271 F.3d 403, 406 (2d Cir. 2001) ("[s]everal courts of appeal have recognized an alternative estoppel theory requiring arbitration between a signatory and nonsignatory ... the circuits have been willing to estop a signatory from avoiding arbitration with a nonsignatory when the issues the nonsignatory is seeking to resolve in arbitration are intertwined with the agreement that the estopped party has signed.") (internal citations omitted).

[83] For choice of law discussion, *see* discussion in Section C.1 of this chapter.

law, notwithstanding the existence of a foreign choice of law clause, and to examine the matter even more closely.[84] This is consistent with the contractual nature of arbitration, according to which a party cannot be forced to arbitrate, or be bound by the terms of an arbitration agreement before it is established that the party, at a minimum, consented to the agreement in the first place.

(b) Who decides scope issues? When determining whether to enforce an arbitration agreement, courts must also determine whether the dispute at issue falls within the scope of the arbitration clause.[85] These rulings are generally based only on preliminary inquiries at the outset of litigation, and as such will not preclude subsequent reexamination of the issue by the arbitrators.[86] The Second Circuit, consistent with the federal presumption in favor of arbitration and the concept of *Kompetenz-Kompetenz*, has developed a multistep test that invokes the federal presumption to compel arbitration where there is a "broad" arbitration clause.[87] **6.24**

(c) Who decides validity issues? Courts at the outset may also rule on the formal and substantive validity of the arbitration agreement before deciding whether to compel arbitration.[88] Despite their general presumption of enforceability, both the FAA § 2 and the New York Convention Article II provide as a condition of enforcement that the agreement be neither invalid nor unenforceable.[89] In keeping with the doctrine of severability, courts will ordinarily, as a precondition to **6.25**

[84] *See, e.g.*, Republic of Ecuador v. ChevronTexaco Corp., 376 F. Supp. 2d 334, 355 (S.D.N.Y. 2005). There is a related trend among courts at the recognition and enforcement stage. *See* discussion in Section F.3(a) of this chapter.

[85] Howsam v. Dean Witter Reynolds, Inc., 537 U.S. 79, 84 (2002) ("a disagreement about whether an arbitration clause ... applies to a particular type of controversy is for the court."); Louis Dreyfus Negoce S.A. v. Blystad Shipping & Trading Inc., 252 F.3d 218, 224 (2d Cir. 2001).

[86] *See* discussion in Section D of this chapter.

[87] The Second Circuit analysis is as follows: first, the court must determine whether the arbitration clause is "broad or narrow"; second, if the clause is "narrow," the court must determine whether the dispute is (a) "on its face within the purview of the [arbitration] clause," or (b) a "collateral issue that is somehow connected to the main agreement," which will generally be presumed to be outside the scope of a narrow arbitration clause; third, if the clause is "broad," the court will invoke the "presumption of arbitrability" and order arbitration even of collateral issues, assuming the arbitration agreement is otherwise valid and enforceable. *Louis Dreyfus Negoce S.A.*, 252 F.3d at 224 (internal citations omitted).

[88] See what is known as the Supreme Court's 1960 "Steelworker Trilogy": United Steelworkers of America v. American Mfg. Co., 363 U.S. 564 (1960); Steelworkers v. Warrior & Gulf Navigation Co., 363 U.S. 574, 582 (1960) ("Arbitration, is a matter of contract and a party cannot be required to submit to arbitration any dispute which he has not agreed to submit."); Steelworkers v. Enter. Wheel & Car Corp., 363 U.S. 593 (1960). The Supreme Court has repeatedly reaffirmed this principle. *See* AT&T Technologies, Inc. v. Communications Workers of America, 475 U.S. 643, 649 (1986) ("unless the parties clearly and unmistakably provide otherwise, the question of whether the parties agreed to arbitrate is to be decided by the court, not the arbitrator."); John Wiley & Sons, Inc. v. Livingston, 376 U.S. 543, 546–47 (1964) ("the duty to arbitrate being of contractual origin, a compulsory submission to arbitration cannot precede judicial determination that that . . . agreement does in fact create such duty.").

[89] The FAA mandates courts to enforce arbitration agreements "save upon such grounds as exist at law or in equity for the revocation of any contract." 9 U.S.C. § 2 (2006). Article II(3) of

enforcement, resolve issues relating exclusively to the validity of the arbitration clause, but generally not those relating equally to the container contract.[90]

6.26 *(d) Who decides arbitrability and "arbitrability-related" issues?* A party may of course seek to bar arbitration on the ground that the underlying dispute is not legally capable of settlement through arbitration. (This is the "arbitrability" issue at its core.) Before a court may compel arbitration, it must determine whether the claims at issue are capable of being adjudicated through arbitration as a matter of statutory law and public policy. Courts will generally decide this issue as part of their arbitral jurisdiction analysis.[91]

6.27 "Arbitrability-related" issues involve similar challenges to arbitral jurisdiction based on the alleged inconsistency between arbitral resolution of a given dispute and the public policies of law applicable to the dispute. We will delay a fuller explanation of the concept of "arbitrability-related" issues until Section E.3(c)(iii), where each of the various "arbitrability-related" issues is most likely to arise. But one "arbitrability-related" issue that arises with some frequency at the compelling stage is the permissibility of class action arbitration. Where the question is whether a broad arbitration clause permits class action arbitration, courts ordinarily do not address the arbitrability-related question directly, namely whether as a matter of federal law class action arbitration is permissible.[92] Rather, courts are likely to treat this as a matter concerning the proper scope of the arbitration agreement.[93] Accordingly, they will compel arbitration where there is a colorable claim that the issue is covered by the arbitration clause, thus allowing the arbitrators to address it.[94] If the arbitration clause itself expressly precludes the

the New York Convention similarly requires enforcement of arbitration agreements except where the agreement is "null and void, inoperative or incapable of being performed." Convention on the Recognition and Enforcement of Foreign Arbitral Awards, June 10, 1958, 21 U.S.T. 2517, 330 U.N.T.S. 3. However, courts may leave issues of procedural validity to the arbitrators. *See* discussion in Section C.4 of this chapter.

[90] *See* discussion in Sections A.4 and C.3 of this chapter.

[91] For a more detailed analysis, *see* Chapter 7.D.2 of this book.

[92] The Supreme Court failed to decide the issue in the *Green Tree* case and lower courts have been unwilling to confront the issue directly. *See* Stolt-Nielsen SA v. AnimalFeeds Int'l Corp., 435 F. Supp. 2d 382, 384–85 (S.D.N.Y. 2006) (stating, on a motion to vacate, "As for the related questions that *Bazzle* failed to resolve—whether the Federal Arbitration Act (which provides for federal enforcement of arbitration provisions in contracts involving commerce, as in Bazzle, or in maritime contracts, as here, see 9 U.S.C. 2, precludes class actions and preempts state law—the Panel here did not reach them; and since they involve unsettled law they are not before this Court on a claim of 'manifest disregard.'" (*citing* Green Tree Financial Corp. v. Bazzle, 539 U.S. 444 (2003)))." For a more detailed analysis, *see* Chapter 11 of this book.

[93] *See* discussion in Section C.3(b) of this chapter.

[94] This is arguably supported by the Supreme Court's holding in the *Green Tree* case. *Green Tree Financial Corp.*, 539 U.S. 444 (holding that the scope question is within the power of the arbitrators to address). A pair of recent New York cases reinforces the *Green Tree* holding: JLM Indus. v. Stolt-Nielsen SA, 387 F.3d 163 (2d Cir. 2004) (Plaintiffs in putative class action file claims against defendants. Prior to class certification, certain defendants successfully move to compel arbitration of plaintiffs' claims); *Stolt-Nielsen SA*, 435 F. Supp. 2d 382

possibility of class action arbitration, a party—usually a plaintiff—will argue that the combination of the arbitration agreement and the class action waiver contained therein effectively forecloses its ability to enforce its legal rights because those legal rights can only be enforced effectively through class action, for example where the value of any individual claim is so small as to render litigation or arbitration unlikely.[95] Consistent with the federal presumption in favor of arbitration, even where the arbitration agreement expressly forecloses the plaintiff's right to engage in any sort of class action, courts generally appear willing to compel arbitration.[96]

Another arbitrability-related issue that may arise is whether an arbitration agreement's exclusion of punitive damages offends a statutory provision such as the provision in the Racketeer Influenced and Corrupt Organizations Act (RICO) providing for treble damages. Following the approach articulated above with respect to class action arbitration, courts are likely to view these assertions as going to the scope of the arbitration agreement and ordinarily will not decline to enforce an arbitration agreement on this ground. For example, in the *PacifiCare* case, the Supreme Court preferred that the arbitrators decide in the first instance whether the punitive damages exclusion would indeed foreclose recovery of treble damages and thus be contrary to public policy.[97] **6.28**

(vacating arbitral award for manifest disregard of the applicable law for incorrectly allowing class action arbitration that was excluded from the scope of the arbitration clause when read in conjunction with applicable maritime and state law). For a more detailed analysis, *see generally* Chapter 11.

[95] Snowden v. CheckPoint Check Cashing, 290 F.3d 631, 638 (4th Cir. 2002) (court rejected plaintiff's argument that "the Arbitration Agreement is unenforceable as unconscionable because without the class action vehicle, she will be unable to maintain her legal representation given the small amount of her individual damages.").

[96] *See, e.g.*, Jenkins v. First American Cash Advance of Georgia, LLC, 400 F.3d 868, 877–78 (11th Cir. 2005), *cert. denied*, 546 U.S. 1214 (2006) (applying Georgia law under the FAA, holding that court would decide the issue where the class action waiver was contained in the arbitration agreement, and that the existence of the waiver did not bar arbitration); Livingston v. Assocs. Fin., Inc., 339 F.3d 553, 559 (7th Cir. 2003); Snowden v. CheckPoint Check Cashing, 290 F.3d 631, 638 (4th Cir. 2002); Johnson v. West Suburban Bank, 225 F.3d 366, 369 (3d Cir. 2000); Levitt v. Lipper Holdings, LLC, 2003 U.S. Dist. LEXIS 11411, at *4 n.3 (S.D.N.Y. July 7, 2003) ("I find that the recently decided Supreme Court case of Green Tree ... allows me to send these cases to arbitration and leave the question of whether putative class actions can be arbitrated under this arbitration clause, to the arbitrator."); Tsadilas v. Providian Nat. Bank, 13 A.D.3d 190 (N.Y. App. Div. 2004); Ragan v. AT&T Corp., 355 Ill. App.3d 1143, 1155 (Ill. App. Ct. 2005) ("[T]he law of New York is clear. Under New York law, 'a contractual proscription against class actions is neither unconscionable nor violative of public policy.' ") (*quoting* Ranieri v. Bell Atlantic Mobile, 304 A.D.2d 353, 354 (N.Y. App. Div. 2003)). *But see* Ting v. AT&T, 319 F.3d 1126, 1150 (9th Cir. 2003) (invalidating class action waiver in an arbitration agreement as unconscionable under state law) *cert. denied*, 540 U.S. 811 (2003).

[97] PacifiCare Health Sys. v. Book, 538 U.S. 401, 406–07 (2003) (deciding that the question of whether an arbitration agreement excluded punitive damages, and was therefore unenforceable as contrary to the federal RICO statutory regime, was a question for the arbitrators in the first instance).

4. Forum-Specific Issues: When and on What Grounds May Courts Avoid Arbitration of Otherwise Arbitrable Disputes?

6.29 In our discussion of severability, we introduced the concept of "forum-specific issues." Even when the initial formal and substantive requirements for enforcing an arbitration agreement have been met, a party resisting arbitration may raise certain forum-specific issues that flow from the arbitration agreement and that severability thinking might ordinarily lead the courts to resolve. We refer here to the second possible exception to the severability doctrine articulated above, labeling these issues "forum-specific" because they directly relate to the procedural mechanics of the arbitral forum.[98] This section will examine how courts handle these issues at the compulsion stage. It is important, of course, to emphasize that the following positions represent what courts have accepted as the default division of decision-making authority, which parties are, in principle, free to alter by agreement.

6.30 In the *Howsam* case, the Supreme Court referred to three of these types of issues—limitation periods, estoppel, and waiver—as issues of "procedural arbitrability."[99] Such issues, it held, are "presumptively for the arbitrator, not for the judge," at least at the stage of compelling arbitration, because the parties are presumed to have allocated decision-making authority over such procedural issues to the arbitrators.[100] Essentially, they relate to whether "conditions that might trigger a duty to arbitrate ... have been fulfilled"[101] (e.g., filing within a limitations period) or whether there are conditions that relieve one of a duty to arbitrate (e.g., the party requesting arbitration has waived its right by commencing litigation in court first). The situation is delicate since, despite their "procedural nature," such issues may be intertwined with the merits of the dispute. Consider, for example, the merits considerations implicated by a claim that the previous judgment of a

[98] Compare, for example, a claim that there was no meeting of the minds on the arbitration agreement. This substantive, contract law challenge does not relate to the procedural mechanics of an arbitral versus a judicial forum.

[99] Howsam v. Dean Witter Reynolds, Inc., 537 U.S. 79, 83–85 (2002). This list does not exhaust the types of forum-specific issues that arise under *Howsam*'s approach. *See, e.g.*, Mulvaney Mechanical, Inc. v. Sheet Metal Workers Intern. Ass'n, Local 38, 351 F.3d 43 (2d Cir. 2003) (analogizing the reasoning in *Howsam* to cover a claim of repudiation, holding that the issue was one for the arbitrators to decide in the first instance).

[100] Howsam v. Dean Witter Reynolds, Inc., 537 U.S. 79, 85 (2002). "Procedural arbitrability" contrasts with "substantive arbitrability," which involves questions such as whether the parties agreed to arbitrate anything at all; under *First Options*, courts presumptively decide such matters. *Id.* The categories of "procedural" versus "substantive" arbitrability are less useful than is the *Howsam* Court's emphasis on presumptive party intent—parties presumably would want arbitrators to resolve issues of interpreting the arbitration agreement in light of issues often intertwined with the merits of the dispute. *Id.*

[101] Richard C. Reuben, First Options, *Consent to Arbitration, and the Demise of Separability: Restoring Access to Justice for Contracts with Arbitration Provisions*, 56 SMU L. Rev. 819, 835 (2003).

court or arbitral tribunal precludes arbitration.[102] To this end, they may be for the arbitrator to determine despite the fact that they exclusively address the arbitration agreement, not the container contract.[103]

(a) Limitation periods The question of limitation periods arises when one party claims that the other's request for arbitration must be refused as untimely because it was made after the expiry of a statutory or contractual limitations period. Under a strict application of the severability doctrine, limitations periods should be adjudicated upfront by the court because they are challenges directed at the arbitration agreement itself rather than the container contract.[104] In New York, however, questions concerning limitation periods have indeed been treated as presumptively for the arbitrators and not for the courts in the first instance.[105] This approach is consistent with the Supreme Court's guidance in *Howsam*, the **6.31**

[102] Relatedly, one can most fairly conceptualize these challenges as "arising under" the arbitration agreement, and involving questions of interpretation that, for reasons of efficiency and presumptive party intent, are properly before the arbitrators. In other words, forum specific issues do not raise the fundamental question of whether a party ever agreed to arbitrate anything at all. *See* Alan Scott Rau, *Everything You Really Need to Know About "Separability" in Seventeen Simple Propositions*, 14 Am. Rev. Int'l Arb. 1, 106–07 (2003) (arguing that Court in *Howsam* "conceptualize[d]" issue as "a matter of contract interpretation that arbitrators are particularly well-placed to address"); Richard C. Reuben, First Options, *Consent to Arbitration, and the Demise of Separability: Restoring Access to Justice for Contracts with Arbitration Provisions*, 56 SMU L. Rev. 819, 836 (2003) (discussing arguments for sending "procedural arbitrability" issues to the arbitrators in the first instance).

[103] The reader should not draw from this description the conclusion that courts handle these issues in the same way. For example, courts may send questions of "compliance with the statute of limitations" to arbitrators while reserving for themselves questions of compliance with "*contractual* time limits." The theory behind this distinction—that statutes of limitations relate to the merits—is questionable given that both statutory and contractual time limits may require "a decisionmaker ... to inquire into the underlying facts or legal theories underpinning a claim." Alan Scott Rau, *The Arbitrability Question Itself*, 10 Am. Rev. Int'l Arb. 287, 326–28 (1999).

[104] *See* discussion in Section C.2 of this chapter.

[105] *See, e.g.*, Mulvaney Mechanical, Inc. v. Sheet Metal Workers Intern. Ass'n, Local 38, 351 F.3d 43 (2d Cir. 2003) (applying the reasoning of *Howsam* to a claim of repudiation by analogy, holding it is for the arbitrators); Office of Supply Government of Republic of Korea v. New York Nav. Co., Inc., 469 F.2d 377, 380 (2d Cir. 1972) (on a motion to vacate) ("In short, where parties have agreed to settle differences by arbitration, they should not be denied access to that forum, regardless of [the statutory] one-year time-bar, provided they invoke arbitration within a reasonable time after their differences have arisen ... Thereafter it is for the arbitrators, not the court, to decide whether a claim is time-barred by their agreement.") (internal citations omitted); Ballard v. Parkstone Energy, LLC, No. 06 Civ. 13099, 2007 U.S. Dist. LEXIS 86957 (S.D.N.Y. Nov. 27, 2007); Goldman, Sachs & Co. v. Griffin, No. 07 Civ. 1313, 2007 U.S. Dist. LEXIS 36674, at *6 (S.D.N.Y. May, 17 2007) (on a motion to stay arbitration) ("The FAA 'establishes that, as a matter of federal law, any doubts concerning the scope of arbitrable issues should be resolved in favor of arbitration, whether the problem at hand is the construction of the contract language itself or an allegation of waiver, delay, or a like defense to arbitrability.' ") (internal citations omitted). Some courts have mentioned the possibility that "unreasonably" untimely requests would be decided upon by courts in the first instance. *See, e.g.*, Office of Supply Government of Republic of Korea v. New York Nav. Co., Inc., 469 F.2d 377 (2d Cir. 1972). Additionally, some earlier cases relied on a distinction between "statutory" limitations being for the court and "contract" limitations for the arbitrators, but this approach does not appear with much frequency in modern cases.

federal presumption in favor of arbitration, and the judicial preference for the efficient resolution of disputes.

6.32 *(b) Waiver of a party's right to arbitrate the dispute* Where a party has acted inconsistently with its right to arbitrate,[106] the doctrine of waiver may bar it from subsequently asserting that right.[107] While the Supreme Court established in *Howsam* that questions of waiver were presumptively for arbitrators to decide,[108] the courts of appeal have not uniformly adopted this approach.[109] In the Second Circuit, courts appear to continue to decide issues of waiver in keeping with pre-*Howsam* precedent without addressing the apparent tension with *Howsam.*[110] However, the standard required to sustain a waiver claim is sufficiently high in New York to justify doubts as to its potency as a bar to arbitration.[111] Parties could presumably avoid any uncertainty about this matter by indicating in the arbitration agreement itself their "clear and unmistakable" intent that this determination be made by the arbitrators.[112]

6.33 *(c) Res judicata and collateral estoppel* A question of preclusion may arise when a party opposing a motion to compel arbitration invokes a prior arbitral award or a prior judgment to exclude claims or issues from the arbitration. (Preclusion itself may be separated into res judicata (claim preclusion)[113] and collateral estoppel

[106] For example, a party may first commence litigation and only later move to compel arbitration of the same dispute.

[107] *See* Application of ABN Intern. Capital Markets Corp., 812 F. Supp. 418 (S.D.N.Y. 1993), *order aff'd.* 996 F.2d 1478 (2d Cir. 1983). *See also* discussion in Chapter 7.C.1(d).

[108] Howsam v. Dean Witter Reynolds, Inc., 537 U.S. 79, 84 (2002) (*quoting* Moses H. Cone Memorial Hospital v. Mercury Constr. Corp., 460 U.S. 1, 24–25 (1983).

[109] In the Eighth Circuit, consistent with *Howsam*, waiver is presumptively to be decided by the arbitrators. *See* National American Ins. Co. v. Transamerica Occidental Life Ins. Co., 328 F.3d 462, 466 (8th Cir. 2003). In the First Circuit, however, waiver is reserved for judicial determination. *See* Marie v. Allied Home Mortgage Corp., 402 F.3d, 1 (1st Cir. 2005).

[110] *See* Bell v. Cendant Corp., 293 F.3d 563, 569 (2d Cir. 2002) (pre-*Howsam*, applying Connecticut law, stating that generally waiver is subject to arbitral determination, but where the party seeking arbitration "had already participated in litigation on the dispute," the district court was correct to decide the issue) (internal citations omitted). Post-*Howsam*, district courts have continued to decide waiver issues. *See, e.g.*, Town of Amherst v. Custom Lighting Servs., L.L.C., No. 07-CV-261S, 2007 U.S. Dist. LEXIS 88296, at *12 (W.D.N.Y. Nov. 30, 2007) (citing Application of Herman Miller, Inc., No. 97 Civ. 7878, 1998 U.S. Dist. LEXIS 5557, at *1 (S.D.N.Y. Apr. 20, 1998) *aff'd*, 173 F. 3d 844 (2d Cir. 1999)) ("A district court may find that a party waived its objection to the arbitrability of a dispute if it participated extensively in arbitration proceedings without asserting a timely objection"); Ballard v. Parkstone Energy, LLC, No. 06 Civ. 13099, 2007 U.S. Dist. LEXIS 86957, at *40–41 (S.D.N.Y. Nov. 27, 2007) (holding that evidence of settlement negotiations was insufficient to maintain a claim of waiver).

[111] *See* PPG Indus. v. Webster Auto Parts, 128 F.3d 103, 107 (2d Cir. 1997) ("a party waives its right to arbitration when it engages in protracted litigation that prejudices the opposing party"); Leadertex v. Morganton Dyeing & Finishing Corp., 67 F.3d 20, 25 (2d Cir. 1995).

[112] *See* First Options of Chicago, Inc. v. Kaplan, 514 U.S. 938, 944 (1995); Coady v. Ashcraft & Gerel, 223 F.3d 1, 9–10 (1st Cir. 2000). *But see* S & R Co. of Kingston v. Latona Trucking, Inc., 159 F.3d 80, 85–86 (2d Cir. 1998) (In a pre-*Howsam* decision, the fact that the arbitration agreement contained a "no waiver" clause did not preclude judicial review).

[113] Benjamin v. Traffic Executive Association Eastern Railroads, 869 F.2d 107, 111 (2d Cir. 1989) ("Under res judicata, a final judgment on the merits bars further claims by parties or their

(issue preclusion)).[114] The threshold question then is whether the court or the arbitrator gets to decide whether the prior decision has the asserted preclusive effect.

When the prior decision is an arbitral award, the clear majority position is that the preclusive effect of the prior arbitral award is properly decided by the arbitrator.[115] The Second Circuit has held that when the prior decision is a judgment, the preclusive effect is also to be decided by the arbitrator,[116] though every other circuit that has addressed this latter question has held that it is to be decided by the court.[117] **6.34**

5. Appealability of Courts' Arbitral Jurisdiction Determinations

Once a court has made its initial ruling on arbitral jurisdiction, various avenues for appeal may be available to the disappointed party.[118] This section discusses the **6.35**

privies from relitigating issues that were or could have been raised in that action.") (*quoting* Kremer v. Chemical Construction Corp., 456 U.S. 461, 466–67 n.6 (1982)).

[114] Postlewaite v. McGraw-Hill, Inc., 333 F.3d 42, 48 (2d Cir. 2003) ("collateral estoppel, or issue preclusion, bars the relitigation of an issue that was raised, litigated, and actually decided by a judgment in a prior proceeding, regardless of whether the two suits are based on the same cause of action.").

[115] *See* National Union Fire Ins. Co. of Pittsburgh v. Belco Petroleum Corp., 88 F.3d 129, 135 (2d Cir. 1996) (holding that the preclusive effect of a prior arbitration was a matter to be decided by the arbitrator); Bishop v. Smith Barney Inc., 1998 U.S. Dist. LEXIS 1239, *26 (S.D.N.Y. 1998) ("the weight of case law indicates that, where the arbitration agreement is broadly inclusive of claims, the question of whether a prior arbitration constitutes a res judicata bar should be resolved by the arbitration panel."). *See also* Consolidation Coal Co. v. United Mine Workers of America, Dist. 12, Local Union 1545, 213 F.3d 404 (7th Cir. 2000) ("the question of the preclusive force of the [prior] arbitration is, like any other defense, itself an issue for a subsequent arbitrator to decide"); Chiron Corp. v. Ortho Diagnostic Sys., Inc., 207 F.3d 1126 (9th Cir. 2000) (same); John Hancock Mutual Life Ins. Co. v. Olick, 151 F.3d 132, 139–40 (3d Cir. 1998) (same). *Cf.* International Union of Operating Engineers v. Flair Builders, Inc., 406 U.S. 487, 490 (1972) (defense of laches to be decided by the arbitrator). ***But see*** Helmsley Spear, Inc. v. Local 32 B-32J Service Employees Int'l Union, 1991 U.S. Dist. LEXIS 10298, *3–4 (S.D.N.Y. 1991) (Under New York law, "the question of whether a second arbitration is precluded by res judicata or collateral estoppel is a question of law for the Court to decide"); Rembrandt Indus., Inc. v. Hodges Int'l, Inc., 344 N.E.2d 383, 384 (N.Y. 1976) ("scope of the award and, therefore, its res judicata effect, is an issue properly determinable by the court and not the arbitrators").

[116] *See* United States Fire Ins. Co. v. National Gypsum Co., 101 F.3d 813, 816 (2d Cir. 1996), *cert. denied*, 521 U.S. 1120 (1997) ("[Appellant] argues that issue preclusion, like other defenses to arbitrability, is arbitrable, and, because issue preclusion can be arbitrated, it must be arbitrated. We agree."). *See also* Shearson Lehman Hutton, Inc. v. Wagoner, 944 F.2d 114, 121 (2d Cir. 1991) (holding that any doubts concerning the scope of arbitrable issues "should be resolved in favor of arbitration, whether the problem at hand is the construction of the contract language or an allegation of waiver, delay, or a like defense to arbitrability.").

[117] *See* John Hancock Mut. Life Ins. Co. v. Olick, 151 F.3d 132, 139 (3d Cir. 1998) (preclusive effect of prior judgments is a matter to be resolved by courts, not arbitrators); *In re* Y & A Group Sec. Litigation, 38 F.3d 380, 383 (8th Cir. 1994) ("The district court, and not the arbitration panel, is the best interpreter of its own judgment."); Kelly v. Merrill Lynch, Pierce, Fenner & Smith, Inc., 985 F.2d 1067 (11th Cir.), *cert. denied*, 510 U.S. 1011 (1993).

[118] These include: 9 U.S.C. § 16, 28 U.S.C. § 1292(b), mandamus certification, and the doctrine of pendent appellate jurisdiction. Gabriel Taran, note, *Towards a Sensible Rule Governing Stays Pending Appeals of Denials of Arbitration*, 73 U. Chi. L. Rev. 399, 403 (2006) (*citing* Mark I. Levy, *Arbitration Appeals II*, Natl L.J. 12 (Aug. 16, 2004)). Interlocutory appeal from an

appealability of judicial determinations of arbitral jurisdiction and the applicable standards of review on appeal.

6.36 Under the FAA, a party may appeal an order declining to enforce an arbitration agreement without judicial permission, but may only appeal an order enforcing an arbitration agreement with express judicial permission. Section 16 of the FAA expressly empowers litigants to immediately appeal as of right and without court approval court orders *declining* to enforce arbitration agreements that fall within the Act's scope.[119] Failure to seek an appeal as of right under FAA § 16 is likely to constitute a waiver[120] of the right to arbitrate and to appeal the denial of arbitration, whereas a failure to seek an appeal under another available procedural avenue, such as 28 U.S.C. § 1292, is less likely to constitute such a waiver.[121] Section 16 of the FAA does not itself permit an immediate appeal, as of right, from an order *enforcing* an arbitration agreement.[122] However, FAA § 16 does permit a party to seek an interlocutory appeal, pursuant to court approval, from an order enforcing an arbitration agreement pursuant to 28 U.S.C. § 1292(b). According to the Second Circuit, "Section 16 is a 'provision governing appeals of orders concerning arbitration, [and] it endeavors to promote appeals from orders barring arbitration and limit appeals from orders directing arbitration,' "[123] which is consistent with the federal presumption in favor of arbitration.

6.37 Even so, a judicial order compelling or denying arbitration may be appealable if it constitutes a "final decision" within the meaning of Section 16(a)(3). The Supreme Court has construed this language to include an order compelling arbitration and dismissing the underlying judicial proceeding, but not an order compelling arbitration while merely staying the litigation.[124] The Second Circuit has

interim arbitral decision is generally unavailable, though similar judicial review may be achieved through other procedural routes.

[119] 9 U.S.C. § 16(a)(1)(A), (B), (C) (2006). Section 16 also applies for purposes of the Panama Convention through its incorporation in 9 U.S.C. § 307.

[120] *See* discussion in Section C.4(b) of this chapter.

[121] The First, Second, Fifth, and Eighth Circuits have held that failure to seek an immediate appeal under 9 U.S.C. § 16 may result in such a waiver. *See* Colon v. R. K. Grace & Co., 358 F.3d 1, 4 (1st Cir. 2003) (acknowledging the possibility of waiver, but refusing to "employ a mechanical forfeiture rule"); Cotton v. Slone, 4 F.3d 176 (2d Cir. 1993) (defendant, who failed to immediately appeal denial of motion to compel arbitration, could not raise the challenge after three years of litigation and entry of an adverse default judgment); Cargill Ferrous Int'l v. Sea Phoenix MV, 325 F.3d 695, 700 (5th Cir. 2003); United Food & Commercial Workers Int'l Union, 37 F.3d 1302, 1303 n.3 (8th Cir. 1994). Courts have been less likely to find waiver arising out of failure to seek interlocutory appeal under 28 U.S.C. § 1292. *See, e.g.*, Clark v. Merrill Lynch, Pierce, Fenner & Smith, Inc., 924 F.2d 550, 553 (4th Cir. 1991).

[122] 9 U.S.C. § 16(b)(1), (3) (2006).

[123] Augustea Impb Et Salvataggi v. Mitsubishi Corp., 126 F.3d 95, 98 (2d Cir. 1997) (*quoting* Filanto, S.p.A. v. Chilewich Int'l Corp., 984 F.2d 58, 60 (2d Cir. 1993)).

[124] Green Tree Fin. Group v. Randolph, 531 U.S. 79, 86–87 & n.2 (2000). *See also* Salim Oleochemicals v. M/V SHROPSHIRE, 278 F.3d 90, 93 (2d Cir. 2002) ("Courts should be aware that a dismissal renders an order appealable under § 16(a)(3), while the granting of a stay is an unappealable interlocutory order under § 16(b) ... Unnecessary delay of the arbitral process

embraced the Supreme Court's approach, thus abandoning prior Second Circuit precedent.[125]

The Second Circuit has consistently held that lower court determinations of arbitrability under federal law are reviewed de novo, while lower court factual determinations are reviewed under a clearly erroneous standard.[126] **6.38**

D. ARBITRAL JURISDICTION BEFORE THE ARBITRATORS

We have thus far imagined courts grappling with whether to defer to the arbitrators in the first instance, before arbitration begins. Now we consider how arbitrators themselves approach the jurisdictional question. Under *Kompetenz-Kompetenz*, arbitrators enjoy authority to determine their own jurisdiction.[127] The severability doctrine as such applies before the arbitrators only in the sense that arbitrators do not undermine their own jurisdiction if they find the container contract to be invalid. **6.39**

We focus here on cases where the matter has already been to court (and the court has presumably referred the parties to arbitration). We look first to the procedures that guide arbitrators' jurisdictional determinations, turn next to choice of law issues, and then delve into the factors that guide their decisions whether to exercise independent judgment on jurisdictional and forum-specific issues that the **6.40**

---

through appellate review is disfavored ... District courts should continue to be mindful of this 'liberal federal policy favoring arbitration agreements,' ... when deciding whether to dismiss an action or instead to grant a stay.") (internal citations omitted). For a more in-depth discussion of the various procedural approaches currently used by courts, *see* Gabriel Taran, note, *Towards a Sensible Rule Governing Stays Pending Appeals of Denials of Arbitration*, 73 U. CHI. L. REV. 399 (2006).

125 Salim Oleochemicals v. M/V Shropshire, 278 F.3d 90, 91 (2d Cir. 2002) (following *Green Tree*, holding that "a dismissal without prejudice in favor of arbitration is an appealable 'final' decision under 9 U.S.C. § 16(a)(3)," and affirming that *Green Tree* has "overruled our precedents that distinguish between 'independent' and 'embedded' actions for purposes of appealability."); Jonesfilm v. Lions Gate Films, Inc., 65 Fed. Appx. 361, 362–63 (2d Cir. 2003).

126 *See* Garten v. Kurth, 265 F.3d 136, 141–42 (2d Cir. 2001). *See also* Harford Accident & Indem. Co. v. Swiss Reinsurance Am. Corp., 246 F.3d 219, 225 (2d Cir. 2001); Chelsea Square Tiles, Inc. v. Bombay Dyeing & Mfg. Co., 189 F.3d 289, 295 (2d Cir. 1998); New York v. Oneida Indian Nation, 90 F.3d 58, 60 (2d Cir. 1996); Leadertex, Inc. v. Morganton Dyeing & Finishing Corp., 67 F.3d 20, 27 (2d Cir. 1995). *See also* First Options of Chicago, Inc. v. Kaplan, 514 U.S. 938, 948–49 (1995).

127 *See, e.g.*, Final Award in ICC Case No. 8938 of 1996, 24 Y.B. Comm. Arb. 174, 176 (1999) (stating that "'competence-competence' is widely recognized by doctrine and jurisprudence"); Antonias Dimolitsa, *Separability and Kompetenz-Kompetenz*, in IMPROVING THE EFFICIENCY OF ARBITRATION AGREEMENTS AND AWARDS: 40 YEARS OF APPLICATION OF THE NEW YORK CONVENTION 217, 228–31 (Albert Jan van den Berg ed., 1999) (discussing national legal systems' general acceptance of the version of *Kompetenz-Kompetenz* that holds that arbitrators have power to decide their own jurisdiction, subject to judicial review at some stage of dispute resolution process).

court may have addressed.[128] We will not distinguish amongst "party," "scope," and "validity" questions, as the relative dearth of publicly available awards makes doing so inappropriate. We will see, however, the effect of the different position arbitrators occupy when considering whether to defer: arbitrators, unlike courts, face the looming threat of vacatur, nonrecognition, or nonenforcement of their awards.

1. Procedural Aspects of Arbitrators' Jurisdictional Determinations

6.41 Though the existence of arbitral jurisdiction is a condition for an arbitration validly to proceed,[129] a jurisdictional ruling need not be made separate from, and prior to, a determination of the merits.[130] This section considers the timing and form of jurisdictional objections and rulings, as well as special procedural issues arising under different institutional regimes.

6.42 *(a) Timing and form of jurisdictional objections* Under institutional arbitration, the timing of jurisdictional objections depends on the institutional regime. The International Centre for Settlement of Investment Disputes (ICSID) rules expressly provide that either the parties or the tribunal itself may raise jurisdictional questions at any stage in the proceedings.[131] The International Chamber of Commerce (ICC) rules make clear that parties may raise jurisdictional questions,[132] and imply that the tribunal may as well.[133] Indeed, the ICC rules have been interpreted to allow either the parties or the tribunal to raise jurisdictional objections at any time.[134] Other institutions' rules affirm the principle that the "tribunal shall have the power to rule on its own jurisdiction,"[135] but do not expressly state that the tribunal may raise jurisdictional issues *sua sponte*. Instead, they focus on the parties' role in raising jurisdictional objections.[136] These

[128] It is important to distinguish these cases from those where an arbitrator is the first decision-maker to consider the propriety of jurisdiction, and will therefore consider the matter independently.

[129] *See, e.g.*, Art. 6(4) of the ICC Rules (stating that if the International Court of Arbitration is not "satisfied" that there is prima facie evidence of an arbitration agreement giving rise to arbitral jurisdiction, "the parties shall be notified that the arbitration cannot proceed").

[130] *See* John Yukio Gotanda, *An Efficient Method for Determining Jurisdiction in International Arbitration*, 40 Colum. J. Transnat'l L. 11, 12 (2001) (noting that arbitrators sometimes defer jurisdictional determinations until the final award).

[131] ICSID Rules, art. 41(2).

[132] ICC art. 6(3) (referring to the situation where "any party raises one or more pleas concerning the existence, validity or scope of the arbitration agreement").

[133] The ICC rules refer to situations where the tribunal may decide on its own jurisdiction when "the Respondent does not submit an Answer." ICC art. 6(3).

[134] ICC art. 6(2). The ICC Rules do not speak to timing; their silence reflects the parties' ability to raise jurisdictional objections at any time. *See* W. Laurence Craig, William W. Park, and Jan Paulsson, Annotated Guide to the 1998 ICC Arbitration Rules with Commentary 60 (1998).

[135] AAA Commercial Rules 7(a).

[136] *See id.*; LCIA Rules, art. 23.1; UNCITRAL Rules, art. 21.

institutions may require a party to raise its jurisdictional objections in the statement of defense, or in the reply to the counterclaim, as the case may be,[137] and consider a failure to raise these objections as a waiver of them.

The parties may also need to examine the *lex arbitri* to determine if it places limits on the timing of jurisdictional objections.[138] The U.N. Commission on International Trade Law (UNCITRAL) Model Law requires parties to raise available jurisdictional objections in the statement of defense, or at least as soon as an issue allegedly lying outside the scope of the arbitrators' jurisdiction is raised.[139] If the arbitrators believe that it is "justified," however, they may hear an ill-timed jurisdictional objection.[140] **6.43**

Jurisdictional objections may be made in writing, but the arbitrators may of course decide to hear the parties on the jurisdictional issue. It is likely they will do so in cases where the predicate facts are in dispute, and in that case they may even ask for the introduction of evidence.[141] **6.44**

When parties challenge arbitral jurisdiction before the arbitrators, they do so on grounds broadly similar to those invocable in court. A party may argue that no arbitration agreement exists,[142] that it was procured by fraud or other vitiating circumstance,[143] that the agreement does not encompass the dispute at hand,[144] or that the arbitration agreement is invalid under the law applicable to it.[145] In considering these challenges, severability may separate challenges going to the container contract from those that go to the arbitration agreement, but the arbitrators will hear both.[146] **6.45**

---

[137] *See, e.g.*, UNCITRAL Rules, art. 21(3), 15 ILM 701 (1976); LCIA Rules, art. 23.3; AAA International Rules, art. 19(3).

[138] *See* John Yukio Gotanda, *An Efficient Method for Determining Jurisdiction in International Arbitration*, 40 Colum. J. Transnat'l L. 11, 18–19 (2001) (noting the importance of national law to the timing question).

[139] UNCITRAL Model Law, art. 16(2), *available at* http://www.uncitral.org/pdf/english/texts/arbitration/ml-arb/07-86998_Ebook.pdf.

[140] *Id.*

[141] Gary B. Born, International Commercial Arbitration: Commentary and Materials 993 (3d ed. 2009).

[142] Interim Award in Case No. 7929 (Fin. v. U.S.) of 1995 (ICC 1995), in 25 Y.B. Comm. Arb. 312, 312–15 (2000), *discussed in* Gotanda, *supra* note 138.

[143] All-Union Export-Import Assoc. Sojuznefteexport (Moscow) v. Joc Oil, Ltd., Arb. No. 109/1980, Foreign Trade Arbitration Commission at the USSR Chamber of Commerce and Industry, Moscow (July 9, 1984), *reprinted in* Gary B. Born, International Commercial Arbitration: Commentary and Materials 59 (2d ed. 2001) (stating in dictum that "[a]n arbitration agreement can be recognized as invalid only in the case where there are discovered in it defects in will (mistake, fraud and so on)").

[144] *See* Tradex Hellas S.A. (Greece) v. Albania, Dec. 24, 1996, reprinted in 25 Y.B. Comm. Arb. 221, 223 (2000), *discussed in* Gotanda, *supra* note 138 (arguing that arbitration agreement only covered expropriation claims, not claims in dispute at hand).

[145] Interim Award in Case No. 6149 of 1990 (ICC 1995), in 20 Y.B. Comm. Arb. 41 (1995), reprinted in Born 2001, 103.

[146] Born, *supra* note 141, at 311–13.

6.46 *(b) Deferring the jurisdictional determination and joining it with the merits* Many institutional rules allow arbitrators to issue partial awards on the jurisdictional issue, or defer ruling on it until issuing a final award encompassing both jurisdiction and the merits.[147] Whether arbitrators defer the jurisdictional ruling appears to depend on (a) what the parties ask them to do; (b) the requirements of the law applicable to the agreement; (c) the requirements, if any, of the arbitration rules governing the arbitration; and (d) considerations of efficiency (such as the arbitrators' sense of the degree to which the jurisdictional facts and the "merits" facts may be intertwined).[148] The question of whether interim awards on jurisdiction are immediately subject to confirmation or vacatur is not as straightforward as it would initially seem. Generally speaking, courts require "finality" before they are willing to entertain a vacatur action; this means, in practice, a necessary condition of immediate review is a "definitive … dispos[ition] of discrete issues."[149] Though a ruling on jurisdiction theoretically could fit this description, U.S. courts generally refuse to review interim awards on jurisdiction.[150]

6.47 *(c) Special jurisdictional procedures for different institutional regimes* Some institutional regimes entail unique procedures governing jurisdictional determinations. The ICC Rules, for example, permit the ICC's International Court of Arbitration to consider a party's objection to the existence, validity, or scope of the arbitration agreement before the arbitrators proceed. If the court is "prima facie satisfied that an arbitration agreement under the Rules may exist," then it remits the jurisdictional objections to the arbitrators.[151] If the court decides the prima facie case has not been met, then it will bar the matter from going to the arbitral tribunal.[152] Of course, the court's finding of a prima facie case does not bar the tribunal from addressing the issue de novo, as the ICC Rules expressly state.[153]

[147] *See, e.g.*, ICSID Convention Rules art. 41(2) ("Any objection by a party to the dispute that that dispute is not within the jurisdiction of the Centre, or for other reasons is not within the competence of the Tribunal, shall be considered by the Tribunal which shall determine whether to deal with it as a preliminary question or to join it to the merits of the dispute.").

[148] Gotanda, *supra* note 138 at 27 (surveying "limited number of decisions that have addressed this issue" and discerning a pattern).

[149] Born, *supra* note 141, at 2433 n.37 (*citing*, *inter alia*, Metallgesellschaft AG v. M/V Capitan Constante, 790 F.2d 280, 283 (2d Cir. 1986)).

[150] Born, *supra* note 143, at 93 n.17 ("Even if an interim jurisdictional award is made by the tribunal, however, then interlocutory review is probably not available under the FAA") (*citing* Transportacion Maritima Mexicana, S.A. v. Companhia de Navegacao Lloyd Brasileiro, 636 F. Supp. 474, 475 (S.D.N.Y. 1983) (stating there is "no authority" for review of interim jurisdictional award)). For a description of ways in which American litigants try to circumvent this rule, *see id.* at 93–94 (describing challenges to ongoing arbitration or decisions to file a separate suit in court, which forces the other party to raise the ongoing arbitration as a defense). Note, however, that there are "few reported decisions" on the matter. *Id.* at 93–94.

[151] ICC Rules Art. 6(4).

[152] *Id.*

[153] *Id.* ("[A]ny decision as to the jurisdiction of the Arbitral Tribunal shall be taken by the Arbitral Tribunal itself.").

2. Choice of Law Governing Arbitrators' Jurisdictional Determinations

Approaches to the choice of law governing arbitral jurisdiction vary, and it is especially difficult to systematize an approach to the issue, given the fact that many arbitral awards go unreported. One commentator has suggested the arbitral case law reflects at least nine possible approaches to deciding what law governs the arbitration agreement.[154] Some commentators suggest that there is a trend toward applying the law of the arbitral situs or some version of transnational law (such as "general principles of an international law merchant").[155] Others strongly disagree, arguing that use of the law of the arbitral situs is "not a majority trend" and that the use of "international trade usages" is "exceptional."[156] Interestingly, both points of view point to ICC awards as their main sources of authority.[157] **6.48**

Commentators agree that the parties may choose a law to apply specifically to the arbitration agreement,[158] and arbitrators have recognized the possibility of subjecting the arbitration agreement to a governing law different from the law governing the container contract.[159] Even in the absence of a separate choice of law to govern the arbitration agreement, the arbitrators may well refuse to apply a general choice of law clause in the container contract to the interpretation and validity of the arbitration agreement.[160] While there appears to be general agreement that, in choosing the law that applies to the arbitration agreement, the **6.49**

---

[154] *See* Marc Blessing, *The Law Applicable to the Arbitration Clause and Arbitrability*, in Improving the Efficiency of Arbitration Agreements and Awards: 40 Years of Application of the New York Convention 168 (Albert Jan van den Berg ed., 1999).

[155] *See id.* at 168, 174 (concluding that there is a "strong tendency" toward choosing the law of the arbitral situs or some "de-nationalized" approach); W. Laurence Craig, William W. Park, and Jan Paulsson, International Chamber of Commerce Arbitration § 5.05, at 53 (2000) (suggesting that trend in ICC arbitration is to use "general principles of an international law merchant," as evidenced in "the growing body of published international awards").

[156] Bernard Hanotiau, *The Law Applicable to Arbitrability*, in Improving the Efficiency of Arbitration Agreements and Awards: 40 Years of Application of the New York Convention 146, 155–57 (Albert Jan van den Berg ed., 1999).

[157] *Compare* W. Laurence Craig, et al., *supra* note 155 at 54 *with* Hanotiau, in Improving the Efficiency of Arbitration Agreements and Awards: 40 Years of Application of the New York Convention, *supra* note 156 at 153–55.

[158] *See* W. Laurence Craig, et al., *supra* note 155 at 54; Hanotiau, in Improving the Efficiency of Arbitration Agreements and Awards: 40 Years of Application of the New York Convention, *supra* note 156 at 153–55; Julian D. M. Lew, *The Law Applicable to the Form and Substance of the Arbitration Clause*, in Improving the Efficiency of Arbitration Agreements and Awards: 40 Years of Application of the New York Convention 114, 140 (Albert Jan van den Berg ed., 1999).

[159] *See* ICC Case No. 6149 (discussing various choice of law possibilities, and ultimately choosing law of the arbitral situs), discussed in Lew, in Improving the Efficiency of Arbitration Agreements and Awards: 40 Years of Application of the New York Convention, *supra* note 158, at 140–41. *See* Craig, et al., *supra* note 155, at 52 (noting that the "autonomy of the arbitration clause" means that a choice of law clause in the container contract need not apply to the arbitration agreement).

[160] Craig, et al., *supra* note 155, at 52.

arbitrators should give effect to party expectations,[161] as well as to the impact of the choice on eventual recognition and enforcement,[162] the question of the arbitrators' choice of law applicable to the arbitration agreement remains contested.

3. *Kompetenz-Kompetenz* and the Scope and Validity of the Arbitrators' Jurisdiction

6.50 If *Kompetenz-Kompetenz* means anything, it surely means that if the parties have gone directly to arbitration and raised jurisdictional issues there, the arbitrators will independently decide whether they possess jurisdiction.[163] As a practical matter, arbitrators will also in effect apply the rule of severability, in that a decision on their part invalidating the container contract will not vitiate their jurisdiction to make such a ruling.[164]

6.51 Two questions arise if the parties have arrived at arbitration via an order from a national court compelling arbitration. The first is whether an order compelling arbitration precludes the arbitrators from independently passing on the question of arbitral jurisdiction.[165] The second is whether the arbitrators will determine a

---

[161] *See, e.g.*, Ad hoc arbitration of April 1982 (Company Z (Republic of Xanadu) v. State Organization ABC (Republic of Utopia)), 8 Yrbk. Comm. Arb. (1983) (looking to what "parties wished" in determining choice of law issues), discussed in Lew, in Improving the Efficiency of Arbitration Agreements and Awards: 40 Years of Application of the New York Convention, *supra* note 158, at 140; ICC Case 4131/1982, I ICC Awards 146, 465 (looking to intent of parties during negotiation and performance, instead of law chosen for container contract, when making choice of law), discussed in Craig, et al., *supra* note 155, at 52–53; Marc Blessing, *The Law Applicable to the Arbitration Clause and Arbitrability*, in Improving the Efficiency of Arbitration Agreements and Awards: 40 Years of Application of the New York Convention 168, 177–78 (Albert Jan van den Berg ed., 1999) (concluding that arbitrators should focus on "fair and legitimate expectations" of parties).

[162] *See* Craig, et al., *supra* note 155, at 53–54 (arguing that "prudent ICC arbitrators ... should deem themselves bound, under [ICC Rules'] Article 35's exhortation that they 'shall make every effort to make sure that the Award is enforceable at law,' to take account of the law of the place of arbitration").

[163] *See* Antonias Dimolitsa, *Separability and* Kompetenz-Kompetenz, in Improving the Efficiency of Arbitration Agreements and Awards: 40 Years of Application of the New York Convention 217, 228 (Albert Jan van den Berg ed., 1999).

[164] Many national laws recognize severability. *See, e.g.*, U.K. Dep't of Trade and Industry Consultation Document on Proposed Clauses and Schedules for an Arbitration Bill, 10 Arb. Int. 189, 227 (1994) ("[I]nternational consensus on autonomy has now grown very broad."). So too do institutional rules. *See, e.g.*, ICC Art. 6(4).

[165] One could also question whether an order staying arbitration binds the arbitrators. If a court in the seat of arbitration enjoins arbitration based on a finding that there is no arbitral jurisdiction, the arbitrators will refuse to hear the matter. *See* Craig, et al., *supra* note 155, at 171 ("[A] direct order emanating from a competent court at the seat of arbitration itself should ordinarily be allowed to affect arbitral proceedings."). If the court staying arbitration is not at the arbitral situs, the arbitrators may ignore the ruling. *See* ICC case 4862/1986, II ICC Awards 308 (refusing to stop arbitration despite an injunction from courts of Yemen, when arbitral situs was Paris), discussed in Craig, et al., *supra* note 155, at 171 n.39; *see also* Telenor Mobile Comms. AS v. Storm LLC, 2007 WL 3274699, at *3– *8 (S.D.N.Y. Nov. 2, 2007) (chronicling refusal of arbitrators in New York to stop arbitration despite multiple injunctions from a Ukrainian court). For discussion of the power of an American court to stay arbitration under both FAA Chapter 1 and the New York Convention,

party has waived its right to object to jurisdiction by not raising jurisdictional challenges before the court compelling arbitration. This second question would most likely arise when a party has raised one objection at the stage of compelling arbitration—for example, the agreement does not cover the dispute at hand—but then raises another before the arbitrators—for example, the party was not a party to the agreement.

(a) Preclusive effect of prior judicial determinations On the first question, arbitrators might conclude that a judicial determination of arbitral jurisdiction should preclude the parties from rearguing jurisdiction or preclude the arbitrators from otherwise declining jurisdiction.[166] One could essentially reason that the initial judicial determination of this issue represents the law of the case.[167] At another extreme, arbitrators could decide the issue independently, on the ground that the court compelling arbitration may have merely indulged in a presumption of validity and breadth of scope of the arbitration agreement, and that those matters remain ripe for de novo review.[168] (Of course, as a practical matter, arbitrators have incentives to agree with a judicial order compelling arbitration.) In general, when a court compels arbitration, "it will rarely occur that an arbitral tribunal holds that it lacks authority to decide the case."[169] On rare occasion, arbitrators have rejected court rulings finding arbitral jurisdiction, resulting in at least one case in vacatur of the award.[170] **6.52**

see Satcom Int'l Group PLC v. Orbcomm Int'l Partners, 49 F. Supp. 2d 331, 342 (S.D.N.Y. 1999), *aff'd*, 205 F.3d 1324 (2d Cir. 1999).

166 *See, e.g., In re* Shea, 132 N.E.2d 864 (N.Y. 1956) (deciding that arbitrators validly concluded that collateral estoppel barred party from rearguing arbitrability challenge based on alleged invalidity of arbitration agreement, given that court had already decided the issue in favor of arbitration); Randy D. Gordon, *Only One Kick at the Cat: A Contextual Rubric for Evaluating Res Judicata and Collateral Estoppel in International Commercial Arbitration*, 18 Fla. J. Int'l L. 549, 563 (2006) ("Once [the parties] have the court's decision, this is clearly a case for collateral estoppel; it would be wasteful to allow either one of the parties to raise the issue of arbitrability before a subsequent tribunal."); Melissa Hope Biren, *Note, Res Judicata/Collateral Estoppel Effect of a Court Determination in Subsequent Arbitration*, 45 Alb. L. Rev. 1029, 1049 (1981) (offering similar argument based upon reading of New York law on collateral estoppel).

167 *See* B-S Steel of Kansas, Inc. v. Texas Industries, Inc., 321 F. Supp. 2d 1214, 1218 (D. Kan. 2004) (concluding, on motion to vacate, that ruling on motion to compel arbitration was law of the case, and refusing to reexamine the validity and scope of the arbitration agreement).

168 Independent review was the rule in West Germany before the reunification. Adam Samuel, Jurisdictional Problems in International Commercial Arbitration: A Study of Belgian, Dutch, English, French, Swedish, Swiss, U.S., and West German Law 192 (1989).

169 *Id.* at 192.

170 Consider Aircraft Braking Systems Corp. v. Local 856, 97 F.3d 155 (6th Cir. 1996). The district court had ordered the parties to arbitration, concluding that there was an agreement to arbitrate. The arbitrator concluded that the court's order compelling arbitration was "not binding upon this arbitrator." *Id.* at 158 (discussing arbitral award (internal quotations omitted)). He then concluded that there was no agreement to arbitrate, and refused to reach the merits. *Id.* The Sixth Circuit affirmed the district court's decision to vacate the award, reasoning that the order compelling arbitration had issue preclusive effect on the issue of arbitral jurisdiction, and that the parties had not agreed under *First Options* to submit the issue to the arbitrator. *Id.* at 161–62. It then confirmed the remand of the case to a new arbitrator. *Id.* at 162–63.

6.53 Various factors may enter into consideration in leading arbitrators to exercise greater or lesser deference to a court determination in favor of arbitral jurisdiction. The *Kompetenz-Kompetenz* doctrine would seem to have its greatest force when the issue is the scope of coverage of the arbitration agreement.[171] Unlike at least some questions of validity, questions of scope—which tend to turn in part on the application of general principles of contract interpretation—do not implicate national courts' expertise on matters of local public policy.[172] This distinction is also consistent with the presumption stated in *First Options* that questions of scope of the arbitration agreement are basically for the arbitrators.[173]

6.54 If the court compelling arbitration is a court at the arbitral situs, the arbitrators will also be mindful of the fact that this may be the same court that will have an opportunity at a later point to vacate the award, and thus be all the more inclined to defer to the court's judgment on jurisdiction.[174] On the other hand, they may pay less respect to the judgment of a court outside the arbitral situs.[175] Choice of law may also be relevant, as the law applicable to the agreement may provide preclusion rules that the arbitrators consider themselves bound to apply.[176] Finally, the tenor of the order compelling arbitration may be relevant. The court compelling arbitration might merely have found there to be prima facie evidence of an agreement to arbitrate, which may in turn encourage the arbitrators to revisit the issue.[177] Given this range of considerations, it is not surprising that arbitrators

[171] This seems to be the thrust of Professor William W. Park's delineation of jurisdictional issues—existence, validity, and public policy versus scope—in his discussion of *Kompetenz-Kompetenz* in William W. Park, *Determining an Arbitrator's Jurisdiction: Timing and Finality in American Law*, 8 Nev. L.J. 135, 149–51 (2007).

[172] One must temper this conclusion with the recognition that certain validity challenges—e.g., fraudulent inducement of the arbitration agreement itself—also involve application of general contract law.

[173] *See* Park, *supra* note 171, at 149–50 ("[T]he arbitrator's authority to address problems of scope might often be addressed in the initial arbitration clause itself.").

[174] *See* Craig, et al., *supra* note 155, at 171 (discussing possibility of an injunction compelling arbitration that has "executory force over the arbitral tribunal itself"); Samuel, *supra* note 168, at 192 (arguing that arbitrators in England and the United States consider themselves bound by orders compelling arbitration when the court compelling arbitration is in England, or the United States, respectively).

[175] *See, e.g.*, Award in ICC Case No. 4862 of 1986, reprinted in S. Jarvin, Y. Derains, and J. Arnaldez, *Collection of ICC Arbitral Awards, 1986–1990*, 508–09 (1994) (determining that a Yemeni court proceeding against the arbitration agreement's validity had no relevance to arbitration in France); Final Award in ICC Case No. 5294 of 1988, 24 Y.B. Comm. Arb. 137 (1989), excerpted in Born *supra* note 143, at 78–80 (stating that Egyptian ruling that there was no arbitral jurisdiction "[does] not have any influence on the arbitrator's jurisdiction").

[176] David LeFevre, Note, *Whose Finding is it Anyway? The Division of Labor Between Courts and Arbitrators with Respect to Waiver*, 2006 J. Disp. Resol. 205, 315 n.127 ("Assuming that the arbitrator does not employ a collateral estoppel-type principle, nothing this author is aware of bars a party from asserting the same argument in arbitration that it argued in front of a judge before being compelled to arbitration.").

[177] The First Circuit's decision in Apollo Computer v. Berg illustrates this possibility. In that case, the court determined that Apollo had agreed to allow the arbitrator to determine jurisdiction so long as there was prima facie evidence of an agreement to arbitrate the issues in dispute.

commonly sidestep the deference question by, for example, analyzing it in the alternative and examining the issue both deferentially and de novo.[178]

(b) Waiver of jurisdictional challenges We must also consider whether the arbitrators will determine that a party has waived its jurisdictional objections by not raising them at the stage of compelling arbitration. For example, suppose a party objects at the compelling stage only on grounds of invalidity, but then objects at the arbitration on grounds of scope. While the dearth of publicly available awards on the topic makes it difficult to say what arbitrators actually do, they may take guidance from judicial statements on the topic. In one case, involving recognition and enforcement under the Convention, a federal district court in New York stated that "[t]he time for [a party] to argue that he could not be compelled to submit to arbitration because he [wasn't a party to the agreement] ... was in [the] action to compel him to arbitrate."[179] One could certainly conceive that arbitrators would adopt this view, given that a doctrine of waiver would discourage strategic behavior and increase the speed of proceedings. On the other hand, as discussed previously, institutional rules only provide for waiver if an objection is not raised at a certain stage *before the arbitrators.* Thus, an arbitrator might not feel constrained to find waiver, despite the obvious advantages. **6.55**

4. Preclusive Effect of Prior Judicial Determinations on Forum-Specific Issues

Lack of reported decisions and scholarly coverage make it difficult to discern a pattern in how arbitrators resolve issues concerning the preclusive effect of prior court rulings on forum-specific issues. As discussed previously,[180] forum-specific issues involve procedural conditions on arbitration that may implicate the merits. By focusing on two such forum-specific issues for which we have court **6.56**

Finding such evidence on the facts before it, the court refused to stay the proceedings. *See* Apollo Computer v. Berg, 886 F.2d 469, 473–74 (1st Cir. 1989).

[178] In PowerAgent Inc. v. Electronic Data Systems Corp., the federal district court compelled arbitration, and refused to allow PowerAgent (the party resisting arbitration) to amend its complaint to avoid arbitration. *See* PowerAgent, Inc. v. United States Dist. Court for the N. Dist. of Cal., 210 F.3d 385, 385 (9th Cir. 2000) (chronicling proceedings in lower court). The dispute proceeded to arbitration with the American Arbitration Association, where PowerAgent requested the arbitrators to independently rule on whether they had jurisdiction, citing a *Kompetenz-Kompetenz* provision in the arbitration agreement. *See* PowerAgent, Inc. v. Elec. Data Sys. Corp., 358 F.3d 1187, 1190 (9th Cir. 2004) (discussing PowerAgent's arguments before the arbitrators). In particular, PowerAgent argued, "The AAA rules, federal arbitration law, and applicable state law all recognize that arbitrators have authority to rule on their own jurisdiction ..."). *Id.* at 1192. The arbitrators considered the issue of jurisdiction, asking for both briefing and a hearing on the matter. They then found they had jurisdiction, but reasoned in the alternative: "Even if this arbitration panel were not bound by the prior orders of the District Court and the Appellate Court, we conclude that the disputes in this action are subject to arbitration." *Id.* at 1190 (*quoting* arbitrators' decision on jurisdiction).

[179] National Dev. Co. v. Khashoggi, 781 F. Supp. 959, 963 (S.D.N.Y. 1992).

[180] *See supra* notes 98–103 and accompanying text.

decisions—namely res judicata and class actions—we can identify two recurring themes. First, arbitrators are likely to be concerned about whether their refusal to give preclusive effect to a prior court ruling will be a ground for vacatur. Second, despite their best efforts, arbitrators may still, by virtue of their handling of these questions, expose an award to vacatur.

6.57 Res judicata issues arise when a party argues that arbitration cannot proceed because there is an existing award or court judgment on the merits that precludes further "litigation" of the dispute.[181] As discussed previously, several circuit courts of appeal recognize the arbitrators' authority to rule upon the preclusive effect of prior awards,[182] but not judicial judgments.[183] In the exercise of that authority, arbitrators will likely apply general notions of preclusion to determine the effect of prior awards.[184] But they will also likely be aware that refusing to give preclusive effect to a prior court judgment may be a ground for vacatur.[185]

6.58 In the class action context, arbitrators may also defer to judicial signals. With respect to permissibility of class action arbitration, the Supreme Court held in *Green Tree Financial Corp. v. Bazzle* that it is for the arbitrators to decide, in the first instance, whether the arbitration agreement permits class arbitration.[186] Even so, preliminary rulings on this issue may be misleading, as the case of *JLM Industries, Inc. v. Stolt-Nielsen SA* illustrates. In that case, the Second Circuit arguably signaled to the arbitrators that class action arbitration would be permissible when it compelled arbitration.[187] The arbitrators, likely acting on this signal,

[181] In this context, then, res judicata does *not* refer to the narrow question of whether an arbitrator will give preclusive effect to a compelling courts' determination that there is (or is not) arbitral jurisdiction over the dispute.

[182] *See* Consolidation Coal Co. v. United Mine Workers of America, 213 F.3d 404, 407 (7th Cir. 2000); John Hancock Mut. Life Ins. Co. v. Olick, 151 F.3d 132, 136–40 (3d Cir. 1998) (concluding that arbitrators have authority to decide preclusive effect of prior arbitral award).

[183] *See* Kelly v. Merrill Lynch, Pierce, Fenner & Smith, Inc., 985 F.2d 1067, 1069 (11th Cir. 1993) (stating, in context of issue of preclusive effect of prior *court judgment*, that "the better rule is that courts can decide res judicata").

[184] *See* Consolidation Coal Co., 213 F.3d at 407.

[185] *See, e.g.*, Aircraft Braking Sys. Corp. v. Local 856, 97 F.3d 155, 159, 161 (6th Cir. 1996) (vacating award and stating, "Arbitrators are not free to ignore the preclusive effect of prior judgments under the doctrines of res judicata and collateral estoppel, although they generally are entitled to determine in the first instance whether to give the prior judicial determination preclusive effect."); John Morrell & Co. v. Local 304A United Food & Comm. Workers, 913 F.3d 544, 563–63 (8th Cir. 1990) (vacating award and emphasizing that arbitrator only has "initial" authority to determine preclusive effect of prior judgment).

[186] *See* Green Tree Fin. Corp. v. Bazzle, 539 U.S. 444, 454 (2003).

[187] *See* JLM Indus., Inc. v. Stolt-Nielsen SA, 387 F.3d 163, 167 (2d Cir. 2004). JLM filed a putative class action under the Sherman Act in federal district court against Stolt-Nielsen, who argued the court should send the parties to arbitration. The Second Circuit ruled that the arbitrators should have first say as to whether the arbitration agreement encompassed these claims. The court noted that JLM was not arguing that the putative class action nature of the claim barred compelling arbitration. It then went on to say, "[w]e would likely view such an argument skeptically." *See* JLM Indus., Inc. v. Stolt-Nielsen SA, 387 F.3d 163, 180 n.9 (2d Cir. 2004).

ruled that class arbitration could go forward. The party that lost in arbitration then sought to vacate the award in the Southern District of New York. The district judge then vacated the award for manifest disregard of the law, determining that the arbitrators reached their conclusion based on a misunderstanding of the applicable law.[188]

The *Stolt-Nielsen* case demonstrates the challenge arbitrators face when they have, on one hand, a prior judgment compelling arbitration, and, on the other hand, the threat of future vacatur. While this difficulty may lead them to consider deferring to the judgment of the compelling court, they cannot be sure of the outcome. **6.59**

5. Appealability of Interim Arbitral Determinations of Arbitral Jurisdiction

One final topic deserves note. The FAA does not, except in extreme circumstances, permit interlocutory appeal from interim arbitral decisions, including decisions on arbitral jurisdiction. Thus, a disappointed party may not seek interlocutory judicial review of the initial determination of arbitral jurisdiction by the arbitrators.[189] The FAA, however, may be read to permit the issuance of injunctive relief from an ongoing arbitration, for example where the disappointed party instead commences a lawsuit in which the opposing party will then likely introduce the arbitration agreement as grounds for staying or dismissing the litigation. If the arbitration agreement is introduced in connection with the motion to dismiss or stay—as it undoubtedly will be—the court will make an independent determination of arbitral jurisdiction.[190] It is unclear what level of deference, if any, will be afforded to the arbitrator's initial jurisdictional findings. (Obviously, a disappointed party may seek judicial review of the final arbitral award.[191]) **6.60**

---

[188] *See* Stolt-Nielsen SA v. AnimalFeeds Int'l Corp., 435 F. Supp. 2d 382, 384–85 (S.D.N.Y. 2006) rev'd, 548 F.3d 85 (2d Cir. 2008), *cert. granted*, 129 S.Ct. 2793 (2009) (vacating the arbitral award).

[189] *See* Transportacion Maritima Mexicana, S.A. v. Compania de Navegacao Lloyd Brasileiro, 636 F. Supp. 474, 475 (S.D.N.Y. 1983) ("It is sufficient to state for the present that the Federal Arbitration Act permits judicial intervention before the arbitration begins and after the award has been rendered. There is no statutory authority for judicial intervention during the course of arbitration proceedings, with the sole exception of a petition if there has been 'a lapse … in filling a vacancy' in the panel of arbitrators."); Glass v. Kidder Peabody & Co., 114 F.3d 446, 454 (4th Cir. 1997) (*citing Transportacion Maritima Mexicana* and Justice Brennan's concurring opinion in United Steelworkers of America v. American Mfg. Co., where Brennan states that "On examining the arbitration clause, the court may conclude that it commits to arbitration any 'dispute, difference, disagreement, or controversy of any nature or character.' With that finding the court will have exhausted its function, except to order the reluctant party to arbitration." 363 U.S. 564, 571 (1960)).

[190] *See* Born, *supra* note 143, at 93.

[191] *See* discussion in Sections E and F of this chapter.

E. ARBITRAL JURISDICTION UPON VACATUR

6.61 Suppose now that an arbitral proceeding has gone forward, resulting in an award that a disappointed party then seeks to have annulled or vacated in a court of the place of arbitration. Among the disappointed party's claims may well be that the arbitrators got the jurisdictional question wrong. The question will arise as to whether, and to what extent, the vacatur court should view itself as in the same position as the court was—or would have been—at the stage of deciding whether to compel arbitration in the first place. While the arbitral award enjoys a general presumption of validity,[192] vacatur courts will not necessarily, or in all circumstances, uphold the arbitrator's assertion of arbitral jurisdiction. We shall see, perhaps unsurprisingly, that vacatur courts neither wholly defer to nor wholly disregard arbitrators' determinations of their own jurisdiction. In practice, this means that a vacatur court—even if it states that it is exercising independent judgment—will often discuss the arbitrator's ruling and reasoning, as opposed to stating that the arbitrator's decision is either decisive or completely irrelevant. A vacatur court, it would seem, is likely to give greater weight to an arbitrator's ruling on the scope of the agreement than to a ruling on the parties subject to the agreement or even the agreement's validity.

1. Confirmation and Vacatur of Awards Rendered in New York

6.62 Both the FAA and New York law provide for confirmation of an award,[193] a procedure which, if successful, enables local enforcement and permits enforcement abroad.[194] Alternatively, the losing party may request a local court to vacate the award,[195] so as to preclude local enforcement and reduce the likelihood of enforcement abroad.[196] The FAA and New York law enumerate a limited number of grounds for vacating an award.[197] The statutory ground that directly addresses arbitral jurisdiction asks whether "the arbitrators exceeded their powers."[198] Though

---

[192] *See* Willeminjn Houdstermcatschappi v. Standard Microsystems, Corp., 103 F.3d 9, 12 (2d Cir. 1997) ("The showing required to avoid summary confirmation of an arbitration award is high ...": "The court's function in confirming or vacating an arbitration award is severely limited."); Goldfinger v. Lisker, 500 N.E.2d 857, 859 (N.Y. 1986) ("Courts are reluctant to disturb the decisions of arbitrators lest the value of this method of resolving controversies be undermined ...").

[193] FAA, 9 U.S.C. § 9 (2000); N.Y. CPLR. § 7510 (2007).

[194] Note, however, that confirmation is not a prerequisite to enforcement abroad. Born, *supra* note 143, at 704. *See also* Chapter 13.A.1.

[195] *See also* Chapter 13.C.1(c). FAA, 9 U.S.C. § 10 (2000) (setting forth four statutory grounds for vacatur); N.Y. CPLR § 7511(b) (2007) (allowing court to vacate an award under enumerated circumstances).

[196] Born, *supra* note 143, at 704.

[197] FAA, 9 U.S.C. § 10 (2000) (setting forth four statutory grounds for vacatur); N.Y. CPLR § 7511(b) (2007) (allowing court to vacate an award under enumerated circumstances).

[198] FAA, 9 U.S.C. § 10(a) (2000); *see also* N.Y. CPLR § 7511(b)(1) (permitting vacatur when arbitrator "exceeded his power").

doing so would be controversial, a court may even be led to inquire into whether the arbitrators' very assertion of jurisdiction was in "manifest disregard" of the law.[199] In any event, the party seeking vacatur bears the burden of proof, which courts often describe as a "high" one, given the presumption in favor of validity.[200] The basic framework of analysis has three parts: (1) the court may vacate the award if there never was an arbitration agreement between the parties, or if the agreement was invalid; (2) the court may vacate the award if the arbitrators exceeded the scope of their authority under the agreement; and (3) the court may vacate the award for arbitrator or party misbehavior or fraud, gross error on the merits, and the like.[201] We are obviously concerned here only with (1) and (2).

Vacatur is also available for New York Convention awards issued within the **6.63**
United States.[202] While the Convention contemplates the possibility that a court may vacate an award rendered within its jurisdiction,[203] it does not specify grounds for or otherwise address vacatur.[204] The Second Circuit has found that the grounds for vacatur under FAA Chapter 1, as well as the nonstatutory "manifest disregard" ground, are available in a challenge to set aside a New York Convention award rendered in the United States.[205]

---

[199] For an encyclopedic account of the statutory and nonstatutory grounds for vacatur, *see* Stephen L. Hayford, *Law in Disarray: Judicial Standards for Vacatur of Commercial Arbitration Awards*, 30 GA. L. REV. 731 (1996). For an early example of searching, nonstatutory review of an arbitrator's decision as to jurisdiction, *see* Swift Industries v. Botany Industries, 466 F.2d 1125, 1125–29 (3d Cir. 1972) (considering whether award was beyond scope of arbitration agreement and therefore was "completely irrational").

[200] Willeminjn Houdstermcatschappi v. Standard Microsystems, Corp., 103 F.3d 9, 12 (2d Cir. 1997) ("The showing required to avoid summary confirmation of an arbitration award is high ..."). The Supreme Court ruled in Hall Street Assocs. L.L.C. v. Mattel, Inc., 552 U.S. 576 (2008), that parties may not under the Federal Arbitration Act contract to expand judicial review of an award on the occasion of an action to vacate the award. The Court left open the possibility that parties might possibly be able to achieve expanded vacatur review by proceeding, not under the Federal Arbitration Act, but under state statutory or common law. The circuits were split on the issue, as were commentators. *See* Hans Smit, *Contractual Modification of the Scope of Judicial Review of Arbitral Awards*, 8 AM. REV. INT'L ARB. 147 (1997) (discussing policy arguments involved in expanded review); Milana Koptsiovsky, Note, *A Right to Contract for Judicial Review of an Arbitration Award: Does Freedom of Contract Apply to Arbitration Agreements?*, 36 CONN. L. REV. 609, 628–43 (2004) (discussing circuit split).

[201] *See* Choice Hotels Intern., Inc. v. Felizardo, 278 F. Supp. 2d 590, 594 (D.Md. 2003) (setting up the framework of analysis).

[202] The New York Convention applies to "awards not considered as domestic awards." New York Convention, art. I(1). In the United States, this category includes awards "pronounced in accordance with foreign law" or those involving "nondomestic parties" and predicate conduct outside the United States. Bergesen v. Joseph Muller Corp., 710 F.2d 928, 932 (2d Cir. 1983).

[203] *See* N.Y. Convention art. V(1)(e) (allowing for nonrecognition or nonenforcement when "[t]he award has not yet become binding on the parties, or has been set aside or suspended by a competent authority of the country, in which, or under the law of which, that award was made").

[204] Susan L. Karamanian, *The Road to the Tribunal and Beyond: International Commercial Arbitration and United States Courts*, 34 GEO. WASH. INT'L L. REV. 17, 41–42 (2002) (discussing vacatur of New York Convention awards in the United States).

[205] *See* Yusuf Ahmed Alghanim & Sons v. Toys "R" Us, Inc., 126 F.3d 15, 21 (2d Cir. 1997). But see Industrial Risk Insurers v. M.A.N. Gutehoffnungshutte, 141 F.3d 1434, 1441–42 (11th Cir. 1998) (concluding that Article V of the New York Convention provides the exclusive grounds for vacating

2. Law Governing the Interpretation and Validity of the Arbitration Agreement

6.64 Choice of law issues at the vacatur stage resemble those at the stage of compelling arbitration.[206] The Supreme Court's *First Options* decision guides the analysis of choice of law on both "party" and "scope" questions. *First Options* instructed lower courts, "when deciding whether parties agreed to arbitrate a certain matter ... [to] apply ordinary state-law principles that govern the formation of contracts."[207] To be sure, courts have not always followed the message, and some continue to apply some version of federal common law.[208] Moreover, in cases involving awards rendered under the auspices of the New York Convention, a vacatur court applying the FAA Chapter 1 grounds for vacatur may apply federal common law to the question of enforcement of the agreement by or against nonsignatories.[209] Applying federal common law in this situation arguably promotes the New York Convention's interest in uniform treatment of Convention awards by avoiding subjecting such awards to the vagaries of fifty different sets of state rules.[210] Finally, the parties' valid choice of law may guide vacatur courts on issues of interpretation and validity.[211]

Convention awards). The Eleventh Circuit's decision to read the Article V grounds—which deal with nonrecognition and nonenforcement—as the bases for vacating a Convention award runs counter to the plain language of the Convention, and the decision of other circuits. For a comparison of the Eleventh Circuit's view with the view of other circuits, *see* Four Seasons Hotels and Resorts, B.V. v. Conscorcio Barr, S.A., 267 F. Supp. 2d 1335, 1340–42 (S.D. Fla. 2003). *See also* Jacada (Europe), Ltd. v. Int'l Mktg. Strategies, Inc., 401 F.3d 701, 709 (6th Cir. 2005) (applying FAA Chapter 1); Merrill Lynch, Pierce, Fenner & Smith, Inc. v Lauer, 49 F.3d 323 (7th Cir. 1995) (grounds for vacatur limited to Convention Article V). In the *Hall Street* case, *supra* note 200, the Supreme Court also cast doubt on the future of manifest disregard as a non-statutory ground for vacatur of awards subject to the Federal Arbitration Act. For further discussion, see James E. Berger & Charlene Sun, The Evolution of Judicial Review under the Federal Arbitration Act, 5 N.Y.U.J.L. & BUS. 745 (2009).

206 *See supra* notes 43–61 and accompanying text. Readers interested in this issue should review the lengthier treatment contained above, and in Chapter 1 of this book.

207 First Options of Chicago, Inc. v. Kaplan, 514 U.S. 938, 944 (1995); *see also In re* Engel (Refco, Inc.), 746 N.Y.S.2d 826, 833–34 (N.Y. Supreme Court, NY County 2002) (stating New York rule, which is same as federal rule).

208 *See* Gold v. Deutsche Aktiengesellschaft, 365 F.3d 144, 149 (2d Cir. 2004) (interpreting *First Options* to direct court to look to "generally accepted principles of contract law" rather than state law, and citing both New York and Second Circuit decisions to find those principles). *See also* Int'l Paper Co. v. Schwabedissen Maschinen & Anlagen GmbH, 206 F.3d 411 (4th Cir. 2000) (FAA and New York Convention "create a body of federal substantive law of arbitrability, applicable to any arbitration agreement within the coverage of the Act") (*quoting* Moses H. Cone Mem'l Hosp. v. Mercury Const. Corp., 460 U.S. 1, 24 (1983)).

209 *See In re* Arbitration between Halcot Navigation Ltd. Partnership and Stolt-Nielsen Trans. Group, BV, 491 F. Supp. 2d 413, 421–22 (S.D.N.Y. 2007). Note, however, that the arbitrators had applied federal law in the first instance in this case. *Id.*

210 *See e.g.*, Certain Underwriters at Lloyd's v. Argonaut Ins. Co., 500 F.3d 571, 579 (7th Cir. 2007); InterGen N.V. v. Grina, 344 F.3d 134, 144 (1st Cir. 2003); Smith/Enron Cogeneration L.P. v. Smith Cogeneration Int'l, Inc., 198 F.3d 88, 96 (2d Cir. 1999).

211 Telenor Mobile Comms. AS v. Storm LLC, 2007 WL 3274699, at *18 (S.D.N.Y. Nov. 2, 2007) (deciding independently whether the agent lacked the authority to sign the arbitration agreement, and determining question under New York law based on parties' choice). *See also* Encyclopaedia Universalis, S.A. v. Encyclopaedia Britannica, Inc., 2003 U.S. Dist. LEXIS 21850

3. *Kompetenz-Kompetenz* and Judicial Review upon Vacatur

Given the FAA's pro-arbitration policy, a party resisting vacatur will almost certainly argue that the court should defer to the arbitrators' judgment in favor of arbitral jurisdiction. However, the Supreme Court's *First Options* decision requires a more careful analysis. That decision directs vacatur courts to ask whether parties "clearly and unmistakably" agreed to arbitrate the question of arbitral jurisdiction.[212] Only if there is a clear and unmistakable agreement by the parties to this effect, should the vacatur court suppose that the parties intended for the arbitrators to enjoy primary authority to determine arbitral jurisdiction, at least in terms of who is bound by the arbitration agreement and whether the arbitration agreements itself is valid.[213] Absent such evidence, the vacatur court should assess the matter of arbitral jurisdiction independently.[214] This is consistent with the notion of severability, according to which questions of the existence and validity of the arbitration agreement are presumptively for the court to decide.[215] The situation may be different when it comes to the scope of the arbitration agreement. Courts would seem more likely to defer to the arbitrators on this issue than on their determination of the parties that are bound by the agreement to arbitrate. **6.65**

Broadly worded arbitration agreements may indicate consent to arbitrate arbitral jurisdiction.[216] But in the international commercial arbitration context, this question often comes down to the effect of incorporation into the agreement of one of the various institutional regimes' arbitral rules,[217] which are understood to authorize the arbitrators to rule on their own jurisdiction, whether this is expressed in terms of *Kompetenz-Kompetenz* or otherwise.[218] Absent some other limiting **6.66**

at *22–24 (S.D.N.Y. Dec. 4, 2003) (applying New York law as specified in general choice-of-law clause to claim impossibility of performance of British arbitration).

212 *See* First Options of Chicago v. Kaplan, 514 U.S. 938, 944–45 (1995); AT&T Technologies, Inc. v. Communications Workers of America, 475 U.S. 643, 649 (1986) ("Unless the parties clearly and unmistakably provide otherwise, the question of whether the parties agreed to arbitrate is to be decided by the court, not the arbitrator.").

213 *See First Options of Chicago*, 514 U.S. at 944. As we shall see below, the matter is more complicated than this brief discussion suggests. The existence of an agreement to arbitrate arbitrability is a prerequisite to *First Options* deference, and vacatur courts are unwilling to give the arbitrators final say on some questions, such as the validity of the agreement as applied to the dispute at hand.

214 *See First Options of Chicago*, 514 U.S. at 944.

215 For a discussion of severability, *see supra* notes 23–27 and accompanying text.

216 *Cf.* PaineWebber Inc. v. Bybyk, 81 F.3d 1193, 1200–02 (2d Cir.1996) (emphasizing broad scope of parties' arbitration agreement).

217 *Compare* Contec Corp. v. Remote Solution Co., Ltd., 398 F.3d 205, 208 (2d Cir. 2005) (relying in significant measure on the incorporation of the rules of the American Arbitration Association's rules in support of holding that parties agreed to arbitrate arbitral jurisdiction) *with* Shaw Group, Inc. v. Triplefine Int'l Corp., 322 F.3d 115, 123 (2d Cir. 2003) (reaching same result based on the International Chamber of Commerce Rules) *and* Telenor Mobile Comms. AS v. Storm LLC, 2007 U.S. Dist. Lexis 81454, at *45–49 (S.D.N.Y. Nov. 2, 2007) (holding that incorporation of the UNCITRAL Arbitration Rules into the agreement does not clearly and unmistakably indicate intent to submit the issue of arbitral jurisdiction to the arbitrators).

218 *See supra* note 134 and accompanying text.

language in the arbitration agreement,[219] incorporation of the ICC Rules,[220] the AAA rules,[221] or the National Association of Securities Dealers (NASD), now the Financial Industry Regulatory Authority (FINRA) rules[222] is thus likely to lead to a finding that the parties agreed to arbitrate arbitral jurisdiction.[223] By contrast, incorporation of the UNCITRAL Arbitration Rules may not constitute clear and unmistakable evidence of this intent.[224]

6.67 We first examine cases where the vacatur court is faced only with the question of deference to the arbitrators' jurisdictional determination. We then turn to the small number of cases in which both the arbitrators and a compelling court have already ruled in favor of arbitral jurisdiction. We will conclude by considering whether parties may waive jurisdictional objections by failing to raise them before compelling courts or the arbitrators.

6.68 *(a) Review of the arbitrators' decision as to the parties bound by the agreement* Upon a petition for vacatur, a party may argue that it is not a party to the arbitration agreement upon which the arbitrators grounded their jurisdiction. A vacatur court in New York will likely assess this question independently, in keeping with *First Options*.[225] Thus, courts have not accepted the reading of *First Options*

---

[219] If, for example, another part of the agreement has "'a specific clause assigning a certain decision' to another decisionmaker," Sunoco, Inc. (R&M) v. Honeywell Int'l, Inc., 2006 U.S. Dist. Lexis 11392, at *9 (S.D.N.Y. Mar. 21, 2006) (*quoting* Katz v. Feinberg, 290 F.3d 95, 97 (2d Cir. 2002), then a court will find that there is no clear and unmistakable evidence of an intent to arbitrate arbitral jurisdiction, notwithstanding *Kompetenz-Kompetenz* references in the arbitration agreement.

[220] *See* Shaw Group, Inc. v. Triplefine Int'l Corp., 322 F.3d 115, 123 (2d Cir. 2003) (ruling that incorporation of ICC Rules evidences clear and unmistakable intent to arbitrate arbitral jurisdiction); *see also* Apollo Computer, Inc. v. Berg, 886 F.2d 469, 472–73 (1st Cir. 1989) (reaching same decision).

[221] *See Contec Corp.*, 398 F.3d at 208 (relying in significant measure on the incorporation of the rules of the American Arbitration Association's rules in support of holding that parties agreed to arbitrate arbitral jurisdiction).

[222] *See* PaineWebber Inc. v. Bybyk, 81 F.3d 1193, 1199 (2d Cir. 1996) (holding that incorporation of the NASD rules indicates intent to arbitrate arbitral jurisdiction); Smith Barney Shearson Inc. v. Sacharow, 689 N.E.2d 884, 888 (N.Y. 1997) (same).

[223] The Draft Restatement rejects this approach. The Reporters' Notes on § 2–7 state: "The Restatement rejects the majority line of cases as based on a misinterpretation of the institutional rules being applied."

[224] Telenor Mobile Comms. AS v. Storm LLC, 2007 U.S. Dist. Lexis 81454, at *45–49 (S.D.N.Y. Nov. 2, 2007) (holding that incorporation of the UNCITRAL Arbitration Rules into the agreement does not clearly and unmistakably indicate intent to submit the issue of arbitral jurisdiction to the arbitrators). The district court distinguished the UNCITRAL rules from the ICC and AAA rules by noting that the UNCITRAL rules "only allow arbitrators to rule on *objections* to [their] authority." *Id.* at *47.

[225] The leading case in the Second Circuit is Orion Shipping & Trading Co. v. Eastern States Petroleum Corp., 312 F.2d 299, 300–01 (2d Cir. 1963) (refusing to confirm an award issued against a nonsignatory to the container contract and stating that the question was "not within the province of the arbitrator himself but only of the court"). Though an older decision, *Orion Shipping* continues to guide assessments of commercial arbitration awards. *See* Compagnie Noga D'Importation et D'Exportation S.A. v. Russian Federation, 361 F.3d 676, 686–87 (2d Cir. 2004) (referring to *Orion Shipping* in context of determining whether party challenging enforcement of award was party to

offered by some commentators who argue that it limits inquiry on vacatur to the question of whether there is *prima facie* evidence of "the simple existence of some written 'clause' or 'provision' to arbitrate."[226] In other words, most vacatur courts examine whether the party resisting the award agreed to arbitrate *something* with the party seeking to have the award upheld.[227]

The district court's decision in *Sea Containers* is a good example of this trend.[228] **6.69**
There, the court reviewed at length the facts of the dispute and the arbitrators' ruling. It first determined that, notwithstanding the arbitrators' ruling, an agreement signed by SCL (the party requesting vacatur) did not incorporate an arbitration agreement from another agreement not signed by SCL. The court also considered whether SCL had implicitly consented to arbitration based on its conduct during the arbitration. On this issue, the court acknowledged that the evidence was somewhat ambiguous. However, the court concluded that the "ambiguities at this stage of the controversy cut in favor" of vacating the award. In sum, the district court's reasoning gives the impression that while the arbitrators' decision was relevant, the matter was for the court to decide more or less independently.[229]

arbitration agreement); District Council No. 9 v. APC Painting, Inc., 272 F. Supp. 2d 229, 238 (S.D.N.Y. 2003) (in context of labor arbitration decision, discussing the Second Circuit's approach to commercial arbitration); In the Matter of the Application to Confirm an Arbitration Award by Chios Charm Shipping Co., 1994 U.S. Dist. Lexis 4517, at *7 (S.D.N.Y. Apr. 11, 1994) (stating that "respondents *incorrectly* assert that the arbitrations have the sole authority to determine who is bound by an arbitral award" and citing *Orion Shipping*); Transrol Navagacao S.A. v. Redir ekommanditselskaber Merc Scandia XXIX, 782 F. Supp. 848, 850 (S.D.N.Y. 1991) (referring to *Orion Shipping* but determining that party's conduct during the arbitration and prior litigation in French courts implied its agreement to arbitrate). Even when not citing *Orion Shipping*, courts in New York independently review the arbitrators' determination of who the parties to the agreement were. *See, e.g.*, Stolt Tankers, Inc. v. Marcus Oil & Chemical, 2001 U.S. Dist. Lexis 19750, at *8–11 (S.D.N.Y. Nov. 28, 2001) (independently reviewing at length whether party challenging confirmation of award was party to arbitration agreement and concluding it was); In the Matter of Arbitration Between Promotora de Navegacion and Sea Containers, 131 F. Supp. 2d 412, 425 (S.D.N.Y. 2000) (vacating award as to party that court independently determined was not a party to the arbitration agreement, despite arbitrators' contrary conclusion). Decisions in other circuits are consistent with this approach. *See, e.g.*, MCI Telecommunications Corp. v. Exalon Indus., Inc., 138 F.3d 426 (1st Cir. 1998) (labeling claim that "nothing is subject to arbitration because there is no agreement to arbitrate … the mother of arbitrability questions").

[226] The quote comes from an article by Professor Alan Rau disagreeing with the *prima facie* reading of *First Options*. *See* Alan Scott Rau, *The Arbitrability Question Itself*, 10 Am. Rev. Int'l Arb. 287, 303 (1999). *But see* Thomas E. Carbonneau, *Beyond Trilogies: A New Bill of Rights and Law Practice Through the Contract of Arbitration*, 6 Am. Rev. Int'l Arb. 1, 21 (1995) (arguing that under *First Options* the presence of a written statement about arbitration is enough to trigger substantial deference to arbitrators on the existence of an agreement between the parties).

[227] Rau, supra note 226, at 312. *But see* Smit, *supra* note 16, at 396 (concluding that because of federal pro-arbitration policy, one could say that "arbitrators named pursuant to the arbitration agreement will have the authority to decide" whether the parties have agreed to arbitrate anything at all).

[228] In the Matter of Arbitration Between Promotora de Navegacion and Sea Containers, 131 F. Supp. 2d 412, 417–19 (S.D.N.Y. 2000).

[229] Citing an earlier Second Circuit decision, the ruling aimed to protect the principle that "a party is bound by an arbitral award only where it has agreed to arbitrate." This language comes from the Second Circuit decision in Gvozdenovic v. United Air Lines, 933 F.2d 1100, 1105

6.70 As in *Sea Containers*, many cases involve the enforcement of an arbitration agreement by or against a nonsignatory. Cases compelling arbitration suggest that courts will more likely enforce an agreement in favor of a nonsignatory than against a non-signatory.[230] When confronted with the issue, vacatur courts may follow similar reasoning, as occurred in *Orion Shipping & Trading Co. v. Eastern States Petroleum Corp.*[231] There, the Second Circuit refused to confirm an award issued against a nonsignatory to the container contract, reasoning that on the facts of the case the nonsignatory "was clearly not a party to the arbitration proceeding."[232] Federal law will likely govern this question.[233]

6.71 Of course, *First Options* recognized the possibility that parties could agree to arbitrate the question of whether one of them ever agreed to arbitrate, though it found that it had not occurred on the facts of the case.[234] Still, vacatur courts will not defer to the arbitrators simply because the party requesting confirmation shows that an agreement to arbitrate the underlying dispute existed between it and someone else. Courts may, however, refuse to reexamine the issue of jurisdiction if the party resisting the award appeared to acquiesce in the arbitrators' authority during the arbitral process. The party requesting vacatur has acquiesced when it has "active[ly] and voluntar[ily] participat[ed] in the arbitration" and has never "objected to the process, refused to arbitrate or made any attempt to seek judicial relief."[235]

(2d Cir. 1991); *see also* In the Matter of Arbitration Between Promotora de Navegacion and Sea Containers, 131 F. Supp. 2d 412, 423 (S.D.N.Y. 2000) ("The analysis of SCL's claim that it was not a party to the arbitration was guided by the principle that arbitration is a creature of contract …").

230 *See* Alan Scott Rau, *Arbitral Jurisdiction and the Dimensions of "Consent,"* Univ. of Texas Law: Law and Economics Research Paper No. 103 47–48 (2007), *available at* SSRN http:// ssrn.com/abstract=1081616 (documenting such cases); *see also supra* note 83–87 (citing cases dealing with a similar issue at stage of compelling arbitration).

231 Orion Shipping & Trading Co. v. Eastern States Petroleum Corp., 312 F.2d 299, 300–01 (2d Cir. 1963) (refusing to confirm an award issued against a nonsignatory to the container contract and stating that the question was "not within the province of the arbitrator himself but only of the court"); *see also* In the Matter of the Arbitration Between Halcot Navigation Ltd. Partnership and Stolt-Nielsen Trans. Group, BV, 491 F. Supp. 2d 413, 421 (S.D.N.Y. 2007) (agreeing with arbitrators' ruling that a nonsignatory could compel signatory to arbitrate with it) (*citing* Choctaw Generation Ltd. Partnership v. American Home Assurance Co., 271 F.3d 403, 406 (2d Cir. 2001)).

232 *Orion Shipping & Trading Co.*, 312 F.2d at 300–01.

233 *See supra* notes 82–83 and accompanying text (discussing choice of law on issue of binding nonsignatories to arbitration agreements).

234 First Options of Chicago v. Kaplan, 514 U.S. 938, 946 (1995). The Second Circuit in dictum in a labor arbitration case has acknowledged the possibility that parties might clearly and unmistakably agree to have an arbitrator decide if "they ever entered into an arbitration agreement." Abram Landau Real Estate v. Bevona, 123 F.3d 69, 73 (2d Cir. 1997).

235 Gvozdenovic v. United Air Lines, 933 F.2d 1100, 1105 (2d Cir. 1991); *cf.* First Options of Chicago v. Kaplan, 514 U.S. 938, 946 (1995) ("[M]erely arguing the arbitrability issue to an arbitrator does not indicate a clear willingness to arbitrate that issue.").

(b) Review of arbitrators' determination of scope of arbitration agreement The FAA expressly recognizes "scope" questions as grounds for vacatur.[236] On questions of scope, much of the argument at the vacatur stage centers on whether the parties have "clearly and unmistakably" submitted these questions to the arbitrators.[237] Nevertheless, a party challenging the arbitrators' decision on grounds of scope has to "overcome a powerful presumption that the arbitral body acted within its powers."[238] Though American courts do not use the words "*Kompetenz-Kompetenz*" when invoking this presumption, one can characterize the presumption as an American version of the doctrine.[239] Obviously, the pro-arbitration presumption is at its most powerful—and will not even need to be invoked—when parties have expressly agreed under *First Options* to arbitrate the scope of arbitral jurisdiction.[240] **6.72**

If a vacatur court satisfies itself that the parties intended for the arbitrators to decide arbitral jurisdiction, its review of that decision will be highly deferential, and the presumption in favor of the arbitration of disputes will likely carry the day.[241] The vacatur court will limit itself to the grounds for vacatur under FAA **6.73**

[236] *See* 9 U.S.C. § 10(a) (2000) (allowing vacatur when arbitrators "exceeded" their powers).

[237] *See, e.g.*, Telenor Mobile Comms. AS v. Storm LLC, 2007 U.S. Dist. Lexis 81454, at *45–49 (S.D.N.Y. Nov. 2, 2007) (holding that incorporation of the UNCITRAL Arbitration Rules into the agreement does not clearly and unmistakably indicate intent to submit the issue of arbitral jurisdiction to the arbitrators).

[238] Parsons & Whittemore Overseas Co., Inc. v. Société Generale de L'industrie du Papier (Ratka), 508 F.2d 969, 976 (2d Cir. 1974) (identifying presumption at stage of recognition and enforcement); *Telenor Mobile Comms. AS*, 2007 U.S. Dist. Lexis 81454, at *45–49 (noting that *Parsons* presumption applies at vacatur stage).

[239] Professor John Barcelo makes a similar argument with respect to the function of American courts' presumptions at the stage of compelling arbitration. *See* John J. Barcelo III, *Who Decides the Arbitrators' Jurisdiction? Separability and Competence-Competence in Transnational Perspective*, 36 Vand. J. Transnat'l L. 1115, 1133–34 (2003).

[240] Though not at the vacatur stage, Ryan, Beck & Co, LLC v. Fakih nicely illustrates the post-*First Options'* distinction between the question of scope and the question of who are parties to the agreement, discussed in the previous subsection. *See* 268 F. Supp. 2d 210 (E.D.N.Y. 2003). One party, Ryan Beck, acknowledged that it had agreed to arbitrate some disputes with Fakih in a pending arbitration, but disputed the scope of the arbitration agreement. *Id.* at 220. The court concluded that by incorporating the NASD arbitration rules into its agreement with Fakih, Beck had agreed to arbitrate arbitral jurisdiction. Beck disputed, however, the claim that it had ever agreed to arbitrate anything with Reich. The court stated, "[u]nder these circumstances, the parties' quarrel as to arbitrability may not be deferred to the arbitrators." *Id.* at 224.

[241] *See, e.g.*, In the Matter of the Arbitration Between Halcot Navigation Ltd. Partnership and Stolt-Nielsen Trans. Group, BV, 491 F. Supp. 2d 413, 421 (S.D.N.Y. 2007) (finding that party requesting vacatur had agreed to arbitrate arbitral jurisdiction, and limiting review to grounds set forth in NY Convention and FAA Chapter 1); Vail-Ballou Press, Inc. v. Graphic Comms. Int'l Union/Int'l Brotherhood of Teamsters, Local 898-M, 480 F. Supp. 2d 568, 573 (N.D.N.Y. 2007) (holding that, because Vail-Ballou had agreed to arbitrate arbitral jurisdiction, it "is bound by the arbitrator's decision that the dispute was indeed arbitrable unless vacatur is warranted under the limited circumstances set forth in § 10(a)"); Sunoco, Inc. (R&M) v. Honeywell Int'l, Inc., 2006 U.S. Dist. Lexis 11392, at *9 (S.D.N.Y. Mar. 21, 2006) (determining that parties had agreed to arbitrate the scope of arbitrators' jurisdiction, and applying limited FAA Chapter 1 grounds of review); In the Matter of the Arbitration of Eric L. Goldstein, 2001 U.S. Dist. Lexis

Chapter 1, which the *First Options* Court described as requiring courts to give "considerable leeway to the arbitrator." These grounds, the Court said, permit vacatur only in "certain narrow circumstances."[242] Thus, even though the grounds for vacatur include "excess of authority," a vacatur court that decides the parties intended to arbitrate arbitral jurisdiction will likely resolve doubts in favor of arbitral jurisdiction.[243]

6.74 The matter is more complicated when the vacatur court concludes under *First Options* that it can "independently" review the propriety of arbitral jurisdiction.[244] This review, while "independent," may very likely still bear something of the pro-arbitration presumptions of federal common law and the FAA. We should expect that these presumptions may lead a court, even when acting de novo, to decide close questions of the scope of arbitral jurisdiction in favor of arbitration.[245] Put differently, a court that is independently reviewing arbitral jurisdiction may nevertheless inject a "weak" dose of *Kompetenz-Kompetenz* deference.[246]

6.75 This is not to say that courts will always defer to arbitrators on the scope of arbitral jurisdiction, or that the pro-arbitration bias will invariably carry the day. For example, courts may find that the arbitrators exceeded their powers by including a provision in the award that is outside the scope of their powers. In one Sixth Circuit case, for example, the arbitrators attempted to protect the validity of their award by including a fallback clause in it. (A *fallback clause* provides that if a court invalidates one remedy in the award, another remedy will take its place.) The Sixth Circuit refused to give effect to the clause.[247]

6.76 *(c) Review of arbitral determinations of the validity of the arbitration agreement* It appears from the cases that, when parties believe that they have a colorable claim that an arbitration agreement is invalid, they are more likely to raise it in attempts to head off arbitration at the outset than in motions for vacatur. Therefore, the

---

7102, at *19 (S.D.N.Y. May 25, 2001) (determining that the parties had agreed to arbitrate arbitral jurisdiction by virtue of the incorporation of NASD rules and deferring to the arbitrators' determination under Chapter 1 of the FAA).

[242] First Options of Chicago v. Kaplan, 514 U.S. 938, 943 (1995).

[243] For a description of the excess of authority ground as narrow, *see* Kerr-McGee Refining Corp. v. M.T. Triumph, 924 F.2d 467, 471 (2d Cir. 1991) (stating that the excess of authority ground is due the "narrowest of readings") (internal quotations omitted).

[244] *See* Telenor Mobile Comms. AS v. Storm LLC, 2007 U.S. Dist. Lexis 81454, at *45–49 (S.D.N.Y. Nov. 2, 2007) (concluding that a court "must make an independent determination of the arbitrability of the dispute").

[245] *See* Kozera v. Westchester-Fairfield Chapter of Nat'l Elec. Contractors Ass'n, Inc., 909 F.2d 48, 53 (2d Cir. 1990) ("The presumed authority of an arbitrator to resolve issues is broad, and courts expansively interpret the scope of an arbitrator's delegated authority by resolving doubts in favor of arbitrability.").

[246] *See* Katz v. Feinberg, 167 F. Supp. 2d 556, 566 (S.D.N.Y. 2001), *aff'd*, 290 F.3d 95 (2d Cir. 2002) (ruling that arbitrability was for court to decide, but then immediately employing the presumption in favor of arbitration to evaluate the issue).

[247] *See* NCR Corp. v. SAC-Co., Inc., 43 F.3d 1076, 1081 (6th Cir. 1995).

comments that follow identify the possibilities more than they report actual patterns of decision. We will reserve for the moment the question of whether vacatur courts will defer on validity questions to a court that compelled arbitration in the same case.

Here we assume the matter did not arise at the stage of compelling arbitration. **6.77**
When a party then argues at the vacatur stage that the arbitration agreement is invalid, the court may choose to decide the matter independently. (It will certainly do so where the party argues that the underlying statutory claim is one that cannot legally be submitted to arbitration, i.e., is not "arbitrable" in the strict sense of the term.) One should shy away from speaking about independence versus deference in this setting as if the two were neatly separated, opposed categories. As we shall see, there appears to be a continuum from aggressive, thorough, and therefore fairly independent review down to mild and deferential review that invokes a pro-arbitration presumption to tip the scale on close questions.

(I) SEVERABILITY AT THE VACATUR STAGE

One way to explain the tendency of vacatur courts to review independently the **6.78**
validity of the arbitration agreement is through the notion of severability,[248] and vacatur courts do seem to take severability seriously.[249] Thus, severability may serve much the same function at the vacatur stage as it does at the stage of compelling arbitration. Parties should be aware, however, that a vacatur court might see itself as performing a crucial "backstop" role,[250] and be tempted to go further than it would when intervening prior to the arbitration. For example, though the Supreme Court suggested in *PacifiCare* that a court should defer on close issues,

[248] *See* Telenor Mobile Comms. AS, 2007 WL 3274699, at *18 (deciding independently whether the agent lacked the authority to sign the arbitration agreement).

[249] *See, e.g.*, Rintin Corp., S.A. v. Domar, Ltd., 476 F.3d 1254, 1259 (11th Cir. 2007) (relying on *Buckeye Check Cashing* for the proposition that the challenge to the validity of the container contract is for arbitrators to decide, even if that challenge would render the contract void, as opposed to voidable); Theis Research, Inc. v. Brown & Bain, 400 F.3d 659, 666 (9th Cir. 2004) (concluding that a claim that container contract was void ab initio was for arbitrators to decide, and that the district court correctly deferred to their judgment); Ferro Corp. v. Garrison, 142 F.3d 926, 938–39 (6th Cir. 1998) (overturning a district court that vacated an arbitration award on the basis of fraudulent inducement of container contract); *see also* Fielding v. Doctor's Assocs., Inc., 2002 WL 32173569, at *2 n.2 (D.Conn. Mar. 30, 2002) (noting in dictum that the party's challenge of fraud went to contract and was a question for the arbitrators to decide). They do not always do so. *See, e.g.*, Ferro Corp. v. Garrison Industries, Inc., 927 F. Supp. 234, 241–44 (N.D. Ohio 1996) (vacating the award because the arbitrators incorrectly determined that they had jurisdiction; "Given that this Court declared the CMA void ab initio, none of the provisions contained within it—including the arbitration clause—remained valid or enforceable."). The Sixth Circuit reversed the district court in this case. Ferro Corp. v. Garrison Industries, Inc., 142 F.3d 926 (6th Cir. 1998). This undoubtedly is the correct result.

[250] *Cf.* Mitsubishi Motors Corp. v. Soler Chrysler-Plymouth, 473 U.S. 614, 637 n.19 (1985) (suggesting that a court may have an important role after arbitration in determining whether "the choice-of-forum and choice-of-law clauses operated in tandem as a prospective waiver of a party's right to pursue statutory remedies for antitrust violations").

allowing arbitrators to rule in the first instance on questions over which they have greater expertise,[251] this does not necessarily mean that a court should not take a somewhat closer look if the same question comes up again on a vacatur motion. The Eleventh Circuit has even suggested in dictum that a vacatur court should also be willing to decide independently a challenge to the container contract if it necessarily also calls into question the existence of the arbitration agreement.[252] This dictum is based on the famous footnote in *Buckeye* which suggested that a court might at the outset refuse to compel arbitration where the container contract was a forgery or for some other reason never came into existence.[253] A fortiori, when a party argues that there never was an offer or acceptance of the arbitration agreement in particular, a court will be justified in independently assuring itself of the agreement's existence before confirming the award.[254] That is of course fully consistent with severability thinking. All such "existence" questions, however, are distinct from questions of the validity of the agreement, which is our focus here.

(II) DEFERENCE ON VALIDITY OF THE ARBITRATION AGREEMENT

6.79 The question of validity of the arbitration agreement is a proper ground for vacatur, and it would not be inconsistent with the principle of severability for a court to exercise full review over the arbitrators' rulings on such issues. In practice, the degree of independent judgment that a vacatur court actually exercises over such questions may vary, however, with the type of challenge involved. By "type of challenge," we mean nothing more than the asserted ground of invalidity. For example, a vacatur court may exercise more deference to the arbitrators when a party argues that the arbitration agreement was the product of unconscionable dealing than when a party argues that the very existence of the arbitration agreement violates public policy.

6.80 Some courts have ruled that "whether the terms and conditions of an arbitration agreement are themselves unconscionable" is a matter for the arbitrators to decide.[255] Yet, vacatur courts are not always comfortable deferring to arbitrators

---

[251] *See* PacifiCare Health Sys. v. Bock, 538 U.S. 401 (2003) (question of whether arbitration agreement excluded punitive damages, and was therefore unenforceable under RICO, was uncertain and thus was a question for the arbitrators in the first instance).

[252] *See* Rintin Corp., S.A. v. Domar, Ltd., 476 F.3d 1254, 1259 n.3 (11th Cir. 2007) (relying on *Buckeye Check Cashing* to recognize in dictum the possibility of entertaining a challenge to the existence of the contract, and therefore the existence of the arbitration agreement, at the vacatur stage).

[253] *See* Buckeye Check Cashing, Inc. v. Cardegna, 546 U.S. 440, 444 n.1 (2006).

[254] *See* Real Color Displays, Inc. v. Universal Applied Technologies Corp., 950 F. Supp. 714, 718–19 (E.D.N.C. 1997) (engaging in straightforward contract analysis to determine if an agreement to arbitrate existed).

[255] *In re* Oakwood Mobile Homes, Inc., 987 S.W.2d 571, 573 n.3 (Tex. 1999); *see* Smith v. Gateway, Inc., 2002 WL 1728615, at *3 (Tex. App.-Austin July 26, 2002) (deferring with very little examination to arbitrators' ruling on "substantive unconscionability").

even on an issue such as this. Thus, a district court in California refused to stay arbitration and vacate an interim ICC jurisdictional award only after exploring at length the merits of one party's arguments that the arbitration agreement was unconscionable.[256] While this decision suggests fairly independent review, vacatur courts, even while exercising what purports to be "independent" judgment, may display a "healthy regard for the federal policy favoring arbitration."[257] Thus, they will at the least resolve close questions in favor of arbitral jurisdiction, which is a form of mild deference to the arbitrators' competence.

Other validity questions invite even more independent review by a vacatur court. *Drayer v. Kramer* is an example of this latter type of case.[258] There, a party argued that the arbitration agreement's very existence violated a significant public policy of the United States, namely, the Sherman Antitrust Act.[259] In particular, it argued that the requirement in the Constitution of the New York Stock Exchange that members agree to arbitration with employees violated the antitrust laws.[260] The Second Circuit affirmed the district court's confirmation of the award, but only after finding, upon lengthy independent review, that there was no illegality.[261] **6.81**

(III) DEFERENCE TO ARBITRATORS ON "ARBITRABILITY-RELATED" ISSUES

We have already introduced the notion of "arbitrability-related" issues. This section explains the concept in greater detail and explores whether vacatur courts defer to arbitrators on this type of issue. As noted, the term *arbitrability*, as used here, refers to the question of whether the law that applies to the arbitration agreement forbids arbitration of the underlying cause of action.[262] To determine **6.82**

---

256 *See* Poponin v. Virtual Pro, Inc., 2006 WL 2691418, at *5–11 (N.D. Cal. Sept. 20, 2006).

257 Real Color Displays, Inc. v. Universal Applied Technologies Corp., 1998 U.S. App. LEXIS 27791, at *8 (4th Cir. Oct. 30, 1998) (*quoting* Moses H. Cone Mem'l Hosp. v. Mercury Const. Corp., 460 U.S. 1, 24 (1983)).

258 572 F.2d 348 (2d Cir. 1978). As will be seen, however, the matter is more complicated if a compelling court has already ruled on the jurisdictional issue; there may be reasons for the vacatur court to defer to the compelling court in this situation.

259 *Id.* at 359–60 (2d Cir. 1978). In distinction, in an as-applied challenge, the party requesting vacatur argues that public policy precludes deciding a particular cause of action through arbitration. *See infra* note 259 and accompanying text. In *Drayer*, no one argued the underlying claim was nonarbitrable.

260 *Id.* at 353.

261 *Id.* at 359–60.

262 For a discussion of "arbitrability," as used here, *see* Chapter 7.D of this book. Commentators sometimes use the phrase "substantive inarbitrability" or "the limits imposed by mandatory law" to refer to this question. *See* Thomas Carbonneau, Cases and Materials on Commercial Arbitration 172 (1997) (distinguishing between "substantive and contractual inarbitrability"); Rau, *supra* note 226 at 308 (referring to "mandatory law"). Of course, the importance of this ground for vacating an award based on federal causes of action has lessened as the U.S. Supreme Court has eroded the nonarbitrability doctrine. *See* Mitsubishi Motors Corp. v. Soler Chrysler-Plymouth, 473 U.S. 614, 637 n.19 (1985) (suggesting that the court may have an important role after arbitration in determining whether "the choice-of-forum and choice-of-law clauses operated in tandem as a prospective waiver of a party's right to pursue statutory remedies for antitrust violations").

whether an underlying right is not arbitrable, courts look to the public policies that support the legal right, asking whether they are inconsistent with arbitral resolution.[263] There are reasons to think that courts—as protectors of statutory policy—will exercise independent review at all stages of this question.[264] Here, we are concerned with challenges to jurisdiction that are merely "arbitrability-related."

6.83 "Arbitrability-related" challenges to arbitral jurisdiction rest on claims that the law applicable to the dispute incorporates policies that limit what the arbitrator can do when resolving the underlying dispute. This is not the same as a straightforward "arbitrability" problem. For example, the antitrust laws create a right to sue for damages that arise from an unlawful horizontal refusal to deal.[265] Such a claim would be "arbitrable": the arbitrator can resolve the dispute between the individual claimant and the individual defendant. But, do the antitrust laws permit *classwide* arbitration of the same claim? This latter question is "arbitrability-related." Similarly, some causes of action permit the prevailing party to obtain attorneys' fees. While the underlying cause of action is arbitrable, a vacatur court may have to consider the propriety of an award that refuses to shift fees based upon a limitation in the arbitration agreement. This question is likewise "arbitrability-related." Though decided at the stage of compelling arbitration, the *PacifiCare* case also raised an arbitrability-related question, namely whether an agreement outlawing the award of punitive damages in arbitration is consistent with a statutory guarantee of treble damages for losses suffered.[266]

6.84 The law is not clear on whether courts will defer to the arbitrators on arbitrability-related issues. The Court's guidance on this matter is mixed. On the one hand, *Mitsubishi Motors* may suggest independent review is appropriate in order to make sure arbitration does not undermine important public policies.[267] On the other hand, the *Mitsubishi* Court also strongly suggested that arbitration merely shifts the forum for determining substantive rights, suggesting courts should merely ensure arbitrators take cognizance of the relevant concerns.[268] *PacifiCare* arguably contemplates judicial review after the arbitration; it merely labeled the question of whether a court should determine the arbitrability-related issue "premature" at the stage of compelling arbitration.[269] Still, some commentators have read *PacifiCare* to suggest that review at the vacatur stage will be "less … than *de novo*."[270]

[263] *See, e.g.*, Wilko v. Swan, 346 U.S. 427, 438 (1953).

[264] *See* Chapter 7.D.2 of this book.

[265] *See* Klor's, Inc. v. Broadway-Hale Stores, Inc., 359 U.S. 207 (U.S. 1959).

[266] PacifiCare Health Sys. v. Book, 538 U.S. 401, 406–07 (2003) (deciding that the question of whether an arbitration agreement excluded punitive damages, and was therefore unenforceable as contrary to the federal RICO statutory regime, was a question for the arbitrators in the first instance).

[267] *See, e.g., Mitsubishi Motors Corp.*, 473 U.S. at 637 n.19.

[268] *Id.* at 638–39.

[269] *PacifiCare Health Sys.*, 538 U.S. at 406–07.

[270] Rau, *supra* note 9 at 104 n.277.

The approach of lower courts suggests that review of such issues on vacatur will in fact be less than de novo, though nevertheless searching. Consider first the issue of the permissibility of classwide arbitration. The First Circuit, in dicta in a case at the stage of compelling arbitration, strongly suggested that a court should closely review an arbitrators' determination on the permissibility of classwide arbitration.[271] The Court, however, did not suggest that the arbitrators' ruling should be irrelevant. On the side of deferential review, however, one can point to a recent decision of the Southern District of New York. There, the district court reviewed in a seemingly perfunctory way the arbitrators' determination that classwide arbitration would be consistent with New York law, reasoning that "arbitrators are well situated to answer" such a question and merely ensuring that they had not committed an "egregious" mistake of law.[272] Consider, as well, the Eighth Circuit's disposition of a closely related scenario: preclusion of attorney-fee shifting in the arbitration agreement. Arguably, an arbitration clause limiting (or requiring) attorney-fee shifting or certain other remedies is invalid as applied to a dispute that is based on a statute that allows for (or prohibits) such a mechanism. The Eighth Circuit suggested that the arbitrators not only have jurisdiction over such a question, but also at the vacatur stage deserve deference as to it.[273] **6.85**

(d) Deference in cases where a court compelling arbitration has ruled on the jurisdictional issue The cases are too few and too unclear to support a conclusion as to **6.86** whether and to what extent a vacatur court will entertain challenges to arbitral

[271] Kristian v. Comcast Corp., 446 F.3d 25, 45 (1st Cir. 2006) (reading *PacifiCare* for the proposition that a compelling court should allow the arbitrator to first determine the scope of the arbitration agreement and its enforceability in light of statutory policy, after which a reviewing court may "decide in light of [the arbitrators'] construction [of the agreement] whether the arbitration agreement is enforceable"). The First Circuit stated:

> Implicit in the *PacifiCare* analysis is the proposition that if the remedies limitation in the arbitration agreement posed a clear conflict with the remedies available in the RICO statute, that clear conflict would pose a question of arbitrability. In other words, in the face of a vindication of statutory rights claim based on such a clear conflict, the court would decide the question of the enforceability of the arbitration clause in the first instance.

The First Circuit's reference to "clear conflict" suggests that a reviewing court should perhaps defer to the arbitrators' determination on ambiguous conflicts. This may be too strong a reading of the case, however, since, in a later discussion, the First Circuit suggested that the "clarity" of the conflict related only to whether to send the matter to the arbitrators first—in other words, ambiguous, possible conflicts between arbitral resolution and statutory policy go to the arbitrator first. *Id.* at 50.

[272] JSC Surgutneftegaz v. President and Fellows of Harvard College, 2007 WL 3019234, at *2–3 (S.D.N.Y. Oct. 11, 2007).

[273] *See* Bob Schultz Motors, Inc. v. Kawasaki Motors Corp., U.S.A., 334 F.3d 721, 727 (8th Cir. 2002). The Eighth Circuit believed its approach in *Kawasaki* to be consistent with the First Circuit's approach. But in Thompson v. Irwin Home Equity Corp., 300 F.3d 88, 92 (1st Cir. 2002), the First Circuit said, "[a]rbitration is the correct *initial forum* for the Thompsons to air their objection to the attorney's fees provisions in the arbitration agreement." *Id.* (emphasis added). This says nothing about the standard of review at the vacatur stage.

jurisdiction where essentially the same challenge was made, and rejected, at the earlier stage of a court's compelling arbitration. The few available cases paint a mixed picture.

6.87 There is precedent to suggest that vacatur courts should defer heavily to compelling courts in the same jurisdiction. In *B-S Steel of Kansas*, a party challenged an award on validity and scope grounds.[274] The district court had compelled arbitration in an earlier ruling. The district court labeled its prior ruling the "law of the case," suggesting it was precluded from reconsidering the matter.[275] At the same time, the court reasoned in the alternative that even if it could reconsider the matter, the dispute at hand fell within the scope of a valid arbitration agreement.[276]

6.88 The Second Circuit's decision in *Orion Shipping* displays a similar ambiguity, though it also strongly suggests a vacatur court should defer to a compelling court in the same jurisdiction. This case involved an issue of the proper parties to an arbitration agreement.[277] In 1960, the Second Circuit compelled Eastern Panama to submit to arbitration.[278] By 1963, the arbitrators' award was before the Second Circuit again, this time on a motion to vacate. The arbitrator had determined that not only Eastern Panama, but a related corporation, Signal, was liable to Orion. The Second Circuit rejected the arbitrators' decision to find Signal liable, reasoning that its 1960 decision made "clear that the liability of Eastern Panama *only* was to be determined by the arbitrator."[279] While this statement suggests deference to its earlier determination, the Second Circuit did not state that its prior ruling was preclusive. Moreover, the parties agreed that the issue was one for the courts.[280] Therefore, while *Orion Shipping* strongly suggests that a vacatur court should show some deference to a compelling court (at least one in the same jurisdiction), it does not clarify what the proper degree of deference is.

6.89 On the other hand, instances can be found where vacatur courts show little or no deference to compelling courts. In one telling case, a federal district court in Louisiana, upon vacatur, fully revisited a claim of invalidity of the arbitration agreement due to lack of consideration even though both the arbitrators and the court itself (on a previous motion to compel arbitration) had already considered

[274] B-S Steel of Kansas, Inc. v. Texas Industries, Inc., 321 F. Supp. 2d 1214, 1218 (D. Kan. 2004) (concluding, on motion to vacate, that ruling on motion to compel arbitration was law of the case).

[275] *Id.* at 1218 (refusing to reexamine the validity and scope of the arbitration agreement).

[276] *Id.* at 1218–19 (concluding, on motion to vacate, that ruling on motion to compel arbitration was law of the case, but also reasoning in the alternative).

[277] Orion Shipping & Trading Co., Inc. v. Eastern States Petroleum Corp. of Panama, S.A., 312 F.2d 299 (2d Cir. 1963).

[278] *Id.*

[279] *Id.* at 300 (emphasis added).

[280] *Id.* at 301.

the matter.[281] The court did not state that it was using de novo review, but it did examine the matter at some length, though it ultimately refused to vacate the award.[282]

(e) Waiver of jurisdictional objections by failure to raise them before vacatur Finally, we should consider briefly the situation where a party has participated in the compulsion stage or at the arbitration without raising certain jurisdictional objections. Consider, for example, the situation where a party objected *only* that it was not a party to the agreement at the stage of compelling arbitration and before the arbitrators. It then comes before a vacatur court, arguing that the dispute at hand lay outside the scope of the agreement. A vacatur court is likely to conclude that the failure to raise the jurisdictional objection earlier resulted in waiver. We have already seen this occur when a party objects that it was not a signatory to the agreement.[283] The policy concerns that drive waiver in that setting could well apply to other jurisdictional objections: waiver prevents sandbagging and foot-dragging to slow the speed of arbitral dispute resolution. **6.90**

4. Deference to Arbitrators on Forum-Specific Issues

With respect to forum-specific issues, vacatur courts confront the same basic policy concerns that courts may be faced with when asked to compel arbitration,[284] and they appear to react in much the same way. The few cases on the subject involve the familiar issue of res judicata and statutes of limitations. With respect to res judicata, a federal court once again is far more likely to defer to an arbitrator's decision about the effect of prior arbitral awards than about the effect of prior court judgments.[285] Specifically, the Second Circuit reviews decisions concerning the preclusive effect of arbitral awards according to a "manifest disregard of the law" standard.[286] **6.91**

As for statutes of limitations, some courts distinguish between limitations periods applicable to the underlying cause of action ("time limits on claims")[287] and **6.92**

[281] *See* Tassin v. Ryan's Family Steakhouse, Inc., 509 F. Supp. 2d 585, 592 (M.D.La. 2007).

[282] *Id.* (M.D.La. 2007).

[283] *See supra* note 235 and accompanying text.

[284] *See supra* notes 98–100 and accompanying text.

[285] *Compare* Nat'l Union Fire Ins. Co. v. Belco Petrol. Corp., 88 F.3d 129, 135 (2d Cir. 1996) (deferring to arbitrators on effect of prior arbitral award) *with* Aircraft Braking Sys. Corp. v. Local 856, 97 F.3d 155, 159, 161 (6th Cir. 1996) ("Arbitrators are not free to ignore the preclusive effect of prior judgments ..."). *See also* related discussion Section C.4(c). *But see* Sutter v. Oxford Health Plans, LLC, 227 Fed. Appx. 135 (3d Cir. 2007) (appearing to review arbitrators' determination of issue preclusive effect of Eleventh Circuit decision for manifest disregard for the law, and affirming arbitrator because "he analyzed the issue ... and provided extensive reasoning").

[286] Bear, Stearns & Co. v. 1109580 Ontario, Inc., 409 F.3d 87, 92 (2d Cir. 2005). On the future of manifest disregard, see note 201, *supra*, and accompanying text.

[287] *See* John J. Barcelo III, *Who Decides the Arbitrators' Jurisdiction? Separability and Competence-Competence in Transnational Perspective*, 36 Vand. J. Transnat'l L. 1115, 1133 (2003).

limitations periods that form part of the lex arbitri ("time limits on arbitration"). With respect to the first type of limitations period, New York law provides that if a party waits to argue a statute of limitations defense, a court will review the arbitrators' decision deferentially.[288] Many federal courts reach the same result by applying a narrow "manifest disregard of the law standard,"[289] ostensibly in the belief that this particular issue is intertwined with the merits.[290] And yet a vacatur court might well conclude that "[s]tatutes of limitations relating to the [*lex arbitri*] ... [are] matters for judges."[291] Obviously the matter remains quite unsettled.

F. ARBITRAL JURISDICTION AT RECOGNITION AND ENFORCEMENT

6.93 The final stage of analysis is reached when a party asks a New York court to recognize or enforce a "foreign" arbitral award.[292] Although the recognition and enforcement court sits in a position similar to that of the vacatur court, the stakes

[288] *See* N.Y.C.P.L.R. § 7502(b) (2007).

[289] Merrill Lynch, Pierce, Fenner & Smith, Inc. v. Jaros, 70 F.3d 418, 421 (6th Cir. 1995) (reasoning, even though "it appears [the] federal securities claims were not timely brought," that confirmation was appropriate because the arbitrators had not acted in "manifest disregard of the law"); Shearson Lehman Hutton, Inc. v. Wagoner, 944 F.2d 114, 121 (2d Cir. 1991) (dealing with motion to compel arbitration; "[W]e have stated emphatically that any limitations defense—whether stemming from the arbitration agreement, arbitration association rule, or state statute—is an issue to be addressed by the arbitrators."); British Ins. Co. of Cayman v. Water Street Ins. Co., Ltd., 93 F. Supp. 2d 506, 520–21 (S.D.N.Y. 2000) (confirming award and stating "it is up to the arbitrators, not the court, to decide the validity of time-bar defenses"). The Court's decision in *Howsam* may support similar deference on waiver and estoppel determinations at the vacatur stage. *See* Howsam v. Dean Witter Reynolds, Inc., 537 U.S. 79, 79 (2002) (referring to arbitrability questions as those bearing on "gateway" matters the parties would likely expect a court to resolve); John J. Barcelo III, *Who Decides the Arbitrators' Jurisdiction? Separability and Competence-Competence in Transnational Perspective*, 36 Vand. J. Transnat'l L. 1115, 1133 (2003) (arguing that *Howsam* suggests that vacatur courts should defer to arbitrators on "time limits on claims and possible waiver or estoppel issues"). But, of course, one should acknowledge that *Howsam* dealt with limits on arbitration under the arbitral rules that the parties had selected. *See* Howsam v. Dean Witter Reynolds, Inc., 537 U.S. 79, 81 (2002). One might distinguish an issue such as what I have called "time limits on arbitration," which seem to go to the judiciary's regulation of its jurisdiction vis-à-vis arbitrators. *See generally* Rau, *supra* note 226, at 327–31 (reviewing arguments on both sides of the issue).

[290] *See* William W. Park, *Determining Arbitral Jurisdiction: Allocation of Tasks Between Courts and Arbitrators*, 8 Am. Rev. Int'l Arb. 133, 139–40 (1997) (discussing policy rationale for deference).

[291] *Id.* at 133, 139.

[292] Note that courts may also use the term "confirmation" when addressing the recognition and enforcement of foreign awards. This confusion stems from FAA § 207's use of the term *confirm*. For purposes of this discussion, the concepts of confirmation, on the one hand, and recognition and enforcement, on the other, shall be kept analytically distinct. The former refers the reduction of a locally-rendered arbitral award to judgment and the latter to the local recognition and enforcement of an arbitral award rendered abroad.

are somewhat different. At the confirmation and vacatur stage, the issue before the court is the continued existence of the arbitral award, whereas at the recognition and enforcement stage, the issue is confined to the enforceability and preclusive effect of the award in the enforcing forum.

The majority of arbitral awards do not require judicial recognition or enforcement, as the losing party will usually comply with the award.[293] However, where there is no voluntary compliance, or where preclusive effect of the judgment is sought, judicial recourse is necessary. The New York Convention, the FAA, and the Panama Convention each provide a framework under which a final award is presumptively entitled to recognition and enforcement,[294] subject to a limited set of formal, procedural, and substantive grounds on which recognition and enforcement may be refused in whole or in part.[295] The precise contours and doctrinal underpinnings of these grounds are often unclear. This is due in part to different conceptions of the court's role as final arbiter or as pro-arbitration enforcer, and in part to complications that arise where enforcement courts freely cite cases from the compelling or vacating stages as if they were interchangeable and the underlying considerations identical. **6.94**

1. The Place of Arbitral Jurisdiction in Recognition and Enforcement

Unsurprisingly, the existence or nonexistence of arbitral jurisdiction remains of central importance at the recognition and enforcement stage.[296] All aspects of **6.95**

---

[293] BORN, *supra* note 53 at 1126 n.136 (*citing* Lalive, *Enforcing Awards*, in ICC, 60 YEARS OF ICC ARBITRATION 317, 319 (1984)).

[294] The Second Circuit declared that there is a "general pro-enforcement bias" manifested in the Convention. Parsons & Whittemore Overseas Co. v. Société Generale de l'Industrie du Papier (RAKTA), 508 F.2d 969, 973 (2d Cir. 1974). This is further supported by the fact that the party opposing confirmation of the award bears the burden of proof. La Société Nationale Pour La Recherche, La Production, Le Transport, La Transformation, et La Commercialisation des Hydrocarbures v. Shaheen Natural Resources Co., Inc., 585 F. Supp. 57, 61 (S.D.N.Y. 1983), *aff'd*, 733 F.2d 260 (2d Cir. 1984), *cert. denied*, 469 U.S. 883, 105 S. Ct. 251, 83 L.Ed.2d 188 (1984).

[295] FAA § 207; New York Convention Article V; Panama Convention Article 5. *See, e.g.*, Parsons & Whittemore Overseas Co., Inc. v. Société Générale de L'Industie du Papier (RAKTA), 508 F.2d 969, 973 (2d Cir. 1974) (discussed but did not decide the exclusivity of the Convention grounds); Fotochrome Inc. v. Copal Co., 517 F.2d 512, 518 (2d Cir. 1975); Management & Technical Consultants S.A. v. Parsons-Jurden Intern. Corp., 820 F.2d 1531, 1533 (9th Cir. 1987); La Societe Nationale Pour La Recherche, La Production, Le Transport, La Transformation, et La Commercialisation des Hydrocarbures v. Shaheen Natural Resources Co., Inc. 585 F. Supp. 57, 61–62 (S.D.N.Y. 1983). *See* Chapter 1 and Chapter 13.C.1 of this book. *See also* BORN, *supra* note 141, at 2730.

[296] *See* China Minmetals Materials Imp. & Exp. Co., Ltd. v. Chi Mei Corp., 334 F.3d 274, 286 (3d Cir. 2003) (stopping short of explicitly incorporating Art. II's "valid written agreement" requirement into Art. V, holding that, "[r]ead as a whole, therefore, the Convention contemplates that a court should enforce only valid agreements to arbitrate and only awards based on those agreements ... We therefore hold that a district court should refuse to enforce an arbitration award under the Convention where the parties did not reach a valid agreement to arbitrate, at least in the absence of a waiver of the objection to arbitration by the party opposing enforcement."). *See also* Robert B. von Mehren, *Enforcement of Foreign Arbitral Awards in the United States*, 771 PLI/COMM 147, 164 (1998) ("The Article V(1)(c) defense reflects the basic assumption upon which

arbitral jurisdiction, including validity and scope of the arbitration agreement, may be raised as possible grounds for denying recognition or enforcement.[297] As discussed later, some courts apply the same level of scrutiny to arbitral jurisdiction questions at the recognition and enforcement stage as they do at the compelling and vacatur stages, while others apply less scrutiny, deferring in large part to prior arbitral and judicial decisions.[298]

2. Choice of Law Governing the Recognition and Enforcement of an Arbitral Award and Defenses Thereto

6.96 The underlying choice of law issues at the recognition and enforcement stage resemble those at the compelling and vacatur stages.[299] While the Convention provides some explicit choice of law guidance, these determinations do not get any less complicated than at the earlier stages of the dispute. Significant complications may arise when analyzing the Convention grounds for non-enforcement because the applicable law can vary based on the ground asserted.[300] For example, challenges to the capacity of the parties to enter the arbitration agreement are governed by the "law applicable to them,"[301] whereas challenges to the validity of the arbitration agreement are either governed by the "law to which the parties ... subjected it or, failing any indication thereon," the law of the arbitral situs,[302] or possibly even the law of place where the contract was performed.[303] Absent express

---

arbitration rests—that the arbitrator's jurisdiction is established by the will of the parties. It can be no more than that to which the parties agreed.").

[297] *See* discussion in Section E.3 of this chapter.

[298] *Compare* Sarhank Group v. Oracle Corp., 404 F.3d 657, 661–62 (2d Cir. 2005) (instructing lower court to review de novo under domestic law whether a nonsignatory party was properly bound under the arbitration agreement by Egyptian arbitral tribunal and confirming court applying the parties' chosen Egyptian law) *with* Interdigital Communs. Corp. v. Samsung Elecs. Co., No. 06 Civ. 6833, 2007 U.S. Dist. LEXIS 91135 (S.D.N.Y 2007) (citing a case decided under the FAA in support of the "extremely deferential standard of review for arbitral awards").

[299] *See* discussion in Sections C.2 and E.2 of this chapter.

[300] Ian R. Macneil, et al., Federal Arbitration Law: Agreements, Awards, and Remedies under the Federal Arbitration Act § 44.40.1 (1994) (enumerating eight possible applicable legal theories).

[301] New York Convention Art. V(1)(a). Determining the "law applicable to them" may also present some interpretive difficulties for courts. One treatise has explained that the Convention language "appears to allow reference to general principles of conflict of laws in determining the applicable law. The law in question appears to be that of status, thus creating the possibility that one law might be applicable to one party, another to another party. In such a case neither law would be applicable to 'them.' A court faced with this situation should look to the law of capacity applicable to the party asserted to lack capacity." Ian R. Macneil, et al., *supra* note 300, at § 44.40.2.1 (*citing* Horacio A. Grigera Naón, Choice-of-Law Problems in International Commercial Arbitration (1992)); Arthur T. von Mehren, *International Commercial Arbitration and Conflict of Laws*, 3 Am. Rev. Int'l Arb. 57 (1992).

[302] New York Convention Art. V(1)(a).

[303] Robert B. von Mehren, *Enforcement of Foreign Arbitral Awards in the United States*, 771 PLI/Comm 147, 165 (1998) ("The validity of the arbitration agreement must be determined with respect to the law governing the contract, which is usually either the law chosen by the parties, the law of the country where the award was made, or the law of the country where the contract was executed.").

guidance from Convention Article V(1)(c), some commentators have hypothesized that the law of the country where the arbitration agreement was formed might reasonably govern questions concerning its scope.[304] Questions concerning whether the subject matter is one that can be submitted to arbitration and matters of public policy are governed by the law of the enforcing forum.[305] Furthermore, the law of the country where the arbitration took place, the law under which the arbitral award was made, and even general principles of international law may all govern different grounds for nonenforcement not directly related to determinations of arbitral jurisdiction.[306] It is worth noting that, while arguably not a majority approach and not without criticism, some courts have subjected arbitral jurisdiction questions to general principles of U.S. law.[307] Notwithstanding the complicated choice of law framework set forth in the Convention, it is important to note that courts may choose to sidestep this complicated issue rather than address it.[308]

3. *Kompetenz-Kompetenz* and Review of Arbitral Jurisdiction in Recognition and Enforcement Proceedings

As shown by the following, all of the grounds on which a party could have contested the existence of arbitral jurisdiction at the outset of the dispute[309] may potentially serve as grounds for the nonrecognition or nonenforcement of a foreign arbitral award under the New York and Panama Conventions. Each of these grounds can be raised simultaneously under one of the specific defenses provided in the Conventions[310] as well as under the more general defenses that the subject matter of the dispute is "not capable of settlement by arbitration"[311] **6.97**

[304] Ian R. Macneil, et al., *supra* note 300, at § 44.40.1 n.53 and accompanying text (suggesting the theoretical possibility but admitting that there are "no clear example[s]").

[305] New York Convention Art. V(2).

[306] Ian R. Macneil, et al., *supra* note 300, at § 44.40.1 & n.57.

[307] *See, e.g.*, Sarhank Group v. Oracle Corp., 404 F.3d 657, 661–62 (2d Cir. 2005) (citing *First Options*, holding that the district court on remand must determine whether the losing American party could be bound, under U.S. law, by the arbitration agreement as a nonsignatory, notwithstanding the presence of an Egyptian choice of law provision and decisions by an Egyptian arbitral tribunal and court binding the nonsignatory party). *See also* Ian R. Macneil, et al., *supra* note 300, at §§ 44.16.6.2, 44.40.2.10 (criticizing courts for applying Article V's "public policy" defense broadly to "provide a basis for virtually any specific defense to enforcement of awards ..." and asserting that "[t]he correct approach ... is to *start* by determining if the issue is one *Prima Paint* requires to be submitted to the arbitrators. If the answer is affirmative that is the end of it, and there is no need to go into questions relating to Article V(2)(b). If it is negative, then and only then, the court applies the public policy defense.").

[308] *See* Born, *supra* note 141, at 2784–85 (noting with respect to decisions under Article V(1)(a), courts "have not ordinarily engaged in any meaningful choice-of-law analysis"). *But cf.* In the Matter of the Arbitration between Overseas Cosmos, Inc. and NR Vessel Corp., No. 97 Civ. 5898, 1997 U.S. Dist. LEXIS 19390 (S.D.N.Y. Dec. 8, 1997) (explicitly analyzing choice of law issues in rejecting Respondent's V(1)(a) defense).

[309] *See* discussion in Section C.3 of this chapter.

[310] New York Convention Article V(1)(a)–(e); Panama Convention Article 5.

[311] New York Convention Article V(2)(a); Panama Convention Article 5.2(a).

under the enforcing forum's law, or that the recognition and enforcement of the award would violate the enforcing forum's public policy.[312] Commentators have expressed concern that the general defenses, particularly that of public policy,[313] can be read to allow broad independent judicial review under forum law of nearly any possible defense, even those that, at the outset, are presumptively for the arbitrators to decide under the doctrine of severability.[314] The same commentators suggest that the doctrine of severability should apply to constrain the scope of the public policy defense and preserve certain arbitral determinations.[315] Though the risk of such expansive judicial review appears minimal given the general pro-enforcement tendencies of courts,[316] the possibility must be addressed in relation to each of the defenses, as analysis under the public policy defense, when accepted by a court, can significantly affect the applicable law and level of judicial review.

6.98 When a party seeks to raise as a defense one of these issues that could have served to bar arbitration at the outset, the issue that arises is whether and to what extent the recognition and enforcement court will treat earlier decisions on these issues by the arbitrators and compelling and vacatur courts as preclusive. Despite the general pro-arbitration and pro-enforcement thrust of the Conventions, courts' responses to this issue are more varied than either a wholesale acceptance or rejection of those earlier determinations and can turn on the particular grounds on which the defense is asserted.

(a) Deference to prior arbitral decision as to the parties bound by the agreement

6.99 A party may object to the recognition and enforcement of an arbitral award on the ground that it is not a party to the arbitration agreement or that its consent to the

[312] New York Convention Article V(2)(b); Panama Convention Article 5.2(b).

[313] It is important to note that arbitral decisions on public policy are generally subject to de novo judicial review. Born, *supra* note 141, at 2644 (*citing* W.R. Grace & Co., v. Local 759, International Union ... 461 U.S. 757, 766 (1983) ("the question of public policy is ultimately one for resolution by the courts"); Transmarine Seaways Corp. of Monrovia v. Marc Rich & Co. A. G., 480 F. Supp. 352, 358 (S.D.N.Y. 1979) ("When public policy is asserted as the basis for vacating an arbitration award, the court is required to make its own, independent evaluation."); Botany Industries, Inc. v. New York Joint Bd., Amalgamated Clothing Workers of America, 375 F. Supp. 485, 491 (S.D.N.Y. 1974) (stating in the context of a domestic arbitration award: "If the agreement is void, it is not legitimatized by the arbitral process; and if the agreement is unenforceable, it is not rendered enforceable by an arbitrator's decision. Simply stated, the court cannot enforce an invalid collective bargaining agreement, either directly, in the context of an action for declaratory judgment, or indirectly, by enforcement of the award.").

[314] Ian R. Macneil, et al., *supra* note 300, at § 44.40.2.10 (*citing* Transmarine Seaways Corp. of Monrovia v. Marc Rich & Co. A. G., 408 F. Supp. 352 (S.D.N.Y. 1979), as an example of a case that violates the separability doctrine by reviewing a claim of "duress" relating to the container contract de novo on the grounds that "[a]greements exacted by duress contravene the public policy of the nation ... accordingly duress, if established, furnishes a basis for refusing enforcement of an award under Article V(2)(b) of the Convention.").

[315] See, *supra* note 306.

[316] *See* Parsons & Whittemore Overseas Co. v. Societe Generale de l'Industrie du Papier (RAKTA), 508 F.2d 969, 973 (2d Cir.1974) (declaring that there is a "general pro-enforcement bias" manifested in the Convention).

agreement was otherwise ineffective due to lack of capacity. This challenge can potentially be raised under several of the Convention grounds, such as Articles V(1)(a) (the parties lacked capacity or the arbitration agreement is otherwise invalid for lack of consent), V(1)(c) (the arbitrator's exceeded the scope of their authority by binding a nonsignatory to the arbitration agreement),[317] and V(2) (enforcing the award against a nonsignatory would be contrary to the enforcing forum's public policy). As at the compelling and vacatur stages, courts take seriously their obligation to determine whether a party consented to arbitrate before enforcing an award.[318] The depth of the court's inquiry at the recognition and enforcement stage appears to be influenced by the Convention ground on which the claim is asserted and the factual disposition of the case. As a general rule, where the party challenging an award fails to assert its defense in prior stages of the dispute, courts will hold that a party has waived its right to challenge the enforcement on that ground, defer to the prior judicial and arbitral determinations on the issue, and conduct at most a summary judicial inquiry reaffirming those prior outcomes.[319]

[317] Fiat S.p.A. v. Ministry of Finance and Planning of Republic of Suriname, No. 88 CIV. 6639, 1989 WL 122891 (S.D.N.Y. Oct. 12, 1989) (analyzing an award under both the FAA and the New York Convention, asserting that "[i]t is usually not within the discretion of the arbitration panel to determine whether a non-signatory to an arbitration agreement should be bound by the arbitrators when that issue is not before the panel," and ultimately vacating the award because the arbitrators exceeded their authority when they bound a nonsignatory party); CBS Corp. v. WAK Orient Power & Light Ltd., 168 F. Supp. 2d. 403 (E.D. Pa. 2001) (challenging party had not signed the arbitration agreement, but had signed a Terms of Reference to Arbitration agreement that both incorporated the ICC Rules and expressly provided for arbitral determination of a number of issues. The arbitrators determined that under English law the challenging party was bound by the arbitration agreement and eventually rendered a decision against the challenging party. The court held that the challenging party had "unmistakably" agreed to submit the question of whether the arbitrators had the authority to join it as a party to the arbitration. The court deferred to the arbitrators' and rejected the challenging party's V(1)(c) argument).

[318] *See* Sarhank Group v. Oracle Corp., 404 F.3d 657, 661 (2d Cir. 2005) ("Under American law, whether a party has consented to arbitrate is an issue to be decided by the Court in which enforcement of an award is sought ... 'If ... the parties did not agree to submit the arbitrability question itself to arbitration, then the court should decide that question just as it would decide any other question that the parties did not submit to arbitration, namely, independently.' ") (*quoting* First Options, Inc. v. Kaplan, 514 U.S. 938, 943 (1995)); In the Matter of the Application to Confirm an Arbitration Award by Chios Charm Shipping Co., No. 93 CIV. 6313 (SS), 1994 U.S. Dist. Lexis 4571 at *7 (S.D.N.Y. Apr. 11, 1994) (stating that "respondents incorrectly assert that the arbitrators have the sole authority to determine who is bound by an arbitral award").

[319] In the Matter of the Arbitration between Overseas Cosmos, Inc. and NR Vessel Corp., No. 97 Civ. 5898, 1997 U.S. Dist. LEXIS 19390 (S.D.N.Y. Dec. 8, 1997) (This was a case involving an arbitration agreement containing an English choice of law clause that was arbitrated in London; respondent argues that the arbitration agreement is unenforceable because they never signed the agreement under V(1)(a). The court first held that respondent waived the issue for failure to raise it before the arbitrators. The court then proceeded with the analysis assuming the parties had not waived the defense. The court found that respondent failed to demonstrate the invalidity of the contract under English law. The court conducted an independent "cursory review" of English law and found respondent's arguments unavailing. Lastly, possibly as an attempt to dissuade a potential claim under Article V(2)(a), or possibly in response to the fact that respondent based its claim on U.S. contract principles, the court ran through a U.S. law analysis under the UCC and found that respondent was properly bound by the arbitration contract and enforced the award.);

However, where a party did not waive its right to object on these grounds, either by objecting to arbitral jurisdiction during the earlier stages of the dispute, or where the issue properly arises for the first time on recognition and enforcement, as when a party tries to enforce the award against an alter ego of its arbitral counterparty, courts tend to engage in fairly rigorous independent analysis to determine whether the party may be bound.[320] Where a nonsignatory repeatedly, but unsuccessfully, challenges the arbitrator's jurisdiction, courts appear most willing to analyze the issue under Article V(2) and disregard prior arbitral or vacatur court rulings and applicable laws in favor of an independent judicial analysis under U.S. law.[321] This is consistent with the hesitancy at the compelling stage to apply the chosen law, if foreign, to determine whether a nonsignatory could be bound by the agreement.[322] The courts in these instances will determine whether the purported nonparty can

National Dev. Co. v. Khashoggi, 781 F. Supp. 959, 963 (S.D.N.Y. 1992) (relying on a prior Second Circuit decision in this case, the court held that, "The time for [respondent] to argue that he could not be compelled to submit to arbitration because he was neither a party to ... nor the alter ego of a party [to the agreement], was in [petitioner]'s action to compel him to arbitrate ... The issue of whether [respondent] was bound by the arbitration agreement was resolved by the October 15, 1987 judgment of this Court ordering him to submit to arbitration by the ICC on the dispute between him and [petitioner], and the denial of [respondent]'s motion to vacate that judgment for a deficiency in service."); La Société Nationale Pour La Recherche, La Production, Le Transport, La Transformation, et La Commercialisation des Hydrocarbures v. Shaheen Natural Resources Co., 585 F. Supp. 57, 62 (S.D.N.Y. 1983) (The court held that the defendant waived its right to challenge enforcement of the award based on an agency theory and reasoning that even if defendant had not waived its right, its argument was still unpersuasive. "Defendant had an affirmative obligation to raise 'any arguments why the arbitration should not proceed' to the panel ... including that it is not a party to the agreement and is not bound by the arbitration provision"; "That Shaheen was merely acting as an agent for NRC and as such is not bound by the agreement to arbitrate is contradicted by the unambiguous language contained in the agreement.") (internal citations omitted).

[320] Compagnie Noga D'Importation Et D'exp. S.A. v. Russian Fed'n, 361 F.3d 676, 680 (2d Cir. 2004) (determining whether an arbitration award rendered against an organ of the Russian Federation can be enforced against the Russian Federation, a sovereign nation; holding that "the Russian Federation and the Government are not separate 'parties'" and as such the Russian Federation could be bound by the award); Chios Charm Shipping Co. v. Rionda, No. 93 CIV. 6313 (SS), 1994 U.S. Dist. LEXIS 4571 (S.D.N.Y. 1994) (petitioner attempted to enforce an award against three contractually related parties. The court held that the award can be enforced only against the one party named in the award).

[321] *See Sarhank Group*, at 658–59 (an American nonsignatory was subject to arbitration in Egypt pursuant to an arbitration agreement containing an Egyptian choice of law clause. The nonsignatory challenged the existence of arbitral jurisdiction first before the arbitrators and again before an Egyptian vacatur court. Both the arbitrators and the vacatur court held the nonsignatory was bound by the arbitration agreement under Egyptian law. The prevailing party sought enforcement in the United States. The District Court accepted the prior arbitral and judicial determinations under Egyptian law and enforced the award. On appeal, the Second Circuit stressed the importance of the judicial role in independently determining whether there was an agreement to arbitrate. Here, the Second Circuit analyzed the nonsignatory issue under Article V(2), and not under V(1)(a) as the district court, and held that under Article V(2), the district court must conduct an independent inquiry under U.S. law as to whether the nonsignatory was bound by the arbitration agreement, notwithstanding the Egyptian choice of law clause and the prior arbitral and judicial decisions.)

[322] *See* discussion in Section C.1 of this chapter.

be bound to the arbitration agreement through doctrines such as piercing the corporate veil, alter ego, estoppel, etc., under either the parties' chosen law, the law of the arbitral situs, or U.S. law.[323]

(b) Deference to the arbitrators' determination of scope of agreement As at the vacatur stage, "scope" questions[324] are expressly permitted as grounds for nonenforcement under the New York and Panama Conventions.[325] This is consistent with the contractual nature of arbitration, where a party can only be compelled to arbitrate issues it has agreed to submit to arbitration. While the scope of the arbitrators' authority is of central importance to arbitral jurisdiction, and parties are generally presumed to have left questions of arbitral jurisdiction to be decided by the courts,[326] recognition and enforcement courts, like vacatur courts, have narrowly construed this defense and invoked a strong presumption that the arbitrators acted within their powers.[327] The presence and force of this presumption in any given case may be dictated by the applicable law.[328] **6.100**

[323] When in doubt, courts may simultaneously analyze the situation under multiple bodies of law. *See* Compagnie Noga D'Importation Et D'exp. S.A. v. Russian Fed'n, 361 F.3d 676, 680 (2d Cir. 2004) ("[W]e hold that regardless of whether Russian law, federal common law, or international law applied, the Russian Federation and the Government are not separate 'parties' for purposes of confirming and enforcing an arbitral award under the Convention.")

[324] *Scope* questions can include claims that the arbitral award covers issues, damages, or even parties not included within the scope of the arbitration agreement.

[325] New York Convention Article V(1)(c) ("The award deals with a difference not contemplated by or not falling within the terms of the submission to arbitration, or it contains decisions on matters beyond the scope of the submission to arbitration."); Panama Convention Art.1(c). According to some commentators, the "scope" defense contained in New York Convention Article V(1)(c) is "merely a reiteration of the invalidity defense" contained in Article V(1)(a), "because both assume that the will and consent of the parties create the bases for the ... arbitration panel's jurisdiction." May Lu, Note, *The New York Convention on the Recognition and Enforcement of Foreign Arbitral Awards: Analysis of the Seven Defenses to Oppose Enforcement in the United States and England*, 23 ARIZ. J. INT'L & COMP. L. 747, 757–58 (2005–2006) (citing Leonard V. Quigley, *Accession by the United States to the United Nations Convention on the Recognition and Enforcement of Foreign Arbitration Awards*, 70 YALE L.J. 1049, 1068 (1961); Robert B. von Mehren, *Enforcement of Foreign Arbitral Awards in the United States*, 771 PLI/COMM 147, 164 (1998)).

[326] First Options of Chicago, Inc. v. Kaplan, 514 U.S. 938 (1995).

[327] *See, e.g.*, Parsons & Whittemore Overseas Co., Inc. v. Société Generale de L'Industrie du Papier (Ratka), 508 F.2d 969, 976 (2d Cir. 1974); American Const. Machinery & Equipment Corp. Ltd. v. Mechanised Const. of Pakistan Ltd., 659 F. Supp. 426, 429 (S.D.N.Y. 1987). *See* discussion Section E.3(b). This is also consistent with the judicial treatment of scope issues at the compelling stage where courts will invoke the presumption in favor of arbitration and compel arbitration where there is a "broad" arbitration clause. *See* discussion Section C.3(b).

[328] Unlike other Convention grounds for nonenforcement, Article V(1)(c) provides no choice of law guidance. Choice of law considerations may be of importance because in the United States there is a presumption that the arbitrators acted within their powers, and this presumption may not be universally accepted. *See* IAN R. MACNEIL, ET AL., *supra* note 300, at § 44.40.2.5. It is unclear how strong a concern this is, however, since courts often do not engage in detailed choice of law analyses, appearing to opt instead to apply some general, frequently unnamed, body of law plus the federal presumption in favor of enforcement. *See, e.g.*, Parsons & Whittemore Overseas Co., Inc. v. Société Generale de L'Industrie du Papier (Ratka), 508 F.2d 969, 976 (2d Cir. 1974); *see also supra* note 311.

6.101 Where a court is presented with a claim that the arbitrators exceeded the scope of their authority, the court must first determine whether the parties intended questions of arbitral jurisdiction, including the scope of such jurisdiction, to be decided by the arbitrators or the court. The level of judicial review of the scope of arbitral jurisdiction can vary from strong deference to the arbitrators' determination[329] to de novo review.[330] Even where the court's review of the arbitrators' jurisdiction determination is de novo, the party challenging the arbitrators' authority is still unlikely to prevail due to the presumption that the arbitrators acted within their authority.[331] Once the court has determined that the parties intended the arbitrators to decide issues of the scope of arbitral jurisdiction, recognition and enforcement courts, like vacatur courts, will likely find that the arbitrators acted within their authority. Though rare, courts have on occasion held that arbitrators did exceed their authority.[332]

6.102 *(c) Deference to arbitrators' determination as to validity of agreement* A party may also seek to prevent recognition or enforcement of an arbitral award by asserting

[329] *See, e.g., Parsons & Whittemore Overseas Co.*, 508 F.2d at 976 (beginning with presumption that arbitrators acted within their scope, invoking deference to arbitrators on their determinations of law and fact, and holding that the appellants' Article V(1)(c) challenge "cannot withstand the most cursory scrutiny"); National Oil Corp. v. Libyan Sun Oil Co., 733 F. Supp. 800, 817, 819 (D. Del. 1990) (applying a deferential standard of review; holding the arbitrators did not exceed their authority because the damage award was "rationally derived" from the arbitration agreement and the awards' terms were not "completely irrational"); Fertilizer Corp. of India v. IDI Management, Inc., 517 F. Supp. 948, 958–61 (S.D. Ohio 1981) (confining itself to narrow judicial review, stating that courts "may not substitute its judgment for that of the arbitrators"; deferring to arbitrators' determination of the scope of their authority and refusing to rely on case law from the compelling stage of arbitration that would have contradicted the arbitrators' determination).

[330] *See, e.g.*, Management & Technical Consultants S.A. v. Parsons-Jurden International Corp., 820 F.2d 1531, 1534 (9th Cir. 1987) (reviewing determination de novo, while invoking the presumption in favor of the arbitrators and holding that the arbitrators did not exceed their authority); Ministry of Def. of Islamic Republic v. Gould, Inc., 969 F.2d 764, 770–71 (9th Cir. 1992) (reviewing the language of an agreement between the United States and Iran, which the court had already deemed constituted a "submission to arbitrate," holding that the broad language of the agreement clearly encompassed the dispute at hand, refusing to bar recognition and enforcement based on respondent's technical pleading claims); Avraham v. Shigur Express, Ltd., No. 91 Civ. 1238 (SWK), 1991 U.S. Dist. LEXIS 12267, at *13–14 (S.D.N.Y. Sept. 4, 1991) (reviewing award "in its entirety"; summarily declaring that "the Award does not exceed the scope of the arbitrator's authority"); American Construction Machinery & Equipment Corporation Ltd. v. Mechanised Construction of Pakistan Ltd., 659 F. Supp. 426, 429 (S.D.N.Y. 1987) (stating presumption that the arbitrators acted within their authority; summarily declaring that they acted within scope because the parties signed the Terms of Reference agreement, which expressly set forth the issues to be arbitrated).

[331] *See, e.g., Management & Technical Consultants S.A.*, 820 F.2d at 1534 (The court stated that it would "review *de novo* a contention that the subject matter of the arbitration lies outside the scope of a contract." The court invoked the presumption that the arbitrators acted within their authority, broadly construed the arbitration agreement language covering "any dispute" to cover "not only the dispute, but the consequences naturally flowing from it" and also "to award costs and fees for obtaining the arbitral decision," and enforced the arbitral award.).

[332] *See, e.g.*, Fiat S.p.A. v. Ministry of Finance and Planning of Republic of Suriname, No. 88 CIV. 6639, 1989 WL 122891 (S.D.N.Y. Oct. 12, 1989) (under both the FAA and the New York Convention, the arbitrators exceeded their scope by rendering an award against a nonsignatory).

that the arbitration agreement that served as the basis of the award is invalid, either because the container contract is invalid or because the arbitration agreement itself is invalid.[333] This challenge can potentially be asserted under both Convention Articles V(1)(a) (the arbitration agreement is invalid under the parties' chosen law or the law of the arbitral situs) or V(2)(b) (enforcing the award would be contrary to the enforcing forum's public policy). When a court is presented with a claim that an arbitral award should not be enforced or recognized because the arbitration agreement is invalid, the court must determine whether and to what extent it will disregard or embrace prior decisions of the arbitral tribunal and vacatur court concerning the validity of the arbitration agreement. Few courts have considered the defense under Article V(1)(a),[334] and while more courts appear to have considered the issue under the rubric of Article V(2)(b), there is insufficient case law to speak in terms of majority and minority approaches. From the limited number of cases examined, the answer to the question of what level of deference is to be accorded to prior arbitral and judicial decisions on the issue appears to be influenced principally by three factors: (1) the particular Convention ground under which the arbitration agreement's validity is challenged; (2) the court's willingness to apply the doctrine of severability as a means of defining the scope of the permissible inquiry under Article V(2)(b); and (3) the court's willingness to incorporate the Convention Article II requirements for a valid arbitration agreement at the compelling stage into Articles V(1)(a) and V(2)(b). Despite these differences, courts are generally reluctant to refuse recognition and enforcement under either Article V(1)(a) or V(2)(b). Courts appear more willing to limit the scope of their inquiry and grant greater deference to prior arbitral tribunal and vacatur court decisions, both with respect to the validity of the agreement and the applicable law, where a challenge is lodged under Convention Article V(1)(a), the Convention's specific invalidity defense.[335] However, where courts entertain

---

333 Recall that these same claims can be asserted at the compelling and vacatur stage. *See* discussion in Sections C.2, C3(c), and E.3(c) of this chapter.

334 *See* Born, *supra* note 141, at 2782–85.

335 For example, in two similar cases, the District Court for the Southern District of New York held that it would defer to the arbitrators under Article V(1)(a) by reviewing their decisions on a manifest disregard standard. In both cases, the challenging party claimed that under the law applicable to it when the arbitration agreement was made, the arbitration agreement was invalid because the challenging party lacked the authority under its national law to enter the agreement. In both cases, the challenging parties presented their claims to the arbitrators. The arbitrators determined that a different law applied to the arbitration agreement, under which the arbitration agreement was valid, thus rejecting the challenging parties' claims. The District Court in both instances deferred to the arbitrators' decisions both as to the applicable law and to the validity of the arbitration agreement thereunder. *See* Buques Centroamericanos, S.A. v. Refinadora Costarricense de Petroleos, S.A., No. 87 Civ. 3256 (DNE), 1989 U.S. Dist. LEXIS 5429 (S.D.N.Y. May, 18, 1989); American Constr. Mach. & Equip. Corp. v. Mechanised Constr. Of Pakistan, 659 F. Supp. 426 (S.D.N.Y. 1987) (rejecting respondent's challenges under both Convention Articles V(1)(a) and V(2)(b)). *See also* Arbitration between Overseas Cosmos, Inc. and NR Vessel Corp., No. 97 Civ. 5898 (DC), 1997 U.S. Dist. LEXIS 19390, at *7–12 (analyzing respondent's claim that there was no valid agreement to arbitrate because it never signed the agreement under both U.K. and

a challenge under the general public policy defense contained in Convention Article V(2)(b), they are more likely to engage in an independent review of the issue under federal law.[336] Even though courts will typically engage in de novo review of the validity issue under Article V(2)(b), they are still unlikely to deny recognition or enforcement on such grounds.[337]

6.103 A court's willingness to apply the doctrine of severability to defining the contours of permissible public policy challenges under Convention Article V(b)(2) can have a significant effect on the level of judicial review of such claims. Some courts appear to reason that if the claim is one that would have been presumptively for the arbitrators to decide at the compelling stage,[338] then a challenge on such a ground cannot form the basis of a public policy defense under Article V(2)(b), and the court will defer to the arbitrators' decision on the issue.[339] This is consistent with the doctrine of severability and with certain commentators'

U.S. law, while ultimately holding that respondent had waived its right to challenge enforcement on this ground).

[336] *See, e.g.*, Sarhank Group v. Oracle Corp., 404 F.3d 657, 661–62 (2d Cir. 2005) (vacating district court decision, holding that the district court must make an independent inquiry to determine the existence of an agreement to arbitrate before recognizing and enforcing an arbitral award; reading "Article V(2)" along with the severability doctrine to permit independent judicial review of the arbitration agreement similar to that at the compelling stage); China Minmetals Materials Imp. & Exp. Co., Ltd. v. Chi Mei Corp., 334 F.3d 274, 286 (3d Cir. 2003) (challenging party sought to bar recognition and enforcement on the grounds that the container contract was the product of forgery. While it is unclear precisely on which section of Convention Article V the court based its decision, the court held that a party may challenge the recognition and enforcement of an award "on the grounds that there never was a valid agreement to arbitrate," and that the district court must independently decide this issue, notwithstanding an arbitral award on the issue.); Transmarine Seaways Corp. of Monrovia v. Marc Rich & Co. A. G., 480 F. Supp. 352 (S.D.N.Y. 1979) (reviewing de novo a claim that an arbitration agreement was invalid because the container contract was "extracted by duress" because "[a]greements extracted by duress contravene public policy of the nation," but ultimately rejecting the challenger's duress claim after independent inquiry).

[337] Consistent with the federal presumption in favor of enforcement, courts generally narrowly construe the Article V(2)(b) defense. See, *e.g.*, Parsons & Whittemore Overseas Co. v. Société Generale de l'Industrie du Papier (RAKTA), 508 F.2d 969, 974 (2d Cir. 1974) ("We conclude, therefore, that the Convention's public policy defense should be construed narrowly. Enforcement of foreign arbitral awards may be denied on this basis only where enforcement would violate the forum state's most basic notions of morality and justice.").

[338] For example, challenges that run to the container contract as opposed to the arbitration agreement alone are presumptively for the arbitrators to decide pursuant to the severability doctrine. *See* discussion Sections A.4 and C.2 of this chapter.

[339] *See, e.g.*, Europcar Italia, S.p.A. v. Maiellano Tours, Inc., 156 F.3d 310, 315–16 (2d Cir. 1998) (rejecting an invitation to use Convention Article V(2)(b) to bar recognition and enforcement on a claim of forgery relating to the container contract; reiterating that "the issue of whether the underlying contract that is the subject of the arbitrated dispute was forged or fraudulently induced—a matter to be determined exclusively by the arbitrators"; deferring to the Italian arbitrators' decision; and holding that "enforcement of the arbitration award would not violate public policy"); China Minmetals Materials Imp. & Exp. Co., Ltd. v. Chi Mei Corp., 334 F.3d 274, 286 (3d Cir. 2003) (relying on the severability doctrine and the reasoning in *First Options* to hold that a claim that the arbitration agreement is invalid because the container contract was a forgery was presumptively a question for the district court to decide).

suggestion that the doctrine of severability is properly applied in this manner to prevent the scope of the Convention Article V(2) defenses from being read so broadly as to render superfluous the other Convention defenses.[340] However, this trend is not universally accepted. Some courts have been willing to grant de novo review of claims that would, under the doctrine of severability, be considered presumptively for the arbitrators to decide, such as a claim of fraud in the factum of the container contract.[341]

The claims of invalidity of the arbitration agreement at the recognition and enforcement stage under Article V(1)(a) or V(2)(b) are closely related, though arguably not identical, to those that may be raised at the compelling stage under Articles II(1) and II(3).[342] Some commentators have suggested that the validity of an arbitration agreement as determined at the compelling stage under Article II is a necessary condition to recognition and enforcement of an award under Article V,[343] while, for others, Article II is wholly irrelevant at the recognition and enforcement stage.[344] There appears to be a similar divide among courts.[345] Where courts read the conditions set forth in Article II as necessary components of, or at least relevant points of departure for, an analysis under either Article V(1)(a) or V(2), they unsurprisingly will engage in de novo review, consistent with their position as the backstop enforcer of the arbitral system.[346] Likewise, it would be **6.104**

[340] *See* Ian R. Macneil, et al., *supra* note 300, at § 44.15.2 (1994) ("The correct approach ... is to *start* by determining if the issue is one *Prima Paint* requires to be submitted to the arbitrators. If the answer is affirmative that is the end of it, and there is no need to go into questions relating to Article V(2)(b). If it is negative, then and only then, the court applies the public policy defense.").

[341] Transmarine Seaways Corp. of Monrovia v. Marc Rich & Co. A. G., 480 F. Supp. 352 (S.D.N.Y. 1979) (reviewing de novo a claim that an arbitration agreement was invalid because the container contract was "extracted by duress").

[342] *See* Born, *supra* note 141, at 2777–78 ("A corollary of the consensual nature of arbitration is the unenforceability of awards that are unsupported by a valid arbitration agreement. Authorities dealing with the existence and validity of the arbitration agreement under Article II are also relevant under Article V(1)(a).").

[343] *See id.* at 2786–87 n.411 856 (2001) (citing with respect to Article II's writing requirement, Albert Jan Van Den Berg, The New York Convention of 1958 284–87 (1981) ("the legislative history of the Convention and its internal consistency require the application of Article II(2) at the award enforcement stage.")).

[344] *See* Born, *supra* note 141, at 2786–87 n.411 (citing Haight, Report on the Convention on the Recognition and Enforcement of foreign Arbitral Awards 17–18 (1958) ("Any form of agreement, express or tacit, would appear to be sufficient").

[345] *Compare* China Minmetals Materials Imp. & Exp. Co., Ltd. v. Chi Mei Corp., 334 F.3d 274, 286 (3d Cir. 2003) (rejecting appellee's claim that validity of the agreement to arbitrate under Article II is irrelevant to the recognition and enforcement inquiry under Article V, which is expressly limited to the defenses listed in the Convention) *with* Slaney v. International Amateur Athletic Federation, 244 F.3d 580 (7th Cir. 2001) (stating in dicta that a written agreement to arbitrate under Convention Article II is not a necessary condition to the recognition and enforcement of an award).

[346] *See, e.g.*, China Minmetals Materials Imp. & Exp. Co., Ltd., 334 F.3d at 286 (stopping short of explicitly incorporating Art. II's "valid written agreement" requirement into Art. V, holding that, "[r]ead as a whole, therefore, the Convention contemplates that a court should enforce only valid agreements to arbitrate and only awards based on those agreements ... We therefore hold that a district court should refuse to enforce an arbitration award under the Convention

reasonable to expect courts that are less willing to inform their invalidity analysis at the recognition and enforcement phase with guidance from the compelling stage to be more likely to defer to the arbitrators' decisions on issues that do not fall expressly within the language of Article V.

6.105 A party might also conceivably argue that, even if an arbitration agreement existed, that party did not consent to be legally bound by the award and that the award should therefore be denied enforcement under Article V(e) as nonbinding or under Article V(1)(a) for lack of a meeting of the minds.[347] Unsurprisingly, a court is unlikely to take this argument very seriously.[348]

6.106 *(d) Deference to arbitrators on arbitrability and "arbitrability-related" issues* A party may also seek to bar enforcement or recognition of an arbitral award on the ground that the underlying subject matter of the dispute cannot be settled through arbitration either under the law chosen by the parties, the law of the arbitral situs,[349] or the law of the enforcing forum.[350] Commentators have concluded that the question of the "arbitrability" of the dispute, narrowly defined, is the same at the compelling stage as at the recognition and enforcement stage, such that "if arbitration of a claim cannot be compelled under Article II(1), because it is non-arbitrable, then an arbitral award dealing with that claim is unenforceable under Article V(2)(a) ..."[351] Just as at the compelling and vacatur stages, courts can be expected to subject these questions to independent review,[352] consistent with the Supreme Court's suggestion in *Mitsubishi* that U.S. courts can take a second look at such issues under Article V(2)(a) and (b) at the recognition and enforcement stage.[353]

---

where the parties did not reach a valid agreement to arbitrate, at least in the absence of a waiver of the objection to arbitration by the party opposing enforcement.").

[347] *See, e.g.*, Europcar Italia, S.p.A. v. Maiellano Tours, Inc., 156 F.3d 310, 315 (2d Cir. 1998).

[348] *Id.* at 315 ("both arbitration agreements stated unambiguously that the arbitration was to finally resolve the dispute and the arbitrators found that the parties intended to be bound by their award. Absent extraordinary circumstances, a confirming court is not to reconsider the arbitrator's findings.").

[349] New York Convention Article V(1)(a); Panama Convention Article 5.1(a).

[350] New York Convention Article V(2)(a); Panama Convention Article 5.2(a).

[351] Born, *supra* note 141 at 2863–64.

[352] *See* discussion in Sections C.3(d) and E.3(c)(iii) of this chapter.

[353] Mitsubishi Motors Corp. v. Soler Chrysler-Plymouth, 473 U.S. 614, 638 (1985) ("Having permitted the arbitration to go forward, the national courts of the United States will have the opportunity at the award-enforcement stage to ensure that the legitimate interest in the enforcement of the antitrust laws has been addressed. The Convention reserves to each signatory country the right to refuse enforcement of an award where the 'recognition or enforcement of the award would be contrary to the public policy of that country.' Art. V(2)(b) ..."). *See* Parsons & Whittemore Overseas Co., Inc. v. Société Generale De L'Industrie Du Papier (RAKTA), 508 F.2d 969 (2d Cir. 1974) (rejecting appellant's defense against recognition and enforcement under Article V(2)(a) as failing to raise a substantial issue of arbitrability, but recognizing that "certain categories of claims may be non-arbitrable because of the special national interest vested in their resolution."); Saudi Iron & Steel Co. v. Stemcor USA Inc., No. 97 CIV. 5976(DLC), 1997 WL 642566 (S.D.N.Y 1997) (rejecting respondent's Article V(2)(a) defense that the award should not be enforced because of respondent's pending third-party petition, noting that "the incapable of

4. Deference to Arbitrators and Vacatur Courts on Forum-Specific Issues

With respect to forum-specific issues,[354] recognition and enforcement courts should in theory conduct a much more limited analysis than vacatur courts.[355] Yet, some recognition and enforcement courts have applied vacatur principles derived from the FAA. They have done so, despite a Second Circuit holding that the Convention prescribes the exclusive grounds for denying effect to an arbitral award, and that the FAA's implied grounds for relief may not be applied at the recognition and enforcement stage.[356] As illustrated previously, the Convention grounds for nonenforcement offer sufficient flexibility to enable a disappointed party to craft an argument based on these forum-specific issues. Even so, just as at the vacatur stage, challenges based on forum-specific issues are unlikely to be successful. **6.107**

Due to the extremely limited number of reported cases on these issues, one cannot speak in terms of general trends, and the description that follows should be considered as only illustrative of possible judicial reactions. **6.108**

Just as a party may challenge a motion to compel arbitration, a party may seek to bar recognition and enforcement where the party that succeeded in compelling arbitration did so after the expiration of a contractual, statutory, or equitable limitations period. Such a challenge can conceivably be raised under various Convention grounds, for example, V(1)(a)[357] or V(2)(b).[358] However, in the limited instances where courts have confronted this issue, they have deferred to the arbitrators' ruling on the issue and declined to bar recognition and enforcement.[359] **6.109**

---

settlement exception has been narrowly construed in light of the strong judicial interest in encouraging the use of arbitration").

[354] *See* discussion in Section C.5 of this chapter.

[355] *See* discussion in Section E.4 of this chapter.

[356] Yusuf Ahmed Alghanim & Sons, W.L.L. v. Toys "R" Us, Inc., 126 F.3d 15, 20 (2d Cir. 1997).

[357] Henry v. Murphy, No. M-82, 2002 WL 24307 (S.D.N.Y. Jan. 8, 2002), *aff'd* 50 Fed.Appx. 55 (2d Cir. 2002) (party challenging recognition and enforcement on the basis that the arbitration was time-barred under the law to which the parties subjected it). *See also* FIA Card Servs., N.A. v. Gachiengu, 571 F. Supp. 2d 799, 803–04 (S.D. Tex. 2008) (describing circuit split over whether FAA Section 9 is a mandatory limitations period).

[358] A. Halcoussis Shipping Ltd. v. Golden Eagle Liberia Ltd., No. 88 CIV. 4500 (MJL), 1989 WL 115941, at *2 (S.D.N.Y. Sept. 27, 1989) (party challenging recognition and enforcement by arguing that the "enforcement of the arbitrators' awards—in the face of its assertion that the underlying claim is barred by laches—would be contrary to this country's public policy"). In any event, the Foreign Sovereign Immunities Act's arbitration exception to immunity is likely to apply in such cases.

[359] *See Henry*, 2002 WL 24307, at *4 (holding that the respondent "should have raised [the statute of limitations defense] to the arbitrator during the arbitration hearing, not to this Court in his submission opposing confirmation under the Convention," and confirming the award under the New York Convention); Quasem Group, Ltd. v. W.D. Mask Cotton Co., 967 F. Supp. 288, 292 (W.D. Tenn. 1997) (holding that the arbitrator's "decision not to hear a claim on the basis that the claim is time barred is, in itself, a decision of the arbitrator and, therefore, subject to the

6.110 By way of further example, a party may seek to defeat recognition or enforcement of an award on the ground that the arbitrators improperly allowed arbitration of an issue or dispute where relitigation should have been precluded under the doctrines of res judicata or collateral estoppel. It seems reasonable to expect a recognition and enforcement court to defer to the prior preclusion determinations of arbitrators and vacatur courts.[360] However, there is insufficient case law to confirm this hypothesis. In a single case addressing the issue of whether an arbitrator's purported failure to apply collateral estoppel to exclude an issue should bar enforcement, the court reached the anticipated result, though by somewhat questionable reasoning.[361] The court in *Interdigital Communications Corp.* decided the issue under the traditional vacatur doctrine of manifest disregard of the law, a judicial doctrine many courts have held is unavailable under the Convention,[362] holding that "because there is absolutely no basis to conclude that the Panel 'manifestly disregarded' the law, the Court rejects [the party's] attempt to supplant the Panel's findings with its own contrary interpretations of the contracts at issue. In sum, applying the extremely deferential standard of review for arbitral awards, the Court concludes that there is no basis to disturb the Panel's findings as set forth in the Award, and, therefore, confirms the Award pursuant to Section 207 of the FAA."[363]

5. Waiver of Jurisdiction Challenges

6.111 A party challenging recognition and enforcement of an award may be deemed to have waived its right to do so on account of its participation in the arbitration without objection.[364] The Second Circuit has held that a party seeking to avoid recognition and enforcement on grounds previously known and available, but not raised until after an award has been rendered, has waived the objection.[365]

---

provisions of the Convention"); *A. Halcoussis Shipping Ltd.*, 1989 WL 115941 (confirming the award under the New York Convention).

[360] *See* discussion in Section E.4 of this chapter.

[361] Interdigital Communs. Corp. v. Samsung Elecs. Co., No. 06 Civ. 6833, 2007 U.S. Dist. LEXIS 91135 (S.D.N.Y. 2007) (deferring to arbitral tribunal's decision to not award collateral estoppel effect to a previous arbitration between the parties).

[362] Yusuf Ahmed Alghanim & Sons, W.L.L. v. Toys "R" Us, Inc., 126 F.3d 15, 20 (2d Cir. 1997).

[363] Interdigital Communs. Corp. v. Samsung Elecs. Co., No. 06 Civ. 6833, 2007 U.S. Dist. LEXIS 91135, *48 (S.D.N.Y. 2007) (internal citations omitted).

[364] See Health Services Mgmt. Corp. v. Hughes, 975 F.2d 1253 (7th Cir. 1992) (concluding that objection to arbitrator was not timely). *See also* Teamsters Local Union No. 764 v. J.H. Merrit & Co., 770 F.2d 40, 42–43 (3d Cir. 1985); Fortune, Alsweet and Eldridge, Inc. v. Daniel, 724 F.2d 1355 (9th Cir. 1983). Having timely objected, a party must not later assert arguments or engage in conduct that suggests that the party has abandoned the objection. See In re Baar & Beards, Inc. v. Oleg Cassini, Inc., 282 N.E.2d 624 (N.Y. 1972).

[365] AAOT Foreign Economic Assoc. (VO) Technostroyexport v. International Dev. and Trade Servs., Inc., 139 F.3d 980, 982 (2d Cir. 1998) (holding that the "settled law of this circuit precludes attacks on the qualifications of arbitrators on grounds previously known but not raised

By the same token, an instrumentality or agent of a New York Convention signatory state may be unsuccessful in asserting foreign sovereign immunity as a bar to recognition and enforcement due to its participation without objection in the arbitration.[366]

until after an award has been rendered"). *Cf.* Henry v. Murphy, No. M-82, 2002 WL 24307, at *4 (S.D.N.Y. Jan. 8, 2002) (holding that failure to raise the defense that the arbitration was time-barred before the arbitral tribunal constitutes a waiver of a limitations period defense at the recognition and enforcement stage).

[366] *See* Seetransport Wiking Trader v. Navimpex Centrala, 989 F.2d 572 (2d Cir. 1993) (holding that defendant, as an instrumentality of a New York Convention signatory, implicitly waived sovereign immunity by participating in arbitration of a dispute arising under a contract to which it had been a party, and thus could not seek to avoid recognition and enforcement on this ground). *But see* Maritime Ventures Int'l, Inc. v. Caribbean Trading & Fidelity Ltd., 689 F. Supp. 1340, 1351 (S.D.N.Y. 1988) (holding that sovereign immunity is not waived simply because a sovereign entered into a contract that named a third country or designated the laws of a third nation to govern the interpretation of the contract).

7

ENFORCING INTERNATIONAL ARBITRATION AGREEMENTS

John Fellas and Hagit Elul

- A. **Proceeding with the Arbitration without Court Intervention** 7.04
- B. **Court Intervention: Introduction** 7.08
  - 1. The Federal Policy in Favor of Arbitration and the New York and Panama Conventions 7.14
    - (a) The federal policy in favor of arbitration 7.14
    - (b) The New York and Panama Conventions 7.16
  - 2. The Jurisdiction of U.S. Federal Courts 7.19
    - (a) Subject-matter jurisdiction 7.20
    - (b) Personal jurisdiction 7.28
  - 3. The Allocation of Power between Arbitrators and Courts 7.29
    - (a) *Kompetenz-Kompetenz* 7.33
    - (b) The separability presumption 7.36
- C. **Reading the *Kompetenz-Kompetenz* Doctrine and the Separability Doctrine Together** 7.42
  - 1. Common Arbitrability Issues 7.55
    - (a) Challenges to the contract 7.57
    - (b) Nonsignatories 7.63
    - (c) The scope of an arbitration clause 7.82
    - (d) Waiver 7.96
- D. **Court Intervention: Compelling Arbitration** 7.98
  - 1. Actions to Compel Arbitration under the Federal Arbitration Act 7.98
  - 2. CPLR § 7503(c) 7.106
- E. **Court Intervention: Staying Litigation Commenced in the United States in Breach of an Arbitration Clause** 7.112
  - 1. Motions to Stay or Dismiss Litigation under the Federal Arbitration Act 7.113
  - 2. The Arbitrability of Claims under U.S. Law 7.121
  - 3. Cases that Include Nonarbitrable Claims 7.124
- F. **Court Intervention: Antisuit Injunctions** 7.129
  - 1. Antisuit Injunctions: An Overview 7.131
  - 2. Circumstances in Which Courts Grant Antisuit Injunctions to Enforce Arbitration Agreements 7.136
  - 3. Circumstances Where Courts Have Denied Antisuit Injunctions in Aid of Arbitration 7.152
- G. **Damages for Breach of an Arbitration Agreement** 7.167
- H. **Conclusion** 7.168

Even though the parties to an international contract may have agreed at the time they entered into it that they would resolve their disputes by arbitration in New York, one or the other party may not abide by that agreement once a dispute actually **7.01** arises. Thus, while one party may commence an arbitration proceeding against the other in accordance with the arbitration clause in the contract, the other may simply refuse to participate in that proceeding. Alternatively, notwithstanding the fact that the parties have agreed to resolve their disputes by arbitration in New York, one party may commence litigation in New York, elsewhere in the United States, or in another country, regarding a subject that falls within the scope of the arbitration agreement. Moreover, occasionally a party to an arbitration agreement may resort to tactics designed to sidestep its obligation to arbitrate by, for example, commencing a lawsuit against a nonparty (e.g., corporate parent) to that agreement, instead of or in addition to suing a related party (e.g., the parent's subsidiary), in connection with an arbitrable dispute. Or it may commence a lawsuit that includes claims, which it asserts fall outside the scope of the arbitration agreement, even though they are connected to the dispute arising out of that agreement. Similarly, a nonparty to an arbitration agreement (e.g., the parent of a subsidiary that is a party to that agreement) may pursue a similar strategy by commencing a lawsuit against a party to that agreement, or advancing claims it asserts to be nonarbitrable.

7.02 This chapter addresses the enforcement of agreements to arbitrate, the question of what one party to an international contract should do when the other fails to comply with its agreement to arbitrate either by refusing to participate in an arbitration, by commencing litigation notwithstanding its agreement to arbitrate, or by engaging in tactics designed to avoid its obligation to arbitrate.[1]

7.03 It will address three basic issues: first, whether one party can proceed with the arbitration and obtain an enforceable award even if the other party fails to participate in the arbitration; second, whether one party can seek the intervention of the courts to enforce its agreement to arbitrate in the event that the other party to the arbitration agreement refuses to arbitrate or commences litigation notwithstanding its agreement to arbitrate; and, third, whether one party can obtain damages against the party that has breached its obligation to arbitrate, for example, by commencing litigation in violation of its agreement to resolve that dispute by arbitration, on the theory that the filing of such a lawsuit is a breach of contract. We consider each of these issues in turn.

A. PROCEEDING WITH THE ARBITRATION WITHOUT COURT INTERVENTION

7.04 If party A commences an arbitration against party B on a subject within the scope of an agreement to arbitrate and party B refuses to participate in that arbitration,

[1] The issue of the choice of law governing the enforcement of agreements to arbitrate is addressed in Chapter 6.C.1 of this book. *See also* Chapter 4.A of this book.

it may not be necessary for party A to seek court intervention if the rules under which the arbitration is being conducted authorize the arbitrators to resolve the case notwithstanding the failure of a party to participate. In such a situation, the party seeking to arbitrate may simply pursue the arbitration without seeking court intervention.

The rules of the major arbitral institutions authorize arbitral tribunals to proceed with an arbitration, and render an award, notwithstanding the failure of one party (almost always the respondent) to participate in the arbitration. Article 23 of the International Centre for Dispute Resolution (ICDR) Rules, which is entitled "Default," is typical:[2] **7.05**

1. If a party fails to file a statement of defense within the time established by the tribunal without showing sufficient cause for such failure, as determined by the tribunal, the tribunal may proceed with the arbitration.
2. If a party, duly notified under these Rules, fails to appear at a hearing without showing sufficient cause for such failure, as determined by the tribunal, the tribunal may proceed with the arbitration.
3. If a party, duly invited to produce evidence or take any other steps in the proceedings, fails to do so within the time established by the tribunal without showing sufficient cause for such failure, as determined by the tribunal, the tribunal may make the award on the evidence before it.

It is important to be clear that such rules do not authorize an arbitral tribunal to issue a default award as a court might render a default judgment in a lawsuit in the United States or elsewhere when a party refuses to appear or participate in that lawsuit. Rather, a tribunal proceeding in the absence of a party will nonetheless be required to make an award based on the evidence, even though it will be presented only by the party that appears. U.S. courts generally enforce awards made in the absence of one party, as long as the nonparticipating party was given notice and an opportunity to be heard.[3] **7.06**

---

[2] *See also* Article 6(3) of the ICC Rules of Arbitration ("If any of the parties refuses or fails to take part in the arbitration or any stage thereof, the arbitration shall proceed notwithstanding such refusal or failure."); Article 15(8) of the LCIA Arbitration Rules ("If the Respondent fails to submit a Statement of Defence or the Claimant a Statement of Defence to Counterclaim, or if at any point any party fails to avail itself of the opportunity to present its case in the manner determined by Article 15(2) to 15(6) or directed by the Arbitral Tribunal, the Arbitral Tribunal may nevertheless proceed with the arbitration and make an award.").

[3] *See, e.g.*, Oh Young Indus. Co. v. E&J Textile Group, Inc., No. B179884, 2005 WL 2470824, at *3 (Cal. Ct. App. Oct. 7, 2005) ("if parties agree to arbitration before an entity whose rules permit proceedings in the absence of one of the parties, then the arbitration provision is self-enforcing or self-executory: arbitration may proceed at a party's request without recourse to the courts for an order to compel arbitration, provided that the other party has adequate notice and an opportunity to participate"); Comprehensive Accounting Corp. v. Rudell, 760 F.2d 138, 140 (7th Cir. 1985); *In re* Transrol Navegacao S.A., 782 F. Supp. 848, 851–53 (S.D.N.Y. 1991).

7.07 However, there are circumstances when it might not be possible for a party seeking to arbitrate to proceed in this manner. One circumstance is when the arbitration clause or the rules it incorporates do not authorize the tribunal to proceed with the case without the participation of all parties. This can occur if the parties agree to arbitrate under an ad hoc clause. Another circumstance is when a signatory to an arbitration agreement commences a case against a nonsignatory. If the nonsignatory fails to appear or participate, the arbitral tribunal might be reluctant to determine whether that nonsignatory is bound by an arbitration agreement purely on the basis of evidence submitted by one side, for fear that any ultimate award against that nonsignatory may be set aside or found to be unenforceable on the ground that the tribunal exceeded its authority. In such a situation, it may be necessary for the party seeking to arbitrate to obtain a court order compelling the nonsignatory to arbitrate. Moreover, if the party resisting arbitration has commenced a lawsuit concerning a dispute that is subject to arbitration notwithstanding the pendency of an arbitration proceeding concerning the same dispute, the party pursuing the arbitration will need to seek the intervention of the courts to stay that litigation.

B. COURT INTERVENTION: INTRODUCTION

7.08 In discussing court intervention to enforce an arbitration agreement, there are three separate situations to consider.

7.09 First, party A commences an arbitration against party B in connection with a dispute which, according to party A, party B is obligated to resolve by arbitration, and party B refuses to participate in that arbitration. Party A may apply for an order from a U.S. court compelling party B to arbitrate, as well as proceeding with the arbitration as discussed previously.

7.10 Second, party B commences litigation against party A in the United States in connection with a dispute which, according to party A, party B is obligated to resolve by arbitration. Party A may seek an order from a U.S. court staying or dismissing that litigation, and may also ask the court to issue an order compelling party B to arbitrate.

7.11 Third, party B commences litigation against party A outside the United States in connection with a dispute which, according to party A, party B is obligated to resolve by arbitration. Party A may seek an antisuit injunction from a U.S. court enjoining party B from pursuing that litigation, as well as an order compelling party B to arbitrate.

7.12 Before discussing the three types of applications for court intervention identified in these scenarios—(1) a motion or petition to compel a party to arbitrate,

(2) a motion to stay or dismiss litigation brought in contravention of an arbitration clause, or (3) a request for an antisuit injunction directed at foreign litigation commenced in violation of an arbitration clause—it is worth considering the context in which these applications would be made. This requires a discussion of four preliminary, but not inconsequential, points.

First, we discuss the fact that any request to a U.S. court to enforce an agreement to arbitrate would be made against the background of those twin peaks that cast a shadow over the entire U.S. arbitration landscape—the federal policy that favors arbitration as an alternative mode of dispute resolution, and the New York and Panama Conventions, as implemented by the Federal Arbitration Act. Second, we address the circumstances in which a U.S. federal court has subject-matter jurisdiction and personal jurisdiction to entertain a case involving the enforcement of an agreement to arbitrate. Third, we discuss the allocation of authority between courts and arbitrators to resolve the various "arbitrability" questions that might arise when courts are called upon to enforce agreements to arbitrate. Finally, we consider some of the common arbitrability questions that arise in actions to enforce agreements to arbitrate. **7.13**

1. The Federal Policy in Favor of Arbitration and the New York and Panama Conventions

(a) The federal policy in favor of arbitration It is well-settled that there is a federal policy in favor of arbitration as an alternative mode of dispute resolution.[4] This policy requires courts to enforce "privately made agreements to arbitrate" as they would other contracts.[5] This policy does not require parties to arbitrate in the absence of their agreement,[6] but it does entail that where parties have agreed to arbitrate they are bound by that agreement.[7] This policy animates the manner in which courts approach the enforcement of agreements to arbitrate. Thus, it is settled that "any doubts concerning the scope of arbitrable issues should be resolved in favor of arbitration," whether the issue concerns construction of the language of the agreement itself, or a defense to arbitrability.[8] **7.14**

[4] *See, e.g.*, Campaniello Imports Ltd. v. Saporiti Italia S.p.A., 117 F.3d 655, 665 (2d Cir. 1997) (Federal Arbitration Act establishes "a liberal policy in favor of arbitration …"); David L. Threlkeld & Co., Inc. v. Metallgesellschaft Ltd., 923 F.2d 245, 248 (2d Cir. 1991) ("[F]ederal policy strongly favors arbitration as an alternative dispute resolution process.").

[5] Dean Witter Reynolds, Inc. v. Byrd, 470 U.S. 213, 219 (1985).

[6] *See* Volt Information Sciences, Inc. v. Board of Trustees of the Leland Stanford Junior Univ., 489 U.S. 468, 478 (1989).

[7] Genesco, Inc. v. T. Kakiuchi & Co. Ltd., 815 F.2d 840, 845 (2d Cir. 1987).

[8] Moses H. Cone Memorial Hospital v. Mercury Construction Corp., 460 U.S. 1, 24–25 (1983). *See also* Mitsubishi Motors Corp. v. Soler Chrysler-Plymouth, Inc., 473 U.S. 614 (1985).

7.15 It is further settled that the federal policy in favor of arbitration is even stronger in international business transactions.[9] As the U.S. Supreme Court put it in the *Scherk* case:

> A contractual provision specifying in advance the forum in which disputes shall be litigated and the law to be applied is ... an almost indispensable precondition to achievement of the orderliness and predictability essential to any international business transaction. Furthermore, such a provision obviates the danger that a dispute under the agreement might be submitted to a forum hostile to the interests of one of the parties or unfamiliar with the problem area involved.
>
> A parochial refusal by the courts of one country to enforce an international arbitration agreement would not only frustrate these purposes, but would invite unseemly and mutually destructive jockeying by the parties to secure tactical litigation advantages.[10]

7.16 *(b) The New York and Panama Conventions* Any request for court intervention to enforce an agreement to arbitrate is also made against the background of two international arbitration conventions to which the United States is a party—the New York Convention[11] and the Panama Convention.[12] The New York Convention, which is viewed as "the cornerstone of current international commercial arbitration,"[13] contains an express provision governing the enforcement of agreements to arbitrate.[14] Article II of the New York Convention provides (with emphasis added):

> 1. Each Contracting State shall recognize an agreement in writing under which the parties undertake to submit to arbitration all or any differences which have arisen or which may arise between them in respect of a defined legal relationship,

---

[9] *Mitsubishi*, 473 U.S. at 629–31.

[10] Scherk v. Alberto-Culver Co., 417 U.S. 506, 516–17 (1974); *see also* Deloitte Noraudit A/S v. Deloitte Haskins & Sells, U.S., 9 F.3d 1060, 1063 (2d Cir. 1993) ("The federal policy favoring arbitration is even stronger in the context of international transactions"); David L. Threlkeld & Co. v. Metallgesellschaft Ltd., 923 F.2d 245, 248 (2d Cir. 1991) ("Enforcement of international arbitral agreements promotes the smooth flow of international transactions by removing the threats and uncertainty of time-consuming and expensive litigation.")

[11] Convention on the Recognition and Enforcement of Foreign Arbitral Awards of 1958, 21 U.S.T. 2517, 330 U.N.T.S. 3, June 10, 1958.

[12] Inter-American Convention on International Commercial Arbitration of 1975, OAS/SERA20 (SEPEF), 14 I.L.M. 336 (1975), January 30, 1975.

[13] Albert Jan Van Den Berg, The New York Arbitration Convention of 1958, Towards a Uniform Judicial Interpretation, Vol. I (1981). These Conventions are discussed in more detail in Chapter 1.B.3 and 1.B.4 of this book.

[14] Article II, New York Convention. The Convention permits contracting states to adopt certain reservations. The United States adopted reservations (i) permitting it, on the basis of reciprocity, to limit the obligation to recognize and enforce awards only to those made in other contracting states, and (ii) to limit the scope of the Convention to disputes that are commercial. *See* Convention, Art. I(3). *See* http://www.uncitral.org/pdf/english/texts/arbitration/NY-conv/XXII_1_e.pdf. *See also* DaPuzzo v. Globalvest Management Company, L.P., 263 F. Supp. 2d 714, 725 n.8 (S.D.N.Y. 2003). The United States adopted the reciprocity reservation in the instrument of ratification of the Panama Convention. *See* http://www.sice.oas.org/dispute/comarb/intl_conv/caicpae.asp.

whether contractual or not, concerning a subject matter capable of settlement by arbitration.

2. The term "agreement in writing" shall include an arbitral clause in a contract or an arbitration agreement, signed by the parties or contained in an exchange of letters or telegrams.
3. *The court of a Contracting State*, when seized of an action in a matter in respect of which the parties have made an agreement within the meaning of this article, *shall, at the request of one of the parties, refer the parties to arbitration*, unless it finds that the said agreement is null and void, inoperative or incapable of being performed.[15]

Each Convention has been implemented in U.S. law in the Federal Arbitration Act.[16] The Federal Arbitration Act is divided into three chapters. The first chapter was enacted in 1925[17] and governs cases involving interstate or foreign commerce. The second chapter contains legislation implementing the New York Convention and applies only to agreements to arbitrate (and arbitration awards) that fall under the New York Convention. The third chapter contains legislation implementing the Panama Convention and applies only to agreements to arbitrate (and arbitration awards) that fall under the Panama Convention. **7.17**

The three chapters do not contain identical provisions, but Chapter 1 of the Federal Arbitration Act is incorporated into Chapter 2[18] and Chapter 3[19] to the extent it does not conflict with other provisions in those chapters or the Convention. Thus, for example, while Chapters 2 and 3 of the Federal Arbitration Act contain provisions governing a court's authority to compel arbitration pursuant to an agreement to arbitrate that falls under the New York Convention and the Panama **7.18**

[15] The Panama Convention contains no provision analogous to Article II(3) requiring courts to refer parties to arbitration, but it has been implemented in U. S. law in a manner requiring that they do so. *See* discussion in Chapter 1.B of this book.

[16] The New York Convention is codified at Chapter 2 of the Federal Arbitration Act, 9 U.S.C. § 201 *et seq*. The Panama Convention is codified at Chapter 3 of the Federal Arbitration Act, 9 U.S.C. § 301 *et seq*.

[17] It was enacted to reverse long-standing opposition by both state and federal courts in the United States to arbitration. Scherk v. Alberto-Culver Co., 417 U.S. 506, 510–11 (1974); Kulukundis Shipping Co., S/A v. Amtorg Trading Corp., 126 F.2d 978, 985 (2d Cir. 1942).

[18] Section 208 of Chapter 2 of the Federal Arbitration Act provides: "Chapter 1 applies to actions and proceedings brought under this chapter to the extent that chapter is not in conflict with this chapter or the Convention as ratified by the United States." *See also* Yusuf Ahmed Alghanim & Sons, W.L.L. v. Toys "R" Us, Inc., 126 F.3d 15, 20 (2d Cir. 1997), *cert. denied*, 522 U.S. 1111 (1998); Oil Basins Ltd. v. Broken Hill Proprietary Co. Ltd., 613 F. Supp. 483, 487 (S.D.N.Y. 1985).

[19] Section 307 of Chapter 3 of the Federal Arbitration Act provides: "Chapter 1 applies to actions and proceedings brought under this chapter to the extent chapter 1 is not in conflict with this chapter or the Inter-American Convention as ratified by the United States." *See also* Siderurgica del Orinoco (Sidor), C.A., v. Linea Naviera de Cabotaje, C.A., No. 99 Civ. 0075 (TPG), 1999 WL 632870, at *4 (S.D.N.Y. Aug. 19, 1999); Productos Mercantiles e Industriales, S.A. v. Faberge USA, 23 F.3d 41, 45 (2d Cir. 1994) ("The legislative history of the Inter-American Convention's implementing statute ... clearly demonstrates that Congress intended the Inter-American Convention to reach the same results as those reached under the New York Convention.").

Convention respectively, neither contains any provision regarding the authority of a court to stay litigation brought in contravention of an arbitration clause. For this, it is necessary for a party to an agreement that falls under the Conventions to rely on Section 3 of Chapter 1 of the Federal Arbitration Act, which is discussed in more detail in Section D of this chapter. Likewise, Chapter 3 incorporates certain provisions of Chapter 2.[20]

2. The Jurisdiction of U.S. Federal Courts

7.19 A U.S. federal court must have subject-matter jurisdiction over the case and personal jurisdiction over the party resisting arbitration before it can enforce an agreement to arbitrate.

7.20 *(a) Subject-matter jurisdiction* Although Chapter 1 of the Federal Arbitration Act established a distinct area of federal law for arbitration, it did not provide an independent basis of federal subject-matter jurisdiction.[21] In other words, even if a case falls under Chapter 1 of the Federal Arbitration Act, it cannot be brought in federal court unless there is an independent basis for federal court jurisdiction. Chapters 2 and 3 of the Federal Arbitration Act, by contrast, provide, first, that cases involving agreements falling under either the New York or the Panama Convention are deemed to raise a federal question such that they may be brought in federal court,[22] and, second, that cases commenced in state court involving such agreements can be removed[23] to federal court.[24]

---

[20] Section 302 of Chapter 3 of the Federal Arbitration Act provides that: "Sections 202, 203, 204, 205 and 207 of this title shall apply to this chapter as if specifically set forth herein, except that for the purposes of this chapter 'the Convention' shall mean the Inter-American Convention."

[21] *Moses H. Cone*, 460 U.S. at 26 n.34; DaPuzzo v. Globalvest Management Company, L.P., 263 F. Supp. 2d 714, 722 (S.D.N.Y. 2003). Thus, a party to a case under Chapter 1 would have to demonstrate that there is diversity of citizenship or that a case raises a federal question. *See* 28 U.S.C. § 1331 and § 1332. The concept of subject matter jurisdiction is discussed in Chapter 2.C.2(a) of this book.

[22] Section 203 of the Federal Arbitration Act provides that any case "falling under" the New York Convention may be brought in federal court. Section 203 states: "An action or proceeding falling under the Convention shall be deemed to arise under the laws and treaties of the United States. The district courts of the United States (including the courts enumerated in Section 460 of title 28) shall have original jurisdiction over such an action or proceeding, regardless of the amount in controversy." Section 302 of the Federal Arbitration Act (by incorporation of Chapter 2 of the Federal Arbitration Act) provides for the same for cases falling under the Panama Convention.

[23] For non-U.S. practitioners, the term *remove* or *removal* is one of legal art referring to the transfer of a case from state court to federal court.

[24] Section 205 of the Federal Arbitration Act provides that any case "falling under" the New York Convention commenced in state court may be removed to federal court at any time before trial. Section 205 states: "Where the subject matter of an action or proceeding pending in a state court relates to an arbitration agreement or award falling under the Convention, the defendant or the defendants may, at any time before the trial thereof, remove such action or proceeding to the district court of the United States for the district and division embracing the place where the action or proceeding is pending. The procedure for removal of causes otherwise provided by law shall apply, except that the ground for removal provided in this section need not appear on the

This raises the question of what conditions need to be satisfied for a case to "fall under" one of the Conventions.[25] Section 202 of the Federal Arbitration Act provides the answer:[26] **7.21**

> An arbitration agreement or arbitral award arising out of a legal relationship, whether contractual or not, which is considered as commercial, including a transaction, contract, or agreement described in section 2 of this title, falls under the Convention. An agreement or award arising out of such a relationship which is entirely between citizens of the United States shall be deemed not to fall under the Convention unless that relationship involves property located abroad, envisages performance or enforcement abroad, or has some other reasonable relation with one or more foreign states. For the purpose of this section a corporation is a citizen of the United States if it is incorporated or has its principal place of business in the United States.

In assessing whether a case falls under the Convention for the purposes of subject-matter jurisdiction, courts look only to whether the claim of subject-matter jurisdiction is "immaterial, frivolous and insubstantial or made solely for the purpose of obtaining jurisdiction."[27] If it is not, a court will conclude that it has subject-matter jurisdiction. **7.22**

Courts have articulated a four-part test for determining whether an agreement falls under the Convention: (1) there must be a written agreement; (2) it must provide for arbitration in the territory of a signatory of the Convention; (3) the subject matter must be commercial; and (4) it cannot be entirely domestic in scope.[28] Each of these four requirements is considered in turn. **7.23**

---

face of the complaint but may be shown in the petition for removal. For the purposes of Chapter 1 of this title any action or proceeding removed under this section shall be deemed to have been brought in the district court to which it is removed." Section 302 of the Federal Arbitration Act (by incorporation of Chapter 2 of the Federal Arbitration Act) provides the same for cases falling under the Panama Convention.

[25] In the discussion that follows, the term *Convention* refers to both the New York Convention and the Panama Convention.

[26] Section 302 of the Federal Arbitration Act has the identical provision for Panama Convention cases by incorporating by reference Section 202.

[27] Sarhank Group v. Oracle Corporation, 404 F.3d 657, 660 (2d Cir. 2005). *Sarhank* concerned an action to enforce an arbitral award under the Convention rather than one to enforce an agreement to arbitrate. But its reasoning applies equally to cases to enforce arbitration agreements that fall under the Convention. There, the court noted that "Sarhank has, for subject matter jurisdiction purposes, adequately pleaded an arbitral award falling under the Convention. Because its allegations are not immaterial, frivolous, or made solely to obtain jurisdiction, the district court had subject matter jurisdiction to resolve the legal and factual questions ancillary to determining whether the Egyptian award could be enforced in the United States against Oracle." *Id.*

[28] Smith/Enron Cogeneration Limited Partnership, Inc. v. Smith Cogeneration International, Inc., 198 F.3d 88, 92 (2d Cir. 1999). If, applying this four-part test, a case is found to fall under both the New York Convention and the Panama Convention, Section 305 of the Federal Arbitration Act provides that the Panama Convention will apply "[i]f a majority of the parties to the arbitration agreement are citizens of a State or States that have ratified or acceded to the [Panama] Convention and are member States of the Organization of American States."

7.24 (1) *Writing.* The Convention applies to an "agreement in writing," which includes "an arbitral clause in a contract or an arbitration agreement, signed by the parties or contained in an exchange of letters or telegrams."[29] While some courts, interpreting this language, have held that a contract containing an arbitration clause need not be signed,[30] the Court of Appeals for the Second Circuit has held that it must be.[31] As discussed in more detail later, however, in the event the arbitration agreement is signed by the parties and thus falls within the scope of the Convention, a nonsignatory can nonetheless rely upon or be bound by it based upon ordinary contract principles.[32]

7.25 (2) *Commercial.* The requirement that the subject matter of the agreement be commercial reflects the United States reservation to the New York Convention. The term *commercial* is viewed broadly by U.S. courts.[33]

7.26 (3) *Territory.* It is important to emphasize that U.S. courts look to the place of arbitration in determining whether a case falls under the Convention, not the nationality of the parties.[34] If the place of arbitration is in a country that is a

[29] Article II(2), New York Convention.

[30] Sphere Drake Ins. PLC v. Marine Towing Inc., 16 F.3d 666, 669 (5th Cir. 1994).

[31] Kahn Lucas Lancaster, Inc. v. Lark Int'l Ltd., 186 F.3d 210, 214–15 (2d Cir. 1999).

[32] "[O]nce a party establishes that … a signed writing … exists, the general rules of contract law apply to determine which parties are subject to arbitration…. The [New York Convention's] writing requirement does not foreclose the application of the … principles under which nonsignatories sometimes can be obligated [to arbitrate] by, or benefit from agreements signed by others." Borsack v. Chalk & Vermilion Fine Arts Ltd., 974 F. Supp. 293, 301 (S.D.N.Y. 1997). *See also* Siderurgica del Orinoco (Sidor), C.A. v. Linea Naviera De Cabotaje, No. 99 Civ. 0075 (TPG), 1999 WL 632870, at *5 (S.D.N.Y. Aug. 19, 1999); Arthur Andersen LLP v. Carlisle, 129 S.Ct. 1896, 1901–02 (2009) (holding that even though Section 3 of the Federal Arbitration Act, which governs motions to stay litigation brought in contravention of an arbitration clause, refers to agreements in "writing," nonparties can nonetheless rely on Section 3, "[b]ecause 'traditional principles' of state law allow a contract to be enforced by or against nonparties to the contract through 'assumption, piercing the corporate veil, alter ego, incorporation by reference, third-party beneficiary theories, waiver and estoppel' ") (citation omitted).

[33] *See* Citizens Bank v. Alafabco, Inc., 539 U.S. 52, 56 (2003) ("We have interpreted the term ['commercial'] in the FAA as the functional equivalent of the more familiar term 'affecting commerce'—words of art that ordinarily signal the broadest permissible exercise of Congress' Commerce Clause power."). *See also* Sumitomo Corp. v. Parakopi Compania Maritima, S.A., 477 F. Supp. 737, 740 (S.D.N.Y. 1979) (definition of "commercial" in Section 202 not limited by definition of "commerce" in Section 1 of the Federal Arbitration Act, and thus includes cases where all the parties involved are foreign entities), *aff'd*, 620 F.2d 286 (2d Cir. 1980); Henry v. Murphy, No. M-82, 2002 WL 24307, at *4 (S.D.N.Y. Jan. 8, 2002) (finding that "a conflict between corporate shareholders regarding the proceeds of a stock transaction" is commercial); Siderius, Inc. v. Compania de Acero del Pacifico, S.A., 453 F. Supp. 22, 24 (S.D.N.Y. 1978) (finding "commercial" requirement satisfied since "this dispute arose out of a classic commercial relationship one involving the purchase and sale of goods by two corporations"); Island Territory of Curacao v. Solitron Devices, Inc., 356 F. Supp. 1, 12–13 (S.D.N.Y. 1973), *aff'd*, 489 F.2d 1313 (2d Cir. 1973); Alexander v. Chesapeake Appalachia, LLC, 839 F. Supp. 2d 544 (N.D.N.Y. 2012) (lease negotiations for interstate oil and gas leases satisfied the commercial requirement).

[34] *Smith/Enron*, 198 F.3d at 92–95 (rejecting view that the Convention requires a "center of gravity" test that looks to whether the subject matter of the arbitration, or the parties to the arbitration, or both, are located in a State that also is a signatory to the Convention, and instead

signatory to the Convention, then the Convention applies. An agreement calling for arbitration in New York, therefore, satisfies this condition.[35]

(4) *Nondomestic.* The requirement that the agreement not be domestic in scope entails that a broad category of cases will fall under the Convention. First, any arbitration agreement involving a non-U.S. party will fall under the Convention, as long as it satisfies the other three conditions. Second, even if there is an arbitration agreement between two U.S. parties, and even if that agreement calls for arbitration in the United States, that agreement would still fall under the Convention if the relationship between the parties "involves property located abroad, envisages performance or enforcement abroad, or has some other reasonable relation with one or more foreign states."[36] **7.27**

(b) Personal jurisdiction Even where a court has subject-matter jurisdiction, it is necessary to establish personal jurisdiction over the defendant in order to enforce an agreement to arbitrate. It is settled that by agreeing to arbitrate in New York, a defendant is "deemed to have consented to the jurisdiction of the court that could compel the arbitration proceeding in New York. To hold otherwise would be to render the arbitration clause a nullity."[37] **7.28**

3. The Allocation of Power between Arbitrators and Courts

The U.S. Supreme Court has stated that "arbitration is a matter of contract and a party cannot be required to submit to arbitration any dispute he has not agreed so to submit."[38] Arbitration under the FAA "is a matter of consent," not coercion.[39] Courts must "give effect to the contractual rights and expectations of the parties."[40] When a party seeks the assistance of a court to enforce an agreement to arbitrate, the party resisting arbitration typically denies that it had agreed to submit that dispute to arbitration, for example, because it never signed the arbitration agreement (or because the party seeking the assistance of the court did not sign the arbitration agreement), or because the dispute in question falls outside the scope of the arbitration agreement, or because the agreement to arbitrate is invalid in some way, or because a related contract contains a contradictory dispute resolution **7.29**

taking the position that the issue is whether the place of arbitration is in a country that is a signatory to the Convention).

[35] *Id.* at 95.

[36] 9 U.S.C. § 202 (2009).

[37] Merrill Lynch, Pierce, Fenner & Smith, Inc. v. Lecopulos, 553 F.2d 842, 844 (2d Cir. 1977). While *Lecopulos* is still good law in the Second Circuit, at least one New York state court has disagreed with its holding, finding that "[s]ome minimal New York nexus is required in order to commence a special proceeding in our courts to stay arbitration." Merrill Lynch, Pierce, Fenner & Smith, Inc. v. McLeod, 622 N.Y.S.2d 954, 955 (N.Y. App. Div. 1995).

[38] Howsam v. Dean Witter Reynolds, Inc., 537 U.S. 79, 83 (2002).

[39] Granite Rock Co. v. Int'l Bhd. of Teamsters, 561 U.S. 287, 299 (2010).

[40] Stolt-Nielsen S.A. v. AnimalFeeds Int'l Corp., 559 U.S. 662, 682 (2010).

clause.[41] Courts typically refer to these issues as questions of "arbitrability"—i.e., whether the dispute in question is subject to arbitration.[42]

7.30 The question arises as to what type of inquiry a court should undertake in order to resolve the type of arbitrability questions that arise when it is called upon to enforce an agreement to arbitrate. On one end of the spectrum, the courts could undertake a full arbitrability inquiry—holding a full evidentiary hearing, if necessary, to resolve the issues raised in an action to enforce an arbitration agreement—and refer the case to an arbitrator only if they conclude that it was indeed arbitrable. On the other end of the spectrum, the courts could refer a case to arbitration based simply on an allegation by the party seeking to arbitrate that the case is arbitrable and leave it to the arbitrators to resolve the objections advanced by the party resisting arbitration.

7.31 On the one hand, if, in an action to enforce an arbitration agreement, a court were to undertake a full arbitrability inquiry to decide, for example, whether an agreement is invalid on the ground that it has been fraudulently induced or whether a particular dispute falls within the scope of an arbitration clause, the result could be a lengthy and costly litigation in the national courts before an arbitration could even get going. This would undermine the efficacy of the arbitration process: parties would be reluctant to agree to arbitrate if protracted litigation were a likely prelude to it. On the other hand, if courts were to refer a case to arbitration based simply on one party's bare allegation that the case was arbitrable, with the understanding that the arbitrators would resolve the arguments advanced by the party resisting arbitration, in many cases (i.e., those where the dispute turned out not to be arbitrable) arbitrators would be exercising authority never granted to them in any agreement to arbitrate, contradicting the bedrock principle of arbitration, namely, that a party cannot be required to arbitrate a dispute absent its agreement.

---

[41] This case involved interrelated contracts with inconsistent dispute resolution clauses, an engineering contract requiring AAA arbitration and a parent guarantee vesting New York courts with exclusive jurisdiction over disputes. The engineering contract contained a supremacy clause stating that in the event of any inconsistency among the transaction agreements, the terms of the engineering contract shall prevail. On this basis the court found that the arbitration agreement in the engineering contract trumped the parent guarantee's dispute resolution clause and compelled arbitration of the dispute.

[42] The term *arbitrability* is also used by United States courts to refer to the question of whether national law prohibits the arbitration of certain subjects. That issue is considered in Section D of this chapter. Commentators have bemoaned the fact U.S. courts have used the term "arbitrability" to refer to different concepts, i.e., on the one hand, whether the parties have agreed to arbitrate a particular dispute and, on the other, whether national law prohibits the arbitration of disputes relating to particular subjects, even if the parties agreed to do so. Rusty Park, for example, writes that this is "regrettable, since it blurs useful distinctions between an arbitrator who may not hear a case because of the parties' drafting choice, and an arbitrator lacking power because nonwaivable legal norms prohibit him to consider the disputed subject matter." William W. Park, *The Contours of Arbitral Jurisdiction*, in ARBITRATION OF INTERNATIONAL BUSINESS DISPUTES: STUDIES IN LAW AND PRACTICE 111–112 n.41 (2006). *See* discussion in Chapter 6.C.3(d) of this book.

Several doctrines and presumptions have evolved to allocate authority between courts and arbitrators to resolve the arbitrability questions raised in actions to enforce arbitration agreements. The two most important are the doctrine of Kompetenz-Kompetenz and the separability presumption. **7.32**

(a) Kompetenz-Kompetenz Although not known by that name in the United States, the Kompetenz-Kompetenz (or competence-competence) doctrine provides "that international arbitral tribunals have the power to consider and to decide disputes concerning their own jurisdiction."[43] While the issue of arbitral jurisdiction is dealt with in detail in Chapter 6 of this book,[44] it is worth saying a little about it in the context of this chapter, since it impacts the question of who, as between the courts and the arbitrators, should resolve the arbitrability issues that arise when a court is called upon to enforce an agreement to arbitrate. **7.33**

The leading case on this issue is *First Options of Chicago, Inc. v. Kaplan*, where the Supreme Court framed the question before it as "who—court or arbitrator—has the primary authority to decide whether a party has agreed to arbitrate."[45] It held that the answer to this question "turns upon what the parties agreed about *that* matter. Did the parties agree to submit the arbitrability question itself to arbitration?"[46] Although it is settled that there is a presumption in favor of arbitration, when it comes to the question of whether the parties agreed to submit the arbitrability question itself to arbitration, the Court held the presumption in favor of arbitrability not to apply.[47] Rather, when it comes to the question of who decides arbitrability, the presumption is in favor of judicial resolution, rather than arbitral resolution.[48] As one court said, "[I]ssues of 'arbitrability' are presumptively for the court to decide, while issues other than 'arbitrability' are presumptively for the arbitrator."[49] **7.34**

This presumption in favor of judicial resolution of arbitrability can be overcome, however, in the event that there is "clea[r] and unmistakabl[e] evidence" that the parties intended for arbitrators to decide questions about their own jurisdiction.[50] It is not necessary that an arbitration clause contain express language empowering an arbitrator to decide issues of arbitrability.[51] Courts in the Second Circuit have found the "clear and unmistakable evidence" necessary in both the **7.35**

---

[43] Gary B. Born, International Commercial Arbitration 1046–47 (2014).

[44] *See* especially Chapter 6.D. *See also* Chapter 3.B.2(a) of this book.

[45] First Options of Chicago, Inc. v. Kaplan, 514 U.S. 938, 942 (1995).

[46] *Id.* at 943.

[47] *Id.* at 944–45.

[48] Howsam v. Dean Witter Reynolds, Inc., 537 U.S. 79, 83 (2002); First Options of Chicago v. Kaplan, 514 U.S. 938, 944–45 (1995); Shaw Group, Inc. v. Triplefine Int'l Corp., 322 F.3d 115, 121 (2d Cir. 2003).

[49] John Hancock Life Ins. Co. v. Wilson, 254 F.3d 48, 53 (2d Cir. 2001) (quotations omitted).

[50] First Options of Chicago Inc. v. Kaplan, 514 U.S. 938, 944 (1995).

[51] Shaw Group, Inc. v. Triplefine, Int'l, 322 F.3d 115, 121 (2d Cir. 2003).

language of an arbitration clause and the rules under which the arbitration is to be conducted. Thus a clause providing that "any and all controversies ... shall be determined by arbitration" was found to be sufficient to encompass arbitrability.[52] Similarly, courts have found that an agreement to arbitrate under the rules of the International Chamber of Commerce (ICC)[53] and the American Arbitration Association (AAA)[54] also constitute such clear and unmistakable evidence.

7.36 *(b) The separability presumption* The other important doctrine that has the effect of allocating authority between arbitrators and courts to resolve disputes that arise when courts are called upon to enforce agreements to arbitrate is the separability, or severability, presumption.[55] In *Prima Paint Corp. v. Conklin Mfg. Co.*,[56] the Supreme Court explained the doctrine in

---

[52] Paine Webber, Inc. v. Bybyk, 81 F.3d 1193, 1199 (2d Cir. 1996) ("The words 'any and all' are elastic enough to encompass disputes over whether a claim ... is within the scope of arbitration."). *See also* Smith Barney Shearson Inc. v. Sacharow, 91 N.Y.2d 39, 46–47 (N.Y. 1997) (holding that language providing for "[a]ny controversy" between the parties to be "settled by arbitration" was sufficiently "plain and sweeping" to indicate an intent to have arbitrability decided by the arbitrators).

[53] In *Shaw Group Inc.*, 322 F.3d at 122, the court found that Article 6(2) of the ICC Rules provided such clear and unmistakable evidence. Article 6(2) of the ICC Rules provides: "If the Respondent does not file an Answer ... or if any party raises one or more pleas concerning the existence, validity or scope of the arbitration agreement, the [ICA] Court may decide, without prejudice to the admissibility or merits of the plea or pleas, that the arbitration shall proceed if it is *prima facie* satisfied that an arbitration agreement under the Rules may exist. In such a case, any decision as to the jurisdiction of the Arbitral Tribunal shall be taken by the Arbitral Tribunal itself. If the [ICA] Court is not so satisfied, the parties shall be notified that the arbitration cannot proceed. In such a case, any party retains the right to ask any court having jurisdiction whether or not there is a binding arbitration agreement." Other courts have reached similar conclusions with respect to the ICC Rules. *See* Oriental Republic of Uruguay v. Chemical Overseas Holdings, Inc., No. 05 Civ. 6151 (WHP), 2006 WL 164967, at *6 (S.D.N.Y. Jan. 24, 2006) (relying on ICC Rules to find that the incorporation of the ICC Rules sufficiently evidences intent of parties to arbitrate questions of arbitrability); Apollo Computer, Inc. v. Berg, 886 F.2d 469, 472–73 (1st Cir. 1989) (same); Daiei, Inc. v. United States Shoe Corp., 755 F. Supp. 299, 303 (D. Haw. 1991) (even where an agreement "does not specifically assign the determination of arbitrability to the arbitrator," a provision to have all disputes resolved according to ICC Rules evidences the parties' "agree[ment] to let the arbitrator decide questions of arbitrability").

[54] Contec Corp. v. Remote Solution Co., 398 F.3d 205, 208 (2d Cir. 2005) ("[W]hen . . . parties explicitly incorporate rules that empower an arbitrator to decide issues of arbitrability, the incorporation serves as clear and unmistakable evidence of the parties' intent to delegate such issues to an arbitrator."). *See also* Qualcomm Inc. v. Nokia Corp., 466 F.3d 1366, 1372–73 (Fed. Cir. 2006) (concluding that the agreement's incorporation of AAA Rules clearly and unmistakably showed the parties' intent to delegate issue of determining arbitrability to arbitrator); Terminix Int'l Co., LP v. Palmer Ranch Ltd. P'ship, 432 F.3d 1327, 1332–33 (11th Cir. 2005) (holding that by incorporating AAA Rules into arbitration agreement, parties clearly and unmistakably agreed that arbitrator should decide whether arbitration clause was valid); Citifinancial, Inc. v. Newton, 359 F. Supp. 2d 545, 549–52 (S.D. Miss. 2005) (holding that by agreeing to be bound by procedural rules of AAA, including rule giving arbitrator power to rule on his or her own jurisdiction, defendant agreed to arbitrate questions of jurisdiction before arbitrator); Sleeper Farms v. Agway, Inc., 211 F. Supp. 2d 197, 200 (D. Me. 2002) (holding arbitration clause stating that arbitration shall proceed according to rules of AAA provides clear and unmistakable delegation of scope-determining authority to arbitrator).

[55] *See* Chapter 1.D.1(a) and Chapter 6.C.2 of this book.

[56] Prima Paint Corp. v. Flood & Conklin Mfg. Co., 388 U.S. 395 (1967).

the following way: "except where the parties otherwise intend … arbitration clauses as a matter of federal law are 'separable' from the contracts in which they are embedded."[57] What this means is that most challenges to the validity of a contract—for example, that it is invalid because it was induced fraudulently or that it is invalid because it is illegal—do not affect the jurisdiction of an arbitral tribunal to resolve a dispute under the arbitration clause in that contract, since by positing that the clause is separate, or severable, from the underlying contract, that clause is insulated from any challenges to the validity of the underlying contract.

The presumption of separability can be explained by considering a hypothetical example. Imagine that A enters into contract with B in circumstances where B fraudulently induced her to do so. B then tries to claim the benefit of that contract, and A asserts as a defense that that contract is invalid because she was fraudulently induced to enter into it. Further suppose that, subsequently, A, this time in the absence of any fraud on the part of B, enters into a separate contract with B to resolve by arbitration their dispute about whether the underlying contract is invalid based on the defense of fraudulent inducement. In this hypothetical case, it is clear that whatever defect may infect the underlying contract, based on the fact that A was fraudulently induced to enter into it, does not affect the subsequent arbitration agreement since the latter was entered into separately and thus not in the circumstances that tainted the underlying agreement. The separability doctrine posits, as a fiction and for the purpose of preserving an arbitral tribunal's jurisdiction to resolve disputes concerning certain challenges to contracts, that where A and B enter into a contract containing an arbitration clause, there is a presumption that that clause was, as in the hypothetical example, entered into separately from the underlying contract. The result is that arbitral jurisdiction under the arbitration clause remains immune from challenges to the validity of the underlying contract. **7.37**

Without the presumption of separability, any challenge to the validity of a contract—for example, that it was fraudulently induced—would, a fortiori, constitute a challenge to an arbitration clause contained within it. As a matter of logic, therefore, an arbitral tribunal could not rely on that clause as the basis of its authority to resolve a dispute between the parties, since the validity of that clause and, thus, the legitimacy of that authority is contested. Without the presumption of separability, in a case where a party resisting arbitration challenged the validity of the contract containing the arbitration clause, a court would, in principle, have to undertake a full arbitrability inquiry to determine the validity of the underlying contract (and thus the arbitration clause contained within it) before a case could be referred to an arbitral tribunal for resolution—assuming **7.38**

[57] *Id.* at 402.

the court found the agreement to be valid. The effect would be to undermine the arbitration process, putting the parties in the position where they might have to engage in a protracted litigation about the validity of their contract before they could arbitrate, and, even then, only if the contract were found by the courts to be valid.

7.39 It would be different, however, to return to the hypothetical, if the subsequent and separate agreement to arbitrate were itself fraudulently induced. In that case, A would have a basis to challenge the validity of the arbitration clause itself, and not simply that of the underlying contract. In such a case, the authority of the arbitrators would be directly at issue, since there would be a challenge to the very agreement that constitutes the basis of that authority. In that situation, the courts rather than the arbitrators would resolve that challenge. As the Supreme Court stated in *Prima Paint*, "if the claim is fraud in the inducement of the arbitration clause itself—an issue which goes to the 'making' of the agreement to arbitrate—the federal court may proceed to adjudicate it."[58] The Supreme Court reiterated this point in the subsequent case of *Buckeye Check Cashing v. Cardegna*[59] stating, "a challenge to the validity of the contract as a whole, and not specifically to the arbitration clause, must go to the arbitrator."[60]

7.40 It is important to stress that the separability presumption is distinct from the doctrine of Kompetenz-Kompetenz.[61] The separability doctrine operates by inoculating an arbitration clause from an attack based on a challenge to the validity of the agreement containing that clause; defects in the underlying agreement will not infect the arbitration clause contained within it because that clause is presumed to be a separate contract. Therefore, whatever authority the arbitrators have under the arbitration clause remains, notwithstanding a challenge to the validity of the contract containing it. The doctrine of Kompetenz-Kompetenz simply does not come into play in this scenario.

7.41 The Kompetenz-Kompetenz doctrine presupposes a challenge to the arbitration clause itself—more specifically a challenge to whether a particular dispute is arbitrable based on that clause (e.g., because a particular dispute falls outside the scope of the clause or because a nonsignatory claims not to be bound to arbitrate by that clause). The Kompetenz-Kompetenz doctrine operates to resolve the question of who, as between the courts and the arbitrators, resolves that question of arbitrability.

58 *Prima Paint*, 388 U.S. 395 at 403–04.

59 Buckeye Check Cashing, Inc. v. John Cardegna, 546 U.S. 440 (2006).

60 *Id.* at 449.

61 *See* William W. Park, *The Arbitrability Dicta in First Options*, in Arbitration of International Business Disputes: Studies in Law and Practice 96–97 (2006); Gary B. Born, International Commercial Arbitration 1071–72 (2014).

C. READING THE *KOMPETENZ-KOMPETENZ* DOCTRINE AND THE SEPARABILITY DOCTRINE TOGETHER

While, as noted above, the Kompetenz-Kompetenz doctrine and the separability doctrine are distinct, in *Rent-A-Center West, Inc. v. Jackson*[62] the Court read together the separability doctrine from *Prima Paint* and the Kompetenz-Kompetenz doctrine from *First Options* (what the Court called the "delegation" doctrine), in a manner that makes it easier for parties seeking to arbitrate to get before an arbitrator. **7.42**

Rent-A-Center is an unusual case in that the arbitration agreement in question was not part of a larger contract dealing with the substantive rights and duties of the parties—in that case an employment relationship—but was itself a separate contract. That agreement also contained a "delegation provision"—a provision explicitly delegating to the arbitrator the exclusive authority to resolve questions about the enforceability of that agreement.[63] **7.43**

The employee, Jackson, argued that his unconscionability challenge to the arbitration agreement had to be decided by a court. The Ninth Circuit agreed. It found that the separability doctrine did not require arbitration of that challenge since it was directed to the arbitration agreement (which happened to be the entire agreement) rather than "to the validity of the contract setting forth other substantive contractual obligations between the parties."[64] It held that the delegation principle of *First Options* was inapplicable because, even though the arbitration agreement delegated to the arbitrator the exclusive authority to resolve questions about the enforceability of the contract, precisely what was in issue was whether Jackson had "meaningfully agreed to the terms of the form of Agreement to Arbitrate."[65] The implication was that the clear and unmistakable evidence required by *First Options* was lacking. Certainly, that is how Justice Stevens, in dissent, read the Ninth Circuit's ruling: "If respondent's unconscionability claim is correct—that is, if the terms of the agreement are so one-sided and the process of its making so unfair—it would contravene the existence of clear and unmistakable assent to arbitrate the very question petitioner now seeks to arbitrate."[66] **7.44**

Whereas the Ninth Circuit dealt with the doctrines from *First Options* and *Prima Paint* separately, Justice Scalia, writing for the Court, read those two doctrines in **7.45**

---

[62] Rent-A-Center West, Inc. v. Jackson, 130 S. Ct. 2722 (2010).

[63] *Id.* at 2777.

[64] Jackson v. Rent-A-Center West, Inc., 581 F.3d 912, 916 n.2 (9th Cir. 2009), *rev'd,* 130 S. Ct. 2772 (2010).

[65] 581 F.3d at 917.

[66] 130 S. Ct. at 2785.

combination and found that the unconscionability challenge had to be resolved by the arbitrator.[67]

7.46 In so far as *First Options* was concerned, Justice Scalia found in the language of the delegation provision clear and unmistakable evidence that the parties intended to delegate to the arbitrator the authority to decide whether that agreement was enforceable. To the objection that this clear and unmistakable textual evidence was outweighed by Jackson's claims of unconscionability, Justice Scalia responded that "[t]his mistakes the subject of *First Options* 'clear and unmistakable' requirement. It pertains to the parties' *manifestation of intent*, not the agreement's validity."[68]

7.47 In so far as *Prima Paint* was concerned, Justice Scalia applied the separability doctrine in a novel way. In the prior separability cases considered by the Court, the arbitration clause was contained in a larger contract dealing with the substantive rights and duties of the parties. "To be sure, this case differs from *Prima Paint*, *Buckeye* and *Preston*, in that the arbitration provisions sought to be enforced in those cases were contained in contracts unrelated to arbitration."[69] Whereas, in these earlier cases, the Court applied the separability doctrine to distinguish *between* the underlying contract and the arbitration clause within it, in *Rent-A-Center*, Justice Scalia applied that doctrine to make distinctions *within* the arbitration clause itself, finding in that clause both "an agreement to arbitrate one controversy (an employment-discrimination claim) … [and] an agreement to arbitrate a different controversy (enforceability)"—the latter being located in the delegation provision.[70]

7.48 Having used the separability doctrine to sever the delegation provision from the rest of the arbitration agreement, Justice Scalia held that in order for Jackson's unconscionability challenge to be resolved by a court, that challenge had to be directed to the delegation provision specifically, rather than the arbitration agreement in its entirety. "[U]nless Jackson challenged the delegation provision specifically, we must treat it as valid under §2 [of the FAA], and must enforce it…."[71] And because the Court found that Jackson had challenged the arbitration agreement as a whole, the Court held that the unconscionability challenge had to be resolved by the arbitrator.

7.49 By combining the delegation and separability doctrines, the effect of *Rent-A-Center* is to make it easier for a party seeking to enforce an arbitration agreement to get before an arbitrator. This is because when a party resists arbitration

[67] *Id.* at 2785.
[68] *Id.* at 2778.
[69] *Id.* at 2779.
[70] *Id.* at 2778 n.1.
[71] *Id.* at 2779.

in a case where the arbitration agreement contains a provision that clearly and unmistakably delegates to the arbitrator the authority to resolve questions about the validity of that agreement (the delegation doctrine), *Rent-A-Center* holds that those questions must be resolved by an arbitrator unless the party challenges the validity of the delegation provision itself (the separability doctrine).

7.50 But it is inevitably more difficult to challenge a delegation provision in an arbitration clause than that clause in its entirety. Justice Scalia acknowledged as much, noting that an argument by Jackson that the delegation provision was unconscionable on grounds that only limited discovery was permitted "would be, of course, a much more difficult argument to sustain than the argument that the same limitation renders arbitration of his fact-bound employment-discrimination claim unconscionable."[72]

7.51 It might have been said that *Rent-A-Center* will have only a limited impact on arbitrability jurisprudence because, first, unlike other arbitration clauses, the arbitration clause there specifically contained a delegation provision, and, second, the arbitration clause in that case was contained in a separate agreement. This view is incorrect.

7.52 The first point overlooks the fact that parties often agree to arbitrate in accordance with arbitration rules like those of the AAA or the ICC, which contain provisions delegating authority to arbitrators to determine objections to the validity of an arbitration agreement. Courts have held that an agreement to arbitrate under such rules satisfies the clear and unmistakable evidence requirement of *First Options*.[73] Thus parties seeking to arbitrate under commonly used arbitration rules will be able to point to a "delegation provision" in those rules similar to that in *Rent-A-Center*. Indeed, in *Brennan v. Opus Bank*,[74] the Ninth Circuit identified a delegation provision in the arbitration clause precisely because the parties had agreed to arbitrate under the AAA Rules. It noted that "these parties' incorporation of the AAA rules constituted 'clear and unmistakable' evidence of their intent to submit the arbitrability disputes to arbitration."[75]

7.53 As far as the second point is concerned, the fact that the arbitration clause in *Rent-A-Center* was itself a separate contract is not material to the holding of that case. The logic of the Court's decision in *Rent-A-Center* is that one can find within an arbitration clause (and thus sever from each other) agreements to arbitrate more than one controversy—for example, an agreement to arbitrate the merits of a dispute about the parties' substantive rights and duties and one to arbitrate a dispute

[72] *Id.* at 2780.

[73] *See, e.g.*, Republic of Ecuador v. Chevron Corp., 638 F.3d 384 (2d Cir. 2011) (UNCITRAL Rules); Contec Corp. v. Remote Solution, Co., Ltd., 398 F.3d 205 (2d Cir. 2005) (AAA Rules); Shaw Group, Inc. v. Triplefine, Int'l, 322 F.3d 115 (2d Cir. 2003) (ICC Rules).

[74] 2015 WL 4731378 (9th Cir. May 8, 2015).

[75] 2015 WL 4731378 at *5.

about the validity of the clause itself. That logic applies whether that arbitration clause is itself a separate contract or part of a larger contract. Indeed, that was precisely the approach taken by the Ninth Circuit in *Brennan*. In that case, there was an employment agreement, which had an arbitration clause incorporating the AAA Rules. The Ninth Circuit stated: "We conclude that *Rent-A-Center* controls the present case. Here, three agreements—each nested inside the other—are relevant to our analysis: (1) Brennan's Employment Agreement, (2) the Arbitration Clause (section 16), and (3) the Delegation Provision (i.e., incorporation of the AAA rules which delegates enforceability questions to the arbitrator). The last two are separate agreements to arbitrate different issues. Thus, just like in *Rent-A-Center*, multiple severable arbitration agreements exist. The arbitration clause at issue, as in *Rent-A-Center*, is the Delegation Provision because that is the arbitration agreement Opus Bank seeks to enforce."[76]

7.54 Parties often agree to arbitrate under rules with a delegation provision, like those of the AAA or the ICC, and the result of *Rent-A-Center* is that it will be harder for a party resisting arbitration in such cases to argue that particular gateway issues should be resolved by a court. What is important is that the party seeking to arbitrate makes clear—either in a petition to compel arbitration or its motion to stay litigation brought in breach of an arbitration clause—that it is asking the court specifically to enforce the delegation provision in its arbitration agreement. The result is that the party resisting arbitration must bear the more difficult burden of challenging the delegation provision itself.

1. Common Arbitrability Issues

7.55 As already discussed, there are three ways in which a party seeking to enforce an arbitration agreement might seek the assistance of a court: by a motion to compel arbitration; a motion to stay or dismiss litigation brought in contravention of an arbitration clause; or a request for an antisuit injunction. There is nothing preventing a party from asking a court for more than one type of relief. Thus, a party might ask a court to stay a lawsuit brought in the United States in contravention of an arbitration clause calling for arbitration in New York and, at the same time, ask it to compel that party to arbitrate in New York. But whether requested separately or together, these types of relief often raise similar issues about whether the dispute in question is arbitrable, such as issues concerning the scope of the arbitration clause or involving nonsignatories.[77]

---

[76] 2015 WL 4731378 at *7.

[77] *See, e.g.*, Collins & Aikman Prods. Co. v. Bldg. Sys. Inc., 58 F.3d 16, 20 (2d Cir. 1995) (issues of scope of arbitration clause in action to compel arbitration); WorldCrisa Corp. v. Armstrong, 129 F.3d 71, 74–76 (2d Cir. 1997) (issues of scope of clause in action to stay litigation brought in alleged contravention of arbitration clause).

We turn to consider some of the common arbitrability challenges raised by parties resisting the enforcement of agreements to arbitrate: (1) disputes concerning challenges to the contract; (2) disputes involving nonsignatories; (3) disputes involving the scope of the arbitration clause; and (4) disputes about whether the party seeking to arbitrate has waived its right to do so. **7.56**

(a) Challenges to the contract There are two distinctions to make when considering a challenge to a contract made by a party resisting arbitration. One distinction is between (1) a claim that the party resisting arbitration is not bound by the arbitration agreement because it never entered into the contract containing that agreement, for example, because its signature on that agreement was forged, and (2) a concession that it entered into the agreement containing the arbitration clause, but a claim that it is nonetheless not bound by it because the contract containing that clause is invalid, for example, because it was fraudulently induced. A second distinction relates to the second prong of the first distinction, and is between (1) a challenge to the validity of a contract as a whole, and (2) a challenge directed specifically to the validity of the arbitration clause contained in the contract. **7.57**

(I) CHALLENGES TO THE VALIDITY OF THE CONTRACT VS. A CLAIM THAT NO CONTRACT WAS EVER CONCLUDED

In *Buckeye*, the Supreme Court stated: "The issue of a contract's validity is different from the issue of whether any agreement between the alleged obligor and obligee was ever concluded."[78] To begin with the former issue, when a party defends against an action to enforce an arbitration agreement by challenging the validity of the contract containing the arbitration clause, the separability presumption requires the courts to refer that matter to the arbitrators for resolution. And courts have held that the separability presumption applies to, among others, challenges that a contract was fraudulently induced, is illegal, or is unconscionable or a contract of adhesion.[79] For example, in *Buckeye*, the party resisting arbitration argued that the underlying loan agreement was void ab initio on grounds of illegality, since it allegedly violated Florida's usury statutes. The trial court denied Buckeye's motion to enforce the arbitration agreement on the ground that a court rather than an arbitrator should resolve a claim that a contract is illegal and void ab initio, a ruling upheld by the Florida Supreme Court. The U.S. Supreme Court reversed, holding that, based on the separability presumption, it was for the arbitrator to resolve the issue.[80] The separability rule applies in equal **7.58**

[78] 546 U.S. 444 n.1.

[79] *See, e.g., Prima Paint*, 388 U.S. 395 (fraudulent inducement); *Buckeye*, 546 U.S. 440 (illegality); Wright v. SFX Entm't Inc., No. 00 Civ. 5354, 2001 WL 103433, at *3 (S.D.N.Y. Feb. 7, 2001) ("Claims of unconscionability and adhesion contracts are similarly included within the *Prima Paint* rule.").

[80] Courts in the Second Circuit and elsewhere had drawn a distinction between a contract that is void and one that is voidable, holding that the presumption of separability applies only in the latter case, but not the former. *See, e.g.*, Sphere Drake Ins. Ltd. v. Clarendon Nat'l Ins. Co., 263

measure to contracts that are themselves arbitration agreements. As noted, in *Rent-A-Ctr., W., Inc. v. Jackson*, the party resisting arbitration claimed that the underlying arbitration agreement was unenforceable under Nevada law on the grounds of unconscionability.[81] The contract explicitly delegated threshold issues concerning enforceability of the agreement to the arbitrator. The party resisting arbitration attacked the arbitration agreement as a whole rather than attacking the delegation provision alone. The Supreme Court held that "[a]pplication of the severability rule does not depend on the substance of the remainder of the contract. Section 2 [of the FAA] operates on the specific 'written provision' to 'settle by arbitration a controversy' that the party seeks to enforce. Accordingly, unless [a party] challenged the delegation provision specifically, we must treat it as valid under § 2, and must enforce it under §§ 3 and 4, leaving any challenge to the validity of the Agreement as a whole for the arbitrator."[82]

7.59 However, if the party resisting arbitration disputes not the validity of the contract but whether a contract was ever concluded in the first place, that matter is for the courts. "[I]t is for the courts to decide whether the alleged obligor ever signed the contract ... whether the signor lacked authority to commit the alleged principal ... and whether the signor lacked the mental capacity to assent."[83]

(II) CHALLENGES TO THE VALIDITY OF THE CONTRACT AS A WHOLE VS. CHALLENGES DIRECTED SPECIFICALLY AT THE ARBITRATION CLAUSE

7.60 In an action to enforce an arbitration agreement, the separability presumption requires that challenges to the validity of a contract as a whole be referred to the arbitrators for resolution, and that challenges directed specifically to the validity of the arbitration clause be resolved by the courts. As the Supreme Court stated in *Buckeye*, "a challenge to the validity of the contract as a whole and not specifically to the arbitration clause must go to the arbitrator."[84]

7.61 It is important to stress, however, that a party disputing the validity of the arbitration clause specifically is required to make more than a conclusory showing to avoid the separability presumption. For example, in the case of a specific

F.3d 26, 31–32 (2d Cir. 2001) (if a contract is "void," a party wishing to avoid arbitration does not have to challenge the arbitration clause specifically; if a contract is "voidable," the party must show that the arbitration clause itself is unenforceable). One New York district court has interpreted the *Buckeye* court as rejecting this distinction, holding that even where the party seeking to avoid arbitration asserts that the agreement as a whole is void, the presumption of separability applies such that the issue of the contract's validity is to be considered by the arbitrator. *See* Rubin v. Soya International Corp., 457 F. Supp. 2d 191, 195 (S.D.N.Y. 2006). However, other New York district courts have continued to rely on that distinction. *See, e.g.*, Simply Fit of North America v. Poyner, 579 F. Supp. 2d 371, 380–81 (E.D.N.Y. 2008).

[81] 561 U.S. 63, 72 (2010).

[82] *Id.* at 72.

[83] *Buckeye*, 546 U.S. at 444 n.1.

[84] *Id.* at 449.

challenge to a clause based on fraud, a party must offer facts to show "some substantial relationship between the fraud or misrepresentation and the arbitration clause in particular. This substantial relationship requires more than a mere claim that the arbitration clause is an element of the scheme to defraud; it must include particularized facts specific to the ... arbitration clause which indicate how it was used to effect the scheme to defraud."[85] Thus, one court enforced an arbitration agreement notwithstanding a claim that the arbitration clause itself was fraudulently induced on the ground that the challenge to that clause was not supported by any facts:

> Aside from characterizing the arbitration provision as "part and parcel" of the larger stock scheme *the plaintiff presents no evidence to support a finding that the arbitration clause was itself induced by fraud.* The plaintiff offers no document or witness statement in support of its theory of the defendants' intent; it offers no evidence regarding any representations made by the defendants about the arbitration provision at the time the Distributorship Agreement was executed; and it offers no evidence regarding the parties' negotiation of the arbitration provision. Thus, *as the question of fraudulent inducement of the Agreement is within the scope of the broad arbitration provision, the question of the validity of the contract itself must go to an arbitrator.*[86]

In other words, courts are unwilling to undertake a full arbitrability inquiry—and thus potentially interfere with the arbitration process—unless the party resisting arbitration satisfies a threshold burden of offering some evidence to support its challenge to the validity of the arbitration clause. **7.62**

(b) Nonsignatories

(I) INTRODUCTION

One specific type of challenge to a contract that often arises in actions to enforce arbitration agreements involves cases where either the party seeking to arbitrate or the party resisting arbitration did not sign the arbitration agreement.[87] It is worth distinguishing two situations when it comes to cases involving nonsignatories. The first is when a nonsignatory seeks to enforce an arbitration agreement against a signatory to a contract, by, for example, asking the court to compel the signatory to arbitrate or to stay a lawsuit commenced by that signatory. The second is when a signatory seeks to enforce an arbitration agreement against a nonsignatory. **7.63**

Some courts rightly draw a distinction between these two situations because, in the case of the first, it is undisputed that the party resisting arbitration (a signatory to the arbitration agreement) agreed to arbitrate with *someone*, and the only issue is whether it agreed to arbitrate with the particular party seeking to enforce **7.64**

[85] *Rubin*, 457 F. Supp. 2d at 195.
[86] *Simply Fit*, 579 F. Supp. 2d at 381 (emphasis added).
[87] For a discussion on how to draft an arbitration clause to avoid it binding nonsignatories, *see* Chapter 3.B.2(c) of this book.

the arbitration agreement. In the second case, however, where the party resisting arbitration never signed an arbitration agreement in the first place, the dispute concerns whether it agreed to arbitrate with *anyone at all*. As the Second Circuit has stated:

> [I]t matters whether the party resisting arbitration is a signatory or not. "[A] court should be wary of imposing a contractual obligation to arbitrate on a non-contracting party ..." Thus a willing non-signatory seeking to arbitrate with a signatory that is unwilling may do so under what has been called an "alternative estoppel theory," which takes into consideration "the relationships of persons, wrongs and issues." But a willing signatory (such as [the investor]) seeking to arbitrate with a *non*-signatory that is unwilling (such as [the fund manager]) must establish at least one of the five theories described in *Thomson-CSF*.[88]

7.65 Because cases involving attempts by a nonsignatory to enforce an arbitration clause against a signatory are viewed as less problematic—since it is undisputed that the signatory resisting arbitration agreed to arbitrate with someone (albeit not necessarily with the person seeking to enforce the arbitration agreement)—courts are more willing to resolve those cases by reference to the Kompetenz-Kompetenz doctrine. In such circumstances, some courts will seek to determine, as a threshold matter, whether there is clear and unmistakable evidence that the arbitration agreement grants the arbitral tribunal the authority to determine its own jurisdiction, and, if so, will refer the case to the tribunal for resolution of the issue of whether the signatory is required to arbitrate with the nonsignatory.

7.66 The case of *Contec Corporation v. Remote Solution Co., Ltd.*,[89] is illustrative. Contec, a nonsignatory to an arbitration agreement, sought to compel arbitration with Remote Solution, a signatory. The arbitration agreement provided that disputes would be resolved in accordance with the Commercial Rules of the American Arbitration Association, Rule 7 of which provides that an arbitrator "shall have the power to rule on his or her own jurisdiction." The court found that this rule constituted clear and unmistakable evidence that the parties to the agreement intended that the arbitral tribunal make a determination of arbitrability. Remote Solution argued, however, that the clear and unmistakable evidence test should not apply to a case involving a nonsignatory. It said that, regardless of what might

[88] Merrill Lynch Investment Managers v. Optibase, Ltd., 337 F.3d 125, 131 (2d Cir. 2003) (citations omitted) (*quoting* Smith/Enron Cogeneration Ltd. v. Smith Cogeneration Int'l, Inc., 198 F.3d 88, 97 (2d Cir. 1999)); Thomson-CSF, S.A. v. American Arbitration Association, 64 F.3d 773, 779 (2d Cir. 1995); and Choctaw Generation Ltd. P'ship v. Am. Home Assur. Co., 271 F.3d 403, 406 (2d Cir. 2001). In Comer v. Micor, Inc., 436 F.3d 1098, 1101 (9th Cir. 2006), the court also drew a distinction between cases where the party that was the object of a motion to compel was a signatory or a nonsignatory. *See also* CD Partners, LLC v. Grizzle, 424 F.3d 795, 798 (8th Cir. 2005) ("[a] non signatory can enforce an arbitration clause against a signatory to the agreement ... when 'the relationship between the signatory and nonsignatory defendants is sufficiently close that only by permitting the nonsignatory to invoke arbitration may evisceration of the underlying arbitration agreement between the parties be avoided.' ").

[89] Contec Corp. v. Remote Solution Co., Ltd., 398 F.3d 205 (2d Cir. 2005).

occur in a dispute between two signatories to an arbitration agreement that incorporated the AAA Commercial Rules, it could not, in this case "be compelled to arbitrate with a stranger to the 1999 Agreement because the contractual language is effective only between the contracting parties," such that the threshold issue of whether the dispute was arbitrable should be resolved by the courts rather than the arbitrator.[90]

The court rejected this argument. It held, in essence, that it need not undertake a full arbitrability analysis in such a case, but need make only a threshold determination that the case should be referred to the arbitrator to rule on arbitrability. In making that threshold determination, the court did more than apply the clear and unmistakable evidence test, although it stopped short of a full arbitrability inquiry. Having found there to be clear and unmistakable evidence in the contract that the arbitrators had jurisdiction to determine their own jurisdiction, it looked to see whether there was a "sufficient relationship" between the signatory and the nonsignatory to warrant referring the case to the tribunal to resolve the arbitrability question. The court noted "[a]s an initial matter, we recognize that just because a signatory has agreed to arbitrate issues of arbitrability with another party, does not mean that it must arbitrate with any non-signatory. In order to decide whether arbitration of arbitrability is appropriate, a court must first determine whether the parties have a sufficient relationship to each other and to the rights created under the agreement."[91] **7.67**

The court found that there was a sufficient relationship between Contec and Remote Solution, in part, because there "is or was an undisputed relationship between each corporate form of Contec and Remote Solution."[92] Thus, the court following the reasoning of the Court of Appeals for the First Circuit in *Apollo Computer, Inc. v. Berg*,[93] held that since Remote Solution was a signatory and had itself agreed to be bound by provisions that clearly and unmistakably allow the arbitrator to determine his or her own jurisdiction, so it followed that the arbitrator should determine whether Remote Solution was bound to arbitrate with Contec. **7.68**

However, courts are, for good reason, reluctant to invoke the Kompetenz-Kompetenz doctrine when it is the nonsignatory who denies being bound by the arbitration agreement. After all, the fact that an arbitration agreement might contain provisions clearly and unmistakably granting an arbitral tribunal the power to determine its own jurisdiction cannot logically serve as a basis for arbitral authority to determine its jurisdiction over a nonsignatory to that agreement. To hold otherwise would be to presume precisely what is in issue, namely that the nonsignatory **7.69**

---

90 398 F.3d at 209.

91 *Id.*

92 *Id.*

93 Apollo Computer, Inc. v. Berg, 886 F.2d 469 (1st Cir. 1989).

has agreed to arbitrate, or has at least agreed to have the arbitrator decide whether the dispute is arbitrable.[94] As the Second Circuit said in a case involving a nonsignatory, *Oracle Corporation*: "An Agreement between Sarhank and Systems which does not mention Oracle does not evidence a 'clear and unmistakable' ... intent by Oracle to arbitrate or to permit the arbitrator to decide the issue of arbitrability."[95] Thus, when it comes to compelling a nonsignatory to arbitrate, rather than referring the issue to an arbitrator, courts tend to undertake a full arbitrability inquiry themselves to determine whether the nonsignatory is bound to arbitrate.[96]

(II) THEORIES BY WHICH NONSIGNATORIES CAN BE OBLIGATED TO ARBITRATE

7.70 Courts have identified six main theories as valid bases on which to compel nonsignatories to arbitrate: (1) incorporation by reference; (2) assumption by conduct; (3) agency; (4) veil piercing/alter ego; (5) estoppel; and (6) third-party beneficiary.[97]

7.71 It is beyond the scope of this chapter to consider these theories in any detail,[98] but a brief overview of each is set forth as follows.

---

[94] In one recent case, a court issued a preliminary injunction enjoining the party seeking to arbitrate from participating in an arbitration about the issue of whether nonsignatories were bound to arbitrate on the ground that this was an issue for the court to resolve. *In re* Lakah, 602 F. Supp. 2d 497, 499 (S.D.N.Y. 2009) ("If the arbitrators proceed to determine their jurisdiction over the Lakahs [the nonsignatories], the Lakahs will be irreparably injured because they will be forced to spend significant time and resources litigating this issue before a body lacking authority to decide that issue.").

[95] Sarhank Group v. Oracle Corp., 404 F.3d 657, 661–62 (2d Cir. 2005) (citation omitted).

[96] *See, e.g., Smith/Enron*, 198 F.3d at 97; Thompson-CSF, S.A. v. American Arbitration Ass'n, 64 F.3d 773, 776 (2d Cir. 1995); InterGen N.V. v. Grina, 344 F.3d 134, 144–50 (1st Cir. 2003); *see also* Trippe Manufacturing Co. v. Niles Audio Corp., 401 F.3d 529 (3rd Cir. 2005) (assumption by conduct a basis to compel nonsignatory to arbitrate); Keytrade USA, Inc. v. Ain Temouchant M/V *in rem*, 404 F.3d 891 (5th Cir. 2005) (incorporation by reference a basis to compel nonsignatory to arbitrate); Int'l Paper Co. v. Schwabedissen Maschinen & Anlagen, GMBH, 206 F.3d 411, 417–18 (4th Cir. 2000) (finding that equitable estoppel was a basis to compel nonsignatory to arbitrate, the court stating: "Equitable estoppel precludes a party from asserting rights 'he otherwise would have had against another' when his own conduct renders assertion of those rights contrary to equity. In the arbitration context, the doctrine recognizes that a party may be estopped from asserting that the lack of his signature on a written contract precludes enforcement of the contract's arbitration clause when he has consistently maintained that other provisions of the same contract should be enforced to benefit him."); Lapina v. Men Women N.Y. Model Mgmt. Inc., 2015 WL 556674, at *5–6 (S.D.N.Y. Feb. 6, 2015) (finding that equitable estoppel was a basis to compel a signatory to arbitrate with a nonsignatory, the court stating: "[t]he purpose of the equitable estoppel doctrine 'is to prevent a plaintiff from, in effect, trying to have [its] cake and eat it too; that is, from relying on the contract when it works to its advantage by establishing the claim and repudiating it when it works to its disadvantage by requiring arbitration").

[97] *Id. See also* Arthur Anderson LLP v. Carlisle, 556 U.S. 624, 631 (2009).

[98] For a thorough discussion *see* Gary B. Born, International Commercial Arbitration 1404–90 (2014). *See also* Carolyn B. Lamm and Joseph A. Aqua, *Defining the Party—Who Is Proper Party in an International Arbitration Before the American Arbitration Association and Other International Institutions*, 34 Geo. Wash Int'l Law Rev. 711 (2003); John M. Townsend, Non-Signatories In International Arbitration—An American Perspective, International

A. INCORPORATION BY REFERENCE

If a dispute arises under a contract that has no arbitration clause, which incorporates by reference a contract containing an arbitration clause, a signatory to the former contract may be required to arbitrate even though she did not sign the latter.[99] The Second Circuit has held that the term incorporating the arbitration clause in a contract need not mention the arbitration agreement specifically, citing the federal policy in favor of arbitration.[100] **7.72**

B. ASSUMPTION BY CONDUCT

If a nonsignatory's conduct indicates an assumption of the obligation to arbitrate, that party may be bound to the agreement. For example, nonsignatories who send representatives to an arbitration or otherwise participate in arbitration proceedings may be bound to arbitrate under the doctrine of assumption.[101] **7.73**

C. AGENCY

A nonsignatory can be held to an arbitration agreement based upon traditional principles of agency law, typically when an agent signs an agreement on behalf of her principal, thereby binding the latter. Agency requires that the agent have been granted express or implied authority by the principal to enter into the agreement in question on the principal's behalf.[102] An agency relationship can also be established through apparent authority, when the putative principal gives a third party a reasonable basis to believe that the putative agent has the authority to act on her behalf.[103] The doctrine of apparent authority often rests upon notions of good faith and estoppel.[104] **7.74**

D. ALTER EGO/PIERCING OF THE CORPORATE VEIL

A nonsignatory can also be held to an arbitration agreement based upon the doctrines of "piercing the corporate veil" or "alter ego." Under these theories, the nonsignatory may be bound to arbitrate if it is the "alter ego" of the signatory to the arbitration agreement. In order to be the alter ego of the signatory, it is necessary to show that the nonsignatory so completely dominated the signatory that the separate corporate forms should be disregarded.[105] U.S. courts presume **7.75**

Arbitration 2006: Back to Basics, International Council for Commercial Arbitration Congress Series 13 (2007).

[99] Coffey v. Dean Witter Reynolds, Inc., 891 F.2d 261 (10th Cir. 1989); R.J. O'Brien & Assoc., Inc. v. Pipkin, 64 F.3d 257 (7th Cir. 1995).

[100] Progressive Casualty Ins. Co. v. CA Reaseguradora Nacional de Venezuela, 991 F.2d 42 (2d Cir. 1993).

[101] Thomson-CSF, S.A. v. American Arbitration Ass'n, 64 F.3d 773, 777 (2d Cir. 1995); Gvozdenovic v. United Air Lines, Inc., 933 F.2d 1100, 1105 (2d Cir. 1991).

[102] Bridas S.A.P.I.C. v. Government of Turkmenistan, 345 F.3d 347, 357 (5th Cir. 2003); Phoenix Canada Oil Co. Ltd. v. Texaco, Inc., 842 F.2d 1466 (3d Cir. 1988); InterGen N.V. v. Grina, 344 F.3d 134, 143 (1st Cir. 2003).

[103] Restatement (Third) Agency § 2.03 (2006).

[104] Biggs v. U.S. Fire Ins. Co., 611 S.W.2d 624, 629 (Tex. 1981).

[105] Arriba Ltd v. Petroleos Mexicanos, 962 F.2d 538 (5th Cir. 1992).

that corporate entities are separate, but this presumption can be overcome with a showing of: (1) domination and control of the affiliate, such that it has no separate existence from the dominating party; and (2) fraud or misuse of that control, to the detriment of other parties.[106] The "alter ego" analysis is a fact-specific analysis, and focuses on a variety of factors to determine domination and control. Some of these factors may include: disregard of corporate formalities; inadequate capitalization; and the extent of financial dealings between the parent and the subsidiary.[107]

E. ESTOPPEL

7.76 U.S. courts have allowed parties to use estoppel as a "sword" to allow a signatory to bind a nonsignatory.[108] Thus courts have generally applied the theory of "equitable estoppel," which prohibits a nonsignatory from exercising some rights under a contract but disavowing certain obligations under the same contract (in this case, the arbitration agreement).[109] A nonsignatory may also be estopped from denying that an agreement applies to them when they receive a "direct benefit" under the contract.[110]

7.77 U.S. courts have also allowed nonsignatories to use the estoppel doctrine as a shield to bind signatories in certain circumstances. This theory has been articulated as follows: the courts "have been willing to estop a signatory from avoiding arbitration with a nonsignatory when the issues the nonsignatory is seeking to resolve in arbitration are intertwined with the agreement that the estopped party has signed."[111]

7.78 *Choctaw Generation Ltd. Partnership v. American Home Assurance Co.*[112] furnishes an example of the "intertwined estoppel theory." That case involved a power plant construction contract between Bechtel Power ("Bechtel"), as contractor, and Choctaw Generation ("Choctaw"), the owner. The construction contract had an arbitration clause. A dispute arose between Bechtel and Choctaw, and Choctaw commenced an arbitration proceeding against Bechtel claiming liquidated damages. To obtain payment of the liquidated damages pending the outcome of the arbitration, Choctaw drew down in full a $33 million letter of credit that the construction contract required Bechtel to post.

7.79 At around the time Choctaw and Bechtel had entered the construction contract, a third party, American Home Assurance Co. ("American Home"), entered into a

---

106 *Bridas SAPIC*, 345 F.3d at 359; *InterGen N.V.*, 344 F.3d at 148–49.
107 Carte Blanche (Singapore) Pte, Ltd v. Diners Club Int'l, Inc., 2 F.3d 24 (2d Cir. 1993).
108 Gary B. Born, International Commercial Arbitration 1471–76 (2014).
109 *Int'l Paper Co.*, 206 F.3d at 417–18.
110 American Bureau of Shipping v. Tencara Shipyard S.p.A., 170 F.3d 349, 353 (2d Cir. 1999).
111 *Thomson-CFS*, 64 F.3d at 779.
112 Choctaw Generation Ltd. Partnership v. American Home Assurance Co., 271 F.3d 403 (2d Cir. 2001).

surety contract to secure performance under the construction contract. The surety contract had no arbitration clause. While the arbitration between Choctaw and Bechtel was pending, Choctaw commenced a lawsuit against American Home to compel serial replenishment of the letter of credit by American Home.

American Home defended by invoking the arbitration clause in the construction contract between Choctaw and Bechtel, arguing that its dispute with Choctaw should be arbitrated. The district court refused to require Choctaw to arbitrate its surety dispute with American Home on the ground that the surety contract signed by American Home did not contain an arbitration clause and that American Home did not sign the construction contract (which does). American Home appealed. The Second Circuit reversed, requiring Choctaw to arbitrate with American Home on the intertwined estoppel theory. It stated: **7.80**

> [S]o the decisive question on this appeal is whether surety American Home can compel Choctaw to arbitrate the present controversy over the surety contract under or by virtue of the arbitration clause of the construction contract to which Choctaw is a signatory and American Home is not. We conclude that this controversy is arbitrable because Choctaw agreed that controversies that are unable to be resolved pursuant to the construction contract "shall be settled by arbitration," and because (under our case law) Choctaw, as signatory, is estopped from avoiding arbitration with a non-signatory "when the issues the nonsignatory is seeking to resolve in arbitration are intertwined with the agreement that the estopped party has signed."[113]

F. THIRD-PARTY BENEFICIARY

The third-party beneficiary doctrine requires a showing that the parties to the contract intended that a third party (i.e., nonsignatory) be able to rely upon or be bound by the contract.[114] Courts will often apply an "estoppel" analysis to cases involving third-party beneficiaries, holding that a party claiming third-party beneficiary status under a contract can be bound by an arbitration clause in that contract on grounds of estoppel.[115] **7.81**

(c) The scope of an arbitration clause Whereas a challenge to the validity of a clause disputes whether there is any basis to arbitrate at all, when a party challenges arbitrability on the basis of scope, it is conceding that there is an agreement to arbitrate *some* dispute, but denying that the agreement applies to the *particular* dispute raised by the party seeking to arbitrate. **7.82**

Courts are not always consistent in the way they have resolved disputes about the scope of an arbitration clause. Some have resolved them on the basis of the Kompetenz-Kompetenz doctrine. For example, in *Bell v. Cendant Corp.*, 293 F.3d 563, 568 (2d Cir. 2002), the court resolved the issue by addressing, first, **7.83**

---

[113] 271 F.3d at 404 (citation omitted.)

[114] *Id.* at 1180.

[115] Spear, Leeds & Kellogg v. Central Life Assur. Co., 85 F.3d 21, 27 (2d Cir. 1996).

whether the dispute about the scope of the clause should be resolved by the arbitrator or the court, and second, upon finding that the arbitration agreement was sufficiently broad that it "clearly and unmistakably evidences the parties' intention to have the arbitrator determine its scope,"[116] it referred the case to the arbitrator to determine whether the dispute fell within the scope of the clause. In *Ibeto Petrochemical Industries Ltd. v. M/T "Beffen,"*[117] by contrast, the court made a decision about whether the dispute fell within the scope of the arbitration clause based on its own interpretation of the language of the clause, without first considering whether, under the arbitration clause, the arbitral tribunal had the authority to determine arbitrability.

(I) REFERRING DISPUTES ABOUT SCOPE TO THE ARBITRATORS

7.84 In *Qualcomm Inc. v. Nokia Corp.*,[118] the Court of Appeals for the Federal Circuit offered a cogent analysis of how, in an action to enforce an arbitration agreement, a court should decide whether a dispute about the scope of an arbitration clause should be resolved by the court itself or referred to the arbitral tribunal for resolution.

7.85 In that case, Qualcomm Inc. and SnapTrack, Inc. (collectively Qualcomm) commenced a lawsuit against Nokia Corporation and Nokia, Inc. (collectively Nokia) claiming patent infringement. Nokia moved to stay the litigation, arguing that the claims asserted in the suit fell within the scope of an arbitration clause contained in a license agreement between the parties. The arbitration clause in question required that disputes be resolved pursuant to the rules of the AAA, which provide that "[t]he tribunal shall have the power to rule on its own jurisdiction, including any objections with respect to the existence, scope or validity of the arbitration agreement," which the court found constitutes "clear and unmistakable" evidence that the parties agreed to authorize the arbitrator to resolve disputes about their jurisdiction.[119]

7.86 The court stated: "[T]his case raises the question of how to reconcile an agreement to delegate arbitrability decisions to an arbitrator in accordance with the language of section 3 of the FAA, which specifies that the district court be 'satisfied' as to the arbitrability of an issue before ordering a stay."[120]

[116] *Bell*, 293 F.3d at 568. Gary Born has noted that: "referring disputes about the scope of an arbitration agreement to the arbitrators makes particular sense. That is because these disputes are (unlike most other jurisdictional issues) inescapably intertwined with the substantive interpretation of the underlying contract and the parties' rights thereunder—matters which are plainly for the arbitral tribunal to resolve under the parties' arbitration agreement." Gary B. Born, International Commercial Arbitration 1187 (2014) (footnote omitted).

[117] Ibeto Petrochemical Industries Ltd. v. M/T "Beffen," 412 F. Supp. 2d 285, 291 (S.D.N.Y. 2005).

[118] Qualcomm Inc. v. Nokia Corp., 466 F.3d 1366 (Fed. Cir. 2006).

[119] *Id.* at 1373 (citations omitted).

[120] *Id.* at 1370.

Nokia argued that the court should merely examine the arbitration agreement to determine whether it clearly and unmistakably evidenced the intent of the parties to delegate arbitrability decisions to an arbitrator. If so, then the court should stay the action. Qualcomm, by contrast, argued that in order to be "satisfied" that the case should be referred to arbitration for the purposes of Section 3 of the Federal Arbitration Act, it was necessary for the court to undertake a full arbitrability inquiry. **7.87**

The court did not follow the position offered by either party, but rather adopted a middle ground. It found that in order to be "satisfied" of the arbitrability of an issue under Section 3 of the Federal Arbitration Act, the district court should first inquire as to who has primary power to decide arbitrability under the parties' agreement. If the court concludes that the parties *did not* clearly and unmistakably intend to delegate arbitrability issues to the arbitrator, the court should undertake "a full arbitrability inquiry in order to be 'satisfied' that the issue involved is referable to arbitration."[121] If, however, the court concludes that the parties *did* clearly and unmistakably decide to delegate arbitrability questions to the arbitrator, then the court should conduct only a limited inquiry into arbitrability, focusing on whether the assertion of arbitrability by the party seeking to stay the litigation is "wholly groundless."[122] The court based its rationale for requiring courts to undertake a modest "wholly groundless" analysis rather than "a full arbitrability inquiry" on the theory that, once it was clear that the parties had agreed to delegate to arbitrators the authority to determine their own jurisdiction, any further inquiry would be a usurpation of the authority of the arbitrators. The court stated: **7.88**

> On remand, in undertaking the "wholly groundless" inquiry, the district court should look to the scope of the arbitration clause and the precise issues that the moving party asserts are subject to arbitration. Because any inquiry beyond a "wholly groundless" test would invade the province of the arbitrator, whose arbitrability judgment the parties agreed to abide by in the 2001 Agreement, the district court need not, and should not, determine whether Nokia's defenses are in fact arbitrable. If the assertion of arbitrability is not "wholly groundless," the district court should conclude that it is "satisfied" pursuant to section 3.[123]

(II) JUDICIAL RESOLUTION OF DISPUTES ABOUT SCOPE

Notwithstanding the analysis by the Court of Appeals for the Federal Circuit in the *Nokia* case, many courts do undertake a full arbitrability inquiry when faced with disputes about the scope of an arbitration clause in an action to enforce an arbitration agreement, although the extensiveness of this inquiry is tempered by certain presumptions in favor of finding arbitrability. **7.89**

---

[121] *Id.* at 1371. *See also* In Paduano v. Express Scripts, Inc., 55 F. Supp. 3d 400, 423–44 (E.D.N.Y. 2014) (adopting the reasoning of the *Qualcomm* court).

[122] *Id.*

[123] *Id.* at 1374.

7.90 Typically, courts will examine the language of the contract to determine whether it covers the dispute. This examination is carried out in the light of "the strong federal policy in favor of arbitration," which states that "the existence of a broad agreement to arbitrate creates a presumption of arbitrability which is only overcome if it may be said with positive assurance that the arbitration clause is not susceptible of an interpretation that covers the asserted dispute. Doubts should be resolved in favor of coverage."[124] Moreover, in deciding "[w]hether a particular claim falls within the scope of the parties' arbitration agreement, [the court] focus[es] on the factual allegations in the complaint rather than the legal causes of action asserted. If the allegations underlying the claims 'touch matters' covered by the parties' ... agreements, then those claims must be arbitrated, whatever the legal labels attached to them."[125]

7.91 The Second Circuit has established a three-part inquiry for determining whether a particular dispute falls within the scope of the arbitration agreement. First, a court should classify the particular clause as broad or narrow. Second, if the clause is narrow, the court must determine whether the dispute is over an issue that is on its face within the purview of the clause or over a collateral issue that is somehow connected to the main agreement that contains the arbitration clause. If an arbitration clause is narrowly worded and the dispute concerns a matter collateral to the contract calling for arbitration "a court should test the presumption [of arbitrability] by reviewing the allegations underlying the dispute and by asking whether the claim alleged implicates issues of contract construction ..."[126] Third, if the arbitration clause is broad, "there arises a presumption of arbitrability and arbitration of even a collateral matter will be ordered if the claim alleged implicates issues of contract construction or the parties' rights and obligations under it or if the allegations underlying the claims touch matters covered by the parties' agreements. In making this determination, courts must focus on the factual allegations in the complaint rather than the legal causes of action asserted."[127]

7.92 As far as the first prong of the test is concerned, courts have acknowledged in recent decisions that imposing a binary opposition—"broad" versus "narrow"—on what is better viewed as a spectrum is not always appropriate. Thus, in the *WorldCrisa* case, the court considered a clause that covered "any dispute" between

---

124 *Smith/Enron*, 198 F.3d at 99; WorldCrisa Corp. v. Armstrong, 129 F.3d 71, 74 (2d Cir. 1997). *See also* Collins & Aikman Prods. Co. v. Bldg. Sys., Inc., 58 F.3d 16, 20 (2d Cir. 1995) (where an arbitration clause is broad, "there is a presumption that the claims are arbitrable").

125 *Smith/Enron*, 198 F.3d at 99.

126 *WorldCrisa*, 129 F.3d at 74–75 (*quoting Collins & Aikman*, 58 F.2d at 19–23).

127 Ibeto Petrochemical Industries, Ltd. v. M/T "Beffen," 412 F. Supp. 2d 285, 289 (S.D.N.Y. 2005); *see also* Louis Dreyfus Negoce S.A. v. Blystad Shipping & Trading, Inc., 252 F.3d 218, 224 (2d Cir. 2001); *WorldCrisa Corp.*, 129 F.3d at 74; *Genesco*, 815 F.2d at 846; *Collins & Aikman*, 58 F.2d at 19–23; Benihana of Tokyo, LLC v. Benihana Inc. 2014 WL 3631759 (S.D.N.Y. July 22, 2014).

the parties to the agreement "over the terms" of the agreement or "any claims of breach" by either of the parties. The court stated:

> The arbitration clause at issue here does not contain the typically broad language that makes arbitrable all disputes "arising out of" or "related to" the contract or its breach ... On the other hand, the clause is by no means narrow. It is not necessary to make the nice determination of exactly where in the range between broad and narrow this clause fits. The clause is close enough to the "broad" end of the spectrum to justify a presumption of arbitrability here. Moreover, we believe that even without resort to the presumption the current dispute falls within the scope of the arbitration clause.[128]

One question that often arises when courts examine arbitration clauses to determine their breadth is whether the clause is limited to disputes concerning only the interpretation or performance of the contract or whether the clause also encompasses other related disputes, such as, for example, claims of fraudulent inducement of contract, Racketeer Influenced and Corrupt Organizations Act (RICO) claims, and tort claims.[129] **7.93**

In the Second Circuit, it had once been settled that if an arbitration clause did not contain the phrase "relating to," "in connection with" or some equivalent, but only the phrase "arising under," the clause was deemed to be narrow. Thus, in *In re Kinoshita*, 287 F.2d 951, 952 (2d Cir. 1961), the Second Circuit considered the following clause: "If any dispute or difference should arise under this Charter" it should be referred to arbitration. It found that this clause was narrow, and did not include within its scope a dispute about whether the agreement was fraudulently induced. However, courts since *Kinoshita* have narrowed its holding to its specific facts, such that only clauses that use the same or almost the same language as of the *Kinoshita* clause are interpreted narrowly. **7.94**

In *S.A. Mineracao Da Trindade-Samitri v. Utah Intern. Inc.*,[130] the Second Circuit held that an arbitration provision requiring arbitration of "any *question* or dispute aris[ing] or *occur[ring]* under" the agreement was broad enough to encompass claims of fraud in the inducement. It distinguished *Kinoshita*, noting: **7.95**

> We decline to overrule *In re Kinoshita*, despite its inconsistency with federal policy favoring arbitration, particularly in international business disputes, because we are concerned that contracting parties may have (in theory at least) relied on that case in their formulation of an arbitration provision. We see no reason, however, why we may not confine *Kinoshita* to its precise facts. We are confident that parties who

---

128 129 F.3d at 75.

129 *See, e.g.*, Shearson/Am. Express Inc. v. McMahon, 482 U.S. 220, 223 (1987) (stating that RICO claims are arbitrable under a clause covering "any controversy arising out of or relating to ... this agreement or the breach thereof"); Genesco v. T. Kakiuchi Ltd., 815 F.2d 840, 848 (2d Cir. 1987) (phrase "relating to" in arbitration clause requires arbitration of fraudulent inducement claim and RICO claims).

130 S.A. Mineracao Da Trindade-Samitri v. Utah Intern. Inc., 745 F.2d 190, 194 (2d Cir. 1984).

> have actually relied on *Kinoshita* in an attempt to formulate a narrow arbitration provision, have adopted the exact language of the arbitration provision involved in *Kinoshita*. The provision involved in *Kinoshita* required arbitration of "any dispute or difference aris[ing] under" the agreement. Thus, to ensure that an arbitration clause is narrowly interpreted contracting parties must use the foregoing phrase or its equivalent, although the better course, obviously, would be to specify exactly which claims are and are not arbitrable.

Id. at 194.[131] However, while *Kinoshita* has been narrowed, it has not been extinguished.[132]

7.96 *(d) Waiver* Another argument sometimes advanced by parties resisting arbitration is that the party seeking to arbitrate has waived its right to do so.[133] The most common argument is that the party seeking to arbitrate has waived its right by engaging in litigation on the subject matter of the dispute. As a threshold matter, it is worth discussing who, as between the courts and the arbitrators, is empowered to resolve allegations of waiver. Courts have not always been consistent in their approach to this issue, but the Second Circuit has held "that, although ordinarily a defense of waiver ... is a matter to be decided by the arbitrator, the district court could properly decide the question when the party seeking arbitration had already participated in litigation on the dispute."[134]

7.97 The federal policy in favor of arbitration applies to assessing an allegation of waiver. Thus, it is settled that the Federal Arbitration Act "establishes that, as a matter of federal law, any doubts concerning the scope of arbitrable issues should be resolved in favor of arbitration, whether the problem at hand is the construction of the contract language itself, *or an allegation of waiver*, delay, or a like defense to arbitrability."[135] As a result, courts have held that a waiver of the right to arbitrate

[131] *See also* Louis Dreyfus Negoce S.A. v. Blystad Shipping & Trading, Inc., 252 F.3d 218, 221 (2d Cir. 2001) ("We have ... since limited [*Kinoshita's*] holding to its facts, declaring that absent further limitation, only the precise language in *Kinoshita* ["arising under"] would evince a narrow clause."); ACE Capital Re Overseas Ltd. v. Central United Life Ins. Co., 307 F.3d 24, 32–33 (2d Cir. 2002) (noting that *Kinoshita* has been criticized); China Auto Care, LLC v. China Auto Care (Caymans), 859 F. Supp. 2d 582 (S.D.N.Y. 2012) (noting that the rationale for confining *Kinoshita* to its precise facts, but not overruling the case altogether, is the concern that contracting parties may have relied on the case to formulate arbitration provisions that were explicitly designed to apply only to a narrow set of issues).

[132] *See* Bristol-Myers Squibb Co. v. SR International Business Insurance Company Ltd., 354 F. Supp. 2d 499 (S.D.N.Y. 2005) (noting that although subsequent decisions of the Second Circuit have had the effect of "eroding [*Kinoshita*] into a tiny island of non-arbitrability in a vast arbitral ocean ... [h]ere ... it appears impossible to distinguish *Kinoshita*, as the operative language of the clause at issue here is substantially identical to that in the *Kinoshita* clause.").

[133] *See also* discussion in Chapter 6.C.4(b) of this book.

[134] *See* S&R Co. of Kingston v. Latona Trucking, Inc., 159 F.3d 80, 82–83 (2d Cir. 1998) (citing Doctor's Associates Inc. v. Distajo, 66 F.3d 438 (2d Cir. 1995)). *See also* Howsam v. Dean Witter Reynolds, 537 U.S. 79, 84 (2002) (noting presumption that arbitrator should decide allegation of waiver).

[135] *See* Progressive Casualty Ins. Co., 991 F.2d at 48 (*quoting* Mitsubishi Motors Corp., 473 U.S. at 626).

is "not to be lightly inferred."[136] Nonetheless, a party is deemed to have waived its right to arbitrate if it "engages in protracted litigation that results in prejudice to the opposing party."[137] Such prejudice is found when the party seeking to enforce the agreement to arbitrate "engages in discovery procedures not available in arbitration, … makes motions going to the merits of an adversary's claims, … or delays invoking arbitration rights while the adversary incurs unnecessary delay or expense."[138] In one case, the Second Circuit affirmed a finding of waiver where the district court had made the following factual findings with respect to the party seeking to enforce the agreement to arbitrate: "(1) they failed to plead the defense of arbitration and award, despite asserting other defenses and S & R's assertion of a counterclaim; (2) they actively participated in the litigation for 15 months before seeking to invoke their right to arbitrate on the eve of trial; (3) they participated in two settlement conferences, and they prejudiced Latona by (4) engaging in extensive discovery—thereby obtaining information that would not have been available in arbitration—and (5) imposing on Latona undue delay and expense."[139]

D. COURT INTERVENTION: COMPELLING ARBITRATION

1. Actions to Compel Arbitration under the Federal Arbitration Act

If a party finds it necessary to seek the assistance of a court to compel a party to arbitrate, the appropriate step is to file a petition or motion to compel arbitration with the court.[140] A motion to compel arbitration "is simply a request for an order compelling specific performance of part of a contract."[141] The failure to comply with such an order constitutes a contempt of court.[142] **7.98**

The Federal Arbitration Act contains three separate provisions empowering courts to compel a party to arbitrate, one in each of its three chapters. It is worth considering each of them in turn to highlight some differences. Section 4 of Chapter 1 of the Federal Arbitration Act provides: **7.99**

> A party aggrieved by the alleged failure, neglect, or refusal of another to arbitrate under a written agreement for arbitration may petition any United States district

[136] Leadertex, Inc. v. Morganton Dyeing & Finishing Corp., 67 F.3d 20, 25 (2d Cir. 1995) (quotations in original).

[137] Cotton v. Slone, 4 F.3d 176, 179 (2d Cir. 1993); *see also* Tech. in P'ship, Inc. v. Rudin, 894 F. Supp. 2d 274 (S.D.N.Y. 2012), *aff'd*, 538 F. App'x 38 (2d Cir. 2013).

[138] *Id.*

[139] *Latona Trucking*, 159 F.3d at 83 (citation omitted).

[140] A petition is the appropriate device where there is no lawsuit already pending, which there may not be in many cases where one party seeks to compel another to arbitrate.

[141] Joseph Muller Corp. Zurich v. Commonwealth Petrochemicals, Inc., 334 F. Supp. 1013, 1018 (S.D.N.Y. 1971).

[142] U.S. Titan Inc. v. Guangzhou Zhen Hua Shipping, Co., 241 F.3d 135 (2d Cir. 2001).

> court which, save for such agreement, would have jurisdiction under title 28, in a civil action or in admiralty of the subject matter of a suit arising out of the controversy between the parties, for an order directing that such arbitration proceed in the manner provided for in such agreement. Five days' notice in writing of such application shall be served upon the party in default. Service thereof shall be made in the manner provided by the Federal Rules of Civil Procedure. The court shall hear the parties, and upon being satisfied that the making of the agreement for arbitration or the failure to comply therewith is not in issue, the court shall make an order directing the parties to proceed to arbitration in accordance with the terms of the agreement. The hearing and proceedings, under such agreement, shall be within the district in which the petition for an order directing such arbitration is filed. If the making of the arbitration agreement or the failure, neglect, or refusal to perform the same be in issue, the court shall proceed summarily to the trial thereof. If no jury trial be demanded by the party alleged to be in default, or if the matter in dispute is within admiralty jurisdiction, the court shall hear and determine such issue. Where such an issue is raised, the party alleged to be in default may, except in cases of admiralty, on or before the return day of the notice of application, demand a jury trial of such issue, and upon such demand the court shall make an order referring the issue or issues to a jury in the manner provided by the Federal Rules of Civil Procedure, or may specially call a jury for that purpose. If the jury finds that no agreement in writing for arbitration was made or that there is no default in proceeding thereunder, the proceeding shall be dismissed. If the jury finds that an agreement for arbitration was made in writing and that there is a default in proceeding thereunder, the court shall make an order summarily directing the parties to proceed with the arbitration in accordance with the terms thereof.

7.100 Section 206 of Chapter 2 of the Federal Arbitration Act, which applies to cases falling under the New York Convention, provides:

> A court having jurisdiction under this chapter may direct that arbitration be held in accordance with the agreement at any place therein provided for, whether that place is within or without the United States. Such court may also appoint arbitrators in accordance with the provisions of the agreement.

7.101 Section 303 of Chapter 3 of the Federal Arbitration Act, which applies to cases falling under the Panama Convention provides:

> (a) A court having jurisdiction under this chapter may direct that arbitration be held in accordance with the agreement at any place therein provided for, whether that place is within or without the United States. The court may also appoint arbitrators in accordance with the provisions of the agreement.
> (b) In the event the agreement does not make provision for the place of arbitration or the appointment of arbitrators, the court shall direct that the arbitration shall be held and the arbitrators be appointed in accordance with Article 3 of the Inter-American Convention.

7.102 One difference between, on the one hand, Section 4 of Chapter 1, and, on the other, Section 206 of Chapter 2 and Section 303 of Chapter 3, is that Section 4 of the Federal Arbitration Act authorizes a court to order arbitration in accordance with the agreement only in the United States, and more specifically only in "the district in which the petition for an order directing such arbitration is filed." Sections 206 and 303, by contrast, authorize a court to "direct that arbitration be held in accordance with the agreement *at any place therein provided for, whether that place is within or without the United States*" (emphasis added). Thus, as one court has noted, the Federal Arbitration Act "makes it clear that in domestic cases a federal district court may only compel arbitration in its own district."[143] Whereas, "in an international dispute covered by Chapter 2 of the Federal Arbitration Act, the rules are broadened by the provisions of Section 206, which permits a court to 'direct that arbitration be held in accordance with the agreement at any place therein provided for, whether that place is within or without the United States.' "[144] If a party wishes to compel arbitration in New York, if its case falls under the Convention, it could rely on Section 206 or 303, depending on which Convention is applicable, or it could rely on Section 4 if it files its motion to compel in the appropriate New York federal district court.

Second, Section 4 operates only in the event that there is "failure, neglect, or refusal of another to arbitrate." Although neither Chapter 2 nor 3 explicitly impose this requirement, courts have held that it is necessary to make this type of showing when making a motion to compel under the Convention.[145] **7.103**

Third, there is a difference between Chapters 2 and 3. Chapter 3—which applies to cases under the Panama Convention—provides that where the contract does not designate the place of arbitration or the number of arbitrators "the court shall direct that the arbitration shall be held and the arbitrators be appointed in accordance with Article 3 of the Inter-American Convention." Article 3 of the Panama Convention provides that "[i]n the absence of an express agreement between the parties, the arbitration shall be conducted in accordance with the rules of procedure of the Inter-American Commercial Arbitration Commission." **7.104**

In order to compel arbitration under the Convention, courts look first to whether the agreement in question "falls under" the Convention, applying the same four-part test used to determine whether an agreement falls under the Convention **7.105**

[143] Oil Basins Ltd. v. Broken Hill Proprietary Co., 613 F. Supp. 483, 486 (S.D.N.Y. 1985); *see also* Klein v. ATP Flight Sch., LLP, 2014 WL 3013294, at *10–11 (E.D.N.Y. July 3, 2014). In a non-Convention case involving an arbitration agreement calling for arbitration in the Bahamas, which thus did not fall under Chapter 2 or 3 of the Federal Arbitration Act, one court held that it lacked the authority to compel arbitration in the Bahamas under Section 4 of the Federal Arbitration Act, since Section 4 permitted a court to compel arbitration only in its own district. *DaPuzzo*, 263 F. Supp. 2d at 728.

[144] *Oil Basins Ltd*, 613 F. Supp. at 486.

[145] *See, e.g.*, Phoenix Aktiengesellschaft v. Ecoplas, Inc., 391 F.3d 433, 437 (2d Cir. 2004) ("[I]t is doubtful that a petition to compel filed before the 'adverse' party has refused arbitration would present an Article III court with justiciable case or controversy in the first instance."); Empresa Generadora de Electricidad ITABO, S.A. v. Corporacion Dominicana de Empresas Electricas Estatales, 2005 WL 1705080, at *6 (S.D.N.Y. July 18, 2005); Hartford Accident & Indemnity Co. v. Equitas Reins Ltd., 200 F. Supp. 2d 102 (D. Conn. 2002).

for the purposes of subject-matter jurisdiction.[146] And in the event that the court finds such an agreement exists, it must compel arbitration of any dispute falling within the scope of the agreement pursuant to the terms of the agreement[147] unless the agreement is "null and void, inoperative or incapable of being performed."[148] It is further settled that "a district court's scope of inquiry in considering a petition to compel arbitration under Chapter 2 of the FAA is 'very limited.' "[149] The most common grounds for resisting a motion to compel arbitration have been discussed previously, but there is an additional issue that may arise in the context of actions to compel arbitration in New York.

2. CPLR § 7503(c)

7.106 A provision of New York State law, Section 7503 of New York Civil Practice Law and Rules (CPLR), provides that a party may, but is not required to, serve a demand for arbitration or a notice of intent to arbitrate explicitly stating that unless the party served applies to a court to stay the arbitration within twenty days after such service, that party will be "precluded from objecting that a valid agreement was not made or has not been complied with and from asserting in court the bar of a limitation of time." Section 7503(c) states in relevant part:

> A party may serve upon another party a demand for arbitration or a notice of intention to arbitrate, specifying the agreement ... and stating that unless the party served applies to stay the arbitration *within twenty days after such service he shall thereafter be precluded from objecting* that a valid agreement was not made or has not been complied with and from asserting in court the bar of a limitation of time.[150]

7.107 The effect of Section 7503(c) is to permit a party commencing an arbitration proceeding to shift to her adversary the burden of promptly seeking a judicial stay of arbitration on the basis of the threshold defenses that a dispute is not arbitrable, that the conditions of the arbitration agreement have not been complied with, or that the arbitration is barred by the statute of limitations. When a party served with a notice of intent to arbitrate does not object to arbitration within the twenty-day period, they are in effect "waiving" their right to raise the threshold defenses in court either through a motion to stay, an opposition to a motion to

---

[146] *Smith/Enron*, 198 F.3d at 92. *See* Section B.2(a) of this chapter.

[147] 198 F.3d at 92.

[148] Article II, paragraph 3, New York Convention. Sphere Drake Ins. Ltd. v. Clarendon Nat'l. Ins. Co., 263 F.3d 26, 30 n.2 (2d Cir. 2001) ("While this case technically arises under the [New York Convention], we may look to precedent discussing 9 U.S.C.A. § 4's requirement that the court be 'satisfied the making of the agreement for arbitration ... is not in issue' in interpreting the [New York Convention's] similar requirement that a court may compel arbitration 'unless it finds that the said agreement is *null and void, inoperative* or incapable of being performed.' ") (alteration in original). U.S. courts have not undertaken much in the way of analysis of the "null and void" language, but rather have included within that term the type of challenges to a contract discussed at Section B.4 of this chapter. *See also* Chapter 1.D.1(b) of this book.

[149] *Smith/Enron*, 198 F.3d at 92.

[150] N.Y. Civil Practice Law and Rules § 7503(c) (McKinney 1998) (emphasis added).

compel, or in an action challenging the award. Courts treat the twenty-day time limit to apply for a stay under Section 7503(c) as a statute of limitations.[151]

Section 7503(c) does not apply to all court challenges to an arbitration. Most notably, the limitation does not apply where the parties "never agreed to arbitrate."[152] A party served with a twenty-day notice under Section 7503(c) may seek a stay, without time limitation, on the ground that no agreement to arbitrate exists between the parties. A nonsignatory to an arbitration agreement should be able to rely on this exception.[153] There is also a public policy exception to the application of Section 7503(c), such that "[a]n untimely application to stay arbitration may … be granted if the agreement for which arbitration is sought is facially illegal or if upon facial examination of the agreement, a court may conclude that it would be against public policy to permit arbitration of the issue sought to be arbitrated."[154] **7.108**

One question that arises is whether Section 7503(c), which, as noted, is a provision of New York state law, applies to arbitrations governed by the Federal Arbitration Act. None of the three chapters of the Federal Arbitration Act contains any explicit limitations period within which a party must seek a stay of arbitration,[155] and neither the Second Circuit nor the New York Court of Appeals (the New York state court of last resort) has addressed this issue. The federal district courts that have considered the question are divided, while the lower state courts have taken the view that Section 7503(c) applies to cases covered by the Federal Arbitration Act. **7.109**

Federal district courts holding that Section 7503(c) does not apply to arbitrations under the Federal Arbitration Act base their view on the ground that the Act preempts state law because, in enacting that statute, Congress intended to occupy the entire field of federal arbitration law and that there is no precedential basis for a federal court to borrow a state law limitations period in the arbitration context.[156] The federal courts that have taken the contrary position rest their view on the ground that the Federal Arbitration Act preempts state arbitration law only to the extent that the two bodies of law conflict. Since the Federal Arbitration Act is silent as to the applicability of any time limit for a motion to stay, these courts reason that there is no conflict between federal and state law, and that courts may **7.110**

[151] *See* Aetna Life & Casualty Co. v. Slekardis, 34 N.Y.2d 182, 185–86 (1974).

[152] *See* Matarasso v. Continental Casualty Co., 56 N.Y.2d 264 (1982).

[153] *See In re* Colonial Co-op. Ins. Co. (Muehlbauer), 46 A.D.3d 1012 (App. Div. Dec. 6, 2007).

[154] *See* Land of the Free, Inc. v. Unique Sanitation, Inc., 93 N.Y.2d 942, 943 (1999).

[155] The FAA also does not contain any explicit procedure for a stay of arbitration. Although the Second Circuit has not expressly addressed whether the FAA allows a district court to stay an arbitration, a number of federal courts have held that, "in appropriate circumstances, § 4 of the FAA may be applied to stay or enjoin arbitration proceedings." United States v. Eberhard, 2004 WL 616122, at *3 (S.D.N.Y. 2004) (*quoting* Westmoreland Capital Corp. v. Findlay, 100 F.3d 263, 266 n.3 (2d Cir. 1996)).

[156] *See* Endriss v. Eklof Marine Corp., No. 96 Civ. 3137 (KMW), 1998 WL 1085911, at *3–4 & n.5 (S.D.N.Y. July 28, 1998); *See also* Sandvik v. Libby, 762 F. Supp. 596, 599 (S.D.N.Y. 1991); Rothberg v. Loeb, Rhoades & Co., 445 F. Supp. 1336 (S.D.N.Y. 1978). The concept of preemption is discussed in Chapter 1.B.1(b).

apply the state limitations period where the party commencing the arbitration has given a notice under CPLR § 7503(c).[157] Some of these courts have relied on the Supreme Court's decision in *Del Costello v. Int'l Bhd. of Teamsters*, a labor arbitration-related case, in which the Supreme Court stated that "resort to state law remains the norm for borrowing of limitations period" for federal causes of action lacking a clear statute of limitations.[158]

7.111 With one exception, the cases addressing the applicability of Section 7503(c) to arbitrations covered by the Federal Arbitration Act have not involved international arbitrations subject to either Convention.[159] However, there is no reason to believe that a court's analysis would differ under these circumstances. In light of the unsettled law, the prudent course for a party served with a Section 7503(c) notice in a case falling under the Conventions would be to seek court intervention within the twenty-day limitations period.

E. COURT INTERVENTION: STAYING LITIGATION COMMENCED IN THE UNITED STATES IN BREACH OF AN ARBITRATION CLAUSE

7.112 As noted, a party may commence litigation in the United States notwithstanding the fact that it agreed to resolve its dispute by arbitration. In such a situation, one remedy open to the party seeking to enforce the agreement to arbitrate is to request the U.S. court to stay or dismiss the litigation. A motion to stay or dismiss litigation is distinct from a motion or petition to compel arbitration—although the two remedies may be, and often are, sought simultaneously. The distinction between the two has been articulated in this way: "The first [motion to stay or

[157] *See, e.g.*, Miller v. Worth Capital, Inc., 1998 WL 193213 (S.D.N.Y. 1998) (noting that Section 7503(c) would apply to FAA arbitration but holding that petitioner waived statute of limitations argument by failing to invoke 20-day limitation its demand for arbitration), *aff'd on other grounds*, 173 F.3d 844 (2d Cir. 1999); Favara, Skahan, Tabaczyk, Ltd. v. Ewing, No. 91 Civ. 7878 (JFK), 1992 WL 80659, at *2 (S.D.N.Y. Apr. 9, 1992); Morgan v. Nikko Sec. Cop. Int'l, 691 F. Supp. 792 (S.D.N.Y. 1992) (noting that CPLR § 7503(c) would apply to FAA cases, but holding Section 7503(c) inapplicable under *Matarasso* exception, where there was no contract containing an arbitration clause). For state court cases holding that the FAA does not preempt CPLR § 7503(c), *see, e.g.*, Propulsora Ixtapa Sur., S.A v. Omni Hotels Franchising Corp., 211 A.D. 2d 546 (1st Dep't 1995); E.D. Jones & Co. v. American Stock Exchange, LLC, 22 A.D.3d 319 (1st Dep't 2005).

[158] Del Costello v. Int'l Bhd. of Teamsters, 462 U.S. 151, 171 (1983) (declining to borrow state limitations period where federal labor law provided a more appropriate limitations period for labor arbitration). *See also* Favara, Skahan, Tabaczyk, Ltd. v. Ewing, 1992 WL 80659, at *2 (citing *Del Costello*); Miller v. Worth Capital, Inc., 1998 WL 193213 (S.D.N.Y. 1998) (same).

[159] Propulsora Ixtapa Sur v. Omni Hotels Franchising Corp., 211 A.D.2d 546 (1st Dep't 1995) involved a dispute between a Mexican and U.S. party and, therefore, was a Convention case. The New York state court held that the Federal Arbitration Act did not preempt Section 7503(c), but did not address the fact that the case fell under the Convention.

dismiss litigation brought in contravention of an arbitration clause] merely arrests further action by the court itself in this suit until something outside the suit has occurred; but the court does not order that it shall be done. The second [motion to compel arbitration] ... affirmatively orders that someone do (or refrain from doing) some act outside the suit."[160]

1. Motions to Stay or Dismiss Litigation under the Federal Arbitration Act

While Chapters 2 and 3 of the Federal Arbitration Act contain no express provisions governing the stay of litigation brought in violation of an arbitration clause, courts have held that the authority of courts to stay such litigation in connection with a case subject to an arbitration agreement that falls under the Convention "exists both implicitly, as well as by incorporation of Chapter 1 into Chapter 2 and the Convention through 9 U.S.C. § 208,"[161] which provides that Chapter 1 of the FAA is incorporated into Chapter 2 "to the extent [that Chapter 1 is] not in conflict with [Chapter 2 or] the Convention."[162] **7.113**

A motion to stay or dismiss litigation is based on Section 3 of Chapter 1 of the Federal Arbitration Act. It provides: **7.114**

> If any suit or proceeding be brought in any of the courts of the United States upon any issue referable to arbitration under an agreement in writing for such arbitration, the court in which such suit is pending, upon being satisfied that the issue involved in such suit or proceeding is referable to arbitration under such an agreement, shall on application of one of the parties stay the trial of the action until such arbitration has been had in accordance with the terms of the agreement, providing the applicant for the stay is not in default in proceeding with such arbitration.

Section 3 is explicit that it applies only in the event that a party seeking to avoid arbitration has brought litigation "in any of the courts of the United States upon any issue referable to arbitration under an agreement in writing for such arbitration." If such litigation is commenced in a court outside the United States, the appropriate remedy to be sought from a U.S. court is to request that it issue an antisuit injunction, which is addressed in Section F of this chapter. **7.115**

In the event litigation is commenced in the United States in violation of an arbitration clause, the party seeking to arbitrate—whether a signatory or a nonsignatory[163]—can rely on Section 3 of the Federal Arbitration Act to request that the court stay or dismiss that litigation on the grounds that the **7.116**

---

160 *Kulukundis Shipping Co.*, 126 F.2d at 987.

161 *DaPuzzo*, 263 F. Supp. 2d at 725.

162 *Id.* at 720–21 (citation omitted). While *DaPuzzo* involves the New York Convention, the same logic would apply to cases that fall under the Panama Convention.

163 In a nonsignatory case, the U.S. Supreme Court held that "a litigant who was not a party to the relevant arbitration agreement may invoke [Section 3 of the Federal Arbitration Act] if the

subject matter of the litigation is "referable to arbitration." A U.S. court would clearly have personal jurisdiction over the party that has commenced litigation in the United States in violation of an arbitration clause, since that party, by having commenced litigation in a U.S. court, has subjected itself to the jurisdiction of that court. Moreover, as discussed earlier in this chapter, if a lawsuit relates to an arbitration agreement that falls under the New York or Panama Conventions, a U.S. federal court has subject-matter jurisdiction over the case. And if such lawsuit were commenced in state court it can be removed to federal court.

7.117 In *Katz v. Cellco Partnership*,[164] the Second Circuit recently held that the Federal Arbitration Act "requires a stay of proceedings when all claims are referred to arbitration and a stay [is] requested."[165] Up until this decision, this issue, on which there is a circuit split, had not been clear in the Second Circuit.[166] Whether a lawsuit is "stayed" or "dismissed" on the ground that it is arbitrable is significant because if a court issues an order staying a lawsuit, that order is an interlocutory order and, as such, is not immediately appealable. If, however, a court issues an order dismissing a lawsuit, that decision is immediately appealable.

7.118 In *Katz*, the Second Circuit rested its decision requiring a grant of a stay if a stay were requested on two grounds. First, it relied on the language of Section 3 of the Federal Arbitration Act, which provides, in mandatory language, that a court "shall" stay proceedings. Second, it relied on the federal policy in favor of arbitration: "[A] mandatory stay is consistent with the FAA's underlying policy 'to move the parties to an arbitrable dispute out of court and into arbitration as quickly and easily as possible.' "[167]

7.119 The Second Circuit has articulated four criteria to determine whether to grant an application pursuant to Section 3 of the Federal Arbitration Act: (1) "whether the parties agreed to arbitrate"; (2) whether the asserted claims fall within the "scope" of the arbitration agreement; (3) "if federal statutory claims" are at issue, whether

relevant state contract law allows him to enforce the agreement." Arthur Andersen v. Carlisle, 129 S. Ct. 1896, 1903 (2009).

[164] 794 F.3d 341 (2d Cir. 2015).

[165] *Id.* at 342.

[166] *Compare* McMahan Sec. Co. v. Forum Capital Mkts. 35 F.3d 82, 85–86 (2d Cir. 1994) ("Under the [FAA], a district court must stay proceedings if satisfied that the parties have agreed in writing to arbitrate an issue or issues underlying the district court proceeding. The FAA leaves no discretion with the district court in the matter.") (citation omitted), *with* Oldroyd v. Elmira Sav. Bank, 134 F.3d 72, 76 (2d Cir. 1998) ("[I]f the court concludes that some, but not all, of the claims in the case are arbitrable, it must then decide whether to stay the balance of the proceedings pending arbitration."), *and* Salim Oleochemicals v. M/V Shropshire, 278 F.3d 90, 93 (2d Cir. 2002) ("We urge district courts in these circumstances to be as clear as possible about whether they truly intend to dismiss an action or mean to grant a stay pursuant to [FAA Section 3], which supplies that power …").

[167] 794 F.3d at 343 (citation omitted).

"Congress intended" such claims to be nonarbitrable; and (4) if only some of the claims are arbitrable, whether to "stay the balance of the proceedings pending arbitration."[168]

The first two parts of the four-part *Oldroyd* test raises similar issues to those discussed in Section B of this chapter, the second two parts of the *Oldroyd* test are addressed below. **7.120**

2. The Arbitrability of Claims under U.S. Law

It was once settled under U.S. law that certain subjects could not be resolved by arbitration.[169] Thus, several decades ago the U.S. Supreme Court held in *Wilko v. Swan*,[170] that claims arising under the federal securities law were not arbitrable, a ruling that was extended by lower courts to include RICO claims,[171] and antitrust claims,[172] among others. However, beginning with the Supreme Court's decision in *Scherk v. Alberto-Culver Co.*,[173] the courts began to reevaluate the holding of *Wilko*. In *Scherk*, the Supreme Court held that claims under the federal securities laws were arbitrable if they arose from an international commercial transaction. In so holding, the Supreme Court noted that, "[a]n agreement to arbitrate before a specified tribunal is, in effect, a specialized kind of forum-selection clause that posits not only the situs of suit but also the procedure to be used in resolving the dispute. The invalidation of such an agreement in the case before us would not only allow the respondent to repudiate its solemn promise but would, as well, reflect a 'parochial concept that all disputes must be resolved under our laws and in our courts ... We cannot have trade and commerce in world markets and international waters exclusively on our terms, governed by our laws, and resolved in our courts.' "[174] **7.121**

Just over a decade later, in *Mitsubishi Motors Corp. v. Soler Chrysler-Plymouth, Inc.*,[175] the Supreme Court held that claims under the federal antitrust laws were also arbitrable in international cases, basing its decision in part on respect for the New York Convention. The Court noted that the **7.122**

> [U]tility of the [New York] Convention in promoting the process of international commercial arbitration depends upon the willingness of national courts to let go

---

[168] *Genesco, Inc.*, 815 F.2d at 844–45; Oldroyd v. Elmira Sav. Bank, FSB, 134 F.3d 72, 75–76 (2d Cir. 1998).

[169] *See also* the discussion of arbitrability in Chapter 6.C.3(d) and Chapter 6.E.3(c)(iii) of this book.

[170] 346 U.S. 427 (1953).

[171] S.A. Mineracao da Trinidade-Samitri v. Utah Int'l Inc., 576 F. Supp. 566 (S.D.N.Y. 1984), *aff'd*, 745 F.2d 190 (2d Cir. 1984).

[172] Am. Safety Equip. v. J.P. Maguire & Co., 391 F.2d 821 (2d Cir. 1968).

[173] 417 U.S. 506 (1974).

[174] *Id.* at 519 (citation and footnote omitted).

[175] 473 U.S. 614 (1985).

of matters they normally would think of as their own. Doubtless, Congress may specify categories of claims it wishes to reserve for decision by our own courts without contravening this Nation's obligations under the [New York] Convention. But we decline to subvert the spirit of the United States' accession to the Convention by recognizing subject-matter exceptions where Congress has not expressly directed the courts to do so.[176]

7.123 And in 1987, in *Shearson/Am. Express, Inc. v. McMahon*,[177] the Court explicitly overruled *Wilko* and held that claims under the federal securities law and the RICO statute were arbitrable even in domestic cases. Since federal statutory claims will generally be deemed to be arbitrable unless the party resisting arbitration can demonstrate that Congress intended otherwise,[178] the third prong of the *Oldroyd* test has little role to play nowadays.[179]

3. Cases that Include Nonarbitrable Claims

7.124 The fourth prong of the *Oldroyd* test concerns the situation where only some of the claims in the lawsuit that is the object of the motion to stay or dismiss are arbitrable. For example, this may arise in a case where a party to an arbitration agreement commences a lawsuit against another party to that agreement, but also joins to that same lawsuit a related nonparty, such as a corporate parent or subsidiary. Alternatively, a party may assert claims arising out of an agreement which

[176] *Id.* at 639 n.21. The Court did, however, emphasize that courts could, at the enforcement stage, examine whether the arbitrators properly resolved any antitrust claims: "[h]aving permitted the arbitration to go forward, the national courts of the United States will have the opportunity at the award-enforcement stage to ensure that the legitimate interest in the enforcement of the antitrust laws has been addressed ... While the efficacy of the arbitral process requires that substantive review at the award-enforcement stage remain minimal, it would not require intrusive inquiry to ascertain that the tribunal took cognizance of the antitrust claims and actually decided them." *Id.* at 638. For a discussion of this "second look" doctrine, *see* Hans Smit, *Mandatory Law in Arbitration*, 18 AM. REV. INT'L ARB. 155 (2007).

[177] 482 U.S. 220 (1987).

[178] *Shearson*, 482 U.S. at 226–27 ("The Arbitration Act, standing alone, therefore mandates enforcement of agreements to arbitrate statutory claims. Like any statutory directive, the Arbitration Act's mandate may be overridden by a contrary congressional command. The burden is on the party opposing arbitration, however, to show that Congress intended to preclude a waiver of judicial remedies for the statutory rights at issue.").

[179] It is worth noting, however, that in one recent case, a court found a case arising out of an arbitration agreement falling under the Convention, which involved personal injury suffered by an employee of a cruise ship, to be not arbitrable on public policy grounds. *See* Thomas v. Carnival Corp., 573 F.3d 1113 (11th Cir. 2009). Specifically, the court found that because the arbitration clause in the employment contract in issue specified that the place of arbitration was the Philippines and, more significantly, was governed by Panamanian law, it constituted a prospective waiver of the employee seaman's statutory rights under the Seaman's Wage Act, and thus was not enforceable under the New York Convention as contrary to United States' public policy, on the ground that there was no assurance of opportunity for review of the seaman's claim. *Id.* at 1123–24. It remains to be seen whether this ruling is the start of a trend reviving the third prong of the *Oldroyd* test, or whether it will be confined to the employment context, where courts tend to be solicitous of the statutory rights of employees.

provides for arbitration, but also assert, in the same lawsuit, claims unrelated to that agreement. It is worth stressing, as already noted, that parties sometimes bring suits that include both arbitrable and nonarbitrable claims as part of a strategy to avoid arbitration. Courts, however, are wise to this tactic.

In *IDS Life Ins. Co. v. SunAmerica, Inc.*, 103 F.3d 524 (7th Cir. 1996), Chief Judge Richard Posner referred to cases **7.125**

> [I]n which a party to an arbitration agreement, trying to get around it, sues not only the other party to the agreement but some related party with which it has no arbitration agreement, in the hope that the claim against the other party will be adjudicated first and have preclusive effect in the arbitration. Such a maneuver should not be allowed to succeed ...[180]

Similarly, *WorldCrisa Corp. v. Armstrong*[181] concerned a case where both a non-party (a parent corporation) and a party (its subsidiary) to an arbitration agreement commenced a lawsuit against the other party to the agreement. Referring to the principle articulated by Chief Judge Posner quoted previously, the Second Circuit stated: "We think the same principle applies in this case, in which a related non-party to an arbitration agreement has apparently brought a suit with the hope of having a similar effect."[182] **7.126**

The question arises as to how courts should resolve a motion to stay a lawsuit that includes some claims that fall within the scope of an arbitration agreement and some that do not. Can they stay the entire lawsuit, including the nonarbitrable claims as well as the arbitrable ones, or must they let the suit go forward as to the nonarbitrable claims? **7.127**

While courts hold that their authority to stay a case under Section 3 of the Federal Arbitration Act applies only to claims subject to arbitration, they nonetheless acknowledge that they also have the power to stay nonarbitrable claims based on their inherent authority to control their docket. Thus, "despite the inapplicability of the [Federal Arbitration Act]," a court "may stay a case pursuant to 'the power inherent in every court to control the disposition of causes on its docket with economy of time and effort for itself, for counsel, and for litigants.' "[183] Courts have held that where "there are arbitrable as well as non-arbitrable claims in a complaint, a stay of the litigation pending arbitration is appropriate where 'the party seeking the stay can demonstrate that he will not hinder the arbitration, that the arbitration will be concluded within a reasonable time; and that the delay will not work an undue hardship ...' "[184] **7.128**

---

180 *IDS Life Ins.*, 103 F.3d at 150.
181 129 F.3d 71 (2d Cir. 1997).
182 *WorldCrisa Corp.*, 129 F.3d at 76.
183 *Id.* at 76.
184 Home Life Ins. Co. v. Kaufman, 547 F. Supp. 833, 835 (S.D.N.Y. 1982) (citation omitted).

F. COURT INTERVENTION: ANTISUIT INJUNCTIONS

7.129 In the prior section, we considered how a party could seek the intervention of a U.S. court to enforce an agreement to arbitrate in the event that a lawsuit is commenced *in the United States* in breach of an arbitration clause calling for arbitration in New York. However, in some cases, the party seeking to avoid an agreement to arbitrate a dispute in New York will not commence litigation in the United States, but rather will commence litigation in the courts of another country, typically its home country. Here, the appropriate remedy for the party seeking to enforce the arbitration agreement is to apply to a New York court for an antisuit injunction.

7.130 The remedy of an antisuit injunction is not one found in either the Convention or in the Federal Arbitration Act. And it is not a remedy that is exclusive to the field of international arbitration. U.S. courts have enjoined a party from proceeding with foreign litigation in various circumstances, such as the commencement of litigation abroad parallel to litigation pending in the United States, and not simply when foreign litigation is brought in contravention of an arbitration clause requiring the case to be arbitrated in the United States.[185] Thus, before considering how the remedy of the antisuit injunction might operate in the arbitration context, it is worth discussing the device of the antisuit injunction more generally.

1. Antisuit Injunctions: An Overview

7.131 It is well settled that U.S. courts have the power to issue an antisuit injunction, that is, an injunction enjoining a person subject to their jurisdiction from prosecuting a foreign lawsuit.[186] It is important to note that this injunction is aimed not at the foreign court, but rather at the party pursuing the foreign lawsuit. Failure to comply with an antisuit injunction, therefore, is a contempt of court, and punishable as such.[187]

[185] *See, e.g.*, China Trade and Dev. Corp. v. M.V. Choong Yong, 837 F.2d 33, 35 (2d Cir. 1987); United States v. Davis, 767 F.2d 1025, 1038 (2d Cir. 1985); Laker Airways Ltd. v. Sabena, Belgian World Airlines, 731 F.2d 909, 926 (D.C. Cir. 1984). Courts in the European Union no longer appear to have the authority to enjoin litigation brought in an E.U. country in contravention of an arbitration clause. Case C-185/07, Allianz S.p.A. v. West Tankers Inc., 2009 WL 303723 (ECJ), Feb. 10, 2009.

[186] *See, e.g.*, Kaepa, Inc. v. Achilles Corp., 76 F.3d 624, 626 (5th Cir. 1996).

[187] *See* Paramedics Electromedicina Comercial, Ltda. v. GE Medical Sys. Information Techs., Inc., 369 F.3d 645, 658 (2d Cir. 2004) (affirming imposition of daily contempt fines on a party that failed to abide by an antisuit injunction, but remanding to district court to reconsider the amount of the daily fine).

Although it is understood that an antisuit injunction is directed at a party to the foreign suit, and not at a foreign court, it is also well recognized that the effect of an antisuit injunction is to interfere with proceedings in a foreign court. U.S. courts, therefore, have acknowledged that the issuance of an antisuit injunction can be problematic, and, thus, can implicate considerations of international comity.[188] "Comity is a recognition which one nation extends within its own territory to the legislative, executive, or judicial acts of another."[189] **7.132**

The circuit courts of appeals vary in the approach they use to decide whether to issue an antisuit injunction. The circuits are generally in agreement that two threshold requirements must be met before a court will consider issuing an antisuit injunction. First, the "parties must be the same in both matters."[190] Second, "resolution of the case before the enjoining court must be dispositive of the action to be enjoined."[191] The circuits differ in how much weight should be accorded to considerations of international comity in the event that the two threshold requirements are satisfied, with some circuits placing great weight on international comity, and granting antisuit injunctions only rarely[192] and other circuits taking a more liberal view of antisuit injunctions.[193] **7.133**

The Second Circuit follows the approach set out in *China Trade and Dev. Corp. v. M.V. Choong Yong*, placing great weight on comity, while considering a variety of other factors in determining whether to issue an antisuit **7.134**

---

[188] *See, e.g.*, *China Trade*, 837 F.2d at 35 ("The fact that the injunction operates only against the parties, and not directly against the foreign court, does not eliminate the need for due regard to principles of international comity, because such an order effectively restricts the jurisdiction of the court of a foreign sovereign."); Garpeg, Ltd. v. United States, 583 F. Supp. 789, 798 (S.D.N.Y. 1984) (an antisuit injunction may be "tantamount to enjoining the tribunal of a foreign sovereign").

[189] Somportex Ltd. v. Philadelphia Chewing Gum Corp., 453 F.2d 435, 440 (3d Cir. 1971), *cert. denied*, 405 U.S. 1017 (1972).

[190] *See China Trade*, 837 F.2d at 35. As noted later, in order to deflect the tactics of a party trying to sidestep its obligations to arbitrate, courts have not applied this requirement strictly when a non-party to the arbitration agreement has been named as a defendant in the foreign lawsuit.

[191] *Id.*

[192] Generally speaking, the Third, Sixth, and D.C. circuits adopt a "conservative" approach. Under this approach, the courts attach great weight to comity considerations and grant antisuit injunction rarely and typically only under two circumstances: (1) when the foreign action is a threat to the jurisdiction of the U.S. court, or (2) on grounds of public policy. *See, e.g.*, Answers in Genesis of Kentucky, Inc. v. Creation Ministries Intern., Ltd., 556 F.3d 459, 471–72 (6th Cir. 2009); Gau Shan Co. v. Bankers Trust Co., 956 F.2d 1349, 1355–58 (6th Cir. 1992); Laker Airways Ltd. v. Sabena, Belgian World Airlines, 731 F.2d 909, 926–27 (D.C. Cir. 1984); Compagnie des Bauxites de Guinea v. Ins. Co. of N. America, 651 F.2d 877, 887 (3d Cir. 1981), *cert. denied*, 457 U.S. 1105 (1982).

[193] The Fifth, Seventh, and Ninth Circuits attach less weight to considerations of international comity, and thus take a more liberal view of when an antisuit injunction should be issued. *See, e.g.*, Kaepa, Inc. v. Achilles Corp., 76 F.3d 624, 626–27 (5th Cir. 1996) ("We decline ... to require a district court to genuflect before a vague and omnipotent notion of comity every time that it must decide whether to enjoin a foreign action."); Allendale Mut. Ins. Co. v. Bull Data Sys., Inc., 10 F.3d 425, 431–32 (7th Cir. 1993); Seattle Totems Hockey Club, Inc. v. Nat'l Hockey League, 652 F.2d 852, 855–56 (9th Cir. 1981), *cert. denied*, 457 U.S. 1105 (1982).

injunction. These factors include whether the foreign litigation would: (1) frustrate a public policy in the enjoining forum; (2) be vexatious; (3) threaten the issuing court's jurisdiction; (4) result in prejudice to other equitable considerations; or (5) result in delay, inconvenience, expense, inconsistency, or a race to judgment.[194] *China Trade* instructs that two of these factors should be accorded "greater significance": whether the foreign action threatens the enjoining forum's jurisdiction, or its "strong public policies."[195] While some courts in the Second Circuit have made determinations as to whether to issue an antisuit injunction by focusing exclusively on these two "greater weight" *China Trade* factors,[196] the Second Circuit recently reiterated that all of the additional *China Trade* factors should be considered when determining whether an antisuit injunction is warranted.[197] *China Trade* also states that "principles of international comity" counsel that injunctions restraining foreign litigation be "used sparingly" and "granted only with care and great restraint."[198]

7.135 It is worth noting that, in some cases, it is necessary for a party to obtain immediate relief to enjoin a foreign lawsuit brought in contravention of an arbitration clause providing for arbitration in New York. This requires the party to apply for a preliminary injunction. Some courts have held that in seeking such an injunction, the party must satisfy not only the standards for an antisuit injunction, but also the specific standards that apply to preliminary injunctions more generally. It is settled that in order to obtain a preliminary injunction, the moving party must show: (1) irreparable harm, and (2) either (a) likelihood of success on the merits, or (b) sufficiently serious questions going to the merits to make them a fair ground for litigation and a balance of hardships tipping decidedly toward the party requesting preliminary relief.[199] In one case, the district court found these standards satisfied in issuing an antisuit injunction enjoining a party from pursuing litigation in the Netherlands in breach of a forum selection clause providing for litigation in New York.[200]

---

[194] *See* Ibeto Petrochem. Indus. Ltd. v. M/T "Beffen," 475 F.3d 56, 64–65 (2d Cir. 2007). The First Circuit follows a similar approach, placing great weight on considerations of international comity, but also considering the "totality of circumstances" generally. According to the First Circuit, there is a rebuttable presumption against an antisuit injunction which "may be counterbalanced by other facts and factors particular to a specific case." *See* Quaak v. Klynveld Peat Marwick Goerdeler Bedrijfsrevisoren, 361 F.3d 11, 19 (1st Cir. 2004).

[195] *China Trade*, 837 F.2d at 36.

[196] 837 F.2d at 35.

[197] *See* Karaha Bodas Co. v. Perusahaan Pertambangan Minyak Dan Gas Bumi Negara, 500 F.3d 111, 119 (2d Cir. 2007) ("we have reiterated that *all* of the additional factors should be considered when determining whether an anti-suit injunction is warranted"). *See also Ibeto Petrochemical*, 475 F.3d at 64.

[198] 837 F.2d at 35–36.

[199] Int'l Fashion Prods. B.V. v. Calvin Klein, Inc., No. 95-CV-0982 (JFK), 1995 WL 92321, at *1 (S.D.N.Y. Mar. 7, 1995). *See also* Beal v. Stern, 184 F.3d 117, 122 (2d Cir. 1999).

[200] Int'l Fashion Prods., 1995 WL 92321, at *2–3.

2. Circumstances in Which Courts Grant Antisuit Injunctions to Enforce Arbitration Agreements

Despite cautioning that antisuit injunctions should be used sparingly, courts in the Second Circuit have granted antisuit injunctions to enjoin foreign litigation brought in contravention of an arbitration clause. **7.136**

One of the leading cases in which the Second Circuit affirmed the grant of an antisuit injunction in an arbitration-related case is *Paramedics Electromedicina Comercial, Ltda. v. GE Medical Systems Information Technologies, Inc.*[201] That case concerned a dispute between a Brazilian company, Paramedics Electromedicina Comercial, Ltd. (known as Tecnimed), and a U.S. medical equipment manufacturer, GE Medical Systems Information Technologies (known as GEMS-IT), an affiliate of General Electric. **7.137**

GEMS-IT entered into two agreements with Tecnimed for the distribution of GEMS-IT's medical equipment in Brazil. Both agreements contained an arbitration clause. After a dispute arose under the agreements, Tecnimed filed a lawsuit in the civil court of Brazil against GEMS-IT and GE Brasil (an affiliate of General Electric based in Brazil). GE Brasil was not a party to the agreements containing the arbitration provisions. In its Brazilian lawsuit, Tecnimed asserted, among other things, that it was not required to arbitrate its dispute with GEMS-IT, and asserted certain breach of contract claims under Brazilian law.[202] **7.138**

GEMS-IT subsequently commenced an arbitration in New York. Tecnimed responded that it would not participate in the arbitration on the ground that the dispute was not arbitrable.[203] The administering institution, the Inter-American Commercial Arbitration Commission (IACAC), nonetheless appointed a panel to hear the case. The arbitral panel ultimately determined that it had jurisdiction to hear the case. **7.139**

Parallel with the arbitration, and in response to Tecnimed's attempt to obtain an order from a New York state court staying the arbitration, GEMS-IT sought an order from the U.S. District Court for the Southern District of New York compelling arbitration and a preliminary injunction enjoining Tecnimed from proceeding with the Brazilian suit. The district court granted both of GEMS-IT's motions and entered an antisuit injunction ordering Tecnimed to "immediately take all steps necessary to cause dismissal of the [Brazilian] Action."[204] Subsequently, the court held Tecnimed in contempt because it did not comply **7.140**

---

[201] No. 02-CV-9369 (DFE), 2003 WL 23641529 (S.D.N.Y. Jun. 4, 2003), *aff'd*, 369 F.3d 645 (2d Cir. 2004).

[202] 369 F.3d at 650.

[203] 2003 WL 23641529, at *4.

[204] 369 F.3d at 650.

with the injunction, and ordered it to pay to GEMS-IT $1,000 for each day of the continued noncompliance, which was later increased to $5,000 per day.

7.141 In finding that the party seeking to arbitrate had met the standard for obtaining a preliminary injunction, the district court started with the premise that demonstrating irreparable harm was "the single most important prerequisite for the issuance of a preliminary injunction."[205] The court found that GEMS-IT met that standard for two reasons. First, it held that the mere fact that it could lose its right to arbitrate, by being forced to litigate in Brazil, alone constituted irreparable harm: "[t]he deprivation of GEMS-IT's contractual right to arbitrate its claims, a right protected by international, federal, and state law, constitutes irreparable harm."[206] Second, the court found that the risk of conflicting judgments resulting from parallel proceedings in Brazil and the United States also gave rise to irreparable harm:

> Tecnimed has submitted the issue of arbitrability to this Court. This Court has ruled on and rejected Tecnimed's contention. If Tecnimed is permitted to proceed in the Brazil Action, the possibility exists of conflicting judgments as to arbitrability. In addition, GEMS-IT faces the prospect of conflicting judgments on the merits from the IACAC Arbitral Tribunal and the Brazilian court.[207]

7.142 The Second Circuit affirmed the district court's issuance of an antisuit injunction. The Second Circuit began its analysis by identifying the two threshold factors used to determine whether a court should grant an antisuit injunction: first, that "the parties are the same in both matters"; second, "that resolution of the case before the enjoining court is dispositive of the action to be enjoined."[208]

7.143 The Second Circuit found that even though the two parties were not identical in both matters—GE Brasil was a party to the Brazilian lawsuit, but not to the New York action—the first factor was nonetheless satisfied. The Second Circuit held that GE Brasil's presence as a party to the Brazilian action did not render the parties any less the same in both actions because "GE Brasil is named in the Porto Alegre action chiefly on the basis of its aspects of identity with GEMS-IT . . ."[209] This is an important holding. As noted earlier, one way in which parties seek to avoid arbitration is by commencing litigation not only against a party to the arbitration agreement, but also against a nonparty in an effort to escape its obligation to arbitrate. The *Paramedics* case makes it clear that courts will take a flexible approach in applying the threshold conditions for the granting of antisuit injunctions so as to enforce agreements to arbitrate.

7.144 The Second Circuit also agreed with the district court that the second threshold consideration—whether the case before the district court was dispositive of

---

205 2003 WL 23641529, at *12.
206 *Id.*
207 *Id.*
208 *Paramedics*, 369 F.3d at 652.
209 *Id.* at 652.

the Brazilian action—was satisfied because "[t]he case before the enjoining court here concerns the arbitrability of the parties' claims; therefore the question ... is whether the ruling on arbitrability is dispositive of the Porto Alegre litigation, even though the underlying disputes are confided to the arbitral panel and will not be decided by the enjoining court."[210] Thus, the Second Circuit focused not on the merits of the underlying claims in the Brazilian action, but on the issue of whether those claims could be arbitrable.

The Second Circuit then turned to consider whether the other factors bearing on the grant of an antisuit injunction were satisfied. Focusing exclusively on the two factors held in *China Trade* to be of "greater importance"—i.e., (1) public policy, and (2) protection of the jurisdiction of the rendering court—the Second Circuit found both criteria were satisfied.[211] **7.145**

As far as public policy was concerned, the Second Circuit invoked the federal policy "favoring the liberal enforcement of arbitration clauses," which "applies with particular force in international disputes."[212] The Second Circuit found that Tecnimed commenced the Brazilian action after GEMS-IT commenced arbitration proceedings as "a tactic to evade arbitration," and found that this justified the injunction.[213] It is important to note, however, that the Second Circuit declined to decide whether the commencement of litigation in an attempt to avoid arbitration alone is sufficient grounds for an antisuit injunction to enjoin that litigation. **7.146**

The Second Circuit also justified the antisuit injunction on the ground that the Brazilian litigation threatened the jurisdiction of the district court. It reasoned as follows: by granting the motion to compel arbitration, the district court had rendered a judgment in a case involving the same issues and parties as the Brazilian court. Having done so, "[a]n anti-suit injunction may be needed to protect a court's jurisdiction once a judgment has been rendered."[214] Thus, while considerations of comity usually weigh heavily against the "extreme measure" of an antisuit injunction, "where one court has already reached a judgment—on the same issues, involving the same parties—considerations of comity have diminished force."[215] **7.147**

Since its decision in *Paramedics*, the Second Circuit has affirmed the grant of an antisuit injunction in two other arbitration cases. In *Ibeto Petrochem.*,[216] the Second Circuit held that an antisuit injunction was appropriate in an international **7.148**

[210] 369 F.3d at 653.
[211] As noted, since *Paramedics*, the Second Circuit has instructed courts to focus on all the *China Trade* factors.
[212] *Id.* at 654.
[213] *Id.*
[214] *Id.*
[215] *Id.* at 654–55.
[216] 475 F.3d at 64–65.

maritime dispute, where a party to an arbitration agreement had brought suit in Nigeria. There are two particularly noteworthy aspects of this decision.

7.149 First, the Second Circuit found that the injunction was appropriate even though there was no threat to the jurisdiction of the federal court. Rather, the Second Circuit held that the injunction was warranted because of the strong federal policy favoring arbitration, and because of other "equitable considerations such as deterring forum shopping" and avoiding "inconvenience, inconsistency [in the application of law] and a possible race to judgment."[217] The Second Circuit specifically noted that *all* the factors set out in *China Trade* should be considered, and not just the two factors relied upon by the court in *Paramedics* (i.e., the threat to the foreign court's jurisdiction and public policy).

7.150 Second, having concluded that an antisuit injunction was appropriate, the Second Circuit nonetheless reiterated that "due regard for principles of international comity and reciprocity require a delicate touch in the issuance of anti-foreign suit injunctions, that such injunctions should be used sparingly, and that the pendency of a suit involving the same parties and same issues does not alone form the basis for such an injunction."[218] Based on these caveats, the Second Circuit concluded that "the injunction in this case cuts much too broadly" because it was not specifically directed at the parties before the court and because there was no need for a permanent injunction; rather the injunction should only have been effective only until the conclusion of the arbitration proceedings.[219]

[217] *Id.*

[218] *Id.* at 65.

[219] *Id.* In another arbitration-related case—Karaha Bodas Co. v. Perusahaan Pertambangan Minyak Dan Gas Bumi Negara (also known as KBC v. Pertamina)—the Second Circuit affirmed the grant of an antisuit injunction. 500 F.3d 111 (2d Cir. 2007). KBC v. Pertamina involved enforcement of an arbitral award, rather than enforcement of an agreement to arbitrate which is the subject of this chapter. However, despite the different procedural stance, it is worth considering the Second Circuit's detailed analysis of the *China Trade* factors as applied to the arbitration context. KBC v. Pertamina involved protracted and complicated multistate and multinational proceedings concerning plaintiff KBC's efforts to confirm and enforce a Swiss arbitration award and defendant Pertamina's efforts to avoid enforcement of and vacate the arbitration award through litigation in various countries, including the Cayman Islands. After Pertamina brought the Cayman Islands action seeking to have the arbitration award vacated on grounds of fraud, KBC sought an antisuit injunction in the U.S. District Court for the Southern District of New York. The district court granted the injunction and the Second Circuit affirmed. The Second Circuit held that an antisuit injunction was appropriate in order to "prevent Pertamina from engaging in litigation that would tend to undermine the regime established by the [New York] Convention for recognition and enforcement of arbitral awards." *Id.* at 125. In reaching this conclusion, the Second Circuit considered all the factors bearing on the grant of an antisuit injunction, including the threat to the jurisdiction of the various courts that had enforced the arbitration award under the New York Convention, the strong public policy favoring arbitration, and the vexatiousness of the Cayman Islands litigation (which the Second Circuit found was a tactic to vitiate the arbitration award). As to the issue of comity, the Second Circuit found it significant that the Cayman Islands vacatur proceedings were not contemplated under the New York Convention. Therefore, it concluded that the principles of international comity were not furthered by allowing the Cayman Islands action to proceed.

There are many decisions by New York federal district courts granting antisuit injunctions in the context of enforcing agreements to arbitrate.[220] These district courts base their decisions in large part on the strong federal public policy favoring enforcement of arbitration agreements in international disputes. As explained by the district court in its well-reasoned opinion in *Storm, LLC v. Telenor Mobile Comm. AS*, "[a]ttempts to interfere with arbitration of international disputes are so powerfully disapproved that the Second Circuit has suggested, albeit not decided, that 'an attempt to sidestep arbitration' might be 'sufficient to support a foreign anti-suit injunction.' Where this factor is present, little else is required to authorize an injunction."[221] **7.151**

3. Circumstances Where Courts Have Denied Antisuit Injunctions in Aid of Arbitration

Despite the strong federal policy favoring enforcement of arbitration agreements in international disputes, courts have, under certain circumstances, denied antisuit injunctions where a party commenced litigation outside the United States in breach of an arbitration clause. While the courts' reasoning has varied, some have found it significant that the party commencing the foreign litigation was not refusing to participate in the arbitration. **7.152**

One case in which the Second Circuit affirmed the denial of a request for an antisuit injunction is *LAIF X SPRL v. Axtel S.A. de C.V.*[222] *Axtel* arose out of a dispute between two shareholders of Axtel: a Mexican telecommunications company, Telinor, and a Belgian partnership, LAIF X. Axtel's bylaws provided that disputes among its shareholders were to be resolved by arbitration in New York. **7.153**

LAIF X commenced an arbitration proceeding against Telinor in New York. Before answering LAIF X's arbitration demand, Telinor filed a lawsuit in Mexico seeking a declaration that LAIF X had obtained its Axtel shares through an invalid assignment, and as a result was not a shareholder of Axtel, and, therefore, had no standing to arbitrate. Telinor then answered the arbitration demand requesting that the arbitration be dismissed because the dispute was not arbitrable, or, alternatively, that it be stayed pending the outcome of the Mexican lawsuit. **7.154**

[220] *See* Storm, LLC v. Telenor Mobile Comms. AS, No. 06-CV-13157 (GEL), 2006 WL 3735657 (S.D.N.Y. Dec. 15, 2006) (enjoining parties to arbitration agreement in shareholder dispute from litigating in Ukraine; finding sufficient similarity between nonidentical parties in parallel proceedings based on alter ego theory); Suchodolski Assocs., Inc. v. Cardell Fin. Corp., (WHP), 2006 WL 3327625 (S.D.N.Y. Nov. 16, 2006) (enjoining party to arbitration agreement from proceeding with litigation in Brazil; noting that to the extent Brazilian action asserted nonarbitrable claims only those claims could proceed through litigation); SG Avipro Fin. Ltd. v. Cameroon Airlines, 2005 WL 1353955 (S.D.N.Y. June 8, 2005) (enjoining party to arbitration agreement from proceeding with litigation in Cameroon).

[221] 2006 WL 3735657, at *9.

[222] 310 F. Supp. 2d 578 (S.D.N.Y. 2004), *aff'd*, 390 F.3d 194 (2d Cir. 2004).

7.155 LAIF X responded by petitioning the U.S. District Court for the Southern District of New York for an order compelling Telinor to arbitrate the dispute and for an antisuit injunction barring Telinor from pursuing the Mexican lawsuit. The district court denied both petitions. LAIF X appealed.

7.156 The Second Circuit affirmed the denial of the petition to compel arbitration on the ground that Telinor's actions—participating in the arbitration and challenging the arbitrability of LAIF X's claim before the tribunal—could not be characterized as a refusal to arbitrate.[223] The Second Circuit stated that a party refuses to arbitrate if it "*commences litigation* or is ordered to arbitrate th[e] dispute [by the relevant arbitral authority] and fails to do so,"[224] but it did not find Telinor's commencement of litigation in Mexico, without an attendant refusal to participate in the arbitration, to warrant an order compelling arbitration.[225]

7.157 The Second Circuit also affirmed the denial of the antisuit injunction after considering three of the *China Trade* factors. The Second Circuit found that "the district court did not abuse its discretion by declining to issue the anti-suit injunction, because: (i) principles of comity counsel against issuing the anti-suit injunction; (ii) the United States federal courts have no interest in enjoining Telinor's Mexican lawsuit; and (iii) Telinor's Mexican lawsuit is not directed at sidestepping arbitration."[226]

7.158 With respect to the first consideration—comity—the Second Circuit found significant that the case before the Mexican court concerned the issue of whether LAIF X was a shareholder of Axtel under Mexican law, in which Mexico had a strong interest. On this basis, the Second Circuit held that "[c]omity militates strongly against an injunction here."[227]

7.159 With respect to the second of the three considerations, the Second Circuit stated that "the United States federal courts have no interest in enjoining Telinor's Mexican

[223] *Id.* at 199 (citing Jacobs v. USA Track & Field, 374 F.3d 85, 89 (2d Cir. 2004) ("the fact that respondents raised before the AAA an objection to petitioner's Demand for Arbitration ... does not constitute a 'refusal to arbitrate' on the part of respondents.")).

[224] *Id.* at 198 (emphasis added) (*quoting* Downing v. Merrill Lynch, Pierce, Fenner & Smith, Inc., 725 F.2d 192, 195 (2d Cir. 1984)).

[225] *Id.* at 199 ("Nor does Telinor's commencement of suit in Mexico constitute a refusal to arbitrate. Telinor's litigation in Mexico of certain claims arguably within the scope of the Axtel arbitration clause suggests that Telinor would prefer not to arbitrate those issues. Without an attendant refusal to arbitrate, however, this preference does not matter. LAIF X complains that a Mexican court might determine whether LAIF X's allegations are arbitrable before the AAA has an opportunity to rule on the issue. However, where foreign law governs an issue that bears on standing to arbitrate, the submission of that issue to the competent foreign court, without more, does not constitute a refusal to arbitrate.").

[226] *Id.* at 200.

[227] *Id.* ("LAIF X invested in a Mexican enterprise, governed by Mexican law. A question has arisen under Mexican law—whether LAIF X is an Axtel shareholder—and that question has been presented to a Mexican court. Mexico has a strong interest in determining who is a shareholder of a Mexican corporation and whether particular transactions were permissible under the bylaws of a Mexican corporation.").

lawsuit" because "the legal relationship between a Belgian investor and a Mexican enterprise in no way implicates 'the strong public policies of the enjoining forum.'"[228] Although there was an agreement to arbitrate in New York (albeit an arbitration agreement of disputed applicability), the Second Circuit did not consider in its analysis the federal public policy favoring arbitration of international disputes.

The third consideration relied upon by the Second Circuit was that Telinor's Mexican lawsuit is "not directed at sidestepping the arbitration," since Telinor was continuing to participate in the arbitration.[229] **7.160**

At first glance, it is difficult to reconcile the result in *Axtel* with the result in *Paramedics*, which also involved questions of foreign law and also involved foreign parties who disputed the application of an arbitration agreement. Yet, despite their similarity, there are significant differences in the cases. First, in *Paramedics*, Tecnimed, the party that had commenced the Brazilian litigation, refused to participate in the arbitration. In *Axtel*, by contrast, Telinor, the party that had commenced the Mexican litigation, did participate, albeit to challenge the jurisdiction of the arbitral tribunal. Indeed, this appears to be the most salient factual distinction between the two cases. **7.161**

Second, in *Paramedics*, the tribunal had decided—prior to the district court's decision to the same effect—that the dispute submitted to the Brazilian court was arbitrable. In reaching the same decision, therefore, the *Paramedics* court was simply echoing the decision of the arbitrators. In *Axtel*, by contrast, while Telinor had challenged the arbitral tribunal's jurisdiction to entertain the case on the ground that the dispute was not arbitrable, the tribunal had not yet ruled on that issue at the time it came before the district court. One suspects that one reason the district court exercised restraint and avoided reaching the issue of whether the claims submitted to the Mexican court were arbitral was that it wanted to leave that issue for the arbitral panel to resolve. Thus, the Second Circuit made it clear that if the panel were to rule that those claims were arbitrable, Telinor could be found to be refusing to arbitrate, the implication being that an antisuit injunction might be warranted: **7.162**

> If the AAA concludes that the issues raised in Telinor's Mexican lawsuit are not arbitrable and need to be decided before arbitration continues, the AAA will issue a stay, in which event Telinor's conduct will be in accord with the arbitral process. *It may be another story if the AAA denies a stay or if Telinor ignores an arbitral order to suspend or discontinue the suit in Mexico; but that has not happened.*[230]

Third, in *Paramedics*, the Second Circuit made it clear that it viewed Tecnimed's Brazilian lawsuit to be "a tactic to evade arbitration."[231] In *Axtel*, by contrast, the Second Circuit found that there was at least a good faith basis for Telinor to **7.163**

---

[228] *Id.*
[229] *Id.*
[230] 390 F.3d at 199 (emphasis added).
[231] 369 F.3d at 654.

have submitted its claims to the Mexican court notwithstanding the arbitration clause, such that "it cannot be said that Telinor's conduct is an evasion of the arbitral forum or an 'attempt to sidestep arbitration.'"[232]

7.164 Following the Second Circuit's lead in *Axtel*, district courts in New York have similarly denied antisuit injunctions where a party to an arbitration agreement participated in the arbitration but nonetheless simultaneously commenced foreign litigation concerning the same dispute. The courts in these cases focused on the threshold question of whether there would be "irreparable harm" if the injunction was not issued. The concept of irreparable harm is a general requirement for preliminary injunctions under federal law, but was not relied upon by the *China Trade* court as one of the factors relevant to antisuit injunctions.

7.165 For example, in *Comverse, Inc. v. American Telecommunications, Inc.*, a dispute arose between Comverse, an American provider of software and telecommunications systems and ATI, a Chilean distributor of telecommunications products under a distribution agreement that contained a broad arbitration clause.[233] Comverse commenced arbitration and ATI participated in the arbitration. At the same time, ATI filed a claim against Comverse Chile SA (an affiliate of Comverse) with a specialized Chilean court having jurisdiction over competition matters. The Chilean action largely reasserted the same counterclaims ATI asserted in the arbitration. Under the applicable Chilean procedures, ATI's claims would be prosecuted not directly by ATI, but rather by a Chilean government body charged with enforcing Chilean competition laws. The New York district court found this fact to be dispositive in denying the antisuit injunction. Rather than proceeding directly to the *China Trade* test, the district court first analyzed whether Comverse would face irreparable harm as a result of the Chilean proceedings. The district court concluded there would not be irreparable harm both because ATI was participating in the arbitration and because ATI would not be the entity prosecuting the Chilean action. Though the district court did not explicitly state so, implicit in the court's decision is its view that the Chilean action would not necessarily have a res judicata effect on the arbitration. The district court also gave significant weight to Chile's public interest in enforcing its competition laws. Having concluded that there was no imminent harm, the district court declined to consider the *China Trade* factors for issuance of an antisuit injunction.[234]

* * *

[232] 390 F.3d at 200.

[233] 2006 WL 3016315 (S.D.N.Y. Oct. 23, 2006).

[234] *See also* Empresa Generadora de Electricidad Itabo, S.A. v. Corporacion Dominica de Empresas Electricas Estatales, 2005 WL 1705080 (S.D.N.Y. July 18, 2005) (denying motion to compel arbitration and request for preliminary antisuit injunction directed at litigation in Dominican Republic in dispute between two Dominican Republic companies on the grounds that there was no irreparable harm where the respondent was participating in the arbitration and arguing before the tribunal that its Dominican Republic claims were not subject to arbitration).

It is clear that New York courts are willing to grant antisuit injunctions in aid of arbitration, but it is also clear that courts will not approach the question of whether to do so mechanically. Rather, they will scrutinize the actions of the party pursuing the litigation to assess whether there is some good faith basis for its actions or whether it is engaged in an illegitimate attempt to avoid arbitration. **7.166**

G. DAMAGES FOR BREACH OF AN ARBITRATION AGREEMENT

A third way in which a party may enforce an agreement to arbitrate is to seek damages against a party that commences litigation in breach of an arbitration clause, on the theory that this is a breach of contract, with the measure of the damages being the attorneys' fees incurred in resisting that litigation. In *Shaw Group Inc. v. Triplefine Int'l Corp.*,[235] the court held that it was for the arbitrator to decide whether damages could properly be awarded in such a situation. **7.167**

H. CONCLUSION

Given the federal policy in favor of arbitration, U.S. courts take a liberal approach to enforcing agreements to arbitrate. Moreover, the recent trend has been for U.S. courts to resolve motions seeking to enforce an agreement to arbitrate by avoiding a full arbitrability inquiry, but, rather, displaying greater deference to the jurisdiction of arbitrators to resolve arbitrability questions. **7.168**

[235] 322 F.3d 115 (2d Cir. 2003).

8

OBTAINING PRELIMINARY RELIEF

Robert H. Smit, Tyler B. Robinson, and Janet M. Whittaker

A. Introduction to Preliminary Relief 8.01
B. Preliminary Relief from Arbitral Tribunals in New York 8.05
1. The Authority of Arbitral Tribunals to Issue Preliminary Relief 8.07
(a) Authority derived from the arbitration clause and the chosen arbitration rules 8.09
(b) Authority derived from applicable arbitration law 8.12
2. Preliminary Relief from Arbitral Tribunals: Types of Relief 8.16
3. Preliminary Relief from Arbitral Tribunals: Procedures 8.17
4. Preliminary Relief from Arbitral Tribunals: Judicial Enforcement 8.20
5. Preliminary Relief from an Emergency Arbitrator 8.24
(a) The need for emergency arbitral relief 8.24
(b) Overview of emergency arbitral relief procedures 8.26
C. Preliminary Relief from Courts in Aid of Arbitration 8.32
1. The New York Convention and Preliminary Relief 8.33
2. Preliminary Relief from Federal Court 8.35
3. Preliminary Relief from New York State Courts 8.40
(a) Preliminary relief under NY CPLR § 7502(c) 8.42
(b) Additional requirements for grant of preliminary relief 8.45

A. INTRODUCTION TO PRELIMINARY RELIEF

This chapter examines the availability of preliminary relief to parties to arbitrations in New York, or who otherwise find the arbitration law or courts of New York involved in the resolution of a dispute that is subject to arbitration. **8.01**

Preliminary relief, also referred to as *interim relief* or *preliminary measures*, broadly refers to the interim prescriptive measures a court or arbitral tribunal may take to ensure that the arbitration will provide an effective forum for the resolution of the parties' dispute. Preliminary relief may contemplate, inter alia, protection of assets or property that is the subject of the dispute, preservation or production of evidence relevant to resolving the dispute, or vindication of the jurisdiction of the arbitral tribunal to decide the dispute. Preliminary relief thus serves to protect **8.02** the efficacy of the arbitral process by equipping parties in arbitration with tools for preventing another party's frustration of the process. In particular, parties to international arbitration may rely on the availability of preliminary relief to ensure the availability of assets or evidence in the other party's control in foreign jurisdictions or to prevent competing parallel proceedings in the courts (or arbitral fora) located in the other party's home country.

8.03 Both arbitrators and national courts can issue preliminary relief in aid of arbitration. Traditionally, arbitral tribunals, cognizant of the contractual source and limited nature of their jurisdiction, have been reluctant to do so. Parties to arbitration historically depended primarily on courts to provide any preliminary relief necessary to protect the arbitral process. The more recent trend is that arbitral tribunals, particularly in international commercial arbitration, are increasingly granting preliminary measures to give effect to their own ability to resolve the matters submitted to them. Several of the principal international arbitration rules have been amended specifically to grant arbitrators the authority to issue preliminary relief. Several arbitral institutions have also established procedures for the appointment of emergency interim arbitrators or referees to provide emergency preliminary relief during the period of time required to select a tribunal to decide the merits of the parties' dispute. At the same time, U.S. federal courts—and state courts, including those of New York—remain available to confirm and enforce preliminary orders issued by arbitral tribunals and to issue preliminary orders of their own in aid of arbitration.

8.04 Preliminary relief will typically take the form of an interim prescriptive order or award requiring a party to perform an action, to refrain from performing an action, or to place assets or funds in escrow. A preliminary (or interim) order or award may be differentiated from a final award order in that it enables or facilitates an ongoing arbitral process, or preliminarily resolves some aspect of the dispute short of final award resolution on the merits. This chapter examines the rules, laws, and practices in New York relating to preliminary measures in support of arbitrations that are international in character.

B. PRELIMINARY RELIEF FROM ARBITRAL TRIBUNALS IN NEW YORK

8.05 In New York, an arbitral tribunal, with broad authority to resolve the merits of a dispute, generally also has broad authority to grant preliminary relief to protect its ability to resolve the dispute. This authority is rooted in—and may be defined, expanded, or limited by—the agreement to arbitrate. It is recognized by federal and New York law as inherent in the authority of the tribunal to resolve the merits of the dispute, and granted under all of the principal institutional and ad hoc arbitration rules.

The following section examines preliminary measures granted by arbitral tribunals. The first part examines the *sources* of arbitrators' authority to grant preliminary measures. The second part considers the *types of preliminary relief* typically sought from arbitrators. The third part briefly sets forth the *procedures* governing the issuance of preliminary relief by an arbitral tribunal. The fourth part addresses *judicial enforcement* of preliminary measures ordered by arbitral tribunals. The fifth and final section outlines the new *emergency arbitrator procedures* recently incorporated into several of the major sets of arbitration rules. 8.06

1. The Authority of Arbitral Tribunals to Issue Preliminary Relief

An arbitral tribunal's authority to grant any form of relief, including preliminary relief, derives first and foremost from the arbitration agreement between the parties.[1] The arbitration clause may contain specific provisions governing preliminary relief or it may designate a set of governing arbitral rules that provide for interim relief. All of the major sets of institutional arbitration rules in use in New York by parties to international arbitration agreements include provisions permitting arbitral tribunals to grant preliminary relief.[2] 8.07

In New York, both federal and state courts have held that an arbitration agreement which grants an arbitral tribunal broad authority to decide the merits of a dispute also affords that tribunal broad authority to grant preliminary relief in aid of the tribunal's jurisdiction over the merits of the dispute.[3] New York does not have any mandatory rules prohibiting arbitral tribunals from issuing preliminary measures.[4] 8.08

(a) Authority derived from the arbitration clause and the chosen arbitration rules Arbitral tribunals may derive authority to grant preliminary relief from the arbitration agreement or from the arbitration rules adopted by the parties to 8.09

---

[1] First Options of Chicago, Inc. v. Kaplan, 514 U.S. 938, 943 (1995) ("[A]rbitration is simply a matter of contract between the parties; it is a way to resolve those disputes—but only those disputes—that the parties have agreed to submit to arbitration."); *see also* Heiges v. J.P. Morgan Chase Bank, N.A., 521 F. Supp. 2d 641, 647 (N.D. Ohio 2007) ("As the Supreme Court of the United States has stressed, 'arbitration is simply a matter of contract between the parties; it is a way to resolve those disputes—but only those disputes that the parties have agreed to submit to arbitration.'" (*quoting* First Options of Chicago, Inc., 514 U.S. at 943)). For clause drafting considerations, *see* Chapter 3 of this book.

[2] International Chamber of Commerce, Rules of Arbitration (2012), Art. 28.1; AAA/ICDR International Arbitration Rules (2014), Art. 24; International Institution for Conflict Prevention and Resolution, Rules for Non-Administered Arbitration, Rule 13.1 (2014); UNCITRAL Arbitration Rules (2010), Art. 26.1.

[3] Sperry Int'l Trade, Inc. v. Gov't of Israel, 689 F.2d 301, 306 (2d Cir. 1982) (holding that tribunals may grant preliminary relief that even a court may not). *See also* Chapter 6.C.

[4] Local New York rules that might curtail the availability of particular remedies may be overcome by arbitration provisions that permit a remedy. Polin v. Kellwood Co., 103 F. Supp. 2d 238, 267–68 (S.D.N.Y. 2000) (holding that broad arbitration clause granting extensive powers to arbitrators to grant remedies renders inapplicable local policy restricting available remedies).

govern the arbitration. All of the principal sets of arbitration rules promulgated by the major institutions supervising or administering arbitrations vest arbitral tribunals with broad discretion to grant such preliminary measures as they deem appropriate. For example, the Rules of Arbitration of the International Chamber of Commerce (ICC Rules) state:

> Unless the parties have otherwise agreed, as soon as the file has been transmitted to it, the arbitral tribunal may, at the request of a party, order any interim or conservatory measure it deems appropriate. The arbitral tribunal may make the granting of any such measure subject to appropriate security being furnished by the requesting party. Any such measure shall take the form of an order, giving reasons, or of an award, as the arbitral tribunal considers appropriate.[5]

8.10 These rules clearly give substantial discretion to International Chamber of Commerce (ICC) tribunals in shaping any form of preliminary relief that they deem necessary. The American Arbitration Association International Center for Dispute Resolution (ICDR) Procedures (ICDR Rules) also provide arbitral tribunals with broad discretion to award preliminary relief:

> 1. At the request of any party, the arbitral tribunal may order or award any interim or conservatory measures it deems necessary, including injunctive relief and measures for the protection or conservation of property.
> 2. Such interim measures may take the form of an interim order or award, and the tribunal may require security for the costs of such measures.
> 3. A request for interim measures addressed by a party to a judicial authority shall not be deemed incompatible with the agreement to arbitrate or a waiver of the right to arbitrate.
> 4. The tribunal may in its discretion allocate costs associated with applications for interim relief in any interim order or award or in the final award.[6]

8.11 Similarly, in ad hoc arbitration, the U.N. Commission on International Trade Law Arbitration Rules (UNCITRAL Rules) vest arbitration tribunals with authority "at the request of a party," to grant interim measures.[7] The Non-Administered Arbitration Rules for International Arbitrations of the International Institute for Conflict Prevention & Resolution (CPR Rules) vest a tribunal with authority to grant "such interim measures as it deems necessary … [and] require appropriate security as a condition of ordering such measures."[8]

---

[5] International Chamber of Commerce, Rules of Arbitration (2012), Art. 28.1.

[6] International Dispute Resolution Procedures (Including Mediation and Arbitration Rules) (2014), Art. 24. The AAA Commercial Arbitration Rules (which often apply to domestic U.S. arbitrations and to some international cases) contain a similar provision. Commercial Arbitration Rules and Mediation Procedures (Including Procedures for Large, Complex Commercial Disputes) (2013), Rule 37.

[7] UNCITRAL Arbitration Rules, Art. 26 (2010); *see also* Georgios Petrochilos, Interim Measures under the Revised UNCITRAL Arbitration Rules, 28 ASA Bulletin 4/2010 (December).

[8] International Institution for Conflict Prevention and Resolution, Rules for Non-Administered Arbitration of International Disputes (2007), Rule 13.1.

(b) Authority derived from applicable arbitration law In the absence of an express provision in an arbitration clause or clear arbitration rules governing interim relief, the law governing the procedure of an arbitration may confer authority to grant interim relief. In most cases, this governing law (or *lex arbitri*) is presumed to be the arbitration law of the place where the arbitration is taking place (the arbitral *situs*, or seat).[9] However, the seat of arbitration may be the subject of dispute if it has not been chosen by the parties ex ante in their arbitration agreement.[10] **8.12**

An international arbitration tribunal sitting in New York is subject primarily to federal arbitration law. The Federal Arbitration Act (FAA) applies to all arbitrable disputes involving interstate or foreign commerce. This means that the FAA will apply to virtually any dispute that can be characterized as an international arbitration.[11] The FAA also incorporates the New York Convention and the Panama Convention, so when the relevant criteria for either of these Conventions are met, they will apply as though part of U.S. domestic law.[12] Federal law preempts state law, so the FAA, if applicable, will trump any contrary state law rules. However, New York law remains relevant to the extent that the FAA is silent on an issue and New York law is not inconsistent with the FAA and the federal policy favoring arbitration.[13] **8.13**

The case law developed by the federal courts of the Second Judicial Circuit (which encompasses New York and other states) vests arbitral tribunals with broad authority to grant preliminary measures provided that the relief is consistent with the grant of authority contemplated under the parties' arbitration agreement. The Second Circuit interprets a broad arbitration clause as a "comprehensive grant of authority" which permits an arbitral tribunal to take whatever steps are necessary **8.14**

---

[9] Gary Born, International Commercial Arbitration §17.02[F]; 2457–61 (2d ed. 2014).

[10] The *lex arbitri* should not be confused with the law selected by the parties to govern the merits of the dispute, sometimes known as the substantive law. The two are separate, and the distinction is important. Mastrobuono v. Shearson Lehman Hutton, Inc., 514 U.S. 52, 60 (1995) (rejecting argument that New York choice of law clause in contract meant that New York law should apply to procedural powers of arbitral tribunal because a choice of New York law referred only to "New York's substantive rights and obligations, and not the State's allocation of power between alternative tribunals"); *Interim ICC Award of 16 July 1986 in Case No. 5029*, XXII Y.B. Comm. Arb. 112 (1987) ("As it is recognized in virtually all legal systems around the world, a basic distinction must be made between the law governing the substance and the law governing the procedure.").

[11] Even a whiff of an interstate or foreign element is sufficient to classify a dispute as involving interstate commerce. *See generally* Alan Scott Rau, *Provisional Relief in Arbitration: How Things Stand in the United States*, 22 J. Int. Arb. 8 (2005). *See also* Chapter 1.B.

[12] Federal Arbitration Act, Chapters II & III, 9 U.S.C. § 201–307.

[13] Southland Corp. v. Keating, 465 U.S. 1, 15–16 (1984) (finding that a state statute that disfavors arbitration of franchisee agreements violates the FAA policy favoring arbitration, and so violates the Supremacy Clause of the U.S. Constitution); Preston v. Ferrer, 128 S.Ct. 978, 983 (2008) (stating that the FAA's policy favoring arbitration "foreclose[s] state legislative attempts to undercut the enforceability of arbitration agreements") (*quoting* Southland Corp., 465 U.S. at 16).

both to resolve the dispute *and* to ensure that the resolution is meaningful.[14] As the Second Circuit stated in upholding an arbitral tribunal's order requiring prehearing security, "[i]t is not the role of the courts to undermine the comprehensive grant of authority to arbitrators by prohibiting an arbitral security award that ensures a meaningful final award" because when "an arbitration clause is broad … arbitrators have the discretion to order remedies they determine appropriate, *so long as they do not exceed the power granted to them by the contract itself*."[15] New York law echoes this basic principle of federal arbitration law. As the Second Circuit recognized in the leading case of *Sperry Int'l Trade, Inc. v. Israel*, "New York law gives arbitrators substantial power to fashion remedies that they believe will do justice between the parties," including "power to fashion relief that a court might not properly grant."[16]

8.15 In *Sperry*, the parties arranged for an irrevocable letter of credit in favor of Israel in the event of Sperry's substantial breach of its contract to design and construct a communication system for the Israeli Air Force. A contract dispute, subject to arbitration, thereafter arose between the parties. When Israel sought to draw down on the letter of credit, Sperry instituted suit to compel arbitration and to preliminarily enjoin access to the funds pending a determination of the parties' contract dispute in arbitration. Ultimately, the federal courts decided that Sperry was not entitled to the requested preliminary injunction because it had not made the requisite showing of irreparable injury. When Sperry thereafter obtained an interim award from an arbitral tribunal that placed the proceeds of the letter of credit in escrow pending resolution of the parties' contract dispute, Israel challenged the award on the ground that it was inconsistent with the federal court's prior determination that Sperry was not entitled to preliminarily enjoin Israel from accessing the funds. In upholding the arbitral award, the Second Circuit, quoting the New York Court of Appeals, observed that

> "Arbitrators may do justice" and the award may well reflect the spirit rather than the letter of the agreement … [A] court may not vacate an award because the arbitrator has exceeded the power the court would have, or would have had if the parties had chosen to litigate, rather than to arbitrate the dispute. Those who have

[14] Banco de Seguros del Estado v. Mut. Marine Office, Inc., 344 F.3d 255, 262 (2d Cir. 2003); ReliaStar Life Ins. Co. of N.Y. v. EMC Nat'l Life Co., 564 F.3d 81, 86 (2d Cir. 2009) (holding that arbitrators had authority to sanction a party for bad faith conduct because the broad arbitration clause granted them the authority to fashion awards or remedies that ensured a meaningful final award).

[15] Banco de Seguros del Estado, 344 F.3d at 262 (emphasis added).

[16] 689 F.2d 301, 306 (2d Cir. 1982); *see also* Rochester City Sch. Dist. v. Rochester Teachers Ass'n, 41 N.Y.2d 578, 582 (1977) ("[A] court may not vacate an award because the arbitrator has exceeded the power the court would have, or would have had if the parties had chosen to litigate, rather than arbitrate the dispute."); Matter of Staklinski (Pyramid Elec. Co.), 6 N.Y.2d 159, 163 (1959) ("The power of an arbitrator to order specific performance in an appropriate case has been recognized from early times.").

chosen arbitration as their forum should recognize that arbitration procedures and awards often differ from what may be expected in courts of law.[17]

2. Preliminary Relief from Arbitral Tribunals: Types of Relief

Neither the FAA nor New York arbitration law defines or restricts the types of interim relief that an arbitral tribunal may grant. As most arbitration clauses and rules do not restrict the power of tribunals to grant interim measures, the power will generally be very broad.[18] The power is implied from the arbitrator's duty to render an effective award: if parties entrust the resolution of their dispute to arbitration, arbitrators may take preliminary measures to prevent the final award from being meaningless.[19] Under New York law, these include: preliminary injunctions prohibiting a party from transferring assets; orders to provide letters of credit, or create and deposit funds in an escrow account;[20] preliminary relief to preserve or gather evidence;[21] preliminary measures to preserve the status quo by preventing one party from taking certain steps such as disclosing trade secrets or using disputed intellectual property or other rights until the merits of the dispute are resolved;[22] and "antisuit" injunctions to prevent a party from engaging in competing parallel proceedings to address the same dispute properly resolved in arbitration.[23] **8.16**

3. Preliminary Relief from Arbitral Tribunals: Procedures

The procedures or standards applied by arbitrators in granting preliminary relief in arbitration often are, but need not be, the same as those applied by the courts. "An arbitrator's paramount responsibility is to reach an equitable result, and the **8.17**

---

[17] Sperry, 689 F.2d 301 at 306 (*quoting* Rochester City Sch. Dist., 41 N.Y.2d at 582).

[18] *Id.* ("New York law gives arbitrators substantial power to fashion remedies that they believe will do justice between the parties.").

[19] Yonir Techs., Inc. v. Duration Sys. (1992) Ltd., 244 F. Supp. 2d 195, 204 (S.D.N.Y. 2002) ("Arbitrators have the authority to award interim relief in order to protect their final award from being meaningless, and equitable awards involving the preservation of assets related to the subject of arbitration are generally considered 'final' arbitral awards subject to judicial review.") (internal citation omitted).

[20] Sperry Int'l Trade, Inc., 689 F.2d 301 at 302, 303 n.2 (arbitrators may order that funds subject to dispute be transferred into an escrow account and remain there pending resolution of the dispute); *see also* Yasuda Fire & Marine Ins. Co. of Europe v. Continental Cas. Co., Ltd., 37 F.3d 345, 349–52 (7th Cir. 1994) (ruling that arbitrators could require letter of credit as interim relief since this would merely preserve the party's stake in the controversy, and was consistent with protecting the bargain that gave rise to arbitration); Pac. Reinsurance Mgmt. Corp. v. Ohio Reinsurance Corp., 935 F.2d 1019, 1025 (9th Cir. 1991) (confirming arbitral award requiring parties to deposit funds in escrow account).

[21] Matter of Schumacher (Genesco, Inc.), 82 A.D.2d 739, 739 (1st Dep't 1981).

[22] *See, e.g.*, Borden Inc. v. Meiji Milk Products Co., 919 F.2d 822 (2d Cir. 1990); Albatross S.S. Co. v. Manning Bros., 95 F. Supp. 459 (S.D.N.Y. 1951).

[23] *See, e.g.*, Ibeto Petrochemical Inds. Ltd. v. M/T Beffen, 475 F.3d 56, 65 (2d Cir. 2007); Storm LLC v. Telenor Mobile Commc'ns AS, No. 06 Civ. 13157(GEL), 2006 WL 3735657, at *12 (S.D.N.Y. Dec. 15, 2006).

courts will not assume the role of overseers to mold the award to conform to their sense of justice."[24] New York federal courts acknowledge that "arbitrators may grant equitable relief that a district court cannot, and they are not required to 'follow all niceties observed by federal courts.'"[25]

8.18 Any arbitral procedures relating to interim measures must comport with fundamental due process. "While the awards of private arbitrators are not subject to substantive Due Process analysis, there is a general requirement under New York law that arbitration procedures comport with due process of law by providing a party with notice and an opportunity to be heard. Under federal law, 'fundamental fairness' requires that each party have an opportunity to present its evidence and argument."[26] In practice, the general requirement that each side have the opportunity to present its case does not mean that specific procedures, such as oral hearings, must be followed.

> It does not violate due process to issue a decision based on a written submission. An arbitrator has the discretion to choose not to hold oral hearings, as long as his decision based on other evidence is reasonable and not fundamentally unfair.[27]

It follows that interim awards should be valid (and confirmed by New York federal and state courts) as long as each relevant party had "an opportunity to submit its evidence and argument."[28]

8.19 Arbitral tribunals wishing to issue preliminary relief that is valid and enforceable under New York law need not comply with any particular form of award when issuing the relief. While most arbitration rules require awards to be reasoned, there is no requirement under the FAA or New York law for an arbitral tribunal to provide an explanation or reasoned opinion when issuing preliminary relief. Thus, courts asked to affirm or vacate preliminary awards are sometimes "left to theorize as to the basis of the Award,"[29] but will affirm the preliminary measure based on any ground they can reasonably identify.[30]

---

[24] Matter of Sprinzen (Nomberg), 46 N.Y.2d 623, 629 (1979); *see also* Banco de Seguros del Estado, 344 F.3d, at 262 ("Where an arbitration clause is broad, as here, arbitrators have the discretion to order remedies they determine appropriate, so long as they do not exceed the power granted to them by the contract itself.").

[25] British Ins. Co. of Cayman v. Water St. Ins. Co., Ltd., 93 F. Supp. 2d 506, 516 (S.D.N.Y. 2000) (*quoting* Bell Aerospace Co. Div. of Textron v. Local 516, 500 F.2d 921, 923 (2d Cir. 1974)) (internal citation omitted).

[26] Yonir Techs., Inc., 244 F. Supp. 2d at 208–09 (internal citation omitted).

[27] *Id.* at 209.

[28] *Id.* (*quoting* Tempo Shain Corp. v. Bertek, Inc., 120 F.3d 16, 20 (2d. Cir 1997)); *see also* Areca, Inc. v. Oppenheimer & Co., Inc., 960 F. Supp. 52, 54-55 (S.D.N.Y. 1997); British Ins. Co. of Cayman, 93 F. Supp. 2d at 517; Cragwood Managers, L.L.C. v. Reliance Ins. Co., 132 F. Supp. 2d 285, 289 (S.D.N.Y. 2001).

[29] Sperry, 689 F.2d 301 at 306 (affirming validity of order issued without any written reasons for decision) (citing cases).

[30] *Id.* ("New York law requires that all reasonable efforts be made to find a ground on which to sustain it.").

4. Preliminary Relief from Arbitral Tribunals: Judicial Enforcement

Provided that it satisfies the criteria of a valid "order" or "award" and resulted from a procedure that comported with due process, an interim order by an arbitral tribunal should be enforceable by a U.S. court. This means that preliminary measures may be enforced by a court if one party refuses to comply with an arbitrator's order. Judicial enforcement can be sought by a party to an arbitration in parallel with an ongoing arbitral procedure. **8.20**

For an award to be ripe for judicial review and enforcement, it must have the element of "finality" in the sense that it either disposes of a separate claim in an arbitration or has actual effects on the property or rights of the parties.[31] When either of these conditions is satisfied, an interim award of preliminary relief is considered sufficiently final for purposes of judicial review and enforcement. For instance, "[c]ourts in this Circuit have generally treated interim arbitration awards that order parties to post some type of prejudgment security, pending the completion of the arbitration proceedings, as sufficiently final to allow for federal court review."[32] If the grant of preliminary relief is deemed to constitute a sufficiently "final" award, it may be vacated, confirmed, or enforced in accordance with the New York Convention.[33] U.S. courts "appear willing to enforce interim arbitral rulings, provided those rulings finally and definitively resolve self-contained issues in the case and regardless of whether the interim rulings take the form of an 'order' or 'award.' "[34] **8.21**

[31] Sperry Int'l Trade v. Gov't of Israel, 532 F. Supp. 901, 909 (S.D.N.Y. 1982), *aff'd*, 689 F.2d 301 (2d Cir. 1982) (holding that arbitrators' order directing defendant to place a letter of credit in escrow pending a final determination of the parties' contract dispute was "a final Award on a clearly severable issue" that was "clearly subject to confirmation"); Metallgesellschaft A.G. v. M/V Capitan Constante, 790 F.2d 280 (2d Cir. 1986) (affirming district court's confirmation of interim arbitration award, as it related to a final and severable issue in the case); Konkar Maritime Enters. v. Compagnie Belge D'Affretement, 668 F. Supp. 267, 272 (S.D.N.Y. 1987) (confirming arbitrators' interim order to establish jointly held escrow account that was intended to establish "security for enforcement of an award in the event that respondent was found liable"); Yonir Techs., Inc., 244 F. Supp. 2d at 204–05 ("The Second Circuit has found that a[n] arbitral decision requiring the establishment of an escrow account pending a decision on the merits is a final award subject to review. Numerous District Courts in the Second Circuit have found that interim, prejudgment security awards are final orders subject to judicial review.") (internal citation omitted); Bailey Shipping Ltd. v. American Bureau of Shipping, No. 12 Civ. 5959 (KPF), 2014 WL 1282504 (S.D.N.Y. Mar. 28, 2014) (discussing finality of arbitration awards, court ultimately decided that it lacked jurisdiction to rule on preliminary relief award as it was not a final award). *But see* Barchha v. TapImmune Inc., No. 12 Civ. 8530 (PKC), 2013 WL 120639, at *2 (S.D.N.Y. Jan. 7, 2013) (denying the requested injunction, as it would be the equivalent of a "final adjudication on the merits of plaintiff's claims").

[32] Great E. Sec., Inc. v. Goldendale Invs., Ltd., No. 06 Civ. 6667 DAB, 2006 WL 3851159, at *4–5 (S.D.N.Y. Dec. 20, 2006) (denying petitioner's motion to vacate arbitral tribunal's interim award, and granting respondents' cross-motion to confirm the interim order pursuant to 9 U.S.C. § 9).

[33] *Supra* note 32.

[34] Robert H. Smit and Emma Lindsay, *Enforcement by U.S. Courts of International Arbitration Interim Orders and Awards Under the New York Convention*: Publicis Communication v. True North Communications, Inc., Stockholm Arbitration Report 201:1.

8.22 Assuming an award satisfies the finality requirement, a New York court will not vacate or reverse a final award, including of preliminary relief, except in very limited circumstances. As one federal court recently noted, for example, "Courts in this Circuit have been reluctant to vacate interim arbitration orders aimed at preserving the ability of parties to pay any final awards that result from the arbitration proceedings."[35] The grounds for vacating an arbitral award of interim relief are strictly limited to the narrow grounds prescribed in the FAA for nonenforcement, including a failure by a tribunal to abide by fundamental due process.[36] As noted above, "due process" merely requires that each of the parties have an opportunity to present their case. Similarly, courts will take "all reasonable efforts" to find rational grounds for sustaining a preliminary award including when the arbitral tribunal has not provided a reasoned decision for the award.[37]

8.23 Finally, foreign arbitral awards are enforceable by American courts in accordance with Article III of the New York Convention. Article III provides that each "Contracting State shall recognize arbitral awards as binding and enforce them in accordance with the rules of procedure of the territory where the award is relied upon ..." Thus, provided that an interim measure by a foreign arbitral tribunal qualifies as an "arbitral award" under the Convention, it should be enforced as such in New York.[38]

5. Preliminary Relief from an Emergency Arbitrator

8.24 *(a) The need for emergency arbitral relief* A party may require preliminary relief before an arbitral tribunal is constituted and therefore in a position to issue the

---

[35] Great E. Sec., Inc., 2006 WL 3851159 at *2.

[36] 9 U.S.C. §§ 10, 11. An arbitration award can also be vacated if an arbitrator acts in "manifest disregard of the law ... leading to an erroneous outcome." Data & Development, Inc. v InfoKall, Inc., 513 Fed.Appx. 117, 117 (2d Cir. 2013). However, "the governing law must clearly apply to the facts of the case, *as those facts have been determined by the arbitrator.*" Westerbeke Corp. v. Daihatsu Motor Co., Ltd., 304 F.3d 200, 213 (2d Cir. 2002) (emphasis in original). *See also* Duferco Int'l Steel Trading v. T. Klaveness Shipping A/S, 333 F.3d 383 (2d Cir. 2003) (explaining reasons for giving arbitrators great deference regarding their awards, and noting that, from 1960–2003, the Second Circuit has only found that arbitrators manifest disregarded the law in four out of forty-eight cases).

[37] Sperry, 689 F.2d 301 at 306.

[38] Existing law indicates that this is the case. *See* Banco de Seguros del Estado, 344 F.3d 255 at 264 (noting that when an award is made pursuant to the New York Convention, "[a] court's power to invoke public policy to reject an arbitral award 'is limited to situations where the contract as interpreted [by the arbitrators] would violate some explicit public policy that is well defined and dominant, and is to be ascertained by reference to the laws and legal precedents and not from general considerations of supposed public interests' ") (United Paperworks Int'l Union, AFL-CIO v. Misco, Inc., 484 U.S. 29, 43, 108 S. Ct. 364, 98 L. Ed. 2d 286 (1987)). However, the UNCITRAL Secretariat has suggested that the prevailing view is that the Convention does not apply to interim awards. *Note by the Secretariat, International Commercial Arbitration: Possible Future Work in the Area of International Commercial Arbitration*, A/CN.9/460 ¶ 121 (April 6, 1999) (discussed in Alan Scott Rau, *Provisional Relief in Arbitration: How Things Stand in the United States*, Vol. 22 No.1 J. INT. ARB., 60 n.272 (2005). *See* Chapter 13.C of this book.

necessary preliminary relief. In the past, a party requiring such relief prior to the formation of a tribunal was constrained to seek it from a court. In recent years, several arbitration rules have been amended to create special procedures whereby emergency relief can be granted by a specially appointed emergency arbitrator.[39] These procedures are designed to make arbitral relief available prior to the constitution of an arbitral tribunal. Such relief is sometimes essential during the weeks or months that tribunal selection may take to prevent parties from causing irreparable harm by, for example, improperly dissipating assets, losing, moving or destroying evidence, wasting or misappropriating property or assets in dispute, or misusing intellectual property.

Emergency arbitrator provisions permit a party to request that the relevant arbitral institution appoint an emergency arbitrator or referee to hear applications for immediate preliminary relief before an arbitral tribunal is empanelled to hear the merits. Typically, the arbitral institution will select the emergency arbitrator from a preconstituted list, and that arbitrator will consider the application for interim relief until relieved of duty by the appointment of an arbitral tribunal in accordance with the parties' arbitration clause. **8.25**

(b) Overview of emergency arbitral relief procedures The emergency relief procedures promulgated by various arbitral institutions share some essential features but also approach certain issues differently. All of the emergency rules require some degree of institutional involvement.[40] The initial application for emergency relief is made to the arbitral institution, and the arbitrator is either selected by that institution or agreed upon by the parties with the assistance of the appointing authority.[41] **8.26**

At least three of the major arbitral institutions that administer arbitrations in New York provide procedures for the appointment of an emergency arbitrator or referee to issue emergency measures before the constitution of an arbitral tribunal. It is worth considering the similarities and differences between the rules promulgated by each institution. **8.27**

The first major international arbitration institution to provide an emergency procedure for interim relief was the ICC. The current ICC rules provide a procedure for a party to request the appointment of an emergency arbitrator with the **8.28**

39 International Institute for Conflict Prevention and Resolution, Rules for Non-Administered Arbitration (2014), Art. 14; International Chamber of Commerce, Rules of Arbitration (2012), Art. 29; International Centre for Dispute Resolution Rules (2014), Art. 6.

40 *Id.*

41 International Chamber of Commerce, Rules of Arbitration (2012), Art. 29; International Institute for Conflict Prevention and Resolution, Rules for Non-Administered Arbitration (2014), Art. 14.5 (providing that if the parties do not agree on an emergency arbitrator, the CPR shall appoint a special arbitrator within one business day of CPR's receipt of the application for interim measures).

authority to order a range of possible interim and conservatory measures, such as payment of security, the preservation of evidence, or even injunctions.[42] While the original ICC Pre-Arbitral Referee Procedure required an explicit "opt in," requiring that parties expressly select the emergency relief provisions for them to apply,[43] the current ICC rules include emergency relief provisions unless the parties expressly exclude them.[44] Under the ICC's new emergency arbitrator procedures, the President of the ICC Court of Arbitration must "appoint an emergency arbitrator within as short a time as possible, normally within two days."[45] The emergency arbitrator has up to fifteen days to issue a decision, which must take the form of an "order" and must be reasoned.[46] The emergency arbitrator's order does not bind the arbitral tribunal subsequently appointed to hear the merits of the dispute, which may "modify, terminate or annul the order or any modification thereto made by the emergency arbitrator."[47]

8.29 The ICDR procedure for emergency arbitral relief is also incorporated directly into the ICDR International Arbitration Rules—parties who do not wish to submit to ICDR's emergency arbitrator procedure must explicitly state that they do not want the procedure to apply.[48] Like the ICC Rules, the ICDR procedure provides for the appointment of an emergency arbitrator to issue emergency interim relief. The ICDR procedure presumes that the emergency arbitrator will be appointed by the ICDR rather than by the parties, as do the ICC rules.[49] There are, however, several noteworthy differences between the ICDR and ICC emergency arbitrator procedures. First, the ICDR process proceeds more quickly. The ICDR must appoint the emergency arbitrator within one business day of the notice requesting the emergency arbitral relief.[50] Second, the emergency arbitrator's decision may take the form of an "interim award" or an "order"—interim awards being more amenable than orders both to judicial enforcement and to judicial challenge.

8.30 The CPR also offers a procedure for "Interim Measures of Protection by a Special Arbitrator."[51] The CPR procedure provides for the appointment of a "special

[42] International Chamber of Commerce, Rules of Arbitration (2012), Art. 29.

[43] *Id.*; International Chamber of Commerce, Rules for a Pre-Arbitral Referee Procedure. For an overview of cases initiated under the ICC Pre-Arbitral Referee Procedure, *see* Emmanuel Gaillard, *ICC Pre-Arbitral Referee: A Procedure into Its Stride*, New York Law Journal (Oct. 5, 2006).

[44] International Chamber of Commerce, Rules of Arbitration (2012), Art. 29(6).

[45] International Chamber of Commerce, Rules of Arbitration (2012), Appendix V, Emergency Arbitrator Rules, Art. 2.1.

[46] *Id.*, Art. 6.1, 6.3, 6.4.

[47] International Chamber of Commerce, Rules of Arbitration (2012), Art. 29.3.

[48] International Centre for Dispute Resolution Rules (2014), Art. 6.

[49] *Id.*, Art. 6.2. The rules do not exclude the possibility of the parties agreeing on an emergency arbitrator prior to an appointment by ICDR.

[50] *Id.*, Art. 6.2.

[51] International Institution for Conflict Prevention and Resolution, Rules for Non-Administered Arbitration (2007), Rule 14. The CPR maintains separate rules for domestic and international arbitrations, but the procedure for appointing a special arbitrator is almost identical in each.

arbitrator" with powers similar to those of the emergency arbitrator under the ICDR procedure.[52] Like the ICC and ICDR procedures, the CPR procedure is an "opt-out" procedure. The procedure is expeditious: "If the parties agree upon a special arbitrator within one business day of the request, that arbitrator shall be appointed ... [and if not,] CPR shall appoint the special arbitrator within one business day of CPR's receipt of the application for interim measures under this Rule."[53] The special arbitrator's "award" or "order" "shall remain in effect until modified or vacated by the special arbitrator or the Tribunal."[54] Finally, the CPR Procedure differs from both the ICC and ICDR procedures by providing that the special arbitrator retains jurisdiction to make a ruling even after the arbitral tribunal is constituted, unless the tribunal directs otherwise.[55]

Significantly, the ICDR's emergency arbitrator provisions have been the subject of a recent case in the New York federal courts, *Yahoo v. Microsoft*.[56] That case concerned a merger of internet search capabilities. Microsoft commenced arbitration because Yahoo halted performance of its duties according to the contract delineating the systematic merger of the two search engines. Microsoft was awarded equitable relief by an emergency arbitrator, aimed at resuming the state of activities between the two companies before the pause in operations. Yahoo moved the district court to vacate the interim award on the grounds that the emergency arbitrator granted what was effectively "final" relief in excess of his authority under the ICDR emergency procedures, and Microsoft cross-moved to confirm the award. The district court confirmed the award, finding that the emergency arbitrator was operating within the authority granted to him by the contract between the parties and that he had a "colorable basis for concluding that an injunction requiring Yahoo to continue to perform ... was necessary."[57] **8.31**

C. PRELIMINARY RELIEF FROM COURTS IN AID OF ARBITRATION

For various reasons, parties to an arbitration agreement may seek preliminary measures from a court rather than from an arbitral tribunal. Court-ordered relief may be **8.32**

[52] *Id.*

[53] *Id.*, Rule 14.5.

[54] *Id.*, Rule 14.13.

[55] *Id.*, Rule 14.13.

[56] 983 F. Supp. 2d 310 (S.D.N.Y. 2013). In this instance, the emergency arbitrator was appointed by the American Arbitration Association (AAA). The ICDR is the international division of the AAA.

[57] *Id.* at 317. Yahoo also argued that the emergency arbitrator lacked jurisdiction because there was no "emergency," however the court stated that they would defer to the emergency arbitrator's determinations that an emergency existed and that immediate irreparable harm could result, based on the evidence presented to him in the arbitration. *Id.* at 317–18.

necessary before a tribunal is constituted, and where an emergency arbitrator procedure is unavailable or ineffective. Unlike arbitrator-ordered interim relief, court-issued interim relief can be granted immediately, and ex parte, and have immediate effect. Importantly, a court can also bind a nonparty to an arbitration agreement, provided that it has personal jurisdiction over the nonparty. Specifically, resort to a court may be necessary to freeze the funds of a party when those funds are held by a third party such as a bank, as arbitral tribunals lack jurisdiction to issue orders binding third parties. Generally, parties to an arbitration clause may seek interim relief from courts without waiving their right to arbitrate the merits of their dispute, provided that they do not engage in "litigation pertaining to 'substantial issues going to the merits.' "[58] This is explicit in the leading sets of arbitration rules.[59]

1. The New York Convention and Preliminary Relief

8.33 In *Borden v. Meiji Milk Prods. Co.*,[60] the Second Circuit addressed the effect of the New York Convention on the jurisdiction of federal courts to issue preliminary injunctions. The Court rejected the argument that Article II(3) of the New York Convention—which requires the courts of member nations to stay adjudication in court of any disputes subject to arbitration—forbids federal courts from granting preliminary relief concerning a dispute governed by the New York Convention, other than ordering the parties to the dispute to arbitrate, or confirming an existing arbitral award.[61] The Court also declined to follow *McCreary Tire & Rubber Co. v. CEAT*, in which the Third Circuit Court of Appeals, through a restrictive reading of the New York Convention, found that the Convention forbade courts from interfering in any way with an international dispute subject to arbitration—and concluded that preliminary measures would constitute such interference.[62] Rather, the Second Circuit held "that entertaining an application for a preliminary injunction in aid of arbitration is consistent with the court's powers pursuant to § 206" of the United States Code implementing the New York Convention.[63] Such an injunction is "not precluded by the Convention but rather is consistent with its provisions and its spirit."[64]

[58] *In re* S & R Co. of Kingston v. Latona Trucking, Inc., 159 F.3d 80, 84 (2d Cir. 1998) (Doctor's Associates, Inc. v. Distajo, 66 F.3d 438 at 457 (2d Cir. 1995)).

[59] ICC Rules of Arbitration (2012), Art. 28.2, ICDR Rules (2014), Art. 24.3, CPR Rules (2014), Art. 13.2.

[60] 919 F.2d 822, 826 (2d Cir. 1990).

[61] 9 U.S.C. §§ 201–208, which adopt and implement the New York Convention.

[62] 501 F.2d 1032, 1037-38 (3d Cir. 1974). Note that prior to the amendment of the New York Civil Practice Laws and Rules (the CPLR) in 2005, the Court of Appeals of New York State had held that the New York Convention—which provides for enforcement of awards but does not mention interim measures—forbade courts from granting interim relief. Cooper v. Ateliers de la Motobecane, 57 N.Y.2d 408, 413–16 (1982). This unfortunate holding was remedied through an amendment of the CPLR.

[63] Borden, 919 F.2d at 826.

[64] *Id.*

Accordingly, an arbitration clause—even in connection with an action under the New York Convention—"does not deprive the promise of the usual provisional remedies."[65] Courts in the Second Circuit have squarely rejected the line of authorities holding that the New York Convention removes jurisdiction from federal courts to issue preliminary measures in relation to arbitration, going so far as to characterize the Third Circuit's reasoning in *McCreary* as "facially absurd"[66] and noting it has "long been harshly criticized by courts and commentators."[67]

Following *Borden*, federal case law in New York holds that the New York Convention gives rise to subject-matter jurisdiction in federal court not only over a petition to confirm an arbitration award or compel arbitration, but also over a petition seeking interim measures in aid of arbitration.[68] Such measures may include an order attaching funds,[69] or prohibiting another party from some action that could cause irreparable harm.[70] A petition for interim measures need not be accompanied by a petition to compel arbitration.[71] However, prudent litigants seeking a host of remedies from a federal court based on jurisdiction derived from **8.34**

65 *Id.* (*quoting* Murray Oil Prods. Co. v. Mitsui & Co., 146 F.2d 381, 384 (2d. Cir. 1944)). *See also* Venconsul N.V. v. Tim Int'l N.V., No. 03 Civ. 5387 (LTS)(MHD), 2003 WL 21804833, at *3 (S.D.N.Y. Aug. 6, 2003) ("In Borden ... the Second Circuit rejected the argument that a court's jurisdiction under the Convention is limited to compelling arbitration or confirming an arbitration award.").

66 Filanto, S.p.A. v. Chilewich Int'l Corp., 789 F. Supp. 1229, 1241 (S.D.N.Y. 1992). The *Filanto* court noted *McCreary*'s holding that "the proper remedy in a Convention case is to refer the parties to arbitration and dismiss for lack of subject matter jurisdiction" is "facially absurd because the enabling legislation gives the district court the power at least to compel arbitration. How could even this limited power be exercised without subject matter jurisdiction?" *Id.* at 1241–42.

67 Bahrain Telecomms. Co. v. Discoverytel, Inc., 476 F. Supp. 2d 176, 180 (D. Conn. 2007) (noting that the "Second Circuit has ... rejected the approach embraced by ... *McCreary*" and holding that the "Convention does not deprive this Court of jurisdiction to issue *pendente lite* orders, such as a prejudgment attachment, in connection with a pending international arbitration" *Id.* at 180, 182). The *Bahrain* court also noted the Second Circuit's rejection of similar reasoning when considering injunctions or provisional remedies under Chapter 1 of the FAA. *Id.* at 179–80; *see also* Jameson v. Pine Hill Dev., LLC, Civ. A. No. 07-0111-WSB, 2007 WL 623807, at *2, n.2 (S.D. Ala. Feb 23, 2007) (agreeing with "overwhelming majority of federal courts" and rejecting "minority view prohibit[ing] the granting of emergency injunctive relief in an action subject to pending arbitration").

68 *See, e.g.*, Venconsul N.V., 2003 WL 21804833, at *2–4 (holding that subject matter jurisdiction existed under New York Convention and denying motion for preliminary injunction seeking to enjoin corporate recapitalization plan); Alvenus Shipping Co. v. Delta Petroleum (U.S.A.), 876 F. Supp. 482, 487 (S.D.N.Y. 1994) ("[E]ntertaining an application for preliminary injunction in aid of arbitration is consistent with the court's powers pursuant to § 206 of the Convention.").

69 Alvenus, 876 F. Supp. at 487–88 (granting order compelling arbitration and attaching funds, based on jurisdiction derived from the New York Convention).

70 Andersen Consulting Business Unit Member Firms v. Andersen Worldwide Societe Co-op., No. 98 CIV. 1030 (JGK), 1998 WL 122590, at *6–7 (S.D.N.Y. March 18, 1998) (finding federal subject jurisdiction under the New York Convention to consider relief including a motion to compel arbitration and a preliminary injunction "in aid of arbitration" seeking to block another party from issuing notices of breach to third parties until an arbitrator was appointed).

71 Venconsul, 2003 WL 21804833 at *3 ("*Borden* has been interpreted as recognizing a court's power to entertain requests for provisional remedies in aid of arbitration even where the request for remedies does not accompany a motion to compel arbitration or to confirm an award.").

the New York Convention should understand that the courts have, in the past, found jurisdiction only with regard to measures linked to compelling or supporting arbitration or confirming an award.[72] As with the New York Convention, federal courts also have federal subject-matter jurisdiction over cases arising under the Panama Convention.[73]

2. Preliminary Relief from Federal Court

8.35 In considering an application for interim measures in aid of arbitration, federal courts generally apply the Federal Rules of Civil Procedure governing applications for interim relief in connection with litigation.[74] Rule 65 governs injunctions, and provides that no preliminary injunction will be issued without notice to the adverse party and without the moving party providing security for the payment of costs or damages incurred by a wrongly enjoined party.[75] To receive ex parte relief in the form of a temporary restraining order, an applicant must demonstrate that "immediate and irreparable injury, loss or damage will result to the movant before the adverse party can be heard in opposition."[76]

8.36 In addition to satisfying Rule 65, the petitioner must demonstrate irreparable harm if the injunction is not granted and, additionally, either a likelihood of

---

[72] *See* Int'l Shipping Co., S.A. v. Hydra Offshore, Inc., 675 F. Supp. 146 (S.D.N.Y. 1987) ("Because this case involved neither an action to compel arbitration nor enforcement of an arbitral award, the Court found that it did not have subject matter jurisdiction pursuant to the [New York] Convention."), *aff'd*, 875 F.2d 388, 391 n.5 (2d Cir. 1989) ("Appellant's contentions that jurisdiction could be premised on the [New York] Convention ... were ... appropriately rejected ... because the party invoking its provisions did not seek either to compel arbitration or to enforce an arbitral award."). Note that this assertion was not followed as dicta in Republic of Ecuador, 638 F.3d at 391 n.6. *See also* Goel v. Ramachandran, 823 F. Supp. 2d 206, 215–16 (S.D.N.Y. 2011) (discussing shift in the Second Circuit's interpretation of subject matter jurisdiction under the New York Convention and the Court's adoption of a "broader view" over time).

[73] Inter-American Convention on International Commercial Arbitration, Jan. 30, 1975, (entered into force June 16, 1976). The Panama Convention was introduced to the FAA as Chapter III: *see* 9 U.S.C. §§ 301–307. *See generally* John P. Bowman, *The Panama Convention and Its Implementation under the Federal Arbitration Act*, 11 Am. Rev. Int'l Arb. 1 (2000).

[74] Unicorn Bulk Traders Ltd. v. Fortune Maritime Enters., Inc., No. 08 Civ. 9710 (PGG), 2009 WL 125751, at *4 (S.D.N.Y. Jan. 20, 2009) ("To show an entitlement to preliminary relief under the Convention, [Plaintiff] would need to meet the requirements of the provisions of the Federal Rules of Civil Procedure pertaining to preliminary relief—*e.g.*, Rule 65, which governs the grant of preliminary injunctions ..." (citing Alvenus, 876 F. Supp. 482 at 487)); Alvenus, 876 F. Supp. 482 at 487 ("Under Rule 65, a preliminary injunction will be issued upon a showing of irreparable harm and the likelihood of success on the merits.").

[75] Fed. R. Civ. P. 65. A petitioner may prevail on the merits but still lose its security if the injunction proves, in hindsight, to have been unnecessary. "The focus of the 'wrongfulness' inquiry is whether, in hindsight, in light of the ultimate decision on the merits after a full hearing, the injunction should not have issued in the first instance." Blumenthal v. Merrill Lynch, Pierce, Fenner & Smith, Inc., 910 F.2d 1049, 1054 (2d Cir. 1990) (awarding damages to plaintiff, who had been subject to preliminary injunction, despite the fact that arbitrators awarded damages to defendants in the eventual arbitration, where arbitrators determined that preliminary injunction had been unnecessary).

[76] Fed. R. Civ. P. 65(b)(1)(A).

success on the merits of the action or an arguable case combined with a balance of hardships tipping toward the petitioner:

> The general standard for issuing a preliminary injunction requires that the movant show "(a) irreparable harm and (b) either (1) likelihood of success on the merits or (2) sufficiently serious questions going to the merits to make them a fair ground for litigation and a balance of hardships tipping decidedly toward the party requesting the preliminary relief."[77]

Under Rule 64 of the Federal Rules of Civil Procedure, New York State law will ordinarily provide the applicable standard for issuing attachments even in federal court.[78] New York State law permits granting attachment in aid of arbitration where the award "may be rendered ineffectual without ... provisional relief."[79] **8.37**

Federal courts will play a limited role in matters of discovery or preservation of evidence for an arbitration. As an initial matter, "allowing discovery on the merits of a case prior to arbitration is inconsistent with the aims of arbitration."[80] "A hallmark of arbitration—and a necessary precursor to its efficient operation—is a limited discovery process."[81] Courts may make exceptions in "limited 'extraordinary circumstances'" and/or where the petitioner seeks "to perpetuate, rather than discover, the evidence."[82] These circumstances might be established if the petitioner can demonstrate that the evidence is "time-sensitive" and "evanescent."[83] **8.38**

---

[77] Maryland Cas. Co. v. Realty Advisory Bd. on Labor Relations, 107 F.3d 979, 984 (2d Cir. 1997) (citation omitted).

[78] Grupo Mexicano de Desarrollo, S.A. v. Alliance Bond Fund, Inc., 527 U.S. 308, 330 (1999). Rule 64 provides that a federal court may use "every remedy ... that, under the law of the state where the court is located, provides for seizing a person or property to secure satisfaction of the potential judgment." Fed. R. Civ. P. 64(a). Federal courts do not have the authority to issue the so-called *Mareva* injunctions and *Anton Pillar* orders of English jurisprudence. Grupo Mexicano de Desarrollo, S.A., 527 U.S. at 327–28, 332.

[79] Drexel Burnham Lambert Inc. v. Ruebsamen, 139 A.D.2d 323, 328 (1st Dep't 1988) (*quoting* N.Y. C.P.L.R. 6201) (holding that party seeking attachment under N.Y. C.P.L.R. 7502(c) need not demonstrate one of the five situations listed in NY CPLR 6201). *See also* County Natwest Sec. Corp., USA v. Jesup, Josephthal & Co., 180 A.D.2d 468, 469 (1st Dep't 1992) ("This court has held that the standard that governs in a case involving arbitration is whether the award 'may be rendered ineffectual without such provisional relief,' and the standards generally applicable to attachments pursuant to CPLR 6201(3), such as sinister maneuvers or fraudulent conduct, are not required to be shown in an application pursuant to CPLR 7502(c).") (*quoting* Habitations Ltd. v. BKL Realty Sales Corp., 160 A.D.2d 423, 424 (1st Dep't 1990)). For a detailed discussion, *see* Section C.3(a) "Preliminary Relief under NY CPLR § 7502(c)," of this chapter.

[80] Mississippi Power Co. v. Peabody Coal Co., 69 F.R.D. 558, 567 (S.D. Miss. 1976).

[81] COMSAT Corp. v. Nat'l Sci. Found., 190 F.3d 269, 276 (4th Cir. 1999); *see also* Burton v. Bush, 614 F.2d 389, 390 (4th Cir. 1980) ("When contracting parties stipulate that disputes will be submitted to arbitration, they relinquish the right to certain procedural niceties which are normally associated with a formal trial. One of these accoutrements is the right to pre-trial discovery." (internal citation omitted)).

[82] Deiulemar Compagnia di Navigazione S.p.A. v. M/V Allegra, 198 F.3d 473, 479, 486 (4th Cir. 1999).

[83] *Id.* at 480.

8.39 Antisuit injunctions are another form of court-ordered preliminary relief sought in aid of arbitration. These injunctions forbid a party from resorting to litigation of issues that are properly subject to arbitration. Different, specialized considerations may apply to this form of injunctive relief. In *Paramedics Electromedicina Comercial, Ltda. v. GE Med. Sys. Info. Techs., Inc.*, a Brazilian entity had commenced litigation in Brazil regarding a contract notwithstanding that an arbitration clause in that contract provided for arbitration in New York.[84] The matter was appealed to the Second Circuit after the federal district court granted an antisuit injunction against the Brazilian entity to end its litigation in Brazil. The Second Circuit began by noting that "principles of comity counsel that injunctions restraining foreign litigation be 'used sparingly' and 'granted only with care and great restraint.'"[85] Nonetheless, the court affirmed the antisuit injunction, noting that the arbitration clause was broad, and "[f]ederal policy strongly favors the enforcement of arbitration agreements."[86] For future cases, the court set forth the following requirements for an antisuit injunction:

> An anti-suit injunction against parallel litigation may be imposed only if: (A) the parties are the same in both matters, and (B) resolution of the case before the enjoining court is dispositive of the action to be enjoined. Once past this threshold, courts are directed to consider a number of additional factors, including whether the foreign action threatens the jurisdiction or the strong public policies of the enjoining forum.[87]

3. Preliminary Relief from New York State Courts

8.40 Applications for preliminary relief in aid of arbitrations that are international in character will typically be made in federal court because international arbitration will generally satisfy the tests for federal jurisdiction. However, at least in some circumstances parties may seek preliminary measures in New York State court where the requirements for federal jurisdiction are not met, or when one party commences an action in state court that is also subject to federal jurisdiction and the other party or parties do not petition for removal.

8.41 New York is the leading center for international arbitration in the United States, and so has adopted a modern, pro-arbitration statute.[88] Also, its courts have adopted a pro-arbitration stance on important issues, recognizing that

[84] 369 F.3d 645, 650 (2d Cir. 2004). Those claims included a claim for "moral damages"—a tort unique to Brazilian law, which the distributor argued was not encompassed by the arbitration clause. *Id.* at 653.

[85] *Id.* at 652 (*quoting* China Trade & Dev. Corp. v. M.V. Choong Yong, 837 F.2d 33, 36 (2d Cir. 1987)).

[86] *Id.* at 653.

[87] *Id.* at 652 (*citing* China Trade & Dev. Corp., 837 F.2d at 35–36).

[88] *See* N.Y. C.P.L.R. Art. 75.

seeking preliminary relief in aid of arbitration does not waive a party's right to arbitrate.[89]

8.42 *(a) Preliminary relief under NY CPLR § 7502(c)* Article 75 of the New York Civil Practice Law and Rules (NY CPLR) contains New York's arbitration statute including a provision dealing with provisional remedies. Under NY CPLR 7502(c), a state supreme court "may entertain an application for an order of attachment or for a preliminary injunction in connection with an arbitration that is pending or that is to be commenced inside or outside this state ... but only upon the ground that the award to which the applicant may be entitled may be rendered ineffectual without such provisional relief."[90] Accordingly, New York courts have jurisdiction to issue preliminary measures in support of arbitration, provided the preliminary measures are necessary to prevent the award from being rendered "ineffectual."

8.43 Until recently, New York State courts offered little assistance to parties seeking preliminary measures in aid of an *international* arbitration encompassed by the New York Convention. In the notorious *Cooper v. Ateliers de la Motobecane, S.A.* case, New York's highest court, the New York Court of Appeals, ruled that "the purpose and policy of the [New York Convention] will be best carried out by restricting prearbitration judicial action to determining whether arbitration should be compelled."[91] This ruling prevented New York courts from issuing attachment orders in aid of most international arbitrations.[92] Following extensive criticism, NY CPLR § 7502(c) was revised in 2005. It now explicitly permits courts to grant preliminary relief in aid of arbitration, even when subject to the New York Convention:

> The supreme court in the county in which an arbitration is pending or in a county specified in [§ 7502(a)], may entertain an application for an order of attachment or for a preliminary injunction in connection with an arbitration that is pending or that is to be commenced inside or outside this state, *whether or not it is subject to the United Nations convention on the recognition and enforcement of foreign arbitral awards, but only upon the ground that the award to which the applicant may be entitled may be rendered ineffectual without such provisional relief.* The provisions of articles 62 and 63 of this chapter [relating to attachments and injunctions] shall apply to the application, including those relating to undertakings and to the time for commencement of an action (arbitration shall be deemed an action for this

[89] Congregation Darech Amuno v. Blasof, 226 A.D.2d 236, 236–37 (1st Dep't 1996) ("There is no merit to [the] claim that ... opposition to [a] motion for a preliminary injunction and appeal from the grant thereof are uses of judicial process indicative of a waiver of any right to arbitrate, given that the court is authorized to grant such an injunction even while an arbitration is pending.").

[90] NY CPLR § 7502(c). For a detailed discussion, *see* Section C.2, "Preliminary Relief from Federal Court," of this chapter.

[91] 57 N.Y.2d 408, 416 (1982).

[92] *See* Drexel Burnham Lambert Inc., 139 A.D.2d at 329–30.

purpose), except that the sole ground for the granting of the remedy shall be as stated above.[93]

8.44 This section further provides that ex parte relief may be available in particular situations, and that if arbitration is not commenced within thirty days of the grant of preliminary relief, the relief shall expire unless extended by the court.[94]

8.45 *(b) Additional requirements for grant of preliminary relief* Just as a petitioner seeking a preliminary injunction in federal court must demonstrate the danger of irreparable harm and other factors, a party seeking preliminary relief in aid of arbitration from a New York State court must satisfy the conditions set forth in the NY CPLR as well as other preconditions pertaining to preliminary relief.[95] A petitioner seeking an order of *attachment* must satisfy the criteria in Article 62, and a petitioner seeking a *preliminary injunction* must satisfy those of Article 63.[96]

8.46 Article 62 states that "[a]n order of attachment may be granted in any action ... where the plaintiff has demanded and would be entitled, in whole or in part, or in the alternative, to a money judgment against one or more defendants" and also one of five specific factual situations has arisen: (1) the defendant is a nondomiciliary or foreign corporation, (2) the defendant cannot be personally served, (3) the defendant has disposed of property with intent to defraud creditors, (4) the action is brought by the victim of a crime, or (5) the cause of action is based on a judgment of another court.[97]

8.47 This ostensibly exhaustive list of criteria indicates that New York courts can order attachment in specifically defined circumstances.[98] However, several decisions by New York courts have disregarded this exhaustive list and granted orders of attachment in aid of arbitration simply because "the possibility that an arbitration award may be rendered ineffectual in the absence of an order of attachment is sufficient under the statute to support provisional relief."[99] This important line of decisions considerably lowers the threshold for parties seeking orders of attachment:

---

[93] N.Y. C.P.L.R. § 7502(c) (emphasis added). For history of the amendment, *see* International Disputes Committee and Committee on Arbitration of the Association of the Bar of the City of New York, *Amendment of New York Civil Practice Law and Rules Section 7502(c) to Permit Attachments and Preliminary Injunctions in Connection with National and International* Arbitrations (New York, Feb. 11, 2005).

[94] N.Y. C.P.L.R. § 7502(c).

[95] *Id.* §§ 7502(c), 6201.

[96] *Id.* § 7502(c); *see also* Continental Chartering & Brokerage, Inc. v. T.J. Stevenson & Co., Inc., 678 F. Supp. 58, 60 (S.D.N.Y. 1987) ("New York law provides for attachments in aid of arbitration in CPLR 7502(c). I read that statute to include in it the requirements of CPLR 6201, which defines the grounds for which attachments are available generally.").

[97] N.Y. C.P.L.R. § 6201.

[98] Continental Chartering & Brokerage, Inc., 678 F. Supp. at 60.

[99] Drexel Burnham Lambert Inc., 139 A.D.2d at 328 (holding that party seeking attachment under NY CPLR 7502(c) need not demonstrate one of the five situations listed in NY CPLR 6201).

> This court has held that the standard that governs in a case involving arbitration is whether the award "may be rendered ineffectual without such provisional relief", and the standards generally applicable to attachments pursuant to CPLR 6201(3), such as sinister maneuvers or fraudulent conduct, are not required to be shown in an application pursuant to CPLR 7502(c).[100]

As federal courts must use state procedures when considering a motion for attachment, these state cases presumptively granting attachment in support of arbitration, are relevant to parties in federal court too.

To obtain a preliminary injunction, a movant must satisfy both the terms of Article 63 of the CPLR (specifically, an affidavit or other evidence regarding potential injury, an undertaking in an amount to be fixed by the court)[101] and demonstrate "(1) a likelihood of ultimate success on the merits, (2) irreparable injury absent granting of the preliminary injunction, and (3) a balancing of the equities in the movant's favor."[102] **8.48**

New York courts have generally held that when an arbitral tribunal is already seized with an action, courts should defer to the tribunal, rather than issue a preliminary injunction at one party's request. In *Meda Int'l v. Salzman*, the Appellate Division reversed a lower court injunction staying defendants' use of a particular trade name.[103] The court did not delve into the merits of the decision, but noted that the matter could be dealt with in arbitration and the arbitral tribunal, if it saw fit, could issue "equitable relief" itself: **8.49**

> It ... appears that in the arbitration proceeding, the issues are almost identical with those alleged in the action. Although all the parties named in the action are not parties to the arbitration agreement, it is obvious that all such parties are effectively controlled by those involved in the arbitration. The arbitrators, who have power to grant equitable relief, can adequately dispose of all of the issues posed in the action. Certainly, any award in the arbitration will resolve the main points of controversy. Therefore, the action should be stayed until completion of the arbitration.[104]

Accordingly, parties to an arbitration subject to the jurisdiction of New York courts should consider seeking emergency relief from the arbitral tribunal in the first instance; a New York court may refuse to grant the relief unless its involvement is actually necessary to preserve the arbitral process.

---

[100] County Natwest Sec. Corp. USA, 180 A.D.2d at 469 (*quoting* Habitations Ltd. v. BKL Realty Sales Corp., 160 A.D.2d 423, 424 (1st Dep't 1990)).

[101] NY C.P.L.R. §§ 6301, 6311.

[102] St. Paul Fire & Marine Ins. Co. v. York Claims Serv., Inc., 308 A.D.2d 347, 348 (1st Dep't 2003) (*quoting* Rosa Hair Stylists v. Jaber Food Corp., 218 A.D.2d 793, 794 (2d Dep't 1995)).

[103] 24 A.D.2d 710, 711 (1st Dep't 1965).

[104] *Id.*

9

DISCOVERY

John L. Gardiner, Lea Haber Kuck, and Julie Bédard

A. Introduction	9.01
B. Framework for Discovery in International Arbitrations Venued in New York	9.03
1. Statutory Framework	9.03
(a) The Federal Arbitration Act	9.04
(b) The New York Civil Practice Law and Rules	9.06
2. Courts in New York Support Party Autonomy: Supremacy of the Parties' Agreement on Discovery	9.07
3. In the Absence of an Agreement to the Contrary, Discovery in Arbitration Will Be More Limited than Discovery in Litigation in State or Federal Court	9.11
4. Arbitration Rules and Guidelines	9.13
(a) International Chamber of Commerce	9.15
(b) International Centre for Dispute Resolution	9.17
(c) JAMS/JAMS International Rules on Evidence	9.18
(d) U.N. Commission on International Trade Law	9.21
(e) International Institute for Conflict Prevention and Resolution	9.22
(f) The International Bar Association's Rules on Taking of Evidence in International Commercial Arbitration	9.25
5. The Discretion of the Arbitral Tribunal	9.30
C. Discovery Between the Parties	9.33
1. Document Discovery	9.33
(a) Documents in "hard copy" form	9.33
(b) Electronically stored documents and information	9.39
(c) Consequences of a party's failure to produce documents	9.51
2. Availability of Depositions	9.54
3. Other Discovery Devices	9.55
4. Privilege	9.56
5. Confidentiality	9.59
D. Obtaining Discovery from Nonparties	9.62
E. Discovery from Expert Witnesses	9.71
F. Discovery when Seeking Preliminary Relief in Aid of Arbitration	9.73
G. Discovery in New York in Aid of a Foreign Arbitration	9.74

A. INTRODUCTION

Discovery refers both to the process whereby the parties exchange information among themselves and also may seek information from third parties in order to assess the merits of their respective cases, prepare for an evidentiary hearing on the merits of their dispute and make necessary submissions to the arbitration **9.01** tribunal.[1] When the arbitration is venued in New York, the first issue for consideration relating to the discovery options that may be available to the parties is what the arbitration agreement itself provides, if anything, about the scope of permissible discovery. This is because, as discussed below, both federal and New York law place party autonomy at the top of the pyramid of considerations when looking at the applicable procedure for the arbitration, including discovery issues. Accordingly, when an arbitration is venued in New York, the scope of discovery provided for in the arbitration clause will be of paramount importance.

9.02 However, given that an arbitration clause most often is silent on discovery matters, what then is the scope of permissible discovery? May the parties assume that discovery is confidential and documents exchanged in discovery will not be disclosed to nonparties during the arbitration? What is the difference between discovery available from the parties and discovery sought from nonparties? Is discovery available when seeking preliminary relief in aid of arbitration? Finally, if the arbitration is venued abroad, may a party to that foreign arbitration obtain discovery in New York under 28 U.S.C. § 1782 in aid of the foreign arbitration? We address these questions in this chapter.

B. FRAMEWORK FOR DISCOVERY IN INTERNATIONAL ARBITRATIONS VENUED IN NEW YORK

1. Statutory Framework

9.03 As discussed in Chapter 1, when an international arbitration is venued in New York, a party to that arbitration must consider two sources of potentially relevant local law for the conduct of the arbitration: (1) the Federal Arbitration Act ("FAA")[2] and (2) Article 75 of the New York Civil Practice Law and Rules ("New York CPLR" or "CPLR").[3]

9.04 *(a) The Federal Arbitration Act* Section 7 of the FAA provides that the arbitrators "may summon in writing any person to attend *before them* or any of them

[1] Some international practitioners would advocate for the use of the term "disclosure" rather than the term "discovery" because, for those practitioners, the latter tends to carry with it a pejorative connotation of the perceived excesses of the judicial system in the United States. The fact remains, however, that international arbitration practitioners commonly use the term "discovery" in connection with U.S. arbitrations, making the use of the term appropriate when discussing international arbitrations venued in New York. For a discussion of how discovery operates in the United States system of civil litigation, *see* Chapter 2.E of this book.

[2] 9 U.S.C. §§ 1–16, 201–208, 301–307 (2012).

[3] N.Y. C.P.L.R. 75 (McKinney 2014).

as a witness and in a proper case to bring with him or them any book, record or document, or paper which may be deemed material as evidence in the case."[4]

As discussed later, a literal reading of Section 7, which addresses the appearance of witnesses at the hearing before the arbitrator, has led some U.S. courts to conclude that it does not cover discovery, because discovery occurs prior to a hearing and is independent of any summoning of witnesses.[5] Other U.S. courts, however, have interpreted Section 7 to encompass discovery.[6] Moreover, considerable debate exists concerning the scope of third-party discovery available under Section 7 before the merits hearing. (*See infra* at Section D.) **9.05**

(b) The New York Civil Practice Law and Rules New York State practice generally recognizes the right of the arbitrator to issue procedural orders directing the parties to exchange documents and to impose adverse inferences against non-compliant parties.[7] Where parties are unable to obtain the discovery they need through the arbitral process,[8] CPLR 3102(c) permits the court to order discovery **9.06**

[4] 9 U.S.C. § 7 (2012) (emphasis added). Under Section 7, the summons must be signed by the arbitrators, or a majority of them, and must be served in the same manner as subpoenas compelling a person to appear and testify before a court. The U.S. district court for the district in which the arbitrators "are sitting," *id.*, is available to enforce arbitrator-issued subpoenas and also to punish for contempt any person who refuses or neglects to obey the arbitrator summons. *See* Stolt-Nielsen SA v. Celanese AG, 430 F.3d 567, 577-81 (2d Cir. 2005) (affirming power of court to enforce subpoenas).

[5] *See* Life Receivables Trust v. Syndicate 102 at Lloyd's of London, 549 F.3d 210, 216 (2d Cir. 2008) ("Documents are only discoverable in arbitration when brought before arbitrators by a testifying witness.") Notably, however, the *Life Receivables* decision does not foreclose the possibility that the tribunal may conduct a preliminary, pre-merits hearing for the sole purpose of calling a third-party witness to appear before it and tender documents. *See id.* at 218. Moreover, Section 7's limitations do not contravene the inherent and separate power of the tribunal to provide for discovery between the parties to the arbitration agreement (including, possibly, parties that may be subject to joinder). *See Life Receivables*, 549 F.3d at 218.

[6] *See* Sec. Life Ins. Co. of Am. v. Duncanson & Holt, Inc., 228 F.3d 865, 870–71 (8th Cir. 2000) ("We thus hold that implicit in an arbitration panel's power to subpoena relevant documents for production at a hearing is the power to order the production of relevant documents for review by a party prior to the hearing.").

[7] See SLG 625 Lessee, LLC v. Neiman Marcus Grp., Inc., 978 N.Y.S.2d 130, 131 (App. Div. 2013) (upholding an award which resolved certain issues against a party when it failed to comply with discovery validly ordered by the tribunal); Sobel v. Charles Schwab & Co., 828 N.Y.S.2d 720, 721 (App. Div. 2007) (refusing to interfere with a tribunal's handling of a disclosure dispute, as "[p]rocedural matters regarding … disclosure … are generally left to the discretion of the arbitrator"); Glen Rauch Sec., Inc. v. Weinraub, 768 N.Y.S.2d 611, 611 (App. Div. 2003) (affirming the lower court decision that granted the petition to confirm an arbitration award, and concluding that the arbitrators' sanction for failure to comply with an arbitral discovery order was proper); Radin v. Kleinman, 750 N.Y.S.2d 276, 277 (App. Div. 2002) (refusing to vacate award and stating that "[t]he arbitrators' limited document production directive was consistent with their 'inherent power to control the course of the arbitration proceedings so as to permit a party to elicit relevant information'" (citation omitted)); Guilford Mills, Inc. v. Rice Pudding, Ltd., 455 N.Y.S.2d 88, 89 (App. Div. 1982) (the arbitrator "has inherent power to control the course of the arbitration proceedings so as to permit a party to elicit relevant information").

[8] *See* De Sapio v. Kohlmeyer, 321 N.E.2d 770, 773 (N.Y. 1974) (noting in dicta that "[u]nder the CPLR, arbiters do not have the power to direct the parties to engage in disclosure proceedings"). *But see* CSP Techs., Inc. v. Hekal, 869 N.Y.S.2d 449, 450 (App. Div. 2008) (although

"to aid in arbitration"[9] although New York courts have limited the application of CPLR 3102(c) to extraordinary circumstances.[10] Additionally, under CPLR 7505, an "arbitrator and any attorney of record in the arbitration proceeding has the power to issue subpoenas"[11] directed to parties and third parties for the hearing.[12] However, much of the case law under the CPLR arises in the context of domestic arbitrations.[13]

2. Courts in New York Support Party Autonomy: Supremacy of the Parties' Agreement on Discovery

9.07 Abundant federal and state case law establishes the important principle that party autonomy is paramount in international arbitration. The U.S. Supreme Court has upheld this cardinal rule on numerous occasions, stating that "parties are

"the CPLR does not itself authorize arbitrators 'to direct the parties to engage in disclosure proceedings'" it does not prohibit parties agreeing to "rules permitting the arbitrators to direct the exchange of information" (citation omitted)).

[9] *See* N.Y. C.P.L.R. 3102(c) (McKinney Supp. 2014) ("Before an action is commenced, disclosure to aid in bringing an action, to preserve information or to aid in arbitration, may be obtained, but only by court order. The court may appoint a referee to take testimony.").

[10] *See* AXA Equitable Life Ins. Co. v. Kalina, 956 N.Y.S.2d 743, 744–45 (App. Div. 2012) (reversing grant of expedited discovery prior to the submission to arbitration as the party failed to show that any discovery received in arbitration would be inadequate for the party to establish its case, nor any other extraordinary circumstances justifying the order); Guilford Mills, 455 N.Y.S.2d at 89 (denying relief under CPLR 3102(c) due to lack of extraordinary circumstances and instructing party to request information sought through the arbitrator); State Farm Mut. Auto. Ins. Co. v. Wernick, 455 N.Y.S.2d 30, 31 (App. Div. 1982) (holding that a "court may order discovery 'to aid in arbitration' pursuant to CPLR 3102 (subd. [c]) only in the presence of 'extraordinary circumstances,'" that the "test is necessity rather than convenience," and further finding in that case that the physical examination of the claimant was a necessity and not a convenience; affirming order that claimant in the arbitration to submit to an examination (citations omitted)).

[11] N.Y. C.P.L.R. 7505 (McKinney 2014). An arbitrator also "has the power to administer oaths." *Id.* However, if the parties expressly choose the FAA or "federal arbitral law" to govern the arbitration (and perhaps even if the FAA governs by default), then counsel may not issue subpoenas under CPLR 7505 because the FAA does not authorize attorneys to issue subpoenas. *See* Kenney, Becker LLP v. Kenney, No. 06 Civ. 2975(JSR), 2008 WL 681452, at *2 n.2 (S.D.N.Y. Mar. 10, 2008).

[12] *See* Integrity Ins. Co. v. Am. Centennial Ins. Co., 885 F. Supp. 69, 71 n.3 (S.D.N.Y. 1995) (CPLR 7505's grant of authority to issue subpoenas "extends only to the hearing before the arbitrators, 'and not, by implication, for the steps preparatory to the hearing'" (*quoting* N.Y. C.P.L.R. 2302(a) cmt. (McKinney 1991) (David D. Siegel, Practice Commentaries, C2302:1)), *abrogated on other grounds by* Life Receivables Trust v. Syndicate 102 at Lloyd's of London, 549 F.3d 210 (2d Cir. 2008); 13 Jack B. Weinstein, Harold L. Korn & Arthur R. Miller, New York Civil Practice: CPLR ¶ 7505.6 (2d ed. 2014) ("[New York's CPLR] merely permits the issuance of subpoenas *ad testificandum* and *duces tecum* to produce evidence at the arbitration hearings in order to relieve them of the necessity of asking a court to issue the subpoena.").

[13] *See Integrity Ins.*, 885 F. Supp. at 71–73 & n.3 (partially granting motion of nonparties to arbitration agreement by quashing that part of the arbitrator's subpoenas requiring nonparties to appear for depositions and to produce documents prior to arbitration hearing under the FAA; noting in passing that an arbitrator's authority under the CPLR to issue subpoenas "extends only to the hearing before the arbitrators" and not to discovery, but holding that the FAA prevails over any inconsistent state arbitration statute (citing Prima Paint Corp. v. Flood & Conklin Mfg. Co., 388 U.S. 395, 401 (1967))).

generally free to structure their arbitration agreements as they see fit."[14] The U.S. Court of Appeals for the Second Circuit also has endorsed the principle of party autonomy in arbitration matters, reiterating that

> [a]rbitration is entirely a creature of contract. The rules governing arbitration, its location, the law the arbitrators will apply, indeed, even which disputes are subject to arbitration, are determined entirely by an agreement between the parties. Any arbitration proceeding is thus an extension of the parties' contract with one another ...[15]

The New York State courts likewise will not interfere with the parties' desire to arbitrate their dispute.[16]

Given the respect of New York courts for party autonomy, discovery rights in an international arbitration venued in New York will be controlled in the first instance by the arbitration agreement itself.[17] If the parties provided for specific types of discovery to be permissible and specific types to be impermissible, then the arbitral tribunal normally should enforce such provisions. **9.08**

The following is an example of an arbitration clause permitting limited discovery at the discretion of the arbitrators: **9.09**

> In addition to the authority conferred on the arbitrator(s) by the above-designated [arbitration] Rules, the arbitrator(s) shall have the authority, upon the showing by either party of a justifiable need, to order production of relevant documents.[18]

[14] Mastrobuono v. Shearson Lehman Hutton, Inc., 514 U.S. 52, 57 (1995); *see also, e.g.*, Am. Express Co. v. Italian Colors Rest., 133 S. Ct. 2304, 2309 (2013) ("[C]ourts must 'rigorously enforce' arbitration agreements according to their terms ..." (citation omitted)); Volt Info. Scis., Inc. v. Bd. of Trs. of Leland Stanford Junior Univ., 489 U.S. 468, 478 (1989) (stating that agreements to arbitrate are enforced "in accordance with their terms").

[15] Sole Resort, S.A. de C.V. v. Allure Resorts Mgmt., LLC, 450 F.3d 100, 104 (2d Cir. 2006); *see also, e.g.*, Schnabel v. Trilegiant Corp., 697 F.3d 110, 118 (2d Cir. 2012) ("With the FAA, Congress sought to counteract an historic judicial hostility toward arbitration, which often trumped the parties' clear intentions."); Vera v. Saks & Co., 335 F.3d 109, 116 (2d Cir. 2003) (stating that the FAA "requires the federal courts to enforce arbitration agreements, reflecting Congress' recognition that arbitration is to be encouraged as a means of reducing the costs and delays associated with litigation" (citation omitted)).

[16] *See, e.g.*, Am. Indep. Ins. Co. v. Art of Healing Med., P.C., 961 N.Y.S.2d 240, 241 (App. Div. 2013) ("There is a strong public policy favoring arbitration, and courts interfere as little as possible with the freedom of parties to submit their disputes to arbitration."); Credit Suisse First Boston Corp. v. Pitofsky, 824 N.E.2d 929, 932 (N.Y. 2005) ("In this context, arbitration is a creature of contract, and it has long been the policy of this State to 'interfere as little as possible with the freedom of consenting parties' in structuring their arbitration relationship." (citation omitted)); Smith Barney Shearson Inc. v. Sacharow, 689 N.E.2d 884, 890 (N.Y. 1997) (same); Siegel v. Lewis, 358 N.E.2d 484, 485 (N.Y. 1976) ("[C]ommercial arbitration is a creature of contract. Parties, by agreement, may substitute a different method for the adjudication of their disputes than those which would otherwise be available to them in public courts of law ... Their quest is usually for a nonjudicial tribunal that will arrive at a private and practical determination with maximum dispatch and at minimum expense.").

[17] For a discussion of drafting considerations for arbitration clauses addressing discovery, *see generally* Chapter 3.B.4(a).

[18] Paul D. Friedland, Arbitration Clauses for International Contracts 236 (2d ed. 2007) (alteration in original).

On the other end of the spectrum, arbitration clauses may contain provisions that permit broad discovery.[19] Such a clause may provide for full blown U.S.-style discovery as follows:

> The parties shall allow and participate in discovery in accordance with the United States Federal Rules of Civil Procedure. Unresolved discovery disputes shall be submitted to the arbitrator(s).[20]

A similar clause might provide for discovery in accordance with the New York CPLR.

In drafting their agreements, parties should use caution when including clauses providing for discovery in accordance with the federal discovery rules or the CPLR. The parties likely will be held to their bargain resulting in an arbitration with U.S. discovery, with depositions of the parties and experts, interrogatories and requests for admissions. Careful consideration needs to be given prior to inviting such discovery devices into an international arbitration.

9.10 Though relatively uncommon in practice, the parties may also agree on certain discovery procedures after the dispute arises.[21]

3. In the Absence of an Agreement to the Contrary, Discovery in Arbitration Will Be More Limited than Discovery in Litigation in State or Federal Court

9.11 The arbitral fact-finding process usually is different from the judicial fact-finding process because rights and procedures common to civil trials, such as discovery, tend to be more limited in arbitration and may sometimes be unavailable. Indeed, the scope and availability of discovery devices is a significant differentiating factor between judicial and arbitral proceedings.

9.12 The limited availability of discovery mechanisms in arbitration clearly does not provide a basis to invalidate an agreement to arbitrate. U.S. courts repeatedly have enforced arbitration agreements despite the limited availability of discovery because "[a]lthough those procedures might not be as extensive as in the federal courts, by

[19] In 2010, the New York State Bar Association issued Guidelines stating that, for international arbitrations in New York, "there is a strong presumption against Pre-Hearing Disclosure which in any way approaches the scope of discovery which one might expect in a case which is litigated in a U.S. court." N.Y. State Bar Ass'n, Guidelines for the Arbitrator's Conduct of the Pre-Hearing Phase of International Arbitration 24 (2010), *available at* http://old.nysba.org/Content/NavigationMenu/Publications/GuidelinesforArbitration/DR_guidelines_booklet_proof_10-24-11.pdf.

[20] *See* Chapter 3.B.4(a) of this book.

[21] Although the arbitration agreement may be silent on discovery, a situation may arise where the parties agree, after the arbitration is commenced, to certain discovery procedures (e.g., extensive discovery and extended deadlines) likely to cause the arbitration to be a lengthy and costly procedure. This may cause concern to the arbitral tribunal, which has a duty under most arbitration rules to conduct the arbitration in an efficient manner. The tension between party autonomy and arbitral efficiency will be resolved on a case-by-case basis.

agreeing to arbitrate, a 'party trades the procedures and opportunity for review of the courtroom for the simplicity, informality, and expedition of arbitration.' "[22]

4. Arbitration Rules and Guidelines

While the language of the arbitration clause will be of primary importance when analyzing the scope of available discovery, international arbitration agreements frequently do not specifically address the scope of discovery in the event of a dispute. This is not surprising because it is difficult for parties to predict, let alone agree on in advance, the type of discovery that would be appropriate in the event of a future dispute. Thus, the parties usually simply specify that a particular set of arbitration rules will govern the arbitral proceedings. In such circumstances, the parties will be held to have incorporated the rules relating to discovery set forth in those arbitration rules, if any, into their arbitration agreement.[23] **9.13**

We consider in the following subsections the relevant provisions of arbitration rules commonly used in international arbitrations venued in New York.[24] Most of the rules discussed in this section have been recently amended to more comprehensively address discovery, including issues related to e-discovery. We also review the International Bar Association Rules on Taking of Evidence in International Commercial Arbitration ("IBA Rules"), which offer guidance to arbitrators and parties alike in matters of discovery even where the parties have not expressly incorporated those rules into their arbitration agreement. **9.14**

(a) International Chamber of Commerce The Rules of Arbitration of the International Chamber of Commerce ("ICC Rules")[25] do not include any express provisions concerning disclosure and discovery. Rather, they provide that "[t]he arbitral tribunal shall ... establish the facts of the case by all appropriate **9.15**

---

[22] Gilmer v. Interstate/Johnson Lane Corp., 500 U.S. 20, 31 (1991) (*quoting* Mitsubishi Motors Corp. v. Soler Chrysler-Plymouth, Inc., 473 U.S. 614, 628 (1985)); *see also* Nat'l Broad. Co. v. Bear Stearns & Co., 165 F.3d 184, 190–91 (2d Cir. 1999) ("The popularity of arbitration rests in considerable part on its asserted efficiency and cost-effectiveness—characteristics said to be at odds with full-scale litigation in the courts, and especially at odds with the broad-ranging discovery made possible by the Federal Rules of Civil Procedure." (citing Allied-Bruce Terminix Cos. v. Dobson, 513 U.S. 265, 280 (1995))); Ciago v. Ameriquest Mortgage Co., 295 F. Supp. 2d 324, 333 (S.D.N.Y. 2003) (dismissing plaintiff's argument that compelling arbitration would cripple plaintiff's ability to prove her claim due to limited discovery and would be tantamount to extinguishing her statutory rights); Commonwealth Ins. Co. v. Beneficial Corp., No. 87 Civ. 5056 (CSH), 1987 WL 17951, at *4–5 (S.D.N.Y. Sept. 29, 1987) (dismissing argument that the broad form of pretrial discovery is essential to the exposure of fraud and staying all proceedings, including pretrial discovery, pending arbitration).

[23] *See In re* Technostroyexport, 853 F. Supp. 695, 697–98 (S.D.N.Y. 1994) ("Whether or not there is to be pre-hearing discovery is a matter governed by the applicable arbitration rules (as distinct from court rules) and by what the arbitrators decide.").

[24] We focus on arbitration rules most likely to be implicated in an international arbitration venued in New York. Other sets of prominent arbitration rules, such as the London Court of International Arbitration's LCIA Arbitration Rules, may also be called into application. *See* LCIA Arb. Rules art. 22 (2014) (enumerating powers of tribunal, including those relating to discovery).

[25] Int'l Chamber of Commerce, Rules of Arbitration (2012) [hereinafter ICC Rules of Arb.].

means" and the tribunal may "[a]t any time during the proceedings ... summon any party to provide additional evidence."[26] The ICC Rules contemplate, but do not require, establishing discovery limitations at the mandatory case management conference such as establishing reasonable time limits for the production of documents and limiting the scope of document requests.[27] In addition, they provide that, where the "Rules are silent," the arbitral tribunal should follow the rules agreed upon by the parties "or, failing them, the arbitral tribunal may settle on" the applicable rules.[28] Finally, the arbitral tribunal must "act fairly and impartially and ensure that each party has a reasonable opportunity to present its case."[29] The ICC Rules therefore grant the arbitrators wide discretion to decide the scope of document discovery (both paper and electronic),[30] if any, in the absence of a specific agreement between the parties.

9.16 The ICC Commission on Arbitration's report, entitled *Techniques for Controlling Time and Costs in Arbitration*, addresses some discovery issues and recommends limiting the number and scope of document requests.[31] Specifically, the report counsels against the production of documentary evidence to prove noncontroversial facts and requests for documents that are not material to the outcome of the case.[32] Additionally, the report recommends that the parties set out the issues in full at an early stage—preferably in advance of the case management conference—with a view to enabling the arbitral tribunal to give appropriate guidance on the topics that should be addressed in documentary, witness, and expert evidence, and "the extent to which disclosure of documents by the parties is needed."[33]

---

[26] ICC Rules of Arb. arts. 25(1), 25(5).

[27] *Id.* Art. 24(1), app. IV, para. (d). Indeed, Appendix IV to the ICC Rules of Arbitration sets forth a number of "case management techniques" which include: (i) "avoiding requests for document production when appropriate in order to control time and cost," (ii) where document production is appropriate, "limiting such requests to documents or categories of documents that are relevant and material to the outcome of the case," (iii) establishing time limits for document discovery, or (iv) "using a schedule of document production to facilitate the resolution of issues in relation to the production of documents." *Id.* app. IV, para. (d)(ii)–(v).

[28] *Id.* art. 19.

[29] *Id.* art. 22(4).

[30] *See* Comm'n on Arbitration & ADR, Int'l Chamber of Commerce, Managing E-Document Production (2012) (hereinafter "ICC E-Document Report"), at 3.1–3.2, *available at* http://www.iccwbo.org/Advocacy-Codes-and-Rules/Document-centre/2012/ICC-Arbitration-Commission-Report-on-Managing-E-Document-Production/. The ICC E-Document Report notes that "a salient characteristic of arbitration is that 'rules of arbitration themselves present a framework for arbitration proceedings but rarely set out detailed procedures for the conduct of the arbitration.' This facilitates the flexibility of arbitration as a method of dispute resolution, and allows the parties and (where they cannot agree) the tribunal to decide the specific procedures for a particular dispute ... This general characteristic of arbitration applies equally to the production of documents (whether paper or electronic)." *Id.*

[31] Comm'n on Arbitration, Int'l Chamber of Commerce, Techniques for Controlling Time and Costs in Arbitration ¶¶ 52, 54 (2d ed. 2012).

[32] *Id.*

[33] *Id.* ¶ 28.

(b) International Centre for Dispute Resolution The International Arbitration Rules forming part of the International Dispute Resolution Procedures of the International Centre for Dispute Resolution (the international arm of the American Arbitration Association) ("ICDR Rules")[34] confer on arbitral tribunals the power to "[a]t any time during the proceedings ... order the parties to produce documents, exhibits, or other evidence it deems necessary or appropriate."[35] This power includes the ability to "require a party to make available to another party documents in that party's possession not otherwise available to the party seeking the documents, that are reasonably believed to exist and to be relevant and material to the outcome of the case."[36] The ICDR Rules also grant broad discretion to the arbitral tribunal, which "may conduct the arbitration in whatever manner it considers appropriate," subject to the ICDR Rules, and "provided that ... each party has the right to be heard and is given a fair opportunity to present its case."[37] **9.17**

(c) JAMS/JAMS International Rules on Evidence The JAMS/JAMS International Arbitration Rules (the "JAMS Rules") likewise confer on arbitral tribunals the authority to "[a]t any time during the proceedings ... order the parties to exchange and produce documents, exhibits or other evidence it deems necessary or appropriate."[38] The tribunal has the power to determine the "admissibility, relevance, materiality and weight of the evidence offered by any party."[39] **9.18**

In February 2011, JAMS/JAMS International adopted the *Efficiency Guidelines for the Pre-Hearing Phase of International Arbitrations* (the "JAMS Guidelines").[40] The JAMS Guidelines aim at ensuring that "JAMS International arbitrators: (i) produce a protocol for Pre-Hearing Disclosure that is specific and appropriate to the given case and is consistent with the accepted norms of international arbitration practice; and (ii) exercise sound judgment to ensure enough Pre-Hearing Disclosure and evidence to permit a fair result, balanced against the need for an efficient process."[41] Although the JAMS Guidelines contemplate that ordinarily the arbitral tribunal has discretion to determine the scope of discovery, **9.19**

[34] The most recent edition of the ICDR Rules came into force on June 1, 2014. *See* INT'L CTR. FOR DISPUTE RESOLUTION, INTERNATIONAL DISPUTE RESOLUTION PROCEDURES (INCLUDING MEDIATION AND ARBITRATION RULES) (June 1, 2014) [hereinafter ICDR ARB. RULES], *available at* https://www.icdr.org/icdr/ShowProperty?nodeId=/UCM/ADRSTAGE2020868&revision=latestreleased.

[35] ICDR ARB. RULES art. 20(4).

[36] *Id.* art. 21(4).

[37] *Id.* art. 20(1).

[38] JAMS INTERNATIONAL ARBITRATION RULES, August 1, 2011 (hereinafter "JAMS RULES"), Art. 25.2.

[39] JAMS RULES, Art. 25.4.

[40] JAMS INT'L, JAMS EFFICIENCY GUIDELINES FOR THE PRE-HEARING PHASE OF INT'L ARB. (Feb. 11, 2011) (hereinafter "JAMS GUIDELINES"), *available at* http://www.jamsadr.com/rules-international-rules/.

[41] *Id.* p. 2.

the JAMS Guidelines also provide that the parties are free to agree to unlimited discovery if they wish.[42]

9.20 The JAMS Guidelines set forth a number of factors that the arbitral tribunal should consider in determining the appropriate scope of discovery including: (i) the agreement of the parties as to the scope and duration of discovery, and the expectations of discovery under the substantive and procedural law(s) agreed upon by the parties; (ii) the characteristics and needs of the parties, including their nationality, the financial resources and financial burden on the parties, whether there is a need for urgent resolution of the matter, and whether the outcome of the dispute may impact the viability of one of the parties; (iii) the nature of the dispute; (iv) the "relevance and reasonable need for pre-hearing disclosure"; and (iv) privilege and confidentiality concerns with respect to the documents requested.[43]

9.21 *(d) U.N. Commission on International Trade Law* The recently amended Arbitration Rules of the U.N. Commission on International Trade Law ("UNCITRAL Rules") contain provisions on the production of evidence before the tribunal that are substantially similar to those included in the ICDR Rules.[44] Likewise, Article 27 of the UNCITRAL Rules provides that the "tribunal may require the parties to produce documents, exhibits or other evidence" at any time during the proceedings.[45]

9.22 *(e) International Institute for Conflict Prevention and Resolution* The International Institute for Conflict Prevention and Resolution has addressed the issue of discovery in its Rules for Administered Arbitration of International Disputes ("CPR International Rules")[46] as well as in its Protocol on Disclosure of Documents and Presentation of Witnesses in Commercial Arbitration ("CPR Protocol").[47]

9.23 The CPR International Rules grant discretion to the arbitral tribunal to "conduct the arbitration in such manner and as it shall deem appropriate,"[48] but also require that the proceedings "be conducted in an expeditious manner."[49] On discovery

---

42 *Id.*, p. 3 ("In any event, where all participants truly desire unlimited discovery, JAMS International arbitrators will respect that decision, as arbitration is governed by the agreement of the parties").

43 *Id.* at Exhibit A.

44 *See* U.N. Comm'n on Int'l Trade Law (UNCITRAL), UNCITRAL Arb. Rules art. 27 (2014) (adopted by G.A. Res. 68/109 (Dec. 16, 2013)).

45 *Id.* art. 27, § 3.

46 *See* Int'l Inst. For Conflict Prevention & Resolution (CPR), Rules for Administered Arbitration of International Disputes R. 11 (2013) [hereinafter CPR Rules for Admin. Arb. of Int'l Disps. R.]; *accord* Int'l Inst for Conflict Prevention & Resolution (CPR), Non-Administered Arbitration Rules R. 11 (2007).

47 Int'l Inst. for Conflict Prevention & Resolution (CPR), CPR Protocol on Disclosure of Documents and Presentation of Witnesses in Commercial Arbitration (2009) [hereinafter CPR Protocol].

48 CPR Rules for Non-Admin. Arb. of Int'l Disps. R. 9.1.

49 *Id.* R. 9.2.

matters, they provide that the arbitral tribunal "may require and facilitate such disclosure as it shall determine is appropriate in the circumstances, taking into account the needs of the parties and the desirability of making disclosure expeditious and cost-effective."[50] The CPR International Rules also require the tribunal to convene an initial prehearing conference, during which the tribunal may consider "the timing and manner of any required disclosure."[51]

The CPR Protocol endeavors to address a concern that the arbitral process lacks predictability, while preserving the need for efficiency and cost-effectiveness.[52] To that end, the CPR Protocol clarifies the boundaries of discovery under Rule 11 of the CPR International Rules by setting out general principles for dealing with requests for the disclosure of documents and electronic information.[53] The CPR Protocol limits disclosure to those items for which a party can demonstrate a substantial, demonstrable need and instructs the tribunal to balance the relative value of the information requested to the issues to be determined against the costs and burdens involved in production.[54] The CPR Protocol also lays out several suggested "modes" of disclosure for documents, from which the parties may choose, before or after a dispute arises, in CPR arbitrations or under other ad hoc or institutional rules.[55] The modes reflect different levels of disclosure, ranging from disclosure only of the information that each side will present at the hearing, to disclosure of information that is relevant and material to a matter of import in the proceeding for which a party has demonstrated a substantial need, or which is in the possession of witnesses, to extensive discovery subject to limitations of reasonableness, duplication and undue burden.[56] Another distinguishing feature of the CPR Protocol is that, unlike the other institutional rules addressed above, it contemplates the possibility of depositions in international arbitration. At the same time, it warns that depositions should be permitted only under limited circumstances.[57] **9.24**

[50] *Id.* R. 11.

[51] *Id.* R. 9.3, 9.3(a).

[52] CPR Protocol, *supra* note 47, at 3 (Introduction); *see also id.* § 1(a), at 5 (the CPR's philosophy underlying document disclosure is that "CPR arbitrators are expected to conduct proceedings before them in accordance with the general principle that arbitration be expeditious and cost-effective as well as fundamentally fair").

[53] *Id.* at 5 (Preamble ¶ 1).

[54] *Id.* § 1(a), (e), at 5–6, 8–9.

[55] *Id.* § 1(d)(2), at 7. Schedule 1 sets forth the various modes as follows: Mode A—No disclosure "other than the disclosure, prior to the hearing, of documents that each side will present in support of its case"; Mode B—prehearing production only of "documents essential to a matter of import in the proceeding for which a party has a substantial, demonstrable need"; Mode C—the production provided for under Mode B plus the production of "documents relating to issues in the case that are in the possession of persons who are noticed as witnesses by the party requested to provide disclosure"; Mode D—prehearing disclosure of "documents regarding non-privileged matters that are relevant to any party's claim or defense, subject to limitations of reasonableness, duplication and undue burden." CPR Protocol Sched. 1, at 10.

[56] *Id.*, Sched. 1, at 10.

[57] *Id.*, § 2(c), at 14.

9.25 *(f) The International Bar Association's Rules on Taking of Evidence in International Commercial Arbitration* Arbitration clauses sometimes provide that the IBA Rules on the Taking of Evidence ("IBA Rules") will apply to discovery. These rules are "intended to provide an efficient, economical and fair process for the taking of evidence in international arbitrations."[58] They are designed to be used in conjunction with and adopted together with institution or ad hoc rules or procedures governing international arbitrations. Even when the IBA Rules do not explicitly govern discovery in an arbitration (because they have not been incorporated by reference in the arbitration agreement), arbitrators and parties often look to them for guidance.

9.26 The IBA Rules adopt a restrictive approach to paper and electronic discovery, authorizing production of "a narrow and specific" category of documents that are "relevant to the case and material to its outcome."[59] This conservative standard was intentional on the part of the drafters who were concerned that U.S.-style discovery not become the norm in international arbitration.[60]

9.27 Article 2 provides for a mandatory consultation between the arbitral tribunal and the parties "at the earliest appropriate time in the proceedings" to address evidentiary issues, such as the "scope, timing and manner of taking of evidence."[61] As the Comment to the 2010 IBA Rules explains, such "[e]arly timing allows the participants to organise the taking of evidence in an efficient, economical and fair manner."[62]

9.28 Article 3.1 provides for the production by each party, within the time ordered by the arbitral tribunal, of all documents on which it intends to rely to support its case.[63] A party may request, and the arbitral tribunal has authority to order, the production

---

[58] Int'l Bar Ass'n, IBA Rules on the Taking of Evidence in International Commercial Arbitration, Preamble (May 29, 2010) [hereinafter IBA R. Evid.], *available at* http://www.ibanet.org/Publications/publications_IBA_guides_and_free_materials.aspx.

[59] IBA R. Evid., Art. 3.3. For information specific to e-discovery, see *supra* Section C.1.(b).

[60] *See* 1999 IBA Working Party & 2010 IBA Rules of Evidence Review Subcommittee, *Commentary on the revised text of the 2010 IBA Rules on the Taking of Evidence in International Arbitration*, [hereinafter "IBA Rules Commentary"], *available at* http://www.ibanet.org/Publications/publications_IBA_guides_ and_free_materials.aspx ("These rules ... represent a well-balanced compromise between the broader view generally taken in common law countries and the more narrow view held generally in civil law countries.").

[61] IBA R. Evid., Art. 2.2. states that "[t]he consultation on evidentiary issues may address the scope, timing and manner of the taking of evidence, including:

(a) the preparation and submission of Witness Statements and Expert Reports;
(b) the taking of oral testimony at any Evidentiary Hearing;
(c) the requirements, procedure and format applicable to the production of Documents;
(d) the level of confidentiality protection to be afforded to evidence in the arbitration; and
(e) the promotion of efficiency, economy and conservation of resources in connection with the taking of evidence."

[62] IBA Rules Commentary, at 5.

[63] IBA R. Evid. Art. 3.1.

of either a specifically identified document, or "a narrow and specific requested category of Documents that are reasonably believed to exist," provided (1) the documents are not in the possession, custody and control of the requesting party, (2) the "Documents requested are relevant to the case and material to its outcome," and (3) production is not objectionable under Article 9.2.[64] Article 9.2 instructs the arbitral tribunal to "exclude from evidence or production any Document" on relevance, materiality, burden, privilege, fairness and other listed grounds.[65]

Parties and arbitrators determine which documents are "relevant and material," as well as what constitutes a "narrow and specific" category of documents for document requests that are not limited to specific documents. Given the guiding principle of "prevent[ing] a broad 'fishing expedition' while [still] permitting parties to request critical documents," broad discovery under the IBA Rules is unlikely to be permitted.[66] **9.29**

5. The Discretion of the Arbitral Tribunal

As is evident from the foregoing discussion of the law and rules, international arbitral tribunals generally have broad discretion to decide procedural matters, including discovery.[67] International arbitration, by its nature, involves parties from different jurisdictions and legal traditions. Indeed, international arbitrations venued in New York may involve not only parties from the United States and other common law jurisdictions, but also parties from civil law jurisdictions. The parties to an international arbitration venued in New York often, but not always, retain U.S. counsel. In addition, the arbitral tribunal may be constituted by arbitrators from different legal traditions. **9.30**

---

[64] IBA R. Evid. Arts. 3.4–7.

[65] IBA R. Evid. Art. 9.2 provides: "The Arbitral Tribunal shall, at the request of a Party or on its own motion, exclude from evidence or production any Document, statement, oral testimony or inspection for any of the following reasons:

(a) lack of sufficient relevance to the case or materiality to its outcome;
(b) legal impediment or privilege under the legal or ethical rules determined by the Arbitral Tribunal to be applicable;
(c) unreasonable burden to produce the requested evidence;
(d) loss or destruction of the Document that has been shown with reasonable likelihood to have occurred;
(e) grounds of commercial or technical confidentiality that the Arbitral Tribunal determines to be compelling;
(f) grounds of special political or institutional sensitivity (including evidence that has been classified as secret by a government or a public international institution) that the Arbitral Tribunal determines to be compelling; or
(g) considerations of procedural economy, proportionality, fairness or equality of the Parties that the Arbitral Tribunal determines to be compelling."

[66] IBA Rules Commentary, at 8.

[67] *See* InterChem Asia 2000 Pte. Ltd. v. Oceana Petrochemicals, AG, 373 F. Supp. 2d 340, 352 (S.D.N.Y. 2005) ("[A]ny and all decisions concerning the procedure of the arbitration, including any discovery procedures, were well within the Arbitrator's discretion."), *amended on other grounds*, 378 F. Supp. 2d 347 (S.D.N.Y. 2005); Mallory Factor Inc. v. W. Coast Entm't Corp., No. 99 CIV.

9.31 Parties, counsel and arbitrators in an international arbitration venued in New York, therefore, may not share a common legal culture, and in fact may have differing approaches to procedural matters and the process of sharing information about a claim and the proof of such claim. While the differences in matters of procedure and underlying assumptions are most significant between broadly defined common law and civil traditions,[68] even among common law jurisdictions, where the concept of discovery generally is known in one form or another, U.S. discovery is unique in its breadth and significance to the proceeding.[69] Different assumptions and practices in matters of discovery come together in international arbitration, and the arbitral tribunal will shape the discovery process based on the arbitration agreement, applicable arbitration rules and guidelines, and, of course, the parties' views.

9.32 Based on the applicable arbitration rules and the submissions of the parties, the arbitral tribunal will prepare a procedural order setting forth the timetable for the arbitration proceeding, including discovery. We next consider a number of specific issues that may arise as discovery proceeds, including the availability of various discovery devices.

C. DISCOVERY BETWEEN THE PARTIES

1. Document Discovery

9.33 *(a) Documents in "hard copy" form* In most international arbitrations venued in New York, parties exchange discovery requests seeking the production of documents[70] and, therefore, questions may arise concerning the permissible

4819(JFK), 1999 WL 1021076, at *3 (S.D.N.Y. Nov. 9, 1999) ("[T]he Arbitrator has wide discretion in determining whether or not to hear evidence at the hearing" and the arbitrator had ensured that "[b]oth parties were permitted to present evidence and to cross-examine adverse witnesses. The Court concludes that there is simply no indication that [the losing party] was denied a fundamentally fair hearing."); Int'l Longshoremen's Ass'n v. W. Gulf Mar. Ass'n, 605 F. Supp. 723, 727 (S.D.N.Y. 1985) ("Resolution of the procedural matters arising out of arbitration are generally left to the arbitrator.").

[68] *See generally* Siegfried H. Elsing & John M. Townsend, *Bridging the Common Law – Civil Law Divide in Arbitration*, 18 Arb. Int'l 59 (2002); 2 Gary B. Born, International Commercial Arbitration 2343–45 (2d ed. 2014).

[69] *See* Robert H. Smit, *Towards Greater Efficiency in Document Production Before Arbitral Tribunals—A North American Viewpoint*, in Document Production in International Arbitration 93, 93 (ICC Int'l Ct. of Arb. Bull. Spec. Supp. 2006) ("Discovery, in the US sense, is a dirty word in international arbitration ... US document production procedures have rarely been viewed as a model for wholesale adoption in international arbitration. Neither, however, can the benefits of US-style document discovery, in terms of truth-finding in particular, be entirely disregarded."); V.V. Veeder, *Document Production in England: Legislative Developments and Current Arbitral Practice*, in Document Production in International Arbitration 57, 57–61 (ICC Int'l Ct. of Arb. Bull. Spec. Supp. 2006) (describing the procedural revolution over the last twenty years in documentary requests in England, in both litigation and international commercial arbitration).

[70] The IBA Rules define "document" as "a writing, communication, picture, drawing, program or data of any kind, whether recorded or maintained on paper or by electronic, audio, visual or any other means." IBA R. Evid. at 4 (Definitions).

scope of document discovery, as well as how one responds to a demand for the production of documents and how discovery disputes should be resolved.

As a preliminary matter, parties usually submit all documents on which they rely to the arbitral tribunal and to the other party within the time ordered by the arbitral tribunal and, in any event, before the hearing.[71] Document discovery requests often precede the production of such documents, but it is also possible that an initial exchange of documents will take place before the parties submit document requests to each other. Document requests may take the form of an informal letter request for the production of documents or may be set forth in a more formal request.[72] Such requests generally will target specific documents or specific categories of documents in order not to be seen as overly broad and violative of the overarching principle that discovery in international arbitration is typically more limited than discovery in civil litigation venued in New York.[73] **9.34**

Using the IBA Rules as an illustration, the documents sought must be described sufficiently to identify them, and if documents are requested by category, then the request must describe "in sufficient detail" a "narrow and specific" category of documents "that are reasonably believed to exist."[74] The requesting party must also explain "how the Documents requested are relevant to the case and material to its outcome."[75] Finally, the requesting party must state that the documents are not in its "possession, custody or control" and the reasons why the requesting party believes the documents "are in the possession, custody or control of another Party."[76] **9.35**

A receiving party should, at a minimum, respond to the document requests with a letter addressing such request; oftentimes, however, the response will consist of a more formal response detailing precisely the requests to which the party is willing to respond and the requests to which it objects and is not willing to respond. If the parties are not able to reach a compromise concerning the request (or certain **9.36**

---

[71] *See, e.g., id.* art. 3(1); ICDR Rules art. 21(3); Am. Arbitration Ass'n (AAA), Commercial Arbitration Rules and Mediation Procedures, R-22 (2013) [hereinafter AAA Commercial Rules], *available at* https://www.adr.org/aaa/ShowProperty?nodeId=/UCM/ADRSTG_004103. This is not unlike what Rule 26(a) of the Federal Rules of Civil Procedure, governing initial disclosures required of parties to federal litigation, was intended to accomplish. *See* Fed. R. Civ. P. 26(a).

[72] Depending on the provisions of the applicable procedural order, the parties may exchange document requests between themselves and possibly provide a copy to the arbitral tribunal, or they will submit the document requests to the arbitral tribunal. Article 3 of the IBA Rules, for example, provides that any party may submit a so-called "Request to Produce," both to the tribunal and to the other parties. IBA R. Evid. art. 3(2).

[73] *See, e.g.,* JAMS Guidelines, *supra* note 40, at 2.

[74] IBA R. Evid. art. 3(3)(a).

[75] *Id.* art. 3(3)(b); *see also* AAA Commercial Rules, R-22(b)(iii) (granting arbitrator authority to impose similar requirements); JAMS Guidelines, *supra* note 40, at 2 ("Arbitrators [should] explain at the first pre-hearing conference that document requests should be limited to documents that are directly relevant to significant issues in the case or to the case's outcome.").

[76] IBA R. Evid., art. 3(3)(c)(i), (ii).

aspects of the request), they will seek the assistance of the arbitral tribunal. Typically, the arbitral tribunal will respond to such disagreements by issuing a written ruling based on the parties' correspondence, sometimes after holding a hearing (in person or by telephone), and determining whether the scope of the request for documents is permissible given the context of the request and the rules governing the arbitration. The IBA Rules set forth specific criteria for making this determination and enumerate grounds on which production of documents shall be denied, such as lack of relevance, privilege, undue burden, confidentiality and unfairness or inequality.[77]

9.37 By contrast, in those uncommon international arbitrations where the parties have agreed that discovery should be governed by the Federal Rules of Civil Procedure or the CPLR, document discovery can be expected to be more formal and more extensive. The request itself would describe the categories of documents sought and specify a time and place of the inspection and might specify the form of production.[78] Document requests under the Federal Rules of Civil Procedure and the CPLR are typically much broader than would be the norm in an arbitration governed by the rules of an arbitral institution or the IBA Rules.

9.38 Additionally, counsel to the parties may themselves have some responsibility for ensuring their clients' compliance with discovery obligations. Recently, the IBA has promulgated Guidelines on Party Representation in International Arbitration, which include a provision on "Information Exchange and Disclosure" stating that a "Party Representative should inform the client of the need to preserve, so far as reasonably possible" documents, if the proceedings "involve or are likely to involve Document production."[79] The IBA Arbitration Committee suggested in its comments that providing a universal standard may help to reduce some of the disparity between parties' respective understandings of the need to preserve

---

[77] The IBA R. Evid., art. 9(2) provide: "The Arbitral Tribunal shall, at the request of a Party or on its own motion, exclude from evidence or production any Document, statement, oral testimony or inspection for any of the following reasons:

(a) lack of sufficient relevance to the case or materiality to its outcome;
(b) legal impediment or privilege under the legal or ethical rules determined by the Arbitral Tribunal to be applicable;
(c) unreasonable burden to produce the requested evidence;
(d) loss or destruction of the Document that has been shown within reasonable likelihood to have occurred;
(e) grounds of commercial or technical confidentiality that the Arbitral Tribunal determines to be compelling;
(f) grounds of special political or institutional sensitivity (including evidence that has been classified as secret by a government or a public international institution) that the Arbitral Tribunal determines to be compelling; or
(g) considerations of procedural economy, proportionality, fairness or equality of the Parties that the Arbitral Tribunal determines to be compelling."

[78] *See* Fed. R. Civ. P. 34(b)(1); N.Y. C.P.L.R. 3120(1), (2) (McKinney 2014).

[79] IBA Guidelines on Party Representation in International Arbitration 10 (May 25, 2013) [hereinafter IBA Guidelines on Party Representation].

documents in international arbitral proceedings.[80] The comments make clear that counsel has an obligation not to encourage bad faith conduct in discovery and "should not make a Request to Produce, or object to a Request to Produce, when such request or objection is only aimed at harassing, obtaining documents for purposes extraneous to the arbitration, or causing unnecessary delay."[81]

(b) Electronically stored documents and information The term "document" is generally defined to include electronically stored information ("ESI").[82] ESI differs in significant ways from traditional paper documents and has important implications for discovery, which warrants separate consideration.[83] The accessibility of ESI depends heavily on the media on which it is stored.[84] It is relatively inexpensive to generate and store ESI, which means companies and individuals tend to accumulate large quantities of ESI with the result that such information is technically "available" to be produced in an appropriate case. **9.39**

Several arbitral institutions have issued rules that deal specifically with e-discovery and would be binding on the parties, while others have issued non-binding, but likely persuasive, guidelines.[85] **9.40**

For example, in 2014, the ICDR updated its Rules to incorporate its previous guidelines to e-discovery. Under the new ICDR Rules, arbitral tribunals must "manage the exchange of information between the parties with a view of maintaining efficiency and economy ... while at the same time avoiding surprise, assuring equality of treatment, and safeguarding each party's opportunity to present its claims and defenses fairly."[86] As such, the ICDR Rules mandate that a **9.41**

[80] *Id.* at 11–12. The comments suggest that a party representative should advise its client to preserve "potentially relevant Documents," which may be broader than the scope of documents actually subject to disclosure. *Id.* at 13.

[81] *Id.* at 13.

[82] *See, e.g.*, IBA R. at 4 (Definition); Fed. R. Civ. P. 34(a)(1)(A); N.Y. C.P.L.R. 3120 cmt. C3120:2A (McKinney Supp. 2014).

[83] *See* Jonathan L. Frank & Julie Bédard, *Electronic Discovery in International Arbitration: Where Neither the IBA Rules Nor U.S. Litigation Principles Are Enough*, Disp. Resol. J., Nov. 2007/Jan. 2008, at 62, 63–65. *See also* Chapter 2.E.4.

[84] In order of accessibility, ESI can be actively stored on hard drives, optical disks and other removable media in robotic storage devices, on manually accessed optical disks and other similar media, or on compressed back-up tapes. ESI can also be found in a fragmented, corrupted or erased state and may only be partially recoverable. *See* Zubulake v. UBS Warburg LLC, 217 F.R.D. 309, 318–20 (S.D.N.Y. 2003). In this regard, ESI is not as easy to dispose of as are paper documents. Even when one deletes a file or an e-mail, it does not mean that the document does not continue to exist in a back-up disk or in some other location. Even data that a user does not intend to retain, such as instant messages, may still exist and be available in discovery. Not only may the final draft be obtainable, but so may all the previous drafts and edits. Moreover, ESI often contains metadata, which can, in certain circumstances, be mined to discover virtually every edit or keystroke entered with regard to a particular document.

[85] *See* Julie Bédard & Jonathan L. Frank, *Electronic Discovery in International Arbitration (Revisited)*, *in* ICDR Awards and Commentaries 35, 48–50 (Grant Hanessian ed., 2012).

[86] ICDR Arb Rules art. 21(1).

party in possession of ESI "may make [it] available in the form (which may be paper copies) most convenient and economical for it, unless the tribunal determines, on application, that there is a compelling need for access to the documents in a different form."[87] Furthermore, requests for ESI "should be narrowly focused and structured to make searching for [it] as economical as possible."[88] Indeed, the "tribunal may direct testing or other means of focusing and limiting any search,"[89] including requiring "a requesting party to justify the time and expense that its request may involve and may condition granting such a request on the payment of part or all of the cost by the party seeking the information."[90]

9.42 JAMS/JAMS International has issued guidelines that deal specifically with limiting e-discovery.[91] The JAMS Guidelines, adopted in February 2011, contemplate that arbitral tribunals will issue an early order addressing the scope of e-discovery,[92] and empower tribunals to either deny an e-discovery request or perform cost-shifting when the burden of compliance becomes "disproportionate to the nature and gravity of the dispute or to the amount in controversy, or to the relevance of the materials requested."[93]

9.43 The *IBA Rules on the Taking of Evidence in International Commercial Arbitration*, were amended in May 2010, in part, to address e-discovery in more detail. The IBA Rules had previously encompassed e-discovery to some degree: the earlier iteration of the IBA Rules defined a "document" as "a writing of any kind, whether recorded on paper, *electronic means*, audio or visual recordings or any other mechanical or electronic means of storing or recording information."[94] The 2010 edition of the rules has further clarified best practices with regard to e-discovery by broadening the definition of terms like "document"[95] and adding specific provisions purporting to address the problems presented by e-discovery.

9.44 Thus, Article 3 provides that "in the case of Documents maintained in electronic form, the requesting Party may, or the Arbitral Tribunal may order that it shall be required to, identify specific files, search terms, individuals or other means

[87] *Id.* art. 21(6).

[88] *Id.*

[89] *Id.*

[90] *Id.* art. 21(8).

[91] JAMS GUIDELINES, *supra* note 40, at 3 ("In any event, where all participants truly desire unlimited discovery, JAMS International arbitrators will respect that decision, as arbitration is governed by the agreement of the parties.").

[92] *See id.* at 3.

[93] *Id.* at 4.

[94] INT'L BAR ASS'N, IBA RULES ON THE TAKING OF EVIDENCE IN INTERNATIONAL COMMERCIAL ARBITRATION art. 1 (1999) (Definitions) (emphasis added), *superseded by* INT'L BAR ASS'N, IBA RULES ON THE TAKING OF EVIDENCE IN INTERNATIONAL ARBITRATION (2010).

[95] Under the most recent iteration of the IBA Rules, "document" is defined as "a writing, communication, picture, drawing, *program or data of any kind*, whether recorded or maintained on paper or by electronic, audio, visual or any other means." IBA R. EVID. at 4 (Definitions) (emphasis added).

of searching for such Documents in an efficient and economical manner"[96] and Article 12(b) states that "Documents that a Party maintains in electronic form shall be submitted or produced in the form most convenient or economical to it that is reasonably usable by the recipients."[97] The 2010 IBA Rules place greater responsibility on arbitral tribunals in resolving e-discovery requests: for example, the IBA Rules now mandate tribunals to confer with parties as early as possible to establish the scope of document discovery, including e-discovery.[98] The IBA Rules also newly empower tribunals to engage in acts such as cost-shifting the expense of e-discovery requests to combat abuse from overly burdensome requirements of compliance with e-discovery.[99]

Other arbitral institutions have set forth non-binding guidelines on e-discovery. For example, the CPR Protocol deals extensively with the problems of electronically stored information and attempts to address the high cost involved in the production of such information.[100] The CPR Protocol also lays out several suggested "modes" of disclosure for electronic documents.[101] The Chartered Institute of Arbitrators *Protocol for E-Disclosure in Arbitration* also provided guidance for electronic disclosure.[102] **9.45**

In its 2012 ICC E-Document Report, the ICC Commission follows the lead of the IBA Rules, noting that "[a]s reflected in the IBA Rules of Evidence, the same principles of specificity, relevance, materiality and proportionality apply to the production of both paper and electronic documents."[103] The ICC E-Document Report serves as a compendium of current international arbitration rules on e-discovery and a primer on considerations, definitions and suggestions for parties **9.46**

---

96 IBA R. Evid., art. 3(3)(a).

97 *Id.* art. 3(12)(b).

98 *Id.* art. 2(1).

99 *Id.* art. 9(7).

100 The CPR Protocol recommends granting production of electronic materials from a wide range of users or custodians only upon a showing of extraordinary need. Similarly, it provides that "[r]equests for back-up tapes, or fragmented or deleted files should only be granted if the requesting party can demonstrate a reasonable likelihood that files were deliberately destroyed or altered by a party in anticipation of litigation or arbitration and outside of that party's document retention policies operated in good faith." CPR Protocol, *supra* note 47, § 1(d), at 7.

101 The various modes of disclosure of electronic information range from disclosure only of the electronic information to be presented in support of that party's case, to disclosure, in reasonably usable form, of electronic information maintained by no more than a specified number of designated custodians and only from primary storage facilities (thus excluding back-up tapes, cell phones, voicemails, etc.) for the time period between the date of the signing of the agreement to the filing of the request for arbitration, to similar disclosure but covering a larger number of custodians and a wider time period, and finally, to disclosure of electronic information regarding nonprivileged matters that are relevant to any party's claim or defense, subject to customary limitations of reasonableness, duplicativeness and undue burden. *Id.* § 1 (Schedule 2), at 11.

102 Chartered Inst. of Arbitrators, Protocol for E-Disclosure in Arbitration (Oct. 2008), *available at* https://www.ciarb.org/docs/default-source/practice-guidelines-protocols-and-rules/e-discolusure-in-arbitration.pdf?sfvrsn=2.

103 *Id.* § 2.1.

and arbitrators less familiar with ESI, but unlike the IBA Rules, the ICDR Rules, and the JAMS Guidelines, the ICC E-Document Report does not purport to be a collection of "rules" or "guidelines" about the conduct of document discovery in arbitral proceedings.[104] The ICC E-Document Report was designed as a collection of resources rather than a source of rules, which aligns with the ICC Rules of Arbitration, which themselves do not feature any provisions on the production of documents.[105]

9.47 Of note, the Federal Rules of Civil Procedure were amended in 2006 to address specifically the production of ESI. With regard to ESI, "a party must produce it in a form or forms in which it is ordinarily maintained or in a reasonably usable form or forms," but in either case need not produce the same ESI in multiple forms.[106] A disclosing party, however, need not produce ESI if it can prove in response to a motion to compel that the ESI "is not reasonably accessible because of undue burden or cost," but the requesting party may, in an appropriate case, trump this for good cause shown.[107]

9.48 In addition, from 2012 to 2014, the U.S. Committee on Rules and Procedure of the Judicial Conference Advisory Committee on Civil Rules suggested further amendments to the Federal Rules of Civil Procedure to deal with electronic discovery.[108] The Committee has recently concluded its review and recommended that the Judicial Conference approve the amendments and transmit them to the United States Supreme Court for approval—the last step before amendments to the Federal Rules are codified into law.[109] Some of the proposed amendments relevant to electronic discovery are:

- Amendments to Federal Rule of Civil Procedure 1 would attempt to introduce the notion of "cooperation" between parties into the Federal Rules of Civil Procedure, which may discourage abusive use of e-discovery.[110]

---

104 *Id.* § 2.2.

105 *Id.* § 3.4.

106 Fed. R. Civ. P. 34(b)(2)(E)(ii), (iii).

107 Fed. R. Civ. P. 26(b)(2)(B); *see also* Fed. R. Civ. P. 26(b)(2)(C).

108 Amendments to Federal Rule of Civil Procedure 34 (along with amendments to Rules 1, 4, 16, 26, 30, 31, 33, 37, and 55) have been recommended by the Judicial Conference Committee on Rules of Practice and Procedure for approval by the Judicial Conference of the United States and transmission to the United States Supreme Court, with a recommendation for their adoption by the Court. *See* Report of the Judicial Conference Committee on Rules of Practice and Procedure 13, 17 (Sept. 2014) (Agenda E-19) [hereinafter "Sept. 2014 Report on Rules of Practice and Procedure"), *available at* http://www.uscourts.gov/uscourts/RulesAndPolicies/rules/Reports/ST09-2014.pdf.

109 *See* Sept. 2014 Report on Rules of Practice and Procedure, *supra* note 108, at 13, 17.

110 *See id.* app. B, at B-13 ("Rule 1 now provides that the civil rules 'should be construed and administered to secure the just, speedy, and inexpensive determination of every action and proceeding.' The proposed amendment would provide that the rules 'be construed, administered, and employed by the court and the parties to secure the just, speedy, and inexpensive determination of every action and proceeding.'").

- Amendments to Rule 26(b)(1) would narrow the scope of discoverable information, requiring that "[p]arties may obtain discovery regarding any nonprivileged matter that is relevant to any party's claim or defense and *proportional to the needs of the case*, considering the importance of the issues at stake in the action, the amount in controversy, the parties' relative access to relevant information, the parties' resources, the importance of the discovery in resolving the issues, and whether the burden or expense of the proposed discovery outweighs its likely benefit."[111]
- Amendments to Rule 26(c) would empower courts to cost-shift.[112]
- Amendments to Rule 37(e) would expand the scope of sanctions for failure to preserve ESI.[113]

However, it is by no means apparent that any Federal Rules amendments will or should have any impact on e-discovery in international arbitrations, particularly where discovery is not governed by the Federal Rules of Civil Procedure. **9.49**

Taken together, when deciding whether to allow discovery of ESI, and if so, how to determine its scope or allocate its cost, arbitral tribunals can be expected to look to the specificity of the request, the materiality of the data sought, the lack of availability to the requesting party, the basis for believing that the other party has the information, and the financial burdens generated by the request. The last factor naturally includes consideration of the cost of producing the documents, which will depend upon their accessibility. Not only is it expensive to conduct searches of easily accessible data, but often outside vendors and data recovery specialists will have to be employed to gather information from less accessible media. Discovery requiring the recovery of data that is not otherwise readily accessible is often considered to be contrary to the goals of economy and efficiency of international arbitration. Nevertheless, it is not unheard of for parties to large and complex international arbitrations venued in New York to engage in extensive discovery involving ESI, including data recovery, especially if they both are represented by U.S. counsel. **9.50**

(c) Consequences of a party's failure to produce documents As in litigation, parties to an arbitration sometimes fail to produce documents in response to unobjectionable document requests or as directed by the arbitral tribunal. Arbitrators do not have the same clear authority as judges to compel production of documents. However, as noted before (*supra* at Section B.1.(a)), Section 7 of the FAA authorizes arbitral tribunals to order witness testimony and document production, and permits arbitrators "to seek judicial assistance" in compelling compliance.[114] In addition, arbitral tribunals have developed other methods to ensure compliance. **9.51**

---

[111] *Id.* app. B, at B-5 (emphasis added).

[112] *Id.* app. B, at B-10–11.

[113] *Id.* app. B, at B-14.

[114] 2 Gary R. Born, International Commercial Arbitration 2327 (2d ed. 2014); *see* 9 U.S.C. § 7 (2012) ("The arbitrators ... or a majority of them, may summon in writing any person to attend before them or any of them as a witness and in a proper case to bring with him or them

9.52 The tribunal's ability to impose negative or adverse inferences against the party that fails to produce may provide the most powerful incentive for the parties to comply with discovery orders.[115] Both the IBA Rules and the ICDR Rules unambiguously provide that the tribunal may draw adverse inferences from a party's failure to produce documents.[116] Although the practice of using adverse

---

any book, record, document, or paper which may be deemed material as evidence in the case ... Said summons shall issue in the name of the arbitrator or arbitrators, or a majority of them, and shall be signed by the arbitrators, or a majority of them, and shall be directed to the said person and shall be served in the same manner as subpoenas to appear and testify before the court; if any person or persons so summoned to testify shall refuse or neglect to obey said summons, upon petition the United States district court for the district in which such arbitrators, or a majority of them, are sitting may compel the attendance of such person or persons before said arbitrator or arbitrators, or punish said person or persons for contempt in the same manner provided by law for securing the attendance of witnesses or their punishment for neglect or refusal to attend in the courts of the United States.").

[115] *See* Jan Paulsson, *Overview of Methods of Presenting Evidence in Different Legal Systems*, in PLANNING EFFICIENT ARBITRATION PROCEEDINGS: THE LAW APPLICABLE IN INTERNATIONAL ARBITRATION 112, 117 (Albert Jan van den Berg, gen. ed., ICCA Cong. Series No. 7, 1996) ("The objection that arbitrators have no powers of coercion is not persuasive; the threat of drawing adverse inferences from the fact of non-production, although not the fearsome weapon some lawyers seem to imagine, given the fact that most arbitrators would be disturbed at the thought of deeming the burden of proof discharged by an inference, is yet not an idle one."). One arbitral tribunal in a domestic arbitration venued in New York sanctioned a party for its failure to comply with an order directing the production of documents by "precluding the testimony of a witness and the introduction of evidence to which the undisclosed documents related." Glen Rauch Sec., Inc. v. Weinraub, 768 N.Y.S.2d 611, 611 (App. Div. 2003); *see also id.* (affirming the lower court decision confirming an arbitration award, and concluding that the arbitrators' sanction for failure to comply with an arbitral discovery order was proper where the arbitrator precluded a witness's testimony and evidence related to the undisclosed documents).

[116] *See* IBA R. EVID. art. 9(5); ICDR ARB. RULES arts. 20(7) and 21(9). The ICDR Rules also provide that the tribunal may take the failure to comply with an order for information exchange "into account in allocating costs." *Id.* art. 21(9). The authority is split on the issue of whether an arbitrator may sanction a party's failure to produce documents in its award on costs. *See, e.g.*, InterChem Asia 2000 Pte. Ltd. v. Oceana Petrochemicals AG, 373 F. Supp. 2d 340, 358 (S.D.N.Y. 2005) ("[F]inding that the Arbitrator had inherent authority to sanction [a party for its failure to produce documents by awarding attorneys' fees to the other party] would directly contradict the principle that an arbitrator's authority is circumscribed by the agreement of the parties."), *amended on other grounds*, 378 F. Supp. 2d 347 (S.D.N.Y. 2005); *but see* Szczepanek v. Dabek, No. 10-cv-2459(SJF)(ARL), 2011 WL 846193, at *3 n.2 (E.D.N.Y. Mar. 7, 2011) (noting that a party may not have been able to challenge award of attorneys' fees for discovery abuses because the "broad arbitration clause" granted the arbitrator authority to sanction parties acting in bad faith), *aff'd*, 465 F. App'x 74 (2d Cir. 2013); McDaniel v. Bear Stearns & Co., 196 F. Supp. 2d 343, 364 (S.D.N.Y. 2002) (confirming an arbitral decision awarding $75,000 in attorneys' fees and prejudgment interest as a discovery sanction under Section VIII of the Notice of the National Association of Securities Dealers, Inc. to members authorizing arbitrators to award attorneys' fees as a sanction for failure of a party to properly make discovery unless they find that there is substantial justification for the failure). *See also* ReliaStar Life Ins. Co. of N.Y. v. EMC Nat'l Life Co., 564 F.3d 81, 86 (2d Cir. 2009) (upholding an arbitral award of fees and costs against a party because the existence of "a broad arbitration clause ... confers inherent authority on arbitrators to sanction a party that participates in the arbitration in bad faith [where bad faith was evidenced by a party's initiation of an action in order to evade obligations under an existing agreement and sanctions] may include an award of attorney's or arbitrator's fees"); Chase Bank USA, N.A. v. Hale, 859 N.Y.S.2d 342, 347, 350-52 (Sup. Ct. 2008) (a recognized exception to the general "American Rule" that each party bears its own costs may be found where one of the parties has engaged in "bad faith" conduct, and Rule 46 of the National Arbitration Forum Code permits arbitrators to sanction offending parties and order payments of fees and costs for violating arbitral rules or orders; affirming an arbitral tribunal's imposition of attorneys' fees).

inferences is well known in international arbitration, the tribunal may provide notice to the parties in the procedural order on document production that failure to comply with the order could result in an adverse inference being drawn against the delinquent party.[117]

More often than not, parties will comply with document production orders in arbitration in order to preserve their credibility. Nonetheless, adverse inferences provide an important sanction for arbitral tribunals in enforcing arbitral discovery orders.[118] **9.53**

2. Availability of Depositions

Depositions, where counsel for one party questions either the opposing party or a third-party under oath and outside the presence of a judicial officer, are a major feature of pretrial discovery in U.S. litigation.[119] However, unless the arbitration agreement provides otherwise,[120] depositions generally are not available in international arbitration. None of the major arbitral rules or the IBA Rules provides for prehearing depositions. The CPR Protocol states that discovery depositions should be permitted "only where the testimony is expected to be material to the outcome of the case and where [certain] exigent circumstances apply,"[121] and the ICDR has gone so far as to take the position that "[d]epositions, interrogatories, and requests to admit as developed for use in [U.S.] court procedures generally are not appropriate procedures for obtaining information in [international arbitration]."[122] The JAMS Guidelines disfavor **9.54**

---

117 A survey of eighty document production orders in ICC arbitrations in 2003–2004 shows that eight procedural orders referred to the practice of drawing negative inferences as a result of a failure to produce, including five that specifically warned that the tribunal "would or could draw appropriate conclusions from a party's refusal to produce the documents requested." Virginia Hamilton, *Document Production in ICC Arbitration*, in Document Production in International Arbitration 80–81 (ICC Int'l Ct. of Arb. Bull. Spec. Supp. 2006).

118 *See* Robert B. von Mehren, *Burden of Proof in International Arbitration, in* Planning Efficient Arbitration Proceedings: The Law Applicable in International Arbitration 123, 129 (Albert Jan van den Berg, gen. ed., ICCA Cong. Series No. 7, 1996).

119 The deposition of a witness occurs before trial and is generally not held before the judge. Rather, it is often held in the office of an attorney in the case; questions are answered under oath and recorded by a court reporter, who creates a deposition transcript. Increasingly, depositions are videotaped. A deponent may be represented by an attorney. At trial, deposition testimony can be used, among other things, to cast doubt on a witness's contradictory trial testimony. If a deposed witness is unavailable when the trial takes place—for example, if he or she has died or otherwise cannot be compelled to appear—the deposition may be read to the jury in place of live testimony.

120 Consider, for example, the following clause: "Depositions may be ordered by the arbitrators upon a showing of need."

121 CPR Protocol, *supra* note 47, § 2(c), at 14. Exigent circumstances are described as follows: "Witness statements are not being used, the parties agree to the taking of the deposition and/or the witness may not be available to testify, in person or by telecommunication, before the tribunal." *Id.* The CPR Protocol further provides that "[t]he tribunal should impose strict limits on the number and length of any depositions allowed." *Id.*

122 ICDR Arb. Rules, art. 21(10).

the use of depositions (or U.S. discovery devices such as interrogatories and requests to admit) in international arbitrations.[123] Parties whose arbitration agreement incorporates the Federal Rules of Civil Procedure or the CPLR, however, should be aware that both sets of rules provide for the taking of depositions, both orally and on written questions.[124] In practice, depositions of parties to an international arbitration are the exception, not the rule, and usually occur only by mutual assent of the parties.[125]

3. Other Discovery Devices

9.55 Discovery under the Federal Rules of Civil Procedure or the CPLR also includes additional discovery devices such as requests to admit and interrogatories.[126] Such devices are rarely employed in an international arbitration and, as noted previously, are generally disfavored.[127]

4. Privilege

9.56 Issues relating to claims of privilege frequently arise during the discovery process in international arbitration, as they do in litigation. In international arbitration, however, privilege issues are complicated by the fact that the arbitrators, and the parties and their counsel, may arrive at arbitration from differing legal traditions. In such circumstances, the tribunal will need to decide whether it will respect the legal privilege rules of the parties (which may be completely different in concept and in scope for each of the parties) or the ethical duties of their counsel (who may be admitted to practice law in jurisdictions where privilege is treated as a professional or ethical obligation as opposed to an evidentiary matter), or whether the tribunal will enforce *sui generis* privilege rules for the purposes of the arbitration.[128]

---

[123] JAMS GUIDELINES, *supra* note 40, at 3.

[124] *See* FED. R. CIV. P. 30, 31; N.Y. C.P.L.R. §§ 3106–16 (McKinney 2014).

[125] The New York State Bar Association, GUIDELINES FOR THE ARBITRATOR'S CONDUCT OF THE PRE-HEARING PHASE OF DOMESTIC COMMERCIAL ARBITRATIONS AND GUIDELINES FOR THE ARBITRATOR'S CONDUCT OF THE PRE-HEARING PHASE OF INTERNATIONAL ARBITRATIONS, *available at* http://old.nysba.org/Content/NavigationMenu/Publications/GuidelinesforArbitration/DR_guidelines_booklet_proof_10-24-11.pdf, reflect the different approaches to depositions which might be found in domestic arbitrations compared to international arbitrations. The NYSBA Domestic Guidelines provide extensive comments and suggestions for the use of depositions in domestic arbitration. *Id.* at 13–14. By contrast, the NYSBA International Guidelines reiterate the JAMS Guidelines verbatim, stating that "[i]n international arbitration, the prevailing practice is that depositions are not permitted. Provision of written direct testimony in advance of the witness' appearance at an arbitration hearing can go far in substituting for the deposition procedure." *Id.* at 28.

[126] *See* FED. R. CIV. P. 33, 36; N.Y. C.P.L.R. 3123, 3130–33 (McKinney 2014).

[127] *See, e.g.*, ICDR ARB. RULES art. 21(10) (noting that "[d]epositions, interrogatories, and requests to admit ... generally are not appropriate procedures ... under these Rules"); JAMS GUIDELINES, *supra* note 40, at 3.

[128] *See generally* James H. Carter, *The Attorney-Client Privilege and Arbitration*, ADR CURRENTS, Winter 1996–97, at 1, 15–17; Javier H. Rubinstein and Britton B. Guerrina, *The Attorney-Client Privilege and International Arbitration*, 18 J. INT'L ARB. 587 (2001).

The IBA Rules allow for the exclusion of documents from evidence or production on the grounds of privilege, such as attorney-client privilege or professional secrecy. Although the IBA Rules do not specify which evidentiary laws an arbitral tribunal should apply or the procedure for excluding documents,[129] they identify issues that tribunals may consider in considering questions or privilege.[130] **9.57**

The ICDR Rules provide that the tribunal should, to the extent possible, apply the same rules of privilege to both sides of a dispute, giving preference to the rules that provide the highest level of protection.[131] Most other arbitral institutions, however, do not expressly address privilege issues, or otherwise do not state how to identify such issues.[132] Accordingly, it is difficult to predict how a tribunal will apply privilege standards in any given international arbitration. **9.58**

5. Confidentiality

Parties should also consider whether steps need to be taken to protect the confidentiality of the information exchanged in discovery between the parties. While arbitration is a private process, confidentiality is not, in fact, guaranteed and some parties have assumed complete confidentiality of all aspects of the proceeding only to be surprised when compelled to negotiate such terms after an arbitration has been set in motion.[133] **9.59**

---

[129] *See* IBA R. Evid. art. 9(2)(a)–(g); Fabian von Schlabrendorff & Audley Sheppard, *Conflict of Legal Privileges in International Arbitration: An Attempt To Find a Holistic Solution*, in Global Reflections on International Law, Commerce and Dispute Resolution 743, 759 (Gerald Aksen et al., eds. 2005).

[130] IBA R. Evid. art. 9(3) ("In considering issues of legal impediment or privilege under Article 9.2(b), and insofar as permitted by any mandatory legal or ethical rules that are determined by it to be applicable, the Arbitral Tribunal may take into account: (a) any need to protect the confidentiality of a Document created or statement or oral communication made in connection with and for the purpose of providing or obtaining legal advice; (b) any need to protect the confidentiality of a Document created or statement or oral communication made in connection with and for the purpose of settlement negotiations; (c) the expectations of the Parties and their advisors at the time the legal impediment or privilege is said to have arisen; (d) any possible waiver of any applicable legal impediment or privilege by virtue of consent, earlier disclosure, affirmative use of the Document, statement, oral communication or advice contained therein, or otherwise; and (e) the need to maintain fairness and equality as between the Parties, particularly if they are subject to different legal or ethical rules.").

[131] *See* ICDR Arb. Rules art. 22 ("The arbitral tribunal shall take into account applicable principles of privilege, such as those involving the confidentiality of communications between a lawyer and client. When the parties, their counsel, or their documents would be subject under applicable law to different rules, the tribunal should, to the extent possible, apply the same rule to all parties, giving preference to the rule that provides the highest level of protection.").

[132] Institutional rules give the tribunal authority over the admissibility and relevance of evidence—thereby granting implicit control over the production of privileged information but not expressly addressing privilege. *See, e.g.*, ICC Rules of Arb., arts. 25(1), 25(5); CPR Rules for Non-Admin. Arb. of Int'l Disps. R. 11; U.N. Comm'n on Int'l Trade Law (UNCITRAL), UNCITRAL Arb. Rules art. 27 (2014) (adopted by G.A. Res. 68/109 (Dec. 16, 2013)).

[133] Parties in many cases negotiate confidentiality agreements after arbitration proceedings commence. *See, e.g.*, Commercial Union Ins. Co. v. Lines, 239 F. Supp. 2d 351, 357 (S.D.N.Y. 2002), *vacated on other grounds*, 378 F.3d 204 (2d Cir. 2004); DiRussa v. Dean Witter Reynolds Inc.,

9.60 Most arbitral rules require confidentiality only from the arbitrators and do *not* prohibit the parties from disclosing information about, or obtained during, the proceeding. The ICC Rules provide that the arbitral tribunal may, if requested by a party, "make orders concerning the confidentiality of the arbitration proceedings ... and may take measures for protecting trade secrets and confidential information."[134] In addition, "persons not involved in the proceedings shall not be admitted."[135] Likewise, the ICDR Rules provide that "[h]earings are private

121 F.3d 818, 826 (2d Cir. 1997); Liberty Re (Bermuda) Ltd. v. Transamerica Occidental Life Ins. Co., No. 04 civ. 5044(NRB), 2005 WL 1216292, at *6 (S.D.N.Y. May 23, 2005). Parties should be aware, however, that documents subject to a confidentiality agreement entered into by the parties in connection with an arbitration may still become public in connection with subsequent court proceedings to confirm or vacate an award, or in any proceedings in which a court deems an arbitration award or supporting documents to be relevant to the underlying cause of action. *See* Istithmar World PJSC v. Amato, No. 12 Civ. 7472(JFK), 2013 WL 66478, at *3 (S.D.N.Y. Jan. 7, 2013) ("Disputants may be drawn to arbitration out of a desire for privacy, but once one side seeks judicial confirmation of an arbitral award, that petition as well as the underlying award become 'judicial documents' to which the common law right of access is presumed to attach."). Courts have held that the presumption of access to arbitration documents trumps confidentiality rules in arbitration, regardless of which arbitration rules govern. *See* Veleron Holding, B.V. v. Morgan Stanley, No. 12 Civ. 5966(CM), 2014 WL 1569610, at *1 (S.D.N.Y. Apr. 16, 2014) ("[A] private agreement to arbitrate [under the LCIA rules] does not ... immunize [documents and other evidence relevant to that dispute] from public disclosure in connection with other, related proceedings ..."); Doscher v. Sobel & Co., No. 14 CV 646(RMB)(GWG), 2014 WL 846773, at *1, *3 (S.D.N.Y. Mar. 3, 2014) ("non-binding statement from the FINRA website" was insufficient to warrant confidential treatment of arbitration proceedings referred to in complaint); Istithmar World PJSC, 2013 WL 66478, at *3 (respondents failed in cross-petition to seal AAA award to rebut presumption of access to award) (AAA governed by the Employment Arbitration Rules and Mediation Procedures). Notably, "[t]he Second Circuit has articulated a three-step process for determining whether documents should be placed [or should remain] under seal." Mut. Marine Office, Inc. v. Transfercom Ltd., No. 08 Civ. 10367(PGG), 2009 WL 1025965, at *4 (S.D.N.Y. Apr. 15, 2009) (citing Lugosch v. Pyramid Co. of Onondaga, 435 F.3d 110, 119 (2d Cir. 2006)). First, a court must determine whether the item is a "judicial document" to which a presumption of access attaches. Lugosch v. Pyramid Co. of Onondaga, 435 F.3d 110, 119 (2d Cir. 2006). A "judicial document" is an " 'item ... relevant to the performance of the judicial function and useful in the judicial process.' " *Id.* (citation omitted). Second, if the court determines that the item is a "judicial document," the court must then determine the weight to be given the presumption of access. *Id.* "Finally, after determining the weight of the presumption of access, the court must 'balance competing considerations against it.' " *Id.* at 120 (citation omitted). "[A]rbitration awards become judicial documents when submitted to [the] Court on a petition to confirm and the presumption of access attaches to them ...." Global Reins. Corp.-U.S. Branch v. Argonaut Ins. Co., No. 07 Civ. 8196(PKC), 2008 WL 126976, at *2 (S.D.N.Y. Jan. 7, 2008) (ordering that arbitration awards remain sealed, but reserving "the right to revisit the issue"), *rev'd in part on other grounds on reconsideration*, 2008 WL 1805459 (S.D.N.Y. Apr. 21, 2008). *See* Global Reins. Corp.-U.S. Branch v. Argonaut Ins. Co., No. 07 Civ. 8196(PKC), 2008 WL 1805459, at *1–2 (S.D.N.Y. Apr. 21, 2008) (reconsidering earlier ruling and unsealing arbitration awards; party advocating continued sealing of awards did "not provide an adequate basis to overcome the presumption of access"). *See also* Aioi Nissay Dowa Ins. Co. v. ProSight Specialty Mgmt. Co., No. 12 Civ. 3274(JPO), 2012 WL 3583176, at *6 (S.D.N.Y. Aug. 21, 2012) ("It is well settled that the petition, memoranda, and other supporting documents filed in connection with a petition to confirm an arbitration award (including the Final Award itself) are 'judicial documents that directly affect ... the Court's adjudication' of that petition." (citations omitted)).

[134] ICC Rules of Arb., art. 22(3).

[135] *Id.* art. 26(3).

unless the parties agree otherwise or the law provides to the contrary."[136] Thus, they do not expressly address the confidential nature of information and documents exchanged prior to the hearing.[137]

Accordingly, at the outset of discovery, if they have not already addressed the issue of confidentiality in their arbitration agreement or the agreement in which the arbitration agreement is contained, the parties may wish to negotiate an agreement concerning the confidentiality of documents produced in discovery (and other information and evidence presented in the arbitration). Should the parties be unable to reach an agreement, the arbitral tribunal has the power to issue confidentiality orders as part of its discretion to direct the procedural aspects of the arbitration.[138] **9.61**

D. OBTAINING DISCOVERY FROM NONPARTIES

Because arbitration is a creature of contract and third parties are generally *not* bound by either the arbitration agreement or any arbitration rules selected by the parties,[139] discovery from third parties presents particular challenges and limitations.[140] **9.62**

[136] ICDR ARB. RULES art. 23(6). *See also* Galleon Syndicate Corp. v. Pan Atl. Grp., Inc., 637 N.Y.S.2d 104, 105 (App. Div. 1996) ("There is no confidentiality privilege precluding disclosure of the material requested as the parties to the arbitration proceedings governed by the [AAA rules] are, in the absence of a confidentiality provision, not prohibited from disclosing documents generated or exchanged during the arbitration and since evidentiary material at an arbitration proceeding is not immune from disclosure."); President & Fellows of Harvard Coll. v. JSC Surgutneftegaz, No. 11 168 T 01654 04, Partial Final Award on Claim Construction at 30–32 (Am. Arb. Ass'n Aug. 1, 2007) (finding that the parties to a New York arbitration are not bound to keep it confidential in the absence of a confidentiality clause in their agreement or a procedural order issued by the tribunal), *attached to* Declaration of Robert A. Skinner *as* Ex. 1, JSC Surgutneftegaz v. President & Fellows of Harvard Coll., No. 1:04-cv-06069-RMB (S.D.N.Y. filed Aug. 14, 2007), ECF Nos. 31, 31–2, 31–3.

[137] By contrast, the arbitration rules of the London Court of International Arbitration explicitly provide that confidentiality of "all awards ... together with all materials in the proceedings created for the purpose of the arbitration and all other documents produced" is assumed, unless disclosure is required by law or the parties otherwise agree to the contrary. LCIA ARB. RULES art. 30.1 (2014).

[138] *See* Bernstein v. On-Line Software Int'l, Inc., 648 N.Y.S.2d 602, 603 (App. Div. 1996) (affirming the Supreme Court's decision to confirm an arbitral award, and finding that the arbitral confidentiality order limiting access to certain subpoenaed material to "'attorney's eyes only' ... in order to protect the confidentiality of trade secrets obtained in the course of discovery" was "not improper").

[139] *See, e.g.*, Hay Grp., Inc. v. E.B.S. Acquisition Corp., 360 F.3d 404, 406 (3d Cir. 2004) ("An arbitrator's authority over parties that are not contractually bound by the arbitration agreement is strictly limited to that granted by the Federal Arbitration Act.").

[140] With regard to nonparties, Article 3(9) of the IBA Rules provides that parties may ask the tribunal "to take whatever steps are legally available to obtain the requested documents." IBA R. EVID. art. 3(9).

9.63 Pursuant to Section 7 of the FAA, "arbitrators ... may summon in writing any person to attend before them or any of them as a witness and ... to bring with him or them any book, record, document, or paper which may be deemed material as evidence in the case."[141] Section 7 further provides that "the United States district court for the district in which such arbitrators, or a majority of them, are sitting may compel the attendance of [witnesses] ... in the same manner provided by law for securing the attendance of witnesses ... in the courts of the United States."[142] Section 7 of the FAA clearly empowers arbitrators to require third parties to attend an arbitration hearing and to bring documentary evidence with them.[143]

9.64 The federal courts are divided, however, over whether Section 7 extends to *prehearing* discovery from third parties (*i.e.*, discovery taking place before the evidentiary hearing on the merits). The Second Circuit has held that no such power exists, thereby joining the Third Circuit's view of the statute and disagreeing with the Eighth and Fourth Circuits, which permit prehearing document discovery where the nonparty is "integrally related to the underlying arbitration" (Eighth Circuit)[144] and sometimes recognize such powers if there is a showing of "special need or hardship" (Fourth Circuit).[145]

9.65 In *Life Receivables Trust v. Syndicate 102 at Lloyd's of London*,[146] the Second Circuit held that "Section 7 of the FAA does not authorize arbitrators to compel pre-hearing document discovery from entities not party to the arbitration proceedings."[147] The Second Circuit found the language of Section 7 of the FAA "straightforward and unambiguous," only permitting discovery of documents when those documents are "brought before arbitrators by a testifying witness."[148] It relied on the Third Circuit's opinion in *Hay Group, Inc. v. E.B.S. Acquisition Corp.*,[149] written by now Supreme Court Justice Samuel Alito, which determined

[141] 9 U.S.C. § 7 (2012). Chapters 2 and 3 of the FAA, 9 U.S.C. §§ 201–208, 301–307 (2012), which govern international arbitrations falling under the Convention on the Recognition and Enforcement of Foreign Arbitral Awards, June 10, 1958, 330 U.N.T.S. 38, and the Inter-American Convention on International Commercial Arbitration, Jan. 30, 1975, S. Treaty Doc. No. 97-12 (1981), O.A.S.T.S. No. 42, 14 I.L.M. 336, respectively, do not speak to discovery or arbitral subpoenas. Section 7 is contained in Chapter 1 of the FAA, 9 U.S.C. §§ 1–16 (2012), which governs domestic arbitrations. Pursuant to 9 U.S.C. §§ 208 and 307, Chapter 1 of the FAA applies in the international setting wherever its provisions do not conflict with the provisions of Chapter 2 or 3 of the FAA.

[142] 9 U.S.C. § 7 (2012).

[143] *See* Paul D. Friedland & Lucy Martinez, *Arbitral Subpoenas Under U.S. Law and Practice*, 14 Am. Rev. Int'l Arb. 197, 228 (2003).

[144] Sec. Life Ins. Co. of Am. v. Duncanson & Holt, Inc., 228 F.3d 865, 871 (8th Cir. 2000).

[145] COMSAT Corp. v. Nat'l Sci. Found., 190 F.3d 269, 278 (4th Cir. 1999); Deiulemar Compagnia Di Navigazione S.p.A. v. M/V Allegra, 198 F.3d 473, 479–80 (4th Cir. 1999).

[146] 549 F.3d 210 (2d Cir. 2008).

[147] *Id.* at 216–17 (reversing a district court decision granting Syndicate 102's motion to enforce an arbitral subpoena seeking documents from a third party).

[148] *Id.* at 216.

[149] 360 F.3d 404 (3d Cir. 2004).

that the FAA confers authority on arbitrators to compel third parties only to appear before the arbitral tribunal and to hand over the requested documents at that time.[150] The Second Circuit added that "section 7 contains no discovery exception for closely related entities" and further concluded that arbitrators do not have the power to compel discovery even from third parties "that signed the underlying arbitration agreement."[151]

Even under the Second Circuit's ruling, however, arbitrators are not powerless to order document production from third parties prior to a hearing on the merits.[152] Any person can be ordered to produce documents "so long as that person is called as a witness *at a hearing*,"[153] and the Second Circuit specifically stated in *Life Receivables Trust* that an arbitrator's authority to call witnesses to "a hearing" "is not limited to witnesses at merits hearings, but extends to hearings covering a variety of preliminary matters."[154] Additionally, it observed that "[a]rbitrators also 'have the power to compel a third-party witness to appear with documents before a single arbitrator, who can then adjourn the proceedings.' "[155] Finally, the Second Circuit noted that, in a prior case, it "carefully distinguishe[d] *hearing testimony* from *depositions*."[156] **9.66**

Accordingly, in order to ensure the enforceability of third-party subpoenas in connection with arbitrations venued in New York, parties should request that the arbitrators issue subpoenas returnable *at a hearing before the arbitral tribunal.* **9.67**

In addition, parties and arbitrators must be mindful of case law from the Second Circuit that limited the territorial scope of a Section 7 subpoena and did not allow for nationwide service of process for such subpoenas: the Second Circuit has previously ruled that, because Section 7 subpoenas issued in the context of an arbitration **9.68**

---

[150] *See id.* at 215–17.

[151] *Id.* at 217.

[152] *See id.* at 218.

[153] *Id.* (emphasis added).

[154] *Id. See also* Stolt-Nielsen SA v. Celanese AG, 430 F.3d 567, 577 (2d Cir. 2005), *aff'g* Odfjell ASA v. Celanese AG, 348 F. Supp. 2d 283 (S.D.N.Y. 2004). In *Stolt-Nielsen*, a third party objected to being called to testify and bring documents to a hearing scheduled in advance of the hearing on the merits, claiming that this was a "ruse" to get third party discovery. *Id.* at 577. The district court found that the FAA does not limit the point during the arbitration process when a third-party witness may be summoned to a hearing before the arbitrators, noting that "Section 7's reference to hearings 'before [the arbitrators] *or any of them*' suggests that the provision authorizes the use of subpoenas at preliminary proceedings even in front of a single arbitrator, before the full panel 'hears the more central issues.'" *Id.* at 579 (alteration in original) (citation omitted).

[155] *Life Receivables Trust*, 549 F.3d at 218 (citing *Hay Group, Inc.*, 360 F.3d at 413). The Second Circuit explained that "Section 7's presence requirement ... forces the party seeking the non-party discovery—and the arbitrators authorizing it—to consider whether production is truly necessary." *Id.*

[156] *Id.* at 218 n.12 ("*Stolt-Nielsen* carefully distinguishes *hearing testimony* from *depositions*, observing that the hearing in question was before all three arbitrators, who ruled on evidentiary issues, and became a part of the arbitration record." (emphasis in original) (citing *Stolt-Nielsen*, 430 F.3d at 578)).

venued in New York could only be issued from the district court of the district where the arbitral tribunal was "sitting," and because a prior version of Federal Rule of Civil Procedure 45(b) contained strict limitations on the territorial service of a subpoena, Section 7 subpoenas were not subject to nationwide service.[157]

9.69 In December 2013, however, Federal Rule of Civil Procedure 45 was substantially amended so as to permit a subpoena to be served to a nonparty located anywhere in the United States, although it "must issue from the [district] court where the action is pending."[158] Nevertheless, a subpoena must direct a nonparty to comply with it at a location within one-hundred miles from the place where that nonparty "resides, is employed, or regularly transacts business" (among others) and that, barring exceptional circumstances, the district court of the place of compliance, not the place of the underlying action, would compel performance with the subpoena.[159]

9.70 Thus, the current version of Rule 45 allows for nationwide service of process of a Rule 45 subpoena, but continues to impose territorial limits on the venue for compliance with that subpoena.[160] To date, the Second Circuit has not revisited the territorial scope of Section 7 in light of the changes to Rule 45, but at

---

[157] Under the former version of Federal Rule of Civil Procedure 45(b)(2), a subpoena could "be served at any place ... within the district of the issuing court," or at any place "outside that district but within 100 miles of the place specified for the deposition, hearing, trial, production, or inspection," or at any place "within the state of the issuing court if a state statute or court rule allows service at that place of a subpoena issued by a state court of general jurisdiction sitting in the place specified for the deposition, hearing, trial, production, or inspection," or at any place "that the court authorizes on motion and for good cause, if a federal statute so provides." Fed. R. Civ. P. 45(b)(2) (2012), *amended and superseded* (2013). The Second Circuit ruled that the territorial limit of Rule 45(b)(2) applies to arbitral subpoenas. *See* Dynegy Midstream Servs. LP v. Trammochem, 451 F.3d 89, 91, 95 (2d Cir. 2006) ("[W]e hold that the Federal Arbitration Act does not authorize nationwide service of process and therefore the district court lacked jurisdiction over appellant."); *see also* Legion Ins. Co. v. John Hancock Mut. Life Ins. Co., 33 F. App'x 26, 27–28 (3d Cir. 2002) (taking similar approach). This, however, was not a universally adopted position. *But see* Sec. Life Ins. Co. of Am. v. Duncanson & Holt, Inc., 228 F.3d 865, 872 (8th Cir. 2000) ("[I]n light of our conclusion that there is no territorial limitation on the panel's authority to order the production of documents, it is apparent that Transamerica suffered no prejudice as a result of the district court's enforcement of the portion of the panel's subpoena ordering the production of documents.").

[158] Fed. R. Civ. P. 45(a)(2).

[159] Fed. R. Civ. P. 45(c).

[160] The potential interplay between the revised Rule 45 and Section 7 of the FAA was highlighted to, but apparently not addressed by, the Committee on the Rules of Practice and Procedure of the Judicial Conference of the United States at the time the revisions to the Rule were being considered. *See* Letter from George A. Davidson to Peter G. McCabe, Secretary, Committee on the Rules of Practice and Procedure of the Judicial Conference of the United States (Jan. 13, 2012), *available at* http://www.uscourts.gov/uscourts/RulesAndPolicies/rules/CV%20Comments%202011/11-CV-011-Comment-Davidson.pdf. Commentators have discussed the issue of whether or not the revisions to Rule 45 impact the interpretation of Section 7 of the FAA, with one finding that "[m]uch may ... depend on the interpretation of the phrase 'sitting' in Section 7, a phrase which, to date, has not been subject to much judicial analysis." Gunjan Sharma, *Proposed Amendments to Rule 45 of the Federal Rules of Civil Procedure May Expand the Territorial Scope of Arbitral Subpoenas under Section 7 of the Federal Arbitration Act*, Mealey's Int'l Arb. Rep., June 2012.

least one Southern District court has indicated that a Section 7 subpoena issued in a New York-venued arbitration and commanding appearance at a hearing in New York (albeit through videoconference) was subject to the territorial limitations of venue for compliance found in Federal Rule of Civil Procedure 45.[161]

E. DISCOVERY FROM EXPERT WITNESSES

Expert testimony has become an essential part of most international arbitrations. Such testimony is usually submitted through a written witness statement or expert report submitted by the expert. The question arises in international commercial arbitration whether the expert is subject to discovery, documentary or deposition. This is in contrast with the Federal Rules of Civil Procedure, which provide specific procedures for the timing and scope of expert discovery.[162] **9.71**

In international arbitrations venued in New York, document discovery is likely to be permitted where necessary, but absent agreement of the parties to mutual depositions of experts, prehearing depositions are not likely. The relatively recent approach to expert witness confrontation in international arbitration may provide a different route to ferreting out the strengths and weaknesses of the expert's position. However, given the paucity of case law addressing the scope of discovery of experts under New York law in connection with international arbitrations, it is unclear what, if any, judicial relief may be available to compel expert discovery outside of the arbitral forum. **9.72**

F. DISCOVERY WHEN SEEKING PRELIMINARY RELIEF IN AID OF ARBITRATION

Where an international arbitration is venued in New York, a party to that arbitration may seek preliminary relief in aid of arbitration in either a federal or state **9.73**

---

[161] *See* Ping-Kuo Lin v. Horan Capital Mgmt, LLC, No. 14 Civ. 5202(LLS), 2014 WL 3974585, at *1–2 (S.D.N.Y. Aug. 13, 2014). Note that, where the third party to be subpoenaed resides outside a 100-mile radius from the district of the seat of the arbitration, the panel may hold a hearing in the district where the third party resides in order to conform with the territorial limits for compliance.

[162] In 2010, Rule 26 of the Federal Rules of Civil Procedure was amended to expressly protect communications between an attorney and an expert witness as well as drafts of expert reports. *See* Fed. R. Civ. P. 26(b)(4)(B)–(C); U.S. Commodity Futures Trading Comm'n v. Newell, No. 12 C 6763, 2014 WL 4179881, at *3 (N.D. Ill. Aug. 25, 2014). Additionally, in U.S. litigation, the expert report by itself does not constitute evidence and, in fact, is used primarily as a discovery device. *See* Blue Cross & Blue Shield United v. Marshfield Clinic, 152 F.3d 588, 595 (7th Cir. 1998) ("[W]hile we have been treating the defendants' experts' reports as if they were evidence, they are not. They are merely discovery materials." (citing Kirk v. Raymark Indus., Inc., 61 F.3d 147, 164 (3d Cir. 1995)); Bryan v. John Bean Div. of FMC Corp., 566 F.2d 541, 544–47 (5th Cir. 1978)). *See generally* Chapter 2.E.3.

court with jurisdiction to hear the matter.[163] In such a proceeding, a party may seek discovery to support (or oppose) the application for interim relief and courts may find discovery necessary to make their determination of whether preliminary relief should issue. Thus, a court potentially could order depositions, including depositions of nonparties, in connection with such a proceeding. Significantly, the discovery application may be merits-based and broader than would be permitted by the arbitrators.

G. DISCOVERY IN NEW YORK IN AID OF A FOREIGN ARBITRATION

9.74 Parties whose arbitration is venued outside the United States should be aware that they may also attempt to enlist the assistance of U.S. courts in obtaining evidence located in the United States for use in their arbitration pursuant to Section 1782 of Title 28 of the U.S. Code.[164]

9.75 Section 1782 states, in pertinent part, that "[t]he district court of the district in which a person resides or is found may order him to give his testimony or statement or to produce a document or other thing for use in a proceeding in a foreign or international tribunal."[165] What exactly constitutes a "foreign or international tribunal" remains subject to interpretation, and courts are divided on whether Section 1782 encompasses assistance to foreign *arbitrations.* A further debate arises over whether Section 1782 may apply to international arbitrations venued in New York and elsewhere in the United States.

9.76 In 1999, the Second Circuit held in *National Broadcasting Co. v. Bear Stearns & Co.*[166] that federal district courts are barred from extending Section 1782(a) assistance to arbitral tribunals sitting outside the United States.[167] The Second Circuit found the phrase "foreign or international tribunal" to be "ambiguous" and upheld the district court's conclusion that a foreign private commercial arbitration

[163] *See* N.Y. C.P.L.R. 3102(c) (McKinney 2005 & Supp. 2014). For a more general discussion of applications for preliminary relief in aid of arbitration, see Chapter 8 of this book.

[164] *See* Comm. On Int'l Commercial Disputes, NYC Bar Ass'n, 28 U.S.C. § 1782 as a Means of Obtaining Discovery in Aid of International Arbitration – Applicability and Best Practices, *available at* http://www.nycbar.org/pdf/report/1782_Report.pdf.

[165] 28 U.S.C. § 1782(a). For an overview of the legislative history of Section 1782, see Brief for the United States as Amicus Curiae Supporting Affirmance, Intel Corp. v. Advanced Micro Devices, Inc., No. 02-572, 2004 WL 214306, at *3–7 (U.S. Jan. 30, 2004). *See also* Act of Mar. 2, 1855, ch. 140, § 2, 10 Stat. 630; Act of Mar. 3, 1863, ch. 95, 12 Stat. 769.

[166] 165 F.3d 184 (2d Cir. 1999).

[167] *Id.* at 191 (holding that private international arbitration falls outside Section 1782's coverage); *accord* Republic of Kazakhstan v. Biedermann Int'l, 168 F.3d 880, 881–83 (5th Cir. 1999). For a prior district court decision in favor of applying Section 1782 to foreign arbitrations, *see* In re Technostroyexport, 853 F. Supp. 695 (S.D.N.Y. 1994). "The court is of the view that an arbitrator

tribunal was not a "foreign or international tribunal" under Section 1782.[168] Upon finding that the legislative intent was to confine the scope of Section 1782 to tribunals established by governments, the Second Circuit determined that the statute's silence regarding arbitral tribunals indicated that Congress did not intend an extension of the statute to include nonsovereign tribunals.[169]

The U.S. Supreme Court's 2004 ruling in *Intel Corp. v. Advanced Micro Devices, Inc.*[170] casts some doubt upon the future application of *National Broadcasting Co.*[171] In *Intel*, the Supreme Court extended Section 1782(a)'s application to nonjudicial bodies, holding that reference to "foreign or international tribunals" extended to the Directorate-General for Competition of the Commission of the European Communities, an administrative body.[172] Although *Intel* did not explicitly address whether assistance under Section 1782 is available in connection with foreign arbitral proceedings, the majority opinion authored by Justice Ruth Joan Bader Ginsburg quoted an article stating that, as used in the text of Section 1782, "[t]he term 'tribunal' ... includes ... arbitral tribunals."[173] Thus, *Intel* seems to re-open the argument that the term "tribunal" includes arbitral tribunals.[174] Notably, since *Intel*, some courts outside of the Second Circuit—including Circuit courts[175]—have differed on **9.77**

or arbitration panel is a 'tribunal' under § 1782. The court further believes that, if Technostroy had obtained a ruling from a foreign arbitrator that discovery should take place, the court would be empowered under § 1782 to enforce that ruling in the United States." *Id.* at 697.

[168] *See* Nat'l Broad. Co., 165 F.3d at 188; *see also* In re Nat'l Broad. Co., No. M-77 (RWS), 1998 WL 1994, at *3–4 (S.D.N.Y. Jan. 21, 1998), *aff'd sub nom.* Nat'l Broad. Co. v. Bear Stearns & Co., 165 F.3d 184 (2d Cir. 1999). In reaching this conclusion, the district court relied on the reasoning of another S.D.N.Y. decision, In re Medway Power Ltd., 985 F. Supp. 402 (S.D.N.Y. 1997). In *Medway Power*, the plaintiffs sought an order under Section 1782 compelling third-party discovery from General Electric for use in a U.K. arbitration. *Id.* at 402–03. First, the court determined that the plain meaning of "tribunal" generally did not include a private arbitration, according to a Webster's dictionary definition. *Id.* at 403. Second, it surveyed the legislative history of the statute, determining that the 1964 revision reflected a legislative intent to extend Section 1782 assistance to "foreign governmental agencies exercising a judicial or quasi-judicial function." *Id.* at 403–04. It also noted that the legislative history contains no suggestion of an intent to include private arbitrations. *Id.* at 403. Thus, the court denied Section 1782 assistance. *Id.* at 405.

[169] *See Nat'l Broad. Co.*, 165 F.3d at 190.

[170] 542 U.S. 241 (2004).

[171] *See* Barry H. Garfinkel and Yuval M. Miller, *The Supreme Court's Reasoning in* Intel *Calls Into Question Circuit Court Rulings on Inapplicability of 28 U.S.C. § 1782 to International Commercial Arbitration*, Mealey's Int'l Arb. Rep., Aug. 30, 2004, at 17 (noting that "*Intel* calls into question the continued validity of the Second and Fifth Circuit opinions" in *National Broadcasting Co.* and *Republic of Kazakhstan*).

[172] *See Intel Corp.*, 542 U.S. at 246, 257–58.

[173] *Id.* at 258 (alteration and first ellipsis in original) (*quoting* Hans Smit, *International Litigation Under the United States Code*, 65 Colum. L. Rev. 1015, 1026 n.71 (1965) (interpreting the term "tribunal" to include arbitral tribunals)).

[174] *See* John Fellas, Outside Counsel, *The U.S. Supreme Court Rules on Section 1782*, 231 N.Y.L.J. 5 (Aug. 18, 2004); *In re* Roz Trading Ltd., 469 F. Supp. 2d 1221, 1224–26 (N.D. Ga. 2006).

[175] The Fifth Circuit has refused to apply Section 1782 to a private, commercial arbitration. *See* El Paso Corp. v. La Comisión Ejecutiva Hidroeléctrica Del Rio Lempa, 341 F. App'x 31, 33–34

the interpretation of Section 1782 and its applicability to international arbitral tribunals.[176]

9.78 To conclude, it remains to be seen whether courts in the Second Circuit will depart from *National Broadcasting Co.* and construe *Intel* to mean that Section 1782 may be used to provide discovery in aid of a foreign arbitration.

(5th Cir. 2009). Notably, the Eleventh Circuit held that a foreign commercial arbitration may constitute a "foreign tribunal" for purposes of Section 1782, but later vacated its prior decision and permitted the same discovery in aid of a related foreign litigation. Consorcio Ecuatoriano de Telecomunicaciones S.A. v. JAS Forwarding (USA), Inc., 747 F.3d 1262 (11th Cir. 2014). The Tenth and Third Circuits have held that an investor-state arbitration, conducted under the auspices of an international treaty (and thus not an arbitration conducted by the agreement of parties, unlike private, commercial arbitrations), will satisfy the requirements of Section 1782—indeed, the Fifth Circuit has also allowed such Section 1782 discovery, albeit on the grounds that a party was judicially estopped from denying that pending investor-state proceedings could not constitute a basis for Section 1782 relief. *See In re* Chevron Corp., 633 F.3d 153, 161–62 (3d Cir. 2011); *In re* Republic of Ecuador, 735 F.3d 1179 (10th Cir. 2013); Republic of Ecuador v. Connor, 708 F.3d 651 (5th Cir. 2013).

[176] *See, e.g., In re* Application of Owl Shipping, LLC, Civ. Act. No. 15-5655 (AET)(DEA), 2014 WL 5320192, at *3 (D.N.J. Oct. 17, 2014) (granting 1782 application in aid of discovery before London Maritime Arbitrators Association); *In re* Oxus Gold PLC, No. Misc. 06-82, 2006 WL 2927615, at *4–6 (D.N.J. Oct. 11, 2006) (ruling that an international investor-state arbitration between a British investor and the Kyrgyz Republic that was venued in London and conducted pursuant to a bilateral investment treaty (BIT) was "a proceeding in a foreign or international tribunal" under Section 1782 and holding that *National Broadcasting Co.* and (by implication) *Republic of Kazakhstan* were distinguishable because they applied to private commercial arbitration, whereas an investor's right to arbitrate under a BIT stems from a binding treaty agreement between two states); *Roz Trading*, 469 F. Supp. 2d at 1222–28 (upholding use of Section 1782 in a purely private international arbitration proceeding venued in Vienna which was brought by Roz Trading, Ltd., a Cayman Islands company, against the Coca-Cola Company, while noting that the Supreme Court in *Intel Corp.* "provided sufficient guidance for this Court to determine that arbitral panels … are 'tribunals' within the statute's scope"); *In re* Roz Trading Ltd., No. 1:06-CV-02305-WSD, 2007 WL 120844, at *1 (N.D. Ga. Jan. 11, 2007) (criticizing the *National Broadcasting Co.* and *Republic of Kazakhstan* decisions as "inconsistent with the Supreme Court's guidance in *Intel*, impos[ing] impermissible judicial limitations into the unambiguous text of § 1782(a)"); *In re* Hallmark Capital Corp., 534 F. Supp. 2d 951, 952 (D. Minn. 2007) (permitting discovery in aid of an arbitration venued in Israel); *In re* Babcock Borsig AG, 583 F. Supp. 2d 233, 238 (D. Mass. 2008) (finding that an ICC arbitration tribunal seated in Dusseldorf is a "tribunal" within the meaning of Section 1782); Comisión Ejecutiva, Hidroeléctrica Del Río Lempa v. Nejapa Power Co., No. 08-135-GMS, 2008 WL 4809035, at *1 (D. Del. Oct. 14, 2008) (allowing discovery in aid of a Geneva arbitration). However, other courts have reached different conclusions concerning Section 1782. *See, e.g., In re* Operadora DB Mex., S.A. de C.V., No. 6:09-cv-383-Orl-22GJK, 2009 WL 2423138, at *12 (M.D. Fla. Aug. 4, 2009) (rejecting the application of Section 1782 to an ICC arbitration venued in Mexico); *In re* Arbitration Between Norfolk S. Corp., Norfolk S. Ry. Co. & Gen. Sec. Ins. Co. & Ace Berm. Ltd., 626 F. Supp. 2d 882, 885 (N.D. Ill. 2009) (denying discovery in aid of London reinsurance arbitration). For a survey of the various district and Circuit courts discussing whether Section 1782 applies to foreign arbitrations, and the legal issues arising therefrom, see Gunjan Sharma, *The Availability of Section 1782 Discovery for Use in Foreign Arbitration: A Survey of U.S. Court Decisions*, MEALEY'S INT'L ARB. REP., Sept. 2012.

10

DAMAGES IN INTERNATIONAL ARBITRATION

Claudia T. Salomon[1]

A. Introduction	10.01
B. Principles Controlling the Proof and Calculation of Damages	10.03
1. Commercial Damages for Breach of Contract	10.03
2. Money Damages vs. Specific Performance	10.06
3. Expectation Damages	10.10
(a) General damages	10.11
(b) Special damages	10.15
(c) Duty to mitigate	10.21
4. Liquidated Damages and Penalties	10.23
5. Punitive Damages	10.27
6. Alternate Theories of Commercial Damages	10.29
(a) Reliance	10.29
(b) Restitution	10.34
7. A Special Case: Demonstrating Damages for Anticipated Future Profits from a Lost Business Opportunity	10.35
C. Calculation of Interest	10.39
1. Prejudgment Interest	10.40
2. Postjudgment Interest	10.46
D. Attorneys' Fees and Costs	10.48
1. Awards of Arbitrator Fees and Costs	10.50
2. Awards of Attorneys' Fees and Costs	10.51

A. INTRODUCTION

In international commercial arbitration, the category of damages, as well as the nature of proof required, is determined by the agreement of the parties. Absent such an agreement, tribunals will be guided by the substantive law of the arbitration. Although an international arbitration venued in New York may be governed by the substantive law of any jurisdiction (or no jurisdiction at all), this chapter will address the implications of the substantive law of the State of New York on the proof and calculation of damages. **10.01**

While causation is an independent element of a breach of contract claim and a predicate for proving liability, causation is frequently informative of both the **10.02**

[1] Peter D. Sharp assisted with a prior version of this chapter.

amount and classes of damages that may be recoverable under New York law. Generally, for damages to be recoverable, an aggrieved party must prove that the opposing party's conduct directly and proximately caused the claimed damages.[2] An injured party is entitled only to reasonable compensation for damage flowing from a breach,[3] i.e., damages that are proximate and certain, not remote, speculative or contingent.[4] Although an in-depth analysis of theories and standards of proof for establishing causation is beyond the scope of this chapter, the requirement that a party prove, with a reasonable degree of certainty, damages proximately caused by a respondent's actions explains New York law's general skepticism about anticipated lost profits for prospective business opportunity as a class of damages because proof of such damages can often be inherently remote or speculative.

B. PRINCIPLES CONTROLLING THE PROOF AND CALCULATION OF DAMAGES

1. Commercial Damages for Breach of Contract

10.03 Under New York law, the injured party should be made whole.[5] New York law thus examines to what extent the injured party has been injured from the breach of contract, rather than to what extent the breaching party benefited from the breach.[6]

[2] Nat'l Mkt. Share, Inc. v. Sterling Nat'l. Bank, 392 F.3d 520, 525 (2d Cir. 2004); Creative Waste Mgmt., Inc. v. Capitol Env't Servs., Inc., 429 F. Supp. 2d 582, 610 (S.D.N.Y. 2006), *opinion supplemented*, 458 F. Supp. 2d 178 (S.D.N.Y. 2006); RCN Telecom Servs., Inc. v. 202 Centre St. Realty LLC, 419 F. Supp. 2d 553, 556 (S.D.N.Y. 2006), vacated on other grounds and remanded, No. US-1508-CV, 2006 WL 3253024 (2d Cir. Nov. 8, 2006); 34–35th Corp. v. 1-10 Indus. Associates, LLC 103 A.D.3d 709, 711 (N.Y. App. Div. 2013), leave to appeal denied, 21 N.Y. 3d 865 (2013) Appellate Division, Second Department, reinforcing that aggrieved party must prove that the opposing party's conduct directly and proximately caused the claimed damages. *See, e.g.*, Pesa v. Yoma Dev. Grp., Inc., 18 N.Y.3d 527, 530 (2012) (holding that a buyer in a real estate transaction must prove that it was ready, willing and able to consummate a real estate transaction to recover damages for an anticipatory breach of contract claim).

[3] Contemporary Mission, Inc. v. Famous Music Corp., 557 F.2d 918, 926, 2 Fed. R. Evid. Serv. 16 (2d Cir. 1977).

[4] Fruition, Inc. v. Rhoda Lee, Inc., 766 N.Y.S.2d 437 (1st Dep't 2003) (*quoting* Booth v. Spuyten Duyvil Rolling Mill Co., 60 N.Y. 487 (1875)); *see also* Xpedior Creditor Trust v. Credit Suisse First Boston (USA) Inc., 341 F. Supp. 2d 258, 271 (S.D.N.Y. 2004) (*quoting* County of Washington v. Counties of Warren & Washington Indus. Dev. Agency, No. 93-CV-0086, 1997 WL 152001 (N.D.N.Y. Mar. 31, 1997), *aff'd*, 2 Fed. Appx. 71, (2d Cir. 2001)); Berley Indus., Inc. v. City of New York, 385 N.E.2d 281 (1978).

[5] Adams v. Linblad Travel, Inc., 730 F.2d 89, 94 (2d Cir. 1984).

[6] *See* Topps Co., v. Cadbury Stani S.A.I.C., 380 F. Supp. 2d 250, 269 (S.D.N.Y. 2005) (noting that disgorgement of profits is not a proper remedy for a breach); Cayuga Harvester, Inc. v. Allis-Chalmers Corp., 465 N.Y.S.2d 606, 618 (4th Dep't 1983) (holding that the plaintiff may recover up to the amount he was damaged).

The nonbreaching party should thus be compensated for its injury without receiving more than it actually bargained for.[7]

An injured party should benefit from its bargain.[8] Therefore, New York law requires the breaching party to compensate the injured party by putting the injured party in as good a position as it would have been had the contract been performed.[9] The injured party is entitled to compensation for the actual losses sustained as a result of the breach or failure to perform the contract,[10] plus—subject to the limitations discussed later—any profits the injured party would have gained had the contract been completed. **10.04**

New York law only allows the nonbreaching party to receive damages up to the amount that both parties would have foreseen at the time they made the contract, even if the breaching party intentionally breached the contract.[11] Because contracts are usually purely economical, New York law favors the concept of an "efficient breach" to allow both parties to receive the optimum profits from their transactions.[12] Thus, if a party may profit more by breaching its contract and paying reasonable damages, the court will not punish the breaching party but only require him or her to compensate the injured party.[13] Consequently, there are only limited circumstances that New York law allows an award of punitive damages for a non-tortuous breach of contract because the purpose of punitive damages is to vindicate public rights rather than remedy private wrongs.[14] **10.05**

---

[7] *See* Freund v. Washington Square Press. Inc., 314 N.E.2d 419, 421 (N.Y. 1974) (noting that the injured party should not receive more than he would have had the contract been performed); Topps, Co., 380 F. Supp. 2d at 269 (noting that looking at the profits that the breaching party gain from the breach is not a suitable remedy).

[8] *See* Bi-Econ. Mkt., Inc. v. Harleysville Ins. Co. of N.Y., 886 N.E.2d 127, 132 (N.Y. 2008) (*quoting* Restatement (Second) of Contracts § 344 cmt. a (1981)) ("Contract damages are ordinarily intended to give the injured party the benefit of the bargain by awarding a sum of money that will, to the extent possible, put that party in as good a position as it would have been in had the contract been performed."); Seidman v. Indus. Recycling Props., Inc., 106 A.D. 3d 983, 985 (N.Y. App. Div. 2013).

[9] Goodstein Constr. Corp. v. City of New York, 604 N.E. 2d 1356, 1360 (N.Y. 1992); *Freund*, 314 N.E.2d at 420 (N.Y. 1974); Bippley v. Hollenback, 644 N.Y.S.2d 852, 853–54 (3d Dep't 1996); New York Water Serv. Corp. v. New York, 163 N.Y.S.2d 538, 544 (1st Dep't 1957).

[10] *See Cayuga*, 465 N.Y.S.2d at 618 (noting that in an action for breach of contract the injured party is entitled to damages for the loss caused by failure to perform the bargain).

[11] Ashland Mgmt. Inc. v. Janien, 624 N.E.2d 1007, 1010 (N.Y. 1993); *Freund*, 314 N.E.2d at 421.

[12] *See* Thyssen, Inc. v. S.S. Fortune Star, 777 F.2d 57, 63 (2d Cir. 1985) (noting that when breaching a contract is more efficient and wealth enhancing, then breaching the contract should be encouraged).

[13] The breaching party may want to breach either because further performance will incur more losses or because there is a more profitable transaction that it can enter into.

[14] *See generally* Rocanova v. Equitable Life Assurance Soc'y of the United States, 634 N.E.2d 940, 943–44 (N.Y. 1994).

2. Money Damages vs. Specific Performance

10.06 New York law rarely allows an award of specific performance, especially when "money damages would be adequate to protect the expectation interest of the injured party."[15] Specific performance is permitted only in instances where money damages are not adequate because the subject of a given contract is unique and has no established market value,[16] or if the contract expressly stipulates a remedy of specific performance.[17] The factors that courts use to determine whether money damages provide an adequate remedy are "the difficulty of proving damages with reasonable certainty and of procuring a suitable substitute performance with a damages award."[18]

10.07 Under New York sales law, governed by New York's Uniform Commercial Code (UCC), a buyer has a statutory right to specific performance under certain, limited circumstances. The New York UCC provides that specific performance may be awarded where "the goods are unique or in other proper circumstances," which may include "payment of the price, damages, or other relief as the court may deem just."[19] Courts, however, have generally confined the remedy of specific performance to reinstating the equivalent of the subject goods that are in a party's possession.[20] While the UCC's provision regarding specific performance leaves the remedy to a court's discretion, New York courts have generally held that specific performance should be declined where "such relief would be a drastic or harsh remedy."[21]

10.08 In cases where the nonbreaching party allows a period of time to lapse before bringing an action for specific performance or when the breach does not occur

---

[15] Sokoloff v. Harriman Estates Dev. Corp., 754 N.E.2d 184, 188 (N.Y. 2001) (*quoting* Restatement (Second) of Contracts § 359 (1981)).

[16] *See* Van Wagner Advert. Corp. v. S & M Enters., 492 N.E.2d 756, 760 (N.Y. 1986).

> What matters, in measuring money damages, is the volume, refinement, and reliability of the available information about substitutes for the subject matter of the breached contract. When the relevant information is thin and unreliable, there is a substantial risk that an award of money damages will either exceed or fall short of the promisee's actual loss. Of course this risk can always be reduced—but only at great cost when reliable information is difficult to obtain. Conversely, when there is a great deal of consumer behavior generating abundant and highly dependable information about substitutes, the risk of error in measuring the promisee's loss may be reduced at much smaller cost. In asserting that the subject matter of a particular contract is unique and has no established market value, a court is really saying that it cannot obtain, at reasonable cost, enough information about substitutes to permit it to calculate an award of money damages without imposing an unacceptably high risk of under compensation on the injured promisee. Conceived in this way, the uniqueness test seems economically sound.

Id. at 760 (*quoting* Anthony Kronman, *Specific Performance*, 45 U. Chi. L. Rev. 351 (1978)).

[17] ESPN, Inc. v. Office of the Commissioner of Baseball, 76 F. Supp. 2d 383, 391 (S.D.N.Y. 1999).

[18] *Sokoloff*, 754 N.E.2d at 188 (*quoting* Restatement (Second) of Contracts § 360 (1981)). *See also* Edge Grp. WAICCS LLC v. Sapir Grp. LLC, 705 F. Supp. 2d 304, 313 (S.D.N.Y. 2010) (in weighing whether to grant specific performance in a breach of contract claim, the principal consideration is not the uniqueness of the products but whether damages can be proved with reasonable certainty).

[19] N.Y.U.C.C. § 2-716 (1)–(2) (2007).

[20] *See, e.g.*, Dexter Bishop Co. v. B. Redmond & Son, Inc., 58 A.D.2d 755 (1st Dep't 1977).

[21] Bander v. Grossman, 161 Misc. 2d 119, 125 (N.Y. Sup. Ct. 1994) (internal citations omitted). *See also* Cole v. Macklowe, 99 A.D.3d 595, 596, 953 N.Y.S.2d 21, 23 (2012).

immediately after the sale of an item, courts are even more reluctant to grant specific performance.[22] Thus, in addition to the requirement that the rest of the contract be sufficiently "unique" to justify the exceptional remedy of specific performance (and support the conclusion that money damages are insufficient as a matter of law), the timeline of the sale of goods, date of breach, and commencement of the action are often times determinative of whether specific performance will be granted.

Notably, specific performance may be barred only by explicit language in the contract.[23] In *Rubinstein v. Rubinstein*,[24] the New York Court of Appeals held that "a liquidated damages provision will not in and of itself be construed as barring the remedy of specific performance ... [f]or there to be a complete bar to equitable relief there must be something more, such as explicit language in the contract that the liquidated damages provision was to be the sole remedy." However, in *L.K. Station*,[25] the First Department held that a clause barring relief in "contract, tort, or otherwise, except for direct damages resulting from gross negligence or willful conduct," curtailed the availability of specific performance as a remedy. The court found that the "or otherwise" language was broad enough to include specific performance, even though specific performance was never explicitly mentioned in the waiver. **10.09**

3. Expectation Damages

Contract damages typically are based upon the party's expectation of how much it would have benefited from the bargain. In other words, compensation should put the nonbreaching party in the same economic position that it expected to be in had the contract been performed.[26] This doctrine, however, is limited by the principle that the nonbreaching party is only entitled to recover damages that were foreseeable at the time the contract was made.[27] There are two types of expectation damages that the nonbreaching party can recover: general damages and special damages.[28] **10.10**

(a) General damages General damages are damages that are the "natural and probable consequence of the breach."[29] This is usually the net revenue that the **10.11**

[22] *Bander*, 161 Misc. 2d at 125 ("With the passage of time, specific performance becomes disfavored. For example, because goods are subject to a rapid change in condition, or the cost of maintenance of the goods is important, time may be found to have been of the essence, and even a month's delay may defeat specific performance.").

[23] L.K. Station Grp., LLC v. Quantek Media, LLC, 62 A.D.3d 487, 494 (2009).

[24] 23 N.Y.2d 293, 298 (1968).

[25] 62 A.D.3d at 494.

[26] *See supra* notes 8–9 and accompanying text.

[27] Freund v. Washington Square Press. Inc., 314 N.E.2d 419, 421 (N.Y. 1974).

[28] Latham Land I, LLC v. TGI Friday's, Inc., 96 A.D.3d 1327, 1330, 948 N.Y.S.2d 147, 151 (2012).

[29] *See* Bi-Econ. Mkt., Inc. v. Harleysville Ins. Co. of N.Y., 886 N.E.2d 127, 132 (N.Y. 2008) (*quoting* Kenford Co. v. Erie, 537 N.E.2d. 176, 178 (N.Y. 1989)).

nonbreaching party would have realized but for the breach and is typically measured by the revenues the nonbreaching party would have gained; usually the contract price, minus the additional cost it would have incurred and/or had incurred in generating those revenues.[30] The nonbreaching party also can collect any expenses incurred from partially performing the contract prior to the breach.[31]

10.12 For example, a seller contracted with a buyer to sell 100 customized widgets for $100. The widgets cost the seller $50 to produce and deliver. If the buyer breached prior to production, the lost profits would be the contract price of $100 minus the cost to produce the widgets of $50, or $50. If the buyer breached the contract after the seller produced half the widgets, the seller would be able to recover the lost profits plus any costs incurred for production worth $25. This outcome is appropriate, however, only if the seller cannot sell those widgets. Otherwise, the seller would be permitted double recovery, as he would receive $50 for lost profits, $25 for costs incurred, plus the $50 worth of widgets, which the seller could sell and gain a $25 profit. This would result in a profit for the seller of $75, which is more than he bargained for.

10.13 In calculating these damages, both common law and the New York UCC follow a lost profit formula. This method of calculation requires the nonbreaching party to make a reasonable attempt to mitigate their damages. A seller who is able to mitigate costs should be limited to the difference between the contract price and his actual resale price.[32]

10.14 Recoverable costs also may include overhead and expenses that would have been incurred from the performance of the contract.[33] However, courts do not include fixed costs in the calculation of lost profits.[34] The reasoning is that the seller would have incurred fixed costs whether or not the breach occurred.[35]

10.15 *(b) Special damages* *Special damages*, also known as *consequential damages*, are damages that do not directly flow from the breach and are only recoverable in limited circumstances.[36] The highest court in New York, the Court of Appeals, has held that in order to recover further liability other than general damages,

---

[30] Adams v. Linblad Travel, Inc., 730 F.2d 89, 93 (2d Cir. 1984).

[31] *See* Harry Kolomick Contractors, Inc. v. Shelter Rock Estates, Inc., 567 N.Y.S.2d 845, 845 (2d Dep't 1991) (holding that a breaching party is liable for part of the performance that had been completed prior to the breach of the contract).

[32] A seller who is able to mitigate costs per § 208(1) is limited to the difference between the contract price and its actual resale price. *See, e.g.*, Tesoro Petroleum Corp. v. Holborn Oil Co., 145 Misc. 2d 715, 718 (N.Y. Sup. Ct. 1989) (noting that "[w]e believe that this is an exact measure of his expectation and that he should not recover more than that.").

[33] *See* R & I Elecs., Inc. v. Neuman, 411 N.Y.S.2d 401, 405 (2d Dep't 1978) (holding that when calculating profits, the nonbreaching party must include in the costs overhead costs that would have been incurred had the contract been performed).

[34] Delchi Carrier SpA. v. Rotorex Corp., 71 F.3d 1024, 1030 (2d Cir. 1995).

[35] *Id.*

[36] Am. List Corp. v. U.S. News & World Report, Inc., 549 N.E.2d 1161, 1164 (N.Y. 1989).

"such extraordinary damages must have been brought within the contemplation of the parties as the probable result of a breach at the time of or prior to contracting."[37] The Court of Appeals explained that the loss that resulted from the breach must be "foreseeable and probable" rather than actually foreseeing "the breach itself or the particular way the loss occurred."[38] This issue of foreseeability is evaluated from the perspective of the defendant.[39]

Where clear, the intent of the parties as expressed in their agreement controls.[40] **10.16** Where the parties' intent is ambiguous from the face of their agreement, however, New York courts consider many factors to determine whether a given class of special damages reasonably was contemplated by the parties. One factor courts consider is "the nature, purpose and particular circumstances of the contract known by the parties."[41] Another factor is "what liability the [breaching party] fairly may be supposed to have assumed consciously, or to have warranted the [nonbreaching party] to supposes that it assumed, when the contract was made."[42] Parties also may point to postcontractual conduct to seek to demonstrate whether the breaching party expressly or impliedly agreed or led the nonbreaching party to assume that the breaching party would take responsibility for any of the extraordinary damages.[43]

As the intent of the parties controls the issue of special damages, parties may include provisions disclaiming any special damages. New York courts enforce such contractual disclaimers unless the disclaimer is deemed unreasonable.[44] "[A]ll claims flowing from the breach of contract," excepting any liabilities of waiver for fraud claims, may be subject to contractual disclaimers.[45] **10.17**

Under the UCC, parties may limit or exclude consequential damages through contractual disclaimers unless the limitation is unfair or unconscionable.[46] **10.18**

[37] Bi-Econ. Mkt., Inc. v. Harleysville Ins. Co. of N.Y., 886 N.E.2d 127, 132 (N.Y. 2008) (*quoting* Kenford Co. v. Erie, 537 N.E.2d. 176, 178 (N.Y. 1989)).

[38] *Id. See also* Fitzpatrick v. Animal Care Hosp., PLLC, 104 A.D.3d 1078, 1081–82, 962 N.Y.S.2d 474, 478–79 (2013).

[39] *See* McLeod v. R.B. Hamilton Moving & Storage, 453 N.Y.S.2d 251, 253 (2d Dep't 1982) (noting the defendant must foresee the damages at the time the contract was made).

[40] *See Kenford*, 537 N.E.2d at 179 (examining the provisions of the contract to demonstrate whether the parties contemplated a certain class of damages); *see also* Chapter 3.B.3.

[41] *McLeod*, 453 N.Y.S.2d at 253.

[42] *Bi-Econ. Mkt.*, 886 N.E.2d at 132.

[43] *See* Lava Trading, Inc. v. Hartford Fire Ins. Co., 365 F. Supp. 2d 434, 445 (S.D.N.Y. 2005) (noting that a court will examine the nonbreaching parties actions).

[44] In some instances, like stock investment brokers, courts in New York have allowed the brokers to relieve themselves of liability in advance of realized loss through exculpatory agreements exonerating them from all liability except caused by willful misconduct. Hunter v. Marine Midland Bank, 143 Misc. 2d 697, 704 (N.Y. City Ct. Rochester 1989), *aff'd*, 48 N.Y.2d 900 (1979) (addressing the liability of investment brokers).

[45] Davis v. A.O. Smith Corp., 262 A.D.2d 752, 753–54 (3d Dep't 1999).

[46] U.C.C. § 2-719 (3) (2005); N.Y.U.C.C. § 2-719 (3) (2007). *See also* Master Lease Corp. v. Manhattan Limousine, Ltd. 177 A.D.2d 85, 86–88 (2d Dep't 1992) (finding that a disclaimer

Whether a contractual disclaimer is unconscionable, and thus unenforceable, depends on the content of the contract. For example, in a dispute involving an injury to a person, the disclaimer is *prima facie* unconscionable. But, where loss is commercial, the disclaimer is not considered *prima facie* unconscionable.[47] New York courts enforce such provisions on a case-by-case basis, and it is the injured parties' burden to prove unfairness or unconscionability.[48]

10.19 In *Biotronik A.G. v. Conor Medsystems Ireland, Ltd.*,[49] the New York Court of Appeals held that lost profits directly resulting from the breach are general damages and not *special* damages that were excluded from recovery in the limitation of liability clause in the distribution agreement at issue in the case. The distribution agreement was not a simple resale contract, where one party buys a product at a set price to sell at whatever the market may bear; rather, the price that the plaintiff paid the defendant reflected the actual sales of the devices. Thus, the court found that any lost profits resulting from a breach would be the natural and probable consequence of that breach. *Biotronik* thus shifts the analysis of whether lost profits are general or special damages to whether the damages are the natural and probable cause of the breach.

10.20 Consequential damages may include money lost due to business interruption,[50] costs due to interest rate increases,[51] or tax consequences arising out of the breach.[52] Anticipated future revenue or lost profits from loss of business opportunity (in any of its many variations) constitutes one of the more frequently disputed elements of damages. When "lost profits" are claimed as the delta between a contracted sales price and the cost to produce the goods, such as in the previous example, they are properly claimed as direct damages. This type of claim is frequently deemed to be within the contemplation of the parties and is easily proven and readily awarded. When parties seek anticipated future lost profits in the context of a lost business opportunity, as the measure of anticipated future revenue streams that would have been realized but for the breach, "lost profits" are usually considered special damages and subject to a much higher burden of proof.[53] In such cases, the claiming party must prove (1) upon a preponderance

---

is valid, unless the contract was unconscionable; in other words, one party must have an absence of a meaningful choice in the contract).

47 *Id.*

48 Royal Indem. Co. v. Westinghouse Elec. Corp., 385 F. Supp. 520, 524 (S.D.N.Y. 1974).

49 22 N.Y.3d 799 (2014).

50 Sabbeth Indus. Ltd. v. Pennsylvania Lumbermens Mut. Ins. Co., 656 N.Y.S.2d 475, 476 (3d Dep't 1997) (awarding consequential damages for business interruption).

51 Int'l Fidelity Ins. Co. v. Rockland, 98 F. Supp. 2d 400, 416 (S.D.N.Y. 2000) (noting that a court can award interest costs incurred by the owner due to a delay).

52 Beggs v. Dougherty Overseas, Inc., 287 F.2d 80, 83 (2d Cir. 1961) (awarding damages attributed to tax benefits lost from termination or employment).

53 DirecTV Latin Am., LLC v. RCTV Int'l Corp., 115 A.D.3d 539, 982 N.Y.S.2d 96, 98 (2014).

of the evidence that recovery of lost profits was within the contemplation of the parties, (2) with certainty that such damages have been caused by the breach, and (3) the alleged loss must itself be capable of proof with reasonable certainty.[54] These types of claims for lost profits may not be recovered if merely speculative, possible, or imaginary.[55] Accordingly, a start-up company or other commercial enterprise without a proven track record of profitability faces a stricter standard when seeking damages for lost profits "for the obvious reason that there does not exist a reasonable basis of experience upon which to estimate lost profits with the requisite degree of reasonable certainty."[56]

(c) Duty to mitigate Parties are obligated to avoid, or mitigate, unnecessary loss. If any benefit or opportunity for benefit arises from the breach, compensable damages will be reduced by the amount which could have been mitigated.[57] New York recognizes that it would be unfair for the nonbreaching party to receive both profits gained from replacing the contract with another and recovery of the lost opportunity to receive profits from the breached contract. Such double recovery is not permitted because contract damages are awarded only to make the injured party whole again, not to award windfall profits.[58] Impermissible double recovery would include an award of two types of damages, such as expectation damages and reliance damages—although pleading of alternate measures of damage is permitted. Moreover, the injured party is required to avoid any unnecessary increase in damages.[59] A court will not award any losses that the injured party could have prevented by using reasonable efforts.[60] **10.21**

---

[54] *See* O'Neill v. Warburg, Pincus & Co., 39 A.D.3d 281, 283–82 (1st Dep't 2007); Kantor v. 75 Worth St., LLC, 95 A.D.3d 718, 945 N.Y.S.2d 245 (2012) (finding that lost profits claim for new veterinary practice based on similar businesses previously located at the same site was too speculative); Blinds to Go (U.S.), Inc. v. Times Plaza Dev., L.P., 88 A.D.3d 838, 840, 931 N.Y.S.2d 105, 108 (2011) (holding that new businesses generally do not have a basis upon which to estimate lost profits with the requisite degree of reasonable certainty, but that there is no per se rule barring new enterprises from recovering lost profits, so long as lost profits may be established with reasonable certainty).

[55] *See* Kenford Co. v. Erie County, 67 N.Y.2d 257 (1986); Wathne Imports, Ltd. v. PRL USA, Inc., 101 A.D.3d 83, 87, (2012) (holding that lost profits may not be recovered if merely speculative, possible or imaginary); Bykowsky v. Eskenazi, 72 A.D.3d 590, (N.Y. App. Div. 2010) (same).

[56] Kenford, 67 N.Y.2d at 261. *See also* Digital Broad. Corp. v. Ladenburg, Thalmann & Co., Inc., 63 A.D.3d 647, 648 (N.Y. App. Div. 2009) (finding that new enterprise in "developmental stage" that never generated any revenue could not meet the stricter standard for the award of lost profits).

[57] *See* Donald Rubin, Inc. v. Schwartz, 594 N.Y.S.2d 193, 195 (1st Dep't 1993) ("gains which were or could have been received by the nondefaulting party by entering into another contract or transaction should be used in reducing damages caused by a breach of contract promise only where the breach gave rise to the opportunity to enter into those other contracts or transactions." (*quoting* 22 Am. Jr. 2d Damages § 34, AT 57 (2008))).

[58] *See* McKesson Automated Healthcare, Inc. v. Brooklyn Hosp. Ctr., 779 N.Y.S.2d 765, 771 (Sup. Ct. 2004) (holding that double recovery is unconscionable and a violation of public policy).

[59] *See* Holy Props. Ltd. v. Kenneth Cole Prods., Inc., 661 N.E.2d 694, 696 (N.Y. 1995) (noting that it is the duty of the injured party to make reasonable exertions to minimize the injury).

[60] Wilmot v. State, 297 N.E.2d 90, 92 (N.Y. 1973).

10.22 A party claiming damages is only required to make reasonable efforts to mitigate the injury; a party is not required to succeed in its mitigation efforts.[61] A court will apply a reasonableness test, considering the nonbreaching party's experience with the particular situation at hand.[62]

4. Liquidated Damages and Penalties

10.23 New York law recognizes the right of contracting parties to stipulate to an amount of liquidated damages to be awarded to the injured party in the event that the contract is breached.[63] Liquidated damages clauses negotiated at arm's length by sophisticated parties represented by experienced counsel are entitled to deference.[64]

10.24 Enforceability of such stipulations, however, will depend on whether they constitute a reasonable method for estimating the recovery that should be paid to make the injured party whole again.[65] If actual damages are easily ascertainable or the liquidated damages disproportionate to the actual damages, then a liquidated damages clause will be deemed an enforceable penalty intended to secure performance and to punish the breaching party, rather than compensating the injured party.[66] In contracts for the sale of goods governed by the UCC (in which valuation estimates are inherently less speculative), provisions that unreasonably estimated the damages at the time of the formation of the contract are frequently unenforceable even if the stipulated damages were proportionate to the actual damage that resulted from the breach.[67]

10.25 As a policy matter under New York law, liquidated damages that penalize the breaching party are unenforceable because they are unconscionable and against public policy.[68] Two types of liquidated damages clauses in particular are usually deemed unenforceable: (1) a provision that requires the breaching party to pay

[61] APL Co. PTE Ltd. v. Blue Water Shipping U.S. Inc. 592 F.3d 108, 111 (2d Cir. 2010).

[62] *Id.*

[63] Truck Rent-A-Center, Inc. v. Puritan Farms 2nd, Inc., 361 N.E.2d 1015, 1018 (N.Y. 1977); *see also* United Air Lines, Inc. v. Austin Travel Corp., 867 F.2d 737, 740 (2d Cir. 1989) (noting it is common for parties to determine in advance the amount of compensation due in a case of breach of contract).

[64] Addressing Sys. & Prods., Inc. v. Friedman, 59 A.D.3d 359 (2009).

[65] *See* McKinley Assocs. v. McKensson HBOC, Inc., 110 F. Supp. 2d 169, 178 (W.D.N.Y. 2000) ("Nevertheless, courts uphold contractual provisions fixing damages for breach when the terms constitute a reasonable mechanism for estimating the compensation which should be paid to satisfy any loss flowing from the breach.").

[66] X.L.O. Concrete Corp. v. John T. Brady and Co., 482 N.Y.S.2d 476, 478–79 (1st Dep't 1984) *aff'd*, 489 N.E.2d 768, 768 (N.Y. 1985); Del Nero v. Colvin, 111 A.D.3d 1250 (2013) leave to appeal denied, 114 A.D.3d 1226 (2014).

[67] Equitable Lumber Corp. v. IPA Land Dev. Corp., 344 N.E.2d 391, 395 (N.Y. 1976) (holding that the UCC only allows anticipated damages if at the time of contracting the compensation was a reasonable estimate).

[68] *X.L.O.*, 482 N.Y.S.2d at 478–79.

the full contract price regardless of how much performance is completed and (2) a provision that requires the breaching party to pay the contract price regardless of whether the breach is material or not.[69]

In *Abacus Fed. Sav. Bank v. ADT Sec. Servs., Inc.*,[70] the New York Court of Appeals held that exculpatory clauses and liquidated damages clauses in contracts are not enforceable against allegations of gross negligence. The court observed that ordinary negligence will not be enough to render the clauses unenforceable but when the conduct "smacks of intentional wrongdoing," the plaintiff will be able to recover in spite of the contractual provisions. Notably, the gross negligence in this context pertains to the breach of contract claim, not to an independent cause of action sounding in tort.[71] **10.26**

5. Punitive Damages

Under New York law, arbitrators are generally prohibited from making awards of punitive damages for an ordinary breach of contract, even if the breach was a deliberate breach of good faith, because the purpose of recovery for a breach is to remedy a private wrong rather than vindicate public rights.[72] While courts are permitted to award punitive damages to vindicate public interests, arbitrators—necessarily appointed to address private contractual rights—are not. **10.27**

However, when an arbitral agreement is governed by the Federal Arbitration Act or arbitral rules that permit awards of punitive damages such as those of the National Association of Securities Dealers, those rules have been held to trump a general New York choice of law provision so as to permit arbitral awards of punitive damages.[73] Thus, while potential conflicts between New York law and an arbitration clause has "engendered some perplexity," "the parties' contractual choice of New York law should not trump the core arbitration provision."[74] "A boilerplate choice of law clause does not necessarily signify the parties' acceptance of limitations imposed by New York law with respect to the contractually **10.28**

[69] Jordache Enter., Inc. v. Global Union Bank, 688 F. Supp. 939, 943 (S.D.N.Y. 1988); NCSPlus Inc. v. WBR Mgmt. Corp., 37 Misc. 3d 227, 235 (N.Y. Sup. Ct. 2012).

[70] 18 N.Y.3d 675, 682–83 (2012).

[71] *Abacus* expands the Court of Appeals holding in Sommer v. Federal Signal Corp, 79 N.Y.2d 540, 553 (1992), in which an exculpatory or liquidated damages provision is unenforceable in tort claims into the breach of contract context. *See also* Wine & Spirits of Am., Inc. v. Impact Envtl. Eng'g, PLLC, 104 A.D.3d 613, 614 (N.Y. App. Div. 2013); Soja v. Keystone Trozze, LLC, 106 A.D.3d 1168, 1169 (2013).

[72] Rocanova v. Equitable Life Assurance Soc'y of the United States, 634 N.E.2d 940, 943 (N.Y. 1994); *see also* Brink's Inc. v. New York, 717 F.2d 700, 705 (2d Cir. 1983) (noting that a party that deliberately breaches a contract in good faith cannot be punished with punitive damages); Kudler v. Truffelman, 93 A.D.3d 549, leave to appeal denied, 19 N.Y.3d 815 (2012).

[73] Mastrobuono v. Shearson Lehman Hutton, Inc., 514 U.S. 52 (1995); Marmet Health Care Ctr., Inc. v. Brown, 132 S. Ct. 1201, 1204 (2012).

[74] Smith Barney Shearson Inc. v. Sacharow, 91 N.Y. 2d 39, 47 (1997).

conferred power of an arbitration to determine all issues."[75] Even when punitive damages are waived by contract, such damages may be awarded if the waiver of punitive damages is contrary to rules or federal laws that may otherwise govern the dispute.[76]

6. Alternate Theories of Commercial Damages

10.29 *(a) Reliance* As an alternative to contractual expectation damages, New York law allows a nonbreaching party to recover reliance damages, also known as *promissory estoppel*, in appropriate cases.[77] *Reliance damages* allow the nonbreaching party to recover any costs incurred in reliance of the breaching party's promise, where the breaching party could reasonably foresee that such costs would be incurred in reliance on the contract.[78] Reliance damages are intended to compensate the nonbreaching party for out-of-pocket loss.[79] In other words, such a measure of damages seeks to place the nonbreaching party in the same position that it was in prior to the execution of the contract.[80] A nonbreaching party cannot collect reliance damages if it is collecting any other type of contractual damages. This would be considered a double recovery, which is prohibited under New York law.[81] Reliance damages, however, may be pled in the alternative.

10.30 In *St. Lawrence Factory Stores v. Ogdensburg Bridge & Port Auth.*,[82] the New York Court of Appeals adopted the Restatement (Second) of Contracts § 349 (Damages Based on Reliance Interest), holding that reliance damages in real property transactions are not limited to expenses ordinarily incurred regarding such a contract (such as a title search, survey, and attorneys' closing fees), but may include any expenditures reasonably made in preparation for or in performance of the agreement. The Court of Appeals clarified that not only ordinary expenses associated with particular types of contracts can be recovered as reliance damages, but a broader range of expenses incurred in the performance of the

---

[75] *Id.*

[76] Lian v. First Asset Mgmt., Inc., 273 A.D.2d 163, 164 (1st Dep't 2000); Kleinberg Elec., Inc. v. E-J Elec. Installation Co., 111 A.D.3d 410, 974 N.Y.S.2d 377, 378–79 (2013).

[77] V.S. Int'l, S.A. v. Boyden World Corp., 862 F. Supp. 1188, 1198 (S.D.N.Y. 1994); *see* Gotham Boxing Inc. v. Finkel, 856 N.Y.S.2d 498, 498 (Sup. Ct. N.Y. County 2008); *see also* Glen Banks, New York Practice Series—New York Contract Law § 23:27 (2008).

[78] *See* Freund v. Washington Square Press. Inc., 314 N.E.2d 419, 421 (N.Y. 1974) (noting that if the nonbreaching party incurred costs because of reliance of the contract and these costs foreseeable and ascertainable, the nonbreaching party would be entitled to recover that expense); 401 Hotel, L.P. v. MTI/Image Group, Inc., 674 N.Y.S.2d 318, 319 (1st Dep't 1998) (holding that plaintiff cannot recover reliance damages because it failed to "demonstrate ... a clear and unambiguous promise by defendants upon which it reasonably and foreseeably relied to its detriment.").

[79] *See Gotham Boxing*, 856 N.Y.S.2d at 498 (noting that a plaintiff was seeking to collect out-of-pocket losses for relying on a promise).

[80] *See V.S. Int'l, S.A.*, 862 F. Supp. at 1198 (noting that reliance damages are intended to place the nonbreaching party in the same position as they were prior to the execution of the contract).

[81] Gosden v. Elmira City Sch. Dist., 90 A.D.3d 1202, 1204 (2011).

[82] 13 N.Y.3d 204, 207 (2009).

agreement are recoverable, provided they are foreseeable and ascertainable at the moment the contract was entered.

The costs that the nonbreaching party can recover under a reliance theory include "preparation and partial performance of the contract, as well as other foreseeable expenses incurred in reliance of the contract."[83] However, the nonbreaching party will not be entitled to collect reliance damages if the breaching party establishes that the nonbreaching party would have lost equal to or more than the reliance expenditures had the nonbreaching party completed performance of the contract.[84] In other words, when recovering reliance damages, the nonbreaching party cannot collect more than it would have collected if it recovered expectation damages.[85] **10.31**

There are two categories in which New York law allows the nonbreaching party to recover reliance damages. The first category is when promissory estoppel is a substitute for consideration.[86] This category only applies to narrow exceptions based on unusual circumstances which include "a pledge of a charitable contribution, marriage settlements, a promise of a gift of land followed by the donee making substantial improvements thereon, a gratuitous bailee's promise to insure the bailed a goods, and a promise by an insurance broker to pay certain premiums to prevent lapse of the policy."[87] The second category is when the nonbreaching party is attempting to bar the breaching party from asserting a defense of the statute of frauds.[88] **10.32**

For the injured party to collect based on promissory estoppel, the injured party must prove the following four elements: (1) the breaching party made a clear and unambiguous promise; (2) the injured party relied on that promise; (3) the reliance on the promise was reasonable and foreseeable; and (4) the injured party asserting the estoppel must have been injured by his reliance.[89] **10.33**

(b) Restitution Similar to reliance, *restitution*, also known as *quantum meruit*, seeks to place the injured party in the same economic position it was in prior to contracting.[90] This is an equitable remedy that restores the injured party in order **10.34**

---

83 Bausch & Lomb Inc. v. Bressler, 977 F.2d 720, 729 (2d Cir. 1992) (*quoting* J. Calimari and J. Perillo, Contracts § 14–19 (3d ed. 1987)).

84 *Id.*

85 *Id.*

86 Murphy v. Gutfreund, 583 F. Supp. 957, 966 (S.D.N.Y. 1984) (citing Swerdloff v. Mobil Oil Corp., 427 N.Y.S.2d 266, 268–69 (2d Dep't 1980)).

87 *Id.*

88 *Id.*

89 *Id.*

90 Farash v. Sykes Datatronics, Inc., 452 N.E.2d 1245, 1248 (N.Y. 1983) (*quoting* J. Calimari and J. Perillo, Contracts § 15–4 (3d ed. 1987)); 23 Laura Dietz et al., 22 N.Y. Jur. 2d Contracts § 586 (2008); Mandarin Trading Ltd. v. Wildenstein, 65 A.D.3d 448, 452 (2009) *aff'd*, 16 N.Y.3d 173 (2011).

to prevent his or her adversary from being unjustly enriched by the performance of the injured party.[91] Restitution damages are measured by the services rendered, goods delivered, or property conveyed by the injured party minus the reasonable value of the performance received by the injured party.[92] As stated previously, New York measures the extent the party was injured rather than the value the breaching party received.[93] Restitution can be awarded even if the breaching party was enriched due to a mistake of the injured party. For example, if the injured party delivered the wrong item, it would probably be able to recover that item.[94]

7. A Special Case: Demonstrating Damages for Anticipated Future Profits from a Lost Business Opportunity

10.35 One of the most difficult tasks of tribunals can be determining an appropriate valuation for lost business, a lost opportunity, or lost profits—particularly for a new or start-up enterprise. Under New York law, these classes of damages may be recoverable as special damages. The very designation of these damages as "special" or "extraordinary," however, is telling indication of their disfavored status under New York law. As discussed previously, such damages must be proven with reasonable certainty in order to be recoverable.

10.36 Under New York law, anticipated future profits for a lost business opportunity may be recoverable as special damages, subject to the limitations discussed previously. New York courts require the party seeking lost profits to prove: (1) that the damages claimed were caused by the breach; (2) that the alleged damages are capable of determination with reasonable certainty; and (3) that the particular damages were fairly within the contemplation of the parties at the time the agreement was made.[95] New York courts often determine these damages by looking at past sales and current and expected future market conditions.[96] This poses difficulties for new businesses, as there is no past basis to make a

---

[91] *See* Brylgrove Ltd. v. Tompkins, PLC, 568 N.Y.S.2d 799, 801 (1st Dep't 1991) (noting that *quantum meriut* is imposed in order to prevent unjust enrichment); Metro. Switch Bd. Mfg. Co., Inc. v. B & G Elec. Contractors, Div. of B & G Indus., Inc., 96 A.D.3d 725, 726 (2012).

[92] Bausch & Lomb Inc. v. Bressler, 977 F.2d 720, 729 (*quoting* J. Calimari and J. Perillo, Contracts §15 –4 (3d ed. 1987)).

[93] *See supra* note 2 and accompanying text; *see also* 22 N.Y. Jur. 2d Contracts § 586 (2008).

[94] *See* First Wall St. Settlement Corp. v. Hart, 590 N.Y.S.2d 81, 852–53 (1st Dep't 1992) (holding a stock broker should recover loss as a result of a misdelivery of the wrong stock even if he was negligent).

[95] Westerbeke Corp. v. Daihatsu Motor Co., 162 F. Supp. 2d 278, 288 (S.D.N.Y. 2001) *rev'd on other grounds*, 304 F.3d 200 (2d Cir. 2002). While New York courts have not expressly defined what constitutes "reasonable certainty," "[p]rojections of future profits based upon a multitude of assumptions that require speculation and conjecture and few known factors do not provide the requisite certainty." Schonfeld v. Hilliard, 218 F.3d 164, 172 (2d Cir. 2000).

[96] Tom Doherty Assocs., Inc. v. Saban Enter., 60 F.3d 27, 38 (2d Cir. 1995).

determination of lost profits, and courts will scrutinize those businesses under a tougher standard.[97]

Courts have frequently found that lost profits claims are too speculative,[98] or that lost profits were not within the contemplation of the parties. Instead of granting lost profit damages, the court will grant lost asset damages. Broadly speaking, this is a default to general damages where special damages are too remote or speculative. A lost asset damages claim is most appropriately used when the defendant's conduct "results in the loss of an income-producing asset with an ascertainable market value."[99] Rather than requiring an estimation of the value of an asset that *may* produce profits in the future, lost asset damages claims measure the market value of the asset at the time of the breach.[100] Courts reason that "[t]he market value of an income-producing asset is inherently less speculative than lost profits because it is determined at a single point in time. It represents what a buyer is willing to pay for the chance to earn the speculative profits."[101] Moreover, calculating lost asset damages for the market loss, as opposed to speculating as to what the plaintiff will lose, is more consistent with the notion of making the plaintiff whole. New York courts commonly follow the theory that while damages are meant to make whole the nonbreaching party, future valuation that is uncertain in its calculation may unfairly award the nonbreaching party beyond what was contemplated at the time of the contract. **10.37**

In *Wathne Imports Ltd. v. PRL USA, Inc.*,[102] the First Department stated that "it is true that a party may only recover damages for loss of future profits if it 'demonstrates with certainty that such damages have been caused by the breach ... the alleged loss must be capable of proof with reasonable certainty ... not merely speculative, possible or imaginary ... and the particular damages [must have been] fairly within the contemplation of the parties.' "[103] However, the court also stated that a "degree of uncertainty is to be expected in assessing lost profits," and an estimate of lost profits necessarily **10.38**

---

[97] *Schonfeld*, 218 F.3d at 172. *See also* Ashland Mgmt. v. Janien, 82 N.Y.2d 395, 404 (2d Cir. 1993) (stating "in the case of a new business seeking to recover loss of future profits, a stricter standard is imposed because there is no experience from which lost profits may be estimated with reasonable certainty and other methods of evaluation may be too speculative."). However, in *Ashland*, the Second Circuit held that where the issue of future earnings were fully debated and analyzed "by sophisticated business professionals at the time of these extended contract negotiations" loss of profits were allowed. *Id.* at 405. Particularly, they were allowed because the proof of contemplation of damages was specific, definite, and was not speculative.

[98] Blinds To Go, Inc. v. Times Plaza Dev., 88 A.D.3d 838 (2d Dep't 2011) (finding that evidence of lost profits was lacking because plaintiff did not have prior operations in the market and because of differences between the alleged comparables and the business at hand); Digital Broadcast corp. v. Ladenburg, Thalmann & Co., Inc., 63 A.D.3d 647 (1st Dep't 2009) (denying lost profits claim because the plaintiff had never generated any revenue and thus could not meet the stricter standard for an award of lost profits).

[99] *Schonfeld*, 218 F.3d at 176 (internal citations omitted).

[100] *Id.* (internal citations omitted).

[101] *Id.* at 177 (internal citations omitted).

[102] 101 A.D.3d 83 (1st Dep't 2012).

[103] *Id.* at 87.

"requires some improvisation, and the party who has caused the loss may not insist on theoretical perfection."[104] Applying these principles, the court concluded that it was appropriate to use a competitor's sales as a basis for establishing lost profits.[105]

C. CALCULATION OF INTEREST

10.39 Under New York law, awards of interest rest on the theory that there has been a deprivation of the use of money or its equivalent, and that an award of interest will make the aggrieved party whole; it is not to provide a windfall.[106]

1. Prejudgment Interest

10.40 The interest component of a damages award is often referred to as *prejudgment interest.* Prejudgment interest is not a penalty. Rather, it "is simply the cost of having the use of another person's money for a specified period."[107] It is intended to indemnify a successful party for the nonpayment of what is due them, and is not meant to punish defendants for delaying the final resolution of the litigation.[108]

10.41 The New York Civil Practice Law and Rules (CPLR) provide for statutory rates of interest in court actions but do not mandate a rate of interest for arbitrations. Arbitrators sometimes, but not always, follow the statutory rates as an exercise of their discretion.

10.42 The CPLR requires that awards of prejudgment interest be made in all breach of contract actions.[109] But in *Stillman v. InService America Inc.*,[110] the court held that prejudgment interest is *mandatory* for breach of contract claims as well as claims arising from "contracts implied in law and quasi-contracts."[111] The court made clear that "even on a claim with equitable underpinnings, such as one for breach of fiduciary duty, [the statutory rate for] prejudgment interest would be mandatory where the only relief sought was compensatory damages."[112]

10.43 According to the CPLR, prejudgment interest is computed from the earliest ascertainable date on which the cause of action existed—most commonly in commercial disputes, the date of the breach.[113] However, interest upon damages

---

[104] *Id.* at 89.
[105] *Id.*
[106] Spodek v. Park Prop. Dev. Assocs., 719 N.Y.S.2d 109, 110 (2d Dep't 2001); Kaiser v. Fishman, 590 N.Y.S.2d 230, 234 (2d Dep't 1992).
[107] Love v. New York, 78 N.Y.2d 540, 533 (1991).
[108] Trimboli v. Scarpaci Funeral Home, 326 N.Y.S.2d 227, 230 (2d Dep't 1971).
[109] N.Y.C.P.L.R. § 5001(a) (2007).
[110] 738 F.Supp. 2d 480 (S.D.N.Y. 2010).
[111] *Id.* at 481.
[112] *Id.* at 482.
[113] N.Y.C.P.L.R. § 5001(b) (2007); Trinity Biotech, Inc. v. Reidy, 665 F. Supp. 2d 377 (S.D.N.Y. 2009): The party who establishes a breach of contract is entitled to prejudgment interest from the date of the breach.

incurred after the cause of action came to exist shall be computed from the date incurred.[114] If damages were incurred at various times, interest may be either computed individually upon each item from the date it was incurred, or upon all of the damages from a single reasonable intermediate date.[115] In a claim for breach of a contractual obligation to pay money, if the contract contains no date when payment is due, prejudgment interest will run from the date plaintiff demanded payment.[116]

The default statutory interest rate awarded by courts in New York is set at 9 percent per year.[117] However, several courts have held that where the contract itself sets forth an interest rate that is higher than 9 percent and the contract states that the given rate governs "until the principal is fully paid," then prejudgment interest on the claim will be at the contract rate.[118] **10.44**

Under New York law, prejudgment interest is calculated on a simple interest basis.[119] "In the absence of an express agreement for either compound interest or interest on interest, or statutory authority, such interest is not recoverable."[120] **10.45**

2. Postjudgment Interest

New York statutory law specifies that court judgments shall accrue postjudgment interest: "every money judgment shall bear interest from the date of its entry."[121] Even if the party is not statutorily entitled to prejudgment interest, all claims reduced to judgment accrue postjudgment until paid. Therefore, if there is a significant delay in the payment of the judgment, the interest may be substantial. As with prejudgment interest, postjudgment interest is normally calculated on a simple interest basis. **10.46**

New York's default rate for postjudgment interest is again the statutory 9 percent. Courts will enforce an agreement to pay postjudgment interest at a rate higher than the statutory rate (up to the legal limit of 25 percent), but only given a "clear, unambiguous, and unequivocal" agreement to do so.[122] **10.47**

---

114 N.Y.C.P.L.R. § 5001(b) (2007).
115 *Id.*
116 Citibank, N.A. v. Barclays Bank, PLC, 2013 WL 6153258 (S.D.N.Y. 2013).
117 N.Y.C.P.L.R. § 5004.
118 Astoria Fed. Sav. & Loan Ass'n v. Rambalakos, 372 N.Y.S.2d 689, 689–90 (2d Dep't 1975).
119 Epstein v. Kalvin-Miller Int'l, Inc., 139 F.Supp 2d 469, 486 (S.D.N.Y. 2001).
120 Rourke v. Fred H. Thomas Assocs., 627 N.Y.S.2d 831, 832 (3d Dep't 1995).
121 N.Y.C.P.L.R. § 5003.
122 Marine Mgmt., Inc. v. Seco Mgmt. Inc., 574 N.Y.S.2d 207, 207 (2d Dep't 1991) *aff'd*, 80 N.Y.2d 886 (1992). *See also* IRB-Brasil Resseguros S.A. v. Portobello Intern. Ltd., 84 A.D.3d 637 (1st Dep't 2011) (applying the statutory interest rate to plaintiff's award of postjudgment interest rather than the contractual rate because the contract did not "clearly and unequivocally" specify a postjudgment rate; the court "merged" the contract into the judgment and applied the statutory interest rate).

D. ATTORNEYS' FEES AND COSTS

10.48 Under New York law (and U.S. law more generally), the default rule in court proceedings requires that parties bear their own costs and fees arising from dispute resolution absent statutory provision, express agreement, or judicially imposed penalty for frivolous conduct to the contrary. In contrast, many jurisdictions outside the United States employ a "loser pays" default rule under which the prevailing party will be awarded its costs and fees as part of its recovery.

10.49 New York courts will not enforce an award of attorneys' fees in an arbitral award without an agreement authorizing the tribunal to do so.[123] In contrast, the arbitrators' fees and expenses, "not including attorneys' fees, incurred in the conduct of the arbitration, shall be paid as provided in the award" unless the arbitration agreement provides otherwise.[124] In short, the award may include tribunal costs unless the agreement precludes it, and may only award attorneys' fees if the agreement permits it (or otherwise is bound by or references rules that permit an award of fees).[125] In all events, where the parties each request an award of attorneys' fees (regardless of the content of their written agreement), the tribunal is certainly empowered to include this in its award.

1. Awards of Arbitrator Fees and Costs

10.50 Unless the agreement between the parties provides otherwise, the arbitrators fees and costs are divided evenly by the parties, pending the arbitral tribunal's final award. However, the manner in which these costs are accounted for and covered at the outset—a procedural rather than substantive issue—is largely dependent on the applicable arbitral rules, not the substantive law of the dispute.

2. Awards of Attorneys' Fees and Costs

10.51 Under New York law, an award of attorneys' fees and costs must be expressly authorized by contract.[126] Parties, however, may contract for an award of

---

[123] *See* Sammy Line Co. v. Altamar Navegacion, S.A., 605 F. Supp. 72, 73–74 (S.D.N.Y. 1985). For clause drafting considerations, see Chapter 3.B.3.(b) of this book.

[124] N.Y.C.P.L.R. § 7513; *see also* Messina & Briante, Inc., v. Blitman Constr. Corp., 32 Misc. 2d 21, (N.Y. Sup. Ct. 1961); *aff'd*, 19 A.D.2d 862 (2d Dep't 1963), *app. dismissed*, 14 N.Y.2d 648 (1964).

[125] The general trend in New York courts is to construe agreements broadly in favor of arbitration, but only when the contractual arbitration provisions allow a broad construction. *See, e.g.*, ACE Capital Re Overseas Ltd. v. Cent. United Life Ins. Co., 307 F.3d 24, 26 (2d Cir. 2002); Oldroyd v. Elmira Sav. Bank, FSB, 134 F.3d 72, 76 (2d Cir. 1998); Collins & Aikman Prods. Co. v. Building Sys., 58 F.3d 16, 19 (2d Cir. 1995); McMahan Sec. Co. v. Forum Capital Mkts. L.P., 35 F.3d 82, 86 (2d Cir. 1994) (all finding that where there is a broad agreement to arbitrate, the presumption of arbitrability will only be overcome if there is clear indication from the language of the agreement that arbitration was not meant to cover the dispute at hand).

[126] Frater v. Tigerpack Capital, Ltd., No. 98 CIV. 3306 1998 WL 851591 (S.D.N.Y. Dec. 9, 1998); Campbell v. Citibank, N.A., 302 A.D.2d 150 (1st Dep't 2003) (fees not recoverable in

attorneys' fees and costs by reference to an arbitral institution's rules which authorize the tribunal to include attorneys' fees in its award.[127] In general, courts will not interfere with an agreement to award attorneys' fees unless such intention is unmistakably expressed in the contract language.[128] The court has an obligation to avoid inferring duties that the parties did not intend to create.[129] It cannot award attorneys' fees based upon what it believes to be the agreement of the parties.[130]

The formula for determining how fees and expenses are allocated between the parties depends on the approach or tradition relied upon in making the decision. The provision of attorneys' fee in the damages award in a particular instance may be influenced by the arbitrators' national backgrounds,[131] which should be considered when selecting applicable rules or arbitrators.[132] There are three broad formulaic approaches: (1) the "loser pays" rule, in which the non-prevailing party covers 100 percent of the attorneys' fees of the prevailing party; (2) consideration of the relative success of the each of the parties and accordingly allocating attorneys' fees between the parties in proportion to the outcome of the case; or (3) each party bears its own fees. Although an arbitral tribunal has wide discretion to order the non-prevailing party to pay the prevailing party's attorneys' fees, the appropriate proportions and awards for attorneys' fees becomes increasingly difficult where neither party succeeds on all the issues in controversy between the parties because it is more difficult to determine who the prevailing party is in fact. **10.52**

The authority to include attorneys' fees within an award for damages is generally granted through express agreement, or statutorily.[133] The parties retain flexibility and remain free to make specific provisions for security of costs within **10.53**

absence of statute, court rule or "written agreement"); Berg v. Berg. 926 N.Y.S.2d 568 (N.Y. App. Div. 2011) (holding that arbitrators erred in awarding attorney's fees because they were not authorized in the arbitration agreement).

[127] Shaw Group Inc. v. Triplefine Int'l Corp., 322 F.3d 115 (2d Cir. 2003).

[128] *See* Hooper Assocs., Ltd. v. AGS Computers, Inc., 548 N.E.2d 903 (1989).

[129] Oscar Gruss & Son, Inc. v. Hollander, 337 F.3d 186, 199 (2d Cir. 2003).

[130] Flores v. Las Americas Comm., Inc., 218 A.D.2d 595 (1st Dep't 1995).

[131] There are three general approaches to developing formulas for attorneys' fee awards: (1) that all fees be borne by one of the parties, usually the losing party, which is essentially England's "costs follow the event" rule; (2) Germany, Switzerland, and Austria's allocation of fees in proportion to the outcome of the case, which takes into consideration the relative success of the claims and defenses; and (3) that the fees be equally shared by the parties or that each party bear their own fees. In Spain, England, Germany, and Switzerland there are also limitations on such attorneys' fee awards, the amount of attorneys' fees permitted is limited by a fixed fee schedule. John Yukio Gotanda, *Awarding Costs and Attorneys' Fees in International Commercial Arbitrations*, 21 Mich. J. Intl L. 1, 8–9 (1999).

[132] Rufus von Thulen Rhoades, Daniel M. Kolkey, Richard Chernick, eds., Practitioner's Handbook on International Arbitration and Mediation: Award of Costs § 7.06 at 263 (2d ed. 2007).

[133] Michael O'Reilly, *Rethinking Costs in Commercial Arbitration*, 69 Arbitration: The Journal of the Chartered Institute of Arbitrators 122 (2003).

agreements or exclude the possibility entirely.[134] Attorneys' fee awards are generally addressed at the time of the final award; however, governing rules may alter this procedure and permit a tribunal to award attorneys' fees at any time during the proceedings.[135]

10.54 Where the arbitration agreement contemplates an award of attorney's fees, courts have held that the issue of whether such an award may include the cost of defending ancillary litigation either to compel arbitration or in defending suits brought in violation of the agreement to arbitrate constitute an arbitral claim within the discretion of the arbitrator.[136]

[134] The autonomy of the parties to an international commercial arbitration proceeding was made clear in *ICC Case*, 5029 (1986), 12 Y. B. Com. Arb. 113 (1987) where the tribunal stated that the parties were free to agree on the applicable rules of procedure. *See also* Noah Rubins, *In God We Trust, All Others Pay Cash: Security for Costs in International Commercial Arbitration*, 11 Am. Rev. Int'l Arb. 307, 316 (2000).

[135] Hilary Heilbron, *Assessing Damages in International Arbitration: Practical Considerations, in* The Leading Arbitrators' Guide to International Arbitration, at 472.

[136] *See, e.g.*, Shaw Group Inc. v. Triplefine Int'l Corp., 322 F.3d 115 (2d Cir. 2003) (award of attorneys' fees for defense of judicial suit brought in alleged violation of agreement to arbitrate within power of arbitrator to decide).

11

CLASS ACTION ARBITRATION

William H. Baker

A. General Principles Governing Class Actions in Courts in the United States 11.04
B. The U.S. Supreme Court's Decision in *Bazzle* 11.08
C. The Class Arbitration Rules Established by the AAA and JAMS Following *Bazzle* 11.29
1. AAA Class Arbitration Rules 11.29
2. JAMS Class Arbitration Rules 11.35
D. The Effect of *Hall St. Associates v. Mattel* on Class Arbitrations 11.37
E. The Different Sources of Law Which One Must Consider in Determining Whether a Silent Arbitration Clause Permits a Class Arbitration 11.48
F. Federal Circuit Court and State Court Decisions Regarding Consolidation of Arbitrations and Class Arbitrations Before *Bazzle* 11.53
G. Clause-Construction Decisions by Arbitral Panels Adjudicating Class Arbitrations After *Bazzle* 11.55
H. The U.S. Supreme Court Decision in *Stolt-Neilsen S.A. v. Animal-Feeds International Corp* 11.65
I. Post-*Stolt-Neilsen* Decisions by Arbitration Tribunals Regarding Whether "Silent Clauses" Permit Class Action Arbitrations 11.71
J. Class-Certification Decisions by Arbitral Tribunals After *Bazzle* 11.73
1. Numerosity 11.76
2. Commonality 11.77
3. Typicality 11.78
4. Adequacy of Class Representative(s) 11.79
5. Adequacy of the Class Representative(s)' Counsel 11.80
6. Substantial Similarity of Arbitration Agreements 11.81
7. Predominance and Superiority of Claims 11.82
K. Arbitral Clauses Prohibiting Class Actions and Public Policy Arguments against Such Clauses Before the Supreme Court Decisions in *AT&T Mobility LLC v. Concepcion* and *American Express Co. v. Italian Colors Restaurant* 11.85
L. Decisions By Courts, Before *AT&T Mobility* and *American Express*, Regarding Whether State Arbitration Laws and Concepts of Public Policy are Preempted by the FAA 11.95
M. The Supreme Court Decisions in *AT&T Mobility* and *American Express* Regarding Whether Clauses Prohibiting Class Arbitrations are Against Public Policy and Whether a State's Public Policy is Preempted by the FAA 11.103
N. Decisions After *AT&T Mobility* and *American Express* Regarding Whether Clauses Prohibiting Class Arbitrations Are Against Public Policy or Whether a State's Public Policy Is Preempted by the FAA 11.110
O. Legislation Regarding Class-Action Arbitrations 11.115
P. Conclusion 11.116

11.01 Class action arbitrations are a relatively recent phenomenon in the United States, but the number of such arbitrations has been expanding at a rapid rate. As of July 2014, the American Arbitration Association (AAA) had administered 323 class action arbitrations, and Judicial Arbitration and Mediation Services, Inc. (JAMS), another major U.S. arbitral institution, had also administered a substantial number of class arbitrations.

11.02 Most such arbitrations are exclusively between domestic parties and often arise out of arbitration clauses inserted in the fine print of consumer or employment contracts. In some cases, however, foreign companies have entered into what may have appeared to be simple, single-party arbitration clauses, only to find themselves embroiled in class action arbitrations. For example, one arbitration panel issued a clause-construction award, which permitted a corporate claimant's antitrust claims against a foreign shipping company to proceed in arbitration as a class action.[1] Another clause-construction award allowed Harvard University to bring a class arbitration on behalf of all investors in a Russian oil and gas company.[2] Another pending class arbitration, *CBR Enterprises, LLC v. Blimpie Int'l, Inc.*,[3] involves several U.S. defendants with substantial international holdings, who could be subject to international enforcement orders, and *Bagpeddler.com v. U.S. Bancorp*[4] could include non-U.S. plaintiffs as part of its class of several hundred thousand Internet vendors. It, therefore, behooves international arbitration practitioners to be aware of class action arbitration law and procedures in New York and in the United States generally.

11.03 There have been significant developments in class arbitration law in the U.S. in recent years due to a series of U.S. Supreme Court decisions. Those decisions nevertheless do not resolve all open issues, and certain of the case law both before and since the key opinions therefore remains important.

A. GENERAL PRINCIPLES GOVERNING CLASS ACTIONS IN COURTS IN THE UNITED STATES

11.04 A class action is a procedure whereby one or more members of a class with similar or identical claims against a common entity may sue as representatives of the other

[1] The Supreme Court of the United States granted *certiorari* in Stolt-Nielsen S. A. v. AnimalFeeds Int'l Corp., 559 U.S. 662 (2010). *See* discussion of this decision at Section H, *infra*.

[2] Harvard Coll. v. Surgutneftegaz, AAA Docket Number 11 168 T 01654 04. The award was affirmed on appeal, JSC Surguntneftegaz v. Harvard Coll., 2007 WL 3019234 (S.D.N.Y. 2007).

[3] CBR Enterprises, LLC v. Blimpie Int'l, Inc. (No current AAA Case Number found).

[4] AAA Case No. 11 181 00322 04.

members of the class. Class actions in federal courts in the United States are governed by Rule 23 of the Federal Rules of Civil Procedure (FRCP). FRCP Rule 23(a) sets forth the prerequisites for asserting a class action:

> One or more members of a class may sue as representative parties on behalf of all only if (1) the class is so numerous that joinder of all members is impracticable, (2) there are questions of law or fact common to the class, (3) the claims or defenses of the representative parties are typical of the claims or defenses of the class, and (4) the representative parties will fairly and adequately protect the interests of the class.

Once these prerequisites have been established, one must also satisfy the requirements of Rule 23(b). Rule 23(b) outlines three different situations in which class actions are appropriate, but the most frequently used basis for a class action is set forth in Rule 23(b)(3). This Rule provides, in pertinent part, that a class may be allowed if the court finds that the prerequisites of Rule 23(a) have been satisfied and further "finds that the questions of law or fact common to class members predominate over any questions affecting only individual members, and that a class action is superior to other available methods for fairly and efficiently adjudicating the controversy."

Rule 23(c) provides that a court must hold a special hearing to determine if the matter is properly certifiable as a class. Rule 23(c)(2)(B) further provides that if a court certifies a class under Rule 23(b)(3), it: **11.05**

> must direct to class members the best notice practicable under the circumstances, including individual notice to all members who can be identified through reasonable effort. The notice must concisely and clearly state in plain, easily understood language:
> - the nature of the action,
> - the definition of the class certified,
> - the class claims, issues, or defenses,
> - that a class member may enter an appearance through counsel if the member so desires,
> - that the court will exclude from the class any member who requests exclusion,
> - the time and manner for requesting exclusion; and
> - the binding effect of a class judgment on class members … [who have not elected to exclude themselves from the class].[5]

Once a class has been certified, if the plaintiff is successful on the merits, whether by judgment or settlement, Rule 23(h) provides that the court may award "reasonable attorney's fees." These fees are often measured by a percentage of the "common fund" recovered on behalf of the class. **11.06**

[5] FRCP 23(b)(2).

11.07 Class actions have been employed in numerous contexts including cases involving civil rights actions,[6] securities fraud claims,[7] and consumer and environmental claims.[8] Some commentators have praised class actions as providing a means of vindicating individual rights in situations where the claims would be too small to bring economically if each person were required to assert his claim on an individual basis.[9] Others have condemned class actions as too often abused by plaintiffs' attorneys, who sometimes bring suits of questionable merit, but are able to force settlement from defendants because of the potentially huge exposure (even if discounted for likelihood of success) arising from the ability to aggregate an enormous number of individual claims.[10] Any comment on the merits or demerits of class actions, however, exceeds the limited purpose of this chapter.

B. THE U.S. SUPREME COURT'S DECISION IN *BAZZLE*

11.08 In *Green Tree Financial Corp. v. Bazzle*,[11] the U.S. Supreme Court reviewed a decision from the Supreme Court of South Carolina.[12] The South Carolina case involved two couples, the Bazzles and the Lackeys. The Bazzles entered into a boilerplate form financing agreement with Green Tree Financial Corporation for a home improvement loan. The financing agreement contained an arbitration clause which provided, in pertinent part, that claims "relating to 'this contract ... will be resolved by binding arbitration by an arbitrator selected by us with the consent of you.' "[13] The Lackeys entered into a similar boilerplate form agreement containing a similar arbitration clause in order to finance the purchase of a mobile home.

11.09 The Lackeys and the Bazzles subsequently filed separate class action lawsuits alleging that Green Tree had failed to comply with applicable law that required that certain attorney and insurance preference forms be included with the loan application. Green Tree moved to stay both cases and to compel separate arbitrations. Eventually, the two cases were consolidated on appeal, and when the

---

[6] *See, e.g.*, Hall v. Werthan Bag Corp., 251 F. Supp 184 (M.D. Tenn. 1966) (discrimination in employment claims); Gantt v. Clemson Agric. Coll. of SC, 320 F.2d 611 (4th Cir. 1963) (discrimination in education claims).

[7] *See, e.g.*, Cary Plastic Packaging Corp. v. Merrill, Lynch, Pierce, Fenner & Smith, Inc., 903 F.2d. 176 (1990).

[8] *See, e.g.*, Mace v. Van Ru Credit Corp, 109 F.3d 338 (7th Cir. 1997) (consumer claims for violation of the Fair Debt Collection Practices Act); Mejdrech v. Met-Coif Sys Corp., 319 F.3d 910 (7th Cir. 2003) (environmental pollution claims).

[9] John Bronsteen and Owen Fiss, *The Class Action Rule*, 78 Notre Dame L. Rev. 1419 (2003).

[10] Gary L. Sasso, *Class Actions: De Minimis Carat Lex?*, 31 Litig. 16 (2005).

[11] 539 U.S. 444 (2003).

[12] Bazzle v. Green Tree Fin. Corp., 569 S.E.2d 349 (S.C. 2002).

[13] *Id.* at 352, note 3.

matter reached the Supreme Court of South Carolina, it posed the issue before it as "whether class-wide arbitration is permissible when the arbitration agreement between the parties is silent regarding class actions."[14] After noting that the law of South Carolina, unlike that of many jurisdictions, permits the consolidation of arbitrations without the parties' express consent, the court ruled that a silent arbitration clause was ambiguous and as such should be construed against the drafter so as to permit a class arbitration:

> If we enforced a mandatory, adhesive arbitration clause, but prohibited class actions in arbitration where the agreement is silent, the drafting party could effectively prevent class actions against it without having to say it was doing so in the agreement.[15]

When the case reached the U.S. Supreme Court, the Court fractured along several lines, resulting in a plurality, rather than a majority opinion. **11.10**

Before discussing the reasoning of the different opinions of the Justices, however, it is first necessary to make a few comments regarding the law in the United States with respect to: (1) whether the courts or arbitrators decide issues of arbitrability; and (2) the circumstances under which the Federal Arbitration Act (FAA) is applicable and preempts a given state's arbitration statute with respect to a particular arbitration issue. **11.11**

With respect to the issue of who decides arbitrability, the law in the United States is different from that in many jurisdictions. In the case of *First Options v. Kaplan*,[16] the U.S. Supreme Court held that the issue of arbitrability may be referred to the arbitrators only if there is "'clear and unmistakable' evidence" from the arbitration agreement that the parties intended the question of arbitrability to be decided by the arbitrators.[17] Determining whether there is "clear and unmistakable evidence" that the parties intended the arbitrators to decide arbitrability requires the court to interpret the arbitration agreement applying relevant state law.[18] The Supreme Court, however, has defined the term "arbitrability" narrowly. In *Howsam v. Dean Witter Reynolds, Inc.*,[19] the Court noted that "[l]inguistically speaking, one might call any potentially dispositive gateway question a 'question of arbitrability,' for its answer will determine whether the underlying controversy will proceed to arbitration on the merits."[20] The Court went on to note, however, that it had found the phrase "question of arbitrability" applicable only in the kind of narrow circumstance where contracting parties would likely have expected a court to have decided the gateway matter, where **11.12**

---

14 *Id.* at 351.
15 *Id.* at 360.
16 514 U.S. 938 (1995).
17 514 U.S. at 944–45 (citation omitted).
18 514 U.S. at 944.
19 537 U.S. 79 (2002).
20 *Id.* at 83.

they are not likely to have thought that they had agreed that an arbitrator would do so, and, consequently, where reference of the gateway dispute to the court avoids the risk of forcing parties to arbitrate a matter that they may well not have agreed to arbitrate.[21]

11.13 Thus, the Supreme Court has decided whether an arbitration agreement bound parties who did not sign it,[22] whether an arbitration agreement survived a corporate merger,[23] or whether a labor-management layoff controversy fell within the arbitration clause of a collective bargaining agreement.[24] By contrast, the Court has indicated that the arbitrator should decide "allegations of waiver, delay, or a like defense to arbitrability,"[25] "whether a condition precedent to arbitrability has been fulfilled,"[26] whether the contract as a whole is void because of "fraud in the inducement,"[27] whether an arbitration agreement is unconscionable where the arbitration agreement explicitly assigned that decision to the arbitrator,[28] and whether a clause in an investment treaty, which requires resort to the local courts before arbitration can be commenced, has been fulfilled or waived.[29]

11.14 Under the law of New York and the Second Circuit Court of Appeals,[30] an arbitration agreement provides "clear and unmistakable evidence" of the parties' intention to submit questions of arbitrability to the arbitrators, even in the absence of an express commitment to do so, if (a) the agreement states that "any and all" controversies arising out of the agreement shall be referred to a particular arbitration forum; and (b) the rules of that forum allow the arbitrators to resolve any

---

21 *Id.* at 83–84.

22 *First Options*, 514 U.S. at 943–46.

23 John Wiley & Sons, Inc. v. Livingston, 376 U.S. 543, 546–47 (1964).

24 AT&T Techs, Inc. v. Communications Workers of Am., 475 U.S. 643, 651–52 (1986).

25 Moses H. Cone Mem. Hosp v. Mercury Constr. Corp., 460 U.S. 1, 24–25 (1983).

26 *Howsam*, 537 U.S. at 85 (*quoting* the Revised Uniform Arbitration Act 2000 § 6(c) and cmt. 2, 7 ULA 12–13 (Supp. 2002), which states that it seeks to "incorporate the holding of the vast majority of state courts and the law that has developed under the [Federal Arbitration Act])."

27 Buckeye Check Cashing, Inc. v. Cardegna, 126 S. Ct. 1204, 1208 (2006). In an earlier case, Prima Paint Corp. v. Flood & Conklin Mfg. Co., 388 U.S. 395 (1967), the Supreme Court had held that the arbitration clause in a contract is severable from the contract itself, and, therefore, the court, as opposed to the arbitrator, may adjudicate fraud in the inducement only if the fraud related to the arbitration clause itself. There was some thought that *First Options* and *Howsam* may have modified, *sub silentio*, the Court's holding in *Prima Paint* because the question of whether the entire contract was induced by fraud might be deemed a gateway issue of arbitrability which the Court should decide. The *Buckeye* decision confirmed *Prima Paint* as good law.

28 Rent-A-Center West, Inc v. Jackson, 561 U.S. 63 (2010) The arbitration clause in question provided that "[t]he Arbitrator, and not any federal, state, or local court or agency, shall have exclusive authority to resolve any dispute relating to the interpretation, applicability, enforceability or formation of this Agreement, including, but not limited to any claim that all or any part of this Agreement is void or voidable." *Id.* at 66.

29 BG Group, PLC v. Republic of Argentina, 133 S. Ct. 2795 (2013).

30 For a map showing the geographical area covered by each of the federal circuit courts of appeals, go to http://www.uscourts.gov and click on Court Links.

disputes about their own jurisdiction.[31] The California,[32] Arkansas,[33] and New Mexico[34] State Courts, the Ninth Circuit,[35] and the Fifth Circuit,[36] and Federal Circuit[37] appear to have joined the Second's Circuit's view. Seven other federal circuit courts of appeals, however, have disagreed with the Second Circuit, holding that incorporation of the rules of an arbitration forum does not by itself provide "clear and unmistakable evidence" that the parties intended the arbitrators to decide the issue of arbitrability.[38]

With respect to the issue of whether the FAA applies to a given arbitration, as opposed to the arbitration statute of the state where the arbitration is sited, courts have held that the FAA governs if the dispute involves interstate commerce.[39] Courts have also held that the FAA governs when the dispute is an international one subject to the Convention on Recognition and Enforcement of Foreign Arbitral Awards[40] (New York Convention).[41] Although the FAA is applicable, state law governing arbitrability can also apply so long as it is not inconsistent with the FAA. If it is inconsistent, then the FAA controls and the state law is preempted.[42] The question of whether a state's law *is* inconsistent, however, is often a murky one. **11.15**

[31] PaineWebber, Inc. v. Bybyk, 81 F.3d 1193, 1199–1200 (2d Cir. 1996); Smith Barney Shearson, Inc. v. Sacharow, 91 N.Y.2d 39, 46–47 (N.Y. 1997) (NASD forum); Shaw Group, Inc. v. Triplefine Int'l Corp., 322 F.3d 115, 120–21 (2d Cir. 2003) (International Chamber of Commerce forum); Contec Corp. v. Remote Solution Co., 398 F.3d 205, 208–09 (2d Cir. 2005) (American Arbitration Association forum); Emilio v. Sprint Spectrum L.P., 508 F. App'x 3, 5–6 (2d Cir. 2013); Alliance Bernstein Inv. Research & Mgmt., Inc. v. Schaffran, 445 F.3d 121 (2d Cir. 2006).

[32] Dream Theater, Inc. v. Dream Theater, 124 Cal. App. 4th 547, 557 (2004).

[33] HPD, LLC v. Tetra Techs., Inc., 2012 Ark. 408.

[34] Felts v. CLK Mgmt., 149 N.M. 681 (2011)

[35] Wynn Resorts v. Atl.-Pac. Capital, Inc. 497 F. App'x 740, 741 (9th Cir. 2012).

[36] Petrofac, Inc. v. Dynmcdermott Petroleum Operations Co., 687 F.3d 671, 675 (5th Cir. 2012).

[37] Qualcomm Inc. v. Nokia Corp., 466 F.3d 1366, 1373 (Fed. Cir. 2006)

[38] Marie v. Allied Home Mortgage Corp., 402 F.3d 1, 15 (1st Cir. 2005); Shank/Balfour Beatty v. IBEW Local 99, 497 F.3d 83, 89 (1st Cir. 2007); Smith Sarno Inc. v. Sarver, 108 F.3d 92, 96–97 (6th Cir. 1997); Miller v. Flume, 139 F.3d 1130, 1134 (7th Cir. 1998); Lebanon Chem. Corp. v. United Farmers Plant Food, Inc., 179 F.3d 1095, 1099 (8th Cir. 1999); Spahr v. Secco, 330 F.3d 1266, 1270 (10th Cir. 2003); Merrill Lynch, Pierce, Fenner & Smith, Inc. v. Cohen, 62 F.3d 381, 384 (11th Cir. 1995); Ehleiter v. Grapetree Shores, Inc., 482 F.3d 207, 221 (3d Cir. 2007).

[39] *See, e.g.*, Citizens Bank v. Alafabco, Inc., 539 U.S. 52, 56 (2003) (noting that the Court has previously interpreted the term "involving commerce" in the FAA, as the functional equivalent of "affecting commerce," which are words of art that ordinarily signal the broadest permissible exercise of Congress' Commerce Clause power); Wien & Malkin LLP v. Helmsley-Spear, Inc., 783 N.Y.S. 2d 339 (NY App. Div. 2004) (holding in light of *Alafabco* that the termination of an agent that managed several buildings in New York City "affects commerce" and therefore brings the FAA into play).

[40] 10 June 1958, 21 UST 2517, 330 UNTS 38, embodied in Chapter 2 of the FAA 9 USC §§ 201–08 (1999).

[41] *See, e.g.*, Smith/Enron Cogeneration Ltd. P'ship, Inc. v. Smith Cogeneration Int'l Inc., 198 F.3d 88, 96 (2d Cir. 1999). *See also* Chapter 1.

[42] Doctor's Assocs., Inc. v. Casarotto, 517 U.S. 681, 687 (1996); Aceros Pefabricados, SA v. TradeArbed, Inc., 282 F.3d 92, 100 (2d Cir. 2002).

11.16 Returning now to the *Bazzle* case before the U.S. Supreme Court, the Court, as noted, split along several lines, resulting in a plurality, rather than a majority opinion. The Chief Justice, writing a dissent on his own behalf as well as on behalf of two other Justices, indicated that they

> would reverse because this determination [of arbitrability] is for the courts, not for the arbitrator, and the holding of the Supreme Court of South Carolina contravenes the terms of the contracts and is therefore pre-empted by the FAA [Federal Arbitration Act].[43]

11.17 The Chief Justice noted that the arbitration clause was a terse one providing that

> all disputes, claims, or controversies arising from or relating to this contract or the relationships which result from this contract ... shall be resolved by binding arbitration by one arbitrator selected by us with consent of you.[44]

He further noted that other aspects of the contract read in the singular, as did each of the contracts signed by other members of the purported class, and that such language made it quite clear

> that petitioner must select, and each buyer must agree to, a particular arbitrator for disputes between petitioner and that specific buyer ... [T]he imposition of class-wide arbitration contravenes the just-quoted provision about the selection of an arbitrator. [P]etitioner had the contractual right to choose an arbitrator for each dispute with the other 3,734 individual class members, and this right was denied when the same arbitrator was foisted upon petitioner to resolve those claims as well.[45]

11.18 The Chief Justice's opinion was that the question of to *whom* to submit the arbitration was closer to the question of *what* should be submitted and that the facts of the case were closer to the Court's decision in *First Options* regarding what gateway questions of arbitrability should be decided by the Court than it was to the decision in *Howsam* regarding what questions should be submitted.[46] The Chief Justice concluded that

> [a]rbitration under the Act [FAA] is a matter of consent, not coercion. Here, the Supreme Court of South Carolina imposed a regime that was contrary to the express agreement of the parties as to how the arbitrator would be chosen. It did not enforce the "agreemen[t] to arbitrate ... according to [its] terms." I would therefore reverse the judgment of the Supreme Court of South Carolina.[47]

11.19 Justice Stephen Breyer, writing the lead opinion on behalf of himself and three other Justices, framed the issue at the outset as follows:

> This case concerns contracts between a commercial lender and its customers, each of which contains a clause providing for arbitration of all contract-related disputes.

[43] *Bazzle*, 539 U.S. at 455.
[44] *Id.* at 456 (citation omitted).
[45] *Id.* at 459.
[46] *Id.* at 456–57.
[47] *Id.* at 459–60 (citations omitted).

> The Supreme Court of South Carolina held (1) that the arbitration clauses are silent as to whether arbitration might take the form of class arbitration, and (2) that, in that circumstance, South Carolina law interprets the contracts as permitting class arbitration. We granted certiorari to determine whether this holding is consistent with the Federal Arbitration Act, 9 U.S.C. § 1 *et seq.*[48]

After framing the issue, Breyer stated that **11.20**

> Green Tree argued [before the court below], as it argues here, that the contracts are not silent—that they forbid class arbitration. And we must deal with that argument at the outset, for if it is right, then the South Carolina court's holding is flawed on its own terms; that court neither said nor implied that it would have authorized class arbitration had the parties' arbitration agreement forbidden it.[49]

Justice Breyer took note of the Chief Justice's dissenting view that the language of the contract, which uses the singular to describe the claimant and respondent, forbids class arbitration, but concluded that "the answer to this question is not completely obvious."[50] At the same time, Breyer indicated that he could not automatically accept the South Carolina Supreme Court's resolution of this contract-interpretation question, nor reach the issue of whether its decision was preempted by the FAA, concluding that "the question—whether the agreement forbids class arbitration—is for the arbitrator to decide."[51] In reaching this conclusion, Breyer noted the parties had definitely agreed on arbitration, and the only issue was what kind of arbitration. Under these circumstances, he viewed the matter as the type of arbitrability questions that an arbitrator should decide under *Howsam*, rather than the question of whether the parties had agreed to arbitrate at all, which under *First Options* would be a question for the Court to decide.[52] Justice Breyer's opinion therefore remanded the case so that the arbitrator could decide the question of whether a silent clause prohibited class arbitration. **11.21**

Justice John Paul Stevens wrote a separate opinion concurring in the judgment and dissenting in part. He noted that the South Carolina Supreme Court had "held as a matter of state law that class-action arbitrations are permissible if not prohibited by the applicable arbitration agreement, and that the agreement between these two parties is silent on the issue."[53] He expressed the opinion that, "[t]here is nothing in the Federal Arbitration Act that precludes either of these determinations,"[54] and stated that "[b]ecause the decision to conduct a class-action arbitration was correct as a matter of law, and because petitioner has merely challenged the merits of that decision without claiming that it was made by the **11.22**

48 *Id.* at 447 (citation omitted).
49 *Id.* at 450.
50 *Id.* at 451.
51 *Id.*
52 *Id.* at 451–53.
53 *Id.* at 454 (citation omitted).
54 *Id.* at 454–55 (citation omitted).

wrong decision-maker, there is no need to remand the case to correct that possible error."[55] He concluded by stating that he would prefer simply to affirm the judgment, but observed, "[w]ere I to adhere to my preferred disposition of the case ... there would be no controlling judgment of the Court. In order to avoid that outcome, and because Justice Breyer's opinion expresses a view of the case close to my own, I concur in the judgment."[56]

11.23 Finally, Justice Clarence Thomas wrote a separate dissent expressing his idiosyncratic view that the FAA does not apply to proceedings in state court. For that reason, he concluded, the FAA cannot be a ground for preempting a state court's interpretation of a private arbitration agreement.[57]

11.24 Following the decision in *Bazzle* most practitioners thought that the case had definitively decided that the question of whether an arbitration clause permits classwide arbitration is for the arbitrator to decide. Seven years later, however, the Supreme Court in *Stolt-Nielsen S.A. v. Animalfeeds International Corp.*,[58] discussed further in Section H, *infra*, noted that the multiple opinions issued in *Bazzle* did not yield a majority decision on this issue:

> Unfortunately, the opinions in *Bazzle* appear to have baffled the parties in this case at the time of the arbitration proceeding. For one thing, the parties appeared to believe that the judgment in *Bazzle* requires an arbitrator, not a court, to decide whether a contract permits class arbitration ... However, only the plurality decided that question. But we need not revisit that question here because the parties supplemental agreement expressly assigned this issue to the arbitration panel, and no party argues that this assignment was impermissible.[59]

11.25 Three years later, the Supreme Court in *Oxford Health Plans v. Sutter*,[60] cast further doubt on the assumption that an arbitrator should decide whether a given contract permits class arbitration. The majority opinion notes:

> We would face a different issue if Oxford had argued below that the availability of class arbitration is a so-called "question of arbitrability." Those questions—which "includes certain gateway matters, such as whether parties have a valid arbitration agreement at all or whether a concededly binding arbitration clause applies to a certain type of controversy"—are presumptively for courts to decide ... *Stolt-Nielsen* made clear that this Court has not yet decided whether the availability of class arbitration is a question of arbitrability. *See* 559 U.S. at 680. But this case gives us no opportunity to do so because Oxford agreed that the arbitrator should determine whether its contract with Sutter authorized class procedures.[61]

---

55 *Id.* at 455.
56 *Id.*
57 *Id.* at 460.
58 559 U.S. 662 (2010).
59 *Id.* at 680.
60 133 S. Ct. 2064 (2013).
61 *Id.* at 2068 fn.2.

Justice Alito, in his concurring opinion, was even more forceful in questioning whether arbitrators should be permitted to decide whether a contract permits class arbitration. He noted that the petitioner consented to the arbitrator's authority by conceding that he should decide whether the contract authorized class arbitration, but unlike petitioner, absent members of the plaintiff class never conceded that the contract authorized the arbitrator to decide whether to conduct class arbitration: **11.26**

> It is true that they signed contracts with arbitration clauses materially identical to those signed by the plaintiff who brought this suit. But an arbitrator's erroneous interpretation of contracts that do not authorize class arbitration cannot bind someone who has not authorized the arbitrator to make that determination.[62]

Justice Alito went on to argue that the distribution of opt-out notices does not cure this flaw and that where absent members have not been required to opt in, it is difficult to see how an arbitrator's decision to conduct class proceedings could bind absent class members who have not authorized the arbitrator to decide on a classwide basis which arbitration procedures are to be used. Such class arbitrations, that are vulnerable to collateral attack, allow absent class members to unfairly claim the benefit from a favorable judgment without subjecting themselves to the binding effect of an unfavorable one. Justice Alito concludes: **11.27**

> [T]his possibility should give courts pause before concluding that the availability of class arbitration is a question the arbitrator should decide. But because that argument was not available to petitioner in light of its concession below, I join the opinion of the Court.[63]

Thus, it remains to be seen whether the Court in the future may conclude that whether a contract permits classwide arbitration is an issue that should be for the court, and not the arbitrator. **11.28**

C. THE CLASS ARBITRATION RULES ESTABLISHED BY THE AAA AND JAMS FOLLOWING *BAZZLE*

1. AAA Class Arbitration Rules

Following the Supreme Court's remand of the cases in *Bazzle* for a determination of whether the arbitration clauses in question permitted class arbitration (which, as noted above, was before the later *Stolt-Nielson* and *Oxford* decisions which indicate that the Court at a later date may decide that such issues of arbitrability are for the Court, and not for arbitrators), the AAA had to decide how **11.29**

[62] *Id.* at 2071.
[63] *Id.* at 2072.

to administer such proceedings. It therefore adopted the American Arbitration Association Policy on Class Arbitrations (Policy)[64] and a set of Supplementary Rules for Class Arbitrations (Rules).[65]

The AAA's Policy states that, in light of the *Bazzle* decision:

> [T]he American Arbitration Association will administer demands for class arbitration pursuant to its Supplementary Rules for Class Arbitrations if (1) the underlying agreement specifies that disputes arising out of the parties' agreement shall be resolved by arbitration in accordance with any of the Association's rules, and (2) the agreement is silent with respect to class claims, consolidation or joinder of claims.
>
> The Association is not currently accepting for administration demands for class arbitration where the underlying agreement *prohibits* class claims, consolidation or joinder, unless an order of a court directs the parties to the underlying dispute to submit any aspect of their dispute involving class claims, consolidation, joinder or the enforceability of such provisions, to an arbitrator or to the Association.

It explained the latter position by noting that

> [t]he Association's determination not to administer class arbitrations where the underlying arbitration agreement *explicitly precludes* class procedures was made because the law on the enforceability of class action waivers was unsettled; the Association takes no position as to whether such clauses are or should be enforceable.
>
> In a recent review of this practice by the Association's Executive Committee it was agreed that this practice should be maintained in light of the continued unsettled state of the law. Courts in different states and different federal circuits have reached differing conclusions regarding the preclusion of class actions by agreement and "gateway" issues generally. However, the courts that have confronted the question have generally concluded that the decision as to whether an agreement that prohibits class actions is enforceable is one for the courts to make, not the arbitrator. In fidelity to its Due Process Protocols, the Association will continue to require all proceedings brought to it for administration to meet the standards of fairness and due process set forth in those protocols, but the Association will not seek to make decisions concerning class action agreements that the courts appear to have reserved for themselves.[66]

---

[64] Am. Arbitration Assoc., AAA Policy on Class Arbitrations *available at* https://www.adr.org/aaa/ShowPDF?doc=ADRSTG_003840.

[65] Am. Arbitration Assoc., AAA Supplementary Rules for Class Arbitrations, *available at* https://www.adr.org/aaa/faces/rules/searchrules/rulesdetail?doc=ADRSTG_004129&_afrLoop=1242094310880503&_afrWindowMode=0&_afrWindowId=null#%40%3F_afrWindowId%3Dnull%26_afrLoop%3D1242094310880503%26doc%3DADRSTG_004129%26_afrWindowMode%3D0%26_adf.ctrl-state%3Di4dxpxr9p_626 [hereinafter AAA Class Arbitration Rules]. Alternatively, click "rules and procedures" then go to "search rules" and click on "Supplementary Rules for Class Arbitrations."

[66] The AAA has published on its website a Consumer Due Process Protocol. These protocols were developed, among other things, to provide relevant standards in situations in which arbitration clauses are inserted into the fine print of consumer contracts that are presented to consumers on a take-it-or-leave-it basis. A copy of the protocols can be found by clicking on "Rules and Procedures" on the AAA's home page and then clicking on "Codes and Protocols."

Although this policy remains on the AAA's website, the Supreme Court recently decided in *American Express Co. v. Italian Colors Restaurant*,[67] discussed at Section M, *infra*, that express prohibition of class arbitration is enforceable even when the plaintiff's cost of individually arbitrating a claim exceeds the potential recovery. This decision would appear to resolve the issue which had conflicted lower courts, and, therefore, remove at least a portion of the stated reasons for the policy of not administering cases containing class action waivers. **11.30**

Having set forth its Policy, the AAA's Rules then provide that class arbitrations shall proceed in three separate stages. Rule 3 provides that as a threshold matter the arbitrator(s) shall determine in a reasoned, partial final award whether the applicable arbitration clause permits the arbitration to proceed on behalf of a class. This clause construction award is then published under the name of the case on the AAA's online, Class Arbitration Case Docket.[68] Any party has thirty days thereafter to appeal the clause construction award if it wishes to do so.[69] **11.31**

If the matter remains alive after any appeal, or after the time to appeal has expired without any party taking an appeal, Rule 5 provides that the arbitrator(s) shall then take evidence and issue a second, reasoned, partial final award determining whether the case meets the standards for proceeding as a class action. These standards are set forth in Rule 4, which are similar to the standards established by Rule 23 of the Federal Rules of Civil Procedure for class action proceedings in a court. This award is likewise posted on the AAA's Web site, and either party is given thirty days to appeal. **11.32**

If the case remains alive after this stage, Rule 7 provides that the arbitrator(s) shall issue a final award on the merits, which shall be reasoned and shall define the class with specificity. The final award also is posted online, and the parties have the normal right to challenge. **11.33**

Although arbitration awards are normally confidential, one assumes that the AAA took the unusual route of posting each of the awards on its Web site and providing the parties with three separate opportunities to appeal because class arbitrations, unlike individual arbitrations, are invested with a public interest and often affect a large number of potential class members beyond the named class representative who is purporting to represent their interests. **11.34**

---

[67] 133 S. Ct. 2304 (2013).

[68] The AAA Class Arbitration Docket can be found at https://www.adr.org/aaa/faces/services/disputeresolutionservices/casedocket?_afrLoop=1245464198752908&_afrWindowMode=0&_afrWindowId=i4dxpxr9p_566#%40%3F_afrWindowId%3Di4dxpxr9p_566%26_afrLoop%3D1245464198752908%26_afrWindowMode%3D0%26_adf.ctrl-state%3D1145c59z0e_4. Alternatively, from the "Services" drop down menu, click "Class Arbitration Case Docket." Cases are listed in the docket chronologically.

[69] Rule 3 also states that "[i]n construing the applicable arbitration clause, the arbitrator shall not consider the existence of these Supplementary Rules, or any other AAA rules, to be a factor either in favor of or against permitting the arbitration to proceed on a class basis."

2. JAMS Class Arbitration Rules

11.35 Following the Supreme Court's decision in *Bazzle*, JAMS also created its own supplementary set of class arbitration rules, called the JAMS Class Arbitration Procedures (JAMS Procedures).[70] Like the AAA Rules, the JAMS Procedures provide for three separate stages of a class arbitration, allowing time for "immediate court review" after each stage. The three-part process of class arbitration under the JAMS Procedures, like that of the AAA, is composed of the Construction of the Arbitration Clause,[71] Prerequisites to a Class Certification,[72] Notice of Class Determination,[73] and the Final Award.[74]

11.36 Like the AAA, the JAMS rules state it will not administer a class action when the agreement contains a class action preclusion clause unless a court orders the matter to arbitration.[75] The rule governing the clause-construction stage states, the Arbitrator "shall determine as a threshold matter whether the applicable arbitration clause permits the arbitration to proceed on behalf of or against a class."[76] Subsequently, at the class-certification stage the arbitrator is guided to allow the class certification if the conditions set forth in Rules 23(a) and (b) of the Federal Rules of Civil Procedure have been met. Notice to the certified class is required, and the guidelines for said notice are also modeled after the notice required by Rule 23, with the additional condition that the identities of and biographical information about the arbitrators, class representative(s), and class counsel shall be included in said notice.[77] The final stage of a class arbitration performed in accordance with the JAMS Procedures, the Final Award, shall be on the merits and reasoned, and it shall contain a specified definition of the class and a description of: (1) those to whom notice of the action was directed; (2) those whom the arbitrators has determined comprise the class; and (3) those who had opted out of the class.[78] Finally, Rule 6 of the JAMS Procedures delineates the procedure and guidelines for arbitrators' approval of settlements, voluntary dismissals, and compromises between the parties.[79]

D. THE EFFECT OF *HALL ST. ASSOCIATES V. MATTEL* ON CLASS ARBITRATIONS

11.37 As discussed previously, the AAA and JAMS rules of arbitration provide for a three-stage process of review of awards.

[70] JAMS Class Action Procedures (2009), *available at* http://www.jamsadr.com/rules-class-action-procedures/ [hereinafter JAMS Procedures].
[71] *Id.* at Rule 2.
[72] *Id.* at Rule 3.
[73] *Id.* at Rule 4.
[74] *Id.* at Rule 5.
[75] *Id.* at Rule 1.
[76] *Id.* at Rule 2.
[77] *Id.* at Rule 4(7).
[78] *Id.* at Rule 5.
[79] *Id.* at Rule 6.

The scope of judicial review of arbitral awards under the FAA is very limited. The only statutory grounds for vacatur and modification in the courts are provided through FAA Sections 10 and 11. FAA Section 10 allows vacatur in the following instances: (1) where there is corruption, fraud, or undue means in the procurement of the award; (2) where there is evident partiality or corruption in an arbitrator; (3) where the rights of a party are prejudiced by an arbitrator's misconduct; and (4) where an arbitrator exceeded her powers.[80] FAA Section 11 provides grounds for modification or correction of an award in the following instances: (1) where there is an evident material miscalculation of figures or material mistake in the description of anything referred to in the award; (2) where an arbitrator awards upon a matter not submitted to arbitration; and (3) where an award is imperfect in a matter or form not affecting the merits of the controversy.[81] **11.38**

In addition to these statutory grounds, there may be common-law ground for vacatur for "manifest disregard for the law."[82] However, the test is very stringent. For example, the Second Circuit, which encompasses New York, requires one to show that: (1) the tribunal had actual knowledge of a governing legal principle and refused to apply it, and (2) the governing legal principle is well-defined, explicit, and clearly applicable to the instant case.[83] **11.39**

Because class actions are invested with the public interest and because the AAA rules provide for review at three separate stages of a class action proceeding, at least one arbitrator had suggested that courts should consider the possibility of expanding the scope of review in order to give arbitrators guidance as to whether they are deciding correctly clause-construction and class-certification issues.[84] **11.40**

However, the Supreme Court eliminated this possibility by its 2008 decision in *Hall Street Associates L.L.C. v. Mattel, Inc.*[85] The issue before the Court was whether parties could contractually expand judicial review of arbitral decisions. The Court held that in actions subject to the FAA, which would include most any class arbitration, FAA Sections 10 and 11 provide the exclusive grounds for vacatur or modification of an award, and that the scope of review provided by these sections cannot be expanded.[86] **11.41**

---

[80] 9 U.S.C. § 10 (2007).

[81] 9 U.S.C. § 11 (2007).

[82] *See, e.g.*, Wallace v. Buttar, 378 F.3d 182, 193 (2d Cir. 2004).

[83] *Id.* at 189. *See also* Duferco Intl. Steel Trading v. T. Klaveness Shipping A/S, 333 F.2d 383 (2d Cir. 2003); Hoeft v. MVL Group, Inc., 343 F.3d 57 (2d Cir. 2003); Westerbeke Corp. v. Daihatsu Motor Co., Ltd., 304 F.3d 200 (2d Cir. 2002); Greenberg v. Bear, Stearns & Co., 220 F.3d 22, 28, (2d Cir. 2000) *cert. denied*, 531 U.S. 1075 (2001). The test in other circuits is also similar, *see, e.g.*, Kashner Davidson Sec. Corp. v. Mscisz, 531 F.3d 68, 74–75 (1st Cir. 2008); Collins v. D.R. Horton, Inc., 505 F.3d 874, 878–79 (9th Cir. 2007); B.L. Harbert Int'l, L.L.C. v. Hercules Steel Co., 441 F. 3d 905, 910 (11th Cir. 2006).

[84] Scher v. Oxford Health Plans, Inc., AAA Case 11 193 00548 05 (Mar. 7, 2006) (W. Baker, dissenting).

[85] 552 U.S. 576, 128 S. Ct. 1396 (2008).

[86] *Id.* at 1401.

11.42 In *dicta*, the Court also cast at least some doubt on the continued viability of "manifest disregard of the law" as a common-law supplement to the FAA statutory grounds of review. Plaintiff Hall Street had argued that because "manifest disregard of the law" had been recognized as an additional common-law ground of review ever since the case of *Wilko v. Swan*,[87] there was no reason why the Court should not permit private parties also to contract for an expanded level of review. In response, the Court stated:

> [T]his is too much for *Wilko* to bear. Quite apart from its leap from a supposed judicial expansion by interpretation to a private expansion by contract, Hall Street overlooks the fact that the statement it relies on expressly rejects just what Hall Street asks for here, general review for an arbitrator's legal errors. Then there is the vagueness of *Wilko's* phrasing. Maybe the term "manifest disregard" was meant to name a new ground of review, but maybe it merely referred to the § 10 grounds collectively, rather than adding to them ... Or as some courts have thought, "manifest disregard" may have been shorthand for § 10(a)(3) or § 10(a)(4), the subsections authorizing vacatur when the arbitrators were "guilty of misconduct" or "exceeded their powers" ... We, when speaking as a Court, have merely taken the *Wilko* language as we found it, without embellishment ... and now that its meaning is implicated, we see no reason to accord it the significance that Hall Street urges.[88]

11.43 At a minimum, the Supreme Court seems to be saying it has never expressly decided whether "manifest disregard" is an additional common-law standard of review or simply another way of referring to the more limited statutory grounds of review.

11.44 Elsewhere in the *Hall Street* opinion, although not expressly referring to "manifest disregard," the Court also notes that FAA Section 9 provides that a court "must" confirm an award "unless the award is vacated, modified or corrected as prescribed in Sections 10 and 11 of this title."[89] Noting that there is "nothing malleable about the words 'must grant,'" the Court states that "[i]nstead of fighting the text, it makes more sense to see the three provisions, §§ 9–11, as substantiating a national policy favoring arbitration with just the limited review needed to maintain arbitration's essential virtue of resolving disputes straightaway."[90]

11.45 The Second Circuit in its opinion in the *Stolt-Nielsen* case[91] discusses the continued viability of the "manifest disregard" doctrine in light of *Hall Street*.[92] It notes that a number of courts, subsequent to *Hall Street*, have concluded or suggested that the "manifest disregard" doctrine does not survive, whereas others have concluded that "manifest disregard" is a simple judicial gloss put on the specific

[87] 346 U.S. 427 (1953).

[88] 128 S. Ct. at 1404 (internal citations omitted).

[89] *Id.* at 1405.

[90] *Id.*

[91] *See* Stolt-Nielsen SA v. AnimalFeeds Int'l Corp., 548 F.3d 85 (2d Cir. 2008), rev'd, 559 U.S. 662 (2010).

[92] *Id.* at 93–94.

grounds for vacatur enumerated in Section 10 of the FAA.[93] The Second Circuit notes its agreement with the latter approach. Citing a pre-*Bazzle*, Seventh Circuit decision for the proposition that "manifest disregard" should more properly be viewed as a mechanism to enforce the parties agreement to arbitrate according to the terms of their contract, rather than as a ground for judicial review of the arbitrator's decision, the Second Circuit states that:

> ... parties do not agree in advance to submit to arbitration that is carried out in manifest disregard of the law. Put another way, the arbitrators have thereby "exceeded their powers, or so imperfectly executed them that a mutual, final, and definite award upon the subject matter submitted was not made." 9 U.S.C. § 10(a)(4).[94]

In any event, regardless of the ultimate status of "manifest disregard of the law" as an additional common-law standard of review, the decision in *Hall Street* means that courts will not be able to use the extra interim appeals—mandated in the AAA and JAMS rules—to provide any substantive guidance to arbitrators regarding Clause Construction and Class Determination Awards. In a way, this leaves parties in class arbitrations worse off than parties in class actions in court. In the latter situation, parties can at least obtain a review on the merits as to whether the court below decided correctly issues relating to class certification and the like. **11.46**

It should be noted, however, that although parties will not be able to obtain expanded judicial review of clause construction and class certification awards, parties can provide in their contract for appellate review on the merits of any interim or final arbitration award, whether in a class arbitration or not, by an appellate tribunal within the arbitral institution. Recommended clauses for expanded review within both the AAA and JAMS institutional schemes are provided on their respective websites. **11.47**

E. THE DIFFERENT SOURCES OF LAW WHICH ONE MUST CONSIDER IN DETERMINING WHETHER A SILENT ARBITRATION CLAUSE PERMITS A CLASS ARBITRATION

In deciding whether a particular "silent" arbitration clause permits class arbitrations, one typically looks to two sources of law: (1) the substantive law chosen by the contract for the interpretation of the agreement, and (2) in cases involving interstate or international commerce, federal common law developed under the FAA, e.g., *Moses H Cone Mem. Hosp.*[95] (FAA Section 2 creates "a body of federal **11.48**

---

[93] *Id.* at 94.

[94] *Id.* at 95.

[95] 460 U.S. 1, 24 (1983). *See also* Chapter 1.D.

substantive law of arbitrability"). As noted previously, however, the federal law of arbitrability under the FAA, which includes decisions regarding whether arbitrations can be consolidated or treated as a class, can be supplemented by law developed under a state's arbitration code, as long as the state arbitration law is not inconsistent with federal law.

11.49 The fact that both state law and federal law regarding arbitrability can potentially be applicable to the same contract raises drafting issues. For example, if a clause states that the contract shall be "governed" by New York law, New York courts have interpreted this as adopting only the substantive contract law of New York, e.g., *Smith Barney Shearson*.[96] However, New York courts have held that a reference to "enforcement" in the choice-of-law clause (as in the phrase, "this contract shall be construed and enforced in accordance with New York law") means that enforcement through arbitration is subject to New York state's special rules regarding arbitrability (including its decisions regarding consolidation of arbitrations), e.g., *Diamond Waterproofing Sys., Inc. v. 33 Liberty Owners Corp.*[97] Even where the choice-of-law clause provided that the agreement and its enforcement were subject to New York law and the FAA, it was held that the arbitrability provisions of New York's state arbitration law still applied, e.g., *Coleman & Co v. Giaquinto Family Trust.*[98]

11.50 Given the above case law, the phrasing of a choice-of-law clause can have an impact on the outcome of a clause construction ruling in a class arbitration. For example, New York state court cases decided under New York's arbitration statute have held that a court has the equitable power to consolidate arbitrations *without* the express consent of the parties.[99] By contrast, in cases decided under the FAA, New York federal cases, as well as most other federal cases, have held that a court has no authority to consolidate arbitrations in the absence of an express agreement among all parties.[100]

11.51 Thus, if the choice-of-law clause merely says that the contract shall be "construed in accordance with the law of New York," then the FAA's more restrictive law

---

[96] 91 N.Y.2d 39; *accord* Mastrobuono v. Shearson Lehman Hutton, 514 U.S. 52, 63–64 (1995) (holding that a "generic" New York choice-of-law clause merely meant that substantive provisions of New York law applied to interpretation of the contract, but such a clause did not make restrictive provisions of New York arbitration law applicable to the arbitration). A number of federal circuits have likewise adopted the rule (under federal common law applicable to interstate and international arbitrations) that a generic choice of law clause does not make the chosen state's law applicable to arbitration procedures unless the parties "clearly" intend that it should do so: Roadway Package Sys., Inc. v. Kayser, 257 F.3d 287 (3d Cir. 2001); Porter Hayden Co v. Century/Mem Co., 136 F.3d 380 (4th Cir. 1998); UHC Mgmt. Co. v. Computer Sew Corp., 148 F.3d 992, 997 (8th Cir. 1998).

[97] 4 N.Y.3d 247, 252 (2005).

[98] 236 F. Supp. 2d 288 (S.D.N.Y. 2002).

[99] *See, e.g.*, County of Sullivan v. Nezelek, Inc., 42 N.Y.2d 123 (NY 1977).

[100] *See, e.g.*, *In re* Cullman Ventura, Inc., 682 N.Y.S. 2d 391 (NY App. Div. 1998); Gov't of U.K. v. Boeing Co., 998 F.2d 68 (2d Cir. 1993).

regarding consolidation is applicable, and one can more easily argue that it was not within the contemplation of the parties at the time they entered into the contract that arbitrations could be consolidated or combined into a class arbitration. On the other hand, if the choice-of-law clause says that the contract shall be "construed and enforced in accordance with the law of New York," then one is deemed to have adopted New York state's more liberal law regarding consolidation, and one can more easily argue that it was within the contemplation of the parties at the time they entered into the contract that arbitrations could be consolidated, or combined into a class arbitration.

The foregoing issues of draftsmanship are more directly relevant to arbitration clauses entered into before *Bazzle* was decided in 2003. Even if the FAA's law in the past was more restrictive regarding consolidation (and, by implication, the permissibility of class arbitrations),[101] one would be wise now to put in a clause expressly forbidding class arbitration in light of the fact that so many arbitrators, at least in the initial post-*Bazzle* era, have ruled that a silent clause permits class arbitration. If one does not insert a clause prohibiting class arbitration, the contract might possibly be considered ambiguous and construed against the drafter so as to permit class arbitration. Even if one does insert such a clause, however, it is possible that a court may hold that such a clause is against public policy and, therefore, unenforceable.[102] **11.52**

F. FEDERAL CIRCUIT COURT AND STATE COURT DECISIONS REGARDING CONSOLIDATION OF ARBITRATIONS AND CLASS ARBITRATIONS BEFORE *BAZZLE*

Before the *Bazzle* plurality ruled that it was for the arbitrator to decide whether separate arbitrations could be consolidated or treated as a class, the vast majority of federal circuit courts, as noted previously, had held that arbitrations could not be consolidated in the absence of an express agreement among all the parties. For example, the Second Circuit stated that concerns of efficiency and inconsistent determinations "do not provide us with the authority to reform private contracts which underlie this dispute. If contracting parties wish to have all disputes that arise from the same factual situation arbitrated in a single proceeding, they can simply provide for consolidated arbitration in the arbitration clauses to which they are a party."[103] Similarly, all of the federal circuit **11.53**

[101] *See* Section F of this chapter, *infra*.
[102] *See* Sections K–N of this chapter, *infra*.
[103] *Gov't of U.K.*, *supra* note 100, at 74. *See also* Am. Centennial Ins. Co. v. Nat'l. Cas. Co., 951 F.2d 207, 208 (6th Cir. 1991) ("a district court is without power to consolidate arbitration

courts considering whether separate arbitrations could be treated as class arbitrations have held that they could not do so in the absence of an express agreement among all the parties.[104] However, a number of state court decisions, mostly in California, had held that a silent arbitration clause did not bar class arbitrations.[105]

11.54 In his dissenting opinion in *Cable Connections, Inc. v. Hughes Elecs. Corp*, arbitrator Richard Chernick noted that California's state arbitration statute was different from that of most other states and, therefore, the rulings in older Supreme Court cases *Keating*[106] and *Blue Cross*[107] were inapplicable to a proceeding governed by the FAA.

---

proceedings, over the objection of a party to the arbitration agreement, *when the agreement is silent regarding consolidation*" (emphasis added)); Baesler v. Cont'l. Grain Co., 900 F.2d 1193, 1194 (8th Cir. 1990) (affirming a refusal to consolidate arbitrations where "[t]he single issue before us is whether a district court has the power to consolidate arbitration proceedings *when the arbitration clause of the parties' agreement* is *silent regarding consolidation*" (emphasis added); Protective Life Ins. Corp. v. Lincoln Nat'l Life Ins. Corp., 873 F.2d 281 (11th Cir. 1989) (vacating the lower court's consolidation of arbitrations where the parties never agreed to it); Del E. Webb Constr. v. Richardson Hosp. Auth., 823 F.2d 145 (5th Cir. 1987). *But see* Pedcor Mgmt. Co. v. Nations Pers. of Tex., 343 F.3d 355, 363 (5th Cir. 2003) (noting that *Bazzle* had effectively overruled *Del E. Webb* to the limited extent of holding that the question of arbitrability is to be decided by the arbitrator, not the court); Weyerhaeuser Co. v. W. Seas Shipping Co., 743 F.2d 635, 637 (9th Cir. 1984) (affirming lower court's refusal to consolidate two arbitrations and noting that "arbitration is a creature of contract, and that [a]n agreement to arbitrate before a special tribunal is, in effect, a specialized forum selection clause that posits not only the situs of suit but also the procedure to be used in resolving the dispute" (internal quotations omitted)). *But see* New England Energy, Inc. v. Keystone Shipping Co., 855 F.2d 1 (1st Cir. 1988) (permitting the consolidation of two arbitrations in a contract subject to the FAA).

[104] *See, e.g.*, Champ v. Siegel Trading Co., 55 F.3d 269, 275 (7th Cir. 1995) ("We find no meaningful basis to distinguish between the failure to provide for consolidated arbitration and class arbitration. We thus adopt the rationale of several other circuits and hold that *section 4 of the FAA forbids federal judges from ordering class arbitration where the parties' arbitration is silent on the matter*" (emphasis added)); Dominium Austin Partners, LLC v. Emerson, 248 F.3d 720, 728–29 (8th Cir. 2001) ("[B]ecause the partnership agreements make no provision for arbitration as a class, the district court did not err by compelling appellants to submit their claims to arbitration as individuals"); Johnson v. W. Suburban Bank, 225 F.3d 366, 373 (3d Cir. 2000) ("[E]ven if plaintiffs who sign valid arbitration agreements lack the procedural right to proceed as part of a class, they retain the full range of rights created by TILA [The Truth In Lending Act]. These rights remain available in individual arbitration proceedings"); Deiulemar Compagnia di Navigazione SpA v. M/V Allegra, 198 F.3d 473, 482 (4th Cir. 1999) (where the parties did not include in their agreement an express term providing for class arbitration, the case must proceed as nonclass arbitration).

[105] *See, e.g.*, Blue Cross of Cal. v. Superior Court of LA County, 67 Cal. App. 4th 42, 60 (Cal. Ct. App. 1998) (ordering class arbitration where the arbitration clause was silent); Keating v. Superior Court, 31 Cal. 3d 584, 609 (1982) (remanding the case to the lower court for consideration of whether a silent clause should be construed to permit class arbitration and noting that "[i]f the right to a classwide proceeding could be automatically eliminated in relationships governed by adhesion contracts through the inclusion of a provision for arbitration, the potential for undercutting these class action principles, and for chilling the effective protection of interests common to a group, would be substantial").

[106] *Keating*, *supra* note 105.

[107] *Blue Cross*, *supra* note 105.

G. CLAUSE-CONSTRUCTION DECISIONS BY ARBITRAL PANELS ADJUDICATING CLASS ARBITRATIONS AFTER *BAZZLE*

After the Supreme Court plurality in *Bazzle* held that it was up to arbitrators rather than the courts to decide whether a silent clause permits class arbitration, but before the April 27, 2010, decision in *Stolt-Neilsen*, which clarified the test to be used in determining when a clause permits class arbitration (*see* discussion in Section H, *infra*), approximately one hundred fifty arbitrators or panels in arbitrations being administered under the AAA's class arbitration rules issued clause construction awards. In approximately 72 percent of the cases, most of which contained a silent clause, the arbitrator or arbitrators determined that the clause permitted class arbitration. This is in marked contrast, as noted previously, to the fact that the vast majority of federal circuits in the pre-*Bazzle* era had ruled that arbitrations could not be consolidated or treated as a class if the arbitration clause was silent on the issue. 11.55

In one case which held that the silent clause before it did not permit a class action arbitration, *Rich v. Rent-A-Center, Inc.*,[108] the arbitrator, retired Judge Louis Bechtle, opted to utilize "traditional principles of contract construction to determine the intent of the parties as to whether or not those procedures should apply." The arbitrator found that the parties had not expressly contracted for the option of class action proceedings in the event of a dispute. Also, the parties were referred to in the singular rather than in the collective throughout the contract, never suggesting the possibility of a class arbitration. The arbitrator also noted that the AAA's Supplementary Rules for Class Arbitrations had not yet been drafted at the time of the parties' contracting. Because the AAA's Supplementary Rules for Class Arbitration did not exist at the time of contracting, the arbitrator found the parties could not have had such rules in mind when they agreed to the arbitration clause. Finally, the arbitrator observed that the contract allowed for the consultation with an attorney, and the putative class representative had availed himself of this opportunity at the signing of the contract. For these reasons, the arbitrator found that the parties had not contracted with the intent to include class arbitrations as a possible form of dispute resolution, and therefore, denied the putative class' claim. 11.56

Another case which held that the silent clause before it did not permit a class action arbitration is *John Ivan Sutter v. Limited Health Care Insurance Company*.[109] The arbitrator in that case, retired Judge Marina Corodenus, noted that most federal and state courts in the pre-*Bazzle* era did not permit class actions where the pre-dispute 11.57

[108] AAA Case No. 11 160 01833 04.
[109] AAA Case No. 11 195 02075 06.

arbitration clause was silent on class actions and that the concept of class actions outside of court began in California with the case of *Keating v. Superior Court.*[110] The arbitrator noted that the AAA's Supplementary Rules for Class Arbitration required the arbitrator to determine if silence in the arbitration clause "permits" class action. The arbitrator concluded that silence under applicable federal and New Jersey law could not be translated into a contractual agreement to permit class arbitration and, therefore, held the arbitration clause did not permit class action treatment. *See also* dissenting opinion of William Baker in *Scher v. Oxford Health Plans, Inc.*[111]

11.58 Three other cases held that the disputes before them could not proceed as class arbitrations. In *Warrior Transportation v. FFE Transportation Servs., Inc.*,[112] the tribunal found that the broadly drafted, silent arbitration clause allowed class arbitrations. However, the tribunal also found that a subparagraph of the clause, requiring that notice of an arbitration claim be given within sixty days, was impermissibly and unconscionably short, and therefore invalid. The tribunal further found that this clause could not be severed from the remainder of the arbitration clause. Therefore, the tribunal found the entire arbitration clause to be invalid and dismissed the case for lack of jurisdiction.

11.59 In *Parham v. Am. Bankers Ins. Co. of Florida*,[113] the tribunal was faced with an arbitration clause which was silent as to class arbitration. The tribunal found that the broad language of the clause, construed against the drafter (in accordance with Alabama law), must allow a class arbitration, and it therefore entered a clause construction award in favor of the class. Upon respondents' appeal to an Alabama circuit court, however, the court concluded that Alabama law dictated that "silence in an arbitration clause on class arbitration means no class arbitration." Therefore, the arbitrator was directed to enter a new clause construction award in accordance with Alabama law.

11.60 In *Cummings v. AT&T Corp.*,[114] the claimant had previously sought to have a court determine that a clause barring class action arbitrations was unconscionable. The Court declined and referred the matter to arbitration, where the claimant then tried to raise the same argument. The arbitrator noted, among other things, that the court had already rejected claimant's arguments. The arbitrator also noted that under applicable New York law, a contractual proscription against class actions is neither unconscionable nor violative of public policy, citing *Tsadilas v. Providian National Bank.*[115] The arbitrator, therefore, ruled that the matter could not proceed as a class arbitration.

[110] 31 Cal. 3d 584, 645 P. 2d 1192 (Cal. 1982).
[111] *Scher*, *supra* note 84.
[112] AAA Case No. 11 118 00365 05 (Aug. 18, 2005).
[113] AAA Case No. 11 195 00157 07 (July 30, 2007).
[114] AAA Case No. 11 181 02586 04 (Mar. 3, 2006).
[115] 786 N.Y.S. 2d 478 (N.Y. App. Div. 2004).

With respect to those decisions which held that a "silent" clause permitted class arbitration, approximately twenty-eight awards, before the *Stolt-Nielsen* decision, relied in whole or in part on California case law, including the *Blue Cross* and *Keating* decisions noted previously.[116] **11.61**

Some of the other clause construction awards were based on idiosyncratic facts. For example, two of the awards were based on the fact that the respondent assured the court that if the matter were transferred to arbitration, it would not assert that the arbitration clause precluded class claims.[117] One decision relied on the fact that at least several of the arbitration clauses expressly permitted class arbitrations,[118] and four merely affirmed stipulated agreements not to contest clause construction.[119] Another case simply considered the state court's referral of the class' claims to arbitration as a binding decision that the clause allowed class actions.[120] The remaining thirty-seven decisions studied relied on various other reasons.[121] **11.62**

[116] Ortiz v. Clougherty Packaging Co. LLC, AAA Case No. 11 160 01241 09 (Apr. 5, 2010); David Rivera v. Corinthian College, Inc., AAA Case No. 11 434 1075 08 (Sep. 11, 2009); Dealer Computer Svcs., Inc. v. Randall Ford, Inc., AAA Case No. 11 117 Y 002788 06 (June 2, 2008); Flaxman v. Terminex, Inc., AAA Case No. 11 434 00701 07 (Jan. 14, 2008); Fannan v. Technisource, Inc., AAA Case No. 11 160 01881 06 (Feb. 25, 2007); Orea v. Tavistock Restaurants LLC, AAA Case No. 11 160 01982 06 (Mar. 2, 2007) (citing Ting v. AT&T, 319 F.3d 1126, 1150 (9th Cir. 2003)); Armstrong v. Ameriquest Mortgage Co., AAA Case No. 11 160 Y 01652 06 (May 23, 2007); Nichols v. Fanfare Media Works, Inc., AAA Case No. 11 160 Y 01780 06 (June 14, 2007); Hlas v. Menard, AAA Case No. 11 160 00131 07 (June 29, 2007); Krastel v. TES Franchising, LLC, AAA Case No. 11 114 00320 05 (July 7, 2006) (citing Gray v. Conseco, Inc., 2001 U.S. Dist. LEXIS 21696 at *7–8 (C.D. Cal. Sept. 6, 2001)); Salcedo v. Cintas Corp., AAA Case No. 11 160 00018 06 (Aug. 16, 2006); Jost v. Sizzler USA Restaurants, Inc., AAA Case No. 11 160 01721 05 (Oct. 25, 2006); Ali v. Morton's of Chicago/Sacramento, Inc., AAA Case No. 11 160 02015 05 (Mar. 22, 2006); Sanchez v. Corinthian Colleges, Inc., AAA Case No. 11 181 00286 5 (Nov. 15, 2005); Groves v. Hemet Manufacturing Co, Inc., AAA Case No. 11 160 00194 05 (Nov. 8, 2005); Olson v. Rent-A-Center, Inc., AAA Case No. 11 160 01831 04 (Oct. 21, 2005); Grayson v. Rent-A-Center, Inc., AAA Case No. 11 160 01823 04 (Aug. 8, 2005); Medina v. GMRI, Inc., AAA Case No. 11 160 02409 04 (July 20, 2005); Anderson v. Check 'N Go of California, Inc., AAA Case No. 11 160 03021 04 (June 20, 2005); Hayes v. MS Carriers, Inc., AAA Case No. 11 118 02907 04 (June 15, 2005); Mitchell v. GMRI, Inc., AAA Case No. 11 160 02939 03 (June 10, 2005); Sidhu v. GMRI, Inc., AAA Case No. 11 160 02273 04 (June 10, 2005); Allen v. Sport & Fitness Clubs of Am., Inc., AAA Case No. 11 160 03041 04 (Apr. 13, 2005); Cable Connection, Ins v. Directu, Inc., AAA Case No. 11 145 00752 04 (Mar. 10, 2005); Hamilton v. Rent-A-Center, Inc., AAA Case No. 11 160 0182 04 (Mar. 10, 2005); Hamilton v. Rent-A-Center, Inc., AAA Case 11 160 01825 04 (Oct. 21, 2004); Milstein v. Protection One Alarm Servus, Inc., AAA Case 11 110 00270 04 (Oct. 11, 2004); Cole v. Long John Silver's Restaurants, Inc., AAA Case 11 160 00194 04 (June 15, 2004); Goldstein v. Ibase Consulting of Fairfield County, LLC, AAA Case No. 11 160 02760 03 (Mar. 29, 2004).

[117] Cotton v. Rent-A-Center, Inc., AAA Case No. 11 160 01819 04 (Aug. 12, 2005); Cook v. Rent-A-Center, Inc., AAA Case No. 11 160 01815 04 (Sept. 19, 2005).

[118] Harris v. Tele Tech Holdings, Inc., AAA Case No 11 160 02701 04 (Dec. 16, 2005).

[119] Brown v. Cellco P'ship, AAA Case No. 11 494 01274 05 (Sept. 15, 2005).

[120] Francis v. United El Segundo, AAA Case No. 11 160 00267 07 (Apr. 30, 2007).

[121] Blackwell v. 24 Hour Fitness USA, Inc., AAA Case No. 11 196 02299 07 (June 20, 2008); Adame v. Fleetwood Enterprises, Inc., AAA Case No. 11 181 01292 07 (Mar. 11, 2008); Walters v. Palm Harbor Homes, Inc., AAA Case No. 11 421 002782 06 (Jan. 17, 2008); Morton

11.63 It should be noted that most of the cases to date have involved arbitration clauses embedded in the fine print of consumer contracts under circumstances where the consumers had no real opportunity to negotiate or change the clauses. Clauses contained in such contracts of adhesions involve special considerations. If there is an arbitration clause in such a contract, it has the effect of prohibiting the consumer from bringing any action in court, including a class action. If a silent arbitration clause is then interpreted as prohibiting a class action in arbitration, the consumer is left without any forum in which to bring class claims. There is an understandable desire not to want to leave a consumer without any forum to assert class claims inasmuch as class actions, in the absence of an arbitration clause, have by this point in time become an accepted part of U.S. jurisprudence.

11.64 To the extent that the above is a valid concern, the answer might lie in narrowly tailored legislation dealing with arbitration clauses in consumer contracts of adhesion.[122] The danger of trying instead to arrive at what may seem to be a just

v. Championcomm.net of Tuscaloosa, Inc., AAA Case No. 11 199 00704 07 (Dec. 26, 2007); Fox Valley Ford v. Dealer Computer Svcs., Inc., AAA Case No. 11 117 01929 06 (Nov. 9, 2007); Hausner v. United Healthcare of Texas, Inc., AAA Case No. 11 193 Y 00447 07 (Oct. 19, 2007); Kinkel v. Cingular Wireless, LLC, AAA Case No. 11 494 02 646 06 (Oct. 12, 2007); Louisiana Health Svc. Indemn. Co. v. DVA Renal Healthcare, Inc., AAA Case No. 11 193 02297 06 (Oct. 5, 2007); Harvard Coll. v. JSC Surgutneftegaz, AAA Case No. 11 168 T 01654 04 (Aug. 1, 2007); Stokes v. AWSM Technology, LLC, AAA Case No. 11 147 02374 06 (June 22, 2007); Crawford v. Labor Ready Northwest, Inc., AAA Case No. 11 160 02264 06 (June 20, 2007); Champion Ford Lincoln Mercury, Inc. v. Dealer Computer Svcs., Inc., AAA Case No. 11 117 01935 06 (June 6, 2007); Travis v. Rhodes Colleges, Inc., AAA Case No. 11 199 01827 06 (June 26, 2007); Zacharias v. Cypress Communications, Inc., AAA Case No. 11 181 00004 06 (Nov. 27, 2006); Tomeldon Co., Inc. v. Medco Health Solutions, Inc., AAA Case No. 11 193 00546 06 (Nov. 22, 2006); Bandler v. Charter One Bank, N.A., AAA Case No. 11 148 02801 04 (Sept. 3, 2006); Terrapin Express, Inc. v. Airborne Express, Inc., AAA Case No. 11 199 01536 05 (May 9, 2006); Hoffman v. Arthur Anderson LLP, AAA Case No. 11 180 01410 05 (Jul. 23, 2006); Scher v. Oxford Health Plans, Inc., AAA Case No. 11 193 00548 05 (Mar. 7, 2006); Hamilton v. Rent-A-Center, Inc., AAA Case No. 11 160 01825 04 (Oct. 21, 2005); Jones v. Genus Credit Mgmt. Corp., AAA Case No. 11 181 00295 05 (Oct. 13, 2005); Addleman v. Ryland Group, Inc., AAA Case No. 11 181 001524 05 (Sept. 15, 2005); Petsch v. Orkin Exterminating Co. v. Rollins, Inc., AAA Case No. 11 181 02541 04 (Aug. 31, 2005); Warrior Transportation v. FFE Transportation Services, Inc., AAA Case No. 11 118 00365 05 (Aug. 18, 2005); Fortuna v. Snap-on Tools Co., LLC, AAA Case No. 11 114 01818 04 (Aug. 12, 2005); Rhodes Colleges, Inc. v. Michael Satz, AAA Case No. 11 18102217 04 (June 23, 2005); Alexander v. GMRI, Inc., AAA Case No. 11 160 02018 05 (June 20, 2005); Hobby v. Snap-on-Tools Co, LLC, AAA Case No. 11 114 01884 04 (June 8, 2005); Awe v. I & M Rail Link, LLC, AAA Case No. 11 160 00026 05 (May 24, 2005); Levitt v. Lipper Holding, LLC, AAA Case No. 11 168 00663 04 (May 20, 2005); Barton v. Cottage Homesteads of Am., Inc., AAA Case No. 11 115 02967 04 (May 11, 2005); Smith v. Tele Tech Holdings, Inc., AAA Case No. 11 160 02726 04 (Apr. 12, 2005); Garrett v. Rollins, Inc., AAA Case No. 11 181 01663 04 (Mar. 23, 2005); Le v. Toshiba Am. Info. Sys, Inc., AAA Case No. 11 160 02033 04 (Mar. 7, 2005); Beazury v. Arbor Homes, LLC, AAA Case No. 11 148 02161 04 (Jan. 31, 2005); Budner v. Oats, AAA Case No. 11 181 00828 04 (Dec. 20, 2004); Bagpeddler.com v. U.S. Bancorp, AAA Case No. 11 181 00322 04 (Sept. 2, 2004); Hearthside Rest., Inc. v. Quest Dex, Inc., AAA Case No. 1I 147 00357 04 (Sept. 2, 2004); Sutter v. Oxford Health Plans, Inc., AAA Case No. 18 193 20593 02 (Sept. 23, 2003).

[122] There is, in fact, legislation pending in Congress on this subject. *See* Section O of this chapter, *infra*.

result by stretching principles of contractual construction is that the case law created has a way of finding its way into situations that involve neither consumers nor contracts of adhesion.

H. THE U.S. SUPREME COURT DECISION IN *STOLT-NEILSEN S.A. V. ANIMALFEEDS INTERNATIONAL CORP*

Following the numerous post-*Bazzle* decisions by arbitration tribunals holding that a silent clause permitted class arbitration, the US Supreme Court finally addressed this issue in the *Stolt-Neilsen* case.[123] More specifically, Justice Alito, writing for the majority noted: "We granted certiorari in this case to decide whether imposing class arbitration on parties whose arbitration clauses are 'silent' on that issue is consistent with the Federal Arbitration Act (FAA), 9 U.S.C. §1 *et seq.*"[124] **11.65**

The petitioners in *Stolt-Neilsen* were shipping companies that served a large share of the world market for parcel tankers—which are seagoing vessels with compartments that are separately chartered to customers wishing to ship liquids in small quantities. The arbitration clause provided, in pertinent part, that any dispute arising out of the making, performance or termination of the charter party shall be settled by arbitration in New York in conformity with the United States Arbitration Act [*i.e.,* the FAA] and that the owner and charterer shall each appoint an arbitrator, and that the two thus chosen shall nominate a third arbitrator if the parties are not able to agree on the third arbitrator.[125] **11.66**

In 2003, a Department of Justice criminal investigation revealed that the shipping companies were engaging in an illegal price-fixing conspiracy. When AnimalFeeds learned of this, it brought a putative class action against the shipping companies. Additional suits were brought by other parties elsewhere. The suits were consolidated, and it was determined that all of the parties must arbitrate their antitrust disputes.[126] **11.67**

When the case reached the Supreme Court, the Court concluded that the parties had stipulated that the arbitration clause was "silent" with respect to class arbitration.[127] It then concluded that because the parties agreed that their agreement was "silent" in the sense that they had not reached any agreement on the issue of class arbitration, the arbitrators' proper task was to identify the rule of **11.68**

[123] 559 U.S. 662 (2010)
[124] *Id.* at 666
[125] *Id.* at 667.
[126] *Id.* at 667–68.
[127] *Id.* at 668. *But see* the Dissent, disputing that there was truly such a stipulation. *Id.* at 698.

law that governs in that situation.[128] The Court concluded that if the tribunal had engaged in that undertaking, they presumably would have looked either to the FAA itself or to one of the two bodies of law that the parties claimed were governing, *i.e.* either federal maritime law or New York law. But rather than inquiring whether the FAA, maritime law, or New York law contained a "default rule" under which an arbitration clause is construed as allowing class arbitration in the absence of express consent, the majority found that the panel instead proceeded as if it had the authority of a common-law court to develop what it viewed as the best rule to be applied in such a situation.[129] It noted that the panel was not persuaded by court cases denying consolidation of arbitrations or by expert opinion that sophisticated, multinational, commercial parties of the type that are sought to be included in the class would never intend that the arbitration clauses permit class arbitration.[130] Instead, the tribunal found no convincing grounds for departing from the post-*Bazzle* arbitral consensus that a class action arbitration is permitted where an arbitration clause is silent. As a result, the Court concluded that "the panel simply imposed its own conception of sound public policy"[131] and therefore "exceeded its powers."[132]

11.69 Having found that the panel exceeded its powers, the Court turned to the question of what rule should be applied in deciding whether an arbitration clause can be construed to permit class arbitration.[133] It started by noting that arbitrators must "give effect to the contractual rights and expectations of the parties,"[134] and that "[n]othing in the [FAA] authorizes a court to compel arbitration of any issues, *or by any parties*, that are not already covered in the agreement."[135] From these principles, it concluded that "a party may not be compelled under the FAA to submit to class arbitration unless there is a contractual basis for concluding that the party *agreed* to do so."[136]

11.70 It explained its holding by noting that "[a]n implicit agreement to authorize class-action arbitration … is not a term that the arbitrator may infer solely from the fact of the parties' agreement to arbitrate … because class action arbitration changes the nature of arbitration to such a degree that it cannot be presumed the parties consented to it by simply agreeing to submit their disputes to an arbitrator."[137] By way of examples, the Court noted that class arbitration changes the number of parties to the dispute, which can involve as many as hundreds

[128] *Id.* at 673.
[129] *Id.* at 673–74.
[130] *Id.* at 674.
[131] *Id.* at 675.
[132] *Id.* at 677.
[133] *Id.* at 681. Slip at 16.
[134] *Id.* at 682. Slip at 18.
[135] *Id.* at 683. Slip at 19.
[136] *Id.* at 684. Slip at 20.
[137] *Id.* at 685. Slip at 21.

or perhaps thousands of parties in the class; it changes the presumption of privacy and confidentiality; and the commercial stakes of class-action arbitration are comparable to those of class-action litigation even though the scope of judicial review is much more limited.[138] In short, the Court concluded that "the differences between bilateral and class-action arbitration are too great for arbitrators to presume, consistent with their limited powers under the FAA, that the parties' mere silence on the issue of class-action arbitration constitutes consent to resolve their disputes in class proceedings."[139]

I. POST-*STOLT-NEILSEN* DECISIONS BY ARBITRATION TRIBUNALS REGARDING WHETHER "SILENT CLAUSES" PERMIT CLASS ACTION ARBITRATIONS

Between the Stolt-Neilsen decision and June 2014, the AAA has overseen sixty-nine arbitrations involving class actions. The clause-construction awards in these cases have varied. Out of thirty-seven clause-construction awards, twenty-two construed the clause in question so as to allow class arbitration.[140] Fifteen, on the other hand, found that the clause in question did not permit class arbitration.[141] Even though many arbitration clauses did not expressly mention class actions, approximately 59 percent found that the arbitration clause in such cases evinced an intent to submit to class arbitration. **11.71**

---

[138] *Id.* at 686–87. Slip at 22–23.

[139] *Id.* at 687. Slip at 23.

[140] In the matter between Luis Maldonado and others similarly situated and Callahan's Express Delivery Inc., AAA Case No. 33 523 00375 13 (Apr. 18, 2014); Timothy A. v. American Dairy Queen Corp. AAA Case No. 65 114 00016 13 (Feb. 18, 2014); Lynn Grande v. Lawrence Recruiting Specialists Inc. d/b/a LRS Healthcare, AAA Case No. 57 160 00080 13 (Dec. 20, 2013); Kissel v. Sirius XM, AAA Case No. 13 516 00198 13 (Dec. 6, 2013) (granted in part); Guzman and AIMCO River Club, LLC, AAA Case No. 18 526 Y 000120 13 (Dec. 4, 2013); Savaria v. Steiner, AAA Case No. 12 460 454 12 (Oct. 30, 2013); Price v. NCR, AAA Case No. 51 160 908 12 (Oct. 24, 2013); Gonazalez and Brand, AAA Case No. 70 160 000270 13 (Oct. 15, 2013); Garcia-Herman v Greystar, AAA Case No. 73 160 00378 12 (Oct. 11, 2013); McCullough v Terminal, AAA Case No. 31 160 00371 12 (Sept. 17, 2013); Harding v. Midsouth, AAA Case No. 69 516 Y 00219 12 (Aug. 29, 2013); Cordova v. United, AAA Case No. 73 516 Y 000065 13 (Aug. 29, 2013); Betts v. Fastfunding, AAA Case No. 33 516 00012 13 (Aug. 21, 2013); Gonzalez v. MMM, AAA Case No. 32 187 Y 000450 12 (Aug. 15, 2013); Her v. Club One, AAA Case No. 74 160 01109 12 (Jul. 29, 2013); Baer v. TruGreen, AAA Case No. 14 160 01482 12 (Jul. 22, 2013); Chae v. Western, AAA Case No. 11 160 424 11 (Sept. 30, 2011); SWLA Hospital Assoc. v. Corvel Corp., AAA Case No. 11 193 02760 06 (Sept. 3, 2010); Danielle Demetriou v. Earthlink, Inc., AAA Case No. 11 117 00273 10 (Sept. 1, 2010); Herman Benson v. Credit Solutions of America, AAA Case No. 11 160 M 02281 08 (Jul. 6, 2010); Francis v. United, AAA Case No. 11 160 00267 07 (Jun. 22, 2010); Knudsen v. North Motors, 11 155 02699 09 (May 18, 2010).

[141] In the matter of: Mary Karen Hoffman and Timothy Lamagna, AAA Case No. 55 160 00251 12 (Apr. 18, 2014); Toney C. Giles v. Legal Helpers Debt Resolution, PLLC, AAA Case No. 11 194 01162 13 (Mar. 16, 2014); Beery v. Quest Diagnostics, AAA Case No. 32 160 00323 13 (Feb. 11, 2014); Muhammad v. Delaware Title Loans Inc., AAA Case No. 18 434 00804 13 (Feb. 10,

11.72 Panels have distinguished their class action cases from *Stolt-Neilson* in a variety of ways in order to find evidence of an intent in the arbitration clause to allow class action arbitration. A common method used to find an intent to allow class arbitration is the principle of *expressio unius est exclusio alterius*. By excluding certain types of cases without excluding class arbitrations, an agreement implicitly allows class arbitration.[142] Some look to the nature of the actions specified in the arbitration clause. Arbitrators have found that if the type of action listed is generally brought as a class, this evinces an intent to allow class arbitrations.[143] Other cases have allowed class arbitrations based on the public policy of the state governing the agreement, such as a significant consumer protection policy.[144]

J. CLASS-CERTIFICATION DECISIONS BY ARBITRAL TRIBUNALS AFTER *BAZZLE*

11.73 Following a decision that the arbitration clause permits class arbitration, the arbitral tribunal must decide whether the standards governing class certification have been satisfied. Class certification in a class arbitration, as discussed previously, involves criteria similar to that of a class action in the U.S. district courts. The rules for class certification in arbitrations performed under the aegis of both the AAA and JAMS are modeled after Rule 23 of the Federal Rules of Civil Procedure, and the decisions in arbitrations in those institutions often rely on relevant state and federal case law in their reasoning. As noted, in order to certify a class, the tribunal must first find that the elements of Rule 23(a) have been satisfied. These are: (1) numerosity; (2) commonality; (3) typicality; (4) adequacy of class representative(s); and (5) adequacy of claimant(s)' counsel. In addition to the requirements of Rule 23(a), the AAA and JAMS rules have a sixth requirement, namely, that the arbitration agreements signed by each member of the class are substantially similar to that signed by the class representative. Once those

2014); Alam v. Charter, AAA Case No. 73 160 00378 12 (Sept. 26, 2013); Curtis Hanna v. Pizza Hut Inc., AAA Case No. 33 160 00281 12 (Jul. 23, 2013); Ormiston v. Red Bull, AAA Case No. 72 160 01077 12 (Apr. 18, 2014); Rivera et al. v. Corinthian Colleges, AAA Case No. 11 434 1075 08 (Nov. 1, 2011); Spalding v. Glass Lewis, AAA Case No. 11 160 00078 11 (Jul. 7, 2011); Emergency v. Proassurance, AAA Case No. 11 195 Y 01789 10 (Apr. 2, 2011); McCalley v. NVR, AAA Case No. 11 110 01323 09 (Feb. 10, 2011); Spradlin v. Trump, AAA Case No. 11 115 Y 01846 09 (Aug. 10, 2010); Benjamin Clark, III v. CHDP Condo LLC, AAA Case No. 11 115 Y 01921 09 (Jul. 22, 2010); Michael Mensch v. Alta Colleges, Inc., AAA Case No. 11 516 00995 09 (Jul. 16, 2010); Maslo v. Oak Pointe, AAA Case No. 11 181 02243 06 (Jun. 15, 2010).

[142] *See, e.g.*, Herman Benson v. Credit Solutions of America, AAA Case No. 11 160 M 02281 08 (Jul. 6, 2010); Guzman and AIMCO River Club, LLC, AAA Case No. 18 526 Y 000120 13 (Dec. 4, 2013).

[143] *See, e.g.*, Timothy A. v. American Dairy Queen Corp. AAA Case No. 65 114 00016 13 (Feb. 18, 2014); Gonzalez and Brand, AAA Case No. 70 160 000270 13 (Oct. 15, 2013).

[144] *See, e.g.*, Danielle Demetriou v. Earthlink, Inc., AAA Case No. 11 117 00273 10 (Sept. 1, 2010); Knudsen v. North Motors, AAA Case No. 11 155 02699 09 (May 18, 2010).

requirements have been met, the "predominance" and "superiority" requirements of FRCP Rule 23(b) must also be met.

As of June 2014, the AAA has overseen forty-nine arbitrations in which the arbitrator or tribunal had entered class-certification awards (numerous other arbitrations have passed the clause-construction phase and are awaiting a hearing or ruling on class certification). Out of the forty class-certification awards, thirty decisions have granted class certification[145] and nineteen have denied it.[146] Eight cases have reached the stage of hearing on the merits.[147] **11.74**

[145] In the matter between Pamela Herrington and others similarly situated and Waterstone Mortgage Corporation, AAA Case No. 51 160 00393 12 (Mar. 4, 2014); Rubio's v. Larke Holden, AAA Case No. 11 160 02787 05 (Jul. 28, 2010); Misty Owens et al. v. Automobile Protection Corp., AAA Case No. 11 188 01140 05 (Jul. 19, 2010); Thomas v. SoutherLinc, AAA Case No. 11 494 01518 08 (Jun. 24, 2010); Francis v. United, AAA Case No. 11 160 00267 07 (Jun. 22, 2010); Rubio's v. Larke Holden, AAA Case No. 11 160 02787 05 (May 12, 2010); Jock v. Sterling, AAA Case No. 11 160 00655 08 (Mar. 8, 2010); Murdock v. Thomas, AAA Case No. 11 148 Y 01805 07 (Sep. 4, 2009); Chavez v. 3P, AAA Case No. 11 145 Y 1839 07 (Jul. 12, 2009); Jones v. Genus, AAA Case No. 11 181 00295 05 (May 7, 2009); John Flores v. Arakelian Enterprises, Inc., AAA Case No. 11 160 02637 05 (Dec. 29, 2008); Herbert Kirsh v. Finova Group, Inc., AAA Case No. 11 148 Y 01381 07 (Nov. 4, 2008); David Godina v. Countrywide Financial Corp., AAA Case No. 11 160 01857 06 (Oct. 24, 2008); Thomas Bundy v. Countrywide Financial Corp., AAA Case No. 11 160 01858 06 (Oct. 24, 2008); Scher v. Oxford Health Plans, AAA Case No. 11 193 00548 05 (Sep.12, 2008); Sutter v. Oxford Health Plans, AAA Case No. 18 193 20593 02 (Sept. 23, 2003). Cole v. Long John Silver's Rest., Inc., AAA Case No. 11 160 00194 04 (Sep. 19, 2005); Barton, *supra* note 121; Addleman v. The Ryland Group, Inc., AAA Case No. 11 181 01524 05 (Dec. 26, 2006); Wolf v. Lakewood Homes, Inc., AAA Case No. 111 181 Y 01244 06 (March 6, 2007); Bagpeddler.com v. U.S. Bancorp, AAA Case No. 11 181 00322 04 (May 4, 2007); Weller v. Sprint Commc'n Co., L.P., AAA Case No. 11 181 00070 06 (May 22, 2007); Johnson v. Morton's Rest. Group, Inc., AAA Case No. 11 160 01513 05 (June 27, 2007); Bryant v. Joel Antunes, LLC, AAA Case No. 111 160 01783 05 (Sept. 17, 2007); Associated Pathology Consultants, S.C. v. United Healthcare of Illinois, Inc., AAA Case No. 11 195 00971 06 (Feb. 25, 2008); McGraw v. Morton's Rest. Group, Inc., AAA Case No. 11 60 02171 06 (April 18, 2008); Maslo v. Oak Pointe Country Club, Inc., AAA Case No. 11 181 02243 06 (May 9, 2008); Kaplan v. Citibank, N.A., AAA Case No. 111 148 1007 07 (June 4, 2008); Brown v. Cellco P'ship, AAA Case No. 11 494 01274 05 and 11 494 0032 05 (Oct. 1, 2008); Smith v. Tele Tech Holdings, Inc., AAA Case No. 11 160 02726 04 (Dec. 26, 2006).

[146] MB & CO., LTD. v. Charter One Bank, N.A., AAA Case No. 11 148 02801 04 (Apr. 24, 2014); John Lear v. Neil Jones Food Company, Inc., AAA Case No. 74 154 Y 00238 11(Aug. 18, 2013); CK Food v. Restaurant, AAA Case No. 11 117 00839 12 (Jul. 10, 2013); Almaraz v. Newbridge College, AAA Case No. 11 434 02001 08 (Jul. 6, 2010); Duran v. Western Exterminator, AAA Case No. 11 160 002055 08 (May 20, 2010); Paul Holland v. ECPI College of Technology, AAA Case No. 11 434 001716 08 (Oct. 22, 2009); Hernandez v. Teletech, AAA Case No. 11 160 01892 06 (Jun. 8, 2009); Tarek, LLC v. Kinkade, AAA Case No. 11 Y 114 00578 04 (Apr. 1, 2005); Milstein v. Protection One Alarm Services, Inc., AAA Case No. 11 110 00270 04 (May 12, 2005); Chavez v. Rent-A-Center, Inc., AAA Case No. 11 160 01817 04 (Aug. 18, 2005); Awe v. I&M Rail Link, LLC, AAA Case No. 11 160 00026 05 (June 23, 2006); Hayes v. M.S. Carriers, Inc., AAA Case No. 11 118 02907 04 (June 26, 2006); Bezaury v. Arbor Homes, LLC, AAA Case No. 11 148 02161 04 (June 30, 2006); Garret v. Rollins, Inc., AAA Case No. 11 181 01663 04 (July 14, 2006); Partners Two, Inc. v. Adecco N. Am., LLC, AAA Case No. 11 114 03042 04 (May 14, 2007); Groves v. Hemet Mfg. Co., Inc., AAA Case No. 11 160 00194 05 (May 30, 2007); Cummings v. Florida Mag Enter., Inc., AAA Case No. 11 188 00203 07 (July 31, 2007); Haro v. NCR Corp., AAA Case No. 111 160 1962 05 (Nov. 9, 2007); Levitt v. Lipper Holdings, AAA Case No. 11 168 00663 04 (Mar. 18, 2008).

[147] Laverne Jones, et al. v. Genus Credit Management Corporation, AAA Case No. 11 181 00295 05 (Apr. 30, 2014); Lear v. Neil Jones Food Co., AAA Case No. 74 154 00238 11 (Jul. 18, 2013);

11.75 A quick review of the bases on which the forty-nine cases have made their class-certification decisions is instructive.

1. Numerosity

11.76 Satisfaction of the numerosity requirement, which stipulates that the putative class must be "so numerous that joinder of separate arbitrations on behalf of all members is impracticable,"[148] has rarely been denied by AAA arbitrators. Certified putative classes in AAA arbitrations have ranged from thousands of members[149] to as few as eighteen members.[150] A class of thirty to fifty persons is "generally viewed" to be the range of claimants necessary to certify a class.[151] Regardless of the size of the putative class, some tribunals have stated that joinder of claims is impossible in AAA arbitrations because there is no joinder device available under AAA procedures, and, therefore, the numerosity requirement is necessarily fulfilled.[152] Circumstances where the numerosity requirement was not fulfilled only arose where there was no evidence to suggest there was another potential class member besides the claimant,[153] there was no unambiguous, definable class to name,[154] or where the tribunal decided to consider the numerosity, commonality, and typicality requirements jointly and found that the entirety had not been fulfilled.[155]

2. Commonality

11.77 The commonality element, requiring that there be "questions of law or fact common to the class,"[156] is also normally satisfied. It is not necessary that all issues of fact and law are common. The standard is, in fact, a very lax one—commonality "requires only that there *be* common questions of law or fact common to the class, not that such issues predominate as required by the more rigorous standard in FRCP Rule 23(b) and AAA Supplementary Rules for Class Arbitrations Rule 4(b)."[157] Therefore, most tribunals have held that one common issue among the class is sufficient.[158] Commonality has been denied in AAA arbitrations only

Jones v. Amerix, AAA Case No. 11 181 00295 05 (Apr. 11, 2014); Flaxman v. Terminix, AAA Case No. 11 434 00701 07 (Jul. 25, 2011); Murdock v. Thomas, AAA Case No. not available (May 2, 2011); Cole v. Long John Silver's, AAA Case No. 11 160 00194 04 (Oct. 7, 2010); Herbert Kirsh v. Finova Group, Inc., AAA Case No. 11 148 Y 01381 07 (Sep. 18, 2009); XM v. Enderlin, AAA Case No. 11 181 00989 06 (Jul. 30, 2009).

148 AAA Class Arbitration Rules, *supra* note 65, at Rule 4(a)(1).
149 *See, e.g., Sutter, supra* note 60.
150 *See Groves, supra* note 146.
151 Bryant v. Joel Antunnes L.L.C., AAA Case No. 11 160 01783 05 (Sept. 17, 2007).
152 *See, e.g., Levitt, L.L.C., supra* note 146; *Awe, supra* note 146.
153 *Cummings, supra* note 146.
154 Chavez v. Rent-A-Center, Inc., AAA Case No. 11 160 01663 04 (Aug. 18, 2005).
155 *See, e.g., Partners Two, supra* note 146.
156 AAA Class Arbitration Rules, *supra* note 75, at Rule 4(a)(2).
157 *Tarek, supra* note 146.
158 *See, e.g.,* Maslo v. Oake Pointe Country Club, Inc., AAA Case No. 11 181 002243 06 (May 9, 2008); *Hayes, supra* note 146.

where the tribunal considered the predominance and commonality requirements in conjunction with each other and the common issues did not predominate,[159] where the claimant's situation was so unique that a class could not be defined,[160] or where the arbitral clause of a nationwide putative class stipulated that the choice of law was the law of the state where each cause of action arose (thereby making the legal issues necessarily different among the class).[161]

3. Typicality

The requirement of the typicality element is that "the claims or defenses of the representative parties are typical of the claims or defenses of the class."[162] Tribunals have held this requirement met where there is no material difference between the named claimants' claims and those of the balance of the class.[163] However, the standard is generally a lax one: "[w]hen it is alleged that the same unlawful conduct was directed at, or affected, both the named plaintiff and the class sought to be represented, the typicality requirement is usually met regardless of varying fact patterns which underlie individual claims."[164] Some tribunals have stated a two-part rule: (1) the claims of the representatives must arise from the same practice or course of conduct giving rise to the claims of all other class members; and (2) the claims of the representative and the class members are based upon the same legal theory.[165] Those circumstances leading to a tribunal's denial of the typicality requirement were found where differences between the representative's factual or legal claims were deemed to be material differences.[166] **11.78**

4. Adequacy of Class Representative(s)

In order to be an adequate representative of a class, the tribunal must conclude that "the representative parties will fairly and adequately protect the interests of the class."[167] This element generally requires two things: (1) the absence of conflicting interests between the class representatives and the unnamed class members; and (2) an assurance of vigorous prosecution on the class' behalf.[168] In order to assure the tribunal of vigorous prosecution of the class' claims, diligence in **11.79**

159 *See, e.g., Hemet, supra* note 146.

160 *Cummings, supra* note 146.

161 *Haro, supra* note 146.

162 AAA Class Arbitration Rules, *supra* note 65, at Rule 4(a)(3).

163 *See, e.g.,* McGraw v. Morton's Rest. Group, Inc., AAA Case No. 11 60 02171 06 (Apr. 18, 2008).

164 *Cole, supra* note 147, *quoting* Newberg On Class Actions, § 3.13, (4th ed. 2002). *See also* Wolf v. Lakewood Homes, Inc., AAA Case No. 11 181 02243 06 (Mar. 2, 2007) (certifying a class even though the defense had raised unique defenses against the named claimant).

165 *See, e.g., Hayes, supra* note 146, citing *In re* Am. Med. Sys., 75 F.3d 1069, 1082 (6th Cir. 1996).

166 *See, e.g., Tarek, supra* note 146; *Haro, supra* note 146; *Garrett, supra* note 121.

167 AAA Class Arbitration Rules, *supra* note 65, at Rule 4(a)(4).

168 Johnson v. Morton's Rest. Group, AAA Class No. 11 160 01513 05 (June 27, 2007).

bringing the claim and preparing for the litigation are factors that weigh strongly in favor of certification.[169] Often, a failure to meet the adequacy of representation element is a function of the failure to meet another element (e.g., the named claimant's claims not being typical of the class because a resulting conflict of interest would limit the representative's ability to protect adequately the class' rights).[170] Other circumstances in which this requirement was not met relied on facts suggesting a conflict of interest or of a lack of vigorous prosecution that were very fact-specific.[171]

5. Adequacy of the Class Representative(s)' Counsel

11.80 The most rarely denied, not to mention the most rarely disputed, element of FRCP Rule 23 and the AAA and JAMS class certification rules is the requirement that "counsel selected to represent the class will fairly and adequately protect the interests of the class." Only one AAA class arbitration had found this requirement unmet. In *Milstein v. Protection One Alarm Services, Inc.*,[172] the class representative's chosen legal counsel was the law firm where his son was a partner. The firm was given unfettered discretion over the case, to the point that the class representative was not entirely familiar with the claim or his attorneys at the time of the hearing. Due to the appearance of divided loyalties of counsel, as well as counsel's failure to even recognize the possible disadvantage to the remaining members of the class, the tribunal denied certification in part on these grounds. In the remainder of the arbitrations, tribunals have accepted claimant's counsel's adequacy based on personal knowledge or reputation of counsel's practice,[173] counsel's performance throughout the arbitral proceedings,[174] submissions regarding experience in class actions,[175] or due to a lack of challenge to counsel's representation by the opposing party or the tribunal.[176]

6. Substantial Similarity of Arbitration Agreements

11.81 The only AAA and JAMS class certification element not modeled after FRCP Rule 23 is the similarity-of-arbitral-agreement element, requiring that "each class member has entered into an agreement containing an arbitration clause which is substantially similar to that signed by the class representative(s) and each of the

[169] *See, e.g., Maslo, supra* note 145; Weller v. Sprint Commc'ns Co., AAA Case No. 11 181 00070 06 (May 22, 2007).

[170] *See, e.g., Tarek, supra* note 146; *Garrett, supra* note 121; *Haro, supra* note 146.

[171] *See, e.g., Milstein, supra* note 146 (denying the adequacy of representation claim where claimant's son's law firm represented the class and was given unfettered discretion as to the claims and where claimant had little or no knowledge regarding the suit).

[172] *Id.*

[173] *See, e.g., Barton, supra* note 121.

[174] *See, e.g., Maslo, supra* note 145.

[175] *See, e.g., Bagpeddler.com, supra* note 121.

[176] *See, e.g., Wolf, supra* note 145.

other class members."[177] Because a class is not defined prior to a class certification hearing, arbitral tribunals have substantial leeway in assessing this requirement. Many tribunals will, where a difference between arbitral clauses arises, simply define the class in a way that excludes those putative class members whose agreements are not similar and would otherwise prevent class certification.[178] Especially where the arbitration clause is part of a larger contract of adhesion, a tribunal may construe the contract and its terms against the drafter in order to interpret the clauses as substantially similar.[179] Circumstances under which a tribunal has found that this requirement was not fulfilled include a situation where there was a lack of evidence that any valid arbitration agreement existed between claimant and respondent at all[180] and where the differences among the contracts were so substantial that the tribunal declined jurisdiction over the matter.[181]

7. Predominance and Superiority of Claims

The key requirement of class certification is the predominance and superiority requirement of FRCP Rule 23(b), AAA Supplementary Rules of Class Arbitration Rule 4(b), and JAMS Class Action Procedures Rule 3(b). AAA Supplementary Rules of Class Arbitration Rules 4(b) states: **11.82**

> An arbitration may be maintained as a class arbitration if the prerequisites of subdivision (a) are satisfied, and in addition, the arbitrator finds that the questions of law or common fact to the members of the class predominate over any questions affecting only individual members, and that a class arbitration is superior to other available methods for the fair and efficient adjudication of the controversy. The matters pertinent to the findings include:
> (1) the interest of members of the class in individually controlling the prosecution or defense of separate arbitrations;
> (2) the extent and nature of any other proceedings concerning the controversy already commenced by or against members of the class;
> (3) the desirability or undesirability of concentrating the determination of the claims in a single tribunal forum and
> (4) the difficulties likely to be encountered in the management of a class arbitration.

Predominance is the crucial question in a class-certification determination, because it meaningfully ties together all of the previous requirements, particularly numerosity, commonality, and typicality. Most tribunals state the requirement simply, requiring that the arbitration be predominated by general, common issues of the class, not individualized issues, such that efficiency would be gained through class arbitration without substantially limiting rights **11.83**

[177] AAA Class Arbitration Rules, *supra* note 65, at Rule 4(a)(6).
[178] *See, e.g., Sutter, supra* note 121; *Barton, supra* note 121; *Bagpeddler.com, supra* note 121.
[179] *McGraw, supra* note 163.
[180] *Cummings, supra* note 146.
[181] *See Milstein, supra* note 146 (declining jurisdiction over the arbitration where some arbitral clauses indicated that the governing arbitral institution would be AAA, some indicated JAMS, and still others indicated the National Arbitration Forum).

protection.[182] Tribunals have clarified this by holding that in order to satisfy the predominance requirement there need be at least one single common issue that is overriding.[183] However, the fact that separate evidence may be required from each claimant regarding matters such as proof or amount of damages generally will not defeat a predominance claim.[184] Where standardized proof is sufficient to prove the claims of the whole class, this is a factor that usually signals the claim is a predominant one.[185] Arbitrations that do not satisfy the predominance requirement are those that would require extensive individualized factual determinations or legal argument. Where a class arbitration would require individualized "mini-trials" to determine whether the respondent is liable to each member of the class, predominance is unlikely to be found.[186]

11.84 Factors considered when determining the superiority of class action include rights protection and efficiency;[187] the manageability of a class in comparison to separate adjudications is a secondary consideration.[188] Often, a finding of lack of predominance correlates to a lack of superiority, because the necessity of individual proof for each individual claim eliminates the arbitration's most beneficial aspects such as expediency and efficiency.[189]

K. ARBITRAL CLAUSES PROHIBITING CLASS ACTIONS AND PUBLIC POLICY ARGUMENTS AGAINST SUCH CLAUSES BEFORE THE SUPREME COURT DECISIONS IN *AT&T MOBILITY LLC V. CONCEPCION* AND *AMERICAN EXPRESS CO. V. ITALIAN COLORS RESTAURANT*

11.85 As noted previously, given the number of clause-construction arbitration awards in the post-*Bazzle* era which have found that a "silent" clause permits class arbitration, one would be wise to draft a clause expressly prohibiting class action arbitrations if one would like to avoid this result. Even if one does insert a no-class-action arbitration clause, however, such a clause may still be held invalid as against public policy. Whether a contract violates public policy is an issue of contract law and has historically been thought to be governed by state law. Until

---

182 *See Maslo*, *supra* note 145.
183 *See Smith*, *supra* note 145.
184 *See Cole*, *supra* note 147.
185 *See Bagpeddler.com*, *supra* note 121.
186 *See, e.g.*, *Garrett*, *supra* note 121; *Tarek*, *supra* note 146; *Hayes*, *supra* note 146.
187 *See* Zobrist v. Verizon Wireless, AAA Case No. 11 494 01274 05, 11 494 0032 05 (Mar. 10, 2008).
188 *Harris Tele Tech Holdings*, *supra* note 118.
189 *See Tarek*, *supra* note 146.

recently, most federal circuits had held that a clause prohibiting class arbitration is not against public policy,[190] but after *Bazzle* federal courts began to find such prohibitions unconscionable.[191] New York federal district courts appear to follow state courts on this public policy issue,[192] but there does not appear to be any Second Circuit opinion on the subject. State courts in New York, have held that a clause prohibiting class action arbitrations is not against public policy.[193]

Immediately after *Bazzle*, however, many other state courts, held that such no-class-action clauses were against the public policies of their respective states.[194] Those state courts which voided no-class-action clauses typically reasoned that **11.86**

---

[190] Jenkins v. First Am. Cash Advance of GA, LLC, 400 F.3d 868 (11th Cir. 2005); Caley v. Gulfstream Aerospace Corp., 428 F.3d 1359 (11th Cir. 2005); Omstead v. Dell, Inc., 473 F. Supp. 2d 1018 (N.D. Cal. 2007); Livingston v. Assocs. Fin., Inc., 339 F.3d 553, 558 (7th Cir. 2003); Snowden v. CheckPoint Check Cashing, 290 F.3d 631, 638 (4th Cir. 2002); Randolph v. Green Tree Fin Corp-Ala., 244 F.3d 814, 818–19 (11th Cir. 2001); Johnson v. W. Suburban Bank, 225 F.3d 366, 377 (3rd Cir. 2000).

[191] *See, e.g.*, Lowden v. T-Mobile USA Inc., 512 F.3d 1213 (9th Cir. 2008); Shroyer v. New Cingular Wireless Services, Inc., 498 F.3d 976 (9th Cir. 2007); Cooper v. QC Fin Services, Inc., 503 F. Supp. 2d 1266 (D. Ariz. 2007); Rollins, Inc. v. Garrett, 176 Fed. Appx. 968, 968 (11th Cir. 2006; Muhummad v. County Bank of Rehobeth Beach, 912 A.2d 88 (N.J. 2006); Kristian v. Comcast Corp., 446 F.3d 25, 53–61 (1st Cir. 2006) (holding a class arbitration ban unconscionable and unenforceable in cases asserting antitrust violations); Ting v. AT&T, 319 F.3d 1126, 1130 (9th Cir. 2003) (deciding that a clause barring class action arbitration was unconscionable under California state law); Szetela v. Discover Bank, 118 Cal. Rptr. 2d 862, 867 (Cal. Ct. App. 2002), *cert. denied* 537 U.S. 1226 (2003).

[192] *See, e.g.*, Chen-Oster v. Goldman, Sachs & Co., 785 F. Supp. 2d 394, 405 (S.D.N.Y. 2011); MQDC, Inc. v. Steadfast Ins. Co., No. CV 2012-1424, 2013 U.S. Dist. LEXIS 172836, at *24 (E.D.N.Y. Sept. 10, 2013).

[193] Tsadilas v. Providian Nat'l Bank, 786 N.Y.S.2d 478, 480 (N.Y. App. Div. 2004) (*quoting* Ranieri v. Bell Atlantic Mobile, 759 N.Y.S.2d 448, 449 (N.Y. App. Div. 2003) ("we are in accord with authorities holding that a contractual proscription against class actions, such as contained in the Agreements, is neither unconscionable nor violative of public policy"); *cf.* Flynn v. Labor Ready, Inc., 751 N.Y.S.2d 721, 722 (N.Y. Sup. Ct. 2002) (sending plaintiffs to arbitration despite finding that "[b]ecause plaintiffs would be precluded from acting as a class in arbitration, the costs they would each incur in arbitration would far outweigh any potential recovery").

[194] *See, e.g.*, Leonard v. Terminix Int'l Co., LP, 854 So. 2d 529 (Ala. 2002); Gentry v. Superior Court, 64 Cal. Rptr. 3d 773 (Cal. Ct. App. 2007); Gatton v. T-Mobile USA, Inc., 61 Cal. Rptr. 3d 344 (Cal. Ct. App. 2007); *In re* Cingular Cases, No. D047603 2007 WL 93229 (Cal. Ct. App. 2007); Firchow v. Citibank (South Dakota), N.A., No. B187081 2007 WL 64763 (Cal. Ct. App. 2007); Mandel v. Household Bank (Nevada), 129 Cal. Rptr. 2d 380 (Cal. Ct. App. 2003); Gutierrez v. Autowest, Inc., 7 Cal. Rptr. 3d 267 (Cal Ct. App. 2003); Szetela v. Discover Bank, 118 Cal. Rptr. 862, 867 (Cal. Ct. App. 2002), *cert. denied* 537 U.S. 1226 (2003); Betts v. McKenzie Check Advance of Florida, Case No. CL 01-320 AI (Fla. Cir. Ct. 2008); Kinkel v. Cingular Wireless, LLC, 828 N.E.2d 812, 820 (Ill. App. Ct. 2005); Whitney v. Alltel Commc'ns, Inc., 173 S.W.3d 200, 313014 (Mo. Ct. App. 2005); Muhummad v. County Bank of Rehobeth Beach, 912 A.2d 88 (N.J. 2006); Tillman v. Commercial Credit Loans, Inc., 655 S.E.2d 362, 373 (N.C. 2008); Eagle v. Fred Martin Motor Co., 809 N.E.2d 1161 (Ohio Ct. App. 2004); Vasquez-Lopez v. Beneficial Or., Inc., 152 P.3d 940 (Or. Ct. App. 2007); Thibodeau v. Comcast Corp., 912 A.2d 874 (Pa. Super. Ct. 2006); Lytle v. Citifinancial Services, Inc., 810 A.2d 643 (Pa. Super. Ct. 2002); Scott v. Cingular Wireless, 161 P.3d 1000 (Wash. 2007); W. Va. ex rel Dunlap v. Berger, 567 S.E.2d 265, 278–79 (W. Va.), *cert. denied*, 527 U.S. 1087 (2002); Coady v. Cross Country Bank, Inc., 729 N.W.2d 732, 745 (Wis. Ct. App. 2007); Wis. Auto Title Loans, Inc. v. Jones, 714 N.W.2d 155 (Wis. 2006).

enforcing a prohibition on class arbitration would be unconscionable because it would put the arbitral forum out of reach for low-dollar claimants. For example, in *Tillman v. Commercial Credit Loans, Inc.*, two plaintiffs with limited financial resources obtained loans from the defendant company and were unaware of the exact terms of the arbitration clause contained in the loan agreement.[195] When the plaintiffs brought a suit alleging violations of state consumer protection law, the lender attempted to compel arbitration pursuant to the arbitration clause contained in the loan agreements. The agreements, which were drafted by defendants, imposed financial barriers to borrowers seeking to bring claims by specifying that borrowers could not arbitrate claims for less than $15,000, that the non-prevailing party would pay for the arbitration proceeding to the extent it exceeded eight hours, and joinder of claims and class actions were prohibited. The trial court found the terms of the arbitration agreement substantively unconscionable because the cost of arbitrating was prohibitively high. The appellate court affirmed, also noting that the prohibition against class action arbitration was a deterrent to plaintiffs seeking to bring a claim against the defendant, as the cost of bringing a claim would inevitably be high, yet the costs could not be shared with other plaintiffs. Other state courts in the immediate years after *Bazzle* also held prohibitions against class action arbitrations unconscionable for largely the same reasons.[196]

11.87 Other courts which during this time period held that no-class-action clauses were against public policy have referred to the fundamental importance of class actions in the enforcement of consumer protection laws. For example, *Fiser v. Dell Computer Corp.* explicitly cites the cost-sharing feature of class actions as providing an opportunity for relief that would otherwise not be economically feasible for an individual plaintiff to obtain.[197] In *Fiser*, the plaintiff alleged that the defendant computer manufacturer systematically misrepresented the memory size of its computers, calculated to be a loss of ten to twenty dollars to each consumer.[198] The arbitration clause between the plaintiff and defendant prohibited class action arbitration. The defendant argued that the plaintiff had not met his burden of proving that the small amount of coverable damages made it economically infeasible to bring an individual claim, but the court disagreed:

> On these facts, enforcing the class action ban would be tantamount to allowing Defendant to unilaterally exempt itself from New Mexico consumer protection laws. It is not hyperbole or exaggeration to say that it is a fundamental principle of

[195] 655 S.E.2d at 373. *See also Kinkel*, 828 N.E.2d at 820 (class arbitration ban unconscionable where cost of filing and pursuing individual claims would offset significant portion of potential recovery, which was capped at $150).

[196] *See, e.g.*, Vasquez-Lopez v. Beneficial Or., Inc., 152 P.3d 940 (Or. Ct. App. 2007); Coady v. Cross Country Bank, Inc., 729 N.W.2d 732 (Wis. Ct. App. 2007); Thibodeau v. Comcast Corp., 912 A.2d 874 (Pa. Super. Ct. 2006).

[197] 188 P.3d 1215, 1219 (N.M. 2008).

[198] *Id.* at 1217.

> justice in New Mexico that corporations may not tailor the laws that our legislature has enacted in order to shield themselves from the potential claims of consumers. Because it violates public policy by depriving small claims consumers of a meaningful remedy and exculpating Defendant from potential wrongdoing, the class action ban meets the test for substantive unconscionability.[199]

In contrast to those post-*Bazzle* state court decisions which found no-class-action arbitration clauses unconscionable, other state courts found such clauses enforceable.[200] They typically reasoned that such clauses were not per se void without additional circumstances. For example, the court held in *Lomax v. Woodmen of World Life Ins. Society*,[201] that an arbitration clause in an agreement between members of a fraternal benefit society and the society itself was not substantively unconscionable and therefore the agreement was enforceable. The society's members argued that the ban on classwide arbitration rendered the clause unconscionable, but the court disagreed, concluding that, without more, the prohibition of classwide arbitration did not render the arbitration clause unconscionable. Other courts upheld such clauses for the sake of efficiency: **11.88**

> Arbitration is meant to resolve private disputes in an expeditious and efficient manner, not to remedy a public wrong. The fact that the procedural device of class treatment is not available in arbitration is part and parcel of arbitration's ability to offer simplicity, informality, and expedition characteristics that generally make arbitration an attractive vehicle for resolution of low-value claims.[202]

Some commentators argued against finding no-class-action clauses "unconscionable" by noting the relative speed, informality, and privacy of individual arbitration in contrast to standard court proceedings.[203] Other commentators pointed out that class arbitration increases the drafting party's cost of doing business, which reduces savings which would otherwise be passed on to consumers and employees in the form of lower product prices and higher employee salaries.[204] **11.89**

---

199 *Id.* at 1221.

200 *See, e.g.*, Cunningham v. Citigroup, Inc., No. Civ. 05-3476 2005 WL 3454312 (D.N.J. 2005) (clause prohibiting class actions upheld because it was clear and unambiguous); Gras v. Associates First Capital Corp., 786 A.2d 886 (N.J. App. Div. 2001); Goetsch v. Shell Oil Co., 197 F.R.D. 574 (W.D. N.C. 2000) (clause upheld because cardholder continued using card after receiving proper notice of changed terms); Mackey v. MBNA America Bank, N.A., 343 F. Supp. 2d 966, 969 (W.D. Wash. 2004) (citing Edelist regarding the enforceability of an amended arbitration clause); Gras v. Associates First Capital Corp., 786 A.2d 886 (N.J. App. Div. 2001) (clause upheld because it was sufficiently clear and specific as to its terms). *See also* Vigil v. Sears Nat'l. Bank, 205 F. Supp. 2d 566 (E.D. La. 2002) (clause upheld because such clauses are routinely included in consumer contracts).

201 228 F. Supp. 2d 1360 (N.D. Ga. 2002).

202 Wing v. Cingular Wireless, LLC, No. A105906 2005 WL 1168363, at *6 (Cal. Ct. App. 2005).

203 Jack Wilson, *No-Class-Action Arbitration Clauses, State-Law Unconscionability, and the Federal Arbitration Act: A Case for Federal Judicial Restraint and Congressional Action*, 23 QLR 737, 759 (2004).

204 Joshua S. Lipshutz, *The Court's Implicit Roadmap: Charting the Prudent Course at the Juncture of Mandatory Arbitration Agreements and Class Action Lawsuits*, 57 Stan. L. Rev. 1677, 1710 (2005).

11.90 While some courts relied on a general statement in favor of enforcing arbitration agreements,[205] courts upholding no-class-action clauses also commonly took into consideration the circumstances surrounding the agreement. These courts found it particularly relevant whether the plaintiff received proper notice of the clause. In *Edelist v. MBNA Am. Bank*,[206] the court held that the no-class-action clause was not unconscionable because the plaintiff credit cardholder had received notice of the arbitration amendment and did not opt out of the amendment. In this and several other credit card cases, courts held in favor of credit card issuers who carefully followed the statutory guidelines for providing proper notice to cardholders about changed terms, as well as the opportunity to opt out of the new terms.[207] Courts also took into account the specific terms of the arbitration agreement, including whether an arbitration agreement entitled a plaintiff to recover attorneys' fees, thus rendering the representation of small claims plaintiffs in arbitration proceedings more attractive to lawyers.[208]

11.91 Even courts in California, the jurisdiction most hostile to no-class-action arbitration clauses, found that such clauses were not per se void as against public policy, but instead their validity depended on the specific facts of each case. In *Szetela v. Discover Bank*,[209] the court held that although adhesive arbitration clauses are not per se unconscionable, the advantages such provisions may give to one party over another may render the clause unfair in practice. In the case before it, the court noted that, because the defendant was also the drafting party, it had effectively written itself a "get out of jail free card" while seriously compromising consumers' rights.[210] The court held that this practice went against the California Legislature's policy of discouraging unfair and unlawful business practices, and undermined the very mechanism by which members of the general public could seek relief for their claims.[211]

11.92 In *Discover Bank v. Superior Court*,[212] the court held that a clause waiving the right to class arbitration in a consumer contract of adhesion could, under certain

---

205 *See, e.g.*, Hutcherson v. Sears Roebuck & Co., 793 N.E.2d 886, 896 (Ill. App. Ct. 2003) (internal citations omitted) (upholding clause, stating that the "strong policy that favors enforcement of arbitration provisions" could not be ignored).

206 790 A.2d 1249, 1258 (Del. Super. Ct. 2001).

207 *See, e.g.*, Jenkins v. First American Cash Advance of Ga., LLC, 400 F.3d 868, 878 (11th Cir. 2005).

208 *See, e.g.*, Billups v. Bankfirst, 294 F. Supp. 2d 1265 (M.D. Ala. 2003) (clause upheld because defendant card issuer would pay administrative fees and clause did not limit recovery of attorney fees); Taylor v. Citibank USA, N.A., 292 F. Supp. 2d 1333 (M.D. Ala. 2003) (clause upheld because Fair Credit Billing Act, as applied to state law, made creditor liable to a successful claimant for attorney fees and costs). *See also* Kathleen M. Scanlon, *Class Arbitration Waivers: The "Severability" Doctrine and Its Consequence*, 62 Disp. Resol. J. 40 (Feb.–Apr. 2007) (noting that the court in *Kristian v. Comcast Corp.*, 446 F.3d 25 (1st Cir. 2006), found that barring class arbitration "would not necessarily choke off the supply of lawyers willing to pursue" certain claims under the federal lending laws).

209 118 Cal. Rptr. 2d at 868 (Cal. Ct. App. 2002).

210 *Id.*

211 *Id.*

212 113 P.3d 1100 (Cal. 2005).

circumstances, be unconscionable and should not be enforced. In that case, the plaintiff alleged that the defendant bank misrepresented to cardholders that late payment fees received by a certain date would not lead to late charges, whereas the bank actually assessed fees for any payment received after 1:00 p.m. on the specified date. The plaintiff's individual damages were small, but aggregating the damages across a class of consumers would have been significantly larger. The credit card agreement prohibited classwide arbitration, making it unlikely that any individual credit cardholder would bring a claim for a small amount of damages. The Supreme Court of California took exception to this, noting that the practices of the defendant bank had rendered the no-class-action clause unconscionable. It further noted, however, that:

> [w]e do not hold that all class action waivers are necessarily unconscionable. But when the waiver is found in a consumer contract of adhesion in a setting in which disputes between the contracting parties predictably involve small amounts of damages, and when it is alleged that the party with the superior bargaining power has carried out a scheme to deliberately cheat large numbers of consumers out of individually small sums of money, then, at least to the extent the obligation at issue is governed by California law, the waiver becomes in practice the exemption of the party "from responsibility for [its] own fraud, or willful injury to the person or property of another." (Civ. Code, § 1668.) Under these circumstances, such waivers are unconscionable under California law and should not be enforced.[213]

In the case of *Kristian v. Comcast Corp.*,[214] the First Circuit took the unusual step of severing a no-class-action clause, which it found unconscionable, from the rest of the arbitration clause, thereby forcing the defendant into a class action arbitration. The court noted that: **11.93**

> Typically, courts prefer declaring an arbitration agreement unenforceable rather than using severance as a remedy when fundamental elements of the arbitration regime are at issue ... However, here, the arbitration agreements do anticipate specifically the severance of the class arbitration bar. Therefore, [defendant] Comcast cannot claim that it did not foresee the possibility that, despite its strong preference for individual arbitration, it would have to arbitrate on a class basis because the contractual bar on class arbitration might, in its application to particular claims, run afoul of controlling law.[215]

To avoid the above result, one should be careful to draft no-class-action arbitration clauses so that such clauses are not severable if one prefers litigating a class action in court, rather than in an arbitration, in the event that such a clause is voided.[216] A well-drafted and explicit provision to this effect should allow a defendant to successfully avoid participating in an undesired class arbitration.[217] **11.94**

---

213 *Id.* at 1110.
214 446 F.3d 25 (1st Cir. 2006).
215 *Id.* at 62–63 (citations omitted).
216 Scanlon, 62 Disp. Resol. J. at 44.
217 *Id.*

L. DECISIONS BY COURTS, BEFORE *AT&T MOBILITY* AND *AMERICAN EXPRESS*, REGARDING WHETHER STATE ARBITRATION LAWS AND CONCEPTS OF PUBLIC POLICY ARE PREEMPTED BY THE FAA

11.95 The FAA is the legislative embodiment of a strong federal policy in favor of arbitration, meant to ensure that courts will treat arbitration agreements in the same manner as other contracts. The motivating principle behind the FAA is that no state should disfavor arbitration agreements in relation to its body of contract law, nor should state courts presume agreements to arbitrate are invalid. This policy of the FAA is most evident in Section 2, which provides that interstate commerce or international transactions with a written provision that disputes be settled by arbitration "shall be valid, irrevocable, and enforceable."[218] Courts have interpreted this as establishing a federal policy favoring arbitration which requires courts to "rigorously enforce agreements to arbitrate."[219]

11.96 As noted previously, ever since the case of *Moses H. Cone*,[220] the Supreme Court has held that there exists a body of federal substantive law of arbitration under the FAA which preempts state common or statutory law, if such state law is inconsistent with federal FAA law. The number of state courts holding that no-class-action arbitration clauses are void under the public policies of their states, raises the question of whether such public policy decisions might be preempted by contrary federal law favoring arbitration.

11.97 The Third Circuit addressed this issue in *Gay v. Creditinform* and held that a no-class-action arbitration clause could not be voided on state public-policy grounds because the state law was preempted by federal law.[221] In that case, the plaintiff made several monthly payments to the defendant for a service she allegedly did not receive. The plaintiff argued that the agreement's arbitration provision was unconscionable under Pennsylvania case law because a clause in the agreement disallowed class actions.[222] In responding to this argument, the court carefully reviewed Supreme Court precedent, and began its analysis by noting that the Pennsylvania cases cited by plaintiff were not the end point of its unconscionability analysis because the federal law that Congress set forth in the FAA was

---

[218] 9 U.S.C. § 2.

[219] Honig v. Comcast of Georgia I, LLC, 537 F. Supp. 2d 1277, 1282 (N.D. Ga. 2008) (citing Shearson/Am. Express, Inc. v. McMahon, 482 U.S. 220, 226, (1987)).

[220] 460 U.S. at 24.

[221] 511 F.3d 369 (3d Cir. 2007).

[222] *Id.* at 392, 393.

controlling and the Pennsylvania law must conform with it. It noted that in *Perry v. Thomas*,[223] the Supreme Court explained how courts should reconcile the promotion of arbitration agreements with competing state interests:

> [T]he text of § 2 provides the touchstone for choosing between state-law principles and the principles of federal common law envisioned by the passage of [the FAA]: An agreement to arbitrate is valid, irrevocable, and enforceable, *as a matter of federal law*, "save upon such grounds as exist at law or in equity for the revocation of *any* contract." Thus state law, whether of legislative or judicial origin, is applicable if that law arose to govern issues concerning the validity, revocability, and enforceability of contracts generally.[224]

The Court distinguished state-law principles that apply to contracts generally from those that are unique to arbitration agreements: **11.98**

> A state-law principle that takes its meaning precisely from the fact that a contract to arbitrate is at issue does not comport with this requirement of § 2. *See Prima Paint Corp. v. Flood & Conklin Mfg. Co.*, 388 U.S. [395,] 404, 87 S. Ct. 1801, 1806 (1967); *Southland Corp. v. Keating*, 465 U.S. 1, 16–17 n. 11 (1984). A court may not, then, in assessing the rights of litigants to enforce an arbitration agreement, construe that agreement in a manner different from that in which it otherwise construes nonarbitration agreements under state law.[225]

The *Gay* court further admonished in a critical explanation that: "Nor may a court rely on the uniqueness of an agreement to arbitrate as a basis for a state-law holding that enforcement would be unconscionable, for this would enable the court to effect what we hold today the state legislature cannot."[226]

The Third Circuit further noted that its own prior decision in *Johnson v. Suburban Bank* compelled the same result: **11.99**

> Addressing the same competing interests that we face in this case, namely, the promotion of arbitration agreements and the protection of class actions prohibited by such agreements, we observed in *Johnson* that the FAA "reflects 'a liberal federal policy favoring arbitration agreements,'" *Johnson*, 225 F.3d at 376 (quoting *Moses H. Cone Mem'l Hosp.*, 460 U.S. at 24), and that "[w]hatever the benefits of class actions, the FAA '*requires* piecemeal resolution when necessary to give effect to an arbitration agreement,'" *id.* at 375 (quoting *Moses H. Cone Mem'l Hosp.*, 460 U.S. at 20). To the extent, then, that *Lytle* and *Thibodeau* hold that the inclusion of a waiver of the right to bring judicial class actions in an arbitration agreement constitutes an unconscionable contract, they are not based "upon such grounds as exist at law or in equity for the revocation of *any* contract" pursuant to section 2 of the FAA, and therefore cannot prevent the enforcement of the arbitration provision in this case. 9 U.S.C. § 2 (emphasis added).[227]

[223] 482 U.S. 483 (1987)

[224] 482 U.S. at 492, n. 9 (internal citations omitted).

[225] *Id.* at 492.

[226] Perry v. Thomas, 482 U.S. 483, 492 n. 9 (1987)

[227] *Id.* at 394.

11.100 Interestingly, the Third Circuit in a footnote also raised the question of whether courts should look to individual state laws at all in deciding whether a contract is against public policy, as opposed to looking to a uniform substantive law of arbitrability under the FAA. It decided, however, that it need not reach this issue on the facts of the case before it:

> We recognize that courts including our court look to the law of the forum state or another state related to the circumstances of the dispute in determining as a matter of federal law whether an issue is referable to arbitration. Yet one might wonder why the consideration of state law is so confined. After all, if, as is the case, federal common law developed under the FAA is at issue then it is logical that the law should be uniform throughout the country. In this regard it could be asked whether federal common law should be one thing in a district court in California but be different in a district court in Pennsylvania. But if a further examination of that point ever is needed it will be at some later day as we have no need to consider it now.[228]

11.101 The Ninth Circuit reached a contrary conclusion regarding preemption in *Lowden v. T-Mobile USA, Inc.*[229] In that case, cellular telephone consumers alleged that T-Mobile had improperly charged them fees and for calls at incorrect rates. T-Mobile moved to compel arbitration in accord with the arbitration provisions in the service agreements, and argued that the FAA mandated enforcement of the no-class-action arbitration clause. To decide the preemption issue, the court first reviewed the issue as follows:

> Where, as here, a party attempts to litigate claims covered by a commercial contract containing an arbitration agreement subject to the FAA, the court must determine (1) whether a valid agreement to arbitrate exists and, if it does, (2) whether the agreement encompasses the dispute at issue. We apply state-law principles that govern the formation of contracts to determine whether a valid arbitration agreement exists.[230]

11.102 Thus, the court applied Washington state law, which, under *Scott v. Cingular Wireless*,[231] had previously considered and rendered unenforceable a similar

[228] *Id.* at 388 n.13. *See also* Joshua S. Lipshutz, *Courts Implicit Roadmap: Charting the Prudent Course at the Juncture of Mandatory Arbitration Agreements and Class Action Lawsuits*, 57 Stan. L. Rev. 1677, 1696–97 (2005) (citing many of the same Supreme Court cases cited by the Third Circuit and further noting that "when there is no state law precluding class action waivers in nonarbitration contracts, invalidating such waivers within arbitration agreements violates the FAA because it singles out arbitration agreements for disfavored treatment"). Other articles which have discussed preemption issues or whether various arbitration clauses are or are not against policy include Robert S. Safi, *Beyond Unconscionability: Preserving the Class Mechanisms Under State Law in the Era of Consumer Arbitration*, 83 Tex. L. Rev. 1715 (2005); Jack Wilson, *No-Class-Action Arbitration Clauses, State-Law Unconscionability, and the Federal Arbitration Act: A Case for Federal Judicial Restraint and Congressional Action*, 23 QLR 737 (2004); Philip Allen Lacovara, *Class Action Arbitrations: The Challenge for the Business Community*, CPR International Institute for Conflict Prevention and Resolution 2008 Annual Meeting (unpublished, on file with author).

[229] 512 F.3d 1213 (9th Cir. 2008).

[230] *Id.* (*citing* Chiron Corp. v. Ortho Diagnostic Sys., Inc., 207 F.3d 1126, 1130 (9th Cir. 2000); *First Options of Chi., Inc. v. Kaplan*, 514 U.S. 938, 944 (1995)).

[231] 161 P.3d 1000 (W.A. 2007). *Id.* at 1006.

cellular telephone service agreement containing a no-class-action arbitration clause. In *Scott*, the court held the class action waiver unconscionable because "it drastically forestall[ed] attempts to vindicate consumer rights" and was, therefore, "substantively unconscionable."[232] In response to T-Mobile's argument that the FAA preempted the Washington rule because it was not a general rule of contracts, the Ninth Circuit looked to one of its own earlier decision, noting that the purpose of the FAA was "to put arbitration clauses on the same footing as other contracts, not make them the special favorites of the law."[233] Thus, the court concluded, because unconscionability was a generally applicable contract *defense*, the FAA did not preempt the state rule.[234]

M. THE SUPREME COURT DECISIONS IN *AT&T MOBILITY* AND *AMERICAN EXPRESS* REGARDING WHETHER CLAUSES PROHIBITING CLASS ARBITRATIONS ARE AGAINST PUBLIC POLICY AND WHETHER A STATE'S PUBLIC POLICY IS PREEMPTED BY THE FAA

In November 2010, the Supreme Court, in the case of *AT&T Mobility LLC v. Conception*,[235] granted certiorari to "consider whether the FAA prohibits States from conditioning the enforceability of certain arbitration agreements on the availability of classwide arbitration procedures."[236] In that case, the plaintiffs had entered into an agreement for the sale of cellular telephones with AT&T Mobility. The plaintiffs later attempted to bring a class action in court because the advertisement had indicated that they would receive free phones, but it had not advised them that they would be charged $30.22 in sales tax based on the phones' retail value. The agreement with AT&T Mobility provided that all claims must go to arbitration but must be brought in the parties' "individual capacity, and not as a plaintiff or class member in any purported class or representative proceeding."[237] The arbitration clause was otherwise a generous one providing that AT&T would pay all the costs for non-frivolous arbitration claims; that the arbitration must take place in the county in which the customer is billed; that, for claims of $10,000 or less, the customer may choose whether the arbitration proceeds in person, by telephone, or based only on submissions; that either **11.103**

[232] *Lowden*, 512 F.3d at 1218 (citing *Scott*, 161 P.3d at 1006).
[233] Shroyer v. New Cingular Wireless Servs., Inc., 498 F.3d 976 (9th Cir. 2007) (citing *Scott*, 161 P.3d at 1008).
[234] *Lowden*, 512 F.3d at 1220.
[235] 131 S. Ct. 1740 (2011).
[236] *Id.* at 1744.
[237] *Id.*

party may bring a claim in a small claims court in lieu of arbitration; and that the arbitrator may award any form of individual relief, including, presumably, punitive damages. The agreement further denied AT&T any ability to seek reimbursement of its attorneys fees, and, in the event that a customer received an arbitration award greater than AT&T's last written settlement offer, it required AT&T to pay a $7500 minimum recovery and twice the amount of the claimant's attorney's fees.[238]

11.104 The Supreme Court of California had found the arbitration clause unconscionable under California law as announced in the *Discover Bank* case and held that the *Discover Bank*[239] case was not preempted by the FAA. The Supreme Court reversed, finding that *Discover Bank* rule was preempted by the FAA. In so doing, it noted that there is a federal body of law reflecting both a liberal federal policy favoring arbitration and the fundamental principle that arbitration is a matter of contract. It noted that "the switch from bilateral to class arbitration sacrifices the principal advantage of arbitration—it's informality—and makes the process slower, more costly, and more likely to generate procedural morass than final judgment."[240] It further noted that class arbitration requires procedural formality and greatly increases risks to defendants because of the aggregation of claims and the limited appellate review available in arbitration.

11.105 Three years later, in *American Express Co. v. Italian Colors Restaurant*,[241] the Court again granted certiorari to "consider whether a contractual waiver of class arbitration is enforceable under the Federal Arbitration Act when the plaintiff's cost of individually arbitrating a federal statutory claim exceeds the potential recovery."[242]

11.106 In that case, the Respondents brought a class action against Petitioners under the federal antitrust laws, alleging that American Express used its monopoly power in the market for credit cards to force merchants to accept credit cards at rates approximately 30% higher than the fees for competing credit cards. Respondents argued that under applicable case law an arbitration clause which compelled arbitration but prohibited class-action arbitration prevented the "effective vindication" of a federal statutory right (i.e., the enforcement of antitrust laws).

11.107 The Supreme Court noted that the text of the arbitration statute "reflects the overarching principle that arbitration is a matter of contract," that courts must rigorously enforce arbitration agreements according to their terms, and that this principle holds true for claims that allege a violation of a federal statute unless

238 *Id.*
239 See, *Discover Bank*, *supra* note 212.
240 *Id.* at 1751.
241 133 S. Ct. 2304 (2013).
242 *Id.* at 2307.

the Federal Arbitration Act's mandate has been overridden by a contrary congressional command.[243] The Court examined the federal antitrust laws and concluded that they do not evince an intention to preclude a waiver of class action procedure.

The Court stated that one might find that an arbitration provision prevented "effective vindication" of a federal statutory right if there were "a provision in an arbitration agreement forbidding the assertion of certain statutory rights," and it "would perhaps cover filing and administrative fees attached to arbitration that are so high as to make access to the forum impractical, but "the fact that it is not worth the expense involved in *proving* a statutory remedy does not constitute the elimination of the *right to pursue* that remedy."[244] It further explained: **11.108**

> [T]o put it differently, the individual suit that was considered adequate to assure "effective vindication" of a federal right before adoption of class-action procedures did not suddenly become "ineffective vindication" upon their adoption.[245]

The Court concluded by reversing the judgment of the Second Circuit, which had held that the waiver of the right to a class action arbitration was unenforceable.[246] **11.109**

N. DECISIONS AFTER *AT&T MOBILITY* AND *AMERICAN EXPRESS* REGARDING WHETHER CLAUSES PROHIBITING CLASS ARBITRATIONS ARE AGAINST PUBLIC POLICY OR WHETHER A STATE'S PUBLIC POLICY IS PREEMPTED BY THE FAA

A number of federal and state decisions following *AT&T Mobility* and *American Express* have ruled on the viability of state public policy prohibitions on class arbitration waivers. Invariably, they have held that the FAA preempts such prohibitions. **11.110**

In the Ninth Circuit case of *Murphy v. DirecTV, Inc.*,[247] an agreement between DirecTV and its customers provided that all disputes would be resolved by arbitration, with a provision that prohibited class arbitration.[248] It also contained a **11.111**

[243] *Id.*

[244] *Id.* at 2310–11.

[245] *Id.* at 2311.

[246] Justice Kagan wrote a forceful dissent, which started with the premise that the effect of the Court's ruling was to insulate American Express from antitrust liability because "[T]he monopolist gets to use its monopoly power to insist on a contract effectively depriving its victims of all legal recourse." *Id.* at 2313.

[247] Murphy v. DirecTV, Inc., 724 F.3d 1218 (9th Cir. 2013).

[248] *Id.* at 1224.

"jettison clause" that rendered the arbitration provision unenforceable if "the law of your state would find this agreement to dispense with class arbitration procedures unenforceable[.]"[249] In attempting to invalidate the arbitration clause, the plaintiffs argued that California law under the *Discover Bank* rule would have found the clause prohibiting class arbitration unenforceable.[250] However, the Ninth Circuit disagreed and clarified the role of federal preemption in interpreting this clause.[251] Under the doctrine of preemption, "state law is *nullified* to the extent that it actually conflicts with federal law."[252] The Supreme Court's ruling in *AT&T Mobility* was the law before, during, and after the agreements in question.[253] Therefore, the arbitration clause was valid because "a valid federal law preempts any state law purporting to regulate the same issue."[254]

11.112 In *Iskanian v. CLS Transportation Los Angeles, LLC*,[255] the California Supreme Court held that where an employment agreement contained a class waiver, the FAA preempted the state's refusal to enforce such a waiver on grounds of public policy.[256] Under a California Supreme Court ruling that pre-dated *AT&T Mobility*, such a provision was against public policy.[257] The plaintiff argued that the pre-*AT&T Mobility* California rule was still valid because it was narrower in that it focused on "whether the class action waiver would 'undermine the vindication of the employees' unwaivable statutory rights' to overtime pay."[258] However, the California Supreme Court reasoned that FAA preemption under *AT&T Mobility* was broad enough to cover even that.[259] Thus, a state law rule against class waivers was preempted even if it would otherwise be desirable for reasons unrelated to "interfer[ing] with fundamental attributes of arbitration[.]"[260] Accordingly, a rule against class waivers in employment agreements was prohibited.[261]

11.113 *Feeney v. Dell, Inc.* involved a Massachusetts Supreme Judicial Court case that was reconsidered after a decision was rendered subsequent to *AT&T Mobility*, but prior to *American Express*.[262] The pre-*American Express* decision held that the FAA "does not foreclose a court 'from invalidating an arbitration agreement that includes a class action waiver where a plaintiff can demonstrate that he or she

---

249 *Id.*
250 *Id.* at 1225.
251 *Id.* at 1225–26.
252 *Id.* at 1226 (*quoting* Fid. Fed. Sav. & Loan Ass'n v. De la Cuesta, 458 U.S. 141, 153 (1982)) (emphasis added to original).
253 *Murphy*, 724 F.3d at 1225–26.
254 *Id.* at 1228 (citations omitted).
255 Iskanian v. CLS Transportation Los Angeles, LLC, 59 Cal. 4th 348 (Cal. 2014).
256 *Id.* at 359–60.
257 *Id.* (citing Gentry v. Superior Court, 42 Cal. 4th 443 (Cal. 2007)).
258 *Iskanian*, 59 Cal. 4th at 362 (*quoting Gentry*, 42 Cal. 4th at 450).
259 *Iskanian*, 59 Cal. 4th at 364.
260 *Id.* (*quoting AT&T Mobility*, 131 S. Ct. at 1753).
261 *Id.* at 366.
262 Feeney v. Dell Inc., 466 1001 (2013).

effectively cannot pursue a claim against [a] defendant in individual arbitration according to the terms of the agreement, thus rendering his or her claim nonremediable.' "[263] However, *American Express* made clear that the mere fact that a remedy under individual arbitration was not worth the expense to prove did not render it invalid.[264] Therefore, the Massachusetts Supreme Court reconsidered its prior decision. While expressing doubt about the Supreme Court's decision, it was bound to decide that a "class waiver may not be invalidated on the grounds that it effectively denies the plaintiffs a remedy."[265]

In *Torrence v. Nationwide Budget Fin.*,[266] the North Carolina Court of Appeals overturned a decision by the trial court that an arbitration agreement was unconscionable for a number of reasons, among them a class arbitration waiver provision.[267] Under North Carolina's Supreme Court case law that pre-dated *AT&T Mobility* and *American Express* a provision was substantively unconscionable if its "collective effect ... was to preclude plaintiffs from effectively vindicating their rights in an arbitration proceeding."[268] Factors relevant to determining substantive unconscionability were 1) potentially high arbitration costs, 2) potentially one-sided terms, and 3) prohibition of joinder of claims and class actions.[269] The North Carolina Court of Appeals concluded that *American Express* precluded analyzing unconscionability under the first factor, which was to perform a cost analysis on whether individual arbitration would be worthwhile for a plaintiff.[270] The logistical, cost, and effort hurdles involved in analyzing "whether or not the parties were to proceed to arbitration 'would undoubtedly destroy the prospect of speedy resolution that arbitration in general and bilateral arbitration in particular was meant to secure.' "[271] Likewise, the Court of Appeals noted that the third unconscionability factor (prohibition of class actions) did not render an arbitration agreement invalid under *AT&T Mobility* and *American Express*.[272] Ultimately, the Court determined that the North Carolina Supreme Court's holdings conflicted with those of the United States Supreme Court.[273] Accordingly, it was improper for the trial court to hold that the arbitration provision was unconscionable because state law could not carve out exceptions where federal law governed.[274] **11.114**

[263] *Id.* (citations omitted)
[264] *Id.* at 1002.
[265] *Id.* at 1003.
[266] Torrence v. Nationwide Budget Fin., 753 S.E.2d 802 (N.C. Ct. App. 2014).
[267] *Id.* at 803–04.
[268] *Id.* at 811 (citing Tillman v. Commercial Credit Loans, Inc., 362 N.C. 93, 104 (2008)).
[269] *Torrence*, 753 S.E.2d at 811–12.
[270] *Id.*
[271] *Id.* (*quoting American Express*, 133 S. Ct. at 2312).
[272] *Torrence*, 753 S.E.2d at 812.
[273] *Id.* at 811.
[274] *Id.* at 818.

O. LEGISLATION REGARDING CLASS-ACTION ARBITRATIONS

11.115 In an effort to address the concerns arising out of arbitration clauses embedded in the fine print of contracts of adhesion, Senator Franken and Representative Hank Johnson, have introduced bills entitled The Arbitration Fairness Act of 2013 (H.R. 1844/S. 878). The bills provide that no pre-dispute arbitration agreement shall be valid or enforceable if it requires arbitration of an employment dispute, consumer dispute, antitrust dispute, or civil rights dispute. However, it appears unlikely that any action on this bill will be taken in the near future.

P. CONCLUSION

11.116 When drafting arbitration clauses that may lead to arbitrations in New York or elsewhere in the United States counsel should be aware of the developing law in the area of class arbitration outlined in this chapter.

12

ARBITRATION HEARINGS IN NEW YORK

Edward G. Kehoe and Jessica Beess und Chrostin

A. Conducting the Arbitration 12.02
1. Major Arbitral Institutions in New York 12.02
2. Arbitral Tribunals 12.04
   (a) Federal and state law 12.05
   (b) Institutional rules 12.09
3. Tribunal Secretaries 12.10
   (a) Federal and state law 12.11
   (b) Institutional rules 12.13
4. Confidentiality and Privacy of Proceedings 12.17
   (a) Federal and state law 12.18
   (b) Institutional rules 12.21
5. Arbitrators' Lack of Authority to Disqualify Counsel in an Arbitration 12.26

B. Who May Appear to Represent Parties in Arbitration in New York 12.29

C. Witnesses 12.35
1. Written Witness Statements and Extent of Live Direct Testimony 12.36
   (a) Federal and state law 12.37
   (b) Institutional rules 12.38
2. Expert Witnesses 12.44
3. Depositions 12.49
4. Witness Attendance 12.52
   (a) Obligation of a party to produce witnesses 12.53
   (b) Subpoenas to compel witness attendance at a hearing 12.58
5. Witness Instructions 12.68
   (a) Administering oaths to witnesses 12.69
   (b) Adjournment and presence during testimony of other witnesses 12.72
6. Use of Exhibits 12.76
   (a) Federal and state law 12.77
   (b) Institutional rules 12.78
7. Closing Proceedings and Post-Hearing Submissions 12.82

D. Logistics 12.86
1. Travel, Accommodation, Catering 12.86
   (a) Travel to and from New York 12.87
   (b) Travel within New York 12.91
   (c) Accommodation and entertainment 12.94
   (d) Catering 12.97
2. Ancillary Services 12.98

New York City is among the major global arbitration centers for international commercial arbitration and is the most favored seat of arbitration in the United States, hosting 63 percent of new U.S. cases according to the International Court of Arbitration of the International Chamber of Commerce (ICC) 2013 Statistics.[1] This chapter provides an overview of relevant administrative and logistical **12.01**

[1] International Court of Arbitration of the International Chamber of Commerce, *2013 Statistical Report*, ICC International Court of Arbitration Bulletin Vol. 25, No. 1 (2014). *See also* John Fellas & Hagit Elul, *United States (New York, Miami, Houston)*, in Choice of Venue in International Arbitration (Michael Ostrove, Claudia Salomon, Bette Shifman

considerations for parties and counsel arbitrating an international dispute in New York City, analyzed under federal and New York state law as well as the arbitration rules of the major arbitration centers with offices in New York City.

A. CONDUCTING THE ARBITRATION

1. Major Arbitral Institutions in New York

12.02 As is discussed in the Introduction to this book, New York is home to a number of prominent arbitral institutions that offer services ranging from administrative assistance to the provision of hearing rooms and technical support. The primary institutions are the American Arbitration Association (AAA) and its International Centre for Dispute Resolution (ICDR); the International Court of Arbitration of the International Chamber of Commerce's North American branch, called the Secretariat of the International Court of Arbitration North America (SICANA); the International Institute for Conflict Prevention and Resolution (CPR) and JAMS, which formerly was named Judicial Arbitration and Mediation Services. The New York International Arbitration Center (NYIAC) is not an administering organization but offers international quality hearing facilities in New York City.

12.03 Table 12.1 provides an overview of these organizations.

2. Arbitral Tribunals

12.04 This section provides a brief overview of the rules applicable to the appointment of arbitral tribunals for international commercial arbitrations seated in New York.

12.05 *(a) Federal and state law* Section 5 of the Federal Arbitration Act provides that, if the parties' agreement specifies a method of naming or appointing the arbitrator(s), such agreement will be given effect. FAA §5 further provides that:

> [I]f no method be provided therein [in the parties' agreement], or if a method be provided and any party thereto shall fail to avail himself of such method, or if for any other reason there shall be a lapse in the naming of an arbitrator or arbitrators or umpire, or in filling a vacancy, then upon the application of either party to the controversy the court shall designate and appoint an arbitrator or arbitrators or umpire, as the case may require, who shall act under the said agreement with the same force and effect as if he or they had been specifically named therein; and unless otherwise provided in the agreement the arbitration shall be by a single arbitrator.

12.06 Accordingly, should the parties fail to agree on a method for appointing the arbitrator(s) or should the agreed-upon method fail, and if the case is international,

eds.), 470–512, 473 (Oxford University Press, 2014) (New York "is the most popular venue for international arbitration in the United States.").

Table 12.1 Arbitration Institutions, New York

Organization	Venue
American Arbitration Association (AAA)/ International Center for Dispute Resolution (ICDR)	Hearing facility: 150 East 42nd Street, 17th Floor New York, NY 10017 Tel: (+1) 212-484-4188 http://www.adr.org http://www.icdr.org Administrative offices: 120 Broadway, 11th Floor New York, NY 10271
International Institute for Conflict Prevention and Resolution (CPR)	30 East 33rd Street, 6th Floor, New York, NY 10016, Tel: (+1) 212-949-6490 http://www.cpradr.org
JAMS (formerly, Judicial Arbitration and Mediation Services)	New York Times Building 620 Eighth Avenue, 34th Floor New York, NY 10018 Tel: (+1) 212-751-2700 http://www.jamsadr.org
Secretariat of the International Court of Arbitration North America (SICANA) and the United States Council for International Business (USCIB)	1212 Avenue of the Americas New York, NY 10036 Tel: (+1) 212-354-4480 http://www.iccwbo.org http://www.uscib.org
New York International Arbitration Center (NYIAC)	150 East 42nd Street New York, NY 10017 Tel: (+1) 917-300-9550 http://nyiac.org

either party may apply to the federal district court at the seat of the arbitration and request that the court appoint the arbitrator(s).

New York Civil Practice Law and Rules §7504 confirms this approach and provides that if the parties do not agree on a method of appointment, or if the agreed method fails, "the court, on application of a party, shall appoint an arbitrator." New York State courts have acknowledged and exercised this power.[2] **12.07**

If the parties agree upon the institutional rules applicable to their arbitral dispute, the method of appointment set forth in the institutional rules will govern, unless the parties explicitly derogate from those rules. **12.08**

[2] *See, e.g.*, Bank v. WorldCom, Inc., 2002 WL 171629, 2002 N.Y. Slip Op. 40009(U) (N.Y. Sup. Ct. Jan. 24, 2002) (acknowledging the court's power to appoint the arbitrator(s) under FAA §5); Basil Castrovinci Associates, Inc. v. District 65 Pension Plan, 16 A.D.3d 493, 791 N.Y.S. 2d 601 (N.Y. App. Div. 2005) (noting with approval the New York Supreme Court's decision to appoint a panel of three arbitrators); Application of Zitner, 286 A.D. 1020, 144 N.Y.S. 2d 905 (N.Y. App. Div. 1955) (holding that the New York Supreme Court properly appointed the third arbitrator where the party-appointed arbitrators failed to make a selection of chair of the tribunal).

12.09 *(b) Institutional rules* The institutional rules of all major arbitration institutions with offices in New York provide extensive guidance on the method and timing of appointing the arbitrator(s). These rules apply to all arbitrations regardless of seat, and a brief overview is provided in Chapter 5 of this book.

3. Tribunal Secretaries

12.10 The use of tribunal secretaries is an increasingly popular practice, and they sometimes are appointed in international arbitrations in New York. According to the *2012 International Arbitration Survey: Current and Preferred Practices in the Arbitral Process*, tribunal secretaries are used more frequently in civil lawyers' arbitrations (46 percent) than in common lawyers' arbitrations (24 percent). Overall, tribunal secretaries were used in only 35 percent of arbitrations.[3] As this chapter is concerned with a discussion of arbitration hearings in New York, this section provides an overview of the use of tribunal secretaries relevant specifically to hearings in New York.

12.11 *(a) Federal and state law* The duties the tribunal delegates to the secretary may have a critical impact on the validity and enforceability of the arbitral award. Pursuant to §10(a)(4) of the FAA, a party may apply to a United States court for vacatur of an arbitral award if the arbitrators "exceeded their powers, or so imperfectly executed them that a mutual, final, and definite award upon the subject matter submitted was not made." Where arbitrators employ secretaries without prior consent of the parties, or delegate decision-making power to the secretary, a court may find an excess of power in violation of FAA §10(a)(4).

12.12 Similarly, a disgruntled party might raise an objection to the enforceability of the award under the United Nations Convention on the Recognition and Enforcement of Foreign Arbitral Awards (the "New York Convention"). Article V.1(c) of the New York Convention provides that recognition and enforcement of an award may be refused if "[the award] contains decisions on matters beyond the scope of the submission to arbitration." In the present context, a party could argue that it agreed to submit the dispute to decision-making by *the tribunal*, not the tribunal secretary. As of September 2014, there is no New York case law addressing this issue.

12.13 *(b) Institutional rules* The ICDR International Arbitration Rules (the ICDR Rules) as amended and effective as of June 1, 2014,[4] do not address the use of tribunal secretaries, which is presumably permissible by agreement of the parties. The AAA's Code

[3] The full survey is available at http://arbitrationpractices.whitecase.com/. *See also Secretaries to International Arbitral Tribunals*, Joint Report of the International Commercial Disputes Committee and the Committee on Arbitration of the New York City Bar Association, 17 Am. Rev. Int'l. Arb. No. 4 (2006).

[4] The ICDR International Dispute Resolution Procedures (including Mediation and Arbitration Rules) are available at https://www.icdr.org/icdr/faces/i_search/i_rule/i_rule_detail?doc=ADRSTAGE2020422&_afrLoop=13317843812118&_afrWindowMode=0&_

of Ethics for Arbitrators in Commercial Disputes,[5] however, provides some guidelines on the use of secretaries and other assistants. Canon VI, Section B, allows an arbitrator to obtain help from "an associate, a research assistant or other persons in connection with reaching his or her decision" under the condition that the arbitrator informs the parties to the dispute of the use of the assistant. Additionally, the assisting party must agree to be bound by the provisions of the Canon. As Canon VI, Section B allows the arbitrator to seek assistance "in connection with reaching his or her decision," the assisting person may provide more than mere organizational support—he or she may provide substantive assistance such as legal research. Notably, the arbitrator is not required to obtain the parties' consent before engaging a secretary or assistant.

The CPR Rules for Administered Arbitration of International Disputes (the CPR Rules)[6] are silent on the use of tribunal secretaries. 12.14

The JAMS Guidelines for Use of Clerks and Tribunal Secretaries in Arbitrations (the JAMS Clerk Guidelines)[7] provide more extensive guidelines on the use of tribunal secretaries. According to the JAMS Clerk Guidelines, the arbitral tribunal must disclose to the parties its intention to engage a tribunal secretary as early as practicable. The use of a tribunal secretary must be approved by the parties and the secretary must complete a separate conflicts disclosure form, which must be made available to the parties. The arbitrators' disclosure regarding the use of a secretary must state the types of tasks assigned to the secretary and expressly permit research and drafting. However, the secretary is not permitted to engage in deliberations or decision-making on behalf of the arbitral tribunal. 12.15

The ICC Rules of Arbitration (the ICC Rules)[8] do not address the appointment or use of tribunal secretaries. However, in 1995, the ICC published a Note setting forth its policies and procedures regarding tribunal secretaries, which it revised and updated in 2012. The revised *Note on the Appointment, Duties and Remuneration of Administrative Secretaries*[9] (the "Note") is a two-page document, 12.16

afrWindowId=ob3ak18w3_57#%40%3F_afrWindowId%3Dob3ak18w3_57%26_afrLoop%3D13317843812118%26doc%3DADRSTAGE2020422%26_afrWindowMode%3D0%26_adf.ctrl-state%3Dob3ak18w3_117&_afr.ts=1410811555070.

[5] The AAA Code of Ethics for Arbitrators in Commercial Disputes is available at https://www.adr.org/aaa/ShowProperty?nodeId=/UCM/ADRSTG_003867.

[6] The CPR Rules for Administered Arbitration of International Disputes became effective December 1, 2014 and are available at http://www.cpradr.org/RulesCaseServices/Arbitration/AdministeredArbitrationofInternationalDisputes/Rules.aspx. The CPR also offers non-administered international arbitration rules, which are substantially similar to the administered rules in the relevant areas discussed in this chapter.

[7] The JAMS Guidelines for Use of Clerks and Tribunal Secretaries in Arbitration are available at http://www.jamsinternational.com/rules-procedures/guidelines-for-use-of-clerks.

[8] The ICC Rules of Arbitration are available at http://www.iccwbo.org/products-and-services/arbitration-and-adr/arbitration/icc-rules-of-arbitration/.

[9] The Note on the Appointment, Duties and Remuneration of Administrative Secretaries is available at http://www.iccwbo.org/products-and-services/arbitration-and-adr/flash-news/introduction-of-revised-note-on-the-appointment,-duties-and-remuneration-of-administrative-secretaries/.

which provides guidance to parties and arbitrators on this topic. According to the Note, administrative secretaries must satisfy the same independence and impartiality requirements as those applicable to arbitrators under the ICC Rules, and may be appointment at any time during the arbitration. At the time the tribunal notifies the parties of its intention to appoint an administrative secretary, it must provide the parties the proposed secretary's curriculum vitae, declaration of independence and impartiality, an undertaking by the secretary to act in accordance with the Note's requirements, and an undertaking by the tribunal to ensure that the secretary meets this obligation. The secretary may perform organizational and administrative tasks, and prepare written notes and memoranda so long as the tribunal personally reviews these writings. Under no circumstances may the tribunal delegate decision-making functions to the secretary or rely on the secretary to perform the essential duties of the arbitrators.

4. Confidentiality and Privacy of Proceedings

12.17 As a preliminary matter, it is important to distinguish confidentiality from privacy. Confidentiality concerns the duty of the arbitrators, parties, witnesses, and counsel not to make unauthorized disclosures regarding the arbitration. Privacy, on the other hand, is concerned with the right of persons other than the arbitrators, parties, witnesses, and counsel, to attend conferences, meetings and hearings, and to know about the arbitration. In general, parties are assured privacy in the proceedings, but confidentiality only by party agreement.

12.18 *(a) Federal and state law* In the U.S., only a handful of cases has addressed the question whether there is a duty of confidentiality absent party agreement. These cases have held that there is no implied duty of confidentiality and therefore no duty of confidentiality in arbitrations absent agreement between the parties to that effect. In *Contship Containerlines, Ltd. v. PPG Industries*,[10] for instance, the District Court for the Southern District of New York refused to recognize an implied duty of confidentiality and instead ordered the production of documents relating to a foreign arbitration proceeding. Similarly, the United States District Court for the District of Delaware held in *United States v. Panhandle E. Corp.*[11] that arbitrations were not confidential without evidence that the parties agreed to keep the proceedings confidential. From these cases it is apparent that parties wishing to submit their dispute to arbitration in New York should expressly agree to hold the proceedings confidential if they wish the protections and obligations of confidentiality to apply.

12.19 Even where the parties have agreed to confidentiality, however, there are certain circumstances in which New York courts may disregard such an imperative. For

[10] Contship Containerlines, Ltd. v. PPG Industries, Inc., 2003 WL 1948807 (S.D.N.Y. 2003).
[11] United States v. Panhandle E. Corp., 118 F.R.D. 346 (D. Del. 1998).

example, in ancillary actions for the enforcement of an arbitral award, the arbitral award itself may be published. In *Global Reinsurance*,[12] for instance, the successful party to an arbitration applied to the New York court for enforcement of the arbitration award. The court initially sealed the arbitration award, but later reconsidered and reversed itself, holding that the plaintiff had failed to make a showing of harm sufficient to justify impinging the presumption of access to judicial materials. Similarly, in *Alexandria Real Estate Equities*,[13] the New York court refused to seal copies of an arbitration award, the record, and the documents that discussed the arbitration. In this case, the District Court for the Southern District of New York reasoned that the First Amendment right of access to judicial documents and proceedings imposes a burden of proof on the party seeking the sealing of the award and related documents to show that higher values overcome the presumption of public access. The plaintiff seeking the sealing of the underlying arbitration award in *Alexandria Real Estate Equities* was motivated by a desire to conceal information about his employment history, which the court found insufficient to overcome the presumption of public access.

New York courts have also refused to honor a confidentiality agreement by parties to an arbitration where public policy supported disclosure of the documents at issue. For example, in *City of Newark v. Law Dep't of the City of N.Y.*,[14] the plaintiff sought to compel disclosure of documents relating to an arbitration between New York City and the Port Authority on the basis of the Freedom of Information Law. The Appellate Court granted the petition, holding that the arbitration tribunal did not have power to deny the public access under the Freedom of Information Law.[15] **12.20**

(b) Institutional rules Arbitral rules tend to impose an obligation of confidentiality of the arbitration absent agreement to the contrary. For example, Article 37 of the ICDR Rules addresses confidentiality and provides that **12.21**

1. Confidential information disclosed during the arbitration by the parties or by witnesses shall not be divulged by an arbitrator or by the Administrator. Except as provided in Article 30, unless otherwise agreed by the parties or required by applicable law, the members of the arbitral tribunal and the Administrator shall keep confidential all matters relating to the arbitration or the award.
2. Unless the parties agree otherwise, the tribunal may make orders concerning the confidentiality of the arbitration or any matters in connection with the arbitration and may take measures for protecting trade secrets and confidential information.

[12] Global Reinsurance Corp.-U.S. Branch v. Argonaut, 2008 WL 1805459 (S.D.N.Y. 2008).

[13] Alexandria Real Estate Equities, Inc. v. Fair, 2011 WL 6015646 (S.D.N.Y. 2011).

[14] City of Newark v. Law Dep't of the City of N.Y., 760 N.Y.S. 2d 431 (N.Y. App. Ct. 2003).

[15] *Id.* at 436–37. *Cf.* Fireman's Fund Ins. Co. v. Cunningham Lindsey Claims Management, 2005 WL 1522783 (E.D.N.Y. 2005) (applying a balancing test, weighing the "ADR confidentiality interest" against the relevance and significance of the evidence relating to the amount awarded in an arbitration proceeding, and finding no compelling reason to impinge the ADR confidentiality in this case).

12.22 Thus, under the ICDR Rules, unless otherwise agreed or required by law, the arbitrators and the administrator are bound to confidentiality. The ICDR Rules do not address any confidentiality restrictions that may exist for the parties, but the arbitral tribunal is empowered to make orders concerning the confidentiality of the arbitration. Article 30, referenced in Article 37(1), concerns arbitral awards and provides, among other things, that arbitral awards may be published if the parties agree to do so or if they have otherwise become public in the course of enforcement proceedings or otherwise.

12.23 Under the CPR Rules, unless the parties agree otherwise, the arbitrators, the CPR and the parties are obligated to treat the arbitral proceeding and any related disclosures as well as the decision of the arbitral tribunal as confidential, except where disclosure is required in ancillary judicial proceedings.[16] Additionally, the tribunal is empowered under Rule 11 to issue "orders to protect the confidentiality of proprietary information, trade secrets and other sensitive information disclosed."

12.24 Under the JAMS International Arbitration Rules (the JAMS Rules), effective as of August 1, 2011,[17] Article 16 provides that, unless otherwise required by law, the tribunal and the administrator of the arbitration shall maintain the confidentiality of the arbitration, including the confidentiality of the award. The award, however, may be published if the parties consent to the publication.[18]

12.25 The ICC Rules take a slightly different approach from the ICDR, CPR, and JAMS Rules, which all provide an apparent default position of confidentiality. Article 22(3) of the ICC Rules simply provides that the arbitral tribunal has the power to make orders "concerning the confidentiality of the arbitration proceedings or of any other matters in connection with the arbitration and may take measures for protecting trade secrets and confidential information." The confidentiality of the proceedings is thus subject to a determination by the tribunal, rather than a default position.

---

[16] Rule 20 of the CPR Rules addresses confidentiality and provides:

> Unless the parties agree otherwise, the parties, the arbitrators and CPR shall treat the proceedings, any related disclosure and the decisions of the Tribunal, as confidential, except in connection with judicial proceedings ancillary to the arbitration, such as a judicial challenge to, or enforcement of, an award, and unless otherwise required by law or to protect a legal right of a party. To the extent possible, any specific issues of confidentiality should be raised and resolved by the Tribunal.

[17] The JAMS International Arbitration Rules are available at http://www.jamsadr.com/international-arbitration-rules/.

[18] Article 16 of the JAMS Rules provides:

> 16.1 Unless otherwise required by law, the Tribunal, the Administrator and the JIAC, if applicable, will maintain the confidentiality of the arbitration.
>
> 16.2 Unless otherwise required by law, an award will remain confidential unless all of the parties consent to its publication.

5. Arbitrators' Lack of Authority to Disqualify Counsel in an Arbitration

An arguable anomaly worth noting in this chapter is that New York courts reserve the authority to disqualify counsel exclusively for themselves. Disqualification of counsel is treated as an aspect of attorney discipline, which, according to New York law, involves enforcing State ethical rules for attorneys. This, however, is a matter reserved for the courts and cannot be delegated or, by mutual agreement of the parties, allocated to the arbitrator(s). This principle is followed by New York state and a number of federal courts. **12.26**

For example, in *Bidermann Indus. Licensing, Inc. v. Avmar N.V.*,[19] the court stayed an arbitration of an attorney disqualification motion, finding that this issue was intertwined with overriding public policy considerations. The court stated that "matters of attorney discipline are beyond the jurisdiction of arbitrators" and "cannot be left to the determination of arbitrators selected by the parties themselves ..."[20] New York federal courts have adopted this approach as well, as noted earlier, holding that there is "some degree of certainty that 'possible attorney disqualification is not capable of settlement by arbitration' ..."[21] **12.27**

This particularity of the New York courts is especially relevant considering the recent increase in requests by parties to international arbitrations to impose disciplinary measures, including disqualification, on a member of the opposing side's legal team,[22] and given the apparent trend in international arbitration toward affording arbitrators greater disciplinary powers over counsel, as evidenced for instance in the IBA Guidelines on Party Representation.[23] **12.28**

B. WHO MAY APPEAR TO REPRESENT PARTIES IN ARBITRATION IN NEW YORK

Many of the world's most renowned law firms have offices in New York, and finding counsel to represent parties to an international commercial arbitration seated in New York therefore will not pose a challenge. However, parties also are **12.29**

---

[19] Bidermann Indus. Licensing, Inc. v. Avmar N.V., 173 A.D.2d 401, 507 N.Y.S.2d 33 (1st Dep't 1991).

[20] *See also* Matter of Erdheim (Selkowe), 51 A.D.2d 705 (1st Dep't 1976); Matter of Shomron v. Fuks, 286 A.D.2d 587 (1st Dep't), *appeal denied*, 97 N.Y.2d 607 (2001).

[21] Munich Re America Inc. v. Ace Property & Casualty Co., 500 F. Supp.2d 272 (S.D.N.Y. 2007).

[22] *See, e.g.*, Hrvatska Elektroprivreda d.d. v. Republic of Slovenia, ICSID Case No. ARB/05/24, Order Concerning the Participation of Counsel dated May 6, 2008; The Rompetrol Group N.V. v. Romania, ICSID Case No. ARB/06/3, Decision on the Participation of a Counsel dated January 14, 2010.

[23] *See, e.g.*, Guidelines 26 and 27.

free to engage counsel not admitted to practice in New York and, under some institutional rules, even individuals who are not attorneys.

12.30 According to Article 15 §478 of the New York Judiciary Law,[24] no natural person may practice law without being admitted to the courts of record of New York and without having taken the constitutional oath. However, in 1982, the District Court for the Southern District of New York held in *Williamson v. John D. Quinn Const. Corp.*,[25] that there is a material difference between arbitration and court proceedings as envisaged in Article 15 §478: "[a]n arbitration tribunal is not a court of record; its rules of evidence and procedures differ from those of courts of record; its fact finding process is not equivalent to judicial fact finding ..."[26] Consequently, the prerequisite of admission to practice in New York set forth in Article 15 §478 is not applicable to counsel appearing in arbitrations seated in New York. In reaching this opinion, the court relied on a prior report by the Association of the Bar of the City of New York regarding labor arbitration,[27] which stated that "representation of a party in an arbitration proceeding by a non-lawyer or a lawyer from another jurisdiction is not the unauthorized practice of law"[28] and is therefore permissible in arbitrations seated in New York. The District Court for the Southern District of New York confirmed this position in *Prudential Equity Group, LLC v. Ajamie* in 2008.[29]

12.31 In 2015, the New York Court of Appeals adopted an amended Rule 523.2 regarding "Temporary Practice," which expressly permits an out-of-state attorney to render services "reasonably related to a pending or potential arbitration[.]" (22 NYCRR § 523)[30] Accordingly, parties may choose to be represented in arbitrations seated in New York by counsel not admitted to practice in New York.

12.32 It is important to note, however, that §7506 of the CPLR provides that a party to an arbitration has the right to be represented by an attorney "and may claim such right at any time as to any part of the arbitration or hearings which have

---

[24] In relevant part, N.Y. Jud. Law § 478: *Practicing or appearing as attorney-at-law without being admitted and registered* provides "[i]t shall be unlawful for any natural person to practice or appear as an attorney-at-law or as an attorney and counselor-at-law for a person other than himself in a court of record in this state, or to furnish attorneys or counsel or an attorney and counsel to render legal services, or to hold himself out to the public as being entitled to practice law as aforesaid, or in any other manner, or to assume to be an attorney or counselor-at-law, or to assume, use, or advertise the title of lawyer, or attorney and counselor-at-law ... without having first been duly and regularly licensed and admitted to practice law in the courts of record of this state [New York], and without having taken the constitutional oath ..."

[25] Williamson v. John D. Quinn Const. Corp., 537 F. Supp. 613 (S.D.N.Y. 1982).

[26] *Id.* at 614.

[27] Committee Report, *Labor Arbitration and the Unauthorized Practice of Law*, The Record of The Association of the Bar of The City of New York, Vol. 30, No. 5/6, May/June 1975.

[28] *Id.*

[29] Prudential Equity Group, LLC v. Ajamie, 538 F. Supp. 2d 605 (S.D.N.Y. 2008).

[30] *Id.* at 607.

not taken place. This right may not be waived." In consequence, even if a party initially chooses a representative who is not an attorney, that party has not thereby waived its right to change its representation and appoint an attorney as counsel at any stage in the proceedings. The only exception to this right regards portions of the proceedings that have already taken place. Thus, if an arbitration is bifurcated and a party was represented by a non-attorney during the procedural phase of the arbitration, which is complete, that party may not invoke its right to counsel as an excuse to re-hear and re-argue the procedural phase of the arbitration.

In accordance with New York law, institutional rules largely permit foreign-admitted lawyers and non-lawyers to represent parties to an arbitration. Article 16 of the ICDR Rules broadly allows representation of the parties to the arbitration without limiting the representation to legal professionals or imposing requirements regarding admission to the local bar.[31] Similarly, Article 19 of the JAMS Rules allows the parties to be represented by "persons of their choice, irrespective of, in particular, nationality or professional qualification."[32] **12.33**

Rule 4 of the CPR Rules also permits parties to be represented by person(s) of their choice. The CPR's official Commentary to Rule 4 of the CPR's domestic arbitration rules provides a clarification that presumably applies to the international rules as well, stating that although parties are normally represented by a law firm or an individual attorney, "the Rules permit parties to be represented or assisted by any persons of their choice."[33] The Commentary further specifies that representatives need not be admitted to the local bar unless local law so requires. Since New York law has no such requirement, parties are free to choose any representative under the CPR Rules. The ICC Rules contain no discussion of requirements for party representatives. **12.34**

---

[31] Article 16 of the International Arbitration Rules is titled "Party Representation" and states that:

> Any party may be represented in the arbitration. The names, addresses, telephone numbers, fax numbers, and email addresses of representatives shall be communicated in writing to the other party and to the Administrator. Unless instructed otherwise by the Administrator, once the arbitral tribunal has been established, the parties or their representatives may communicate in writing directly with the tribunal with simultaneous copies to the other party and, unless otherwise instructed by the Administrator, to the Administrator. The conduct of party representatives shall be in accordance with such guidelines as the ICDR may issue on the subject.

[32] JAMS Rules Article 19 on "Representation" provides in full:

> The parties may be represented by the persons of their choice, irrespective of, in particular, nationality or professional qualification. The names, addresses and telephone, facsimile, email or other communication references of representatives will be communicated to the Administrator, the other party and, after its establishment, the Tribunal.

[33] CPR Administered Arbitration Rules and Commentary, available at http://www.cpradr.org/RulesCaseServices/CPRRules/AdministeredArbitrationRules.aspx. Rule 4 is titled "Representation" and provides that:

C. WITNESSES

12.35 Considerations of due process and fundamental fairness require the arbitral tribunal to give the parties to the dispute the opportunity to be heard and to present evidence. One important form of evidence is the submission of witness testimony. This comprises fact witnesses, who have personal knowledge of the facts underlying the dispute and are by virtue of this knowledge qualified to submit testimony, and expert witnesses, who are usually experts in a complex field relevant to the specific dispute at issue. Witnesses can submit testimony in either written form, or oral, or both. This section provides an overview of the federal, state, and institutional rules that govern the submission of witness testimony in international commercial arbitrations seated in New York.

1. Written Witness Statements and Extent of Live Direct Testimony

12.36 In international commercial arbitration, the use of written witness statements in the stead of providing oral direct testimony is a frequent practice that permits parties to control and limit the time and cost of the arbitration without sacrificing their right to be fully heard. In New York, institutional rules provide more guidance on how and when to provide written witness statements and/or oral direct testimony than federal and state law. Importantly, even if the direct examination is submitted in the form of a written witness statement, oral cross examination will still be allowed.

12.37 *(a) Federal and state law* Neither federal nor state law prescribes the use of witness statements and/or direct testimony, and parties are therefore generally free to agree on a course of conduct. The tribunal, however, is subject to some limited constraints under federal law regarding the hearing of witness testimony. Section 10(a)(3) of the FAA provides that a United States court in the district in which an arbitration award was rendered may vacate the award upon application of a party to the arbitration where the arbitrators were guilty of misconduct "in refusing to hear evidence pertinent and material to the controversy."[34] This, however, does not mean that arbitrators are required to hear immaterial or redundant evidence, and courts have rejected challenges to awards that declined to entertain testimony on

4.1 The parties may be represented or assisted by persons of their choice.
4.2 Each party shall communicate the name, address, telephone number and email address, and function of such persons in writing to the other party, to the Tribunal and to CPR.

[34] FAA § 10(a)(3) permits a United States court in and for the district wherein an arbitral award was made to vacate the award upon the application of any party to the arbitration "where the arbitrators were guilty of misconduct in refusing to postpone the hearing, upon sufficient cause shown, or in refusing to hear evidence pertinent and material to the controversy; or of any other misbehavior by which the rights of any party have been prejudiced[.]"

these grounds.[35] The relevant test is whether the arbitrator(s) refused to hear pertinent and material evidence to the prejudice of one of the parties such that this refusal amounted to a denial of fundamental fairness in the arbitration proceeding.[36] New York state law provides no additional guidance on this issue.

(b) Institutional rules Institutional rules provide more guidance than federal and New York state law. The ICDR Rules permit parties to submit witness testimony in the form of a written witness statement and to designate witnesses of the opposing party whom they wish to cross-examine. Article 23.4 states: **12.38**

> Unless otherwise agreed by the parties or directed by the tribunal, evidence of witnesses may be presented in the form of written statements signed by them. In accordance with a schedule set by the tribunal, each party shall notify the tribunal and the other parties of the names of any witnesses who have presented a witness statement whom it requests to examine. The tribunal may require any witness to appear at a hearing. If a witness whose appearance has been requested fails to appear without a valid excuse as determined by the tribunal, the tribunal may disregard any written statement by that witness.

Thus, pursuant to the ICDR Rules, either party may submit written witness statements and either party as well as the tribunal may designate witnesses to be examined at the oral hearing. If a party intends to present a witness at the hearing, it must give the tribunal and the other parties to the dispute notice of this intent at least fifteen days prior to the hearing, and must specify the subject of the witnesses' testimony and the language(s) in which the witness will testify (Article 23.1). Whether to call a witness to present live testimony or to designate a witness to be cross-examined will be a question of strategy dependent on the facts of the case. **12.39**

Under CPR Rule 12, parties are, unless otherwise agreed or determined by the tribunal, required to submit a pre-hearing memorandum including a statement of the facts, applicable law, authorities, relief requested, and "[t]he evidence to be presented, including documents relied upon and the name, capacity and subject of testimony of any witnesses to be called, and the language in which each witness will testify." In practice, the documentary portion of this information is often submitted in the form of a joint exhibit binder, which typically includes all exhibits either party intends to use at the hearing. If either party requests or the tribunal so orders, a hearing may be held and "[t]estimony may be presented in written and/or oral form as the Tribunal may determine is appropriate." The **12.40**

[35] *See, e.g.*, Areca, Inc. v. Oppenheimer & Co., Inc., 960 F. Supp. 52 (S.D.N.Y. 1997) (holding inter alia that arbitrators' refusal to allow investors to present testimony of brokerage firm's chief financial officer was not misconduct warranting vacatur of arbitration award). *Cf.* Tempo Shain Corp. v. Bertek, Inc., 120 F. 3d 16 (2d Cir. 1997) (vacating arbitral award under FAA § 10(a)(3) on basis of tribunal's refusal to continue hearings to allow company's official to testify).

[36] *Areca*, 960 F. Supp. 52–53; Transit Cas. Co. v. Trenwick Reins. Co., 659 F. Supp. 1346, 1354–55 (S.D.N.Y. 1987), *aff'd*, 841 F. 2d 1117 (2d Cir. 1988); Bell Aerospace Co. Div. of Textron, Inc. v. Local 516, UAW, 500 F.2d 921, 923 (2d Cir. 1974).

tribunal has discretion under the CPR Rules to determine the manner in which witnesses are examined and the tribunal has the right to order witnesses excluded from the hearing during the testimony of other witnesses.

12.41 The JAMS Rules provide comparatively extensive guidance on the use of witnesses in international arbitrations. Under Article 23, either party may request a hearing to present evidence by witnesses and the tribunal has discretion to determine the manner in which witnesses are examined. If neither party requests a hearing, the tribunal may decide whether to proceed solely on the basis of the written record, which would include written witness statements. If a hearing takes place, Article 24 governs "Experts and Other Witnesses."

12.42 Under Article 24.1, the tribunal may require that the parties give notice in advance of the hearing of the identity, purpose, and relevance of witnesses they intend to call. The tribunal has power to subpoena witnesses pursuant to Article 24.2, and conversely, has discretion under Article 24.3 to limit or refuse the appearance of any witness, whether fact or expert, on the ground of redundancy or irrelevance. Pursuant to Article 24.4, the tribunal may permit witnesses to present their testimony in the form of written witness statements, which must be signed by the witness, and may condition the admissibility of such written statements on the witness's agreement to appear for cross-examination. Rather exceptionally, the JAMS Rules specifically address pre-hearing witness interviews in Article 24.5. According to this rule, the parties and their legal representatives are permitted to interview any witness or potential witness "for the purpose of presenting his or her testimony in written form or producing him or her as an oral witness" subject to any contrary local law or applicable ethics rules. Under the JAMS Rules, parties thus have broad discretion to present witness testimony in written or oral form, or both.

12.43 The ICC Rules do not expressly state that written witness statements and oral testimony are permitted, but this is implied in Article 25, which addresses "Establishing the Facts of the Case." Article 25(2) provides that the parties make written submissions, including all documents relied upon, which would include written witness statements. Article 25(3) further states that the arbitral tribunal is authorized to hear witnesses in the presence of the parties or in their absence. Moreover, Appendix IV: Case Management Techniques, lists limiting the length and scope of written submissions and written and oral witness evidence as a method for controlling the time and cost of the arbitration. Beyond these provisions, however, the ICC Rules do not address written witness statements or the extent of live direct testimony.

2. Expert Witnesses

12.44 The use of expert witnesses increasingly is a necessary part of international commercial arbitrations due to the complexity of disputes, and often due to the need for assistance in damages calculations. Although the qualifications of experts and the admissibility of expert testimony are highly regulated under federal and New York state law, neither regulates the use of experts in arbitration. Institutional rules, however, provide some guidance.

The ICDR Rules have only limited provisions regarding the use of experts. ICDR Rule 25 gives the tribunal authority to appoint "one or more independent experts to report to it, in writing, on issues designated by the tribunal and communicated to the parties" after consultation with the parties. In order to assist the expert, the parties are obligated to provide the expert any relevant information or documents the expert may require. The parties have an opportunity to express their opinion on the expert's report in writing, and may, upon request, question the expert at the arbitration hearing. The parties also may present expert witnesses to testify on the points at issue at the hearing. The ICDR Rules do not specify whether parties have the right to submit expert witness testimony in other circumstances, although this right may be implied in Article 20, which provides for each party to have the right to be heard and given a fair opportunity to present its case. **12.45**

Pursuant to CPR Rule 9.3, the need for expert witnesses, the manner and form of presentation of expert testimony, and the possibility of the appointment of a neutral expert by the tribunal are matters for discussion at the pre-hearing conference. Should the tribunal appoint a neutral expert, the expert's testimony is subject to examination by the parties and the tribunal in accordance with Rule 12.3. Importantly, the Commentary to Rules 12.3 clarifies that, should the tribunal appoint a neutral expert, such expert is not intended to give advice to the Tribunal ex parte. **12.46**

The JAMS Rules clearly envision the parties' need, depending on the specific case at issue, to submit expert testimony. Article 22.2 on "Pre-hearing Conferences" provides that the need for expert witnesses and the manner of presentation of expert testimony should be discussed at the pre-hearing conference. Moreover, Articles 23 and 24 as discussed, *supra*, in the context of fact witnesses, apply equally to expert witnesses. With respect to experts, Article 24.7 provides additionally that the tribunal may, after consultation with the parties, appoint expert witness(es) and define the scope of the expert(s)' work. Should the tribunal appoint one or more experts, the parties will have an opportunity to question the expert(s) at a hearing and to comment in writing on any reports. **12.47**

The ICC Rules permit parties to submit expert testimony and allow the arbitral tribunal discretion to hear testimony of the experts appointed by the parties (Article 25). Further, the tribunal may appoint one or more experts upon consultation with the parties. If a party requests to cross-examine the tribunal-appointed expert(s), he or she must be given an opportunity to do so under Article 25(4). **12.48**

3. Depositions

12.49 A deposition is an out-of-court interrogation of a witness, in which the party seeking discovery and any other party may ask the witness questions, which the witness must testify to under oath. The interrogation is recorded by a court reporter and oftentimes also by video. Depositions are a common discovery tool in U.S. litigation and may be used under limited circumstances at trial.[37] They sometimes are used in U.S. domestic arbitrations by counsel accustomed to U.S. litigation practice. In international commercial arbitration, by contrast, depositions are rare although sometimes used, for example, to secure testimony of witnesses who might not be available at a hearing. Neither federal nor New York state law provides for the availability of depositions in international arbitrations and the international rules of the arbitration institutions discussed in this chapter have few provisions relating to them.[38]

12.50 Article 21.10 of the ICDR Rules provides that "[d]epositions, interrogatories, and requests to admit as developed for use in the U.S. court procedures generally are not appropriate for obtaining information in an arbitration under these Rules." While the ICDR Rules impose no absolute prohibition on the use of depositions, they expressly discourage the practice as unsuitable to international arbitrations under the ICDR Rules.

12.51 Thus, even though depositions are frequent practice in U.S. court litigations, parties to arbitrations seated in New York will not automatically have the right to take depositions absent express party agreement to apply the relevant federal or New York procedures.[39]

4. Witness Attendance

12.52 As already noted, witnesses often play a key role in the effective and just resolution of arbitral disputes. Under some institutional rules, the parties to the arbitration bear the obligation to produce witnesses whose attendance has been requested either by the tribunal or by another party to the dispute. Stronger than the parties' obligation, however, is the arbitral tribunal's power to subpoena a witness.

---

[37] *See* Fed. R. Civ. P. 32; N.Y. CPLR §3117(a) and Chapter 2 of this book.

[38] Some of the arbitral institutions covered in this chapter have rules for domestic arbitrations that envision possible depositions. *See, e.g.*, CPR Employment Arbitration Procedure, Article 11.4 ("Upon request, the Employee shall be entitled, at least (30) days in advance of the commencement of the hearing, to take one deposition of an Employer representative designated by the Employee. Upon request, the Employer shall be entitled, at least thirty (30) days in advance of the commencement of the hearing, to take the deposition of the Employee. The Arbitrator upon a showing of good cause may direct that other depositions be taken."); JAMS Streamlined Arbitration Rules, Rule 17(e) ("The Arbitrator shall receive and consider relevant deposition testimony recorded by transcript or videotape, provided that the other Parties have had the opportunity to attend and cross-examine."). These rules are not discussed in detail here as they are outside the scope of this chapter on international commercial disputes.

[39] *See* Gilmer v. Interstate/Johnson Lane Corp., 500 U.S. 20, 31 (1991).

(a) Obligation of a party to produce witnesses Neither federal nor state law discusses the potential obligation of a party to produce witnesses. Institutional rules, on the other hand, address this issue. **12.53**

The ICDR Rules recognize a party's duty to produce evidence, which may include witnesses depending on the facts of the case, upon the request of the tribunal. Article 20.4 provides that the tribunal may order the parties to produce "documents, exhibits, or other evidence it deems necessary or appropriate" at any time during the proceedings. "Other evidence" may include witnesses. Article 20.7 incentivizes compliance with the tribunal's orders by authorizing the tribunal to draw adverse inferences and allocate costs in consideration of a party's efforts to avoid unnecessary delay and expense in the arbitration. **12.54**

The CPR Rules permit the tribunal to require the parties to produce evidence in addition to that already offered (Rule 12.3). Such evidence may include further witnesses. Similar to the ICDR Rules, CPR Rule 16 incentivizes compliance by permitting the tribunal to "impose a remedy it deems just, including an award on default" should the party ordered to produce evidence fail to comply with the order. **12.55**

The JAMS Rules are comparable to the CPR Rules and allow the tribunal to order the parties "to exchange and produce documents, exhibits or other evidence it deems necessary or appropriate" (Article 25.2). "Other evidence" may include witnesses. **12.56**

The ICC Rules do not impose an obligation on the parties to produce witnesses. **12.57**

(b) Subpoenas to compel witness attendance at a hearing A subpoena is an order that a person appear for testimony in court. Federal and state law as well as institutional rules afford arbitrators discretion to summon witnesses, including in the form of a summons or subpoena, for appearance at an arbitral hearing. **12.58**

Both the Federal Arbitration Act and New York law recognize the right of the arbitral tribunal to compel witness testimony and to impose sanctions in case the summoned witness refuses to appear and testify at a hearing. Section 7 of the Federal Arbitration Act gives the arbitrators broad discretion: **12.59**

> Section 7. Witnesses before arbitrators; fees; compelling attendance
>
> The arbitrators selected either as prescribed in this title or otherwise, or a majority of them, may summon in writing any person to attend before them or any of them as a witness and in a proper case to bring with him or them any book, record, document, or paper which may be deemed material as evidence in the case. The fees for such attendance shall be the same as the fees of witnesses before masters of the United States courts. Said summons shall issue in the name of the arbitrator or arbitrators, or a majority of them, and shall be signed by the arbitrators, or a majority of them, and shall be directed to the said person and shall be served in the same manner as subpoenas to appear and testify before the court; if any person or persons so summoned to testify shall refuse or neglect to obey said summons,

upon petition the United States district court for the district in which such arbitrators, or a majority of them, are sitting may compel the attendance of such person or persons before said arbitrator or arbitrators, or punish said person or persons for contempt in the same manner provided by law for securing the attendance of witnesses or their punishment for neglect or refusal to attend in the courts of the United States.[40]

12.60 Section 7 of the Federal Arbitration Act not only gives arbitrators broad discretion to order witness attendance at a hearing, it also expressly grants U.S. district courts in the district in which the arbitration is seated power to compel witness attendance and punish witnesses who fail to appear in spite of a summons. Notably, the power to compel witness testimony at a hearing is not limited to entities that are party to the arbitral proceedings. Section 7 of the FAA empowers the tribunal to issue a summons for *any* witness, along with *any* material evidence.[41]

12.61 Moreover, following the December 2013 amendment to Rule 45 of the FRCP, which governs the manner of service of a subpoena (see, *infra*, note 43), subpoenas may be served "at any place within the United States,"[42] i.e. nationwide. Regarding service in a foreign country of subpoenas on United States nationals or residents, 28 U.S.C. §1783 governs[43] and provides, among other things, that such subpoenas are permissible if "it is not possible to obtain [the witness's] testimony in admissible form without his personal appearance or to obtain the production of the document or other thing in any other manner."[44] Given the currently widespread availability of phone- and video-conferencing technology, §1783 imposes a high bar to international service of subpoenas.

12.62 New York state law addresses the tribunal's power to subpoena witnesses in CPLR §7505, which provides simply that "[a]n arbitrator and any attorney of record in the arbitration proceeding has the power to issue subpoenas." The New York courts confirmed this broad authority of the arbitral tribunal in *Radin*

[40] FAA § 7 uses the term "summons," as opposed to subpoena, and states that they shall be issued in the same manner as subpoenas. In substance, the terms summons and subpoena denote the same action—the compulsion of a witness's attendance at a hearing or other proceeding—and may be used interchangeably. *See, e.g.*, The International Commercial Disputes Committee and the Arbitration Committee of the New York City Bar Association's Report, *A Model Federal Arbitration Summons to Testify and Present Documentary Evidence at an Arbitration Hearing*, ARIA Vol. 26, No. 2 (Oct. 2015), Introduction & p. 4 (see Appendix 7). The manner of issuing a subpoena is detailed in Rule 45 of the Federal Rules of Civil Procedure (the FRCP).

[41] *See generally* Paul D. Friedland & Lucy Martinez, *Arbitral Subpoenas under U.S. Law and Practice*, 14 Am. Rev. Int'l Arb. 197 (2003) (providing a thorough discussion of the use of arbitral subpoenas under U.S. law and institutional rules, but noting that in practice, when directed to the parties, arbitrators generally request witness attendance through arbitral orders rather than subpoenas).

[42] FRCP 45(b)(2). *See also*, Armand M. Paré, Jr., *Nationwide Arbitration Subpoenas Under the United States Arbitration Act*, 25 Am. Rev. Intl. Arb. No. 2 (2014).

[43] FRCP 45(b)(3).

[44] 28 U.S.C. §1783(a).

v. Kleinman, which held that arbitrators have "inherent power to control the course of arbitral proceedings so as to permit a party to elicit the relevant information."[45] FAA §7, by contrast, appears to give authority to issue subpoenas only to arbitrators; not to counsel or the parties. It is an open question, therefore, whether the FAA preempts the reference to subpoenas from an attorney under state laws. To the authors' knowledge, as of the date of this publication, no federal court has directly answered this question.

Some federal district courts, however, have addressed whether state laws permitting attorneys or parties to issue subpoenas in an arbitration to which the FAA applies. These federal court decisions suggest that such state laws are not applicable, at least where the parties have not expressly agreed upon the use of state law rules of arbitral procedure. For example, the Second Circuit held in *NBC v. Bear Stearns & Co.*,[46] that §7 of the FAA "explicitly confers authority only upon *arbitrators*; by necessary implication, the *parties* to an arbitration may not employ this provision to subpoena documents and witnesses[.]"[47] Other federal districts, including the Fourth and Seventh Districts, have reached the same or similar conclusions.[48] **12.63**

In view of the detailed federal and state rules on the arbitral tribunal's power to issue subpoenas, it is hardly surprising that institutional rules tend to raise the issue either summarily by referring to the applicable law, or not at all. **12.64**

Neither the ICDR Rules nor the CPR Rules address the tribunal's power to issue subpoenas.[49] **12.65**

Article 24.2 of the JAMS Rules gives the tribunal power to "summon witnesses and to compel the production of relevant documents by subpoena or other compulsory process where authorized to do so by the law of the location where the testimony of the witness is to be heard ... whether such location is at the place of arbitration or in another location designated by the Tribunal pursuant to Article 14.2." Accordingly, tribunals hearing a case under the JAMS Rules have authority to issue subpoenas and, importantly, to subpoena a witness to testify in New York, even if the seat of the arbitration is abroad. **12.66**

---

45 Matter of Radin (Kleinman), 299 A.D.2d 236 (App. Div. 2002).

46 NBC v. Bear Stearns & Co., 165 F.3d 184 (2d Cir. 1999).

47 *Id.* at 187 (emphasis in original).

48 *See, e.g.*, Burton v. Bush, 614 F.2d 389, 390 (4th Cir. 1980); St. Mary's Medical Center v. Disco Aluminum Prods., 969 F.2d 585, 591 (7th Cir. 1992). For a more detailed discussion of this issue, *see* The International Commercial Disputes Committee and the Arbitration Committee of the New York City Bar Association's Report, *A Model Federal Arbitration Summons to Testify and Present Documentary Evidence at an Arbitration Hearing*, ARIA Vol. 26, No. 2 (Oct. 2015), pp. 7–10 (see Appendix 7).

49 The CPR only addresses the tribunal's subpoena power in the official Commentary to the CPR's domestic Rules, in particular to Rule 12, stating that "[t]he Tribunal's powers with respect to subpoenas are determined by applicable law and are not dealt with specifically in the [CPR] Rules." The complete CPR Commentary is available at http://www.cpradr.org/RulesCaseServices/CPRRules/AdministeredArbitrationRules.asp.

12.67 The ICC Rules provide in Article 25.3 that the arbitral tribunal may "hear witnesses, experts appointed by the parties or any other person, in the presence of the parties, or in their absence provided they have been duly summoned." The ICC Rules also allow "the tribunal [to] require any witness to appear at a hearing. If a witness whose appearance has been requested fails to appear without valid excuse as determined by the tribunal, the tribunal may disregard any written statement by that witness" (Article 23.4).

5. Witness Instructions

12.68 Once a witness has been successfully compelled, or has voluntarily agreed, to attend the hearing, it may be incumbent on the arbitrator to require the witness to testify under oath, to exclude the witness during the testimony of other witnesses, or to provide instructions during adjournments. In all three cases federal and state law as well as institutional rules provide little guidance and the parties and tribunal are consequently at liberty to determine a course of conduct.

12.69 *(a) Administering oaths to witnesses* The Federal Arbitration Act does not address the issue of the tribunal's authority, or the necessity, to administer witness oaths. New York state law, however, expressly recognizes the arbitrators' power to administer oaths in § 7505 of the New York Civil Procedure Law. Beyond this brief provision, stating simply that "[a]n arbitrator has the power to administer oaths," there is no discussion of the content of the oath or manner of administration. Court reporters transcribing arbitration hearings typically are notaries and also are authorized to administer oaths, and they often are asked by the arbitrators to do so. The oath is a statement, in words or substance, that the witness swears or affirms that the testimony he or she is about to give will be the truth, the whole truth and nothing but the truth.

12.70 New York CPLR §7506 provides that the arbitrator him or herself must take an oath to hear and decide the dispute faithfully and fairly. The arbitrator's oath must be administered by an officer authorized to administer oaths. There is no such requirement in the Federal Arbitration Act. In practice, this means that arbitrators in New York generally sign an oath faithfully to hear and decide the case before a notary as part of the papers accepting their appointments from an institution and/or sign the award before a notary (or separately before three different notaries), under oath, that the award is the arbitrator's, and the notary affixes a certification to that effect.

12.71 The ICDR Rules do not address the issue of testimony under oath, but absent express derogation from § 7505 of the CPLR, the state law's grant to the arbitrator of power to administer oaths will apply to ICDR arbitrations as well. The CPR Rules follow the same principle and do not expressly discuss the administration of witness oaths. Neither the JAMS Rules nor the ICC Rules address this issue at all.

(b) Adjournment and presence during testimony of other witnesses New York law and institutional rules do not provide guidance on witness instructions during adjournments of the hearing. However, it is common practice in U.S. litigation, and therefore by extension in international commercial arbitrations seated in New York, that a witness may not discuss the case with the lawyers of either side while the witness is continuing his or her testimony, including during lunch breaks, coffee breaks, or overnight if the witness' testimony continues from one day of the hearing to the next. Ordinarily, if requested to do so, arbitrators will give the witness and counsel instructions to this effect. **12.72**

With regard to the permissibility of a witness' presence during the testimony of other witnesses, neither federal nor state law provides any guidance on this point. In U.S. litigation, fact witnesses ordinarily are excluded from the hearing until after they have testified, if an opposing party requests this exclusion, but experts normally are not excluded. A party nevertheless is entitled to have one representative present throughout the proceedings, and this person may be present at all times even if he or she is a potential fact witness. These litigation practices often are followed, by analogy, in arbitrations in New York. **12.73**

The ICDR Rules permit the tribunal to determine both the manner in which witnesses are examined and "who shall be present during witness examination" (Article 23.3). Similarly, CPR Rule 12.4 provides that "[t]he Tribunal shall have the right to exclude witnesses from hearings during the testimony of other witnesses." **12.74**

Article 23.4 of the JAMS Rules states that hearings shall be private unless the parties agree otherwise (or the law provides to the contrary), and the tribunal may determine the manner of witness examination and whether the witness(es) shall retire during the testimony of other witnesses. Interestingly, Article 24.6 clarifies that "[a]ny person intending to testify to the Tribunal on any issue of fact or expertise will be treated as a witness under these Rules even if that person is a party to the arbitration or was or is an officer, employee or shareholder of any party." This provision implies that the tribunal has authority under the JAMS Rules to exclude parties to the arbitration from hearing other witnesses' testimony if those parties also intend to testify at the hearing. **12.75**

The ICC Rules do not address the tribunal's power to exclude witnesses during the testimony of other witnesses, though it is common practice that this is permitted.

6. Use of Exhibits

The use of exhibits in international arbitration is an important topic for parties to consider as they choose the seat of the arbitration and the applicable institutional rules. Federal and New York state law do not provide guidance or regulations specific to the use of exhibits in arbitration. Instead, they afford the parties **12.76** full authority to determine the applicable procedures. Institutional rules, on the other hand, regulate the use of exhibits to varying degrees. As a general matter, unless the institutional rules require otherwise, parties to international commercial arbitrations seated in New York frequently agree reciprocally to permit the use of electronic displays of exhibits and PowerPoint presentations for opening and closing statements, so long as any exhibits referred to in the presentations or used in the course of the arbitration were previously disclosed to the other party and are tied to the exhibits already in evidence. As a matter of practice, tribunals in international cases commonly treat all documents proposed as exhibits as part of the record, without regard to procedures to "introduce them in evidence" as required in U.S. litigation.

12.77 *(a) Federal and state law* While federal and New York state laws have extensive rules on the use of exhibits in commercial litigation, neither federal nor state law specifically addresses the subject of the use of exhibits in arbitration. Unless otherwise agreed by the parties, international arbitrations are not subject to the evidentiary rules of commercial litigation in the United Sates. As the Supreme Court stated in *Gilmer v. Interstate/Johnson Lane Corp.*, when a party agrees to arbitrate a dispute, he or she "trades the procedures and opportunity for review of the courtroom for the simplicity, informality, and expedition of arbitration."[50] In consequence, the parties and the arbitrators are free to determine a mutually agreeable course of conduct. The parties are, of course, free to agree voluntarily to conduct their arbitration in accordance with the Federal Rules of Civil Procedure and courts will enforce such an agreement where it exists. However, parties to international arbitrations rarely agree to the extensive U.S. procedural rules.[51] In fact, the extensive procedures are one reason parties frequently turn to arbitration to begin with.

12.78 *(b) Institutional rules* The ICDR Rules provide only minimal guidance on the use of exhibits in arbitration. Article 20 governs the "Conduct of Proceedings" and gives the arbitral tribunal discretion to conduct the proceedings as the tribunal sees fit. Specifically, Article 20.1 states that "[s]ubject to these Rules, the arbitral tribunal may conduct the arbitration in whatever manner it considers appropriate, provided that the parties are treated with equality and that each party has the right to be heard and is given a fair opportunity to present its case." The ICDR Rules further provide that the tribunal shall hold a preparatory conference with the parties to consult, and if possible agree, on organization, scheduling, and procedures for the conduct of the arbitration. With regard to exhibits, Article 20.4 provides that the tribunal may "order the parties to produce documents, exhibits, or other evidence it deems necessary or appropriate." Under the ICDR Rules, the

[50] Gilmer v. Interstate/Johnson Lane Corp., 500 U.S. 20, 31 (1991).

[51] The conduct of U.S. litigation and its impact on arbitration is not discussed further here as it is the subject of Chapter 2 of this book. Discovery under U.S. rules is the topic of Chapter 9.

tribunal thus has discretion to conduct the proceedings in the manner it deems appropriate, including with respect to the production and use of exhibits.

Similar to the ICDR Rules, the CPR Rules afford the tribunal primary authority and responsibility for setting the procedural rules governing the arbitration proceeding and hearing. Rule 12 of the CPR Rules governs "Evidence and Hearings" and provides that the tribunal "shall determine the manner in which the parties shall present their cases." The tribunal is not bound to apply the rules of evidence used in judicial proceedings. Rather, the "[t]ribunal shall determine the applicability of any privilege or immunity and the admissibility, relevance, materiality and weight of the evidence offered."[52] These rules hence leave the parties and the tribunal flexibility to determine the procedures appropriate for the specific case. **12.79**

The JAMS Rules also provide only minimal guidance on the use of exhibits. Article 25 on "Evidence" empowers the tribunal to order the parties to "exchange and produce documents, exhibits or other evidence it deems necessary or appropriate." Further, the tribunal has authority to determine the "time, manner and form in which written exhibits are to be exchanged between the parties and presented to the [t]ribunal."[53] **12.80**

The ICC Rules do not specifically address the use of exhibits. Rather, the ICC Rules simply provide in Article 22.1 that "[t]he arbitral tribunal and the parties shall make every effort to conduct the arbitration in an expeditious and cost-effective manner, having regard to the complexity and value of the dispute." Further, Article 22.4 requires the tribunal to act "fairly and impartially and [to] ensure that each party has a reasonable opportunity to present its case." Apart from these provisions, the ICC Rules do not provide any guidance or regulations that would affect the use of exhibits during the arbitration hearing. **12.81**

7. Closing Proceedings and Post-Hearing Submissions

At the conclusion of the hearing, the arbitral tribunal must close the proceedings and the record before issuing its final award. In some circumstances, the tribunal **12.82**

---

[52] CPR Rule 12.2.

[53] It is noteworthy that the JAMS Streamlined Arbitration Rules provide more extensive guidance on the use of exhibits than the JAMS International Arbitration Rules. Under JAMS Streamlined Arbitration Rule 13, regarding the "Exchange of Information," parties are obligated to cooperate in good faith in the voluntary and informal exchange of non-privileged documents and must provide the other party "copies of all documents in their possession or control on which they rely in support of their positions or *that they intend to introduce as exhibits at the Arbitration Hearing* …" Further, Rules 15 on "Pre-Hearing Submissions" requires that each party, unless otherwise agreed, exchange at least seven calendar days prior to the arbitration hearing, "a list of all exhibits intended to be used at the Hearing." The parties must pre-mark the exhibits and exchange copies them if they have not done so already. Additionally, the parties must attempt to resolve any dispute regarding the admissibility of exhibits prior to the Hearing. The JAMS Streamlined Arbitration Rules are evidently concerned with ensuring the early exchange of information and avoiding any delay in the arbitration hearing due to disagreement regarding exhibits. They are available at http://www.jamsadr.com/rules-streamlined-arbitration/.

may permit the parties to submit post-hearing briefs and may specify, if it so wishes, certain questions for the parties to address. Neither federal nor state law has specific provisions on closing the proceedings.

12.83 The ICDR Rules provide in Article 27 that the tribunal may close the arbitral hearing by asking the parties if they have any further submissions and, upon a negative answer, declaring the arbitral hearing closed. However, the tribunal may, upon its own motion or upon application of a party, reopen the hearing at any time before it renders its final award. The CPR Rules do not provide any specific guidance regarding the closing of proceedings or the permissibility of post-hearing briefs.

12.84 Article 29 of the JAMS Rules governs "closing of the Proceedings." It provides that the tribunal will declare the proceedings closed when it is "satisfied that the parties have had a reasonable opportunity to present their cases." The reasonable opportunity to present one's case may include the submission of post-hearing briefs. However, once the tribunal closes the proceedings, "no further submission or argument may be made, or evidence produced, unless requested or authorized by the Tribunal" (Article 29).

12.85 Article 27 of the ICC Rules discusses, among other matters, the requirements for closing the arbitral proceedings. As soon as possible after the last hearing regarding issues to be decided by the tribunal, or after the latest filing (i.e. post-hearing filings), whichever is later, the arbitral tribunal must "declare the proceedings closed with respect to the matters to be decided in the award; and … inform the [ICC] Secretariat and the parties of the date by which it expects to submit a draft award to the Court for approval …" Following closure of the proceedings, no further submissions may be made and no additional evidence may be submitted regarding the issues to be decided in the award "unless requested or authorized by the arbitral tribunal."

D. LOGISTICS

1. Travel, Accommodation, Catering

12.86 New York City is one of the prime holiday and business destinations in the world and thus offers extensive travel, accommodation, and catering options.

12.87 *(a) Travel to and from New York* Three major airports service New York, which together create the largest airport system in the United States and the second largest in the world as measured by passenger traffic.

12.88 **John F. Kennedy International Airport** (JFK) is an international airport located in Jamaica, Queens, approximately fifteen miles from midtown Manhattan. Over ninety (90) airlines operate out of JFK, and in 2013, the airport accommodated over fifty (50) million passengers. Daily flights to and from JFK are available to almost any destination in the world, making New York travel convenient and flexible. Bus, train, taxi, airport shuttle, and rental car services are available for transportation between JFK Airport and New York City. Although the distance from the airport to midtown Manhattan is only fifteen (15) miles, the trip by taxi can take forty-five minutes to one hour depending on traffic.

Newark Liberty International Airport (EWR) is the second major international airport servicing New York. The airport is located in New Jersey and is approximately fifteen miles (24 km) southwest of Midtown Manhattan. Over thirty (30) airlines offer flights to and from Newark and in 2013, Newark Airport handled thirty-five (35) million passengers. Bus, train, taxi, airport shuttle, and rental car services are available for transportation between Newark Airport and New York City. The trip by taxi from the airport to midtown Manhattan is approximately fifty minutes to an hour and fifteen minutes depending on traffic. **12.89**

La Guardia Airport (LGA) is located in Queens, New York. Around twenty airlines offer flights to and from La Guardia, and in 2013, La Guardia handled almost twenty-seven (27) million passengers. Notably, however, La Guardia does not provide any non-stop services to destinations in Europe. Bus, train, taxi, airport shuttle, and rental car services are available for transportation between La Guardia and New York City. The trip by taxi from the airport to midtown Manhattan is approximately thirty-five to fifty minutes depending on traffic. **12.90**

(b) Travel within New York Travel within New York City is easy and relatively inexpensive. New York boasts an extensive public transportation system, with bus and subway service in all of the city's five boroughs. As of September 2014, a single-ride MetroCard costs $2.75, a 7-Day unlimited ride MetroCard costs $30, and a 30-Day unlimited ride MetroCard costs $112. MetroCards may be used for subway and bus rides. **12.91**

Yellow cab rides cannot be pre-booked, but limousine services with pre-set prices are widely available and accept pre-booking. Additionally, Uber, Lyft, Via, Gett, and other ridesharing services that allow passengers to order a car via Smartphone app are now available in New York City. Rides ordered through these apps are usually charged directly to the user's Smartphone app account. **12.92**

Finally, New York City's grid plan layout makes it easy to navigate on foot. Since traffic in New York can be heavy, walking is oftentimes a quicker option. **12.93**

(c) Accommodation and entertainment New York City offers hundreds of hotels located around the city. *NYC: The Official Guide* offers easy tools to customize hotel searches at http://www.nycgo.com/hotels/. Hotels close to the NYIAC and AAA/ICDR hearing facilities include the Grand Hyatt New York (109 East 42nd Street), the Roosevelt Hotel New York (45 East 45th Street), and the Westin New York Grand Central (212 East 42nd Street). Understanding the need for **12.94**

flexibility in arbitration hearings, many hotels offer special rates and cancelation options to accommodate business needs.

12.95 New York also is home to some of the world's most renowned entertainment providers. To name but a few: Broadway houses forty (40) major professional theaters; the Lincoln Center for the Performing Arts is home to the Metropolitan Opera, the New York City Ballet, the New York Philharmonic, and Jazz at Lincoln Center; Carnegie Hall is a prestigious venue for both classical and popular music; and Madison Square Garden is home to the New York Knicks and the New York Rangers, and is a popular venue for leading entertainers. The following Web sites, among others, offer tickets for advance purchase:

www.abt.org
www.broadway.com
www.metopera.org
www.telecharge.com
www.ticketmaster.com

12.96 Additionally, hotels often provide a concierge service to their guests, which includes booking tickets to shows, sporting events, and concerts.

12.97 *(d) Catering* Thousands of restaurants are located in New York with prices ranging from cheap to very expensive, and offering every type of cuisine. Many restaurants, especially those located in the city's business centers, offer catering and will deliver to offices and hearing rooms. Most restaurants accept catering orders via phone or online.

2. Ancillary Services

12.98 As a leading business and legal center, New York has a well-developed market of providers of ancillary services, such as court reporting and interpretation services. While prices depend on the specific services requested, they are generally competitive and on part with comparable service providers in other major arbitral centers like Paris and London. The New York International Arbitration Center offers advice concerning ancillary support providers whose services are available for arbitration hearings in New York.

13

CHALLENGING AND ENFORCING INTERNATIONAL ARBITRAL AWARDS IN NEW YORK

John V. H. Pierce, Janet R. Carter, and David N. Cinotti

A. Introduction	13.03
1. Options for the "Winner" and the "Loser" in International Arbitration	13.03
2. The Legal Regime Applicable to Actions to Challenge or Enforce International Arbitral Awards in New York	13.07
B. Procedural Issues Involved in Challenging and Enforcing International Arbitral Awards in New York	13.12
1. Actions in the Federal Courts in New York	13.13
(a) General procedural considerations	13.14
(b) Subject-matter jurisdiction	13.29
(c) Personal jurisdiction	13.40
(d) Establishing venue	13.60
(e) Removal of enforcement proceedings from state to federal court	13.65
2. Actions in New York State Courts	13.73
(a) Form and location of action	13.74
(b) Statute of limitations	13.76
C. Substantive Issues Involved in Challenging International Arbitral Awards in New York	13.78
1. Grounds for Nonrecognition under the New York Convention	13.78
(a) Absence of a valid arbitration agreement (Article V(1)(a))	13.81
(b) Denial of opportunity to present one's case (Article V(1)(b))	13.96
(c) Excess of authority (Article V(1)(c))	13.98
(d) Violations of arbitral procedures or the law of the arbitral situs (Article V(1)(d))	13.101
(e) Awards that are not binding or have been set aside (Article V(1)(e))	13.104
(f) Awards that address nonarbitrable issues (Article V(2)(a))	13.106
(g) Awards that violate public policy (Article V(2)(b))	13.108
2. FAA Chapter 1 Grounds for Vacating International Arbitral Awards	13.111
(a) Award procured by corruption, fraud, or undue means (Section 10(a)(1))	13.113
(b) Partiality or corruption of the arbitrators (Section 10(a)(2))	13.115
(c) Failure to adjourn or hear evidence; prejudicial misbehavior (Section 10(a)(3))	13.119
(d) Exceeding jurisdiction (Section 10(a)(4))	13.124
(e) Manifest disregard of the law	13.126
(f) Public policy	13.135
(g) Sanctions for frivolous attacks on arbitral awards	13.136
3. New York State Law Grounds for Vacating Awards	13.138
4. Choice of Arbitral Law When Resisting Enforcement of an Award Made in the United States	13.142

13.01 This chapter addresses the key issues involved in challenging and enforcing international arbitral awards in New York. It is divided into two principal sections. First, it addresses the procedural issues that a party must consider when seeking to challenge or enforce an international arbitral award in New York. Such issues include, among other things, the form, timing, and service of the application, and the satisfaction of subject-matter jurisdiction, personal jurisdiction, and venue requirements.

13.02 Second, this chapter examines the substantive grounds available to a party that seeks to vacate, or resist recognition and enforcement of, an international arbitral award in New York. Depending on the circumstances, including the jurisdiction in which the award was made and the terms of the parties' arbitration agreement, these grounds may be those set forth in the Federal Arbitration Act (the FAA),[1] the United Nations Convention on the Recognition and Enforcement of Foreign Arbitral Awards (New York Convention),[2] and the New York Civil Practice Law and Rules (CPLR).[3]

A. INTRODUCTION

1. Options for the "Winner" and the "Loser" in International Arbitration

13.03 In the great majority of cases, once an international arbitral award has been issued, the losing party (award-debtor) voluntarily complies with the award, thus obviating the need for the prevailing party (award-creditor) to seek to "confirm" or "enforce" the award against the award-debtor. In large part, such compliance is due to the existence of an international legal regime that is highly supportive of arbitration and that promotes the enforcement of international arbitral awards. This regime—the central component of which is the New York Convention—makes it very difficult, in most cases, to successfully resist recognition and enforcement of an international arbitral award.

13.04 In some cases, however, the award-debtor decides that the award is fundamentally unfair, abusive, or otherwise unacceptable and refuses to comply with it. In these instances, the award-creditor has several options. It may seek to have the arbitral award "confirmed" in the place in which it was rendered (the legal situs of the arbitration), thereby converting the award into a court judgment that may be enforced either at the arbitral situs or in another state. Alternatively, it may forego confirmation of the award in the arbitral situs and immediately seek to

[1] 9 U.S.C. §§ 1–307. *See generally* Chapter 1 for a discussion of applicable law.
[2] June 10, 1958, 21 U.S.T. 2517, 330 U.N.T.S. 3.
[3] N.Y. CPLR 7509–7511.

have the award recognized and enforced in a foreign jurisdiction where, for example, the award-debtor may have assets that could be used to satisfy the award.[4] If the award-creditor is successful in having the award "confirmed" or "recognized," the award will be afforded the status of a national court judgment and may be enforced by application of the full panoply of coercive measures available to enforce such judgments.[5]

The award-debtor also has several options to consider.[6] It may choose to await **13.05**
an action brought by the award-creditor to confirm or recognize the award and then resist recognition and enforcement of the award in those proceedings. Or, it may seek proactively to "vacate" or "annul" the award in the place in which, or under the law of which, the award was made. This choice has significant strategic ramifications. First, whereas an award-debtor that seeks to resist recognition and enforcement of an international arbitral award will generally be limited to the seven express grounds set forth in the New York Convention, the award-debtor that seeks to vacate an international award in the state in which, or under the law of which, the award was made may benefit from the "full panoply of express and implied grounds for relief" available in the national arbitration law of the forum state.[7] In such actions, the award-debtor is not limited by the grounds for nonrecognition set forth in the New York Convention.

Second, if an action to vacate or annul an arbitral award is successful, the award **13.06**
is of no legal effect in the forum in which it was vacated and, in most cases, will not be enforced outside of that forum.[8] This is in contrast to the successful

[4] Unlike the Geneva Convention for the Execution of Foreign Arbitral Awards of 1927 (Geneva Convention), the predecessor to the New York Convention, the New York Convention does not mandate *double exequatur*, the requirement that an award be confirmed in the country in which it was rendered, before the award-creditor can seek recognition of the award elsewhere. *See, e.g.*, Kenneth R. Davis, *Unconventional Wisdom: A New Look at Articles V and VII of the Convention on the Recognition and Enforcement of Foreign Arbitral Awards*, 37 Tex. Int'l L.J. 43, 45 (2002).

[5] *See, e.g.*, Karaha Bodas Co. v. Perusahaan Pertambangan Minyak Dan Gas Bumi Negara, 500 F.3d 111, 124 (2d Cir. 2007) (approving antisuit injunction to protect judgment confirming international arbitral award). A party that successfully *defended* against claims in an international arbitration may also seek to have the resulting award recognized by a national court in order to preclude the claimant from bringing the same claims again in another forum. *See generally* 3 Gary B. Born, International Commercial Arbitration 3746–62 (2d ed. 2014).

[6] *Id.* at 2344–46.

[7] *See* Yusuf Ahmed Alghanim & Sons v. Toys "R" Us, Inc., 126 F.3d 15, 21–23 (2d Cir. 1997) (holding that an award-debtor resisting recognition and enforcement of an arbitral award made in the United States and subject to the New York Convention may rely on the FAA Chapter 1 grounds to vacate awards, including those implied grounds developed by U.S. case law). *See generally* Chapter 1.E of this book.

[8] Thai-Lao Lignite (Thailand) Co. Ltd. & Hongsa Lignite (Lao Pdr) Co., Ltd. v. Government of the Lao People's Democratic Republic, 997 F. Supp. 2d 214 (S.D.N.Y. 2014). But *see* Corporacion Mexicana de Mantenimiento Integral ("COMMISA") v. Pemex Exploracion y Produccion ("PEP"), 962 F. Supp. 2d 642 (S.D.N.Y. 2013) (award vacated at seat enforced in New York under Panama Convention); Chromalloy Aeroservs. v. Arab Repub. of Egypt, 939 F. Supp. 907, 909 (D.D.C. 1996); Baker Marine (Nig.) Ltd. v. Chevron (Nig.) Ltd., 191 F.3d 194, 197 n.3 (2d Cir. 1999)

effort to resist recognition and enforcement in the forum selected by the award-creditor. In these circumstances (unlike a successful annulment action) the award continues to exist and may be recognized and enforced in other jurisdictions.[9] The proactive effort to vacate an arbitral award also has the significant advantage of permitting the award-debtor to select the forum in which a challenge to the award will be heard.

2. The Legal Regime Applicable to Actions to Challenge or Enforce International Arbitral Awards in New York

13.07 Actions brought in New York to enforce or challenge international arbitral awards are ordinarily subject to federal law.[10] First, such actions will generally be subject to the FAA, which governs written arbitration agreements that pertain to contracts involving foreign or interstate commerce.[11] The FAA is divided into three chapters. Congress passed Chapter 1 of the FAA in 1925, with the intent of ending the traditional judicial hostility to arbitration that had been inherited from the courts of England.[12] Chapter 1 thus requires courts to enforce arbitration agreements as they would other contracts.[13] Chapter 1 also directs courts to enforce arbitral awards unless certain narrow bases to vacate or modify an award are present.[14] FAA Chapter 2 implements the New York Convention,[15] while Chapter 3 implements the Inter-American Convention on International Commercial Arbitration (Inter-American Convention).[16]

13.08 Second, most international arbitral awards for which recognition and enforcement are sought in New York will be subject to the New York Convention. Opened for signature in 1958, the Convention is a multilateral treaty to which more than 150 states, including the United States, are parties.[17] Its purpose was "to encourage the recognition and enforcement of commercial arbitration

(distinguishing *Chromalloy* on the ground that the respondent did not violate any express promise by seeking to annul the award in Nigeria, where it was rendered).

[9] *See* Karaha Bodas Co. v. Perusahaan Pertambangan Minyak Dan Gas Bumi Negara, 335 F.3d 357, 367 (5th Cir. 2003) ("[E]nforcement proceedings in multiple secondary-jurisdiction states can address the same substantive issues.").

[10] Where the award is "foreign" in the sense that it was rendered or "made" in another country, the application of federal law is clear. *See* Ocean Warehousing B.V. v. Baron Metals & Alloys, Inc., 157 F. Supp. 2d 245, 249 (S.D.N.Y. 2001) ("A court's decision whether to recognize and enforce a foreign arbitral award is governed by federal law—specifically, the [New York] Convention.").

[11] *See* 9 U.S.C. §§ 1–2. The FAA's scope is coextensive with Congress's Commerce Clause power. Allied-Bruce Terminix Cos. v. Dobson, 513 U.S. 265, 277 (1995).

[12] Circuit City Stores, Inc. v. Adams, 532 U.S. 105, 111 (2001).

[13] *See* Scherk v. Alberto-Culver Co., 417 U.S. 506, 511 (1974).

[14] *See* 9 U.S.C. §§ 9–11.

[15] *See id.* §§ 201–208.

[16] *See id.* §§ 301–307; Jan. 30, 1975, S. Treaty Doc. No. 97–12, 1438 U.N.T.S. 245 (sometimes called the Panama Convention).

[17] *See* Jens Dammann & Henry Hansmann, *Globalizing Commercial Litigation*, 94 Cornell L. Rev. 1, 33 & n.92 (2008).

agreements in international contracts and to unify the standards by which agreements to arbitrate are observed and arbitral awards are enforced in the signatory countries."[18]

The Convention applies to the recognition and enforcement of both "foreign" awards (i.e., those "made in the territory of a State other than the State where the recognition and enforcement of such awards are sought") and awards that are "not considered as domestic awards in the State where their recognition and enforcement are sought."[19] Chapter 2 of the FAA defines nondomestic awards broadly. Pursuant to FAA Section 202, an arbitral award arising out of a commercial legal relationship falls under the New York Convention unless: (1) the award is entirely between citizens of the United States, (2) the parties' relationship involves no property abroad, (3) the parties' relationship does not envisage performance or enforcement abroad, and (4) the parties' relationship lacks some other reasonable connection to a foreign state.[20] Courts in New York have accordingly found that an arbitral award made in the United States is "non-domestic" and subject to the Convention so long as it bears some reasonable relation to a foreign state.[21] In many cases, where the award is made in the United States, the award will be subject to the overlapping coverage of the FAA and the New York Convention. Parties in such cases may have "more than one remedy available and may choose the most advantageous."[22] **13.09**

Parties seeking to challenge or enforce international arbitral awards in New York should also be aware that the award may be subject to the Inter-American Convention. This treaty, which largely tracks the New York Convention (at least as far as enforcement of awards is concerned), was meant to ensure the enforcement of **13.10**

---

[18] *Scherk*, 417 U.S. at 520 n.15.

[19] N.Y. Convention, art. I(1).

[20] *See* 9 U.S.C. § 202. Section 202 provides in full: "An arbitration agreement or arbitral award arising out of a legal relationship, whether contractual or not, which is considered as commercial, including a transaction, contract, or agreement described in section 2 of this title, falls under the Convention. An agreement or award arising out of such a relationship which is entirely between citizens of the United States shall be deemed not to fall under the Convention unless that relationship involves property located abroad, envisages performance or enforcement abroad, or has some other reasonable relation with one or more foreign states. For the purpose of this section a corporation is a citizen of the United States if it is incorporated or has its principal place of business in the United States."

[21] *See, e.g.*, Bergesen v. Joseph Muller Corp., 710 F.2d 928, 933 (2d Cir. 1983) (finding that award rendered in the United States in an arbitration involving two foreign parties was "non-domestic" and thus subject to the New York Convention); Shanghai Foodstuffs Imp. & Exp. Corp. v. Int'l Chem., Inc., No. 99 Civ. 3320 (RCC), 2004 WL 213019, at *1–2 (S.D.N.Y. Feb. 4, 2004) (holding the award made in United States fell under New York Convention because one of the parties was a foreign corporation and the parties' agreement involved the international shipment of goods); *see also* Lander Co. v. MMP Invests., Inc., 107 F.3d 476, 478, 481–82 (7th Cir. 1997) (holding that New York Convention applied to award made in New York resolving dispute between U.S. companies regarding the sale of products in Poland).

[22] *Bergesen*, 710 F.2d at 934 (noting that there "is no reason to assume that Congress did not intend to provide overlapping coverage between the Convention and the Federal Arbitration Act").

arbitration agreements and awards in Latin America.[23] Adopted by the Organization of American States (OAS), it was opened for signature in 1975.[24] Currently, nineteen countries, including the United States, are parties.[25] In U.S. courts, the Inter-American Convention applies instead of the New York Convention if "a majority of the parties to the arbitration agreement are citizens of a State or States that have ratified or acceded to the Inter-American Convention and are members of the [OAS]."[26]

13.11 Although New York state law provides its own statutory framework for challenging and enforcing arbitral awards,[27] it is unlikely that New York state law would apply in an action to challenge or enforce an international arbitral award—even where the action is originally brought in state court.[28]

B. PROCEDURAL ISSUES INVOLVED IN CHALLENGING AND ENFORCING INTERNATIONAL ARBITRAL AWARDS IN NEW YORK

13.12 This section considers the procedural issues that arise when a party seeks to challenge or enforce an international arbitral award in New York. First, the section addresses procedural issues for a party filing an action in federal court: (1) the timing of applications to confirm or vacate awards, (2) the form of the action, (3) service of process, (4) the requirement of a written arbitration agreement, (5) subject-matter jurisdiction, (6) personal jurisdiction, (7) venue, and (8) removal from state to federal court. Second, the section reviews the procedures for actions to challenge or enforce international arbitral awards in New York state courts.

1. Actions in the Federal Courts in New York

13.13 Parties in actions to challenge or enforce international arbitral awards in New York will more often than not choose to be in federal court. Indeed, it is difficult to

---

[23] *See* John P. Bowman, *The Panama Convention and Its Implementation Under the Federal Arbitration Act*, 11 Am. Rev. Int'l Arb. 1, 6–7, 20 (2000). For the differences between the two Conventions, see *id.* at 24–69.

[24] *Id.* at 1. The legislative history of FAA Chapter 3 suggests that Congress believed "courts in the United States would achieve a general uniformity of results under the two conventions." H.R. Rep. No. 101–501, at 5 (1990), *reprinted in* 1990 U.S.C.C.A.N. 675, 678.

[25] *See* Dep't of Int'l Law, OAS, Multilateral Treaties, Inter-American Convention on International Commercial Arbitration, *at* http://www.oas.org/juridico/english/sigs/b-35.html (last visited Feb. 9, 2015).

[26] 9 U.S.C. § 305(1).

[27] N.Y. CPLR 7509–7511.

[28] *See* Corcoran v. Ardra Ins. Co., 567 N.E.2d 969, 969 (N.Y. 1990). Note that the FAA contains a specific provision for the removal of cases from state to federal court that "relate" to an arbitration agreement or award falling under the Conventions. *See* 9 U.S.C. §§ 205, 302; section B.1(e) of this chapter, *infra*.

imagine a case in which both parties would prefer a state to a federal forum when addressing the enforceability of an international arbitral award. Even where a party seeking to challenge or enforce an international arbitral award initially files an application in state court, the FAA specifically contemplates removal to federal court of actions "relate[d] to" an agreement or award falling under the New York or Inter-American Convention.[29] The bulk of this section, therefore, is devoted to the procedural issues involved in bringing an action to challenge or enforce an international arbitral award in the federal courts in New York.

(a) General procedural considerations

(I) TIMING OF APPLICATION TO CONFIRM OR VACATE AWARD

An action to confirm an award under the New York Convention or Inter-American Convention must be brought within three years after the award is "made."[30] An award is "made" at the time it is "originally decided by the arbitrators," not when it "becomes final according to the law that governs" the arbitration.[31] To avoid ambiguity about this important date, some institutional arbitration rules require that an award expressly set forth the date on which the award was "made."[32] **13.14**

With respect to actions to vacate arbitral awards, FAA Section 12 provides that "*notice* of a motion to vacate ... must be served upon the adverse party or his attorney within three months after the award is filed or delivered."[33] The Seventh Circuit has relied on this section's plain language to hold that an action to vacate was untimely where the petitioner *filed* his motion within three months but did not *serve* notice of the motion until one day after the three-month period expired.[34] Under this reasoning, a petitioner could apparently preserve the application to vacate by serving the petition on the respondent within three months after receipt of the award, without actually filing the petition within the three-month period. **13.15**

The three-month time limit for initiating a vacatur or annulment action is absolute and applies even where the party seeking vacatur raises it as a defense to a petition to confirm an award. The Second Circuit has said, "We have made clear that 'a party may not raise a motion to vacate, modify or correct an arbitration award after the three month period has run, even when raised as a defense to a **13.16**

29 *See* 9 U.S.C. §§ 205, 302.

30 *Id.* §§ 207, 302; *see also* Seetransport Wiking Trader Schiffarhtsgesellschaft MBH & Co. v. Navimpex Centrala Navala, 989 F.2d 572, 581 (2d Cir. 1993) (holding that an action to confirm an award brought more than three years after the award was made is time-barred). In contrast, an action to enforce an award under FAA Chapter 1 must be brought within one year. *See* 9 U.S.C. § 9; Photopaint Techs., LLC v. Smartlens Corp., 335 F.3d 152, 158 (2d Cir. 2003). The parties may agree, however, to toll this limitations period. *See Photopaint Techs.*, 335 F.3d at 160–61.

31 *Seetransport*, 989 F.2d at 581.

32 For example, the ICC Rules state: "The Award shall be deemed to be made ... on the date stated therein." ICC Rules of Arbitration, art. 31(3) (2012); *see also* LCIA Arbitration Rules, art 26(2) (2014); UNCITRAL Arbitration Rules, art. 32(4) (revised 2010).

33 9 U.S.C. § 12 (emphasis added).

34 *See* Webster v. A.T. Kearney, Inc., 507 F.3d 568, 571–72 (7th Cir. 2007).

motion to confirm.'"[35] Thus, an award-debtor must act quickly if it intends to seek vacatur, even if it expects the award-creditor to move to confirm the award.

13.17 Courts have interpreted the phrase "filed or delivered" in FAA Section 12 to refer to the date the moving party receives the award, rather than the date it is sent to the parties by the arbitrators.[36] If the parties' arbitration agreement or the rules under which the arbitration was conducted define the filing or delivery date, the agreement or rules should control.[37]

(II) FORM OF APPLICATION TO CONFIRM OR VACATE AWARD

13.18 Parties seeking to confirm or to vacate an arbitral award in federal court should not file a complaint, as one would typically do to commence a civil action in federal court, but rather should proceed as if filing a motion.[38] As the FAA makes clear, "any application [under the FAA] shall be made and heard in the manner provided by law for the making and hearing of motions."[39] Because the application is a motion and not a complaint, the court need not require a case management conference pursuant to Federal Rule of Civil Procedure 16.[40] Parties should check the individual practices of the district judge assigned to the case to determine matters such as timing of briefing and the need for premotion conferences. Many federal judges in New York require a premotion conference prior to the filing of dispositive motions, but some judges exempt arbitration matters from that rule.[41]

13.19 Courts have held that Federal Rules of Civil Procedure 12(b) and 56, which govern motions to dismiss and for summary judgment, respectively, do not apply in actions to confirm or vacate arbitral awards.[42] As the Seventh Circuit has put it, in an action to enforce or to vacate an award "[n]o 'complaint' or 'motion to dismiss' or any other filing conceived by the Federal Rules of Civil Procedure

---

[35] Wallace v. Buttar, 378 F.3d 182, 197–98 (2d Cir. 2004) (*quoting* Florasynth, Inc. v. Pickholz, 750 F.2d 171, 175 (2d Cir. 1984)).

[36] *See, e.g.*, Sargent v. Paine Webber Jackson & Curtis, Inc., 882 F.2d 529, 531 (D.C. Cir. 1989).

[37] *See Webster*, 507 F.3d at 573 (holding that the rules applicable to the arbitration provided for service by mail and defined delivery of an award as "the placing of the award … in the mail").

[38] *See* D.H. Blair & Co. v. Gottdiener, 462 F.3d 95, 108 (2d Cir. 2006); Encyclopaedia Universalis S.A. v. Encyclopaedia Britannica, Inc., 403 F.3d 85, 89 n.2 (2d Cir. 2005).

[39] 9 U.S.C. § 6. FAA Section 6 applies to actions brought under the New York and Inter-American Conventions. *See* 9 U.S.C. §§ 208, 307 (providing that FAA Chapter 1 applies to cases under Chapters 2 or 3 "to the extent that [Chapter 1] is not in conflict with" the Conventions).

[40] *See* Health Servs. Mgmt. Corp. v. Hughes, 975 F.2d 1253, 1258 (7th Cir. 1992).

[41] *See, e.g.*, Individual Practices of Chief Judge Loretta A. Preska, S.D.N.Y., ¶ 2.A., *link available at* http://www.nysd.uscourts.gov/judge/Preska (last visited Feb. 9, 2015) (exempting petitions to compel arbitration or confirm or modify awards from promotion conference requirement).

[42] *See, e.g., Webster*, 507 F.3d at 570-71 (holding that neither Rule 12 nor Rule 56 applies to petition to vacate); IFC Interconsult, AG v. Safeguard Int'l Partners, LLC, 438 F.3d 298, 308 (3d Cir. 2006) (holding that Rule 12(b) does not apply to enforcement action); Productos Mercantiles e Industriales, S.A. v. Faberge USA, Inc., 23 F.3d 41, 46 (2d Cir. 1994) (same with regard to vacatur action). Some district courts in New York, however, have analogized a petition to confirm an award to a motion for summary judgment. *See, e.g.*, Franklin Hamilton, LLC. v. Creative Ins. Underwriters, Inc., No. 08 Civ. 7449 (JFK), 2008 WL 4837680, at *1 (S.D.N.Y. Nov. 6, 2008).

need [be] filed."[43] Instead, parties may submit "affidavits, legal briefs, and documentary evidence in support of the order sought."[44]

A district court should treat an action under the FAA that is originally filed in state court and removed to federal court "as a motion rather than a complaint."[45] Parties should take heed, however, that "[r]emoved proceedings arrive in federal court in the procedural posture they had in state court"; thus, if a response is due to a petition filed in state court, parties must adhere to the state-court deadline after the petition is removed unless ordered otherwise by the federal court.[46] **13.20**

(III) SERVICE OF APPLICATION TO CONFIRM OR VACATE AWARD

The rule that an action to confirm or to vacate an international arbitral award under the New York or Inter-American Convention should be initiated by way of motion, not complaint, raises issues regarding service of process. FAA Section 9 contains instructions for service of process in an action to enforce an award.[47] Section 9 applies to Convention cases because there is no service-of-process provision in FAA Chapters 2 or 3.[48] Section 12 contains identical instructions for service of process in an action to vacate an award.[49] Sections 9 and 12 are anachronistic and poorly drafted, which creates difficulties of application.[50] **13.21**

Sections 9 and 12 provide for different methods of service depending on whether the adverse party is a resident or nonresident of the district *in which the award was made*. Service on a resident of the district in which the award was made is accomplished "as prescribed by law for service of notice of motion in an action in the same court."[51] If the adverse party is not a resident of the district in which the award was made, however, the FAA provides that "notice of the application shall be served by the marshal of any district within which the adverse party may be found in like manner as other process of the court."[52] **13.22**

Accordingly, if the adverse party resides in the district in which the arbitration was conducted, the petition to enforce may be served as a motion pursuant to **13.23**

---

[43] *Webster*, 507 F.3d at 571; *see also* Fed. R. Civ. P. 81(a)(6) (providing that the procedural rules in the FAA control in arbitration cases).

[44] Moses H. Cone Mem'l Hosp. v. Mercury Constr. Corp., 460 U.S. 1, 22 n.26 (1983); *see also Webster*, 507 F.3d at 571 (noting that a moving party should "provid[e] the Court with all matters that it desires the Court to consider in support of" its motion (internal quotation marks omitted)).

[45] *D.H. Blair*, 462 F.3d at 108 n.2.

[46] *Id.* at 108 (holding that Fed. R. Civ. P. 81(c) regarding removed actions does not apply to petitions to confirm or vacate arbitral awards).

[47] *See* 9 U.S.C. § 9.

[48] *See id.* §§ 208, 307; InterCarbon Berm., Ltd. v. Caltex Trading & Transp. Corp., 146 F.R.D. 64, 67 (S.D.N.Y. 1993).

[49] *See* 9 U.S.C. § 12.

[50] *See InterCarbon*, 146 F.R.D. at 67 (describing Section 12 as "an anachronism").

[51] 9 U.S.C. §§ 9, 12.

[52] *Id.*

Federal Rule of Civil Procedure 5.[53] This rule makes sense because Congress contemplated that an action to vacate or confirm an arbitral award under FAA Chapter 1 would, unless otherwise agreed by the parties, be brought in the district in which the award was made.[54] There is little chance that a party which has already arbitrated a dispute in the district in which it resides would be surprised by a notice of motion to enforce or to vacate the resulting award in the same district.

13.24 When the respondent to a petition to confirm an award resides *outside* the district where the award was made, the petitioner should serve the petition pursuant to Federal Rule of Civil Procedure 4.[55] District courts have so held after concluding that the language of FAA sections 9 and 12—requiring service by U.S. marshal—was anachronistic and unworkable.[56]

13.25 Sections 9 and 12 do not on their face make any provision for service on respondents who reside outside the United States, and so cannot be "found" in *any* U.S. "district."[57] Requiring petitioners to satisfy Section 9 and 12 in these circumstances "might amount to requiring them to do the impossible."[58] Thus, where the respondent resides outside the United States, courts have found that service should be made in accordance with Federal Rule of Civil Procedure 4.[59]

---

[53] *See* Bricklayers & Allied Craftworkers Int'l Union v. Jocanz, Inc., No. 07-2562 (GEB), 2007 WL 1876508, at *2 n.1 (D.N.J. June 27, 2007) (upholding service of application to enforce award by certified mail pursuant to Federal Rule of Civil Procedure 5(b)).

[54] *See* 9 U.S.C. §§ 9, 12. The Supreme Court has interpreted the FAA's venue provisions to be permissive, not mandatory. *See* Cortez Byrd Chips, Inc. v. Bill Harbert Constr. Co., 529 U.S. 193, 204 (2000).

[55] For a discussion of Rule 4, *see, e.g.*, Moore's Federal Practice, §§ 4.01–4.121 (Matthew Bender 3d ed.).

[56] *InterCarbon*, 146 F.R.D. at 67 n.3 (explaining that amendments to the Federal Rules of Civil Procedure in the early 1980s abandoned U.S. marshals as routine process-servers); *see also* Hancor, Inc. v. R&R Eng'g Prods., Inc., 381 F. Supp. 2d 12, 15–16 (D.P.R. 2005) (holding that U.S. service on a nonresident of the district in which the award was made need not be via U.S. marshal but may be valid if accomplished by a means of permissible service under Rule 4); Dobco, Inc. v. Mery Gates, Inc., Civ. No. 06-0699 (HAA), 2006 WL 2056799, at *2 (D.N.J. July 21, 2006) (same).

[57] *See InterCarbon*, 146 F.R.D. at 67; Can. Life Assurance Co. v. Converium Ruckversicherung (Deutschland) AG, Civ. No. 06-3800 (GEB), 2007 WL 1726565, at *4 (D.N.J. Jun. 13, 2007); Lucent Techs., Inc. v. Tatung Co., No. 02 Civ. 8107 (JSR), 2003 WL 402539, at *1 (S.D.N.Y. Feb. 20, 2003) (holding that Section 9 "is an irrelevancy in a case ... where the respondent, being a foreign entity, cannot necessarily be found in any United States district").

[58] *InterCarbon*, 146 F.R.D. at 67.

[59] *See* Technologists, Inc. v. MIR's Ltd., 725 F. Supp. 2d 120, 127 (D.D.C. 2010); *InterCarbon*, 146 F.R.D. at 67; *Can. Life Assurance Co.*, 2007 WL 1726565, at *4; Fed. R. Civ. P. 4(h)(2) (incorporating Rule 4(f) for service made outside the United States). One district court held that service need only "provide[] the fair notice required by due process," but that case involved a respondent that had agreed to arbitrate in New York and was therefore subject to the court's personal jurisdiction by consent. *Lucent Techs.*, 2003 WL 402539, at *1. Judge Rakoff found that due process was satisfied when the respondent was served by: (1) hand on its arbitration counsel; (2) hand at its mailroom in Taiwan; (3) hand on its president's secretary; and (4) mail to its headquarters, with return receipt requested and received. *Id.*

Sections 9 and 12 are also silent about arbitrations sited outside the United States, as they only address service in cases in which an award was made in a U.S. district. Nothing in FAA Chapter 2 or 3 speaks to service. The most prudent practice would be for parties to adhere to Rule 4 when their action concerns an award made abroad. **13.26**

(IV) REQUIREMENT OF A WRITTEN ARBITRATION AGREEMENT

The New York Convention requires that parties seeking to recognize and enforce an arbitral award supply a copy of "an [arbitration] agreement in writing" pursuant to which the award was issued.[60] FAA Chapter 1 mandates that the arbitration agreement be filed by the party "moving for an order confirming, modifying, or correcting an award."[61] Some courts have held that the failure to supply an applicable agreement in writing is fatal to an enforcement action.[62] **13.27**

(V) ENFORCING A JUDGMENT CONFIRMING AN ARBITRAL AWARD

A petitioner who obtains a judgment confirming an arbitral award will hope that the respondent will pay the amount owed without further litigation. If the respondent does not do so, the petitioner can return to court for assistance in enforcing the judgment.[63] Under Federal Rule of Civil Procedure 69, federal courts apply the execution procedures of the state in which they sit,[64] and will allow discovery (including third-party discovery) in aid of execution.[65] Execution procedures in New York are governed by Article 52 of the CPLR.[66] **13.28**

---

[60] *See* N.Y. Convention, art. IV(1)(a) (incorporating Article II, which in turn provides that "[e]ach Contracting State shall recognize an agreement in writing"). The Second Circuit has held that the agreement, "whether it be an arbitration agreement or an arbitral clause in a contract, [must] be signed by the parties or contained in a series of letters or telegrams." Kahn Lucas Lancaster, Inc. v. Lark Int'l Ltd., 186 F.3d 210, 215 (2d Cir. 1999).

[61] 9 U.S.C. § 13. No similar requirement expressly applies to actions to vacate.

[62] *See* Czarina, L.L.C. v. W.F. Poe Syndicate, 358 F.3d 1286, 1292 (11th Cir. 2004). The Second Circuit has clarified that the failure to supply a written agreement does not affect a court's subject-matter jurisdiction but is an issue as to the merits of whether an award should be enforced. *See* Sarhank Group v. Oracle Corp., 404 F.3d 657, 660 n.2 (2d Cir. 2005).

[63] *See, e.g.*, Universitas Educ., LLC v. Nova Grp., Inc., No. 11 CIV. 1590, 2013 WL 57892 (S.D.N.Y. Jan. 4, 2013).

[64] Fed. R. Civ. P. 69(a)(1) ("A money judgment is enforced by a writ of execution, unless the court directs otherwise. The procedure on execution … must accord with the procedure of the state where the court is located, but a federal statute governs to the extent it applies.").

[65] Fed. R. Civ. P. 69(a)(2) ("In aid of the judgment or execution, the judgment creditor … may obtain discovery from any person—including the judgment debtor—as provided in these rules or by the procedure of the state where the court is located.").

[66] N.Y. CPLR 5201–5253. For example, CPLR 5222 addresses restraining notices; CPLR 5223 and 5224 address subpoenas that may assist a judgment creditor in determining the existence and location of the judgment debtor's property; CPLR 5228 provides for a receiver to assist in enforcing the judgment; CPLR 5230, 5232, 5233, 5236 and 5237 address execution on personal and real property.

13.29 *(b) Subject-matter jurisdiction* For international arbitral awards subject to the New York Convention, the FAA provides federal district courts with federal-question jurisdiction over "[a]n action or proceeding falling under the [New York] Convention" without regard to the amount in controversy.[67] FAA Section 302 extends this jurisdiction to actions falling under the Inter-American Convention.[68] These jurisdictional grants are notable because FAA Chapter 1, which governs domestic awards and arbitration agreements, creates substantive federal arbitration law but not federal-question jurisdiction.[69] Thus, parties seeking to enforce awards under FAA Chapter 1 in federal court must identify another source of subject-matter jurisdiction, such as diversity of citizenship or maritime jurisdiction.[70]

13.30 Although these jurisdictional complications need not trouble parties seeking to confirm international arbitral awards under FAA Section 203 or 302, they may be relevant to award-debtors seeking to vacate international arbitral awards in New York. As will be explained in more detail, subject-matter jurisdiction over actions to vacate international arbitral awards remains somewhat unclear.[71]

13.31 A commercial arbitral award "falls under" the New York and Inter-American Conventions when the legal relationship between the parties, "whether contractual or not,"[72] is not "entirely domestic in scope."[73] An award resolving a dispute entirely between U.S. citizens still falls under the Conventions if the legal relationship out of which the arbitral award arises "involves property located abroad, envisages performance or enforcement abroad, or has some other reasonable

[67] 9 U.S.C. § 203; Vaden v. Discover Bank, 556 U.S. 49, 59 n.9 (2009). It is beyond this chapter's scope to address enforcement of awards against foreign sovereigns, which is the subject of Chapter 14 of this book. The practitioner should be aware, however, that the Foreign Sovereign Immunities Act (FSIA), 28 U.S.C. §§ 1330, 1605–1607, contains jurisdictional provisions particular to such actions. For a further discussion of enforcement of awards against sovereigns, see R. Doak Bishop, ed., Enforcement of Arbitral Awards Against Sovereigns (2009).

[68] *See* 9 U.S.C. § 302.

[69] *See* Southland Corp. v. Keating, 465 U.S. 1, 15 n.9 (1984) ("While the [FAA] creates federal substantive law requiring the parties to honor arbitration agreements, it does not create any independent federal-question jurisdiction under 28 U.S.C. § 1331 ... or otherwise."); *see also* Durant, Nichols, Houston, Hodgson & Cortese-Costa P.C. v. Dupont, 565 F.3d 56, 63 (2d Cir. 2009).

[70] *See* Perpetual Secs., Inc. v. Tang, 290 F.3d 132, 140 (2d Cir. 2002); *see also* Victory Transp. Inc. v. Comisaria General de Abastecimientos y Transportes, 336 F.2d 354, 364 (2d Cir. 1964) (finding admiralty jurisdiction over an action to compel arbitration arising from a dispute between parties to a charter-party). The Supreme Court has held that, in actions to compel arbitration under FAA Section 4, "[a] federal court may 'look through' a § 4 petition to determine whether it is predicated on an action that 'arises under' federal law," but the court may not consider an anticipated counterclaim. Vaden v. Discover Bank, 556 U.S. 49, 62 (2009).

[71] *See generally* Chapter 6.E of this book for a discussion of arbitral jurisdiction in vacatur proceedings.

[72] 9 U.S.C. § 202.

[73] Smith/Enron Cogeneration Ltd. P'ship, Inc. v. Smith Cogeneration Int'l, Inc., 198 F.3d 88, 92–93 (2d Cir. 1999).

relation with one or more foreign states."[74] The FAA's "reasonable-relation" requirement was modeled on a provision of the Uniform Commercial Code that "permits the parties to a transaction that bears a reasonable relationship to any other state or nation to specify that the law of that state or nation will govern their rights and duties."[75] Awards made in the United States also fall under the Conventions when there is a sufficient connection to a foreign state.[76]

Although Sections 202 and 203 are broadly written, the Second Circuit has held that the New York Convention does not apply when the arbitration is among U.S. citizens and the sole foreign connection is that the agreement calls for arbitration abroad under foreign law.[77] As commentators have suggested, the court's reasoning is dubious because an agreement that calls for arbitration outside the United States appears to "envisage[] performance or enforcement abroad,"[78] and a refusal to apply the Convention to foreign awards, even where all parties are U.S. citizens, would violate U.S. obligations to recognize and enforce "awards made in the territory of [another] State."[79] However questionable the holding, it appears to remain Second Circuit law.[80] **13.32**

Consistent with Article I(3) of the New York Convention, the United States declared that it would apply the Convention only to awards made in the territory of a signatory state.[81] The United States similarly qualified its accession to the **13.33**

[74] 9 U.S.C. § 202; *see also id.* § 302 (applying Section 202 to Inter-American Convention cases). A corporation is a U.S. citizen under the statute if it is incorporated or has its principal place of business in the United States. *Id.* § 302.

[75] S. Rep. No. 91-702, at 6 (1970) (statement of Richard D. Kearney, Chairman of the Secretary of State's Advisory Committee on Private International Law) (noting that FAA Section 202's provision that the New York Convention applies to an award between U.S. parties if the parties' relationship has a reasonable connection to a foreign state was modeled on Section 1-105(1) of the Uniform Commercial Code).

[76] *See Bergesen*, 710 F.2d at 932–34 (New York Convention); *Productos Mercantiles*, 23 F.3d at 44 (Inter-American Convention).

[77] *See* Jones v. Sea Tow Servs. Freeport NY Inc., 30 F.3d 360, 365 (2d Cir. 1994).

[78] 9 U.S.C. § 202.

[79] *See* Born, 3 International Commercial Arbitration (2d ed. 2014), *supra* note 5, at 2952–53; Richard W. Hulbert, *Comment on a Proposed New Statute for International Arbitration*, 13 Am. Rev. Int'l Arb. 153, 158 (2002); Alan Scott Rau, *The New York Convention in American Courts*, 7 Am. Rev. Int'l Arb. 213, 242–51 (1996). Professor Rau suggests that Section 202 defines awards that the United States considers to be "nondomestic" within the terms of New York Convention Article I(1), but that awards made outside the United States need not comply with Section 202 because they always fall under the Convention and therefore provide federal courts with subject-matter jurisdiction under FAA Section 203. *See* Rau, *The New York Convention in American Courts, supra*, at 248–50. Both Professor Rau's interpretation and a construction that would apply Section 202 to foreign awards because the parties' relationship calls for performance abroad would comport with the longstanding principle that "an act of congress ought never to be construed to violate the law of nations if any other possible construction remains." Murray v. Schooner Charming Betsy, 6 U.S. (2 Cranch) 64, 118 (1804).

[80] *See* Best Concrete Mix Corp. v. Lloyd's of London Underwriters, 413 F. Supp. 2d 180, 188 (E.D.N.Y. 2006) (relying on *Jones* to define scope of jurisdiction in Convention case).

[81] *See* N.Y. Convention, art. I(3) ("When signing, ratifying or acceding to this Convention ... any State may on the basis of reciprocity declare that it will apply the Convention to the recognition and

Inter-American Convention.[82] The place at which an award is "made" is the place "designated for the arbitration in the agreement to arbitrate; if no place is mentioned, the place of the award is determined in accordance with the agreement to arbitrate by the arbitrators" or by the authority that is designated to appoint the arbitrators.[83]

13.34 Accordingly, FAA Sections 203 and 302 would not provide subject-matter jurisdiction to enforce an award made in a state which is not a party to either the New York or Inter-American Convention.[84] It is irrelevant for jurisdictional purposes that the *parties* to an action under the New York or Inter-American Conventions are not nationals of states that have acceded to the treaties.[85] However, when the court has jurisdiction under Sections 203 and 302, the nationality of the parties is relevant to determining whether the New York or Inter-American Convention is controlling in the action.[86]

13.35 There is some uncertainty in the Second Circuit as to the scope of jurisdiction in Convention cases. In particular, neither the New York nor the Inter-American Convention provides grounds to vacate an arbitral award; they only provide grounds to refuse enforcement of an award.[87] The question therefore arises whether a court has jurisdiction pursuant to FAA Sections 203 and 302 over an action to vacate an award.

13.36 The authority to vacate or annul an award is distinct from the power to refuse recognition of an award. In *Yusuf Ahmed Alghanim & Sons v. Toys "R" Us, Inc.*, the Second Circuit held that "the [New York] Convention mandates very different regimes for the review of arbitral awards (1) in the state in which, or under the law of which, the award was made, and (2) in other states where recognition and enforcement are sought."[88] The court noted that "many commentators and foreign

enforcement of awards made only in the territory of another Contracting State."); N.Y. Convention, 21 U.S.T. 2517 (declaration of the United States of America). Although Article I(3) and the U.S. reciprocity declaration limit recognition to "awards made … in the territory of another Contracting State," courts have held that this language merely means that the United States will not apply the Convention to awards made in nonsignatory states, not that the Convention is inapplicable to U.S. awards. *See, e.g., Productos Mercantiles*, 23 F.3d at 44; *see also* Rau, *The New York Convention in American Courts*, *supra* note 79, at 225–28 (discussing interpretation of reciprocity declaration).

[82] *See* 9 U.S.C. § 304 (codifying declaration as to Inter-American Convention).

[83] Restatement (Third) of Foreign Relations Law § 487 cmt. b (1987).

[84] *See* Ministry of Def. of Islamic Republic of Iran v. Gould Inc., 887 F.2d 1357, 1363 (9th Cir. 1989) (holding that the reciprocity declaration limits courts' jurisdiction under FAA Section 203).

[85] *See* Restatement (Third) of Foreign Relations Law § 487 cmt. b ("[T]he critical element is the place of the award: if that place is in the territory of a party to the [New York] Convention, all other Convention states are required to recognize and enforce the award, *regardless of the citizenship or domicile of the parties to the arbitration*." (emphasis added)).

[86] *See* 9 U.S.C. § 305.

[87] *See* N.Y. Convention, art. V ("[r]ecognition and enforcement of the award may be refused"); Inter-American Convention, art. 5 ("[t]he recognition and execution of the decision may be refused").

[88] 126 F.3d at 23.

courts have concluded that an action to set aside an award can be brought only under the domestic law of the arbitral forum, and can never be made under the Convention."[89] The Second Circuit built upon this reasoning in *Karaha Bodas Co. v. Perusahaan Pertambangan Minyak Dan Gas Bumi Negara*, in which it suggested that the New York Convention contemplates that only the state in which the award was made has authority to set aside an award: "[T]he country in which, or under the [arbitration] law of which, [an] award was made is said to have *primary* jurisdiction over the arbitration award. All other signatory States are *secondary* jurisdictions, in which parties can only contest whether the State should enforce the arbitral award."[90] Courts outside the Second Circuit have expressly held that "a United States court sitting in secondary jurisdiction lacks subject matter jurisdiction over claims seeking to vacate, set aside, or modify a foreign arbitral award."[91]

Because FAA Sections 203 and 302 only provide jurisdiction over actions that fall under the Conventions, and an action to vacate an award falls under national law, not the Conventions, some courts have indicated that Chapters 2 and 3 do not provide subject-matter jurisdiction over an action to vacate an award.[92] The Second Circuit, however, in a recent decision involving a petition to vacate an award made in the United States, stated, without analysis, that "the district court had subject-matter jurisdiction under 9 U.S.C. § 203, which *provides federal jurisdiction* over actions to confirm *or vacate* an arbitral award that is governed by the … New York Convention."[93] The court did not mention *Karaha Bodas* or otherwise address the argument that vacatur is permissible only under national law, not under the Convention. To date, no Second Circuit decision has attempted to reconcile these analyses. **13.37**

[89] *Id.* at 22.

[90] 500 F.3d at 115 n.1 (*quoting Karaha Bodas Co.*, 335 F.3d at 364 (internal quotation marks omitted)); *see also* Int'l Shipping Co. v. Hydra Offshore, Inc., 875 F.2d 388, 391 n.5 (2d Cir. 1989) (approving district court's decision that New York Convention did not apply to action to vacate an award).

[91] Gulf Petro Trading Co. v. Nigerian Nat'l Petroleum Corp., 512 F.3d 742, 753 (5th Cir. 2008); *see also* M&C Corp. v. Erwin Behr GmbH & Co., 87 F.3d 844, 847–48 (6th Cir. 1996) (holding that district courts have no jurisdiction to vacate awards made outside the United States); Int'l Standard Elec. Corp. v. Bridas Sociedad Anonima Petrolera, Industrial y Comercial, 745 F. Supp. 172, 178 (S.D.N.Y. 1990) ("[S]ince the … forum of the arbitration is Mexico, and the governing procedural law is that of Mexico, only the courts of Mexico have jurisdiction under the Convention to vacate the award.").

[92] *See, e.g.*, Ingaseosas Int'l Co. v. Aconcagua Investing Ltd., No. 09-23078-CIV, 2011 WL 500042, at *5 (S.D. Fla. Feb. 10, 2011) (holding that court does not have jurisdiction pursuant to 9 U.S.C. § 205 or 28 U.S.C. § 1331 over petition to vacate Convention award); HSMV Corp. v. ADI Ltd., 72 F. Supp. 2d 1122, 1127 n.8 (C.D. Cal. 1999) (noting that FAA Chapter 2 does not provide subject-matter jurisdiction over an action to vacate an award because "[t]he Convention contains no provision that expressly permits a losing party to initiate suit to vacate an award that would otherwise fall under the scope of the Convention"); Tesoro Petro. Corp. v. Asamera (S. Sumatra) Ltd., 798 F. Supp. 400, 404–05 (W.D. Tex. 1992) (holding that the New York Convention does not authorize a suit to vacate an award).

[93] Scandinavian Reinsurance Co. v. Saint Paul Fire & Marine Ins. Co., 668 F.3d 60, 71 (2d Cir. 2012) (emphasis added).

13.38 Meanwhile, some commentators have argued that courts should exercise jurisdiction under section 203 and 302 over petitions to vacate Convention awards. They have pointed out that an action to vacate a Convention award originally filed in state court would be subject to removal to federal court under FAA Section 205,[94] and have argued that it therefore would make no sense to interpret FAA Sections 203 and 302 not to provide original subject-matter jurisdiction over an annulment action.[95] In any event, even if it did not have original jurisdiction, a court would likely have supplemental jurisdiction over a party's cross-petition to vacate an award in an action to enforce an award falling under either Convention.[96]

13.39 In practice, an award that a court refuses to enforce under the New York or Inter-American Convention will have no legal effect in the United States.[97] As discussed above, however, the issue of subject-matter jurisdiction over an action to vacate a Convention award has strategic significance if a party that lost in a U.S.-based arbitration faces the threat of enforcement proceedings in an undesirable foreign jurisdiction. In those circumstances, a party might file an action to vacate in the United States and, if successful, use the U.S. judgment as a defense to enforcement abroad. As discussed, the Conventions permit refusal of enforcement in secondary jurisdictions when an award "has been set aside or suspended by a competent authority of the country in which, or under the law of which, that award was made."[98]

(c) Personal jurisdiction

(I) THE NEED TO ESTABLISH A BASIS FOR JURISDICTION

13.40 It might be argued that the application of the New York or Inter-American Convention to an international arbitral award obviates any need to demonstrate personal jurisdiction because the Conventions' grounds for refusing recognition are exclusive,[99] and lack of personal jurisdiction is not among them.[100]

---

[94] *See* 9 U.S.C. § 205 (providing for removal when an action "relates to an arbitration agreement or award falling under the Convention").

[95] *See* Marc J. Goldstein, *International Legal Developments in Review: 1998 Business Transactions & Disputes*, 33 INT'L LAW. 389, 393 (1999).

[96] *See* 28 U.S.C. § 1367(a); *cf. Ingaseosas Int'l Co.*, 2011 WL 500042, at *5 (where a petition to vacate is filed first, and petition to confirm is subsequently filed as a cross-motion, court does not have supplemental jurisdiction over petition to vacate).

[97] *See* Hulbert, *supra* note 79, at 157.

[98] N.Y. Convention, art. V(1)(e); *see also* Inter-American Convention, art. 5(1)(e).

[99] *Encyclopaedia Universalis*, 403 F.3d at 90.

[100] Some commentators have argued that rejecting actions to enforce Convention awards for lack of personal jurisdiction and other grounds not found in the Conventions (for example, *forum non conveniens*) violates U.S. treaty obligations. *See, e.g.*, William W. Park & Alexander A. Yanos, *Treaty Obligations and National Law: Emerging Conflicts in International Arbitration*, 58 HASTINGS L.J. 251 (2006); Linda Silberman, *International Arbitration: Comments from a Critic*, 13 AM. REV. INT'L ARB. 9, 15–16 (2002). Article III of the New York Convention does provide that "Contracting State[s] shall recognize arbitral awards as binding and *enforce them in accordance with the rules of procedure*" of the state in which enforcement is sought, N.Y. Convention, art. III (emphasis added), but commentators have argued that Article III's "reference to 'rules of

The Second Circuit has held, however, that personal jurisdiction over an award-debtor is a prerequisite to an action to confirm an award.[101] The court reasoned that U.S. courts are of limited jurisdiction and may not exercise jurisdiction over parties unless both statutory and constitutional requirements are met.[102] The Second Circuit also rejected the argument that Article V of the New York Convention prohibits U.S. courts from refusing to confirm awards based on lack of personal jurisdiction. The court explained that even though Article V provides the exclusive means to decline to enforce an award under the Convention, "Article V's exclusivity ... does nothing to alter the fundamental requirement of jurisdiction over the party against whom enforcement is being sought."[103]

The First,[104] Third,[105] Fourth,[106] Fifth,[107] and Ninth Circuits[108] have also held that a petitioner in an action falling under the Conventions must establish personal jurisdiction over the respondent. **13.41**

The following sections discuss three means to establish personal jurisdiction in an arbitration case: (1) jurisdiction by consent, (2) jurisdiction through minimum contacts, and (3) *quasi in rem* jurisdiction. **13.42**

(II) JURISDICTION BY CONSENT

Personal jurisdiction may be established by consent where the parties have expressly consented to jurisdiction in an arbitration agreement. For example, such language might state: "[The parties] consent to the jurisdiction of the state and federal courts in the City of New York for the purpose of ... enforcing any award."[109] Courts in the Second Circuit would likely construe such consent as applying to actions to vacate as well as to confirm awards because, in the Second Circuit's view, "it is irrational to consent to jurisdiction in a court for purposes of confirming an award but not for purposes of vacating all or part of it."[110] **13.43**

procedure' relates simply to formalities for an application to confirm or enforce, including fees and the pro forma structure of the request," and that "there is no evidence that the language was intended to incorporate doctrines that permit or require courts to prune their dockets in normal commercial litigation." Park & Yanos, *supra*, at 259, 262.

[101] *See* Frontera Res. Azer. Corp. v. State Oil Co. of Azer. Republic, 582 F.3d 393, 397–98 (2d Cir. 2009).

[102] *See id.*

[103] *Id.* at 397.

[104] *See* InterGen N.V. v. Grina, 344 F.3d 134, 142 (1st Cir. 2003).

[105] *See* Telcordia Tech, Inc. v. Telkom SA, 458 F.3d 172, 178-79 (3d Cir. 2006).

[106] *See* Base Metal Trading, Ltd. v. OJSC "Novokuznetsky Aluminum Factory," 283 F.3d 208, 212 (4th Cir. 2002).

[107] *See* First Inv. Corp. of Marshall Islands v. Fujian Mawei Shipbuilding, Ltd., 703 F.3d 742, 748 (5th Cir. 2012).

[108] *See* Glencore Grain Rotterdam B.V. v. Shivnath Rai Harnarain Co., 284 F.3d 1114, 1128 (9th Cir. 2002).

[109] *D.H. Blair*, 462 F.3d at 103; *see* Chapter 3.B of this book.

[110] *Id.* at 104.

13.44 A respondent may also be found to have waived objections to personal jurisdiction by virtue of a contractual forum-selection clause. In *Bank Julius Baer & Co. v. Waxfield, Ltd.*,[111] the Second Circuit interpreted a forum-selection clause providing that the parties "irrevocably submit[] to the jurisdiction of any New York State or Federal court sitting in New York City" as a waiver of any objection to personal jurisdiction in an action to compel arbitration.[112] The court explained:

> The Forum Selection Clause merely requires [the parties] to submit to suit in the courts of New York. It may be read, consistent with the Arbitration Agreement, in such a way that [the parties] are required to arbitrate their disputes, but that, to the extent [a party] files suit in a court of New York—for example, to enforce an arbitral award or to challenge the validity or application of the arbitration agreement—[the other party] will not challenge either jurisdiction or venue.[113]

13.45 The federal common-law rule that doubts about arbitrability should be resolved in favor of arbitration appears to have influenced this result.[114] Such a presumption in favor of arbitration has since been ruled inapplicable to the question the *Bank Julius Baer* court faced—whether the parties had agreed to arbitrate.[115]

13.46 In the absence of express consent, courts have found language in arbitration agreements to constitute implied consent to personal jurisdiction. As the Fifth Circuit has explained, "in certain circumstances, an arbitration agreement may alter an otherwise decisive jurisdictional analysis by evidencing a nonresident's implied consent to personal jurisdiction."[116] In the Second Circuit, "[a] party who agrees to arbitrate in a particular jurisdiction consents ... to personal jurisdiction [and] venue of the courts within that jurisdiction."[117] Although the majority of cases applying this rule involve petitions to compel arbitration, it is arguable that the rule should apply in enforcement and vacatur actions as well; at least two New York district courts have so held.[118]

[111] 424 F.3d 278 (2d Cir. 2005), *described as abrogated in part on other grounds*, Goldman, Sachs & Co. v. Golden Empire Sch. Fin. Auth., 764 F.3d 210, 215 (2d Cir. 2014).

[112] *Id.* at 282, 285.

[113] *Id.* at 285.

[114] *See id.*

[115] *See* Applied Energetics, Inc. v. NewOak Capital Markets, LLC, 645 F.3d 522, 526 (2d Cir. 2011) (explaining that, under Granite Rock Co. v. International Brotherhood of Teamsters, 561 U.S. 287 (2010), "while doubts concerning the scope of an arbitration clause should be resolved in favor of arbitration, the presumption does not apply to disputes concerning whether an agreement to arbitrate has been made").

[116] Freudensprung v. Offshore Tech. Servs., Inc., 379 F.3d 327, 345 (5th Cir. 2004).

[117] Doctor's Assocs. v. Stuart, 85 F.3d 975, 983 (2d Cir. 1996); *see also* Merrill Lynch, Pierce, Fenner & Smith Inc. v. Lecopulos, 553 F.2d 842, 844 (2d Cir. 1977); *Victory Transp. Inc.*, 336 F.2d at 363–64.

[118] *See* Lucent Technologies, Inc. v. Tatung Co., No. 02 CIV. 8107, 2003 WL 402539 (S.D.N.Y. Feb. 20, 2003) (petition to confirm); Marine Trading Ltd. v. Naviera Comercial Naylamp S.A., 879 F. Supp. 389, 391 (S.D.N.Y. 1995) (petition to confirm; concluding that respondent had consented to personal jurisdiction in New York courts by agreeing to arbitration in New York and to court enforcement of award, given that Convention "contemplates court enforcement in the venue in which the arbitration takes place"). Note, however, that in a case concerning an award issued in an arbitration seated in Geneva, the Second Circuit held that consent to court enforcement "in

Finally, it may be argued that the mere fact of agreeing to arbitrate in the territory of a country which is a party to the New York or Inter-American Convention waives objections to the jurisdiction of any signatory nation's courts. The Fifth and D.C. Circuits have rejected this argument.[119] As explained later, however, it is arguable that consent to arbitrate in a New York Convention jurisdiction should affect whether a party should reasonably anticipate being haled into a U.S. court in a recognition action.[120] **13.47**

(III) JURISDICTION THROUGH MINIMUM CONTACTS

Where no argument is available that a respondent has consented to personal jurisdiction, either expressly or impliedly, a New York court considering an enforcement action involving an international arbitral award will apply a traditional personal-jurisdiction analysis to determine whether it has personal jurisdiction over the respondent. To establish jurisdiction over an out-of-state defendant, a plaintiff must demonstrate that: (1) the defendant is "subject to jurisdiction under the law of the forum state," and (2) the exercise of jurisdiction would comport with constitutional due process.[121] This test applies in cases that are based on federal question jurisdiction and in those based on diversity jurisdiction.[122] This section discusses the application of that test in actions to challenge and enforce international arbitral awards. **13.48**

With respect to the first prong of the test, the requirements differ somewhat depending on the basis for subject matter jurisdiction. Cases based on diversity jurisdiction rely on the applicable statute of the forum state to establish jurisdiction. In New York, the relevant statute—C.P.L.R. 302(a), commonly referred to as the "long-arm statute"—sets out circumstances which will permit a New York court to exercise personal jurisdiction over a party, such as where the defendant transacts business within the state.[123] **13.49**

Cases grounded in federal question jurisdiction, such as actions to enforce an award falling under the Conventions, can look to both federal and state law for a **13.50**

any court having jurisdiction over the award" did not constitute contractual consent to personal jurisdiction in New York. *See* Sonera Holdings B.V. v. Çukurova Holding A.Ş, 750 F.3d 221, 226–27 (2d Cir. 2014).

[119] *See First Inv. Corp. of Marshall Islands*, 703 F.3d at 752 n.6; Creighton Ltd. v. Gov't of Qatar, 181 F.3d 118, 126–27 (D.C. Cir. 1999); *see also* Int'l Commercial Disputes Comm. of Ass'n of Bar of City of N.Y., *Lack of Jurisdiction and Forum Non Conveniens as Defenses to the Enforcement of Foreign Arbitral Awards*, 15 Am. Rev. Int'l Arb. 407, 415–16 (2004) ("NYC Bar Report").

[120] *See* section B.1(c)(iv) of this chapter, *infra*.

[121] Sonera Holding B.V. v. Cukurova Holding A.S., 750 F.3d 221, 224 (2d Cir. 2014).

[122] *See id.* (discussing the test for personal jurisdiction in cases based on federal question jurisdiction); Metro. Life Ins. Co. v. Robertson-Ceco Corp., 84 F.3d 560, 567 (2d Cir. 1996) (discussing the same for diversity actions).

[123] *See* N.Y. CPLR 302(a). The Second Circuit has held that "New York contacts underlying a contract that provides for arbitration have the requisite relationship under section 302(a)(1) to a claim challenging the results of that arbitration." *Sole Resort*, 450 F.3d at 104.

statutory basis for personal jurisdiction. Federal Rule of Civil Procedure 4(k)(2) states that, if the respondent is not subject to the jurisdiction of *any* U.S. state and the claim arises under federal law, the petitioner may establish personal jurisdiction through proper service of process, if "exercising jurisdiction is consistent with the United States Constitution and laws."[124] In such cases, the constitutionality of jurisdiction turns on the respondent's contacts with the United States as a whole, not just New York.[125] Rule 4(k)(2) acts as a kind of federal long-arm statute which can satisfy the first, statutory prong of the test for personal jurisdiction. Given that Rule 4(k)(2) only applies in limited circumstances, however, courts will more often look to the applicable state statute—such as the New York long-arm statute—as a basis of personal jurisdiction.[126]

13.51 It should be noted that Rule 4 also provides that service of process establishes personal jurisdiction "when authorized by a federal statute."[127] FAA Section 9 provides that "[n]otice of [an] application [to enforce an award] shall be served upon the adverse party, *and thereupon the court shall have jurisdiction of such party* as though he had appeared generally in the proceeding."[128] Some have argued that this provision, which would apply to cases under FAA Chapters 2 and 3 pursuant to FAA Sections 208 and 307,[129] authorizes personal jurisdiction in actions to enforce awards.[130] The Second Circuit has agreed that Section 9 is a personal-jurisdiction statute.[131] A number of district courts in New York have accepted this view.[132]

13.52 Even if Section 9 does contain a statutory grant of personal jurisdiction, it likely does not authorize international service of process.[133] The statute authorizes service in "any district within which the adverse party may be found."[134] Thus, unless

[124] Fed. R. Civ. P. 4(k)(2); *see also* Glencore Grain Rotterdam B.V. v. Shivnath Rai Harnarain Co., 284 F.3d 1114, 1126–27 (9th Cir. 2002).

[125] Dardana Ltd. v. Yuganskneftegaz, 317 F.3d 202, 207 (2d Cir. 2003).

[126] *See Sonera Holding*, 750 F.3d at 224.

[127] Fed. R. Civ. P. 4(k)(1)(C).

[128] 9 U.S.C. § 9 (emphasis added).

[129] *See id.* § 208 ("Chapter 1 applies to actions and proceedings brought under this chapter to the extent that [Chapter 1] is not in conflict with [Chapter 2] or the [New York] Convention."), § 307 (same with regard to FAA Chapter 3 and the Inter-American Convention).

[130] *See* Gary B. Born, International Commercial Arbitration 891 (2d ed. 2001).

[131] *See* Reed & Martin, Inc. v. Westinghouse Elec. Corp., 439 F.2d 1268, 1276–77 (2d Cir. 1971) (upholding personal jurisdiction because Section 9 "provides for a specific means of obtaining personal jurisdiction ... which procedures were followed here").

[132] *See, e.g.*, Stolt-Nielsen Transp. Group B.V. v. Edible Oil Trading Corp., No. 06 Civ. 0703 (NRB), 2007 WL 194182, at *2 n.6 (S.D.N.Y. Jan. 24, 2007); Hausman v. Earlswood Enters., Ltd., No. 95 Civ. 9088 (JSM), 1996 WL 527335, at *6 (S.D.N.Y. Sept. 16, 1996); LeJacq Pub., Inc. v. Am. Soc'y Contemporary Medicine, Surgery & Ophthalmology, No. 88 Civ. 7242 (MJL), 1989 WL 37673, at *3 (S.D.N.Y. Apr. 11, 1989).

[133] *See Marine Trading Ltd.*, 879 F. Supp. at 391 (holding that Section 9 "does not provide for service ... at any location that does not lie within a judicial district of the United States").

[134] 9 U.S.C. § 9. By contrast, statues such as Section 12 of the Clayton Act, which permit worldwide service, state that a defendant may be served "wherever it may be found." 15 U.S.C. § 22; *see also id.* § 77v(a).

a petitioner can establish that the respondent can be "found" in a U.S. district, Section 9 will not provide a basis for establishing personal jurisdiction.

The second prong of the test asks whether the exercise of personal jurisdiction comports with constitutional due process.[135] "Due process mandates that a 'defendant's conduct and connection with the forum State are such that he should reasonably anticipate being haled into court there.'"[136] Whether the relevant contacts are those with the state or the nation, the constitutional test looks to whether the defendant has "certain minimum contracts [with the state or the nation] ... such that the maintenance of the suit does not offend traditional notions of fair play and substantial justice."[137] **13.53**

A petitioner can establish constitutionally-sufficient contacts with a state as a matter either of "specific jurisdiction" or of "general jurisdiction." Specific jurisdiction "depends on an affiliatio[n] between the forum and the underlying controversy, principally, activity or an occurrence that takes place in the forum State and is therefore subject to the State's regulation."[138] Under recent Supreme Court jurisprudence, general jurisdiction exists when a party's affiliations with the state are "so 'continuous and systematic' as to render them essentially at home in the forum State[139]—a high bar unlikely to be met outside the party's domicile (which, for corporations, is the state in which it is incorporated and the state in which it has its principal place of business).[140] The Second Circuit has recently applied these standards in the enforcement context.[141] **13.54**

(IV) *QUASI IN REM* JURISDICTION

Personal jurisdiction in an action to enforce an international arbitral award may also be premised on the respondent's ownership of property in the forum state, without any other contacts with the forum. This is so even where the property has no relation to the parties' controversy, other than as a means to satisfy an award. **13.55**

---

135 *See* Best Van Lines, Inc. v. Walker, 490 F.3d 239, 242 (2d Cir. 2007).

136 *In re* Terrorist Attacks on Sept. 11, 2001, 538 F.3d 71, 93 (2d Cir. 2008) (*quoting* World-Wide Volkswagen Corp. v. Woodson, 444 U.S. 286, 297 (1980)).

137 Bank Brussels Lambert v. Fiddler Gonzales & Rodriquez, 305 F.3d 120, 127 (2d Cir. 2002) (internal quotation marks omitted).

138 Goodyear Dunlop Tires Operations, S.A. v. Brown, 131 S. Ct. 2846, 2851 (2011) (internal quotation marks omitted).

139 *Goodyear Dunlop Tires Operations, S.A.*, 131 S. Ct. at 2851 (citation omitted).

140 Daimler AG v. Bauman, 134 S. Ct. 746, 761 n.19 (2014) (leaving open possibility of general jurisdiction outside states of incorporation and principal place of business as an "exceptional case").

141 Sonera Holdings B.V. v. Çukurova Holding A.Ş, 750 F.3d 221, 224–26 (2d Cir. 2014). In light of the Supreme Court's decision in *Daimler*, which made it more difficult to establish general jurisdiction over an award-debtor, commentators have called into question the requirement that personal jurisdiction must be established over the award-debtor in an action to enforce an arbitral award. *See, e.g.*, John Fellas, *Enforcing Foreign Arbitral Awards: Should Jurisdictional Defenses Apply?* New York Law Journal, Volume 253, No. 25, February 6, 2015.

13.56 In *Glencore Grain Rotterdam B.V. v. Shivnath Rai Harnarain Co.*, the Ninth Circuit determined that "[c]onsiderable authority supports [the] position that [a party] can enforce [an arbitral] award against ... property in the forum even if that property has no relationship to the underlying controversy between the parties."[142] The *Glencore* court relied on *Shaffer v. Heitner*,[143] in which the Supreme Court observed in dicta:

> Once it has been determined ... that the defendant is a debtor of the plaintiff, there would seem to be no unfairness in allowing an action to realize on that debt in a State where the defendant has property, whether or not that State would have jurisdiction to determine the existence of the debt as an original matter.[144]

13.57 The Fourth Circuit came to a different conclusion in *Base Metal Trading, Ltd. v. OJSC "Novokuznetsky Aluminum Factory,"* holding that the "basic [personal-jurisdiction] analysis is not altered when the defendant's property is found in the forum state."[145] The Fourth Circuit read *Shaffer* to permit property ownership to be considered as part of the inquiry, but not to resolve the inquiry entirely. Under that view, when claims to the property are the source of the dispute, "it would be unusual for the State where the property is located not to have jurisdiction."[146] But, the Fourth Circuit concluded, when the property is unrelated to the cause of action, the property alone is insufficient to convey jurisdiction.[147]

13.58 The Second Circuit appears to agree with the Ninth Circuit. In *Frontera Resources Azerbaijan Corp. v. State Oil Co. of the Azerbaijan Republic*, the court noted the suggestion in *Shaffer* that personal jurisdiction could be based on a defendant's property in the forum and held that the district court had "appropriately considered whether it could assert jurisdiction over [the respondent's] property."[148] Thus, it appears that courts in the Second Circuit can assert *quasi in rem* jurisdiction over award-debtors that possess assets in the forum state.

13.59 This rule makes sense in the arbitration context. An award-debtor that consented to arbitrate in a New York Convention jurisdiction should reasonably anticipate being haled into court in an action to recognize the award in any other New York Convention jurisdiction where the award-debtor has assets. After all, the portability of an award under the Convention—which avoids the need to relitigate in various jurisdictions—is a central reason for the attractiveness of arbitration as a form of international commercial dispute resolution. That portability is also a benefit (and potential burden) of which parties to an arbitration agreement are

---

142 284 F.3d at 1127.
143 433 U.S. 186 (1977).
144 *Id.* at 210 n.36.
145 283 F.3d at 213.
146 *Id.* (*quoting Shaffer*, 433 U.S. at 207).
147 *Id.*
148 582 F.3d at 398.

presumably aware. As the Third Circuit has suggested, "[a]lthough the New York Convention does not diminish the Due Process constraints in asserting jurisdiction over a nonresident alien, the desire to have portability of arbitral awards prevalent in the Convention influences the answer as to whether [the respondent] 'reasonably anticipate[d] being haled into'" a court in the forum.[149]

(d) Establishing venue The FAA provides that venue is proper in a Convention case in any court "in which[,] save for the arbitration[,] an action or proceeding with respect to the controversy between the parties could be brought, or in such court for the district and division which embraces the place designated in the agreement as the place of arbitration if such place is within the United States."[150] **13.60**

Accordingly, in actions to recognize an international arbitral award subject to the Conventions, venue would be proper in: (1) the district in which the parties' underlying dispute could have been litigated pursuant to the general venue statute, 28 U.S.C. § 1391, *or* (2) the federal district that served as the legal seat of the arbitration.[151] With respect to an action to vacate an award, FAA Chapter 1 contains its own venue provisions. Section 10 states that venue in an action to vacate an award is proper in "the United States court in and for the district wherein the award was made."[152] The Supreme Court has held that FAA Chapter 1's venue provision is permissive, not exclusive, so that an action under Chapter 1 may be brought "*either* where the award was made or in any district proper under the general venue statute."[153] **13.61**

District courts in the Second Circuit may apply the doctrine of *forum non conveniens* to decline jurisdiction over an action falling under the Conventions even when venue is otherwise appropriate.[154] *Forum non conveniens* is a common-law doctrine that permits a district court to decline to exercise jurisdiction over a case even where the case satisfies the formal requirements for venue.[155] The rationale for applying *forum non conveniens* in arbitration cases is found in Article III of the New York Convention, which provides: **13.62**

> Each Contracting State shall recognize arbitral awards as binding and enforce them in accordance with the rules of procedure of the territory where the award is relied upon ... There shall not be imposed substantially more onerous conditions ... on the recognition or enforcement of arbitral awards to which this Convention applies than are imposed on the recognition or enforcement of domestic arbitral awards.[156]

---

149 *Telcordia Tech*, 458 F.3d at 178–79 (*quoting World-Wide Volkswagen Corp.*, 444 U.S. at 297).

150 9 U.S.C. § 204.

151 *See* Am. Constr. Mach. & Equip. Corp. v. Mechanised Constr. of Pak. Ltd., No. 85 Civ. 3765 (JFK), 1986 WL 2973, at *4–5 (S.D.N.Y. Mar. 5, 1986).

152 9 U.S.C. § 10.

153 *Cortez Byrd Chips, Inc.*, 529 U.S. at 195 (emphasis added).

154 *See* Monegasque de Reassurances S.A.M. v. Nak Naftogaz of Ukr., 311 F.3d 488, 496–97 (2d Cir. 2002).

155 *See* Sinochem Int'l Co. v. Malaysia Int'l Shipping Corp., 549 U.S. 422, 428–29 (2007).

156 N.Y. Convention, art. III.

The Inter-American Convention contains a similar provision.[157]

13.63 Based on this language, the Second Circuit has taken the view that the New York Convention does not prohibit application of *forum non conveniens* as a basis to refuse to compel arbitration or enforce an international arbitral award.[158] Commentators have challenged this reasoning,[159] but it remains the law of the Second Circuit.[160]

13.64 Thus, a respondent in the federal courts in New York may move to dismiss an enforcement action for *forum non conveniens* because the case can be heard in an alternative forum abroad and the balance of public and private interest factors supports overturning the petitioner's choice of forum.[161] In *Monegasque*, the Second Circuit affirmed dismissal of an action to enforce a Russian award because: (1) "the jurisdiction provided by the [New York] Convention [was] the only link between the parties and the United States"; (2) an adequate alternative forum for the enforcement action existed in the Ukraine; (3) the action involved a third party, the Ukraine itself, that was not a signatory to the arbitration agreement; and (4) resolving "the question of whether the Ukraine [was] bound as a non-signer of the ... agreement" required application of Ukrainian law.[162] It is arguable that *Monegasque* should be limited to cases in which there are nonsignatory respondents.[163]

13.65 *(e) Removal of enforcement proceedings from state to federal court* Where a petitioner brings an action to challenge or confirm an international arbitral award in state court, the FAA permits the removal of such actions to federal court. FAA Section 205, which is incorporated by reference into FAA Chapter 3 for cases under the Inter-American Convention,[164] provides:

> Where the subject matter of an action or proceeding pending in a State court relates to an arbitration agreement or award falling under the Convention, the defendant or the defendants may, at any time before the trial thereof, remove such action or proceeding to the district court of the United States for the district and division embracing the place where the action or proceeding is pending. The procedure for

---

[157] *See* Inter-American Convention, art. 4.

[158] *See Monegasque*, 311 F.3d at 495–96.

[159] *See, e.g.*, Fellas, *supra* note 141; Park & Yanos, *supra* note 100, at 262; NYC Bar Report, *supra* note 119, at 429–33. The NYC Bar Report supports the view, however, that "*[f]orum non conveniens* should be available as a defense in an action to enforce an award *against a non-party to the arbitration*." NYC Bar Report, *supra* note 119, at 433 (emphasis added).

[160] *See also* Figueiredo Ferraz E Engenharia de Projeto Ltda. v. Republic of Peru, 665 F.3d 384, 393–94 (2d Cir. 2011) (dismissing petition to confirm arbitral award covered by Inter-American Convention on *forum non conveniens* grounds).

[161] *See* Norex Petroleum Ltd. v. Access Indus., Inc., 416 F.3d 146, 153 (2d Cir. 2005).

[162] 311 F.3d at 498–501.

[163] *See* NYC Bar Report, *supra* note 119, at 433 (supporting the view that "*[f]orum non conveniens* should be available as a defense in an action to enforce an award against a non-party to the arbitration").

[164] 9 U.S.C. § 302.

removal of causes otherwise provided by law shall apply, except that the ground for removal provided in this section need not appear on the face of the complaint but may be shown in the petition for removal.[165]

Three aspects of the FAA removal provision are noteworthy: (1) it includes an exception to the well-pleaded complaint rule; (2) removal is permitted if an action "relates to" a Convention agreement or award; and (3) removal may be accomplished "at any time before trial." **13.66**

(I) EXCEPTION TO WELL-PLEADED COMPLAINT RULE

First, the FAA creates an exception to the well-pleaded complaint rule,[166] under which a state-court defendant normally cannot remove an action on federal-question grounds unless a federal cause of action appears on the face of the complaint.[167] The presence of a federal defense is insufficient.[168] The well-pleaded complaint rule ordinarily "makes the plaintiff the master of the claim; he or she may avoid federal jurisdiction by exclusive reliance on state law."[169] An exception to this rule applies when the complaint presents a "claim based on preempted state law."[170] Thus, when a state-court plaintiff bases its claim on state law that is completely preempted by federal law, the complaint necessarily raises a federal question and may be removed to federal court.[171] Section 205 eliminates the need to resolve any questions as to preemption in the removal context because a party can remove the case if it alleges a defense based on the Conventions, whether or not the Conventions were ever mentioned in the state-court action. **13.67**

(II) REMOVAL AUTHORIZED IF AN ACTION "RELATES TO" A CONVENTION AGREEMENT OR AWARD

The second notable feature of the FAA's removal provision is that removal is permitted whenever an action "*relates to* an arbitration *agreement or award* falling under" the Conventions.[172] In contrast, FAA Section 203 grants original jurisdiction over "an action or proceeding *falling under*" the Conventions.[173] Thus, while Section 203 requires that the action itself fall under the Conventions, Section 205 is written more broadly and permits removal of any action related to an arbitral agreement or award that falls under the Conventions. This difference in language could, in theory, be read to suggest that Congress granted federal courts greater removal jurisdiction over Convention-related cases than it granted **13.68**

---

165 *Id.* § 205.

166 *Vaden*, 556 U.S. at 59 n.9 ("FAA § 205 … overrides the well-pleaded complaint rule *pro tanto*.").

167 *See* Vera v. Saks & Co., 335 F.3d 109, 113 (2d Cir. 2003) (per curiam).

168 *See id.*

169 Caterpillar Inc. v. Williams, 482 U.S. 386, 392 (1987).

170 *Vera*, 335 F.3d at 113 (internal quotation marks omitted).

171 *See id.* at 113–14.

172 9 U.S.C. § 205 (emphasis added).

173 *Id.* § 203 (emphasis added).

the courts original jurisdiction over such cases. But it is difficult to imagine why Congress would have intended that result.[174]

13.69 Courts have generally interpreted Section 205 broadly. The Fifth Circuit has held that "whenever an arbitration agreement [or award] falling under the Convention could *conceivably* affect the outcome of the plaintiff's case, the agreement 'relates to' the plaintiff's suit."[175] That conclusion was based in part on a comparison to the bankruptcy-jurisdiction statute, which the Fifth Circuit has construed as providing for federal jurisdiction over any state proceeding that could conceivably affect the bankruptcy estate.[176] The Ninth Circuit has adopted the Fifth Circuit's approach, finding that "the phrase 'relates to' is plainly broad, and has been interpreted to convey sweeping removal jurisdiction in analogous statutes," and, moreover, that "[n]othing in § 205 urges a narrower construction."[177] Although the Second Circuit has not interpreted the "relates to" language in Section 205, it shares the Fifth Circuit's expansive view of bankruptcy jurisdiction and may therefore adopt the same test for Section 205.[178]

13.70 While district court interpretations of Section 205 in New York were, for a time, somewhat inconsistent, recent cases have moved toward adopting the broad approach of the Fifth Circuit in *Beiser*. In 2006, the district court in *Banco de Santander Central Hispano, S.A. v. Consalvi International Inc.*[179] appeared to adopt the *Beiser* standard. There, a petitioner had filed a claim in state court to vacate an arbitral award made in New York on the ground that the arbitrators acted in manifest disregard of Spanish law.[180] The defendant removed the case to federal court and the district court held that removal was proper under Section 205 (though the basis for the court's approval of removal is somewhat unclear).[181]

13.71 Most recently, in *Kolel Beth Yechiel Mechil of Tartikov, Inc. v. YLL Irrevocable Trust*,[182] the court based its holding that removal was proper upon *Beiser*'s broad interpretation of Section 205. The court found that "the contents of the Arbitration Agreement could 'conceivably' affect the outcome of the Removed Action because the allegations necessarily involve the Arbitration Agreement's provision for a neutral arbitrator, the proper procedures for the arbitration, and

---

174 *See, e.g.*, Born, International Commercial Arbitration (2d ed. 2001), *supra* note 130, at 383–84 (arguing that Sections 203 and 205 "probably were intended to have an identical meaning"); Goldstein, *supra* note 95, at 393 (maintaining that it would be nonsensical for Congress to have intended such a result). The legislative history of FAA Chapter 2 sheds no light on this issue. *See* H.R. Rep. No. 91-1181 (1970); S. Rep. No. 91-702 (1970).

175 Beiser v. Weyler, 284 F.3d 665, 669–70 (5th Cir. 2002).

176 *See id.* (relying on 28 U.S.C. § 1334(b)).

177 Infuturia Global Ltd. v. Sequus Pharms., Inc., 631 F.3d 1133, 1138 (9th Cir. 2011).

178 *See In re* Cuyahoga Equip. Corp., 980 F.2d 110, 114 (2d Cir. 1992).

179 425 F. Supp. 2d 421 (S.D.N.Y. 2006).

180 *See id.* at 422.

181 *See id.* at 433–34.

182 863 F. Supp. 2d 351, 356 (S.D.N.Y. 2012).

the Arbitration Decision itself."[183] In so holding, the court explicitly incorporated the Fifth Circuit's "conceivably affect" test into its reasoning.

(III) TIMING OF REMOVAL

Third, unlike the general removal statute, which requires removal within thirty days after service of the initial pleading or other paper from which it can be ascertained that the case is removable, Section 205 permits removal "at any time before trial."[184] Failure to remove the action before trial will result in remand.[185] Courts have construed "trial" to mean "adjudication of the entirety of the claim," whether or not by actual trial.[186] One district court in New York held that an action may not be removed after the state court has resolved all issues that would have required a hearing, whether or not the state court has resolved the entire dispute between the parties.[187] 28 U.S.C. § 1447(d), which provides that "[a]n order remanding a case back to the State court from which it was removed is not reviewable on appeal," applies to decisions remanding cases removed under Section 205.[188] **13.72**

2. Actions in New York State Courts

New York's Civil Practice Law and Rules (CPLR) contain several procedural provisions regarding actions to confirm and to vacate arbitral awards.[189] Because most international cases fall under the Conventions and are brought in, or removed to, federal court, case law is severely limited on the application of these provisions in the context of international arbitrations. Indeed, at the time of this writing, there are no reported New York state cases applying the New York or Inter-American Convention's grounds to resist enforcement of awards, and very few New York state cases that discuss those treaties at all. The following discussion of New York state procedure is based on New York state cases pertaining to domestic arbitrations, and applies with equal force to actions that are subject **13.73**

[183] *Kolel*, 863 F. Supp. 2d at 356.

[184] *Id.* at 427 (contrasting 9 U.S.C. § 205 and 28 U.S.C. § 1446(b)).

[185] LaFarge Corp. v. Venezolana de Cementos, S.A., 31 F.3d 70, 72 (2d Cir. 1994).

[186] *See id.* at 72–73 (holding that state-court resolution of petition for injunction in aid of arbitration, the only relief sought in the action, was the trial for purposes of Section 205).

[187] *See* Pan Atl. Group, Inc. v. Republic Ins. Co., 878 F. Supp. 630, 639–40 (S.D.N.Y. 1995). The petitioners in that case commenced a special proceeding under N.Y. CPLR 7502 to confirm an interim arbitral award and sought an order from the state court compelling the respondents to arbitrate. *See id.* at 633. The state court compelled the respondents to arbitrate—the only issue that could have required a hearing—but had not ruled on the motion to confirm the interim award. *See id.* at 639–40. The district court determined that Section 205 barred removal after *commencement* of trial, not after completion of trial, and that adjudication of the motion to compel was the beginning of trial for Section 205 purposes. *See id.* At least one other district court has disagreed with this reasoning. *See* Acosta v. Master Maint. & Constr., Inc., 52 F. Supp. 2d 699, 705 (M.D. La. 1999).

[188] *LaFarge*, 31 F.3d at 71.

[189] The CPLR refers to actions "to confirm," and thus this section uses that term. *See, e.g.*, N.Y. CPLR 7502.

to the FAA.[190] The substantive grounds for confirming or vacating international awards in state court are addressed later in this chapter.[191]

13.74 *(a) Form and location of action* CPLR 7502 instructs parties in a confirmation or vacatur action to initiate a special proceeding "in the county where at least one of the parties resides or is doing business or where the arbitration was held or is pending."[192] Similar to confirmation or vacatur actions in federal court, "[a] special proceeding is commenced by filing a petition."[193] The petitioner obtains an index number from the clerk of the court[194] and has 120 days to serve notice of the petition. Notice of a petition *to vacate* must be served no later than fifteen days after the ninety-day limitations period for such actions expires.[195] "Confirmation [of an award] may be opposed on the same grounds that provide a basis for a vacatur," however, "even if the ninety-day period [to move to vacate] has expired."[196]

13.75 It bears noting that, in the context of enforcement of foreign *judgments*, New York's Appellate Division, First Department, has held that a party seeking recognition in New York of a judgment issued either in another U.S. state or in a foreign country need not establish that the New York courts have personal jurisdiction over the judgment-debtor.[197] This rule stands in stark contrast to the federal appellate courts' position with respect to foreign arbitral awards,[198] a context to which the New York state courts do not appear to have applied the rule.[199]

13.76 *(b) Statute of limitations* New York law provides that an action to confirm must be made within one year after the award is delivered to the victorious party.[200]

---

[190] *See* Keilly v. Sands Bros., 803 N.Y.S.2d 385, 386 (N.Y. Sup. Ct. 2005) (finding that in a confirmation proceeding governed by the FAA but brought in state court, New York state procedural rules govern procedural issues such as service of process).

[191] *See* section C.3 of this chapter, *infra*.

[192] N.Y. CPLR 7502(a).

[193] *Id.* 304(a).

[194] *Id.* 306–a.

[195] *See id.* 306–b; *see also id.* 7511 (providing for ninety-day limitations period on petitions to vacate).

[196] N.Y. CPLR 7511(a) 1998 practice commentary (citing Karlan Constr. Co. v. Burdick Assocs. Owners Corp., 560 N.Y.S.2d 480, 481 (App. Div. 1990)). This is a significant difference between practice under the New York CPLR and the FAA. Under the FAA, the three-month time limit for initiating a vacatur action is absolute and applies even where the party seeking vacatur raises it as a defense to a petition to confirm an award. *See* Wallace v. Buttar, 378 F.3d 182, 197 (2d Cir. 2004) ("We have made clear that [, under the FAA,] 'a party may not raise a motion to vacate, modify or correct an arbitration award after the three month period has run, even when raised as a defense to a motion to confirm.' " (*quoting* Florasynth, Inc. v. Pickholz, 750 F.2d 171, 175 (2d Cir. 1984))).

[197] Abu Dhabi Comm. Bank PJSC v. Saad Trading, Contracting & Fin. Servs. Co., 986 N.Y.S.2d 454 (1st Dep't 2014).

[198] *See* section B.1(c) of this chapter, *supra*.

[199] For a critique of this difference between enforcement of foreign judgments and foreign arbitral awards, *see* Fellas, *supra*, note 141.

[200] N.Y. CPLR 7510.

This statute of limitations is shorter than the three years provided by federal law for actions to confirm Convention awards.[201] Although no court has decided whether the FAA's statute of limitations supersedes the New York statute of limitations in an action to confirm under federal law brought in state court, the U.S. Supreme Court has recognized that "where state courts entertain a federally created cause of action, the federal right cannot be defeated by the forms of local practice."[202] Moreover, New York courts routinely apply federal statutes of limitations to federal claims.[203] Therefore, the longer federal statute of limitations should apply in an action to confirm brought under the New York or Inter-American Convention.

The statute of limitations for a vacatur action under CPLR 7511 is ninety days after delivery of the award to the moving party.[204] This statute normally will not present a conflict with federal law because the FAA similarly provides three months for notice of an action to vacate under Section 10.[205] **13.77**

C. SUBSTANTIVE ISSUES INVOLVED IN CHALLENGING INTERNATIONAL ARBITRAL AWARDS IN NEW YORK

1. Grounds for Nonrecognition under the New York Convention

The "basic thrust" of the New York Convention "was to liberalize procedures for enforcing foreign arbitral awards."[206] Consistent with this pro-arbitration bias, the New York Convention requires only a few, simple steps on the part of the award-creditor to prove the existence of an enforceable international arbitral award. The party seeking recognition and enforcement of an award subject to the Convention need only supply to the court (1) the "duly authorized original award or a duly certified copy thereof," (2) the original arbitration agreement "or a duly certified copy thereof," and (3) if the award or arbitration agreement is in a language other than English, a certified translation of these documents.[207] **13.78**

---

201 *See* 9 U.S.C. §§ 207, 302.

202 Felder v. Casey, 487 U.S. 131, 138 (1988) (*quoting* Brown v. W. Ry. Co. of Ala., 338 U.S. 294, 296 (1949) (internal quotation marks omitted)).

203 *See, e.g.*, World-Link, Inc. v. Mezun.com, Inc., 827 N.Y.S.2d 642, 653 (Sup. Ct. 2006); Holder v. Gen. Motors Corp., 732 N.Y.S.2d 545, 548 (Sup. Ct. 2001).

204 *See* N.Y. CPLR 7511(a).

205 *See* 9 U.S.C. § 12.

206 Parsons & Whittemore Overseas Co. v. Societe Generale de l'Industrie du Papier, 508 F.2d 969, 973 (2d Cir. 1974).

207 N.Y. Convention, art. IV. Mindful of the pro-arbitration purposes of the New York Convention, courts in New York have resisted efforts to complicate the proof requirements of Article IV. *See, e.g., Bergesen*, 710 F.2d at 934 (rejecting claim that, under Article IV of the Convention, a petitioner is required to provide "a duly authenticated original [of the award and

13.79 Once these materials have been furnished to the court, and the petitioner has satisfied the requisite jurisdiction and venue requirements, the burden shifts to the party resisting recognition and enforcement.[208] Under Articles III and V of the New York Convention, the court "*shall* recognize arbitral awards as binding and enforce them in accordance with the rules of procedure of the territory where the award is relied upon"[209] unless (1) the party against whom the award is invoked provides "proof" that one of five grounds for nonrecognition exists;[210] or (2) the court decides that (a) the subject matter of the award is not capable of settlement by arbitration under the laws of the United States, or (b) the recognition or enforcement of the award would be contrary to the public policy of the United States.[211] "Given the strong public policy in favor of international arbitration, review of arbitral awards under the New York Convention is 'very limited ... in order to avoid undermining the twin goals of arbitration, namely, settling disputes efficiently and avoiding long and expensive litigation.' "[212]

13.80 Each of the grounds for nonrecognition under the New York Convention is discussed more fully in the following sections.[213] Importantly, none of them permits nonrecognition of an arbitral award on the ground that the tribunal's decision was simply wrong on the facts or the law.[214]

13.81 *(a) Absence of a valid arbitration agreement (Article V(1)(a))* Article V(1)(a) of the New York Convention provides that a court may refuse to recognize and enforce

---

arbitration agreement] or a duly certified copy of *a duly authenticated* original"; holding that copies of the award and agreement certified by an arbitrator are sufficient).

[208] Consistent with its pro-enforcement bias, the New York Convention places the burden on the party *resisting* enforcement of the award to establish that one of the exclusive grounds for nonrecognition in Article V the Convention applies. This was an important departure from the Geneva Convention, the predecessor to the New York Convention, which placed the burden of proof on the party seeking recognition and enforcement. *See Parsons & Whittemore*, 508 F.2d at 973.

[209] N.Y. Convention, art. III.

[210] *Id.*, art. V(1). In summary, these are: the absence of a valid arbitration agreement (art. V(1)(a)); the inability to present one's case (art. V(1)(b)); the award deals with a difference that falls outside the submission to arbitration (art. V(1)(c)); the arbitral procedure was not in accordance with the agreement of the parties (art. V(1)(d)); the award was set aside in the place in which it was made (art. V(1)(e)).

[211] *Id.*, art. V(2).

[212] *Encyclopaedia Universalis*, 403 F.3d at 90.

[213] This discussion focuses on the key aspects of the grounds for nonrecognition under the New York Convention and focuses on the law applicable in courts in New York. For a complete discussion of these grounds, including an analysis of common and civil-law jurisdictions around the world, see 3 Born, International Commercial Arbitration (2d ed. 2014), *supra* note 5, at 3443–717. Note that the grounds for nonrecognition under the Inter-American Convention are substantially similar.

[214] Note that in actions to confirm or vacate arbitral awards made in the United States, the express and implied terms of the FAA are available to vacate an arbitral award. *See Yusuf Ahmed*, 126 F.3d at 21. These grounds, which include a finding that the arbitral tribunal acted in "manifest disregard of the law," are not available in connection with the review of a foreign arbitral award under the New York Convention. *See id.* at 20.

an award where the parties to the arbitration agreement "were, under the law applicable to them, under some incapacity, or the said agreement is not valid under the law to which the parties have subjected it or, failing any indication thereon, under the law of the country where the award was made." Article V(1)(a) specifically cross-references Article II of the Convention, which requires contracting states to "recognize an agreement in writing under which the parties undertake to submit to arbitration all or any differences which have arisen or which may arise between them" and which are capable of being settled by arbitration.[215] Although most New York decisions in which defenses to recognition under Article V(1)(a) have been raised have rejected the defense,[216] some decisions have refused to recognize arbitral awards in circumstances where the existence of a valid agreement to arbitrate was not established.[217]

In U.S. case law, questions about an arbitral tribunal's jurisdiction are often referred to as questions of "arbitrability." U.S. courts have used this term to mean different things;[218] it can refer to whether: (1) a party is bound by an arbitration agreement; (2) an arbitration agreement is valid and legal; (3) the dispute at issue falls within the scope of a binding arbitration agreement; or (4) the dispute is of a type (*e.g.*, violation of a particular statute) that applicable law allows to be **13.82**

[215] N.Y. Convention, art. II.

[216] *See, e.g.*, Telenor Mobile Commc'ns AS v. Storm LLC, 524 F. Supp. 2d 332, 367–68 (S.D.N.Y. 2007), *aff'd*, 584 F.3d 396 (2d Cir. 2009) (rejecting Article V(1)(a) defense to recognition on the ground that the arbitration agreement was valid under the applicable law); Encyclopaedia Universalis, S.A. v. Encyclopaedia Britannica, Inc., No. 03 Civ. 4363 (SAS), 2003 WL 22881820, at *6–7 (S.D.N.Y. Dec. 4, 2003), *vacated in part on other grounds*, 403 F.3d 85 (2d Cir. 2005) (rejecting argument that arbitration agreement was invalid under New York state contract law); Overseas Cosmos, Inc. v. NR Vessel Corp., No. 97 Civ. 5898 (DC), 1997 WL 757041, at *2–3 & n.2 (S.D.N.Y. Dec. 8, 1997) (rejecting claim that arbitration agreement was invalid under English and U.S. law); Am. Constr. Mach. & Equip. Corp. v. Mechanised Constr. of Pak. Ltd., 659 F. Supp. 426, 429 (S.D.N.Y. 1987), *aff'd*, 828 F.2d 117 (2d Cir. 1987); (rejecting Article V(1)(a) defense to recognition on the ground that it "would require this Court to reverse one of the Arbitrator's express findings of law"); Buques Centroamericanos, S.A. v. Refinadora Costarricense de Petroleos, S.A., No. 87 Civ. 3256 (DNE), 1989 U.S. Dist. LEXIS 5429, at *2–4 (S.D.N.Y. May 18, 1989) (deferring to arbitrators' finding on the validity of the arbitration agreement and rejecting Article V(1)(a) defense to recognition).

[217] *See, e.g.*, *Sarhank*, 404 F.3d at 661–62 (vacating judgment confirming international arbitral award on the ground that there was no "clear and unmistakable evidence" that Oracle submitted the issue of arbitrability to the arbitrators, and remanding to district court for a determination whether Oracle had agreed to arbitrate).

[218] The term "arbitrability" is used more broadly in U.S. law than in the laws of most other jurisdictions. Outside the United States, the term "arbitrability" is generally used to refer only to the question whether a particular type of dispute is capable of being arbitrated. The imprecision of the term as used in U.S. jurisprudence has been noted in case law and commentary. *See, e.g.*, Howsam v. Dean Witter Reynolds, Inc., 537 U.S. 79, 83 (2002) ("Linguistically speaking, one might call any potentially dispositive gateway question a 'question of arbitrability' ..."); Alan Scott Rau, *Everything You Really Need to Know About "Separability" in Seventeen Simple Propositions*, 14 Am. Rev. Int'l Arb. 1, 120 (2003) (decrying the term as an "unnecessary and incoherent formulation[] that ... apparently serve[s] only as [an] obstacle[] to thought"). The term is used here because it consistently appears in U.S. arbitration case law.

arbitrated.[219] Questions as to the scope of an arbitration agreement are best reviewed under Article V(1)(c), while the question whether the subject matter of the dispute is arbitrable falls within Article V(2)(a). This discussion, therefore, focuses on the question whether a valid arbitration agreement exists between the parties (*i.e.*, numbers (1) and (2) above).

13.83 In the context of a petition to confirm an award, an arbitral tribunal has already decided its jurisdiction. The question for the court under Article V(1)(a) is the extent to which it can review that decision. The seminal Supreme Court case on judicial review of arbitrators' jurisdictional decisions is *First Options of Chicago, Inc. v. Kaplan.*[220]

13.84 In *First Options*, an arbitral tribunal had found that an arbitration agreement between MK Investments, Inc. and First Options of Chicago, Inc. bound the Kaplans, who owned MK Investments; the tribunal had also ruled in favor of First Options on the merits.[221] The Kaplans moved to vacate the award under FAA Section 10, arguing that they were not parties to the arbitration agreement and therefore had not agreed to arbitrate the dispute.[222] The Supreme Court, in a decision by Justice Breyer, resolved a narrow question: "who—court or arbitrator—has the primary authority to decide whether a party has agreed to arbitrate."[223]

13.85 The Court explained that the answer to this question depends on the parties' arbitration agreement and conduct during the arbitration.[224] Thus, a court reviewing arbitral jurisdiction must first decide whether the parties agreed to arbitrate the question of whether a party has agreed to arbitrate. If so, "the court should give considerable leeway to the arbitrator, setting aside his or her decision [as to jurisdiction] only in certain narrow circumstances," that is, on the FAA's grounds for vacatur.[225] If, however, the parties did not agree to arbitrate the question of arbitrability, then the court should decide the jurisdictional issue *de novo.*[226]

13.86 The Supreme Court established background principles to guide lower courts in this analysis. Unless there is "clear and unmistakable" evidence that the parties agreed to arbitrate the question of arbitrability, the court has primary authority to decide whether a dispute is subject to arbitration.[227] "In this manner the law treats

---

219 The U.S. Supreme Court has distinguished between arbitrability issues and procedural preconditions to arbitration; the latter involve "*when* the contractual duty to arbitrate arises, not *whether* there is a contractual duty to arbitrate at all." BG Grp. plc v. Republic of Argentina, 134 S. Ct. 1198, 1206 (2014).

220 514 U.S. 938 (1995); *see generally* Chapter 6.F of this book.

221 *Id.* at 941.

222 *Id.*

223 *Id.* at 942.

224 *See id.* at 943, 946.

225 *Id.*

226 *Id.*

227 *See id.* at 944.

silence or ambiguity about ... *who* (primarily) should decide arbitrability differently from the way it treats silence or ambiguity about ... *whether* a particular merits-related dispute is arbitrable because it is within the scope of a valid arbitration agreement."[228] In the latter circumstance, courts presume that a dispute is subject to arbitration if the parties' arbitration agreement is silent or ambiguous on the matter.[229] To determine whether the dispute was subject to arbitration, the Supreme Court looked to the Kaplans' conduct during the arbitral proceedings and found that, because the Kaplans objected to the arbitrators' jurisdiction over them, there was no clear and unmistakable evidence of their intent to be bound by the arbitrators' decisions.[230]

Two important questions arise when considering the impact of *First Options* on cases under the New York and Inter-American Conventions. First, does *First Options* apply in cases under FAA Chapters 2 and 3? Second, does *First Options* shield arbitral rulings on jurisdiction from judicial review in the many cases where the arbitration clause confers on the arbitrators the power to decide their own jurisdiction? **13.87**

As to the first question, a notable feature of Article V(1)(a) is that it contains a choice-of-law provision.[231] If the parties have not specifically chosen a law to govern the arbitration agreement (as opposed to the contract in general), the applicable law is that of the arbitral seat, the place "where the award was made."[232] Awards made in the United States will therefore likely be subject to the *First Options* analysis in actions to recognize or vacate an award. **13.88**

The U.S. Supreme Court appears to have adopted this approach. In *BG Group plc v. Republic of Argentina*, the U.S. Supreme Court applied the *First Options* presumptions to decide whether an UNCITRAL award rendered in the United States should be annulled because of alleged noncompliance with a provision in a bilateral investment treaty that required a period of litigation in the local courts before arbitration could be initiated. The Court explained: "[W]here ... a federal court is asked to interpret [the parties'] intent pursuant to a motion to vacate or confirm an award made in the United States under the Federal Arbitration Act, it should normally apply the presumptions supplied by American law."[233] **13.89**

228 *Id.* at 944–45.

229 *See id.*

230 *See id.* at 946.

231 *See* Born, 3 International Commercial Arbitration (2d ed. 2014), *supra* note 5, at 3462 ("Some commentators have called Article V(1)(a)'s choice-of-law provision the crowning achievement of the Convention.").

232 *Id.* at 3462–63.

233 *BG Grp.*, 134 S. Ct. at 1208; *see also* Telenor Mobile Commc'ns AS v. Storm LLC, 584 F.3d 396, 406 (2d Cir. 2009) (holding that the presumption that a court determines arbitrability applies in cases under the New York Convention); Schneider v. Kingdom of Thailand, 688 F.3d 68, 74 (2d Cir. 2012) (applying *First Options* in FAA Chapter 2 case); *Sarhank Group*, 404 F.3d at 661. In *Sarhank Group*, the respondent argued that it was not a party to the arbitration agreement and that

13.90 If, as appears to be the case, *First Options* applies under FAA Chapters 2 and 3, it should not be read so broadly as to prohibit judicial review of arbitrators' jurisdictional rulings when a party claims that it is not bound by an existing arbitration agreement or that no valid agreement exists. Under Second Circuit law, "clear and unmistakable evidence" of the parties' intent to submit the question of arbitrability to the arbitrators may either be express or implied.

13.91 It may be implied by the incorporation into the arbitration agreement of a set of institutional rules that confer the authority on the arbitrators to decide their own jurisdiction.[234] Most institutional or ad hoc rules give the arbitral tribunal the authority to decide whether it has jurisdiction over a dispute presented to it, the so-called *compétence-compétence* doctrine.[235] But "where one party denied ever having made a valid arbitration agreement or ever having submitted any dispute, jurisdictional or otherwise, to arbitration,"[236] the analysis changes.

13.92 In circumstances where a party argues that it is not bound to an arbitration agreement or an existing agreement is invalid or illegal, the court must first determine whether a valid arbitration agreement exists between the parties, notwithstanding an arbitral judgment on the matter.[237] "[A]s arbitration depends on a valid contract[,] an argument that the contract does not exist can't logically be resolved by the arbitrator (unless the parties agree to arbitrate this issue after the dispute arises)."[238] Therefore, the court should review *de novo* whether a valid arbitration agreement exists between the parties, unless the objecting party manifested some intent to be bound by the arbitration agreement during the arbitration itself.

13.93 U.S. courts (like the courts of most developed jurisdictions) recognize the so-called "separability presumption," which provides that the arbitration agreement is

---

therefore the award should not be enforced. The arbitral tribunal, in a proceeding sited in Egypt, had found that the respondent was bound by the arbitration agreement, but the Second Circuit held that it would not defer to that ruling because there was no clear and unmistakable evidence that the respondent had agreed to arbitrate jurisdictional issues. *See* 404 F.3d at 661–62. Other courts have expressly found *First Options* applicable to international arbitration cases. *See* Gen. Elec. Co. v. Deutz AG, 270 F.3d 144, 155 (3d Cir. 2001) ("the international nature of the present litigation does not affect the application of *First Options*' principles"); *see also* Born, 1 International Commercial Arbitration (2d ed. 2014), *supra* note 5, at 1141 n.523 (collecting cases).

234 *See, e.g.*, Contec Corp. v. Remote Solution, Co., 398 F.3d 205, 208 (2d Cir. 2005).

235 *See, e.g.*, AAA Rules (2013), Rule 7; AAA/ICDR International Arbitration Rules (2014), art. 19; ICC Rules of Arbitration (2012), art. 6(3); LCIA Arbitration Rules (2014), art. 23; UNCITRAL Arbitration Rules (revised 2010), art. 23; *see also* Chapter 6.F.3 of this book.

236 Born, 3 International Commercial Arbitration (2d ed. 2014), *supra* note 5, at 3479.

237 Under the FAA, where the party challenging arbitral jurisdiction has "some evidence" to supports its position, the decision as to the existence or validity of an arbitration agreement should ordinarily be made after holding a trial. *See* Sphere Drake Ins. Ltd. v. Clarendon Nat'l Ins. Co., 263 F.3d 26, 30 (2d Cir. 2001) (holding that "if the making of the agreement to arbitrate is placed in issue ... the court must set the issue for trial," provided that the party challenging the agreement has "some evidence" to support its claim); 9 U.S.C. § 4 ("If the making of the arbitration agreement ... be in issue, the court shall proceed summarily to the trial thereof.").

238 Sphere Drake Ins. Ltd. v. All Am. Ins. Co., 256 F.3d 587, 591 (7th Cir. 2001).

separable from the underlying contract with which it is associated.[239] Separability explains how arbitrators can find a contract invalid without "thereby destroying their power to render an award pursuant to the arbitration clause."[240] Based on this principle, the Supreme Court has held that challenges to the validity of the underlying contract (such as, for example, a claim that the contract was fraudulently induced) are for the arbitrators to consider in the first instance, even if a successful challenge would also render the arbitration agreement invalid.[241] But this holding does not mean that a court is barred from reviewing an arbitrator's decision that an underlying contract (and, accordingly, the arbitration clause contained in it) exists.[242] Indeed, "[s]eparability ... says nothing about the validity of the arbitration clause itself."[243]

After the arbitrators render an award, a court can review challenges to the validity of the arbitration agreement pursuant to Article V(1)(a).[244] Accordingly, the Third Circuit has held: **13.94**

> [U]nder the rule of *First Options*, a party that opposes enforcement of a foreign arbitration award under the Convention on the grounds that the alleged agreement containing the arbitration clause on which the arbitral panel rested its jurisdiction was void *ab initio* is entitled to present evidence of such invalidity to the district court, which must make an independent determination of the agreement's validity and therefore of the arbitrability of the dispute ...[245]

It bears emphasis that Article V(1)(a) only applies where the agreement is incapable of being enforced "under the law to which the parties have subjected **13.95**

[239] *See* Buckeye Check Cashing, Inc. v. Cardegna, 546 U.S. 440, 445 (2006); Prima Paint Corp. v. Flood & Conklin Mfg. Co., 388 U.S. 395, 403–04 (1967); ACE Capital Re Overseas Ltd. v. Cent. United Life Ins. Co., 307 F.3d 24, 29 (2d Cir. 2002); Campaniello Imps., Ltd. v. Saporiti Italia S.p.A., 117 F.3d 655, 667 (2d Cir. 1997).

[240] William W. Park, *Determining Arbitral Jurisdiction: Allocation of Tasks Between Courts and Arbitrators*, 8 Am. Rev. Int'l Arb. 133, 143 (1997) (hereinafter, *Arbitral Jurisdiction*).

[241] *See Buckeye Check Cashing*, 546 U.S. at 445–46. In *Buckeye*, the Court did not decide whether challenges to the existence of an arbitration agreement were similarly for the arbitrators to decide in the first instance. *See id.* at 444 n.1. The Seventh Circuit has observed that "[a] person whose signature was forged has never agreed to anything ... in [such] cases ... the arbitrator's authority to resolve the dispute would depend on one particular answer to that very dispute. Only a court can break that circle." *Sphere Drake*, 256 F.3d at 590–91. In circumstances like forgery, the challenge of the party objecting to arbitration "rests ... on the simple 'nonexistence' of the agreement to arbitrate itself." Rau, *Everything You Really Need to Know About "Separability" in Seventeen Simple Propositions*, *supra* note 219, at 15 (emphasis omitted); *see also id.* at 17–18 ("[I]sn't there something terminally silly about an analysis which permits arbitration just because the respondent has taken the pains to cover with his hand—not merely the arbitration clause—but *all the other provisions in the contract as well*?").

[242] *See, e.g., id.* at 54–55 ("It does not at all follow that entrusting the issue of contract validity to arbitrators under [the separability principle] necessarily and in all cases entails giving them the final word."); Park, *Arbitral Jurisdiction*, *supra* note 240, at 143 ("[C]ompétence-compétence principles would permit the arbitrators to examine the power of the person who signed the contract, albeit subject to subsequent court challenge.").

[243] Park, *Arbitral Jurisdiction*, *supra* note 240, at 143.

[244] *See id.* at 957–58.

[245] China Minmetals Materials Imp. & Exp. Co. v. Chi Mei Corp., 334 F.3d 274, 288 (3d Cir. 2003).

it."[246] Thus, even if the arbitration agreement could not be enforced under the laws of certain jurisdictions, so long as it can be enforced under the laws applicable to the arbitration proceedings, Article V(1)(a) does not provide a basis for nonrecognition.[247]

13.96 *(b) Denial of opportunity to present one's case (Article V(1)(b))* Article V(1)(b) of the New York Convention permits nonrecognition of an award in circumstances in which the "party against whom the award is invoked was not given proper notice of the appointment of the arbitrator or of the arbitration proceedings or was otherwise unable to present his case." The Second Circuit has determined that Article V(1)(b) "essentially sanctions the application of the forum state's standards of due process."[248] Courts in New York have recognized that the "fundamental requirement of due process is the opportunity to be heard at a meaningful time and in a meaningful manner."[249] Accordingly, in order to successfully resist recognition of an international arbitral award under Article V(1)(b), the award-debtor must prove "that it was denied a full and fair opportunity to be heard."[250] In applying this standard, courts have sometimes relied on domestic precedent in vacatur actions under the FAA.[251]

13.97 While it is difficult to generalize about the types of cases in which courts have considered whether a party to an international arbitration was denied fundamental due process, certain procedural issues are raised more often than others in this context. These include: denial of the right to be heard in an oral proceeding;[252] denial of the opportunity to comment on evidence or

---

[246] N.Y. Convention, art. V(1)(a).

[247] *See Telenor*, 524 F. Supp. 2d at 367–68 (denying nonrecognition under Article V(1)(a) where the arbitration agreement was valid and enforceable under New York law, which was applicable to the arbitration agreement, even assuming that the agreement would be invalid under Ukrainian law).

[248] *Parsons & Whittemore*, 508 F.2d at 975–76 (applying party's "due process rights under American law"). *But see* Born, 3 International Commercial Arbitration (2d ed. 2014), *supra* note 5, at 3502–06 (arguing that in recognition proceedings, as opposed to proceedings to vacate an award, contracting states should not impose their own national standards of due process but should apply international standards of procedural fairness).

[249] Iran Aircraft Indus. v. Avco Corp., 980 F.2d 141, 146 (2d Cir. 1992) (*quoting* Mathews v. Eldridge, 424 U.S. 319, 333 (1976)); *see also* Ukrvneshprom State Foreign Econ. Enter. v. Tradeway, Inc., No. 95 Civ. 10278 (RPP), 1996 WL 107285, at *5 (S.D.N.Y. Mar. 12, 1996) ("[I]n order to invoke the Article V(1)(b) defense, Tradeway must establish that it was denied the opportunity to be heard at a meaningful time or in a meaningful manner.").

[250] *Id.; see also Iran Aircraft Indus.*, 980 F.2d at 146 ("[I]f Avco was denied the opportunity to be heard in a meaningful time or in a meaningful manner, enforcement of the Award should be refused pursuant to Article V(1)(b).").

[251] *See* Slaney v. Int'l Amateur Athletic Fed'n, 244 F.3d 580, 592 (7th Cir. 2001); Generica Ltd. v. Pharm. Basics, Inc., 125 F.3d 1123, 1129–30 (7th Cir. 1997).

[252] *See, e.g., InterCarbon*, 146 F.R.D. at 72 (accepting that "the failure to hear live testimony compromised the fullness of InterCarbon's hearing" but rejecting claim "that those facts prevent confirmation of the award").

arguments;[253] failure to provide notice of hearings;[254] and failure to postpone or adjourn the proceedings.[255]

(c) Excess of authority (Article V(1)(c)) Article V(1)(c) of the New York Convention permits nonrecognition of an international arbitral award when the award: **13.98**

> deals with a difference not contemplated by or not falling within the terms of the submission to arbitration, or it contains decisions on matters beyond the scope of the submission to arbitration, provided that, if the decisions on matters submitted to arbitration can be separated from those not so submitted, that part of the award which contains decisions on matters submitted to arbitration may be recognized and enforced.

Article V(1)(c) applies in circumstances where a valid arbitration agreement exists but the tribunal exceeds the matters that were submitted to it or fails to address matters that were submitted to it. It also applies in circumstances where an award may be said to exceed the scope of a valid arbitration agreement. Consistent with "the enforcement-facilitating thrust" of the New York Convention, the Second Circuit has read this ground for nonrecognition narrowly.[256] In order to successfully resist recognition of an international arbitral award under Article V(1)(c), a petitioner must "overcome a powerful presumption that the arbitral body acted within its powers."[257] In addition, courts will be wary of arguments that are made in the guise of an excess-of-authority argument under Article V(1)(c) but are, in essence, attempts to attack the substantive decision-making of the arbitral tribunal.[258] **13.99**

[253] *See, e.g., Overseas Cosmos*, 1997 WL 757041, at *4 (finding that "respondent cannot seriously contend that it lacked notice of the London arbitration so as to justify this Court's refusal to confirm the award pursuant to Article V(1)(b) of the Convention," and concluding that the "[r]espondent's alleged lack of participation in the arbitration proceeding, even if true, could only be interpreted as intentional").

[254] *See, e.g.*, Geotech Lizenz AG v. Evergreen Sys., Inc., 697 F. Supp. 1248, 1253 (E.D.N.Y. 1988) (rejecting Article V(1)(b) defense to recognition on the ground that party "was given ample notice of the arbitration and an adequate opportunity to present its defenses. Evergreen's failure to participate was a decision that was reached only after the Company had full knowledge of the peril at which it acted").

[255] *See, e.g.*, P.T. Reasuransi Umum Indon. v. Evanston Ins. Co., No. 92 Civ. 4623, 1992 WL 400733, at *2 (S.D.N.Y. Dec. 23, 1992) (rejecting claim that "the Panel's refusal to grant an extension" constituted "an act of misconduct which justifies vacating the arbitration award").

[256] *Parsons & Whittemore*, 508 F.2d at 976 (Article V(1)(c)'s "defense to enforcement ... should be construed narrowly"); *see also* Fiat S.p.A. v. Ministry of Fin. & Planning, No. 88 Civ. 6639 (SWK), 1989 WL 122891, at *5 (S.D.N.Y. Oct. 12, 1989) (noting that "authority also exists to support the proposition that 'any issue that is "inextricably tied up with the merits of the underlying dispute" may properly be decided by the arbitrator'" (*quoting* DiGhello v. Busconi, 673 F. Supp. 85, 87 (D. Conn. 1987))). In *Fiat*, the court appears to have erred in deciding under Article V(1)(c), rather than Article V(1)(a), that the arbitrators should not have asserted jurisdiction over a nonsignatory to the arbitration agreement.

[257] *Parsons & Whittemore*, 508 F.2d at 976; *see also* Whirlpool Corp. v. Philips Elecs., N.V., 848 F. Supp. 474, 480 (S.D.N.Y. 1994) (finding that a tribunal's "decision as to the scope of its arbitral authority is entitled to deference").

[258] *See Parsons & Whittemore*, 508 F.2d at 977 ("Although the Convention recognizes that an award may not be enforced where predicated on a subject matter outside the arbitrator's

13.100 An initial question for a reviewing court under Article V(1)(c) is whether the parties intended the court or arbitrator to decide whether a dispute falls within the scope of their arbitration agreement. If the parties have agreed that arbitrators will determine the scope of their own jurisdiction by, for example, agreeing to institutional rules that confer this authority on the arbitral tribunal, a good argument exists that the tribunal's decision as to the scope of the agreement cannot be upset by a reviewing court under Article V(1)(c). In such cases, questions as to the scope of the arbitration agreement are "contemplated by or ... fall[] within the terms of the submission to arbitration." If the arbitrators have jurisdiction to decide issues of scope, that should be the end of the court's review under Article V(1)(c).

13.101 *(d) Violations of arbitral procedures or the law of the arbitral situs (Article V(1)(d))* An international arbitral award may be denied recognition under Article V(1)(d) where:

> The composition of the arbitral authority or the arbitral procedure was not in accordance with the agreement of the parties, or, failing such agreement, was not in accordance with the law of the country where the arbitration took place.

13.102 Article V(1)(d) establishes the important principle that the arbitral procedure must first be determined by the agreement of the parties, and—only failing such agreement—by the law of the arbitral situs. In order to rely on Article V(1)(d) as a defense to recognition, a party must establish either that (1) the tribunal failed to comply with the parties' agreed arbitral procedure (such as time limits imposed by the parties' arbitration agreement or the means by which the arbitral tribunal should be composed);[259] or (2) the tribunal failed to comply with the procedural law of the arbitral seat.

13.103 Compliance with the law of the arbitral seat does not mean compliance with the rules of civil procedure of the arbitral seat. Rather, it means compliance with the arbitration law of the arbitral seat, which, in most developed jurisdictions, provides wide latitude to international arbitrators to decide procedural issues as they deem appropriate. It is therefore difficult to resist enforcement of an arbitral award on the ground that the tribunal failed to comply with the procedural law of the arbitral situs. Moreover, in light of the pro-enforcement bias of the New York Convention, courts have rejected attempts to resist enforcement of

---

jurisdiction, it does not sanction second-guessing the arbitrator's construction of the parties' agreement."); Capgemini v. Sorensen, No. 04 Civ. 7584 (JGK), 2005 WL 1560482, at *9 (S.D.N.Y. July 1, 2005) (rejecting argument under FAA § 10(a)(4) that tribunal exceeded its authority where claim was "that the Panel mistakenly failed to account for the restrictions on the stock when calculating its value").

[259] *See Encyclopaedia Universalis*, 403 F.3d at 90–92 (finding that district court properly refused to confirm arbitral award "on the grounds that the appointment of the third arbitrator was premature, and, therefore, the composition of the arbitral authority was not in accordance with the parties' agreement").

arbitral awards based on a failure to comply with the parties' agreement absent a showing of "substantial prejudice to the complaining party."[260]

13.104 *(e) Awards that are not binding or have been set aside (Article V(1)(e))* Article V(1)(e) permits nonrecognition of an international arbitral award in circumstances where the award "has not yet become binding on the parties, or has been set aside or suspended by a competent authority of the country in which, or under the law of which, that award was made." As discussed previously, one of the principal shortcomings of the Geneva Convention of 1927—the predecessor to the New York Convention—was the requirement of so-called "double exequatur," by which an award first had to be confirmed in the rendering state before it could be enforced abroad.[261] Although the Convention eliminated this requirement, it did not "provide any international mechanism to insure the validity of the award where rendered. This was left to the provisions of local law ... [and the] Convention provides no restraint whatsoever on the control functions of local courts at the seat of arbitration."[262] Indeed, Article V(1)(e) "allow[s] a court in the country under whose law the arbitration was conducted to apply domestic arbitral law ... to a motion to set aside or vacate that arbitral award."[263] Once an award has been set aside in the arbitral seat, Article V(1)(e) permits courts in any future forum in which enforcement proceedings are brought to refuse recognition.

13.105 With respect to the requirement that the award be "binding" on the parties, the elimination of the "double exequatur" requirement clearly eliminates the requirement that the award-creditor confirm the arbitral award in the arbitral situs in order for the award to become "binding." Nor is an award not "binding" simply because proceedings to vacate the award are ongoing at the arbitral seat.[264]

[260] *Evanston*, 1992 WL 400733, at *1–2; Karaha Bodas Co., L.L.C. v. Perusahaan Pertambangan Minyak Dan Gas Bumi Negara, 190 F. Supp. 2d 936, 945 (S.D. Tex. 2001); Compagnie des Bauxites de Guinee v. Hammermills, Inc., No. 90-0169, 1992 WL 122712, *5 (D.D.C. May 29, 1992).

[261] *Yusuf Ahmed*, 126 F.3d at 22.

[262] *Id.*

[263] *Id.* at 21.

[264] *See Karaha Bodas*, 335 F.3d at 367 n.42 ("[U]nder the Convention, a court maintains the discretion to enforce an arbitral award even when nullification proceedings are occurring in the country where the award was rendered."); Fertilizer Corp. of India v. IDI Mgmt., Inc., 517 F. Supp. 948, 957 (S.D. Ohio 1981) (concluding that award was binding under Indian law even pending annulment proceedings). However, courts may stay enforcement actions pending annulment proceedings in the primary jurisdiction. *See* N.Y. Convention, art. VI; *Telcordia Tech*, 458 F.3d at 181 (affirming dismissal without prejudice of action to enforce South African award pending completion of annulment proceedings in South Africa); Europcar Italia, S.p.A. v. Maiellano Tours, Inc., 156 F.3d 310, 317 (2d Cir. 1998) ("[W]here a parallel proceeding is ongoing in the originating country and there is a possibility that the award will be set aside, a district court may be acting improvidently in enforcing the award prior to the completion of the foreign proceedings."); Jorf Lasfar Energy Co. v. AMCI Exp. Corp., No. Civ. A. 05-0423, 2005 WL 3533128, at *2 (W.D. Pa. Dec. 22, 2005) (staying confirmation proceeding pending annulment action in country where arbitration took place); Spier v. Calzaturificio Tecnica S.p.A., 663 F. Supp. 871, 875 (S.D.N.Y. 1987) (same). The Second Circuit in *Europcar Italia* instructed district courts to consider various factors when deciding whether to delay confirmation proceedings under Article

Rather, courts will broadly interpret arbitral awards as "binding" for purposes of Article V(1)(e) so long as the arbitral proceedings have ended and there are no further steps left for the arbitral tribunal to take.[265]

13.106 *(f) Awards that address nonarbitrable issues (Article V(2)(a))* Article V(2) of the New York Convention provides two additional grounds for nonrecognition of international arbitral awards that may be raised by the party resisting recognition or by the court itself. The first of these, Article V(2)(a), permits nonrecognition where the court finds that the "subject matter of the difference is not capable of settlement by arbitration under the law of that country."

13.107 In other words, under Article V(2)(a), the party resisting recognition and enforcement of an international arbitral award must demonstrate that the subject matter of dispute is not arbitrable in the place where recognition and enforcement are sought.[266] The same "nonarbitrability" grounds that can be used to support a defense to an arbitration agreement under Article II of the New York Convention can generally be used to support a defense to recognition under Article V(2)(a). The U.S. Supreme Court has "decline[d] to subvert the spirit of the United States' accession to the Convention by recognizing subject-matter exceptions [to arbitration] where Congress has not expressly directed the courts to do so,"[267] leaving the defense under Article V(2)(a) to be narrowly construed.[268]

13.108 *(g) Awards that violate public policy (Article V(2)(b))* One of the grounds most widely (and improperly) invoked to attempt to resist recognition and enforcement of international arbitral awards is the assertion, under Article V(2)(b) of the Convention, that the award is not enforceable because "recognition or enforcement of the award would be contrary to the public policy of" the forum state.

13.109 The Second Circuit has rejected an expansive reading of the public policy defense on the ground that such a reading "would vitiate the Convention's basic effort to remove preexisting obstacles to enforcement."[269] Instead, the Second Circuit has determined, consistent with the "general pro-enforcement bias" of the Convention, that the defense should be read "narrow[ly]" and that "considerations

VI of the New York Convention, including: (1) the goal of avoiding delay and expensive litigation, (2) the status of the annulment proceedings, and (3) the possible hardships to the parties. *See* 156 F.3d at 317–18.

[265] *See, e.g.*, Publicis Commc'n v. True N. Commc'ns, Inc., 206 F.3d 725, 729–30 (7th Cir. 2000) (finding that award was final as to a particular issue when the tribunal had decided "the whole ball of wax" and would not need to make any further decision as to that issue); *Ukrvneshprom*, 1996 WL 107285, at *4 ("The award will be considered 'binding' for the purpose of the Convention if no further recourse may be had to another arbitral tribunal (that is, an appeals tribunal).") (*quoting Fertilizer Corp.*, 517 F. Supp. at 958).

[266] *See Sarhank Group*, 404 F.3d at 661.

[267] Mitsubishi Motors Co. v. Soler Chrysler-Plymouth, Inc., 473 U.S. 614, 639 n.21 (1985).

[268] Saudi Iron & Steel Co. v. Stemcor USA Inc., No. 97 CIV. 5976 (DLC), 1997 WL 642566, at *3 (S.D.N.Y. Oct. 17, 1997).

[269] *Parsons & Whittemore*, 508 F.2d at 974.

of reciprocity—considerations given express recognition in the Convention itself—counsel courts to invoke the public policy defense with caution lest foreign courts frequently accept it as a defense to enforcement of arbitral awards rendered in the United States."[270]

Accordingly, the Second Circuit has determined that "[e]nforcement of awards may be denied on [the] basis [of public policy] only where enforcement would violate the forum state's most basic notions of morality and justice."[271] Applying these standards, courts in New York have frequently rejected attempts to resist recognition of international arbitral awards on grounds of public policy under Article V(2)(b).[272] **13.110**

2. FAA Chapter 1 Grounds for Vacating International Arbitral Awards

Whether the FAA or the New York Convention grounds for resisting enforcement of an award apply depends on whether the award was made under U.S. or foreign law. As discussed previously, Article V(1)(e) of the New York Convention states that recognition and enforcement of an award may be denied if the award "has been set aside or suspended by a competent authority of the country in which, or under the law of which, that award was made."[273] The **13.111**

[270] *Id.; see also* Waterside Ocean Navigation Co. Inc. v. Int'l Navigation Ltd., 737 F.2d 150, 152 (2d Cir. 1984) (finding that the public policy defense "must be construed in light of the overriding purpose of the Convention, which is to encourage the recognition and enforcement of commercial arbitration agreements in international contracts and to unify the standards by which agreements to arbitrate are observed and arbitral awards are enforced in the signatory countries"); MGM Prods. Group, Inc. v. Aeroflot Russian Airlines, No. 03 Civ. 0500 (RMB), 2003 WL 21108367, at *3 (S.D.N.Y. May 14, 2003), *aff'd*, 91 F. App'x. 716 (2d Cir. 2004) ("Courts construe the public policy limitation in the Convention very narrowly and apply it only where enforcement would violate the forum state's 'most basic notions of morality and justice.'" (*quoting Europcar Italia*, 156 F.3d at 313)).

[271] *Parsons & Whittemore*, 508 F.2d at 974. An unpublished Second Circuit order emphasizes that "the [public policy] exception applies only where enforcement of the arbitration award, as opposed to enforcement of the underlying contract, would violate public policy," and that a claim "that the underlying contract violates public policy ... is 'to be determined exclusively by the arbitrators.'" Yukos Capital S.A.R.L. v. Samaraneftegaz, No. 13-3357, 2014 WL 5572696, at *3 (2d Cir. Nov. 4, 2014).

[272] *See, e.g., Telenor*, 584 F.3d at 410–11 (rejecting argument that public policy prevented confirmation of award that was inconsistent with a foreign-court judgment, which the respondent had obtained through "improper collateral litigation"); *Europcar Italia*, 156 F.3d at 315 (holding that public policy defense not warranted where issue was not a fraudulently obtained award but rather "whether the underlying contract that is the subject of the arbitrated dispute was forged or fraudulently induced"); *Parsons & Whittemore*, 508 F.2d at 974 (holding that a violation of U.S. foreign policy does not rise to the level of a violation of public policy under Article V(2)(b)); *MGM Prods.*, 2003 WL 21108367, at *5 (holding that violation of U.S. foreign policy vis-à-vis Iran not a violation of public policy that would support defense to enforcement under Article V(2)(b)); Henry v. Murphy, No. M-82, 2002 WL 24307, at *4 (S.D.N.Y. Jan. 8, 2002); Saudi Iron & Steel Co. v. Stemcor USA Inc., No. 97 Civ. 5976 (DLC), 1997 WL 642566, at *2–3 (S.D.N.Y. Oct. 17, 1997) (rejecting public policy defense based on alleged denial of due process); Brandeis Intsel Ltd. v. Calabrian Chem. Corp., 656 F. Supp. 160, 167 (S.D.N.Y. 1987) (holding that "manifest disregard" of the law does not rise to the level of a public policy violation).

[273] N.Y. Convention, art. V(1)(e).

Second Circuit held in *Yusuf Ahmed* that "Article V(1)(e) of the Convention … allow[s] a court in the country under whose law the arbitration was conducted to apply domestic arbitral law, in this case the FAA, to a motion to set aside or vacate that arbitral award."[274] "[T]he Convention is equally clear," however, "that when an action for enforcement is brought in a foreign state, the state may refuse to enforce the award only on the grounds explicitly set forth in Article V of the Convention."[275] Thus, U.S. awards that fall under the Conventions can be subject to the FAA Chapter 1 grounds to vacate, while awards made outside the United States may only be denied enforcement under the Conventions.[276]

FAA Section 10(a) provides four grounds to vacate an arbitral award:

(1) where the award was procured by corruption, fraud, or undue means;
(2) where there was evident partiality or corruption in the arbitrators …
(3) where the arbitrators were guilty of misconduct in refusing to postpone the hearing, upon sufficient cause shown, or in refusing to hear evidence pertinent and material to the controversy; or of any other misbehavior by which the rights of any party have been prejudiced; or
(4) where the arbitrators exceeded their powers, or so imperfectly executed them that a mutual, final, and definite award upon the subject matter submitted was not made.[277]

Courts have also recognized implied grounds to vacate when an arbitral tribunal manifestly disregards the law or when the award violates public policy. Both of these grounds are discussed below.[278]

13.112 In practical terms, many of the FAA Chapter 1 grounds are substantially similar to those under the New York and Inter-American Conventions. They each permit nonrecognition if the arbitral tribunal exceeded its jurisdiction,[279]

[274] 126 F.3d at 21. The court came to this conclusion despite the language of FAA Section 207, which provides that a U.S. court "shall confirm [an award to which the Convention applies] unless it finds one of the grounds for refusal or deferral of recognition or enforcement of the award specified in [the New York] Convention." 9 U.S.C. § 207; *see* William W. Park, *The Specificity of International Arbitration: The Case for FAA Reform*, 36 Vand. J. Trans. L. 1241, 1246 (2003).

[275] *Id.* at 23.

[276] A U.S. court can only vacate an award made in the United States pursuant to the grounds specified, or implied, in FAA Chapter 1; it cannot vacate, but can only refuse to confirm, a U.S. award under the grounds in Article V of the New York Convention. Zeiler v. Deitsch, 500 F.3d 157, 166 n.6 (2d Cir. 2007).

[277] 9 U.S.C. § 10(a).

[278] *See* sections C.2(e), (f) of this Chapter *infra*.

[279] *See* N.Y. Convention, art. V(1)(c); Inter-American Convention, art. 5(1)(c); 9 U.S.C. § 10(a)(4); *Lander Co.*, 107 F.3d at 481 ("The wording [between FAA Section 10(a)(4) and New York Convention Article V(1)(c)] is slightly different but there is no reason to think the meaning different."). However, in *Encyclopaedia Universalis*, the Second Circuit reversed a district court for refusing to enforce an award made in Luxembourg because the arbitrators "exceeded their powers." *Id.* at 92. The Second Circuit explained, "That an arbitration panel exceeded its powers is not … one of the seven exclusive grounds for denying enforcement under the New York Convention." The court did not address whether the award could have been denied enforcement under New York Convention Article V(1)(c).

for violations of due process[280] and, in some circuits, for violations of public policy.[281] Just as with the Conventions' grounds to refuse enforcement, courts have narrowly interpreted the grounds to vacate awards under FAA Chapter 1.[282] Because of these similarities, case law interpreting the FAA Chapter 1 grounds may be useful to a party that asks a court to refuse enforcement under the Conventions. Federal courts have recognized this overlap.[283] The following sections briefly discuss the grounds to vacate arbitral awards set forth in FAA Chapter 1.

(a) Award procured by corruption, fraud, or undue means (Section 10(a)(1)) There are few New York cases addressing the circumstances in which a court can vacate an award that is procured by corruption, fraud, or undue means under Section 10(a)(1). Some district courts have held that a party must "(1) establish the existence of the alleged fraud or undue means by clear and convincing evidence, (2) demonstrate due diligence in attempting to discover the fraud before entry of the award, and (3) demonstrate that the fraud was material to the arbitrators' decision."[284] Other district courts in New York have adopted a similar standard, but have not required clear and convincing evidence of fraud.[285] **13.113**

All three bases for vacatur—corruption, fraud, and undue means—require intentional misconduct by a party that led to the award.[286] Courts have noted that an award based on perjured testimony that was material to the decision and credited by the arbitrator may be vacated under this section.[287] **13.114**

---

[280] *See* N.Y. Convention, art. V(1)(b); Inter-American Convention, art. 5(1)(b); 9 U.S.C. § 10(a)(3).

[281] *See* N.Y. Convention, art. V(2)(b); Inter-American Convention, art. 5(2)(b); *Greenberg*, 220 F.3d at 27 (noting implied public policy ground for vacating awards).

[282] *See, e.g.*, Banco de Seguros del Estado v. Mut. Marine Office, Inc., 344 F.3d 255, 262 (2d Cir. 2003).

[283] *See Lander Co.*, 107 F.3d at 481; Mgmt. & Tech. Consultants S.A. v. Parsons-Jurden Int'l Corp., 820 F.2d 1531, 1534 (9th Cir. 1987) ("In interpreting the grounds specified [in the New York Convention], it is generally recognized that the Convention tracks the Federal Arbitration Act."); *Parsons & Whittemore*, 508 F.2d at 976 (noting that New York Convention article V(1)(c) "tracks in more detailed form" the similar ground under FAA Chapter 1).

[284] Houston Gen. Ins. Co. v. Certain Underwriters at Lloyd's London, No. 02 Civ. 7599 (JSR), 2003 WL 22480058, at *1 (S.D.N.Y. Oct. 31, 2003) (citing A.G. Edwards & Sons, Inc. v. McCullough, 967 F.2d 1401, 1404 (9th Cir. 1992)); *accord* Red Apple Supermkts./Supermkts. Acquisitions v. Local 338, Retail, Wholesale & Chain Store Food Employees Union, No. 98 Civ. 2303 (LMM), 1999 WL 596273, at *6 (S.D.N.Y. Aug. 9, 1999).

[285] *See* Hakala v. Deutsche Bank AG, No. 01 Civ. 3366 (MGC), 2004 WL 1057788, at *3 (S.D.N.Y. May 11, 2004); McCarthy v. Smith Barney Inc., 58 F. Supp. 2d 288, 293 (S.D.N.Y. 1999); Master's Choice, Inc. v. Cowie, No. 96-CV-0554E(F), 1997 WL 211368, at *3 (W.D.N.Y. Apr. 23, 1997).

[286] *See* Nat'l Cas. Co. v. First State Ins. Group, 430 F.3d 492, 499 (1st Cir. 2005) (construing "undue means" as requiring "conniving ways of procuring an award ... similar to corruption or fraud"); Delta Mine Holding Co. v. AFC Coal Props., Inc., 280 F.3d 815, 822 (8th Cir. 2001) ("A party seeking vacation of an award [under Section 10(a)(1)] must demonstrate that the conduct influenced the outcome of the arbitration.").

[287] *See Red Apple*, 1999 WL 596273 at *6.

13.115 *(b) Partiality or corruption of the arbitrators (Section 10(a)(2))* A court can vacate an award under Section 10(a)(2) based on corruption or bias of an arbitrator.[288] There need not be proof of actual bias, but in the Second Circuit it is insufficient to show merely an appearance of bias.[289] Instead, the award may be vacated only "where a reasonable person would have to conclude that an arbitrator was partial to one party to the arbitration."[290] The Second Circuit has held that a court cannot hear a challenge to an arbitrator until after the award is rendered.[291]

13.116 The failure to disclose a material relationship with a party to the arbitration may result in vacatur under this section.[292] "A reasonable person would have to conclude that an arbitrator who failed to disclose [a material relationship with a party] was partial to one side."[293] Arbitrators should investigate potential conflicts,[294] but an imperfectly-performed investigation that failed to identify a conflict has been found not to warrant vacatur under Section 10(a)(2) where the arbitrator lacked actual knowledge of the conflict.[295] When an arbitrator has reason to believe that he or she has a nontrivial conflict of interest, the arbitrator must "(1) investigate the conflict (which may reveal information that must be disclosed …) or (2) disclose his reasons for believing there might be a conflict and his intention not to investigate."[296] When an arbitrator knows of a potential conflict and fails either to investigate or to disclose his or her intent not to investigate, a court may take this fact as evidence of partiality.[297]

13.117 Courts will not vacate an award based on an undisclosed relationship, however, when the complaining party should have known of the relationship or could have learned of the relationship during the arbitration proceedings.[298] Thus, the Second Circuit refused to vacate an award rendered by an arbitrator who had previously served as an expert witness for the winning party because the arbitrator disclosed the relationship on a form filed with the AAA.[299] Although the opposing party never received the form from the AAA, the Second Circuit reasoned

[288] 9 U.S.C. § 10(a)(2).
[289] Morelite Constr. Corp. v. N.Y. City Dist. Council Carpenters Benefit Funds, 748 F.2d 79, 84 (2d Cir. 1984).
[290] *Id.*
[291] *See* Aviall, Inc. v. Ryder Sys., Inc., 110 F.3d 892, 895–96 (2d Cir. 1997).
[292] *See* Commonwealth Coatings Corp. v. Cont'l Cas. Co., 393 U.S. 145, 149–50 (1968).
[293] Applied Indus. Materials Corp. v. Ovalar Makine Ticaret Ve Sanayi, A.S., 492 F.3d 132, 137–38 (2d Cir. 2007).
[294] *Id.*
[295] Ometto v. ASA Bioenergy Holding A.G., No. 12 CIV 1328, 2013 WL 174259, at *2–4 (S.D.N.Y. Jan. 9, 2013), *aff'd*, 549 F. App'x 41 (2d Cir. 2014).
[296] Applied Indus. Materials Corp., 492 F.3d at 137–38.
[297] *Id.* (finding "evident partiality" when an arbitrator on a three-member tribunal, whose vote was dispositive, failed to investigate fully and disclose that the company for which he worked was a party to a lucrative contract with the parent company of one of the parties to the arbitration).
[298] Lucent Techs. Inc. v. Tatung Co., 379 F.3d 24, 28 (2d Cir. 2004).
[299] *See id.* at 28–29.

that the opposing party knew of the AAA rules requiring disclosure and knew of the AAA form that each arbitrator had to fill out; thus, the party should have inquired about the missing form.[300]

Arbitrator bias is not an express ground to refuse enforcement under the New York and Inter-American Conventions. An award rendered by biased arbitrators, however, might conceivably be refused recognition under the Conventions as a matter of public policy.[301] Furthermore, the Conventions permit nonrecognition if the "composition of the arbitral authority or the arbitral procedure was not in accordance with the agreement of the parties, or failing such agreement, was not in accordance with the law of the country where the arbitration took place."[302] Thus, when the parties' arbitration agreement incorporates institutional rules that require arbitrator independence, bias or corruption may provide a basis to refuse enforcement on the ground that the composition of the tribunal is contrary to the parties' agreement. And, in the absence of an agreement that incorporates any rules on arbitrator conduct, the court could look to the arbitration law of the arbitral seat to determine whether bias or corruption is a ground to refuse enforcement.[303] **13.118**

(c) Failure to adjourn or hear evidence; prejudicial misbehavior (Section 10(a)(3)) **13.119**
Section 10(a)(3) permits a court to vacate an award if the arbitrators engaged in: (1) "misconduct" in refusing to postpone a hearing when sufficient cause was shown, (2) "misconduct" in refusing to hear pertinent and material evidence, or (3) other "misbehavior" that prejudiced the rights of a party.[304] A refusal to postpone a hearing or to hear particular evidence only constitutes misconduct sufficient to vacate an award if it deprives a party of a fundamentally fair proceeding.[305] Arbitrators have broad discretion in granting or denying adjournments, and New York district courts have refused to vacate awards "[a]s long as there is at least a 'barely colorable justification' for the arbitrators' decision not to grant an adjournment."[306] Other courts have looked for a "reasonable basis" for denials

[300] *See id.* at 30.

[301] *See* York Hannover Holding A.G. v. Am. Arbitration Ass'n, No. 92 Civ. 1643 (CSH), 1993 WL 159961, at *3 n.4 (S.D.N.Y. May 11, 1993).

[302] N.Y. Convention, art. V(1)(d); *see also* Inter-American Convention, art. 5(1)(d); section C.1(d) of this Chapter, *supra.*

[303] *See* Chapter 5.C of this book; *see generally* Catherine A. Rogers, *Regulating International Arbitrators: A Functional Approach to Developing Standards of Conduct,* 41 Stan. J. Int'l L. 53, 78 & n.139 (2005).

[304] 9 U.S.C. § 10(a)(1); *see* Tempo Shain Corp. v. Bertek, Inc., 120 F.3d 16, 20 (2d Cir. 1997).

[305] *See Tempo Shain,* 120 F.3d at 20; Delgado v. A. Korenegay Senior House HDFC, No. 07 Civ. 7761 (DC), 2008 WL 748848, at *3 (S.D.N.Y. Mar. 21, 2008). This standard essentially requires due process. *Cf.* Lisenba v. California, 314 U.S. 219, 236 (1941) ("[D]enial of due process is the failure to observe that fundamental fairness essential to the very concept of justice.").

[306] Alexander Julian, Inc. v. Mimco, Inc., No. 00 Civ. 4131(DC), 2001 WL 477010, at *2 (S.D.N.Y. May 4, 2001) (*quoting* Prozina Shipping Co. v. Elizabeth-Newark Shipping, Inc., No. 98 Civ. 5834, 1999 WL 705545, at *2 (S.D.N.Y. Sept. 10, 1999)); *see also* Cong. Secs., Inc. v. Fiserv Secs., Inc., No. 02 Civ. 6593 (JSM), 2003 WL 21664678, at *2 (S.D.N.Y. July 15, 2003).

of adjournments.[307] For example, a district court in New York found the denial of a one-week adjournment unreasonable when the party requesting the adjournment had previously informed the tribunal that it was unavailable on particular dates, but the tribunal nevertheless scheduled the hearings on those dates.[308] The court vacated the award, which was issued without the party's participation, and ordered the hearing to be rescheduled.[309]

13.120 Arbitrators also are not required to hear all evidence that the parties proffer or follow the same procedural rules that courts apply, but they must provide an adequate opportunity for the parties to present their case.[310] One district court found fundamental unfairness when the arbitrator refused to reopen the proceedings after a party failed to appear at a hearing of which it lacked notice.[311]

13.121 District courts have held that arbitrators are not compelled to hold oral hearings in every case, so that the failure to conduct an oral hearing will not constitute misconduct under Section 10(a)(3), provided that deciding the case on documentary submissions is fundamentally fair.[312]

13.122 The Second Circuit found that vacatur under Section 10(a)(3) was appropriate where an arbitral tribunal refused to postpone a hearing so that a witness with pertinent and material evidence, whose wife had cancer and was therefore not available to testify on the date of the scheduled hearing, could testify.[313] The tribunal refused the adjournment because it concluded that the witness's testimony would have been cumulative of other evidence.[314] Although the court noted that "[i]n making evidentiary determinations, an arbitrator 'need not follow all the niceties observed by the federal courts,' "[315] it concluded that there was no reasonable basis for finding that the witness's evidence was cumulative.[316]

---

[307] *See, e.g.*, Ottawa Office Integration Inc. v. FTF Bus. Sys., Inc., 132 F. Supp. 2d 215, 220 (S.D.N.Y. 2001).

[308] *See* Tube Steel Corp. of Am. v. Chicago Carbon Steel Prods., 319 F. Supp. 1302, 1302–04 (S.D.N.Y. 1970).

[309] *See id.* at 1302, 1304.

[310] *See Tempo Shain*, 120 F.3d at 20; Bell Aerospace Co. Div. of Textron v. Local 516, Int'l Union of United Auto., Aerospace & Agric. Implement Workers of Am., 500 F.2d 921, 923 (2d Cir. 1974); Smith v. Positive Prods., 419 F. Supp. 2d 437, 444–45 (S.D.N.Y. 2005).

[311] *See* Kaplan v. Alfred Dunhill of London, Inc., No. 96 Civ. 0258 (JFK), 1996 WL 640901, at *6 (S.D.N.Y. Nov. 4, 1996).

[312] *See* Yonir Techs., Inc. v. Duration Sys. (1992) Ltd., 244 F. Supp. 2d 195, 209 (S.D.N.Y. 2002); Griffin Indus., Inc. v. Petrojam, Ltd., 58 F. Supp. 2d 212, 219 (S.D.N.Y. 1999); *InterCarbon*, 146 F.R.D. at 74; Teamsters, Chauffeurs, Warehousemen & Helpers, Local Union No. 506 v. E.D. Clapp Corp., 551 F. Supp. 570, 578 (S.D.N.Y. 1982).

[313] *See Tempo Shain*, 120 F.3d at 17–18, 20.

[314] *See id.* at 20.

[315] *Id.* (*quoting Bell Aerospace Co.*, 500 F.2d at 923).

[316] *See id.* at 20; *see also* Hoteles Condado Beach, La Concha & Convention Ctr. v. Union de Tronquistas Local 901, 763 F.2d 34, 40 (1st Cir. 1985) (finding misconduct where the arbitrator refused to give any weight to witness's testimony from a related criminal trial after a witness refused to testify at the arbitration hearing); *cf.* Bisnoff v. King, 154 F. Supp. 2d 630, 634, 638–39 (S.D.N.Y. 2001) (refusing to vacate award where tribunal denied adjournment of hearing because

The third basis for vacatur under Section 10(a)(3)—other misbehavior that prejudices a party—has not often been discussed, but may be seen as a catch-all provision to ensure basic procedural due process.[317] In *Stefano Berizzi Co. v. Krausz*,[318] the New York Court of Appeals, applying New York's arbitration statute (on which the FAA was modeled), explained that "misbehavior, though without taint of corruption or fraud, may be born of indiscretion."[319] Judge Benjamin Cardozo, writing for the court, held that an arbitrator committed prejudicial misbehavior when he based the award on his own personal investigation of the facts of the case, which he conducted without notice to the parties.[320] **13.123**

(d) Exceeding jurisdiction (Section 10(a)(4)) Section 10(a)(4) permits vacatur where "the arbitrators exceeded their powers, or so imperfectly executed them that a mutual, final, and definite award upon the subject matter submitted was not made."[321] Because arbitral jurisdiction depends on the scope of the parties' agreement to arbitrate, this section "focuses on whether the arbitrators had the power, based on the parties' submissions or the arbitration agreement, to reach a certain issue."[322] **13.124**

As FAA Section 10(a)(4) and New York Convention Article V(1)(c) have generally been interpreted consistently,[323] readers should refer to the previous discussion of Article V(1)(c).[324] **13.125**

(e) Manifest disregard of the law One of the most widely discussed but rarely applied grounds for vacatur under FAA Chapter 1 is the judicially-implied ground of manifest disregard of the law. This ground originated in the U.S. Supreme Court case *Wilko v. Swan*,[325] in which the Supreme Court stated that "interpretations of the law by the arbitrators in contrast to manifest disregard are not subject … to judicial review for error in interpretation."[326] *Wilko*'s dictum has blossomed **13.126**

tribunal found incredible petitioner's claim that he could not testify due to medical condition and offered petitioner chance to testify via telephone or videotaped deposition).

317 *See* Schoenduve Corp. v. Lucent Techs., Inc., 442 F.3d 727, 734 (9th Cir. 2006) (holding that there was no "due process violation" under Section 10(a)(3) when arbitrators allegedly decided an issue not properly presented to them by the parties); Lourdes Med. Ctr. of Burlington County v. JNESO, No. 04-Civ-4494 (JCL), 2007 WL 1040961, at *6–7 (D.N.J. Apr. 5, 2007) (rejecting argument that arbitrator engaged in misbehavior by violating party's due-process rights); Lovell v. Harris Methodist Health Sys., No. Civ. A. 3:99CV2809G, 2000 WL 351384, at *3 (N.D. Tex. Mar. 10, 2000) (rejecting misbehavior claim based on evidentiary rulings).

318 146 N.E.2d 436 (N.Y. 1925).

319 *Id.* at 437.

320 *See id.* at 436–38.

321 9 U.S.C. § 10(a)(4).

322 Westerbeke Corp. v. Daihatsu Motor Co., 304 F.3d 200, 220 (2d Cir. 2002).

323 *See Lander Co.*, 107 F.3d at 481; Ludgate Ins. Co. v. Banco de Seguros del Estado, No. 02 Civ. 3653 (DC), 2003 WL 443584, at *4 (S.D.N.Y. Jan. 6, 2003); Bowman, *supra* note 23, at 107 & n.285.

324 *See* section C.1(c) of this chapter, *supra*.

325 346 U.S. 427 (1953).

326 *Id.* at 436–37.

into an implied ground to review awards under FAA Chapter 1, though one that is "severely limited."[327] Indeed, it is noteworthy that no court in the Second Circuit has ever set aside an international arbitral award made in New York on the ground of manifest disregard of the law.[328]

13.127 The Second Circuit has noted that, because it so infrequently finds that arbitrators have manifestly disregarded the law, the doctrine's "precise boundaries are ill defined, although its rough contours are well known."[329] A party seeking to vacate an award on the basis of manifest disregard of the law must show: "(1) the arbitrator ... knew of a governing legal principle yet refused to apply it or ignored it altogether, and (2) the law ignored by the arbitrator ... was well defined, explicit, and clearly applicable to the case."[330] Thus, manifest disregard involves a subjective and an objective component.[331]

13.128 The subjective component focuses on "whether the arbitrator was aware of the governing law, and whether he consciously decided to ignore it."[332] Because "the term 'disregard' implies that the arbitrator appreciates the existence of a clearly governing legal principle but decides to ignore or pay no attention to it,"[333] a party challenging an award "must demonstrate that the arbitrator actually knew about the relevant rule of law."[334] It is not enough that a reasonable arbitrator would have known of, and applied, the relevant law; instead, the court looks only to the law that was expressly cited to the arbitrator by the parties.[335] The Second Circuit has held that a reviewing court "cannot presume that the arbitrator is capable of understanding and applying legal principles with the sophistication of a highly skilled attorney" because there is no requirement that arbitrators have any particular legal expertise or be attorneys at all.[336] Instead, "[a]n arbitrator (even an

---

[327] Gov't of India v. Cargill Inc., 867 F.2d 130, 133 (2d Cir. 1989) (internal quotation marks omitted).

[328] *See generally* Report by the Committee On International Commercial Disputes, "The 'Manifest Disregard of Law' Doctrine and International Arbitration in New York," August 2012, *available at* http://www2.nycbar.org/pdf/report/uploads/20072344-ManifestDisregardofLaw--DoctrineandInternationalArbitrationinNewYork.pdf.

[329] Duferco Int'l Steel Trading v. T. Klaveness Shipping A/S, 333 F.3d 383, 389 (2d Cir. 2003). The panel noted that the Second Circuit had arguably vacated awards based on manifest disregard of the law in only four out of approximately forty-eight cases that had raised the issue. *See id.* The court explained, however, that all but one of the four cases "involved an arbitral decision that exceeded the legal powers of the arbitrators," suggesting "that manifest disregard need not have been the basis for vacating the award[s], since vacatur would have been warranted under the FAA." *Id.* Since *Duferco*, the Second Circuit has vacated, for manifest disregard, at least one other arbitral award. *See* Porzig v. Dresdner, Kleinwort, Benson, N.Am. LLC, 497 F.3d 133, 140 (2d Cir. 2007).

[330] Hoeft v. MVL Group, Inc., 343 F.3d 57, 69 (2d Cir. 2003) (internal quotation marks omitted).

[331] *Id.* at 67.

[332] *Id.* at 67–68.

[333] Merrill Lynch, Pierce, Fenner & Smith, Inc. v. Bobker, 808 F.2d 930, 933 (2d Cir. 1986).

[334] *Gottdiener*, 462 F.3d at 111.

[335] *See Duferco*, 333 F.3d at 390.

[336] Wallace v. Buttar, 378 F.3d 182, 190 (2d Cir. 2004); *accord Duferco*, 333 F.3d at 390.

arbitrator who is a lawyer) is often selected for expertise in the commercial aspect of the dispute or for trustworthiness, rather than for knowledge of the applicable law, and under the test of manifest disregard is ordinarily assumed to be a blank slate unless educated in the law by the parties."[337] To prove arbitrators' knowledge and disregard of the law, a party may not seek to depose the arbitrators.[338]

To establish the objective component that the disregarded law was "well defined, explicit, and clearly applicable," "[i]t is not enough to demonstrate that the arbitrators ... erred."[339] Instead, "[o]nly after a[n arbitration] panel has been presented with binding authority in a way that compels relief can it be said that the panel exhibited manifest disregard of the law."[340] An award will not be set aside for manifest disregard if the law or its application to the case is ambiguous.[341] Thus, an arbitrator does not manifestly disregard the law if the issue calls for application "of an unclear rule of law to a complex factual situation."[342] **13.129**

Federal courts in New York have very rarely found an award to be in manifest disregard of the law (and, as noted, have never done so in the context of an international arbitral award made in New York[343]). The Second Circuit has found manifest disregard where arbitrators expressly rejected controlling precedent from which the case was indistinguishable,[344] and where the losing party had "carefully and accurately explained to the arbitral panel the prevailing law" on attorneys' fees (after the district court had vacated the panel's prior award for manifestly disregarding the law on attorneys' fees) and the panel once again failed to award appropriate fees.[345] **13.130**

Manifest disregard does not permit courts to vacate an award for flawed fact-finding. In *Halligan v. Piper Jaffray, Inc.*,[346] the Second Circuit affirmed vacatur of an award that rejected a claim of age discrimination where there was "overwhelming evidence" of discrimination.[347] The basis for the award was unclear, as the tribunal failed to provide any reasoning. The parties had agreed on the controlling law before the arbitrators, and thus the court found that the tribunal was aware of the applicable authority.[348] The court's decision seemed to broaden **13.131**

---

337 Goldman v. Architectural Iron Co., 306 F.3d 1214, 1216 (2d Cir. 2002).
338 *See Hoeft*, 343 F.3d at 68–69.
339 Bear, Stearns & Co. v. 1109580 Ontario, Inc., 409 F.3d 87, 92 (2d Cir. 2005).
340 *Id.* at 93.
341 *See Duferco*, 333 F.3d at 390; *Bobker*, 808 F.2d at 934.
342 *Goldman*, 306 F.3d at 1217 (internal quotation marks omitted).
343 *See infra* notes 368–70 and accompanying text (findings of New York City Bar Association report).
344 *See* N.Y. Tel. Co. v. Comm'cns Workers of Am. Local 1100, 256 F.3d 89, 93 (2d Cir. 2001) (per curiam).
345 *See Porzig*, 497 F.3d at 141–43.
346 148 F.3d 197 (2d Cir. 1998).
347 *See id.* at 203–04.
348 *See id.*

the standard from manifest disregard of the law to manifest disregard of "the law or the evidence or both."[349] But, the court's holding might have rested on the assumption that an award so contrary to the relevant evidence must have rejected the controlling law cited by the parties.[350] A later Second Circuit panel clarified that the court "does not recognize manifest disregard of the evidence as proper ground for vacating an arbitrator's award."[351]

13.132 The Supreme Court has called into question the doctrine of manifest disregard as a basis to deny recognition of an award. In *Hall Street Associates, L.L.C. v. Mattel, Inc.*,[352] the Court held that parties may not contractually expand grounds to review an arbitral award under FAA Chapter 1.[353] In so holding, it rejected an argument that the judicially implied manifest-disregard standard was "the camel's nose: if judges can add grounds to vacate (or modify), so can contracting parties."[354] Although the Court suggested that judicially implied grounds may be as invalid as contractually expanded grounds, it did not expressly hold that lower courts cannot review awards for manifest disregard of the law. Instead, the Court wrote in reference to *Wilko*: "Maybe the term 'manifest disregard' was meant to name a new ground for review, but maybe it merely referred to the § 10 grounds collectively, rather than adding to them. Or ... [it] may have been shorthand for § 10(a)(3) or § 10(a)(4) ..."[355]

13.133 The Second Circuit has held that *Hall Street* did not overrule the manifest-disregard doctrine.[356] Instead, the doctrine survives, "reconceptualized as a judicial gloss on the specific grounds for vacatur enumerated in section 10 of the FAA."[357] Courts in the Second Circuit thus retain authority to vacate awards "in the rare instances in which the arbitrator knew of the relevant [legal] principle, appreciated that this principle controlled the outcome of the disputed issue, and nonetheless willfully flouted the governing law by refusing to apply it," because arbitrators exceed their powers when they engage in manifest disregard of

[349] *Id.* at 204.

[350] The court explained that "where a reviewing court is inclined to find that the arbitrators manifestly disregarded the law or the evidence and that an explanation, if given, would have strained credulity, the absence of explanation may reinforce the reviewing court's confidence that the arbitrators engaged in manifest disregard." *Id.*

[351] *Wallace*, 378 F.3d at 193 (internal quotation marks omitted); *see also Westerbeke*, 304 F.3d at 213 n.9 ("*Halligan* does not stand for the proposition that factual findings put on the record by the arbitrator are subject to an independent judicial review ...").

[352] 552 U.S. 576 (2008).

[353] *See id.* at 590–91.

[354] *Id.* at 585.

[355] *Id.* at 585 (citations omitted).

[356] *See, e.g.*, Schwartz v. Merrill Lynch & Co., 665 F.3d 444, 452 (2d Cir. 2011). At least two other circuits have disagreed. *See* Frazier v. CitiFinancial Corp., 604 F.3d 1313, 1324–25 (11th Cir. 2010); Citigroup Global Mkts. Inc. v. Bacon, 562 F.3d 349, 349 (5th Cir. 2009).

[357] Stolt-Nielson SA v. AnimalFeeds Int'l Corp., 548 F.3d 85, 94 (2d Cir. 2008), *reversed on other grounds*, 559 U.S. 662 (2010).

the law.[358] It does not appear that this "reconceptualization" of the doctrine has changed the way in which the Second Circuit will analyze claims of manifest disregard of the law after *Hall Street*.[359] In practice, the doctrine remains "severely limited."[360]

In 2012, mindful of concerns in the arbitration community surrounding the availability of "manifest disregard" as a potential basis for vacating an award, the International Commercial Disputes Committee of the New York City Bar Association issued a report addressing the doctrine.[361] It examined the Second Circuit's application of "manifest disregard" both empirically and analytically, and compared it to the approach taken in leading arbitral seats outside the United States to vacating an award on comparable grounds. Having found that, "to date, *no* international arbitral award rendered in New York has *ever* been set aside in the Second Circuit on the ground of manifest disregard,"[362] the committee concluded that "United States law, especially as applied by the federal courts in New York, is no less favorable to international arbitral awards than the laws of other major centers of international arbitration.[363] **13.134**

(f) Public policy Some courts have recognized in FAA Chapter 1 cases an implied ground to vacate arbitral awards that violate public policy.[364] The Second Circuit, however, has held that it "will vacate an award only upon finding a violation of one of the four statutory bases [in FAA Chapter 1], or, more rarely, if [it] find[s] a panel has acted in manifest disregard of the law."[365] Thus, in the Second Circuit, public policy is not a valid basis on which to vacate an award in FAA cases. There is some confusion on this point in Second Circuit case law because the court does permit labor arbitration awards to be vacated if they violate a "well-defined and dominant public policy."[366] But labor arbitration under section 301 of the Labor Management Relations Act of 1947 is "a substantive body of federal law ... that is 'analytically distinct from the FAA.' "[367] Thus, the **13.135**

[358] *Id.* at 95 (internal quotation marks omitted).

[359] *See Telenor*, 584 F.3d at 407, 408–10.

[360] *See, e.g.*, Sotheby's Int'l Rlty., Inc. v. Relocation Grp., LLC, 588 F. App'x 64, 65 (2d Cir. 2015) (reversing District of Connecticut decision that had vacated a domestic award on "manifest disregard" grounds, upon finding that lower court had failed to apply the Second Circuit's very narrow test).

[361] Report by the Committee On International Commercial Disputes, "The 'Manifest Disregard of Law' Doctrine and International Arbitration in New York," August 2012, *available at* http://www2.nycbar.org/pdf/report/uploads/20072344-ManifestDisregardofLaw--Doctrineand InternationalArbitrationinNewYork.pdf.

[362] *Id.* at 2 (emphasis added).

[363] *Id.* at 4.

[364] *Porzig*, 497 F.3d at 139 (citing cases).

[365] *Id.*

[366] IBEW Local 97 v. Niagara Mohawk Power Corp., 143 F.3d 704, 713 (2d Cir. 1998).

[367] *Westerbeke*, 304 F.3d at 221 (*quoting* Coca-Cola Bottling Co. v. Soft Drink & Brewery Workers Union Local 812, 242 F.3d 52, 54 (2d Cir. 2001)).

grounds for vacating labor arbitration awards and awards under the FAA are not the same.[368]

13.136 *(g) Sanctions for frivolous attacks on arbitral awards* Federal courts are becoming increasingly likely to award sanctions in response to frivolous attempts to vacate or oppose confirmation of arbitral awards. A district court in New York has observed that "[f]rivolous claims are particularly egregious when brought to frustrate arbitration,"[369] because they directly undermine the interest in preserving the efficiency and finality of arbitration as an alternative to litigation.[370] As the Eleventh Circuit observed in a frequently-cited case, "the promise of arbitration is broken" when a losing party "drags the dispute through the court system without an objectively reasonable belief it will prevail."[371]

13.137 Courts have focused on two sources of authority for imposing sanctions in arbitration cases: 28 U.S.C. § 1927, which authorizes courts to sanction attorneys who "so multipl[y] the proceedings in any case unreasonably and vexatiously"[372]; and Rule 11 of the Federal Rules of Civil Procedure, which authorizes sanctions against both attorneys and parties for violating the Rule's standards of conduct.[373] In the Second Circuit, courts have sanctioned parties for behavior that falls generally into two categories: (a) raising inappropriate or meritless motions and arguments,[374] and (b) misrepresenting the record or the arbitral proceedings.[375]

---

[368] Public policy remains an applicable ground to refuse enforcement of awards under the Conventions. *See* N.Y. Convention, art. V(2)(b); Inter-American Convention, art. 5(2)(b); section C.1(g) of this Chapter, *supra*.

[369] Prospect Capital Corp. v. Enmon, No. 08 CIV. 3721 (LBS), 2010 WL 907956, at *7 (S.D.N.Y. Mar. 9, 2010), *aff'd*, 675 F.3d 138 (2d Cir. 2012).

[370] *See id.*; DigiTelCom, Ltd. v. Tele2 Sverige AB, 2012 WL 3065345, at *7 (S.D.N.Y. July 25, 2012) ("[W]here parties agree to arbitration as an efficient and lower-cost alternative to litigation, both the parties and the system itself have a strong interest in the finality of those arbitration awards.")

[371] B.L. Harbert Int'l v. Hercules Steel Co., 441 F.3d 905, 913–14 (11th Cir. 2006).

[372] Decisions regarding arbitral awards that have considered § 1927 sanctions include *Prospect Capital Corp.*, 2010 WL 907956; DigiTelCom, Ltd. v. Tele2 Sverige AB, 2012 WL 3065345 (S.D.N.Y. July 25, 2012); and Smiga v. Dean Witter Reynolds, Inc., 766 F.2d 698 (2d Cir. N.Y. 1985).

[373] Fed. R. Civ. P. 11 (submissions must "not be[] presented for any improper purpose, such as to harass [or] delay," must contain claims and legal contentions that are "warranted by existing law or by a nonfrivolous argument for extending ... [the] law," and must contain supported (or likely supportable) factual contentions). Decisions regarding arbitral awards that have considered Rule 11 sanctions include Fairchild Corp. v. Alcoa, Inc., 510 F. Supp. 2d 280, 298 (S.D.N.Y. 2007) (declining to award sanctions where arguments, though unsuccessful, were not the kind of "extreme misconduct that warrant[s] sanctions" under Rule 11); Manning v. Smith Barney, Harris Upham & Co., 822 F. Supp. 1081, 1083–84 (S.D.N.Y. 1993) (awarding $250 sanction under Rule 11); and Quick & Reilly v. Jacobson, 126 F.R.D. 24 (S.D.N.Y. 1989) (awarding $25,000 under Rule 11).

[374] *See, e.g.*, *Smiga*, 766 F.2d at 708 (affirming district court's imposition of sanctions under § 1927 where party had raised "arguments which were not only inappropriate upon a motion to confirm but were also without merit"); *Manning*, 822 F. Supp. at 1083–84 ("[S]anctions are peculiarly appropriate in the context of a challenge to an arbitration award which appears to be a largely dilatory effort."); *Quick & Reilly, Inc.*, 126 F.R.D. at 27 ("[T]he claims advanced by [party seeking to vacate award] were so totally devoid of merit as to warrant imposition of Rule 11 sanctions.").

[375] *See, e.g.*, Enmon v. Prospect Capital Corp., 675 F.3d 138, 145–46 (2d Cir. 2012) ("We see no abuse of discretion in the District Court's decision to sanction [law firm for party who opposed

3. New York State Law Grounds for Vacating Awards

The grounds for vacating arbitral awards under New York law are similar to the grounds for vacating awards under the FAA and the Conventions. The Civil Practice Law and Rules provide that a party to an arbitration, or one who was served with notice of arbitration, may move to vacate an award based on: **13.138**

(i) corruption, fraud or misconduct in procuring the award; or
(ii) partiality of an arbitrator appointed as a neutral, except where the award was by confession; or
(iii) an arbitrator ... exceed[ing] his power or so imperfectly execut[ing] it that a final and definite award upon the subject matter submitted was not made; or
(iv) failure to follow the procedure of [the CPLR governing arbitration proceedings], unless the party applying to vacate the award continued with the arbitration with notice of the defect and without objection.[376]

A person who did not participate in an arbitration and was not served with notice of arbitration may move to vacate an award if: **13.139**

(i) the rights of that party were prejudiced by one of the grounds specified [above]; or
(ii) a valid agreement to arbitrate was not made; or
(iii) the agreement to arbitrate had not been complied with; or
(iv) the arbitrated claim was barred by [the statute of] limitation[.][377]

Generally speaking, New York state courts also favor arbitration[378] and thus "are reluctant to disturb the decisions of arbitrators lest the value of this method of resolving controversies be undermined."[379] Like the FAA and Convention grounds for vacatur, courts narrowly construe the basis to vacate awards under CPLR 7511.[380] The New York Court of Appeals has admonished that awards should not be vacated "for errors of law and fact committed by the arbitrator and the courts **13.140**

petition to confirm arbitral award] for its gross mischaracterization of the arbitral proceedings."); *DigiTelCom, Ltd.*, 2012 WL 3065345, at *7 ("Plaintiffs' representation of what facts were undisputed and, particularly, its selective quoting of the agreement in question, are disingenuous at best"; granting attorneys' fees under § 1927).

376 N.Y. CPLR 7511(b)(1).

377 *Id.* 7511(b)(2). New York courts may also order awards to be modified if: (1) there was a miscalculation of figures or description of any person, thing, or property in the award; (2) the arbitrators addressed a matter outside their jurisdiction that "may be corrected without affecting the merits of the decision upon the issues submitted"; or (3) the award contains imperfections in form that do not affect the merits of the controversy. *Id.* 7511(c).

378 *See* Union Free Sch. Dist. No. 15 v. Lawrence Teachers Ass'n, 822 N.Y.S.2d 767, 768 (App. Div. 2006).

379 Goldfinger v. Lisker, 500 N.E.2d 857, 859 (N.Y. 1986). New York has a long history of supporting arbitration. Indeed, FAA Chapter 1 was modeled on New York's 1920 arbitration statute. *See Southland Corp.*, 465 U.S. at 25 n.8; Red Cross Line v. Atl. Fruit Co., 264 U.S. 109, 118 (1924).

380 N.Y. CPLR 7511(b)(1), (2) 1998 practice commentary.

should not assume the role of overseers to mold the award to conform to their sense of justice."[381] Many of the state-law grounds are similar to those in the FAA and the Conventions.[382]

13.141 Unlike the FAA and the Conventions, the CPLR contains provisions regarding procedures to be followed during the arbitration.[383] CPLR Article 75 dictates the content and service of the notice of arbitration,[384] authorizes a court to appoint the arbitrators if the arbitration agreement does not set the method of selection,[385] grants arbitrators and attorneys the power to issue subpoenas during arbitration,[386] recognizes arbitrators' authority to conduct hearings and receive evidence,[387] governs the form and timing of awards,[388] permits awards by confession or consent,[389] and grants arbitrators the power to modify awards.[390] For the violation of a procedural rule to form a basis to vacate, the violation must be both preserved by objection during the arbitration and prejudicial.[391] The party seeking vacatur bears the burden of proving prejudice.[392]

4. Choice of Arbitral Law When Resisting Enforcement of an Award Made in the United States

13.142 If the arbitral award subject to judicial review was made outside the United States and the New York or Inter-American Convention applies, the Conventions will provide the basis for judicial review.[393] This is true whether the action to enforce the award is brought in federal or state court.[394] If the

[381] Wien & Malkin LLP v. Helmsley-Spear, Inc., 846 N.E.2d 1201, 1206 (N.Y. 2006).

[382] *See* A.G. Edwards & Sons v. Lobacz, 831 N.Y.S.2d 346 (App. Div. 2006) (table decision).

[383] *See* N.Y. CPLR 7503–7509.

[384] *See id.* 7503(c).

[385] *See id.* 7504.

[386] *See id.* 7505.

[387] *See id.* 7506.

[388] *See id.* 7507.

[389] *See id.* 7508.

[390] *See id.* 7509.

[391] *See id.* 7511(b)(iv); Silverman v. Benmor Coats, Inc., 461 N.E.2d 1261, 1265 (N.Y. 1984).

[392] *See* Meisels v. Uhr, 593 N.E.2d 1359, 1363 (N.Y. 1992).

[393] *See Yusuf Ahmed*, 126 F.3d at 20–21. It should be noted, however, that the New York Convention provides that it does not "deprive any interested party of any right he may have to avail himself of an arbitral award in the manner and to the extent allowed by the law ... of the country where such award is sought to be relied upon." N.Y. Convention, art. VII(1). Thus, the New York Convention does not itself require displacement of U.S. state law to the extent that such law is more favorable to the recognition of arbitral awards. In addition, based on the language of the Supreme Court in *Hall Street*, it is at least conceivable that parties could agree in their arbitration clause that the CPLR, rather than the Conventions, would govern judicial review of an arbitral award resulting from their arbitration. *See Hall St.*, 552 U.S. at 590 ("The FAA is not the only way into court for parties wanting review of arbitration awards: they may contemplate enforcement under state statutory or common law, for example, where judicial review of different scope is arguable.").

[394] *Cf. Corcoran*, 567 N.E.2d at 969 (recognizing application of New York Convention in state-court action to compel arbitration); Drexel Burnham Lambert Inc. v. Ruebsamen, 531 N.Y.S.2d

award was made in the United States, however, the court may vacate the award under domestic law.[395] In such cases, the court may need to decide whether federal or state arbitration law applies because, although they often overlap, there are some inconsistencies.[396] For example, under New York law, an arbitrator exceeds his or her authority by granting punitive damages,[397] while federal arbitral law does not prohibit an award of punitive damages when the parties have not agreed to restrict the types of damages available.[398] Resolution of this choice-of-law problem depends on both principles of federal preemption and state contract law.

The FAA does not preempt all state arbitration law.[399] Instead, it only preempts state law to the extent the relevant state law "stands as an obstacle to the accomplishment and execution of the full purposes and objectives of Congress" in the FAA.[400] Although the FAA manifests a pro-arbitration policy, "[t]here is no federal policy favoring arbitration under a certain set of procedural rules; the federal policy is simply to ensure the enforceability, according to their terms, of private agreements to arbitrate."[401] Thus, parties may agree by contract that New York arbitral law will apply to an arbitration that would otherwise fall under the FAA.[402] As the Supreme Court explained in *Volt Information Sciences, Inc. v. Board of Trustees of Leland Stanford Junior University*, the FAA does not prevent "the enforcement of agreements to **13.143**

547, 550 (App. Div. 1988) (rejecting request for order of attachment in aid of arbitration because the New York Convention does not provide for such relief).

395 *See Yusuf Ahmed*, 126 F.3d at 20–21.

396 *See* Johnson v. Summit Equities, Inc., 864 N.Y.S.2d 873, 885 (Sup. Ct. 2008) ("While application of the FAA is easily triggered, it is not necessarily exclusive, and only displaces state law when the latter is inconsistent with the FAA or its policies favoring arbitration. Hence, both federal and state law may govern the same case." (citations omitted)).

397 *See* Garrity v. Lyle Stuart, Inc., 353 N.E.2d 793, 832 (N.Y. 1976) ("Punitive damages is a sanction reserved to the State [and] … enforcement of an award of punitive damages as a purely private remedy would violate strong public policy [; thus] an arbitrator's award which imposes punitive damages should be vacated.").

398 *See* Barbier v. Shearson Lehman Hutton Inc., 948 F.2d 117, 122 (2d Cir. 1991); *see also* JSC Surgutneftegaz v. President & Fellows of Harv. Coll., No. 04 Civ. 6069 (RCC), 2005 WL 1863676, at *5 (Aug. 3, 2005) (holding that "the FAA preempts any principles of New York State public policy that are less favorable to arbitration [than the FAA itself]"), *aff'd*, 167 F. App'x. 266 (2d Cir. 2006).

399 *See* Volt Info. Scis., Inc. v. Bd. of Trustees of Leland Stanford Jr. Univ., 489 U.S. 468, 477 (1989) ("The FAA contains no express pre-emptive provision, nor does it reflect a congressional intent to occupy the entire field of arbitration.").

400 *Id.* (*quoting* Hines v. Davidowitz, 312 U.S. 52, 67 (1941)).

401 *Id.* at 476.

402 *See id.* at 479; *see also Hall St.*, 552 U.S. at 590 ("The FAA is not the only way into court for parties wanting review of arbitration awards: they may contemplate enforcement under state statutory or common law, for example, where judicial review of different scope is arguable."); Hackett v. Milbank, Tweed, Hadley & McCloy, 654 N.E.2d 95, 100 (N.Y. 1995) (holding that CPLR 7511, and not FAA Section 10, applied to a motion to vacate an award that would otherwise have fallen under the FAA because the parties' arbitration agreement expressly provided that the only grounds for vacating an award would be those found in the CPLR).

arbitrate under different rules than those set forth in the Act itself. Indeed, such a result would be quite inimical to the FAA's primary purpose of ensuring that private agreements to arbitrate are enforced according to their terms."[403] Although this precedent involved domestic arbitration, there appears to be no case law suggesting that parties could not contract to apply New York law instead of the FAA to the grounds for reviewing an international award made in the United States.

13.144 What remains unclear is the degree to which state arbitration law that the parties have agreed will apply to their arbitration will nevertheless be preempted under the FAA. In *Volt*, the Supreme Court deferred to a state court's interpretation of a choice-of-law clause as incorporating state arbitral law, but went on to decide whether a particular provision of that state law was preempted because it "would undermine the goals and policies of the FAA."[404] The Court concluded that the FAA's main goal was to require judicial enforcement of arbitration clauses according to their terms and that enforcing the parties' agreement to apply state arbitral law instead of the FAA was consistent with that goal.[405] Thus, preemption of party-chosen state arbitration law may be limited to unusual situations in which the state law is so unfavorable to arbitration agreements that it violates the FAA's objective of "plac[ing] [arbitration] agreements upon the same footing as other contracts."[406]

13.145 In the absence of an express agreement to incorporate state law, state and federal courts will likely apply the FAA. The New York Court of Appeals appears to have adopted a default rule that when the FAA applies by its terms to a dispute, the FAA, and not the CPLR, governs the arbitration unless the parties have expressly provided to the contrary.[407] Thus, in *Salvano v. Merrill Lynch, Pierce, Fenner & Smith*, the Court of Appeals held that the FAA applied to a dispute concerning employment in the securities industry in the absence of an express choice of New York arbitral law.[408] Many federal courts, including the Second Circuit, appear to have adopted a similar rule.[409]

---

403 *Volt*, 489 U.S. at 479.

404 *See id.* at 476–78.

405 *See id.* at 478–79.

406 *Id.* at 478 (internal quotation marks omitted).

407 *See* Salvano v. Merrill Lynch, Pierce, Fenner & Smith, Inc., 647 N.E.2d 1298, 1301 (N.Y. 1995). Of course, a choice-of-law analysis will often be unnecessary because the grounds for vacating an award under the CPLR and the FAA Chapter 1 are similar.

408 *See id.* at 1301–02.

409 *See, e.g.*, Action Indus., Inc. v. U.S. Fid. & Guar. Co., 358 F.3d 337, 341 (5th Cir. 2004) ("In general, this Court permits arbitration under non-FAA rules if a contract expressly references state arbitration law, or if its arbitration clause specifies with certain exactitude how the FAA rules are to modified."); Sovak v. Chugai Pharm. Co., 280 F.3d 1266, 1270 (9th Cir. 2002) (noting presumption that "FAA supplies the rules for arbitration" when it applies); Doctor's Assocs., Inc. v. Distajo, 107 F.3d 126, 131 (2d Cir. 1997) (holding that the FAA governs "unless it is clear that the parties intended state arbitration law to apply on a particular issue").

This rule would appear to have greater force in Convention cases. As the Second Circuit has explained, there are "compelling reasons to apply federal law" to determining the enforceability of arbitration agreements in Convention cases.[410] Applying state law in the absence of an express party agreement would, the court noted, "introduce a degree of parochialism and uncertainty into international arbitration that would subvert the goal of simplifying and unifying international arbitration law."[411] The court was addressing an international arbitration *agreement*, but its reasoning appears equally applicable to the enforceability of international arbitral *awards*. Accordingly, courts will likely apply the FAA, not the CPLR, to determine the enforceability of an award made in New York, unless the parties agree to apply New York arbitral law.[412] **13.146**

It is not always a simple matter to decide whether the parties agreed to apply state arbitral law, especially when parties include both a choice-of-law clause—for example, "this Agreement shall be governed by the laws of the State of New York"—and an arbitration clause. In *Volt*, the Supreme Court accepted the California state court's interpretation that a choice-of-law clause incorporated state arbitral law.[413] In *Mastrobuono v. Shearson Lehman Hutton, Inc.*, however, the Supreme Court, reviewing the decision of a federal court of appeals *de novo*, interpreted a New York choice-of-law clause and held that it did not incorporate New York arbitral law.[414] The parties' contract also contained a clause calling for arbitration under the rules of the National Association of Securities Dealers (NASD).[415] The Court explained that "the best way to harmonize the choice-of-law provision with the arbitration provision is to read 'the laws of the State of New York' to encompass the substantive principles that New York courts would apply, but not to include special rules limiting the authority of arbitrators."[416] Therefore, "the choice-of-law provision cover[ed] the rights and duties of the parties, while the arbitration clause cover[ed] arbitration."[417] The Court distinguished *Volt* on the ground that *Volt* did not interpret the contract *de novo*, but deferred to the California court's interpretation of state law.[418] **13.147**

410 *Smith/Enron Cogeneration*, 198 F.3d at 96.

411 *Id.*

412 In one case, however, the Second Circuit upheld the district court's vacatur of an arbitral award of punitive damages based on New York arbitral law even though the FAA applied to the award and the parties did not expressly agree to New York law. *See* Fahnestock & Co. v. Waltman, 935 F.2d 512, 516–18 (2d Cir. 1991). The court reasoned that jurisdiction was based on diversity, thus making state law applicable to the issue of damages. *See id.* at 518. Because district courts have federal-question jurisdiction over most, if not all, actions regarding the enforceability of Convention awards, the *Fahnestock* court's rationale will not often apply to international awards.

413 *See Volt*, 489 U.S. at 474 (noting that "the interpretation of private contracts is ordinarily a question of state law, which this Court does not sit to review").

414 *See* 514 U.S. 52, 63–64 (1995).

415 *Id.* at 59.

416 *Id.* at 63–64.

417 *Id.* at 64.

418 *Id.* at 60 n.4.

13.148 *Volt* and *Mastrobuono* create some uncertainty for courts deciding whether a choice-of-law clause incorporates state arbitral law, including the grounds for judicial review. It is unclear whether *Mastrobuono* interpreted the choice-of-law clause purely as a matter of state law, as was done in *Volt*,[419] or established a federal common-law rule.[420] Although the *Mastrobuono* Court did cite the law of New York and Illinois (the forum state) for standard rules of contract interpretation,[421] it did not discuss a New York Court of Appeals case, decided a short time earlier, that construed a choice-of-law clause providing that New York law governed "the agreement and its enforcement." The Court of Appeals held that such a clause incorporated New York state arbitral law.[422]

13.149 Some courts appear to read *Mastrobuono* as adopting a federal common-law rule regarding the scope of choice-of-law clauses, rather than as merely following state contract law.[423] Both the Second Circuit and the New York Court of Appeals have issued decisions that suggest this approach. For example, in one case, the Second Circuit rejected application of the New York Court of Appeals' interpretation of a New York choice-of-law clause because it held that *Mastrobuono* was controlling.[424] In another case, the Second Circuit followed California law in construing a California choice-of-law clause to incorporate state arbitral law governing "the efficient order of proceedings," but reasoned that *Mastrobuono* established a federal rule that "federal policy favoring arbitration requires a specific reference to [state-law] restrictions on the parties' substantive rights or the arbitrator's powers."[425] In addition, the New York Court of Appeals followed *Mastrobuono* and held that "a choice of law clause incorporates substantive New York principles, [but] does not also pull in conflicting restrictions on the scope of the authority of arbitrators and the competence of parties to contract for plenary alternative

[419] *See Volt*, 489 U.S. at 476; *cf. Mastrobuono*, 514 U.S. at 71–72 (Thomas, J., dissenting) (describing majority opinion as "nothing more than a federal court applying [state] contract law").

[420] *See* Note, *An Unnecessary Choice of Law: Volt, Mastrobuono, and Federal Arbitration Act Preemption*, 115 Harv. L. Rev. 2250, 2260 (2002) (suggesting that lower courts incorrectly read *Mastrobuono* as establishing a federal rule that preempts state contract law).

[421] *See Mastrobuono*, 514 U.S. at 62–64 & n.9.

[422] Smith Barney, Harris Upham & Co. v. Luckie, 647 N.E.2d 1308, 1313 (N.Y. 1995). It is likely that a choice-of-law clause without the word "enforcement" does not incorporate state arbitral law under New York law. *See* Smith Barney, Inc. v. Hause, 655 N.Y.S.2d 489, 492–93 (App. Div. 1997).

[423] *See* Note, *An Unnecessary Choice of Law*, *supra* note 420, at 2266 (noting that some lower courts "have simply cited *Mastrobuono* as resolving the meaning of generic choice-of-law clauses for all contracts").

[424] *See* PaineWebber Inc. v. Bybyk, 81 F.3d 1193, 1200 (2d Cir. 1996).

[425] Sec. Ins. Co. of Hartford v. TIG Ins. Co., 360 F.3d 322, 327–28 (2d Cir. 2004) (internal quotation marks omitted); *see also* Shaw Group Inc. v. Triplefine Int'l Corp., 322 F.3d 115, 124 (2d Cir. 2003) (contrasting general choice-of-law clause with contracts calling for arbitration "under the prevailing *arbitration laws* of the State of New York," and for arbitration to be "conducted pursuant to … the laws of the State of New York" (internal quotation marks omitted)).

dispute resolution."[426] The Court of Appeals was not clear as to whether it considered itself bound by *Mastrobuono*.[427]

The Supreme Court addressed the tension between *Volt* and *Mastrobuono* in *Preston v. Ferrer*.[428] In that case, the Court explained that *Volt* did not consider whether the parties' choice of arbitral rules evinced an intent that the state choice-of-law clause be read merely to govern substantive, and not arbitral, law.[429] By contrast, the Court in *Mastrobuono* considered the parties' inclusion of the NASD rules in the arbitration agreement as an indication that the choice-of-law clause did not affect the arbitral law under which the arbitration was to be conducted.[430] Although the *Preston* Court did not indicate whether its interpretation of the parties' contract was a matter of state contract law or federal common law, it is notable that *Preston*, like *Volt*, involved a California choice-of-law clause that had been interpreted by a California state court. Therefore, *Preston* could be read to support the view that federal law, at least in part, controls interpretation of a standard choice-of-law clause in arbitration cases and that, under federal law, a choice-of-law clause does not speak to arbitral law. *Preston* could also be read to establish a federal rule of interpretation that choice-of-law clauses do not include state arbitral law when the parties have agreed to arbitrate according to particular rules, such as those of the AAA or the International Chamber of Commerce (ICC). **13.150**

Thus, it appears that both the Second Circuit and the New York Court of Appeals would require an express agreement to incorporate the CPLR grounds to review an international arbitral award made in the United States. A standard choice-of-law clause stating that New York law governs the contract will not be sufficient, especially if the arbitration clause refers to institutional or ad hoc arbitration rules. In such cases, the courts would likely apply the default rule that the FAA grounds for review apply. **13.151**

Ambiguous arbitration agreements that specifically refer to state law can also subject parties to uncertainty and expand the scope of litigation. In one case, for example, the parties' contract was governed by New York law, while the arbitration agreement stated that arbitration was to be conducted "pursuant to the Federal Arbitration Act and the laws of the State of New York."[431] The district court held that the substantive choice-of-law clause did not itself incorporate New York arbitral law.[432] The district court construed the arbitration clause, however, to require **13.152**

[426] Smith Barney Shearson Inc. v. Sacharow, 689 N.E.2d 884, 889 (N.Y. 1997).
[427] *See id.* at 889 (stating that "attention must also be paid to" *Mastrobuono*).
[428] 552 U.S. 346 (2008).
[429] *See id.* at 361–62.
[430] *See id.* at 362.
[431] Coleman & Co. Secs., Inc. v. Giaquinto Family Trust, No. 00 Civ. 1632(DC), 2000 WL 1683450, at *3 (S.D.N.Y. Nov. 9, 2000).
[432] *Id.* at *3 (relying on *Mastrobuono*, 514 U.S. at 63).

application of both the FAA and New York arbitration law, to the extent that New York law was not inconsistent with the FAA.[433] Under federal arbitration law, application of a statute of limitations is a matter for the arbitrators to decide, while New York law reserves the issue for courts.[434] Because the court found that the rule requiring it to decide the statute-of-limitations issue was procedural and did not interfere with the FAA's pro-enforcement policy, the court concluded that New York law was not preempted and that it, rather than the arbitrators, should decide that statute-of-limitations issue.[435]

433 *See id.* at *3–4.
434 *See id.* at *2, 3.
435 *See id.* at *4.

14

ENFORCING AWARDS INVOLVING FOREIGN SOVEREIGNS

Brian King and Alexander Yanos[1]

A. **Introduction: The Unique Characteristics of Arbitrations Involving Sovereigns** 14.01
B. **The Legal Regime Applicable to the Enforcement of Arbitral Awards Against Sovereigns in New York** 14.04
1. Sovereigns Usually Pay Arbitral Awards 14.05
2. The Recognition of Awards Rendered Against Sovereigns 14.12
(a) Recognition of awards subject to the New York Convention 14.12
(b) Recognition of ICSID awards in the United States is "automatic" 14.15
(c) A potential alternative track: recognition of a foreign court's recognition of the award 14.17
3. Sovereigns Enjoy Significant Immunities With Respect to the Enforcement of Arbitral Awards Against Them 14.19
4. Foreign Sovereigns Are Not Immune From Personal Jurisdiction and Service 14.27
C. **Dealing With the Problem of Recalcitrant States** 14.31
1. Predispute Protections 14.31
2. Prearbitration Attachment 14.33
(a) The requirement of explicit waiver 14.34
(b) Procedure for prearbitration attachment 14.40
3. Interim Measures from the Arbitral Tribunal 14.41
4. Prerecognition Attachment and Explicit Waiver 14.42
5. Postrecognition Attachment and Execution 14.51
6. What Kind of Assets May Be Attached? 14.56
(a) Debt and property subject to attachment 14.63
(b) Attaching the property of state-owned companies 14.64
(c) Garnishment of royalties or taxes 14.69
(d) Attachment of trust accounts 14.74

[1] Brian King is a partner in the international arbitration group in the New York office of Freshfields Bruckhaus Deringer US LLP, and Alexander Yanos is a partner and co-chair of the treaty arbitration group in the New York office of Hughes Hubbard & Reed LLP. The views expressed in this chapter are the authors' alone and do not reflect any views of Freshfields Bruckhaus Deringer US LLP or Hughes Hubbard & Reed LLP.

Jessica Bannon Vanto and Phillip Riblett contributed to a previous version of this chapter. The authors also wish to thank Charline Yim and Dean Rosenberg for their assistance in the preparation of this chapter.

A. INTRODUCTION: THE UNIQUE CHARACTERISTICS OF ARBITRATIONS INVOLVING SOVEREIGNS

14.01 Arbitrations involving sovereigns are fundamentally different from arbitrations involving private individuals. Practitioners for either side, investor or state, would be wise to bear these differences in mind from the outset of the representation. In particular, practitioners should be aware that: (1) arbitrations involving sovereigns tend to take longer due to the deliberative process inherent in all governmental bodies; (2) due to the combination of the sovereign's need to protect the public fisc and the relative difficulty in procuring funds for settlements, arbitrations involving sovereigns tend to continue further into the arbitral process than commercial disputes (often to the conclusion of the process); (3) due to the public nature of a sovereign's business, sovereigns generally pay their debts; (4) sovereigns generally enjoy a number of immunities not applicable to private individuals, so that sovereigns that decide not to pay have powerful weapons at their disposal to shield their assets from enforcement;[2] and (5) unique rules for personal jurisdiction and service apply to sovereigns in the context of enforcement actions.

14.02 In this chapter, we outline the strategies employed by counsel to address these unique differences. In particular:

- Private parties have sought to insert certain provisions in the arbitration agreement to facilitate enforcement of an eventual award. Such provisions have ranged from requirements that the state post a letter of credit against which the private party can draw in the event of a favorable award, to express waivers of immunity with respect to arbitration, award enforcement and efforts to obtain preaward attachment. States have acquiesced in such requirements—particularly states in need of foreign investment—where doing so was perceived as necessary to get the deal done.
- At the time a dispute arises, private parties have gone to the New York courts to attempt to attach sovereign assets, in order to ensure that an eventual award is paid. However, it is quite difficult to obtain a preaward attachment of sovereign

[2] In the United States, foreign sovereigns are immune from attachment and execution of their property in the United States, subject to certain exceptions. 28 U.S.C. §§ 1602, *et seq.* (2012) (Foreign Sovereign Immunities Act or FSIA). In particular, Section 1609 of the FSIA provides:

> Subject to existing international agreements to which the United States is a party at the time of enactment of this Act the property in the United States of a foreign state shall be immune from attachment arrest and execution except as provided in sections 1610 and 1611 of this chapter.

The exceptions to immunity from attachment or execution specified in Section 1610 provide award creditors with the ability to enforce an award by attaching sovereign assets in certain circumstances.

assets. Under the Foreign Sovereign Immunities Act (FSIA), prejudgment attachment (which is analogous to preaward attachment) of sovereign assets is possible only where it is first established that the sovereign has *expressly* waived its immunity from such attachment. Even if such an express waiver has been given, only commercial assets are subject to attachment.

- At the time a dispute arises, litigants also have gone to their arbitral tribunal and sought interim measures, such as the posting of security for costs. It has been held that such interim measures are enforceable where the arbitration agreement selected the rules of a particular arbitration institution, such as the International Chamber of Commerce (ICC) or London Court of International Arbitration (LCIA), which expressly allow the arbitral tribunal to issue such interim measures.
- After the award has been rendered, private parties have sought to attach sovereign assets before the relevant award is recognized by the New York courts, although there too the FSIA creates difficulties.
- After recognition of the applicable award (and assuming the sovereign has refused to pay beyond a reasonable period of time), private parties have sought to identify attachable commercial assets and seize them.

Because of the primacy of New York as an international financial center, the strategies outlined above are played out more frequently in New York courts than any other U.S. jurisdiction.[3] Compared to other jurisdictions around the world, New York tends to be an hospitable environment for enforcement of arbitral awards against foreign sovereigns.[4] It is likely that the law in this area will continue to develop in the coming years due to the growing number of recognition and enforcement actions being taken against sovereigns.[5] **14.03**

---

[3] Of the approximately forty U.S. court decisions examined by the authors involving efforts by an arbitral award creditor to enforce an award against the assets of a foreign sovereign, two-thirds were from the Second Circuit (including its district courts).

[4] Of the decisions examined from the Second Circuit, the award creditors successfully enforced their award in over half of these cases. This record contrasts with, for example, China, Hong Kong, and India, where enforcement against the assets of a foreign sovereign would not be permitted, and other jurisdictions, for example in continental Europe, where claimants face more significant obstacles to enforcement against a sovereign's assets. Generally, the United States is considered to be a "favorable enforcement forum." Edward G. Kehoe, *The Enforcement of Arbitral Awards Against Foreign Sovereigns – the United States*, in Enforcement of Arbitral Awards Against Sovereigns 241, 242 (R. Doak Bishop ed., 2009).

[5] For example, following a number of arbitral awards against the Republic of Argentina arising out of measures taken by Argentina during its 2001–2002 economic crisis—and Argentina's refusal to pay those awards—recognition and enforcement actions against Argentina proliferated. *See, e.g.*, Blue Ridge Invs., LLC v. Republic of Arg., 902 F. Supp. 2d 367 (S.D.N.Y. 2012), *aff'd*, 735 F.3d 72 (2d Cir. 2013); Cont'l Cas. Co. v. Argentine Republic, 893 F. Supp. 2d 747 (E.D. Va. 2012); Republic of Arg. v. BG Group PLC, 715 F. Supp. 2d 108 (D.D.C. 2010); Argentine Republic v. Nat'l Grid Plc, 2010 U.S. Dist. LEXIS 142052 (D.D.C. June 7, 2010). Additionally, the U.S. government took action to pressure Argentina to comply with its international obligations. In particular, in September 2011, the United States voted against financing projects for Argentina worth $232 million at the Inter-American development Bank. Sandrine Rastello & Eric Martin, *U.S. Opposes Loans to Argentina in Bid to Step Up Pressure for Debt Accord*, BLOOMBERG

B. THE LEGAL REGIME APPLICABLE TO THE ENFORCEMENT OF ARBITRAL AWARDS AGAINST SOVEREIGNS IN NEW YORK

14.04 To facilitate the discussion below it is useful to divide the arbitral process into four distinct temporal phases:

(i) *preaward judicial proceedings*: this refers to requests for interim measures submitted to the New York courts before an award has been rendered in the arbitration;
(ii) *preaward arbitral proceedings*: this refers to requests for interim measures submitted to the arbitral tribunal before an award has been rendered in the arbitration;
(iii) *prerecognition judicial proceedings*: this refers to requests for the attachment of sovereign assets submitted to the New York courts after an award (other than an award rendered under the auspices of the International Centre for Settlement of Investment Disputes (ICSID), an organ of the World Bank, which does not require recognition) has been rendered but before the award has been recognized by a court with jurisdiction over the award; and
(iv) *postrecognition judicial proceedings*: this refers to requests for the attachment of sovereign assets submitted to the New York courts after an award has been issued in the ICSID context or after a non-ICSID award has been recognized by a court with jurisdiction.[6]

1. Sovereigns Usually Pay Arbitral Awards

14.05 Most sovereigns, like most private parties, voluntarily pay their debts without the need for judicial enforcement proceedings. Indeed, even states that take a

(Sept. 28, 2011), http://www.bloomberg.com/news/2011-09-28/u-s-opposes-loans-to-argentina-in-bid-to-boost-pressure-for-debt-accord.html. Also, on March 26, 2012, the United States revoked Argentina's status as a favored trading partner and removed Argentina from the list of United States Generalized System of Preference (GSP)-eligible countries in response to its failure to pay arbitral awards to two U.S. companies, a demotion that put Argentina in the unenviable company of countries such as Syria and Belarus. It also meant that Argentina was exposed to tariffs on the $477 million in Argentine goods that were previously exported to the United States duty-free. *See* U.S. Trade Representative Ron Kirk Comments on Presidential Actions Related to the Generalized System of Preferences (http://www.ustr.gov/about-us/press-office/press-releases/2012/march/us-trade-representative-ron-kirk-comments-presidenti). Argentina ultimately agreed to a settlement relating to a number of awards following U.S. litigation. Douglas Thomson, *Argentina Agrees to Settle Treaty Awards*, Global Arbitration Review (Oct. 11, 2013), http://globalarbitrationreview.com/news/article/31961.

[6] Generally speaking, *recognition* is a court's "formal certification that an … award is a final and binding disposition of contested claims" decided therein. *Enforcement* follows recognition and consists of the award creditor's efforts to collect the award. *See* Lucy Reed, Jan Paulsson & Nigel Blackaby, Guide to ICSID Arbitration 179–80 (Kluwer Law International 2010).

superficially recalcitrant position against international arbitration tend to pay. This is because, following award recognition, states face considerable pressure from claimants, the investment community and the global community in general to pay awards. In the short term, states may consider themselves to be immune to such pressure, but history has taught claimants to take a longer view.

For example, all but a few of the final awards rendered under the auspices of ICSID have been paid or settled. This is partly due to the public nature of ICSID arbitration (the commencement of ICSID proceedings is publicly disclosed on ICSID's Web site, and most ICSID awards are published) and may also be related to the idea that failure to perform an ICSID award will have consequences in terms of World Bank funding. **14.06**

At the same time, beyond the influence of the World Bank, many states are motivated to pay adverse arbitral awards because failure to do so can transform the state into an inhospitable environment for investment, have serious repercussions with the international investment community, and restrict access to the capital markets. While this may not be a motivating factor immediately after an award is rendered or recognized, eventually a state will seek foreign direct investment. Payment of adverse awards may be the only option for achieving a state's economic goals. The stature of a claimant bears on this issue. An unpaid award in favor of a large multinational company would be a thorn in a state's side. States often conclude, in time, that paying awards is a wise use of their money. **14.07**

As an example, in the 1970s three significant arbitral awards resulted from then-President Moammar Kadafi's nationalization of Libya's oil industry. In each case, Libya initially offered to pay the expropriated entities net book value and offered the companies the right to purchase the expropriated oil at a price halfway between the posted price and the tax-paid cost to the companies (buy-back price); but after losing the arbitrations, Libya paid the investors the value of their awards.[7] **14.08**

---

[7] *See* Texaco Overseas Petroleum Co. (TOPCO) & Cal. Asiatic Oil Co. v. Gov't of the Libyan Arab Republic, 53 I.L.R. 389 (1977) (awarding the investor specific performance, i.e., an order that Libya abide by its contract and restore the parties to their original position—several months later, a settlement was reached whereby Libya agreed to transfer to the claimants $76 million in oil over fifteen months); BP Exploration Co. (Libya) v. Gov't of the Libyan Arab Republic, 53 I.L.R. 297 (1973) (awarding BP the full value of its investments in Libya on a discounted cash flow basis shortly after the award was issued, Libya reached a full and final settlement with BP, whereby the latter received a net payment of £17.4 million, representing £62.44 million compensation for the value of the assets seized, less £45 million retroactive payments assessed as due from BP according to a prior agreement); Libyan Am. Oil Co. (LIAMCO) v. Gov't of the Libyan Arab Republic, 20 I.L.M. 1 (1977) (deciding that Libya unjustly seized LIAMCO's property and awarding LIAMCO the full value ($13,882,667) for the loss of its physical plant, as well as $66 million in lost profits, for a total of $79,882,667—shortly thereafter, Libya agreed to pay the full value of the award in crude). *See also* Andrew B. Derman, *Nationalization and the Protective Arbitration Clause*, 5 J. Int'l Arb. 131 (1988).

14.09 Similarly, although Argentina initially declared itself to be immune from pressure to pay adverse awards rendered against it with regard to measures adopted during its economic crisis in 2001 and 2002, in October 2013, Argentina settled five final awards rendered against it at that time.[8]

14.10 In addition, even "rogue" states face the prospect of eventual regime change and/or a change of heart that could lead to a decision to pay adverse arbitral awards. A new or changed government may consider payment of an award, or a portion of an award coupled with investment incentives, in line with its new agenda. Libya is an example of a regime that engaged in such a dramatic reversal of policy.[9]

14.11 It should also be noted that failure to pay an award after exhaustion of existing challenge rights is not simply a breach of an obligation toward a claimant, but in the case of arbitrations pursuant to treaty obligations, a serious breach of international obligations toward the other signatory states of the relevant convention. In the event of nonpayment, separately from the right to forced execution in signatory states, a parallel diplomatic incident could result.

2. The Recognition of Awards Rendered Against Sovereigns

14.12 *(a) Recognition of awards subject to the New York Convention* Arbitral awards rendered against foreign sovereigns in a commercial arbitration that took place in a state that has adhered to the 1958 U.N. Convention on the Recognition and Enforcement of Foreign Arbitral Awards (New York Convention)[10] generally are enforceable in the United States pursuant to the New York Convention, implemented in the United States through the Federal Arbitration Act (FAA), 9 U.S.C. §§ 201–08.[11] The same procedures for obtaining recognition of a foreign arbitral award against a private defendant apply to a foreign sovereign. Under the New York Convention as implemented in the United States, the award creditor

---

[8] Douglas Thomson, *Argentina Agrees to Settle Treaty Awards*, Global Arbitration Review (Oct. 11, 2013, http://globalarbitrationreview.com/news/article/31961).

[9] Christopher Boucek, *Libya's Return To The Fold?* Foreign Policy in Focus Policy Report (Apr. 2004), *available at* http://fpif.org/libyas_return_to_the_fold/.

[10] Convention on the Recognition and Enforcement of Foreign Arbitral Awards, June 10, 1958, 21 U.S.T. 2517, 330 U.N.T.S. 3 [hereinafter the New York Convention]. The United States became a party to the New York Convention in 1970. Currently there are 154 parties to the New York Convention. *See* Status of the Convention on the Recognition and Enforcement of Foreign Arbitral Awards, http://www.uncitral.org/uncitral/en/uncitral_texts/arbitration/NYConvention_status.html (last visited Jan. 7, 2015). *See* Chapter 1.B.3 of this book.

[11] In the United States, the New York Convention applies not only to awards rendered in foreign countries, but also to so-called "nondomestic awards": those awards rendered in the United States but involving at least one non-U.S. party, or dealing with property abroad or performance abroad. 9 U.S.C. § 202 (2012). An award rendered in the United States involving a foreign sovereign will almost certainly constitute a "nondomestic" award. Zeiler v. Deitsch, 500 F.3d 157, 164 (2d Cir. 2007); Yusuf Ahmed Alghanim & Sons, W.L.L. v. Toys "R" Us, Inc., 126 F.3d 15, 18–19 (2d Cir. 1997); Bergeson v. Joseph Muller Corp., 710 F.2d 928, 933 (2d Cir. 1983).

has three years to have the award recognized by a U.S. court.[12] The court will recognize an award unless it concludes that one of the grounds for refusal specified in Article V of the New York Convention (concerning primarily due process and public policy violations) is present.[13]

Federal courts in New York exercise subject-matter jurisdiction over the foreign sovereign in proceedings for the recognition of an award subject to the New York Convention pursuant to 9 U.S.C. § 9 (providing for recognition in the district in which the award was rendered), 9 U.S.C. §§ 203 and 204 (providing federal courts with subject-matter jurisdiction and venue over recognition applications), and also 28 U.S.C. § 1330(a) (providing the federal district courts with subject-matter jurisdiction over disputes involving foreign states if the foreign state is not immune with respect to such dispute pursuant to the terms of the FSIA). This last section enables U.S. federal courts to exercise subject-matter jurisdiction over all actions for the recognition of arbitral awards rendered against a foreign sovereign because Section 1605(a)(6)(B) of the FSIA provides that a foreign sovereign shall not be immune from the jurisdiction of the U.S. courts in any action to recognize an arbitration award governed by an international treaty. **14.13**

An additional ground for subject-matter jurisdiction can be found in Section 1605(a)(1) of the FSIA, which provides jurisdiction over a foreign sovereign where the foreign state has waived its immunity from suit either explicitly or implicitly. Award creditors may benefit from New York jurisprudence that deems foreign sovereigns that are signatories to the New York Convention to have waived implicitly through the Convention their immunity from recognition actions.[14] **14.14**

(b) Recognition of ICSID awards in the United States is "automatic" Foreign investors who have successfully arbitrated claims against a foreign sovereign under **14.15**

[12] Federal Arbitration Act (FAA), 9 U.S.C. § 207 (2012) ("Within three years after an arbitral award falling under the Convention is made, any party to the arbitration may apply to any court having jurisdiction under this chapter for an order confirming the award as against any other party to the arbitration."). For arbitral awards to which the New York Convention does not apply, the statute of limitations for confirmation is only one year. 9 U.S.C. § 9 (2012). *See* Chapter 1.B of this book.

[13] 9 U.S.C. § 207. Also, in the case of international arbitrations taking place in the United States, some courts recognize the applicability of the "manifest disregard of the law" standard as a basis for vacatur. *See, e.g., Yusuf Ahmed Alghanim & Sons*, 126 F.3d at 23–24. *But see, e.g.*, Industrial Risk Insurers v. M.A.N. Gutehoffnungshutte GmbH, 141 F.3d 1434, 1441 (11th Cir. 1998) (holding that an award must be confirmed "unless appellants can successfully assert one of the seven defenses against enforcement of the award enumerated in Article V of the New York Convention").

[14] *See, e.g.*, Seetransport Wiking Trader Schiffahrtsgesellschaft MBH & Co., Kommanditgesellschaft v. Navimpex Centrala Navala, 989 F.2d 572, 578–79 (2d Cir. 1993) (implicit waiver was found because the arbitral award to be enforced was subject to the New York Convention, which expressly permits recognition and enforcement actions in Contracting States).

the 1966 Convention on the Settlement of Investment Disputes Between States and Nationals of Other States (ICSID Convention)[15] will have their awards recognized.[16] Just as in the case of awards subject to the New York Convention, New York courts have determined that signatories to the ICSID Convention have implicitly waived their sovereign immunity.[17] Article 54 of the ICSID Convention (as implemented in U.S. law) confers subject-matter jurisdiction on the courts of the United States to enforce immediately the pecuniary obligations of an ICSID award against a foreign sovereign as if it were a final judgment of a court of the United States.[18] As discussed further below, U.S. District Courts disagree as to whether ICSID awards may be recognized on an *ex parte* basis, or whether a plenary action is required.

14.16 Under Article 54(2) of the ICSID Convention, a party seeking enforcement of an ICSID award must provide a certified copy of the award to a designated competent court or authority. The United States has designated all of its federal district courts as such.[19] An award creditor thus can present a certified copy of the award to a U.S. District Court in New York for the purpose of enforcement, and move simultaneously to execution procedures under New York law to attach assets.[20]

14.17 *(c) A potential alternative track: recognition of a foreign court's recognition of the award* Depending upon an award creditor's global enforcement

[15] Convention on the Settlement of Investment Disputes Between States and Nationals of Other States, Mar. 18, 1965, 17 U.S.T. 1270, 575 U.N.T.S. 159 [hereinafter the ICSID Convention].

[16] *See, e.g.*, Mobil Cerro Negro Ltd. v. Bolivarian Republic of Venezuela, 87 F. Supp. 3d 573, 597 (S.D.N.Y. 2015) ("Such a court therefore is to review only the award's authenticity; recognition thereafter is mechanistic and effectively 'automatic.' ").

[17] *See* Blue Ridge Invs. v. Republic of Arg., 735 F.3d 72, 84 (2d. Cir. 2013).

[18] Article 54 of the ICSID Convention is implemented in U.S. law by 22 U.S.C. § 1650a (2012). Section 1650a provides:

> (a) Treaty rights; enforcement; full faith and credit; nonapplication of Federal Arbitration Act
>
> An award of an arbitral tribunal rendered pursuant to chapter IV of the convention shall create a right arising under a treaty of the United States. The pecuniary obligations imposed by such an award shall be enforced and shall be given the same full faith and credit as if the award were a final judgment of a court of general jurisdiction of one of the several States. The Federal Arbitration Act (9 U.S.C. 1 et seq.) shall not apply to enforcement of awards rendered pursuant to the convention.
>
> (b) Jurisdiction; amount in controversy
>
> The district courts of the United States (including the courts enumerated in section 460 of Title 28) shall have exclusive jurisdiction over actions and proceedings under subsection (a) of this section, regardless of the amount in controversy.

[19] *See* Contracting States and Measures Taken By Them for the Purpose of the Convention (2014), https://icsid.worldbank.org/apps/ICSIDWEB/icsiddocs/Documents/ICSID%208%20-%20latest%20-%20Nov%2010%202014.pdf.

[20] New York Civil Practice Law and Rules (N.Y. C.P.L.R.) § 5201 (Consol. 2009).

strategy, an award creditor may engage the recognition process with respect to a foreign arbitral award in a foreign jurisdiction and achieve the status of a final judgment in that jurisdiction. In such a case, the award creditor may bring the recognized arbitral award to New York and have it recognized under New York law as a foreign judgment that is "final, conclusive and enforceable where rendered."[21] In such a case, a U.S. District Court in New York would be seized with subject-matter jurisdiction pursuant to implicit waiver under Section 1605(a)(1) of the FSIA.[22]

The award creditor successfully pursued this approach in *Seetransport Wiking Trader Schiffahrtsgesellschaft MBH & Co., Kommanditgesellschaft v. Navimpex Centrala Navala*, decided by the Second Circuit in 1993.[23] The award creditor, a German shipbuilding company, secured recognition in a French court of a favorable ICC award against an instrumentality of the Romanian government. The award creditor sought to have the French court judgment that recognized the ICC award subsequently recognized under New York law. The Second Circuit held that a final judgment of a French court recognizing the ICC award could be recognized under New York law as a final foreign judgment. The court reasoned that in such a case, subject-matter jurisdiction would arise under the FSIA, and the foreign sovereign's immunity would be deemed implicitly waived because the cause of action was so closely related to a claim for recognition of the arbitral award. In such a case, the district court could exercise supplemental jurisdiction pursuant to 28 U.S.C. § 1367.[24] **14.18**

3. Sovereigns Enjoy Significant Immunities With Respect to the Enforcement of Arbitral Awards Against Them

Generally, the assets of a foreign sovereign are immune from execution. However, there are limited exceptions to this rule, set forth in Sections 1610 and 1611 of the FSIA. FSIA Section 1610(a) through (d) constructs a regime for attachment of the sovereign's assets. Opportunities and limitations are determined **14.19**

[21] N.Y. C.P.L.R. § 5302 (Consol. 2009). *See, e.g.*, Commissions Imp. Exp. S.A. v. Republic of the Congo, 757 F.3d 321 (D.C. Cir. 2014) (holding that the three-year statute of limitations period in the FAA does not preempt the longer limitation period in the D.C. Uniform Foreign-Country Money Judgments Recognition Act, in a case in which a judgment creditor sought recognition of a U.K. judgment enforcing an arbitral award).

[22] *See supra* note 14 and accompanying text.

[23] *See* Transport Wiking Trader Schiffahrtsgesellschaft MBH & Co., Kommanditgesellschaft v. Navimpex Centrala Navala, 989 F.2d 572 (2d Cir. 1993).

[24] *Id.* at 581–83; 28 U.S.C. § 1367(a) (2012) provides in part: "... in any civil action of which the district courts have original jurisdiction, the district courts shall have supplemental jurisdiction over all other claims that are so related to claims in the action within such original jurisdiction that they form part of the same case or controversy under Article III of the United States Constitution."

by the procedural posture of the arbitration and the recognition process in the U.S. courts:

- Subsection (a) addresses postjudgment[25] attachment against a foreign state.
- Subsection (b) addresses postjudgment attachment against an agency or instrumentality[26] of a foreign state (working as a supplement to subsection (a)).
- Subsection (c) provides that executions or attachments under subsections (a) or (b) are permitted only after the court has determined that a reasonable period of time has elapsed following the entry of judgment and the giving of any notice required under Section 1608(e).
- Subsection (d) addresses prejudgment attachment[27] against a foreign state.[28]

---

[25] We note that for the purposes of Section 1610 of the FSIA, "judgment" refers to a U.S. court judgment. As set out below, "postjudgment" attachment corresponds, in this chapter, to post-recognition attachment.

[26] Under Section 1603 of the FSIA, an agency or instrumentality of a foreign state is also considered to be a "foreign state" for the purposes of the FSIA. Thus, subsection (a) would include agencies and instrumentalities, but the subsection (b) exception is particular to agencies and instrumentalities only.

[27] *See* Sections C.2 and C.4 of this Chapter for a discussion of the relevance of the concept of "prejudgment" attachment in the arbitral context.

[28] Section 1610(a)–(d), in relevant part provides:

> (a) The property in the United States of a foreign state, as defined in *section 1603(a)* of this chapter, used for a commercial activity in the United States, shall not be immune from attachment in aid of execution, or from execution, upon a judgment entered by a court of the United States or of a State after the effective date of this Act, if—
>
> (1) the foreign state has waived its immunity from attachment in aid of execution or from execution either explicitly or by implication, notwithstanding any withdrawal of the waiver the foreign state may purport to effect except in accordance with the terms of the waiver, or
>
> (2) the property is or was used for the commercial activity upon which the claim is based, or
>
> (3) the execution relates to a judgment establishing rights in property which has been taken in violation of international law or which has been exchanged for property taken in violation of international law, or
>
> * * *
>
> (6) the judgment is based on an order confirming an arbitral award rendered against the foreign state, provided that attachment in aid of execution, or execution, would not be inconsistent with any provision in the arbitral agreement ...
>
> * * *
>
> (b) In addition to subsection (a), any property in the United States of an agency or instrumentality of a foreign state engaged in commercial activity in the United States shall not be immune from attachment in aid of execution, or from execution, upon a judgment entered by a court of the United States or of a State after the effective date of this Act, if—
>
> (1) the agency or instrumentality has waived its immunity from attachment in aid of execution or from execution either explicitly or implicitly, notwithstanding any withdrawal of the waiver the agency or instrumentality may purport to effect except in accordance with the terms of the waiver, or
>
> (2) the judgment relates to a claim for which the agency or instrumentality is not immune by virtue of *section 1605(a) (2), (3),* or *(5)* or *1605(b)* of this chapter, regardless of whether the property is or was involved in the act upon which the claim is based; or

The FSIA attachment regime does not prevent an award creditor from attaching the assets of a foreign sovereign, but the award creditor will be challenged by the boundaries of immunity. Considering first enforcement of arbitral awards subject to the New York Convention, the FSIA can work harshly to the disadvantage of claimants even though the New York Convention facilitates the enforcement of international arbitral awards in contracting states. From an award creditor's perspective, the FSIA's structure impedes the enforcement of arbitral awards in two significant ways: (1) in the context of New York Convention awards, the FSIA fails to distinguish between preaward attachment and prerecognition attachment—meaning that, arguably, both are prohibited absent an explicit waiver of sovereign immunity; and (2) the "reasonable time" requirement imposed by Section 1610(c) provides the sovereign with an opportunity to evade enforcement by moving assets out of the jurisdiction. **14.20**

With respect to the first issue, the distinction drawn in the FSIA between prejudgment and postjudgment attachment disadvantages New York Convention award creditors because it prevents them from attaching a sovereign's commercial assets, even after a "win" in the arbitration, until the creditor is able to obtain recognition of the award (or an explicit waiver of sovereign immunity from prerecognition attachment). Some have criticized this state of affairs because the U.S. courts treat the creditor of an unrecognized New York Convention award the same way they treat any plaintiff who has yet to obtain a judgment or award in its dispute with a sovereign.[29] If an award creditor is dealing with a recalcitrant sovereign, this creates a significant disadvantage. **14.21**

---

(3) the judgment relates to a claim for which the agency or instrumentality is not immune by virtue of *section 1605A* of this chapter or section 1605(a)(7) of this chapter (as such section was in effect on January 27, 2008), regardless of whether the property is or was involved in the act upon which the claim is based.

(c) No attachment or execution referred to in subsections (a) and (b) of this section shall be permitted until the court has ordered such attachment and execution after having determined that a reasonable period of time has elapsed following the entry of judgment and the giving of any notice required under *section 1608(e)* of this chapter.

(d) The property of a foreign state, as defined in *section 1603(a)* of this chapter, used for a commercial activity in the United States, shall not be immune from attachment prior to the entry of judgment in any action brought in a court of the United States or of a State, or prior to the elapse of the period of time provided in subsection (c) of this section, if—

(1) the foreign state has explicitly waived its immunity from attachment prior to judgment, notwithstanding any withdrawal of the waiver the foreign state may purport to effect except in accordance with the terms of the waiver, and

(2) the purpose of the attachment is to secure satisfaction of a judgment that has been or may ultimately be entered against the foreign state, and not to obtain jurisdiction.

[29] Alexander Yanos, Cassandra Marshall & Daina Bray, *Getting the Money: When Can a Sovereign's Assets Be Attached Before a Judgment Has Been Obtained on a Successful Arbitral Award?*, 21 Mealey's Int'l Arb. Rep. 14 (2006).

14.22 As noted above, the ICSID award creditor is spared this problem because Article 54(1) of the ICSID Convention requires each contracting state to enforce an ICSID award as if it were a final judgment of its own courts. In the United States, 22 U.S.C. § 1650a specifically provides that "[t]he pecuniary obligations imposed by [an ICSID] award shall be enforced and shall be given the same full faith and credit as if the award were a final judgment of a court of general jurisdiction of one of the several States." In other words, ICSID awards are *automatically* recognized in the United States and treated as if they were final judgments issued in one of the 50 states.[30]

14.23 As such, in New York, ICSID awards are subject to the same streamlined enforcement procedure available for the enforcement of judgments issued in other U.S. jurisdictions.[31] In particular, Claimants need only follow the procedures outlined in Article 54 of the N.Y.C.P.L.R. before the underlying award is considered a "judgment,"[32] which can be done on an *ex parte* basis.[33]

14.24 However, a recent decision in the D.C. District Court has disagreed with the precedent set in New York courts. In *Viorel Micula v. The Government of Romania*, Viorel Micula filed a petition with the court seeking confirmation, on an *ex parte* basis, of a $116.3 million ICSID award received by Micula and

[30] *See* Mobil Cerro Negro Ltd. v. Bolivarian Republic of Venezuela, 87 F. Supp. 3d 573, 593–602 (S.D.N.Y. 2015) (reviewing statutory history of 22 U.S.C. § 1650a and emphasizing distinction from awards subject to New York Convention). *See also* New York City Bar, *Report by the Comm. on Int'l Commercial Disputes: Recommended Procedures for Recognition & Enforcement of Int'l Arbitration Awards Rendered Under the ICSID Convention*, 2–3 (July 2012) (emphasizing different status of ICSID awards due to lack of possibility for judicial review), *available at* http://www2.nycbar.org/Publications/reports/index_new.php?type=subject&alpha=I.

[31] *See* Siag v. Arab Republic of Egypt, 2009 WL 1834562, at *3 (S.D.N.Y. June 19, 2009).

[32] These requirements include: filing an authenticated copy of the award; submitting an affidavit to the effect that the award was not obtained by default, that it remains unsatisfied, and that its enforcement has not been stayed; and serving notice of filing of the judgment on the award debtor at its last known address within thirty days of filing the judgment and the affidavit. N.Y.C.P.L.R. §§ 5402, 5403 (Consol. 2009). Article 54 of the N.Y.C.P.L.R. is New York's version of the Uniform Enforcement of Foreign Judgments Act (the UEFJA). Generally speaking, under the UEFJA, a judgment of any state or federal court may be registered by filing an exemplified copy of the foreign judgment with the appropriate office of the Court and notifying the debtor of the filing. An exemplified judgment is a copy of the judgment to which a certificate has been attached and signed in three places, once by the judge and twice by the clerk, attesting to the authenticity and validity of the judgment.

[33] Mobil Cerro Negro Ltd. v. Bolivarian Republic of Venezuela, 87 F. Supp. 3d 573 (S.D.N.Y. 2015) (holding that award creditor need not comply with the FSIA's requirements as to process, personal jurisdiction, and venue to have an ICSID award recognized in New York courts, and that New York law permits *ex parte* recognition of ICSID awards). *See also* Grenada v. Grynberg, No. 11 Misc. 45 (S.D.N.Y. Apr. 29, 2011); Siag v. Arab Republic of Egypt, 2009 WL 1834562, at *3 (S.D.N.Y. June 19, 2009); Enron Corp. & Ponderosa Assets L.P. v. Argentine Republic, No. M-82 (S.D.N.Y. Nov. 20, 2007); Sempra Energy Int'l v. Argentine Republic, No. M-82 (S.D.N.Y. Nov. 14, 2007). Note, however, that some creditors have chosen not to avail themselves of this streamlined procedure for the enforcement of an ICSID award in New York. Blue Ridge Invs., LLC v. Republic of Argentina, 902 F. Supp. 2d 367, 370 (S.D.N.Y. 2012) *aff'd*, 735 F.3d 72 (2d Cir. 2013); Funnekotter v. Republic of Zimbabwe, No. 09 Civ. 8168 (CM) (Dkt. 11) (S.D.N.Y. Feb. 1, 2010).

four co-petitioners against Romania.[34] Engaging in a textual analysis and review of the legislative history of 22 U.S.C. § 1650a, the Court held that § 1650a does not permit *ex parte* confirmation of an ICSID award, which rather can be achieved only through a plenary action with proper service under the FSIA.[35] In doing so, the Court rejected the rulings of the New York District Courts as well as an earlier ruling of the D.C. District Court, which held that *ex parte* proceedings suffice for recognition of ICSID awards.[36] Immediately thereafter, Micula's co-petitioners sought *ex parte* recognition of the same ICSID award before the District Court for the Southern District of New York.[37] Here, the Southern District explicitly disagreed with the reasoning of the D.C. District Court, and again held that ICSID awards can be recognized by *ex parte* proceedings.[38] At the time of this publication, no appellate court has ruled on this issue.

The second impediment to post-recognition attachment is the requirement that a "reasonable period of time" elapse following the entry of the judgment and the giving of notice pursuant to Section 1608(e) of the FSIA.[39] This requirement affords a foreign sovereign additional time to secrete its assets out of the United States prior to enforcement. In at least one case, the Southern District of New York has found thirty days to be a reasonable period of time.[40] However, in light of the legislative history of the FSIA,[41] an award creditor may argue that a court's calculation of the "reasonable period of time" should take into account the time that has elapsed since the award was rendered and the state ignored the award creditor's demands for payment. In particular, the legislative history provides that: **14.25**

> In determining whether the period has been reasonable, the courts should take into account procedures, including legislation, that may be necessary for payment of a

[34] Micula v. Gov't of Romania, No. 1:14-CV-00600 (APM), 2015 WL 2354310, at *2–3 (D.D.C. May 18, 2015).

[35] *Id.* at *4–7 (D.D.C. May 18, 2015). In its decision, the court further held that this plenary action requirement does not conflict with the United States' obligations under Article 54 of the ICSID Convention. *Id.* at *7.

[36] Miminco, LLC v. Dem. Rep. Congo, 79 F. Supp. 3d 213, 216 (D.D.C. 2015).

[37] Micula v. Gov't of Romania, No. 15 MISC. 107, 2015 WL 4643180, at *1–2 (S.D.N.Y. Aug. 5, 2015), *reconsideration denied*, No. 15 MISC. 107 LGS, 2015 WL 5257013 (S.D.N.Y. Sept. 9, 2015).

[38] *Id.* at *3–4 ("[G]iven the spirit of the ICSID Convention (to which the United States is a party), the language of its enabling statute, the clear exceptions to the FSIA that apply and precedent in this District, the expensive and time-consuming process of a plenary proceeding to recognize an ICSID award in the United States is unnecessary as a matter of law.").

[39] *See* 28 U.S.C. § 1610(c).

[40] Order Granting Motion to Execute on Judgment, FG Hemisphere Assocs. v. Republique du Congo, No. 01 Civ. 8700 (S.D.N.Y. Sept. 5, 2002). In any event, all judgment creditors are subject to Rule 62(a) of the U.S. Federal Rules of Civil Procedure, which imposes an automatic fourteen-day stay on execution of any judgment in a U.S. federal court.

[41] H.R. Rep. 94–1487, at 30 (1976). Of course, a state is likely to argue that a reasonable time period is still needed after the conclusion of annulment proceedings because: (a) payment was not due during the pendency of its challenge to the award; and (b) the bureaucratic machinery of the state takes some time to organize payment once it finally comes due.

judgment by a foreign state, which may take several months; representations by the foreign state of steps being taken to satisfy the judgment; or any steps being taken to satisfy the judgment; or evidence that the foreign state is about to remove assets from the jurisdiction to frustrate satisfaction of the judgment.[42]

14.26 These considerations—the state's ability and willingness to pay—can be assessed by a court on a case-by-case basis and, in certain circumstances, merit calculations based upon the timing of the issuance of the award. Therefore, in the context of postrecognition attachment, in certain cases it would be unreasonable to make the award creditor wait any more to begin attachment proceedings than it already has.

4. Foreign Sovereigns Are Not Immune From Personal Jurisdiction and Service

14.27 Although the Southern District of New York has recently held that the FSIA's requirements regarding personal jurisdiction and service do not apply in the context of the enforcement of ICSID awards, in all other contexts, the unique characteristics of foreign sovereigns bring additional complexities to the threshold issues of personal jurisdiction and service that must be respected in the award enforcement context.[43] In particular, the FSIA provides that personal jurisdiction shall exist over foreign states "as to every claim for relief over which the district courts have jurisdiction," provided that service is made in accordance with Section 1608 of the FSIA.[44] Section 1608 sets forth several alternatives for serving foreign sovereigns in U.S. court proceedings.[45]

---

[42] *Id.*

[43] Mobil Cerro Negro Ltd. v. Bolivarian Republic of Venezuela, 87 F. Supp. 3d 573 (S.D.N.Y. 2015) (holding that award creditor need not comply with the FSIA's requirements as to process, personal jurisdiction, and venue to have an ICSID award recognized in New York courts).

[44] 28 U.S.C. § 1330(b) (2012); *see also* 4B Charles Alan Wright & Arthur R. Miller, Federal Practice and Procedure §1111, at 123 (3d ed. 2002) (citing the legislative history behind the FSIA for the proposition that Section 1608 provides the exclusive procedure for service of process on a foreign state). The U.S. Court of Appeals for the Second Circuit has held that foreign states do not enjoy protection under the Due Process Clause, so a petitioner need not satisfy constitutional "minimum contacts" requirements to establish a court's personal jurisdiction over a foreign state. Frontera Res. Azer. Corp. v. State Oil Co. of the Azer. Republic, 582 F.3d 393, 397–98 (2d Cir. 2009); *see also* TMR Energy Ltd v. State Prop. Fund of Ukraine, 411 F.3d 296, 300 (D.C. Cir. 2005) (citing Price v. Socialist People's Libya Arab Jamahiraya, 294 F.3d 82 (D.C. Cir. 2002) for the proposition that states are not "persons" within the meaning of the due process clause). *But see* S.I. Strong, *Enforcement of Arbitral Awards Against Foreign States or State Agencies*, 24 Nw. J. Int'l L. & Bus. 335 (2006) (noting contrary arguments).

[45] Section 1608(a) specifies that service upon a foreign sovereign may be made:

(1) by delivery of a copy of the summons and complaint in accordance with any special arrangement for service between the plaintiff and the foreign state or political subdivision; or

(2) if no special arrangement exists, by delivery of a copy of the summons and complaint in accordance with an applicable international convention on service of judicial documents; or

(3) if service cannot be made under paragraphs (1) or (2), by sending a copy of the summons and complaint and a notice of suit, together with a translation of each into the official language of the foreign state, by any form of mail requiring a signed receipt,

Where relevant, strict adherence to the service requirements under Section 1608 is important in any proceeding against a sovereign.[46] For this reason, it is wise to ensure at the contracting stage that a party and the sovereign counterparty agree on special arrangements for service of process. Importantly, if a state is a signatory to the 1965 Hague Convention on the Service Abroad of Judicial and Extrajudicial Documents in Civil or Commercial Matters,[47] service can be completed pursuant to its basic methods. **14.28**

A question arises as to what an award creditor can do in the event that a foreign sovereign has not appointed an agent for service of process in the United States, and no international convention on service of documents applies. In that case, the award creditor must rely on a special arrangement between the parties for service.[48] Notice provisions in the relevant contract might suffice, as long as they are specific with regard to the address to which notices are to be sent, and the sovereign receives timely notice. For example, in *Concord Reinsurance Co. v. Caja Nacional de Ahorro y Seguro*, the claimant attempted to rely on the notice provision in its agreement with the defendant, an agent of the Argentine government.[49] The U.S. District Court for the Southern District of New York rejected service as deficient because the notice provision in the agreement failed to specify an address for service.[50] **14.29**

Even if jurisdiction is established, a problem can arise where the court concludes that, for prudential reasons, the action ought to be dismissed on grounds of *forum non conveniens*. That is, the court concludes that it should decline jurisdiction over the petition to enforce an award because another forum is better suited to **14.30**

---

to be addressed and dispatched by the clerk of the court to the head of the ministry of foreign affairs of the foreign state concerned, or

(4) if service cannot be made within 30 days under paragraph (3), by sending two copies of the summons and complaint and a notice of suit, together with a translation of each into the official language of the foreign state, by any form of mail requiring a signed receipt, to be addressed and dispatched by the clerk of the court to the Secretary of State in Washington, District of Columbia, to the attention of the Director of Special Consular Services—and the Secretary shall transmit one copy of the papers through diplomatic channels to the foreign state and shall send to the clerk of the court a certified copy of the diplomatic note indicating when the papers were transmitted.

[46] Of equal importance for the sovereign is that it raise any challenges to service under Section 1608 at the appropriate juncture. *See* Democratic Republic of Congo v. FG Hemisphere Assocs., LLC, 508 F.3d 1062, 1065 (D.C. Cir. 2007) (finding that the Congo waived its claim to improper service of process by not raising this defense in a timely manner).

[47] Hague Convention on the Service Abroad of Judicial and Extrajudicial Documents in Civil or Commercial Matters, Nov. 15, 1965, 20 U.S.T. 361, 658 U.N.T.S. 263.

[48] *See* 28 U.S.C. § 1608(a)(1).

[49] Concord Reinsurance Co. v. Caja Nacional de Ahorro y Seguro, No. 93 Civ. 6606, 1994 WL 86401 (S.D.N.Y. Mar. 16, 1994).

[50] *Id.* at *3. *See also* Seven Seas Shipping (UK) Ltd. v. Tondo Limitada, No. 99 Civ. 1164, 2000 WL 60208 (S.D.N.Y. Jan. 24, 2000), in which the award creditor's effort at securing postjudgment attachment was unsuccessful due to its failure to provide adequate notice of confirmation pursuant to Section 1610(c), which cross-references Section 1608(e), *id.* at *3.

the resolution of the dispute. The Second Circuit has twice declined jurisdiction over awards being enforced against sovereigns in New York on grounds of *forum non conveniens*.[51] In both cases, the decisions may have turned on the fact that the plaintiffs were seeking to enforce the award against the state, although the state was not a signatory to the underlying arbitration agreement, based on corporate veil piercing arguments. The use of the *forum non conveniens* doctrine to decline jurisdiction in the arbitral context has been the subject of a fair amount of criticism.[52]

C. DEALING WITH THE PROBLEM OF RECALCITRANT STATES

1. Predispute Protections

14.31 There are several steps that a party can take at the time of its investment that can facilitate later enforcement of an arbitral award. First, the state may be required to post a letter of credit or performance bond against which the private party can draw in the event of a favorable award. Such a provision may be difficult to negotiate, but if possible it will provide security to a potential award creditor.

14.32 Second, a party can seek an explicit waiver of sovereign immunity from the state in the arbitration agreement. Not all waivers are equally effective, however, and it is important for a party to ensure that the sovereign spells out precisely which immunities it is waiving. A waiver of immunity from the jurisdiction of the U.S. courts, for example, does not necessarily constitute a waiver of immunity from attachment; a waiver of immunity from attachment, moreover, does not necessarily constitute a waiver of immunity from prejudgment attachment. Thus, a private party should seek a broad waiver that covers all immunities that might be relevant in enforcing an award. In the case of contracts with ICSID arbitration clauses, it would also be prudent to seek an agreement that either party could pursue preaward interim measures in the municipal courts, as is required in Rule 39(6) of the ICSID Arbitration Rules in order for court-ordered interim measures to be available.

2. Prearbitration Attachment

14.33 Prior to the formation of an arbitral tribunal, the only means for a party to seek interim relief is to petition a national court directly. Most widely-used arbitral

[51] Figueiredo Ferraz e Engenharia de Projecto Ltda. v. Republic of Peru, 665 F.3d 384 (2d Cir. 2011) (*Figueiredo*); Monegasque de Reassurances S.A.M. v. Nak Naftogaz of Ukraine, 311 F.3d 488 (2d Cir. 2002).

[52] *Figueiredo*, 665 F.3d at 401 (Lynch, J. dissenting); William W. Park & Alexander A. Yanos, *Treaty Obligations and National Law: Emerging Conflicts in International Arbitration*, 58 Hastings

rules permit such a remedy. The ICC Rules permit a party to seek interim measures from courts without limitation in the period prior to filing the Request for Arbitration, and "in appropriate circumstances" thereafter.[53] Similarly, the LCIA Rules permit a party to apply to a national court for interim measures "(i) before the formation of the Arbitral Tribunal; and (ii) after the formation of the Arbitral Tribunal, in exceptional cases and with the Arbitral Tribunal's authorisation, until the final award."[54] Meanwhile, the rules of the Arbitration Institute of the Stockholm Chamber of Commerce,[55] American Arbitration Association,[56] and Permanent Court of Arbitration[57] provide that a request for interim measures to a judicial authority is not deemed to be incompatible with the arbitration agreement or the applicable rules. In contrast, the ICSID Rules prevent the parties from seeking attachments or other interim measures from any national court, unless the parties have expressly agreed otherwise.[58]

(a) The requirement of explicit waiver All prearbitration attachment actions—as well as (as discussed previously) all arbitration and prerecognition attachment actions—have the same statutory requirements as the "prejudgment" attachment action governed by Section 1610(d) of the FSIA. The claimant must show that: (1) the property at issue is used for commercial activity in the United States; (2) the foreign state has explicitly waived its immunity from attachment prior to judgment; and (3) the purpose of the attachment is to secure satisfaction of a judgment, not to secure jurisdiction. **14.34**

The crux of the issue lies in the sovereign's waiver. It has been said that "[t]he only way to place a sovereign party on an equal footing with a private one is to ensure that there is a waiver of immunity from *execution* as well as immunity from *jurisdiction*, the latter implied by the arbitration clause itself."[59] **14.35**

An explicit waiver of immunity from prejudgment attachment need not use the phrase "prejudgment attachment." The Second Circuit reached this conclusion in 1982 in *Libra Bank Ltd. v. Banco Nacional de Costa Rica, S.A.*, finding an explicit waiver where the sovereign had agreed to "irrevocably and unconditionally waiv[e] any right or immunity from legal proceedings including suit judgment and execution on grounds of sovereignty which it or its property may now or hereafter enjoy."[60] **14.36**

L. Rev. 251 (2006); Ben Juratowitch, Fora Non Conveniens *for Enforcement of Arbitral Awards Against States*, 63 Int'l and Comp. L. Q. 477 (2014).

[53] International Chamber of Commerce Rules of Arbitration, Article 28(2) (2012).

[54] London Court of International Arbitration Rules, Article 25.3 (2014).

[55] Arbitration Institute of Stockholm Chamber of Commerce Rules, Article 32 (2010).

[56] American Arbitration Association Commercial Arbitration Rules, Rule 37 (2013).

[57] Permanent Court of Arbitration Arbitration Rules, Article 26(9) (2012).

[58] International Centre for Settlement of Investment Disputes Arbitration Rules, Rule 39(6).

[59] Jan Paulsson, Nigel Rawding & Lucy Reed, The Freshfields Guide to Arbitration Clauses in International Contracts 105 (3d ed. Kluwer Law International 2010).

[60] Libra Bank Ltd. v. Banco Nacional de Costa Rica, S. A., 676 F.2d 47, 49 (2d Cir. 1982).

14.37 New York courts have found explicit waiver in the provisions of the contracts giving rise to the arbitration. For example, the Second Circuit in *Banco de Seguros del Estado v. Mutual Marine Office, Inc.*[61] held that Banco de Seguros del Estado, a company wholly owned by the Uruguayan government, had explicitly waived its immunity in the United States through the umbrella agreements at issue in two separate reinsurance arbitrations. The agreements provided that the arbitrators "are relieved of all judicial formalities and may abstain from following the strict rules of law."[62] On this basis, the court concluded that each of the arbitral tribunal's orders granting prehearing security was enforceable in New York.[63] In reaching its conclusion, the Second Circuit noted that the Ninth Circuit and other courts had held similar clauses to constitute a waiver of immunity from prejudgment attachment.[64]

14.38 In a case outside of the Second Circuit, *Enron Equipment Procurement Co. v. The M/V Titan 2*, the U.S. District Court for the Western District of Louisiana permitted prearbitration attachment in connection with a Texas arbitration involving an instrumentality of Ukraine.[65] The sovereign's agent had agreed in the underlying contract that the counterparty was entitled to a statutory lien to secure payment of money owed under the contract. The court noted that "agreeing to arbitration and consenting to be governed by laws in a certain country are not explicit waivers."[66] The court nonetheless found that the agreement to grant a lien constituted an explicit waiver of immunity against prejudgment attachment.[67]

14.39 Similarly, in *Venus Lines Agency v. CVG Industria Venezolana de Aluminio, C.A.*,[68] the Eleventh Circuit, citing *Libra Bank Ltd.*, found an explicit waiver of immunity from prejudgment attachment relating to an arbitration against an instrumentality of the Venezuelan government. In that case, the instrumentality had agreed that the claimant would "have the right to attach the cargo for the payment of the freight, dead freight, demurrages and losses due to detention"; this was held to be sufficiently clear to constitute an explicit waiver.[69]

14.40 *(b) Procedure for prearbitration attachment* Pursuant to Federal Rule of Civil Procedure 64, state law governs prejudgment attachment. In New York, under N.Y. C.P.L.R. § 6212(a), in order to obtain an order of attachment, the movant

[61] Banco de Seguros del Estado v. Mut. Marine Office, Inc., 344 F.3d 255 (2d Cir. 2003).
[62] *Id.* at 258.
[63] *Id.*
[64] *Id.* at 261–62 (*citing* Pac. Reins. Mgmt. Corp. v. Ohio Reins. Corp., 935 F.2d 1019 (9th Cir. 1991) and British Ins. Co. of Cayman v. Water St. Ins. Co., 93 F. Supp. 2d 506 (S.D.N.Y. 2000)). Note that there was no question that the property at issue (a letter of credit in a commercial arbitration) was used for commercial activity.
[65] Enron Equip. Procurement Co. v. The M/V TITAN 2, 82 F. Supp. 2d 602 (W.D. La. 1999).
[66] *Id.* at 608.
[67] *Id.*
[68] 210 F.3d 1309 (11th Cir. 2000).
[69] *Id.* at 1311–12.

must show that: (1) there is a cause of action; (2) it is probable that the plaintiff will succeed on the merits; (3) one or more grounds for attachment provided in section 6201 exist;[70] and (4) the amount demanded from the defendant exceeds all counterclaims known to the movant.[71] With respect to a pending arbitration, N.Y. C.P.L.R. § 7502(c) qualifies § 6212(a) by limiting the grounds available for prearbitral attachment. Namely, provisional remedies may be granted for a pending arbitration "only upon the ground that the award to which the applicant may be entitled may be rendered ineffectual without such provisional relief."[72]

3. Interim Measures from the Arbitral Tribunal

Once an arbitral tribunal has been formed, parties may seek interim measures from the tribunal itself. If those measures are granted, parties may then turn to New York courts to enforce or challenge such measures. For example, in *Banco de Seguros del Estado v. Mutual Marine Office, Inc.*, also discussed in Section C.2(a), two arbitral tribunals had issued orders granting the claimants' motions to require the respondent to post security.[73] The respondent challenged the orders in the United States District Court for the Southern District of New York. The District Court,[74] and then the Second Circuit,[75] confirmed the arbitral tribunals' orders, finding that the tribunals had acted within their authority and that the respondent was not immune from prejudgment attachment under the FSIA. **14.41**

4. Prerecognition Attachment and Explicit Waiver

Some award creditors may wish to attach the assets of a foreign sovereign award debtor as soon as a favorable award is rendered by a foreign arbitral tribunal. As discussed previously, however, in the context of New York Convention awards, the terms of the FSIA are at odds with an award creditor's goal of speedy attachment. In this procedural posture, the award creditor is required to seek attachment under the prejudgment attachment rule set forth in Section 1610(d) of the FSIA. Despite the fact that a tribunal has already issued the award, the award creditor has the difficult task of demonstrating that the sovereign has explicitly waived its immunity from prejudgment attachment. **14.42**

---

[70] *See, e.g.*, N.Y. C.P.L.R. § 6201(3), which provides that "the defendant, with intent to defraud his creditors or frustrate the enforcement of a judgment that might be rendered in plaintiff's favor, has assigned, disposed of, encumbered or secreted property, or removed it from the state or is about to do any of these acts."

[71] N.Y. C.P.L.R. § 6212(a); *see also* Sivault Sys., Inc. v. Wondernet, Ltd., No. 05 Civ. 890, 2005 WL 681457, at *3 (S.D.N.Y. Mar. 25, 2005). *See also* Chapter 8.C.3 of this book.

[72] *See* Swift Splash, Ltd. v. Rice Corp., 2010 U.S. Dist. LEXIS 101324, at *5 (S.D.N.Y. 2010).

[73] Banco de Seguros del Estado v. Mut. Marine Office, Inc., 344 F.3d 255, 258 (2d Cir. 2003).

[74] Banco de Seguros del Estado v. Mut. Marine Offices, Inc., 230 F.Supp.2d 362 (S.D.N.Y. 2002).

[75] *Banco de Seguros del Estado*, 344 F.3d at 262–64.

14.43 That being said, if a sovereign that has signed the New York Convention challenges the arbitral award in the country in which the award is issued, courts may well construe this action to be an explicit waiver under Section 1610(d) under certain circumstances.[76] This approach is based upon Article VI of the New York Convention, which provides:

> If an application for the setting aside or suspension of the award has been made to a competent authority [of the country in which, or under the law of which, that award was made], the authority before which the award is sought to be relied upon may, ... on the application of the party claiming enforcement of the award, order the other party to give suitable security.

14.44 *Skandia America Reinsurance Company v. Caja Nacional de Ahorro y Seguro* provides an example of such a case arising in the Southern District of New York.[77] The claimant initiated an arbitration in New York against Caja Nacional de Ahorro y Seguro (Caja), a company wholly owned by the government of Argentina. Caja failed to file any responsive pleading or make an appearance at the hearing, and the arbitral tribunal found for Skandia on the merits of the claim. Skandia filed a motion in the Southern District of New York to recognize the award, and further requested that Caja post "prejudgment" security.

14.45 Caja challenged the recognition proceedings, arguing that the New York Convention applied and that the FSIA protected Caja from prejudgment attachment. While Caja later argued that its challenge did not constitute an "application for the setting aside or suspension of the award" under Article VI of the New York Convention, the court found that based upon Caja's attack on the manner in which Skandia submitted the award and the nature of the relief sought, Caja's failure to pay, and the Second Circuit's recommendation that the New York Convention be interpreted broadly,[78] Caja "ha[d] in effect moved to suspend the award."[79] Because Argentina is a signatory to the New York Convention and Caja had challenged the confirmation of the award in its response to Skandia's motion, the court held that Caja had explicitly waived its immunity from prejudgment attachment.[80]

---

[76] *See* Int'l Ins. Co. v. Caja Nacional de Ahorro y Seguro, 293 F.3d 392, 399–400 (7th Cir. 2002); Skandia Am. Reinsurance Corp. v. Caja Nacional de Ahorro y Seguro, No. 96 Civ. 2301, 1997 WL 278054 (S.D.N.Y. May 23, 1997).

[77] *Skandia*, 1997 WL 278054.

[78] *See* Cargill Int'l S.A. v. M/T Pavel Dybenko, 991 F.2d 1012, 1018 (2d Cir. 1993).

[79] *Skandia*, 1997 WL 278054 at *5.

[80] *Id.* at *6. The court also found that, under Section 1609 (which provides the general rule of immunity from attachment or execution, except where otherwise provided in existing international agreements or in the exceptions enumerated in Sections 1610 and 1611), the New York Convention, to which the United States acceded in 1970, was an "existing international agreement" at the time of enactment of the FSIA in 1976. *Id.* at *4. Thus, the FSIA's prohibition on prejudgment attachment is "subject to" Article VI of the New York Convention, and immunity was inapplicable even without reference to Sections 1610 or 1611.

Another case brought against Caja, *Concord Reinsurance Co. v. Caja Nacional de Ahorro y Seguro*,[81] decided by the Southern District in 1994, presents an interesting contrast. In this case Concord Reinsurance Company (Concord) sought recognition of its arbitral award, secured by default in a Bermuda arbitration, against Caja in the Southern District of New York, concurrently moving for attachment of a bank account in New York City. Caja argued that it was immune from attachment under Section 1610(d) of the FSIA. **14.46**

While Concord argued that Article VI of the New York Convention constituted waiver of immunity from prejudgment attachment, the court found there had been no waiver because Article VI "concerns a situation in which the party against whom an award has been entered seeks affirmative relief from the court. That situation is not at all the same as that here, in which the party that obtained an award seeks prejudgment security in a court of its own choosing."[82] **14.47**

Thus, based on the discussion above, sovereign defendants should carefully consider challenging an award, as doing so may risk effecting an explicit waiver of immunity from prejudgment attachment, rendering assets in the United States and potentially other jurisdictions susceptible to attachment. **14.48**

In a 2006 case before the Southern District, *Libancell S.A.L. v. Republic of Lebanon*, Libancell had prevailed in a United Nations Commission on International Trade Law (UNCITRAL) arbitration in Beirut and secured recognition of its award in France.[83] Libancell then sought recognition of the award in the Southern District, also moving to attach the proceeds of a pending bond offering by Lebanon. The court found that because Lebanon had not challenged the award in Lebanon, no explicit waiver had occurred.[84] Importantly, the court noted that the situation would be different *after* recognition of the award, in which case Libancell could rely upon Section 1610(a)(6) of the FSIA, rendering explicit waiver unnecessary.[85] **14.49**

A more recent example of such an approach was seen in the efforts by BG Group to collect on an UNCITRAL award against Argentina in the U.S. District Court for the District of Columbia. Argentina sought to set aside the award and also contested BG Group's attempt to seek recognition and enforcement. In response, **14.50**

---

[81] Concord Reinsurance Co. v. Caja Nacional De Ahorro y Seguro, No. 93 Civ. 6606, 1994 WL 86401 (S.D.N.Y. Mar. 16, 1994).

[82] *Id.* at *2. In any event, because the arbitration was based in Bermuda, Caja could have challenged the award only in a Bermuda court. Thus, even if Caja had objected to confirmation of the award in New York, the court could not have deemed this a challenge to the award or request for suspension falling within the meaning of Article VI of the New York Convention.

[83] Libancell S.A.L. v. The Republic of Lebanon, No. 06 Civ. 2765, 2006 WL 1321328 at *1 (S.D.N.Y. May 16, 2006).

[84] *Id.* at *5.

[85] Section 1610(a)(6) allows for postjudgment attachment of property of a foreign state that is used for commercial activity in the United States when "the judgment is based on an order confirming an arbitral award rendered against the foreign state, provided that attachment in aid of execution, or execution, would not be inconsistent with any provision in the arbitral agreement."

BG Group requested that Argentina post security pursuant to Article VI of the New York Convention.[86] Similar applications have also been made in the context of annulment proceedings brought before ICSID.[87]

5. Postrecognition Attachment and Execution

14.51 In the event that a foreign sovereign refuses to pay a recognized foreign arbitral award, the FSIA provides the terms on which an award creditor can proceed to execution procedures to force a state to pay its obligations.

14.52 An award creditor with an arbitral award that has been recognized (i.e., under the New York Convention), or an award creditor with an award that is automatically enforceable (i.e., an ICSID award), may move to enforce its award by attaching

[86] BG Group's case was subsequently appealed to the Supreme Court due to questions of jurisdiction. The Court ultimately found that the district court did have jurisdiction to enforce the award. *See* BG Group PLC v. Republic of Arg., 134 S. Ct. 1198 (2014). Note, Freshfields Bruckhaus Deringer US LLP was counsel to BG in this proceeding.

[87] In CMS Gas Transmission Co. v. Argentine Republic, ICSID Case No. ARB/01/8, the annulment committee refused to require Argentina to post a bond based upon a letter from Argentina's attorney general promising that, in the event that the award was not annulled, Argentina would pay it. Note, Freshfields Bruckhaus Deringer US LLP was counsel to CMS in this proceeding. Following the committee's decision to uphold the award, Argentina did not initially pay the award and was subject to domestic litigation in the United States. Blue Ridge Invs., LLC v. Republic of Arg., 902 F. Supp. 2d 367 (S.D.N.Y. 2012), *aff'd*, 735 F.3d 72 (2d Cir. 2013). It eventually settled the case after losing an appeal in the Second Circuit. In Enron Creditors Recovery Corp. (formerly Enron Corp.) and Ponderosa Assets, L.P. v. Argentine Republic, ICSID Case No. ARB/01/3, the annulment committee (in a decision dated October 7, 2008) gave Argentina sixty days to indicate whether it intended to pay the award promptly if its annulment request proved unsuccessful, noting that, if necessary, it would reconsider at a later date the issue of a continuance of the stay of enforcement of the award and the issue of security. However, in a decision dated May 20, 2009, the committee decided to continue the stay of enforcement without requiring Argentina to post security, despite acknowledging that there was a "high risk" that Argentina would not voluntarily pay the award. In reaching its decision, the committee cited its concern that interim measures would "have an irreversible effect for one of the parties" and that third-party creditors in unrelated claims would seek to attach any funds posted by Argentina as security in the case at hand. Argentina was ultimately successful in the annulment proceedings. In contrast, in a March 5, 2009 decision in Sempra Energy International v. Argentine Republic, ICSID Case No. ARB/02/16, the annulment committee conditioned a continued stay of enforcement of the award upon Argentina's placement of US$75 million into an escrow account within 120 days of the decision, as proof of future performance in the event the award was not annulled. Following Argentina's failure to comply with the committee's March 5 decision, the claimant again requested the committee to lift the stay of enforcement. In a decision dated August 7, 2009, the committee terminated the stay of enforcement based on Argentina's non-compliance. In doing so, it also rejected the concerns cited by the annulment committee in the *Enron Creditors* case discussed above. Nevertheless, that award too was ultimately annulled by the ad hoc committee. Finally, in Compañia de Aguas del Aconquija S.A. and Vivendi Universal S.A. v. Argentine Republic, ICSID Case No. ARB/97/3, the annulment committee demanded a detailed commitment from Argentina that it would pay the award, days following the initiation of efforts by Vivendi to enforce the award (assuming that the award was not annulled). The committee noted that Argentina's failure to assure the committee regarding its commitment would lead it to require Argentina to arrange a bank guarantee. If Argentina then failed to post the bank guarantee within sixty days, the committee would lift the stay on enforcement of the award. That annulment application was rejected, and Argentina subsequently settled domestic litigation in the United States relating to the enforcement of the award.

assets of a foreign state under Section 1610(a) or (b) of the FSIA after a reasonable period of time has elapsed.[88] This procedural posture is more favorable to the award creditor because the explicit waiver requirement disappears. While the award creditor still must demonstrate that the property is used for commercial activity in the United States and is located in the United States, Section 1610(a) provides the award creditor with seven options for demonstrating an exception to immunity, only one of which must be established.[89]

Section 1610(a)(6) allows for the postjudgment attachment of the property of a foreign state that is used for commercial activity in the United States when "the judgment is based on an order confirming an arbitral award rendered against the foreign state, provided that attachment in aid of execution, or execution, would not be inconsistent with any provision in the arbitral agreement."[90] As an example, the U.S. District Court for the Northern District of Georgia relied upon the Section 1610(a)(6) exception in *Lloyd's Underwriters v. AO Gazsnabtranzit*, a case involving a requested writ of execution in order to enforce a previously recognized arbitral award against the Republic of Moldova.[91] **14.53**

Also common, even when the court could rely upon Section 1610(a)(6), is for the court to rely on the Section 1610(a)(1) or 1610(b)(1) waiver exceptions instead.[92] These exceptions apply where "the foreign state has waived its immunity from attachment in aid of execution or from execution either explicitly or by implication."[93] **14.54**

However, it is important to remember that this is not the end of the story. In the case of a confirmed New York Convention award or any ICSID award: (1) a reasonable period of time must have passed following the entry of judgment, pursuant to Section 1610(c) of the FSIA (this element is discussed further in Section B.3 above); and (2) the award creditor must demonstrate that the sovereign uses **14.55**

---

88 *But see* discussion in Section B.3 of this chapter, as to whether the reasonable time period requirement should be truncated in the arbitral context.

89 *See supra* note 27.

90 Other important exceptions potentially relevant for enforcing arbitral awards against a foreign sovereign include where: (1) the foreign state has waived its immunity from attachment in aid of execution, either explicitly or implicitly (Section 1610(a)(1)); (2) the property is or was used for the commercial activity upon which the claim is based (Section 1610(a)(2)); (3) the execution relates to a judgment establishing rights in property which has been taken in violation of international law or which has been exchanged for property taken in violation of international law (Section 1610(a)(3)); and (4) the additional exceptions available against agencies and instrumentalities under Section 1610(b) apply.

91 Lloyd's Underwriters v. AO Gazsnabtranzit, No. 00 Civ. 242, 2000 WL 1719493 (N.D. Ga., Nov. 2, 2000).

92 *See* Karaha Bodas Co. v. Pertamina, 313 F.3d 70 (2d Cir. 2002) (Section 1610(b)(1)); Birch Shipping Corp. v. Embassy of United Republic of Tanzania, 507 F. Supp. 311 (D.D.C. 1980) (Section 1610(a)(1)).

93 28 U.S.C. §1610(a)(1). The wording in Section 1610(b)(1) is identical except for using the phrase "implicitly" rather than "by implication."

the property at issue for commercial activity in the United States. These criteria cannot be waived by the sovereign.[94] In fact, in many cases where an exception might otherwise apply in a postrecognition effort to enforce an arbitral award, courts have found that the property at issue was not used for commercial activity in the United States.[95] If any veil piercing issues are raised in the enforcement context, the doctrine of *forum non conveniens* could present an additional obstacle.[96]

6. What Kind of Assets May Be Attached?

14.56 Award creditors and judgment creditors are growing increasingly creative in their efforts to collect. For example, NML Capital, Ltd. and EM Ltd., holders of defaulted Argentine bonds, temporarily secured a restraining order on asset pledge accounts maintained for the benefit of the New York State Banking Department by Banco de la Nación Argentina, a bank wholly owned by Argentina.[97] In addition, other bondholders obtained temporary attachment orders with respect to pension funds that Argentina declared would later be expropriated, on the basis that the Argentine government had acquired an interest in this property.[98] More recently, the Export-Import Bank of China, which held defaulted Grenadian bonds, sought unsuccessfully to attach funds awarded to Grenada following an unrelated ICSID arbitration, in addition to other funds owed to Grenada.[99]

[94] Thai Lao Lignite (Thailand) Co. v. Gov't of Lao People's Democratic Republic, No. 10 CIV. 5256 KMW DCF, 2013 WL 1703873, at *6 (S.D.N.Y. Apr. 19, 2013) (citing Aurelius Capital Partners, LP v. Republic of Arg., 584 F.3d 120, 130 (2d Cir. 2009)).

[95] *See* Liberian E. Timber Corp. v. Republic of Liberia, 650 F. Supp. 73, 77–78 (S.D.N.Y. 1986) (finding that tax revenues were not used for commercial activity), aff'd without comment, 854 F.2d 1314 (2d Cir. 1987). *See also* FG Hemisphere Assocs. v. Democratic Republic of Congo, 447 F.3d 835 (D.C. Cir. 2006) (finding that diplomatic dwellings were not used for commercial activity); Walker Int'l Holdings Ltd. v. Republic of Congo, 395 F.3d 229 (5th Cir. 2004) (finding that signing bonuses and other payments owed to the Congo had not been used for commercial activity); and Liberian E. Timber Corp. v. Republic of Liberia, 659 F. Supp. 606 (D.D.C. 1987) (finding that an embassy bank account had not been used for commercial activity).

[96] *See, e.g.*, Figueiredo Ferraz e Engenharia de Projecto Ltda. v. Republic of Peru, 665 F.3d 384 (2d Cir. 2011); Monegasque de Reassurances S.A.M. v. Nak Naftogaz of Ukraine, 311 F.3d 488 (2d Cir. 2002).

[97] Order of Attachment, NML Capital, Ltd. v. The Republic of Arg., No. 05 Civ. 2434 (S.D.N.Y. Sept. 12, 2008); *see also* NML Capital, Ltd. v. Republic of Arg., 680 F.3d 254, 255 (2d Cir. 2012) (affirming the District Court's attachment and restraining orders).

[98] Order to Show Cause, Aurelius Capital Partners, LP et al. v. The Republic of Argentina, No. 07 Civ. 2715 (S.D.N.Y. Oct. 30, 2008). Although these temporary orders were confirmed by the District Court upon finalization of Argentine legislation authorizing the transfer of the funds to Argentina, the attachment was later overturned by the U.S. Court of Appeals for the Second Circuit on the basis that the exception to immunity in Section 1610(a) of the FSIA was inapplicable because the Republic had not used the funds for commercial activity in the United States. Aurelius Capital Partners, LP v. Republic of Argentina, 2008 U.S. Dist. LEXIS 101764 (S.D.N.Y. Dec. 11, 2008); Aurelius Capital Partners, LP v. The Republic of Argentina, 584 F.3d 120 (2d Cir. 2009).

[99] Exp.-Imp. Bank of the Republic of China v. Grenada, 768 F.3d 75 (2d Cir. 2014). Note, Freshfields Bruckhaus Deringer US LLP was counsel to Grenada in the underlying arbitration proceeding.

Notably, the Supreme Court recently found in *Republic of Argentina v. NML Capital, Ltd.* that the requirements for *discovery* of a foreign state's assets prior to attachment are less strict than those for attachment.[100] Contrary to the arguments set forth by Argentina and the United States, as amicus curiae, the Court held that the FSIA does not provide an implied immunity from postjudgment discovery of information concerning a foreign state's extraterritorial assets in aid of execution.[101] While some property subject to discovery might ultimately be immune from execution, such as diplomatic or military property, the Court emphasized that it would be illogical to presumptively immunize states from being subjected to discovery in relation to such property, since the plaintiff in such cases "*does not yet know* what property [the state] has and where it is, let alone whether it is executable under the relevant jurisdiction's law."[102] Thus, plaintiffs seeking to enforce awards may make use of the United States' broad discovery allowances in identifying and attaching assets worldwide.[103] **14.57**

No matter the stage of the proceeding, any party attempting to enforce an arbitral award against a foreign sovereign must demonstrate that the property is used by the foreign state for a commercial activity in the United States.[104] An award creditor attempting to attach the assets of an agency or instrumentality of the foreign sovereign under Section 1610(b) of the FSIA must show merely that the agency or instrumentality is engaged in commercial activity in the United States, but need not make any showing with respect to the particular property at issue.[105] **14.58**

In determining whether an asset is used for commercial activity in the United States, courts are careful to note that the relevant consideration is not how the government generated the asset, but rather how the government has used the asset. The term *commercial* refers to situations where the state acts in the manner **14.59**

---

[100] Republic of Arg. v. NML Capital, Ltd., 134 S. Ct. 2250 (2014).

[101] *See id.* at 2256–57.

[102] *Id.* at 2257.

[103] *See, e.g.*, Aurelius Capital Master, Ltd. v. Republic of Arg., No. 13-4054, 2014 WL 7272279 (2d Cir. Dec. 23, 2014).

[104] The award creditor must also carefully identify the assets it is seeking to attach. For example, in CMS Gas Transmission Company v. Republic of Argentina, CMS sought to enforce its ICSID award against Argentina. No. 08 Civ. 3169 (S.D.N.Y.). Following news reports that Argentina was repatriating certain funds from Switzerland—via New York—CMS moved for an ex parte attachment of the funds in New York. Following the issuance of an order freezing Argentina's New York bank accounts, one week later, on April 2, 2008, the court overturned the freeze order on the ground that the order was insufficiently specific regarding the assets to be attached. Order, CMS Gas Transmission Company v. Republic of Argentina, No. 08 Civ. 3169 (S.D.N.Y. Apr. 2, 2008). Note, Freshfields Bruckhaus Deringer US LLP was counsel to CMS in this proceeding. *See also* Thai-Lao Lignite (Thail.) Co., 997 F. Supp. 2d at 228–29 (finding that the petitioner had failed to identify specific U.S. assets of Laos that met the Section 1610(a) criteria).

[105] *See* Conn. Bank of Commerce v. Republic of Congo, 309 F.3d 240, 252 (5th Cir. 2002) (drawing a distinction between the commercial activity requirement in Section 1610(a) and that in Section 1610(b)).

of a private player in the market, rather than as a regulator.[106] The FSIA defines "commercial activity" as "either a regular course of commercial conduct or a particular commercial transaction or act. The commercial character of an activity shall be determined by reference to the nature of the course of conduct or particular transaction or act, rather than by reference to its purpose."[107] The existence of a profit motive is irrelevant to the analysis. As the Second Circuit recently reaffirmed, "[w]hen a foreign sovereign engages in [conduct in which a private party would customarily engage for profit], that activity retains its commercial nature, even though the foreign sovereign acts without a profit motive."[108] However, both the Fifth Circuit and the Ninth Circuit have also agreed that property is only used for a commercial activity in the United States "when the property in question is put into action, put into service, availed or employed *for* a commercial activity, not *in connection* with a commercial activity or *in relation* to a commercial activity."[109]

14.60 According to Federal Rules of Civil Procedure 64 (in the case of prejudgment attachment) and 69 (in the case of postjudgment attachment), the law of the state in which the district court is located dictates the relevant standards for attachment. In other words, while federal law (the FSIA) will be determinative with respect to whether particular property is amenable to attachment (through the commercial activity standard), state law determines the procedure for attachment, and in some cases exempts certain types of property from attachment. Therefore, once an award creditor meets the commercial activity standard under the FSIA, it still must satisfy the relevant New York law requirements to attach the assets at issue. Cases from other states have demonstrated that, even when all FSIA requirements have been met, state law can be a final obstacle to enforcement.

14.61 For example, considering the Texas garnishment statute, the Fifth Circuit has ruled that royalties qualify as nonmonetary obligations, which under Texas law cannot be garnished. In *Af-Cap Inc. v. Republic of Congo*,[110] a case in which Af-Cap Inc. (Af-Cap) sought to collect upon an English judgment (which was subsequently entered in New York and registered in Texas and California) against the Republic of Congo, the Congo had the option of accepting royalty payments in cash or in kind. Without explanation, the Fifth Circuit found that the royalty payments

---

[106] Republic of Arg. v. Weltover, Inc., 504 U.S. 607, 614 (1992).

[107] 28 U.S.C. § 1603(d).

[108] *NML Capital*, 680 F.3d at 259–60 (*citing* Weltover, Inc. v. Republic of Arg., 941 F.2d 145, 150 (2d Cir. 1991) *aff'd*, 504 U.S. 607, 112 S. Ct. 2160, 119 L. Ed. 2d 394 (1992), alterations in original).

[109] Af-Cap Inc. v. Chevron Overseas (Congo) Ltd., 475 F.3d 1080, 1091 (9th Cir. 2007) (emphasis in original) (adopting the test articulated by the Fifth Circuit in Conn. Bank of Commerce v. Republic of Congo, 309 F.3d 240 (5th Cir. 2002)). This language has also been endorsed by at least one New York court. *See* In re 650 Fifth Ave., No. 08 CIV. 10934 KBF, 2014 WL 1516328, at *17 (S.D.N.Y. Apr. 18, 2014).

[110] Af-Cap Inc. v. Republic of Congo, 462 F.3d 417 (5th Cir. 2006).

were nonmonetary obligations. Noting that "[t]he Texas garnishment statute contemplates garnishment of (1) debts, money owed to a defendant, and (2) effects, tangible property owned by the defendant in possession of the garnishee," the Fifth Circuit found that Texas law does not permit garnishment of nonmonetary obligations.[111] Because the garnishee "d[id] not owe money to the Congo; [it] owe[d] oil," the court affirmed the district court's dissolution of the writs of garnishment.[112]

Additionally, the Fifth Circuit reversed the district court's issuance of a turnover order directing the Congo to accept its royalty payments in cash and require its debtors to make those payments to the court registry. Due to the dissolution of the writs of garnishment, the court found that it had lost its basis for jurisdiction over the Congo. Previously, the location of the garnishees in Texas had provided a foothold for jurisdiction under the FSIA. The turnover order, however, "bypasses the [garnishees] and directly orders the Congo to act."[113] Because that order was not one for attachment of property and it was not "based upon a commercial activity carried on in the United States by the foreign state," as required by 28 U.S.C. §1605(a), the Congo was immune from the turnover order. **14.62**

(a) Debt and property subject to attachment Award creditors must also take into account specific rules pertaining to the attachment of certain kinds of property. The relevant New York procedural rules utilize extremely broad language regarding debt and property that may be attached. With respect to debt, N.Y.C.P.L.R. § 5201(a) provides that "[a] money judgment may be enforced against any debt, which is past due or which is yet to become due, certainly or upon demand of the judgment debtor." With respect to property, N.Y.C.P.L.R. § 5201(b) provides that "[a] money judgment may be enforced against any property which could be assigned or transferred, whether it consists of a present or future right or interest and whether or not it is vested, unless it is exempt from application to the satisfaction of the judgment."[114] N.Y.C.P.L.R. § 6202, meanwhile, makes clear that "[a]ny debt or property against which a money judgment may be enforced as provided in section 5201 is subject to [prejudgment] attachment." Thus, the relevant standard set forth in Section 5201 applies for either prejudgment or post-judgment attachment. **14.63**

(b) Attaching the property of state-owned companies Award creditors ideally will target assets directly owned by a state to satisfy arbitral awards. However, because many of a state's commercial assets are held by state-owned companies, award creditors often attempt to pursue the assets of state-owned companies. **14.64**

---

[111] *Id.* at 424.

[112] *Id.* at 425.

[113] *Id.* at 426.

[114] N.Y.C.P.L.R. § 5205 (personal property) and § 5206 (real property) provide certain exemptions from application to the satisfaction of money judgments, none of which is particularly relevant for the purposes of this book.

14.65 In order to attach assets of state-owned companies, the award creditor must overcome the general rule that state agencies and instrumentalities are considered to be distinct legal entities from the state.[115] There are two exceptions to this rule, each of which can be difficult to establish: (1) the "corporate entity is so extensively controlled by its owner that a relationship of principal and agent is created" (i.e., the parent is an alter ego of the corporation); or (2) recognition of the separate corporate status "would work fraud or injustice" on the other party.[116]

14.66 The implications of this issue were highlighted in a case involving the efforts of a telecommunications company (ETI) to attach several New York bank accounts owned by the Bolivian national telecommunications company (Entel) as pre-award security for ETI's arbitration against Bolivia.[117] The court overturned the *ex parte* order of attachment by the District Court on the ground that the plaintiff had failed to identify a valid basis for the attachment of the assets of the Bolivian-owned entity in aid of foreign arbitral proceedings against the state.[118]

14.67 In a separate case, *Figueiredo Ferraz Consultoria E Engenharia de Projeto Ltda v. Republic of Peru*, a Brazilian corporation was originally successful in its argument that an organization created to coordinate Peruvian sanitation programs was a political organ that was not legally distinguishable from the Peruvian state for the purpose of confirming an arbitral award.[119] The court took note of the entity's status under Peruvian law and of the fact that the entity's assets were not distinct from those of the state.[120] However, this decision was ultimately reversed by the Second Circuit on grounds of *forum non conveniens*.[121]

14.68 Attempting to attach assets owned by a state-owned company can greatly increase the number of U.S.-based assets available to satisfy an arbitral award against a sovereign. However, the award creditor must have a viable theory to justify "piercing the corporate veil" between the State and the state-owned company.

---

[115] First Nat'l City Bank v. Banco Para El Comercio Exterior de Cuba, 462 U.S. 611, 626–27 (1983) (*Bancec*). This rule is also recognized in other jurisdictions, such as England. Uzma Balkiss Sulaiman, *Nigerian Oil Company Escapes Payment Order for Government Bill*, Global Arbitration Review (November 27, 2009), http://globalarbitrationreview.com/news/article/19507/.

[116] *Bancec*, 462 U.S. at 629.

[117] E.T.I. Euro Telecom International N.V. v. Republic of Bolivia, No. 08 Civ. 4247, 2008 WL 2940583 (S.D.N.Y. July 30, 2008). ETI contended that the bank accounts constituted a debt that Entel owed to Bolivia. When the court rejected this argument, the only way for the court to uphold the attachment would be if ETI could "pierce the corporate veil" and establish that Entel's assets are actually assets of Bolivia.

[118] *Id.* at *2.

[119] Figueiredo Ferraz Consultoria E Engenharia de Projeto Ltda v. Republic of Peru, 655 F. Supp. 2d 361, 371 (S.D.N.Y. 2009) *rev'd* 665 F.3d 384 (2d Cir. 2011). The arbitration involved the breach of an agreement entered into between the plaintiff and the government-created organization. Peru argued that the award could not be enforced against the state because it itself was not a signatory to the agreement. *Id.* at 368.

[120] *Id.* at 368–71.

[121] Figueiredo Ferraz e Engenharia de Projecto Ltda. v. Republic of Peru, 665 F.3d 384 (2d Cir. 2011).

(c) Garnishment of royalties or taxes One option that some award creditors pursue against foreign states is to seek garnishment of royalties or taxes. Keeping in mind that only property located in the United States is subject to attachment and that royalties and taxes are "intangible in nature," the law has developed favorably to award creditors.[122] As the Fifth Circuit has stated, "courts consistently hold that the situs of a debt obligation is the situs of the debtor."[123] This determination is based upon the situs of the debtor at the time when the district court determines whether sovereign immunity applies.[124] The New York Appellate Division, First Department, has effectively reached a similar conclusion to the Fifth Circuit.[125] However, in a recent case in New York federal district court, the court distinguished between the situation where plaintiffs seek to attach the *beneficial interests* of a bond or similar asset, in which case the situs of the property is that of the debtor,[126] and the case where plaintiffs seek to attach the *asset itself*.[127] As the court determined the plaintiffs were seeking the bonds themselves, which were clearly tendered in Argentina, and not Argentina's beneficial interest in the bonds, the court found that Argentina was not required to turn them over to the plaintiff debtors as the situs of the bonds was in Argentina, not the United States.[128] **14.69**

It is important to note that many courts have considered the use of tax revenues to be inherently noncommercial.[129] However, several prominent cases have recently addressed the garnishment of royalties and taxes, involving the efforts of Af-Cap to garnish royalties and taxes owed to the Congo for oil production. **14.70**

In *Af-Cap Inc. v. Republic of Congo*, Af-Cap attempted to garnish tax and royalty obligations owed by CMS Nomeco Congo, Inc. and affiliated companies to the Congo.[130] The Fifth Circuit found that the Congo had consistently used the tax and royalty obligations at issue for commercial activity (as part of a **14.71**

[122] Af-Cap Inc. v. Republic of Congo, 383 F.3d 361, 371 (5th Cir. 2004).

[123] *Id.*

[124] FG Hemisphere Assocs. v. Republic of Congo, 455 F.3d 575, 589–90 (5th Cir. 2006).

[125] Breezevale Ltd. v. Dickinson, 262 A.D.2d 248 (N.Y. App. Div. 1999) (finding that the relevant jurisdictional consideration was whether the court had jurisdiction over the third-party debtor, not the judgment debtor).

[126] *See, e.g.*, EM Ltd. v. Republic of Arg., 389 Fed. Appx. 38, 44 (2d Cir. 2010) ("[T]he situs of intangible property, such as beneficial interests, is 'the location of the party of whom performance is required by the terms of the contract.'" (*citing* ABKCO Indus., Inc. v. Apple Films, Inc., 39 N.Y.2d 670, 675 (1976))).

[127] Aurelius Capital Partners, LP v. Republic of Arg., No. 07 CIV. 11327 (TPG), 2010 WL 2925072, at *3–4 (S.D.N.Y. July 23, 2010).

[128] *Aurelius*, 2010 WL 2925072, at *3–4.

[129] *See, e.g.*, LNC Invs., Inc. v. Republic of Nicaragua, No. 96 Civ. 6360, 2000 WL 745550 (S.D.N.Y. June 8, 2000); *see also* Liberian E. Timber Corp. v. Republic of Nigeria, 650 F. Supp. 73, 77–78 (S.D.N.Y. 1986) (finding that "[t]he levy and collection of taxes intended to serve as revenues for the support and maintenance of governmental functions are an exercise of powers particular to the sovereign").

[130] Af-Cap Inc. v. Republic of Congo, 383 F.3d 361 (5th Cir. 2004).

settlement to pay a debt), so sovereign immunity would not prevent their garnishment. The court noted that rare commercial use would be insufficient, and placed particular emphasis on consideration of commercial use "holistically and in context":

> As the facts of the NUFI settlement indicate, for nearly half of the twenty-four years that these obligations existed, the Congo has used at least fifty percent of them to repay a commercial debt. The amount of the debt repaid was not insignificant.... Such a continuing, extended and monetarily significant use is neither exceptional nor de minimis. ... Indeed, on at least one other occasion, the Congo contemplated engaging in the same type of use again. Although such contemplated use is not actual use, it is strongly suggestive that the proceeds of these tax and royalty obligations were not cordoned off for use of the Congo in its sovereign capacity. Instead, it indicates the availability of this property for whatever purpose—commercial or otherwise—the Congo deems appropriate.[131]

14.72 In an earlier stage of appeal for the same case, the Fifth Circuit provided another suggestion as to a factual scenario that would demonstrate use for commercial activity by the Congo. The court noted that "the royalty and tax obligations would be used for a commercial activity in the United States if the Congo used them as collateral for loans obtained from United States banks."[132]

14.73 A separate Af-Cap proceeding in California, *Af-Cap Inc. v. Chevron Overseas (Congo) Ltd.*, also provides an example of the application of the commercial activity standard, although in this case the Ninth Circuit found that the Congo had not used the assets at issue for commercial activity in the United States.[133] Of particular relevance, the court found that the fact that the obligations (which included taxes, other payments, and in-kind royalties) were pledged as security for a loan agreement "between the Congo and a bank located in the Bahamas for the financing and construction of a highway in the Congo, to be managed by an English contractor" did not establish their use for a commercial activity *in the United States*.[134] Additionally, Chevron's obligation to pay approximately $7 million to the Congo for an interest in a joint venture located entirely in the Congo did not constitute commercial activity by the Congo in the United States. In any event, the court noted that the relevant inquiry is how the Congo has used this intangible asset, not how the intangible asset was generated.[135] This inquiry, which focuses on the state's *use* of the asset rather than how the state *generated*

[131] *Id.* at 370–71.
[132] Conn. Bank of Commerce v. Republic of Congo, 309 F.3d 240, 259 (5th Cir. 2002).
[133] Af-Cap, Inc. v. Chevron Overseas (Congo) Ltd., 475 F.3d 1080 (9th Cir. 2007).
[134] *Id.* at 1091–92.
[135] *Id.* at 1094.

the asset, has been adopted more recently by the Second Circuit in *Export-Import Bank of the Republic of China v. Grenada.*[136]

(d) Attachment of trust accounts Award creditors also have the option of seeking attachment of trust accounts or other similar accounts or instruments into which proceeds are routed by the foreign state. Trust accounts present an excellent opportunity for attachment because the funds at issue are clearly related to commercial activity, unlike bank accounts held for an embassy, for example.[137] *Karaha Bodas Co. v. Pertamina* provides an example of a court permitting attachment of a trust account.[138] **14.74**

Karaha Bodas Co. (KBC) attempted to attach funds held in New York trust accounts that were derived from sales of liquefied natural gas (LNG) extracted in Indonesia. Pertamina, the Indonesian state-owned oil and gas company, had breached its contract with KBC for the construction of extraction facilities, and KBC had prevailed in arbitral proceedings in Switzerland. **14.75**

In the normal course of business, Pertamina had entered into numerous contracts with private contractors for the exploration and extraction of natural gas, which it would sell—or convert to LNG and sell—to foreign buyers. Payment for the LNG and natural gas was made directly into trust accounts in New York. The trustee then distributed the proceeds among Pertamina's lenders, the private contractors, and Pertamina. Pertamina had instructed the trustee to direct Pertamina's entire share of the proceeds to the Indonesian government; Pertamina was then entitled to retain only a small percentage. The court found that under Indonesian law, gas **14.76**

[136] Exp.-Imp. Bank of the Republic of China v. Grenada, 768 F.3d 75, 88–89 (2d Cir. 2014) (finding that funds, which included payments of taxes, fees, and other charges, were not attachable because "once generated, they are *used* to serve public purposes, and that use takes place in Grenada").

[137] With respect to bank accounts utilized to operate an embassy—used for what would otherwise be commercial purposes such as paying employees and purchasing goods and services—courts have asserted conflicting views regarding whether such accounts are commercial in nature. *See* Liberian E. Timber Corp. v. Republic of Liberia, 659 F.Supp. 606 (D.D.C. 1987) (stating that the "incidental" or "auxiliary" use for commercial activities of bank account funds of the foreign state's embassy did not cause the entire account to lose its immunity from attachment, and holding that the account was immune from attachment under the Vienna Convention on Diplomatic Relations and that the same result would obtain under the FSIA regardless of a finding of diplomatic immunity); *but see* Birch Shipping Corp. v. Embassy of United Republic of Tanzania, 507 F. Supp. 311 (D.D.C. 1980) (holding that a checking account used by the foreign state's embassy to pay staff salaries and to pay for incidental purchases and services necessary for the operation of the embassy was used for commercial purposes and therefore was not immune from attachment under the FSIA). In Germany, on the other hand, Franz Sedelmeyer—whose interest in a Russian company had been confiscated by the Russian government over a decade earlier—has succeeded in forcing an auction of a Kremlin-owned estate in Cologne, Germany. Nikolaus von Twickel, *German Wins Right To Kremlin Property*, Moscow Times (Mar. 21, 2008), http://www.themoscowtimes.com/sitemap/free/2008/3/article/german-wins-right-to-kremlin-property/360985.html.

[138] Karaha Bodas Co. v. Perusahaan Pertambangan Minyak Dan Gas Bumi Negara ("Pertamina"), 313 F.3d 70 (2d Cir. 2002).

and oil belonged to the state.[139] Thus, the plaintiff could recover that small proportion of the trust accounts that would ultimately go to Pertamina. The court upheld the district court's order of attachment against Pertamina's portion of the proceeds.[140]

[139] *Id.* at 88.

[140] *Id.* at 92–93. Similarly, the Second Circuit affirmed the attachment of assets in a trust established by Argentina to sell securities in a state-owned bank. *See* EM Ltd. v. Republic of Arg., 389 Fed. Appx. 38, 42 (2d Cir. 2010). Upon the order of the trust, the trust proceeds were to be distributed to funds established by the Argentinian government to support infrastructure projects. *See* EM Ltd. v. Republic of Argentina, No. 03 CIV. 2507 (TPG), 2009 WL 2568433, at *1–3 (S.D.N.Y. Aug. 18, 2009). The Second Circuit found that the assets in the trust were predominantly controlled directly by Argentina. *EM Ltd.*, 389 Fed. Appx. at 42. The court further held that under New York law, the trust was invalid and could not be protected from creditors because Argentinian government had the authority to direct the trust for its own benefit, violating principles of public policy. *See Id.* at 42–43.

APPENDIX 1

Schedule of International Arbitration Conventions

The International Arbitration Conventions important in New York arbitrations are:

I. The United Nations Convention on the Recognition and Enforcement of Foreign Arbitral Awards (also known as the "New York Convention") (1958), available at: http://www.uncitral.org
Guide to interpretation available at: http://www.arbitration-icca.org
Cases available at: http://newyorkconvention.org
http://www.newyorkconvention1958.org

II. The Inter-American Convention on International Commercial Arbitration (also known as the "Panama Convention") (1975), available at: http://www.oas.org

APPENDIX 2

Federal Arbitration Act

Title 9, US Code, Section 1–14, was first enacted February 12, 1925 (43 Stat. 883), codified July 30, 1947 (61 Stat. 669), and amended September 3, 1954 (68 Stat. 1233). Chapter 2 was added July 31, 1970 (84 Stat. 692), two new Sections were passed by the Congress in October of 1988 and renumbered on December 1, 1990 (PLS 669 and 702); Chapter 3 was added on August 15, 1990 (PL 101–369); and Section 10 was amended on November 15.

Arbitration

Chapter 1. General Provisions

Section 1. "Maritime transactions" and "commerce" defined; exceptions to operation of title

"Maritime transaction", as herein defined, means charter parties, bills of lading of water carriers, agreements relating to wharfage, supplies furnished vessels or repairs to vessels, collisions, or any other matters in foreign commerce which, if the subject of controversy, would be embraced within admiralty jurisdiction; "commerce", as herein defined, means commerce among the several States or with foreign nations, or in any Territory of the United States or in the District of Columbia, or between any such Territory and another, or between any such Territory and any State or foreign nation, or between the District of Columbia and any State or Territory or foreign nation, but nothing herein contained shall apply to contracts of employment of seamen, railroad employees, or any other class of workers engaged in foreign or interstate commerce.

Section 2. Validity, irrevocability, and enforcement of agreements to arbitrate

A written provision in any maritime transaction or a contract evidencing a transaction involving commerce to settle by arbitration a controversy thereafter arising out of such contract or transaction, or the refusal to perform the whole or any part thereof, or an agreement in writing to submit to arbitration an existing controversy arising out of such a contract, transaction, or refusal, shall be valid, irrevocable, and enforceable, save upon such grounds as exist at law or in equity for the revocation of any contract.

Section 3. Stay of proceedings where issue therein referable to arbitration

If any suit or proceeding be brought in any of the courts of the United States upon any issue referable to arbitration under an agreement in writing for such arbitration, the court in which such suit is pending, upon being satisfied that the issue involved in such suit or proceeding is referable to arbitration under such an agreement, shall on application of one of the parties stay the trial of the action until such arbitration has been had in accordance with the terms of the agreement, providing the applicant for the stay is not in default in proceeding with such arbitration.

Section 4. Failure to arbitrate under agreement; petition to United States court having jurisdiction for order to compel arbitration; notice and service thereof; hearing and determination

A party aggrieved by the alleged failure, neglect, or refusal of another to arbitrate under a written agreement for arbitration may petition any United States district court which, save for such agreement, would have jurisdiction under Title 28, in a civil action or in admiralty of the subject matter of a suit arising out of the controversy between the parties, for an order directing that such arbitration proceed in the manner provided for in such agreement. Five days' notice in writing of such application shall be served upon the party in default. Service thereof shall be made in the manner provided by the Federal Rules of Civil Procedure. The court shall hear the parties, and upon being satisfied that the making of the agreement for arbitration or the failure to comply therewith is not in issue, the court shall make an order directing the parties to proceed to arbitration in accordance with the terms of the agreement. The hearing and proceedings, under such agreement, shall be within the district in which the petition for an order directing such arbitration is filed. If the making of the arbitration agreement or the failure, neglect, or refusal to perform the same be in issue, the court shall proceed summarily to the trial thereof. If no jury trial be demanded by the party alleged to be in default, or if the matter in dispute is within admiralty jurisdiction, the court shall hear and determine such issue. Where such an issue is raised, the party alleged to be in default may, except in cases of admiralty, on or before the return day of the notice of application, demand a jury trial of such issue, and upon such demand the court shall make an order referring the issue or issues to a jury in the manner provided by the Federal Rules of Civil Procedure, or may specially call a jury for that purpose. If the jury find that no agreement in writing for arbitration was made or that there is no default in proceeding thereunder, the proceeding shall be dismissed. If the jury find that an agreement for arbitration was made in writing and that there is a default in proceeding thereunder, the court shall make an order summarily directing the parties to proceed with the arbitration in accordance with the terms thereof.

Section 5. Appointment of arbitrators or umpire

If in the agreement provision be made for a method of naming or appointing an arbitrator or arbitrators or an umpire, such method shall be followed; but if no method be provided therein, or if a method be provided and any party thereto shall fail to avail himself of such method, or if for any other reason there shall be a lapse in the naming of an arbitrator or arbitrators or umpire, or in filling a vacancy, then upon the application of either party to the controversy the court shall designate and appoint an arbitrator or arbitrators or umpire, as the case may require, who shall act under the said agreement with the same force and effect as if he or they had been specifically named therein; and unless otherwise provided in the agreement the arbitration shall be by a single arbitrator.

Section 6. Application heard as motion

Any application to the court hereunder shall be made and heard in the manner provided by law for the making and hearing of motions, except as otherwise herein expressly provided.

Section 7. Witnesses before arbitrators; fees; compelling attendance

The arbitrators selected either as prescribed in this title or otherwise, or a majority of them, may summon in writing any person to attend before them or any of them as a witness and in a proper case to bring with him or them any book, record, document, or paper which may be deemed material as evidence in the case. The fees for such attendance shall be the same as the fees of witnesses before masters of the United States courts. Said summons shall issue in the name of the arbitrator or arbitrators, or a majority of them, and shall be signed by the arbitrators, or a majority of them, and shall be directed to the said person and shall be served in the same manner as subpoenas to appear and testify before the court; if any person or persons so summoned to testify shall refuse or neglect to obey said summons, upon petition the United States district court for the district in which such arbitrators, or a majority of them, are sitting may compel the attendance of such person or persons before said arbitrator or arbitrators, or punish said person or persons for contempt in the same manner provided by law for securing the attendance of witnesses or their punishment for neglect or refusal to attend in the courts of the United States.

Section 8. Proceedings begun by libel in admiralty and seizure of vessel or property

If the basis of jurisdiction be a cause of action otherwise justiciable in admiralty, then, notwithstanding anything herein to the contrary, the party claiming to be aggrieved may begin his proceeding hereunder by seizure of the vessel or other property of the other party according to the usual course of admiralty proceedings, and the court shall then have jurisdiction to direct the parties to proceed with the arbitration and shall retain jurisdiction to enter its decree upon the award.

Section 9. Award of arbitrators; confirmation; jurisdiction; procedure

If the parties in their agreement have agreed that a judgment of the court shall be entered upon the award made pursuant to the arbitration, and shall specify the court, then at any time within one year after the award is made any party to the arbitration may apply to the court so specified for an order confirming the award, and thereupon the court must grant such an order unless the award is vacated, modified, or corrected as prescribed in sections 10 and 11 of this title. If no court is specified in the agreement of the parties, then such application may be made to the United States court in and for the district within which such award was made. Notice of the application shall be served upon the adverse party, and thereupon the court shall have jurisdiction of such party as though he had appeared generally in the proceeding. If the adverse party is a resident of the district within which the award was made, such service shall be made upon the adverse party or his attorney as prescribed by law for service of notice of motion in an action in the same court. If the adverse party shall be a nonresident, then the notice of the application shall be served by the marshal of any district within which the adverse party may be found in like manner as other process of the court.

Section 10. Same; vacation; grounds; rehearing

a. In any of the following cases the United States court in and for the district wherein the award was made may make an order vacating the award upon the application of any party to the arbitration:
   1. Where the award was procured by corruption, fraud, or undue means.
   2. Where there was evident partiality or corruption in the arbitrators, or either of them.
   3. Where the arbitrators were guilty of misconduct in refusing to postpone the hearing, upon sufficient cause shown, or in refusing to hear evidence pertinent and material to the controversy; or of any other misbehavior by which the rights of any party have been prejudiced.
   4. Where the arbitrators exceeded their powers, or so imperfectly executed them that a mutual, final, and definite award upon the subject matter submitted was not made.
   5. Where an award is vacated and the time within which the agreement required the award to be made has not expired the court may, in its discretion, direct a rehearing by the arbitrators.
b. The United States district court for the district wherein an award was made that was issued pursuant to section 590 of title 5 may make an order vacating the award upon the application of a person, other than a party to the arbitration, who is adversely affected or aggrieved by the award, if the use of arbitration or the award is clearly inconsistent with the factors set forth in section 582 of title 5.

Section 11. Same; modification or correction; grounds; order

In either of the following cases the United States court in and for the district wherein the award was made may make an order modifying or correcting the award upon the application of any party to the arbitration—

a. Where there was an evident material miscalculation of figures or an evident material mistake in the description of any person, thing, or property referred to in the award.
b. Where the arbitrators have awarded upon a matter not submitted to them, unless it is a matter not affecting the merits of the decision upon the matter submitted.
c. Where the award is imperfect in matter of form not affecting the merits of the controversy.

The order may modify and correct the award, so as to effect the intent thereof and promote justice between the parties.

Section 12. Notice of motions to vacate or modify; service; stay of proceedings

Notice of a motion to vacate, modify, or correct an award must be served upon the adverse party or his attorney within three months after the award is filed or delivered. If the adverse party is a resident of the district within which the award was made, such service shall be made upon the adverse party or his attorney as prescribed by law for service of notice of motion in an action in the same court. If the adverse party shall be a nonresident then the notice of the application shall be served by the marshal of any district within which the adverse party may be found in like manner as other process of the court. For the purposes of the motion any judge who might make an order to stay the proceedings in an action brought in the same court may make an order, to be served with the notice of motion, staying the proceedings of the adverse party to enforce the award.

Section 13. Papers filed with order on motions; judgment; docketing; force and effect; enforcement

The party moving for an order confirming, modifying, or correcting an award shall, at the time such order is filed with the clerk for the entry of judgment thereon, also file the following papers with the clerk:

a. The agreement; the selection or appointment, if any, of an additional arbitrator or umpire; and each written extension of the time, if any, within which to make the award.
b. The award.
c. Each notice, affidavit, or other paper used upon an application to confirm, modify, or correct the award, and a copy of each order of the court upon such an application.

The judgment shall be docketed as if it was rendered in an action. The judgment so entered shall have the same force and effect, in all respects, as, and be subject to all the provisions of law relating to a judgment in an action; and it may be enforced as if it had been rendered in an action in the court in which it is entered.

Section 14. Contracts not affected

This title shall not apply to contracts made prior to January 1, 1926.

Section 15. Inapplicability of the Act of State doctrine

Enforcement of arbitral agreements, confirmation of arbitral awards, and execution upon judgments based on orders confirming such awards shall not be refused on the basis of the Act of State doctrine.

Section 16. Appeals

a. An appeal may be taken from
   1. an order—
      A. refusing a stay of any action under section 3 of this title,
      B. denying a petition under section 4 of this title to order arbitration to proceed,
      C. denying an application under section 206 of this title to compel arbitration,
      D. confirming or denying confirmation of an award or partial award, or
      E. modifying, correcting, or vacating an award;
   2. an interlocutory order granting, continuing, or modifying an injunction against an arbitration that is subject to this title; or
   3. a final decision with respect to an arbitration that is subject to this title.
b. Except as otherwise provided in section 1292(b) of title 28, an appeal may not be taken from an interlocutory order—
   - granting a stay of any action under section 3 of this title;
   - directing arbitration to proceed under section 4 of this title;
   - compelling arbitration under section 206 of this title; or
   - refusing to enjoin an arbitration that is subject to this title.

Chapter 2. Convention on the Recognition and Enforcement of Foreign Arbitral Awards

Section 201. Enforcement of Convention

The Convention on the Recognition and Enforcement of Foreign Arbitral Awards of June 10, 1958, shall be enforced in United States courts in accordance with this chapter.

Section 202. Agreement or award falling under the Convention

An arbitration agreement or arbitral award arising out of a legal relationship, whether contractual or not, which is considered as commercial, including a transaction, contract, or agreement described in section 2 of this title, falls under the Convention. An agreement or award arising out of such a relationship which is entirely between citizens of the United States shall be deemed not to fall under the Convention unless that relationship involves property located abroad, envisages performance or enforcement abroad, or has some other reasonable relation with one or more foreign states. For the purpose of this section a corporation is a citizen of the United States if it is incorporated or has its principal place of business in the United States.

Section 203. Jurisdiction; amount in controversy

An action or proceeding falling under the Convention shall be deemed to arise under the laws and treaties of the United States. The district courts of the United States (including the courts enumerated in section 460 of title 28) shall have original jurisdiction over such an action or proceeding, regardless of the amount in controversy.

Section 204. Venue

An action or proceeding over which the district courts have jurisdiction pursuant to section 203 of this title may be brought in any such court in which save for the arbitration agreement an action or proceeding with respect to the controversy between the parties could be brought, or in such court for the district and division which embraces the place designated in the agreement as the place of arbitration if such place is within the United States.

Section 205. Removal of cases from State courts

Where the subject matter of an action or proceeding pending in a State court relates to an arbitration agreement or award falling under the Convention, the defendant or the defendants may, at any time before the trial thereof, remove such action or proceeding to the district court of the United States for the district and division embracing the place where the action or proceeding is pending. The procedure for removal of causes otherwise provided by law shall apply, except that the ground for removal provided in this section need not appear on the face of the complaint but may be shown in the petition for removal. For the purposes of Chapter 1 of this title any action or proceeding removed under this section shall be deemed to have been brought in the district court to which it is removed.

Section 206. Order to compel arbitration; appointment of arbitrators

A court having jurisdiction under this chapter may direct that arbitration be held in accordance with the agreement at any place therein provided for, whether that place is within or without the United States. Such court may also appoint arbitrators in accordance with the provisions of the agreement.

Section 207. Award of arbitrators; confirmation; jurisdiction; proceeding

Within three years after an arbitral award falling under the Convention is made, any party to the arbitration may apply to any court having jurisdiction under this chapter for an order confirming the award as against any other party to the arbitration. The court shall confirm the award unless it finds one of the grounds for refusal or deferral of recognition or enforcement of the award specified in the said Convention.

Section 208. Chapter 1; residual application

Chapter 1 applies to actions and proceedings brought under this chapter to the extent that chapter is not in conflict with this chapter or the Convention as ratified by the United States.

Chapter 3. Inter-American Convention On International Commercial Arbitration

Section 301. Enforcement of Convention

The Inter-American Convention on International Commercial Arbitration of January 30, 1975, shall be enforced in United States courts in accordance with this chapter.

Section 302. Incorporation by reference

Sections 202, 203, 204, 205, and 207 of this title shall apply to this chapter as if specifically set forth herein, except that for the purposes of this chapter "the Convention" shall mean the Inter-American Convention.

Section 303. Order to compel arbitration; appointment of arbitrators; locale

(a) A court having jurisdiction under this chapter may direct that arbitration be held in accordance with the agreement at any place therein provided for, whether that place is within or without the United States. The court may also appoint arbitrators in accordance with the provisions of the agreement.

(b) In the event the agreement does not make provision for the place of arbitration or the appointment of arbitrators, the court shall direct that the arbitration shall be held and the arbitrators be appointed in accordance with Article 3 of the Inter-American Convention.

Section 304. Recognition and enforcement of foreign arbitral decisions and awards; reciprocity

Arbitral decisions or awards made in the territory of a foreign State shall, on the basis of reciprocity, be recognized and enforced under this chapter only if that State has ratified or acceded to the Inter-American Convention.

Section 305. Relationship between the Inter-American Convention and the Convention on the Recognition and Enforcement of Foreign Arbitral Awards of June 10, 1958

When the requirements for application of both the Inter-American Convention and the Convention on the Recognition and Enforcement of Foreign Arbitral Awards of June 10, 1958, are met, determination as to which Convention applies shall, unless otherwise expressly agreed, be made as follows:

1. If a majority of the parties to the arbitration agreement are citizens of a State or States that have ratified or acceded to the Inter-American Convention and are member States of the Organization of American States, the Inter-American Convention shall apply.
2. In all other cases the Convention on the Recognition and Enforcement of Foreign Arbitral Awards of June 10, 1958, shall apply.

Section 306. Applicable rules of Inter-American Commercial Arbitration Commission

a. for the purposes of this chapter the rules of procedure of the Inter-American Commercial Arbitration Commission referred to in Article 3 of the Inter-American Convention shall, subject to subsection (b) of this section, be those rules as promulgated by the Commission on July 1, 1988.
b. In the event the rules of procedure of the Inter-American Commercial Arbitration Commission are modified or amended in accordance with the procedures for amendment of the rules of that Commission, the Secretary of State, by regulation in accordance with section 553 of title 5, consistent with the aims and purposes of this Convention, may prescribe that such modifications or amendments shall be effective for purposes of this chapter.

Section 307. Chapter 1; residual application

Chapter 1 applies to actions and proceedings brought under this chapter to the extent chapter 1 is not in conflict with this chapter or the Inter-American Convention as ratified by the United States.

APPENDIX 3

NY Civil Practice Law and Rules, Article 75

§ 7501. Effect of arbitration agreement

A written agreement to submit any controversy thereafter arising or any existing controversy to arbitration is enforceable without regard to the justiciable character of the controversy and confers jurisdiction on the courts of the state to enforce it and to enter judgment on an award. In determining any matter arising under this article, the court shall not consider whether the claim with respect to which arbitration is sought is tenable, or otherwise pass upon the merits of the dispute.

§ 7502. Applications to the court; venue; statutes of limitation; provisional remedies

(a) Applications to the court; venue. A special proceeding shall be used to bring before a court the first application arising out of an arbitrable controversy which is not made by motion in a pending action.

(i) The proceeding shall be brought in the court and county specified in the agreement. If the name of the county is not specified, proceedings to stay or bar arbitration shall be brought in the county where the party seeking arbitration resides or is doing business, and other proceedings affecting arbitration are to be brought in the county where at least one of the parties resides or is doing business or where the arbitration was held or is pending.

(ii) If there is no county in which the proceeding may be brought under paragraph (i) of this subdivision, the proceeding may be brought in any county.

(iii) Notwithstanding the entry of judgment, all subsequent applications shall be made by motion in the special proceeding or action in which the first application was made.

(iv) If an application to confirm an arbitration award made within the one year as provided by section seventy-five hundred ten of this article, or an application to vacate or modify an award made within the ninety days as provided by subdivision (a) of section seventy-five hundred eleven of this article, was denied or dismissed solely on the ground that it was made in the form of a motion captioned in an earlier special proceeding having reference to the arbitration instead of as a distinct special proceeding, the time in which to apply to confirm the award and the time in which to apply to vacate or modify the award may, notwithstanding that the applicable period of time has expired, be made at any time within ninety days after the effective date of this paragraph, and may be made in whatever form is appropriate (motion or special proceeding) pursuant to this subdivision.

(b) Limitation of time. If, at the time that a demand for arbitration was made or a notice of intention to arbitrate was served, the claim sought to be arbitrated would have been barred by limitation of time had it been asserted in a court of the state, a party may assert the limitation as a bar to the arbitration on an application to the court as provided in section 7503 or subdivision (b) of section 7511. The failure to assert such bar by such application shall not preclude its assertion before the arbitrators, who may, in their sole discretion, apply or not apply the bar. Except as provided in subdivision (b) of section 7511, such exercise of discretion by the arbitrators shall not be subject to review by a court on an application to confirm, vacate or modify the award.

(c) Provisional remedies. The supreme court in the county in which an arbitration is pending, or, if not yet commenced, in a county specified in subdivision (a), may entertain an application for an order of attachment or for a preliminary injunction in connection with an arbitrable controversy, but only upon the ground that the award to which the applicant may be entitled may be rendered ineffectual without such provisional relief. The provisions of articles 62 and 63 of this chapter shall apply to the application, including those relating to undertakings and to the time for commencement of an action (arbitration shall be deemed an action for this purpose) if the application is made before commencement, except that the sole ground for the granting of the remedy shall be as stated above. The form of the application shall be as provided in subdivision (a).

§ 7503. Application to compel or stay arbitration; stay of action; notice of intention to arbitrate

(a) Application to compel arbitration; stay of action. A party aggrieved by the failure of another to arbitrate may apply for an order compelling arbitration. Where there is no substantial question whether a valid agreement was made or complied with, and the claim sought to be arbitrated is not barred by limitation under subdivision (b) of section 7502, the court shall direct the parties to arbitrate. Where any such question is raised, it shall be tried forthwith in said court. If an issue claimed to be arbitrable is involved in an action pending in a court having jurisdiction to hear a motion to compel arbitration, the application shall be made by motion in that action. If the application is granted, the order shall operate to stay a pending or subsequent action, or so much of it as is referable to arbitration.

(b) Application to stay arbitration. Subject to the provisions of subdivision (c), a party who has not participated in the arbitration and who has not made or been served with an application to compel arbitration, may apply to stay arbitration on the ground that a valid agreement was not made or has not been complied with or that the claim sought to be arbitrated is barred by limitation under subdivision (b) of section 7502.

(c) Notice of intention to arbitrate. A party may serve upon another party a demand for arbitration or a notice of intention to arbitrate, specifying the agreement pursuant to which arbitration is sought and the name and address of the party serving the notice, or of an officer or agent thereof if such party is an association or corporation, and stating that unless the party served applies to stay the arbitration within twenty days after such service he shall thereafter be precluded from objecting that a valid agreement was not made or has not been complied with and from asserting in court the bar of a limitation of time. Such notice or demand shall be served in the same manner as a summons or by registered or certified mail, return receipt requested. An application to stay arbitration must be made by the party served within twenty days after service upon him of the notice or demand, or he shall be so precluded. Notice of such application shall be served in the same manner as a summons or by registered or certified mail, return receipt requested. Service of the application may be made upon the adverse party, or upon his attorney if the attorney's name appears on the demand for arbitration or the notice of intention to arbitrate. Service of the application by mail shall be timely if such application is posted within the prescribed period. Any provision in an arbitration agreement or arbitration rules which waives the right to apply for a stay of arbitration is hereby declared null and void.

§ 7504. Court appointment of arbitrator

If the arbitration agreement does not provide for a method of appointment of an arbitrator, or if the agreed method fails or for any reason is not followed, or if an arbitrator fails to act and his successor has not been appointed, the court, on application of a party, shall appoint an arbitrator.

§ 7505. Powers of arbitrator

An arbitrator and any attorney of record in the arbitration proceeding has the power to issue subpoenas. An arbitrator has the power to administer oaths.

§ 7506. Hearing

(a) Oath of arbitrator. Before hearing any testimony, an arbitrator shall be sworn to hear and decide the controversy faithfully and fairly by an officer authorized to administer an oath.
(b) Time and place. The arbitrator shall appoint a time and place for the hearing and notify the parties in writing personally or by registered or certified mail not less than eight days before the hearing. The arbitrator may adjourn or postpone the hearing. The court, upon application of any party, may direct the arbitrator to proceed promptly with the hearing and determination of the controversy.
(c) Evidence. The parties are entitled to be heard, to present evidence and to cross-examine witnesses. Notwithstanding the failure of a party duly notified to appear, the arbitrator may hear and determine the controversy upon the evidence produced.
(d) Representation by attorney. A party has the right to be represented by an attorney and may claim such right at any time as to any part of the arbitration or hearings which have not taken place. This right may not be waived. If a party is represented by an attorney, papers to be served on the party shall be served upon his attorney.
(e) Determination by majority. The hearing shall be conducted by all the arbitrators, but a majority may determine any question and render an award.
(f) Waiver. Except as provided in subdivision (d), a requirement of this section may be waived by written consent of the parties and it is waived if the parties continue with the arbitration without objection.

§ 7507. Award; form; time; delivery

Except as provided in section 7508, the award shall be in writing, signed and affirmed by the arbitrator making it within the time fixed by the agreement, or, if the time is not fixed, within such time as the court orders. The parties may in writing extend the time either before or after its expiration. A party waives the objection that an award was not made within the time required unless he notifies the arbitrator in writing of his objection prior to the delivery of the award to him. The arbitrator shall deliver a copy of the award to each party in the manner provided in the agreement, or, if no provision is so made, personally or by registered or certified mail, return receipt requested.

§ 7508. Award by confession

(a) When available. An award by confession may be made for money due or to become due at any time before an award is otherwise made. The award shall be based upon a statement, verified by each party, containing an authorization to make the award, the sum of the award or the method of ascertaining it, and the facts constituting the liability.
(b) Time of award. The award may be made at any time within three months after the statement is verified.
(c) Person or agency making award. The award may be made by an arbitrator or by the agency or person named by the parties to designate the abitrator.

§ 7509. Modification of award by arbitrator

On written application of a party to the arbitrators within twenty days after delivery of the award to the applicant, the arbitrators may modify the award upon the grounds stated in subdivision (c) of section 7511. Written notice of the application shall be given to other parties to the arbitration. Written objection to modification must be served on the arbitrators and other parties to the arbitration within ten days of receipt of the notice. The arbitrators shall dispose of any application made under this section in writing, signed and acknowledged by them, within thirty days after either written objection to modification has been served on them or the time for serving said objection has expired, whichever is earlier. The parties may in writing extend the time for such disposition either before or after its expiration.

§ 7510. Confirmation of award

The court shall confirm an award upon application of a party made within one year after its delivery to him, unless the award is vacated or modified upon a ground specified in section 7511.

§ 7511. Vacating or modifying award

(a) When application made. An application to vacate or modify an award may be made by a party within ninety days after its delivery to him.
(b) Grounds for vacating. 1. The award shall be vacated on the application of a party who either participated in the arbitration or was served with a notice of intention to arbitrate if the court finds that the rights of that party were prejudiced by: (i) corruption, fraud or misconduct in procuring the award; or (ii) partiality of an arbitrator appointed as a neutral, except where the award was by confession; or (iii) an arbitrator, or agency or person making the award exceeded his power or so imperfectly executed it that a final and definite award upon the subject matter submitted was not made; or (iv) failure to follow the procedure of this article, unless the party applying to vacate the award continued with the arbitration with notice of the defect and without objection. 2. The award shall be vacated on the application of a party who neither participated in the arbitration nor was served with a notice of intention to arbitrate if the court finds that: (i) the rights of that party were prejudiced by one of the grounds specified in paragraph one; or (ii) a valid agreement to arbitrate was not made; or (iii) the agreement to arbitrate had not been complied with; or (iv) the arbitrated claim was barred by limitation under subdivision (b) of section 7502.
(c) Grounds for modifying. The court shall modify the award if: 1. there was a miscalculation of figures or a mistake in the description of any person, thing or property referred to in the award; or 2. the arbitrators have awarded upon a matter not submitted to them and the award may be corrected without affecting the merits of the decision upon the issues submitted; or 3. the award is imperfect in a matter of form, not affecting the merits of the controversy.
(d) Rehearing. Upon vacating an award, the court may order a rehearing and determination of all or any of the issues either before the same arbitrator or before a new arbitrator appointed in accordance with this article. Time in any provision limiting the time for a hearing or award shall be measured from the date of such order or rehearing, whichever is appropriate, or a time may be specified by the court.
(e) Confirmation. Upon the granting of a motion to modify, the court shall confirm the award as modified; upon the denial of a motion to vacate or modify, it shall confirm the award.

§ 7512. Death or incompetency of a party

Where a party dies after making a written agreement to submit a controversy to arbitration, the proceedings may be begun or continued upon the application of, or upon notice to, his executor or administrator or, where it relates to real property, his distributee or devisee who has succeeded to his interest in the real property. Where a committee of the property or of the person of a party to such an agreement is appointed, the proceedings may be continued upon the application of, or notice to, the committee. Upon the death or incompetency of a party, the court may extend the time within which an application to confirm, vacate or modify the award or to stay arbitration must be made. Where a party has died since an award was delivered, the proceedings thereupon are the same as where a party dies after a verdict.

§ 7513. Fees and expenses

Unless otherwise provided in the agreement to arbitrate, the arbitrators' expenses and fees, together with other expenses, not including attorney's fees, incurred in the conduct of the arbitration, shall be paid as provided in the award. The court, on application, may reduce or disallow any fee or expense it finds excessive or allocate it as justice requires.

§ 7514. Judgment on an award

(a) Entry. A judgment shall be entered upon the confirmation of an award.
(b) Judgment-roll. The judgment-roll consists of the original or a copy of the agreement and each written extention of time within which to make an award; the statement required by section 7508 where the award was by confession; the award; each paper submitted to the court and each order of the court upon an application under sections 7510 and 7511; and a copy of the judgment.

APPENDIX 4

Supreme Court, New York County Commercial Division, Charles E. Ramos, Justice, International Arbitration Rules (2013) International Arbitration Part Rules—Part 53

These International Arbitration Part Rules supplement the Part 53 Practice Rules, which shall govern any matters not specifically addressed to these rules.

Parties to international arbitration-related matters before this court should familiarize themselves with the following rules and resources:

a. The Part 53 Practice Rules and Rule 202.5-b of the Uniform Rules for the New York State Trial Courts, which addresses electronic filing.
b. CPLR Article 75—Arbitration.
c. The Federal Arbitration Act, (FAA) 9 U.S.C. § 1 et seq.
d. The Convention on the Recognition and Enforcement of Foreign Arbitral Awards ("New York Convention"), June 10, 1958, 21 U.S.T. 2517, 330 U.N.T.S. 38, if applicable.
e. The Inter-American Convention on International Commercial Arbitration ("Panama Convention"), Jan. 30, 1975, S. Treaty Doc. No. 97–12, O.A.S.T.S. No. 42, 14 I.L.M. 336, if applicable.

If the parties wish to avail themselves of these International Arbitration Rules, they are strongly advised to include a forum selection clause in their contracts that explicitly waives the right of removal to Federal court, which is otherwise available under the New York Convention on the Recognition and Enforcement of Foreign Arbitral Awards and chapter 2 of the FAA. In this regard, please see *Yakin v Tyler Hill Corp.* (566 F3d 72 [2d Cir 2009] ["Parties are free to bind themselves to forum selection clauses that trump what would otherwise be a right to remove cases to federal courts"]).

It is the policy of New York State to enforce arbitration agreements and awards, as set out in CPLR 7501: "A written agreement to submit any controversy thereafter arising or any existing controversy to arbitration is enforceable without regard to the justiciable character of the controversy and confers jurisdiction on the courts of the state to enforce it and to enter judgment on an award."

This Court will enforce the parties written agreements and applicable conventions governing international arbitrations with regard to all matters, including restrictions or limitations on the right to discovery, provisional remedies and the rules of evidence.

In all regards, it is preferable that the applicable convention be incorporated by reference in the agreement to arbitrate.

1. A Special Proceeding in accordance with CPLR 7502 shall be used to bring before the Court the first application arising out of an arbitrable controversy which is not otherwise made by motion in a pending action. All subsequent applications shall be made by motion in the special proceeding or in the action in which the first application was made.
2. Any party making an application arising out of an arbitrable controversy, whether or not it is the first such application, shall include with the application the full text of the arbitration agreement and any other contractual provisions that govern the dispute resolution process.
3. Applications for the following relief shall be made by motion on notice or on an expedited basis by Order to Show Cause:
   a. Orders to compel arbitration or to stay an action. CPLR 7503(a).
   b. Orders to confirm an award. CPLR 7510.
   c. Orders to vacate or modify an award. CPLR 7511.

The following applications should be made only by order to show cause:
a. Preliminary injunction
b. A stay of arbitration
c. Disclosure to aid in arbitration
d. An Order of Attachment

4. Unless the parties stipulate to the contrary or extraordinary circumstance are present, all motions and applications shall be decided within 60 days of oral argument and any party may for any reason request an expedited decision.
   a. Applications by letter may be on consent for the appointment of an arbitration and for a direction that the arbitrator proceed promptly with the hearing. Absent consent, a motion is required.
5. In the event the Court appoints an arbitrator, the Court will appoint a sole arbitrator unless the parties have agreed otherwise. Arbitrators shall be selected by this Court from a list or source agreed by the parties or from the Unified Court System's Fiduciary Eligibility List.
6. Counsel should note that The United States is a party to two significant international conventions that promote the enforcement of arbitral awards. They are:
   a. The Convention on the Recognition and Enforcement of Foreign Arbitral Awards, June 10, 1958, 21 U.S.T. 2517, 330 U.N.T.S. 38 ("New York Convention"), and the Inter-American Convention on International Commercial Arbitration, Jan. 30, 1975, S. Treaty Doc. No. 97-12, O.A.S.T.S. No. 42, 14 I.L.M. 336 ("Panama Convention").
   b. The New York Convention refers to the laws of its member states to determine whether an arbitration should be considered international. See New York Convention, Art. I(1) (covering "awards made in a territory of an State other than the State where the recognition and enforcement of such awards are sought" and awards "not considered as domestic awards in the State where their recognition and enforcement are sought").

   The Federal Arbitration Act sets forth the following test to determine whether a matter falls under the New York Convention:

   > An arbitration agreement or arbitral award arising out of a legal relationship, whether contractual or not, which is considered as commercial, including a transaction, contract, or agreement described in section 2 of this title, falls under the Convention. An agreement or award arising out of such a relationship which is entirely between citizens of the United States shall be deemed not to fall under the Convention unless that relationship involves property located abroad, envisages performance or enforcement abroad, or has some other reasonable relation with one or more foreign states. For the purpose of this section a corporation is a citizen of the United States if it is incorporated or has its principal place of business in the United States.

7. Counsel are reminded that any request to assign or to transfer an action or proceeding to Part 53 requires that a copy of the Administrative Order of the Administrative Judge for Civil Matters of the First Judicial District must accompany such request. A copy of said order is available from the Commercial division website at:

   http://www.nycourts.gov/courts/comdiv/PDFs/Practices_in_Part_53.pdf.

APPENDIX 5

Schedule of Arbitration Rules and Guidelines

There are many choices for arbitration rules, and arbitral institutions publish guidelines and fact sheets offering additional assistance. Among those used in New York international arbitrations are:

I. American Arbitration Association/International Centre for Dispute Resolution (all rules and guidelines available at: http://www.adr.org)
   A. International Arbitration Rules (2014)
   B. Commercial Arbitration Rules (2013), including Procedures for Large, Complex Commercial Disputes)
   C. Optional Appellate Arbitration Rules (2013)
   D. Procedures for Cases Under the UNCITRAL Arbitration Rules (2005)
   E. The Code of Ethics for Arbitrators in Commercial Disputes (2004)
   F. Fact Sheet: Enhanced Neutral Selection Process For Large Complex Cases

II. International Chamber of Commerce (ICC), (rules available at: http://www.iccwbo.org)
   A. Arbitration Rules (2012)

III. JAMS (all rules and guidelines available at http://www.jamsadr.com)
   A. Comprehensive Arbitration Rules and Procedures (2014)
   B. International Arbitration Rules (2011)
   C. Arbitration Discovery Protocols (2010)
   D. Efficiency Guidelines for the Pre-Hearing Phase of International Arbitrations (2011)
   E. Optional Appeal Procedures (2003)

IV. International Institute for Conflict Prevention & Resolution (CPR) (all rules and guidelines available at: http://www.cpradr.org)
   A. Rules for Administered Arbitration of International Disputes (2014)
   B. Administered Arbitration Rules (2013)
   C. Non-Administered International Arbitration Rules (2007)
   D. Non-Administered Arbitration Rules (2007)
   E. Appellate Arbitration Procedure
   F. Protocol on Determination of Damages in Arbitration
   G. Guidelines on Early Disposition of Issues in Arbitration
   H. Guidelines for Arbitrators Conducting Complex Arbitrations
   I. Protocol on Disclosure of Documents and Presentation of Witnesses in Commercial Arbitration

V. International Bar Association (IBA) (all rules and guidelines available at: http://www.ibanet.org/Publications/publications_IBA_guides_and_free_materials.aspx)
   A. Guidelines on Conflicts of Interest in International Arbitration (2014)
   B. Guidelines on Party Representation in International Arbitration (2013)
   C. Rules on the Taking of Evidence in International Arbitration (2010)

APPENDIX 6

AAA/ABA Code Of Ethics For Arbitrators in Commercial Disputes

The Code of Ethics for Arbitrators in Commercial Disputes was originally prepared in 1977 by a joint committee consisting of a special committee of the American Arbitration Association and a special committee of the American Bar Association. The Code was revised in 2003 by an ABA Task Force and special committee of the AAA.

Preamble

The use of arbitration to resolve a wide variety of disputes has grown extensively and forms a significant part of the system of justice on which our society relies for a fair determination of legal rights. Persons who act as arbitrators therefore undertake serious responsibilities to the public, as well as to the parties. Those responsibilities include important ethical obligations.

Few cases of unethical behavior by commercial arbitrators have arisen. Nevertheless, this Code sets forth generally accepted standards of ethical conduct for the guidance of arbitrators and parties in commercial disputes, in the hope of contributing to the maintenance of high standards and continued confidence in the process of arbitration.

There are many different types of commercial arbitration. Some proceedings are conducted under arbitration rules established by various organizations and trade associations, while others are conducted without such rules. Although most proceedings are arbitrated pursuant to voluntary agreement of the parties, certain types of disputes are submitted to arbitration by reason of particular laws. This Code is intended to apply to all such proceedings in which disputes or claims are submitted for decision to one or more arbitrators appointed in a manner provided by an agreement of the parties, by applicable arbitration rules, or by law. In all such cases, the persons who have the power to decide should observe fundamental standards of ethical conduct. In this Code, all such persons are called "arbitrators," although in some types of proceeding they might be called "umpires," "referees," "neutrals," or have some other title.

Arbitrators, like judges, have the power to decide cases. However, unlike full-time judges, arbitrators are usually engaged in other occupations before, during, and after the time that they serve as arbitrators. Often, arbitrators are purposely chosen from the same trade or industry as the parties in order to bring special knowledge to the task of deciding. This Code recognizes these fundamental differences between arbitrators and judges. In those instances where this Code has been approved and recommended by organizations that provide, coordinate, or administer services of arbitrators, it provides ethical standards for the members of their respective panels of arbitrators. However, this Code does not form a part of the arbitration rules of any such organization unless its rules so provide.

Note on Neutrality

In some types of commercial arbitration, the parties or the administering institution provide for three or more arbitrators. In some such proceedings, it is the practice for each party, acting alone, to appoint one arbitrator (a "party-appointed arbitrator") and for one additional arbitrator to be designated by the party-appointed arbitrators, or by the parties, or by an independent institution or individual. The sponsors of this Code believe that it is preferable for all arbitrators including any party-appointed arbitrators to be neutral, that is, independent and impartial, and to comply with the same ethical standards. This expectation generally is essential in arbitrations where the parties, the nature of the dispute, or the enforcement of any resulting award may have international aspects. However, parties in certain domestic arbitrations in the United States may prefer that party-appointed arbitrators be non-neutral and governed by special ethical considerations. These special ethical considerations appear in Canon X of this Code.

This Code establishes a presumption of neutrality for all arbitrators, including party-appointed arbitrators, which applies unless the parties' agreement, the arbitration rules agreed to by the parties or applicable laws provide otherwise. This Code requires all party-appointed arbitrators, whether neutral or not, to make pre-appointment disclosures of any facts which might affect their neutrality, independence, or impartiality. This Code also requires all party-appointed arbitrators to ascertain and disclose as soon as practicable whether the parties intended for them to serve as neutral or not. If any doubt or uncertainty exists, the party-appointed arbitrators should serve as neutrals unless and until such doubt or uncertainty is resolved in accordance with Canon IX. This Code expects all arbitrators, including those serving under Canon X, to preserve the integrity and fairness of the process.

Note on Construction

Various aspects of the conduct of arbitrators, including some matters covered by this Code, may also be governed by agreements of the parties, arbitration rules to which the parties have agreed, applicable law, or other applicable ethics rules, all of which should be consulted by the arbitrators. This Code does not take the place of or supersede such laws, agreements, or arbitration rules to which the parties have agreed and should be read in conjunction with other rules of ethics. It does not establish new or additional grounds for judicial review of arbitration awards.

All provisions of this Code should therefore be read as subject to contrary provisions of applicable law and arbitration rules. They should also be read as subject to contrary agreements of the parties. Nevertheless, this Code imposes no obligation on any arbitrator to act in a manner inconsistent with the arbitrator's fundamental duty to preserve the integrity and fairness of the arbitral process.

Canons I through VIII of this Code apply to all arbitrators. Canon IX applies to all party-appointed arbitrators, except that certain party-appointed arbitrators are exempted by Canon X from compliance with certain provisions of Canons I–IX related to impartiality and independence, as specified in Canon X.

Canon I: An Arbitrator should Uphold the Integrity and Fairness of the Arbitration Process

A. An arbitrator has a responsibility not only to the parties but also to the process of arbitration itself, and must observe high standards of conduct so that the integrity and fairness of the process will be preserved. Accordingly, an arbitrator should recognize a responsibility to the public, to the parties whose rights will be decided, and to all other participants in the proceeding. This responsibility may include pro bono service as an arbitrator where appropriate.

B. One should accept appointment as an arbitrator only if fully satisfied:
   (1) that he or she can serve impartially;
   (2) that he or she can serve independently from the parties, potential witnesses, and the other arbitrators;
   (3) that he or she is competent to serve; and
   (4) that he or she can be available to commence the arbitration in accordance with the requirements of the proceeding and thereafter to devote the time and attention to its completion that the parties are reasonably entitled to expect.

C. After accepting appointment and while serving as an arbitrator, a person should avoid entering into any business, professional, or personal relationship, or acquiring any financial or personal interest, which is likely to affect impartiality or which might reasonably create the appearance of partiality. For a reasonable period of time after the decision of a case, persons who have served as arbitrators should avoid entering into any such relationship, or acquiring any such interest, in circumstances which might reasonably create the appearance that they had been influenced in the arbitration by the anticipation or expectation of the relationship or interest. Existence of any of the matters or circumstances described in this paragraph C does not render it unethical for one to serve as an arbitrator where the parties have consented to the arbitrator's appointment or continued services following full disclosure of the relevant facts in accordance with Canon II.

D. Arbitrators should conduct themselves in a way that is fair to all parties and should not be swayed by outside pressure, public clamor, and fear of criticism or self-interest. They should avoid conduct and statements that give the appearance of partiality toward or against any party.

E. When an arbitrator's authority is derived from the agreement of the parties, an arbitrator should neither exceed that authority nor do less than is required to exercise that authority completely. Where the agreement of the parties sets forth procedures to be followed in conducting the arbitration or refers to rules to be followed, it is the obligation of the arbitrator to comply with such procedures or rules. An arbitrator has no ethical obligation to comply with any agreement, procedures or rules that are unlawful or that, in the arbitrator's judgment, would be inconsistent with this Code.

F. An arbitrator should conduct the arbitration process so as to advance the fair and efficient resolution of the matters submitted for decision. An arbitrator should make all reasonable efforts to prevent delaying tactics, harassment of parties or other participants, or other abuse or disruption of the arbitration process.

G. The ethical obligations of an arbitrator begin upon acceptance of the appointment and continue throughout all stages of the proceeding. In addition, as set forth in this Code, certain ethical obligations begin as soon as a person is requested to serve as an arbitrator and certain ethical obligations continue after the decision in the proceeding has been given to the parties.

H. Once an arbitrator has accepted an appointment, the arbitrator should not withdraw or abandon the appointment unless compelled to do so by unanticipated circumstances that would render it impossible or impracticable to continue. When an arbitrator is to be compensated for his or her services, the arbitrator may withdraw if the parties fail or refuse to provide for payment of the compensation as agreed.

I. An arbitrator who withdraws prior to the completion of the arbitration, whether upon the arbitrator's initiative or upon the request of one or more of the parties, should take reasonable steps to protect the interests of the parties in the arbitration, including return of evidentiary materials and protection of confidentiality.

Comment to Canon I

A prospective arbitrator is not necessarily partial or prejudiced by having acquired knowledge of the parties, the applicable law or the customs and practices of the business involved. Arbitrators may also have special experience or expertise in the areas of business, commerce, or technology which are involved in the arbitration. Arbitrators do not contravene this Canon if, by virtue of such experience or expertise, they have views on certain general issues likely to arise in the arbitration, but an arbitrator may not have prejudged any of the specific factual or legal determinations to be addressed during the arbitration.

During an arbitration, the arbitrator may engage in discourse with the parties or their counsel, draw out arguments or contentions, comment on the law or evidence, make interim rulings, and otherwise control or direct the arbitration. These activities are integral parts of an arbitration. Paragraph D of Canon I is not intended to preclude or limit either full discussion of the issues during the course of the arbitration or the arbitrator's management of the proceeding.

Canon II: An Arbitrator should Disclose any Interest or Relationship Likely to Affect Impartiality or which might Create an Appearance of Partiality

A. Persons who are requested to serve as arbitrators should, before accepting, disclose:

   (1) any known direct or indirect financial or personal interest in the outcome of the arbitration;

   (2) any known existing or past financial, business, professional or personal relationships which might reasonably affect impartiality or lack of independence in the eyes of any of the parties. For example, prospective arbitrators should disclose any such relationships which they personally have with any party or its lawyer, with any co-arbitrator, or with any individual

whom they have been told will be a witness. They should also disclose any such relationships involving their families or household members or their current employers, partners, or professional or business associates that can be ascertained by reasonable efforts;

(3) the nature and extent of any prior knowledge they may have of the dispute; and

(4) any other matters, relationships, or interests which they are obligated to disclose by the agreement of the parties, the rules or practices of an institution, or applicable law regulating arbitrator disclosure.

B. Persons who are requested to accept appointment as arbitrators should make a reasonable effort to inform themselves of any interests or relationships described in paragraph A.

C. The obligation to disclose interests or relationships described in paragraph A is a continuing duty which requires a person who accepts appointment as an arbitrator to disclose, as soon as practicable, at any stage of the arbitration, any such interests or relationships which may arise, or which are recalled or discovered.

D. Any doubt as to whether or not disclosure is to be made should be resolved in favor of disclosure.

E. Disclosure should be made to all parties unless other procedures for disclosure are provided in the agreement of the parties, applicable rules or practices of an institution, or by law. Where more than one arbitrator has been appointed, each should inform the others of all matters disclosed.

F. When parties, with knowledge of a person's interests and relationships, nevertheless desire that person to serve as an arbitrator, that person may properly serve.

G. If an arbitrator is requested by all parties to withdraw, the arbitrator must do so. If an arbitrator is requested to withdraw by less than all of the parties because of alleged partiality, the arbitrator should withdraw unless either of the following circumstances exists:

(1) An agreement of the parties, or arbitration rules agreed to by the parties, or applicable law establishes procedures for determining challenges to arbitrators, in which case those procedures should be followed; or

(2) In the absence of applicable procedures, if the arbitrator, after carefully considering the matter, determines that the reason for the challenge is not substantial, and that he or she can nevertheless act and decide the case impartially and fairly.

H. If compliance by a prospective arbitrator with any provision of this Code would require disclosure of confidential or privileged information, the prospective arbitrator should either:

(1) Secure the consent to the disclosure from the person who furnished the information or the holder of the privilege; or

(2) Withdraw.

Canon III: An Arbitrator should Avoid Impropriety or the Appearance of Impropriety in Communicating with Parties

A. If an agreement of the parties or applicable arbitration rules establishes the manner or content of communications between the arbitrator and the parties, the arbitrator should follow those procedures notwithstanding any contrary provision of paragraphs B and C.

B. An arbitrator or prospective arbitrator should not discuss a proceeding with any party in the absence of any other party, except in any of the following circumstances:

(1) When the appointment of a prospective arbitrator is being considered, the prospective arbitrator:

(a) may ask about the identities of the parties, counsel, or witnesses and the general nature of the case; and

(b) may respond to inquiries from a party or its counsel designed to determine his or her suitability and availability for the appointment. In any such dialogue, the prospective arbitrator may receive information from a party or its counsel disclosing the general nature of the dispute but should not permit them to discuss the merits of the case.

(2) In an arbitration in which the two party-appointed arbitrators are expected to appoint the third arbitrator, each party-appointed arbitrator may consult with the party who appointed the arbitrator concerning the choice of the third arbitrator;

(3) In an arbitration involving party-appointed arbitrators, each party-appointed arbitrator may consult with the party who appointed the arbitrator concerning arrangements for any compensation to be paid to the party-appointed arbitrator. Submission of routine written requests for payment of compensation and expenses in accordance with such arrangements and written communications pertaining solely to such requests need not be sent to the other party;

(4) In an arbitration involving party-appointed arbitrators, each party-appointed arbitrator may consult with the party who appointed the arbitrator concerning the status of the arbitrator (i.e., neutral or non-neutral), as contemplated by paragraph C of Canon IX;

(5) Discussions may be had with a party concerning such logistical matters as setting the time and place of hearings or making other arrangements for the conduct of the proceedings. However, the arbitrator should promptly inform each other party of the discussion and should not make any final determination concerning the matter discussed before giving each absent party an opportunity to express the party's views; or (6) If a party fails to be present at a hearing after having been given due notice, or if all parties expressly consent, the arbitrator may discuss the case with any party who is present.

C. Unless otherwise provided in this Canon, in applicable arbitration rules or in an agreement of the parties, whenever an arbitrator communicates in writing with one party, the arbitrator should at the same time send a copy of the communication to every other party, and whenever the arbitrator receives any written communication concerning the case from one party which has not already been sent to every other party, the arbitrator should send or cause it to be sent to the other parties.

Canon IV: An Arbitrator should Conduct the Proceedings Fairly and Diligently

A. An arbitrator should conduct the proceedings in an even-handed manner. The arbitrator should be patient and courteous to the parties, their representatives, and the witnesses and should encourage similar conduct by all participants.

B. The arbitrator should afford to all parties the right to be heard and due notice of the time and place of any hearing. The arbitrator should allow each party a fair opportunity to present its evidence and arguments.

C. The arbitrator should not deny any party the opportunity to be represented by counsel or by any other person chosen by the party.

D. If a party fails to appear after due notice, the arbitrator should proceed with the arbitration when authorized to do so, but only after receiving assurance that appropriate notice has been given to the absent party.

E. When the arbitrator determines that more information than has been presented by the parties is required to decide the case, it is not improper for the arbitrator to ask questions, call witnesses, and request documents or other evidence, including expert testimony.

F. Although it is not improper for an arbitrator to suggest to the parties that they discuss the possibility of settlement or the use of mediation, or other dispute resolution processes, an arbitrator should not exert pressure on any party to settle or to utilize other dispute resolution processes. An arbitrator should not be present or otherwise participate in settlement discussions or act as a mediator unless requested to do so by all parties.

G. Co-arbitrators should afford each other full opportunity to participate in all aspects of the proceedings.

Comment to Paragraph G

Paragraph G of Canon IV is not intended to preclude one arbitrator from acting in limited circumstances (e.g., ruling on discovery issues) where authorized by the agreement of the parties, applicable rules or law, nor does it preclude a majority of the arbitrators from proceeding with any aspect of the arbitration if an arbitrator is unable or unwilling to participate and such action is authorized by the agreement of the parties or applicable rules or law. It also does not preclude ex parte requests for interim relief.

Canon V: An Arbitrator should make Decisions in a just, Independent and Deliberate Manner

A. The arbitrator should, after careful deliberation, decide all issues submitted for determination. An arbitrator should decide no other issues.
B. An arbitrator should decide all matters justly, exercising independent judgment, and should not permit outside pressure to affect the decision.
C. An arbitrator should not delegate the duty to decide to any other person.
D. In the event that all parties agree upon a settlement of issues in dispute and request the arbitrator to embody that agreement in an award, the arbitrator may do so, but is not required to do so unless satisfied with the propriety of the terms of settlement. Whenever an arbitrator embodies a settlement by the parties in an award, the arbitrator should state in the award that it is based on an agreement of the parties.

Canon VI: An Arbitrator should be Faithful to the Relationship of Trust and Confidentiality Inherent in that Office

A. An arbitrator is in a relationship of trust to the parties and should not, at any time, use confidential information acquired during the arbitration proceeding to gain personal advantage or advantage for others, or to affect adversely the interest of another.
B. The arbitrator should keep confidential all matters relating to the arbitration proceedings and decision. An arbitrator may obtain help from an associate, a research assistant or other persons in connection with reaching his or her decision if the arbitrator informs the parties of the use of such assistance and such persons agree to be bound by the provisions of this Canon.
C. It is not proper at any time for an arbitrator to inform anyone of any decision in advance of the time it is given to all parties. In a proceeding in which there is more than one arbitrator, it is not proper at any time for an arbitrator to inform anyone about the substance of the deliberations of the arbitrators. After an arbitration award has been made, it is not proper for an arbitrator to assist in proceedings to enforce or challenge the award.
D. Unless the parties so request, an arbitrator should not appoint himself or herself to a separate office related to the subject matter of the dispute, such as receiver or trustee, nor should a panel of arbitrators appoint one of their number to such an office.

Canon VII: An Arbitrator should Adhere to Standards of Integrity and Fairness when making Arrangements for Compensation and Reimbursement of Expenses

A. Arbitrators who are to be compensated for their services or reimbursed for their expenses shall adhere to standards of integrity and fairness in making arrangements for such payments.
B. Certain practices relating to payments are generally recognized as tending to preserve the integrity and fairness of the arbitration process. These practices include:
   (1) Before the arbitrator finally accepts appointment, the basis of payment, including any cancellation fee, compensation in the event of withdrawal and compensation for study and preparation time, and all other charges, should be established. Except for arrangements for the compensation of party-appointed arbitrators, all parties should be informed in writing of the terms established;
   (2) In proceedings conducted under the rules or administration of an institution that is available to assist in making arrangements for payments, communication related to compensation should be made through the institution. In proceedings where no institution has been engaged by the parties to administer the arbitration, any communication with arbitrators (other than party appointed arbitrators) concerning payments should be in the presence of all parties; and
   (3) Arbitrators should not, absent extraordinary circumstances, request increases in the basis of their compensation during the course of a proceeding.

Canon VIII: An Arbitrator may Engage in Advertising or Promotion of Arbitral Services which is Truthful and Accurate

A. Advertising or promotion of an individual's willingness or availability to serve as an arbitrator must be accurate and unlikely to mislead. Any statements about the quality of the arbitrator's work or the success of the arbitrator's practice must be truthful.
B. Advertising and promotion must not imply any willingness to accept an appointment otherwise than in accordance with this Code.

Comment to Canon VIII

This Canon does not preclude an arbitrator from printing, publishing, or disseminating advertisements conforming to these standards in any electronic or print medium, from making personal presentations to prospective users of arbitral services conforming to such standards or from responding to inquiries concerning the arbitrator's availability, qualifications, experience, or fee arrangements.

Canon IX: Arbitrators Appointed by One Party have a Duty to Determine and Disclose their Status and to Comply with this Code, Except as Exempted by Canon X

A. In some types of arbitration in which there are three arbitrators, it is customary for each party, acting alone, to appoint one arbitrator. The third arbitrator is then appointed by agreement either of the parties or of the two arbitrators, or failing such agreement, by an independent institution or individual. In tripartite arbitrations to which this Code applies, all three arbitrators are presumed to be neutral and are expected to observe the same standards as the third arbitrator.
B. Notwithstanding this presumption, there are certain types of tripartite arbitration in which it is expected by all parties that the two arbitrators appointed by the parties may be predisposed toward the party appointing them. Those arbitrators, referred to in this Code as "Canon X arbitrators," are not to be held to the standards of neutrality and independence applicable to other arbitrators. Canon X describes the special ethical obligations of partyappointed arbitrators who are not expected to meet the standard of neutrality.
C. A party-appointed arbitrator has an obligation to ascertain, as early as possible but not later than the first meeting of the arbitrators and parties, whether the parties have agreed that the party-appointed arbitrators will serve as neutrals or whether they shall be subject to Canon X, and to provide a timely report of their conclusions to the parties and other arbitrators:
   (1) Party-appointed arbitrators should review the agreement of the parties, the applicable rules and any applicable law bearing upon arbitrator neutrality. In reviewing the agreement of the parties, party-appointed arbitrators should consult any relevant express terms of the written or oral arbitration agreement. It may also be appropriate for them to inquire into agreements that have not been expressly set forth, but which may be implied from an established course of dealings of the parties or well-recognized custom and usage in their trade or profession;
   (2) Where party-appointed arbitrators conclude that the parties intended for the partyappointed arbitrators not to serve as neutrals, they should so inform the parties and the other arbitrators. The arbitrators may then act as provided in Canon X unless or until a different determination of their status is made by the parties, any administering institution or the arbitral panel; and
   (3) Until party-appointed arbitrators conclude that the party-appointed arbitrators were not intended by the parties to serve as neutrals, or if the party-appointed arbitrators are unable to form a reasonable belief of their status from the foregoing sources and no decision in this regard has yet been made by the parties, any administering institution, or the arbitral panel, they should observe all of the obligations of neutral arbitrators set forth in this Code.
D. Party-appointed arbitrators not governed by Canon X shall observe all of the obligations of Canons I through VIII unless otherwise required by agreement of the parties, any applicable rules, or applicable law.

Canon X: Exemptions for Arbitrators Appointed by One Party who are not Subject to Rules of Neutrality

Canon X arbitrators are expected to observe all of the ethical obligations prescribed by this Code except those from which they are specifically excused by Canon X.

A. Obligations under Canon I

Canon X arbitrators should observe all of the obligations of Canon I subject only to the following provisions:

(1) Canon X arbitrators may be predisposed toward the party who appointed them but in all other respects are obligated to act in good faith and with integrity and fairness. For example, Canon X arbitrators should not engage in delaying tactics or harassment of any party or witness and should not knowingly make untrue or misleading statements to the other arbitrators; and

(2) The provisions of subparagraphs B(1), B(2), and paragraphs C and D of Canon I, insofar as they relate to partiality, relationships, and interests are not applicable to Canon X arbitrators.

B. Obligations under Canon II

(1) Canon X arbitrators should disclose to all parties, and to the other arbitrators, all interests and relationships which Canon II requires be disclosed. Disclosure as required by Canon II is for the benefit not only of the party who appointed the arbitrator, but also for the benefit of the other parties and arbitrators so that they may know of any partiality which may exist or appear to exist; and

(2) Canon X arbitrators are not obliged to withdraw under paragraph G of Canon II if requested to do so only by the party who did not appoint them.

C. Obligations under Canon III

Canon X arbitrators should observe all of the obligations of Canon III subject only to the following provisions:

(1) Like neutral party-appointed arbitrators, Canon X arbitrators may consult with the party who appointed them to the extent permitted in paragraph B of Canon III;

(2) Canon X arbitrators shall, at the earliest practicable time, disclose to the other arbitrators and to the parties whether or not they intend to communicate with their appointing parties. If they have disclosed the intention to engage in such communications, they may thereafter communicate with their appointing parties concerning any other aspect of the case, except as provided in paragraph (3);

(3) If such communication occurred prior to the time they were appointed as arbitrators, or prior to the first hearing or other meeting of the parties with the arbitrators, the Canon X arbitrator should, at or before the first hearing or meeting of the arbitrators with the parties, disclose the fact that such communication has taken place. In complying with the provisions of this subparagraph, it is sufficient that there be disclosure of the fact that such communication has occurred without disclosing the content of the communication.

A single timely disclosure of the Canon X arbitrator's intention to participate in such communications in the future is sufficient;

(4) Canon X arbitrators may not at any time during the arbitration:

(a) disclose any deliberations by the arbitrators on any matter or issue submitted to them for decision;

(b) communicate with the parties that appointed them concerning any matter or issue taken under consideration by the panel after the record is closed or such matter or issue has been submitted for decision; or

(c) disclose any final decision or interim decision in advance of the time that it is disclosed to all parties.

(5) Unless otherwise agreed by the arbitrators and the parties, a Canon X arbitrator may not communicate orally with the neutral arbitrator concerning any matter or issue arising or expected

to arise in the arbitration in the absence of the other Canon X arbitrator. If a Canon X arbitrator communicates in writing with the neutral arbitrator, he or she shall simultaneously provide a copy of the written communication to the other Canon X arbitrator;

(6) When Canon X arbitrators communicate orally with the parties that appointed them concerning any matter on which communication is permitted under this Code, they are not obligated to disclose the contents of such oral communications to any other party or arbitrator; and

(7) When Canon X arbitrators communicate in writing with the party who appointed them concerning any matter on which communication is permitted under this Code, they are not required to send copies of any such written communication to any other party or arbitrator.

D. Obligations under Canon IV

Canon X arbitrators should observe all of the obligations of Canon IV.

E. Obligations under Canon V

Canon X arbitrators should observe all of the obligations of Canon V, except that they may be predisposed toward deciding in favor of the party who appointed them.

F. Obligations under Canon VI

Canon X arbitrators should observe all of the obligations of Canon VI.

G. Obligations under Canon VII

Canon X arbitrators should observe all of the obligations of Canon VII.

H. Obligations under Canon VIII

Canon X arbitrators should observe all of the obligations of Canon VIII.

I. Obligations under Canon IX

The provisions of paragraph D of Canon IX are inapplicable to Canon X arbitrators, except insofar as the obligations are also set forth in this Canon.

APPENDIX 7

Schedule of New York City Bar Association Arbitration Reports

The New York City Bar Association's International Commercial Disputes Committee has published reports on issues relevant to international arbitrations, all available at: http://www2.nycbar.org/Publications/reports/reportsbycom.php?com=101.

I. Advance Waivers of Arbitrator Conflicts of Interest in International Commercial Arbitrations Seated in New York (2016)
II. A Model Federal Arbitration Summons to Testify and Present Documentary Evidence at an Arbitration Hearing (2015), also published in 26(2) AMERICAN REVIEW OF INTERNATIONAL ARBITRATION (2015)
III. Publication of International Arbitration Awards and Decisions (2014)
IV. Purchase Price Adjustment Clauses and Expert Determinations: Legal Issues, Practical Problems and Suggested Improvements (2013)
V. The "Manifest Disregard of Law" Doctrine and International Arbitration in New York (2012)
VI. Recommended procedures for Recognition and Enforcement of International Arbitral Awards Rendered Under the ICSID Convention (2012)
VII. Obtaining Evidence from Non-Parties in International Arbitration in the United States (2010)
VIII. 28 U.S.C. 1782 as a Means of Obtaining Discovery in Aid of International Commercial Arbitration—Applicability and Best Practices
IX. Lack of Jurisdiction and Forum non Conveniens as Defenses to the Enforcement of Foreign Arbitral Awards

INDEX

References to footnotes will be followed by the letter 'n' and number of the Note.

A

AAA *see* **American Arbitration Association (AAA)**
Acceptance 4.15–4.16
see also Breach of contract; Contract law; New York contract law
Action to challenge or enforce arbitral award *see* **International arbitral awards, challenging and enforcing**
Adjourn, failure to 13.119–13.133
Administered Arbitration Rules, issue by International Institute for Conflict Prevention and Resolution 0.14
Adversarial model
discovery in 2.55–2.56
U.S. legal system as 2.04–2.07
Advertising and promotion, truthful Appendix 6
Affirmative defenses 2.33
Agency, nonsignatories 7.74
Agreement to arbitrate 1.02, 1.09, 1.28, 1.32
see also Arbitration agreement(s)
allocation of power between arbitrators and courts 7.29
arbitrability 3.16, 7.30
arbitral jurisdiction 6.05
under Conventions 1.50, 1.51, 1.52, 7.16, 7.18
court intervention 7.13
proceeding without 7.04
deciding of party issues 6.23
failure to comply with 7.02
under Federal Arbitration Act 1.54, 1.55
internationally recognized minimum standards, consideration of 1.72, 1.73
invalid 7.29
jurisdiction of U.S. courts 7.19
Kompetenz-Kompetenz doctrine 6.65, 7.33
limiting of time to object to validity 1.40–1.42
preclusive effect of prior judicial determinations 6.52n170, 6.54
provisional measures 3.53
review of arbitrator's decision as to the parties bound by the agreement 6.71
scope 6.16
Second Circuit case law 1.61, 1.63, 1.65, 1.66, 1.67, 1.69
selection of arbitrators 5.29n23
separability doctrine 1.45, 1.46, 1.47
specialist advice 1.110
time limits 1.40
Alter ego
awards based on 6.99
of corporations 14.65
deciding of party issues 6.23
international arbitration agreements, enforcing 7.75
nonsignatories, jurisdiction over 3.24n36
American Arbitration Association (AAA)
AAA/ABA Code of Ethics and rules 5.57–5.59, Appendix 6
class arbitration rules established following *Bazzle* judgment 11.29–11.34
Commercial Arbitration Rules 0.10, 5.16–5.18
conducting arbitration 12.02
international caseload administered through 0.09
on New York as an arbitration site 0.01
numbers of cases administered 0.08
offices 0.08
selection of arbitrators 5.57–5.59
services 0.08
American Bar Association 0.27
***American Express Co. v Italian Colors Restaurant* judgment**
arbitral clauses prohibiting class actions (and public policy arguments against such clauses)
decisions following judgment 11.110–11.114
effect of judgment 11.103–11.109
prior to judgment 11.85–11.94
decisions whether state arbitration laws/ concepts of public policy are preempted by FAA
decisions following judgment 11.110–11.114
effect of judgment 11.103–11.109
prior to judgment 11.95–11.102
Anticipated future profits, damages for lost business opportunity 10.35–10.38
Antisuit injunctions
circumstances in which courts grant to enforce arbitration agreements 7.136–7.151
circumstances in which courts have denied in aid of arbitration 7.152–7.166
overview 7.131–7.135

Appeals 2.96–2.101
appellate-level courts 2.22
arbitral jurisdiction determinations of court, appealability 6.35–6.38
civil procedure 2.26
"final judgment" rule 2.98
to higher court 0.19, 2.99
interim arbitral determinations of arbitral jurisdiction, appealability 6.60
review, scope 2.100–2.101
Applicable law
arbitrability 1.79–1.81
capacity and competence 1.83
foreign sovereigns, enforcing awards involving 14.04–14.30
formal validity of agreement to arbitrate pursuant to terms of Conventions 1.74–1.78
formation and substantive validity of the agreement to arbitrate 1.57–1.73
case law from Second Circuit applying law of forum 1.61–1.64
case law from Second Circuit applying law of underlying contract 1.69–1.71
internationally recognized minimum standards, consideration of 1.72–1.73
state contract law principles, considering when applying law of forum in Second Circuit 1.65–1.68
international arbitral awards, challenging and enforcing 13.07–13.11
interpretation and scope, regarding 1.82
recognition and enforcement of Convention awards 1.84–1.102
application of Conventions 1.86–1.87
arbitral awards rendered outside the United States/pursuant to a foreign law, may not be vacated under U.S. law 1.95–1.99
nondomestic awards rendered in the United States/pursuant to U.S. arbitration law vacated under U.S arbitration law 1.88–1.94
relevance of New York arbitration law to arbitral awards 1.100–1.102
recognition of arbitration agreement under Conventions 1.44–1.83
Federal Arbitration Act 1.54–1.56
New York Convention 1.48–1.53
separability doctrine 1.45–1.47
Arbitrability
see also Arbitrability-related issues
agreement to arbitrate 3.16, 7.30
of ancillary claims 4.45–4.48
applicable law 1.79–1.81
cases including nonarbitrable claims 7.124–7.128
of claims under U.S. law 7.121–7.123
common issues, in enforcement of international agreements 7.55–7.97
deference to arbitrators on 6.106
those deciding arbitrability and arbitrability-related issues 6.26–6.28
Arbitrability-related issues
deference to arbitrators on 6.82–6.85, 6.106
those deciding 6.26–6.28
Arbitral awards against foreign sovereigns *see* **Foreign sovereigns, enforcing awards involving**
Arbitral determination
deference to prior arbitral decision 6.99
preservation 6.97
of validity of arbitration agreement 6.76
waiver subject to 6.32n110
Arbitral jurisdiction
see also Jurisdiction
appealability of court's arbitral jurisdiction determinations 6.35–6.38
appealability of interim arbitral determinations of 6.60
before the arbitrators 6.39–6.60
assisting in judicial proceedings prior to arbitration 6.11–6.38
choice of law governing jurisdictional determinations 6.48–6.49
deferring the jurisdictional determination and joining it with the merits 6.46
existence and scope 6.03–6.04
forum-specific issues 6.29–6.34
deference to arbitrators on 6.91–6.92
limitation periods 6.31
preclusive effect of prior judicial determinations 6.56–6.59
res judicata and collateral estoppel 6.33–6.34
waiver of a party's right to arbitrate the dispute 6.32
interim arbitral determinations of, appealability 6.60
in judicial proceedings *see* Arbitral jurisdiction in judicial proceedings
Kompetenz-Kompetenz principle 6.06, 6.09, 6.22–6.28
scope and validity of arbitrators' jurisdiction 6.50–6.55
those deciding party issues 6.23
those deciding scope issues 6.24
those deciding validity issues 6.25
policy dimensions 6.05
preclusive effect of prior judicial determinations 6.52–6.54, 6.56–6.59
preliminary issues 3.20–3.23
procedural aspects of arbitrators' determinations 6.41–6.47
at recognition and enforcement *see* Arbitral jurisdiction at recognition and enforcement
scenarios 6.10

severability doctrine 6.06, 6.07, 6.08, 6.09
severability as guide to validity questions 6.18–6.21
special jurisdictional procedures for different institutional regimes 6.47
timing and form of jurisdictional objections 6.42–6.45
upon vacatur *see* Arbitral jurisdiction upon vacatur
waiver of jurisdictional challenges 6.55

Arbitral jurisdiction at recognition and enforcement 6.93–6.111
see also Arbitral jurisdiction; International arbitral awards, challenging and enforcing
choice-of-law rules 6.96
deference
to arbitrators and vacatur courts on forum-specific issues 6.107–6.110
to arbitrators' determination as to validity 6.102–6.105
to arbitrators' determination of scope of agreement 6.100–6.101
to arbitrators on arbitrability and arbitrability-related issues 6.106
to prior arbitral decision as to the parties bound by the agreement 6.99
Kompetenz-Kompetenz and review of arbitral jurisdiction 6.97–6.106
place of arbitral jurisdiction 6.95
waiver of jurisdictional challenges 6.111

Arbitral jurisdiction in judicial proceedings 6.11–6.38
see also Arbitral jurisdiction
choice of law governing interpretation and enforcement of arbitration agreement 6.14–6.17
Kompetenz-Kompetenz doctrine 6.22–6.28
severability as guide to validity questions 6.18–6.21
those deciding arbitrability and arbitrability-related issues 6.26–6.28

Arbitral jurisdiction upon vacatur 6.61–6.92
see also Arbitral jurisdiction
confirmation and vacatur of awards rendered in New York 6.62–6.63
deference
to arbitrators on "arbitrability-related" issues 6.82–6.85
to arbitrators on forum-specific issues 6.91–6.92
in cases where a court compelling arbitration has ruled on the jurisdictional issue 6.86–6.89
on validity of arbitration agreement 6.79–6.81
law governing interpretation and validity of arbitration agreement 6.64
review of arbitrator's decision as to the parties bound by the agreement 6.68–6.71
review of arbitrator's determination of scope of arbitration agreement 6.72–6.75
review of arbitrator's determinations of the validity of the arbitration agreement 6.76–6.85
severability at vacatur stage 6.78
waiver of jurisdictional objections by failure to raise them before vacatur 6.90

Arbitral process 3.38–3.50
see also Civil procedure
confidentiality 3.49–3.50
consolidation of proceedings 3.44–3.48
discovery 3.38–3.43
upholding integrity and fairness of Appendix 6
violations of arbitral procedures 13.101–13.103

Arbitral tribunal(s)
allocation of costs and fees 3.29–3.33
arbitral process 3.38–3.50
authority to issue preliminary relief 8.07–8.15
class certification decisions by, following *Bazzle* 11.73–11.84
class proceedings 3.37
discretion of 9.30–9.32
federal and state law 12.05–12.08
institutional rules 12.09
interim measures from 14.41
powers and duties 3.27–3.37
punitive damages 3.34–3.36
structure *see* Structure of tribunal
tribunal secretaries 12.10–12.16

Arbitration
see also specific entries
applications to compel or stay (N. Y. CPLR) Appendix 3
discovery in, limited nature compared to in state litigation/federal courts 9.11–9.12
drafting of clauses 3.06
fair conduct of proceedings Appendix 6
notice of intention to arbitrate Appendix 3
rules and guidelines *see* Rules and guidelines, arbitration

Arbitration agreement(s)
see also Agreement to arbitrate; Validity of arbitration agreement
applicable law
formation and substantive validity of the agreement to arbitrate 1.57–1.73
recognition of arbitration agreement under Conventions 1.44–1.83
deference
to arbitrators' determination as to validity 6.102–6.105
to arbitrators' determination of scope of agreement 6.100–6.101
to prior arbitral decision as to the parties bound by the agreement 6.99

Arbitration agreement(s) (*cont.*)
enforcement *see* Enforcement
jurisdiction 6.02
parties bound by, deference to prior arbitral decision as to 6.99
predispute, state law prohibiting 1.43
scope, deference to arbitrators' determination of 6.100–6.101
standard form agreements, global 0.05
substantial similarity 11.81
written requirement, challenging and enforcing of awards 13.27
Arbitration awards *see* **Awards**
Arbitration clauses
see also Force majeure clause; Merger clauses, contract law
challenges to contract 7.60–7.62
detailed arbitrator selection clauses 5.05–5.06
drafting *see* Drafting considerations, arbitration clauses
dysfunctional, referring to non-existent or unavailable arbitral institutions 5.29
governing law 1.103–1.110
judicial resolution of disputes 7.89–7.95
referring disputes to the arbitrators 7.84–7.88
scope 7.82–7.95
silent, effect on class action arbitration 11.48–11.52
post-*Stolt-Neilsen decisions* 11.71–11.72
sole option 3.26
staying litigation commenced in U.S. in breach of 7.112–7.128
Arbitration Committee, New York City Bar Association 0.26
Arbitration Committee of the U.S. Council for International Business (U.S. National Committee) 0.12, 5.51
Arbitration Fairness Act, class action arbitrations 11.115
Arbitration hearings *see* **Hearings, arbitration**
Arbitration institutions
see also specific institutions, such as American Arbitration Association (AAA)
leading (New York) 0.06, 0.07–0.16
non-existent or unavailable, dysfunctional clauses referring to 5.29
Arbitrators
see also Arbitral jurisdiction
allocation of power between arbitrators and courts 7.29–7.41
appointment Appendix 3
arbitral jurisdiction before 6.39–6.60
challenges and replacement of 5.86–5.93
corruption 13.115–13.118
deference to *see* Deference
disclosures by, and conflicts checks 5.82–5.85
emergency *see* Emergency arbitrators, preliminary relief from
fees and costs 10.50
impartiality 3.27–3.28
lack of authority to disqualify counsel in an arbitration 12.26–12.28
partiality of 13.115–13.118
party-appointed *see* Party-appointed arbitrators
powers Appendix 3
referring disputes to, in arbitration clauses 7.84–7.88
selection *see* Selection of arbitrators
Assets, attachment of 14.56–14.76
debt and property subject to attachment 14.63
garnishment of royalties or taxes 14.69–14.73
property of state-owned companies 14.64–14.68
trust accounts 14.74–14.76
***AT&T Mobility LLC v. Conception* judgment**
arbitral clauses prohibiting class actions (and public policy arguments against such clauses)
prior to judgment 11.85–11.94
effect of judgment 11.103–11.109
decisions following judgment 11.110–11.114
decisions whether state arbitration laws/concepts of public policy are preempted by FAA
prior to judgment 11.95–11.102
effect of judgment 11.103–11.109
decisions following judgment 11.110–11.114
Attachment
assets attached 14.56–14.76
debt and property subject to 14.63
garnishment of royalties or taxes 14.69–14.73
postrecognition 14.51–14.55
prearbitration
explicit waiver requirement 14.34–14.39
procedure 14.40
recalcitrant states 14.33–14.40
prerecognition 14.42–14.50
property of state-owned companies 14.64–14.68
of trust accounts 14.74–14.76
Attorneys
see also Lawyers
attorney-client privilege
see Privilege, discovery
fees and costs 10.51–10.54
Awards
action to challenge or enforce *see* International arbitral awards, challenging and enforcing
by confession Appendix 3
confirming/vacating of 6.62–6.63, Appendix 3
form of application 13.18–13.20
service of application 13.21–13.26
timing of application 13.14–13.17
vacatur of awards rendered in New York 6.62–6.63
corruption, procured by 13.113–13.114
delivery Appendix 3
enforcement of judgment confirming 13.28
form Appendix 3
fraud, procured by 13.113–13.114

judgment Appendix 3
modification by arbitrator Appendix 3
non-arbitrable issues, addressing 13.106–13.107
not binding 13.104–13.105
sanctions for frivolous attacks on 13.136–13.137
setting aside 13.104–13.105
time Appendix 3
undue means, procured by 13.113–13.114

B

Bar association committees 0.25, 0.26
***Bazzle* judgment (*Green Tree Financial Corporation vs. Bazzle*)** 11.08–11.28
see also Class action arbitrations
AAA class arbitration rules established following 11.29–11.34
class certification decisions by arbitral tribunals following 11.73–11.84
clause-construction decisions by arbitral panels adjudicating class arbitrations following 11.55–11.64
federal court decisions regarding consolidation of arbitrations/class arbitrations prior to 11.53–11.54
Bench trial, judgment in 2.89–2.91
Best efforts vs. reasonable efforts, contract law 4.64–4.66
Bilateral investment treaty (BIT) 0.45
discovery in aid of foreign arbitration 9.77n176
international arbitral awards, challenging and enforcing 13.89
Book value 14.08
Breach of contract 4.22–4.28
see also Contract law
anticipatory 4.26–4.27
claims ancillary to
arbitrability of 4.45–4.48
under New York law 4.49–4.58
consequences 4.29–4.44
damages 10.03–10.05
divisible or installment contracts 4.28
effect on performance of the non-breaching party 4.29–4.33
equitable relief 4.42–4.44
material 4.23–4.24
measure of damages 4.34–4.41
repudiation 4.26–4.27
substantial performance 4.25

C

Capacity, applicable law 1.83
Case management, procedural calendar 2.45
Case presentation 2.26, 2.76–2.82
Causation, damages 10.02
Center of gravity (significant contracts) test, choice-of-law rules 4.09
Chairperson
convincing to serve 5.75–5.76
negotiations 5.70–5.74
role of party-appointed arbitrators in selecting 5.66–5.69
Challenging of judgment 2.26
Chartered Institute of Arbitrators, Guideline on selection of arbitrators 5.60–5.63
Choice-of-law rules
see also Forum-specific issues; Law of forum
arbitral jurisdiction before the arbitrators 6.48–6.49
contract law 4.06–4.11
enforcement of arbitration agreement 6.14–6.17
international arbitral awards, challenging and enforcing 6.96
Circuit courts, appeals to, from district courts 0.19
Civil Practice Law and Rules (CPLR) *see* **New York Civil Practice Law and Rules (N. Y. CPLR)**
Civil procedure 2.18–2.20, 2.26
see also Federal Rules of Civil Procedure (FRCP)
Claims ancillary to breach of contract
see also Breach of contract
arbitrability of ancillary claims 4.45–4.48
fraud in the inducement 4.53–4.54
good faith, implied covenant 4.49–4.50
under New York law 4.49–4.58
third-party beneficiaries 4.57–4.58
unjust enrichment 4.51–4.52
Class action arbitrations
see also Class certification decisions by arbitral tribunals
arbitral clauses prohibiting class actions (and public policy arguments against such clauses)
prior to *AT&T Mobility/American Express Co.* 11.85–11.94
effect of *AT&T Mobility/American Express Co.* 11.103–11.109
following *AT&T Mobility/American Express Co.* 11.110–11.114
in post-*Bazzle* era 11.85–11.86
case law/Supreme Court judgments *see American Express Co. v Italian Colors Restaurant* judgment; *AT&T Mobility LLC v. Conception* judgment; *Bazzle* judgment (*Green Tree Financial Corporation vs. Bazzle*); *Hall St. Associations v Mattel* judgment; *Stolt-Neilsen S.A. v AnimalFeeds International Corp* judgment
federal court decisions regarding consolidation of arbitrations/class arbitrations prior to *Bazzle* 11.53–11.54
general principles governing in U.S. courts 11.04–11.07
JAMS Class Arbitration Procedures 11.35–11.36
legislation 11.115

Class action arbitrations (*cont.*)
public policy considerations
arbitral clauses prohibiting class actions 11.85–11.94, 11.103–11.109
whether preempted by FAA 11.95–11.109
and silent arbitration clause 11.48–11.52
post-*Stolt-Neilsen decisions* 11.71–11.72
whether state arbitration laws/concepts of public policy preempted by FAA
prior to *AT&T Mobility/American Express Co.* 11.95–11.102
effect of *AT&T Mobility/American Express Co.* 11.103–11.109
decisions following *AT&T Mobility/American Express Co.* 11.110–11.114
Class certification decisions by arbitral tribunals 3.37
see also Class action arbitrations
class representative(s), adequacy
counsel 11.80
requirements 11.79
commonality 11.77
numerosity 11.76
predominance and superiority of claims 11.82–11.84
standards for 11.73–11.84
substantial similarity of arbitration agreements 11.81
typicality 11.78
Clauses, arbitration *see* **Arbitration clauses**
Clear and unmistakable evidence test, nonsignatories 7.66, 7.67
CLPR *see* **Federal Rules of Civil Procedure (FRCP)**
Collateral estoppel 6.33–6.34
Collateral order doctrine 2.98n103
College of Commercial Arbitrators (CCA) 0.28
Comity *see* **International comity**
Commencement of litigation 2.27–2.43
civil procedure 2.26
court jurisdiction 2.38–2.43
pleadings 2.28–2.37
staying litigation commenced in U.S. in breach of an arbitration clause 7.112–7.128
Commercial Arbitration Rules (AAA) 0.10, 5.16–5.18
Commercial damages
alternate theories
reliance 10.29–10.33
restitution 10.34
breach of contract 10.03–10.05
Common law, U.S. litigation 2.14–2.15
Compelling arbitration
actions to compel under FAA 7.98–7.105
arbitral jurisdiction upon vacatur 6.86–6.89
New York Practice Law and Rules, s. 7503(c) 7.106–7.111
Compensation
arbitrator compensation and conflicts waivers 5.77–5.81
standards for Appendix 6
Competence
see also Kompetenz-Kompetenz (compétence-compétence)
applicable law 1.83
death or incompetency of a party Appendix 3
Confession, awards by Appendix 3
Confidentiality
arbitral process 3.49–3.50
conducting arbitration 12.17–12.25
discovery 9.59–9.61
distinguished from privacy 12.17
upholding Appendix 6
Conflicts, waivers, and arbitrator compensation 5.77–5.81
Consent, personal jurisdiction by 13.43–13.47
Consequential (special) damages 10.15–10.20
Consideration 4.17–4.18
see also Breach of contract; Contract law; New York contract law
promissory estoppel as substitute for 10.32
Consulting firms 0.30
Consumer contracts 1.43
Contract law
see also Breach of contract; Consumer contracts; New York contract law
authority to enter contracts 4.20–4.21
best efforts vs. reasonable efforts 4.64–4.66
challenges to contract 7.57–7.62
challenges to validity of contract as a whole vs. challenges directed specifically at arbitration clause 7.60–7.62
challenges to validity of contract vs. a claim that no contract was ever concluded 7.58–7.59
changed circumstances and *force majeure* 4.67–4.70
choice-of-law rules in New York 4.06–4.11
divisible or installment contracts 4.28
elements of a contract 4.14–4.18
formation of contracts 4.12–4.21
future contracts 4.19
grouping of contracts theory *see* Center of gravity (significant contacts) test
merger clauses 4.60–4.63
predispute arbitration agreements in consumer contracts, state law prohibiting 1.43
significant contacts test *see* Center of gravity (significant contacts) test
state contract law principles, considering when applying law of forum in Second Circuit 1.65–1.68
underlying contract, applying law of 1.69–1.71
Corruption
of arbitrators 13.115–13.118
award procured by 13.113–13.114

Costs
allocation by arbitral tribunal 3.29–3.33
of arbitrators 10.50
of attorneys 10.51–10.54
and fees *see* Fees and costs
litigation 2.26, 2.92–2.95
Court(s)
see also Enforcement; Federal courts
allocation of power between arbitrators and courts 7.29–7.41
appellate-level 2.22
arbitral jurisdiction determinations of, appealability 6.35–6.38
circuit 0.19
compelling arbitration, ruling on the jurisdictional issue 6.86–6.89
court system supporting arbitration 0.17–0.21
district 0.18, 0.19
enforcement of international arbitration agreements, intervention with 7.08–7.41
local court rules 2.22
preliminary relief from 8.32–8.49
proceeding with arbitration without intervention of 7.04–7.07
structure 2.08–2.11
Supreme Court 0.20
CPR *see* **International Institute for Conflict Prevention and Resolution (CPR)**

D

Damages
for anticipated future profits from lost business opportunity 10.35–10.38
causation 10.02
commercial
alternate theories 10.29–10.34
for breach of contract 10.03–10.05
determination by agreement of parties, in commercial arbitration 10.01
duty to mitigate 10.21–10.22
expectation 10.10–10.22
fees and costs 10.48–10.54
of arbitrators 10.50
of attorneys 10.51–10.54
general 10.11–10.14
and good faith 4.39, 10.27
interest calculation 10.39–10.47
liquidated 10.23–10.26
measure of 4.34–4.41
money damages, vs. specific performance 10.06–10.09
principles controlling proof, and calculation of 10.03–10.38
punitive 3.34–3.36, 10.27–10.28
reasonableness test 10.22
special 10.15–10.20
"Daubert challenge," expert discovery 2.70
***De novo* review**
deference issues 6.86, 6.101, 6.102, 6.103, 6.104
preclusive effect of prior judicial determinations 6.52
scope of appellate review 2.101
Death or incompetency Appendix 3
Decision and judgment *see* **Judgment**
Defenses, recognition and international arbitral awards, challenging and enforcing 6.96
Deference
see also Arbitral jurisdiction; Arbitral jurisdiction at recognition and enforcement; Arbitral jurisdiction in judicial proceedings; Arbitral jurisdiction upon vacatur; Arbitrators; Selection of arbitrators
to arbitrators and vacatur courts on forum-specific issues 6.107–6.110
to arbitrators' determination of scope of agreement 6.100–6.101
to arbitrators on arbitrability and arbitrability-related issues 6.82–6.85, 6.106
to arbitrators on forum-specific issues 6.91–6.92, 6.107–6.110
in cases where a court compelling arbitration has ruled on the jurisdictional issue 6.86–6.89
to prior arbitral decision as to parties bound by agreement 6.99
on validity of arbitration agreement
arbitral jurisdiction at recognition and enforcement 6.102–6.105
arbitral jurisdiction upon vacatur 6.79–6.81
Delegation doctrine 0.44
Depositions
discovery 2.63, 9.54
witnesses 12.49–12.51
Director of Arbitration and Alternative Dispute Resolution, Arbitration Committee administered by 0.12
Disclosures, by arbitrators 5.82–5.85
Discounted cash flow method (DCF) 14.08
Discovery 2.52–2.75
see also Litigation, U.S.
in adversarial model 2.55–2.56
arbitral process 3.38–3.43
arbitration rules and guidelines 9.13–9.29
civil procedure 2.26
confidentiality 9.59–9.61
depositions 2.63, 9.54
discretion of arbitral tribunal 9.30–9.32
document *see* Document discovery
document requests 2.63
electronic 2.71–2.72
expert 2.68–2.70
from expert witnesses 9.71–9.72
Federal Arbitration Act 9.04–9.05
Federal Rules of Civil Procedure 2.59–2.61
framework for international arbitrations venued in New York 9.03–9.32

Discovery (*cont.*)
initial disclosures 2.62
limited
example of clause permitting, at discretion of arbitrators 9.09
limited nature of discovery in arbitration compared to state litigation/Federal Court 9.11–9.12
New York Civil Practice Law and Rules 9.06
in New York, in aid of a foreign arbitration 9.74–9.78
obtaining from non-parties 9.62–9.70
between the parties 9.33–9.61
depositions 2.63, 9.54
document discovery *see* Document discovery
Federal Rules of Civil Procedure 9.55
privilege 9.56–9.58
party autonomy
New York State courts supporting 9.07–9.10
paramount in international arbitration 9.07
supremacy of parties' agreement on discovery 9.08
preliminary relief, when seeking 9.73
production, requests for 2.63
rules, methods and mechanisms, in U.S. litigation 2.57–2.67
statutory framework 9.03–9.06
summary judgment 2.74–2.75
supremacy of parties' agreement on 9.08
third-party subpoenas 2.63
using the evidence 2.73–2.75
District courts
appeals from, to circuit courts 0.19
courts of first instance as 0.18
in New York City 0.19
Document
definition 9.33n70, 9.39, 9.43
requests for 2.01, 2.63, 9.35, 9.36
Document discovery 9.33–9.53
see also Discovery
consequences of a party's failure to produce documents 9.51–9.53
documents in "hard copy" form 9.33–9.38
electronically stored documents and information 9.39–9.50
Drafting considerations, arbitration clauses
arbitral process 3.38–3.50
arbitral tribunal 3.27–3.37
arbitration as designated dispute settlement method 3.06
essential elements 3.04–3.07
judicial powers, considerations relating to 3.51–3.61
jurisdictional issues 3.16–3.26
Kompetenz-Kompetenz 3.16–3.19
law governing, for New York arbitration 3.11–3.15
nonsignatories, jurisdiction over 3.24–3.25
not particular to arbitration in New York 3.04–3.10
preliminary issues, arbitral jursidiction to resolve 3.20–3.23
recommended elements 3.08–3.10
sole option clauses, validity 3.26
Due process
AAA Protocols 11.29
civil procedure rules 2.18
clauses 14.27
constitutional 13.48, 13.53
denial of opportunity to present case 13.96, 13.97
foreign sovereigns, enforcing awards involving 14.12
litigation 2.18, 2.43
preliminary relief 8.18, 8.20, 8.22
procedural 13.123
witnesses 12.35
Duty to mitigate 10.21–10.22

E
E-discovery (electronic discovery) *see* **Electronically stored Information (ESI)**
Electronically stored information (ESI) 2.51n63, 9.39–9.50
Emergency arbitrators, preliminary relief from 8.24–8.31
need for emergency arbitral relief 8.24–8.25
procedures 8.26–8.31
Energy Arbitrators List 5.48, 5.50
Enforcement
of arbitration agreement *see* International arbitration agreements, enforcing
of awards *see* Foreign sovereigns, enforcing awards involving; International arbitral awards, challenging and enforcing
preliminary relief 8.20–8.23
Equity
damages, equitable relief 4.42–4.44
U.S. litigation 2.16–2.17
Estoppel
collateral 6.33–6.34
nonsignatories 7.76–7.80
promissory 4.19, 10.29, 10.32, 10.33
Ethical obligations and codes Appendix 6
AAA/ABA Code of Ethics and rules 5.57–5.59
U.S. litigation 2.24–2.25
Evidence
discovery 2.73–2.75
failure to hear 13.119–13.133
rules of 2.22
Exclusivity, drafting considerations 3.07
Exhibits, use 12.76–12.81
Expectation damages 10.10–10.22
see also Damages
general damages 10.11–10.14

Expert witnesses
see also Discovery; Witnesses
arbitration hearings 12.44–12.48
discovery 2.68–2.70, 9.71–9.72

F

FAA *see* **Federal Arbitration Act (FAA)**
Fair dealing 4.49–4.50
Federal Arbitration Act (FAA)
see also Inter-American Convention on International Commercial Arbitration of 1975 (Panama Convention); New York Convention
actions to compel under 7.98–7.105
discovery 9.04–9.05
and Federal Law of Arbitration (Chapter 1) 1.11–1.21
Cable Connection judgment 1.28
Hall Street judgment 1.27
provisions 1.21–1.26
motions to stay or dismiss litigation under 7.113–7.120
and New York Convention (Chapter 2) 1.01, 1.30–1.33
and Panama Convention 1.01, 1.34–1.35
recognition of arbitration agreement, applicable law regarding 1.54–1.56
role 1.04–1.05
scope 1.04
text Appendix 2
vacation of international arbitral awards, grounds under Chapter 1 13.111–13.137
award procured by corruption, fraud or undue means 13.113–13.114
exceeding jurisdiction 13.124–13.125
failure to adjourn or hear evidence 13.119–13.133
partiality or corruption of arbitrators 13.115–13.118
prejudicial behavior 13.119–13.133
public policy considerations 13.135
sanctions for frivolous attacks on arbitral awards 13.136–13.137
whether state arbitration laws/concepts of public policy preempted by 11.95–11.102
Federal courts
see also Court(s)
actions in 13.13–13.72
decisions regarding consolidation of arbitrations/class actions 11.53–11.54
enforcement of international arbitration awards 13.65–13.72
jurisdiction 1.10, 7.19–7.28
commercial 7.25
nondomestic 7.27
personal 7.28
subject-matter 7.20–7.27
territorial 7.26
in writing 7.24
preliminary relief from 8.35–8.39
Federal Rules of Appellate Procedure 2.22, 2.100
Federal Rules of Civil Procedure (FRCP)
discovery 2.59–2.61, 9.55
sources of law 2.18–2.20
Fees and costs
see also Costs
allocation by arbitral tribunal 3.29–3.33
of arbitrators 10.50
of attorneys 10.51–10.54
New York Civil Practice Law and Rules (CPLR) Appendix 3
"Final judgment" rule 2.98
***Force majeure* clause** 4.67–4.70
Foreign sovereigns, enforcing awards involving
forum non conveniens 14.30, 14.55, 14.67
immunities
enjoyed by sovereigns with respect to enforcement of awards against them 14.19–14.26
foreign sovereigns not immune from personal jurisdiction and service 14.27–14.30
interim measures from arbitral tribunal 14.41
legal regime applicable to arbitration awards against sovereigns in New York 14.04–14.30
postrecognition judicial proceedings 14.04
preaward arbitral proceedings 14.04
preaward judicial proceedings 14.04
prerecognition judicial proceedings 14.04
recalcitrant states, problem of 14.31–14.76
assets attached 14.56–14.76
interim measures from arbitral tribunal 14.41
postrecognition attachment and execution 14.51–14.55
prearbitration attachment 14.33–14.40
predispute protections 14.31–14.32
prerecognition attachment 14.42–14.50
recognition of awards rendered against sovereigns
recognition of a foreign court's recognition of the award 14.17–14.18
recognition of ICSID awards "automatic" 14.15–14.16
subject to New York Convention 14.12–14.14
unique characteristics of arbitrations involving 14.01–14.03
usual payment of awards by sovereigns 14.05–14.11
Formation of tribunal, incorporation of arbitral rules regarding 5.07–5.27
AAA Commercial Arbitration Rules 5.16–5.18
ICC International Rules 5.19–5.21
ICDR International Rules 5.08–5.15
International Institute for Conflict Prevention and Resolution (CPR) Rules 5.24–5.26
UNCITRAL Rules 5.22–5.23

Forum non conveniens
foreign sovereigns, enforcing awards involving 14.30, 14.55, 14.67
international arbitral awards, challenging and enforcing 13.62, 13.63, 13.64
motion for 2.34n47
personal jurisdiction 13.40
Forum-specific issues 6.29–6.34
see also Choice of law rules; Law of forum
deference to arbitrators on 6.91–6.92, 6.107–6.110
limitation periods 6.31
preclusive effect of prior judicial determinations 6.56–6.59
res judicata and collateral estoppel 6.33–6.34
waiver of a party's right to arbitrate the dispute 6.32
Fraud
award procured by 13.113–13.114
claims ancillary to breach of contract 4.53–4.56
in the inducement 4.53–4.54
in the performance 4.55–4.56
***Frye* test, expert discovery** 2.70n75
Fulbright Annual Litigation Trends Survey Report (2013) 0.03
***Functus officio* doctrine** 1.94

G
General damages 10.11–10.14
see also Damages; Expectation damages
Good faith
antisuit injunctions 7.166
best efforts vs. reasonable efforts 4.64
and damages 4.39, 10.27
drafting considerations, arbitration clauses 3.33n45
and estoppel 7.74
future contracts 4.19n56
implied covenant 4.45, 4.49–4.50
breaches of 4.48
litigation 2.32, 2.36n50
and material breach of contract 4.23
substantial performance 4.25
Governing law
effective clauses 1.103–1.110
of New York 0.05

H
***Hall St. Associates v Mattel* judgment, effect on class arbitrations** 11.37–11.47
Hearings, arbitration
accommodation and entertainment 12.94–12.96
ancillary services 12.98
arbitral tribunals 12.04–12.09
catering 12.97
closing proceedings and post-hearing submissions 12.82–12.85
confidentiality 12.17–12.25
entitlement to represent parties 12.29–12.34
federal and state law
arbitral tribunals 12.05–12.08
confidentiality 12.18–12.20
tribunal secretaries 12.11–12.12
witnesses 12.77
written witness statements/extent of live direct testimony 12.37
institutional rules
arbitral tribunals 12.09
confidentiality 12.21–12.25
tribunal secretaries 12.13–12.16
witnesses 12.78–12.81
written witness statements/extent of live direct testimony 12.38–12.43
lack of authority of arbitrators to disqualify counsel in an arbitration 12.26–12.28
locations 0.32–0.33
logistics 12.86–12.98
major arbitral institutions 12.02
New York Civil Practice Law and Rules (CPLR) Appendix 3
travel to and from New York 12.87–12.90
tribunal secretaries 12.10–12.16
witnesses *see* Witnesses

I
ICC *see* **International Chamber of Commerce (ICC)**
ICDR *see* **International Centre for Dispute Resolution (ICDR)**
Impartiality of arbitrators 3.27–3.28
disclosure of any interest/relationship likely to affect Appendix 6
Inducement, fraud in 4.53–4.54
Institutions *see* **Arbitration institutions**
Inter-American Convention on International Commercial Arbitration of 1975 (Panama Convention)
enforcement of international arbitration agreements 7.16–7.18
and Federal Arbitration Act 1.01, 1.34–1.35
Interest, damages 10.39–10.47
prejudgment 10.40–10.45
postjudgment 10.46–10.47
Interim relief *see* **Preliminary relief**
International arbitral awards, challenging and enforcing 1.84–1.102
see also Applicable law; Awards; New York Convention on the Recognition and Enforcement of Foreign Arbitral Awards (1958)
actions in federal courts in New York *see* Federal courts
application of Conventions 1.86–1.87
arbitral awards rendered outside the United States/pursuant to a foreign law, may not be vacated under U.S. law 1.95–1.99

award procured by corruption, fraud or undue means 13.113–13.114
challenging awards in New York, substantive issues involved 13.78–13.152
choice of arbitral law when resisting enforcement of award made in U.S. 13.142–13.152
FAA Chapter 1 grounds for vacating awards 13.111–13.137
New York State law grounds for vacating awards 13.138–13.141
nonrecognition grounds 13.78–13.110
choice of arbitral law when resisting enforcement of award made in U.S. 13.142–13.152
choice-of-law rules 6.96
exception to well-pleaded rule 13.67
FAA Chapter 1 grounds for vacating awards 13.111–13.137
award procured by corruption, fraud or undue means 13.113–13.114
exceeding jurisdiction 13.124–13.125
failure to adjourn or hear evidence 13.119–13.133
"manifest disregard of the law" 13.126–13.134
partiality or corruption of arbitrators 13.115–13.118
prejudicial behavior 13.119–13.133
public policy considerations 13.135
sanctions for frivolous attacks on awards 13.136–13.137
form of application to confirm/vacate award 13.18–13.20
forum non conveniens 13.62, 13.63, 13.64
judgment confirming an arbitral award, enforcing 13.28
judicial powers 3.58–3.61
legal regime applicable, in New York 13.07–13.11
New York State law grounds for vacating awards 13.138–13.141
nondomestic awards rendered in the United States/pursuant to U.S. arbitration law vacated under U.S arbitration law 1.88–1.94
options for "winner" and "loser" 13.03–13.06
procedural issues 13.12–13.77
recognition and enforcement
applicable law 1.84–1.102
arbitral jurisdiction 6.93–6.111
choice of law rules 6.96
Kompetenz-Kompetenz and review of arbitral jurisdiction 6.97–6.106
nonrecognition *see* Nonrecognition of international arbitral award, New York Convention
place of arbitral jurisdiction 6.95
relevance of New York arbitration law to arbitral awards 1.100–1.102
removal
authorized if an action "relates to" a Convention agreement/award 13.68–13.71
from state to federal courts 13.65–13.72
timing 13.72
service of application to confirm or vacate award 13.21–13.26
significant contacts test 7.26n34
substantive issues involved in challenging awards in New York 13.78–13.152
timing of application to confirm or vacate award 13.14–13.17
venue, establishing 13.60–13.64
written arbitration agreement requirement 13.27
International arbitration agreements, enforcing
allocation of power between arbitrators and courts 7.29–7.41
antisuit injunctions
circumstances in which courts grant to enforce arbitration agreements 7.136–7.151
circumstances in which courts have denied in aid of arbitration 7.152–7.166
overview 7.131–7.135
challenges to contract 7.57–7.62
challenges to validity of contract as a whole vs. challenges directed specifically at arbitration clause 7.60–7.62
challenges to validity of contract vs. a claim that no contract was ever concluded 7.58–7.59
choice of law rules governing interpretation and enforcement 6.14–6.17
compelling arbitration 7.98–7.111
court intervention 7.08–7.41, 7.129–7.166
federal policy in favor of arbitration 7.14–7.15
jurisdiction of U.S. federal courts 7.19–7.28
Kompetenz-Kompetenz doctrine 7.33–7.35
reading together with separability doctrine 7.42–7.97
New York Convention 7.16–7.18
nonsignatories 7.63–7.81
theories by which obligated to arbitrate 7.70–7.83
Panama Convention 7.16–7.18
proceeding with arbitration without court intervention 7.04–7.07
scope of arbitration clause 7.82–7.95
separability doctrine 7.36–7.41
reading together with *Kompetenz-Kompetenz* doctrine 7.42–7.97
staying litigation commenced in U.S. in breach of an arbitration clause 7.112–7.128
arbitrability of claims under U.S. law 7.121–7.123
cases including nonarbitrable claims 7.124–7.128
motions to stay or dismiss litigation under the FAA 7.113–7.120
waiver 7.96–7.97

International Arbitration Committee, International Section of New York State Bar Association 0.26
International Arbitration Part Rules Appendix 4
Commercial Division (Supreme Court) 0.21
International Bar Association (IBA), Rules on Taking of Evidence in International Commercial Arbitration 9.25–9.29
International Centre for Dispute Resolution (ICDR)
conducting arbitration 12.02
International Arbitration Rules 0.10, 5.08–5.15, 9.17
offices 0.09
selection of arbitrators 5.50
staff 0.10
International Centre for Settlement of Investment Disputes (ICSID), recognition of awards "automatic" 14.15–14.16
International Chamber of Commerce (ICC)
International Court of Arbitration
administration of cases in New York 0.02
Secretariat 0.11, 12.02
location 0.11
numbers of cases administered 0.11
Rules 5.19–5.21, 9.15
U.S. National Committee (Arbitration Committee of the U.S. Council for International Business) 0.12, 5.51
International comity
antisuit injunctions 7.132, 7.133, 7.147, 7.157
principles 7.134, 7.150, 8.39
International Commercial Disputes Committee, New York City Bar Association 0.26
International Court of Arbitration
administration of cases in New York 0.02
Secretariat 0.11
International Institute for Conflict Prevention and Resolution (CPR)
Administered Arbitration Rules issued by 0.14
appointment services 0.15
conducting arbitration 12.02
and finding of arbitrator candidates 5.47
role and services 0.13
Rules 9.22–9.24
tribunal formation rules 5.24–5.26
International Swaps and Derivatives Association (ISDA) 0.05
Investment value *see* **Costs**

J
JAMS (*formerly* Judicial Arbitration and Mediation Service)
Class Arbitration Procedures (JAMS Procedures) 11.35–11.36
conducting arbitration 12.02
International Arbitration Rules 9.18–9.20
role and services 0.16
selection of arbitrators 5.49
Streamlined Arbitration Rules 12.80n53
"Jettison clause" 11.111
John F. Kennedy International Airport (JFK) 12.88
Judgment 2.83–2.91
see also Litigation, U.S.
in bench trial 2.89–2.91
civil procedure 2.26
"final judgment" rule 2.98
in jury trial 2.85–2.88
summary 2.74–2.75
Judicial powers, considerations relating to 3.51–3.61
international arbitral awards, challenging and enforcing 3.58–3.61
judicial review, modifying scope 3.55–3.57
provisional measures 3.51–3.54
Judicial review
appeals 2.100–2.101
of arbitrator's decision as to the parties bound by the agreement 6.68–6.71
of arbitrator's determination of scope of arbitration agreement 6.72–6.75
of arbitrator's determinations of the validity of the arbitration agreement 6.76–6.85
Kompetenz-Kompetenz and judicial review upon vacatur 6.65–6.90
modification of scope 3.55–3.57
Jurisdiction
see also Arbitral jurisdiction
arbitration agreements 6.02
international, enforcement of 7.19–7.28
commercial 7.25
exceeding 13.124–13.125
of federal courts 1.10
nondomestic 7.27
personal *see* Personal jurisdiction
quasi in rem 13.55–13.59
subject-matter *see* Subject-matter jurisdiction
territorial 2.42–2.43, 7.26
of U.S. federal courts 7.19–7.28
in writing 7.24
Jury trial, judgment in 2.85–2.88

K
***Kompetenz-Kompetenz* (*compétence-compétence*)**
allocation of power between arbitrators and courts 7.33–7.35
arbitral jurisdiction 6.06, 6.09, 6.22–6.28
drafting considerations, arbitration clauses 3.16–3.19
and judicial review upon vacatur 6.65–6.90
reading together with separability doctrine 7.42–7.97

and review of arbitral jurisdiction in recognition and enforcement proceedings 6.97–6.106
scope and validity of arbitrators' jurisdiction 6.50–6.55
those deciding party issues 6.23
those deciding scope issues 6.24
those deciding validity issues 6.25

L
La Guardia Airport (LGA) 12.90
Law firm international groups 0.31
Law of forum
see also Forum-specific issues
consideration of state contract law principles when applying in Second Circuit 1.65–1.68
Second Circuit case law applying 1.61–1.64
Lawyers
see also Attorneys
lawyer directories 5.53
vs. non-lawyers, tripartite tribunal 5.35–5.36
Limitation *see* **Time limits**
Liquidated damages 10.23–10.26
Litigation, U.S.
adversarial model 2.04–2.07, 2.55–2.56
appeals *see* Appeals
civil procedure 2.26
commencement 2.27–2.43
costs 2.92–2.95
court structure 2.08–2.11
discovery *see* Discovery
judgment *see* Judgment
motions to stay or dismiss under the FAA 7.113–7.120
Oldroyd test 7.120, 7.123
overview 2.03–2.26
presentation of case 2.26, 2.76–2.82
pretrial matters 2.26, 2.76–2.82
privilege 2.64–2.67
procedural calendar 2.26, 2.44–2.51
sources of law governing *see* Sources of law, litigation
staying litigation commenced in U.S. in breach of an arbitration clause 7.112–7.128
Lost business opportunity, damages for anticipated future profits 10.35–10.38

M
"Manifest disregard of the law" 1.97
class action arbitrations 11.45
as grounds for vacating arbitral awards 13.126–13.134
vacatur 11.39
Merger clauses, contract law 4.60–4.63
Model arbitration clauses 0.05
Money damages, vs. specific performance 10.06–10.09
see also Damages
Motion
forum non conveniens 2.34n47
to stay or dismiss litigation under FAA 7.113–7.120

N
N. Y. CPLR *see* **New York Civil Practice Law and Rules (N. Y. CPLR)**
National Committee (Arbitration Committee of the U.S. Council for International Business) 0.12, 5.51
Nationality considerations, tripartite tribunal 5.40–5.42
Net asset approach to damages *see* **Book value**
Neutrality
AAA/ABA Code of Ethics and rules Appendix 6
exceptions for arbitrators not subject to rules Appendix 6
of party-appointed arbitrators 5.43–5.45
New York
see also New York Convention on the Recognition and Enforcement of Foreign Arbitral Awards (1958)
arbitration statute *see* New York State arbitration statute
challenging awards in, substantive issues involved 13.78–13.152
Civil Practice Law and Rules *see* New York Civil Practice Law and Rules (N. Y. CPLR)
confirmation and vacatur of awards rendered in 6.62–6.63
contract law *see* New York contract law
discovery in, in aid of a foreign arbitration 9.74–9.78
federal judicial districts 0.18
as a financial and legal capital 0.05
governing law of 0.05
idiosyncratic appointing authorities 5.28
law applicable to international arbitration in *see* Applicable law
leading arbitration institutions based in 0.06, 0.07–0.16
New York City Bar Association 0.25, 0.26
New York State Bar Association 0.25, 0.26
as preferred arbitration site 0.01, 0.03
travel to and from 12.87–12.90
travel within 12.91–12.93
New York City Bar Association Appendix 7
New York Civil Practice Law and Rules (N. Y. CPLR)
actions in New York State courts 13.73–13.77
applications to compel or stay arbitration Appendix 3
applications to the court Appendix 3
compelling arbitration under s. 7503(c) 7.106–7.111
discovery 9.06

New York contract law
see also Breach of contract; Contract law
choice-of-law rules 4.06–4.11
claims ancillary to breach of contract 4.49–4.58
special issues arising under 4.59–4.70
New York Convention on the Recognition and Enforcement of Foreign Arbitral Awards (1958)
enforcement of international arbitration agreements 7.16–7.18
and Federal Arbitration Act 1.01, 1.30–1.33
nonrecognition grounds under *see* nonrecognition of international arbitral award, New York Convention
and preliminary relief 8.33–8.34
recognition of arbitration agreement, applicable law regarding 1.48–1.53
recognition of awards rendered against sovereigns 14.12–14.14
New York International Arbitration Center (NYIAC) 0.22
conducting arbitration 12.02
New York International Arbitration Club 0.24, 5.52
New York State arbitration statute
see also Federal Arbitration Act (FAA)
and Federal Arbitration Act 1.36–1.43
predispute arbitration agreements in consumer contracts, prohibiting 1.43
statute of limitations as threshold matter, authority to decide 1.38–1.39
validity of agreement to arbitrate, limiting time to object to 1.40–1.42
New York State Court E-Filing (NYSCEF) 2.23
New York State courts
see also Court(s)
actions in 13.73–13.77
form and location 13.74–13.75
statute of limitations 13.76–13.77
federal judicial districts 0.18
grounds for vacating awards 13.138–13.141
New York Civil Practice Law and Rules (N. Y. CPLR) 13.73
party autonomy, supporting 9.07–9.10
preliminary relief 8.39–8.49
Newark Liberty International Airport (EWR) 12.89
Nonrecognition of international arbitral award, New York Convention 13.78–13.110
see also International arbitral awards, challenging and enforcing
absence of valid arbitration agreement 13.81–13.95
awards not binding or have been set aside 13.104–13.105
excess of authority 13.98–13.100
non-arbitrable issues, awards addressing 13.106–13.107
violation of public policy 13.108–13.110
violations of arbitral procedures or law of arbitral situs 13.101–13.103
Nonsignatories
clear and unmistakable evidence test 7.66, 7.67
jurisdiction over 3.24–3.25
theories by which obligated to arbitrate 7.70–7.83
agency 7.74
alter ego 7.75
assumption by conduct 7.73
estoppel 7.76–7.80
incorporate by reference 7.72
third-party beneficiaries 7.81
veil piercing 7.75
Notice pleading 0.38
see also Pleadings
purpose 2.30
requirements 2.37
standards for 2.27, 2.61

O

Offer 4.14
see also Breach of contract; Contract law; New York contract law
***Oldroyd* test**
cases that include nonarbitrable claims 7.124
motions to stay or dismiss litigation 7.120, 7.123
Organization of American States (OAS) 1.35, 13.10

P

Panama Convention *see* **Inter-American Convention on International Commercial Arbitration of 1975 (Panama Convention)**
Party autonomy
example of clause permitting limited discovery at discretion of arbitrators 9.09
New York State courts supporting 9.07–9.10
paramount in international arbitration 9.07
supremacy of parties' agreement on discovery 9.08
Party-appointed arbitrators
see also Arbitrators; Selection of arbitrators
communications with 5.56–5.65
neutrality of 5.43–5.45
role in selecting a chairperson 5.66–5.69
Penalties, and liquidated damages 10.23–10.26
Pendent appellation jurisdiction doctrine 6.35n118
Performance
effect of non-breaching party on 4.29–4.33
fraud in 4.55–4.56
money damages, vs. specific performance 10.06–10.09
substantial 4.25
Personal jurisdiction
by consent 13.43–13.47
in federal courts 7.28

foreign sovereigns not immune from 14.27–14.30
need to establish a basis for jurisdiction 13.40–13.42
quasi in rem 13.55–13.59
through minimum contacts 13.48–13.54
Pleadings
see also Notice pleading
commencement of litigation 2.28–2.37
exception to well-pleaded rule 13.67
Postjudgment interest 10.46–10.47
Prearbitration attachment
explicit waiver requirement 14.34–14.39
procedure 14.40
Preclusive effect of prior judicial determinations 6.52–6.54
forum-specific issues 6.56–6.59
Predispute protections, recalcitrant states 14.31–14.32
Preemption
class action arbitrations 11.111
and conflicts between laws affecting arbitration 1.05
defined 1.06–1.09
Prejudgment interest 10.40–10.45
Prejudicial behavior 13.119–13.133
Preliminary measures *see* **Preliminary relief**
Preliminary relief
from arbitral tribunals in New York 8.05–8.31
authority of arbitral tribunals to issue 8.07–8.15
from courts in aid of arbitration 8.32–8.49
defined 8.02
discovery 9.73
emergency arbitral relief
emergency arbitrators 8.24–8.31
need for 8.24–8.25
procedures 8.26–8.31
entitlement to issue 8.03
from federal courts 8.35–8.39
form 8.04
judicial enforcement 8.20–8.23
and New York Convention 8.33–8.34
from New York State courts 8.39–8.49
procedures 8.17–8.19
types 8.16
Presentation of case
civil procedure 2.26
denial of opportunity in challenging international arbitral awards in New York 13.96–13.97
pretrial matters 2.76–2.82
Pretrial conferences 2.46–2.49
Pretrial matters 2.26
and presentation of case 2.76–2.82
Privacy, distinguished from confidentiality 12.17
Privilege, discovery 2.64–2.67, 9.56–9.58
Procedural calendar 2.26, 2.44–2.51
see also Litigation, U.S.
case management 2.45
pretrial conferences 2.46–2.49
scheduling order 2.50–2.51
Production, requests for 2.63
Professional qualifications, tripartite tribunal 5.37–5.39
Promissory estoppel
future contracts 4.19
and reliance 10.29, 10.32, 10.33
as substitution for consideration 10.32
Public policy considerations
see also Class action arbitrations
arbitral clauses prohibiting class actions 11.85–11.94, 11.103–11.109
awards violating public policy 13.108–13.110
vacation of international arbitral awards, grounds under FAA Chapter 1 13.135
whether preempted by FAA 11.95–11.109
Punitive damages 10.27–10.28
arbitral tribunal 3.34–3.36

Q

Quantum meruit *see* **Restitution damages**
Quasi in rem **jurisdiction** 13.55–13.59
see also Jurisdiction

R

Racketeer Influenced and Corrupt Organizations Act (RICO) 0.41, 6.28, 7.93
Reasonableness test, damages 10.22
Recalcitrant states, problem of 14.31–14.76
prearbitration attachment 14.33–14.40
predispute protections 14.31–14.32
Reliance damages 10.29–10.33
Renvoi 4.11
***Res judicata*, forum-specific issues** 6.33–6.34
Restitution damages 10.34
Rules and guidelines, arbitration 9.13–9.29
see also Arbitration; Discovery
CPR Rules 9.22–9.24
ICDR International Arbitration Rules 0.10, 5.08–5.15, 9.17
International Bar Association (IBA) Rules of Evidence 9.25–9.29
International Chamber of Commerce Rules of Arbitration (ICC Rules) 9.15
JAMS/JAMS International Arbitration Rules 9.18–9.20
Techniques for Controlling Time and Costs in Arbitration Report 9.16
UNCITRAL Rules 9.21
Rules of evidence, U.S. litigation 2.22

S

Schedule of International Arbitration Conventions Appendix 1
Scheduling order 2.50–2.51

Second Circuit Court of Appeals
see also Appeals; Court(s); Federal courts
law of forum, applying
case law 1.61–1.64
consideration of state contract law principles 1.65–1.68
underlying contract, applying law of 1.69–1.71
"Second look" doctrine 7.122n176
Secretariat of the International Court of Arbitration North America (SICANA, Inc) 0.11
conducting arbitration 12.02
Selection of arbitrators
see also Arbitral tribunal; Arbitrators; Party-appointed arbitrators
AAA/ABA Code of Ethics and rules 5.57–5.59, Appendix 6
Arbitration Committee of U.S. Council for International Business 5.51
arbitrator compensation and conflicts waivers 5.77–5.81
chairperson
convincing to serve 5.75–5.76
negotiations 5.70–5.74
role of party-appointed arbitrators in selecting 5.66–5.69
Chartered Institute of Arbitrators, Guideline 5.60–5.63
communications with party-appointed arbitrators 5.56–5.65
conflicts checks and arbitrator disclosures 5.82–5.85
and CPR 5.47
detailed arbitrator selection clauses 5.05–5.06
and Energy Arbitrators List 5.48, 5.50
finding of candidates 5.46–5.53
formation of tribunal, incorporation of arbitral rules regarding 5.07–5.27
and ICDR 5.50
idiosyncratic appointing authorities, New York 5.28
JAMS roster 5.49
lawyer directories 5.53
time limits 5.64–5.65
tribunal structure *see* Structure of tribunal
tripartite tribunal, strategy in selection of members *see* Tripartite tribunal
Separability doctrine
reading together with *Kompetenz-Kompetenz* doctrine 7.42–7.97
recognition of arbitration agreement under Conventions 1.45–1.47
Severability doctrine
arbitral jurisdiction 6.06, 6.07, 6.08, 6.09
severability as guide to validity questions 6.18–6.21
severability at vacatur stage 6.78
Situs, arbitral 13.101–13.103
Sources of law, litigation 2.12–2.25
appellate-level courts 2.22
common law 2.14–2.15
constitutions 2.21
equity 2.16–2.17
ethical obligations and codes 2.24 2.25
local court rules 2.22
New York State Court E-Filing system 2.23
rules of civil procedure 2.18–2.20
rules of evidence 2.22
Special damages 10.15–10.20
see also Damages
Specific performance, vs. money damages 10.06–10.09
Standard form agreements, global 0.05
***Stare decisis* doctrine** 2.14
***Stolt-Neilsen S.A. v AnimalFeeds International Corp* judgment** 11.65–11.70
decisions following regarding whether silent clauses permit class action arbitrations 11.71–11.72
Structure of tribunal 5.03–5.31
see also Arbitral tribunal; Selection of arbitrators
detailed arbitrator selection clauses 5.05–5.06
dysfunctional clauses referring to non-existent/unavailable institutions 5.29
incorporation of arbitral rules governing tribunal formation 5.07–5.27
statutory default procedures 5.30–5.31
Subject-matter jurisdiction
challenging and enforcing international arbitral awards 13.29–13.39
enforcement of international arbitration agreements 7.20–7.27
U.S. litigation 2.39–2.41
Subpoenas
to compel attendance at a hearing 12.58–12.67
third-party 2.63
Summary judgment 2.74–2.75
Supporting organizations 0.23–0.31
bar association committees 0.25, 0.26
New York International Arbitration Club 0.24, 5.52
Supreme Court
Bazzle judgment 11.08–11.28
Commercial Division 0.20, 0.21

T

***Techniques for Controlling Time and Costs in Arbitration* Report** 9.16
Territorial jurisdiction 2.42–2.43, 7.26
Third-party beneficiaries
claims ancillary to breach of contract 4.57–4.58
nonsignatories 7.81
Third-party subpoenas 2.63

Time limits
agreement to arbitrate 1.40
enforcement of arbitral awards 13.72
forum-specific issues 6.31
selection of arbitrators 5.64–5.65
statute of limitations as threshold matter, court authority to decide 1.38–1.39
validity of agreement to arbitrate, limiting time to object to 1.40–1.42
Trial
see also Pretrial conferences; Pretrial matters
bench 2.89–2.91
jury 2.85–2.88
Tribunal secretaries 12.10–12.16
federal and state law 12.11–12.12
institutional rules 12.13–12.16
Tripartite tribunal
default mechanisms, role 5.33–5.34
lawyers vs. non-lawyers 5.35–5.36
nationality 5.40–5.42
special professional qualifications 5.37–5.39
strategy in selection of members 5.32–5.42
Trust accounts, attachment of 14.74–14.76

U

UCC *see* **Uniform Commercial Code (UCC)**
U.N. Commission on International Trade Law (UNCITRAL)
Rules 9.21
tribunal formation 5.22–5.23
U.N. Convention on Contracts for the International Sale of Goods 4.02
Undue means, award procured by 13.113–13.114
Uniform Commercial Code (UCC)
contract law 4.02
money damages, vs. specific performance 10.07
subject-matter jurisdiction 13.31
Universities 0.29
Unjust enrichment, claims ancillary to breach of contract 4.51–4.52

V

Validity
of arbitration agreement *see* Validity of arbitration agreement
of contract
challenges to contract as a whole vs. challenges directed specifically at arbitration clause 7.60–7.62
challenges to, vs. a claim that no contract was ever concluded 7.58–7.59
formal validity of agreement to arbitrate pursuant to terms of Conventions 1.74–1.78
limiting of time to object to 1.40–1.42
severability as guide to questions of 6.18–6.21
sole option clauses 3.26
substantive validity of the agreement to arbitrate 1.57–1.73
case law from Second Circuit applying law of forum 1.61–1.64
case law from Second Circuit applying law of underlying contract 1.69–1.71
internationally recognized minimum standards, consideration of 1.72–1.73
state contract law principles, considering when applying law of forum in Second Circuit 1.65–1.68
those deciding issues (*Kompetenz-Kompetenz* principle) 6.25
Validity of arbitration agreement
see also Validity
absence of valid agreement and nonrecognition of award 13.81–13.95
arbitral determination 6.76
arbitral jurisdiction upon vacatur
arbitral determinations, review of 6.76–6.85
deference 6.79–6.81
law governing interpretation and validity 6.64
severability at vacatur stage 6.78
deference on
arbitral jurisdiction at recognition and enforcement 6.102–6.105
arbitral jurisdiction upon vacatur 6.79–6.81
formation and substantive validity, applicable law 1.57–1.73
pursuant to terms of Conventions 1.74–1.78
Veil piercing
deciding of party issues 6.23
foreign sovereigns, enforcing awards involving 14.30, 14.55, 14.68
international arbitration agreements, enforcing 7.75
nonsignatories 3.24n36, 7.75
Venue
establishing 13.60–13.64
framework for international arbitrations venued in New York 9.03–9.32
New York as leading venue for international commercial arbitration in United States 0.01
Voir dire 2.79

W

Waivers
arbitrator compensation and conflicts waivers 5.77–5.81
explicit
prearbitration attachment 14.34–14.39
prerecognition attachment 14.42–14.50
forum-specific issues 6.32
international arbitration agreements, enforcing 7.96–7.97

Waivers (*cont.*)
of jurisdiction objections 6.90
jurisdictional challenges 6.55, 6.111
"Wholly groundless" test, disputes on scope 7.88
Witnesses
arbitration hearings 12.35–12.85
attendance at hearing 12.52–12.67
depositions 12.49–12.51
due process 12.35
exhibits, use 12.76–12.81
expert 9.71–9.72, 12.44–12.48
instructions 12.68–12.75
obligation of a party to produce 12.53–12.57
subpoena to compel attendance 12.58–12.67
written statements/extent of live direct testimony 12.36–12.43
Work-product doctrine 2.65, 2.66